Marketing Research

In a Digital Information Environment

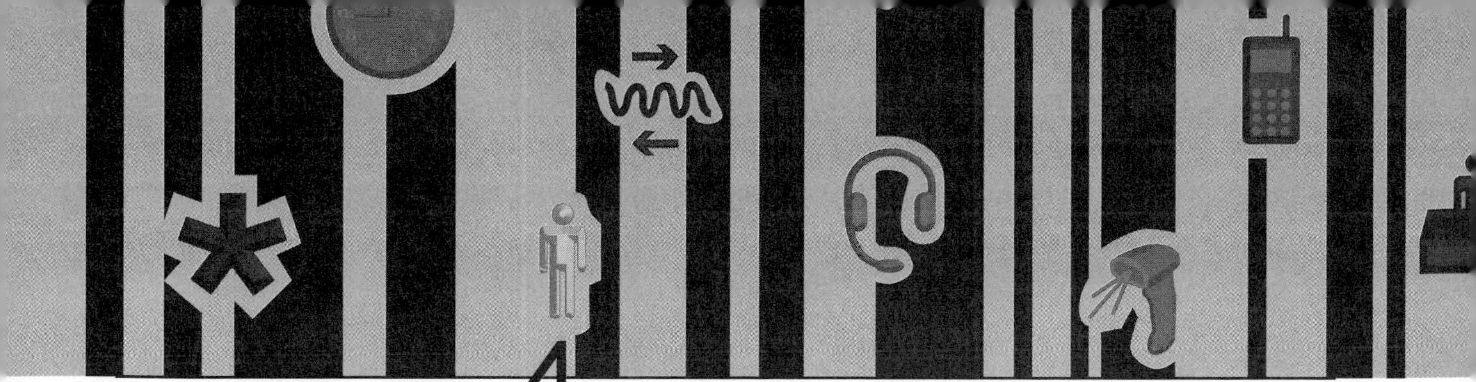

edition 4

Marketing Research

In a Digital Information Environment

JOSEPH F. HAIR, JR.
Kennesaw State University

ROBERT P. BUSH
Louisiana State University at Alexandria

DAVID J. ORTINAU
University of South Florida

McGraw-Hill Irwin

Boston Burr Ridge, IL Dubuque, IA New York San Francisco St. Louis
Bangkok Bogotá Caracas Kuala Lumpur Lisbon London Madrid Mexico City
Milan Montreal New Delhi Santiago Seoul Singapore Sydney Taipei Toronto

WB

The McGraw-Hill Companies

McGraw-Hill Irwin

MARKETING RESEARCH: IN A DIGITAL INFORMATION ENVIRONMENT Published by McGraw-Hill/Irwin, a business unit of The McGraw-Hill Companies, Inc., 1221 Avenue of the Americas, New York, NY, 10020.

This book is printed on acid-free paper.

1 2 3 4 5 6 7 8 9 0 QPD/QPD 0 9 8

ISBN 978-0-07-340470-7
MHID 0-07-340470-5

Vice president and editor-in-chief: *Brent Gordon*
Publisher: *Paul Ducham*
Managing developmental editor: *Laura Hurst Spell*
Editorial assistant: *Jane Beck*
Associate marketing manager: *Dean Karampelas*
Project manager: *Kathryn D. Mikulic*
Full service project manager: *Jodi Dowling, Aptara®, Inc.*
Production supervisor: *Gina Hangos*
Lead designer: *Matthew Baldwin*
Media project manager: *Suresh Babu, Hurix Systems Pvt. Ltd.*
Cover designer: *Brittany Skwierczynski*
Cover image: *©Getty Images*
Typeface: *10/12 Times Roman*
Compositor: *Aptara®, Inc.*
Printer: *Quebecor World Dubuque Inc.*

Library of Congress Cataloging-in-Publication Data

Hair, Joseph F.
Marketing research : in a digital information environment / Joseph F. Hair Jr., Robert P. Bush, David J. Ortinau. — 4th ed.
p. cm. — (McGraw-Hill/Irwin series in marketing)
Subtitle on 3rd ed., 2006 varies.
Includes bibliographical references and index.
ISBN-13: 978-0-07-340470-7 (alk. paper)
ISBN-10: 0-07-340470-5 (alk. paper)
1. Marketing research. I. Bush, Robert P. II. Ortinau, David J. III. Title.
HF5415.2.H258 2009
658.8'3—dc22

2008039035

11/20/12

www.mhhe.com

dedication

To my wife, Dale, my son Joe III and his wife Kerrie, and to my grandson Joe IV.

—Joseph F. Hair, Jr., Kennesaw, GA

This book is dedicated to my wife, Donny, and to my two boys, Robert Jr. and Michael.

—Robert P. Bush, Sr., Lafayette, LA

This edition is dedicated to Carol V. Livingstone, to my mom Lois, to my wonderful sister Nancy and her husband Jim Sasaki, to my great brothers Dean and Denny along with their families, with thanks for their unconditional love and support, and to all my past, present, and future students for enriching my life experiences as an educator and researcher on a daily basis.

—David J. Ortinau, Tampa, FL

about the authors

Joseph F. Hair, Jr., is Professor of Marketing at Kennesaw State University. He previously held the Copeland Endowed Chair of Entrepreneurship and was Director, Entrepreneurship Institute, Louisiana State University. He was a United States Steel Foundation Fellow at the University of Florida, Gainesville, where he earned his Ph.D. in Marketing in 1971. He has published over 40 books, including *Marketing,* South-Western Publishing Company, 10th edition, 2010 (South African, Portuguese, Malaysian, Australian, and Spanish-language editions also available); *Marketing Essentials,* South-Western Publishing Company, 6th edition, 2009; *Multivariate Data Analysis,* Prentice Hall, 6th edition, 2006 (this text cited over 7,000 times according to Google Scholar, January 2008); *Research Methods for Business,* Wiley, UK, 2007; *Essentials of Marketing Research,* McGraw-Hill/Irwin, 2007; and *Sales Management,* Houghton-Mifflin, 2008. He also has published numerous articles in professional journals such as the *Journal of Marketing Research, Journal of Academy of Marketing Science, Journal of Business/Chicago, Journal of Advertising Research, Journal of Business Research, Journal of Marketing Theory and Practice, Journal of Personal Selling and Sales Management, Industrial Marketing Management,* and others.

He is a Distinguished Fellow of the Academy of Marketing Sciences, the Society for Marketing Advances, and Southwestern Marketing Association. In 2007 he was recognized as the Innovative Marketer of the Year in 2007 by the Marketing Management Association. In 2004 he was awarded the Academy of Marketing Science Outstanding Marketing Teaching Excellence Award. The Louisiana State University Entrepreneurship Institute under his leadership was recognized nationally by *Entrepreneurship* magazine in 2003 as one of the top 12 programs in the United States, and was ranked number 3 in the United States in 2004 and 2005 by *Forbes* magazine/*Princeton Review.* He has been retained as a consultant for numerous companies in a wide variety of industries, as well as by the U.S. Department of Agriculture and the U.S. Department of the Interior. Finally, he is often invited to give lectures on research techniques, data analysis, and marketing issues for organizations in the United States, Europe, and the Pacific Rim region.

Robert P. Bush earned a B.A. in Psychology and Economic History from St. Mary's University and an M.A. and Ph.D. in Marketing at Louisiana State University. He began his teaching career at the University of South Florida before moving on to the University of Mississippi, the University of Memphis, and then the University of Louisiana, Lafayette. He was chairman of the committee on Grants and Research for the Fogelman College of Business from 1991 to 1997 and Director of the Ph.D. program at Memphis from 1995 to 1997. He has been a consultant for a wide range of corporations and institutes, as well as for the U.S. Department of Defense. Robert P. Bush is the coauthor of *Retailing for the 21st Century,* Houghton Mifflin, 1993; and a co-editor of *Advances in Marketing* (LSU Press, 1994). He is a regular contributor to such academic publications as *Journal of Advertising, Journal of Consumer Marketing, Journal of Marketing Education, Journal of Direct Marketing, Journal of Health Care Marketing,* and *Marketing Education Review.*

David J. Ortinau earned his B.S. in Management from Southern Illinois University, Carbondale, an M.S. in Business Administration, with a specialty in marketing research, from Illinois State University, and his Ph.D. in Marketing from Louisiana State University. He began his teaching career at Illinois State University and is currently Professor of Marketing at the University of South Florida, Tampa, where he continues to win awards for both outstanding research and excellence in teaching. His scholarly research is acknowledged both nationally and internationally in the areas of consumer satisfaction and value evaluation/models; research methods and scale measurements; services marketing and service quality within selected market segments; and marketing education issues. Professor Ortinau specializes in attitudinal, motivation, and value issues and his scholarly contributions have appeared in the *Journal of the Academy of Marketing Science, Journal of Retailing, Journal of Business Research, Journal of Health Care Marketing, Journal of Service Marketing, Journal of Marketing Education,* and others. He actively publishes in a variety of professional/educational-based proceedings. He is coauthor of several textbooks including *Essentials of Marketing Research,* Irwin/McGraw-Hill, 2008, and is co-editor of *Marketing: Moving toward the 21st Century,* SMA Press, 1996. He served as an editorial review board member for the *Journal of the Academy of Marketing Science* from 1988 through 2006 (named "Outstanding Reviewer" in 1992 and for 1997–2000) and currently serves on the editorial review boards of the *Journal of Business Research* ("Outstanding Reviewer" in 2002 and 2005) and the *Journal of Marketing Theory and Practice,* as well as serving as an ad hoc reviewer for several other journals. Professor Ortinau remains an active leader in the Marketing discipline. He has held many leadership positions in the Society for Marketing Advances (SMA), served as co-chair of the 1998 SMA Doctoral Consortium in New Orleans and the 1999 SMA Doctoral Consortium in Atlanta, co-chaired the 2006 and 2007 SMA/Retail Management and Patronage Behavior Research Symposium, served as the program co-chair of the 2004 Academy of Marketing Science Conference, and served as the 2008 American Marketing Association Conference's Marketing Research Track Co-chair. He is past president of SMA, president of the SMA Foundation, and was recognized as the 2001 SMA Fellow. He has consulted for a number of corporations and small businesses, with specialties in customer satisfaction, customer service quality and value, retail loyalty, and imagery.

preface

Since we wrote the first edition of *Marketing Research,* the world has become global, highly competitive, and increasingly influenced by information technology, particularly the Internet. With its steadily growing market share, *Marketing Research* has become a premier source for new and essential marketing research knowledge. Many of you, our customers, have provided feedback on the first three editions. Some of you like to do applied research projects while others emphasize case studies or exercises at the end of the chapters. Others have requested additional coverage of qualitative methods. Students and professors alike are concerned about the price of textbooks. This fourth edition, *Marketing Research: In a Digital Information Environment,* was written to meet the needs of our customers. The text is concise, highly readable, and it delivers the basic knowledge needed for an introductory text. We provide you and your students with an exciting, up-to-date text and an extensive supplement package. We summarize below what you will find when you examine, and we hope adopt, this book. There are several innovative features of our new book.

First, it is the only text that includes a separate chapter on **qualitative data analysis.** Other texts discuss qualitative data collection, such as focus groups and in-depth interviews, but then say little about what to do with this kind of data. In contrast, we dedicate an entire chapter to the topic, referencing the seminal work in this area by Miles and Huberman, and enabling professors to provide a more balanced approach in their classes. In addition, we explain important tasks such as coding qualitative data and identifying themes and patterns.

Second, other texts include little coverage of the task of conducting a **literature review** to find background information on the research problem. Our text has a chapter that includes substantial material on this topic, including guidelines on how to conduct a literature review and the sources to search. Since students these days rely so heavily on the Internet, the emphasis is on using Google, Yahoo!, and other search engines to execute the background research. The fourth edition of *Marketing Research* provides an excellent foundation for students learning to conduct background searches for relevant information.

Third, more so than other texts, we emphasize the **role of secondary data,** particularly as part of a company's CRM (Customer Relationship Management) efforts. Increasingly companies turn to their internal data warehouses that contain already collected secondary information both from within the firm as well as from external sources such as syndicated studies and data enhancement vendors. Enterprise software systems such as SAP that have achieved significant market penetration in recent years, as well as many CRM systems, enable companies to quickly access this information and use it to improve decision making. Other texts have only limited coverage of this important development.

Fourth, as one component of the "applied" emphasis of our text, the fourth edition of *Marketing Research* has retained and refined two popular pedagogical features. One is boxes in all chapters titled **A Closer Look at Research** that summarize an applied research example and pose questions for discussion. The second is the **Marketing Research in Action** exercise at the end of each chapter that enables students to apply what was covered in the chapter to a real world situation or challenge.

Fifth, our text has an excellent *continuing case* throughout the book that enables the professor to illustrate applied concepts using a realistic example. Our continuing case, the **Santa Fe Grill Mexican Restaurant,** is an example students can relate to because virtually all of them have eaten in a Mexican restaurant! The case is relevant too because the story setting is two college student entrepreneurs who start their own business—a goal of many students these days. This case study has been expanded in the fourth edition and the Santa Fe Grill now has a competitor, Jose's Southwestern Café. Both restaurants are located on outparcels of a large regional mall but Jose's is more successful. The task for students then is to analyze the competitive situation using actual data and to recommend research solutions for gaining competitive advantage. In addition, we include specific mini-case studies based on this example in almost every chapter.

Since the Santa Fe Grill is a continuing case, the professor does not have to familiarize students with a new example every chapter. Instead, students build upon what has been covered earlier. This has the effect of bringing a research challenge into focus in its various aspects. When the case is used in later chapters on quantitative data analysis, a data set (in SPSS format) is provided that actually works as it should when students use it. For example, there are statistically significant differences between male and female customers as well as between the customers of the two competing restaurants—and lifestyle attitudes influence satisfaction with both restaurants. Thus, students can truly see how marketing research information can be used to improve decision making.

Sixth, in addition to the Santa Fe Grill case, there are **five other data sets in SPSS format.** The data sets can be used to assign research projects or as additional exercises throughout the book. These databases cover a wide variety of topics that all students can identify with and offer an excellent approach to enhance teaching of concepts:

Deli Depot is an expanded version of the Deli Depot case included in previous editions. An overview of this case is provided as part of the Marketing Research in Action in Chapter 14. The sample size is 200.

Remington's Steak House is introduced as the Marketing Research in Action in Chapter 15. Remington's Steak House competes with Outback and Longhorn. The focus of the case is analyzing data to identify restaurant images and prepare perceptual maps to facilitate strategy development. The sample size is 200.

QualKote is a business-to-business application of marketing research based on an employee survey. It is introduced as the Marketing Research in Action in Chapter 16. The case examines the implementation of a quality improvement program and its impact on customer satisfaction. The sample size is 57.

Consumer Electronics is based on the rapid growth of the DVD market and focuses on the concept of innovators and early adopters. The case overview and variables as well as some data analysis examples are provided in the Marketing Research in Action for Chapter 17. The sample size is 200.

Backyard Burgers is based on a nationwide survey of customers. The database is rich with potential data analysis comparisons and covers topics with which students can easily identify. The sample size is 300.

Seventh, the text's coverage of **quantitative data analysis** is more extensive and much easier to understand than other books'. Specific step-by-step instructions are included on how to use SPSS to execute data analysis for all statistical techniques. This enables instructors to spend much less time teaching students how to use the software the first time. It also saves time later by providing a handy reference for students when they forget how to use the software, which they often do. For instructors who want to cover more advanced statistical techniques, our book is the only one that includes this topic.

Eighth, **online marketing research techniques** are rapidly changing the face of marketing, and the authors have experience with and a strong interest in these techniques. For the most part other texts' material on this subject often is an "add-on" that does not fully integrate online research considerations and their impact. Our text does a better job presenting this material because it was extensively updated in the last year when many of these trends are now evident and information is available to document them.

Pedagogy

Many marketing research texts are readable enough. But a more important question is "Can students comprehend what they are reading?" This book offers a wealth of pedagogical features, all aimed at answering that question positively. Below is a list of the major elements:

Learning Objectives

Each chapter begins with clear learning objectives that students can use to assess their expectations for the chapter in view of the nature and importance of the chapter material.

Real-World Chapter Openers

Each chapter opens with an interesting, relevant example of a real-world business situation that illustrates the focus and significance of the chapter materials.

Key Terms and Concepts

These are bold-faced in the text and defined in the page margins. They are listed at the end of the chapters along with page numbers to make reviewing easier and are also found in the Glossary at the end of the book.

A Closer Look at Research

These illustrative boxes, found frequently throughout the chapters, cover three different types of marketing research challenges: Using Technology, Small Business Implications, and In the Field. They are intended to expose students to real-world marketing research issues.

Ethics

Ethical issues are treated at the outset in the first chapter to provide students with a basic understanding of ethical challenges in marketing research—for research providers, clients, and respondents. Ethical issues are revisited throughout the text and illustrated in Ethics boxes.

Global Insights

Global Insights boxes encourage students to consider the international implications of and opportunities for marketing research.

Chapter Summaries

End-of-chapter Summaries of the chapter discussions are organized by the learning objectives presented at the beginning of the chapter. This approach to organizing the Summaries helps students remember the key concepts and issues. The Summaries also serve as an excellent study guide to prepare for in-class exercises or exams.

Questions for Review and Discussion

The Review and Discussion Questions are carefully designed to enhance the self-learning process and to encourage application of the concepts learned in the chapter to real business decision-making situations. There are two or three questions in each chapter directly related to the Internet and designed to provide students with opportunities to enhance their electronic data gathering and interpretative skills.

Marketing Research in Action

These short cases at the end of the chapters provide students with additional insights into how key concepts in each chapter can be applied to real-world situations. The Marketing Research in Action cases serve as in-class discussion tools or applied case exercises.

Santa Fe Grill Continuing Case

The Santa Fe Grill continuing case is a specially designed business scenario embedded throughout the book for the purpose of illustrating chapter topics. The case is introduced in Chapter 1, and in each subsequent chapter it builds upon the concepts previously learned. Santa Fe Grill uses a single research situation to illustrate various aspects of the marketing research process. More than 30 class-tested examples are included as well as SPSS and Excel formatted databases covering a customer survey of the restaurant and its competitor.

Supplements

The fourth edition *of Marketing Research* provides an extensive and rich ancillary package. Below is a brief description of each element in the package.

Instructor's Resources

Specially prepared Instructor's Manual, electronic Test Bank, and PowerPoint slide presentations provide an easy transition for instructors teaching with the book the first time. For those who have used previous editions, there are many new support materials to build upon the teaching enhancements available previously. A wealth of extra student projects and real-life examples are available as additional classroom resources. These resources may be found on the book's Web site (www.mhhe.com/hair4e).

Web Site

Students can use their Internet skills to log on to the book's dedicated Web site (www.mhhe.com/hair4e) to access additional information about marketing research and evaluate their understanding of chapter material by taking the sample quizzes. Students also can prepare their marketing research projects with our online support system. Additional resources are offered for each chapter—look for prompts in the book that will guide you to the Web site for more useful information on various topics.

Data Sets

Six data sets in SPSS format are available at the book's Web site (www.mhhe.com/hair4e). The data sets can be used to assign research projects or with exercises throughout the book. (The concepts covered in each of the data sets are summarized earlier in this preface.)

SPSS Student Version

Through an arrangement with SPSS, we offer the option of purchasing the textbook packaged with a CD-ROM containing an SPSS Student Version for Windows. This powerful software tool enables students to analyze up to 50 variables and 1,500 observations. It contains all data sets and can be used in conjunction with data analysis procedures included in the text.

Acknowledgments

The authors took the lead in preparing the new fourth edition, but many other people must be given credit for their significant contributions in bringing our vision to reality. We thank our colleagues in academia and industry for their helpful insights over many years on numerous research topics. And again we thank the following reviewers of all the previous editions:

David Andrus
Kansas State University
Mark J. Arnold
Saint Louis University
Barry Babin
Louisiana Tech University
Joseph K. Ballanger
Stephen F. Austin State University
Kevin Bittle
Johnson and Wales University
Mike Brady
Florida State University
John R. Brooks, Jr.
Houston Baptist University
Mary L. Carsky
University of Hartford
Gabriel Perez Cifuentes
University of the Andes
Sam Cousley
University of Mississippi
Vicki Crittenden
Boston College
Carolyn Curasi
Georgia State University
Frank Franzak
Virginia Commonwealth University
Susan Geringer
California State University, Fresno
Timothy Graeff
Middle Tennessee State University
Harry Harmon
Central Missouri State University

Mark E. Hill
Montclair State University
Beverly Jones
Kettering University
Karen Kolzow-Bowman
Morgan State University
Michel Laroche
Concordia University
Bryan Lukas
University of Melbourne
Amro Maher
Old Dominion University
Erika Matulich
University of Tampa
Peter McGoldrick
University of Manchester
Martin Meyers
University of Wisconsin, Stevens Point
Arthur Money
Henley Management College
Tom O'Connor
University of New Orleans
Ossi Pesamaa
Jonkoping University
Herve Queneau
Brooklyn College-CUNY
Molly Rapert
University of Arkansas
John Rigney
Golden State University
Jean Romeo
Boston College
Lawrence E. Ross
Florida Southern University
Phillip Samouel
Kingston University
Carl Saxby
University of Southern Indiana
Steven Silver
San Jose State University
Bruce Stern
Portland State University
Goran Svensson
University of Oslo
Gail Tom
California State University, Sacramento
John Tsalikis
Florida International University
Ann Veeck
Western Michigan University
Steve Vitucci
University of Central Texas
John Weiss
Colorado State University
Beverly Wright
East Carolina University
Tsu-Hong Yen
San Jose State University

Finally, we would like to thank our editors and advisors at McGraw-Hill/Irwin. Thanks go to Paul Ducham, our publisher; Laura Hurst Spell, our sponsoring editor; and Dean Karempalas, our marketing manager. We are also grateful to our very professional production team—Kathryn Mikulic, project manager; Matthew Baldwin, designer; and Gina Hangos, production supervisor.

Joseph F. Hair, Jr.
Robert P. Bush
David J. Ortinau

brief contents

part 1
The Role and Value of Marketing Research 1

chapter 1
Marketing Research and Managerial Decision Making 2

chapter 2
Overview of the Research Process and Research Proposals 34

chapter 3
Information-Driven Technology and the Research Process 64

chapter 4
Market Intelligence and Database Research 82

part 2
Designing Marketing Research Projects 111

chapter 5
Secondary Research: Designs, Searches, and Sources 112

chapter 6
Exploratory Research Using Qualitative and Observation Methods 150

chapter 7
Analyzing and Reporting Qualitative Research 204

chapter 8
Descriptive Research Designs Using Surveys 230

chapter 9
Causal Research Designs and Test Markets 272

part 3
Designing and Conducting Surveys 309

chapter 10
Sampling: Theories, Designs, and Plans 310

chapter 11
Overview of Measurement: Construct Development and Scaling 332

chapter 12
Advanced Measurement Designs for Survey Research 366

chapter 13
Questionnaire Design: Concepts and Issues 402

part 4
Data Preparation, Analysis, and Reporting Results 451

chapter 14
Preparing Survey Data for Analysis 452

chapter 15
Data Analysis: Testing for Significant Differences 480

chapter 16
Data Analysis: Testing for Associations 516

chapter 17
Overview of Multivariate Analysis Methods 558

chapter 18
Preparing and Presenting Marketing Research Reports 598

Glossary 627
Endnotes 651
Name Index 663
Subject Index 665

contents

part 1

The Role and Value of Marketing Research 1

chapter 1

Marketing Research and Managerial Decision Making 2

MARKETING RESEARCH AND DECISION MAKING: SAAB CARS USA 3

Value of Marketing Research Information 4

Relationship Marketing and the Marketing Research Process 4

Relationship Marketing and Customer Relationship Management 5

Marketing Planning and Decision Making 7

Marketing Situation Analysis 8

Market Analysis 8

Market Segmentation 8

Competitive Analysis 9

Marketing Strategy Design 9

Target Marketing 9

Positioning 9

New-Product Planning 10

Marketing Program Development 10

Product Portfolio Analysis 11

Distribution Decisions 11

Pricing Decisions 13

Integrated Marketing Communications 14

Marketing Program Implementation and Control 15

Marketing Program Control 16

Information Analysis 16

The Marketing Research Industry 16

Types of Marketing Research Firms 17

A CLOSER LOOK AT RESEARCH—IN THE FIELD: YAHOO! AND AC NIELSEN: A MARKETING RESEARCH MARRIAGE THROUGH TECHNOLOGY 18

Changing Skills for a Changing Industry 19

Ethics in Marketing Research Practices 20

Unethical Activities by the Client/Research User 20

Unethical Activities by the Research Provider or Research Company 20

Unethical Activities by the Respondent 21

Marketing Research Codes of Ethics 21

Emerging Trends and Organization of This Book 24

Continuing Case: The Santa Fe Grill Mexican Restaurant 25

MARKETING RESEARCH IN ACTION: CONTINUING CASE: THE SANTA FE GRILL 26

Summary of Learning Objectives 28

Key Terms and Concepts 29

Review Questions 29

Discussion Questions 29

Appendix 1.A: Careers in Marketing Research with a Look at Federal Express 31

chapter 2

Overview of the Research Process and Research Proposals 34

SOLVING MARKETING PROBLEMS USING A SYSTEMATIC PROCESS 35

Value of the Research Process 36

Changing View of the Marketing Research Process 36

Determining the Need for Information Research 38

A CLOSER LOOK AT RESEARCH—IN THE FIELD: MANAGEMENT DECISION MAKERS AND MARKETING RESEARCHERS 39

Overview of the Research Process 42

Transforming Data into Knowledge 42

Interrelatedness of the Steps and the Research Process 44

Phase I: Determine the Research Problem 45

Step 1: Identify and Clarify Information Needs 45

A CLOSER LOOK AT RESEARCH—IN THE FIELD: "CAN I GET A NEW COKE PLEASE?" 46

Step 2: Define the Research Problem and Questions 48
A CLOSER LOOK AT RESEARCH—SMALL BUSINESS IMPLICATIONS: FORD FOUNDATION 50
Step 3: Specify Research Objectives and Confirm the Information Value 50
Phase II: Select the Research Design 51
Step 4: Determine the Research Design and Data Sources 51
Step 5: Develop the Sampling Plan and Sample Size 52
Step 6: Examine Measurement Issues and Scales 53
Step 7: Design and Pretest the Questionnaire 54
Phase III: Execute the Research Design 54
Step 8: Collect and Prepare Data 54
Step 9: Analyze Data 56
Step 10: Interpret Data to Create Knowledge 56
Phase IV: Communicate the Research Results 56
Step 11: Prepare and Present the Final Report 56
Develop a Research Proposal 56
MARKETING RESEARCH IN ACTION: WHAT DOES A RESEARCH PROPOSAL LOOK LIKE? EXCELSIOR HOTEL PREFERRED GUEST CARD RESEARCH PROPOSAL 58
Summary of Learning Objectives 61
Key Terms and Concepts 62
Review Questions 62
Discussion Questions 62

chapter 3
Information-Driven Technology and the Research Process 64
GOOGLE FOR KNOWLEDGE 65
Value of New Technology in Marketing Research Practices 66
Technology and the Marketing Research Process 66
Research Problems, Objectives, and Technological Approaches 66
Portals as Problem Detectors and Opportunity Assessors 67
Influence of Technology on Research Designs and Data Sources 68
Benefits of Transactional and Analytical Customer Data 68
Technology and Data Enhancement: Biometrics and Smartcards 69
Technology and Primary Data Collection 70
Nontraditional Technology-Driven Data Collection Methods 73
Social Networking as a Marketing Research Tool 73
Social Networks and Focus Group Interviews 74
A CLOSER LOOK AT RESEARCH—USING TECHNOLOGY: ONLINE OPTIONS FOR FOCUS GROUP RESEARCH 75
Technology-Driven Data Analysis in Marketing Research 76
Disseminating Marketing Research Results through Research Portals 77
MARKETING RESEARCH IN ACTION: CONTINUING CASE: THE SANTA FE GRILL AND TECHNOLOGY 79
Summary of Learning Objectives 80
Key Terms and Concepts 81
Review Questions 81
Discussion Questions 81

chapter 4
Market Intelligence and Database Research 82
CONSUMER DATABASES ENHANCE CUSTOMER RETENTION 83
Value of Market Intelligence and Database Information 84
Databases and Market Intelligence 84
Transforming Marketing Research into Market Intelligence 85
A CLOSER LOOK AT RESEARCH—IN THE FIELD: MARKETING INTELLIGENCE IN THE FINANCIAL SERVICES INDUSTRY 86
Strategic Use of Customer Information 86
Information Based on a Transactional Focus 87
Companywide Approach to Using Database Information 87
Technology Support of Market Intelligence 87
Marketing Databases 88
Purposes of a Customer Database 89

Marketing Research and Data Enhancement 90
Effective Development of Enhanced Databases 91
Dynamics of Database Development 92
Rules of Thumb in Database Development 93
Database Technology 93
Data Warehousing 96
Marketing-Related Data and Data Warehousing 97
Data Mining: Transforming Data into Knowledge 98
The Data Mining Process 98
Database Modeling 100
A CLOSER LOOK AT RESEARCH—IN THE FIELD: DATABASE AMERICA INTRODUCES SALESLEADS™—FIRST WEB-BASED LEAD-GENERATING SERVICE FOR CONSUMERS AND SMALL BUSINESSES 101
Scoring Models 102
Lifetime Value Models 103
MARKETING RESEARCH IN ACTION: THE FUNCTION OF DATABASES WITHIN THE FINANCIAL SERVICES INDUSTRY: LEADING WITH DATA 105
Summary of Learning Objectives 109
Key Terms and Concepts 109
Review Questions 110
Discussion Questions 110

part 2
Designing Marketing Research Projects 111

chapter 5
Secondary Research: Designs, Searches, and Sources 112
SECONDARY RESEARCH GOES GLOBAL 113
Value of Secondary Research 114
Nature and Scope of Secondary Research 114
Role of Secondary Data in Marketing Research 116
Secondary Data and Customer Relationship Management 116
Secondary Data and the Marketing Research Process 117
Secondary Research Designs 118
Literature Reviews 118
A CLOSER LOOK AT RESEARCH—IN THE FIELD: GOOGLE AND EBAY FORM NEW "CLICK-TO-CALL" ALLIANCE 119
Electronic Searches: Popular Sources 121
Scholarly Research 123
Online Electronic Searches for Secondary Data 124
Advantages and Limitations of Using Secondary Data 129
Advantages of Secondary Data 129
Limitations of Secondary Data 130
Internal and External Sources of Secondary Data 131
Internal Secondary Data Sources 131
External Secondary Data Sources 133
North American Industry Classification System (NAICS) 134
Government Documents 136
Secondary Sources of Business Information 137
A CLOSER LOOK AT RESEARCH—IN THE FIELD: SECONDARY DATA AND THE MARKET INTELLIGENCE PROCESS: PLACING A VALUE ON CUSTOMER INFORMATION 138
Continuing Case: Using Secondary Data for the Santa Fe Grill 139
Syndicated Sources of Secondary Data 140
Characteristics of Syndicated Data Sources 140
Consumer Panels 140
Store Audits 142
The Internet as a Growing Source of Secondary Data 143
A CLOSER LOOK AT RESEARCH—IN THE FIELD: CUSTOMIZED DATA 145
MARKETING RESEARCH IN ACTION: CONTINUING CASE: SANTA FE GRILL CONSIDERING EXPANSION 146
Summary of Learning Objectives 147
Key Terms and Concepts 148
Review Questions 148
Discussion Questions 149

chapter 6
Exploratory Research Using Qualitative and Observation Methods 150
CULTURE CODES BRING INSIGHTS TO CHRYSLER'S JEEP 151
Value of Exploratory Research 152

Observation and Questioning as Methods of Collecting Primary Data 152
Overview of Qualitative and Quantitative Research Methods 153
Quantitative Research Methods 154
Qualitative Research Methods 154
When to Use Qualitative Research Methods in Exploratory Designs 155
Advantages and Disadvantages of Qualitative Research Methods 156
Questioning Techniques in Qualitative Research 158
In-Depth Interviews 158
A CLOSER LOOK AT RESEARCH—IN THE FIELD: INSIGHTS INTO BUSINESS CUSTOMERS' HOTEL NEEDS AND WANTS 160
Focus Group Interviews 161
A CLOSER LOOK AT RESEARCH—IN THE FIELD: DIMENSIONS OF SERVICE QUALITY 165
Conducting Focus Group Interviews 165
A CLOSER LOOK AT RESEARCH—SMALL BUSINESS IMPLICATIONS: MODERATOR'S GUIDE FOR VAIL PERFORMING ARTS PROGRAM FOCUS GROUP INTERVIEW SESSIONS 173
Impact of New Technologies on Focus Group Research 179
GLOBAL INSIGHTS: UNDERSTANDING FOCUS GROUP RESEARCH ABROAD 180
Other Qualitative Research Methods 182
GLOBAL INSIGHTS: CUSTOM DOORS, INC., ENTERS THE JAPANESE COMMERCIAL MARKET 183
Continuing Case: Santa Fe Grill Mexican Restaurant 189
Overview of Observation Methods 189
Appropriate Conditions for Using Observation Techniques 190
Unique Characteristics of Observation Techniques 191
Selecting the Appropriate Observation Method 195
Benefits and Limitations of Observation Methods 196
ETHICS: MINIMIZING BIAS IN RESEARCH DESIGNS: SUBJECTS' UNAWARENESS CAN RAISE MANY QUESTIONS 197
MARKETING RESEARCH IN ACTION: CONTENT ANALYSIS: THE FUTURE OF FOR-PROFIT HIGHER EDUCATION 198
Summary of Learning Objectives 199
Key Terms and Concepts 200
Review Questions 201
Discussion Questions 201

chapter 7
Analyzing and Reporting Qualitative Research 204
WIRELESS COMMUNICATION'S IMPACT ON SOCIAL BEHAVIOR 205
Nature of Qualitative Data Analysis 206
Qualitative versus Quantitative Analysis 206
The Process of Analyzing Qualitative Data 208
Managing the Data Collection Effort 208
Step 1: Data Reduction 208
Step 2: Data Display 215
Step 3: Conclusion Drawing/Verification 217
Writing the Report 222
Introduction 222
Analysis of the Data/Findings 223
Conclusions and Recommendations: Marketing Implications 223
Continuing Case: Using Qualitative Research for the Santa Fe Grill 224
MARKETING RESEARCH IN ACTION: ANALYZING QUALITATIVE DATA: HOTEL TRAVELERS' CHEERS AND JEERS AT THEIR EXPERIENCES 225
Summary of Learning Objectives 227
Key Terms and Concepts 228
Review Questions 228
Discussion Questions 228

chapter 8
Descriptive Research Designs Using Surveys 230
MALES LIKE MALL SHOPPING: INSIGHTS TO THEIR SHOPPING INTERESTS 231
Value of Descriptive Survey Research Designs 232
Descriptive Designs and Surveys in Quantitative Research 232
Overview of Constructs, Variables, and Relationships 233
Overview of Survey Research Methods 235
Advantages of Survey Methods 235
Disadvantages of Survey Methods 236

Types of Errors in Survey Research 237
Sampling Error 237
Nonsampling Errors 237
Types of Survey Methods 244
Person-Administered Surveys 244
Telephone-Administered Surveys 246
ETHICS—USING TECHNOLOGY: SUGGING IS A FEDERAL OFFENSE 248
Self-Administered Surveys 252
Online Survey Methods 255
A CLOSER LOOK AT RESEARCH—USING TECHNOLOGY: VIRTUAL REALITY IN MARKETING RESEARCH 259
Selecting the Appropriate Survey Method 260
Situational Characteristics 261
Task Characteristics 263
Respondent Characteristics 264
MARKETING RESEARCH IN ACTION: CONTINUING CASE: SANTA FE GRILL MEXICAN RESTAURANT: DEVELOPING RESEARCH QUESTIONS, FORMING HYPOTHESES, AND SELECTING A SURVEY METHOD 267
Summary of Learning Objectives 268
Key Terms and Concepts 269
Review Questions 270
Discussion Questions 270

chapter 9
Causal Research Designs and Test Markets 272

TEST MARKETING TO GAUGE NEW-PRODUCT ACCEPTANCE: LEE APPAREL COMPANY 273
Value of Experimentation and Test Marketing 274
Overview of Causal Research Designs 274
The Nature of Experimentation 275
A CLOSER LOOK AT RESEARCH—USING TECHNOLOGY: BEHAVIORSCAN: A DEVICE USED FOR TESTING NEW PRODUCTS AND MARKETING PROGRAMS 276
How Variables Are Used in Experimental Designs 277
The Role of Theory in Experimental Designs 279
Laboratory and Field Experiments 280
Validity and Reliability Concerns with Experimental Designs 280
Internal Validity 281
External Validity 282
Construct Validity 283
Reliability of Experimental Research Designs 285
Improving the Internal and External Validity of Experimental Designs 285
Types of Experimental Research Designs 286
Pre-experimental Designs 287
True Experimental Designs 288
Quasi-experimental Designs 291
Field Experiments 293
Factorial Designs 293
Latin Square Designs 294
Considerations in Using Field Experiments 295
Validity Concerns 295
Test Marketing 296
Traditional Test Markets 296
Controlled Test Markets 297
A CLOSER LOOK AT RESEARCH—IN THE FIELD: GOOD TEST MARKET RESULTS DO NOT GUARANTEE NEW-PRODUCT SUCCESS: COORS GIVES THE COLD SHOULDER TO WINE COOLERS 298
Electronic Test Markets 298
A CLOSER LOOK AT RESEARCH—IN THE FIELD: STARBUCKS HAS UPSCALE CONCEPT PERCOLATING 299
Simulated Test Markets 299
Web-Based TV Test Markets 300
Virtual Test Markets 301
A CLOSER LOOK AT RESEARCH—IN THE FIELD: GOODYEAR STEPS OUT OF ITS OWN STORES 302
Other Issues in Test Marketing 302
MARKETING RESEARCH IN ACTION: RIDERS FITS NEW DATABASE INTO BRAND LAUNCH: THE INITIAL LAUNCH 304
Summary of Learning Objectives 306
Key Terms and Concepts 307
Review Questions 307
Discussion Questions 308

part 3
Designing and Conducting Surveys 309

chapter 10
Sampling: Theories, Designs, and Plans 310

TECHNOLOGY AND SAMPLING PROCEDURES—CAN THE TWO EVER CO-EXIST? 311
The Value of Sampling Methods in Marketing Research 312
Types of Probability Sampling Designs 313
Simple Random Sampling 313
Systematic Random Sampling 314
Stratified Random Sampling 316
Cluster Sampling 317
ETHICS—SAMPLING METHODS: U.S. CENSUS BUREAU MISLEADS CONGRESS 319
Types of Nonprobability Sampling Designs 322
Convenience Sampling 322
Judgment Sampling 322
Quota Sampling 323
Snowball Sampling 323
Determining the Appropriate Sampling Design 324
Research Objectives 325
Degree of Accuracy 325
Resources 325
Time Frame 325
Knowledge of the Target Population 325
Scope of the Research 325
A CLOSER LOOK AT RESEARCH—USING TECHNOLOGY: THE INTERNET PROVIDES VALUABLE INTELLIGENCE INFORMATION 326
Statistical Analysis 326
Steps in Developing a Sampling Plan 326
Step 1: Define the Target Population 327
Step 2: Select the Data Collection Method 327
Step 3: Identify the Sampling Frame(s) Needed 327
Step 4: Select the Appropriate Sampling Method 328
Step 5: Determine Necessary Sample Sizes and Overall Contact Rates 328
Step 6: Create an Operating Plan for Selecting Sampling Units 328
Step 7: Execute the Operational Plan 328
MARKETING RESEARCH IN ACTION: CONTINUING CASE: SANTA FE GRILL: DEVELOPING A SAMPLING PLAN FOR A NEW MENU INITIATIVE SURVEY 329
Summary of Learning Objectives 330
Key Terms and Concepts 330
Review Questions 331
Discussion Questions 331

chapter 11
Overview of Measurement: Construct Development and Scaling 332
SANTA FE GRILL MEXICAN RESTAURANT: PREDICTING CUSTOMER LOYALTY 333
Value of Measurement in Information Research 334
Overview of the Measurement Process 334
Construct Development 335
Abstractness of the Construct 336
Determining Dimensionality of the Construct 336
Assessing Construct Validity 337
Construct Operationalization 338
A CLOSER LOOK AT RESEARCH—IN THE FIELD: PROBLEM IN CONSTRUCT DEVELOPMENT 339
Basic Concepts of Scale Measurement 340
Types of Data Collected in Research Practices 340
The Nature of Scale Measurement 342
Properties of Scale Measurements 342
Basic Levels of Scales 344
Developing and Refining Measurement Scales 348
Criteria for Scale Development 349
A CLOSER LOOK AT RESEARCH—USING TECHNOLOGY: MACRO CONSULTING, INC. 358
MARKETING RESEARCH IN ACTION: PART 1: WHAT YOU CAN LEARN FROM A CUSTOMER LOYALTY INDEX 359
Summary of Learning Objectives 362
Key Terms and Concepts 363
Review Questions 363
Discussion Questions 364

chapter 12
Advanced Measurement Designs for Survey Research 366
ATTITUDE AND IMAGE MEASUREMENTS IN MARKETING RESEARCH 367
Value of Attitude Measurement 368
Nature of Attitudes and Marketplace Behaviors 368
Components of Attitudes 369
Measuring Attitudes and Behaviors 370
Likert Scale 370
Semantic Differential Scale 372

Behavior Intention Scale 377
Strengths and Weaknesses of Attitude and Behavior Intention Scales 378
Other Types of Comparative and Noncomparative Scales 379
A CLOSER LOOK AT RESEARCH—SMALL BUSINESS IMPLICATIONS: INSTANT ON-SITE CUSTOMER SATISFACTION FEEDBACK 380
Comments on Single-Item and Multiple-Item Scales 384
Measurement Design Issues 384
MARKETING RESEARCH IN ACTION: PART 2: SCALE MEASUREMENTS USED IN CREATING A CUSTOMER LOYALTY INDEX 387
Summary of Learning Objectives 389
Key Terms and Concepts 390
Review Questions 390
Discussion Questions 391
Appendix 12.A: Trilogy and Affect Global Approaches 392

chapter 13
Questionnaire Design: Concepts and Issues 402
CAN SURVEYS BE USED TO DEVELOP UNIVERSITY RESIDENCE LIFE PLANS? 403
Value of Questionnaires in Marketing Research 404
Questionnaire Design 405
Theoretical Components of a Questionnaire 405
Description versus Prediction 409
A CLOSER LOOK AT RESEARCH—USING TECHNOLOGY: COMPUTERIZED QUESTIONNAIRES 410
Accuracy versus Precision 410
Value of a Good Survey Instrument 410
Flowerpot Approach to Questionnaire Design 411
Impact of the Flowerpot Approach on Questionnaire Development 415
Developing a Flowerpot-Designed Questionnaire 416
Developing Cover Letters 426
The Role of a Cover Letter 426
Guidelines for Developing Cover Letters 426
A CLOSER LOOK AT RESEARCH—IN THE FIELD: COVER LETTER 432
ETHICS: TELEPHONE SURVEY GOES SOUR 434
Other Documents Associated with Survey Instrument Designs 434
Supervisor Instructions 435
Interviewer Instructions 436
Screening Forms 436
Quota Sheets 438
Rating Cards 438
Call Record Sheets 439
MARKETING RESEARCH IN ACTION: CONTINUING CASE: DESIGNING A QUESTIONNAIRE TO ASSESS THE DINING HABITS AND PATTERNS OF THE SANTA FE GRILL'S CUSTOMERS 442
Summary of Learning Objectives 448
Key Terms and Concepts 449
Review Questions 449
Discussion Questions 450

part 4
Data Preparation, Analysis, and Reporting Results 451

chapter 14
Preparing Survey Data for Analysis 452
WAL-MART AND SCANNER TECHNOLOGY 453
Value of Preparing Data for Analysis 454
Data Validation 455
Editing and Coding 456
Asking the Proper Questions 456
Accurate Recording of Answers 456
Correct Screening Questions 456
Responses to Open-Ended Questions 456
The Coding Process 461
Data Entry 464
Error Detection 466
Data Tabulation 467
A CLOSER LOOK AT RESEARCH—IN THE FIELD: DATA COLLECTION SHOULD NOT BE MANUAL LABOR 468
One-Way Tabulation 468
Descriptive Statistics 471
Graphical Illustration of Data 471
MARKETING RESEARCH IN ACTION: EXAMINING DATA: DELI DEPOT 474
Summary of Learning Objectives 478
Key Terms and Concepts 478

Review Questions 478
Discussion Questions 479

chapter 15
Data Analysis: Testing for Significant Differences 480

STATISTICAL SOFTWARE MAKES DATA ANALYSIS EASY 481
Value of Testing for Differences in Data 482
Analyzing the Santa Fe Grill Database 482
Analyzing Groups 482
Select Cases Analysis 483
Measures of Central Tendency 483
Mean 483
Mode 484
Median 484
SPSS Applications—Measures of Central Tendency 484
Measures of Dispersion 486
Range 486
Standard Deviation 487
SPSS Applications—Measures of Dispersion 487
Analyzing Relationships in Sample Data 488
Sample Statistics and Population Parameters 489
Univariate Statistical Tests 489
SPSS Application—Univariate Hypothesis Test 490
Bivariate Statistical Tests 490
Comparing Means: Independent versus Related Samples 497
Using the *t*-Test to Compare Two Means 497
SPSS Application—Independent Samples *t*-Test 498
SPSS Application—Paired Samples *t*-Test 498
Analysis of Variance (ANOVA) 499
Perceptual Mapping 504
Perceptual Mapping Applications in Marketing Research 504
Continuing Case: The Santa Fe Grill 505
MARKETING RESEARCH IN ACTION: EXAMINING RESTAURANT IMAGE POSITIONS: REMINGTON'S STEAK HOUSE 506
Summary of Learning Objectives 513
Key Terms and Concepts 513
Review Questions 513
Discussion Questions 514

chapter 16
Data Analysis: Testing for Associations 516

DATA MINING HELPS REBUILD PROCTER & GAMBLE AS A GLOBAL POWERHOUSE 517
Examining Relationships between Variables 518
Covariation and Variable Relationships 519
Correlation Analysis 521
Pearson Correlation Coefficient Assumptions 523
SPSS Application—Pearson Correlation 523
Substantive Significance of the Correlation Coefficient 524
Influence of Measurement Scales on Correlation Analysis 525
SPSS Application—Spearman Rank Order Correlation 526
SPSS Application—Calculating Median Rankings 526
Regression Analysis 527
Fundamentals of Regression Analysis 528
Developing and Estimating the Regression Coefficients 530
SPSS Application—Bivariate Regression 532
Significance 535
Multiple Regression Analysis 535
Statistical Significance 536
Substantive Significance 537
SPSS Application—Multiple Regression 537
Multicollinearity and Multiple Regression Analysis 539
SPSS Application—Multicollinearity 540
Dummy Variables and Multiple Regression 543
SPSS Application—Use of Dummy Variables in Regression 543
MARKETING RESEARCH IN ACTION: CUSTOMER SATISFACTION SURVEY: THE ROLE OF EMPLOYEES IN DEVELOPING A CUSTOMER SATISFACTION PROGRAM 545
Summary of Learning Objectives 548
Key Terms and Concepts 548
Review Questions 549

Discussion Questions 549
Appendix 16.A: Formulas for Calculating Correlation and Regression Issues 551
Appendix 16.B: Examining Residuals 553

chapter 17
Overview of Multivariate Analysis Methods 558

MULTIVARIATE METHODS IMPACT OUR LIVES EVERY DAY 559
Value of Multivariate Techniques in Data Analysis 560
A CLOSER LOOK AT RESEARCH—SMALL BUSINESS IMPLICATIONS: XLSTAT 561
Classification of Multivariate Methods 561
- Dependence and Interdependence Methods 562
- Influence of Measurement Scales 562

GLOBAL INSIGHTS: ANALYSIS FROM GLOBAL RESEARCH MAY YIELD INTERESTING FINDINGS 563
Interdependence Methods 563
- Factor Analysis 563
- Cluster Analysis 572

Dependence Methods 579
- Discriminant Analysis 579

A CLOSER LOOK AT RESEARCH—USING TECHNOLOGY: DISCRIMINANT ANALYSIS—SPSS 580
- Conjoint Analysis 587

MARKETING RESEARCH IN ACTION: CLUSTER AND DISCRIMINANT ANALYSIS: DVD RECORDERS REMAIN POPULAR 591
Summary of Learning Objectives 596
Key Terms and Concepts 596
Review Questions 597
Discussion Questions 597

chapter 18
Preparing and Presenting Marketing Research Reports 598

IT TAKES MORE THAN NUMBERS TO COMMUNICATE 599
Value of Preparing the Marketing Research Report 600
Marketing Research Reports 600
Format of the Marketing Research Report 603
- Title Page 603
- Table of Contents 603
- Executive Summary 603
- Introduction 605
- Research Methods and Procedures 605
- Data Analysis and Findings 605
- Conclusions and Recommendations 618
- Limitations 618
- Appendices 619

Problems in Preparing the Marketing Research Report 619
The Critical Nature of Presentations 620
- Guidelines for Preparing the Visual Presentation 620

MARKETING RESEARCH IN ACTION: REPORTING RESEARCH FINDINGS: WRITING THE MARKETING RESEARCH REPORT FOR A FOCUS GROUP INTERVIEW 621
Summary of Learning Objectives 625
Key Terms and Concepts 625
Review Questions 625
Discussion Questions 626

Glossary 627
Endnotes 651
Name Index 663
Subject Index 665

Marketing Research

In a Digital Information Environment

part 1

The Role and Value of Marketing Research

chapter 1

Marketing Research and Managerial Decision Making

Learning Objectives

After reading this chapter, you will be able to:

1. Describe the impact of marketing research on marketing decision making.
2. Demonstrate the relationship between marketing research and marketing planning.
3. Provide examples of marketing research studies.
4. Understand the scope and focus of the marketing research industry.
5. Explain the ethical dimensions of marketing research.
6. Discuss emerging trends and new skills needed in marketing research.

"I don't know how you're supposed to make intelligent decisions without facts."

—WILLIAM DILLARD SR.,
Founder and Chairman,
Dillard's Department Stores[1]

Marketing Research and Decision Making: Saab Cars USA

Saab Cars USA imports more than 37,000 Saab sedans, convertibles, and wagons annually and distributes the cars to 220 U.S. dealerships. Saab competes in the premium automotive market with rivals who attract customers through aggressive marketing campaigns, reduced prices, and inexpensive financing. Saab decided that the answer to beating its competition was not to spend capital on additional promotion, but to invest in a highly sophisticated marketing research program.

Until recently, the company collected customer and dealer information from traditional surveys and focus group research through three primary channels: (1) dealer networks, (2) customer assistance centers, and (3) regional financial centers. At each level Saab obtained a wealth of data ranging from customer satisfaction data, to service improvement information, performance data on various models, and promotional effectiveness data. All of this data was stored independently by each channel in its own customer database of information. This splintered approach to managing customer information caused numerous problems for the company. For example, a prospective customer might receive a direct mail promotion from Saab one week, then an e-mail with an unrelated promotion from the financial center the next week. The local dealer might not know of either activity, and therefore might use an inappropriate sales approach when the customer visited the showroom that weekend. Al Fontova, marketing research director with Saab Cars USA, stated that he had information on over 3 million customers and files for over 100 dealers at three different levels within the company. Analyzing this data in aggregate was complicated, inefficient, and costly.[2]

Saab required a solution that would provide a consolidated customer view from all three data collection points. As a result, Saab implemented a data warehouse and data mart solution that provides key customer contact employees within the company a 360-degree view of each customer, including prior service-related information, satisfaction data, and feedback on quality improvement issues. The system is shared with dealers through a Web-based portal allowing them to coordinate national and local sales and marketing activities. These tracking capabilities have enabled Saab to measure the sales results of specific promotional campaigns, implement more effective vehicle service processes, and even obtain direct customer input on certain features and options built into Saab cars.

Based on the new system, promotional costs have decreased by 5 percent, customer visits to dealers have increased by 20 percent, customer satisfaction has increased 25 percent, and Saab has been able to gain a single view of its customers across the multiple data collection channels.

Value of Marketing Research Information

The Saab example illustrates how properly organized marketing research operates to solve business problems and clarify emerging trends. Developing a sound research process based on customer feedback whose analysis is accessible and usable enables any size business to make confident, cost-effective decisions, whether identifying new product opportunities or designing new approaches for communicating with customers.

Marketing research The function that links an organization to its market through the gathering of information.

The American Marketing Association defines **marketing research** as the function that links an organization to its market through the gathering of information. This information facilitates the identification and definition of market-driven opportunities and problems, as well as the development and evaluation of marketing actions. It enables the monitoring of marketing performance and improved understanding of marketing as a business process.[3]

Applying this definition to Saab Cars USA, we can see that Saab used marketing research information to identify product improvements, develop promotional strategies, and implement new data-gathering methods to better understand customers, activities that are part of *relationship building* and *customer relationship management,* discussed later in the chapter.

Marketing research is a systematic process. Tasks in this process include designing methods for collecting information, managing the information collection process, analyzing and interpreting results, and communicating findings to decision makers. This chapter provides an overview of marketing research as well as a fundamental understanding of its relationship to marketing. We first explain why firms use marketing research and give some examples of how marketing research can help companies make sound marketing decisions. Next we discuss who should use marketing research, and when.

The chapter also provides a general description of the activities companies use to collect marketing research information. We present an overview of the marketing research industry in order to clarify the relationship between the providers and the users of marketing information. The chapter closes with a discussion of the important role of ethics in marketing research. At the end of the chapter is an appendix on careers in marketing research.

Relationship Marketing and the Marketing Research Process

Marketing The process of planning and executing the pricing, promotion, and distribution of products, services, and ideas in order to create exchanges that satisfy both the firm and its customers.

The fundamental purpose of **marketing** is to enable firms to plan and execute the pricing, promotion, and distribution of products, services, and ideas in order to create exchanges that satisfy both the firm and its customers. Creating this exchange is the responsibility of the firm's marketing manager. Marketing managers focus on getting the right goods and services (1) to the right people, (2) at the right place and time, (3) with the right price, (4) through the use of the right blend of promotional techniques. By doing their job marketing managers enhance the likelihood of a successful marketing effort. But this does not eliminate the element of uncertainty. Uncertainty emerges to a great extent from unpredictable consumers and competitors. In order to reduce uncertainty, marketing managers must have accurate, relevant, and timely information. Marketing research generates that information.

Relationship marketing The strategy of forging long-term relationships with customers.

Today, successful businesses follow a business strategy known as **relationship marketing.** Companies pursuing relationship marketing build long-term relationships with customers by offering real value for the price. The company is rewarded with repeat purchases, increased sales, and higher market share and profits. Apple, for example, is highly focused on relationship marketing. Apple views its customers as individuals having unique needs and desires. Its marketing research programs are directed toward measuring these aspects of the customer, then developing its entire marketing program around these metrics to build long-term relationships with customers by offering them the value they desire.

The success of any relationship marketing program depends on knowledge of the market, effective training programs, and employee empowerment and teamwork:

- **Knowledge of the market.** For an organization to build relationships with customers, it must possess relevant information about those customers. The company must understand customer needs and desires in order to deliver satisfaction to the customer. Gaining a solid and detailed knowledge of the market is the basic function of those with marketing research responsibilities in the company.
- **Effective training programs.** Building excellence in relationships with customers begins with the employee. In the eyes of many consumers, the employee *is* the company. Therefore, it is critical that the actions and behaviors of employees throughout the entire company, not just those charged with marketing research responsibilities, be marketing oriented. Many organizations such as McDonald's, Disney, and American Express have corporate universities designed to train employees in customer relations. Moreover, these universities train employees in the proper ways to gather data from customers. For example, emphasizing paying attention to informal customer comments, discussing with customers issues related to competing products, and encouraging customers to use comment cards are data gathering practices American Express teaches its employees.
- **Employee empowerment and teamwork.** Many successful companies encourage their employees to be more proactive in solving customer problems. On-the-spot problem solving is known as **empowerment.** Organizations are now developing cross-functional teams of employees dedicated to proactively developing and delivering customer solutions. Teamwork designed to accomplish common goals was evident in the chapter opening example about Saab Cars USA, which used teamwork to consolidate three levels of customer data, collected independently across three divisions of the company, into a more efficient system for improving customer satisfaction.

Empowerment Employees can solve problems immediately without requesting permission

Employee empowerment and teamwork facilitate relationship building with a company's customers. These along with the dimensions of training and knowledge of the market form the catalyst for implementing the relationship marketing strategy commonly referred to as *customer relationship management.*

Relationship Marketing and Customer Relationship Management

Customer relationship management, or CRM, is the process used to implement a relationship marketing strategy. CRM gathers market-driven data to learn more about customers' needs and behaviors for the purpose of delivering added value and satisfaction to

Customer relationship management The process used for implementing a relationship marketing strategy.

the customer. The data, in conjunction with information technology, are then used to develop stronger relationships with customers. Fundamentally, CRM is based on a number of concepts focusing on the marketplace and the consumer. Specifically, these concepts address the following:

Customer/market knowledge is the starting point of any CRM process. The role of marketing research is to collect and gather information from multiple sources about the customer. Key data to be captured include demographics, psychographics, buying and service history, preferences, complaints, and other communications the customer has with the company. Data can be internal through customers' interaction with the company, or external through surveys or other data collection methods.

Data integration involves setting up a data warehouse to integrate information from multiple sources into a single shared depository of data. The data are used to understand and predict customer behavior and are made available to all functional areas of the company so that anyone who interacts with the customer will have a history of the customer.

Information technology has facilitated the expansion of marketing research activities. The role of marketing research is to facilitate data integration through technology-driven techniques. These techniques perform functions such as basic reporting on customers, data mining, and statistical analysis.

Customer profiles are created and used to improve marketing decisions. Data are collected, integrated into data warehouses, and used to develop customer profiles. Profiles are then made available to all functional areas of the company utilizing the appropriate information technology.

These concepts are embodied in a variety of outcomes based on the decision making and planning objectives of the company (introducing new products, growing new market segments, evaluating advertising campaigns). The overriding goal is to provide the necessary data and technology to monitor customer changes while building and maintaining long-term customer relationships.

Information sharing All functional areas of the business have the information they need to improve decision making.

Executive dashboard An interactive computer terminal or screen that organizes and presents information in a way that is easy for executives to read and understand.

Information sharing ensures that all functional areas of the business have the information they need to improve decision making. Increasingly information is being shared through the effective use of *executive dashboards*. An **executive dashboard** is an intranet for a select group of managers who are the main decision makers in the company. Dashboards display the key metrics on which the company wants everyone to focus. Their purpose is to give managers a snapshot of the current status of their business, including recent positive and negative trends, so they can react quickly. This on-screen display of metrics is similar to the driver's console in a car, as the name implies. Just as the automobile's dashboard provides all the critical information needed to operate the vehicle at a glance, a business intelligence dashboard serves a similar purpose whether managers are using it to make strategic decisions, run the daily operations of a team, or perform tasks that involve only their area of responsibility. Dashboards typically are used for displaying metrics defined by the organization, such as products sold by region, defects per thousand shipped, or student grades by faculty. These metrics often are displayed as key performance indicators (KPIs), and a typical dashboard brings several KPIs together across critical aspects of the business. Dashboards are a key component of information sharing and they increase the likelihood of successful customer relationship management programs. Additional discussion of dashboards is provided in Chapter 3.

Marketing Planning and Decision Making

Marketing managers make many marketing decisions. These decisions vary dramatically in both focus and complexity. For example, managers must decide which new markets to penetrate, which products to introduce, and which new business opportunities to pursue. Such broad decisions usually require consideration of a variety of alternative approaches. Conversely, decisions regarding advertising effectiveness, product positioning, or sales tracking, while still very complex, are somewhat narrower in focus. Such decisions usually concentrate on a specific advertising campaign, a particular brand, or a specific market segment, as well as monitoring performance.

Regardless of the complexity or focus of the decision-making process, managers must have accurate information to make the right decisions. The entire marketing planning process is a series of decisions that must be made with high levels of confidence about the outcome. It is therefore not surprising that a sound marketing research process is the foundation of market planning.

Exhibit 1.1 lists some of the research-related tasks necessary for marketing decision making. While the list is by no means exhaustive, it illustrates the relationship between

eXHIBIT 1.1 Marketing Decision Making and Related Marketing Research Tasks

Marketing Planning Process	Marketing Research Task
Marketing Situation Analysis	**Situation Research Efforts**
Market analysis	Opportunity assessment
Market segmentation	Benefit and lifestyle studies
	Descriptive studies
Competition analysis	Importance-performance analysis
Marketing Program Design	**Program-Driven Research Efforts**
Target marketing	Target market analysis
Positioning	Positioning (perceptual mapping)
New-product planning	Concept and product testing
	Test marketing
Marketing Program Development	**Program Development Research**
Product portfolio decisions	Customer satisfaction studies
	Service quality studies
Distribution decisions	Cycle time research
	Retailing research
	Logistic assessment
Pricing decisions	Demand analysis
	Sales forecasting
Integrated marketing communications	Advertising effectiveness studies
	Attitudinal research
	Sales tracking
Program Implementation and Control	**Performance Analysis**
Marketing control	Product analysis
	Environmental forecasting
Critical information analysis	Marketing decision support systems

marketing planning and marketing research. The following sections describe these relationships in more detail.

Marketing Situation Analysis

The purpose of a situation analysis is to monitor marketing programs and determine whether changes are necessary. A situation analysis includes three decision areas: market analysis, market segmentation, and competition analysis. When conducting a situation analysis, marketing researchers should:

1. Locate and identify new market opportunities for a company (use *opportunity assessment*).
2. Identify groups of customers in a product/market who possess similar needs, characteristics, and preferences (use *benefit and lifestyle studies, descriptive studies*).
3. Identify existing and potential competitors' strengths and weaknesses (use *importance-performance analysis*).

Market Analysis

Opportunity assessment Involves collecting information on product markets for the purpose of forecasting how they will change.

The research task related to market analysis is **opportunity assessment.** Opportunity assessment involves collecting market information to forecast changes. Companies gather information relevant to macroenvironmental trends (political and regulatory, economic and social, and cultural and technological) and assess how those trends will influence the product market.

The role of marketing research is to gather information on macroenvironmental variables, and then interpret the information in terms of strategic consequences to the firm. Marketing researchers use three common approaches in the collection of macroenvironmental information:

1. Content analysis, in which researchers analyze various trade publications, newspaper articles, academic literature, or computer databases for information on trends in a given industry.
2. In-depth interviews, in which researchers conduct formal, structured interviews with experts in a given field.
3. Formal rating procedures, in which researchers use structured questionnaires to gather information on environmental occurrences.

These procedures will be discussed further in other chapters.

Market Segmentation

Benefit and lifestyle studies Examine similarities and differences in consumers' needs. Researchers use these studies to identify two or more segments within the market for a particular company's products.

A major component of market segmentation is **benefit and lifestyle studies,** which examine similarities and differences in consumers' needs. Researchers use these studies to identify segments within the market for a particular company's products. The objective is to collect information about customer characteristics, product benefits, and brand preferences. This data along with information on age, family size, income, and lifestyle is then compared to purchase patterns of particular products (cars, food, electronics, financial services) to develop market segmentation profiles.

Creating customer profiles and understanding behavioral characteristics are major focuses of any marketing research project. Determining why consumers behave as they do becomes the critical interaction between marketing research and program development. Chapter 8 will focus on this issue as well as selected marketing research approaches.

Competitive Analysis

Importance-performance analysis A research approach for evaluating competitors' strategies, strengths, limitations, and future plans.

Competitive analysis involves **importance-performance analysis,** an approach for evaluating competitors' strategies, strengths, limitations, and future plans. Importance-performance analysis asks consumers to identify key attributes that drive their purchase behavior. These attributes might include price, product performance, product quality, accuracy of shipping and delivery, or convenience of store location. Consumers are then asked to rank the importance of the attributes.

Following the importance rankings, researchers identify and evaluate competing firms. Highly ranked attributes are viewed as strengths, and lower ranked attributes are weaknesses. When competing firms are analyzed together, a company can see where its competitors are concentrating their marketing efforts and where they are falling below customer expectations.

Importance-performance analysis is just one technique for analyzing competition. This and other techniques for analyzing competition are discussed in Chapters 15 through 17.

Marketing Strategy Design

Information collected during a situation analysis is used to design a marketing strategy. At this stage of the planning process, companies identify target markets, develop positioning strategies for products and brands, test new products, and assess market potential.

Target Marketing

Target market analysis Information for identifying those people (or companies) that an organization wishes to serve.

Target market analysis provides useful information for identifying people (or companies) an organization wants to serve. In addition, it helps management determine the most efficient way of serving the targeted group. Target market analysis attempts to provide information on the following issues:

- New-product opportunities.
- Demographics, including attitudinal or behavioral characteristics.
- User profiles, usage patterns, and attitudes.
- The effectiveness of a firm's current marketing program.

To provide such information, marketing researchers must measure certain key variables as outlined in Exhibit 1.2.

Positioning

Positioning A process by which a company seeks to establish a meaning or general definition of its product offering that is consistent with customers' needs and preferences.

Positioning, or *perceptual mapping,* is a process by which a company seeks to establish perceptions of its product offering that are consistent with customers' needs and preferences. Companies accomplish this task by combining elements of the marketing mix in a manner that meets or exceeds the expectations of targeted customers.

EXHIBIT 1.2 Target Market Characteristics and Associated Variables Measured in Target Market Analysis

Target Market Characteristics	Key Variables to Measure
Demographics	Age, gender, race, income, religion, occupation, family size, geographic location, and zip code
Psychographics	Consumer activities, interests, and opinions
Product usage	Occasion (special use, gift); situation (climate, time of day, place); and usage context (heavy, medium, or light)
Brand preferences	Level of brand loyalty, salient product attributes, and product/brand awareness
Decision process	Size and frequency of purchase; propensity to purchase; risk of purchase (high, medium, low); and product involvement

The task of the marketing researcher is to provide an overview of the relationship between competitive product offerings based on a sample of respondents familiar with the product category being investigated. Consumers are asked to indicate how they view the similarities and dissimilarities among relevant product attributes for competing brands. For example, positioning among beers may indicate that customers decide between "popular versus premium" or "regional versus national" brands.

The information is then used to construct perceptual maps that transform the positioning data into "perceptual space." Perceptual mapping reflects the criteria on which brands are evaluated, typically representing product features viewed as important in a customer's selection process.

New-Product Planning

Concept and product testing and **test marketing** Information for decisions on product improvements and new-product introductions.

Research tasks related to new-product planning are **concept and product testing** and **test marketing,** which provide information for decisions on product improvements and new-product introductions. Product testing attempts to answer two fundamental questions: "How does a product perform for the customer?" and "How can a product be improved to exceed customer expectations?" In product tests, ideas are reshaped and redefined to identify those that not only meet but exceed market expectations. Specifically, product tests

1. Provide necessary information for designing and developing new products.
2. Determine whether new or improved products should replace current products.
3. Assess the appeal of alternative products for new target segments.
4. Identify products that are most preferred or actively sought compared to existing competitive offerings.

Marketing Program Development

The information requirements for marketing program development involve all the familiar components of the marketing mix: product, distribution, price, and promotion. Managers combine these components to create the total marketing effort for each market targeted.

While all this at first might seem self-evident, the success of the marketing program relies heavily on its *synergy.* That is, it is critical not only that the marketing mix contain the right elements but that they are delivered in the right amount, at the right time, and in the proper sequence. Ensuring this synergy, or optimal blend of marketing elements, is the responsibility of market researchers.

Product Portfolio Analysis

The total product line typically is the focal point of product portfolio analysis. Market researchers design studies that help product managers make decisions about reducing costs, altering marketing mixes, and changing or deleting product lines. Examples include customer satisfaction studies and service quality studies.

Customer satisfaction studies These studies assess the strengths and weaknesses that customers perceive in a firm's marketing mix.

Customer satisfaction studies assess the strengths and weaknesses customers perceive in a firm's marketing mix. While these studies are usually designed to analyze the marketing mix collectively, many firms elect to focus on customer responses to one element at a time (e.g., satisfaction with pricing policy). Regardless of their scope, customer satisfaction studies measure customer attitudes. Research reveals that customers' attitudes are linked to purchase intentions, brand switching, perceptions of company image, and brand loyalty.[4] Attitude information enables management to make decisions regarding product or brand repositioning, new-product introductions, new market segments, and the deletion of ineffective products. Chapters 11, 12, and 13 discuss the design of attitudinal research studies.

Service quality studies These studies are designed to measure the degree to which an organization conforms to the quality level customers expect.

Service quality studies measure the extent to which an organization conforms to the quality levels customers expect. Service quality studies examine physical facilities and equipment, appearance and behavior of company personnel, and dependability of products and programs. Specifically, employees are rated on their general willingness to help customers and provide them with prompt, friendly, courteous treatment.

A popular service quality study involves the use of *mystery shoppers* in which trained professional shoppers visit retail stores, restaurants, or financial institutions, for example, and "shop" for various goods and services. Atmosphere, friendliness, and customer appreciation are just a few of the dimensions evaluated by mystery shoppers. Some firms also patronize their competitors to see how their own performance compares. Data from service quality studies have been invaluable for decision making related to products or services. Companies can anticipate problems in product or service offerings before they create problems. Also, the data enable firms to assess themselves relative to competitors on key strengths and weaknesses.

Distribution Decisions

Distribution decisions involve distributors and retailers that link producers with end users. The distribution channel used by a producer can influence a buyer's perception of the brand. For example, Rolex watches are distributed through a limited number of retailers that project a prestigious image consistent with the Rolex brand name. Three common types of distribution-related research studies focus on cycle time, retailing store image, and supply chain efficiency.

Cycle time research A research method that centers on reducing the time between the initial contact and final delivery (or installation) of the product.

Many businesses trying to control inventory costs use *automatic replenishment systems* and *electronic data interchange*. Such inventory systems are based on **cycle time research,** which looks for ways of reducing the time between the initial contact with a customer and the final delivery (or installation) of the product.[5] This research is most often concerned with large distribution networks (manufacturers, wholesalers, retailers) but cycle time research does not ignore shorter channels of distribution (direct to retailer or end user), for in many cases, such as direct marketing channels, cycle time research also becomes critical in exploring ways to increase customer satisfaction and fulfillment. This type of marketing research collects information that helps reduce costs at critical points in the total cycle time, including exploring alternative methods of distribution to reduce the time for shipping and installation of goods.

Two typical research projects are *delivery expense studies* and *alternative delivery systems studies.* Both seek to obtain information related to expense and other analysis for alternative forms of delivery (USPS, FedEx, UPS) with the aim of increasing customer satisfaction. These studies are becoming common. Such studies are unique in that they rely heavily on internal company records or databases, or *secondary* research. Chapter 5 discusses information-gathering procedures for secondary data.

Retailing research
Studies on retailing topics such as trade area analysis, store image/perception, in-store traffic patterns, and location analyses.

Retailing research includes a variety of studies. Because retailers often are independent businesses, most of the studies we discuss are applicable to the retail environment. At the same time, the information needs of retailers are unique. Market research studies peculiar to retailers include trade area analysis, store image/perception studies, in-store traffic patterns, and location analyses.

Because retailing is a high-customer-contact activity, much retailing research focuses on database development through optical scanning procedures. As illustrated in Exhibit 1.3, every time a transaction is recorded using an optical scanner, the scanner notes the type of product, its manufacturer and vendor, and its size and price. Marketing research then categorizes the data and combines it with other relevant information to form a database. Retailers can determine the television programs their customers watch, the kinds of neighborhoods they live in, and the types of stores they prefer to patronize. Such information helps retailers determine the kind of merchandise to stock and what factors may influence purchase decisions.

Traditional brick-and-mortar retailers with an online presence as well as purely online retailers collect lots of information on online customer behavior. The information includes

EXHIBIT 1.3 Information Collection Process through Retail Optical Scanning Techniques

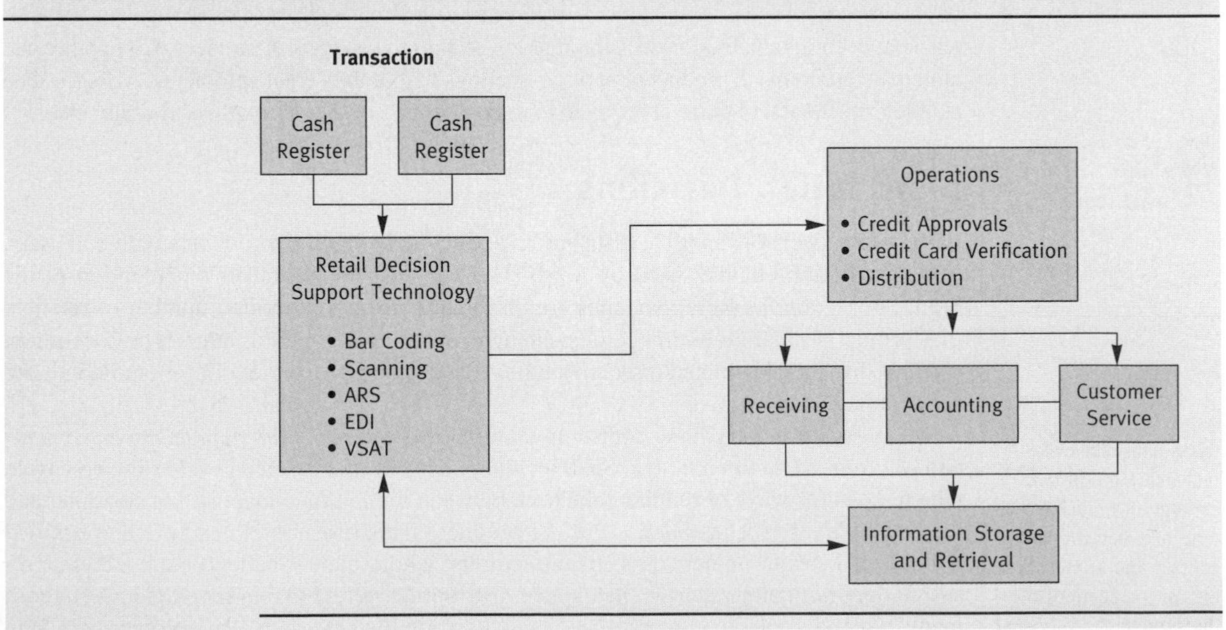

when a Web site is visited, which pages are viewed and for how long, the products examined and ultimately purchased, and how the visitor got to the Web site. This is critical information for retailers and other businesses because more than 50 percent of the time customers go online to obtain information about products and services before they purchase them, no matter how they make the purchase.

Logistics assessment Studies in logistics allow market researchers to conduct total cost analysis and service sensitivity analysis.

Marketing research related to **logistics assessment** is an often overlooked area in distribution decisions. One reason is that traditionally it has been driven by secondary data, which although cheaper may be more difficult to find. Logistics information enables market researchers to conduct total cost and service sensitivity analyses.

Total cost analysis explores alternative logistics system designs a firm can use to achieve its performance objectives at the lowest total cost. The role of marketing research is to develop an activity-based cost information system by identifying key factors that affect transportation, inventory, and warehousing costs.

Service sensitivity analysis helps organizations design basic customer service programs by evaluating cost-to-service trade-offs. In conducting this type of analysis, market researchers look for ways to increase various basic services by making adjustments in transportation activities, inventory levels, or location planning. Each adjustment is analyzed relative to its impact on corresponding total costs.

Pricing Decisions

Pricing decisions involve pricing new products, establishing price levels in test-market situations, and modifying prices for existing products. Marketing research provides answers to questions such as the following:

1. How large is the demand potential within the target market?
2. How sensitive is demand to changes in price levels?
3. What nonprice factors are important to customers?
4. What are sales forecasts at various price levels?

Two common approaches to pricing research are demand analysis and sales forecasting. When a company evaluates a new-product idea, develops a test market, or plans changes for existing products, an important research challenge is estimating how customers will respond to different price levels. **Demand analysis** seeks to estimate the level of customer demand for a given product and the underlying reasons for that demand.

Demand analysis A research method that seeks to estimate the level of customer demand for a given product and the underlying reasons for that demand.

Pricing decisions are not always straightforward. For example, demand analysis has indicated that customers often buy more of certain products at *higher* prices, which suggests that price may be an indication of quality.[6] The influence of price on perception of quality seems to occur most often when customers are unable to evaluate the product themselves.

The chemical firm Du Pont, using demand analysis, also obtains measures of nonprice factors for its products. Among these factors are delivery, service, innovation, brand name, and quality. This places the pricing decision in an overall demand context.

Demand analysis often incorporates a test-marketing procedure involving the actual marketing of a product in one of several cities with the intent of measuring customer sensitivity to changes in a firm's marketing mix. Demand analysis can also incorporate end-user research studies and analysis of historical price and quality data for specific products.

Sales forecasting Uses variables that affect customer demand to provide estimates of financial outcomes for different price strategies.

Closely associated with demand analysis is **sales forecasting.** After demand analysis identifies the variables that affect customer demand, sales forecasting uses those variables to provide estimates of financial outcomes for different price strategies. Although a variety of sales forecasting techniques exist, most can be placed in one of two categories: qualitative or quantitative. *Qualitative* techniques include user expectation studies, sales-force composites, juries of executive opinion, and Delphi techniques. *Quantitative* forecasting techniques include market testing, time series analysis, and statistical demand analysis.

Integrated Marketing Communications

Promotional decisions are important influences on any company's sales. Billions of dollars are spent yearly on various promotional activities in this country. Given that heavy level of expenditure on promotional activities, it is essential that companies know how to obtain optimum returns from their promotional budgets. This is particularly important as a result of the rapid movement of businesses into online advertising whose effect is not as well understood yet.

Three key concerns in conducting promotional research are using the appropriate methodology, estimating adequate sample sizes, and developing the proper scaling techniques. We will study these in later chapters.

Marketing research that examines the performance of a promotional program must consider the entire integrated marketing communications program. The three most common research tasks related to assessing integrated marketing communications are advertising effectiveness studies; attitudinal research; and sales tracking.

Because advertising serves so many purposes, *advertising effectiveness studies* often vary across situations. Advertising effectiveness studies may be qualitative, quantitative, or both. They may take place in laboratory-type settings or in real-life settings. Measures of an ad's effectiveness may be taken before or at various times after media placement. Regardless, the key elements of advertising effectiveness studies are what is being measured, when the measurement is made, and which medium is being used.

Advertising effectiveness studies may focus on measuring a particular ad's ability to generate brand awareness, communicate product benefits, or create a favorable impression of a product or service. To measure these aspects, market researchers often use *attitudinal research* as part of an advertising effectiveness study. In addition, researchers increasingly are monitoring online behavior and making advertising media decisions using approaches such as pay-per-click (pay for advertising based on number of clicks on an ad) or pay-per-action (pay for advertising based on some action, such as providing contact information or an e-mail address).

Personal selling plays a major role in a firm's promotional mix. The goals assigned to salespeople frequently involve expected sales results or sales quotas. Related nonsales objectives also are important and may include increasing new accounts, evaluating middlemen, or achieving set levels of customer service. All these objectives are commonly tied to the evaluation of a salesperson's overall performance and must be considered in the evaluation process, which is referred to as *sales tracking*. Sales-tracking procedures facilitate measurement of both objective and subjective performance dimensions. Information must be gathered to evaluate factors beyond the control of individual salespeople as well. Exhibit 1.4 depicts data collected using a sales-tracking form. Some of the key variables are industry classification codes, annual sales, and number of employees. The form illustrates the effectiveness of the selling function by documenting who sold the product, the number of sales calls required to close the sale, and the profit generated. This and similar information is entered into the marketing information system so it can be used to improve decision making. A well-designed sales-tracking system helps managers diagnose performance-related problems and determine corrective actions that may be necessary.

eXHIBIT 1.4 Computerized Sales Tracking Form Illustrating Key Sales Tracking Variables

Company Id:	5012	Job No:	7012
Name:	HERSHEY CHOCOLATE USA		
Address:	27 WEST CHOCOLATE AVE		
City ST Zip:	HERSHEY	PA	17033-0819
Phone:	717-534-6488	DIV:	
SIC Code:	2066	**Employees:**	5
Annual Sales:	4	**Region:**	1
Primary Bus:	4		
No. of Plants:	8		
Projected Growth:	7		
Primary Market:	2		
No. of Product Line:	4		
End Product:	4		
Facility Address:	HERSHEY		
Key Contact Person:	GARY HOMMEL		
Division No.:		**Location:**	1
System Price:	1	**System Profit:**	
Sales Call/Close Ratio:		**Sales Rep:**	52

Marketing Program Implementation and Control

The key to marketing program implementation and control for any organization is the *marketing plan.* This plan specifies strategic goals and how they will be accomplished. Marketing research creates the foundation for such a plan by providing information needed to analyze product markets, the competition, market performance, strategy implementation, and long-term planning. Once the plan is put in place, the concern is to measure and control progress.

Marketing Program Control

Product analysis Identifies the relative importance of product selection criteria to buyers and rates brands against these criteria.

Environmental forecasting A research method used to predict external occurrences that can affect the long-term strategy of a firm.

Two key means of control are product analysis and environmental forecasting. **Product analysis** identifies the relative importance of product selection criteria to buyers and rates brands against these criteria. It is conducted throughout the life cycle of the product or brand; it is particularly useful in assessing strengths and weaknesses. Many standardized information services such as Information Resources and AC Nielsen monitor the performance of competing brands across a wide variety of products.

Environmental forecasting is used to predict external developments that can affect the long-term strategy of a firm. This technique involves a three-phase process that begins with a survey of customers and industry experts. Market tests follow to measure customer response to a particular marketing program and, finally, internal company records are analyzed to determine past buying behaviors. The net result is a collection of data pertaining to industry trends, customer profiles, and environmental changes that enable a company to adapt its strategy to anticipated future events.

Information Analysis

Information is vital to the market planning process. Just as market planning is the key to the long-term survival of the firm, information is the key to the accuracy of the marketing plan. Critical information allows firms to develop a competitive advantage. The role of marketing research is not only to collect and analyze data, but to organize the data for maximum benefit. This task is achieved through the development of a system referred to as a **marketing decision support system (MDSS).**

Marketing decision support system (MDSS) A company-developed database used to analyze company performance and control marketing activities.

An MDSS is a company-developed database used to analyze company performance and control marketing activities. It includes standardized marketing research reports, sales and cost data, product-line sales, advertising data, and price information. The information is organized to correspond to specific units of analysis (market segments, geographic locations, particular vendors) and is used for various small and large decisions from reordering inventory to launching new products. The value of an MDSS becomes apparent when managerial decision making focuses on the needs of specific market segments. Northwest Airlines' system, which determines mileage awards for frequent flyers and provides a reservation support database organized according to market segments, reveals that the top 3 percent of the company's customers account for almost 50 percent of its sales. These key customers are highlighted on all service screens and reports. Customer contact individuals are alerted when one of these customers calls so they can offer a variety of special services, such as first-class upgrades.[7] This information is also stored in Web site databases to be used when the customer contact point is over the Internet.

New technologies for collecting, processing, and analyzing market research data are rapidly changing organizations in a variety of ways. In the future information technology such as that used with the MDSS will likely increase the use of secondary data from internal data warehouses and reduce primary data collection.[8]

The Marketing Research Industry

The marketing research industry has experienced unparalleled growth in recent years. According to an *Advertising Age* study, revenues of U.S. research companies have grown substantially in recent years.[9] The growth in revenues of international research firms has been even more dramatic. Marketing research firms have attributed these revenue increases to post-sale customer satisfaction studies (one-third of research company revenues), retail-driven product scanning systems (also one-third of all revenues), database development for long-term brand management, and international research studies.

Types of Marketing Research Firms

Marketing research providers can be classified as internal or external, custom or standardized, or brokers or facilitators. Internal research providers are normally organizational units that reside within a company. For example, General Motors, Procter & Gamble, and Kodak all have internal marketing research departments. Kraft Foods realizes many benefits by keeping the marketing research function internal; these benefits include research method consistency, shared information across the company, minimized spending on research, and ability to produce actionable research results.

Other firms choose to use external sources for marketing research. External sources, usually referred to as marketing research suppliers, perform all aspects of the research, including study design, questionnaire production, interviewing, data analysis, and report preparation. These firms operate on a fee basis and commonly submit a research proposal to be used by a client for evaluation and decision purposes. An example of such a proposal is provided in the Marketing Research in Action at the end of Chapter 2.

Many companies use external research suppliers because, first, the suppliers can be more objective and less subject to company politics and regulations than internal suppliers, and second, many external suppliers provide specialized talents that, for the same cost, internal suppliers cannot provide. Finally, companies can choose external suppliers on a study-by-study basis and thus gain greater flexibility in scheduling studies and matching specific project requirements to the talents of specific research firms.

The services of marketing research firms can be customized or standardized. Customized research firms provide specialized, highly tailored services to the client. Many firms in this line of business concentrate their research activities in one specific area such as brand-name testing, test marketing, or new-product development. For example, Namestormers (namestormers.com) assists companies in brand-name selection and recognition. Survey Sampling International (surveysampling.com) concentrates solely on sampling development. In contrast, standardized research firms provide more general services. These firms also follow a more common approach in research design so the results of a study conducted for one client can be compared to norms established by studies done for other clients. Examples of these firms are Burke Market Research, which conducts day-after advertising recall; AC Nielsen (separate from Nielsen Media Research), which conducts store audits for a variety of retail firms; and Arbitron Ratings, which provides primary data collection on television commercials.

Many standardized research firms also provide syndicated business services, which include purchase diary panels, audits, and advertising recall data made or developed from a common data pool or database. A prime example of a syndicated business service is a database established through retail optical scanner methods. This database, available from AC Nielsen, tracks the retail sales of thousands of brand-name products. The data can be customized for a variety of industries (snack foods, over-the-counter drugs) to indicate purchase profiles and volume sales in a given industry. The nearby A Closer Look at Research (In the Field) box based on a Yahoo! press release illustrates how Yahoo! and AC Nielsen together provide customized data on Internet business developments.

A Closer Look at Research

Yahoo! and AC Nielsen: A Marketing Research Marriage through Technology

Yahoo! Inc., a leading global Internet company, and AC Nielsen, the world's leading market research firm, today released the results of the most recent Yahoo!/AC Nielsen Internet Confidence Index, a quarterly study designed to measure confidence levels in Internet products and services. The results of the Index show that consumer confidence and attitudes about the Internet and online shopping are up substantially over the same period last year. The survey also shows that consumers intend to spend more than $20 billion online in the holiday season, an increase of over 20 percent from last year. The strong confidence level is driving an increased intent to spend more online, especially among broadband users, pointing to the growing mainstream acceptance and reliance on the Internet as a medium for commerce. Year over year, there has been a statistically significant increase in the Yahoo!/AC Nielsen Internet Confidence Index. The results of this current wave show that the steady rise in confidence among Internet users can be attributed in part to a greater confidence in the security of personal information online. The increase in Internet confidence from last year's holiday season is good news for marketers who are utilizing the Internet for holiday shopping campaigns," said Travyn Rhall, managing director, AC Nielsen International. "Our data indicates that there is a strong correlation between higher confidence and higher consumer spending. Marketers should therefore focus on bringing down the perceived barriers to e-commerce, including comfort regarding personal information online."

BROADBAND CONSUMERS HIGHLY CONFIDENT This quarter's Internet Confidence Index examined broadband usage and those consumers' confidence in Internet products and services. Consumers with faster Internet access are the most confident in e-commerce transactions and have the highest intent to shop and spend during the next quarter. Three key motivators driving the increased confidence include convenience, high comfort levels with credit card usage, and a strong sense of security with personal information online.

Age also plays a factor in confidence level and spending habits. The confidence of the 25–34-year-old age group (currently the most confident demographic), and the 45+ year-old group have both increased significantly. The 25–34 age group shows an 11-point leap since last year and is up 16 points since the last quarter. Additionally, the 45+ age group has shown a 19-point increase in confidence levels in the last year and a 13-point increase since the last quarter.

ABOUT THE YAHOO!/AC NIELSEN INTERNET CONFIDENCE INDEX The Yahoo!/AC Nielsen Internet Confidence Index measures consumers' attitudes related to potential motivators and barriers to e-commerce, as well as various facets of purchasing behavior within the U.S. The index score for the initial Yahoo!/AC Nielsen Internet Confidence Index was set at 100 for use as a baseline, allowing subsequent survey data to be converted into trended, indexed scores. Further information can be accessed at http://docs.yahoo.com/docs/info/yici/.

AC Nielsen, on behalf of Yahoo!, conducts research for the Index through computer-aided telephone interviewing with random digit dialing and utilizes a sample size audience of 1,000 adults, who may or may not be currently utilizing the Internet. Yahoo! publishes Index results on a quarterly basis, four times per calendar year, and when special circumstances merit close examination of changes in consumer attitudes.

ABOUT AC NIELSEN AC Nielsen, a VNU business, is the world's leading marketing information company. Offering services in more than 100 countries, the company provides measurement and analysis of marketplace dynamics and consumer attitudes and behavior. Clients rely on AC Nielsen's market research, proprietary products, analytical tools, and professional service to understand competitive performance, to uncover new opportunities, and to raise the profitability of their marketing and sales campaigns.

Source: Reprinted by permission: Yahoo! Inc., Yahoo media relations, June 24, 2002.

Finally, marketing research firms can be distinguished as either brokers or facilitators. Broker services provide the ancillary tasks that complement many marketing research studies. For example, marketing research suppliers and clients who do not have the resources for data entry, tabulation, or analysis will typically use a broker service to facilitate the data management process. Brokers usually offer specialized programming, canned statistical packages, and other data management tools at low cost. P-Shat, Inc., for example, is a marketing research broker service that performs only three functions: data entry, data tabulation, and statistical analysis.

Facilitating agencies
Businesses that perform marketing research functions as a supplement to a broader marketing research project.

Facilitating agencies perform marketing research functions as a supplement to a company's broader marketing research project. Advertising agencies, field services, and independent consultants are usually classified as facilitators because they help companies to complete broader marketing projects. Advertising agencies, for example, are in the business of designing, implementing, and evaluating advertising campaigns for individual clients. Many agencies use their own research services to guide the development of the campaign and test for effectiveness. In this instance, the ad agency provides marketing research to facilitate the ad campaign process.

Marketing research suppliers frequently employ field services, whose primary responsibilities are to schedule, supervise, and complete interviews. As a facilitating agency, a field service contributes data collection services toward the completion of the marketing research project. In addition, many independent consultants are hired ad hoc to complement strategic planning activities for clients. Many consultants, offering unique and specialized research skills, are hired by firms to facilitate a total quality management program, develop a marketing information system, or train employees in the procedures of marketing research.

As this discussion shows, marketing research is a diverse industry. Diversity, coupled with increased revenue growth in the industry, has created job opportunities for people with a variety of skills. Furthermore, as more and more marketing research projects take on international flavor, these opportunities will continue to expand. The following section addresses what skills will be needed in the industry.

Changing Skills for a Changing Industry

Marketing research employees represent a vast diversity of cultures, technology, and personalities. As marketing research firms expand their geographic scope to Europe, Asia, and the Pacific Rim, the requirements for successfully executing marketing research projects will change dramatically. Many fundamental skill requirements will remain in place, but new and innovative practices will require a totally unique skill base that is more comprehensive than ever before.

In a survey of 100 marketing research executives, basic fundamental business skills were rated high for potential employees. Communication skills (verbal and written), interpersonal skills (ability to work with others), and statistical skills were the leading attributes in basic job aptitude.[10] More specifically, the top five skills executives hope to find in candidates for marketing research positions are (1) the ability to understand and interpret secondary data, (2) presentation skills, (3) foreign-language competency, (4) negotiation skills, and (5) computer proficiency.[11] Results of this survey indicate there has been a shift from analytical to execution skill requirements in the marketing research industry. In the future, analyzing existing databases, multicultural interaction, and negotiation are likely to be important characteristics of marketing researchers. Marketing research jobs are discussed further in the careers appendix at the end of this chapter.

Ethics in Marketing Research Practices

There are many opportunities for both ethical and unethical behaviors to occur in the research process. The major sources of ethical dilemmas in marketing research are the interactions among the three key groups: (1) the research information user (decision maker, sponsoring client, management team, practitioner); (2) the research information provider (researcher, research organization or company, project supervisor, researcher's staff representative or employees); and (3) the selected respondents (subjects or objects of investigation).

Unethical Activities by the Client/Research User

Decisions and practices of the client or decision maker (like most human situations) present various opportunities for unethical behavior. One such behavior is the client/decision maker requesting detailed research proposals from several competing research providers with no intention of selecting a firm to conduct the research, the purpose being to learn how to conduct the necessary marketing research themselves. Decision makers can obtain first drafts of questionnaires, sampling frames and sampling procedures, and knowledge on data collection procedures. Then, unethically, they can use the information to either perform the research project themselves or bargain for a better price among interested research companies.

Unfortunately, another common behavior among unethical decision makers is promising a prospective research provider a long-term relationship or additional projects in order to obtain a very low price on the initial research project. Then, after the researcher completes the initial project, the decision maker forgets about the long-term promises.

Unethical Activities by the Research Provider or Research Company

There are of course numerous opportunities for the researcher, the research company, or its representatives to act unethically in the process of conducting a study. First, a policy of unethical pricing practices is a common source of conflict. For example, after quoting a set overall price for a proposed research project, the researcher may tell the decision maker that variable-cost items such as travel expenses, monetary response incentives, or fees charged for computer time are extra, over and above the quoted price. Such "soft" costs can easily be used to manipulate the total project cost.

Second, all too often research firms do not provide the promised incentive (contest awards, gifts, money) to respondents for completing the interviews or questionnaires. Also, many firms delay indefinitely the fees owed to field workers (interviewers, data tabulators, data entry personnel). Usually, these parties are paid at the project's completion and thus lose any leverage they have with the research provider to collect on services rendered.

Third is respondent abuse. Research companies have a tendency to state to respondents that interviews will be very short when in reality they may last up to one hour. Other respondent abuse includes selling the respondents' names and demographic data to other companies without their approval, using infrared dye on questionnaires to trace selective respondents for the purpose of making a sales call, or using hidden tape recorders in a personal interviewing situation without the respondent's permission.

Finally, an unethical practice found all too often in marketing research is the selling of unnecessary or unwarranted research services. While it is perfectly acceptable to sell follow-up research that can aid the decision maker's company, selling bogus or unneeded services is completely unethical.

Within the execution of the research design, researcher-related unethical practices include (1) falsifying data, (2) duplicating actual response data, and (3) consciously manipulating the data structures inappropriately.

A practice of data falsification known to many researchers and field interviewers is *curbstoning,* or *rocking-chair* interviewing, when the researcher's trained interviewers or observers, rather than conducting interviews or observing respondents' actions as directed in the study, complete the interviews themselves or make up "observed" respondents' behaviors. Other falsification practices include having friends and relatives fill out surveys, not using the designated sample of sample respondents but rather anyone who is conveniently available to complete the survey, or not following up on the established call-back procedures indicated in the research procedure.

Another variation of data falsification is duplication of responses or the creation of "phantom" respondents, whereby a researcher or field personnel (interviewer, field observer, or data entry personnel) duplicate an actual respondent's data to represent a second set of responses. This practice artificially creates responses from people who were scheduled to be in the study but for some reason were not actually interviewed.

To minimize the likelihood of data falsification, research companies typically randomly verify 10 to 15 percent of the interviews.

Finally, researchers act unethically when they either (1) consciously manipulate data structures from data analysis procedures for the purpose of reporting a biased picture to the decision maker or (2) do not report selected findings at all.

Unethical Activities by the Respondent

The primary unethical practice of respondents or subjects in any research endeavor is providing dishonest answers or faking behavior. The general expectation is that when subjects have freely consented to participate, they will provide truthful responses, but truthfulness might be more difficult to achieve than one thinks. Some procedures are available to researchers to help evaluate the honesty of respondents' answers or actions. For example, bipolar questioning is used as a consistency check in surveys. Here the first question is framed in a positive way and the second question is framed in a negative way. The respondent's answers, if consistent, will be inversely related.

Other areas of possible ethical concerns within a researcher–respondent relationship that are beyond the scope of our present discussion include (1) the respondent's right to privacy; (2) the need to disguise the true purpose of the research; and (3) the respondent's right to be informed about certain aspects of the research process, including the sponsorship of the research.

Marketing Research Codes of Ethics

Today's marketing researchers must be proactive in their efforts to ensure an ethical environment, and the first step in being proactive is to develop a code of ethics. Such codes as part of ethics awareness programs offer perhaps the best chance of minimizing unethical behavior. Many marketing research companies have established internal company codes of ethics derived from the ethical codes formulated by larger institutions that govern today's marketing research industry. Exhibit 1.5 displays the code developed by the American Marketing Association.[12] This code provides a framework for identifying ethical issues and arriving at ethical decisions in situations researchers sometimes face.

EXHIBIT 1.5 Code of Ethics of the American Marketing Association

The American Marketing Association, in furtherance of its central objective of the advancement of science in marketing and in recognition of its obligation to the public, has established these principles of ethical practice of marketing research for the guidance of its members. In an increasingly complex society, marketing research is more and more dependent upon marketing information intelligently and systematically obtained. The consumer is the source of much of this information. Seeking the cooperation of the consumer in the development of information, marketing management must acknowledge its obligation to protect the public from misrepresentation and exploitation under the guise of research.

Similarly the research practitioner has an obligation to the discipline he practices and to those who provide support of his practice—an obligation to adhere to basic and commonly accepted standards of scientific investigation as they apply to the domain of marketing research. It is the intent of this code to define ethical standards required of marketing research in satisfying these obligations.

Adherence to this code will assure the user of marketing research that the research was done in accordance with acceptable ethical practices. Those engaged in research will find in this code an affirmation of sound and honest basic principles which have developed over the years as the profession has grown. The field interviewers who are the point of contact between the profession and the consumer will also find guidance in fulfilling their vitally important roles.

AMA CODE OF ETHICS

Members of the American Marketing Association are committed to ethical professional conduct. They have joined together in subscribing to this Code of Ethics embracing the following topics:

Responsibilities of the Marketer

Marketers must accept responsibility for the consequences of their activities and make every effort to ensure that their decisions, recommendations and actions function to identify, serve and satisfy all relevant publics: customers, organizations and society.

Marketers' Professional Conduct must be guided by:

1. The basic rule of professional ethics: not knowingly to do harm;
2. The adherence to all applicable laws and regulations;
3. The accurate representation of their education, training and experience; and
4. The active support, practice and promotion of this Code of Ethics.

Honesty and Fairness

Marketers shall uphold and advance the integrity, honor and dignity of the marketing profession by:

1. Being honest in serving consumers, clients, employees, suppliers, distributors, and the public;
2. Not knowingly participating in conflict of interest without prior notice to all parties involved; and
3. Establishing equitable fee schedules including the payment or receipt of usual, customary and/or legal compensation for marketing exchanges.

Rights and Duties of Parties in the Marketing Exchange Process

Participants in the marketing exchange process should be able to expect that

1. Products and services offered are safe and fit for their intended uses;
2. Communications about offered products and services are not deceptive;
3. All parties intend to discharge their obligations, financial and otherwise, in good faith; and
4. Appropriate internal methods exist for equitable adjustment and/or redress of grievances concerning purchases.

It is understood that the above would include, but is not limited to, the following responsibilities of the marketer:

EXHIBIT 1.5 *continued*

In the area of product development and management:

- disclosure of all substantial risks associated with product or service usage;
- identification of any product component substitution that might materially change the product or impact on the buyer's purchase decision;
- identification of extra cost-added features.

In the area of promotions:

- avoidance of false and misleading advertising;
- rejection of high-pressure manipulations, or misleading sales tactics;
- avoidance of sales promotions that use deception or manipulation.

In the area of distribution:

- not manipulating the availability of a product for the purpose of exploitation;
- not using coercion in the marketing channel;
- not exerting undue influence over the reseller's choice to handle a product.

In the area of pricing:

- not engaging in price fixing;
- not practicing predatory pricing;
- disclosing the full price associated with any purchase.

In the area of marketing research:

- prohibiting selling or fundraising under the guise of conducting research;
- maintaining research integrity by avoiding misrepresentation and omission of pertinent research data;
- treating outside clients and suppliers fairly.

Organizational Relationships

Marketers should be aware of how their behavior may influence or impact the behavior of others in organizational relationships. They should not demand, encourage or apply coercion to obtain unethical behavior in their relationships with others, such as employees, suppliers, or customers.

1. Apply confidentiality and anonymity in professional relationships with regard to privileged information;
2. Meet their obligations and responsibilities in contracts and mutual agreements in a timely manner;
3. Avoid taking the work of others, in whole, or in part, and representing this work as their own or directly benefiting from it without compensation or consent of the originator or owner; and
4. Avoid manipulation to take advantage of situations to maximize personal welfare in a way that unfairly deprives or damages the organization of others.

Any AMA member found to be in violation of any provision of this Code of Ethics may have his or her Association membership suspended or revoked.

AMERICAN MARKETING ASSOCIATION CODE OF ETHICS FOR MARKETING ON THE INTERNET

Preamble

The Internet, including online computer communications, has become increasingly important to marketers' activities, as they provide exchanges and access to markets worldwide. The ability to interact with stakeholders has created new marketing opportunities and risks that are not currently specifically addressed in

continued

eXHIBIT 1.5 Code of Ethics of the American Marketing Association, *continued*

the American Marketing Association Code of Ethics. The American Marketing Association Code of Ethics for Internet marketing provides additional guidance and direction for ethical responsibility in this dynamic area of marketing. The American Marketing Association is committed to ethical professional conduct and has adopted these principles for using the Internet, including on-line marketing activities utilizing network computers.

General Responsibilities

Internet marketers must assess the risks and take responsibility for the consequences of their activities. Internet marketers' professional conduct must be guided by:

1. Support of professional ethics to avoid harm by protecting the rights of privacy, ownership and access.
2. Adherence to all applicable laws and regulations with no use of Internet marketing that would be illegal, if conducted by mail, telephone, fax or other media.
3. Awareness of changes in regulations related to Internet marketing.
4. Effective communication to organizational members on risks and policies related to Internet marketing, when appropriate.
5. Organizational commitment to ethical Internet practices communicated to employees, customers and relevant stakeholders.

Privacy

Information collected from customers should be confidential and used only for expressed purposes. All data, especially confidential customer data, should be safeguarded against unauthorized access. The expressed wishes of others should be respected with regard to the receipt of unsolicited e-mail messages.

Ownership

Information obtained from the Internet sources should be properly authorized and documented. Information ownership should be safeguarded and respected. Marketers should respect the integrity and ownership of computer and network systems.

Access

Marketers should treat access to accounts, passwords, and other information as confidential, and only examine or disclose content when authorized by a responsible party. The integrity of others' information systems should be respected with regard to placement of information, advertising or messages.

While the codes of ethics advocated by marketing and survey research associations have given proactive guidance and the appearance of integrity to the marketing research industry, some researchers believe they are not enough in themselves to guarantee ethical behavior. Acting honestly and avoiding ethical dilemmas remain a never-ending concern for the parties involved with research practices.

Emerging Trends and Organization of This Book

The general consensus in the marketing research industry today is that five major trends are becoming evident: (1) increased emphasis on secondary data collection methods; (2) movement toward technology-related data management (optical scanning, database technology, customer relationship management); (3) expanded use of digital technology for information acquisition and retrieval; (4) a broader international client base; and (5) movement beyond data analysis toward a data interpretation/information management environment.

The organization of this book is consistent with these trends. Part 1 (Chapters 1–4) explores marketing research information and technology from the client's perspective, including how to evaluate marketing research projects. Part 2 (Chapters 5–9) provides an innovative overview of the emerging role of secondary data, with emphasis on technology-driven approaches for the design and development of research projects. This part also discusses traditional marketing research project design issues (survey methods and research designs) as well as collection and interpretation of qualitative data. Practical examples illustrating how qualitative data is used today in industry facilitate the discussion. While these methods are fundamental to the marketing research process, recent developments have changed the focus of these issues. Part 3 (Chapters 10–13) covers sampling, attitude measurement and scaling, and questionnaire design. Part 4 (Chapters 14–18) prepares the reader for management, categorization, and analysis of marketing research data, particularly quantitative methods. Applications of the SPSS statistical software give readers a hands-on guide to analyzing quantitative data. This part concludes by showing how to effectively present marketing research findings. Key elements in preparing a written marketing research report and planning an oral presentation are treated succinctly.

Each chapter concludes with an illustrative example called *Marketing Research in Action* whose goal is to facilitate the reader's understanding of chapter topics and to provide the reader with a "how-to" approach for marketing research methods.

Continuing Case: The Santa Fe Grill Mexican Restaurant

To illustrate the marketing research principles and concepts presented in this text, a Continuing Case study will be followed along throughout the book in most chapters. The Continuing Case may appear in a main feature or be explored in other ways in a chapter. For instance after establishing the case in Chapters 1 and 3, some Review Questions in Chapter 4 ask you to explore the Case in terms of what you have read there. The case is about the Santa Fe Grill Mexican Restaurant, which was started 18 months ago by two former business students at the University of Nebraska, Lincoln. They had been roommates in college and both had an entrepreneurial desire. After graduating they wanted to start a business instead of working for someone else. The students worked in restaurants while attending college, both as waiters and one of them as an assistant manager, and they felt they had the knowledge and experience necessary to start their own business.

The focus on a single case study of a typical business research problem will enable you to more easily understand the benefits and pitfalls of using research to improve business decision making. In the early chapters we use the continuing case to illustrate concepts and principles. Then, in the data analysis chapters the case study data is used to illustrate statistical software and the various statistical techniques for analyzing data. For example, Chapter 5 has a secondary data assignment. When sampling is discussed in Chapter 10, different sampling approaches are evaluated and we point out sample size issues as well as why the research company recommended exit interviews. Similarly, the questionnaire used to collect primary data in Chapter 13 illustrates measurement and questionnaire design principles. The Marketing Research in Action exercise that follows in this chapter provides more details about this continuing case.

Marketing Research in Action

Continuing Case

The Santa Fe Grill

During their senior year at college the owners prepared a business plan in their entrepreneurship class for a new Mexican restaurant concept. They initially intended to start the restaurant in Lincoln, Nebraska, where they were at college. But a demographic analysis of that market revealed that Lincoln did not match their target demographics.

After researching the demographic and competitive profile of several markets, they decided Dallas, Texas, would be the best place to start their business. In examining the markets, they were looking for a town that would best fit their target market of singles and families in the age range of 25 to 50. The population of Dallas was almost 5.5 million people, of which about 50 percent were between the ages of 25 and 60. This indicated there were a lot of individuals in their target demographic in the Dallas area. They also found that about 55 percent of the population earned between $35,000 and $75,000 a year, which indicated the market would have enough income to eat out regularly. Finally, 56 percent of the population was married and many of them had children at home, which was consistent with their target market.

The new restaurant concept was based on providing the freshest ingredients for their menu offerings, complemented by a festive atmosphere, friendly service, and cutting-edge advertising and marketing strategies. The key idea would be to prepare and serve the freshest "made-from-scratch" Mexican foods possible—everything fresh every single day. In addition to their freshness concept, they wanted to have a fun, festive atmosphere and fast, friendly service. The atmosphere would be open, brightly lit and bustling with activity. Their target market would be mostly families with children and generally individuals aged 18 to 49. Their marketing programs would be ahead of the pack, with the advertising designed to provide an appealing, slightly off-center, unrefined positioning in the market.

The Santa Fe Grill was successful, but not as quickly as the owners had anticipated. Their restaurant is located on an outparcel near the main entrance on the east side of the Cumberland Mall, which has 75+ stores in it and is considered very successful for the area. Another Mexican restaurant that has been in business longer and appears to be more successful is on another outparcel on the west side of the same mall. The owners believe this other Mexican restaurant, Jose's Southwestern Café, is their primary competitor. In recent weeks, the owners have observed people standing in line waiting to eat there during both lunch and dinner hours. They have also eaten at the restaurant to observe the menu, taste the food, and develop a feeling for their competitor's operations and atmosphere.

To improve business at the Santa Fe Grill, the owners have decided they need to better understand what aspects of restaurant operations drive customer satisfaction and loyalty. Some of the questions they have come up with include: Are our customers satisfied with the restaurant? Are there problems with the food, the atmosphere, or some other aspect of restaurant operations (e.g., employees or service)? Is the target market correctly defined or do we need to focus on a different niche? What are the common characteristics of satisfied customers? What do the Santa Fe Grill customers think about their dining experiences compared to the customers of Jose's Southwestern Café? Answering these and other similar questions will help the owners to focus their marketing efforts, improve operations, and be in a position to expand their restaurant concept to other markets.

Hands-On Exercise

1. Based on your understanding of Chapter 1, and specifically using Exhibit 1.1, what type(s) of research program(s) should the owners of Santa Fe Grill consider?
2. Is a research project actually needed? If yes, what kind of project? What areas should the research focus on?
3. Are there any potential ethical issues that need to be considered in determining what kind of research project is needed?

Summary of Learning Objectives

■ **Describe the impact of marketing research on marketing decision making.**

Marketing research is the set of activities central to all marketing-related decisions regardless of the complexity or focus of the decision. Marketing research is responsible for providing managers with accurate, relevant, and timely information so that they can make marketing decisions with a high degree of confidence. Within the context of strategic planning, marketing research is responsible for the tasks, methods, and procedures a firm will use to implement and direct its strategic plan.

■ **Demonstrate the relationship between marketing research and marketing planning.**

Marketing research is the backbone of any relationship marketing process through the data collection operations of the research process. Specifically, marketing research facilitates the CRM process through the generation of customer/market knowledge, data integration, information technology, and the creation of customer profiles. The key to successful planning is accurate information. Information related to product performance, distribution efficiency, pricing policies, and promotional efforts is crucial for developing the strategic plan. The primary responsibility of any marketing research endeavor is to design a project that yields the most accurate information possible in aiding the development of a marketing plan.

■ **Provide examples of marketing research studies.**

The scope of marketing research activities extends far beyond examination of customer characteristics. The major categories of marketing research tasks include, but are not limited to, (1) situation research efforts (which include opportunity assessment, benefit and lifestyle studies, descriptive studies, and importance-performance analysis); (2) strategy-driven research efforts (which include target market analysis, positioning or perceptual mapping, concept and product testing, and test marketing); (3) program development research (which includes customer satisfaction studies, service quality studies, cycle time research, retailing research, logistic assessment, demand analysis, sales forecasting, advertising effectiveness studies, attitudinal research, and sales tracking); and (4) performance analysis (which includes product analysis, environmental forecasting, and marketing decision support systems).

■ **Understand the scope and focus of the marketing research industry.**

Generally, marketing research projects can be conducted either internally by an in-house marketing research staff or externally by independent or facilitating marketing research firms. External research suppliers are normally classified as custom or standardized, or as brokers or facilitators.

■ **Explain the ethical dimensions of marketing research.**

Ethical dilemmas in decision making are faced by all industries, including marketing research. The research information user, the research information provider, and the selected respondents may all engage in unethical behavior in marketing research. Unethical behavior by clients includes requesting research proposals with no intent to follow through and unethical practices to secure low-cost research services. Specific unethical practices among research providers include unethical pricing practices, failure to meet obligations to respondents, respondent abuse, and selling unnecessary services. The falsification of data and duplication of actual responses are unethical practices sometimes associated with the research firm. Respondents may falsify or fake their responses.

■ **Discuss emerging trends and new skills needed in marketing research.**

Today's dynamic business environment dictates change in the marketing research industry. Far-reaching technological and societal changes will affect how marketing research will be conducted in the future. Necessary skills required to adapt to these changes include (1) the ability to understand and interpret secondary data, (2) presentation skills, (3) foeign-language competency, (4) negotiation skills, and (5) computer proficiency.

Key Terms and Concepts

Benefit and lifestyle studies 8
Concept and product testing and **test marketing** 10
Customer relationship management 6
Customer satisfaction studies 11
Cycle time research 11
Demand analysis 13
Environmental forecasting 16
Empowerment 5
Executive dashboard 6
Facilitating agencies 19
Information sharing 6
Importance-performance analysis 9
Logistics assessment 13
Marketing 4
Marketing decision support system (MDSS) 16
Marketing research 4
Opportunity assessment 8
Positioning 9
Product analysis 16
Relationship marketing 5
Retailing research 12
Sales forecasting 13
Service quality studies 11
Target market analysis 9

Review Questions

1. Provide three examples of how marketing research helps marketing personnel make sound managerial decisions.
2. What improvements in marketing planning can be attributed to the results obtained from customer satisfaction studies?
3. Discuss the importance of target market analysis. How does it affect the development of marketing planning for a particular company?
4. What are the advantages and disadvantages of companies' maintaining an internal marketing research department? What are the advantages and disadvantages of hiring an external marketing research supplier?
5. As the marketing research industry expands, what skills will future research practitioners need to possess? How do these skills differ from those currently needed to function successfully in the marketing research field?
6. Identify and explain four potential unethical practices within the marketing research process and their contribution to deceptive research results.

Discussion Questions

1. **EXPERIENCE THE INTERNET.** Go online to one of your favorite search engines (Yahoo!, Google, etc.) and enter the following search term: marketing research. From the results, access a directory of marketing research firms. Select a particular firm and comment on the types of marketing research studies it performs.
2. **EXPERIENCE THE INTERNET.** Using the Yahoo! search engine, specifically, the Get Local section, select the closest major city in your area and search for the number of marketing research firms there. Select and e-mail a marketing research firm. Ask to

have any job descriptions for positions in that company e-mailed back to you. Once you obtain the descriptions, discuss the particular qualities needed to perform each job.

3. You have been hired by McDonald's to lead a mystery shopper team. The goal of your research is to improve the service quality at the McDonald's restaurant in your area. What attributes of service quality will you attempt to measure? What customer or employee behaviors will you closely monitor?

4. Contact a local business and interview the owner/manager about the types of marketing research performed for that business. Determine whether the business has its own marketing research department, or if it hires an outside agency. Also, determine whether the company takes a one-shot approach to particular problems or is systematic over a long period of time.

5. **EXPERIENCE THE INTERNET.** As the Internet continues to grow as a medium for conducting various types of marketing research studies, there is growing concern about ethical issues. Identify and discuss three ethical issues pertinent to research conducted using the Internet. Now go online and validate your ethical concerns. Using any search engine go to the Internet Fraud home page, at www.fraud.org/ifw.htm. Click on the other links and browse the information. What unethical practices are plaguing the Net?

appendix 1.A

Careers in Marketing Research with a Look at Federal Express

Career opportunities in marketing research vary by industry, company, and size of company. Different positions exist in consumer products companies, industrial goods companies, internal marketing research departments, and professional marketing research firms. Marketing research tasks range from the very simple, such as tabulation of questionnaires, to the very complex, such as sophisticated data analysis. Exhibit A.1 lists some common job titles and their functions as well as compensation ranges for marketing research positions.

EXHIBIT A.1 Marketing Research Career Outline

Position*	Duties	Compensation Range (Annual)
Account executive research director	Responsible for entire research program of the company. Works as go-between for the company and client. Employs personnel and supervises research department. Presents research findings to company and/or clients.	$75,000 to $100,000
Information technician statistician	Acts as expert consultant on application of statistical techniques for specific research problems. Many times responsible for research design and data analysis.	$45,000 to $75,000
Research analyst	Plans research project and executes project assignments. Works with analyst in preparing questionnaire. Makes analysis, prepares report, schedules project events, and sets budget.	$40,000 to $65,000
Assistant research analyst	Works under research analyst supervision. Assists in development of questionnaire, pretest, preliminary analysis.	$40,000 to $45,000
Project coordinator Project director Field manager Fieldwork director	Hires, trains, and supervises field interviewers. Provides work schedules and is responsible for data accuracy.	$30,000 to $40,000
Librarian	Builds and maintains a library of primary and secondary data sources to meet the requirements of the research department.	$35,000 to $45,000
Clerical and tabulation assistant	Handles and processes statistical data. Supervises day-to-day office work.	$22,000 to $35,000

*Positions are generalized, and not all companies have all of the positions.

Most successful marketing research people are intelligent and creative; they also possess problem-solving, critical-thinking, communication, and negotiation skills. Marketing researchers must be able to function under strict time constraints and feel comfortable with working with large volumes of data. Federal Express, for example, seeks individuals with strong analytical and computer skills to fill its research positions. Candidates should have an undergraduate degree in business, marketing, or information systems. Having an MBA will usually give an applicant a competitive advantage.

As is the case with many companies, the normal entry-level position in the marketing research area at Federal Express is the assistant research analyst. While learning details of the company and the industry, these individuals receive on-the-job training from a research analyst. The normal career path includes advancement to information technician and then research director and/or account executive.

Marketing research at Federal Express is somewhat unusual in that it is housed in the information technology division. This is evidence that, while the research function is integrated throughout the company, it has taken on a high-tech orientation. Marketing research at FedEx operates in three general areas:

1. *Database development and enhancement.* Establishing relationships with current FedEx customers to obtain information for the planning of new products.

2. *Cycle time research.* Providing more information for the efficient shipping of packages, tracking of shipments, automatic replenishment of customers' inventories, and enhanced electronic data interchange.

3. *Market intelligence system.* Primarily a logistical database and research effort to provide increased customer service to catalog retailers, direct marketing firms, and electronic commerce organizations.

The entire research function is led by a vice president of research and information technology, to whom four functional units report directly. These four units are responsible for the marketing decision support system operation, sales tracking, new business development, and special project administration.

If you are interested in pursuing a career in marketing research, a good way to start is to obtain the following career guide published by the Marketing Research Association:

Career Guide: Your Future in Marketing Research
Marketing Research Association
2189 Silas Deane Highway, Suite 5
Rocky Hill, CT 06067
MRAH@aol.com

It is also a wise idea to obtain the *Marketing and Sales Career Directory,* available at your university library or by writing:

Marketing and Sales Career Directory
Gale Research Inc.
835 Penobscot Building
Detroit, MI 48226-4094

Exercise

1. Go to the home Web page for Federal Express and identify the requirements that FedEx is seeking in marketing research personnel. Write a brief description of these requirements and report your finding to the class.
2. If you were seeking a marketing research position at FedEx, how would you prepare yourself through training and education for such a position? Put together a one-year plan for yourself identifying the college courses, special activities, interests, and related work experience you would engage in to obtain a marketing research position at FedEx.

chapter 2

Overview of the Research Process and Research Proposals

Learning Objectives

After reading this chapter, you will be able to:

1. Describe the major environmental factors influencing marketing research.
2. Discuss the research process and explain its various steps.
3. Distinguish between exploratory, descriptive, and causal research designs.
4. Identify and explain the major components of a research proposal.

"How do I determine whether Rosetta Technologies, Inc., is meeting the printing needs and requirements of our customers?"

—ROB HULLAR,
Co-founder and President,
Rosetta Technologies

Solving Marketing Problems Using a Systematic Process

Bill Shulby is president of Carolina Consulting Company, a marketing strategy consulting firm based in Raleigh-Durham, North Carolina. He was recently working with the owners of a regional telecommunications firm located in Texas on improving service quality processes. Toward the end of their meeting, one of the owners, Dan Carter, asked him about customer satisfaction and perceptions of the company's image as they related to service quality and customer retention. During the discussion, Carter stated that he was not sure how the company's telecommunications services were viewed by current or potential customers. He said, "Just last week, the customer service department received eleven calls from different customers complaining about everything from incorrect bills to taking too long to get DSL (high speed internet service) installed. Clearly, none of these customers were happy about our service." Then he asked Shulby, "What can I do to find out how satisfied our customers are overall and what can be done to improve our image?"

Shulby indicated that answers could be obtained to his questions by conducting a marketing research study. Dan Carter responded that the company had not done research in the past so he did not know what to expect from such a study. Shulby then gave several examples of studies the Carolina Consulting Company had conducted for other clients and explained how the information had been used, making sure not to disclose any confidential information. Carter then asked, "How much would it cost me to do this study and how long would it take to complete?" Shulby explained he would like to ask a few more questions so he could better understand the issues, and then he would prepare a research proposal summarizing the approach to be used, the deliverables from the study, the cost, and the time frame for completion. The proposal would be ready in about a week and they would meet to go over it in detail.

Value of the Research Process

Business owners and managers often identify problems they need help to resolve. In such situations what is needed to make a decision or solve the problem typically is additional information. Onc solution for gaining the necessary information to deal with the problem is a marketing research study based on a scientific research process. This chapter provides an overview of the research process as well as a preview of some of the core topics in the text.

Changing View of the Marketing Research Process

Organizations, both for-profit and not-for-profit, increasingly are confronted with new and ever more complex challenges and opportunities as a result of changing legal, political, cultural, technological, and competitive environments. Exhibit 2.1 summarizes several key environmental factors that are significantly impacting business decision making and the marketing research process.

Perhaps the most influential factor creating change today is the Internet. The rapid technological advances associated with it and its growing use by people worldwide are

EXHIBIT 2.1 Environmental Factors That Affect Marketing Research Practices

Factors	Impact on Practices
Internet and e-commerce	Revolutionizing the methods and opportunities for data collection. *Examples:* increasing need for and integration of online and offline data; quicker and cheaper data collection; growing multimedia capabilities; increased availability of user-generated content (MySpace, Facebook, blogs, newsgroups, brand communities) that can be analyzed; increasing use of clickstream analysis.
Gatekeeper technologies	Increasing difficulty in reaching respondents amid rising concerns about consumers' right to privacy. *Examples:* increased use of caller ID, electronic answering, and voice messenger devices; increases in intrusive telemarketing practices and scam artists; more restrictive data privacy laws; mandated opt-out opportunities.
Global market expansion	Creating multicultural interaction problems, opportunities, and questions for marketing decision makers as well as new language and measurement challenges for researchers. *Examples:* different cultural-based market needs and wants; different global data requirements for segmentation; use of different, yet compatible measurement schemes for market performance, attitude, and behavior data.
Growing need for information	Leading businesses to reposition marketing research activities with more emphasis on strategic implications. *Examples:* use of marketing research for developing CRM and customer and competitor intelligence strategies; marketing researchers' deeper involvement in developing online/offline databases.

making the Internet a driving force in many current and future developments in marketing research. Traditional research philosophies are being challenged as never before. For example, partly as a result of the Internet there is a growing emphasis on *secondary* data collection, analysis, and interpretation as a basis of making business decisions. **Secondary data** is information previously collected for some other problem or issue. That is, it is "out there" in, among other places, cyberspace. In contrast, **primary data** is information (usually more expensive) specifically collected for a current research problem or opportunity.

Secondary data Information previously collected for some other problem or issue.

Primary data Information specifically collected for a current research problem or opportunity.

A by-product of the technology advances is the ongoing collection of data that is placed in data warehouses and is available as secondary data to help understand business problems and to improve decisions. Many large businesses (for example, Dell Computers, Bank of America, Marriott Hotels, Coca-Cola, IBM, McDonald's, Wal-Mart) are linking purchase data collected in-store and online with customer profiles already in company databases, thus enhancing their ability to understand shopping behavior and better meet customer needs. But even medium-sized and small companies are building databases of customer information to serve current customers more effectively and to attract new customers.

A second change factor is increased use of **gatekeeper technologies** (for example, caller ID and automated screening and answering devices) as a means of protecting one's privacy against intrusive marketing practices such as telemarketers and illegal scam artists. Similarly, many Internet users either block the placement of cookies on their computers or periodically erase them in order to keep marketers from tracking their behavior. Marketing researchers' ability to collect consumer data using traditional methods like mail and telephone surveys has been severely limited by the combination of gatekeeper devices and recent Federal and state data privacy legislation. Indeed, marketing researchers must contact almost four times more people today to complete a single interview than was true five years ago. Online marketers and researchers must provide opt-in/opt-out opportunities when soliciting business or collecting information. Advances in gatekeeper technologies, along with new privacy concerns and laws, will continue to challenge marketers to be more creative in developing new ways to reach respondents.

Gatekeeper technologies Automated screening and/or answering devices that protect an individual against intrusive business practices.

The third environmental challenge facing marketing decision makers today is widespread expansion of businesses into global markets. Global expansion introduces marketing decision makers to new cultural issues that force researchers to focus not only on data collection tasks, but also on data interpretation and information management activities. For example, one of the largest full-service global marketing information firms, NFO (National Family Opinion) Worldwide, Inc., located in Greenwich, Connecticut, with subsidiaries in North America, Europe, Australia, Asia, and the Middle East, has adapted many of its measurement and brand tracking services to accommodate specific cultural and language differences encountered in global markets.

A fourth development is marketing research being repositioned in businesses to play an ever more important role in strategy development. Information created by marketing research increasingly is being used to identify new business opportunities and to develop new product, service, and delivery ideas. It is viewed as a mechanism to more efficiently execute CRM (customer relationship management) strategies and also as a critical component in developing competitive intelligence. For example, Sony uses its PlayStation Web site (www.playstation.com) to collect information on PlayStation gaming users and to build closer relationships with them. The PlayStation Web site is designed to create a community of users who can join PlayStation Underground where they will "feel like they belong to a subculture of intense gamers." To achieve this objective the Web site offers online shopping, opportunities to try new games, customer support, and information on news, events, and promotions. Interactive relationship-building features include online gaming and message boards. Marketing researchers at Sony and other companies are becoming more like cross-functional information experts, assisting in collecting not only marketing information but also information on all types of business functions.

Collectively, these key influences increasingly are forcing managers and researchers to view marketing research as an *information management* function. The term *information research* reflects the evolution occurring in the market research industry affecting organizational decision makers. Indeed, a more appropriate name for the traditional marketing research process is now the *information research process*. The **information research process** is a systematic approach to collecting, analyzing, interpreting, and transforming data into decision-making information. While many of the specific tasks involved in marketing research remain the same, understanding the process of transforming data into usable information from a broader information processing framework expands the applicability of the research process in solving organizational problems and creating opportunities.

Information research process A systematic approach to collecting, analyzing, interpreting, and transforming data into decision-making information.

Determining the Need for Information Research

Before we introduce and discuss the phases and specific steps in the information research process, it is important that you understand when research is needed and when it is not.

While many marketing research texts suggest the first step in the marketing research process is for the *researcher* to establish the need for marketing research, this places too much responsibility and control in the hands of a person who might not be trained in understanding the management decision-making process. Decision makers and researchers frequently are trained differently in their approach to identifying and solving business problems, questions, and opportunities, as illustrated in the nearby A Closer Look at Research (In the Field) box. Until decision makers and marketing researchers become closer to each other in their thinking, the initial recognition of a problem or opportunity should be the primary responsibility of the *decision maker,* not the researcher.

Nevertheless increasingly researchers must interact closely with managers in recognizing and identifying business problems and opportunities. Decision makers often initiate the research process because they recognize that more information is needed before a good plan of action can be developed. It is at this point, especially, that the help and advice of the researcher are required. Once the research process is initiated, in most cases decision makers will need assistance in defining the problem, collecting and analyzing the data, and interpreting the data. But when is it advisable to initiate the research process? For decision makers given the responsibility of recognizing and defining a problem or opportunity, a good rule of thumb is to ask, "Can the decision-making problem (or question) be resolved based on past experience and managerial judgment?" Only if the response is "no" should research be considered and perhaps implemented.

A key to knowing when the information research process should be undertaken is to understand that marketing research no longer focuses on primary data to solve management's problems. Increasingly, secondary research and data warehouse information are being used to address decision making. Technological advances in the Internet, high-speed communication systems, and faster secondary and primary data acquisition and retrieval systems are dramatically changing marketing research practices in that more problems are being resolved with secondary data instead of collecting primary data.

Four situations in which the decision to commission a marketing research project may be ill advised are when sufficient secondary information already is available, when time is of the essence, when resources are inadequate, and when costs of research are too high (see Exhibit 2.2).[1] However, an important caveat to these cautions is that the decision maker is assumed to have precise knowledge about the true availability of existing information, the necessary time, staff, and adequate resources should a research project be initiated, and the expected value or cost/benefit trade-off of the resulting information. But such knowledge is

A Closer Look at Research

Management Decision Makers and Marketing Researchers

MANAGEMENT DECISION MAKERS . . . Tend to be decision-oriented, intuitive thinkers who want information to confirm their decisions. They want additional information now or "yesterday," as well as results about future market component behavior ("What will sales be next year?"), while maintaining a frugal stance with regard to the cost of additional information. Decision makers tend to be results-oriented, do not like surprises, and tend to reject the information when they are surprised. Their dominant concern is market performance ("Aren't we number one yet?"); they want information that allows certainty ("Is it or isn't it?") and advocate being proactive but often allow problems to force them into reactive decision-making modes.

MARKETING RESEARCHERS . . . Tend to be scientific, technical, analytical thinkers who love to explore new phenomena; accept prolonged investigations to ensure completeness; focus on information about past behaviors ("Our trend has been . . ."); and are not cost conscious with additional information ("You get what you pay for"). Researchers are results-oriented but love surprises; they tend to enjoy abstractions ("Our exponential gain . . ."), the probability of occurrences ("May be," "Tends to suggest that . . ."); and they advocate the proactive need for continuous inquiries of market component changes, but feel most of the time that they are restricted to doing reactive ("quick and dirty") investigations due to management's lack of vision and planning.

a rare thing. And as technology advances, bearing on all the factors in decision making unpredictably, this assumption becomes more not less suspect, complicating the decision still further. For instance, the time and money needed to conduct an interview may go down with new technology, even while the availability of secondary data increases. Here the research expert can be of great assistance to managers trying to decide the nature of the research effort to be conducted or whether or not sufficient internal information exists already.

eXHIBIT 2.2 Situations When Marketing Research Might Not Be Needed

Situation Factors and Comments

Information already available When the decision maker has substantial knowledge about markets, products and services, and the competition, enough information may exist to make an informed decision without doing marketing research. Improvements in information processing technology mean more information is available, ensuring the right information gets to the right decision makers in a timely fashion.

Insufficient time frames When the discovery of a problem situation leaves inadequate time to execute the necessary research activities, a decision maker may have to use informed judgment. Competitive actions/reactions sometimes emerge so fast that marketing research studies are not a feasible option.

Inadequate resources When there are significant limitations in money, manpower, and/or facilities, then marketing research typically is not feasible.

Costs outweigh the value When the benefits to be gained by conducting the research are not significantly greater than the costs, then marketing research is not feasible.

EXHIBIT 2.3 Determining When to Undertake the Information Research Process

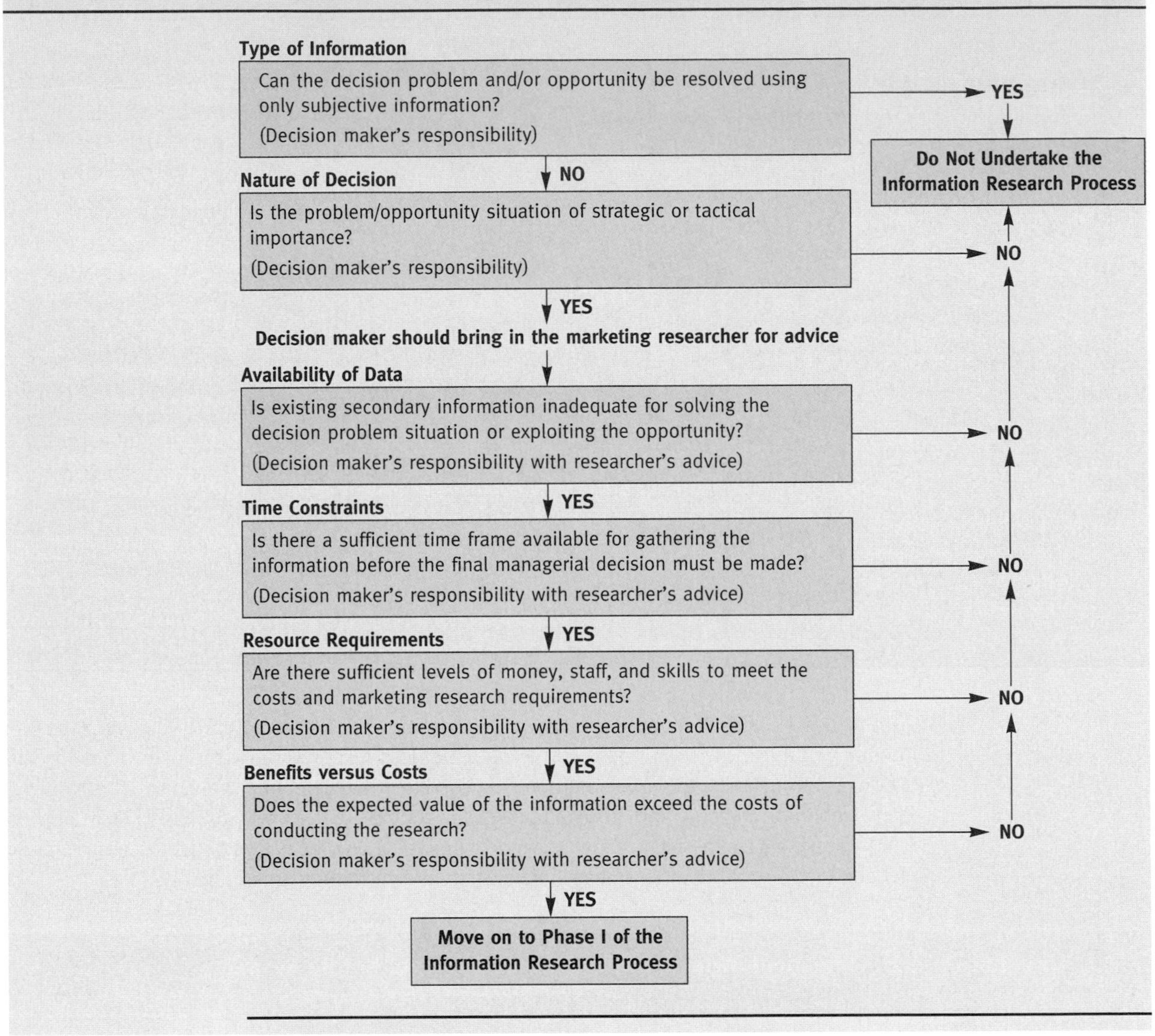

Type of Information
Can the decision problem and/or opportunity be resolved using only subjective information?
(Decision maker's responsibility)
YES
Do Not Undertake the Information Research Process
NO
Nature of Decision
Is the problem/opportunity situation of strategic or tactical importance?
(Decision maker's responsibility)
NO
YES
Decision maker should bring in the marketing researcher for advice
Availability of Data
Is existing secondary information inadequate for solving the decision problem situation or exploiting the opportunity?
(Decision maker's responsibility with researcher's advice)
NO
YES
Time Constraints
Is there a sufficient time frame available for gathering the information before the final managerial decision must be made?
(Decision maker's responsibility with researcher's advice)
NO
YES
Resource Requirements
Are there sufficient levels of money, staff, and skills to meet the costs and marketing research requirements?
(Decision maker's responsibility with researcher's advice)
NO
YES
Benefits versus Costs
Does the expected value of the information exceed the costs of conducting the research?
(Decision maker's responsibility with researcher's advice)
NO
YES
Move on to Phase I of the Information Research Process

Exhibit 2.3 displays a framework for determining whether the research process is necessary. To repeat, the initial responsibility of the decision maker is to determine if research should be used to collect the needed primary information. Or *can the problem or opportunity be resolved using existing (secondary) information and managerial judgment?* The focus is on deciding what type of information (secondary or primary) is really required to answer the research question(s). In reality, conducting either secondary or primary research costs time, effort, and money. So the bottom line is that if there is an opportunity, but decision makers do not have the right information or are unwilling to rely on the information at hand, a research effort may be warranted.

A related question is: *Does the problem/opportunity have strategic or significant tactical importance?* Strategic decisions generally have longer time horizons and are more complex than tactical decisions. Most strategic decisions are critical to the company's profit objectives, but tactical decisions can be important as well. For example, Outback Steakhouse recently made a tactical decision to update its menu both in appearance and food offerings. Researching the opinions of customers proved very helpful in determining new food items to be included and items that should be offered as occasional "chef's specials." Thus, if the problem has strategic or significant tactical importance, a research expert should be consulted and perhaps a research process implemented.

With the assistance of the research expert, decision makers are in a better position to answer the question: *Is adequate information available within the company's internal record systems to resolve the problem?* In the past, if the necessary marketing information was not available in the firm's internal record system, then a customized marketing research project was undertaken to obtain the information. The resources today available on the Internet may allow a problem to be solved with secondary data.

With input from the research expert, decision makers must assess the "time constraints" associated with the problem/opportunity: *Is there enough time to conduct the necessary research before the final managerial decision must be made?* Today's decision makers often need information in real time. But in many cases, systematic research that delivers high-quality information can take months. If the decision maker needs the information immediately, there may not be enough time to complete the research process. Another fundamental question focuses on the availability of marketing resources such as money, staff, skills, and facilities. Many small businesses lack the funds necessary to consider doing formal primary research even if it would be valuable.

A cost-benefit assessment should ask: *Do the benefits of having the additional information outweigh the costs of gathering the information?* While the costs of doing marketing research vary from project to project, generally they can be estimated accurately. But predetermining the benefits and true value of the expected information remains difficult.

Other questions to consider before starting a research project include:

- What is the perceived importance and complexity of the problem?
- Is the problem realistically researchable? Can the critical variables in the proposed research be adequately designed and measured?
- Will conducting the needed research give valuable information to the firm's competitors?
- Will the research findings be implemented?
- Will the research design and data represent reality?
- Will the research results and findings be used as legal evidence?
- Is the proposed research politically motivated?

Finally, it is useful to go back to the firm's broadest strategic considerations in answering the most basic question: *Why should the decision maker conduct information research?*

1. If the information will clarify the problem or identify marketplace changes that directly influence the company's product/service responsibilities.
2. If the information helps the company to acquire meaningful competitive advantages within its market environment.
3. If the information leads to marketing actions that will achieve marketing objectives.
4. If the information provides proactive understanding of future market conditions.

If the research process will likely throw good light on any of these, then it is probably worth it.

Overview of the Research Process

The research process consists of four distinct but related phases as shown in Exhibit 2.4: (1) determine the research problem, (2) select the appropriate research design, (3) execute the research design, and (4) communicate the research results. All the phases of the process must be completed properly to provide accurate information for decision making. Each phase consists of several steps.

Scientific method Research procedures are logical, objective, systematic, reliable, and valid.

The four phases are guided by the **scientific method.** This means the research procedures should be logical, objective, systematic, reliable, and valid.

Transforming Data into Knowledge

Knowledge A combination of information and judgment used to make decisions that emerges after data has been collected, analyzed, and interpreted.

Raw data Actual responses obtained about a topic of investigation by asking questions or observing actions.

The primary goal of the research process is to provide decision makers with knowledge that will enable them to resolve problems or pursue opportunities. **Knowledge** is created only after the data have been collected, analyzed, and interpreted so decision makers can make decisions.

To understand this process, decision makers need to know the difference between raw data, data structures, information, and knowledge. First, **raw data** are the actual responses that are obtained about an object or topic of investigation by asking questions or observing actions. These initial responses have not been analyzed or given an interpretive meaning. Some examples of raw data are (1) the responses on a questionnaire; (2) the words recorded during a focus group interview; (3) the number of vehicles that pass through a specified intersection; and (4) the list of purchases, by product type, recorded by an electronic cash register at a local supermarket.

All secondary and primary marketing information is derived from the following process: *gather raw responses; apply some form of data analysis to create usable data structures; and then have someone (a researcher or decision maker) interpret those data structures.*

Gather raw data → Create data structures → Provide interpretation

Data structures The combination of raw responses into groups of data using quantitative or qualitative analysis to reveal patterns or trends.

Data structures are the result of combining individual raw responses into groups of data using some type of quantitative or qualitative analysis procedure (e.g., content analysis, calculation of sample statistics). The results reveal data patterns or trends, which in turn can be simple or complex. Some examples are (1) the average number of times 500 moviegoers patronize their favorite movie house; (2) the frequency distribution of 1,000 college students eating at several predetermined restaurants in a 30-day time frame; (3) the sampling

eXHIBIT 2.4 The Four Phases of the Information Research Process

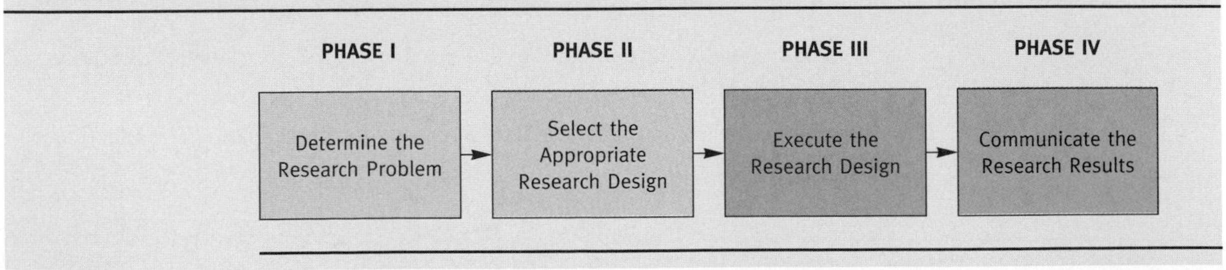

error associated with the overall satisfaction of 250 new Acura 3.2TL automobile owners; and (4) the analysis of variance statistical results of comparing hotel selection criteria means for first-time and repeat customers of a particular hotel.

Information Data used by researchers to created knowledge for decision making.

Information becomes knowledge when someone (either the researcher or the decision maker) interprets the data and attaches meaning. To illustrate this process, consider the Excelsior Hotel. Corporate executives were assessing ways to reduce costs and improve profits. The VP of finance suggested cutting back on the "quality of the towels and bedding" in the rooms. Before making a final decision, the president asked the marketing research department to interview business customers.

Exhibit 2.5 summarizes the key results. A total of 880 people were asked to indicate the degree of importance they placed on seven criteria when selecting a hotel. Respondents used a six-point importance scale ranging from "Extremely Important = 6" to "Not At All Important = 1." The average importance of each criterion was calculated for both first-time and repeat customers and statistically significant differences were identified. These results do not confirm, however, whether "quality towels and bedding" should be cut back to reduce operating costs.

When shown the results, the president asked this question: "I see a lot of numbers, but what are they really telling me?" The director of marketing research quickly responded by explaining: "Among our first-time and repeat business customers, the quality of the hotel's towels and bedding is considered one of the three most important selection criteria impacting their choice of a hotel to stay at when an overnight stay is required. In addition, they feel cleanliness of the room and offering preferred guest card options are of comparable importance to the quality of towels and bedding. But, first-time patrons place significantly higher importance on cleanliness of the room than do repeat patrons (5.75 vs. 5.50). Moreover, repeat customers place significantly more importance on the availability of our preferred guest card options than do business patrons ($x = 5.71$ vs. 5.42)."

Based on these comments, the executives decided they should not cut back on the quality of towels or bedding as a way to reduce expenses and improve profitability.

EXHIBIT 2.5 Summary of Differences in Selected Hotel-Choice Criteria: Comparison of First-Time and Repeat Business Customers

Hotel Selection Criteria	Total (n = 880) Mean[a] Value	First-Time Customers (n = 440) Mean Value	Repeat Customers (n = 440) Mean Value
Cleanliness of the room	5.65	5.75	5.50[b]
Good-quality bedding and towels	5.60	5.55	5.62
Preferred guest card options	5.57	5.42	5.71[b]
Friendly/courteous staff and employees	5.10	4.85	5.45[b]
Free VIP services	5.06	4.35	5.38[b]
Conveniently located for business	5.04	5.25	4.92[b]
In-room movie entertainment	3.63	3.30	4.56[b]

[a]Importance scale: a six-point scale ranging from 6 (extremely important) to 1 (not at all important).
[b]Mean difference in importance between the two customer groups is significant at $p < .05$.

Interrelatedness of the Steps and the Research Process

Exhibit 2.6 shows the steps included in each phase of the research process. Although in many instances researchers follow the four phases in order, individual steps may be shifted or omitted. The complexity of the problem, the urgency of solving the problem, the cost of alternative approaches, and the clarification of information needs will directly impact how many of the steps are taken and in what order. For example, secondary data or "off-the-shelf" research studies may be found that could eliminate the need to collect primary data. Similarly, pretesting the questionnaire (step 7) might reveal weaknesses in some of the scales being considered (step 6), resulting in further refinement of the scales or even selection of a new research design (back to step 4).

What might happen if the research process is not followed? Substantial time, energy, and money can be spent with the result being incomplete, biased, or wrong information. For example, the Food and Beverage Committee at the Alto Lakes Golf and Country Club in Alto, New Mexico, wanted to determine members' satisfaction with the "beverage cart" services being provided on the golf course and learn how to improve services. Not knowing the research process, the committee asked members to rate the beverage cart service using a six-point scale ranging from (6) "Outstanding" to (1) "Terrible" and provided space for written comments. After reviewing only 50 cards returned, the committee found that some members' comments were related to beverage cart satisfaction. But the rating scale was measuring performance rather than satisfaction. The committee did obtain information about the beverage cart service, but it was not what they wanted. Although the committee included some of the key activities in the research process, the data did not answer their questions.

eXHIBIT 2.6 Phases and Steps in the Information Research Process

Phase I: Determine the Research Problem
Step 1: Identify and clarify information needs
Step 2: Define the research problem and questions
Step 3: Specify research objectives and confirm the information value
Phase II: Select the Research Design
Step 4: Determine the research design and data sources
Step 5: Develop the sampling plan and sample size
Step 6: Examine measurement issues and scales
Step 7: Design and pretest the questionnaire
Phase III: Execute the Research Design
Step 8: Collect and prepare data
Step 9: Analyze data
Step 10: Interpret data to create knowledge
Phase IV: Communicate the Research Results
Step 11: Prepare and present the final report

Phase I: Determine the Research Problem

The process of determining the research problem involves three interrelated activities: (1) identify and clarify information needs; (2) define the research problem and questions; and (3) specify research objectives and confirm the information value. These activities bring researchers and decision makers together based on management's recognition of the need for information to improve decision making.

Step 1: Identify and Clarify Information Needs

Generally, decision makers prepare a statement of what they believe is the problem before the researcher becomes involved. Then researchers assist decision makers to make sure the problem or opportunity has been correctly defined and the information requirements are known.

For researchers to understand the problem, they use a problem definition process such as shown in Exhibit 2.7. There is no one best process. But any process undertaken should include the following activities: (1) agree on the decision maker's purpose for the research, (2) understand the complete problem, (3) identify measurable symptoms, (4) select the unit of analysis, and (5) determine the relevant variables. Correctly defining the problem is an important first step in determining if research is necessary. A poorly defined problem can produce research results that are of little value, as in the New Coke example in the nearby A Closer Look at Research (In the Field) box.

Purpose of the Research Request

Problem definition begins by determining the research purpose. Decision makers must decide whether the services of a researcher are needed. Then, the researcher begins to define the problem by asking the decision maker why the research is needed. Through questioning, researchers begin to learn what the decision maker believes the problem is. Having a

eXHIBIT 2.7 Integrated Decision Problem Definition Process

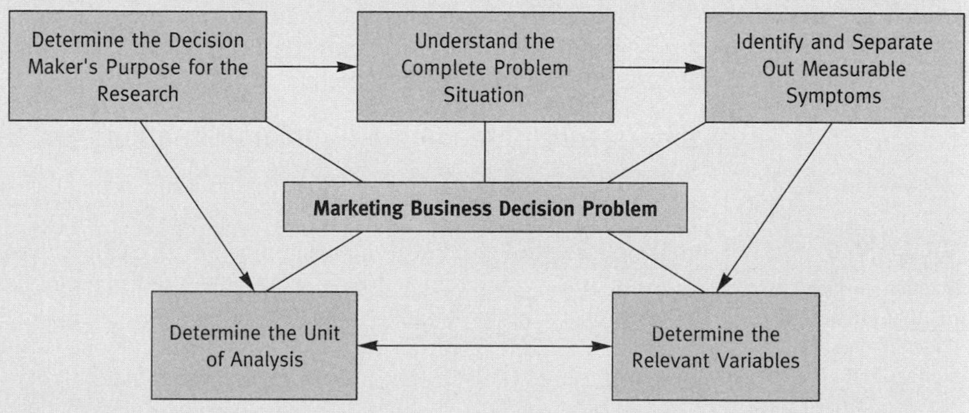

A Closer Look at Research

"Can I Get a New Coke Please?"

In an effort to gain market share, the Pepsi-Cola Company conducted a series of blind taste tests and determined that soft-drink consumers preferred the sweetness of Pepsi to the crisper taste of Coke. On the basis of what was called the Pepsi Challenge, Pepsi developed a marketing program concentrating on younger soft-drink customers and labeling them the Pepsi Generation.

The Coca-Cola company's initial response was to increase its advertising budget and develop a claim of product superiority. Nonetheless, Coke's own taste tests validated Pepsi's claims that customers preferred a sweeter product. Using information obtained in the development of Diet Coke, Coca-Cola created a new, sweeter Coke product and embarked on one of the most extensive marketing research programs in the history of the soft-drink industry.

Coke's market research lasted three years and asked over 200,000 customers to participate in blind taste tests conducted in shopping malls across the country. The information research question that guided Coca-Cola's research program was: "What will be the ultimate consumer reactions to the taste of the new Coke product?" Results of the marketing research indicated that when asked to compare unmarked beverages, consumers favored the new Coke formula over the original Coke product by a margin of 55 percent to 45 percent. When both soft drinks were identified, 53 percent of those taking the test still preferred the new Coke formula over the original Coke.

Based on these research results, Coca-Cola decided to introduce a new sweeter-formula coke. The product was introduced with the name New Coke and the original Coke was discontinued. Within three months, however, old Coke was put back on the market. By the end of the year, the new Coke formula, the one marketing research showed to be preferred by drinkers, was discontinued. What happened? Where did Coca-Cola go wrong? What should have been measured? What if Coca-Cola had put the new product under the old label? These remain good topics of discussion within marketing research. The Coca-Cola research question and problem definition had been too narrow and researchers investigated and tested only one aspect—consumers' taste preferences. Researchers did not investigate others aspects of consumer preference, including emotional attachment and brand loyalty. Moreover, Coca-Cola's research failed to ask respondents if the new Coke product should replace the original Coca-Cola.[2]

general idea of why research is needed focuses attention on the circumstances surrounding the problem. Using the *iceberg principle* displayed in Exhibit 2.8 helps researchers to distinguish between the symptoms and the causes.

Understand the Complete Problem Situation

The decision maker and the researcher both must understand the complete problem. This is easy to state but quite often difficult to execute. To gain an understanding of the complete problem, researchers and decision makers should do a situation analysis of the problem. A **situation analysis** is a tool that focuses on gathering background information to familiarize the researcher with the overall complexity of the problem. A situation analysis attempts to identify the events and factors that have led to the situation, as well as any expected future consequences. Awareness of the complete problem situation provides better perspectives on the decision maker's needs, the complexity of the problem, and the factors involved.

Situation analysis A tool that focuses on gathering background information to familiarize the researcher with the overall complexity of the research problem.

A situation analysis enhances communication between the researcher and the decision maker. The researcher must understand the client's business, including factors such as the

EXHIBIT 2.8 The Iceberg Principle

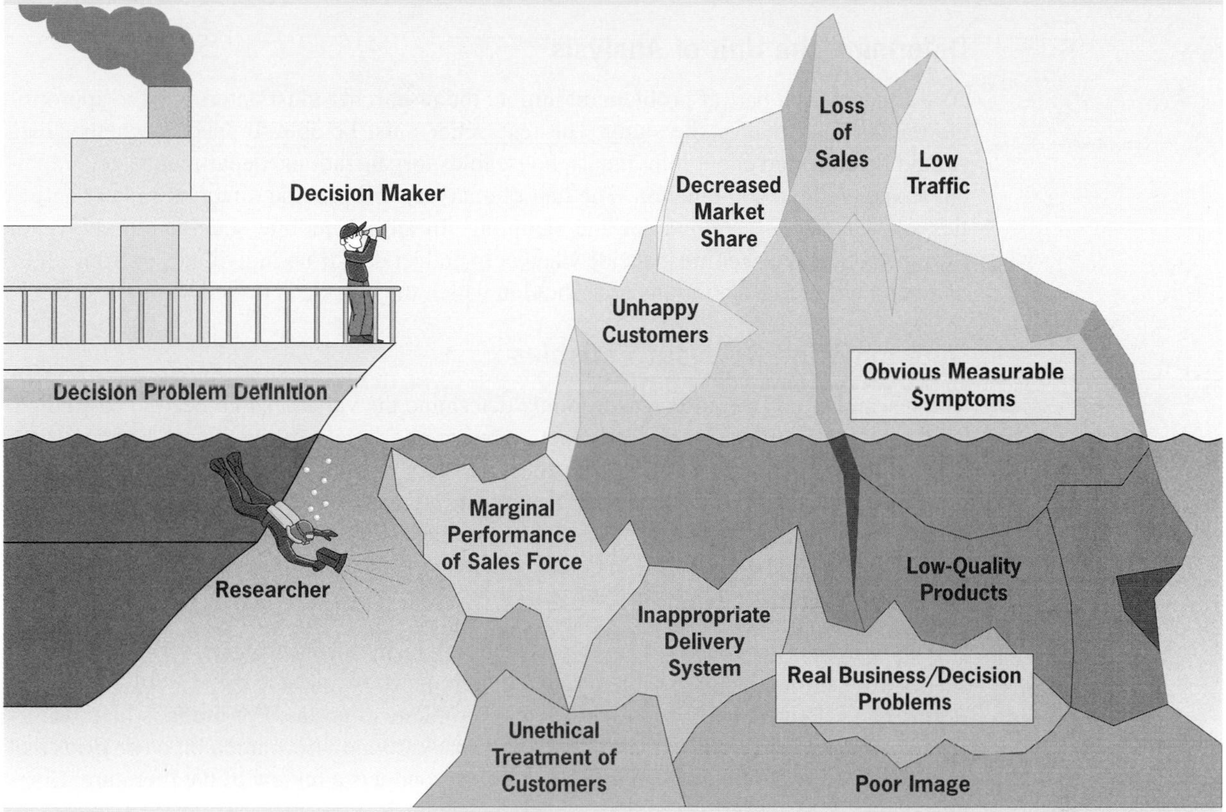

The iceberg principle holds that decision makers are aware of only 10 percent of the true problem. Frequently the perceived problem is actually a symptom that is some type of measurable market performance factor, while 90 percent of the problem is not visible to decision makers. For example, the problem may be defined as "loss of market share" when in fact the problem is ineffective advertising or a poorly trained sales force. The real problems are below the waterline of observation. If the submerged portions of the problem are omitted from the problem definition and later from the research design, then decisions based on the research may be incorrect.

industry, competition, product lines, markets, and in some cases production facilities. To do so, the researcher cannot rely solely on information provided by the client because many decision makers either do not know or will not disclose the information needed. Only when the researcher views the client's business objectively can the true problem be clarified.

Identify and Separate Out Symptoms

Once the researcher understands the overall problem situation, he or she must work with the decision maker to separate the possible basic problems from the observable and measurable symptoms that may have been initially perceived as being the problem. For example, many times managers view declining sales or loss of market share as problems. After examining these issues, the researcher may see that they are really symptoms—the result of more specific issues such as poor advertising execution, lack of sales force motivation, or inadequate distribution. The challenge facing the researcher is one of clarifying the real problem by separating out possible causes from symptoms. Is a decline in sales truly the problem or merely a symptom of lack of planning, poor location, or ineffective sales management?

Determine the Unit of Analysis

As a fundamental part of problem definition, the researcher must determine the appropriate unit of analysis for the study. The researcher must be able to specify whether data should be collected about individuals, households, organizations, departments, geographical areas, or some combination. The unit of analysis will provide direction in later activities such as scale development and sampling. In an automobile satisfaction study, for example, the researcher must decide whether to collect data from individuals or from a husband and wife representing the household in which the vehicle is driven.

Determine the Relevant Variables

The researcher and decision maker jointly determine the variables that need to be studied. The types of information needed (facts, predictions, relationships) must be identified. Exhibit 2.9 lists examples of variables that are often investigated in marketing. Variables are often measured using several related questions on a survey and may be called constructs. In some situations we refer to these variables as constructs.

Step 2: Define the Research Problem and Questions

Next, the researcher must reformulate the problem in scientific terms. That is, the researcher must redefine the problem as a research question because the scientific approach ensures a systematic approach to developing problem solutions. For the most part, this is the responsibility of the researcher. To provide background information on other firms that may have faced similar problems, the researcher conducts a review of the literature. Literature reviews are described in more detail in Chapter 5.

Breaking down the problem into research questions is one of the most important steps in the marketing research process because how the research problem is defined influences all of the remaining research steps. The researcher's task is to restate the initial variables

eXHIBIT 2.9 Examples of Variables/Constructs Investigated in Marketing

Variables/Constructs	Description
Brand awareness	Percentage of respondents having heard of a designated brand; awareness could be either unaided or aided.
Brand attitudes	The number of respondents and their intensity of feeling positive or negative toward a specific brand.
Satisfaction	How people evaluate their postpurchase consumption experience with a particular product, service, or company.
Purchase intention	The number of people planning to buy a specified object (e.g., product or service) within a designated time period.
Importance of factors	To what extent do specific factors influence a person's purchase choice?
Demographics	The age, gender, occupation, income level, and other characteristics of individuals providing the information.

associated with the problem in the form of key questions: how, what, where, when, and why. For example, management of Lowe's Home Improvement Inc. was concerned about the overall image of Lowe's retail operations as well as its image among customers within the Atlanta metropolitan market. The initial research question was "Do our marketing strategies need to be modified to increase satisfaction among our current and future customers?" After Lowe's management met with consultants at Corporate Communications and Marketing, Inc., to clarify the firm's information needs, the consultants translated the initial problem into the specific questions displayed in Exhibit 2.10. With assistance of management, the consultants then identified the attributes in each research question. For example, specific "store/operation aspects" that can affect satisfaction included convenient operating hours, friendly/courteous staff, and wide assortment of products and services.

When research questions are written, two approaches can be taken to determine the level of detail to use. One approach is to phrase the questions to include only the general category of possible factors. For example, with the demographic question in the Lowe's example (Exhibit 2.10), the phrasing is somewhat ambiguous because it expresses only the need for a "demographic/psychographic profile" of customers without specifying which particular demographic characteristics (e.g., age, income, education level, marital status) or psychographic factors (e.g., price conscious, do-it-yourself, brand loyalist, information seeker) should be investigated. The other approach is to be more specific in phrasing the research questions. For example, if Lowe's management team is interested in determining the price range for a particular Black & Decker power drill, the research questions would be phrased as follows: "What are the price ranges customers expect to pay for the Black & Decker RX power drill?" and "What are the price ranges customers are willing to pay for the Black & Decker RX power drill?" Here each research question focuses on a specific data requirement—expected price ranges and then actual price ranges.

After redefining the problem into research questions and identifying the information requirements, the researcher must determine the types of data (secondary or primary) that will best answer each research problem. Although a final decision on types of data is part of Step 4 (Determine the Research Design and Data Sources), the researcher begins the process in Step 2. The researcher asks the question "Can the specific research question be addressed with data that already exist or does the question require new data?" To answer this question, researchers consider other issues such as data availability, data quality, and budget and time constraints.

eXHIBIT 2.10 Initial and Redefined Research Questions for Lowe's Home Improvement, Inc.

Initial research question

Do our marketing strategies need to be modified to increase satisfaction among our current and future customer segments?

Redefined research questions

- What store/operation aspects do people believe are important in selecting a retail hardware/lumber outlet?
- How do customers evaluate Lowe's retail outlets on store/operation aspects?
- What are the perceived strengths and weaknesses of Lowe's retail operations?
- How do customers and noncustomers compare Lowe's to other retail hardware/lumber outlets within the Atlanta metropolitan area?
- What is the demographic/psychographic profile of the people who patronize Lowe's retail outlets in the Atlanta market?

A Closer Look at Research

Small Business Implications

Ford Foundation[3]

Several years ago, the Ford Foundation of the Performing Arts, located in Vail, Colorado, successfully completed a $5 million fund-raising drive to build an amphitheater to house performing arts events. The Foundation's Amphitheater Design Team faced some difficult decisions. They were not sure which design features should be included in the structure to handle different types of events (theatrical productions, music concerts, dance productions, and so on). Further, they could not decide if the structure should accommodate indoor events, outdoor events, or a combination.

They questioned the seating capacity and worried about ticket prices, parking requirements, availability of refreshments, and types of events most desired by local residents and visitors. The foundation hired a marketing research consultant to assist in gathering both primary and secondary data needed to address the team's questions and concerns. After several meetings with the design team, the researcher presented his research proposal, which stated that the "primary research objective focused on the collection of attitudinal and behavioral information to be used in addressing several questions posed by the Ford Amphitheater Design Team. The questions focused on performing arts events and possible design features for the proposed amphitheater structure." Three of the key research questions were:

1. What type of performing arts programs would residents and guests most prefer to see offered in the Vail Valley area?
2. What prices should be charged for the various types of events?
3. What type of summer-evening performing arts programs would people prefer attending at an indoor versus outdoor facility? If outdoors, what type of protection should be provided to the audience and the performers?

These questions were then transformed into the following research objectives:

1. To determine how often people attended performing arts events in the past 12 months and what three types of events (dance productions, theatrical productions, music concerts, and so on) they would be most interested in attending while staying in Vail Valley.
2. To determine, by event type, the average price range a person would expect and be willing to pay for an adult-reserved-seat ticket to the events presented in Vail Valley.
3. To determine the extent to which people would prefer to attend a specific type of event at an indoor or outdoor facility and the specific type of protection that should be offered the audience if the event was held at an outdoor facility.

Finally, in Step 2 the researcher determines whether the information being requested is necessary. This step must be completed before going on to Step 3.

Step 3: Specify Research Objectives and Confirm the Information Value

The research objectives should be based on the definition of the research problem in Step 2. Formally stated research objectives provide guidelines for determining other steps that must be taken. The assumption is if the objectives are achieved, the decision maker will have the information needed to solve the problem.

Research objectives serve as the justification for management and researchers to undertake a research project. Consider the Ford Foundation example in the nearby A Closer Look at Research (Small Business Implications) box. Notice that the objectives listed at the end are different from the foundation's statement of the research problem and the researcher's problem. Before researchers move beyond Phase I of the research process, they must make sure each factor in the study has been defined. There also must be justification for the relevance of each factor. For example, what does the Ford Foundation really mean by "protection"? Protection from what—rain or cold or snow, or perhaps something else?

Before moving to Phase II of the research process, the decision maker and the researcher must evaluate the expected value of the information. This is not an easy task because a number of factors come into play. "Best guess" answers have to be made to the following types of questions:

"Can the information be collected at all?"

"Can the information tell the decision maker something not already known?"

"Will the information provide significant insights?"

"What benefits will be delivered by this information?"

In most cases, research should be conducted only when the expected value of the information to be obtained exceeds the cost.

Phase II: Select the Research Design

The main focus of Phase II is to select the most appropriate research design to achieve the research objectives. The steps in this phase are outlined below.

Step 4: Determine the Research Design and Data Sources

The research design serves as an overall plan of the methods used to collect and analyze the data. Determining the most appropriate research design is a function of the research objectives and information requirements. The researcher must consider the types of data, the data collection method (for example, survey, observation, in-depth interview), sampling method, schedule, and budget. There are three broad categories of research designs: exploratory, descriptive, and causal. An individual research project may sometimes require a combination of exploratory, descriptive, and/or causal techniques in order to meet research objectives.

Exploratory research Generates insights that help define the problem and increase the understanding of consumer motivations, attitudes, and behavior.

Exploratory research has one of two objectives: (1) generating insights that will help define the problem situation confronting the researcher or (2) deepening the understanding of consumer motivations, attitudes, and behavior that are not easy to access using other research methods. Examples of exploratory research methods include literature reviews of already available information; qualitative approaches such as focus groups and in-depth interviews; or pilot studies. Literature reviews are described in Chapter 5 and exploratory research in Chapters 6 and 7.

Descriptive research Provides answers to who, what, when, where and how questions.

Descriptive research involves collecting numeric data to answer research questions. Descriptive information provides answers to who, what, when, where and how questions. In marketing, examples of descriptive information include consumer attitudes, intentions, preferences, purchase behaviors, evaluations of current marketing mix strategies, and demographics.

Descriptive studies may provide information about competitors, target markets, and environmental factors. For example, many chain restaurants conduct annual studies that describe customers' perceptions of their restaurant as well as perceptions of primary competitors. These studies, referred to as either image assessment surveys or customer satisfaction surveys, describe how customers rate different restaurants' customer service, convenience of location, food quality, and atmosphere. Some qualitative research is descriptive in the sense of providing rich or "thick" narrative description of phenomena. However, the term "descriptive research" usually means numeric rather than textual data. Descriptive designs are discussed in Chapter 8.

Causal research Enables decision makers to determine cause-and-effect relationships between two or more varibles.

Causal research collects data that enable decision makers to determine cause-and-effect relationships between two or more variables. Causal research is most appropriate when the research objectives include the need to understand which variables (for example, advertising, number of salespersons, price) affect a dependent variable (sales, customer satisfaction).

Understanding cause–effect relationships among market performance factors enables the decision maker to make "If–then" statements about the variables. For example, as a result of using causal research methods, the owner of a men's clothing store in Chicago can predict, "If I increase my advertising budget by 15 percent, then overall sales volume should increase by 20 percent." Causal research designs provide an opportunity to assess and explain causality among market factors. But they often can be complex, expensive, and time-consuming. Causal research designs are discussed in Chapter 9.

Secondary and Primary Data Sources

The sources of data needed to address research problems can be classified as either secondary or primary. The sources used depend on two fundamental issues: (1) whether the data already exist, and (2) the extent to which the researcher or decision maker knows the reason(s) why the data were collected. Sources of secondary data include "inside" the company—a company's data warehouse—or "outside" the company—public libraries and universities, the Internet, or commercial data purchased from firms specializing in providing secondary information. Chapter 5 covers secondary information research designs.

Primary data are collected directly from first-hand sources to address the current information research problem. The nature and collection of primary data are covered in Chapters 6 through 9.

Step 5: Develop the Sampling Plan and Sample Size

Target population A specified group of people for which questions will be asked or observations made to obtain the desired information.

Census Questioning or observing all the members of a defined target population.

When conducting primary research, consideration must be given to the sampling design. When conducting secondary research, the researcher must still determine that the population represented by the secondary data is relevant to the current research problem. Relevancy of secondary data is covered in Chapters 4 and 5.

If predictions are to be made about market phenomena, the sample must be representative. Typically, marketing decision makers are most interested in identifying and resolving problems associated with their target markets. Therefore, researchers need to identify the relevant **target population.** In collecting data, researchers can choose between collecting data from a census or sample. In a **census,** the researcher attempts to question or observe all the members of a defined target population. For small populations a census may be the best approach.

eXHIBIT 2.11 Questions and Issues in the Development of a Sampling Plan

- Given the problem, research objectives, and information requirements, who would be the best person (or object) to question or observe?
- What demographic (gender, occupation, age, marital status, income levels, education) and/or behavioral traits (regular shopper/occasional shopper/nonshopper; heavy user/light user/nonuser; customer/noncustomer) should be used to identify population membership?
- How many population elements must be in the sample to ensure it is representative of the population?
- How reliable does the information have to be for the decision maker?
- What are the data quality concerns and acceptable levels of sampling error?
- What technique should be used in the actual selection of sampling units?
- What are the time and cost constraints associated with executing the appropriate sampling plan?

Sample A group of people or objects selected from the target population.

A second approach, used when the target population is large, involves the selection of a **sample** from the defined target population. Researchers must use a representative sample of the population if they wish to generalize the findings. To achieve this objective, researchers develop a sampling plan as part of the overall research design. A sampling plan serves as the blueprint for defining the appropriate target population, identifying the possible respondents, establishing the procedures for selecting the sample, and determining the appropriate sample size. Exhibit 2.11 lists the questions and issues researchers typically face when developing a sampling plan.

Sampling plans can be classified into two general types: probability and nonprobability. In *probability sampling,* each member of the defined target population has a known chance of being selected. Also, probability sampling gives the researcher the opportunity to assess sampling error. In contrast, *nonprobability sampling* plans cannot measure sampling error and limit the generalizability of the research findings. Qualitative research designs often use small samples, so sample members are usually hand-selected.

Sample size affects data quality and generalizability. Researchers must therefore determine how many people to include or how many objects to investigate. We discuss sampling in more detail in Chapter 10.

Step 6: Examine Measurement Issues and Scales

Step 6 is an important step in the research process for descriptive and causal designs. It involves identifying the concepts to study and measuring the variables related to the problem. Given the importance of measurement to the process of creating information, researchers must be able to answer questions such as:

> "How should a variable such as customer satisfaction or service quality be defined and measured?"
>
> "Should researchers use single-item or multi-item measures to quantify variables?"

In Chapters 11 and 12 we discuss measurement and scaling.

Although most of the activities involved in Step 6 are related to primary research, understanding these activities is important in secondary research as well. For example, when using data mining with database variables, researchers must consider the measurement issues. They must understand the measurement approach used in creating the database as well as any measurement biases. Otherwise, secondary data may be misinterpreted.

Step 7: Design and Pretest the Questionnaire

Designing good questionnaires is difficult. Researchers must select the correct type of questions, consider their sequence and format, and pretest the questionnaire. Pretesting obtains information from people representative of those who will be questioned in the actual survey. In a pretest respondents are asked to complete the questionnaire and comment on issues like clarity of instructions and questions, sequence of the topics and questions, and anything that is potentially difficult or confusing. Chapter 13 covers questionnaire design.

If qualitative research is being conducted, interview guides and exercises are developed by researchers. If the data is preexisting "found" data (for example, posted consumer opinions of a book at Amazon.com), then categories or themes are emergent. That is, they are identified by researchers as they review the data. Measurements for observational research may be emergent or predetermined. For example, observers of babies at the Fisher Price toy lab may determine prior to observation that they will count the number of times babies play with each toy as well as the amount of time spent with each toy. Forms will be designed when categories are predetermined to enable researchers to collect the required data.

Phase III: Execute the Research Design

The main objectives of the execution phase are to finalize all necessary data collection forms, gather and prepare the data, and analyze and interpret the data to understand the problem or opportunity. As in the first two phases, researchers must be cautious to ensure potential biases or errors are either eliminated or at least minimized.

Step 8: Collect and Prepare Data

Data Collection Methods

There are two approaches to gathering data. One is to have interviewers ask questions about variables and market phenomena or to use self-completion questionnaires. The other is to observe individuals or market phenomena. Self-administered surveys, personal interviews, computer simulations, telephone interviews, and focus groups are just some of the tools researchers use to collect data (see Exhibit 2.12).

A major advantage of questioning approaches over observation is they enable the researcher to collect a wider array of data. Questioning approaches can collect information about attitudes, intentions, motivations, and past behavior, which are usually invisible in observational research. In short, questioning approaches can be used to answer not just how persons are behaving, but why persons are behaving as they are.

Observation methods can be characterized as natural or contrived, disguised or undisguised, structured or unstructured, direct or indirect, and human, electronic, or mechanical. For example, researchers might use trained human observers or a variety of mechanical devices such as a video camera, audiometer, eye camera, or pupilometer to record behavior or events.

eXHIBIT 2.12 Data Collection Tools Used in Marketing Research

Observation Tools	Description
Trained observers	Highly skilled people who use their senses (sight, hearing, smell, touch, taste) to observe and record physical phenomena. *Examples:* mystery shoppers; traffic counters; ethnographers.
Mechanical/electronic	Devices that can observe and record physical phenomena. *Examples:* security cameras; videotaping equipment; scanning devices; Internet technology; tape recorders; air-hose traffic counters.
Questioning Tools	
Trained interviewers	Highly trained people who ask respondents specific questions and accurately record their responses. *Examples:* face-to-face interviewers; telephone interviewers; group survey leaders; focus group moderators.
Interviewer/electronic devices	Highly skilled people who use technology devices when surveying respondents. *Examples:* computer-assisted personal interviews; computer-assisted telephone interviews.
Fully automatic devices	High-tech devices that interact with respondents without the presence of a trained interviewer. *Examples:* on-site fully automatic interviews; fully automatic telephone interviews; Internet surveys.
Direct self-administered questionnaires	Survey instruments that are designed to have the respondent serve the roles of both interviewer and respondent. *Examples:* direct mail surveys; most group self-administered surveys.

As technology advances, researchers are moving toward integrating the benefits of technology with existing questioning tools that enable faster data acquisition. Online primary data studies (e-mail surveys, online focus group interviews, Internet surveys) are increasing as well as secondary database research studies. Data collection approaches and instruments are covered in Chapters 5 to 13.

Preparation of Data

Once primary data are collected, researchers must perform several activities before data analysis. A coding scheme is needed so the data can be entered into computer files. Typically, researchers assign a logical numerical descriptor (code) to all response categories. After the responses are entered, the researcher inspects the computer files to verify they are accurate. The data then must be examined for coding or data-entry errors. Chapter 14 discusses data preparation.

Data preparation in secondary research studies is somewhat different from that used with primary research. Researchers focus on evaluating the use of a single or multiple databases to obtain the needed information. When the data exist in multiple databases, different databases must be merged into a combined database. At times, merging one database with another can be challenging and may require restructuring one or more databases to achieve compatibility. Another activity is determining which data should be included in the analysis. Chapter 5 covers secondary data and sources.

Step 9: Analyze Data

In Step 9, the researcher analyzes the data and may create summated variables, ratios, constructs, and so on. Analysis procedures vary widely in sophistication and complexity, from simple frequency distributions (percentages) to statistics (mean, median, and mode) and perhaps even multivariate data analysis. Different procedures enable the researcher to statistically test hypotheses for significant differences or correlations among several variables, evaluate data quality, and test models of cause–effect relationships. Chapters 15 through 17 provide an overview of data analysis techniques.

Step 10: Interpret Data to Create Knowledge

Knowledge is created for decision makers in Step 10. *Knowledge* (as we discussed it earlier in the chapter) is information combined with judgment and interpretation to facilitate accurate decisions. Researchers and decision makers interpret the results of the data analysis. Interpretation is more than a narrative description of the results. It involves integrating several aspects of the findings into conclusions that can be used to answer the research questions.

Phase IV: Communicate the Research Results

The last phase of the information research process focuses on reporting the research findings to management. The overall objective often is to prepare a report that is useful to a non-research-oriented person.

Step 11: Prepare and Present the Final Report

Step 11 is preparing and presenting the final research report to management. The importance of this step cannot be overstated. There are some sections that should be included in any research report: executive summary/key findings, introduction, problem definition and objectives, methodology, results and findings, and limitations of study. The researcher asks the decision maker whether specific sections need to be included or expanded, such as recommendations for future actions or further information needs. In some cases, the researcher not only submits a written report but also makes an oral presentation of the major findings. Chapter 18 describes how to write and present research reports.

Develop a Research Proposal

Research proposal A document that serves as a written contract between the decision maker and the researcher regarding the research to be conducted.

By understanding the four phases of the research process, a researcher can develop a research proposal that communicates the research framework to the decision maker. A **research proposal** is a specific document that serves as a written contract between the decision maker and the researcher. It lists the activities that will be undertaken to develop the needed information, the research deliverables, how long it will take, and what it will cost.

The research proposal is not set up the same as a final research report. But some of the sections are similar. There is no best way to write a research proposal. Exhibit 2.13 shows the sections that should be included in most research proposals. The exhibit presents only a general outline; an actual proposal can be found in the Marketing Research in Action at the end of this chapter.

eXHIBIT 2.13 General Outline of a Research Proposal

TITLE OF THE RESEARCH PROPOSAL

I. Purpose of the Proposed Research Project
Includes a description of the problem and research objectives.

II. Type of Study
Discusses the type of research design (exploratory, descriptive, or causal), and secondary versus primary data requirements, with justification of choice.

III. Definition of the Target Population and Sample Size
Describes the overall target population to be studied and determination of the appropriate sample size, including a justification of the size.

IV. Sample Design and Data Collection Method
Describes the sampling technique used, the method of collecting data (for example, observation or survey), incentive plans, and justifications.

V. Specific Research Instruments
Discusses the method used to collect the needed data, including the various types of scales.

VI. Potential Managerial Benefits of the Proposed Study
Discusses the expected value of the information to management and how the initial problem might be resolved, including the study's limitations.

VII. Proposed Cost for the Total Project
Itemizes the expected costs for completing the research, including a total cost figure and anticipated time frames.

VIII. Profile of the Research Company Capabilities
Briefly describes the researchers and their qualifications as well as a general overview of the company.

IX. Optional Dummy Tables of the Projected Results
Gives examples of how the data might be presented in the final report.

MARKETING RESEARCH IN ACTION

What Does a Research Proposal Look Like?

Excelsior Hotel Preferred Guest Card Research Proposal

The purpose of the proposed research project is to collect attitudinal, behavioral, motivational, and general demographic information to address several key questions posed by management concerning the Excelsior Hotel Preferred Guest Card, a recently implemented marketing strategy. Key questions are as follows:

1. Is the Preferred Guest Card being used by cardholders?
2. How do cardholders evaluate the privileges associated with the card?
3. What are the perceived benefits and weaknesses of the card, and why?
4. Is the Preferred Guest Card an important factor in selecting a hotel?
5. How often and when do cardholders use their Preferred Guest Card?
6. Of those who have used the card, what privileges have been used and how often?
7. What improvements should be made regarding the card or the extended privileges?
8. How did cardholders obtain the card?
9. Should the Preferred Guest Card membership be complimentary or should cardholders pay an annual fee?
10. If there should be an annual fee, how much should it be? What would a cardholder be willing to pay?
11. What is the demographic profile of the people who have the Excelsior Hotel Preferred Guest Card?

To collect the data needed to examine these questions, the research should have a structured, nondisguised design that includes both exploratory and descriptive research. The study will be descriptive to the extent that most of the questions focus on identifying the perceived awareness, attitudes, and usage patterns of the Excelsior Hotel Preferred Guest Card holders as well as the demographic profiles of the current cardholders. It will be exploratory since it is looking for possible improvements to the card and its privileges, the pricing structure, and the perceived benefits and weaknesses of the current card's features.

The target population to be studied consists of adults who are known to be current cardholders of the Excelsior Hotel Preferred Guest Card. At present, this population frame is approximately 17,000 individuals across the United States. Statistically a conservative sample size would be 387. But realistically a sample of approximately 1,500 should be used to enable examination of sample subgroups. The bases for this approximation are the likely response rate based on the sampling method and questionnaire design, a predetermined level of precision of ± 5% sampling error and a desired confidence level of 95%, general administrative costs and trade-offs, and the desirability of having a prespecified minimum number of randomly selected cardholders for the data analyses.

Probability sampling will be used to draw the sample from the central cardholder database. Using a mail survey, cardholders randomly selected as prospective respondents will be mailed a personalized self-administered questionnaire. Attached to the questionnaire will be a carefully designed cover letter that explains the generalities of the study as well as inducements for respondent participation. Given the nature of the study, the perceived type of cardholder, the general trade-offs regarding costs and time considerations, and the utilization of updated incentives to induce respondent participation, a mail survey would be more appropriate than other methods.

The questionnaire will be self-administered. That is, respondents will fill out the survey in the privacy of their home and without the presence of an interviewer. All survey questions will be pretested using a convenience sample to assess clarity of instructions, questions, and administrative time dimensions. Response scales for the questions will conform to questionnaire design guidelines and industry judgment.

Given the scope and nature of this proposed research project, the study's findings will enable Excelsior Hotel's management to answer questions regarding the Preferred Guest Card as well as other marketing strategy issues. Specifically, the proposed study will help management to:

- Better understand the types of people that use the Preferred Guest Card and the extent of usage;
- Identify issues that suggest evaluating (and possibly modifying) current marketing strategies or tactics for the card and its privileges; and
- Develop insights concerning the promotion and distribution of the card to additional segments.

Additionally, the proposed research project will initiate a customer-oriented database and information system to assist management in better understanding its customers' hotel service needs and wants. Customer-oriented databases will be useful in developing promotional strategies as well as pricing and service approaches.

Proposed Project Costs

Questionnaire/cover letter design and reproduction	$ 4,800
Development, typing, pretest, reproduction (1,500)	
Envelopes (3,000)	
Sample design and plan	2,750
Administration/data collection	5,800
Questionnaire packet assembly	
Postage and P.O. box	
Address labels	
Coding and pre–data analysis costs	4,000
Coding and data entry	
Tab development	
Computer programming	
Data analysis and interpretation	7,500
Written report and presentation	4,500
Total proposed project cost*	$29,350

*Costing policy: Some items may cost more or less than what is stated on the proposal. Cost reductions, if any, will be passed on to the client. Additionally, there is a ± 10% cost margin associated with the pre- and actual data analysis activities depending on client changes of the original tab and analyses requirements.

Research for this proposed project will be conducted by the Marketing Resource Group (MRG), a firm that specializes in a wide array of research approaches. MRG is located in Tampa, Florida, and has conducted research studies for many Fortune 1000 companies. The principal researcher and project coordinator will be Mr. Alex Smith, Senior Project Director at MRG. Mr. Smith holds a Ph.D. in Marketing from Louisiana State University, an MBA from Illinois State University, and a BS from Southern Illinois University. With 25 years of marketing research experience, he has conducted numerous projects within the consumer packaged-goods products, hotel/resort, retail banking, automobile, and insurance industries, to name a few. He specializes in projects that focus on customer satisfaction, service/product quality, market segmentation, and general consumer attitudes and behavior patterns as well as interactive electronic marketing technologies. In addition, he has published numerous articles on theoretical and pragmatic researching topics.

Hands-On Exercise

1. If this proposal is accepted, will it achieve the objectives of management?
2. Is the target population being interviewed the appropriate one?
3. Are there other questions that should be asked in the project?

Summary of Learning Objectives

■ **Describe the major environmental factors influencing marketing research.**

Several key environmental factors have significant impact on changing the tasks, responsibilities, and efforts associated with marketing research practices. Marketing research has risen from a supporting role within organizations to being integral in strategic planning. The Internet and e-commerce, gatekeeper technologies and data privacy legislation, and new global market structure expansions are all forcing researchers to balance their use of secondary and primary data to assist decision makers in solving decision problems and taking advantage of opportunities. Researchers need to improve their ability to use technology-driven tools and databases. There are also greater needs for faster data acquisition and retrieval, analysis, and interpretation of cross-functional data and information among decision-making teams within global market environments.

■ **Discuss the research process and explain its various steps.**

The information research process has four major phases, identified as (1) determine the research problem, (2) select the appropriate research design, (3) execute the research design, and (4) communicate the results. To achieve the overall objectives of each phase, researchers must be able to successfully execute eleven interrelated task steps: (1) identify and clarify information needs, (2) define the research problem and questions, (3) specify research objectives and confirm the information value, (4) determine the research design and data sources, (5) develop the sampling plan and sample size, (6) examine measurement issues and scales, (7) design and pretest questionnaires, (8) collect and prepare data, (9) analyze data, (10) interpret data to create knowledge, and (11) prepare and present the final report.

■ **Distinguish between exploratory, descriptive, and causal research designs.**

The main objective of exploratory research designs is to create information that the researcher or decision maker can use to (1) gain a clear understanding of the problem; (2) define or redefine the initial problem, separating the symptoms from the causes; (3) confirm the problem and objectives; or (4) identify the information requirements. Exploratory research designs are often intended to provide preliminary insight for follow-up quantitative research. However, sometimes qualitative exploratory methods are used as standalone techniques because the topic under investigation requires in-depth understanding of a complex web of consumer culture, psychological motivations, and behavior. For some research topics, quantitative research may be too superficial or it may elicit responses from consumers that are rationalizations rather than true reasons for purchase decisions and behavior.

Descriptive research designs produce numeric data to describe existing characteristics (for example, attitudes, intentions, preferences, purchase behaviors, evaluations of current marketing mix strategies) of a defined target population. The researcher looks for answers to how, who, what, when, and where questions. Information from descriptive designs allows decision makers to draw inferences about their customers, competitors, target markets, environmental factors, or other phenomena.

Finally, causal research designs are most useful when the research objectives include the need to understand why market phenomena happen. The focus of causal research is to collect data that enables the decision maker or researcher to model cause-and-effect relationships between two or more variables.

■ **Identify and explain the major components of a research proposal.**

Once the researcher understands the different phases and task steps of the information research process, he or she can develop a research proposal. The proposal serves as a contract between the researcher and decision maker. There are nine sections suggested for inclusion: (1) purpose of the proposed research project; (2) type of study; (3) definition of the target population and sample size; (4) sample design, technique, and data collection method; (5) research instruments; (6) potential managerial benefits of the proposed study; (7) proposed cost structure for the project; (8) profile of the researcher and company; and (9) dummy tables of the projected results.

Key Terms and Concepts

Causal research 52
Census 52
Data structures 42
Descriptive research 51
Exploratory research 51
Gatekeeper technologies 37
Information 43
Information research process 38
Internet 36
Knowledge 42
Primary data 37
Raw data 42
Research proposal 56
Sample 53
Scientific method 42
Secondary data 37
Situation analysis 46
Target population 52

Review Questions

1. Identify the significant changes taking place in today's business environment that are forcing management decision makers to rethink their views of marketing research. Also discuss the potential impact that these changes might have on marketing research activities.
2. In the business world of the 21st century, will it be possible to make critical marketing decisions without marketing research? Why or why not?
3. How are management decision makers and information researchers alike? How are they different? How might the differences be reduced between these two types of professionals?
4. Comment on the following statements:
   a. The primary responsibility for determining whether marketing research activities are necessary is that of the marketing research specialist.
   b. The information research process serves as a blueprint for reducing risks in making marketing decisions.
   c. Selecting the most appropriate research design is the most critical task in the research process.
5. How can the iceberg principle be used to help decision makers better understand problems or opportunities?

Discussion Questions

1. For each of the four phases of the information research process, identify the corresponding steps and develop a set of questions that a researcher should attempt to answer within each step.
2. What are the differences among the exploratory, descriptive, and causal research designs? Which design type would be most appropriate to address the following question: "How satisfied or dissatisfied are customers with the automobile repair service offerings of the dealership from which they purchased their new 2009 BMW?"

3. When should a researcher use a probability sampling method rather than a nonprobability method?

4. **EXPERIENCE THE INTERNET.** Go to the Gallup Poll organization's Web home page at www.gallup.com. Select the "Take poll" option and review the results by selecting the "Findings" option. After reviewing the information, outline the different phases and task steps of the information research process that might have been used in the Gallup Internet Poll.

chapter 3

Information-Driven Technology and the Research Process

Learning Objectives

After reading this chapter, you will be able to:

1. Describe how changing technology influences the marketing research process.
2. Discuss how portals help in the problem definition process.
3. Explain how technology influences research designs and data sources.
4. Explain the influence of technology on methods of primary data collection.
5. Know the differences between data warehouses and data marts.
6. Distinguish between pull and push portals for research presentations.

> "Technology will kill us or cure us, hopefully the latter."
>
> —ANONYMOUS

Google for Knowledge

Google recently reported a 200 percent increase in sales of its new Enterprise Search Appliance tool. Companies are using the tool in their information portal to search corporate data to answer customer questions, fill sales orders, analyze customer comments, and explore reasons for product failures. Xerox, Hitachi, Nextel, Procter and Gamble, and Boeing are just a few of Google's hundreds of customers. These companies recognize that the ability to search, analyze, and comprehend customer data is vital to success. The incredible 200 percent growth in sales for Google's new Search Appliance tool is one strong indicator among many that companies are adopting new technologies that will help them increase the efficiency of their marketing research efforts.[1]

Value of New Technology in Marketing Research Practices

Information is everywhere in an organization. Employees must be able to access and analyze this information to make the best business decisions. Collecting, compiling, sorting, and analyzing customer data from multiple sources provides tremendous insights into how a business is performing. Examining customer data yields exciting and even unexpected results, including knowledge about emerging market segments, new methods of reaching customers, and recognition of major flaws in business strategies.

Technology is affecting all businesses. Some of the most notable changes are occurring in traditionally low technology areas. One example is marketing research, which encompasses many activities that new technology can improve. Using technology as a research mechanism and data management tool, companies are expediting the marketing research process and reducing the cost of marketing research.

As illustrated in Chapter 2, the marketing research process has several phases and steps and technology can provide benefits at each stage of the research process. This chapter explores how technology is creating change across the marketing research industry in general as well as within the marketing research process specifically.

Technology and the Marketing Research Process

New technology is affecting the marketing research process in four basic areas. First, technology is changing the way companies define the research problem and specify research objectives. Second, innovations in technology are determining the most effective research designs and the best data sources to use in achieving research objectives. Third, technology is dramatically changing sampling of participants, scale measurement designs, and questionnaires, and is expediting the data collection process. Finally, the processes of compiling, storing, and analyzing data and the dissemination of research results have become more precise and user-friendly.

Research Problems, Objectives, and Technological Approaches

Using new technology, Samsung Electronics examined 10,000 detailed reports from vendors, resellers, and customers to determine where they were "losing deals or orders" to the competition. Examination of the reports showed that 80 percent of lost sales took place within a single strategic business unit—health care. Furthermore, Samsung identified that 40 percent of lost sales in this business unit were to one competitor. After analyzing its current selling approach and customer relationship building techniques, Samsung realized its current strategy was not working and needed to be retooled. The research problem was redefined as a lack of information and problem solving directed at hardware vendors. Research objectives were adopted to obtain the needed data and define the activities to better serve this critical supply chain partner. Samsung's new strategy was made possible through an Enterprise Informational Portal.[2]

Portals as Problem Detectors and Opportunity Assessors

Portal is a Web site that offers a broad array of resources and services, such as e-mail, online discussion groups, search engines, and online shopping.

Enterprise Informational Portal (EIP) is an Internet site owned and operated by an organization to support its total business operation.

Dashboards An interactive computer terminal or screen that organizes and presents information in a way that is easy for the user to read and understand.

A **portal** is a Web site that offers a broad array of resources and services, such as e-mail, online discussion groups, search engines, and online shopping. Some major general portals include Yahoo!, Excite, and AOL. Specialized portals include Garden.com for gardeners and Fool.com for investors. An **Enterprise Informational Portal (EIP)** is an Internet site owned and operated by an organization to support its total business operation. Often referred to as a **dashboard,** the EIP is a single point of connection between a business, its supply chain partners, and customers. Like popular consumer portals, the EIP organizes information using indexes and visual presentation.

While most organizations use EIPs or dashboards for enterprisewide data integration purposes, many organizations are finding them useful for detecting problems in business operations and for marketing research purposes. Harrah's, for example, uses the real-time data capabilities of the EIP for overcoming problems in customer satisfaction and addressing customer loyalty issues. Through its dashboard system called "Winners Information Network," which collects and visually presents customer information from all the company's transactions, gaming machines, and hotel reservation systems, Harrah's recognized that marketing research was needed in the areas of gambler security, new menu initiatives for its restaurants, and customer preferences regarding types of rewards received for being a registered "Total Rewards" member. Harrah's developed a programmatic research agenda to identify problem areas that could be solved regarding the issues of security, food service, and rewards preferences.[3]

EIPs are designed to track flows of information in the total business process. Users can graphically view information as pie-charts, bullet graphs, sparklines, and gauges. Portals also can "drill down" into lower-level data to identify both negative and positive business trends. Using its portal known as "Talon," Harley-Davidson found its $500 million aftermarket sales were declining rapidly even though average length of ownership of motorcycles was increasing. Drilling further into dealer inventory and automatic parts replenishment systems revealed no answers. Harley then decided to examine aftermarket dynamics with further marketing research on motorcycle owners. After collecting and analyzing data, they learned from motorcycle owners that dealers were difficult to locate, not conveniently located, and aftermarket parts prices were perceived as high. The company decided to add an e-commerce option selling aftermarket parts and accessories online. Thus, Harley's dashboard helped define the research problem and suggest research actions to solve the business problem.[4]

Dashboards enable decision makers to gauge how well an organization is performing overall and to capture and report specific performance data in a "snapshot" format. The benefits of using dashboards in marketing research are:

1. Visual presentation of marketing and customer performance data.
2. Improved problem definition and identification of negative and positive trends.
3. More detailed reports on markets, products, and segments.
4. Better informed decisions on marketing research plans.

Influence of Technology on Research Designs and Data Sources

Transactional customer data the information contained in a strategic business unit.

Analytical customer data data used in performing analyses as the basis for managerial decision making.

Technology is impacting how marketing researchers define and categorize customer data. While the data itself has remained relatively unchanged (purchase behavior, demographic characteristics, lifestyle dimensions), the methods used to obtain the data are dramatically changing how customer data is being interpreted. In a marketing research context two broad forms of customer data exist: transactional and analytical. **Transactional customer data** includes all the information contained in a strategic business unit, whose purpose is to support the daily operations of that unit.[5] Examples of transactional customer data include cash withdrawals from an ATM, hotel or airline reservations, and sporting goods purchases from an online store. Some of the primary uses of transactional customer data are to generate sales reports, facilitate inventory control procedures, and enable tracking of product and service sales.

Analytical customer data is customer data used in performing analyses as the basis for managerial decision making. Analytical data includes market and industry trends, competitor information, and macroenvironmental changes, as well as transactional customer data.[6] Analytical data is primarily used in making marketing strategy or planning decisions. Typical decisions made with analytical customer data include expanding product lines, moving into new market segments, evaluating new distribution methods, or repositioning a current brand.

Anheuser-Busch (AB) uses both transactional and analytical customer data in its marketing operations. Every time a six-pack moves off the shelf, AB's BudNet knows about it. BudNet is AB's data system that integrates both transactional and analytical customer data on a daily basis. Every AB sales rep collects data for the system and utilizes it for decisions. When a sales rep enters one of his customers' stores, he already knows what products are selling, which promotional campaigns are successful, and what needs to be done to help the customer's business. Every time an AB sales rep enters a store, he checks his handheld PC, which displays information about the store. Sales reps check the stores' accounts receivable making sure everything is current, then check a four-week inventory history to examine past sales and package placements, and sales during in-store promotional campaigns. The reps also input competitive data such as product displays, pricing strategies, and in-store promotions.[7]

AB uses BudNet data to revise marketing strategies, design promotions to fit the ethnic makeup of its markets, and as an early warning to detect where competition may be making inroads into the market. According to beer industry analysts, AB has made a science out of determining what beer drinkers are buying, as well as when, where, and why. At a transactional customer data level, AB records what a customer paid for the beer, when the beer was brewed, if the beer was chilled or warm, and whether the customer could have gotten it cheaper at another store.[8]

Benefits of Transactional and Analytical Customer Data

Understanding transactional and analytical customer data can significantly improve marketing decisions and increase the effectiveness of marketing programs. Lillian Vernon Corp., a catalog company, used customer data to discover that men preferred to shop at Lillian Vernon's Web site rather than use its traditional catalog. This insight derived from the data was used to design the Web site around more male products and the result was a 15 percent growth in sales.[9] Similarly, Calloway Golf discovered that Phoenix, Arizona, was not a good market for selling golf clubs, even with its high number of golf courses. Transactional customer data showed that the typical golfers in Phoenix were tourists or conventioneers who usually brought their clubs with them when visiting Phoenix. The data further revealed that a high number of individuals visiting Phoenix came from Rochester, New York, and Detroit, Michigan.

Real time data is immediate, up to date, and maintained on a 24-hour/365-day reporting period.

Web traffic analysis measures the traffic generated by a company's Web site.

Click-stream data reflects the exact pattern of a customer's navigation through a particular Web site and reveals a number of basic data points on how customers interact with the Web site.

The success of any marketing program depends on leveraging high-quality data that is also timely. *Timeliness* is a critical aspect of any data, but particularly of transactional and analytical customer data. The factor that makes these data forms unique is the real-time nature of the data. **"Real time"** means the data is immediate, up to date, and maintained on a 24-hour/365-day reporting period.

A major trend in marketing research is movement away from traditional customer behavioral intention measures (*probability* of purchase-related behavior) to more robust real-time measures of transaction-related behavior (the actual *outcome* of the purchase-related behavior). Actual outcome data is obtained from **Web traffic analysis,** which measures the traffic generated by a company's Web site. The primary objective of Web traffic analysis is to record customer visits, purchases, revenue, service calls generated, traffic reduction, and so forth. The type of data analyzed is typically called click-stream data. **Click-stream data** reflects the exact pattern of a customer's navigation through a particular Web site and reveals a number of basic data points on how customers interact with the Web site. These data points are known as behavioral metrics and commonly include:

1. The number of pages viewed by a visitor.
2. The pattern of Web sites visited.
3. Length of stay on the Web site.
4. Dates and times of visits.
5. Number of registrations filled out per 100 visitors.
6. Number of abandoned registrations.
7. Demographics of registered visitors.
8. Number of customers with shopping carts.
9. Number of abandoned shopping carts.

Click-stream data captures real-time behavioral metrics that can be tracked over any given period of time. Click-stream data will soon be available from communication devices such as mobile phones, personal digital assistants (PDAs), and tablet computers.

Technology and Data Enhancement: Biometrics and Smartcards

Biometrics automatic identification of a person based on his/her physiological or behavioral characteristics.

Biometrics refers to the automatic identification of a person based on his/her physiological or behavioral characteristics. Biometrics is a pattern recognition system that determines authenticity by two types of traits: physiological (fingerprint, face recognition, hand geometry, iris recognition) and behavioral (signature, keystroke dynamics, voice).[10] For example, Pay By Touch is used in retail grocery chain Piggly Wiggly to enable a customer to pay by simply touching her finger to a fingerprint sensor and providing her phone number. If the two match, Pay By Touch automatically performs a transfer of funds to the merchant's account using electronic check clearing.[11] Disney World recently installed biometric hand scanners to identify patrons upon admission to its theme parks in Orlando, Florida.[12]

Using biometrics to gather data isn't new in the field of marketing research. There is a large body of published work in advertising research that correlates a subject's physiological responses to advertisements by measuring skin conductance, heart rate, and eye movement. More modern biometrics technology uses state-of-the-art head sets to monitor multiple physiological responses that measure moment-by-moment metrics among subjects. Most measures focus on how engaged or excited individuals become when exposed to specific events in commercials, humor appeals, or comparative advertising claims. The data collected is then used to build models describing how physiological signals change in response to specific advertising events. Many of these physiological signals describe the specific emotional or attitudinal feeling the subjects experience when viewing commercials or advertisements. As an example, brain scans recently showed that individuals react more favorably to the taste of wine when they believe it is more expensive.

Smart card chip card, or integrated circuit card (ICC) is defined as any pocket-sized card with embedded integrated circuits that can process information about people.

Closely associated with biometric technology are smart cards. A **smart card,** chip card, or integrated circuit card (ICC) is defined as any pocket-sized card with embedded integrated circuits that can process information about people. Smart card and biometric technologies have a substantial advantage over past information gathering systems because they provide a macro view of what has taken place within a shopping mall, retail store, themepark, or casino. At Harrah's casino, for example, when visitors register for "Total Rewards," they receive a credit-card-sized plastic card with a computer chip containing up to 512 characters of personal demographic information embedded in it, typically data that has been collected from a registration form. The value of the smart card is that, unlike earlier technologies, the progress of each casino visitor can be tracked when the smart card is inserted into any gaming device. Data obtained from smart card users tells casino managers the most popular gaming devices, amounts being wagered, traffic flow around the various gaming devices, time spent in restaurants and shops, and overall time the visitor spends in the casino.[13]

Technology and Primary Data Collection

Technology has brought greater speed and productivity to marketing research through online interviewing methods and more efficient data processing. The result is richer insights through more sophisticated analytic techniques. Use of new marketing research technology and methods creates many positive benefits for marketing research providers, principally, more efficiently collected and reported data and easier integration of primary and secondary data into the research process.

Technology-based tools such as the Internet are primarily used for survey and focus group design, recruitment of subjects, data collection, and data analysis. Use of the Internet as a preferred data collection tool, both qualitative and quantitative, has dramatically changed marketing research methodologies as well as client/user expectations. The greatest impact on client/user expectations has been that many methodologies are now considered Internet-appropriate without compromising results and the potential decrease in fieldwork equates to reduced analytic time. For many client/users of marketing research, the need for speed has superseded the need for comprehensive data analysis and interpretation and, in some cases, analytic precision.

eXHIBIT 3.1 Comparing Traditional and Internet Data Collection and Analysis

Survey Design

Traditional approach

Questionnaire is developed by professionals. When completed, questionnaire is printed and sent to the participants by mail or fax, or a survey is given over the phone by a staff person. Mailed surveys include postage costs; faxed surveys include phone charges.

Internet approach

Questionnaire is developed by professionals. When completed, questions are converted into a form that can be accessed online by participants.

Recruitment

Traditional approach

Participants are contacted by mail, phone, or fax, and asked to complete the survey. Multiple contacts may be required to speak directly to a participant or get a fax to the desk of the participant.

Internet approach

Cooperative participant panels are assembled and alerted by e-mail when studies are available online. Only eligible participants are contacted for any particular study.

Data Collection

Traditional approach

When surveys are completed, they must be returned by mail or fax. Phone survey results are available immediately. All results must be entered into a database, which can be used for analysis.

Internet approach

When participants complete a survey, the data are automatically entered into a database that can be used for analysis.

Analysis

Traditional approach

Customer receives tabulated results that have been analyzed by consultants to make recommendations.

Internet approach

The database automatically generates aggregate data (bar graphs, pie charts, cross-tabs) in addition to a raw data set that can be used for other forms of analysis.

Technology-based tools, such as the Internet, provide benefits at each stage of the marketing research process. For example, 24/7 accessibility to the Internet facilitates effective communication between the marketing research firm and consumer panels or focus groups, facilitating maximum participation and reducing the time required to complete the research. Increasing accessibility brings greater efficiency to both primary and secondary research. Exhibit 3.1 compares traditional marketing research approaches with Internet approaches for data collection and analysis.

The advantage of using the Internet to collect research data is greater control of the survey. For example, respondents to Internet surveys are allowed to select only from the given responses to each question. Participants cannot write in another answer or select more than one answer. Also, respondents are not able to skip ahead, as is possible with traditional surveys. Internet approaches yield surveys that are more complete and reduce bias that can develop if participants are able to look ahead at question topics.

Getting participation from respondents is critical to the success of any marketing research project. Participants generally respond favorably to Internet surveys. The ability to

EXHIBIT 3.2 Characteristics of U.S. Internet Users

- Total U.S. population is about 300 million people with 225 million of them over the age of 17. (U.S. Census)
- There are 178.8 million Web users in the U.S. (comScore, June 2007)
- 71% of all adults are online. (www.pewinternet.org)
- 87% of 18–24-year-olds, 83% of 30–49-year-olds, 65% of those 50–64, and 32% of those over 65 are online. (www.pewinternet.org)
- 73% of whites, 62% of blacks, and 78% of English-speaking Hispanics are online. (www.pewinternet.org)
- 73% of people living in urban/suburban environments and 60% living in rural areas are online. (www.pewinternet.org)
- 93% of those earning $75K+, 82% of those earning $50K–$74K, 69% of those earning $30K–$49K, and 55% of those earning less than $30K are online. (www.pewinternet.org)
- Total number of U.S. households is 105.4 million. (U.S. Census)
- Almost 70% of U.S. households have Internet access at home. (Leichtman Research Group Q1 2007)
- 53% of U.S. households have high-speed access (Leichtman Research Group Q1 2007)

take part in surveys at any time of the day or night is a convenience that most individuals enjoy. Also an international sample can be obtained much more easily via the Internet. Exhibit 3.2 illustrates that a majority of people, at least in the United States, have Internet capabilities and engage in online activities quite often. However, the Internet after all is a relatively new technology. Sampling and sample bias has been an issue with Internet-based surveys. A caution is that in any Internet-based survey the question arises whether the sample obtained is representative of the population you wanted to target. If not, your results could be misleading.

Use of online methods for data collection is not new in marketing research. But recent technological advances in software are changing the way online surveys are executed. New software will do everything from generating and creating the online survey to analyzing the data and even preparing research reports. This software also develops online surveys in multilingual formats to reach international respondents, modifies surveys for different methods of delivery (phone, media rich, mobile), and even enables information from outside databases to be merged with the collected data for analysis purposes.

SPSS Dimensions 4.0 is an excellent example of how software is changing the execution of online surveys.[14] SPSS Dimensions isn't so much an individual software package as a platform of several independent software packages working together in a seamless fashion. Using its interactive software, SPSS Dimensions performs the following tasks:

- Automated dialing for phone surveys
- Creation and execution of online, phone, and paper surveys.
- Scanning of paper surveys
- Managing and manipulating data
- Creation of tables from local data
- Interaction with tables on the desktop
- Translation of surveys and reports

- Collection of data via handheld devices
- Data analysis, including data mining
- Preparation of reports and presentations

The most unique characteristic of SPSS Dimensions 4.0 is its multimodal deployment capability enabling potential respondents to answer surveys via paper, Web, phone, or other channels such as instant messaging or mobile phones.

Nontraditional Technology–Driven Data Collection Methods

Software advances like SPSS Dimensions 4.0 provide innovative approaches for survey deployment and data collection. Research firms now have new options available for survey deployment, specifically mobile phones and personal digital assistants (PDAs). The obvious benefit of this technology is the immediacy of results so researchers can get an instant reflection of respondent opinions. Moreover, many mobile-based surveys are quick and easy to complete, and the respondent has options as to the device used in completing the survey. Finally, there are no restrictions on when and where the survey is completed, the cost is lower when large numbers of respondents are needed, and respondents who may normally be difficult to contact, for example, the youth market, are much more easily contacted.

Atlanta-based Mobile Transit Authority recently launched a new mobile opinion solution called "mDive." This is a mobile-based research tool that interacts with respondents on mobile phones. The technology facilitates surveying respondents through text messaging, mobile Internet connections, or click-to-call voice-driven methods. Once the data is collected, the system analyzes and interprets the data, and then generates reports for the client.[15] Embrace Mobile, a UK-based survey company, employs similar technology for completing questionnaires with mobile phones. Embrace's approach uses short questionnaires delivered to respondents through instant messaging, mobile Web browsers, or downloadable applications. Embrace primarily conducts surveys for opinion polls, customer satisfaction surveys, and employee satisfaction surveys.[16]

A similar approach for obtaining customer data involves using mobile phones and PDAs to collect data for consumer panels. MTV/Nickelodeon has announced the development of a mobile community, MBuzzy.com, which is a teen wireless research panel. Called "Teens Everywhere," this research panel has over 10,000 teens who provide opinions on a variety of topics ranging from network programming to advertising effectiveness.[17]

Social Networking as a Marketing Research Tool

Social network a service that uses software to build online social networks for communities of people who share mutual interests and activities or who are interested in exploring the interests and activities of others.

A **social network** is a service that uses software to build online social networks for communities of people who share mutual interests and activities or who are interested in exploring the interests and activities of others. Most of these services are primarily Web based and provide a collection of ways for users to interact, such as chat, messaging, e-mail, video, voice chat, file sharing, blogging, and discussion groups. Social networking has revolutionized the way many people communicate and share information with one another. Various social networking Web sites are regularly used by millions of people every day and are rapidly becoming a part of everyday life for many individuals.

The main types of social networking services contain directories of selected categories, such as classmates.com, or are recommender-based systems linked to trust, such as

WebMD.com. More popular social networks now combine the two types, with MySpace and Facebook being the most popular. Social networks connect people at a low cost, and many businesses are using social networks for advertising and customer relationship management. Increasingly, social networking is used in marketing research, particularly for online focus groups and intelligence gathering techniques.

Social Networks and Focus Group Interviews

For several years online focus groups have been used in the marketing research industry. Advances in software technology have given marketing researchers more options in the way they design and implement online focus groups. Indeed, individuals increasingly make friends and share comments and information through social networks such as Second Life, MySpace, and Facebook. Operating under a similar concept of social networking, a new approach for the design and setting of focus group research has emerged known as "nQual Rich Focus Research Platform." Rich Focus is a Web-based online focus group technique that operates in real time and in virtual space. In many ways it resembles Web conferencing traditionally used for business meetings such as "webex" or "GoToMeeting," but without the cumbersome nature of telephone conversations. Rich Focus assumes all conversations are completed using instant messaging or chat and can be completed through a research literate dialogue.

The process starts where the researcher develops a topical guide centered around the global issues to be addressed in the focus group. Then, the information is uploaded and stored on the Rich Focus platform. Next, the researcher recruits participants either in a conventional offline approach or through some previously developed consumer panel. Once respondents have agreed to participate in the research, they are sent an initial e-mail with a Rich Focus software download. The software is compatible with Internet Explorer, but also can be used with its own dedicated "nQual" plug in and browser which avoids problems with participants' browser settings.

Invitations are then sent to participants with an embedded link and the time the group research will begin. Participants use the embedded link to log on to the system and begin the focus group process. Once logged on, all participants are identified by a name and color (for instance, Sandy, color "red"). The participants' screen is then generated in three sections: (1) in one section participants see their name and those of other group members, (2) in another section the questions, answers, and discussion take place, and (3) the third area is where stimulus material such as a package design, advertisement, or new products can be presented and viewed by all participants.[18] When the focus group session is over, a full transcript of the group discussion is available in a Word or Excel file. The Excel file is organized with comments in one column and the respondent's name in another. If any data analysis is required the files can be imported in SPSS or SAS.

Blog a Web site where individuals can communicate with each other and comments are displayed in a reverse chronological order.

Another nontraditional approach for gathering customer data is through blogs. A **blog** or Web log is a Web site where individuals can communicate with each other and comments are displayed in a reverse chronological order. Many blogs provide commentary or news on a particular subject, or even video games. Others function as more personal online diaries. A typical blog combines text, images, and links to other blogs, Web pages, and other media related to its topic. The ability for readers to leave comments in an interactive format is the unique dimension of blogs. Micro-blogging is another type of blog that consists of blogs with very short information posts. As of 2008, blog search engine Technorati reported tracking more than 112 million blogs.[19]

As illustrated in the nearby A Closer Look at Research (Using Technology) box, marketing researchers use blogs as a way of capturing customer data and opinions. This

A Closer Look at Research

Online Options for Focus Group Research

Sometimes Craig Jolley just needs to confirm a hunch. He has at his disposal all the traditional tools of marketing research as customer segment manager for Mead Data Central, the company that provides NEXIS, the online information retrieval service. But to clarify a position or find a basis for that gut instinct, he goes online to get opinions.

Call it a sort of online focus group. Jolley frequents several CompuServe forums to get to know people and identify those who might offer useful perspectives. Then, when a question or issue arises on which he needs feedback, he will direct a few questions to them.

He calls it the direct approach. "I send e-mail questions to selected individuals, primarily those who I've corresponded with on the forums and who have proved to be knowledgeable about the subject matter I am interested in exploring," Jolley said.

Another strategy he calls the group grope. "I'll post a message in a forum that masks a specific product idea but attempts to solicit feedback regarding the concept." He has used forums as varied as the White House Forum, the Outdoors Forum, the Legal Forum, and the Public Relations and Marketing Forum.

Jolley calls his third use of online research *I spy.* "I'll lurk to view the interaction in a chat room or online forum without participating by typing in any comments. I visit message boards and monitor conversations related to programs, products or services I'm working on. I'll inject comments every now and then to direct the conversation and receive input," he said. Whether for formal research or fun, "lurking" is a common online pastime and one reason electronic bulletin boards are so popular.

"The ability to lurk online and read others' posts is a great complement to the traditional environmental scanning approach available via NEXIS and other methods. It is amazing what people will say in posts that they probably wouldn't say in a formal focus group setting. I think it has something to do with the feeling of anonymity that they feel interacting with their screen," Jolley explained.

Lurking and other online research will not replace scientific methods. "Because the sample size is too small, too polarized—it includes only those with access to the service—and is not random, it cannot take the place of formal focus group research—yet," Jolley said. "On the other hand, it does provide a very cost efficient way to gather input from a geographically diverse and eclectic group in a manner impossible by other, traditional methods."

In his efforts to market the NEXIS service, Jolley spends a great deal of time targeting public relations and communication managers. "The only way I can even begin to try to keep my fingers on the pulse of this market is to use online communication and bulletin boards. It almost defies imagination how much in time, energy, and money it would require to do this on a manual basis. In one respect, I don't think enough money could be spent to adequately replicate what can be accomplished through online opportunities," he said.

Does he sound like an evangelist? Actually, he points out disadvantages, too, particularly in relying on online veterans to figure out how to approach people who are not yet online. "Online veterans are very helpful in determining if there is real value in a potential product idea, but, unfortunately, it seems there is no one who can put their finger on why so many in the public relations and communication management field are shunning technology integration. We know they should use it. We know it will offer a wealth of value and benefits. We know it is in the interests of the profession. We just don't know the one switch that made some of us very technology adept and others technology averse," he said.

Yes, an evangelist he is. It's not just because the company he works for provides online services. "I would say that online research would prove valuable for just about any product, service, or industry. It certainly helps that my service ties into the medium I am using to find out information, but I don't see this as offering any substantial advantages over someone who might be in another business altogether," he said.

So if you're looking to augment your current marketing research, online strategies may serve you well. In fact, this may be the switch about which Jolley speaks to "turn on" some of the technology-averse in the profession.[20]

method of data collection has become so popular in marketing research that AC Nielsen Research has developed a tracking system designed primarily for blogs, referred to as "Buzzmetrics."[21] The software measures consumer-generated media and online word of mouth, and enables companies to track consumer "buzz" including opinions, preferences, and trends for a variety of products and services. "Buzzmetrics" is a tracking tool that manages consumer-driven discussions from online content, discussion boards, blogs, forums, review sites, and Usenet newsgroups. The software tracks and reports customer information across a variety of industries including, consumer electronics, automotive, health, nutrition, and entertainment.[22]

Technology-Driven Data Analysis in Marketing Research

Data warehouse a logical aggregation of information stored in a single data location.

Data mart contains all the types of data included in a data warehouse but in a format relating to only one product of a company.

Data mining the process of analyzing data to extract patterns and relationships not easily visible from simply looking at the data.

Most customer data is recorded and stored in a **data warehouse.** A data warehouse is a logical aggregation of information stored in a single data location. The primary purpose of the data warehouse is to aggregate information from all sources of the business into a single data storage area in such a way that managers can use the data for further analysis and decision making. For example, data relating to customer satisfaction, product sales, sales by store type, and sales by differing price levels may exist in different areas of a company. A data warehouse aggregates all the data in a single area and converts the data to a format more suited for supporting decision making. The data warehouse then sends subsets of customer information to **data marts.** To distinguish between data warehouses and data marts, think of data warehouses as having a broad marketing focus and containing secondary data, competitive information, sales data, environmental information, and primary data on customers. Data marts have a more focused approach and contain all the types of data just described but in a format relating to only one product a company may have. Apple has a data warehouse that contains customer data for all the products produced and marketed by Apple. This data is then sent to data marts that contain data relevant to a single Apple product, such as iPods, iPhones, laptops, or desktops.

The unique characteristic of both the data warehouse and the data mart is that the customer information stored in them is multidimensional. A *dimension* is a particular attribute of a customer, product, brand, or store. Customer attributes could be demographic information such as age, gender, and education. Product attributes could be factors such as style, features, and quality levels. Brand attributes are color, price, package size, and taste, and store attributes typically represent the type of store selling the product (discount, department store, convenience store), its geographical location, and product inventory levels. When the information is aggregated and sent to the data mart, for example, for Apple iPhones, the data represents the multidimensional description of all information relevant to the Apple iPhones. This multidimensional description is unique to the data mart for Apple iPhones and differs from the multidimensional description of data in the data mart for Apple iPods. The benefit of multidimensional data is that it enables researchers to develop customer profiles and buying behaviors across products or brands. For example, if a researcher wishes to compare the iPod buyer with the iPhone buyer, she would simply access the data mart for each product and compare the attributes among buyers for each product line.

The ability to generate customer profiles or buyer behavior characteristics is typically accomplished through data mining. **Data mining** is the process of analyzing data to extract patterns and relationships not easily visible from simply looking at the data. For example,

Ruf Strategic Solutions helps organizations employ data mining approaches in data warehouses to identify customer segments that display common buying traits.[23] Once generated, the segments are sent to data marts, and marketers use the data to target these segments with specially designed products, promotional programs, and pricing strategies.

To perform data mining, researchers need data mining tools. Data mining tools use a variety of techniques to find patterns and relationships in large volumes of data and infer rules from them that predict future behavior and guide decision making. Data mining tools for data warehouses and data marts typically include multidimensional analysis as well as a variety of statistical tools. Sega of America, one of the largest publishers of video games, uses statistical tools to allocate its promotional budget of more than $50 million a year. Sega marketing researchers and product managers "drill" into its data marts to find trends in each retail store chain. Their goal is to find buying trends that determine which promotional campaigns are working best and how to reallocate promotional resources by media, territory, and store type.[24]

Disseminating Marketing Research Results through Research Portals

Technology has greatly enhanced the way marketing research results and reports are disseminated to clients. A *portal* is a Web site that offers a broad array of resources and services provided by marketing research firms for their clients. We discussed portals earlier in our discussion in this chapter. Many research firms are implementing portals to provide clients with information on research projects, to view data that has been collected for the client, and for reporting results and recommendations from the research study. Marketing research portals, often referred to as *reportals,* exist in either a push environment or a pull environment. A **push portal** is one in which the research firm *pushes* marketing research information to the client. The classic push approach is e-mail; the research firm sends the marketing research results, or a link to the results, to the client with the anticipation that the client will read and utilize the information for decision purposes.

Push portal one used by the research firm to push marketing research information to the client.

Pull portal one used by the client to search for and extract only the information the client believes is necessary.

Via a **pull portal** the client can search for and extract only the information that the client deems necessary. Examples of pull portals include file transfer protocols (FTPs) and the online reporting built into many Internet-based data collection systems. These systems enable the client to search and trawl the information, collecting only the information the client may need. Pull portals are considered very client-friendly. They provide the most benefit when clients want only bits and pieces of marketing research information and not the data streams in the full scope of the total study that may not be relevant to their current problem.

A major disadvantage of pull portals is that many clients do not have the time to visit a number of different provider sites to access the various elements of research information they may need. Also, clients often are unsure of exactly which pieces of information or data they may need to answer an urgent question about their business. In fact, several marketing research firms have reported that when they provide information or reports in a pull portal environment, some clients never access it, making it a poor value.

Pull portals appear to be most effective when they deliver access to certain types of data rather than recommendations or conclusions, or when the information is necessary for the client as opposed to just being desirable. Pull portals also work effectively when the amount of information is so large the client might be overwhelmed if all the information is sent to them. The most well-known example of an effective pull portal is the AC Neilsen marketing research audit data.

Push portals, such as e-mailing the results to clients, are based on marketing research firms' wanting clients to access the information. The research firm knows the most important information and has a financial obligation to ensure the client is aware of and reads the important information generated by the research. Push portals appear to have a distinct advantage over pull portals when the material delivered is more conclusion or recommendation oriented rather than data driven or analysis based. Many marketing research firms are now beginning to develop a hybrid pull-push portal. Information is sent to the client in a pull portal mode, but key findings and recommendations are e-mailed to the client in the form of dashboard results.

MARKETING RESEARCH IN ACTION

Continuing Case

The Santa Fe Grill and Technology

The owners of the Santa Fe Grill have met with their marketing research consultants. The consultants reviewed with them the ways new technology is impacting marketing research and particularly how restaurant industry operations and marketing are changing as a result of this new technology. The ideas and information the consultants shared with the owners very much reflected the chapter discussion you have just read. Since you have studied this material, the owners would like your input on how to use new technology in marketing research to improve their restaurant.

Hands-On Exercise

1. Which new technology developments are likely to impact the restaurant industry the most?
2. In your opinion which two technological developments are most likely to help the owners of the Santa Fe Grill research ways to improve their business? Explain your choice.

Summary of Learning Objectives

■ Describe how changing technology influences the marketing research process.

First, technology is changing the manner in which companies are able to define the research problem and establishing research objectives. Second, innovations in technology are determining the most effective research designs to employ and efficiently developing the best type of data sources to procure for achieving the research objectives. Third, technology is becoming most pronounced in the sampling of participants, designing scales and questionnaires, and expediting the data collection process. Finally, how data is compiled, stored, and analyzed, along with the dissemination of research results, have become more defined and user-friendly due to technological advances.

■ Discuss how portals help in the problem definition process.

EIP, or dashboards, allow decision makers to gauge exactly how well an organization is performing overall, and allow the decision maker to capture and report specific performance data in a "snapshot" format. The benefits of using the EIP or dashboard in a marketing research capacity are:

1. Visual presentation of marketing and customer performance data.
2. Ability to define problems and correct negative trends.
3. Ability to generate detailed reports on markets, products, and segments.
4. Ability to make better informed decisions regarding marketing research plans.

■ Explain how technology influences research designs and data sources.

Technology is having a great impact on how marketing researchers define and categorize customer data. While the data itself is remaining relatively unchanged (purchase behavior, demographic characteristics, lifestyle dimensions), the methods used to obtain the data is dramatically changing how customer data are being interpreted. In a marketing research context two broad forms of customer data exist, transactional and analytical customer data. Transactional customer data encompasses all the information contained within a strategic business unit, and its purpose is to support the daily operations of that unit. Analytical customer data encompasses customer data that is used in performing analysis for managerial decision making. Analytical data includes transactional customer data along with other information such as market and industry trends, competitor information, or macroenvironmental changes.

■ Explain the influence of technology on methods of primary data collection.

Use of the Internet as a preferred data collection tool, both qualitatively and quantitatively, has had the greatest impact on changing marketing research methodologies and client/users' expectations. The greatest impact has been on client/users' expectations that all methodologies are Internet-appropriate without compromising results and that the potential decrease in fieldwork equates to reduced required analytic time. For many client/users of marketing research, the need for speed has superseded the need for comprehensive data analysis and interpretation and, in some cases, analytic precision.

■ Know the differences between data warehouses and data marts.

Most customer data, collected by various methods as described earlier, is recorded and stored in a data warehouse, which is a logical aggregation of information housed in a single data repository. The primary purpose of the data warehouse is to aggregate information from all sources of the business into a single data storage area in such a way that managers can use the data for further analysis and decision making. The data warehouse then sends subsets of customer information to data marts. A data mart contains subsets of customer information.

■ Distinguish between pull and push portals for research presentations.

Many research firms are implementing portals to provide clients with information on research projects, view data collected for the client, and report results and recommendations from the research study. Marketing research portals, many times referred to as "reportals," exist either in a pull environment or a push environment. A push portal environment is one where the research firm pushes marketing research information to the client. The classic push approach is e-mail, where the research firm sends the marketing research results, or a link to the results, to the client with the anticipation that the client will read and utilize the information for decision purposes.

Key Terms and Concepts

Analytical customer data 68
Biometrics 69
Blog 74
Click-stream data 69
Dashboards 67
Data mart 76
Data mining 76
Data warehouse 76
Enterprise Informational Portal 67
Portal 67
Pull portal 77
Push portal 77
Real time 69
Smart card 70
Social network 73
Transactional customer data 68
Web traffic analysis 69

Review Questions

1. Identify three ways in which new technology is changing the way in which businesses conduct marketing research.
2. Explain what an Enterprise Informational Portal is, and how they are used in marketing research.
3. What is the difference between transactional customer data and analytical customer data. Provide an example of how each type of data is used.
4. Illustrate how biometrics and smartcards can be used to provide businesses with information about their customers.
5. Discuss four of the unique features associated with SPSS Dimensions 4.0.
6. Explain how the concepts of data warehousing and data marts operate in providing customer information to businesses.
7. Explain the differences between a push and pull portal environment as they relate to the communication of marketing research results.

Discussion Questions

1. Red Bull, the energy drink manufacturer, has asked you to prepare a brief outline on data they could use to better serve their customers. They have specifically asked you to identify what transactional data you would recommend they use, as well as what analytical data they should collect. Identify these data sets for Red Bull and provide them with your reasoning for making your data selection.
2. Provide a brief description on how a social network like MySpace could be used as a method of data collection for a cosmetics company such as Revlon. What type of customer information could Revlon collect from users of MySpace?

3. **EXPERIENCE THE INTERNET.** Go to Technorati.com and identify five blogs that could be used for marketing research purposes. In your discussion illustrate why you chose the particular blogs and what information you could possibly obtain from them.
4. **EXPERIENCE THE INTERNET.** Go to MySpace.com and view some of the profiles that are available. After viewing these profiles, develop a brief discussion on how MySpace could operate as a platform for a focus group discussion.

chapter 4

Market Intelligence and Database Research

Learning Objectives

After reading this chapter, you will be able to:

1. Understand the essential elements of market intelligence designs.
2. Explain the development of customer databases.
3. Discuss the elements of enhanced marketing databases.
4. Explain the role of data mining in marketing research.
5. Understand modeling in database analysis.

"As few as 10 percent of your customers contribute 90 percent to the company's profits. The problem is finding out who they are!"

—DAVID OGILVY,
President,
Ogilvy & Mather

Consumer Databases Enhance Customer Retention

Many companies are turning to market intelligence methods to better understand consumers and reshape their retail operations. Customer-oriented databases provide companies like Samsonite Corporation with unique marketing research capabilities and tools to improve decision making. Its market intelligence positions Samsonite to deal with the challenges of retail consolidation, blurring channel leadership, improving distribution systems, and creating better informed, proactive consumers.

The overall mission of marketing research is to provide management with quality information on customers' attitudes, feelings, and consumption behaviors, as well as tracking sales. Advances in communication and related technologies provide innovative database-oriented techniques for gathering and analyzing the information. The resulting market intelligence is key to Samsonite's achieving leading-edge capabilities in product quality and development, communications, customer service, and strategic planning.

Samsonite uses project teams made up of personnel from marketing research, marketing, advertising, engineering, production, and sales to develop solutions to research problems, placing emphasis on shorter, more targeted online surveys to gain actionable information faster and examination of customers' behaviors because Samsonite's researchers realize that actions speak louder than words and are more accurate predictors of future behavior.

Consumer databases are the main research tools and repositories of market information for Samsonite and are used for decision making in several areas.

1. **Market planning.** By analyzing customers' characteristics, Samsonite targets its products more precisely. After examining customers against the defined target population, the company develops new products for neglected segments, such as high-end luggage for professional women.
2. **Sales.** Data available from consumer databases enables better planning and tracking of retail account sales activities. Analysis of Samsonite purchasers in different retail

accounts helps the sales force to understand how different retailers operate as well as how selling additional lines of Samsonite luggage can reach different shoppers.

3. **Customer satisfaction.** Samsonite conducts customer satisfaction studies for new and existing products more quickly and efficiently with the databases. Because luggage is purchased relatively infrequently, database approaches enable targeted, cost-efficient data collection. For example, Samsonite conducts quarterly customer satisfaction studies for all new products as well as existing luggage items. Database information enables marketing researchers to interact more directly with customers, resulting in better understanding of different markets and improved products.

Value of Market Intelligence and Database Information

Responding to the individual needs and wants of customers in order to develop and nurture long-term customer relationships is a major objective behind market intelligence research endeavors. As the Samsonite example illustrates, creating market intelligence, the process of systematically categorizing timely customer data, is a critical function of marketing research. Marketing research has evolved from a process of merely collecting data to one of generating information through shared dialogue with customers. Customer databases enhance marketing researchers' opportunities and ability to better identify individual customers, rank those customers' transactions over time, and predict what those customers might buy in the future. Market intelligence based on database research ensures long-term profitability and survival for both product and service businesses.

Databases and Market Intelligence

Customer relationship management (CRM) A strategy of managing customer relationships based on the integration of customer information throughout a company in order to achieve maximum customer satisfaction and retention.

Market intelligence The use of real-time customer information (customer knowledge) to achieve a competitive advantage.

The growing use of databases can be directly linked to the evolution of **customer relationship management (CRM),** the strategy of managing customer relationships based on the integration of customer information throughout a company to achieve maximum customer satisfaction and retention. A primary function of marketing research in the CRM process is to collect, store, and analyze customer interaction information (customer knowledge), transforming the practice of marketing research into **market intelligence.** Market intelligence goes beyond traditional market research to data acquisition that is strategic and transactional in focus. In short, market intelligence seeks competitive advantage based on real-time customer information.

Market intelligence begins with the notion of *customer knowledge.* A company cannot meet its customers' needs and wants, and thereby offer value, unless it understands the evolution of the customer. Customer knowledge is used to assess profitability and provide increased value to targeted customer segments. From a market intelligence perspective, some of the major questions to answer are:

1. What kind of relationships will add value to customers (e.g., loyalty programs, preferred customer status, etc.)?
2. What is the value perception of the customer segment, and how can the value be enhanced (e.g., direct communication to customers, new services, etc.)?

3. What products and services and mode of delivery have value to the customer segment (e.g., stock market alerts via Web-enabled mobile phones)?

4. What are customers' responses to marketing and sales campaigns?

To answer these questions, marketing researchers capture and integrate information about customers from multiple data sources and create internal databases that can be shared by many users, both within and outside the company. The information includes customer demographics, psychographic data, behavioral and preference data, complaint behavior, sales and inventory levels, and direct and indirect communications with the company. Once compiled and analyzed the data is used for two key objectives: to create customer profiles that can be used to tailor interactions with customers and to segment customers in order to develop appropriate product and service offerings, marketing campaigns, and growth and retention programs.

Capturing the information involves the development of a *market intelligence culture* that ensures that collected data is integrated into all facets of the company. For example, late payment notices from accounting are often shared with customer service departments attempting to introduce customers to a new product or program. Data sharing with all departments improves customer understanding by everyone interacting with the customer. This level of integration of knowledge comes only through market intelligence.

Transforming Marketing Research into Market Intelligence

Market intelligence helps retain and regain customers. For example, when AT&T lost almost 27 percent of its intrastate long-distance telephone customers to other long-distance providers, it used highly refined information on the profitability of those customers to identify defectors and tailor a strategy to win them back. The company was able to re-sign 7 percent of those who left for another service provider. This resulted in the retention of almost 50 percent of AT&T's most profitable customers, leaving the unprofitable customers with the competition. Through additional research, AT&T gained important other information from those customers, including how competitors lured them away and how they rated the service quality of AT&T. The company learned that its service was weak and needed to be enhanced quickly.

This example illustrates a well-known premise that typically 20 percent of a company's customer base provides a large percentage of revenues and profit. For example, Coca-Cola found that one-third of its Diet Coke drinkers consumed 84 percent of total Diet Coke sales.[1] Data in internal databases enables businesses to execute strategies to increase profits from high-consumption customers. Market intelligence using internal databases helps businesses transform themselves from viewing marketing research as primarily information acquisition oriented to viewing it as information sharing to facilitate being proactive and responsive to customers.

Granular data Highly detailed, highly personalized data specifically structured around an individual customer.

Market intelligence activities enable businesses to create competitive advantages by using customer information at the **granular data** level. That is, data are detailed, highly personalized, and specifically structured around the individual customer. Companies like Coca-Cola, Google, and Apple embrace the vision and long-term goal of capturing and retaining customers. With granular customer information, market intelligence helps them and other companies anticipate changing customer desires and thus to refine their offerings. From a CRM perspective, experts commonly refer to this type of data acquisition and use

A Closer Look at Research

Marketing Intelligence in the Financial Services Industry

MIECO, a financial services company, tailors its products to each customer's needs. One particular customer's package includes a money market fund, a mutual fund, a credit card, a home mortgage, and home, life, and auto insurance. MIECO knows the customer travels frequently for work and relays this information to its credit card partner to prevent unnecessary calls to the customer for authorization when there are periods of heavy use.

Having accumulated knowledge of customer preferences by learning habits and trends through each transaction, MIECO sends offers that have a high degree of acceptance (e.g., information on vacation home real estate opportunities and car lease changes). The company also provides information on the tax implications of owning a second home and reviews the customer's financial holdings, offering suggestions on how to finance a second mortgage. And when interest rates drop, MIECO e-mails the customer to see if he or she wants to speak with a MIECO representative about refinancing the first mortgage. Using family information from the insurance policy, the company sends timely information on college loan programs, something the customer has agreed to receive. The customer may ask to be contacted by e-mail, never by phone, and MIECO makes sure that this happens.

Customer-centric approach Use of granular data to anticipate and fulfill customers' desires.

as a customer-centric approach. A **customer-centric approach** facilitates convenience and efficiency for customers in their interactions (touchpoints) with the company. Interactions are used to obtain information from the customer in order to build and solidify long-term relationships. The nearby A Closer Look at Research (In the Field) box illustrates how the process works in the financial services industry.

Similar to a CRM framework, market intelligence possesses four unique characteristics that shape and define its character: (1) strategic use of customer information; (2) transaction-based information; (3) companywide approach to sharing information; and (4) advanced Internet and telecommunications technology.

Strategic Use of Customer Information

Two key questions guiding the use of market intelligence are "What does my customer value?" and "What is the value of my customer?" Fortune 500 companies, like Bank of America, Verizon, and Procter and Gamble, address these questions through their proactive efforts to strategically sort customers into profitable and unprofitable segments.

Information from many sources is organized and categorized in the firm's data warehouse. Some examples of key data and sources include customer identification information and purchase transactions (purchase frequency, credit information), salespeople (competitive information), call centers (customer service lines), sales promotions (purchase habits), survey data (customer satisfaction), in-store interactions, the Internet, kiosks, demographic information, service bureaus, external database marketing companies, and even motor vehicle registrations. Marketing researchers perform statistical analysis of customers' value, preferences, profitability, and lifetime value. With this information, management refines product and service strategies to meet the changing needs of the most profitable customer segments, manage relationships, and build loyalty.

Using databases developed for the consumer electronics industry, companies like Best Buy better understand that young single adults purchase DVD players for home and auto; childless newlyweds buy small appliances for the home; new parents often want digital cameras; and established families look for multiple televisions and home computers. Retired adults buy electronics for second homes; divorced couples spend to set up new households. Database marketing insights like these can be profitable for companies that use strategic market intelligence approaches.

Information Based on a Transactional Focus

Every interaction with customers provides an opportunity to capture customer information, invest in the customer relationship, and build loyalty. Real-time communication between buyers and sellers enables firms to enhance interactions with customers and capture information beyond the transaction. For example, if Seven-Eleven customers have to buy a Pepsi when a Coke is not available, store management shares that information with others in the company and soft drink suppliers so inventory adjustments can be made. Marketing intelligence provides information that uncovers what each customer actually desires and why, not just what the customer purchases when a desired item is not available.

In addition to purchase transaction data, companies collect information regarding the context of the interaction. For example, Capital One uses contextual marketing to learn that a particular customer generally phones the bank's call center on Sunday evenings between 7:00 p.m. and 9:30 p.m. This information is then used by Capital One to communicate with that customer on Sunday evenings during that time frame, and the telephone is chosen as the best way to complete the interaction.

Companywide Approach to Using Database Information

Capturing information during every transaction or at each contact with customers and using that information are the foundation of a market intelligence program. A corollary is that information not remain in the marketing research or advertising departments but be disseminated throughout the company. Successful marketing intelligence requires information to be available across all business units to manage the supply chain, create customized products and pricing strategies, acquire new customers, and improve service quality. In this context, information availability to all departments is referred to as "information at every touchpoint." That is, all individuals throughout the company having direct or indirect contact with customers must have access to the same customer information.[2] Thus, all business units—accounting, engineering, production, marketing, distribution—share the same information about customers. This community of shared information extends even beyond the firm to include all facets of the company—suppliers, independent contractors, facilitating agencies, and retailers.

Technology Support of Market Intelligence

Technology support makes it possible to develop a strategic, information-rich market intelligence infrastructure. Technology provides the platform for turning customer data into customer knowledge. Advances in Internet and related technologies are the driving force behind the successful acquisition, recording, integration, storing, and sharing of information by many businesses today. In short, information technology plays a pivotal role enabling companies to maximize profitability through precise targeting of market segments.

Information technology drives the collection of customer data relating to demographics, billings, transactions, satisfaction levels, and service quality. These data are combined with additional primary and secondary data, integrated, and stored in a centralized data warehouse where they are then analyzed with data mining tools.

Companies are now leveraging technology so that information itself becomes a primary product and a prerequisite for doing business. For example, Wal-Mart and Target require all vendors not only to use information in their database warehouse, but to cooperate in capturing information by using Radio Frequency Identification tags (RFID), a tracking technology designed to manage the supply chain.

MARKETING DATABASES

Database Collection of information indicating what customers are purchasing, how often they purchase, and the amount they purchase.

A marketing database is a central repository of all relevant information concerning a company's customers. Specifically, a **database** is a collection of information indicating what customers are purchasing, how often they purchase, and the amount they purchase. A well-designed database incorporates information from a multitude of diverse sources, including actual transactions, history of promotional effectiveness, consumer surveys, secondary data, and other past marketing research project data. Unlike operational databases that reflect accounting and financial data, a true marketing database enables users to analyze purchase behavior, not intentions, over some predetermined time frame, event, or business situation.

A typical database is structured around transactional information that is chronologically arranged to reflect each purchase occasion. Additional information such as customers' demographics, lifestyles, and media habits is integrated with transactional data so a company can develop a complete picture of its customers. The outcome is a complete customer profile based on actual purchase frequency and amount at any given point in time. When categorized effectively, the information provides a total customer portfolio to be used in making product or brand decisions, resource allocations, and decisions on communication tools and distribution channels.

The customer information obtained from sales invoices, warranty cards, telephone calls, market research projects, and so forth generates the data stored in a marketing database. The information is logically arranged to allow for instant access whenever the customer contacts a company or vice versa. Such databases typically are linked to an interactive computer system that can automatically display a customer profile on demand. This enables the user of the database to recognize customers by name, purchase history, general interests, and product uses, as well as future product needs. In addition, most marketing databases are enhanced with information on the company's product mix. Database users then know exactly what a company makes or sells, which items are the most popular, and which are most suitable for certain customers.

At the core of the database is a network that provides specific information on each and every product or service offered by the company. With such information, companies can tell customers which replacement parts to order for their dishwasher, how to change a filter on their air conditioner, what games are available for their Nintendo system, and what each would cost. Even technical questions, such as those regarding installation of a home television satellite system, can be routed to a company expert.

Airlines and travel agencies provide excellent examples of marketing database development and usage. These service providers book customers on complicated tours around the world, have hotel rooms and rental cars waiting at each destination, and deliver tickets, boarding passes, and itineraries within hours, or perhaps minutes. This happens because of a networked database that links airlines, hotels, car rental services, and express delivery systems. With database information, the service provider knows a particular customer prefers a window seat, usually travels with Delta Airlines, always flies first class, is a Crown Room member, and uses Hertz Number One Gold Club Auto Rentals. The service provider knows the address where the tickets are sent, the spouse's name, and the home, office, and mobile phone numbers. All of the customer's information is stored in the database and can be accessed instantly anytime the service provider needs it.

Purposes of a Customer Database

In the broadest sense, the purpose of any customer database is to help a firm develop meaningful, personal communication with its customers. This level of communication deals with the proper products or brands, the various prices of the product offering, the level of customer service to be built into the total offering, and how much access customers have to the product. In short, a customer database allows a company to communicate at the right place, at the right time, with the right product, to the right customer. Lands' End, Dell, Nike, Coca-Cola, Target, Procter and Gamble, and most other consumer goods companies have extensive databases to better serve their customers.

More specific purposes of the customer database are (1) to improve the efficiency of market segmentation, (2) to increase the probability of repeat purchase behavior, and (3) to enhance sales and media effectiveness. To fulfill these purposes, the successful customer database must enable users to measure, track, and analyze customer buying behaviors. The role of marketing research, then, becomes one of generating, developing, and sustaining the database.

In a real sense, marketing databases bring back the level of individual service lost with the onset of mass merchandising. In the past, local retailers knew each customer and his or her family members. They established a bond with customers that included two-way communication, and that instilled customer loyalty, increased customer satisfaction, and fostered the growth of the business. Mass merchandising and discount retailing ended this relationship. Price, not loyalty, began to drive customers' purchase decisions. While quality of merchandise went up, personal service went down. Today the situation is reversing itself. By giving a firm access to information on each customer's family demographics, leisure activities, purchase history, media interests, and personal socioeconomic factors, the modern database can help that firm re-create personal service.

Four fundamental areas in which the database benefits the firm are (1) exchanging information with customers, (2) determining heavy users, (3) determining lifetime customer value, and (4) building segment profiles. One of the most valuable benefits is the exchange of information between a firm and its customers. Information on product availability, special features, competitive product comparisons, repairs, and warranties are critical information requirements for customer service. Most businesses, through internal secondary data, have this information available. The task becomes providing it to customers so they have better decision-making capabilities.

At the same time, customers possess a wealth of information essential for any business. Why do customers buy a certain product? What features and benefits do they seek? What other products are they likely to purchase? Successful databases constantly provide such exchange of information. Every contact with a customer becomes an occasion to provide more information to a database. Also, as a business learns more about its customers, it understands what information customers want from it.

Information exchange tells a business that all customers are not alike. With a database, businesses can distinguish heavy, medium, and light users of their product or service and adjust their strategy accordingly. The database's ranking system for all customers can help the business tailor products, benefits, and services to each class to keep heavy users loyal and stimulate medium and light users to buy more.

Within each user class, the business can also determine the expected lifetime value per customer. When a customer is acquired, the database enables the business to determine what it can expect from that customer. Calculating contribution to profit and overhead over a customer's lifetime with the company is a major task. Using this lifetime value, the company can determine how much to spend on marketing activities to keep the customer satisfied and loyal.

Finally, a marketing database enables the business to answer the crucial question: "Why do some consumers buy our products or services regularly while others do not?" The simple premise behind a database is that consumers themselves can provide the information necessary to answer this question. Other questions that can be answered using the database include:

- How do our products compare with the competition?
- What is the relationship between perceived value and price of the product?
- How satisfied are customers with the service level and support for the product?
- What are the comparisons among lifestyles, demographics, attitudes, and media habits among heavy, medium, and light users of the product?

Through various modeling techniques, individuals can be profiled on the basis of selected characteristics that will likely distinguish buyers from nonbuyers.

Marketing Research and Data Enhancement

Data enhancement The overlay of information about customers to better determine their responsiveness to marketing programs.

The primary role of a database is to serve as an information and intelligence resource for a company. Central to this objective is the process of **data enhancement,** which is defined as the overlay (adding) of information about customers to better determine their responsiveness to marketing programs. Data enhancement gives organizations three distinct advantages:

More knowledge of customers. Knowing exactly who buys products or services is extremely valuable in adjusting a company's marketing plan. Most databases are built with this purpose and concentrate on internal company data for current users of a product or service. Data enhancement enables external primary data to be woven into current internal data to gain a more accurate categorization of customers based on their true value to the company. The external data normally contain, but are not limited to, demographic, psychographic, behavioral, and motivational data about various consumers.

Increased effectiveness of marketing programs. Through data enhancement, the marketing function of an organization can gain greater insights into communications, distribution, and new-product development. When internal data about customers are enhanced with external data, usage profiles by consumer can be tailored to reflect the unique desires of various customer groups.

Predicting responses to changing marketing programs. Having concise information on various customer groups allows for increased targeting efficiency. Efficiency is increased when current customer profiles are used to predict the probability of targeting new yet similar customers with a new marketing plan. In short, the probability of success regarding new programs and procedures can be calculated according to the enhanced data.

Effective Development of Enhanced Databases

A typical database contains three critical data units that can be interactively categorized for unique customer profile reports: geodemographic factors, attribute data, and target market dimensions. Exhibit 4.1 shows the interactive properties of these data units.

Two levels of geodemographic factors are generally used: geographic market and residential area. At the residential level, information requirements center on the individual, the household, and the zip code where current customers reside. The geographic market level requires data at a more aggregate level representing metropolitan or regional market areas.

Attitudinal data Reflect a consumer's preferences, views, and feelings toward products and services.

Typically, **attitudinal data** reflect an individual's preferences, views, and feelings toward a particular product or service offering. Attitudinal data reflect a person's overall attitude toward the product, specific brands, and product features and are an important component of database development because they are related to purchase behavior. When individuals prefer a product or brand, they are more inclined to buy it than when they have no preference.

Motivational data Refer to the drive, desire, or impulse that channels a person's behavior.

Motivational data refer to the drive, desire, or impulse that channels an individual's behavior toward a goal. Motivational data typically involve those factors behind why people behave as they do. Seeking particular product benefits, shopping at stores that are convenient and comfortable, or simply enjoying the interaction with certain salespeople may all constitute motivational characteristics that drive a purchase decision. In short, motivational data reflect the activities behind the purchase. Whether the issue is brand loyalty, store loyalty, or media influence, motivational data describe those circumstances that direct a customer's behavior toward a goal.

Target market characteristics Describe selective demographic, purchase volume, and frequency factors used to categorize consumers or businesses.

Target market characteristics describe heavy product users versus light users on such dimensions as demographics, purchase volume, and purchase frequency. Other data reveal household consumption patterns, shopping patterns, advertising effectiveness, and price sensitivity information.

The key to database enhancement, of course, is the availability of data to increase the interactive efficiency of the data units. In most database development, the geodemographic unit is called the *driver dimension* because it determines (or drives) the type and amount of additional data that can be generated for cross-reference purposes. For example, a company may have a limited database of its current customers. But it wants to use a promotional campaign to increase awareness of its product offering among potential new users. Analysis of its database based on geodemographic factors reveals useful

eXHIBIT 4.1 Interactive Components of a Database

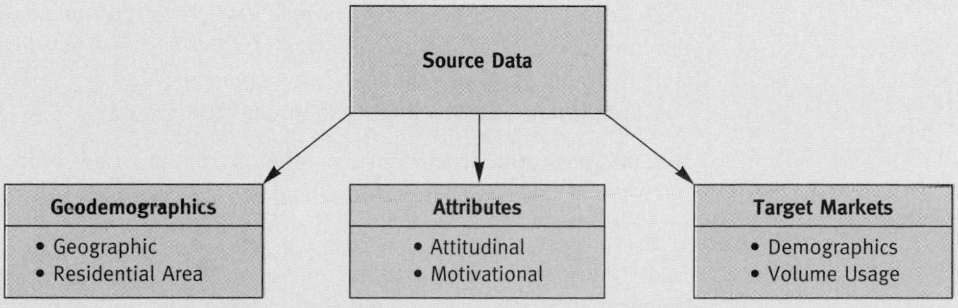

information on where current customers reside. However, it provides little value regarding the targeting of new customers except for similar residential locations. Therefore, the data requirement shifts to obtaining external data on attributes and target market characteristics of current users in order to enhance the transferability of current customer profiles to potential new customers.

Geodemographic data Characteristics (factors) that serve as the driver for determining additional data requirements.

In this simple example, **geodemographic data** serve as the driver for determining additional data requirements. Depending on the level and amount of information available on a geodemographic level, additional data requirements are then determined.

Dynamics of Database Development

The data in a database come from many sources both internal and external to the company. Regardless of where the information comes from, a database is only as good as the information it contains. If the information required to make marketing decisions is not in the database, or if the accessible information is not relevant, the database is useless. From a marketing perspective, information generated for a database must possess the following characteristics:

Affinity. Data must reflect prior usage of the product or service in question. Data reflecting past usage by current customers are one of the best predictors of future purchases.

Frequency. Information reflected in a database must give users the ability to categorize customers by frequency of purchase. Available information should reflect the amount of business each individual has conducted with the company.

Recency. Length of time between purchases is a very powerful predictor of future purchases. Because of this, recency of purchase is a critical factor in database dynamics. Recency assumes that a customer who purchased from a particular business last month has a greater probability of repurchase than a customer whose last purchase occurred six months ago.

Using recency, customers are profiled on the basis of their most recent purchase, the most recent having the highest probability and the least recent having the lowest probability of repurchase. Each customer is assigned a recency code (1 = most recent, 5 = least recent, for example) and sorted into groups based on the assigned codes.

Once the profiles are established, decision makers view these customers in a totally different light. Certain customer groups can receive new-product promotions, while others may be targeted with specially designed marketing efforts to increase repeat purchases. Understanding recency enables the business to build better relationships with different customer classes. Researchers also can determine which groups are most important and which need additional cultivation.

Amount. How much a customer purchases from any one company is a good predictor of future usage status. Therefore, the data must facilitate categorization of customers into specific usage groups (light, medium, heavy users).[3]

Many companies go beyond the above guidelines and consider *profitability* as well. A customer may purchase frequently and in large amounts, but if she purchases only items that are on sale or deeply discounted she is less profitable to the firm. Wachovia National Bank groups its customers into 10 segments based on profitability. Customer relationship managers call the bank's customers in more profitable segments to make them aware of new products and services or just to tell them they appreciate their business. Less profitable customers are encouraged to use less costly approaches like the Internet,[4] with some banks even charging customers a fee to talk with a bank representative.

Although the information in a database must have certain common and useful characteristics, researchers must never lose sight of the fact that database development is unique to each company. Database development maximizes the relevancy of the information but is highly specific. The amount and type of information relevant to one business may not be relevant to another.

Rules of Thumb in Database Development

Given the value a well-developed database can add to a company, management should view the total process of database development as a commitment to a long-term data acquisition plan. Thus, the development of a database should be budgeted as a multiyear process. Researchers should begin with collecting the data that will have the greatest amount of predictive power.

Database depth The overall number of key data fields or key variables that will make up the data record.

Database width The total number of records contained in the database (also referred to as sample size).

Second, management should view the data acquisition process in terms of the depth and width of the database. **Database depth** refers to the overall number of key data fields or variables that make up the data record (all data pertaining to the individual or company). **Database width,** in contrast, refers to the total number of records contained in the database (total number of individuals or companies in the database).

Finally, companies should avoid jumping onto the database bandwagon (developing a database just because everyone else is doing so) and then failing to commit the necessary resources. A marketing research database is a constant and ongoing process. A database will not succeed unless the company makes a commitment to long-term data acquisition and enhancement.

Database Technology

Database technology The tools that are used to transform data into information.

Database management system A computerized program that creates, modifies, and controls the flow of data.

Data dictionary Provides descriptions of data in a database.

Most companies have data on almost every aspect of their operations. Many companies even have data on how much data they have. What are data? *Data* are verbal or numerical facts that can be used for reasoning or calculating. In database terminology, a data item or data field is a basic characteristic about a customer or client (e.g., sex, age, name, address). Data fields have little value when treated individually. But when they are combined in a manner that makes them useful for making decisions, they acquire value and can be regarded as market information.

Database technology refers to the tools used to transform data into useful information. Database technology processes data and stores it in a single databank. It consists of two unique features: a database management system and a data dictionary. A **database management system** is a computer program that creates, modifies, and controls access to the data in the database. Users of these programs follow basic instructions to combine data and produce a desired output. The output of a typical database management system is shown in Exhibit 4.2. A **data dictionary** provides descriptions of the data in the database. It formats the data and assigns meaning to the data fields or variables. Together, the

EXHIBIT 4.2 Typical Output of a Database Management System

PRIMARY BUSINE	KEY CONTACT PE	DELIVERY STREET	STATE	ZIP CODE	PHONE	FAX	CUSTOMER PO	ORDER NO.
	Douglas				2882231	0	100541	52117
banks	Ernest Stevens		AL	35203-	2052521161	2053266220	020890-2	299568
snack food	DENNY TAVERES				7176324477	7176327207	VERBAL PER DEN	572117
	Richard Trotter						2179	342422
food	John Lock		W	54467	7153415960	7153415966	21259	59571
food			W	54467	715341596	7153415566	29060	127397
	DALE COWART				5014245403	5014245228	MH51114	376271
			OR	97220-	5036664545	5036692223	DM90099	222620
pers care			PR	00709	3154322287	0	BM00030	54200
pers care			PR	00709	0	0	BM	109800
pers care	FRANCK		PR	00709	3154322287	315432411	VERBAL	96175
pers care	Ben Sepulveda		PR	00709	8098340185	8098331095	20464	48541
pers care	Ben Sepulveda		PR	00709	8098340185	8098001095	20464	48541
pers care	JERRY WOOSTER		VA	22021	2019266786	2019266782	M-01202	60067
	MILLOS CIKASA				8185494	8185496638	101071	53582
	OLIVIER DULAUN				6096632260	6096650474	5586	407602
					6096632260	0	1187	780000
building products					2154858959		72748	74000
					2068728400	2063957701	F-35580	145560
	MARK MIKA		WA	98032	2063957596	2063957591	D67428	3977000
							84007	194076
	CAROL COLLINS		MI	48043	6144386312	0	LMT104737	48897
			PA	19363	7088332900	7088331025	K-53167	43188
	PAUL MORGAN				6155976700	6155975243	13362	42009
	ALLEN RANSOM		IN	46041	8032815292	0	B883D150061	312743
snack foods			IN	46041	2143534893	0		375954
snack foods					0	0	U9914	383478
snack foods			NC		0	0		360140
snack foods			MD		0	0	EU10443	403937
snack foods	Royce Shafer							957600
snack foods					0	0	U9914	383478
snack foods								42960
snack foods	Engineering Accou		IN	46041-	2143534893	0	EU-7308	375954
snack foods	BRUCE FISHER/II		MD		2143344940	2143345175	EU-14060	997554
snack foods	DAN PREMUS		OR	97005	2143344940	2145345175	EV14247	596553
snack foods	Bruce Fisher	Aberdeen	MD	21001			EV15168	325766
food	ED CASSATERI		IL	60185	7082311140	7082316968	WC-072810	189319
	D. WHEL		KS	66031	9137648100	9137646520	VERBAL	550691
	NANCY HOLLAND				8002556837	0	H2924	56861
		Burlingame	CA	94010			1717	222430
	Roland Gage						1717	787745
snack food					2159329330	2159325698	SM12067	98481
food	CHRISTINE ALLEN	HERSHEY	PA	17033			2R5076221	49428

eXHIBIT 4.3 An Example of a Data Pattern of a Sequential Database

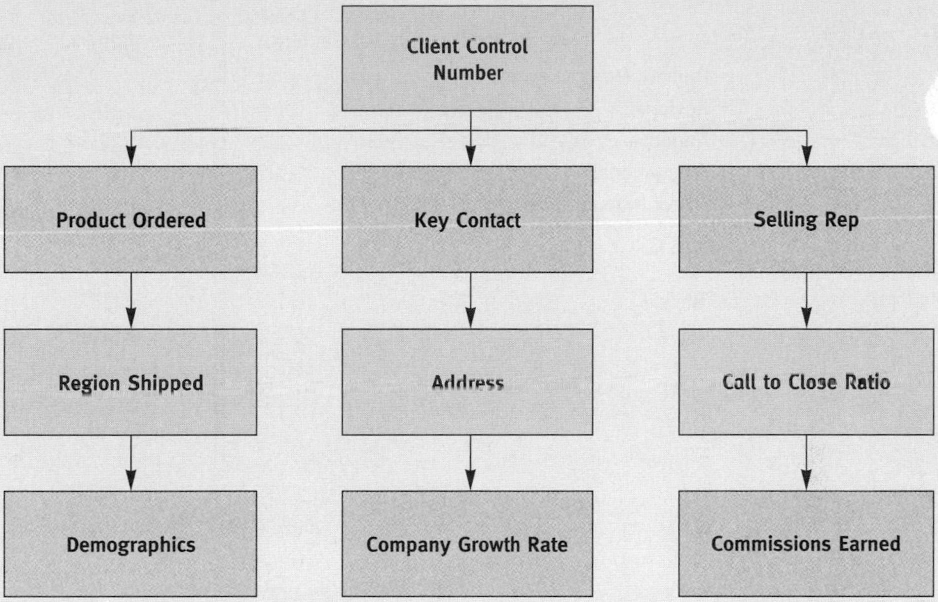

database management system and data dictionary constitute what is called the *database processing system.*

Sequential database system Organizes data in a very simple pattern, that is, a simple path, linkage, or network.

Two types of database processing systems exist: sequential and relational. A **sequential database system** organizes data in a very simple pattern, that is, a simple path, linkage, or network. In a sequential database only two single data fields can be paired. Once paired, they can be linked to a third data field. Once this group is connected, it can be linked to a fourth, and then to a fifth, and so on, as illustrated in Exhibit 4.3.

Many companies choose to develop sequential databases because they allow users to easily access detailed data linked to a specific data field or variable (e.g., region of country). Also, database systems are commonly used in companies that require reports based on consistent data in a given format.

Relational database system A system that structures a database in tables with rows and columns, with the tables (not data fields) being linked together depending on the output desired.

A **relational database system** operates somewhat differently from a sequential database system. The major difference is that relational databases require no direct relationship between data fields or variables. Data are structured in tables with rows and columns, with the tables (not the data fields) being linked together depending on the output desired. With a relational database system, the table becomes an individual file, rows correspond to records (width), and columns represent data fields or variables (depth) within each record.

In Exhibit 4.4, for example, each row represents the number of customers for that particular field. The primary market attribute is divided into regional, national, and international fields. Each column contains the breakdown of each customer by primary business (bakery, chemical, pharmaceutical, and so on). The rows and columns together constitute the table, which profiles customers by industry segment.

EXHIBIT 4.4 A Relational Database That Shows a Customer Profile by Industry Segment

	Bakery (15)	Chemical (7)	Pharmaceutical (35)	Snack food (42)	Other (11)
Primary Market Served					
Regional	1(6.7)	1(14.3)		3(7.1)	1(9.1)
National		2(28.6)	7(20)	37(88.1)	3(27.3)
International	3(20)	2(28.6)	8(22.9)		5(45.5)
No. of Product Lines					
One	(6.7)	1(14.3)	1(2.9)		3(27.3)
Two	6(40)		2(5.7)	2(4.8)	2(18.2)
Three		1(14.3)	5(14.3)	1(2.4)	1(9.1)
Four	1(6.7)	3(42.9)	4(11.4)	4(9.5)	—
Five		1(2.9)			—
Six	1(6.7)				1(9.1)
Seven					
Region					
N.E.	5(33.3)		13(37.1)	9(21.4)	2(18.2)
S.E.	1(1.7)	6(85.7)	4(11.4)	1(2.4)	5(45.5)
M.W.	4(26.7)	1(14.3)	3(8.6)	23(54.8)	2(18.2)
West	5(33.3)		1(2.9)	2(4.8)	2(18.2)
CAN/Other			13(37.1)	7(16.7)	

Relational databases offer greater flexibility than sequential databases in examining complex data relationships. In addition, relational databases enable the analyst to look at all variables or data fields simultaneously rather than one variable at a time. Overall, relational databases are best for dynamic situations in which the database must expand over time and in which multiple variable applications are needed.

Data Warehousing

Data warehouse Central repository for all significant parts of information that an organization collects.

Operational data Data for the daily operations of the business.

A **data warehouse** is a central repository for the information an organization collects. Data from various functions of the organization are stored in a central computer so that the information can be shared across all functional departments of the business. The major significance of a data warehouse is its purpose. From the standpoint of data collection, a data warehouse serves two purposes. First, the data warehouse collects and stores data for the daily operations of the business. This type of data is called **operational data** and the system used to collect operational data is *online transaction processing (OLTP)*. Operational data represent not only information collected from customers, but also data collected from suppliers and vendors.[5]

The second purpose of the data warehouse is to collect, organize, and make data available for analysis. This enables the business to use the data warehouse as a decision-making tool for marketing programs. This type of data is commonly referred to as

Informational data Data available for analysis purposes.

informational data and the system used to collect and organize informational data is *online analytical processing (OLAP)*. This process involves the development of customer categories based on relationships among the data.[6] For example, purchase history, frequency, store visits, and brand preference may all share a common relationship among a group of customers and are therefore grouped and categorized to form a profile of a particular customer group, similar to that of a market segment profile. The data warehouse provides the company with a system that is driven toward shared information, that is, information that can be used by any and all functional departments of the business.

A data warehouse is comparable to a campus library, both as a resource for and as a service to the entire university. The value of your campus library resources is determined by the variety and assortment of books, periodicals, and professional information it contains. The value of your campus library service is based on how quickly and easily the staff can assist you in finding and using what you need. In a data warehouse, the value of the resource is determined by the amount and variety of data collected and stored in the warehouse. The value of the service is determined by the ease of use and the extent to which the information can be shared throughout the entire business.

Marketing-Related Data and Data Warehousing

The type of data collected and stored is a key determinant in the success of any data warehouse. Data collected for a warehouse are highly specific to the business, yet the common feature of all data, regardless of the business, is that they are centered on the customer. Hospitals collect data on patient procedures, financial institutions collect data on financial services used, and insurance companies collect data on types of policies and risk associated with types of events that might occur. Although all three differ in their product/service offerings, they are similar in collecting data related to the customer. Aside from secondary and primary data stored in the warehouse, two unique forms of customer data most commonly collected for a data warehouse are (1) real-time transactional data and (2) customer-volunteered data.

Real-time transactional data Data collected at the point of sale.

Real-time transactional data are collected at the point of sale. This type of data is usually collected through a customer loyalty program or preferred buying program. Customer loyalty cards identify who the customer is, what the customer is buying and in what quantity and frequency, and at what retail outlet (either brick and mortar or online). The key dimension is that data are collected at the time of purchase, so manufacturers can identify how customers respond to a specific marketing program being used at that point in time. For example, sales of Miller beer may be tracked via point-of-sale data where price may vary over certain days along with point-of-sale promotional activities. In this case, the retailer can identify the impact of price and promotional variations on the sale of Miller beer.

Customer-volunteered information Data provided by the customer without any solicitation.

Customer-volunteered information is provided by customers without any direct solicitation. This type of data includes customer comment cards or complaints, customer registration information from Web sites, customer communications via chat rooms, and data obtained through customer advisory groups.

Wal-Mart has both real-time and customer-volunteer information in its data warehouse. Its data warehouse, second in size only to the Pentagon, contains over 200 terabytes (trillions of characters) of transaction data. Among other things, Wal-Mart uses its warehouse database to help stores select and adapt merchandising mixes to match local neighborhood preferences.

Data Mining: Transforming Data into Knowledge

Many businesses have implemented systematic processes for collecting data from a variety of sources. Justification for these efforts focuses on specific marketing questions facing the business. Data warehouses are designed to answer marketing-related questions. Many businesses are drowning in data while starving for useful knowledge about customers. This data overload has led to widespread interest in data mining.

Data mining Process of finding hidden patterns and relationships among variables/characteristics contained in data stored in the data warehouse.

Data mining is the process of finding "hidden" relationships among variables contained in data stored in the data warehouse. Data mining is an analysis procedure known primarily for the recognition of significant patterns of data for particular customers or customer groups. Marketing researchers have used data mining for many years. But the procedures usually were performed on small data sets containing 1,000 or fewer respondents. Today, with the development of sophisticated data warehouses, the size of data sets being analyzed has increased to millions, even billions of respondent records. For example, Nokia examined over 6 billion pieces of data in designing its N-Series mobile phone. Ford Motor Company's database has over 50 million names, Kraft Foods has more than 25 million names, Citi Bank has over 35 million names, American Express has 30 million names, and so on. Special data mining tools have been developed for the specific purpose of analyzing customer patterns found in very large databases.

Data mining finds relationships that are hidden or not easily identifiable among several customer dimensions within large data warehouses. The procedure is used when the market researcher has limited knowledge of a particular subject. For example, management in a casino business might ask the question "What are the characteristics of the gaming customers who spent the most in our casino last year?" Data mining techniques are used to search the data warehouse, capture the relevant data, categorize the significant characteristics, and develop a profile of the high-budget gambler.

The Data Mining Process

Exhibit 4.5 provides a framework of the four steps in the data mining process: the marketing research question, data mining approaches, the data mining implementation process, and the visual data mining product.

Marketing Research Question

The marketing research question is the starting point in any data mining analysis. For example, management might want an answer to a question such as "Which customers are most likely to visit our casino in the month of July and why?" To provide an answer, data mining tools analyze two key requirements: description and prediction.

Description The process of discovering patterns, associations, and relationships among key customer characteristics.

Prediction Uses patterns and relationships to predict future trends and behaviors.

Description is the process of discovering patterns, associations, and relationships among key customer characteristics such as demographic variables, gambling expenditures, frequency of casino visits, amount of wagers won/lost, day of the week, month, time of day, number of hours engaged in gambling, and so forth. **Prediction** uses these patterns and relationships to predict future trends and behaviors, such as why customers visit during a given month, what activities they engage in during that month, how much they gamble during the month, and what special events they attended, if any, during that particular time.

EXHIBIT 4.5 Data Mining Framework for Marketing Decisions

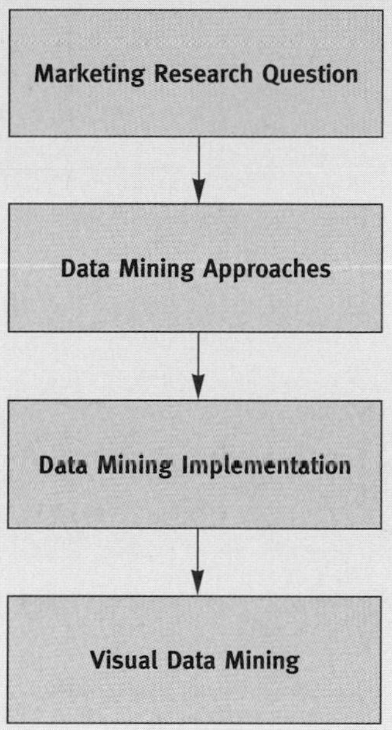

Data Mining Approaches

Data mining uses several approaches for description and prediction. One or more of these approaches can be used, for example, to profile groups based on age, sex, income, race, and lifestyle using consistent or sequential behavior patterns, or to predict customer satisfaction levels based on friendliness of employees, cleanliness of surroundings, quality of services, and reputation of the business. Exhibit 4.6 lists the most commonly used data mining approaches and some business applications in which they are applied.

Data Mining Implementation

In this process the researcher first identifies how the data contained in the warehouse are stored and categorized. Categorization and storage determine which data mining approach is most appropriate to find answers to the marketing question.

Visual Data Mining Product

No matter which data mining approach is used, deciding how the results will be presented is a critical part of any data mining activity. Remember, data mining is the combination of two concepts: automatic pattern discovery among customer characteristics and visual presentation of those patterns. A data mining approach may be very good at discovering patterns, but if those patterns are not effectively visualized, the power to make strategic decisions using the information is lost. Thus, the success of any data mining procedure relies on the ability of the researcher to access and comprehend the results of the analysis relative to the marketing research question.

eXHIBIT 4.6 Commonly Used Approaches in Data Mining

Decision Trees

This is a set of rules that uses a tree-like structure to classify customers into segments or other relevant groups. Examples of this approach include:

Retail: What are the differences between frequent and infrequent shoppers at Wal-Mart?

Medical: Which factors affect kidney transplant survival rates?

Telemarketing: Which prospects are good risks and therefore an attempt should be made to sell them a mortgage?

Rule Induction

This process develops "If . . . then . . . " rules to classify individuals in a database. While decision trees use a set of rules, rule induction methods generate a set of independent rules that are unlikely to form a tree and may form better classification patterns. Examples include:

Retail: Will the likelihood of purchase of a one-year extended warranty on a new digital camera from Best Buy be greater than, equal to, or less than 10 percent?

Medical: What are the "good risk" criteria that must be met before trying a particular treatment on a cancer patient?

Direct mail: Will the response to a mail campaign for Office Depot be greater than 5 percent?

Neural Networking

This is a nonlinear predictive model that learns how to detect patterns that match a particular profile. The name comes from the fact that the process resembles that of the human brain. The results typically are based on clustering or sequencing of patterns. Examples include:

Retail: Which brand of DVD player is a prospect most likely to purchase?

Medical: What disease is a person likely to contract?

Direct Mail: Who will respond to a particular mailing?

Fuzzy Logic

This approach handles imprecise concepts like "small, large, big, young, old, high, and low" and is more flexible. It examines fuzzy types of data classifications rather than those with more precise boundaries.

Retail: Who is a likely customer for our new line of HDTV products?

Medical: Which smokers are likely to develop lung cancer?

Direct Mail: Who might be a likely person to respond to our new promotional campaign?

Genetic Algorithms

These are not used to find patterns, but rather to guide the learning process of neural networking. The approach loosely follows the pattern of biological evolution in which members of one generation compete to pass on their characteristics to the next generation until the best model is found. Examples include:

Retail: What is the optimal store layout for a particular location?

Medical: What is the optimal treatment for a particular disease?

Direct Mail: What is the optimal demographic profile of an individual who is likely to invest $20,000 or more in a mutual fund this year?

Database Modeling

Before conducting any modeling, the researcher needs to review, refine, and format the raw data in the database so it can be easily processed using statistical packages. This data interface process is necessary for successful query and modeling activities.

A Closer Look at Research

Database America Introduces SalesLeads™—First Web-Based Lead-Generating Service for Consumers and Small Businesses

Database America markets SalesLeads™, a Web-based direct marketing database designed to generate sales leads for small to medium-sized businesses. SalesLeads provides anyone with access to the Internet a cost-effective means of building targeted prospect lists from Database America's file of in-depth information on more than 14 million U.S. and Canadian businesses and over 200 million people in 104 million households. While on the Web site users can develop highly customized mailing lists paying a minimal charge for the names they download.

Anyone with a computer and an Internet connection can access SalesLeads via the Database America Web site (www.databaseamerica.com). The system provides an easy interface for selecting marketing criteria such as geographic and demographic attributes and honing the list to specify details such as sales volume or employee size. Uses for SalesLeads range from students researching employment prospects, to hobbyists building a list of regional churches or associations sponsoring craft fairs, to commercial real estate agents generating leads to sell properties. There is no charge for looking and no minimum requirements. Customers pay only a few cents for each prospect they download and can pay via a secure credit card transaction on the system.

"Database America is drawing on more than 40 years of expertise in business-to-business direct mail marketing. We pride ourselves on leading the market with the latest technology," said Al Ambrosino, president of Database America. "As an online service, SalesLeads provides the small business and home office audience access to the identical database information previously geared towards much larger organizations."

SalesLeads is the first lead-generating product of its kind on the Web offering real-time delivery of information that can be easily updated. Users can conduct their searches by filling in criteria in an easy-to-use graphical form on the Database America Web page. Criteria include business name, business type via NAICS (North American Industry Classification System) codes, geography, ZIP code, number of employees, and sales volume.

Once users have determined their search criteria and built a mailing or telemarketing list, they can download the file to their computers. The list is created in a standard character file format that is compatible with virtually all desktop word processing and spreadsheet programs. The list includes business names, addresses, and phone numbers for printing out as address labels. Database America also offers users the option of purchasing the data for shipment in hardcopy labels.

Source: www.databaseamerica.com.

Database modeling A framework used to summarize what a company already knows about its best customers and what else is needed.

Database modeling and analysis are designed to summarize what companies already know about their best customers and at the same time indicate what else they need to learn about these individuals. When a database model fails to predict a customer's future behavior, the database analyst needs to ask whether the company truly knows enough about its customers. The nearby A Closer Look at Research (In the Field) box highlights one of the largest database firms in the world.

Many companies find themselves data rich and information poor. Customer database modeling often points to a company's information shortages and triggers new ideas for future marketing research endeavors. An effective approach to handling database modeling is to start where the process will end and then work backward. The question then becomes: "How will the information be used?" or "What will the information enable us to do?" With this approach the researcher knows how the modeling output will be usable for the decision maker. Among the many modeling procedures that exist in database analysis, two of the more traditional are scoring models and lifetime value models.

Scoring Models

Scoring model Ranking system that judges the desirability of a customer based on that customer's propensity to purchase products or services.

Scoring models are used to predict consumption behavior. Each individual in the database is assigned a score based on his or her propensity to respond to a marketing variable or make an actual purchase. High scores are indications of very desirable customers; low scores represent less desirable segments. The initial objective is to rank customer segments based on their potential profitability to the company. The primary feature of scoring models is called the gains table. An example of a gains table is presented in Exhibit 4.7.

Using a gains table, a database analyst can project and manage the profitability of various customer segments. For example, according to the data in Exhibit 4.7, the customer base is composed of 500,000 persons divided into five equal segments of 100,000, or five segments of 20 percent of the market. The gains table ranks each of these segments based on its profit potential. Group 1 customers have the highest profit potential, and group 5 the lowest. Group 1 is estimated to draw approximately $2 million in future profit, or an estimated $20 per customer, and so on. Combined, groups 1, 2, and 3 are expected to generate $4.5 million in total future profits, or an estimated $20, $17.50, and $3.50, respectively, per customer. As you move through the gains table, you see the percentage of profitability per segment begin to decrease. This approach reinforces the basic marketing principle that customers are not homogeneous and, more specifically, the conventional wisdom that 20 percent of customers represent 80 percent of a company's profits.

Key Variables in Scoring Models

Key variables in the scoring model enable researchers to determine which factors can be used to separate customers into purchase groups. Scoring models use weights to multiply assigned values in each customer's record. For example, suppose five factors are useful in separating heavy users from light users of hair spray: age, income, occupation, number of children under 18, and home value. On the basis of customer characteristics in the database, the scoring model determines that for heavy users of hair spray, the variables are arranged in the following order and assigned a corresponding weight: home value, .130; age, .050; occupation, .042; number of children under 18, .022; and income, .012. Obviously, the real weights produced by the model would be quite different, since they are to be multiplied by numbers (e.g., age in years, occupation in assigned coded value, income in thousands of dollars). For our discussion, however, let's assume these are real values.

EXHIBIT 4.7 Example of the Data Output from a Gains Table

Group Number	Number of Customers	Percentage of Customers	Cumulative Number of Customers	Cumulative Percentage	Average Profile per Customer	Predicted Total Profit	Cumulative Total	Cumulative Average per Customer
1	100,000	20%	100,000	20%	$20	$2,000,000	$2,000,000	$20.00
2	100,000	20	200,000	40	15	1,500,000	3,500,000	17.50
3	100,000	20	300,000	60	10	1,000,000	4,500,000	3.50
4	100,000	20	400,000	80	5	500,000	5,000,000	1.25
5	100,000	20	500,000	100	1	100,000	5,100,000	.20

In this example, home value is an important factor, with income being a less important factor for classifying customers into a heavy user group. The model permits a researcher to run a program that takes each of the relevant factors in the customer record and multiplies it by the appropriate weight. The weights are then added together to get an overall score. The score represents the likelihood of a customer's being a heavy user (or a medium user, etc.) of the product.

Variables used to generate scoring model gains tables should be from actual purchase behavior data. Key variables include demographics, psychographics, lifestyle data, and purchase habits including frequency, volume, and amount spent at a given time. These variables would then be assigned weights or scores depending on their ability to predict purchase behavior. For example, men may purchase more power tools than women. Therefore, on the basis of the single demographic variable of gender, men would be assigned a 10, women a 4. Each variable classification is assigned a weight or score. The scoring weight structure for two customer groups based on gender may look like the following:

Customer Group A		Customer Group B	
Female	2 pts	Male	10 pts
Volume: $100	5 pts	Volume: $50	10 pts
Frequency: 2 weeks	4 pts	Frequency: 1 month	8 pts
Product purchased: Dry cleaning	6 pts	Product Purchased: Dry cleaning	6 pts
Total:	17 pts	Total:	34 pts

As can be seen, Group B (with 34 points) has better matching variables than Group A (with only 17 points). The total scores for each group are then converted to dollars. So 34 points would become $34, and 17 points would become $17. This conversion becomes the foundation for predicting future profitability in gains table analysis.

Scoring models have a limited period of effectiveness. The life of the model is directly related to changes in customer demand. Therefore, scoring models need to be revised and changed as the market changes.

Lifetime Value Models

Lifetime value model Database model developed on historical data, using actual purchase behavior, not probability estimates, to predict future actions.

The fundamental premise behind **lifetime value models** is that customers, just like physical and tangible machinery, represent company assets. Moreover, customers represent a continuous stream of cash flow based on transactions they conduct with the business. All too often, the outcome of many marketing research projects is to obtain information that can be used to generate new customers only. Lifetime value models demonstrate that it is more valuable for businesses to concentrate on qualified customers first, then focus on growing them rather than constantly seeking new customers. Database information in most lifetime value models includes the following:

Price variables: The initial product or service cost and any price changes that occur.

Sales promotional variables: Type used, cost of the incentive, value to the customer.

Advertising expenditures: Direct costs of advertising expenses.

Product costs: Direct costs, plus quality of goods/services.

Relationship-building efforts: Type and costs of relationship-building devices and value of building long-term relationships.

EXHIBIT 4.8 A Hypothetical Lifetime Value Model for a Fast-Food Restaurant

PERIOD	1	2	3	4
CUSTOMERS	10,000			
REPEAT		3,500	1,225	428
REPEAT %		35%	35%	35%
REVENUE				
AVE, TICKET	$4.30	$4.50	$4.75	$4.75
PRICE INC.	.90			
TOTAL	34,000	15,750	5,818	2,033
EXPENSES				
DIRECT COSTS	60%	60%	60%	60%
TOTAL	20,400	9,450	3,491	1,219
REPEAT EFFORT				
TARGET	10,000	3,500	1,225	428
REPEAT %	35%	35%	35%	35%
RATE	3,500	1,225	428	150
TOTAL MAIL	10,000	3,500	1,225	428
COST	$3,800	$1,330	$465	$162
TOTAL EXP.	$24,200	$10,780	$3,956	$1,381
CONTRIB.	9,800	4,970	1,862	652
INVEST.	3,800	1,330	465	162
TOTAL LIFETIME VALUE	$6,000	$9,460	$11,037	$11,527
CUSTOMER VALUE	$.60	$.96	$1.10	$1.15

Database information is used to identify the most profitable customers. Exhibit 4.8 represents the output from a hypothetical lifetime value model for a fast-food restaurant. In this example 10,000 new customers are targeted for the marketing effort. The average amount spent by customers is about $4.30, and a free sandwich (with a cost of 90 cents) is the incentive to attract the customers. Therefore, the estimated revenue is about $34,000. Expenses amount to approximately 60 percent of total revenues, for a total expense of $20,400.

The business averages a 35 percent return rate of its customers. Therefore, mailing out 10,000 free sandwich coupons should yield 3,500 responses at a cost of $3,800. Total expenses for this planned effort are now estimated at $24,200. With an initial investment of $3,800, the total contribution should result in a $9,800 return to the business. This, in turn, equates to a total lifetime customer value of $6,000, or 60 cents per customer during the first period of the promotion. Given expected rates of return for customers over the next three promotional periods, total contribution would fall to $652, with investment costs down to $162. Total lifetime value over four periods would increase to $11,527, or $1.15 per customer. The four-period lifetime value for an individual customer is $1.15.

As a database tool, lifetime value models examine the asset value of customers over time. In contrast to purchase intention data, lifetime value models are based on actual purchase data and are often a better predictor of customer behavior.

MARKETING RESEARCH IN ACTION

The Function of Databases within the Financial Services Industry

Leading with Data[7]

Credit card issuers and bankers have big appetites for customer data and are using it to drive their businesses. As a representative of Jackson, MS–based Trustmark National Bank recently said, "If we don't know our customers and their behavior patterns, we can't make decisions that harness those behavior patterns into desired actions."

Never has such knowledge been more crucial. The banking industry is in transition, with new electronic delivery channels changing traditional banker–client relationships, replacing them with a fluid market system in which consumers can shop for products and services on price. Loyalty is difficult to come by, as products become increasingly commoditized, and channels of delivery more abundant. In this environment, banks are grooming a new breed of data-savvy executives who can lead by following the data trail.

Courting Profitable Customers

According to Acxiom Corporation (www.acxiom.com), bankers are at different levels in their mastery of the data basics of segmentation and data enhancement. But competition is forcing quick transformations of those who are not on board. The collection, integration, enhancement, and analysis of customer data have become must-do disciplines for improving marketing efficiency. Major credit card issuers have been using advanced database techniques for years. But other financial services businesses are just beginning to use such information technology. Mutual fund issuers are beginning to take advantage of consumer data sources. Retail bankers also are very involved in customer databases (called master customer information files or MCIFs), while commercial banking is only beginning to use these approaches.

Many banks are concerned with the warehousing of multiple streams of customer and prospect data and with providing analytical tools to their executives to support customer acquisition and retention efforts. Some of this work is being outsourced to service bureaus and consultants to help bring projects to rapid completion. And new data service providers are cropping up in unexpected places. MasterCard International, for example, has thousands of member banks that access consumer transaction data by account number.

While data is driving more acquisition and retention programs, New York City–based research firm First Manhattan Consulting Group (www.fmcy.com) reports that only 10 percent of America's top 50 banks use data for the more sophisticated profitability analysis at the account or household level. Profitability analysis involves obtaining operating costs, by product, identifying profit components from each transaction file, creating a formula for each product, and validating the accuracy of the calculated data. For example, CoreStates Bank (www.corestatesbank.com) uses profitability analysis to measure a customer's return. CoreStates' initial profitability analysis showed that 20 percent of customers were very profitable, 20 percent were very unprofitable, and 60 percent were marginal. Going further, CoreStates analyzed two of its branches. Branch "A" was in an affluent neighborhood and very profitable, while Branch "B" was in a blue-collar area and losing money.

To management's surprise, the two branches were comparable in loan ratios and all other areas except one: no-fee checking. That product alone pushed Branch "B" into the red. This knowledge allowed the product manager to change the minimum balance, raise fees, and use other alternatives to improve the profitability of both the accounts and the branch. Conventional wisdom holds that blue-collar customers are a bank's bread and butter because affluent customers often establish more than one banking relationship, but analysis showed that wasn't true in this case. Because the affluent customers' balances were so much higher—double that of other households, even without the total banking relationship, they produced a much better return.

At the other end of the spectrum is a small, 15-branch community bank that was very proficient at identifying the most profitable branch portfolios. They used an MCIF system to determine who the most profitable customers were in each branch, and to evaluate product profitability by customer. The analysis has enabled the bank to generate multimillion-dollar returns in customer acquisition and retention campaigns.

Mastering the Basics

Acxiom recommends that all banks use the following:

- **RFM Segmentation.** Segmenting customers by the three key variables of behavior: recency, frequency, and monetary value (RFM). Transaction data remains the most powerful predictor of future behavior, and can help banks identify the best prospects and possible defectors.

- **Data Enhancement.** Appending demographic and geographic data to customer records permits various modeling and mining efforts to be undertaken, including:
  1. **Profiling.** Create a profile of individual customers and households in each of your key segments, comparing the incidence of a particular type of buyer in your customer universe to the larger marketplace.
  2. **Cross-selling the existing customer base.** Identify best customers and target those who are prime candidates for additional products and services. Analytical models pinpoint variables that will lift response—which means you can mail to fewer people and get a greater response on what you do mail.
  3. **Upselling or reactivating customers.** Low-balance depositors and noncredit customers can be upgraded to more profitable status with appropriate product targeting. Inactive customers may likewise be viable prospects for other offerings.
  4. **Retention.** Reduce churn in your customer base by identifying factors predictive of defection and testing programs to turn likely defectors into your most loyal customers.
  5. **Acquisition.** Data can be used in various ways to improve acquisition. Your profile of your best customers points the way to the prospect most likely to respond and be profitable over time. This data can drive your offer, your creative, your media selection, and your fulfillment approach. Large mailers or telemarketers can also screen prospect lists by running them through a regression model, since they have considerable bargaining power in the list rental marketplace.

The Loyalty Connection

Developing deeper customer loyalty is an ongoing challenge for every financial institution. It is compounded by the industry's increasing reliance on technology, both for developing products and for executing transactions. As reliance on brick-and mortar branch infrastructures and personal relationships decreases, low-cost, high-tech options such as automated teller machines (ATMs) and online banking are increasingly homogenizing product offerings, and banks may lose the opportunity to cross-sell and upsell to their own customers because newcomers, not tied to banking's traditional branch infrastructure, can deliver services more cheaply. While it may be hard to think of bank products and services as commodities that we can shop around for like bread or milk, that mindset is changing.

Newcomers to banking such as Net Bank (www.netbank.com) are making some inroads with Internet-happy customers. But there is an upside for established players who are expanding their own online offerings. Electronic transactions generate transactional data which, when handled proactively, can help banks stand out from the crowd. For example, data captured on which ATM locations a customer uses, where the ATM is located in relation to the consumer's home and work, and what type of transactions each consumer conducts by time of day, week, or month can be very illuminating. Banks can use such data resources to increase overall ATM usage, to redirect traffic to underutilized sites, or to increase usage during low-peak evening and weekend hours.

Designing Win-Win Situations

Leading with data in financial services is not without its challenges. One of the key problems is that a model profitable customer—one who runs high balances on credit cards or other revolving loan programs—is also a model candidate for bankruptcy. That problem has been worsened by industry practice in issuing preapproved credit cards, which has contributed to rising bad debt for both consumers and issuers.

The delinquency crunch has attracted some nonbank innovators to the marketplace. Merchandise cataloger Fingerhut of Minnetonka, MN (www.fingerhut.com) decided to pursue high-risk customers as a lucrative credit card market. Using the company's catalog database containing 500 pieces of information on the cataloger's 50-million-name file, Fingerhut opened 670,000 credit card accounts with $500 million in receivables in less than a year, making it one of the largest card issuers in the U.S. Factoring in the inherent risk of extending credit to low to middle income families, Fingerhut allowed a 6 percent write-off for bad debt, and a competitive interest rate on its co-branded Visa and MasterCard. Fingerhut attributed the company's success to data—"It all goes back to the database," said their CEO.

Sensitivity Prevails

Another sophisticated use of data is segmented pricing based on customers' and prospective customers' risk and return profiles. Such customization, however, while used successfully in the insurance industry, faces consumer resistance when it comes to accessing credit. In fact, some issuers have raised consumer ire by offering preapproved cards without revealing all of the facts about the offered rate. Variable rates and "as low as" offers are clearly on shaky ethical and legal ground (federal law requires issuers to disclose in writing the interest rate in preapproved offers). And recent amendments to the Fair Credit Reporting Act require all companies using credit bureau lists to inform consumers of their opt-out rights. Issuers must factor in these business realities as they experiment with data-driven programs.

Data can also help bankers to think about customers in fresh ways. Data helps banks to develop traditional or emerging channels and to glean all the information they possibly can. Trustmark National Bank (www.trustmark.com), for example, offers senior citizens, who generally appreciate high-touch over high-tech service, the opportunity to have someone reconcile their check registers with their bank statements. Does that sound time consuming and unprofitable? It could be, but Trustmark added a relational database field to track which seniors opened savings accounts for their grandchildren and markets to them accordingly.

Banks are entering a new era of relationship-oriented strategies. Intensely transaction-driven, they have realized that product-oriented strategies will give way to more targeted and focused marketing efforts. Gemini Consulting (www.gemini.com) outlines the benefits banks derive as they adopt relationship-building strategies that lead with data:

- They efficiently sell the maximum amount of the banking products targeted to the right segments of their databases.
- Basic segmentation and cross-selling become easier, as preferred pricing and service strategies emerge for customers who buy multiple products and keep their business close to home.
- They build multiple product relationships with targeted customer segments, as sophisticated modeling techniques and profitability analysis at the account level allow customized value offerings and pricing.

To overcome the increasing homogenization of banking products via Internet banking and other online services, banks must position and distribute distinct initiatives associated with a bank's brand identity.

Hands-On Exercise

1. Using the database model in Exhibit 4.1, what elements are used by the financial services firms in your community? Give examples of some banks that are appealing to students using enhanced database marketing practices and how.
2. Using the knowledge you acquired in this chapter about market intelligence research practices, suggest ways banks and other companies can use market intelligence research to better serve their customers.

Summary of Learning Objectives

■ Understand the essential elements of market intelligence designs.

While market intelligence studies are similar to CRM frameworks, this specific type of secondary research design possesses four unique characteristics that shape and define its character: (1) the strategic use of customer information, (2) the use of transactional-based information, (3) companywide sharing of the information, and (4) support of advanced Internet and telecommunication technologies. In many cases, conducting a market intelligence study requires the researcher to integrate secondary data that are stored on both internal and external electronic databases containing *geodemographics*, customer *attitudinal* and *motivational attributes*, and *target market* characteristics. With such information, researchers can determine highly profitable customer segments compared to less profitable segments by using *scoring models* and/or *lifetime value modeling* approaches.

■ Explain the development of customer databases.

A marketing research database is a central repository of information on what customers are purchasing, how often, and in what amount. The fundamental purpose of any customer database is to help a firm develop meaningful, personal communication with its customers. Other, more specific purposes of this database are to improve efficiency of market segment construction, increase the probability of repeat purchase behavior, and enhance sales and media effectiveness.

■ Discuss the elements of enhanced marketing databases.

Typically a marketing database contains three critical types of data units that can be interactively categorized for unique customer profile reports: geodemographic factors, attribute data, and target market dimensions. The geodemographic factors focus on both geographic and residential units of measures, while both attitudinal and motivational characteristics of customers form the "attribute" elements of the database. Target market variables typically are concerned with the demographic facts about customers as well as those customers' purchase behaviors. Information generated for an enhanced database must possess elements of affinity, frequency, recency, and amount in order to provide both information "depth" and "width."

■ Explain the role of data mining in marketing research.

Data mining is the process of finding hidden relationships among variables contained in data stored in the data warehouse. Data mining is a data analysis procedure known primarily for the recognition of significant patterns of data as they pertain to particular customers or customer groups. Researchers must be aware of what the research questions are, the different data mining approaches, their implementation, and visualization of the potential relationships so they are usable.

■ Understand modeling in database analysis.

The purpose of database modeling is twofold: (1) to summarize what companies already know about their customers, and (2) to show companies what they need to learn about their customers. Two common modeling techniques exist in database analysis. Scoring models are designed to predict consumption behavior. Lifetime value models measure the value customers represent to the firm. Both models rely on actual purchase behavior.

Key Terms and Concepts

Attitudinal data 91
Customer-centric approach 86
Customer relationship management (CRM) 84
Customer-volunteered information 87
Database 88
Database depth 93
Database management system 93
Database modeling 101
Database technology 93
Database width 93
Data dictionary 93
Data enhancement 90
Data mining 98
Data warehouse 96
Description 98
Geodemographic data 92
Granular data 85
Informational data 97
Lifetime value model 103
Market intelligence 84
Motivational data 91
Operational data 96

Prediction 98
Real-time transactional data 97
Relational database system 95
Scoring model 102
Sequential database system 95
Target market characteristics 91

Review Questions

1. How have advances in Internet and telecommunication technologies impacted database marketing activities leading to market intelligence programs?
2. What is market intelligence research and why are many companies undertaking this type of research?
3. What are the major benefits that a consumer product/service company can realize from using market intelligence research?
4. List the three main advantages that database enhancement provides and explain how Nike (www.nike.com) can use each one.
5. Discuss the differences between a sequential database and a relational database. What advantages are associated with each database?
6. Describe how data mining works and how it helps companies to improve their decision-making practices.
7. What is the value of database modeling in understanding customers' behaviors?

Discussion Questions

1. Identify and discuss the ways in which marketing researchers can achieve database enhancements, including the dynamics that need to be incorporated into database development activities.
2. What specific industry information could executives at Procter and Gamble (P&G) obtain from the *Source Book of Demographics and Buying Power for Every Zip Code in the U.S.A.*? Discuss how this information would improve P&G's marketing strategies.
3. **EXPERIENCE THE INTERNET.** Conduct an Internet search on "market intelligence" research. In your research, identify 10 Fortune 500 companies that regularly utilize market intelligence research practices.
4. **EXPERIENCE THE INTERNET.** Conduct an Internet search for consulting firms that provide "market intelligence" research assistance to businesses. Select a firm and provide a brief [two-page] write-up on what that firm provides regarding "market intelligence" information.
5. Briefly discuss the differences between lifetime value models and scoring models as described in the chapter. In what situations would each type of modeling procedure be most appropriate?
6. Refer to our Continuing Case from the previous chapters concerning the Santa Fe Grill Mexican restaurant. What are the major types of information the Santa Fe Grill Mexican restaurant should include in building a data warehouse?
7. How might the Santa Fe Grill restaurant benefit from using database modeling in its operations?

part 2

Designing Marketing Research Projects

chapter 5

Secondary Research: Designs, Searches, and Sources

Learning Objectives

After reading this chapter, you will be able to:

1. Determine when secondary research is the best approach.
2. Understand the role of secondary data in marketing research.
3. Explain why researchers conduct literature reviews and electronic searches.
4. Describe how to conduct secondary research.
5. Identify and use internal and external secondary data sources.

"In today's competitive environment, the key word is fast. Faster in obtaining results, faster in disseminating results. Therefore, we now conduct marketing research with priority given to secondary data. Why? It's faster."

—ROBERT BENGEN,
Director of Marketing and Research,
Samsonite Corporation

Secondary Research Goes Global

With continuous advances in technology and rapid increases in availability and accessibility of electronic databases, many more small and medium-sized companies can use secondary data to develop product and service strategies. Marketing researchers can obtain secondary data on worldwide market, demographic, socioeconomic, political, and cultural characteristics to pursue global opportunities. The U.S. and many foreign governments as well as other organizations (single-source suppliers) compile and update business, industry, and market databases that are Internet accessible and that enable researchers to better understand global markets.

Many governments produce a wealth of secondary data on global markets. For example, the U.S. government publishes the *World Fact Book* (www. worldfactbook.com) and the *National Trade Data Bank* (www.NTDA.com), which are both useful sources for electronic access to business/marketing databases and are centralized, inexpensive, and ease to use. With NTDB, companies can find secondary data on topics such as export opportunities by country, industry, and/or product categories; socioeconomic, demographic, political, and cultural conditions; foreign-based import companies by products; and much more. Similarly, many foreign governments compile databases, and secondary sources such as the *European Union in the U.S.* (www.eurunion.org) provide detailed profiles for European Union members on financial topics such as investment opportunities, grant sources, and related business information.

Whether a company is already operating in global markets (Sony, McDonald's, FedEx, Roper Starch Worldwide) or is a smaller company exploring the idea of expanding to global markets (for instance, Custom Doors in El Paso, Illinois), the growing availability and Internet accessibility of secondary data in combination with companies' own internal databases enable researchers to identify and understand changes in global market structures and a wealth of details about buyer behaviors and customer characteristics. At the same time, researchers must recognize potential weaknesses of global market and cross-cultural secondary data, just as they do with domestic secondary data, particularly problems of relevancy, availability, and reliability.

Value of Secondary Research

The trend is upward in the use of secondary research designs to collect and store data to solve business problems and pursue opportunities. Improvements in information technology enable most companies to use secondary research designs to capture a wide variety of customer, competitor, and industry data. One example of an emerging secondary data source is *customer-volunteered information,* sometimes referred to as *customer knowledge,* information gathered from electronic customer councils, customer usability labs, e-mail comments, chat sessions, and so forth. With electronic search engines such as Google and Yahoo!, companies increasingly can find this type of information.

As internal and external databases become more available and accessible, decision makers are realizing secondary data can be the basis for making sound marketing decisions. Secondary data are not only more readily available, but sometimes more valid and frequently less expensive than primary data.

This chapter focuses on the types of secondary data available to researchers, how secondary data can be used, and the benefits and the impact of the Internet on the use of secondary data.

Nature and Scope of Secondary Research

The essential goal of marketing research is to obtain information that enables management to make the best possible decisions. Some of the key steps in conducting secondary research are similar to those in the marketing research process. Before determining whether secondary research should be undertaken, management and the researcher must clarify the research problem or opportunity. To do so, they must (1) *identify and clarify the information needs,* (2) *define the research problem and questions,* and (3) *specify the research objectives and confirm the information value*. Once these activities are completed, the next step is *determining whether secondary data can be used* to answer the research questions. Here the researcher, with the help of management, determines whether useful secondary data already exist, the relevance of the data, and how to obtain the data. Working with management the researcher must answer "yes" to the following questions:

1. Can the data help answer the specified research questions?
2. Are the data relevant to the time period and population of interest?
3. Is the unit of measurement comparable to the current situation?
4. Can the original source of the data be accessed?
5. Are data acquisition costs reasonable?
6. Can data bias be assessed?
7. Can data collection accuracy be verified?
8. If accuracy cannot be verified, should the data be used?

Secondary data Data not gathered for the immediate study; the data already exists, having been collected for some other purpose.

The term **secondary data** refers to data that *already exists* and was gathered for purposes other than the current research project. In many cases secondary data is historical in nature and already assembled or published. Moreover, secondary data is available in many different forms, including data tables, full text, summary statistics, broadcast video streams (TV ads or news reports), online and offline databases, and so on.

Internal secondary data Data collected by the individual company for accounting purposes or marketing activity reports.

Customer knowledge Customer interaction information collected to create customer profiles that can be used to tailor interactions, segment customers, and build strong customer relationships.

External secondary data Data collected by outside agencies such as the federal government, trade associations, or periodicals.

Marketing researchers often classify secondary data into two categories: internal and external. **Internal secondary data** is collected in-house by a company for accounting purposes, marketing activity reports, customer knowledge, and so forth. **Customer knowledge** is data provided by customers for marketing purposes as well as use in other areas in an organization. For example, information may be provided to engineers, logistical support personnel, or information technology departments on issues relating to product improvement, packaging, or Web registration. Data of this type, if properly warehoused and categorized, can be an invaluable form of secondary data for marketing decisions as they relate to customer relationship management (CRM). **External secondary data** is collected by outside organizations such as federal and state governments, trade associations, nonprofit organizations, marketing research services, consulting companies, consumer purchase panels, store audits, and academic and popular periodicals.

Secondary data is also available from computerized data sources. Computerized secondary data sources typically are designed by research companies or specialty consulting or information service groups and include internal and external data combined with online information sources. Examples of these computerized information sources include information vendors, commercial Web sites, mailing lists, or direct marketing clearing and fulfillment services.

To obtain the desired secondary data, researchers must prepare a "systematic pathway" (or search procedure). In many cases the search needs to be across multiple sources. For example, if the focus of a secondary research project is to identify and assess the financial strength of the Procter and Gamble Corporation (P&G), you must look at the financial data not only found on P&G's Web site (www.P&G.com) but also from outside sources such as *The Wall Street Journal* (www.wsj.com) and the Fortune 500 (www.fortune.com). When multiple sources are used to obtain data, the next step is *data integration and creating new summary tables and charts*. The researcher must develop a "labeling" format to describe the key elements displayed in each table, chart, and/or figure. Once the new summary data results are integrated, the researcher then *provides interpretive meaning* to the data. Here, the researcher focuses on developing an overall picture of the data as well as important "subpictures" that directly relate to the initial research questions. The interpretive language must be clear and pragmatic so that non–research oriented people can understand the findings. The last step in the process is to *write and present the research findings*. Chapter 18 covers this topic in detail, but the key elements of the final report are: (1) an "Executive Summary" that highlights the key findings and answers the research questions as well as the initial questions/problems; (2) a logical "Overview" of the key elements of the report, making good use of *headings* and *subheadings*; and (3) summary data covering the main findings and conclusions. Exhibit 5.1 summarizes the steps in collecting and assembling secondary data.

eXHIBIT 5.1 Steps in Secondary Research

Step 1: Confirm the problem and research objectives.
Step 2: Clarify information needs and evaluate information value.
Step 3: Determine whether secondary data can solve the problem.
Step 4: Develop a systematic search plan and procedures.
Step 5: Combine data from multiple sources.
Step 6: Interpret and summarize the data.
Step 7: Write and present research findings.

Role of Secondary Data in Marketing Research

The role of secondary data in the marketing research process has expanded in recent years. Traditionally, research based on secondary data was viewed as having limited value. Identifying and retrieving secondary data were outsourced to a corporate librarian, syndicated data collection firm, or junior research analyst. The main functions of secondary data research were to provide historical background for a current primary research endeavor and to allow longitudinal trend analysis within an industry. With the increased emphasis on business and competitive intelligence, target marketing, marketing segmentation, strategic performance analysis, customer relationship management (CRM) programs, and the ever-increasing availability of information from offline and online databases, secondary data is gaining importance in the marketing research process.

Secondary data is increasingly used to examine a wide variety of marketing and business problems because of the relative speed and cost-effectiveness of obtaining the data. The role of the market researcher (market analyst) is being redefined and modified to that of a business information service professional or information technology specialist. Some of the main responsibilities of this individual relate to creating contact and sales databases, preparing competitive trend reports, developing customer retention strategies, and so forth.

Secondary Data and Customer Relationship Management

Customer relationship management (CRM) programs help companies learn about customers' needs and behaviors in order to develop stronger relationships with customers. CRM combines technology and human insights to better understand customer behavior and the value of customers to the organization. For CRM to be effective, an organization must first determine its information needs and what it intends to do with the information. For example, many retail financial institutions keep track of customer life cycle stages in order to determine the right time to market appropriate financial products like mortgages, equity loans, or retirement products. Similarly, consumer product companies like Procter and Gamble maintain lists of expectant mothers so they can target them for a variety of baby products, and Pizza Hut maintains detailed customer identification and past purchase behavior information to help in cross-selling food products.

Companies using CRM programs carefully examine the different ways customer information comes into the business, where and how the data is stored, and how data is currently being used. For example, a large retail business like Best Buy may interact with customers in a variety of ways including mail campaigns, Web sites, brick-and-mortar stores, call centers, salespersons, and advertising efforts. CRM links these different sources of secondary data and data flow between operational units (for instance, sales and inventory), and analytical software systems sort through the data for customer patterns. Trained marketing information specialists (analysts) integrate the data to identify understandable buying trends or patterns as well as develop an overview of each customer to pinpoint strengths and weaknesses in sales and service operations. While many CRM activities are initially supported by primary data, the vast network of secondary data collection and storage points is the real foundation of a CRM system and provides the nucleus for the overall CRM process.

Secondary Data and the Marketing Research Process

Marketing research, publishing, communications, marketing and distribution of products/services, advertising, and financial markets are all being directly affected by the Internet and related technologies. The Internet now defines the information infrastructure for dealing with secondary data. Search engines such as Google (www.google.com), Yahoo! (www.yahoo.com), Fast Search (www.alltheweb.com), MSN Search (www.search.msn.com), AltaVista (www.altavista.com), and Northern Light (www.northernlight.com), as well as proprietary search engines, are how researchers find secondary information. Similarly, electronic mail, file transfers, and Web downloads are how secondary data is distributed. Electronic reproduction costs are small and storage is inexpensive.

As secondary information becomes more widely available, traditional marketing research providers face new nontraditional competition such as consultants and accounting firms as well as changing client information needs. Today, businesses are turning to secondary data to better understand market size, market growth, and trends in targeted industries as well as other elements relevant to developing and implementing business strategies. Industry experts like Thomas Miller, president of Research Publishers LLC in Madison, Wisconsin, predict that success for many companies in the 21st century will depend on their ability to utilize secondary data made available through computer and communication technologies and the integration of secondary research and information services.[1]

Until recently, secondary data played a smaller role relative to primary marketing research activities. In product and concept testing, focus groups, and customer satisfaction surveys, primary research was used to analyze marketing problems. In other words, companies commissioned original unique (primary) research to help them with their decision making. But in a growing number of cases today, secondary data can solve research problems. Secondary data often is the starting point in defining the research that needs to be conducted. If the problem can be solved based on available secondary data alone, then the company can save time, money, and effort. Only if the availability of secondary data is not sufficient to solve the specific research problems is primary data collection considered.

If the research focus is business and competitive intelligence, secondary data collection is vital in the acquisition of information on all aspects of competitors' marketing and business activities. If the focus is potential new customers, researchers may use internal company documents to profile the current customer base. The existing customer base can be used to identify significant characteristics of potential customers. Similarly, customer need/want analysis, which identifies problems or requirements of specific customer groups, may be satisfied by secondary data. Finally, companies need to know how markets are changing for successful strategic planning, and researchers rely on identification and integration of secondary data to support planning activities. Internal secondary data collection also plays a significant support role for sales presentations, a myriad of minor decision-making functions, and those cases where documentation for necessary primary research activities is called for.

To clarify the role of secondary research in marketing research, a survey of research firms conducted by the Society of Competitive Intelligence Professionals reported that about 60 percent of the sample used secondary research on a regular basis. The survey also revealed the following uses of secondary data:[2]

- Monitoring competitive and business intelligence—82 percent.
- Providing functional support for primary research projects—75 percent.
- Managerial presentations—59 percent.

- Specific business decisions—57 percent.
- Validating internal data and primary data collection—48 percent.

As the importance and value of secondary data in the marketing research process continue to grow, the researchers' skills required for working with these new forms of data will evolve and job opportunities multiply.

Secondary Research Designs

The steps in the research process presented earlier serve as a basic framework for all secondary research designs. However, differences in the research focus and information search plans often result in different types of research designs. Two types of research designs frequently used by marketing researchers are *literature reviews* and *electronic searches*.

Literature Reviews

Literature review A comprehensive examination of available information relating to a topic of interest.

A **literature review** is a comprehensive examination of available information related to your research topic. When conducting a literature review, researchers locate information relevant to the research problems and issues at hand. Literature reviews have the following objectives: provide background information for the current study; clarify thinking about the research problem and questions; reveal whether information already exists about the issue of interest; help define important constructs of interest to the study; and suggest sampling and other methodological approaches that have been successful in studying similar topics.

Reviewing available literature helps researchers stay abreast of the latest thinking related to their topic of interest. In most industries there are some widely known and cited studies. For example, the Internet Advertising Bureau (IAB) is an industry organization whose members are a Who's Who of online publishers and advertisers. The IAB has conducted a number of high profile studies that are well known to industry members and available on their Web site. The studies report what works and doesn't work in online advertising. An analyst conducting research on online advertising who is not familiar with major published studies, such as those conducted by the IAB, would likely have difficulty establishing her expertise with her clients, many of whom would be familiar with these studies.

Literature reviews provide information that enables researchers to better understand a research problem or opportunity. The nearby A Closer Look at Research (In the Field) box reports on an example of researchers defining a business opportunity after an extensive literature review. Often researchers develop ideas from their review of the literature that lead to working hypotheses, but whether such hypotheses are developed or not, literature reviews at a minimum provide background information for beginning the research process.

Reasons for Conducting a Literature Review

An important reason for completing a literature review is that it can help clarify and define the research problem and research questions. Suppose an online advertiser, Verizon, for instance, wants to study how consumer engagement with online advertising affects attitudes toward brands of mobile phones, Web site visits, and actual purchase behavior. A literature review would identify published studies on the topic of consumer engagement, as well as the different ways to define and measure consumer engagement. Some researchers might define consumer engagement as any interaction with an ad, which may include every interactive action from a simple accidental mouseover of an ad, to participating in a question and answer quiz within an ad, to clicking the ad to visit the Web site. Other

A Closer Look at Research

Google and eBay Form New "Click-To-Call" Alliance

After extensive secondary research and a literature review concerning online customers' attitudes, preferences, and search and purchase behaviors, researchers at prominent Internet players Google and eBay met to form a "Click-To-Call" alliance. The alliance calls for Google to begin selling text advertising exclusively for eBay outside the United States to help buyers instantly call an online seller to do business. Advanced "click-to-call" technology will enable eBay customers to call eBay merchants or Google advertisers by simply clicking a link on a Web page. eBay's CEO believes the alliance will provide a whole new way for buyers and sellers to connect online and create a significant revenue stream for both eBay and Google. After their secondary research process and literature review, both organizations concluded the available research information strongly supports their view that an opportunity exists to provide a new online service that lets Web surfers place telephone calls through their computers or handheld devices when they click on a link in an Internet ad.

experts might define consumer engagement in a way that excludes passive interaction such as an accidental mouseover and includes only active involvement with an ad. Through a review of the literature together with conversations with the client, Verizon in this case, researchers can decide how to conceptualize consumer engagement in a way that is relevant to the research problem at hand.

A literature review can also suggest research hypotheses to investigate. For example, a literature review may show that frequent Internet shoppers are more likely to be engaged with online advertising; that engagement increases positive attitudes toward the brand; that younger people are more likely to become engaged with an online ad; or that high involvement product categories, such as cell phones, are more likely to result in consumer engagement than are low involvement categories, such as paper towels. Although the studies may not be definitive, and may not provide answers to specific research questions, they are likely to provide some issues and relationships—hypotheses—to investigate.

Literature reviews can identify scales with which to measure variables and research methodologies that have been used successfully to study topics similar to the problem at hand. For instance, suppose a researcher wants to measure the usability of a Web site. A literature review will locate published studies that suggest checklists of important features of usable sites. Reviewing previous studies will save the researcher time and effort because new scales will not need to be developed from scratch. Similarly, researchers can review successful published studies to see what methodologies (focus groups, surveys, experiments) have been used to research the topic or similar topics. Reviewing published work, researchers interested in Web site usability would quickly find that *observation* and *moderated interaction* are preferred methods to study this particular topic and that experiments using different versions of the Web site (an experimental method called A/B testing) can be useful. Reviewing the literature they would find that focus groups and surveys are not preferred methods of research in this case because participants' memories are not good enough to give experts the specific information regarding the Web site's usability they need to improve the Web site. Apparently what users think they might like when asked is different from what they actually like when observed in practice.[3]

EXHIBIT 5.2 Guidelines for Conducting Literature Reviews[4]

Step 1: Identify Relevant Literature to Review for Your Topic

Issues: keep the topic manageable, search an appropriate database, shorten reference list (if too long) or increase the size of reference list (if too short), search for unpublished studies, develop first draft of topic statement, get familiar with different online databases, select relevant databases for the field of study, get familiar with the organization of each relevant database, record a general description of each source, redefine the topic more narrowly, begin with most current study and work backwards, search for related theoretical articles, look for "review" articles, identify landmark or classic studies and theories.

Step 2: Analyze Literature and Sources

Issues: scan literature sources (studies) for an overview, group sources by categories, organize material prior to reading, take consistent notes, look for explicit term definitions and statistics, pay attention to "review" articles, assess methodological strengths and weaknesses, differentiate between "assertions" and "evidence," identify major result trends and patterns, identify possible "gaps" in the literature and relationships among studies, make notes on the relevancy of a study to your topic, assess reference list for currency (within the last 10 years, unless a classic study) and coverage.

Step 3: Analyze Quantitative Research Literature/Sources (if needed)

Issues: classify study as quantitative or qualitative research and as experimental or nonexperimental design, specify cause–effect issues, reliability and validity of measurement instruments, differences in measures across studies, sampling design, respondent demographics, differences and statistical significance of findings, note the flaws associated with each study.

Step 4: Analyze Qualitative Research Literatures/Sources (if needed)

Issues: specify individual or team data collection, assess independence of data analysis, check involvement of outside experts, determine sampling design, respondents' input on data interpretation, respondent demographics, method of analysis used, and full disclosure in results of quantitative factors.

Step 5: Prepare Tables That Summarize Literature Sources

Issues: prepare list of definitions and research methods including summary of results, establish criteria for inclusion of articles in summary table, create tables for complex material, number and give descriptive title to each table, and summarize all tables.

Step 6: Synthesize Literature Prior to Writing a Review

Issues: consider purpose and voice tense, reassemble notes, develop topic outline that traces the main argument, clearly and conveniently support your argument, for each topic report differences in studies, identify the gaps and needs for more research, present relevant theories, discuss how included studies relate and/or advance theory, summarize findings, present clear meaningful conclusions and implications, suggest future research directions, and prepare outline with details from analysis.

Step 7: Write First Draft of the Review

Issues: begin by identifying broad problem but avoid "global" statements, build a convincing argument for the topic's importance, discuss the importance to key studies, reference classic studies and indicate if a study was replicated, integrate other pertinent literature reviews, refer reader to other reviews on interesting topics not being discussed in detail, avoid list of nonspecific references, cite studies with contradictory results separately, include relevant references, and emphasize the need for current research. Toward the front of the review state explicitly what will be and what will not be covered and specify key points of view, avoid annotations, make good use of "headings" and "subheadings," use transitions to trace the main argument, consider reviewing studies from across disciplines separately, include a conclusion at the end of the review, and double check the flow of the main argument for coherence.

Step 8: Check Style, Mechanics, and Language Usage

Issues: cross check draft with topic outline, avoid direct and long quotes, check correct style for citations, spell out acronyms first time, put "coined terms" in quotations, limit idioms, colloquialisms, and slang expressions, check for common writing conventions, make sure title is concise yet descriptive, and be very careful to avoid plagiarism.

Conducting the Review

Literature reviews may include a search of both popular and scholarly sources. With the advent of the Internet, preparing a literature review has become both easier and harder. It is easier in the sense that a wide variety of material is instantly available. Thus, finding relevant published studies has become easier than ever. But wading through the results to find the studies that are actually of interest can be overwhelming. Thus, it is important to narrow your topic so that you can focus your efforts before conducting a search for relevant information. Exhibit 5.2 provides some guidelines for conducting and writing a literature review.

Electronic Searches: Popular Sources

Many popular sources are available both in the library and on the Internet. Examples of popular sources include *The Wall Street Journal* (www.wsj.com), *BusinessWeek* (www.businessweek.com), *Forbes* (www.forbes.com), *Harvard Business Review* (www.hbr.com), *Business 2.0* (www.business2.com), and so on. Journalists, industry experts, and freelance writers write popular articles for newspapers and periodicals. Popular sources are often more current than scholarly sources and are written using less technical language. However, the findings and ideas expressed in popular sources often involve secondhand reporting of information. Moreover, prior to publication peers review scholarly findings, while findings reported in journalistic publications receive much less scrutiny.[5]

Many business students are already familiar with the business articles and resources offered by ABI/Inform and Lexis/Nexis. These databases can be searched through online library gateways at most colleges and universities. The databases cover many publications that are "walled off" and thus not available through major search engines. For example, both the *New York Times* (www.newyorktimes.com) and *The Wall Street Journal* (www.wsj.com) provide excellent business news. However, search engines currently do not access the archives of these and other prominent newspapers. While the archives of these and other publications are often available through the newspapers' Web sites, the articles are usually offered on a pay-per-view basis. Most libraries pay for access to many newspaper and business publications through arrangements with ABI/Inform and Lexis/Nexis.

A great deal of information is available on the Internet without subscription to library databases. Search engines continually catalog this information and return the most relevant and most popular Web sites for particular search terms. Google (www.google.com), Yahoo! (www.yahoo.com), and MSN (www.search.msn.com) are good at locating published studies. Before performing an online search, it is useful to brainstorm several relevant keywords to use in search engines. As an example, if you were interested in word-of-mouth marketing, several terms might make useful search terms: *buzz marketing, underground marketing,* and *stealth marketing.*

Some popular sources are publications staffed by writers who are marketing practitioners and analysts. For instance, contributors to www.Clickz.com who write articles about a wide variety of online marketing issues are specialists in the areas they cover. Therefore, the opinions and analyses they offer are timely and informed by experience. Nevertheless, their opinions, while reflective of their experience and in-depth knowledge, have not been investigated with the same level of care as those available in scholarly publications.

Another possible source is marketing blogs. Many marketing writers and analysts have their own blogs. These sources must be chosen very carefully, however, since anyone can write and post a blog. Only blogs written by respected experts are worthy of mention in

EXHIBIT 5.3 MarketingSherpa.Com's Best Marketing Blogs[6]

Best Blog on General Marketing Topics
Seth Godin's Blog, by Seth Godin
http://sethgodin.typepad.com/

Best B-to-B Marketing Blog
B2B Lead Generation Blog, by Brian Carroll
http://blog.startwithalead.com/weblog/

Best Blog on Email Marketing
Chris Baggott's Email Marketing Best Practices, by Chris Baggott
http://exacttarget.typepad.com/chrisbaggott/

Best Blog on Search Marketing
Search Engine Roundtable by Bloggers include: Barry Schwartz, Benjamin Pfeiffer, Chris Boggs, Kim Krause, Shawn Hogan, Ignacio Hernandez, Morgan Carey & Dan Thies
http://www.seroundtable.com/

Best Blog on Advertising
Adrants, by Steve Hall
http://www.adrants.com/

Best Blog on Marketing to a Specific Consumer Demographic
Andy Wibbels, the Original Blogging Evangelist, by Andy Wibbels
http://andywibbels.com/

Best Blog on Affiliate Marketing
ReveNews, by Larry Adams et al.
http://www.revenews.com/

Best Blog on the Topic of PR
Active Voice, by Matt "PodBoy"
http://podboy.typepad.com/techvoice/

Best Blog on Small Business Marketing
Duct Tape Marketing, by John Jantsch
http://www.ducttapemarketing.com/weblog.php

Honorable Mentions: Five More Blogs That Deserve Your Attention
Adland, by (Nom de Guerres): Åsk Dabitch, Clayton Claymore, Caffeinegoddess and Robblink
http://commercial-archive.com/

Future Now: A Day in the Life of a Persuasion Architect, by Howard Kaplan, Anthony C. Garcia Jr., Dave Young & Jim Novo
http://persuasion.typepad.com/

StartupNation, by Joel Welsh, Jonathan Hudson, Joan Isabella & Sloan Brothers
http://www.startupnation.com/blog/

The WebMarketCentral Blog, by Tom Pick
http://webmarketcentral.blogspot.com/

Ypulse, by Anastasia Goodstein
http://www.ypulse.com/

your literature review. MarketingSherpa.com has an annual list of best marketing blogs. Some of them may be relevant to your topic (see Exhibit 5.3). Blogs written by high profile practitioners and analysts are often provocative and up-to-date. They frequently suggest perspectives worthy of consideration in the design and execution of a study. Blog writers also may provide insightful commentary and critical analysis of published studies and practices currently being discussed by experts in the field. However, even blogs written by the most respected analysts express viewpoints that are often speculative and unproven. When preparing a literature review you must be clear in noting that these blogs frequently are more opinion than fact.

Popular sources on the Web must be carefully evaluated. Check the "About Us" portion of the Web site to see who is publishing the articles or studies to see if the source of the material is reputable. Another issue to consider is that marketing studies found on Web sites sometimes promote the business interest of the publisher. For instance, studies published by the Internet Advertising Bureau have to be carefully scrutinized for methodological bias because the IAB is a trade organization representing businesses that will benefit when Internet advertising grows. Ideally, you are looking for the highest quality information by experts in the field. When sources are cited and mentioned more often, they are more likely to be credible.[7]

Scholarly Research

You may want to search your library for scholarly articles that are relevant to your research topic. But an online search for the same information is easier and more consistent with the way you are used to searching. Google has a specialized search engine dedicated to scholarly articles called Google Scholar. Using Google's home page search function rather than Google Scholar will identify some scholarly articles, but many other kinds of results are shown that make scholarly articles difficult to identify. You can find Google Scholar by following the "more" link from their home page. If you go to Google Scholar, and type "online shopping," for instance, Google Scholar (www.scholar.google.com) lists published studies that address online shopping. Google Scholar counts how many times a study is referenced by other documents on the Web and lists that number in the search results (the results say "cited by" and list the number of Web site citations). The number of citation counts on the Web is one measure of the importance of an article to the field.

Some of the studies listed by Google Scholar will be available online from any location. You may have access to others only when you are at school or through a library gateway. Most colleges and universities pay fees for access to scholarly published papers. If you are on campus while you are accessing these sources, many journal publishers read the IP address of the computer you are using and grant access based on your location. In particular, articles in JSTOR (www.jstor.com), which hosts many of the top marketing journals, may be accessible through any computer linked to your campus network. However, some journals require you to go through the library gateway to obtain access whether you are on or off campus.

Both popular and scholarly sources can be tracked using Web-based bookmarking tools like Del.icio.us.com and Linksnarf.com that will help you organize your sources. Using these bookmarking tools, you can keep track of the links for research projects, take notes about each of the sites, and "tag" the links with your choice of search terms to make future retrieval of the source easy. Bookmarking tools also allow exchanges with a social network, so they can be very helpful in sharing sources with multiple members of the research team.

Divergent perspectives and findings need to be included in your literature review. It is likely the findings of some studies will be inconsistent with each other. These differences may include estimates of descriptive data, for example, the percentage of people who buy from catalog marketers, the amount of dollars spent on advertising, or online retail sales numbers. Reports may also disagree as to the nature of theoretical relationships between variables. You need to dig into the details of the methodology that is used to define variables and collect data. For example, differences in estimates of online retail spending are caused by several factors. Three major causes of discrepancies in online retail estimates are: (1) the inclusion (or not) of travel spending, which is a major category of online spending; (2) methodological differences, for instance, some reports make estimates based on surveying retailers while others survey customers; and (3) there is always some degree of sampling error. It is not enough to say that reports differ in their findings. You want to make intelligent judgments about the sources that may be causing the differences.

Online Electronic Searches for Secondary Data

The procedures used to conduct *online electronic data searches* are similar to the general steps shown in Exhibit 5.1. The primary differences for electronic data searches are the research objectives and the types of sources. There are an almost infinite number of problems and research objectives that may rely on secondary data. But typical problems for which marketing researchers use electronic data searches focus on *fact-finding, database marketing,* and *predictive modeling*. The types of fact-finding projects that incorporate secondary data include (1) personal intelligence projects, (2) environmental intelligence projects, (3) consumer intelligence activities, and (4) competitive intelligence studies. We discuss fact-finding first and then database marketing and predictive modeling.

Personal intelligence Information that is most relevant to an individual's personal and/or professional well-being.

Personal intelligence refers to information that is relevant to an individual's personal and/or professional well-being.[8] The focus of personal intelligence is on gathering secondary data that will answer everyday questions or resolve some type of problem, thus achieving a personal or professional goal. The main objective of personal intelligence is to customize information so the individual can operate in a more efficient manner. With electronic search capabilities, an individual can customize his methods of obtaining important information. For example, many Web sites can be customized to allow registration with category-specific mailing lists, as well as participation in chat, blog, or news groups dedicated to special topics. Advanced Internet technologies have created a variety of tools that can improve the effectiveness and efficiency in finding, downloading, filtering, displaying, and managing information use for personal or professional advantage. Exhibit 5.4 displays examples of technology-based tools used in customizing secondary information for personal intelligence designs.

Environmental intelligence Online electronic search design that focuses on information relating to an organization's environmental factors.

Environmental scan Electronic search of trends, events, and emerging issues from external operating environments.

Environmental intelligence is online electronic search that focuses on gathering and analyzing secondary information relating to the political, legal, economic, sociocultural, and technological elements making up an organization's macroenvironment. The relationship between an organization and its macroenvironment is highly interactive and has a direct bearing on the organization's survival. Monitoring and understanding the macroenvironment are critical for determining trends and events that pose marketing threats and/or opportunities. Researchers need to be able to conduct **environmental scans** involving gathering, evaluating, and incorporating recognized trends, events, and emerging issues from the

EXHIBIT 5.4 Examples of Different Customizing Tools and Sources[9]

ZDNet.com	Provides a comprehensive listing of downloadable search tools and add-on browser utilities.
Finding Information	
Atomica.com (www.atomica.com)	Free downloadable browser add-on that allows a person to query such information as general definition, technical definitions and explanations, maps, relevant new stories, acronyms, foreign language translations, relevant Web sites, Internet keywords, and search words.
Exchanging Information	
iRemember (www.researchsoftwar.com)	Browser plug-in that indexes the Web sites visited by a user. When searching for an item seen during other Internet searches, the user can enter a few relevant words and iRemember will display Web sites previously visited that contain those words.
NetSonic (www.netsonic.com)	NetSonic stores the main parts of Web sites (i.e., pictures) on the user's hard drive more effectively than the browser, reducing the amount of downloadable the next time it is visited.
Gator (www.gator.com)	Gator saves time for online shoppers, by automatically filling in forms with standard information such as name, e-mail address, and credit card number as well as tracking the sites visited.
Filtering Information	
Ad-Ware (www.adware.com)	To limit the number of pop-up ads, blinking banners, and cookies during information search and retrieval activities, Ad-Ware scans the researcher's computer for the most common spyware programs such as Adware, Comet Cursor, and Web 3000, helping the researcher find and remove programs that might be tracking online behavior.
Displaying Information	
Katiesoft (www.katiesoft.com)	Enables researchers to view multiple Web pages from the same browser window. In addition to displaying the usual browser navigation tools, Katiesoft provides quick access to Windows Explorer and Media Player programs.
Managing Information	
eNotes (www.my-enotes.com)	When researching multiple sites and related information sources eNotes adds an intelligent "cut and paste" capability that provides a quick and simple way to gather information from the Internet. As a researcher identifies anything of interest, eNotes automatically captures and organizes the material (i.e., text and images) into a personalized "Knowledge Cart."

Consumer intelligence Online search design that produces aggregate results on consumers' tastes, desires, media habits, and other attitudinal factors.

organization's external environment into decision making and strategic planning.[10] In today's digital information world, numerous online data sources are available for information acquisition and use in performing environmental intelligence research. Exhibit 5.5 shows some examples of secondary information sources useful when conducting environmental intelligence projects.

Consumer intelligence is an online search design that produces aggregated results about customers by gathering, analyzing, and synthesizing secondary information on consumers' tastes, desires, preferences, attitudes, interests, opinions, media habits, and product/

eXHIBIT 5.5 Environmental Intelligence Information Sources

GlobalEDGE (www.globaledge.msu.edu)	A database produced and maintained by Michigan State University that provides numerous international links to newspapers and periodicals, regional/country data and information, and indexes to business resources.
World Factbook (www.worldfactbook.com)	Makes available secondary information on the geography, demographics, government, and economy of countries, territories, and regions of interest.
Online Intelligence Project (www.interaccess.com)	Specializes in international information, news, and commerce, and provides hundreds of useful links to databases and info-sources for every region and country in the world.
FedStats (www.fedstats.gov)	Contains official statistical information put together by over 100 U.S. federal agencies on numerous industries.
American Law Sources Online (www.law-sources.com)	Provides numerous links to other law-oriented sources and reviews of the American legal systems as well as Canada and Mexico.
Bureau of Labor Statistics (www.stats.bls.gov)	U.S. government-generated source that provides a wealth of information on U.S. household income, employment, and related economic factors.
Eurostat (www.europa.eu.int/comm/eurostat)	Provides detailed databases on the economies, finances, populations, social conditions, industry and trade, transport, and technology of every member of the European Union.
United Nations Global Trends (www.0.un.org)	Includes a wide range of global indicators and regional statistics on population, health, agriculture, economic development, climate, environment, housing, literacy, demographics, and social indicators.

service consumption patterns in a real-time framework.[11] The focus of consumer intelligence is to provide decision makers and researchers with understandable insights into the changing needs and wants of customers, their shopping and purchasing trends/patterns, as well as psychographic and demographic characteristics that can serve as indicators in predicting changes in market structures. Secondary data compiled through this type of design is critical for marketing researchers in developing customer segments and creating or modifying marketing mix strategies. Some marketing experts say consumer intelligence is a precursor to conducting consumer research studies. The types of questions that researchers address with consumer intelligence designs are: "What are the markets? "What, how, when, where, and why does the market buy?" and "Who participates in the buying?" Technological advances and the proliferation of online and offline databases have contributed to the growing importance and use of consumer intelligence research. Exhibit 5.6 provides examples of online data sources used by marketing researchers.

Competitive intelligence A secondary research design that gathers data from both online and offline sources about competitors and potential competitors.

Competitive intelligence is an online secondary data research design that uses systematic searching to identify and gather timely, relevant information about a company's existing and potential competitors.[12] Data requirements range from information about a competitor's structure, operations, and personnel to its position within the industry. For this research to be effective there must be a constant flow of information that can be disseminated

eXHIBIT 5.6 Consumer Intelligence Information Sources

U.S. Census Bureau (www.census.gov)	Provides PDF downloadable files containing a wide variety of demographics, income, housing, and socioeconomic characteristics of the U.S. population.
USA Data (www.usadata.com)	Subscription fee–based online databases on a wide range of market-specific information on topics including consumer demographics, Internet usage, shopping, lifestyle issues, health, and transportation.
Claritas (www.claritas.com)	Provides PRIZM, a segmentation tool, which combines detailed demographics with specialized product, media, and purchase data as well as lifestyle preferences to create portraits of different consumer groups.
Consumer Trends Institute (www.trendsinstitute.com)	Provides an ongoing series of consumer reports, for a user's fee, that contain information on a variety of consumer trends, preferences (i.e., consumers' inner thoughts, behaviors, opinions, and values), and product typologies.
Service Intelligence (www.serviceintelligence.com)	Provides customer stories about unpleasant experiences with restaurants, banks, airlines, and other service businesses.
American Consumer Satisfaction Index (ACSI) (www.bus.mich.edu/research)	Produced and maintained at the University of Michigan, ACSI provides premiere national economic indicators of customer satisfaction toward numerous products and services.
AC Nielsen (www.acnielsen.com)	One of the world's leading marketing research and syndicated data services that provide detailed information on the lifestyle, culture, politics, infrastructure, and economy, as well as retail, media, and consumer panel services in over 95 countries.
Information Resources, Inc. (IRI) (www.infores.com)	Syndicated international research firm that provides a wide variety of consumer and marketing intelligence information. The company's InfoScan, a store-tracking service, provides firms with data on electronic point-of-purchases from thousands of domestic and international retail businesses.
Bureau of Labor Statistics (BLS) (www.stats.bls.gov)	U.S. government agency providing information on consumers' buying habits including their expenditures, income, and credit ratings. Data is presented using different consumer and household characteristics.
Burke, Inc. (www.burke.com)	Leading full-service international marketing research and consulting firm that produces and sells customized information relating to topics such as product testing, brand equity, pricing, segmentation, image positioning useful in developing both tactical and strategic business planning activities.
Arbitron, Inc. (www.arbitron.com)	International syndicated media and marketing research firm specializing in providing detailed information in the areas of radio, TV broadcast, cable companies, advertisers/ad agencies, magazines, newspapers, and online media.
eMarketer (www.emarketer.com)	One of the world's leading research companies providing Internet and e-business statistics.
Survey-Net (www.survey.net)	Provides up-to-date secondary information, opinions, and demographics from the NET Communities.

to decision makers and transformed into actionable strategies and tactics. Most competitive intelligence focuses on gathering data on financial, market, and product performance indicators; price positions; inbound and outbound logistics; advertising and promotions; trade relations; production and sales force processes, and executive profiles. While much of the data is secondary, competitive intelligence can integrate primary data, if available. For example, primary information can be obtained from sources such as industry experts, suppliers that deal with competitors, the government, or any other source with first-hand knowledge of the competition. Secondary sources for information include trade associations, manufacturer and/or wholesale prices, published annual company reports, news items, and industrial reports or other sources in the public domain. Effective competitive intelligence research is characterized as ongoing, with competitive profiles continually being updated and reanalyzed. The intelligence benefits the company by reducing costs, adding value, lowering risk, and improving productivity and reaction time.[13] Exhibit 5.7 outlines the steps followed in conducting competitive intelligence research.

EXHIBIT 5.7 Steps in Conducting Competitive Intelligence Research[14]

Step 1: Determine research objective(s)

Reason(s) for conducting competitive intelligence are clarified.

Step 2: Identify competing companies and factors of interest

Competing companies for which information profiles will be developed are determined.

Step 3: Conduct online search

- Check competitive intelligence research sources. Two useful sources are: Competitive Intelligence Resource Index (www.bidigital.com) and Peppers and Rogers Group Consulting (www.1to1.com).
- Search for competing company information through independent sources such as OneSource Information Services, Inc. (www.onesource.com), Report Gallery (www.reportgallery.com), American Business Information (ABI) (www.abii.com), Harris InfoSource (www.harrisinfo.com), or Streetlink (www.streetlink.com).
- Search for trade associations and conferences using Google (www.google.com) and Yahoo (www.yahoo.com/Business_and_Economy/Organizations/Trade_Associations/).
- Utilize Comparative Shopping Services such as mySimon (www.mysimon.com), DealTime (www.dealtime.com), RoboShopper (www.roboshopper.com), and Consumer Reports (www.consumerreports.org).
- Search electronic newspapers, newsgroups, and eLibraries. Some examples of useful Web sites are: OnlineNewspapers (www.onlinenewspapers.com), PR Newswire (www.prnewswire.com), and eLibrary (www.elibrary.com).

Step 4: Compile data in summary tables

After locating the relevant data, summary tables must be created. The summary tables display the results in an easy-to-understand format.

Step 5: Interpret results

Interpretations answer each of the initial research questions. They also identify similarities and differences between competitors and discuss the resulting profiles.

Step 6: Prepare and present findings to management

Key elements included are: (1) an "Executive Summary" that highlights the key findings and the research questions, (2) an overview of the key elements in the report, and (3) summary data supporting each objective.

Advantages and Limitations of Using Secondary Data

With the increased availability of secondary data in today's digital information world, marketing researchers must understand the advantages as well as the limitations of using secondary data.

Advantages of Secondary Data

The main advantage of secondary data is its *availability*. There are literally millions of sources of secondary data. Advances in Internet and related technology as well as improvements in electronic search engines reduce the *time* and *cost* of retrieving, storing, and sharing secondary data. Secondary data collection typically involves locating the appropriate source or sources, extracting the necessary data, and recording it. This process usually takes several days but may take as little as a few hours.

In contrast, primary data acquisition may take months. Considering the requirements of designing and testing questionnaires, developing a sampling plan, collecting the data, and then analyzing and tabulating it, it is not surprising that primary data collection is a time-consuming and expensive process. Fees for services by market research firms typically range from $10,000 to $500,000 depending on the scope and magnitude of the research project. With any primary data collection project it is difficult to avoid wages and expenses, transportation and data collection costs, and clerical and field services charges.

Costs associated with many secondary data sources are minimal. Expenses usually are incurred by the original data source, as with published secondary data sources (the U.S. census, corporate surveys of buying power, state and county demographic data), or shared between the user and the commercial provider of the data. Even when this is not the case, obtaining secondary data generally costs significantly less than obtaining primary data.

Because of time and cost savings, research projects should first exhaust all potential sources of secondary data. Indeed, by 2010 almost half of all marketing research projects are expected to be completed using secondary data.[15] As secondary information becomes more widely available and technology enables greater refinement and categorization for electronic searches, the emphasis on secondary data will increase. Moreover, secondary data will be more accurate. Bar coding, optical scanning, and point-of-purchase data often provide companies with much of the information needed for marketing decisions.

In certain situations, researchers find that secondary data is the only available information when primary data cannot be obtained. For example, when American Multi-Cinema, Inc. (AMC), a private movie entertainment company in Kansas City, Missouri, was interested in building a new movie theatre megaplex in Wesley Chapel, Florida, they did not have information on population trends in that geographic area. AMC could not duplicate the geodemographic data available on Wesley Chapel, Florida, available from the U.S. Census Bureau because a lot of the data (median household income, dollar taxes paid, population density levels) was not accessible using primary data collection. As digital sources of secondary data become more accessible, researchers are using secondary information more often to (1) gain clearer insight and understanding of problems/opportunities; (2) provide guidance in evaluating and designing data collection methods and/or addressing measurement issues; (3) identify sampling and response rate difficulties; (4) obtain background information and justification for research findings; and (5) provide solutions to problems without the need to collect any primary data, thus reducing the time, money, and effort.

Limitations of Secondary Data

While the advantages of abundant, accessible secondary information are clear, there are some potential drawbacks. Before using any secondary data, several considerations must be addressed by the researcher, including (1) prior data manipulation, (2) data relevancy, and (3) data accuracy.

The fact is that secondary data has been previously collected, manipulated, and reported by other researchers for their own purposes—for purposes other than the research at hand. Consequently, the data must be carefully evaluated for how well the current research purpose matches the original purpose for collecting the data. In other words **prior data manipulation** may render the data unfit for present purposes. The more the data has been manipulated to fit previous research objectives, the less likely the data will be suitable for use in the current project.

Prior data manipulation previous organizing, reformatting, and/or presenting the data in a manner that fits the organization's objectives.

Data relevancy How well available secondary data matches the data needs of a current problem.

Data relevancy relates to how well the secondary data matches the needs of the current problem. Relevancy is based on three factors: (1) the *time period* during which the original data was collected, (2) the *categories* or *definitions* for which the data is reported, and (3) the *unit of measure*. The time frame secondary data was collected for directly impacts the relevancy and usability of the data. Use of outdated data to resolve current marketing problems can be more dangerous and misleading than using no data at all, especially in situations involving rapidly changing market conditions. Consider the recent U.S. housing market crisis. Market experts using median house prices and single-family home mortgage values reported by the U.S Census Bureau from the 2000 census data will most certainly have difficulty estimating the number of home foreclosures in 2009 or later as well as property values. Secondary data from the 2000 census is too old to be relevant in estimating housing prices, mortgage values, and foreclosure rates.

Secondary data may also be unusable if the categories used to summarize and report the data are not consistent over different reporting periods, or are not defined by the sources in the same way as in the current research project. Mismatching of category names for the desired variable also creates problems in locating secondary data through electronic searching procedures. Differences in how variables of interest are defined by different secondary sources can easily lead to collecting the wrong data and making incorrect inferences. Great care must be taken in judging this. For example, when the Nike Corporation attempts to collect industry dollar sales data, do researchers consider the industry to be "shoes" or "footwear"? Thus, researchers must examine variable names to determine whether differences are important.

The different units of measurement used by secondary data sources in reporting data must be closely compared. For example, sales figures for products like soft drinks can be measured in terms of dollar sales (gross or net) or by physical units (individual or cases); a company such as UPS can measure its volume of shipments in terms of number of packages (volume), weight, truckload, or dollar value. Similarly, with regard to personal income, the unit of measure could be total family income, personal disposable income, median family income, head-of-household income, per capita income, or other different units of measures.

Data conversion A modification process that changes the original unit of measure to a format that is compatible with the current study.

In some cases when secondary data are not reported in the desired unit of measure, researchers can do data conversions. One solution to inconsistent units of measurement is **data conversion**—the process of changing the original unit of measure to a format that is compatible for achieving the research objective. For example, the seafood department at

Fresh Market Stores can report its sales of shrimp in pounds, pieces, or dollars. A comparable estimate of dollars per pound may be used to convert dollar volume data to pounds or some other suitable format, like price per shrimp, assuming you know how many shrimp represent a pound. But data conversion often is not an option because the original units the data was reported in cannot be converted to the ones needed in the new study.

Data accuracy The extent to which a researcher can trust secondary data.

Data accuracy refers to whether the researcher can trust the secondary data. While data relevance describes the *suitability* of the data, accuracy focuses on data *trustworthiness*. When assessing secondary data, researchers need to keep in mind what was actually measured. For example, if actual purchases in a test market were measured, were they first-time trial purchases or repeat purchases? Were the data presented as a total of responses from all respondents or were they categorized by age, gender, or socioeconomic status?

Part of the accuracy issue is determining how *consistent* the data are across different sources. When evaluating any source of secondary data, a good strategy is to search multiple sources for the same data to determine consistency. For example, when evaluating the economic characteristics of a foreign market, a researcher may gather the same information from government sources, private business publications (*Fortune, BusinessWeek*), and specialty import/export trade publications. Then the secondary information from different sources would be compared to determine if it is consistent, that is, the same from the different sources.

Additional key elements of accuracy are *source credibility, appropriateness of methodology,* and *source bias*. Researchers should always question the credibility of the secondary data source. Technical competence, service quality, reputation, training, and expertise of personnel in the organization are some of the credibility indicators. The quality of secondary data is very important in establishing the trustworthiness of secondary data, and data quality is only as good as the methodology employed to gather it. Flaws in methodological procedures can produce results that are invalid, unreliable, or nongeneralizable. Therefore, the researcher must evaluate the size and description of the sample, the response rate, the questionnaire, and the overall procedure for collecting the data (telephone, Internet, or personal interview). Finally, researchers must determine the underlying motivation or hidden agenda, if any, behind secondary data. It is not uncommon to find secondary data sources published to advance the interests of commercial, political, or other special interest groups. Sometimes secondary data are published to incite controversy or refute other data sources. Researchers must determine if the organization reporting the data is motivated by a certain purpose. For example, statistics on animal extinction reported by the National Hardwood Lumber Association or, alternatively, by the People for the Ethical Treatment of Animals (PETA) should be validated before they can be relied on as unbiased sources of information.

Next we discuss internal and external secondary data sources, but at this point please review Exhibit 5.8 for a summary of some operating tools and strategies for conducting online electronic searches for secondary data.

Internal and External Sources of Secondary Data

Internal Secondary Data Sources

The logical starting point in searching for secondary data is the company's own *internal* information sources. Many organizations are not aware of the wealth of information in their own records. Moreover, internal data is the most readily available and can be accessed at little or no cost. But while this appears to be a good rationale for using internal data, researchers must remember that much of the information comes from past business activities.

EXHIBIT 5.8 Tools and Strategies Used in Online Electronic Data Searches

Boolean Logic	Use of "AND," "OR," and "NOT" as operators to establish relationships between search words and terms in many databases. (1) use of "AND" will retrieve all denoted search terms specified. *Examples:* Fast food AND restaurant; AC Nielsen AND surveys (2) use of "OR" will retrieve either search word. *Examples:* Footwear OR walking shoes; survey OR questionnaire (3) use of "NOT" eliminates records containing the search term. *Examples:* restaurant NOT fast food; detergents NOT clothes
Proximity Operators	Use of "ADJ," "NEAR," and "SAME" as operators to indicate how close and in what order two or more search terms should appear on the record. (1) use of "ADJ" will retrieve adjoining words in a specified order. *Examples:* Nike ADJ golf clubs; residential ADJ air conditioning (2) use of "NEAR" will retrieve specified adjoining search terms in any order. *Examples:* Sony NEAR HDTV; market share NEAR Custom Door (3) use of "SAME" retrieves records when both search terms are located in the specified record field. *Examples:* Insane Shine SAME tire coating; cat litter SAME Tidy Cat
Limiting	Typically associated with advanced search screen functions; restricts searches to only database record meeting specified criteria such as a date, or location. *Examples:* "2010 Chicago Illinois housing prices"; "Texas public hospitals"
Field Searches	Searching of database records by one or more of the specified "field" descriptors. Research must be able to identify the various fields making up a database record. Normally the researcher will use " " around the field search terms. *Examples:* "professors at UF"; "commercial banks"
Truncation	Use of "root word?" that enables the retrieval of all records with words beginning with the specified root term. *Examples:* – market? would retrieve records with marketing, marketability, etc. – control? would retrieve controllable, controlled, controller, controlling, etc.
Nesting	Use of parentheses "( )" in combination with boolean logic, proximity, and/or truncation operators to indicate the order that the search should follow. *Examples:* To search for movie theatre megaplex or retail DVD in Ohio, the researcher would submit the following; Ohio AND (movie ADJ theatre ADJ megaplex? OR retail ADJ DVD?)

This is not to say that internal data is not usable for future business decisions, because it can be effective in preparing marketing strategies and plans. Generally, internal secondary data consists of sales or cost information. Exhibit 5.9 lists key variables found in each of these internal sources of secondary data.

Other types of internal secondary data obtained from company records can complement the sales and cost data. Exhibit 5.10 outlines other potential sources of internal data.

Often substantial internal company information is available. If maintained and categorized properly, internal data can be used to analyze product performance, customer satisfaction, distribution effectiveness, and target market strategies. These forms of internal data also are useful for planning new-product introductions, product deletions, promotional strategies, competitive intelligence, or customer service tactics.

EXHIBIT 5.9 Common Sources of Internal Secondary Data

1. **Sales invoices:**
   a. Customer name
   b. Address
   c. Class of product/service sold
   d. Price by unit
   e. Salesperson
   f. Terms of sales
   g. Shipment point

2. **Accounts receivable reports:**
   a. Customer name
   b. Product purchased
   c. Total unit and dollar sales
   d. Customer as percentage of sales
   e. Customer as percentage of regional sales
   f. Profit margin
   g. Credit rating
   h. Items returned
   i. Reason for return

3. **Quarterly sales reports:**
   a. Total dollar and unit sales by:
      - Customer
      - Customer segment
      - Product
      - Product segment
      - Geographic segment
      - Sales territory
      - Sales rep
   b. Total sales against planned objectives
   c. Total sales against budget
   d. Total sales against prior periods
   e. Actual sales percentage increase/decrease
   f. Contribution trends

4. **Sales activity reports:**
   a. Classification of customer accounts
      - Mega
      - Large
      - Medium
      - Small
   b. Available dollar sales potential
   c. Current sales penetration
   d. Existing bids/contracts by customer location or product

External Secondary Data Sources

After examining internal secondary data, the researcher searches for *external* secondary data. Three primary sources of external secondary data are: (1) published or online data in periodicals, directories, or indexes; (2) data compiled by outside vendors (syndicated or commercial) that can be purchased on an as-needed basis; and (3) data from online and offline databases.

A major challenge associated with external secondary data is finding and securing the appropriate source. U.S. Department of Defense researchers say there is enough information available today to solve a majority of managers' questions and problems. But 90 percent of that information is not categorized properly.[16] Thus, the problem often is not finding out whether information exists, but finding out where the information resides.

EXHIBIT 5.10 Additional Internal Sources of Secondary Data

Source	Information
Customer letters	General satisfaction/dissatisfaction data
Customer comment cards	Overall performance data
Mail-order forms	Customer name, address, items purchased, quality, cycle time of order
Credit applications	Detailed biography of customer segments (demographic, socioeconomic, credit usage, credit ratings)
Cash register receipts	Dollar volume, merchandise type, salesperson, vendor, manufacturer
Salesperson expense reports	Sales activities, competitor activities in market
Employee exit interviews	General internal satisfaction/dissatisfaction data, internal company performance data
Warranty cards	Sales volume, names, addresses, zip codes, items purchased, reasons for product return
Past marketing research studies	Data pertaining to the situation in which the marketing research was conducted
Internet-provided information	Customer registration information, tracking, Web site visits, e-mail correspondence

The amount of secondary information is indeed vast. But the information needs of many researchers are connected by a common theme. Data most often sought by researchers includes demographic characteristics, employment, economic statistics, competitive and supply assessments, regulations, and international market characteristics. Exhibit 5.11 provides examples of specific variables within these categories.

Several key sources of secondary data enable the researcher to create a hierarchy of information sources to guide a secondary data search, regardless of the variables sought. Several broad to narrow data sources are described below to help guide the researcher through the jungle of secondary information.

North American Industry Classification System (NAICS)

NAICS codes Numerical industrial listings designed to promote uniformity in data reporting procedures for the U.S. government.

An initial step in any secondary data search is to use the numeric listings of the **North American Industry Classification System (NAICS) codes.** NAICS codes were designed to promote uniformity in data reporting by federal and state government sources and private business. The federal government assigns every industry an NAICS code. Businesses within each industry report all activities (sales, payrolls, taxation) according to their code. Currently, there are 99 two-digit industry codes representing everything from agricultural production of crops to environmental quality and housing. Within each two-digit industry classification code is a four-digit industry group code representing specific industry groups. All businesses in the industry represented by a given four-digit code report detailed information about the business to various sources for publication. For example, as shown in Exhibit 5.12, NAICS code 12 is assigned to coal mining and NAICS code 1221 specifies bituminous coal and lignite, surface extraction. It is at the four-digit level where the researcher will concentrate most data searches.

eXHIBIT 5.11 Key Variables Sought in Secondary Data Search

Demographics

- Population growth: actual and projected
- Population density
- In-migration and out-migration patterns
- Population trends by age, race, and ethnic background

Employment Characteristics

- Labor force growth
- Unemployment levels
- Percentage of employment by occupation categories
- Employment by industry

Economic Data

- Personal income levels (per capita and median)
- Type of manufacturing/service firms
- Total housing starts
- Building permits issued
- Sales tax rates

Competitive Characteristics

- Levels of retail and wholesale sales
- Number and types of competing retailers
- Availability of financial institutions

Supply Characteristics

- Number of distribution facilities
- Cost of deliveries
- Level of rail, water, air, and road transportation

Regulations

- Taxes
- Licensing
- Wages
- Zoning

International Market Characteristics

- Transportation and exporting requirements
- Trade barriers
- Business philosophies
- Legal system
- Social customs
- Political climate
- Cultural patterns
- Religious and moral backgrounds

EXHIBIT 5.12 Sample List of North American Industry Classification System Codes

Numeric—Listing

10—Metal Mining

1011	Iron Ores
1021	Copper Ores
1031	Lead & Zinc Ores
1041	Gold Ores
1044	Silver Ores
1061	Ferroalloy Ores except Vanadium
1081	Metal Mining Services
1094	Uranium, Radium & Vanadium Ores
1099	Metal Ores Nec*

12—Coal Mining

1221	Bituminous Coal & Lignite—Surface
1222	Bituminous Coal—Underground
1231	Anthracite Mining
1241	Coal Mining Services

13—Oil & Gas Extraction

1311	Crude Petroleum & Natural Gas
1321	Natural Gas Liquids
1381	Drilling Oil & Gas Wells
1382	Oil & Gas Exploration Services
1389	Oil & Gas Field Services Nec*

14—Nonmetallic Minerals except Fuels

1411	Dimension Stone
1422	Crushed & Broken Limestone
1423	Crushed & Broken Granite
1429	Crushed & Broken Stone Nec*
1442	Construction Sand & Gravel
1446	Industrial Sand

Source: Ward Business Directory of U.S. Private and Public Companies, 2006.

*Not elsewhere classified

Government Documents

Detail, completeness, and consistency are major reasons for using U.S. government documents. In fact, U.S. Bureau of the Census reports are the statistical foundation for most of the information available on U.S. population and economic activities. Exhibit 5.13 lists some of the common sources of secondary data available from the U.S. government. These include specific census data (e.g., censuses of agriculture or construction), census reports (e.g., the County and City Data Book), U.S. Department of Commerce data, and a variety of additional government reports.

There are two notes of caution about census or other secondary data. First, census data is collected only every 10 years with periodic updates, so researchers always need to consider the timeliness of census data. Second, census data can be misleading. Not every person or household is reflected in census data. Those who have recently changed residences or were simply not available for contact at census time are not included in census data.

EXHIBIT 5.13 Common Government Documents Used as Secondary Data Sources

U.S. Census Data

- Census of Agriculture
- Census of Construction
- Census of Government
- Census of Manufacturing
- Census of Mineral Industries
- Census of Retail Trade
- Census of Service Industries
- Census of Transportation
- Census of Wholesale Trade
- Census of Housing
- Census of Population

U.S. Census Reports

- Guide to Industrial Statistics
- County and City Data Book
- Statistical Abstract of the U.S.
- Fact Finders for the Nation
- Guide to Foreign Trade Statistics

U.S. Department of Commerce Data

- U.S. Industrial Outlook
- County Business Patterns
- State and Metro Area Data Book
- Business Statistics
- Monthly Labor Review
- Measuring Markets: Federal and State Statistical Data

Additional Government Reports

- Aging America: Trends and Population
- Economic Indicators
- Economic Report of the President
- Federal Reserve Bulletin
- Statistics of Income
- Survey of Current Business

A final source of information available through the U.S. government is the Catalog of Government Publications compiled by Marcive, Inc. (www.marcive.com). This catalog indexes major market research reports for a variety of domestic and international industries, markets, and institutions. It also provides an index of publications available to researchers from July 1976 to the current month and year.

Secondary Sources of Business Information

It is virtually impossible to document all of the sources of secondary data available from businesses. Most sources are, however, classified by some index, directory, or standardized guidebook, so researchers should consult a directory of business information. These direc-

A Closer Look at Research

Secondary Data and the Market Intelligence Process: Placing a Value on Customer Information

Organizations practicing market intelligence are now treating secondary data as a valuable balance sheet asset. Industry leaders in market intelligence processes are placing a clear value on customer information in order to size, rank, and cost overall investment. Companies that do not articulate a clear business rationale—based on customer information, revenue sources, and exit barrier considerations—for market intelligence applications and integration priorities are wasting their significant investment.

In directing their market intelligence investment, catalog retailers such as Lands' End and JC Penney use large amounts of secondary data to calculate the lifetime value of customers. Knowing, for example, that a specific type of customer will likely buy $1,000 in merchandise over 10 transactions allows these companies to place a clear value on that relationship and budget for CRM/ market intelligence programs that will retain or enhance customer relationship value by building exit barriers and cross-selling campaigns. Analytical applications that improve data quality, such as data warehousing and data mining, are of course critical components of the process.

tories identify statistical information, trade associations, trade journals, market characteristics, and environmental trends.

A key source of business information is the ABI Inform Database (www.cas.org). This database is available both online and on CD-ROM. It provides indexes and abstracts of business periodicals relating to a broad range of business topics. Electronic access to most business articles is also available. Gathering market information through business sources frequently leads the researcher to three widely used sources of data: *Sales and Marketing Management's Survey of Buying Power, Editors and Publishers Market Guide,* and *Source Book of Demographics and Buying Power for Every Zip Code in the U.S.A.* As illustrated in the nearby A Closer Look at Research (In the Field) box, secondary data often come from selected business sources and are very carefully chosen.

Editors and Publishers Market Guide

An additional source of secondary information on buying potential is the *Editors and Publishers Market Guide.* This guide provides unique city-by-city variables useful in making comparisons as well as information on infrastructure, transportation, principal industries, banks, and retail outlets. The data provides a detailed profile of economic activity within a given geographic area and is used for comparison purposes when selecting markets for new stores or product introductions. For more information on this guide, go to: http://www.editorandpublisher.com/eandp/resources/market_guide.jsp.

Source Book of Demographics and Buying Power for Every Zip Code in the U.S.A.

This source book provides information on population, socioeconomic characteristics, buying power, and other demographic characteristics for zip code areas across the United States. Each zip code area is analyzed relative to its consumption potential across a variety of product categories, and a purchasing potential index is calculated. The index is based on a national average score of 100.[17] For example, if zip code 55959 generates a score of 110 for furniture consumption, then that zip code area has a 10 percent greater potential to purchase furniture than the U.S. average.

Statistical Sources of Information

Statistical sources of secondary data can lead the researcher to specific statistical publications or can provide actual reprints of data extracted from numerous other secondary data sources. If actual data are located in the sourcebook, rather than in indexed references, these sources can save considerable research time. The following are examples of statistical data sources:

- Merchandising: "Statistical and Marketing Report."
- Standard and Poor's Industrial Surveys.
- Data Sources for Business and Market Analysis.
- American Statistics Index.
- Statistical Reference Index.
- Federal Statistical Directory.

Commercial Publications and Newspapers

Newspapers and commercial publications (*Time, Newsweek, BusinessWeek, Forbes, Fortune*) are important sources of secondary information. Because these publications are circulated on a daily, weekly, or monthly basis, the information they contain is very recent. In addition, many publications are archived enabling the researcher access to historical information. The **Business Periodical Index** is the primary index for commercial publications.

Business Periodical Index A list of business publications showing typical topics covered in the periodical.

The problem with commercial publications and newspapers is volume. There are probably more than 1,000 business-related commercial publications available. Many of these publications, especially newspapers, are not indexed in traditional reference books. Those that do provide indexing are usually associated with major metropolitan markets. Many of these publications now have archives online, but some of them charge for access.

Continuing Case: Using Secondary Data for the Santa Fe Grill

As you recall from our ongoing case study, the Santa Fe Grill Mexican restaurant is a new restaurant concept that currently operates in Dallas, Texas. The owners of the Santa Fe Grill believe secondary data may be useful in better understanding how to run their restaurant and also to expand their concept. The Marketing Research in Action at the end of the chapter contains an exercise in using secondary research for the Santa Fe Grill. Based on what you have learned in this chapter about secondary data, to get prepared for that exercise, think about and answer the following questions.

1. What kinds of secondary data are likely to be useful?
2. Conduct a search of secondary data sources for material that could be used by the Santa Fe Grill owners to better understand the problems/opportunities facing them. Use the Google, Yahoo!, or other search engines to do so.
3. What key words would you use in the search?

   Summarize what you found in your search.

Syndicated Sources of Secondary Data

A major trend in marketing research is toward a greater dependency on syndicated (or commercial) data sources. The rationale for this is that companies can obtain substantial information from a variety of industries at a relatively low cost. Also, because most of the data contained in these sources is collected at the point of purchase, the information represents actual purchase behavior rather than purchase intentions.

The Society of Competitive Intelligence Professionals reports that over 80 percent of marketing research firms purchase and use secondary research reports from commercial vendors. In addition, firms spend thousands of dollars annually for syndicated reports and devote many hours per week to analyzing the data.[18] Indeed, syndicated reports available online are rapidly replacing traditional paper-based sources.

Characteristics of Syndicated Data Sources

Syndicated (commercial) data Data that has been compiled according to some standardized procedure; customized data is provided for companies, such as market share, ad effectiveness, and sales tracking.

Syndicated (commercial) data is information that has been collected and compiled according to some standardized procedure. In most cases the information is collected for a particular business or company, with a specific reason or purpose motivating the data collection procedure. The information is then sold to different companies in the form of tabulated reports prepared specifically for a client's research needs, often tailored to specific reporting units. For example, reports can be organized by geographic region, sales territory, market segment, product class, or brand. For these data sources to be effective, suppliers of commercial/syndicated data must have in-depth knowledge of the industry and generate timely data. Suppliers traditionally have used two methods of data collection: consumer panels and store audits.

Consumer Panels

Consumer panel Large samples of households that provide specific, detailed data for an extended period of time.

Consumer panels consist of large samples of households that have agreed to provide detailed data for an extended period of time. Information provided by these panels typically consists of product purchase information or media habits, often on the consumer package goods industry. But information obtained from optical scanners is increasingly being used as well.

Panels are typically developed by marketing research firms and integrate a rigorous data collection approach. Respondents are required to record detailed behaviors at the time of occurrence on a highly structured questionnaire. The questionnaire contains a large number of questions related directly to actual product purchases or media exposure. Most often this is an ongoing procedure whereby respondents report data back to the company on a weekly or monthly basis. Panel data are then sold to a variety of clients after being tailored to the client's research needs.

A variety of benefits are associated with panel data. These include (1) lower cost than primary data collection methods; (2) rapid availability and timeliness; (3) accurate reporting of socially sensitive expenditures, for example, beer, liquor, cigarettes, generic brands; and (4) high level of specificity, for instance, actual products purchased or media habits, not merely intentions or propensities to purchase. In contrast, researchers must stay aware of the three main weaknesses of data generated through consumer panel groups. First, most consumer panels tend to underrepresent minority consumers, thereby creating sampling error/bias. In fact, many panels have sampling distributions that are highly skewed toward white, middle-class respondents. Second, there are problems with significant "turnover" among panel members because no one member is obligated to stay on the panel for the entire duration. Many members leave this type of panel or have other family members perform the response activities, and some members simply do not respond at all. This "turnover" seriously jeopardizes the representativeness and internal validity of panel data. In some cases, response bias becomes a problem when too many panel respondents answer questions in what they believe is the "socially desirable" manner, knowing that their purchases are being scrutinized. Also, when panel members either leave certain questions unanswered (blank) or record the wrong answers, these actions lead to higher levels of response bias.

There are two types of panel-based data sources: those reflecting actual purchases of products and services and those reflecting media habits. The discussion below provides examples of both types.

Examples of Consumer Panel Data Sources

A variety of companies offer panel-based purchasing data. Two of the largest companies are National Family Opinion (NFO) and the NPD Group (www.npd.com). NPD collects continuous data from a national sample consisting of approximately 15,000 members. Data collection centers on consumer attitudes and awareness of such products as toys, apparel, textiles, sporting goods, athletic footwear, automotive products, home electronics, and cameras.[19]

Three of NPD's most commonly used data sources are the Consumer Report on Eating Share Trends (CREST), National Eating Trends (NET), and a service that provides data on the food service industry in general. CREST is based on over 14,000 households that report data on restaurant habits. NET provides continuous tracking of in-home food and beverage consumption patterns. ISL, a Canadian subsidiary of the NPD Group, provides similar purchase data through the Consumer Panel of Canada.

National Family Opinion (NFO) maintains a consumer panel of over 450,000 households to conduct product tests, concept tests, and attitude, awareness, and brand-usage studies. The NFO panel offers a proprietary software program called Smart-System. This system enables clients to access and analyze complex information quickly, with easy cross-referencing on major data variables. In addition, NFO maintains highly targeted panels referred to as the Hispanic Panel, the Baby Panel, the Mover Panel, and SIP (Share of Intake Panel on Beverage Consumption). The following list describes additional companies and the consumer panels they maintain:

- Market Facts, Inc. (www.marketfacts.com) provides panel data for forecasting models, brand equity/loyalty models, and brand tracking information.
- J. D. Power and Associates (www.jdpower.com) maintains a consumer panel of car and light-truck owners to provide data on product quality, satisfaction, and vehicle dependability.
- Roper Starch Worldwide (www.roper.com) provides data on consumption patterns for the 6–18-year-old age market.
- Creative and Response Research Services has a consumer panel called Kidspeak (www.kidspeak.com) that provides advertising and brand tracking among children.

Examples of Media Panel Data Sources

Media panels and consumer panels are similar in procedure, composition, and design. They differ only in that media panels primarily measure media consumption habits as opposed to product or brand consumption. As with consumer panels, numerous media panels exist. This section provides examples of the most commonly used syndicated media panels.

Nielsen Media Research is by far the most widely known and accepted source of media panel data. The flagship service of Nielsen is the National Television Index (NTI). Based on a 5,000-household sample, the NTI provides an estimation of national television audiences measuring "ratings" and "share." Ratings refer to the percentage of households that have at least one television set tuned to a program for at least 6 of every 15 minutes a program is aired. Share constitutes the percentage of households that have a television tuned to one specific program at one specific time.[20] Data are collected on television, cable, and home video viewing habits through an electronic device, called a people meter, connected to a television set. The people meter continuously monitors and records when a television set is turned on, what channels are being viewed, how much time is spent on each channel, and who is watching. The data are communicated back to the central computer by telephone or the Internet.

The primary purpose of the NTI data is to assist media planners in determining audience volume, demographics, and viewing habits. This information is then used to calculate media efficiency measured as cost per thousand (CPM), that is, how much it costs to reach 1,000 viewers. CPM measures a program's ability to deliver the largest target audience at the lowest cost.

While most data are collected by the people meter, Nielsen still maintains diary panels in selected markets measuring the same media habits. In addition, Nielsen also operates an 800-household sample of Hispanic TV viewers designed to measure Spanish-language media usage in the United States. Arbitron Inc. is primarily a media research firm that conducts ongoing data collection for electronic media. Arbitron is organized into five media research business units.[21] Arbitron Radio provides radio audience data for more than 250 local market areas. Utilizing a 2 million-plus customer panel, Arbitron Radio collects over 1 million weekly listening diaries that are the basis of Arbitron Radio's station rating reports. The data are used primarily by media planners, advertising agencies, and advertisers. Arbitron also sells syndicated data on local media, consumer listening habits, and retail advertising impact data across 58 of the major U.S. markets. Currently, 600 newspapers, radio stations, television stations, and cable systems are predominant users of this syndicated data source.

Store Audits

Store audits Formal examination and verification of how much of a particular product or brand has been sold at the retail level.

Store audits consist of formal examination and verification of how much of a particular product or brand has been sold at the retail level. Based on a collection of participating retailers (typically discount, supermarket, and drugstore retailers), audits are performed on product or brand movement in return for detailed activity reports and cash compensation to the retailer. The audits then operate as a secondary data source. Clients can purchase the data relative to industry, competition, product, or specific brand. Store audits provide two unique benefits: precision and timeliness. Many of the biases of consumer panels are not found in store audits. By design, store audits measure product and brand movement directly at the point of sale (usually at the retail level). Also, sales and competitive activities are reported when the audit is completed, making the data timely and readily available to potential users.

Key variables being measured in the store audit typically include beginning and ending inventory levels, sales receipts, price levels, price inducements, local advertising, and point-of-purchase (POP) displays. Collectively, these data allow users of store audit services to generate information on the following factors:

- Product/brand sales in relation to competition.
- Effectiveness of shelf space and POP displays.
- Sales at various price points and levels.

- Effectiveness of in-store promotions and point-of-sale coupons.
- Direct sales by store type, product location, territory, and region.

Two of the major providers of in-store audit services are AC Nielsen (www.acnielsen.com/ retail/index) and Information Resources (www.Infoscan.com). Collectively, these two organizations conduct over 150,000 store audits in more than 40,000 separate retail locations. The Nielsen Retail Index provides information on a wide range of causal marketing factors that affect consumer responses to grocery, health and beauty, drug, and beverage products. Nielsen audits are developed on a stratified sampling procedure of store size, type, population, and geographic location. Actual stores used in the audit are randomly selected from designated strata. Audits typically are performed on a monthly basis at the point-of-sale level.

Infoscan provides census-based information rather than information based on a sample of representative stores. Through the Infoscan census, all stores within a particular retail chain (Wal-Mart, Kroger, Target) are audited. Information from the audit is then compiled and disseminated to each store within the chain for store-level marketing applications. The data are also used within specific industries to develop customer response programs at the manufacturer or wholesale level.

A variety of smaller audit services exists, such as Audits and Surveys, Inc., which provides syndicated product movement data in the automotive, sporting goods, home improvement, and entertainment industries. Through the audit service called National Total Market, Audits and Surveys provides a retail census of distribution for any specific company (AutoZone, Hand City, etc.) and in-store data on shelf-space availability, brand-name sales, mystery-shopper programs, and in-store promotional impacts.

The Internet as a Growing Source of Secondary Data

Advances in Internet and telecommunication technologies have dramatically accelerated the speed at which anyone can obtain secondary information. Web sites describe products and services and provide information that can be used to evaluate corporate structure and marketing positioning strategies. Finding a company's Web page can be fairly easy when companies use their name as the URL. Many times, however, multiple companies have the same or a similar name, although operating in different industries. A solution to this problem is to search for competitive companies using KnowThis (www.knowthis.com), a specialty search engine for a virtual marketing library that contains Internet addresses for more than a million companies.

Company management, financial, and marketing information are necessary components for any business intelligence program (BIP) and most of the information can be found easily on the Internet. An excellent starting point is a specialty Web site known as "Corporate Information" (www.corporateinformation.com). This site contains links to public and private companies in more than 100 countries and recently added a search engine for accessing a database of 100,000 companies.

As discussed earlier in designing and conducting a competitive intelligence study, the Internet can be used to track and monitor current alerts about competitors. Press releases and news stories contain a wealth of information about a competitor's services, products, and markets. Two valuable sources for this type of information are Excite's News-tracker Clipping Service (www.news.excite.com) and Company Sleuth (www.companysleuth.com).

One of the greatest assets of the Internet is the powerful search engines. Engines such as Google (www.google.com), AltaVista (www.altavista.com), Yahoo! (www.yahoo.com),

eXHIBIT 5.14 Selected Online Internet Information Sources

Source	Description of Data
International Business Research (www.infotoday.com)	Provides international business information and links to useful data sources
BUSLIB-L (www.montague.com)	Collection of business research articles and e-mail discussion groups
BRINT (www.brint.com)	Guide to business research sites with editorial comments
CI Resource Index (www.ciseek.com)	Listing of sites by category for finding competitive intelligence sources
European Research Gateways (www.cordis.lu/ergo/home)	Stores 60,000 records of R&D projects currently in operation in Europe
Intellifacts.com (www.intellifact.com)	230,000 company profiles and business locators
International Business Resource (www.globaledge.msu.edu)	Vast directory of regional trade and trade-related statistics
The Internet for Competitive Intelligence (www.freeprint.com)	Web resources for finding corporate and industry intelligence
Internet Intelligence Index (www.fuld.com)	600 intelligence-related sites
Powerize.com (www.powerize.com)	Version of Hoover.com, contains over 32 million business filings
PR Webpress Database (www.prweb.com)	Press releases of business and industry over the preceding 90 days
American Demographics/ Marketing Tools www.marketingtools.com)	Searches the full text of *American Demographics* and *Marketing Tools*
EconData (www.econdata.net)	An excellent site for researchers interested in economics and demographics
Harris Info Service (www.harrisinfo.com)	Provides business-to-business data on American manufacturers
Nielsen Media Research (www.nielsenmedia.com)	Data on media usage in the United States
U.S. Census Bureau (www.census.gov)	Useful source for all census data
World Opinion (www.worldopinion.com)	Excellent site for the marketing research industry; many research studies referenced
USA Data (www.usadata.com)	Consumer lifestyle data on a local, regional, and national basis

and Excite (www.excite.com) have made it easy for researchers to gather secondary information on the Internet.

With advances in technologies, the Internet will continue to be a significant tool for secondary data gathering and may become the only one needed to supply information for any type of intelligence program. Exhibit 5.14 provides additional sources of useful secondary marketing and business information on the Internet. It is essential to proceed with caution, though, as we have emphasized throughout, since the quality and reliability

A Closer Look at Research

Customized Data

As computer technology continues to change and more people become versed in Boolean search strategies for databases, the role of secondary research will continue to evolve. Secondary data researchers will become more involved with a company's internal technology department as they begin to tap into real-time inventory and client or production systems to add more customization of information to the secondary data that they find online. Try it for yourself. Go to the Internet and contact www.freeedgar.com. You will find hundreds of documents on U.S. companies that are not only updated daily but also highly customized from a secondary data perspective.

of Internet information—or for that matter, any information—must be questioned and its quality and reliability confirmed.

As more and more organizations begin to realize the full value of database development and information systems management, they will be able to customize secondary data sources. For a short discussion of this development see the nearby A Closer Look at Research (In the Field) box.

MARKETING RESEARCH IN ACTION

Continuing Case

Santa Fe Grill Considering Expansion

The owners of the Santa Fe Grill Mexican restaurant, in Dallas, Texas, when developing their five-year plan, anticipated the opening of two additional locations in Texas, after five years of successful operation at the Dallas location. The owners considered expanding to Houston, and possibly San Antonio as well.

After revisiting the five-year plan, the owners realized they lacked data and information relevant to these two cities. In fact, the only information they had was their population size and growth. Realizing this, they decided to develop area profiles of Houston and San Antonio relative to the restaurant market. For this they need professional help.

Following on their decision, key secondary data must now be collected. Population characteristics, economic conditions, competitive trends in the restaurant industry, and market factors appear to be the starting point of the secondary data search. The owners, realizing these factors may be too broad for facilitating an expansion decision, have requested the help of a local university marketing research class (suppose it's your own) to conduct a secondary data search for the most relevant and specific information on Houston and San Antonio, Texas.

Hands-On Exercise

The owners need your help in designing the approach, collection of data, types of data, and conclusive evidence to be featured in a secondary research search. Specifically, the following issues should be addressed:

1. Develop a list of the specific variables that need to be examined regarding demographic characteristics, economic characteristics, competitive dimensions of the restaurant market, and other relevant customer data as pertains to Houston and San Antonio, Texas.
2. Based on the discussion in this chapter, perform a secondary data search on all key variables you identified in your answer to question 1.
3. Develop a comparative profile of the two cities (Houston, San Antonio) based on your secondary data and provide the owners with a report showing evidence that one, both, or neither of the cities would be desirable for possible restaurant expansion.

Summary of Learning Objectives

■ **Determine when secondary research is the best approach.**

Prior to any determination of whether secondary research should be undertaken, management and the researcher must engage in dialogue with one another to determine the research problems. This entails that management and the researcher must (1) *identify and clarify the information needs*, (2) *define (possibly refine) the research problem and questions*, and (3) *clearly specify the research objectives and confirm the information value*. Once these activities are completed, the next task step focuses on *determining whether secondary data can be used* to answer the specified research questions. Here the researcher, with the help of management, determines whether useful information/data already exists, the relevance of the information/data, its availability, and method of capturing the information/data. Working with management the researcher must address and answer "yes" to the following types of questions:

1. Can the data help answer the specified research questions?
2. To what extent are the data relevant to the time period of interest?
3. Are the data relevant to the population of interest?
4. Are there other variables available that are relevant to the research project?
5. Will the variables' unit of measurement be comparable to the current situation?
6. Can the original source of the data be accessed?
7. Are the data acquisition costs worth it?
8. Can the data bias be determined?
9. Can data collection accuracy be verified?
10. If accuracy cannot be verified, is using the data worth the risks?

■ **Understand the role of secondary data in marketing research.**

The task of a marketing researcher is to solve the problem in the shortest time, at the least cost, with the highest level of accuracy. Therefore, before any marketing research project is conducted, researchers must find existing information that can facilitate a decision or outcome for a company. Existing data are commonly called secondary data.

■ **Explain why researchers conduct literature reviews and electronic searches.**

A literature review is a comprehensive examination of available information that is related to your research topic. When conducting a literature review, researchers locate information relevant to the research problems and issues at hand. Literature reviews have the following objectives: provide background information for the current study; clarify thinking about the research problem and questions you are studying; reveal whether information already exists that addresses the issue of interest; help to define important constructs of interest to the study; and suggest sampling and other methodological approaches that have been successful in studying similar topics. Advancements in Internet and telecommunication technologies have made online electronic searches for existing information to solve management problems much faster, easier, and less costly than ever before. With the expanding availability of secondary data and powerful search engines like Google and Yahoo!, electronic searches increase the speed of locating information while significantly reducing the cost and time required to capture and retrieve needed data. In addition, secondary data is becoming more accurate than ever before. For example, bar coding, optical scanning, and point-of-purchase data provide many consumer-product and retail companies with all the information they need for many of their marketing decisions.

■ **Describe how to conduct secondary research.**

Conducting a literature review is tedious and time consuming, often taking much longer than originally anticipated. The objective of a literature review is to summarize the existing research related to your problem. The review includes findings reported by different authors, their methodology, and how their findings are similar as well as different from your own. For research findings that are similar, you likely will point out why. Where the findings are different, you should suggest reasons for this as well. In all cases you should indicate how their findings influenced your own research. A good literature review demonstrates the researcher has an excellent understanding of previous work and how it is related. Citing an extensive list of references is not good enough, and could be risky. Researchers must clearly interpret previous research and show the linkages. To search online for secondary data, researchers must clearly understand the research objectives, types of electronic-based sources, as well as the internal and external nature of those sources. For example, in conducting a competitive intelligence study, researchers focus on gathering topics such as financial, market, and product performance indicators, price positions, inbound and outbound logistics, advertising and promotions, trade relations, production and salesforce processes, as well as executive profiles. For this type of research to be effective, there must be a constant flow of timely and accurate information that can be disseminated to decision makers and transformed into actionable strategies and tactics. Exhibit 5.7 lists the six steps researchers follow in conducting competitive intelligence studies.

■ **Identify and use internal and external secondary data sources.**

Internal secondary data include company internal accounting and financial information sources. These typically consist of sales invoices, accounts receivable reports, and quarterly sales reports. Other forms of internal data include past marketing research studies, customer credit applications, warranty cards, and employee exit interviews. External secondary data can be obtained from a wide variety of sources. The most common forms of external data are North American Industry Classification System (NAICS) codes, government documents (which include census reports), business directories, trade journals, statistical sources, commercial publications, and newspapers. Syndicated (or commercial) data sources consist of data that have been systematically collected and compiled according to some standardized procedure. Suppliers of syndicated data have traditionally used one of two approaches in collecting data: consumer panels and store audits. (A third approach, optical-scanner technology, will be discussed in a later chapter.) With most syndicated data sources, the objective is quite clear: to measure point-of-sale purchase behaviors or to measure media habits.

Key Terms and Concepts

Business Periodical Index 139
Competitive intelligence 126
Consumer intelligence 125
Consumer panel 140
Customer knowledge 115
Data accuracy 131
Data conversion 130
Data relevancy 130
Environmental intelligence 124
Environmental scan 124
External secondary data 115
Internal secondary data 115
Literature review 118
NAICS codes 134
Personal intelligence 124
Prior data manipulation 130
Secondary data 114
Store audit 142
Syndicated (commercial) data 140

Review Questions

1. What process would a researcher undertake to determine whether secondary research would be the best approach for gathering data to address a decision maker's problem or opportunity?
2. What role should secondary information research designs play in marketing research today?
3. What are the various reasons to conduct a literature review?
4. What are the major sources of information for a literature review? What are the advantages and limitations of using these sources?
5. What are the major types of online electronic data search designs? How do they differ from each other?
6. What are the general steps involved in conducting any type of secondary research project?

7. How have advances in Internet and telecommunication technologies impacted database marketing activities leading to market intelligence programs?
8. What are the main advantages and limitations associated with secondary data?
9. List the major differences between internal and external secondary data sources.
10. How have browsers like Google and Yahoo! changed the ways market researchers search for online secondary information?

Discussion Questions

1. **EXPERIENCE THE INTERNET.** Go online to your favorite browser (e.g., Google or Yahoo!) and find the home page for your particular state. For example, www.texas.com would get to the home page for the state of Texas. Once there, seek out the category that gives you information on county and local statistics. Select the county where you reside and obtain the vital demographic and socioeconomic data available. Provide a demographic profile of the residents in your community.
2. **EXPERIENCE THE INTERNET.** Visit four or five of the marketing blogs listed in Exhibit 5.3. Do these blogs have any information that might be relevant to practitioners who are conducting research in the topic areas that the blogs address? Why or why not?
3. It is possible to design a study, collect and analyze data, and write a report without conducting a literature review. What are the dangers and drawbacks of conducting your research without doing a literature review? In your judgment, do the drawbacks outweigh the advantages? Why or why not?
4. Identify and discuss the ways in which marketing researchers can achieve database enhancements, including the dynamics that need to be incorporated into database development activities.
5. What specific industry information could executives at Procter and Gamble (P&G) obtain from the *Source Book of Demographics and Buying Power for Every Zip Code in the U.S.A.*? Discuss how this information would improve P&G's marketing strategies.
6. You are planning to open a new casual dining restaurant in one of two areas in your local community. Conduct an online electronic secondary data search on some key variables that would allow you to make a logical decision on which area is best suited for your proposed restaurant.

chapter 6

Exploratory Research Using Qualitative and Observation Methods

Learning Objectives

After reading this chapter, you will be able to:

1. Identify the major differences between qualitative and quantitative research.
2. Describe the pros and cons of using qualitative data collection techniques.
3. Understand in-depth interviewing and focus groups as questioning techniques.
4. Explain other qualitative data collection methods such as ethnography, case studies, protocol interviews, and projective interviewing techniques.
5. Discuss observation methods and explain how they are used to collect primary data.

"What new banking services or changes in existing service offerings does Barnett Bank need to consider to assure customer service quality and satisfaction?"

—LAURA W. GAUTHIER,
Vice President and Sales Manager,
Barnett Bank of Pasco County

Culture Codes Bring Insights to Chrysler's Jeep

Clotaire Rapaille was hired by Chrysler to help understand how the Jeep Wrangler could be more successfully positioned in the American marketplace. Although Chrysler managers had already conducted plenty of traditional research and were skeptical of Rapaille's methodology, the researcher convinced the company that he could help them to better understand consumers' emotional connections to Jeep. The research was performed in three stages. In the first hour, Rapaille told focus group participants that he was a visitor from another planet and had never seen a Jeep. He asked group members to explain to an extraterrestrial what a Jeep is and how it is used. In the second hour, group members made collages about Jeep using scissors and pictures cut from magazines. In the last hour, they lay down on the floor with pillows while soothing music played and the lights were dimmed, and were asked about their earliest memories of the Jeep.

Rapaille's goal in using a multistage qualitative method is to get past rational, conscious filters into more emotional and unconscious mental territory. Among participants, several stories and images about the Jeep recurred: "being out in the open land" . . . "going where no ordinary car could go" . . . "riding free of the restraints of the road." Consistent with these stories, many consumers invoked the image of the American West and the open plains.

Rapaille returned to a skeptical group of Chrysler executives and explained to them that the "Code" for the Jeep in America is "Horse." Thus, designing and positioning the Jeep to be an SUV would be a strategic mistake. "SUVs are not horses. Horses don't have luxury appointments." Chrysler executives weren't impressed because they had done a great deal of research that suggested that consumers wanted something else. But Rapaille asked them to test his theory by changing the Jeep's square headlights to be round instead. His reasoning was that horses have round eyes rather than square ones. When Chrysler tested the new design, the response from consumers was immediately positive. Sales rose and the new appearance of the Wrangler became its most marketable feature. The company also positioned the car as a horse in its new advertising. In one execution of the ad campaign, a dog falls off a cliff and hangs onto a tree. A child runs for help, passing various vehicles until he reaches a Jeep Wrangler. In this "product as hero" ad, the Jeep is able to negotiate the difficult terrain and rescue the dog. Like a Western hero, the Jeep heads off into the sunset before the child can thank the driver. The campaign was a huge success for Jeep.[1]

Value of Exploratory Research

Management is often faced with situations in which important questions cannot be adequately addressed or resolved with secondary information. Meaningful insights can be gained only through the collection of primary data. Recall that primary data are typically collected using a set of formal procedures in which researchers question or observe individuals and record their findings. The method employed may involve qualitative or quantitative research or both.

As the journey through Phase II of the research process (Select the Appropriate Research Design) continues, attention moves from secondary data to primary data collection techniques. This chapter begins a series of chapters that discuss research designs used in collecting primary data. Research objectives and information requirements are the keys to determining the appropriate type of research design for collecting data. For example, *qualitative* research is often used in exploratory research designs when the research objectives are to gather background information and clarify the research problems and to create hypotheses or establish research priorities. *Quantitative* research may then be used to follow up and quantify the qualitative findings.

Qualitative research results may be sufficient for decision making in certain situations. For example, if the research is designed to assess customer responses to different advertising approaches while the ads are still in the storyboard phase of development, qualitative research is effective. Qualitative research may also be sufficient when feedback in focus groups or in-depth interviews is consistent, such as overwhelmingly favorable (or unfavorable) toward a new product concept. Last, some topics are more appropriately studied using qualitative research. This is particularly true for complex consumer behaviors that may be affected by factors that are not easily reducible to numbers, such as consumer choices and experiences involving cultural, family, and psychological influences that are difficult to tap into using quantitative methods. Occasionally, qualitative research is conducted as a follow-up to quantitative research. This happens when quantitative findings are contradictory or ambiguous and do not fully answer research questions. This chapter introduces several qualitative research methods used in exploratory research designs.

Observation and Questioning as Methods of Collecting Primary Data

Prior to discussing the different methods used by researchers to collect primary data, it is important to remember that there are actually two basic ways to collect primary data. Researchers can use either some form of *observation* to record human behavior or market phenomena, or some form of *questioning* and *recording* to capture a person's attitudes, feelings, and/or behaviors. Observation methods require the use of either a human observer or some type of mechanical or electronic device to capture and record specific human behaviors or phenomena of interest that take place during the observing time. In contrast, questioning/recording methods of capturing data ask specific questions and record the responses and may or may not require an interviewer. In some situations, researchers may use both forms in order to obtain the required primary data to answer the research questions. Although some marketing researchers consider observation methods to be primarily an exploratory research design, they are also used in both descriptive and causal research designs. As you learn about exploratory, descriptive, and causal research designs, you will see how researchers can use both observation and questioning in many research designs.

Overview of Qualitative and Quantitative Research Methods

There are differences in qualitative and quantitative approaches, but all researchers interpret data and tell stories about the research topics they study.[2] Prior to discussing qualitative techniques used in exploratory research we summarize some of the differences between qualitative and quantitative research methods. The factors listed in Exhibit 6.1 summarize the major differences.

eXHIBIT 6.1 Major Differences between Qualitative and Quantitative Research

	Qualitative Methods	Quantitative Methods
Goals/Objectives	Discovery/identification of new ideas, thoughts, feelings; preliminary understanding of relationships, ideas, and objects	Validation of facts, estimates, relationships, and predictions
Type of Research	Exploratory	Descriptive and causal
Type of Questions	Open-ended, unstructured, probing	Mostly structured
Time of Execution	Relatively short time frame	Typically significantly longer time frame
Representativeness	Small samples, only the sampled individuals	Large samples, with proper sampling, can represent population
Type of Analysis	Debriefing, subjective, content analysis, interpretive	Statistical, descriptive, and causal predictions
Researcher Skills	Interpersonal communications, observation, interpretation of text or visual data	statistical analysis and interpretation of numbers
Generalizability	Limited	Generally very good, can infer facts and relationships

Quantitative Research Methods

Quantitative research Survey designs that place heavy emphasis on using formal standardized questions and predetermined response options in questionnaires or surveys administered to large numbers of respondents.

Quantitative research uses formal questions and predetermined response options in questionnaires administered to large numbers of respondents. For example, when you think of quantitative research, think of J. D. Power and Associates conducting a nationwide survey of customer satisfaction among new car purchasers or American Express doing a global survey on travel behaviors. With quantitative methods, the research problems are specific and well defined, and the decision maker and researcher have agreed on precise information needs.

Quantitative research methods are most often used with descriptive and causal research designs but are occasionally associated with exploratory designs. For example, a researcher may pilot test items on a questionnaire to see how well they measure a construct before including them in a larger study. Success in collecting quantitative data is more a function of correctly designing and administering the questionnaire than of the communication and interpretive skills of an interviewer or observer.

The main goals of quantitative research are to obtain information to (1) make accurate predictions about relationships between market factors and behaviors, (2) gain meaningful insights into those relationships, (3) validate relationships, and (4) test hypotheses. Quantitative researchers are well trained in construct development, scale measurement, questionnaire design, sampling, and statistical data analysis. In addition, quantitative researchers must be able to translate numerical data into meaningful narrative information, telling a compelling story that is supported by data. Finally, quantitative methods are statistically projectible to the target population of interest and relatively more reliable because every question is asked of all respondents in precisely the same way and sample sizes are much larger. Exhibit 6.2 displays some of the main guidelines for determining when it is appropriate to use quantitative research methods. These guidelines are by no means exhaustive and are discussed in later chapters.

Qualitative Research Methods

Qualitative research The collection of data in the form of text or images using open-ended questions, observation, or "found" data.

While qualitative research data collection and analysis can be careful and rigorous, most practitioners regard qualitative research as being less reliable than quantitative research. **Qualitative research** seeks to *understand* research participants rather than to fit their answers into predetermined categories with little room for qualifying or explaining their

EXHIBIT 6.2 Guidelines for Using Quantitative Research

Quantitative research methods are appropriate when decision makers or researchers are:

- Validating or answering a business problem or information requirements.
- Obtaining detailed descriptions or insights into the motivation, emotional, attitudinal, and personality factors that influence marketplace behaviors.
- Testing theories and models to explain marketplace behaviors or relationships between two or more marketing variables.
- Assessing the reliability and validity of scales for investigating market factors, consumer qualities (e.g., attitudes, emotional feelings, preferences, beliefs, perceptions) and behavioral outcomes.
- Assessing the effectiveness of marketing strategies on marketplace behaviors.
- Examining new-product/service development or repositioning of current products or service images.
- Segmenting and/or comparing large or small differences in markets, new products, services, or evaluation and repositioning of current products or service images.

choices. Thus, qualitative research often uncovers unanticipated findings and reactions. Therefore, one common objective of qualitative research is to gain preliminary insights into research problems. These preliminary insights are sometimes followed up with quantitative research to verify the qualitative findings.

A second use of qualitative research is to probe more deeply into areas that quantitative research may be too superficial to access, such as subconscious consumer motivations.[3] Qualitative research enables researchers and clients to get closer to their customers and potential customers than does quantitative research. For example, video and textual verbatims enable participants to speak and be heard in their own words in the researcher's report.

Qualitative researchers usually collect detailed data from relatively small samples by asking questions or observing behavior. Researchers trained in interpersonal communications and interpretive skills use open-ended questions and other materials to facilitate in-depth probing of participants' thoughts. Some qualitative research involves analysis of "found" data, or existing text. For example, qualitative researchers who want to better understand teen consumer culture might analyze a sample of MySpace entries posted by teens. In most cases, qualitative data is collected in relatively short time periods. Data analysis typically involves content analysis and interpretation. To increase the reliability and trustworthiness of the interpretation, researchers follow consistent approaches that are extensively documented.

The semistructured format of the questions and the small sample sizes limit the researcher's ability to generalize qualitative data to the population. Nevertheless, qualitative data have important uses in identifying and understanding business problems. For example, qualitative data can be invaluable in providing researchers with initial ideas about specific problems or opportunities, theories and relationships, variables, or the design of scale measurements. Finally, qualitative research can be superior for studying topics that involve complex psychological motivations not easily reduced to survey formats and quantitative analyses.

When to Use Qualitative Research Methods in Exploratory Designs

In most exploratory research projects, the raw data are gathered through qualitative data collection practices. Exhibit 6.3 lists some guidelines for determining when it is appropriate to use qualitative research methods for collecting information with exploratory designs.

eXHIBIT 6.3 Guidelines for Using Qualitative Research

Qualitative research methods are appropriate when researchers are:

- Identifying a business problem or opportunity situation, or establishing information requirements.
- Obtaining preliminary insights into the motivation, emotional, attitudinal, and personality factors that influence marketplace behaviors.
- Building theories and models to explain marketplace behaviors or relationships between two or more marketing constructs.
- Developing valid scales for investigating specific market factors, consumer qualities (e.g., attitudes, emotional feelings, preferences, beliefs, perceptions), and behavioral outcomes.
- Determining the preliminary effectiveness of marketing strategies on actual marketplace behaviors.
- Developing new products and services, or repositioning current product or service images.

EXHIBIT 6.4 Advantages and Disadvantages of Using Qualitative Research Methods

Advantages of Qualitative Research	Disadvantages of Qualitative Research
Except for ethnography, data can be collected relatively quickly	Lack of generalizability
Richness of the data	Difficulty in estimating small-magnitude differences of the phenomena being investigated
Accuracy of recording marketplace behaviors (validity)	Low reliability
Preliminary insights into building models investigators, and scale measurements	Difficulty finding well-trained interviewers and observers
Insights from qualitative researchers with skills training in social and behavioral sciences	Reliance on subjective interpretive of qualitative researcher

Advantages and Disadvantages of Qualitative Research Methods

Qualitative research data collection methods have both advantages and disadvantages. Exhibit 6.4 summarizes the main advantages and disadvantages.

Advantages

One advantage of qualitative research, particularly for focus groups and in-depth interviews, is that it can be completed relatively quickly. Partly because of the use of small samples, researchers can complete their investigations more quickly and sometimes at a lower cost than is the case with quantitative research data collection methods. Another advantage is the *richness of the data*. The unstructured approach of qualitative techniques enables researchers to collect in-depth data about the respondents' attitudes, beliefs, emotions, and perceptions, all of which may strongly influence their behaviors as consumers.

The richness of the qualitative data can often supplement the facts gathered through other primary data collection techniques. Qualitative techniques enable decision makers to gain *first-hand experiences* with customers and can provide revealing information that is contextualized to their thoughts. For example, an ethnographic study of Thanksgiving traditions conducted in consumers' homes during their celebrations discovered that the term "homemade" is often applied to dishes that are not made from scratch, but instead use at least some pre-made, branded ingredients.[4] Such rich data can be invaluable in gaining an understanding of consumers' thoughts and behaviors.

Qualitative research methods often provide researchers with preliminary insights useful in developing ideas about how variables are related. Similarly, qualitative research can help *define constructs or variables* and suggest items that can be used to measure those constructs. For example, before they can successfully measure the perceived quality of online shopping experiences from their customers' perspective, retailers must first ascertain the factors or dimensions that are important to their customers when shopping online. Qualitative data also play an important role in identifying *marketing problems and opportunities*. The in-depth information enhances the researcher's ability to understand consumer behavior.

Finally, many qualitative researchers have backgrounds in the social sciences, such as sociology, anthropology or psychology, and thus bring knowledge of theories from their disciplines to enhance their interpretation of data. A study of grooming behavior of young adults conducted by an anthropologist described grooming behavior as "ritual magic."[5] Qualitative insights like this have implications for advertising and marketing.

The legacy of psychology and psychiatry in developing qualitative techniques is seen in the emphasis on subconscious motivations and the use of probing techniques that are designed to uncover motives.[6] In addition, qualitative data play a critical role in *building marketing models and scale measurements*. The in-depth information enhances the researcher's ability to predict consumer behavior in the marketplace and enables the researcher to develop better marketing constructs and more reliable and valid scale measurements of those constructs.

Disadvantages

Although qualitative research produces useful information, it has some potential disadvantages, including sample sizes and the need for well-trained interviewers or observers. The sample size in a qualitative study may be as few as 10 (individual in-depth interviews), and is rarely more than 60 (the number of participants in 5–6 focus groups). Occasionally, companies will undertake large-scale qualitative studies involving thousands of in-depth interviews and hundreds of focus groups, as Forrester Research did to support the development of their e-commerce consulting business.[7] But this is the exception, not the rule. While researchers often handpick respondents to represent their target population, the resulting samples are not representative in the statistical sense. Qualitative researchers emphasize that their samples are made up of "relevant" rather than representative consumers. The *lack of representativeness* of the defined target population may limit the use of qualitative information in selecting and implementing final action strategies. The attitudes and behaviors of a group of 8 to 12 of your classmates are unlikely to be representative of all college students at your university, or even business majors or marketing majors at your university, much less all college students in the United States. Small sample sizes make it difficult for researchers to generalize findings beyond the group used to collect the data.

Another disadvantage is that the data generated through qualitative methods are limited by their *inability to distinguish small differences*. Many times marketing successes and failures are based on small differences in marketing mix strategies. Using small samples of subjects to provide critical information does not allow researchers to evaluate the impact of small differences. Moreover, researchers are forced to analyze qualitative data at aggregate, not disaggregate, levels. Aggregation of the findings eliminates the opportunity to study individual differences. In most cases, the reliability of data collected using qualitative research methods cannot be assessed. Decision makers often are reluctant to use information that cannot be assessed for reliability.

Finally, the *difficulty of finding well-trained interviewers and observers* to conduct qualitative research can be a potential disadvantage. A high level of expertise is required to practice informal, unstructured methods of obtaining qualitative data, and few marketing researchers have the extensive formal training needed to be an expert in the qualitative field. Moreover, it is difficult for the unsuspecting practitioner to discern the researcher's qualifications or the quality of the research.

In spite of these disadvantages, the benefits of qualitative research, particularly in the exploratory stage, are clear. Researchers should integrate qualitative and quantitative techniques in order to make the research program complete.

Questioning Techniques in Qualitative Research

In today's technology-driven business environment many marketing problems can be solved only by looking beyond secondary data. Frequently decision makers need current information that can be obtained only through *real-time observations* of individual behaviors or by *directly asking people questions.* Observation and interviewing techniques play important roles in exploratory research designs. Since observation methods can be used to capture both qualitative and quantitative data, we will discuss observation methods later on in the chapter. The focus here is on introducing and detailing the interviewing techniques and activities associated with collecting primary data using qualitative methods. There is a distinct "family" of interviewing approaches that can be used to collect primary qualitative data, including in-depth interviews, focus groups, case studies, experience interviews, and projective interviewing techniques. The use of observation, projective techniques, ethnography, and similar approaches has been growing in recent years. All these approaches are useful in providing information to decision makers, but we will focus primarily on in-depth interviews and focus group interviews, techniques that are the most popular methods among many decision makers and researchers, while highlighting the others (see Exhibit 6.5).

In-Depth Interviews

In-depth interview A formal process in which a well-trained interviewer asks a subject a set of semistructured questions in a face-to-face setting.

The **in-depth interview,** also referred to as a "depth" or "one-on-one" interview, involves a trained interviewer asking a respondent a set of semistructured, probing questions usually in a face-to-face setting. The typical setting for this type of interview is either the respondent's home or office, or some type of centralized interviewing center convenient for the respondent. Some research firms use hybrid in-depth interviews involving a combination of Internet and phone interviewing. In these cases, the conversation can be extended over several days, giving participants more time to consider their answers.[8] The Internet also enables consumers to be exposed to visual and audio stimuli, thus overcoming a major limitation of phone interviewing. Exhibit 6.6 lists the primary objectives of in-depth interviews.

eXHIBIT 6.5 Interviewing Techniques

Primary Qualitative Method	Frequency of Use
Traditional focus groups	51.8%
Hybrids (2 or more methods)	14.3
In-depth interviews	7.8
Netnography	4.2
Ethnography	2.0
Chat-based online focus groups	1.2
Video-based online focus groups	1.0
Other	5.0
None	12.7

Source: Research Industry Trends, 2006 Report, Pioneer Marketing Research, GreenBook, Rockhopper Research, and Dialtech.

EXHIBIT 6.6 Primary Objectives of In-Depth Interviewing

- To discover preliminary insights into what a respondent thinks or believes about the topic of concern or why they exhibit certain behaviors.
- To obtain unrestricted and detailed comments including feelings, beliefs, and opinions that can help better understand the different elements of the respondent's thoughts and the reasons why they exist.
- To have the respondent communicate as much detail as possible about his or her knowledge and behavior toward a given topic or object.

Probing questions Specific questions that result when an interviewer takes the subject's initial response to a question and uses that response as the framework for the next question (the probing question) in order to gain more detailed responses.

In-depth interviewing enables the researcher to collect both attitudinal and behavioral data from the respondent that spans all time frames (past, present, and future). A unique characteristic of this data collection method is that the interviewer uses **probing questions** as the mechanism to get more data on the topic from the subject. By taking the subject's initial response and turning it into a question, the interviewer encourages the subject to further explain the first response and creates natural opportunities for a more detailed discussion of the topic. The general rule of thumb is that the more a subject talks about a topic, the more likely he or she is to reveal underlying attitudes, motives, emotions, and behaviors. To illustrate the technique of using probing questions, read the nearby A Closer Look at Research (In the Field) box to see how Marriott Hotels employs in-depth interviewing as a method of collecting detailed information from its business customers.

By interpreting the responses from respondent M14 and those of other participants, the researcher can create theme categories that reveal not only *what* hotel services the guests used, but also *why* those particular services were used during their stay at the Marriott. For example, from just respondent M14's responses, management learns the property's *fitness center, availability of in-room movie entertainment,* and *on-property car rental service* are some of the hotel features that must be in place to attract business travelers to the hotel. In addition, the movie entertainment and fitness center features could be promoted with a theme aimed toward "stress reduction" activities during the customer's stay at the hotel.

A word of caution about probing questions: it is critically important that the interviewer avoid framing questions that allow the subject to reply with a simple but logical "no." Unless the interviewer intends to bring closure to the discussion, probing questions should not be framed in formats like "Can you tell me more about that point?" "Could you elaborate on that?" "Do you have some specific reasons?" or "Is there anything else?" All these formats allow the subject to logically say no. Once a "no" response is given, it becomes very difficult to continue probing the topic for more detailed data.

Skills Required for Conducting In-Depth Interviews

Interpersonal communication skills The interviewer's ability to articulate questions in a direct and clear manner.

Listening skills The interviewer's ability to accurately interpret and record the subject's responses.

For in-depth interviewing to be an effective data collection tool, interviewers must have excellent interpersonal communication and listening skills. **Interpersonal communication skills** relate to the interviewer's ability to ask the questions in a direct and clear manner so the subjects understand exactly what they are responding to. **Listening skills** include the ability to accurately hear, record, and interpret the subject's responses. Depending on the complexity of the topic and the desired data requirements, most interviewers ask permission from the subject to record the interview using either a tape recorder or possibly a video recorder rather than relying solely on handwritten notes.

Without excellent probing skills, interviewers may allow the discussion of a specific topic to end before all the potential information is revealed. Most interviewers have to

A Closer Look at Research

Insights into Business Customers' Hotel Needs and Wants

Recently corporate management of Marriott Hotels wanted to understand how to deliver better on-site services to business customers. Marriott's researchers conducted 1,000 on-site, in-depth interviews with selected business travelers at selected Marriott hotel properties across the country. Several of the initial research questions that management wanted insight on included the following:

1. What were the specific factors you used in selecting Marriott for overnight accommodations during your business trip to San Diego, California? (Motives.)
2. What hotel services did you use during your stay? (Behavior.)
3. How satisfied or dissatisfied are you with those services? (Current feelings.)
4. How likely are you to stay at a Marriott Hotel next time you are in San Diego for business, and why? (Future intended behavior.)

Focusing on the second question above, the dialogue between the trained interviewer and respondent M14 went as follows:

Interviewer: "What hotel services did you use during your stay?"

Respondent M14: "I used the *front desk, restaurant,* and the hotel's *fitness center.*"

Interviewer: "With regard to the *front desk,* what were some of the actual services you requested?"

Respondent M14: "Well, besides *checking in,* I inquired about the *availability of a fitness room* and *car rental.*"

Interviewer: "Why were you interested in information about the hotel's *fitness center* and *car rental service?*"

Respondent M14: "When I am away on business, I *enjoy a good workout* to help *relieve stress buildup* and I find my *energy level improves.*"

Interviewer: "While at the hotel, how did *renting a car* fit into your plans?"

Respondent M14: "I had a *business meeting* at 9:30 A.M. across town, after which I *played a round of golf.*"

Interviewer: "Which *rental car company* do you usually prefer to use?"

Respondent M14: *"Hertz—they are the best!* I have *Gold VIP status* with them and I receive *frequent flier miles.*"

Interviewer: "Besides using the fitness center and renting a car, what *other hotel services* might you request during your stay?"

Respondent M14: "I will probably *rent a movie.*"

Interviewer: "Renting a movie? What *kinds of movies* do you prefer?"

Respondent M14: "When away from home, I enjoy watching *action-oriented movies* as a means to *relax* after a long day on the road. I do not get much of a chance when I am *at home* with the wife and the kids."

Interviewer: "Are there any *other services* you would consider using?"

Respondent M14: "No." (With this response, the interviewer would move on to the next topic.)

work at learning to ask good probing questions. Probing questions need to be precise and include some aspect of the subject's previous reply. **Interpretive skills** refer to the interviewer's ability to accurately understand the respondent's responses. Interpretive skills are important for transforming the data into usable information. Weak interpretive skills will have a negative impact on the quality of the information collected. Finally, the personality of the interviewer plays a significant role in establishing a "comfort zone" for the subject during the question/answer process. Interviewers should be easygoing, flexible, trustworthy, and professional. Respondents who feel at ease with an interviewer are more likely to reveal their hidden attitudes, feelings, motivations, and behaviors.

Interpretive skills Interviewer's ability to accurately understand the respondent's responses.

Advantages of In-Depth Interviews

As a qualitative data collection method, in-depth interviewing offers researchers several benefits. First is flexibility. One-on-one personal interviews enable the researcher to ask questions on a wide variety of topics. The question-and-answer process gives the researcher the flexibility to collect data not only on the subject's activities and behavior patterns, but also on the attitudes, motivations, and opinions that underlie those reported behaviors. Probing questions allow researchers to collect highly detailed data from the subject regarding the topic at hand. Once a certain comfort zone is reached in the interviewer–subject relationship, subjects willingly reveal their inner thinking.

Disadvantages of In-Depth Interviews

Data collected by in-depth interviews is subject to the same general limitations as all qualitative methods. Although in-depth interviews can generate a lot of detailed data, the findings lack generalizability, reliability, and the ability to distinguish small differences. Inaccurate findings may be caused by the introduction of interviewer–respondent artifacts (e.g., interviewer illustrates empathy toward the respondent's answers); respondent bias (faulty recall, concern with social acceptability, fatigue); or interviewer errors (inadequate listening, faulty recording procedures, fatigue). Other factors that limit the use of this questioning approach are the costs for both setup and completion and the extensive length of time required.

Steps in Conducting an In-Depth Interview

In planning and conducting an in-depth interview, there are a number of logical and formalized steps for the researcher to carry out. Exhibit 6.7 highlights those necessary steps.

Focus Group Interviews

Nature of Focus Group Interviews

Focus group research A formal process of bringing a small group of people together for an interactive, spontaneous discussion on one particular topic or concept.

The most widely used qualitative data collection method in marketing is focus group research, sometimes referred to as *group depth interview.* The focus group interview has its roots in the behavioral sciences. **Focus group research** involves bringing a small group of people together for an interactive and spontaneous discussion on a particular topic or concept. Focus groups typically consist of 8 to 12 participants who are guided by a professional moderator through a semistructured discussion that most often lasts about two hours. By encouraging group members to talk in detail about a topic, the moderator draws out as many ideas, attitudes, and experiences as possible about the specified issue. The fundamental idea behind the focus group approach is that one person's response will spark comments from other members, thus creating synergy among participants.

The overall goal of focus group research is to give researchers, and ultimately decision makers, as much information as possible about how people regard the topic of interest. That topic is typically a product, service, concept, or organization. Unlike many other types of questioning techniques, focus group research is not restricted to just asking and answering questions posed by an interviewer. Its success relies heavily on the group dynamics, the willingness of members to engage in an interactive dialogue, and the professional moderator's ability to keep the discussion on track. The overall cost of conducting a focus group can vary from $2,000 to $5,000 per session.[9]

EXHIBIT 6.7 Steps in Conducting an In-Depth Interview

Steps — **Description and Comments**

Step #1 — **Understand Initial Decision Question(s)/Problems**

- Define and understand management's problem situation and decision question(s).
- Engage in dialogue with decision makers that focuses on bring clarity and understanding to the problem situation (factors, thoughts, and concerns) and research problem(s).

Step #2 — **Create a Set of Research Questions**

- Develop a set of research questions (like an interviewer guide) directly related to the major elements of the questions or problems. These questions will serve as the "backbone" of the in-depth interview.
- Arrange the research questions using a logical flow from "general" to "specific" within topic areas.

Step #3 — **Decide on the Best Environment for Conducting the Interview**

- Determine best location for the interview based on the characteristics of the participant and select a relaxed, comfortable interviewing setting.
- Setting must facilitate private conversations without outside distractions.

Step #4 — **Select, Screen, and Secure the Prospective Subjects**

- Select participants using specified criteria for the situation being studied.
- Decision maker and researcher make a joint decision on the critical qualifying criteria.
- Sometimes particular demographic, attitudinal, emotional, and/or behavioral factors are used.
- Screen participants to assure they meet a set of specified criteria.

Step #5 — **Greet Respondent, Give interviewing Guidelines, Create a Comfort Zone**

- Interviewer meets participant and provides the appropriate introductory guidelines for the interviewing process.
- Obtains permission to tape record and/or video record the interview.
- Use the first few minutes prior to the start of the questioning process to create a "comfort zone" for the respondent, using warmup questions.
- Begin the interview by asking the first research question.

Step #6 — **Conduct the In-Depth Interview**

- Use probing questions to obtain as many details as possible from the participant on the topic before moving to the next question.
- Ask and probe all the research questions.
- When interview is completed, thank respondent for participating, debrief as necessary, and give incentives, if any.

Step #7 — **Analyze Respondent's Narrative Responses**

- Summarize initial thoughts after each interview. In particular, write down themes and ideas that may be used later in coding transcripts, a process referred to as "memoing."
- After all the data is collected, code each participant's transcript by classifying responses into categories.
- Interpret the responses of each respondent interviewed using predetermined classification systems or by using the responses to first create a classification system and then go back and code the responses.
- This analysis is very similar to that of a focus group.

Step #8 — **Write Summary Report of the Results**

- Prepare a summary report.
- The report is similar to writing a report for a "focus group."

Focus Group Research Objectives

There are many reasons focus group research is the most popular qualitative research method. As noted earlier, data collected in focus groups can offer preliminary insights into hidden marketing phenomena. Exhibit 6.8 lists some other pertinent objectives of focus group research. Each of these is described in more detail below.

To Provide Data for Defining and Redefining Marketing Problems. In situations where managers or researchers experience difficulties in identifying and understanding the marketing problem, focus groups can help to identify the differences between symptoms and problems. For example, the marketing department chairperson at a major southwestern university was not sure why undergraduate enrollment levels were continually declining. The chairperson called for a departmental faculty meeting using a focus group format. The discussion revealed several unexpected factors that provided the marketing department preliminary insights into why enrollment levels were declining. One of these had to do with whether the current marketing curriculum was offering marketing majors the kinds of skills currently demanded by businesses. The marketing department investigated this issue and found significant gaps between the two perspectives as to which skills undergraduate marketing majors needed. The department began a reassessment of its own curriculum in an attempt to realign the skills being taught to those being mandated by the business world.

To Identify Specific Hidden Information Requirements. In some cases, decision makers and researchers are not totally sure what specific types of data or information should be investigated. Focus groups can reveal unexpected aspects of the problem and thus can directly help researchers determine what specific data should be collected. For example, the directors of the Ford Foundation of Performing Arts in Vail, Colorado, were faced with the difficulty of deciding what design features should be included in the construction of a new $5 million Performing Arts Center. The foundation's research team conducted several focus groups consisting of local residents and seasonal visitors. From the groups' spontaneous, unstructured discussions, specific features and concerns such as different types of indoor and outdoor events, parking requirements, availability of refreshments, seating design and capacity, pricing of tickets, and protection from bad weather were revealed as being important factors that needed further understanding.

To Provide Data for Better Understanding Results from Quantitative Studies. There are quantitative research investigations that leave the decision maker or researcher asking *why* the results came out the way they did. Focus groups can be conducted to help

eXHIBIT 6.8 Primary Focus Group Objectives

1. To provide data for defining and redefining marketing problems.
2. To identify specific hidden information requirements.
3. To provide data for better understanding results from quantitative studies.
4. To reveal consumers' hidden needs, wants, attitudes, feelings, behaviors, perceptions, and motives regarding services, products, or practices.
5. To generate new ideas about products, services, or delivery methods.
6. To discover new constructs and measurement methods.
7. To help explain changing consumer preferences.

explain the findings of other surveys. For example, corporate management of Excelsior Hotels, Inc., conducted a survey among business guests at its hotels concerning free in-room entertainment services. The results indicated that 85 percent of the business guests were aware of the availability of the entertainment services but only 15 percent actually used them. Not understanding this gap between awareness and actual use, Excelsior Hotels conducted several focus groups among its business guests regarding these services. The focus group discussions revealed that business travelers were either too busy doing necessary paperwork or too exhausted to watch any type of TV at night. They preferred to read or listen to music as a means of relaxing after a long workday.

To Reveal Consumers' Hidden Needs, Wants, Feelings, Perceptions, Motives, Behaviors. Focus group interviews provide researchers with excellent opportunities to gain preliminary insights into what consumers think or feel about a wide array of products and services. For example, a manufacturer such as Procter & Gamble uses focus groups to obtain data that reveal consumers' attitudes for and against using Crest toothpaste. These data help the company understand how consumer brand loyalty is developed and what marketing factors are necessary to reinforce it.

To Generate New Ideas about Products, Services, or Delivery Methods. This particular objective has long been a mainstay among decision makers and researchers. Here, focus groups generate interactive discussions about new or existing products and services. Data collected through these discussions provide valuable preliminary insights into new-product development, new usages of existing products and services, possible changes for improving products or services, or identifying better delivery systems. A classic example is how Arm & Hammer discovered new in-home uses for baking soda. Periodically, the company conducts focus group interviews among known users of Arm & Hammer baking soda. Data generated from these discussions revealed that baking soda is used for such things as cleaning kitchens and bathrooms, cleaning around babies, deodorizing everything from carpets to cat litter boxes, freshening laundry, soothing and conditioning skin, and cleaning teeth. Today, Arm & Hammer baking soda is marketed as a natural product with "a houseful of uses."

To Discover New Constructs and Measurement Methods. For academicians and practitioners alike, focus group interviews play a critical role in the process of developing new marketing constructs and creating reliable and valid construct measurement scales. In the exploratory stage of construct development, researchers may conduct focus groups concerning a particular marketing idea to reveal additional insights into the underlying dimensions that may or may not make up the construct. These insights can help researchers develop scales that can be tested and refined through larger survey research designs. Take the important construct of service quality, for example. Researchers have been trying to refine the measurement of this construct for the past 20 years. They continue to ask such questions as "What does service quality mean to consumers, practitioners, and academicians?" "What is the underlying dimensionality of the construct—is it unidimensional or multidimensional?" and "What is the most appropriate way of measuring service quality?" Read the nearby A Closer Look at Research (In the Field) box to see how these questions have been investigated.

To Help Explain Changing Consumer Preferences. This objective refers to the use of focus group interviews to collect data that can be useful in understanding how customers describe their experiences with different products and services. This type of qualitative data can be valuable in improving marketing communications as well as in creating more

A Closer Look at Research

Dimensions of Service Quality

Researchers at the University of South Florida conducted exploratory research in an effort to bring clarity to the dimensionality controversy that plagues the "service quality" construct. Using available secondary information from earlier research on service quality reported in the literature, several focus group interviews were conducted among known patrons of retail commercial banking services. A trained professional moderator led the participants through unstructured and spontaneous discussions using a predetermined series of topical questions relating to the generic aspects of service quality. The qualitative data resulting from the discussions revealed seven possible sets of interpersonal behavior activities that consumers relied on when assessing the existence of service quality. These activities were subjectively described as service providers' communication/listening capabilities; diagnostic competence—understanding customers' needs/wants; empathy with customers' needs/wants; tactful responsiveness to customers' questions; reliability/credibility of the service provider; technical knowledge; and interpersonal social skills. In addition, the data supplied the researchers with preliminary insights into specific behavioral interchanges between service providers and customers. In turn, the interchanges were useful in building a 75-item inventory of interpersonal behavior activities and were used in a quantitative survey designed to test which behavioral interchanges were associated with these behaviors.[10]

effective marketing segmentation strategies. For example, a manufacturer of a brand-name line of lawn care products may be interested in such questions as "What do consumers like about lawn care and gardening?" "What words or terms do they use in describing lawn care/gardening products and their use?" "Why do they do their own lawn work?" and "How do they take care of their lawns and gardens?"

Conducting Focus Group Interviews

Focus group interview An interactive group discussion on selected topic issues.

Focus group interviews can be viewed as a process divided into three logical phases: planning the study, conducting the focus group discussions, and analyzing and reporting the results (see Exhibit 6.9).

Phase 1: Planning the Focus Group Study

As with most other types of marketing research, the planning phase is most critical for successful focus group interviews. In this phase, researchers and decision makers must have a clear understanding of the purpose of the study, a precise definition of the problem, and specific data requirements. There must be agreement on such questions as: "Why should such a study be conducted?" "What kinds of information will be produced?" "What types of information are of particular importance?" "How will the information be used?" and "Who wants the information?" Answers to these questions can help eliminate the obstacles (organizational politics, incomplete disclosure, and hidden personal agendas) that can delay agreement and create problems between decision makers and researchers. Other important factors in the planning phase relate to decisions about who the participants should be, how to select and recruit respondents, and where to have the focus group sessions.

EXHIBIT 6.9 Three-Phase Process for Developing a Focus Group Interview

Phase 1: Planning the Focus Group Study

- This is the most critical phase.
- Researchers must have an understanding of the purpose of the study, a precise definition of the problem, and specific data requirements.
- Key decisions focus on who the appropriate participants would be; how to select and recruit respondents; what size the focus group should be; and where to have the sessions.

Phase 2: Conducting the Focus Group Discussions

- One of the key players in this phase is the focus group moderator.
- To ensure a successful interactive session, the moderator's role and pertinent characteristics must be clearly understood by everyone involved.
- A necessary activity in this phase is the development of a moderator's guide that outlines the topics, questions, and subquestions that will be used in the session.
- The actual focus group session should be structured with beginning, main, and closing sections.

Phase 3: Analyzing and Reporting the Results

- After the actual session is completed and if the sponsoring client's representatives are present, the researcher should conduct a debriefing analysis with all the key players involved to compare notes.
- The researcher should conduct a content analysis on the raw data obtained from the participants during the interviewing session and write a formal report that communicates the findings.
- Key to the researcher here is to remember who will be the reading audience, the purpose of the report, and the nature of reporting the results as well as an appropriate report style format.

Focus Group Participants. In deciding who should be included as participants in a focus group, researchers must give strong consideration to the purpose of the study and think as well about who can best provide the necessary information. The first step is to consider all participants who should be represented in the study. While there is no one set of human characteristics that can guarantee the right group dynamics, the focus group must be as homogeneous as possible yet with enough variation to allow for contrasting opinions. Central factors in the selection process are the potential group dynamics and the willingness of members to engage in dialogue. Demographics such as age, gender, education level, family structure and product-related behaviors such as purchase and usage behavior are often considered in the sampling plan. The underlying concern is the degree to which these factors influence members' willingness to share ideas within group discussions. A focus group in which participants recognize and feel comfortable with their commonalities will create a more natural and relaxed group environment than a heterogeneous group. Furthermore, participants with common traits are less likely to be eager to present contrived or socially acceptable responses just to impress other group members or the moderator. Remember that in most cases, focus group participants are neither friends nor even acquaintances but typically strangers. Many people can feel intimidated or hesitant to voice their opinions, feelings, or suggestions to strangers.

A factor often overlooked in selecting participants is the individuals' existing knowledge level of the topic. Researchers must determine whether prospective participants have enough prior knowledge about the topics to be discussed in the interview. Lack of knowledge on the part of participants severely limits the opportunities for creating spontaneous, interactive discussions that will provide detailed data about a specific topic. For example, bringing together a group of people who sell women's shoes for a discussion about the operations of a nuclear power plant is likely to produce few meaningful insights pertinent to that topic.

Selection and Recruitment of Participants. Selecting and recruiting appropriate participants are keys to the success of any focus group. We have already noted the necessity for homogeneous groups. Now it becomes critical to understand the general makeup of the target audience that needs to be represented by the focus group. Exhibit 6.10 lists some general rules for the selection process.

To select participants, researchers first develop a screening form that specifies the characteristics respondents must have to qualify for group membership. Researchers choose a method for contacting prospective participants. They can use lists of potential participants supplied by the company sponsoring the research project, a screening company that specializes in focus group interviewing, or a direct mail list company. Other methods are piggyback focus groups, on-location interviews, snowball sampling, random telephone screening, and placing ads in newspapers and on bulletin boards. Regardless of the method used to obtain the names of prospective participants, the key to qualifying a person is the screening form. A sample telephone screening form is shown in Exhibit 6.11. This form illustrates the format, key information questions, and screening instructions.

EXHIBIT 6.10 Guidelines for the Selection of Focus Group Participants[11]

Factors	Guidelines
Specify exact selection criteria	Interacting with the decision maker, the researcher needs to identify, as precisely as possible, the desired characteristics of the group members.
Maintain control of the selection	The researcher must maintain control of the selection process. A screening mechanism that contains the key demographic or socioeconomic characteristics must be developed and used to ensure consistency in the selection process. In those situations where the researcher allows someone else to do the selection, precise instructions and training must be given to that individual.
Beware of potential selection bias	Selection bias tends to be overlooked by researchers and decision makers alike. Biases can develop in subtle ways and seriously erode the quality of the data collected. Beware of participants picked from memory, or because they expressed an interest or concerns about the topic, or because they are clones of the person doing the selection.
Incorporate randomization	Whenever possible, randomize the process. It will help ensure a nonbiased cross section of prospective participants. This will work only if the pool of respondents meets the established selection criteria.
Check respondents' knowledge	For any given topic, prospective participants may differ in knowledge and experience. Lack of experience and knowledge may directly affect respondents' abilities to engage in spontaneous topical discussions.
No selection process is perfect	Researchers have to make the best choices they can with the knowledge they have at the time of selection. The process may overlook certain aspects of the problem and inadvertently neglect individuals with unique points of view.

eXHIBIT 6.11 Telephone Screener to Recruit Focus Group Participants: Performing Arts Programs among Adults in Vail, Colorado*

Respondent's Name: ______________________ Date: ______________
Mailing Address: ______________________ Phone #: ______________
______________________ Cell #: ______________
(City) (State) (Zip Code) Fax #: ______________

Hello, my name is ______________, and I'm calling for the Marketing Resources Group in Tampa, Florida. We are conducting a short interesting survey in your area and would like to include your opinions. The Marketing Resources Group is conducting a study on performing arts programs offered in your metropolitan area and I would like to ask you a few questions. The questions will take less than two minutes. Let me begin by asking . . .

1. Do you or any member of your immediate household work for a research firm, an advertising agency, or a firm that produces or markets performing arts programs or events?
(__) Yes **[THANK THE PERSON AND TERMINATE AND TALLY]**
(__) No **[CONTINUE]**

2. Have you attended a performing arts event in the past month?
(__) Yes **[CONTINUE]**
(__) No **[THANK THE PERSON AND TERMINATE AND TALLY]**

3. Are you a permanent resident of Summit County?
(__) Yes **[CONTINUE]**
(__) No **[THANK THE PERSON AND TERMINATE AND TALLY]**

4. Are you currently employed full-time or part-time outside the home?
(__) Full-time **[CONTINUE]**
(__) Part-time **[THANK THE PERSON AND TERMINATE AND TALLY]**
(__) Not currently employed **[THANK THE PERSON AND TERMINATE AND TALLY]**

5. Please stop me when I come to the age category to which you belong.
(__) Under 20 **[THANK THE PERSON AND TERMINATE AND TALLY]**
(__) 21 to 35 **[RECRUIT AT LEAST 12]**
(__) 36 to 50 **[RECRUIT AT LEAST 12]**
(__) 51 to 65 **[RECRUIT AT LEAST 12]**
(__) Over 65 **[THANK THE PERSON AND TERMINATE AND TALLY]**

[PARTICIPANT RECRUITMENT PART—READ BY INTERVIEWER]

(Mr., Mrs., Ms.) **(Person's Last Name Here)**, the **Marketing Resources Group (MRG)** is sponsoring a meeting with people, like yourself, to discuss performing arts programs and events. We understand that **many people are busy yet enjoy attending performing arts events and have opinions about different topics concerning the arts.** We would like you to join a group of people, like yourself, to **discuss** and **get your opinions** about some performing arts topics. This **is not** a sales meeting, **but strictly a research project.** The group will meet on **Wednesday evening, August 15th, at the Vail Chamber of Commerce Office,** in downtown Vail. We would like you to be our guest. The **session will start promptly at 7:00 P.M.,** there will be refreshments, and the **session will be over by 9:30 P.M.** Those people **who participate will receive $100** as our token of appreciation for participating in this important discussion session. Will you be able to attend?

(__) Yes **[CONFIRM NAME, ADDRESS, PHONE/CELL, AND FAX NUMBERS]**
(__) No **[THANK THE PERSON AND TERMINATE AND TALLY]**

[If YES], I will be sending you a **letter and information packet in a few days confirming the meeting and your participation.**

If you have **any questions or need to cancel,** please telephone our office at **[GIVE OFFICE PHONE NUMBER].** On behalf of MRG, **thank you and have a pleasant (day or evening).**

**Author's note:* The items that absolutely must be included in a screening/recruitment form are in boldface type for identification purposes.

Sampling Procedures for Focus Groups. Sampling requires some special thought when planning focus group interviews. Traditionally, researchers try to randomize the process of identifying prospective subjects. While randomization is critical in quantitative surveys, it is not as necessary in qualitative studies. Focus groups tend to require a more flexible research design. While a degree of randomization is desirable, it is not the primary factor in selection. Participant credibility during the focus group discussions is a key factor researchers want to achieve. Randomization helps reduce the selection bias inherent in some forms of personal recruitment, but there is never total assurance.

Once a prospective participant is identified, contacted, and qualified for group membership, the task becomes one of obtaining that person's willingness to actually join the group. Securing the respondent's willingness to participate is not an easy process. The researcher invites the respondent to participate in the discussion of an interesting and important topic. There is no one best method of achieving this task, but there are some key factors that must be incorporated in the process. Only professionally trained people as recruiters with good interpersonal communication skills, as well as such characteristics as a positive, pleasant voice, a professional appearance, polite and friendly manners, and a "people-to-people" personality should be used. The recruiter needs to establish a comfort zone with the respondent as quickly as possible.

To bring legitimacy to the research project, the recruiter must communicate the general interest and importance of the topic, making it clear that because of the small group size participants' opinions and feelings are very important to the success of the project. It must be made clear that the group meeting is not a sales meeting, but strictly a research project. Other information factors include the date, starting/ending times, location of the focus group, the incentives for participating, and a method of contacting the recruiter if the prospective participant has any questions or problems concerning the meeting. Exhibit 6.11 shows an example of the recruitment part of a screening form for a focus group session.

After the respondent commits to participating in the focus group, researchers send out a formal confirmation/invitation letter that includes all the critical information about the focus group meeting. The main purpose of this type of letter is to reinforce the person's commitment to participate in the focus group. Exhibit 6.12 displays a hypothetical confirmation letter. The last activity in the recruiting process is that of calling the respondent the day before (or the morning of) the actual focus group session to further reinforce his or her commitment to participate in the session.

Size of the Focus Group. Most experts agree that the optimal number of participants in any type of focus group interview is from 8 to 12. Any size smaller than 8 participants is not likely to generate the right type of group dynamics or energy necessary for a beneficial group session. Too few participants create a situation where one or two people can dominate the discussion regardless of the efforts of the moderator. Also there is the increased probability of the moderator's having to become too active and talkative to keep the discussions flowing. In contrast, having too many participants can easily limit each person's opportunity to contribute insights and observations.

Another reason for the need for a wide range of members (8 to 12) is that it is difficult to predict just how many respondents will actually show up at the focus group session. It is not uncommon for 12 people to agree to participate but for only 8 to show up. Some researchers may try to hedge on actual response rates by inviting more people than necessary, in hopes that only the right number will show up. In cases where too many respondents show up, the researcher is forced to decide whether or not to send some home. The greatest fear of a focus group researcher is that no one will show up for the session, despite promises they will attend.

EXHIBIT 6.12 Sample of Confirmation/Invitation Letter*

[USE OFFICIAL LETTERHEAD]

[Date]

[Name of the Participant]
[Mailing Address]
[City, State, Zip]

Dear **[First Name of Participant]:**

Thank you for accepting our invitation to attend the discussion on Performing Arts Programs and Events at the Vail Chamber of Commerce Office in Vail, Colorado, on Wednesday evening, August 15. The Chamber of Commerce Office is **located** at 1240 Windsor Pine Drive in downtown Vail. For your convenience, **please find the enclosed map and specific directions to the Commerce Office,** if needed. We would like **you to be at** the office **between 6:45 P.M. and 7:00 P.M.;** the discussion session **will begin at 7:00 P.M.** There will be refreshments and the **session will end by 9:30 P.M.**

Since we are talking to a limited number of people, t**he success and quality** of the discussion **will be based on the cooperation and participation of the people who attend.** Your opinions and feelings are **very important, and attendance** at the session will help **make the research project a success.**

As mentioned during our earlier telephone conversation, the discussion will focus on several critical issues and topics concerning Performing Arts Programs and Events, and **we would like to get your opinions and feelings on these topics.** Your **candid thoughts on the topics** will be **very important to the success of the study.** Remember, this session is **strictly a research project,** and **no sales or solicitations** will be made. At the **conclusion** of the discussion session, we will be **giving you $100** to cover your expenses in attending. If necessary, child care will be provided.

If **by chance you find you are not able** to attend the session or **have any questions,** please call us to let us know **as soon as possible** at our office. That **phone number is (813) 974-6236.**

Again, on behalf of MRG I thank you for your willingness to participate in the study. I am looking forward to meeting you on August 15 and sharing your important thoughts and feelings on the performing arts topics and events.

Sincerely,

Thomas G. Smith
MRG Moderator

**Author's note:* All parts that are in boldface type are information that must be included in the letter.

Focus Group Incentives. While using screening forms, professionally trained recruiters, personalized invitations, and follow-up phone calls can help secure a person's willingness to participate, incentives are needed because participation requires both time and effort. Participants usually must reserve time out of a busy schedule and are likely to incur expenses such as for child care, travel, and meals. Finally, participants will typically spend time (between 90 minutes and two hours) in the actual session. In some cases the total time is three hours—two hours for the session and an additional hour for pre- and postinterviewing activities.[12] As a result group members need to be compensated for their "investments" associated with their willingness to participate.

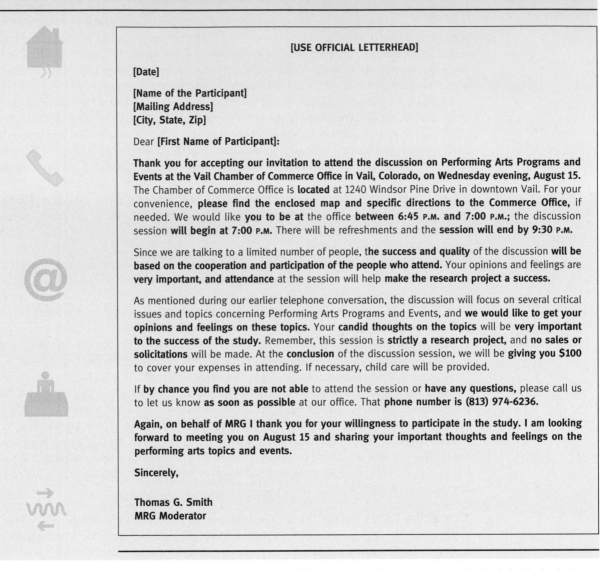

Incentives Monetary or nonmonetary compensation for an individual's willingness to participate in a focus group session.

The **incentive** should not be viewed as a reward or salary, but rather as a stimulus to get prospective participants to attend the scheduled session on time. Incentives help remind people that their commitment to participate is worth the effort, help them to keep the promised time slot from being preempted by other factors, and communicate to the participants that the discussion session is important. While different types of incentives have different effects on participation, money is the best incentive choice. The advantages of using money as an incentive are (1) it is immediately recognized and understood by the participants, (2) it is portable and fits into small spaces, (3) most people like to receive immediate cash, and (4) it has a proven track record of working. The dollar amount per participant will vary from project to project, mostly ranging between $75 and $200.

Number of Focus Group Sessions. Depending on the complexity of the issues to be discussed, one or more focus group sessions are held. "How many sessions should be conducted?" is an elusive question. There is no set standard. The number usually increases with the number of participant variables (age, geographic area) of interest. Many research issues can be covered with 4 to 8 groups. Use of more than 10 groups seldom uncovers new information on the same topic. Although some differences in opinion among participants are desirable because they facilitate conversation, participants should be separated into different groups when differences are likely to result in opinions being withheld or modified. For example, including top management with middle management in the same focus group can inhibit discussion. Similarly, multiple groups are used to obtain information from different market segments. Depending on the topic, desirable commonalities among participants may include occupation, education, income, age, or sex. A good rule of thumb is that there should be a minimum of two sessions and that sessions should continue until no more new ideas, thoughts, or feelings are offered by different groups of respondents.

Focus Group Locations. Focus groups can be held in the client's conference room, the moderator's home, a meeting room at a church or civic organization, or an office or hotel meeting room, to name a few. While all of the sites listed above are acceptable, in most instances the best location is a *professional focus group facility*. Such facilities provide specially designed rooms for conducting focus group interviews. Typically, the room has a large table and comfortable chairs for up to 13 people (12 participants and a moderator), a relaxing atmosphere, built-in recording equipment, and a one-way mirror so that researchers and the client can view and hear the discussions without being seen. Also available is videotaping equipment that captures the participants' nonverbal communication behaviors. Since a focus group session can last between 90 minutes and two hours, it is necessary to ensure that the setting is comfortable and conducive to spontaneous, unrestricted dialogue among all group members. A professional focus group facility usually adds to the overall data collection costs. Depending on which services are used, extra costs can range between $800 and $2,500 per focus group session.

Phase 2: Conducting the Focus Group Discussions

Focus group moderator A person who is well trained in the interpersonal communication skills and professional manners required for a focus group.

The Focus Group Moderator. The success of the actual focus group session depends heavily on the *moderator's* communication, interpersonal, probing, observation, and interpretive skills. The **focus group moderator** must be able not only to ask the right questions but also to stimulate and control the direction of the participants' discussions over a variety of predetermined topics. The moderator is responsible for creating positive group dynamics and a comfort zone between himself or herself and each group member as well as among the members themselves. The moderator needs interpersonal communication skills and professional manners to draw from the participants the best and most innovative ideas about the

EXHIBIT 6.13 Important Traits of a Focus Group Moderator

The following descriptions represent some of the important traits that a researcher must consider in the selection of an excellent moderator for the focus group session:

1. The person must be *well trained* in interpersonal communications and have excellent listening, observation, and interpretive skills.
2. The moderator must *display professional mannerisms* and *personality,* have a good memory for names, create positive group dynamics and a comfort zone for spontaneous and interactive dialogue.
3. The moderator must be *comfortable and familiar with group dynamics* and processes, and must be able to exercise mild, unobtrusive control over participants.
4. The moderator must have *good understanding and background knowledge* of the specified topics and questions and the ability to guide the participants from one topic to the next.
5. The person must be *well trained in asking follow-up probing questions,* and must demonstrate respect and sensitivity for the participants and their expressed opinions and feelings.
6. The moderator must be able to *communicate clearly and precisely both in writing and verbally,* and must be objective, self-disciplined, and focused.
7. The person should exhibit a *friendly, courteous, enthusiastic,* and *adaptive personality,* along with a *sense of humor.*
8. The person should be *experienced* in focus group research.
9. The moderator must have a *quick mind* capable of noting new ideas that come from the group.
10. The moderator must know *how and when to bring closure* to one topic and move the discussion to the next.

assigned topic or question through spontaneous interactive and detailed discussions. While there is no one set of traits that best describes the characteristics of a good group moderator, Exhibit 6.13 lists some of the traits used in selecting focus group moderators.

Moderator's guide A detailed outline of the topics, questions, and subquestions used by the moderator to lead the focus group session.

Preparing a Moderator's Guide. To ensure that the actual focus group session is productive, a moderator's guide must be prepared. A **moderator's guide** is a detailed outline of the topics and questions used to generate the spontaneous interactive dialogue among the participants. The nearby A Closer Look at Research (Small Business Implications) box shows a moderator's guide that was incorporated in the Vail Performing Arts example mentioned earlier. A moderator's guide uses a structured outline format—a sequence of opening, introductory, transition, substantive, and ending questions. *Opening questions* are answered quickly to identify characteristics participants have in common. They are typically factual and important in establishing the group's comfort zone and internal dynamics. *Introductory questions* introduce the first general topic of discussion and provide participants with the opportunity to reflect on past experiences and their connection with the overall topic. While these questions are not critical to the final analysis, they are important in creating spontaneous, interactive discussions. The main objective of transition questions is to direct the conversation toward the main topics of interest. *Transition questions* help participants view the topic in a broader scope and let them know how others feel about the topic. These questions are the logical link between introductory and substantive questions. From a context perspective, *substantive questions* drive the overall study. The moderator uses them to get to the heart of discussing the topic and critical issues. Finally, *ending questions* are used to bring closure to the discussion. They allow participants to reflect on previous comments and feelings, and they encourage members to summarize any final thoughts.

A Closer Look at Research

Moderator's Guide for Vail Performing Arts Program Focus Group Interview Sessions

I. INTRODUCTION

a. Welcome the participants.

b. Briefly highlight the focus group format . . . get consent forms signed and turned in (if necessary).

c. Explain ground rules for session:

No correct answers—only your opinions and feelings . . . you are speaking for other people like yourself . . . want to hear from everyone.

Briefly explain the audio taping of the session and why . . . so I don't have to take many notes. If necessary, mention the one-way mirror and that some of my associates are observing the session . . . because they are extremely interested in your opinions.

Only one speaks at a time . . . please no side discussions . . . I do not want to miss anyone's comments.

Do not worry if you do not know much about a particular topic we talk about . . . it is OK and important for me to know . . . if your views are different from someone else's that's all right . . . it is important for me to know that too . . . please do not be afraid of having different opinions, just express them . . . remember there is no one right answer.

This is an informal discussion . . . a research project, not a sales meeting . . . I will not be contacting you later on to try to sell you anything . . . I want you to be comfortable and relax . . . just express your opinions and feelings.

d. Any questions? [Answer all questions of participants.] Let's begin.

II. WARMUP [Use opening question format.]

Tell us your name and one or two things about yourself. [Ask this of each participant.] (Build group dynamics and comfort zone among group members.)

III. INTRODUCE FIRST TOPIC

[Use an introductory question format.]

"FROM YOUR VIEWPOINT, TO WHAT EXTENT DO YOU ENJOY ATTENDING PERFORMING ARTS PROGRAMS AND/OR ENTERTAINMENT EVENTS?"

Probe for:

a. Types of programs and events that have been attended in the past and would attend in the future.

b. Types of programs and events most preferred to see offered in the Vail Valley area.

[Use transition question format to move to next topic.]

IV. SECOND MAJOR TOPIC

[Use a critical question format.]

Now I want you to think about how people make their decisions to attend performing arts events.

"WHAT PERFORMING ARTS/ ENTERTAINMENT FEATURES DO PEOPLE DEEM IMPORTANT IN DECIDING TO ATTEND A PROGRAM OR EVENT?"

Probe for:

a. Detail and clarification of features.

b. Understanding of importance of identified features. [Use transition question format to move to the next topic.]

V. SPECIFIC DESIGN FEATURES

[Use a critical question format.]

Now think about the facilities used to present performing arts programs and events.

"WHAT FACTORS SHOULD BE INCLUDED IN FACILITY STRUCTURE DESIGN?"

Probe for:

a. Specific design features and why.

b. Thoughts and feelings about indoor versus outdoor event capabilities.

c. Types of protection features for outdoor events for the audience, the performers.

[Use transition question format to move to closure of session.]

Small Business Implications

Continued

A Closer Look at Research

Continued

VI. CLOSE SESSION WITH SUGGESTIONS AND FINAL THOUGHTS [Use ending question format.]
"TAKING INTO CONSIDERATION OUR DISCUSSIONS, WHAT SPECIFIC ACTIONS WOULD YOU SUGGEST OR RECOMMEND TO THE DESIGN TEAM TO HELP MAKE VAIL'S NEW PERFORMING ARTS FACILITY THE BEST POSSIBLE?"
Probe for clarity of specific ideas and details as to why.
Features:
___ structure designs
___ seating requirements
___ theater style vs. auditorium style
___ quality of sound system/ acoustics
___ outdoor event protection features

"ANY LAST THOUGHTS, FEELINGS, OR COMMENTS?"
[Ask and probe for each participant.]

VII. END THE FOCUS SESSION
a. Thank the participants for their cooperation and input.
b. Give each participant his or her gift of appreciation.
c. Extend a warm wish to drive home carefully.

Beginning the Focus Group Session. As the participants arrive for the session, the moderator warmly greets them and gives them name cards. Prior to seating the participants, the moderator uses his or her observation skills to notice how well group members interact and talk with one another. For example, if the moderator can identify dominant talkers and shy listeners, this can be used to place members strategically around the table. After the participants sit down, there should be an opportunity (about 10 minutes) for sociable small talk, coupled with refreshments. The purpose of these pre-session activities is to create a friendly, warm, comfortable environment in which participants feel at ease. The moderator briefly discusses the ground rules for the session. Participants are told that only one person should speak at a time, everyone's opinion is valued, and there are no wrong answers. If consent forms are required, participants sign them and give them to the moderator before the session begins. If a one-way mirror or audio/video equipment is being used, the moderator informs participants they are being taped and that the clients are sitting behind the one-way mirror. Sometimes group members are asked to introduce themselves with a few short remarks. This approach breaks the ice, gets each participant to talk, and continues the process of building positive group dynamics and comfort zones. After completing the ground rules and introductions, the moderator asks the first question using an opening question format. This question is designed to engage all participants in the discussion.

Main Session. Using the moderator's guide, the first topic area is introduced to the participants. The first topic should be interesting and easy to talk about. As the discussion unfolds, the moderator uses probing techniques to gain as many details as possible. If there is a good rapport between group members and the moderator, little time is spent on merely asking selected questions and receiving answers. In a well-run focus group, participants interact and comment on each other's answers. There are no hard-and-fast rules on how long the discussion should last on any one particular topic. The moderator uses his or her judgment in deciding when to bring closure to one topic and move on to the next. In general, the session should move toward the study's critical questions at a pace that ensures enough time for deep probing of as many ideas and opinions as possible.

Closing the Session. After all of the prespecified topics have been covered, participants should be asked a closing question that encourages them to express final ideas or opinions. The moderator may present a final overview of the discussion and then ask the participants, "Have we missed anything?" or "Do you think we've missed anything in the discussion?" Responses to closing questions may reveal some thoughts that were not anticipated. Also the moderator should observe the body language of the participants for signs of agreement, disagreement, hesitation, or confusion. Upon final closure, participants should be given a short debriefing of the session, thanked for participating, given the promised incentive gift or cash, and wished a safe journey home.

Phase 3: Analyzing and Reporting the Results

Debriefing analysis An interactive procedure in which the researcher and moderator discuss the subjects' responses to the topics that outlined the focus group session.

Debriefing. The researchers, the moderator, and the sponsoring client's representatives should conduct a debriefing and wrap-up activities as soon as possible after the focus group members leave the session. **Debriefing analysis** gives the researchers, clients, and moderator a chance to compare notes. The other individuals who have heard the discussions need to know how their impressions compare to those of the moderator. In this type of analysis, insights and perceptions are expressed concerning the major ideas, suggestions, thoughts, and feelings from the session.

One beneficial outcome from debriefing is uncovering ways for improving the session that can be useful in future focus group sessions. For example, strong points can be identified and emphasized, and errors noted, while they are fresh in everyone's mind. Sometimes debriefing analysis (1) provides an opportunity to include the opinions of marketing experts with those of the moderator; (2) allows the sponsoring client's representatives or researcher to learn, understand, and react to the moderator's top-of-mind perceptions about what was said in the group discussion; and (3) can offer opportunities for brainstorming new ideas and implications of the main points expressed in the discussion. In contrast, potential shortcomings of debriefing include (1) a clear possibility of creating interpretive bias; (2) faulty recall on the part of the moderator due to recency or limited memory capabilities; and (3) misconceptions due to lack of time for reflecting on what was actually said by the participants.[13]

Content analysis A systematic procedure of taking individual responses and grouping them into larger theme categories or patterns.

Content Analysis. Qualitative researchers use content analysis to create meaningful findings from focus group discussions. **Content analysis** requires the researchers to systematically review transcripts of individual responses and categorize them into larger thematic categories or patterns. Although first "topline" reactions are shared during debriefing, more formalized analysis will reveal greater detail and identify themes and relationships that were not remembered and discussed during debriefing. Exhibit 6.14 displays some of interpretive factors researchers use in analyzing focus group data. Qualitative data analysis procedures are discussed in greater detail in the next chapter.

Reporting Focus Group Results. In reporting the findings, researchers must understand the audience, the purpose of the report, and the expected format. For example, researchers must have a strong understanding of the people who will be using the results, their preferences in receiving information, and their demographic profile, including

EXHIBIT 6.14 Interpretive Factors in Analyzing Focus Groups Data[14]

Interpretive Factors	Description and Comments
Consider the words	Thought must be given to both the words used by the participants and the meanings of those words. Because there will be a variety of words and phrases used by the group members, the researcher will have to determine the degree of similarity and classify them accordingly. It should be remembered that editing messy quotations is a difficult but necessary task.
Consider the context	The researcher will have to gain an understanding of the context in which participants expressed key words and phrases. The context includes the actual words as well as their tone and intensity (voice inflection). It must be remembered that nonverbal communication (body language) can also provide meaningful bits of data worth analyzing.
Consider the frequency of comments	In most situations, some of the topics presented in the session will be discussed more (extensiveness) and some comments made more often (frequency) than others. However, the researcher should not assume that extensiveness and frequency of comments are directly related to their importance.
Consider the intensity of comments	Sometimes group members will talk about specific aspects of a topic with passion or deep feelings. While left undetected in transcripts alone, the intensity factor can be uncovered in audio- or videotapes by changes in voice tone, talking speed, and emphasis placed on certain words or phrases.
Consider the specificity of responses	Those responses that are associated with some emotional first-hand experience probably are more intense than responses that are vague and impersonal. For example, "I feel that the new McDonald's McArch burger is a rip-off because I ate one and it tasted just terrible, especially at the price they are charging" should be given more weight than "The new McArch burger does not taste very good, considering what it costs."
Consider the big picture	Because data from focus groups come in many different forms (words, body language, intensity, etc.), the researcher needs to construct an aggregate theme or message of what is being portrayed. Painting a bigger picture of what group members are actually saying can provide preliminary insights into how consumers view the specified product, service, or program. Caution should be used when trying to quantify the data. Use of numbers can inappropriately convey the impression that the results can be projected to a target population, which is not within the capabilities of qualitative data.

educational level, occupation, and age, to name only a few. Overall, the report should stress clarity, demonstrate understanding, and support the findings. In many cases, the writing style is informal and the vocabulary familiar. Typically active rather than passive voice expressions are used, incorporating quotations, illustrations, and examples where appropriate.

The report is guided by the basic purpose of conducting the research. First, the report needs to *communicate useful insights* and *information* to the audience. It should be a *clear and precise presentation* tailored to the specific user's information needs. It must offer a *logical sequence of findings, insights, and recommendations*. The report is a historical record that likely will be reviewed at some point in the future.

EXHIBIT 6.15 Components of a Written Focus Group Research Report[15]

Components	Description and Comments
Cover page	The front cover should include the title, the names of people receiving or commissioning the report, the names of the researchers, and the date the report is submitted.
Executive summary	A brief, well-written executive summary should describe why the focus group session was conducted and list the major insights and recommendations. It should be limited to two pages and be able to stand alone.
Table of contents	This section provides the reader with information on how the report is organized and where various parts can be located. (It is optional for short reports.)
Statement of the problem, questions, methods	This section describes the purpose of the study and includes a brief description of the focus interviews, critical questions, the number of focus group sessions, the methods of selecting participants, and the number of people included in each session.
Results and findings	The results are most often organized by critical questions or overall ideas. The results can be presented in a number of ways using bulleted lists or narrative formats, listing raw data, summarizing the discussion, or using an interpretative approach.
Summary of themes	Statements in this section are not limited to specific questions but rather connect several questions into a larger picture.
Limitations and alternative explanations	This section can be placed within the results section, if it is brief. Limitations reflect those aspects of the study that reduce the application of the findings or affect different interpretations of the findings.
Recommendations	This optional section is not automatically included in all focus group reports. The recommendations suggest what might be done with the results.
Appendix	The appendix should include any additional materials that might be helpful to the reader. Most often a copy of the moderator's guide, screening form, or other relevant material would go into the appendix.

Format of the Report. The focus group report is typically presented in a narrative style that uses complete sentences supported by direct quotes from the group discussion. An alternative style is to use an outline format supported with bulleted statements that use key words or phrases to highlight the critical points from the group discussion. Regardless of the style, the report must be written in a clear, logical fashion and must look professional. Although there is no one best format, Exhibit 6.15 describes the essential components of a typical report.

Advantages of Focus Group Interviews

There are five major advantages to using focus group interviews: They (1) stimulate new ideas, thoughts, and feelings about a topic; (2) foster understanding of why people act or how they behave in certain market situations; (3) allow client participation; (4) elicit wide-ranging participant responses; and (5) can bring together hard-to-reach subject groups.

New Ideas. The spontaneous, unrestricted interaction among focus group participants can stimulate new ideas, thoughts, and feelings that may not be raised in one-on-one interviews. There is a high likelihood that participants will offer creative opinions about a subject topic. Participants are more at ease in expressing their candid opinions than in a one-on-one situation with an interviewer. The spontaneous, interactive environment encourages participants to freely engage in group creativity that induces a "snowballing" process where additional responses are triggered by someone else's comments.

Underlying Reasons for Behavior. Using focus groups, researchers collect detailed data about the underlying reasons people act as they do in different market situations. A trained moderator directs the discussions that reveal why participants hold certain beliefs or feel the way they do about particular discussion topics such as the product's attributes, service components, brand images, or particular marketing practices, to name a few.

Client Participation. Decision makers (the clients) have the opportunity to be involved in the overall process from start to finish. Clients have an interactive role in creating the research objectives and setting the focus group's overall agenda and initial research questions. The energetic atmosphere during the actual sessions enables the client's representatives and researchers to observe first-hand (from behind a one-way mirror) the group dynamics and how participants respond to information on the topics and questions of interest. This participation leads to impressions and results that suggest specific marketing actions. In some cases, clients formulate and begin action plans based on their observations even before the data are analyzed and submitted as a final report.

Breadth of Topics Covered. Focus group interviews can range over an unlimited number of topics and management issues as well as very diverse groups of subjects (children, teenagers, senior citizens). Sessions can incorporate prototypes of new products to be demonstrated or advertising copy being evaluated. In addition, other types of projective data collection methods could be included (for example, balloon tests, role-playing activities, word association tests, picture tests) to stimulate spontaneous discussions of a topic. Recent technology has added new flexibility to the process by allowing clients located in different geographic regions to participate in and observe the live sessions without having to be at the specific facility location.

Special Market Segments. Focus groups offer a unique ability to bring together groups of individuals, such as doctors, lawyers, and engineers, to name a few, who might not otherwise be willing to participate in a study. The format allows these hard-to-interview individuals an opportunity to interact with their peers and compare thoughts and feelings on common topics and issues of interest.

Disadvantages of Focus Group Interviews

As with any exploratory research design, focus group interviews are not a perfect data collection method. The major weaknesses are inherently similar to all qualitative methods: the findings lack generalizability to the target population, the reliability of the data is limited, the trustworthiness of the interpretation is based on the care and insightfulness of researchers, and there are high dollar costs connected with focus group data.

Inability to Generalize Results. Focus group interviews lack representativeness with regard to the target population. This makes it difficult for researchers to generalize the results to larger market segments. For example, Procter & Gamble's brand manager of Crest toothpaste as well as the researcher might run substantial risks in believing that the attitudes and feelings toward a new formula change in the product obtained from 12 Crest users in a focus group are truly representative of the typical attitudes and feelings of the millions of Crest users in the market.

Questions of Data Reliability. In addition to having to deal with extremely small sample sizes, the semistructured nature of the data (nominal nature of the verbalized comments and nonverbal body language) precludes analyzing the results in standard statistical formats (e.g., percentage and mean values). Adding to this weakness is the possibility that some degree of the well-known "Hawthorne effect" has impacted the data collected from the participants—that is, the focus group process can easily create an environment that makes some of the participants think they are "special" and act accordingly when offering their comments.

Moderator interaction bias is another potential problem. Because of the social dynamics and interaction between participants and the moderator, the moderator must guard against behaving in ways that might prejudice participants' responses. For example, a moderator who is aggressive (or confrontational) could systematically lead participants to say whatever they think the moderator wants to hear. On the other hand, a moderator's attempt to play dumb or be too supportive of participants' comments might create a false atmosphere and cause some respondents to draw back and stop making comments. While difficult to measure, these conditions may reduce the reliability of the data.

Subjectivity of Interpretations. Given the subjective nature of the data collected, the researchers or the clients can misinterpret the data. For example, if the clients enter the focus group process with preconceived ideas of what will emerge from a focus group, they often can find something in the data (the participants' comments) that can be subjectively interpreted as being supportive of those predetermined views while ignoring any opposing data. Again, there is always the possibility of moderator interpretation bias, which can quickly reduce the credibility and trustworthiness of the information being provided to marketing decision makers.

High Cost per Participant. The costs of identifying, recruiting, and compensating focus group participants along with the costs of the moderator(s) and facilities are overall quite high (ranging from $3,000 to $8,000 per session), resulting in a cost-per-participant average of between $300 and $800 (assuming the data came from 10 participants). This dollar average per participant is significantly greater than the cost of other qualitative methods.

Despite their limitations, focus groups are popular not only in the United States, but also globally. The nearby Global Insights box describes focus group research practices in other countries and compares them with those in the United States.

Impact of New Technologies on Focus Group Research

Online focus group
A focus group that is conducted in an online setting.

With growing advances in Internet, multimedia, and telecommunication technologies, **online focus groups** are becoming more widely used. With this approach, a special group of service application providers (SAPs), not marketing researchers, have successfully integrated many of the benefits of the high-speed computer and telecommunication technologies into focus group research. For example, interactive marketing technologies (IMTs)

GLOBAL INSIGHTS

Understanding Focus Group Research Abroad[16]

As more companies enter the global market, there is an increasing need for qualitative research information, both to help assess the demand for items and to identify the optimal way of marketing in foreign countries. Many U.S. companies are expanding their use of focus group research to their overseas markets. There are some major differences in doing focus groups outside the United States and Canada, according to Thomas L. Greenbaum, President of Groups Plus, Inc. One cannot simply take the same materials used to conduct focus groups in the United States and send them to a research organization in a foreign country and expect to get comparable, or even reliable, results. The following insights are offered within seven key components of focus group research:

1. **Time frame.** Whereas many companies are accustomed to developing a project on Monday and having it completed by the end of the following week, this is almost impossible to do in foreign countries. Lead times tend to be much longer, with the Far East being particularly troublesome. If it takes two weeks to set up groups in the United States, figure almost double that in most of Europe and even more than that in Asia.
2. **Structure.** Eight to 10 people in a group is a large number for most foreign groups, which often consist of 4 to 6 people, our minigroup. Further, the length of sessions outside the United States can be up to four hours. Be very specific when arranging for international focus groups. Most foreign research organizations seem to adapt well to our format if properly informed and supervised.
3. **Recruiting and rescreening.** In general, the United States is much more rigid in adhering to specifications both in recruiting and screening. These processes must be monitored very carefully.
4. **Approach.** Foreign moderators tend to be much less structured and authoritative, which can result in a great deal of downtime during the sessions. Also they tend to use fewer writing exercises and external stimuli such as concept boards and photos. This must be considered when planning foreign sessions.
5. **Project length.** Projects can take much longer to execute. In the United States, we are accustomed to doing two, sometimes three or four, groups a day, but in many overseas markets, one group is the limit because of the time they are scheduled, the length of the sessions, or the demands of the moderators. Also, some moderators have a break in the middle of the group, which would be very unusual in U.S. sessions.
6. **Facilities.** The facility environment outside the United States and Canada is much like the setup here 20 years ago. For example, it is more common than not to watch a group in a residential setting on a television which is connected to the group room by cable. Many of the facilities with one-way mirror capabilities simply do not have the amenities we are accustomed to in the United States.
7. **Costs.** Finally, the cost of conducting focus group research varies considerably by region and country. It would not be unusual to pay almost twice as much per group for sessions conducted in Europe and almost three times as much for many areas in Asia.

In light of these differences, it is important that companies take action to ensure that they get the results needed from foreign research. Greenbaum suggests having the international research managed by the same people who run the U.S. studies or use a U.S.-based foreign research company that can be a central point of contact and will handle the details abroad. So if you are going to conduct qualitative research outside the United States, spend the extra time and money, and do it right. It will be a small investment over the long term.

facilitate conducting telephone, video, and Internet focus group interviews through such formats as teleconference networks. TeleSessions, FocusVision Networks, and itracks Internet software use videoconferencing and online Internet systems to complete focus groups.[17] Research firms like Market Opinion Research (MOR), FocusVision Worldwide,

Inc., Interactive Tracking Systems, Inc. (hppt://www.itracks.com), and others offer interactive focus group research systems that allow customization to any business's needs, whether they involve testing new TV ads or product or advertising concepts, or observing consumers' reactions to words, phrases, or visuals.[18]

The rapid expansion and improvements of Internet technologies are driving how, what, when, where, and how fast qualitative data are collected, analyzed and disseminated to researchers and decision makers. High-speed Internet-assisted approaches are making it easier to reach today's hard-to-reach subjects and are shortening the time cycle in completing focus group research projects, while allowing decision makers to interact with the process in real time.[19] In turn, these technology-driven online approaches for conducting focus groups and videoconferencing have increased the costs of collecting qualitative data, at least in the short run.

Online versus Offline Focus Group Research

Debate remains on whether the future of focus group research will be online or offline methods (traditional focus group practices as discussed earlier in this chapter). For now, it is important to understand the driving forces behind new online practices. The push is coming not from marketing researchers, but rather from the new breed of specialized focus group data collection facilities. Once limited to providing researchers with a professional taping facility for conducting focus group sessions, these service providers are shortening the data acquisition, analysis, and reporting activities of focus groups through the integration of high-speed technologies. Decision makers have embraced the real-time dimension and flexibility these service providers offer.

Overall, the processes, guidelines, and decisions required in the "planning" and "execution" stages of an online focus group session are, for the most part, the same as for conducting a traditional offline focus group session. Both methods require that the decision maker and researcher fully understand the nature of focus group interviews and together develop the focus group objectives. Identifying the appropriate type of people for inclusion in the focus group, the sampling, selection, and recruitment of the prospective participants, and the critical decisions concerning size and number of focus groups, incentives, and location remain a joint undertaking by the researcher and decision maker.

It is during the actual focus group session that differences begin to appear. For example, the data-capturing activities during the focus group session are much more sophisticated for online than offline methods, requiring online moderators to have a greater technological aptitude and understanding of the devices used to gather the data in real time. Online sessions provide significantly greater flexibility to client participation before, during, and after the session. Offline traditional methods enable the client's representatives to be at the focus group session, located behind a one-way mirror, and communication capabilities with the moderator are limited and rather antiquated (moderator headset, handwritten notes, or specified breaks in the session). On the other hand, online methods use advanced communication technologies that enable clients to directly participate from anywhere in the world; all they need is a computer and Internet access. A disadvantage is that in certain forms of online group interviews (chat room discussions, bulletin boards, newsgroups, discussion lists), the lack of face-to-face interaction makes obtaining nonverbal communication clues and body language information impossible. However, the lack of face-to-face exposure may make online participants feel more comfortable in giving more candid responses than in an offline group interview. In online methods (excluding those that use some form of face-to-face interactions), incentives needed to recruit participants are typically cheaper or less extensive than the incentives needed to secure participants in offline group interviews.

The greatest differences between the two methods are in the last phase of the process (analyzing and reporting of the results). Online focus group interviewing facilitates data manipulation, retrieval, and reporting of the qualitative data results in real time, whereas offline methods typically take researchers days, if not weeks, to manipulate and understand the data and report the findings to decision makers. For more insights into new online focus group research practices visit the book's Web site at www.mhhe.com/hair4e.

Other Qualitative Research Methods

Case Studies

Case study An exploratory research technique that intensively investigates one or several existing situations similar to the current problem/opportunity situation.

Case studies are exploratory research designs that involve intense investigation of one or a few past problem situations that are viewed as being similar to the researcher's current problem situation. The premise underlying the case study approach is that for any current research issue there are probably several past situations that have some very similar elements. The case study approach requires the researcher or decision maker to conduct an in-depth examination of the element of interest. The specific element can be a customer, salesperson, store, firm, market area, and so forth. This approach of gathering data is best when researchers need to obtain substantial detail about the issue or when they do not know exactly what they are looking for or are trying to find important clues and ideas concerning a current research problem.

Very often success in using the case study method is a function of the investigator's ability to use common sense and imagination during the data gathering process. Typical objectives of the case study method are to: (1) identify relevant variables, (2) indicate the nature and order of the existing relationships between the variables, and (3) identify the nature of the problem and/or opportunity present in the original decision. The overall goal is to develop a comprehensive description of the issues leading to a better understanding of the current problem situation and the potential impact of the interacting elements. Read the nearby Global Insights box to learn how one medium-size U.S firm researched the situation before it went into the Japanese commercial market.

Experience Interviews

Experience interview A face-to-face questioning technique to gather opinions from people considered to be knowledgeable on the issues of the research problem.

Experience interviews gather opinions and insights informally from people considered to be knowledgeable on the issues associated with the research problem. For example, if the research problem involves difficulties in purchasing books online from Amazon.com, then researchers would identify and interview dissatisfied online Amazon purchasers, or if Procter & Gamble has concerns dealing with estimating future demand for its new Web site, "Consumer Corner" (http://www.consumercorner.com), the company could obtain helpful insights by contacting several Web site experts and asking their opinions on the issues. Experience interviews differ from other types of interviewing approaches in that there is no attempt to ensure that the findings are representative of any overall defined group of subjects. Yet the findings may still prove very useful. To illustrate this point, let's take an instructor at your institution who is teaching a marketing research course for the first time. The fundamental research problem here simply deals with which topics should be covered in what detail within a specified time frame. The instructor could contact several other people who have experience in teaching a marketing research course and ask their opinions about topics and depth of coverage. Although these "experts" may provide useful information, there is a high likelihood their opinions and suggestions would differ from the collective opinions of all people who have experience teaching marketing research.

GLOBAL INSIGHTS

Custom Doors, Inc., Enters the Japanese Commercial Market

Custom Doors, Inc., a medium-size commercial building-grade door manufacturer located in central Illinois, wanted to expand its market to include commercial businesses in Japan but was unaware of the key factors necessary to be successful. The executives at Custom Doors researched several of the leading Japanese construction companies using their annual financial reports and available information on their distribution systems. They also had detailed discussions with several of their own current material suppliers that had experience in Japanese commercial markets as well as interviews with two architects at one of the largest Japanese architectural firms in Tokyo. As a result of their in-depth analysis of the information obtained, management gained a better understanding of the key elements for landing Japanese ventures. The key elements focused on the company's ability to (1) secure high quality raw materials, (2) produce commercial doors that met very strict product specifications, (3) be adaptable with design changes, and (4) make assurances on the delivery of the final product on time. As a consequence of their successful research, Customer Doors, Inc. (1) developed strong relationships with four U.S.-based suppliers that guaranteed the needed high quality raw material, (2) spent about $2 million to purchase laser-guided manufacturing equipment for improving their ability to meet product specifications, (3) developed a system for handling short notice architectural specification changes, and (4) contracted with a Japanese-based delivery company. Today, Custom Doors, Inc., has expanded its annual commercial door business to about $12 million just within the Japanese market.

Protocol Interviews

Protocol interview
A data collection technique that places a person in a specific decision-making situation and asks him or her to verbalize how to make the decision.

Protocol interviewing places a person in a specified decision-making situation and asks the person to verbally express the process and activities that are considered in making a decision. This method is useful when the research problem focuses on selected aspects (motivational or procedural) of making a purchase decision. For example, suppose Dell Computer Company wants to understand the difficulties associated with the various decision criteria customers use when making online purchases of Dell PCs. By asking several Dell PC purchasers to verbalize the steps and activities they went through, the researcher is able to work backwards and identify the different processes used in making online purchase decisions. This can provide the researcher with insights and understanding of those motivational and/or procedural activities that might be potential obstacles keeping other potential customers from making an online purchase from Dell.

Articulative Interviews

Articulative interview
A face-to-face questioning technique for listening for and identifying key conflicts in a person's orientation values toward products and services.

Articulative interviews are qualitative group interviews that focus on listening for and identifying key conflicts in a person's orientation values toward products and services. This method gets participants to articulate their orienting values as well as their inherent conflicts with those values that otherwise might seem inexpressible. An articulative interview is structured to elicit narratives as opposed to gaining factual truths. The interview focuses on uncovering what respondents find worthy and unworthy in their lives, how they live in particular roles and in certain domains of activity. The type of questioning requires respondents to express narrative responses which incorporate a past-present-future structure of the topic of concern. During the story-telling process, the interviewer raises questions about the parts of the story that were left out and tends to bring out expressions of conflict. By questioning their narrative context, respondents are encouraged to describe how the ideas they hold are in conflict, resulting in seemingly insoluble dilemmas.

When conducting articulative interviews, researchers must be able to achieve two goals: identify the respondents' orienting values toward the product or service being investigated; and clarify existing value conflicts. To identify these orienting values, researchers must be able to: (1) question the obvious and listen for differences, (2) study the present, (3) know the past, and (4) learn the descriptive vocabulary used by the respondents. For example, researchers interviewing parents from different cultures and economic classes about the values they taught to their children initially found that most parents universally expressed "I want what is best for my children. And that is that they 'do well' in life." By questioning the obvious, it was learned that among parents in middle-class Mexican culture, "doing well" meant visibly achieving the next economic class status, but in low-income Mexican culture, "doing well" meant the children would have their own home without regard to whether it came by good fortune or hard work. As a result, the researchers were able to identify significantly different shadings of "doing well."[20]

In order to expose a respondent's value conflicts, researchers must be able to (1) listen for confusion, awkwardness, resignations, and contradictions among the subjects, (2) listen for invidious distinctions and self-righteous expressions, (3) identify the roles the subject plays in relation to the product or service category, and (4) elicit defining narratives of life changes. To illustrate, researchers studied female college graduates regarding their orienting value of "being taken seriously." When asked to reflect back as undergraduate students, many of the respondents thought their future careers would mean everything to them. Being taken seriously meant doing anything to get ahead in a career. But after entering the workforce, a new value arose, that of being able to live a balanced, good quality life. For most this meant having a family, engaging in healthy physical activities, taking vacations, as well as being a "serious" person. To better understand the changing meaning of "being taken seriously" and the conflicts of living a "quality life," researchers used follow-up questions such as "Where do you see your professional life moving in the future?" "What do you wish you could keep from the old way of being serious?" "How does having a family fit in?" and "How do you view yourself in comparison to your mother?"

Ethnography

Ethnography A form of qualitative data collection that records behavior in natural settings to understand how social and cultural influences affect individuals' behaviors and experiences.

Participant observation An ethnographic research technique that involves extended observation of behavior in natural settings in order to fully experience cultural or subcultural contexts.

Most qualitative methods do not allow researchers to actually see consumers in their natural setting. But ethnography is increasingly being used to help researchers better understand how cultural trends influence consumer choices. Ethnography is a distinct form of qualitative data collection that seeks to understand how social and cultural influences affect people's behavior and experiences. **Ethnography** records behavior in natural settings, often involves extended experience in a cultural or subcultural context, called **participant observation,** produces accounts of behaviors that are credible to the persons who are studied, and involves triangulation among multiple sources of data.[21] For example, one ethnographic study of skydiving employed multiple methods, using observation of two skydiving sites over a two-year period, participant observation by one researcher who made over 700 dives during the research, and in-depth interviews with skydiving participants with varying levels of experience.[22]

There is no one given set of data collection tools used in ethnography. Participant observation is often used because observers can uncover insights by being part of a culture or subculture that informants cannot always articulate in interviews. However, some research questions do not require participant involvement to provide answers to questions. In

Nonparticipant observation An ethnographic research technique that involves extended contact with a natural setting, but without participation by the researcher.

nonparticipant observation, the researcher observes without entering into events. For example, Whirlpool's corporate anthropologist, Donna Romero, conducted a study for a line of luxury-jetted bathtubs. She interviewed 15 families in their homes and videotaped participants as they soaked in bathing suits. Last, Romero asked participants to create a journal of images that included personal and magazine photos. From her research, Romero concluded that bathing is a "transformative experience . . . it's like getting in touch with the divine for 15 minutes."[23]

Netnography

Netnography A research technique that draws on ethnography but uses "found data" on the Internet that is produced by virtual communities.

Netnography draws on ethnographic techniques. The difference is that netnography uses "found data" on the Internet that is produced by virtual communities. Online communities are often organized around interests in industries, products, brands, sports teams, or music groups, for instance. Moreover, these communities often contain fanatic consumers who are "lead users" or innovators. The data occurs naturally and is thus not affected by the researcher who collects the data. Rob Kozinets, who developed Netnography, used the technique to study an online community of coffeephiles. Kozinets concluded that the devotion to coffee among the members of <alt.coffee> was almost religious: "Coffee is emotional, human, deeply and personally relevant—and not to be 'commodified' . . . or treated as just another product."[24]

In Netnography, researchers must (1) gain entry into the culture/community, (2) gather and analyze data, (3) ensure trustworthy interpretation, and (4) provide opportunities for feedback from members of the community (see Chapter 7 for interpretation and analysis of qualitative data). Before gaining entry, researchers must develop research questions and use search to identify online forums that will provide the answers to their research questions. Generally, researchers prefer to collect data from higher traffic forums with larger numbers of discrete message posters and greater between-member interactions.[25]

Projective Interviewing Methods

Projective method An indirect method of questioning that enables a subject to project beliefs and feelings onto a third party, into a task situation, or onto an inanimate object.

Projective methods constitute a "family" of qualitative data collection methods. Some of the methods have respondents project themselves into specified buying situations, then are asked questions about the situations. The main objective is to learn more about the respondents in situations where they might not reveal their true thoughts in a direct questioning process. Yet other projective methods use indirect questioning to encourage participants to freely project beliefs and feelings into a situation or stimulus provided by the researcher. Participants are asked to talk about what "other people" would feel, think or do; interpret or produce pictures; or project themselves into an ambiguous situation. Indirect questioning methods are designed to more nearly reveal a participant's true thoughts than direct questioning approaches which often tend to prompt people to give rational, conscious, and socially desirable responses.

Projective methods were developed by clinical psychologists and can be used in conjunction with focus groups or in-depth interviews. These techniques include word association tests, sentence completion tests, picture tests, the thematic appreciation test (TAT), cartoon or balloon tests, role-playing activities, and the Zaltman Metaphor Elicitation Technique (ZMET). The stimuli should be ambiguous enough to invite individual participant interpretation, but still specific enough to be associated with the topic of interest.

Word association test A projective technique in which the subject is presented with a list of words or short phrases, one at a time, and asked to respond with the first thoughts or word that comes to mind.

Word Association Tests.

In a **word association test,** a participant is read a preselected set of words, one at a time, and asked to respond with the first thing that comes to her or his mind regarding that word. For example, what comes to your mind when you hear the word

EXHIBIT 6.16 From the Mouths of Teens

Word/Phrase	Definition	Used in a Sentence
"Be easy"	Relax, calm down	"Yo, son, be easy. Sit down."
"Jump off"	Hot: really happening	"That party is the jump off."
"Mad" or "Madd"	A lot: very	"This shirt is mad cool."
"Shorty"	A girl	"She's my shorty."
"Cheesin'"	Smiling broadly	"Yo. That chick is cheesin'."

Source: The Discovery Group and *American Demographics,* May 2003.

"red"? Some people might respond with hot; others might either say danger, apple, stop, fire truck, or Santa Claus. After completing the list of words, researchers then look for hidden meanings and associations between the responses and the words being tested on the original list. Advertising researchers employ word association tests in efforts to develop meaningful ad copy that a target market can quickly identify with the message. For example, a research company like the Discovery Group, a New England–based youth firm, uses word association techniques to find out the latest slang words or phrases peculiar to East Coast kids 11 to 17 years of age. Exhibit 6.16 illustrates some of the new words and phrases most popular in teen-speaking today. Marketers and advertisers can gain better insight into how to communicate more effectively to teens by understanding the latest teen lexicons.

Sentence completion test A projective technique where subjects are given a set of incomplete sentences and asked to complete them in their own words.

Sentence Completion Tests. In **sentence completion tests,** respondents are presented with a set of incomplete sentences and asked to complete them in their own words. When successful, sentence completion tests reveal hidden aspects of individuals' thoughts and feelings toward the object studied. From the data collected, researchers interpret the completed sentences to identify meaningful themes or concepts. For example, let's say the local Chili's restaurant in your area wants to find out what modifications to its current image are needed to attract a larger portion of the college student market segment. Researchers could interview college students in the area and ask them to complete the following sentences:

People who eat at Chili's are ______________________________.

Chili's reminds me of ______________________________.

Chili's is the place to be when ______________________________.

College students go to Chili's to ______________________________.

My friends think Chili's is ______________________________.

After collecting the completed sentences, the researcher separately identifies different themes from the data provided from each question. Then the data from all the sentences are integrated together to reveal overall themes that might prove more useful in creating a dining experience likely to attract significantly more college students. For example, an interpretation of the data from the first sentence might reveal the theme of "older, more mature restaurant patrons," suggesting that serious changes would be needed to attract those college students not interested in spending their dining experience in a restaurant setting where mature people eat. The theme for the second sentence might be "family-oriented," suggesting that Chili's is perceived as an eating establishment where there are a lot of small children, not appealing to many college students. The next sentence might support a theme of "great place to take a date," indicating college students think of Chili's as a place to eat dinner when out on a date. Data from the next sentence might suggest the theme of "a place to hang out with friends and watch sporting events." Here, it would be important for the restaurant to make sure its advertisements convey this theme to college students. The final sentence might generate data that support the theme "fun atmosphere," indicating that students like going to Chili's when they want to have fun. Now combining the information, Chili's management will know the college market perceives the restaurant as being an enjoyable place to meet friends, watch sporting events, and have dinner with a date, but a place that is too family oriented and caters to noncollege patrons.

Picture test A qualitative interviewing method where the subjects are given a picture and instructed to describe their reactions by writing a short narrative story about the picture.

Picture Tests. In a **picture test,** respondents are given a picture and instructed to describe their reactions by writing a short narrative story about the picture. Researchers interpret the content of the written stories to identify the respondents' positive, neutral, or negative feelings or concerns generated by the picture. This method is very useful to ad agencies testing the impact of pictures for use on product packaging, print advertisements, and brochures. For example, a test print advertisement for a Virgin Mobile Cell Phone designed to possibly attract more college student consumers depicted a fogged up back window of a car with the ad headline written on the window that said, "Hello Lovers: get a Hot Virgin Mobile cell phone for as low as $59." A picture test may divulge some aspects about the ad that are negative or not believable. Perhaps some college students might not make the connection because they do not have a significant other or they just went through a tough relationship breakup. In turn, the picture may be perceived as not having much relevance to college students or the $59 rate as not being a bargain or not generating the types of feelings toward staying connected as intended by Virgin Mobile's ad agency. Regardless of the stories communicated by the respondents, without the picture test it would be difficult for management at Virgin Mobile to determine the audience's reactions to the ad.

Thematic apperception test (TAT) A specific projective technique that presents the subjects with a series of pictures and asks them to provide a description of or a story about the pictures.

Thematic Apperception Test (TAT). Similar to, yet different from, the picture test is the **Thematic Apperception Test (TAT).** Instead of asking the participant to write a short story about what a single picture is communicating, the TAT method presents a series of pictures where the consumer and/or products/services are the main focus in each picture. Typically there is some level of continuity among the pictures. Participants are asked to provide their descriptive interpretation of what is happening in the pictures or a story about the pictures and what the people might do next. Researchers then conduct a content analysis of the descriptions and stories. The goal is to create interpretable themes based on the descriptions or stories attached to the pictures.

One of the keys in using TAT is that pictures or cartoon stimuli must be sufficiently interesting to the participants to induce discussions, yet ambiguous enough not to give away the nature of the research project. It is important that hints not be given to the picture characters' positive or negative predispositions. For example, a designer clothing manufacturer wanting to test the potential of a new pair of jeans having a positive appeal to female college students might use TAT by showing selected females a set of pictures with the first one portraying three college-age females at the local department store discussing the jeans. The second picture might show one of the females getting dressed in the jeans, and the final picture may have a female dancing in the jeans at a party. After viewing the pictures, participants are asked to provide their interpretation of what is going on in each picture. Researchers then do a content analysis of the descriptions or stories to uncover latent themes that might represent either positive or negative elements of the jeans. While TATs are fun to do, the complexity factor of the picture or stimuli used can cause difficulties in analysis. Insights gained from TAT research can prove useful in better understanding elements used in product design, packaging, print advertisements, and brochures.

Cartoon (balloon) test A qualitative data collection method in which the subject is given a cartoon drawing and suggests the dialogue in which the character(s) might engage.

Cartoon or Balloon Tests. A **cartoon (balloon) test** involves the use of cartoons similar to those in your local newspaper. Typically, one or two characters are arranged in a setting, sometimes predescribed and other times ambiguous. Typically the characters are presented in a vague manner, without expression, to ensure the respondent is not given any clues regarding a suggested type of response. Researchers place an empty balloon above one or both of the characters and instruct respondents to write in the balloon(s) what they believe the character(s) are saying. Then researchers interpret these written thoughts to identify the respondent's latent feelings about the situation being portrayed in the cartoon. For example, when shown a cartoon situation of a male and female character in a pet store in which the female is making the statement, "Here is a multilevel cat condo on sale for $165," the respondents are asked how the male character in the drawing would respond and asked to write their thoughts in the balloon above the male character. After the response is provided, researchers then use their interpretive skills to evaluate the respondents' reactions.

Role-playing interview Subject is asked to act out someone else's behavior in a specified setting.

Role-Playing Interviews. In **role-playing interviews,** participants are asked to take on the identity of a third person, such as a neighbor or friend, placed into a specific, predetermined situation, and then asked to verbalize how they would act in the situation. In other cases where the research interest lies in how participants would respond to a specific statement, rather than asking directly what they think, the statement is phrased in terms of "your neighbors" or "most people" or another third-party format. For example, rather than asking a person why she does not use the Internet more frequently to purchase online consumer products for her home, researchers would ask, "Why don't many people use the Internet more often to purchase online consumer products for their home?"

ZMET (Zaltman Metaphor Elicitation Technique) A visual research technique used in in-depth interviewing that encourages research participants to share emotional and subconscious reactions to a particular topic.

Projective hypothesis The belief that a good deal of thoughts and emotions are processed in images and metaphors rather than just words.

Zaltman Metaphor Elicitation Technique (ZMET). The **Zaltman Metaphor Elicitation Technique (ZMET)** is the first marketing research tool to be patented in the United States. It is based on the **projective hypothesis** which holds that a good deal of thought, especially thought with emotional content, is processed in images and metaphors rather than words.[26] In contrast to the visual method used in the ZMET, both surveys and focus groups, the most widely used techniques in marketing research, rely heavily on verbal stimuli. Gerald Zaltman of Olson Zaltman Associates explains that "consumers can't tell you what they think because they just don't know. Their deepest thoughts, the ones that account for their behavior in the marketplace, are unconscious [and] . . . primarily visual."[27]

Several steps are followed in the ZMET. When recruited, participants are told the topic of the study, for example, Coke. Participants are asked to spend a week collecting 10–15 pictures or images that describe their reaction to the topic (in this case, Coke) and to bring the pictures to their interview. Each participant is asked to compare and contrast pictures and to explain what else might be in the picture if the frame were to be widened. Then, participants construct a "mini-movie" which strings together the images they have been discussing and describes how they feel about Coke, the topic of interest. At the end of the interview, participants create a "digital image" which is a summary image of their feelings. When the ZMET was used to study Coke, the company discovered something they already knew—that the drink evokes feelings of invigoration and sociability. But it also found something they did not know—that the drink could bring about feelings of calm solitude and relaxation. This paradoxical view of Coke was highlighted in an ad that showed a Buddhist monk meditating in a crowded soccer field, an image taken from an actual ZMET interview.[28]

Continuing Case: Santa Fe Grill Mexican Restaurant

Recently the owners of the Santa Fe Grill hired an experienced restaurant industry consultant. After an initial consultation, the consultant recommended two areas that needed to be examined. The first area focused on the restaurant's operations. The proposed variables to be investigated included:

- Prices being charged.
- Menu items being offered.
- Interior decorations and atmosphere.
- Average dollar amount spent per customer.

The second area to be studied was to learn more about what factors the Santa Fe Grill customers considered in selecting a restaurant at which to dine. Variables to be examined included:

- Food quality.
- Food variety.
- Servers and other restaurant employees.
- Pricing.
- Atmosphere.
- Dining out habits.
- Customer characteristics.

Using your knowledge and understanding of exploratory research methods, address the following two questions:

1. Do the two research projects proposed by the consultant include all the areas that need to be researched? If yes, why? If no, which others need to be studied and why?
2. Can these topics be fully understood with qualitative data research methods? Why or why not? Or is quantitative research needed as well? Why or why not?

Overview of Observation Methods

Observation methods The tools researchers use to collect primary data about human behavior and marketing phenomena.

Observation methods are tools researchers can use to collect primary data about human behavior and marketing phenomena regardless of the nature of research designs, whether exploratory, descriptive, or causal. The primary characteristic of observation methods is that researchers must rely on their *observation skills* rather than using respondents' reports of their behavior. Researchers watch and record what people (or objects) do rather than relying on them to report their behaviors. A great deal of information about the behavior of people and objects can be observed: *physical actions* (consumers' shopping patterns or automobile driving habits), *expressive behaviors* (tone of voice and facial expressions), *verbal behavior* (phone conversations), *temporal behavior patterns* (amount of time spent online shopping or at a particular Web site), *spatial relationships and locations* (number of vehicles that move through a traffic light or movements of people at a theme park), *physical objects* (which brand name items are purchased at supermarkets or which make/model SUVs are driven), and so on. Observation data can be added to data collected using other research designs by providing direct evidence about individuals' actions.

Observation The systematic activities of witnessing and recording the behavioral patterns of objects, people, and events without directly communicating with them.

Observation involves systematic watching and recording of the behavioral patterns of objects, people, events, and other phenomena. Observation methods require two elements: a behavior or event that is observable and a system of recording it. Behavior patterns are recorded using trained human observers or devices such as cameras, audiotapes, computers, handwritten notes, or some other recording mechanism. Traditionally, observation was considered predominantly a qualitative data collection method. But since the emergence of the Internet and related digital technology, much observation research can be considered quantitative. For example, observation of click-stream behavior online is clearly a quantitative approach to research.

The main weakness of observation methods is they cannot be used to obtain information on attitudes, preferences, beliefs, emotions, or similar internal information. Researchers see *what* people do, but not *why* they do it. Some research efforts combine observation with other methods to overcome this particular limitation. One example of a combined methodological approach is **usability studies.** Moderators give participants activities to complete at a Web site, and then talk with them about any problems they are having in completing their task.

Usability study A study that combines observation and interviewing in which a moderator gives participants activities to complete at a Web site, and then talks with them about any problems they are having in completing their task.

Appropriate Conditions for Using Observation Techniques

Several conditions are required for the successful use of observation. Research objectives must specify that some event or behavior is to be observed. For the most part, the event or behavior must be repetitive, frequent, and relatively predictable. Finally, the behavior typically takes place in some type of public setting that enables the researcher to observe the behavior directly.

Information Condition

Collecting current-behavior data using any other method might lessen the data's accuracy and meaningfulness due to respondents' faulty recall. For example, people might not accurately recall the number of times they zap commercials while watching their favorite one-hour TV program on Monday nights. New technology available and used by research companies like AC Nielsen Media Research can capture commercial zapping behavior among those members of its Nielsen Television Index (NTI) consumer panel groups.

Type-of-Data Condition

If researchers want to know *why* an individual purchased one brand of cereal over the other brands available, observation techniques will not provide the answers. Thus, observation is used only when a respondent's feelings are relatively unimportant to the research objective or believed to be readily inferable from the behavior. For example, in studying children playing with toys, it is possible to use facial expressions as an indicator of a child's attitudes or preferences toward the toys because children often react with conspicuous physical expressions. However, this type of observation method means the observer must have excellent interpretive skills.

Time-Frame Condition

For observation methods to be feasible, the behaviors or events being observed need to happen within a relatively short time span. This means behaviors or events must be repetitive and frequent. For example, attempting to observe all the activities involved in the process of buying a new home or automobile would not be feasible in terms of data collection costs and time. In turn, behaviors associated with someone purchasing food items in a supermarket, people waiting in line inside a bank, or children watching a TV program could lend themselves to observation methods.

Setting

Activities are limited to those investigators can readily observe first-hand or through a device such as a video camera. Typically, activities such as private worshiping or using inhome products (products used when cooking, turning up and down air conditioning controls, or washing clothes) are not readily observable. It is important to recognize that the four observational conditions apply to capturing *current* events/ behaviors. These conditions do not apply when researchers are interested in collecting data on past events. Some experts suggest that indirect observations can be used to accurately infer past behaviors or events. What researchers normally observe in those situations is some type of artifact (a videotape or audiotape, a written transcript).[29] These artifacts are often like secondary data. The main emphasis would be on interpreting the reported outcomes and making preliminary inductive statements about the actual behavior.

Unique Characteristics of Observation Techniques

Observation can be described in term of four characteristics: (1) directness, (2) awareness, (3) structure, and (4) type of observing/recording mechanism. These characteristics directly influence the framework for conducting the observations. With good designs, researchers can eliminate, or at least control for, methodological problems that could prevent the gathering of consistent and generalizable data. Exhibit 6.17 is an overview of the characteristics of observation techniques and their impact.

Directness of Observation

Direct observation The process of observing actual behaviors or events and recording them as they occur.

Direct observation is the process of observing actual behavior, activities, or events and recording them as they occur.[30] Direct observations use either trained human observers or mechanical/electronic devices. For example, researchers interested in conducting a field experiment to find out how often people read tabloid magazines while waiting to check out at a supermarket could use several different direct observation methods.

EXHIBIT 6.17 Unique Characteristics of Observation

Characteristic	Description
Directness	The degree to which the researcher or trained observer actually observes the behavior/event as it occurs. Observation can be either direct or indirect.
Awareness	The degree to which individuals consciously know their behavior is being observed and recorded. Observation can be either disguised or undisguised.
Structure	The degree to which the behavior, activities, or events to be observed are known to the researcher before doing the observations. Observation can be either structured or unstructured.
Observing mechanism	How the behavior, activities, or events are observed and recorded. Alternatives include trained human observers and mechanical or electronic devices.

Indirect observation The process of directly observing the recorded artifacts of past behaviors.

Some experts believe that indirect observation techniques can be used to capture and understand individuals' past behaviors in certain situations.[31] **Indirect observation** uses methods to observe the artifacts that represent behaviors from earlier time periods. One can argue that this direct observing of artifacts of past human behavior is really nothing more than a trained investigator interpreting a form of secondary data. While indirect observations provide researchers with insight into past behaviors, those insights should be viewed cautiously. For example, management of Tech Data, a company that sells computer systems worldwide, can review and interpret the company's telephone logs to find out how many long-distance telephone calls its sales department made during the previous month. After interpreting the logs, management might make general inferences concerning the impact of cold-calling behaviors between highly productive salespeople and less productive salespeople. Secondary sources that record past behavior are referred to as archives, physical audits, or traces.[32] These artifacts represent tangible evidence of some past event. For example, a retail chain looking to expand its operations to new locations might directly observe the amount of graffiti on existing buildings around proposed locations to estimate the potential crime factor in those areas.

Subjects' Awareness

Awareness The degree to which subjects consciously know their behavior is being observed and recorded.

Disguised observation A data collection technique where the subjects of interest are completely unaware that they are being observed.

Mystery shopper technique A technique in which trained, professional shoppers visit stores, financial institutions, or companies and "shop" for various products and assess service quality factors or levels.

Awareness refers to the degree to which subjects consciously know their behavior is being observed and recorded. When the subjects are completely unaware they are being observed, the observation method is termed **disguised observation.** A popular example of disguised observation is the **mystery shopper technique** used by many retailers.[33] For example, Wal-Mart periodically hires a research firm to send in observers disguised as ordinary shoppers to observe how well the stores' employees and staff interact with customers. The observers look for interpersonal behaviors that demonstrate attributes like friendliness, courtesy, helpfulness, and store/product knowledge. The information gained helps management in determining how its employees' interpersonal skills can enhance the customers' overall shopping experience. Additionally, Wal-Mart uses other methods (one-way mirrors and hidden cameras) to prevent its employees from finding out they are being observed. Disguised observations are used because when people know they are being watched, they naturally tend to modify their normal behavior, resulting in atypical behaviors. Case in point, how would Wal-Mart's sales associates act if they were told they were going to be watched for the next several hours? Most likely the associates would be on their best behavior for that time period.

New consumer right-to-privacy legislation limits the use of disguised observing methods. Federal laws restrict the conditions for which disguised methods can be used by requiring the approval of the individual. For example, 28 states currently have "stalking" laws while another 16 states have pending laws that make it a crime to track people unknowingly.

There are situations in which it is impossible to keep the individuals from knowing they are being observed, for example, observing the interpersonal behavior of a new waiter or waitress with customers at a restaurant like T.G.I.F. in Washington, D.C., or textbook sales representatives' behavior with faculty members on sales calls. Similarly, AC Nielsen Media Research would find it difficult to use its audiometers on in-home TV sets without individuals' knowledge. Whenever people are aware they are being watched, the process is termed **undisguised observation.** Researchers should minimize the presence of the observer to avoid the possibility of atypical behavior by subjects.

Undisguised observation Data recording method where the subjects are aware that they are being watched.

Structure of Observation

Structure refers to the degree to which the behaviors or events are known to the researcher prior to the observation. When researchers know which behaviors or events are to be

Structured observation The degree to which behaviors or events are specifically known prior to observing them.

recorded, a **structured observation** method is most appropriate. With this method, trained observers look for specific prespecified behaviors and ignore all others. Checklist or standardized recording forms are used to help observers restrict their attention to just those prespecified behaviors or events.

For example, the produce manager at a local Safeway supermarket was deciding whether to prepackage the tomatoes or display them individually. He was concerned about the extent to which customers handle and squeeze the tomatoes in selecting which ones to buy. Using a structured observation, he assigned a store employee to hang out in the produce department and observe 100 customers as they selected tomatoes. The employee simply focused on the following behaviors: number of times individual tomatoes were picked up and handled; number of times prepackaged tomatoes were picked up and handled; and any noticeable squeezing of individual and prepackaged tomatoes. The tallied results showed that 75 percent of the observed customers picked up and handled the individual tomatoes, while only 35 percent picked up and handled the prepackaged ones. Also, 55 percent of those observed actually squeezed the individual tomatoes, while only 40 percent did the same to the prepackaged ones. Even though individual tomatoes got handled and squeezed more frequently, the produce manager felt uncomfortable going to the store manager suggesting that all tomatoes should be prepackaged to reduce spoilage. Eventually the decision involved increasing prepackaging by a certain amount. Think about what other behaviors should have been recorded to make this decision.

Unstructured observation Data recording format that does not place any restrictions on the observer regarding what behaviors or events should be recorded.

On the other hand, **unstructured observation** methods place no restrictions on the observer regarding what should be recorded. Typically, all behaviors, activities, and events are observed and recorded. When using unstructured observation, researchers brief the trained observers on the research objectives and information requirements and then allow them to use their own discretion in determining what behaviors are actually recorded. For example, the director of parks and recreation in Tampa, Florida, developed a proposal for renovating several of the city's aging parks. Not sure what type of equipment should be included in the renovations, he sent out two park supervisors to observe people using the facilities at several of the city's most popular parks. The collected data were useful not only in redesigning the aging parks but also in providing ideas about how to make the parks safer for people.

Type of Observing Mechanism

Observation mechanism Any nonhuman device used to observe and record current behaviors or events.

Observation mechanism relates to how the behaviors or events will be observed/recorded. Researchers can choose between human observers and mechanical or electronic devices. With human observation, observers are either people hired and trained by the researcher or members of the research team. To be effective, observers must have a good understanding of the research objectives and strong observation and subjective interpretive skills. For example, the professor of a marketing research course can use observation skills to capture not only students' classroom behavior but also nonverbal communication symbols exhibited by students during class (facial expressions, body postures, movement in chairs, hand gestures), which allows him or her to determine, in real time, if students are paying attention to what is being discussed, when students become confused about a concept, or if boredom begins to set in.

Mechanical/electronic observation Data collection using some type of mechanical device to capture human behavior, events, or marketing phenomena.

In many situations the use of a mechanical or electronic device is more suitable than a person in collecting the primary data. **Mechanical/electronic observation** uses a mechanical or electronic device to capture human behavior, events, or marketing phenomena. Devices commonly used include video cameras, traffic counters, optical scanners, eye tracking monitors, pupilometers, audio voice pitch analyzers, and psychogalvanometers.

The devices often reduce the cost and improve the flexibility and accuracy of data collection. For example, when the Department of Transportation (DOT) conducts traffic-flow studies, air pressure lines are laid across the road and connected to a counter box that is activated every time a vehicle's tires roll over the lines. Although the data are limited to the number of vehicles passing by within a specified time span, this method is less costly and more accurate than using human observers to record traffic flows. Other examples of situations where mechanical/electronic observations are appropriate include using security cameras at ATM locations to detect problems that customers might have in operating the ATM, optical scanners and bar-code technology (which relies upon universal product code or UPC) to count, in real time, the number and types of products purchased at a retail establishment, turnstile meters to count the number of fans at major sporting or entertainment events, and placing "cookies" on computers to track Internet usage behavior (click-stream analysis).

Advances in Internet, telecommunication, and computer technologies are making electronic observation more useful and cost-effective for monitoring human behaviors and marketing phenomena.[34] For example, AC Nielsen upgraded its U.S. Television Index (NTI) system by integrating its People Meter technology into the NTI system. The **People Meter** is a technology-driven TV rating system that replaces handwritten diaries electronic measuring devices. When the TV is turned on, a symbol appears on the screen to remind viewers to indicate who is watching the program using a handheld electronic device similar to a TV remote control. Another device attached to the TV automatically sends prespecified information (for example, viewer's age, gender, program tuned to, time of program) to Nielsen's computers. Data are used to generate overnight ratings for shows as well as demographic profiles of the audiences for various shows.

People Meter A technology-driven TV rating and data collection system.

Another technology-driven element is new software used to monitor people's interactive behavior with Internet Web sites. Companies such as itracks, FocusVision Worldwide, Inc., HarrisInteractive, and Burke have developed new tracking software that monitors participants' interactive Web site behavior including clicking of multiple pages, page by page, as well as the paths or sequence of pages visitors follow as well as tracking the popularity of participating Web sites and online Internet providers such as Google, America Online, Yahoo!, and MSN.

Additionally, advanced scanner technology, a type of electronic observation, is rapidly replacing traditional consumer purchase diary methods. **Scanner-based panels** involve groups of participating households that are assigned unique bar-coded cards that are presented to the clerk at the checkout register. The household's code number is matched with information obtained from scanner transactions during a defined time period. Scanner systems enable researchers to observe and develop a purchase behavior database on each household. Researchers also can combine offline tracking information with online-generated information for households providing more complete customer profiles. Studies that integrate online and offline data can show, for instance, if panel members exposed to an online ad or Web site made an offline purchase after the exposure. Scanner data provide marketers with week-by-week information on how products are doing in individual stores and track sales against price changes and local ads or promotion activities. Scanner technology is also used to observe and collect data from the general population. Market research companies work with drug stores, supermarkets, and other types of retail stores to collect data at checkout counters. The data include products purchased, time of day, day of week, and so forth. Data on advertising campaigns as well as in-store promotions are integrated with the purchase data to determine effectiveness of various marketing strategies.

Scanner-based panel A group of participating households that have a unique bar-coded card as an identification characteristic for inclusion in the research study.

Perhaps the fastest growing observation approach is tracking *click-stream behavior* on the Internet. Online merchants, content sites, and search engines all collect information about online behavior. These companies maintain databases with customer profiles and can predict probable response rates to ads, the time of day and day of week the ads are likely to be most effective, the various stages of potential buyers in the consideration process for a particular product or service, and the type and level of engagement with a Web site.

Mechanical Devices for Measuring Physiological Actions and Reactions. Traditionally, there are a variety of mechanical observations used to evaluate consumers' physical and physiological reactions to various stimuli such as ad copy, packaging, and new products. Researchers use technology-based devices to record actions and reactions that participants are unaware of or unwilling to provide honest responses about in regard to the effects of the stimulus being studied. There are four categories of mechanical observation devices used to measure physiological reactions: voice pitch analyzers, pupilometers, eye tracking monitors, and psychogalvanometers.

Voice pitch analyzer A computer system that measures emotional responses by changes in the subject's voice.

The **voice pitch analyzer** is a computer-based system that measures emotional responses by changes in the participant's voice. Sophisticated audio-adapted computers are used to detect abnormal frequencies in the participant's voice caused by changes in the person's autonomic nervous system. It is similar to a lie detector test, but the participant is not hooked up to a lot of wires. Computerized analysis compares the participant's voice pitch patterns during a warm-up session (benchmarked as the normal range) to those patterns obtained from the recorded verbal responses to a given stimulus such as a TV commercial.

Pupilometer A mechanical instrument that observes and records changes in the diameter of a subject's pupils.

The **pupilometer** mechanically observes and records changes in the diameter of a participant's pupils. The individual views a screen on which the stimulus is projected. As the distance and brightness of the stimulus to the participant's eyes are held constant, changes in pupil sizes are recorded and are interpreted as some type of unobservable cognitive activity. The assumption underlying the data produced by a pupilometer is that increases in pupil size within a controlled environment reflect a positive attitude or interest in the stimulus.

Eye tracking monitor A mechanical device that observes and records a person's unconscious eye movements.

The **eye tracking monitor** observes and records a person's unconscious eye movements. Invisible infrared light beams record the participant's eye movements while reading or viewing the stimulus (magazine ad, TV commercial, package design) and a video camera records what part of the given stimulus is being viewed at the movement. Then the two databases are overlaid for determining what parts of the stimulus were seen and which components were overlooked. In advertising, this type of data can provide insights to possible points of interest and impacts to selling points.

Psychogalvanometer An electronic instrument that measures changes in a subject's involuntary electronic skin resistance, also referred to as the galvanic skin response (GSR).

The **psychogalvanometer** measures a participant's involuntary changes in electronic skin resistance, referred to as the galvanic skin response (GSR). This observation method indicates when the person's emotional arousal or tension level changes toward the stimulus. Any recorded changes are presumed to be the result of the presence of the stimulus.

While these mechanical observation methods are interesting, they are based on the unproven assumption that physiological actions and reactions are predictors of people's thoughts or emotions. There is no theoretical consensus that this assumption is valid. Moreover, the accuracy of the measurements obtained from these observation methods remains questionable, and required technology is expensive. Also, external validity remains an issue because these types of physiological observations require that participants be brought into controlled artificial laboratory environments, which do not represent reality.

Selecting the Appropriate Observation Method

As mentioned earlier, determining the most appropriate type of observation method for collecting primary data requires researchers to integrate their knowledge and understanding of the research objectives, information requirements, conditions for using observations, and characteristics of observation methods.

The first step in determining the observation method is to understand the information requirements and consider how that information will be used later on. Without this understanding, selecting the observation method is significantly more difficult. First, researchers must answer the following questions:

1. What types of behaviors are relevant to the research problem?
2. How simple or complex are the behaviors?
3. How much detail of the behavior needs to be recorded?
4. What is the most appropriate setting, natural or artificial?

Then the various methods for observing behaviors must be evaluated. Issues to be considered include:

1. How *complex* is the required public setting?
2. Is a setting *available* to observe the behaviors or events?
3. To what extent are the behaviors or events *repetitious* and *frequently exhibited*?
4. What degrees of *directness* and *structure* are needed to observe the behaviors or events?
5. How *aware* should the subjects be that their behaviors are being observed?
6. Are the observable behaviors or events complex enough to require the use of a mechanical/electronic device for observing the behavior? If so, which specific method would be most appropriate?

Researchers can now determine the proposed method's ability to accurately observe and record the behavior or activity. The costs involved—time, money, and manpower—also must be determined and evaluated. Finally, potential ethical issues associated with the proposed observation method must be considered. See the nearby Ethics box, which discusses ethical issues associated with observation methods.

Benefits and Limitations of Observation Methods

Observation methods have strengths and weaknesses, as summarized in Exhibit 6.18. A major benefit is that observation methods enable researchers to capture actual behavior, events, and/or activities rather than reported ones. This is especially true in situations where individuals are observed in a natural setting using a disguised technique. In situations

EXHIBIT 6.18 Benefits and Limitations of Observation Techniques

Benefits of Observation	Limitations of Observation
Accuracy of actual behavior	Difficult to generalize findings
Reduces biases found in other data	Cannot explain behaviors, events, collection methods, or activities unless combined with other methods
Provides detailed behavioral data	Problems in setting up and recording behavior(s), events, and/or activities

ETHICS

Minimizing Bias in Research Designs

Subjects' Unawareness Can Raise Many Questions

Subjects' awareness of observation methods raises some ethical questions worth noting. When using observations to collect primary behavior data, should the subjects be informed that they are being observed? If so, what changes in their natural behavior might occur? Remember, the researcher wants to capture the subjects' natural behavior as it actually occurs and relates to the specified situation. Subjects being observed might feel uncomfortable about their true behavior or actions and try to behave in a more socially acceptable manner. For example, a marketing professor at a university is told by his department chair that as part of his annual performance review, an outside observer will be in class Monday to observe the professor's teaching style. How likely will the professor be to modify his "normal" classroom behavior for that Monday's class session to make doubly sure his effectiveness meets or exceeds the standards? Would you behave in a more socially acceptable manner if you knew someone was going to be observing you? In disguised observations, the researcher uses some degree of deceit in order to observe behavior without the subjects' knowledge. In this situation, the ethical questions focus on the subjects' right to privacy. Are there certain public or private behaviors that are protected by U.S. law? Is spying on people an acceptable norm of our society? These are tough but pertinent questions that a researcher must address prior to conducting research with observational techniques, and there are no easy, clear-cut answers. In part, ethical issues surrounding the use of disguised techniques might be related to whether or not the investigated behaviors are legal versus illegal. However, beyond that, questions of ethics may confront the researcher as well.

where the behaviors or events are complex and unstructured, mechanical/electronic observation methods such as video cameras or traffic counters are useful. In addition, observation methods reduce recall error, response bias, and refusal to participate, as well as interviewer/observer errors. Finally, data can be collected in less time and at a lower cost than through other types of procedures.

One of the inherent limitations of observation methods is that they produce data that are difficult to generalize beyond the individuals who were actually observed. For example, observation methods are used in research projects that focus on a small number of subjects (between 5 and 60) under unique or special circumstances, thus reducing the representativeness to larger groups of people.[35] The nature of observation makes it extremely difficult for researchers to logically explain *why* the observed behaviors or events took place. Not being able to question the individuals on their attitudes, motives, feelings, and other nonobservable factors restricts researchers to applying subjective "educated guesses" to understand observed behaviors, events, and/or activities.

In cases where the natural setting includes a large number of subjects, it is difficult for even trained observers to note all the activities occurring at the same time. For example, while the observer is focused on the behavior of one particular subject, she or he is likely to completely miss the behavior of the other subjects in the setting during that same time frame. Disguised observation methods pose an additional limitation in that human observers cannot instantaneously or automatically record the behavior activities as they occur. There is some amount of lag time between observing the behavior or event and recording what was observed. With this lag time, there is the possibility of faulty recall on the part of the observer. One way to overcome these potential limitations is to make the observations with mechanical/electronic devices, when possible.

MARKETING RESEARCH IN ACTION

Content Analysis

The Future of For-Profit Higher Education

As over 74 million Gen Yers reach college age and beyond, surging demand for higher education is forcing state universities and community colleges to cap enrollment. For-profit institutions have stepped in to fill the growing need.

The following dialogue is part of an in-depth interview on higher education and where it is heading recently conducted by *American Demographics* reporter Sandra Yin with Sean Gallagher, senior analyst with Eduventures, a consulting firm in Boston that serves the education industry. The dialogue relates only to the for-profit higher education portion of the topic.

AD: How much will for-profit higher education grow over the next five years?
SG: It is forecasted that total growth from 2005 to 2010 will be about 91 percent based on current growth in enrollment and increases in pricing.
AD: What factors will contribute to this continued growth?
SG: The growth drivers vary. One is the demographic bulge of Gen Y. Another is that more people recognize the economic value of a degree. Also, what formerly could be learned through on-the-job training may now require a degree. For example, one might need an associate degree to do specific kinds of health care work. Because of automation and computers, vocational disciplines like auto repair have become more technical than ever.
AD: What distinguishes for-profit schools from the nonprofits?
SG: They are managed as businesses, with all profits coming from tuition. Program offerings are aligned with the demand and employers' needs as well as convenience, accessibility, and flexible scheduling of courses. For-profits often centralize the development of their curriculum and syndicate it throughout their campuses.

Hands-On Exercise

1. Conduct a "content analysis" of Sean Gallagher's responses to the in-depth interview questions posed by Sandra Yin of *American Demographics* and identify main themes. Be sure you include support for each of the themes you identify.
2. Given the specific topic of the above interview, what other questions might have been asked to create a richer database? (Review Exhibit 6.14.)
3. What specific conclusions about the themes of the interview data, if any, can you draw from your analysis of the above transcript? Any limitations to what you can conclude?

Summary of Learning Objectives

■ **Identify the major differences between qualitative and quantitative research.**

In business problem situations where secondary information alone cannot answer management's questions, primary data must be collected and transformed into usable information. Researchers can choose between two general types of data collection methods: qualitative or quantitative. There are many differences between these two approaches with respect to their research objectives and goals, type of research, type of questions, time of execution, generalizability to target populations, type of analysis, and researcher skill requirements.

Qualitative methods may be used to generate exploratory, preliminary insights into decision problems or address complex consumer motivations that may be difficult to study with quantitative research. Qualitative methods are also useful to understanding the impact of culture or subculture on consumer decision making and for probing unconscious or hidden motivations that are not easy to access using quantitative research. Qualitative researchers collect detailed amounts of data from relatively small samples by questioning or observing what people do and say. These methods require that researchers be well trained in interpersonal communication, observation, and interpretation. Data typically are collected using open-ended or semistructured questioning formats that allow for probing attitudes or behavior patterns or human/mechanical/electrical observation techniques for current behaviors or events. In Netnography, qualitative researchers analyze text and images produced in online communities. While qualitative data can be collected quickly (except in ethnography), it requires good interpretive skills to transform data into useful findings. The small nonrandom samples that are typically used in qualitative research make generalization to a larger population of interest questionable.

In contrast, quantitative or survey research methods place heavy emphasis on using formalized, structured questioning practices where the response options have been predetermined by the researcher. These questions tend to be administered to large numbers of respondents. Quantitative methods are directly related to descriptive and causal types of research projects where the objectives are either to make more accurate predictions about relationships between market factors and behaviors or to validate the existence of relationships. Quantitative researchers are well trained in scale measurement, questionnaire design, sampling, and statistical data analyses.

■ **Describe the pros and cons of using qualitative data collection techniques.**

The main advantages of qualitative data collection methods include the economy and timeliness of data collection; richness of the data; accuracy of recording marketplace behaviors; preliminary insights into building models and scale measurements; and researchers' training skills from the social and behavioral sciences. In contrast, the main limitations include difficulty in generalizing data findings to larger target groups; difficulty in estimating small magnitude differences of the phenomena being investigated; low data reliability; difficulty of finding well trained investigators, interviewers, and observers; and heavy reliance on subjective interpretive skills.

■ **Understand in-depth interviewing and focus groups as questioning techniques.**

An in-depth interview is a formal process of asking a subject a set of semistructured, probing questions in a face-to-face setting. Focus groups involve bringing a small group of people together for an interactive and spontaneous discussion of a particular topic or concept. While the success of in-depth interviewing depends heavily on the interpersonal communication and probing skills of the interviewer, success in focus group interviewing relies more on the group dynamics of the members, the willingness of members to engage in an interactive dialogue, and the moderator's abilities to keep the discussion on track.

In-depth interviewing and focus groups are both guided by similar research objectives: (1) to provide data for defining and redefining marketing problem situations; (2) to provide data for better understanding the results from previously completed quantitative survey studies; (3) to reveal and understand consumers' hidden or unconscious needs, wants, attitudes, feelings, behaviors, perceptions, and motives regarding services, products, or practices; (4) to generate new ideas about products, services, or delivery methods; and (5) to discover new constructs and measurement methods.

A focus group is a small group of people (8 to 12) brought together for an interactive, spontaneous discussion. The three phases of a focus group study are planning the study, conducting the actual focus group discussions, and analyzing and reporting the results. In planning a focus group, critical decisions have to be made regarding who should participate, how to select and recruit the appropriate participants, what size the group should be, what incentives to offer to encourage and reinforce participants' willingness and commitment to participate, and where the group sessions should be held.

■ **Explain other qualitative data collection methods such as ethnography, case studies, protocol interviews, and projective interviewing techniques.**
There are several useful qualitative data collection methods other than in-depth interviews and focus groups. These methods include ethnography and case studies, which both involve extended contact with research settings. Other types of interviews that produce qualitative data structures include experience interviews, protocol interviews, and articulative interviews. Researchers may also use projective techniques such as word association tests, sentence completion, picture and cartoon tests, thematic apperception tests, role-playing, and the ZMET, which use indirect techniques to access consumers' feelings, emotions, and unconscious motivations. These techniques are less frequently used than are in-depth interviews, focus groups, and observation methods but are still considered useful approaches.

■ **Discuss observation methods and explain how they are used to collect primary data.**
Observation methods can be used by researchers in all types of research designs (exploratory, descriptive, causal). The unique characteristics that underlie observation data collection methods are their (1) directness, (2) subject's degree of awareness, (3) structure, and (4) observing mechanism. For observation methods to be successful there are some conditions that must exist that relate to key elements such as information needs, type of data, time-frame requirements, and the observing environmental setting. In addition to the general advantages of observation, major benefits are the accuracy of collecting data on actual behavior, reduction of confounding factors, and amount of detailed behavioral data that can be recorded. The unique limitations of observation methods are lack of generalizability of the data, inability to explain current behaviors or events, and complexity of accurately observing the behavior.

Key Term and Concepts

Articulative interview 183
Awareness 192
Cartoon (balloon) test 188
Case study 182
Content analysis 175
Debriefing analysis 175
Direct observation 191
Disguised observation 192
Ethnography 184
Experience interview 182
Eye tracking monitor 195
Focus group interview 165
Focus group moderator 171
Focus group research 161
Incentives 171
In-depth interview 158
Indirect observation 192
Interpersonal communication skills 159
Interpretive skills 160
Listening skills 159
Mechanical/electronic observation 193
Moderator's guide 172
Mystery shopper technique 192
Netnography 185
Nonparticipant observation 185
Observation 190
Observation mechanism 193
Observation methods 189
Online focus group 179
Participant observation 184
People Meter 194
Picture test 187
Probing questions 159
Projective hypothesis 188
Projective method 185
Protocol interview 183
Psychogalvanometer 195
Pupilometer 195
Qualitative research 154
Quantitative research 154
Role-playing interview 188
Scanner-based panel 194
Sentence completion test 186
Structured observation 193
Thematic apperception test (TAT) 187
Undisguised observation 192
Unstructured observation 193
Usability study 190
Voice pitch analyzer 195
Word association test 185
ZMET (Zaltman Metaphor Elicitation Technique) 188

Review Questions

1. What are the major differences between quantitative and qualitative research methods? What skills must a researcher have to develop and implement each type of design?
2. Compare and contrast the *unique characteristics*, *main research objectives,* and *advantages/disadvantages* of the in-depth and focus group interviews.
3. Explain the pros and cons of using qualitative research methods as the means of developing raw data structures for each of the following situations:
   a. Adding carbonation to Gatorade and selling it as a true soft drink.
   b. Finding new consumption usages for Arm & Hammer baking soda.
   c. Inducing customers who have stopped shopping at Wal-Mart to return to Wal-Mart.
   d. Advising Southwest Airlines when it wants to enter the cruise ship vacation market.
4. What are the characteristics of a good focus group moderator? What is the purpose of a moderator's guide?
5. Why are the screening activities so important in the selection of focus group participants? Develop a screening form that would allow you to select participants for a focus group on the benefits and costs of owning a cell phone with Internet capabilities.
6. What are the advantages and disadvantages of online focus group interviews compared to "offline" (traditional) focus group interviews?
7. What are the advantages and limitations of using disguised observations compared to undisguised observations?
8. What are the main differences between articulative interviews and in-depth interviews?
9. Develop a word association test that will provide some insight to the following information research question: "What are college students' perceptions of their university's Student Union?
10. Comment on the ethics of the following situations:
   a. You are unaware that a marketing researcher goes around on garbage day in your neighborhood and collects your trash prior to the trash person's arrival. The purpose is to determine your alcohol consumption behavior during the past month.
   b. You are invited by a researcher to be a test user for a new food item at a mall testing site and the researcher plans to secretly videotape your actions and reactions from behind a one-way mirror.

Discussion Questions

1. What type of exploratory research design (observation, projective technique, in-depth interview, focus group, case study, ethnography, netnography, ZMET) would you suggest for each of the following situations and why?
   a. Zales jewelry retailer wants to better understand why men buy jewelry for women and how they select what they buy.

b. The owner of the local McDonald's store located by your university is planning to build a playland and wants to know which play equipment is most interesting to children.
c. Victoria's Secret wants to better understand women's body images.
d. The director of on-campus housing at your university proposes some significant changes to the physical configuration of the current on-campus dorm rooms for freshmen and new transfer students.
e. The corporate V.P. of Merchandising for Whole Foods Supermarkets would like to know the popularity of a new brand of cereal that is produced by General Mills.

2. Develop a moderator's guide that could be used in a focus group interview to investigate the following question: What does "cool" mean to teens and how do the teens decide what products are "cool"?

3. Thinking about how most participants are recruited for focus groups, identify and discuss three ethical issues the researcher and decision maker must consider when using a focus group research design to collect primary data.

4. Conduct an "in-depth" interview and write a brief summary report that would enable you to answer the following question: "What do students want from their education?"

5. OutBack Steak, Inc., is concerned about the shifting attitudes and feelings of the public toward the consumption of red meat. Chris Sullivan, CEO and co-founder of OutBack Steak, Inc., thinks that the "red meat" issues are not that important because his restaurants also serve fish and chicken entrees. Select any two "projective interviewing" techniques that you feel would be appropriate in collecting data for the above situation. First, defend your choice of each of your selected projective interviewing techniques. Second, describe in detail how each of your two chosen techniques would be applied to Sullivan's research problem.

6. **EXPERIENCE THE INTERNET.** Go to the Internet and find a college-student-oriented bulletin board and conduct a focus group interview among some college students at universities in Illinois, Michigan, and Nebraska regarding decision factors they use when choosing a destination in Colorado for a spring break skiing trip.

7. Identify a retail office supply store and develop and execute a "mystery shopper" method that enables you to collect observation data to answer the research questions below. Then analyze the data and write a brief (one or two pages) summary report of your findings.
   a. How well do the office supply store's employees and service staff *interact with* the customers?
   b. How *friendly* are the office supply store's employees and service staff to customers?
   c. How *courteous* are the office supply store's employees and service staff to customers?
   d. How *helpful* are the office supply store's employees and service staff in meeting customers' needs and wants?
   e. What is the level of *product/service knowledge* exhibited by the office supply store's employees and service staff?
   f. How *satisfying or dissatisfying* was your retail office supply store shopping experience?

8. Recall the Continuing Case about the Santa Fe Grill Mexican restaurant. The owners are interested in determining the possibility of offering "Mexican chicken wings" as a new finger food item on the menu. But the owners do not want to just add this item to the menu and hope customers will buy into the idea; they want to do some type of exploratory research prior to making the investment. As a marketing research student, what type of exploratory research design might you suggest be used? Make sure you provide a detailed discussion of the elements that would be included in the proposed design and why you feel your proposed design would capture the needed information and insights.

chapter 7

Analyzing and Reporting Qualitative Research

Learning Objectives

After reading this chapter, you will be able to:

1. Contrast qualitative and quantitative data analysis.
2. Explain the steps in qualitative data analysis.
3. Describe the processes of categorizing and coding data as well as developing theory.
4. Clarify how credibility is established in qualitative data analysis.
5. Discuss the steps involved in writing a qualitative research report.

> **"We are drowning in information and starved for knowledge."**
>
> **—TOM PETERS,**
> ***Thriving on Chaos***

Wireless Communication's Impact on Social Behavior

Mobile phones were once all business. But today they are all in the family. A recent survey of Americans between the ages of 18 and 64 conducted by Knowledge Networks, a market research firm in Cranford, New Jersey, revealed that most respondents underscore "family" as the top reason to go wireless. Young respondents, more so than older ones, cite "reaching friends" as their second leading reason to go wireless, with "work-related calls" being the overall third most important reason for having a wireless phone. The survey also reported some interesting descriptive information. For example, men tend to make more calls on mobile phones per day (8.3 calls) than women (5.5 calls). Although both put family first, women were more partial to calling friends, whereas men were three times as likely to use their phones for work. In addition, 65 percent of African Americans had mobile phones, compared to 62 percent of Caucasians. Hispanics remain well behind in mobile phone usage, with just 54 percent penetration.

Traditional surveys produce this type of information about cell phone usage; their findings are limited to aggregate descriptive interpretations and meaning. In contrast, *qualitative research* on wireless phone usage offers greater opportunities to gain more in-depth understanding of what lies beyond those descriptive numbers. With over 190 million Americans now owning mobile phones, the new phone technology reaches further into our lives. Robbie Blinkoof, principal anthropologist and managing partner at Context-Based Research Group in Baltimore, Maryland, and other ethnographers believe that wireless communication is beginning to create a deeper impression on the American psyche and to have a notable impact on Americans' social behavior, one that could have a long-lasting effect on society and the world around us. Recent ethnographic studies have yielded significant clues about cell phone users' communication habits and related behavior. In general, observed changes relate to how mobile phone customers form relationships and define a sense of time and place. In one study, researchers watched newly connected users at work and play and found that one of the biggest differences was these users became more accessible to their social networks. Mobile phones now supported entire social networks of relationships and were being used to sustain social ties for purely psychological and emotional value. Participants were more flexible in how they arranged their communication schedules and gradually more willing to speak on a mobile phone in public.

In another ethnographic study, context researchers observed changes in how the subjects related to their mobile life. Participants were far more concerned with wireless as an enabler rather than as a toy. They learned to use the wireless features they needed while ignoring those they didn't need. Other interpretive findings of qualitative research have been that wireless phones give people new opportunities for spontaneity. They can change their plans at the last minute more easily or call friends and colleagues to tell them they are running behind schedule. Wireless phones create flexibility by loosening time and place parameters, for instance, enabling people to merely suggest a time and place to meet and then pin down a location or fine-tune the time as they approach the moment.

Nature of Qualitative Data Analysis

Students and researchers alike often think of data analysis as involving numbers. But the data qualitative researchers analyze consists of text (and sometimes images) rather than numbers. Some researchers criticize qualitative research as "soft," lacking rigor and thus being inferior. But measurement and statistical analysis do not ensure that research is useful or accurate. What increases the likelihood of good research is a deliberate, thoughtful, and knowledgeable approach to both gathering and understanding the data, whether qualitative or quantitative research methods are used.

When the sample size and statistical projectability are important, quantitative research should be used to verify and extend qualitative findings. But when the purpose of a research project is to better understand psychoanalytical or cultural phenomena, quantitative research may not offer a great deal of insight or depth. For these topics, qualitative research and analysis often are superior to quantitative research in providing useful knowledge for decision makers.

In this chapter, you will learn the processes used by researchers to analyze and interpret qualitative data and form insights about their meaning. The chapter details a process that can be followed to ensure qualitative data analyses are careful and rigorous. We first compare qualitative and quantitative analysis. While the reliability and validity of quantitative analysis can be evaluated numerically, the judgment that qualitative analysis is trustworthy is based fundamentally on the rigor of the *processes* used for collecting and analyzing data. In this regard, we explain the steps involved in careful qualitative data analysis. Topics such as categorizing, coding, and assessing trustworthiness and credibility of the data are explained. The chapter concludes by providing guidelines on writing a qualitative research report.

Qualitative versus Quantitative Analysis

Marketing researchers construct "stories" based on whatever data they have collected. The goal of these stories, whether they are based on qualitative or quantitative data, is to provide actionable answers to research questions. To arrive at their useful conclusions researchers may travel very different roads depending on whether they are manipulating qualitative or quantitative data. The most apparent difference between the processes of analyzing and interpreting qualitative and quantitative data stems from the nature of the data itself. Qualitative data is textual (and occasionally visual) rather than numerical. While the goal of quantitative analysis is quantifying the magnitude of variables and relationships, or explaining causal relationships, the goal of qualitative analysis is *understanding*.

Qualitative analyses tend to be ongoing and iterative. This means the data is analyzed as it is collected, which may affect further data collection efforts in terms of who is sampled and what questions are asked. While quantitative analyses are guided entirely by the researchers, good qualitative researchers employ member checking. **Member checking** involves asking key informants to read the researchers' report to verify that the story they are telling about the focal problem or situation is accurate.

Member checking Asking key informants to read the researcher's report to verify that the analysis is accurate.

Qualitative data analysis is largely *inductive:* The categories, themes and patterns analysts describe in their reports emerge from the data, rather than being defined prior to data collection, as in quantitative analyses. Because an inductive process is used, the theory that emerges is often called "grounded theory."[1] The categories and corresponding codes for categories are developed as researchers go along, working through the texts and images and finding what is there. Of course, the development of categories and theory is rarely completely inductive. Researchers bring with them knowledge, theory, and training that suggest categories, themes, and theories which might exist in the data they have collected.

There is no one process for analyzing qualitative data, although the three-step process described in this chapter has been useful to the thinking of many qualitative researchers. Some researchers prefer a more impressionistic approach to qualitative analysis and do not go through transcripts and other documents with the degree of care that we suggest here. Nevertheless, *careful and deliberate analysis remains crucial to sound qualitative research.*[2]

Qualitative researchers differ in their beliefs about how useful it may be to quantify their data. Some feel that quantification is completely useless and likely misleading. But others find that quantification can be useful in both counting responses and in model development.[3] Tabulation (counting) in qualitative research is discussed later in this chapter.

Qualitative researchers use different techniques for data collection. These differences affect the kinds of analyses that can be performed with the data. Ethnographic analysis usually results in a **thick description** that contextualizes behavior within a culture or subculture.[4] In marketing research thick description explains consumer behavior more fully than other methods because it connects the behavior to the larger social context in which it occurs. For example, a thick description of urban culture would contextualize the purchase and display of the Timberland brand, stylish automobile tire rims, Courvoisier, or other products and brands that have symbolic properties in the urban subculture that would not be immediately understandable to outsiders.

Thick description An ethnographic research report that contextualizes behavior within a culture or subculture.

Focus group and in-depth interview data typically do not produce thick descriptions because the data gathered are not as extensive and are not collected in context. As in thick description, however, analysts use the collected and transcribed textual data to develop themes, categories, and relationships between variables. Categories are usually developed as the transcripts (and images) are reviewed by researchers. Codes are attached to the categories, which are then used to mark the portions of text (or images) where the category is mentioned. You will understand this better as you read this chapter.

In this chapter, we review the three-step process of analyzing qualitative data: data reduction, data display, and conclusion making and verification. We explain how qualitative researchers develop analyses that are credible, that is, authentic and believable. Finally, we explain how to write a qualitative research report.

The Process of Analyzing Qualitative Data

After data is collected, researchers engage in a three-step process of analysis: data reduction, data display, and conclusion drawing/verification.[5] The three steps as well as relationships between the steps and data collection efforts are pictured in Exhibit 7.1.

Managing the Data Collection Effort

In online focus groups and netnography, the text is produced automatically and is immediately available for analysis. For other methods, audiotapes or videotapes have to be transcribed. Notes and memory may be used to fill in sections of the transcript that are inaudible and to make corrections to the transcription. Qualitative researchers also enter any of their observations and notes, including notes from debriefing sessions, into the data set. Ethnographers take field notes that contain their observations. These field notes also become part of the data set. Any pictures taken by researchers or brought to interviews by participants (as in the ZMET) become part of the data set as well. Material should be indexed and related material should be cross-indexed.

Step 1: Data Reduction

The amount of data collected in a qualitative study can be extensive. Researchers must make decisions about how to categorize and represent the data. We call this process *data reduction.* The most systematic method of analysis is to read through transcripts and develop categories to represent the data. When similar topics are encountered, they are coded as belonging to a similar category. Researchers may simply write codes in the margins of their transcripts. But increasingly software such as QSR NVIVO and Atlas/ti is used to code data and track the passages that are coded. Computer coding enables

eXHIBIT 7.1 Components of Qualitative Data Analysis: An Interactive Model

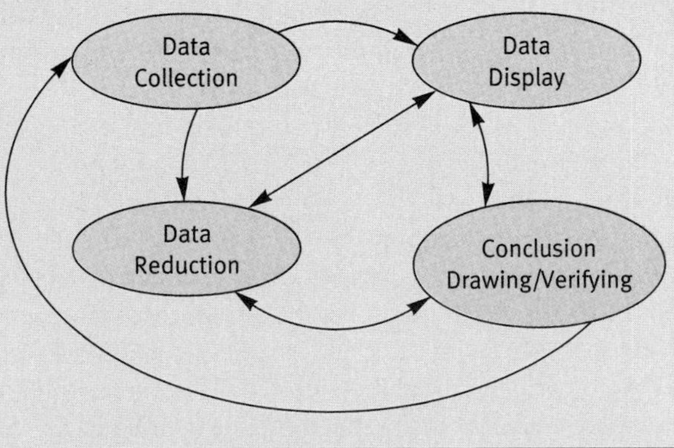

Source: Matthew B. Miles and A. Michael Huberman, *Qualitative Data Analysis: An Expanded Sourcebook* (Thousand Oaks, CA: Sage Publications, 1994), p. 12.

researchers to view all similarly coded passages at the same time, which facilitates comparison and deeper coding. Computer coding makes it easier to study relationships in the data. **Data reduction** consists of several interrelated processes: categorization and coding; theory development; and iteration and negative case analysis.

Data reduction The categorization and coding of data that is part of the theory development process in qualitative data analysis.

Data Reduction: Categorization and Coding

Categorization Placing portions of transcripts into similar groups based on their content.

The first step in data reduction is **categorization.** Researchers categorize sections of the transcript and label them with names and sometimes code numbers. There may be some categories that are determined before the study begins because of existing researcher knowledge and experience. However, most often the codes are developed inductively as researchers move through transcripts and discover new themes of interest and code new instances of categories that have already been discovered. The sections that are coded can be one word long or several pages. The same sections of data can be categorized in multiple ways. If a passage refers to several different themes that have been identified by researchers, the passage will be coded for all the different relevant themes. Some portions of the transcripts will not contain information that is relevant to the analysis, and will not be coded at all.[6]

Code sheet A sheet of paper that lists the codes for different themes or categories for a particular study.

Codes Labels or numbers that are used to track categories in a qualitative study.

A **code sheet** is a piece of paper with all the categories and codes on it (see Exhibit 7.2 for an example from a Senior Internet adoption study). The coded data may be entered into a computer, but the first round of coding usually occurs in the margins (see Exhibit 7.3). The **codes** can be words or numbers that refer to categories on the coding sheet.

As an example of the process of data coding, consider an online shopping study based on data collected from both online and offline focus groups. One theme that emerged from the data was the importance of freedom and control as desirable outcomes when shopping online.[7] The following are some examples of passages in the textual data that were coded as representing the "freedom and control" theme:

- "You're not as committed [online]. You haven't driven over there and parked and walked around so you have a little more flexibility and can get around a lot faster."
- ". . . when I go to a store and a salesperson's helping me for a long time and it's not really what I wanted . . . I'll oblige them, [since] they spent all this time with me . . . but . . . online, I know I will get to the point and be ready to order but I know I don't have to, I can come back anytime I want to."
- You can sit on your arse and eat while you shop. You kin even shop nekked!"
- For me, online browsing is similar [to offline browsing], but I have more of a sense of freedom. I'll browse stores I might not go into offline . . . Victoria's Secret comes to mind . . . also I'll go into swank stores that I might feel intimidated in going into offline . . . when you're a 51 year old chubby gramma, online Victoria's Secret just feels a bit more comfortable."

Abstraction Collapsing some categories or themes into a larger category or higher order conceptual construct.

Categories may be modified and combined as data analysis continues. The researcher's understanding evolves during the data analysis phase, and often results in revisiting, recoding, and recategorizing data. In the process of **abstraction,** some categories are collapsed into higher order conceptual constructs.[8] For instance, in the study of senior adoption of the Internet, researchers initially had separate categories for "curiosity," "lifelong learning," "proactive coping," and "life involvement." After reviewing the data, researchers believed the concepts were related to each other and reviewed research in psychology, which also suggested the categories previously labeled as curiosity, lifelong learning,

EXHIBIT 7.2 Senior Adoption of the Internet, Initial Code Sheet

I. Antecedents

- **A.** Observability
  - **1.** Seeing others use the Internet
  - **2.** Having an "a-ha" experience
  - **3.** Marketing influences
- **B.** Trialability
  - **1.** Family
  - **2.** Community centers
  - **3.** Friends
  - **4.** Work
- **C.** Complexity
  - **1.** Physical challenges
  - **2.** Learning challenges
  - **3.** Initial fear
- **D.** Relative advantage
  - **1.** Cultural currency
  - **2.** Ability to engage in hobbies
  - **3.** Finding information
  - **4.** Communication
  - **5.** Creativity
- **E.** Compatibility
  - **1.** Openness to experience/life involvement
  - **2.** Technology optimism
  - **3.** Self-efficacy/proactive coping
  - **4.** Financial resources
  - **5.** Time in retirement
  - **6.** Previous experience w/computing

II. Processes

- **1.** Attend formal classes
- **2.** Consult published sources
- **3.** Mentors
- **4.** Bricolage (learning by doing)
- **5.** Ancillary systems (e.g., handwritten notes)
- **6.** Flow
- **7.** Multitasking

III. Uses

- **A.** Communication (e-mail, jokes, support groups)
- **B.** Gather info
  - **1.** health
  - **2.** hobbies
  - **3.** places
  - **4.** news
  - **5.** financial
  - **6.** product
  - **7.** travel
- **C.** Banking
- **D.** Shop selectively
- **E.** Later life uses (keeper of the meaning, generativity, integrity)
- **F.** Intended uses
- **G.** Acting as an intermediary/proxy
- **H.** Entertainment
- **I.** Word processing etc.
- **J.** Creativity

IV. Outcomes

- **A.** Connectedness
  - **1.** Companionship
  - **2.** Social support
  - **3.** Linkages to places visited, lived
- **B.** Self-efficacy/Independence
- **C.** Cultural currency
  - **1.** Computer skills
  - **2.** Increased knowledge
- **D.** Excitement
- **E.** Evangelism
- **F.** Fun
- **G.** Self-extension

V. Coping strategies

- **A.** Security—personal info
- **B.** Protecting privacy
- **C.** Flow/limiting flow
- **D.** Ease
- **E.** Satisfying

Codes for Senior Characteristics

B = Broadband
M = Modem
OO = Old Old 75 +
Y = Young Old 65–74

S = Self adopted
O = Other adopted
SA = Self Assisted

self-efficacy, and life involvement could be subsumed in a category called "self-directed values and behavior."[9]

Not all categories can be combined with others. The decision to combine categories is based on the perception that subcategories are related to each other in some meaningful way, and the higher order construct has theoretical significance.[10]

EXHIBIT 7.3 Coding Transcripts in the Margins

Moderator: What's a typical session like? You sit down at the computer and . . .

III 1

III 2D Nisreen: I sit down at the computer and then I go into my emails. I check my emails and I make
III 2C the replies. Then I want to find out about certain things, then I find out about those things and then I go to World News. Then I go to the different countries I'm interested in, then I go to the newspapers. I get the news about Pakistan right now. I go into Asia and then I go into Pakistan and then I get the news right there before I think my relatives know in Pakistan. I know the news before that. So isn't <u>it wonderful</u>? IV D

Moderator: Yes. It really is. It's amazing.

IV A1

Nisreen: My cousin in Australia . . . before he thought he was leaving Australia from Sydney and I knew all about it, it's faster than telegram. It's so wonderful. I almost feel like I'm sitting
IV D <u>on a magic carpet</u> and I <u>press a button and boom, I'm there</u>. IV C
IV F

Moderator: That's interesting. Just reading the paper makes you feel like you are there.

III 2D

Nisreen: And then I want to read the viewpoint of different newspapers, so I go into different
III 2C countries like India, Bangladesh or Pakistan or the Middle East. In the Middle East I used to be a voluntary assistant of the "Perspective," which is the only women's magazine in the Middle East. At that time, Jordan was a very peaceful place. The rest of the world was up in arms and that kind of thing. So you see, I feel like <u>I'm in touch with the whole world.</u> It's such a <u>wonderful</u> feeling at my age to be in
IV A <u>touch with the world.</u> I wish more and more . . . because I think in the near future, that would be the
IV C2 order of the day.

In the senior Internet adoption study, the set of self-directed values and behaviors identified through analysis of the transcripts were strongly related to adoption and extent of Internet usage by seniors. Thus, the construct possessed theoretical significance.

Data Reduction: Comparison

Comparison The process of developing and refining theory and constructs by analyzing the differences and similarities in passages, themes, or types of participants.

Comparison of differences and similarities is a fundamental process in qualitative data analysis. There is an analogy to experimental design, in which various conditions or manipulations (for instance, price levels, advertising appeals) are compared to each other or to a control group. Comparison first occurs as researchers identify categories. Each potential new instance of a category or theme is compared to already coded instances to determine if the new instance belongs in the existing category. When all transcripts have been coded and important categories and themes identified, instances within a category will be scrutinized so that the theme can be defined and explained in more detail. For example, in a study of employee reactions to their own employers' advertising, the category "effectiveness of advertising with consumers" was a recurring theme. Because of the importance of advertising effectiveness in determining employees' reactions to the ad, employees' views of what made ads effective were compared and contrasted. Employees most often associated the following qualities with effective organizational ads to consumers: (1) likely to result in short-term sales, (2) appealing to the target audience, (3) attention-grabbing, (4) easily understandable, and (5) portrays the organization and its products authentically.[11]

Comparison processes are also used to better understand the differences and similarities between two constructs of interest. In the study of online shopping, two types of shopping motivations emerged from analyses of transcripts: goal-oriented behavior (shopping to buy or find information about specific products) and experiential behavior (shopping to shop). Comparison of shopper motivations, descriptions, and desired outcomes from each type of behavior revealed that consumers' online shopping behavior is different depending on whether or not the shopping trip is goal-oriented or experiential.[12]

Comparisons can also be made between different kinds of informants. In a study of high-risk leisure behavior, skydivers with different levels of experience were interviewed. As a result of comparing more and less experienced skydivers, the researchers were able to show that motivations changed and evolved, for example, from thrill, to pleasure, to flow, as skydivers continued their participation in the sport.[13] Similarly, in a study of post-socialist eastern European women who were newly exposed to cosmetics and cosmetics brands, researchers compared women who embraced cosmetics to those who were either ambivalent about cosmetics or who rejected them entirely.[14]

Data Reduction: Theory Building

Integration The process of moving from the identification of themes and categories to the development of theory.

Axial coding Specifying the conditions, context, or variables that lead to a particular category or construct, and the outcomes from the construct.

Integration is the process through which researchers build theory that is grounded, or based on the data collected. The idea is to move from the identification of themes and categories to the development of theory.

Two techniques are useful for developing theory: axial coding and selective coding.[15] When they use **axial coding** researchers can specify the conditions, context, or variables that lead to a particular category or construct, the actions needed for informants to carry out the construct, and the outcomes from the construct. In axial coding researchers learn that particular conditions, contexts, and outcomes cluster together. For example, self-directed seniors (conditions) tend to be technology optimists (conditions) who adopt the Internet (a central concept of interest). They either adopt themselves, or if they have high levels of technology discomfort, get help to adopt (actions or strategies to carry out the construct). Adoption can lead to heavier or lighter use (outcome). Not only are self-directed seniors more likely to adopt the Internet, but they use it more often after adoption (outcome).

Recursive A relationship in which a variable can both cause and be caused by the same variable.

In qualitative research, relationships may or may not be conceptualized and pictured in a way that looks like the traditional causal model employed by quantitative researchers. For instance, relationships may be portrayed as circular or **recursive.** In recursive relationships, variables may both cause and be caused by the same variable. A good example is the relationship between job satisfaction and financial compensation. Job satisfaction tends to increase performance and thus compensation earned on the job, which in turn increases job satisfaction.

Selective coding Building a storyline around one core category or theme; the other categories will be related to or subsumed to this central overarching category.

Qualitative researchers may look for one core category or theme to build their storyline around, a process referred to as **selective coding.** All other categories will be related to or subsumed to this central category or theme. Selective coding is evident in the following studies that all have an overarching viewpoint or frame:

- A study of personal Web sites finds that posting a site is an imaginary digital extension of self.
- A study of an online Newton (a discontinued Apple PDA) user group finds several elements of religious devotion in the community.
- A study of Hispanic consumer behavior in the United States uses the metaphor of boundary crossing to explore Hispanic purchase and consumption.[16]

Given its role as an integrating concept, it is not surprising that selective coding generally occurs in the later stages of data analysis. Once the overarching theme is developed, researchers review all their codes and cases to better understand how they relate to the larger category, or central storyline, that has emerged from their data.

Data Reduction: Iteration and Negative Case Analysis

Iteration Working through the data several times in order to modify early ideas and to be informed by subsequent analyses.

Iteration means working through the data in a way that permits early ideas and analyses to be modified by choosing cases and issues in the data that will permit deeper analyses. The iterative process may uncover issues that the already collected data do not address. In this case, the researcher will collect data from more informants, or may choose specific types of informants that he or she believes will answer questions that have arisen during the iterative process. The iterative procedure may also take place after an original attempt at integration. Each of the interviews (or texts or images) may be reviewed to see whether it supports the larger theory that has been developed. This iterative process can result in revising and deepening constructs as well as the larger theory based on relationships between constructs.

Memoing Writing down thoughts as soon as possible after each interview, focus group, or site visit.

Negative case analysis Deliberately looking for cases and instances that contradict the ideas and theories that researchers have been developing.

An important element of iterative analysis is note taking or **memoing.** Researchers should write down their thoughts and reactions as soon after each interview, focus group, or site visit as circumstances will allow. Researchers may want to write down not only what participants say they feel, but whether or not what they say seems credible.

Perhaps most important, during the iterative process researchers use **negative case analysis,** which means that they deliberately look for cases and instances that contradict the ideas and theories that they have been developing. Negative case analysis helps to establish boundaries and conditions for the theory that is being developed by the qualitative researcher. The general stance of qualitative researchers should be skepticism toward the ideas and theory they have created based on the data they have collected.[17] Otherwise they are likely to look for evidence that confirms their preexisting biases and early analysis. Doing so may result in important alternative conceptualizations that are legitimately present in the data being completely overlooked.

Iteration and negative case analysis begin in the data reduction stage. But they continue through the data display and conclusion drawing/verification stages. As analysis continues in the project, data displays are altered. Late in the life of the project, iterative analysis and negative case analysis provide verification for and qualification of the themes and theories developed during the data reduction phase of research.

Data Reduction: The Role of Tabulation

The use of tabulation in qualitative analysis is controversial. Some analysts feel that any kind of tabulation will be misleading. After all, the data collected are not like survey data where all questions are asked of all respondents in exactly the same way. Each focus group or in-depth interview asks somewhat different questions in somewhat different ways. Moreover, frequency of mention is not always a good measure of research importance. A unique answer from a lone wolf in an interview may be worthy of attention because it is consistent with other interpretation and analysis, or because it suggests a boundary condition for the theory and findings.[18]

Exhibit 7.4 shows a data tabulation from the study of senior adoption of the Internet. The most frequently coded response was "communication," followed by "self-directed values/behavior." While this result may seem meaningful, a better measure of the importance

EXHIBIT 7.4 Tabulation of Most Frequently Appearing Categories in the Senior Adoption of the Internet Study

Themes	Passages	Documents (Participants)
Communication—Uses	149	27
Self-Directed Values and Behavior	107	23
Shopping/Conducting Biz—Uses	66	24
Gather Information—Uses	65	25
Classes to Learn the Internet	64	22
Future Intended Uses	63	20
Mentors/Teachers Helping to Learn	55	20
Difficulty in Learning	50	20
Self-efficacy/Proactive Coping—Outcome	46	16
Later Life Cycle Uses (e.g., Genealogy)	45	19
Entertainment—Uses	43	24
Excitement about the Internet	40	14
Adopting to Facilitate Hobbies	40	15
Technology Optimism	40	18
Proactive Coping	38	19
Health Information on Internet—Uses	34	19
Bricolage (tinkering to learn the Internet)	34	20

of communications to seniors over the Internet is likely to be found using surveys. But the result does provide some guidance. All 27 participants in the study mentioned the use of the Internet for communication, so researchers are likely to investigate this theme in their analysis even if the tabulations are not included in the final report. Note that qualitative researchers virtually never report percentages. For example, they seldom would report 4 out of 10 that are positive about a product concept as 40 percent. Using percentages would inaccurately imply that the results are statistically projectible to a larger population of consumers.

Tabulation can also keep researchers honest. For example, researchers involved in the senior Internet adoption study were initially impressed by informants who made the decision to adopt the Internet quickly and dramatically when someone showed them an Internet function that supported a preexisting interest or hobby (coded as "a-ha"). But the code only appeared three times across the 27 participants in the study. While researchers may judge the theme worthy of mention in their report, they are unlikely to argue that "a-ha" moments are central in the senior adoption decision process. Counting responses can help keep researchers honest in the sense that it provides a counterweight to biases they may bring to the analysis.[19]

Another way to use tabulation is to look at co-occurrences of themes in the study. Exhibit 7.5 shows the number of times selected concepts were mentioned together in the same coded passage. In the table categories most often mentioned together with curiosity were technology optimism, proactive coping skills ("I can figure it out even if it makes me feel stupid sometimes"), and cultural currency (adopting to keep up with the times). The

EXHIBIT 7.5 Relationships between Categories: Co-mentions of Selected Constructs in the Senior Adoption of the Internet Study

	Co-mentions of Selected Constructs			
	Curiosity	Technology Optimism	Proactive Coping Skills	Cultural Currency
Curiosity	**107***			
Technology Optimism	16	**40**		
Proactive Coping Skills	19	10	**38**	
Cultural Currency	12	8	7	**26**

*Diagonal contains total number of mentions of each concept.

co-mentions with curiosity suggest that qualitative analysts would consider the idea that curious people are more likely to be technology optimists, to be interested in keeping up with the times, and to have strong proactive coping skills. But interpreting these numbers too literally is risky. Further iterative analysis is required to develop these conceptual ideas and to support (or refute) their credibility. Whenever the magnitude of a finding is important to decision makers, well-designed quantitative studies are likely to provide better measures than are qualitative studies.

Some researchers suggest a middle ground for reporting tabulations of qualitative data. They suggest using "fuzzy numerical qualifiers" such as "often," "typically," or "few" in their reports.[20] Marketing researchers usually include a section in their reports about limitations of their research. A caution about the inappropriateness of estimating magnitudes based on qualitative research typically is included in the limitations section of the report. Therefore, when reading qualitative findings, readers would be cautioned that any numerical findings presented should not be read too literally.

Step 2: Data Display

Qualitative researchers typically use visual displays to summarize data. Data displays are important because they help reduce and summarize the extensive textual data collected in the study in a way that conveys major ideas in a compact fashion. There is no one way to display and present data in qualitative analysis. Any perusal of qualitative reports will find a wide variety of formats, each developed in response to the combination of research problem, methodology (ethnography, case study, focus group or in-depth interview, for instance), and focus of analysis. Coming up with ideas for useful data displays is a creative task that can be both fun and satisfying. Some data displays provide interim analysis and thus may not be included in the final report. In any case, the displays will probably change over the course of analysis as researchers interpret and reread their data and modify and qualify their initial impressions. The displays also evolve as researchers seek to better display their findings.

Displays may be tables or figures. Tables have rows or row by column formats that cross themes and/or informants. Figures may include flow diagrams; traditional box and arrow causal diagrams (often associated with quantitative research); diagrams that display circular or recursive relationships; trees that display consumers' taxonomies of products, brands

eXHIBIT 7.6 Eight Central Paradoxes of Technological Products

Paradox	Description
Control/chaos	Technology can facilitate regulation or order, and technology can lead to upheaval or disorder
Freedom/enslavement	Technology can facilitate independence or fewer restrictions, and technology can lead to dependence or more restrictions
New/obsolete	New technologies provide the user with the most recently developed benefits of scientific knowledge, and new technologies are already or soon to be outmoded as they reach the marketplace
Competence/Incompetence	Technology can facilitate feelings of intelligence or efficacy, and technology can lead to feelings of ignorance or ineptitude
Efficiency/inefficiency	Technology can facilitate less effort or time spent in certain activities, and technology can lead to more effort or time in certain activities
Fulfills/creates needs	Technology can facilitate the fulfillment of needs or desires, and technology can lead to the development or awareness of needs or desires previously unrealized
Assimilation/isolation	Technology can facilitate human togetherness, and technology can lead to human separation
Engaging/disengaging	Technology can facilitate involvement, flow, or activity, and technology can lead to disconnection, disruption, or passivity

Source: David Glen Mick and Susan Fournier, "Paradoxes of Technology: Consumer Cognizance, Emotions and Coping Strategies," *Journal of Consumer Research* 25 (September 1998), p. 126.

or other concepts; consensus maps, which picture the collective connections that informants make between concepts or ideas; and checklists that show all informants and then indicate whether or not each informant possesses a particular attitude, value, behavior, ideology, or role. While displays of qualitative findings are quite diverse, some common types of displays are:

- A table that explains central themes in the study; for example, a study of technology products uncovered eight themes that represent the paradoxes or issues in technology adoption and use (see Exhibit 7.6).
- A diagram that suggests relationships between variables. An example of a diagram that pictures relationships between themes comes from the earlier mentioned study of skydiving (see Exhibit 7.7). The diagram pictures how three sets of motivations evolve over time as skydivers become more experienced. The arrows are double sided because movement to a higher level is not complete, since skydivers revisit and experience the lower-level motivations.
- A table with a comparison of key categories in the study. An example is a table that compares goal-oriented and experiential shopping in an online environment (see Exhibit 7.8).
- A matrix including quotes for various themes from representative informants. An example comes from the previously mentioned study of involvement with cosmetics and brand attitudes in post-socialist Europe. The table in Exhibit 7.9 shows attitudes of women who

eXHIBIT 7.7 Evolution of Motives for High-Risk Consumption in Relation to Risk Acculturation and Experience

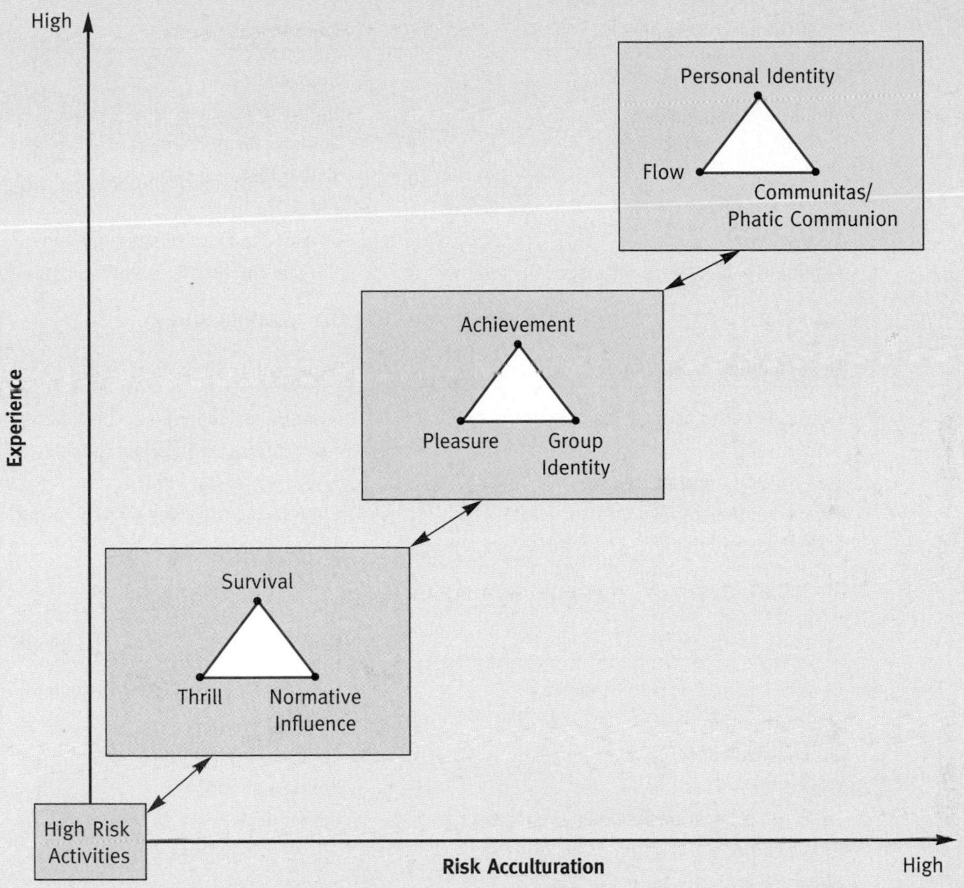

Source: Richard L. Celsi, Randy L. Rose, and Tom W. Leigh, "An Exploration of High Risk Leisure Consumption through Skydiving," *Journal of Consumer Research* 20 (June 1993), p. 14.

are ambivalent about cosmetics. Other tables included in the study contain parallel verbatims for women who have embraced cosmetics and women who have rejected cosmetics.

- A consensus map that shows the relationships between ideas and concepts informants collectively express. An example in Exhibit 7.10 is based on a ZMET study of the issues that surround privacy. The data display appeared online, and users could drill down and see representative verbatims for each concept and for the connections between concepts.

Step 3: Conclusion Drawing/Verification

The iterative process and negative case analysis continue through the verification phase of the project. The process includes checking for common biases that may affect researcher

eXHIBIT 7.8 Goal-Oriented vs. Experiential Behavior in Online Shopping

FOCUS GROUP PARTICIPANT DESCRIPTORS OF:

Goal-Oriented Shopping	Experiential Shopping
Accomplishment	Enjoyment
Going to specific site	Surfing/trying new sites
Looking for specific product	Looking for new things
Saving time	Killing time
I have a purpose in mind	I look for ideas
I make repeat purchases	I check my favorite sites regularly
Finding the best price for a specific item	Bargain hunting for what's on sale

FOCUS GROUP PARTICIPANT DESIRES WHEN:

Goal-Oriented Shopping	Experiential Shopping
I want to get in and out quickly (fewest clicks)	I want a welcoming site that draws me in
Do-it-myself	I can interact with other consumers
Don't waste my time	Show me lots of choices
I want immediate response to questions	I like to browse sites related to my hobby
I want ease of use	I want a unique experience

FOCUS GROUP PARTICIPANT DESCRIPTORS OF:

Freedom and Control	Fun
Control what information I receive	Read reviews (but don't believe them)
No salespeople	I get drawn in
No lines/crowds	Excitement of bidding
Only brands/sites I know	Window shopping
I can come back anytime/delay purchase	I'm impulsive
I have options	I have to limit myself
Show me what I want	Surprise me

Source: Mary Wolfinbarger and Mary C. Gilly, "Shopping Online for Freedom, Control and Fun," *California Management Review* 43, no. 2 (Winter 2001), p. 39.

conclusions. A list of the most common biases to watch out for is shown in Exhibit 7.11. In addition to actively considering the possibility of bias in the analysis, researchers also must establish credibility for their findings. We explain credibility next.

Verification/Conclusion Drawing: Credibility in Qualitative Research

Quantitative researchers establish credibility in data analysis by demonstrating that their results are reliable (measurement and findings are stable, repeatable, and generalizable) and valid (the research measures what it was intended to measure). In contrast, the credibility of qualitative data analysis is based on *the rigor of the actual strategies used for collecting, coding, analyzing, and presenting data when generating theory.*[21] The essential question in developing credibility in qualitative research is "How can [a researcher] persuade his or her audiences that the research findings of an inquiry are worth paying attention to?"[22]

eXHIBIT 7.9 Post-Socialist Eastern European Women's Product Involvement and Brand Commitment: Informants Who Were Ambivalent about Cosmetics

	Alexandra	Laura
Cosmetics use and Involvement	3.1: Normally I wash my hair twice a week. But . . . I knew we would meet, so I washed it yesterday. It depends on my mood. I use corrector and cream powder in winter when I am not so brown, but in the summer. . . . It is disgusting. If I go to the theater then I always use makeup, but if I go to a movie I don't. So, I always say, "Okay, you have to have a nice look, but you don't have to prepare for the next beauty contest every morning."	3.8: Only if something bad happened, a disaster, and then I wouldn't think about appearance. Mascara, this is something that I always use, and powder everyday for my face. I like it. . . . Mascara, I can put that on myself. But I can't put on makeup. I can give advice, but I don't know how to do it for myself. Maybe I am too stressed, I won't get the effect that I want. I feel better without makeup.
Consumer as Interpreter	3.2: When I'll be the grandparent then it will be okay for the parent, because I've changed my way of thinking. I will give it to my children.	3.9: I buy things that I don't really need. I know that I don't need it, but I buy it, and then I am sorry. . . . Those things can wait.
Cultural ideologies and intermedieries	3.3: I mean during the socialist communist regime there wasn't a choice. People weren't conscious about cosmetics. The only thing that was important was to have a workplace and to meet the requirement of the socialist men and women.	3.10: Romanian women are more attractive than five years ago because they have the chance to find out new things from TV and magazines—how to put on makeup and how to dress. For instance, my mother doesn't take care of herself. . . . You know we didn't learn how to use cosmetics from her. We watched TV. read books. My moher didn't tell me anything.
Local context and social networks	3.4: There is *Cosmopolitan* in Hungary, but it is not as good as in English. It is thinner, and there are only advertisements in it and about sex and that is all. I am lucky because we have an English teacher at the university, and they subscribe to this megazine, and I can read it. And there are fashion models, as well and cooking advice and so on. So, it is much nicer.	3.11: They judge you according to appearance. Even in the job, women discuss . . . and then you also have to buy it, because you want to be at the same level, I saw this, and after they buy the products, they show off. Look what I have. Those who cannot buy suffer, even if they don't admit it. It is painful. . . . After the Revolution, I guese this is when it started—with jeans.
Ideological positions	3.5: We have to forget about communism, and we have to change our way of thinking, but it is very, very hard to change the thinking of the whole country.	3.12: If you look good, you get a good guy, a good job, even though you are not very smart. But many have problems because of this . . . It is risky to look good. Everyone wants to look better than the other. They think that if you are dressed according to the latest fashion, everyone will think that you have money and have a good life.
Involvement with branded products	3.6: If I have money I get cosmetics at a pharmacy, if I don't have much money I go to a drugstore. Usually [pharmacists] have creams that they do themselves. They are good ones because they know what to put in them, but they don't have names. And they are cheaper. . . . The name isn't important to me, what is important is quality. If I find an unknown product, but it is good for me, I buy it. . . . And I don't trust these [products] . . . it would be cheaper to buy them, but I haven't heard about them. I don't trust them.	3.13: I saw many women that want to use branded products, not because they know it is good, but because they saw a commercial, or they want to show off. They don't think it is possible that the products don't fit you. Branded products might not fit you. At some point, we had Pantene shampoos. All the commercial breaks had ads with Pantene. I didn't want to buy. I got it as a gift and used it, and I wasn't happy with it. I didn't like. It might be a good brand, but it didn't fit me, so brand is not enough.
Brand commitment and brand experimentation	3.7: This is my favorite. I just found it. . . . It is brand new. I tried Wash & Go. It was advertised very frequently, and everybody ran to the shops and bought it. But I said, "OK, it's very popular, but it is not good for me [it tangled my hair]."	3.14: I prefer L'Oreal, and Avon and Oriflame have good body lotion. I still like to try other things. I like to try only things that I have heard of.

Source: Robin A. Coulter, Linda L. Price, and Lawrence Feick, "Rethinking the Origins of Involvement and Brand Commitment: Insights from Postsocialist Europe," *Journal of Consumer Research* 30 (September 2003), p. 159.

EXHIBIT 7.10 Consensus Map of the Concept of Privacy along with Drilldown of the Relationship between Scrutiny and Invasion

Consensus Map for Consumer Thoughts about Privacy

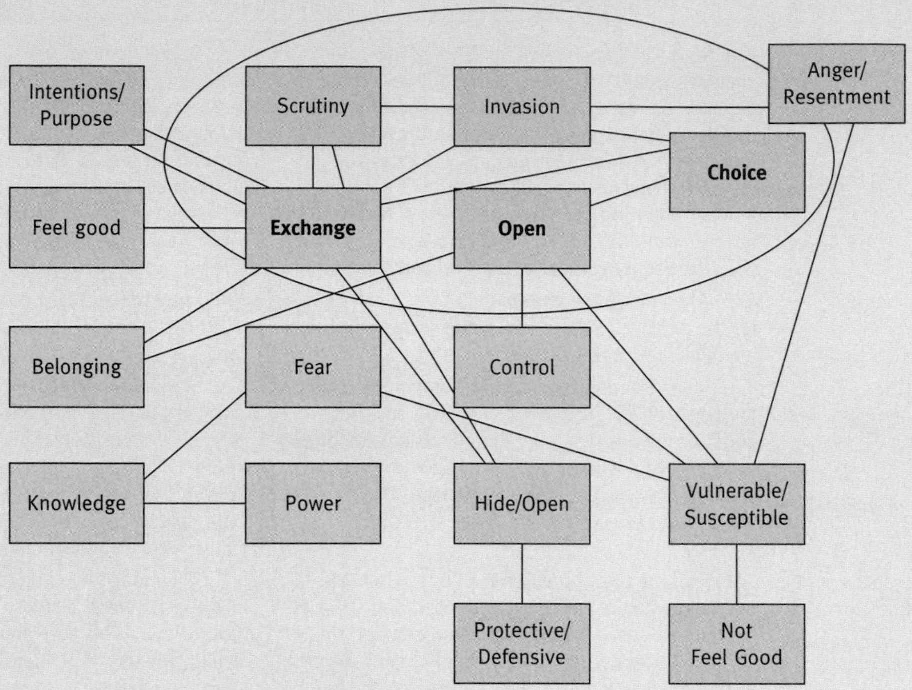

The Reasoning Process Involving Scrutiny and Invasion

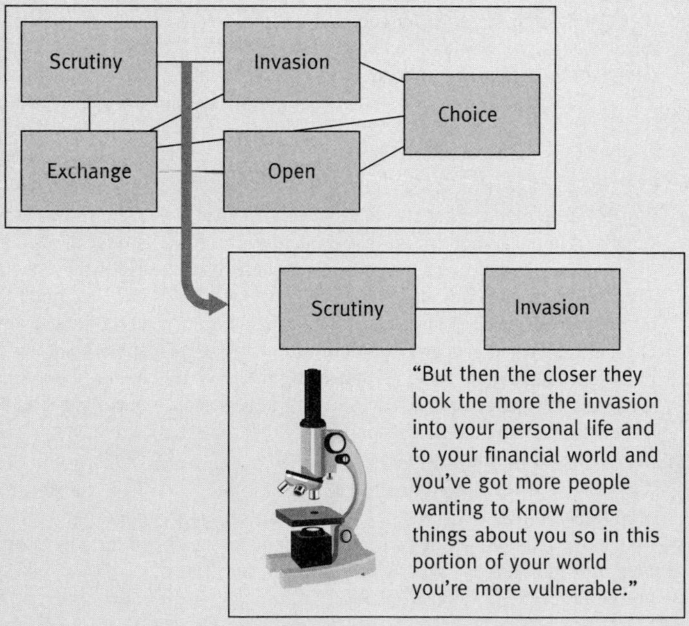

Source: Gerald Zaltman, *How Consumers Think: Essential Insights into the Mind of the Market* (Boston: Harvard Business School Press, 2003), pp. 152 and 154.

eXHIBIT 7.11 Threats to Drawing Credible Conclusions in Qualitative Analysis

- Salience of first impressions or of observations of highly concrete or dramatic incidents.
- Selectivity which leads to overconfidence in some data, especially when trying to confirm a key finding.
- Co-occurrences taken as correlations or even as causal relationships.
- Extrapolating the rate of instances in the population from those observed.
- Not taking account of the fact that information from some sources may be unreliable.

Source: Adapted from Matthew B. Miles and A. Michael Huberman, *Qualitative Research: An Expanded Sourcebook* (Thousand Oaks, CA: Sage Publications, 1994), p. 438.

Emic validity An attribute of qualitative research that affirms that key members within a culture or subculture agree with the findings of a research report.

Cross-researcher reliability The degree of similarity in the coding of the same data by different researchers.

Credibility The degree of rigor, believability, and trustworthiness established by qualitative research.

Triangulation Addressing the topic analysis from multiple perspectives, including using multiple methods of data collection and analysis, multiple data sets, multiple researchers, multiple time periods, and different kinds of relevant research informants.

Peer review A process in which external qualitative methodology or topic area specialists are asked to review the research analysis.

The terms *validity* and *reliability* have to be redefined in qualitative research. For example, in qualitative research the term **emic validity** means the analysis presented in the report resonates with those inside the studied culture or subculture, a form of validity established by *member checking*. Similarly, **cross-researcher reliability** means the text and images are coded similarly among multiple researchers. However, many qualitative researchers prefer terms such as "quality," "rigor," "dependability," "transferability," and "trustworthiness" to the traditionally quantitative terms "validity" and "reliability." Moreover, some qualitative researchers completely reject any notions of validity and reliability, believing there is no single "correct" interpretation of qualitative data.[23] In this chapter, we use the term **credibility** to describe the rigor and believability established in qualitative analysis.

Triangulation is the technique most often associated with establishing credibility in qualitative research.[24] Triangulation requires that research inquiry be addressed from multiple perspectives. Several kinds of triangulation are possible:

- Multiple methods of data collection and analysis.
- Multiple data sets.
- Multiple researchers analyzing the data, especially if they come from different backgrounds or research perspectives.
- Data collection in multiple time periods.
- Providing selective breadth in informants so that different kinds of relevant groups that may have different and relevant perspectives are included in the research.

Credibility is also increased when key informants and other practicing qualitative researchers are asked to review the analyses. As earlier mentioned, soliciting feedback from key informants or member checking strengthens the credibility of qualitative analysis. Seeking feedback from external expert reviewers, called **peer review,** also strengthens credibility. Key informants and external qualitative methodology and topic area experts often question the analyses, push researchers to better clarify their thinking, and occasionally change key interpretations in the research. When member checking and peer review are utilized in a qualitative design, it is reported in the methodological section of the report.

Writing the Report

Researchers should keep in mind that research reports are likely to be read by people in the company who are not familiar with the study. Moreover, the study may be reviewed years later by individuals who were not working at the company at the time the research was conducted. Therefore, the research objectives and procedures should be well explained both to current and future decision makers. Qualitative research reports typically contain three sections:[25]

1. Introduction
   a. Research objectives
   b. Research questions
   c. Description of research methods
2. Analysis of the Data/Findings
   a. Literature review and relevant secondary data
   b. Findings displayed in tables or charts
   c. Interpretation and summary of the findings
3. Conclusions and Recommendations

Introduction

The *introductory* portion of the report should present the research problem, the objectives of the research, and the methodology used. As do quantitative researchers, qualitative researchers report the procedures they used to collect and analyze data. The methodology section of a qualitative report usually contains:

- Topics covered in questioning and other materials used in questioning informants.
- If observational methods are used, the locations, dates, times, and context of observation.
- Number of researchers involved and their level of involvement in the study. Any diversity in background or training of researchers may be highlighted as positive for the study because multiple viewpoints have been brought to the analysis.
- Procedure for choosing informants.
- Number of informants and informant characteristics, such as age, gender, location, level of experience with the product/service. This information is often summarized in a table.
- The number of focus groups, interviews, or transcripts.
- The total number of pages of the transcripts, number of pictures, videos, number and page length of researcher memos.
- Any procedures used to ensure the data collection and analysis were systematic, for example, coding, iterative analysis of transcripts, member checking, peer reviews, and so forth.
- Procedures used for negative case analyses and how the interpretation was modified.
- Limitations of qualitative methodology in general, and any limitations that are specific to the particular qualitative method used.

Two examples of explaining the general limitations of qualitative methodology in a report are the following:

> "The reader is cautioned that the findings reported here are qualitative, not quantitative in nature. The study was designed to explore *how* respondents feel and behave rather than to determine *how many* think or act in specific ways."

> "Respondents constitute a small nonrandom sample of relevant consumers and are therefore not statistically representative of the universe from which they have been drawn."[26]

Analysis of the Data/Findings

The sequence of reported findings should be written in a way that is logical and persuasive. Secondary data may be brought into the analysis to help contextualize the findings. For instance, in the senior adoption of the Internet study, the percentage and demographics of senior adopters were covered in the report to contextualize the qualitative findings. Also, general topics precede more specific topics. For example, a discussion of findings related to seniors' general attitudes toward and adoption of technology will precede the discussion of senior Internet adoption.

Verbatims Quotes from research participants that are used in research reports.

Data displays that summarize, clarify, or provide evidence for assertions should be included with the report. **Verbatims,** or quotes from research participants, should be used judiciously in the textual report as well as in data displays. When they are well chosen, verbatims are a particularly powerful way to underscore important points because they express consumers' viewpoints in their own voice. Video verbatims can be used in live presentations. Of course, the power of verbatims is a double-edged sword. Colorfully stated, interesting verbatims do not always make points that are well grounded in the body of data collected. Researchers need to take care that they do not select, analyze, and present verbatims that are memorable rather than revealing of patterns in their data.

Conclusions and Recommendations: Marketing Implications

Researchers should provide information that is relevant to the research problem articulated by the client. As two qualitative researchers stated, "A psychoanalytically rich interpretation of personal hygiene and deodorant products is ultimately of little value to the client if it cannot be linked to a set of actionable marketing implications—for example, a positioning which directly reflects consumer motivations or a new product directed at needs not currently addressed."[27] As with quantitative research, knowledge of both the market and the client's business is useful in translating research findings into managerial implications.

When the magnitude of consumer response is important to the client, researchers are likely to report what they have found and suggest follow-up research. Even so, qualitative research should be reported in a way that reflects an appropriate level of confidence in the findings. Exhibit 7.12 lists three examples of forceful, but realistic, recommendations based on qualitative research.

eXHIBIT 7.12 Making Recommendations Based on Qualitative Research When Magnitude Matters

- "The qualitative findings give reason for optimism about market interest in the new product concept. . . . We therefore recommend that the concept be further developed and formal executions be tested."
- "While actual market demand may not necessarily meet the test of profitability, the data reported here suggest that there is widespread interest in the new device."
- "The results of this study suggest that ad version #3 is most promising because it elicited more enthusiastic responses and because it appears to describe situations under which consumers actually expect to use the product."

Source: Alfred E. Goldman and Susan Schwartz McDonald, *The Group Depth Interview* (Englewood Cliffs, NJ: Prentice Hall, 1987), p. 176.

Continuing Case: Using Qualitative Research for the Santa Fe Grill

The business consultant hired by the owners of the Santa Fe Grill has recommended a quantitative survey of lunch and dinner customers. He has not recommended any qualitative research. The owners are not experts in research methods, but they do know the difference between qualitative and quantitative research. They are wondering if some kind of *qualitative* research approach would be better to help them understand the challenges facing them. Or perhaps *both* qualitative and quantitative research should be undertaken?

1. Could observation be used to collect qualitative information?
2. If yes, when and how could observation be used?
3. Are there topics that could be explored better using focus groups?
4. If yes, suggest topics to be used in the focus group studies.

MARKETING RESEARCH IN ACTION

Analyzing Qualitative Data

Hotel Travelers' Cheers and Jeers at Their Experiences

After braving airport security or a tedious long drive, travelers do not want to endure hassles at a hotel. Recently, ethnographers at American Demographics (AD) investigated the following research question: "What are travelers' good and bad experiences with the hospitality industry?" Using content analysis and procedures for triangulation, researchers sifted through a sample of nearly 2,000 letters submitted by consumers to hotels and resorts through Planetfeedback, a division of Intelliseek, a Cincinnati-based market research firm. Of all the letters submitted to Planetfeedback's online forum, 78 percent were complaints and 16 percent were compliments, with the remaining 6 percent being either questions or suggestions. Through qualitative analysis, the researchers identified several themes, including "personalized service," "fair deal," "extra perks," "cleanliness/hygiene," "unsatisfactory facilities," and "poor customer service." Here is what they discovered: Travelers overwhelmingly agree that hotel housekeeping needs to clean up its act. Among the 150 letters submitted on the topic of "cleanliness/hygiene," almost all of them were complaints. The billing and check-in departments also received a large share of complaints. Despite the efforts of the hospitality industry to personalize reservations and add amenities, nothing wins guests over like a friendly staff. The highest percentage of complimentary letters fell into the "hotel staff performance" category. Here are some examples of what consumers wrote:

Customer 1

"I would like to compliment the employees of your Peoria, IL hotel. They greet me by name, ask how my day has been and if they can do anything to help me out. They always phone after I've gone to my room to see that it's adequate. When I've neglected to get a reservation, they have been kind enough to reserve a room for me at another hotel. That's going the extra mile for a guest!"

Customer 2

"My partner and I are very price-conscious and tend to shop around for the best hotel rates. On one of the popular travel Web sites, I found a much cheaper rate than I was quoted by your hotel on the phone or on your own site. I pointed this out to the staff and they honored the Web rate, plus they knocked an additional 10 percent off. The entire process was very efficient."

Customer 3

"When we arrived at your hotel, we asked about receiving a room upgrade, never imagining we could afford it, and we received it for free. We were absolutely thrilled. The employees at the front desk went out of their way to make it a pleasant stay for our family and us. It really made our day, month, and probably our year."

Customer 4

"When we returned to our room, the beds were not made, towels were not replaced, and were wet on the floor, and the waste receptacles were overflowing. The front desk person informed us that there was a form in the room that we were supposed to fill out to identify the level of housekeeping we needed. It seems that a minimum level of cleaning should be assumed in the absence of any formal request form."

Customer 5

"My husband has a heart condition and is supposed to exercise every day. I chose your hotel in St. Louis because it had an exercise facility. When we got there, the equipment was rusty and nonfunctional."

Customer 6

"I called your toll-free reservation line and was quoted $92.65 per night. When I checked out of the hotel, I was billed $92.65 for Friday night but $143.65 for Saturday night. The attendant called the 800-number and handed me the phone. The representative took my number and told me someone from Guest Relations would call me. I did not receive a call. I am very upset by the brush-off."

Hands-On Exercise

1. Using your understanding of the chapter material and the theme topics presented above, reanalyze each of the given examples and categorize them into what you believe to be the most appropriate "theme."
2. Using the six customer examples, is there any evidence that would allow you to determine if "triangulation" of the data occurs? If yes, explain how. If no, why not?
3. What other possible themes, if any, could be identified from the given customers' letters? Make sure you label the topics and support your choices.

Summary of Learning Objectives

■ **Contrast qualitative and quantitative data analysis.**
There are many differences between qualitative and quantitative data analysis. The data that are analyzed in qualitative research include text and images, rather than numbers. In quantitative research, the goal is to quantify the magnitude of variables and relationships, or explain causal relationships. In qualitative analysis, the goal of research is deeper understanding. A second difference is that qualitative analysis is iterative, with researchers revisiting data and clarifying their thinking about each iteration. Third, quantitative analysis is driven entirely by researchers, while good qualitative research employs member checking, or asking key informants to verify the accuracy of research reports. Last, qualitative data analysis is inductive, which means that the theory grows out of the research process rather than preceding it, as in quantitative analysis.

■ **Explain the steps in qualitative data analysis.**
After data collection, there are three steps in analyzing qualitative data. Researchers move back and forth between these steps iteratively rather than going through them one step at a time. The steps are data reduction, constructing data displays, and conclusion drawing/verification. Data reduction consists of several interrelated processes: categorization and coding, theory development and iteration, and negative case analysis. Categorization is the process of coding and labeling sections of the transcripts or images into themes. Then, the categories can be integrated into a theory through iterative analysis of the data. Data displays are the second step. Data displays picture findings in tables or figures so that the data can be more easily digested and communicated. After a rigorous iterative process, researchers can draw conclusions and verify their findings. During the verification/conclusion drawing stage, researchers work to establish the credibility of their data analysis.

■ **Describe the processes of categorizing and coding data as well as developing theory.**
During the categorization phase, researchers develop categories based on both preexisting theory and the categories that emerge from the data. They code the data in the margins and develop a code sheet that shows the various labels that they are developing. The codes are revised and revisited as the theory develops. In the process of abstraction, related categories are collapsed into higher-order conceptual constructs. Comparison of differences and similarities between instances of a category, between related categories, and between different participants is particularly useful in better defining constructs and refining theory.

Integration is the process of moving from identification of themes and categories to the investigation of relationships between categories. Two techniques are used in the integration/theory development process. One is axial coding in which researchers specify the conditions, context, or variables that lead to a particular category or construct; the actions needed for informants to carry out the construct; and the outcomes from the construct. In axial coding researchers learn that particular conditions, contexts, and outcomes cluster together. In selective coding, researchers develop an overarching theme or category around which to build their storyline.

■ **Clarify how credibility is established in qualitative data analysis.**
Credibility in data analysis is established through (1) careful, iterative analysis in categorization and theory development, (2) the use of negative case analysis, and (3) triangulation. In negative case analysis, researchers systematically search the data for information that does not conform to their theory. This helps both to establish the credibility of their analysis and to identify boundary conditions for their theory. Triangulation is especially important in developing credibility for qualitative data analyses. There are several forms of triangulation, including using multiple methods of data collection and analysis; multiple data sets, multiple researchers; data collection in multiple time periods; and use of informants with different perspectives and experiences. Credibility is also enhanced with member checking, which is soliciting feedback about the accuracy of the analysis from key informants. In peer review, qualitative methodology experts are asked to critique the qualitative report.

■ **Discuss the steps involved in writing a qualitative research report.**
A qualitative report has three sections: (1) Introduction, (2) Analysis of the Data/Findings, and (3) Conclusions: Marketing Implications. In the introductory portion of the report, the objectives of the research and methodology are explained as well as the methods employed. In the data analysis section, the reported findings are written in a way that is logical and

persuasive. Data displays and verbatims may be used to enhance the communication of the findings. The last part of the report is the marketing implications section. In this final part of the report, researchers provide conclusions that are relevant to the research problems articulated by the client.

Key Terms and Concepts

Abstraction 209
Axial coding 212
Categorization 209
Code sheet 209
Codes 209
Comparison 211
Credibility 221
Cross-researcher reliability 221
Data reduction 209
Emic validity 221
Integration 212
Iteration 213
Member checking 207
Memoing 213
Negative case analysis 213
Peer review 221
Recursive 212
Selective coding 212
Thick description 207
Triangulation 221
Verbatims 223

Review Questions

1. How are quantitative and qualitative data analysis different?
2. Describe the three steps in qualitative data analysis and explain how and why these steps are iterative.
3. What are the interrelated steps in data reduction?
4. How do you build theory in qualitative analysis?
5. What is negative case analysis and why is it important to the credibility of qualitative analysis?
6. What are the different kinds of data displays? Give some specific examples of how they may be used in qualitative data analysis.
7. What are some of the threats to drawing credible conclusions in qualitative data analysis?
8. What is triangulation and what is its role in qualitative analysis?
9. What are the various ways that credibility can be established in qualitative analysis?

Discussion Questions

1. Compare and contrast reliability and validity in quantitative analysis with the concept of credibility used in qualitative analysis. Do you believe the concepts are really similar? Why or why not?
2. Let's say your college has as a goal increasing the participation in student activities on your college campus. As part of this study, you are doing an ethnographic study to better understand why students do or do not participate in student activities. How would you plan for triangulation in this study?

3. **EXPERIENCE THE INTERNET.** Ask permission from three people to analyze the content of their MySpace, Facebook, or similar site (of course, you should promise them anonymity). If the sites are extensive, you may need a plan to sample a portion

of the site (at least 5–10 representative pages). As you go through the sites, develop a coding sheet. What content categories are the most frequently occurring? What do you conclude from the fact that these categories are the most frequently occurring at these three sites? Are there any implications of your findings for advertisers that are considering advertising on MySpace?

4. An anthropology professor over the age of 50 took a year of leave and spent the year undercover as a student at her college. She did not take classes in her own department, but instead signed up, attended classes, took exams, and wrote papers just like any other freshman. She lived in the dorm for a year. At the end of a year, she wrote a book entitled *My Freshman Year*[28] which details her findings. In reporting the research methodology of her study, what methodological strengths and weaknesses should the anthropology professor address?

5. Conduct 3 or 4 in-depth interviews with college students who are not business majors. You will be conducting an investigation of the associations that college students make with the word "marketing." You can ask students to bring 5–10 images of any type (pictures, cut-outs from magazines) that most essentially picture what they think marketing is all about. You may also conduct a word association exercise with the students. During the interview, you may want to tell informants that you are an alien from another planet and have never heard of marketing. Based on your interviews, develop a consensus map that shows the concepts that students relate to marketing. Draw a circle around the most frequently occurring connections in your diagram. What did you learn about how college students view marketing?

6. Conduct an interview on the topic of soft drinks. Your task is to create a tree diagram that shows how your informant conceptualizes the soft drink market. As the diagram goes from top to bottom, the categories will go from more general to more specific types and brands of soft drinks.

7. You are conducting a small-scale qualitative project about the nature of product dissatisfaction. You will need to follow the steps below.
   a. Write a 2-page narrative about a time that you purchased a product or service with which you were very dissatisfied. You should include in your narrative the following points: (1) the product or service, (2) your expectations when you bought the product or service, (3) any interactions with salespeople or customer service people before, during, or after the purchase, (4) the feelings and emotions that accompanied your dissatisfaction, and (5) the outcomes of your dissatisfaction. You may include other details as well.
   b. Collect narratives written by four of your classmates. You are now going to engage in axial coding of the narratives. Create a matrix. Across the top you will list the product or service, the conditions that led to dissatisfaction, any actions that are related to the creation of dissatisfaction, and the outcomes of dissatisfaction (you may separate the emotions accompanying dissatisfaction from other outcomes in two or more separate outcome columns). Down the left side you will name each person (using a pseudonym).
   c. If you were to engage in selective coding, what overarching theme or perspective do you think would integrate your categories?
   d. What did you learn about dissatisfaction? What are the managerial implications of your findings; that is, how can companies lessen or prevent dissatisfaction? Be as complete as possible in drawing managerial implications.

chapter 8

Descriptive Research Designs Using Surveys

Learning Objectives

After reading this chapter, you will be able to:

1. Discuss the role of constructs, variables, and relationships in survey research.
2. Identify and explain the types of errors that occur in survey research.
3. Describe the types of survey methods.
4. Assess the strengths and weaknesses of different survey methods.
5. Explain the impact of technology on survey research designs.
6. Discuss factors influencing the choice of survey methods.

"The basic techniques of market research—interview, focus groups, surveys, observation—are used in all corners of the globe."

—MICHAEL R. CZINKOTA AND ILKKA A. RONKAINEN[1]

Males Like Mall Shopping: Insights to Their Shopping Interests

One elusive question retailers and advertisers have yet to fully answer is "Do men really hate shopping?" While some experts say yes, others remain unsure. So, recently *Men's Health Magazine* hired Harris Interactive (HI), one of the world's largest marketing research firms, to find out. Using an online descriptive research design, Harris polled 1,000 men across the country asking "how," "what," "when," "where" questions about their shopping habits and preferences. The findings offer direct insight into some misperceptions about how men shop or don't shop as well as some lessons for marketers and advertisers.

Here are some of the results: Regarding men's interest in personal grooming products, over a third of the respondents had not purchased any grooming products such as exfoliant body scrub or anti-aging products, with about 70 percent indicating they "just do not have interest" in those types of products. Yet, 37 percent do buy shower gel and about 35 percent indicated they will buy cologne in the next year. With respect to fashions, about 60 percent said they typically purchase clothing items only to replace those that have worn out. More than 50 percent of the respondents have clothing that needs replacement, while 35 percent indicate they have out-of-style clothes in their closets but wear them anyway. Only 17 percent follow current fashion trends in style, color, or brands. About 25 percent of men buy casual clothes on a monthly basis but about a third have never purchased a suit. Among the suit owners, about half admit their suits are out of style but they basically do not care.

Concerning food shopping habits, 65 percent of the men surveyed said they do at least half of the household food shopping, 80 percent going alone to the store for quick trips, 48 percent alone for supplemental trips, but only about 30 percent alone for the big shopping trips. When asked about what they did with their food purchases, almost 80 percent make their own breakfast, 60 percent make their own dinners, and 47 percent make dinner for others in the household or for special friends. About a third like cooking, another 21 percent do not enjoy cooking, and only 9 percent avoid it, saying that activity is "woman's work."

Some of the interpretive results of this study suggest that in fact (1) men do not hate shopping,

(2) men shop for casual clothing more so than ever before, and (3) men buy many of the household grocery items and regularly buy shower gel and cologne grooming products for themselves. Given that about 80 percent of all marketing dollars for food and personal grooming products goes to targeting women, marketers and advertisers of food and personal grooming products are missing a real opportunity in not trying harder to attract male consumers to their products.[2]

Value of Descriptive Survey Research Designs

The chapter opener example about male shoppers shows that sometimes the research problem requires primary data that can be gathered only by questioning a large number of respondents who are representative of the defined target population. Survey research plays an important role in providing the necessary primary information to guide a firm's development of new marketing strategies. This chapter is the third of four chapters devoted to methods of collecting and analyzing primary data. Whereas Chapter 6 discussed qualitative methods used in exploratory research, this chapter will focus on survey designs used in descriptive research.

We begin this chapter by noting when descriptive research is called for and how descriptive research designs and survey methods are interdependent, followed by a discussion of the importance of constructs, variables, and relationships in the research process. Then we provide a brief overview of survey research methods, their objectives and advantages and disadvantages. The next section highlights the type of errors (or biases) common in survey research. Finally, survey methods are classified by communication means and discussed in detail, followed by a discussion of factors that play in survey method selection.

Descriptive Designs and Surveys in Quantitative Research

Descriptive research deals with quantitative data. Quantitative research practices are driven by the need to collect substantial information from a large number (typically 200 or more) of members of the defined target population so that accurate inferences can be made about the market factors and phenomena under investigation.

Determination of whether the research design should be *descriptive* is based on three factors: (1) the nature of the initial decision problem/opportunity, (2) the set of research questions, and (3) the research objectives. When the nature of the initial research problem/opportunity is either to *describe specific characteristics* of existing market situations or to *evaluate current marketing mix strategies,* then descriptive research design is an appropriate choice. Second, if the management's research questions focus on issues such as *who, what, where, when, and how* of target populations or market structures, then a descriptive research design is appropriate. Finally, if the task is to *identify meaningful relationships,* determine whether true differences exist, or *verify the validity of relationships* among the marketing phenomena, then descriptive research designs should be considered. Although taken separately, these factors are not automatically determinative; if all three characterize the research challenge, they suggest the need to use descriptive research designs.

All research designs must focus on how to collect the data. As we have brought out in previous chapters, there are two basic approaches to collecting primary data: observation and asking questions. While both may be elements in most types of research designs, descriptive designs frequently feature the latter and use data collection procedures that heavily emphasize asking respondents structured questions about what they think, feel, and do, rather than observing what they do. Thus, descriptive research designs use survey data collection methods for gathering quantitative data from large groups of people through the question/answer process.

Overview of Constructs, Variables, and Relationships

Researchers may use both secondary and exploratory (primary) research activities to define (or redefine) research questions and objectives, as well as to identify specific information requirements. Each approach has its requirements. *When using descriptive research methods to collect primary data,* it is important for researchers to fully understand what *constructs, variables,* and *relationships* are being investigated. This section offers a brief overview of constructs, variables and relationships. In those cases where one or more research questions require investigating relationships between constructs or variables, researchers need to conceptualize these hypothesized relationships. The conceptualization process is aided by developing a *model* (or framework) that shows the predicted causal relationships.

Variable Any observable, measurable element (or attribute) of an object or event.

Construct Hypothetical variables composed of a set of component responses or behaviors that are thought to be related.

A **variable** is an observable, measurable element (or attribute) of an object. Variables have concrete properties and are measured *directly.* Examples of variables include gender, marital status, company name, number of employees, and how frequently a particular brand is purchased, among a world of others. In contrast, a **construct** is an unobservable, abstract concept that is measured *indirectly* by a group of related variables. Some examples of commonly measured constructs in marketing include service quality, value, customer satisfaction, brand attitude, and product loyalty. People (or consumer) characteristics that represent indirectly measurable constructs include innovativeness, opinion leadership, personality, and deal proneness. For example, Exhibit 8.1 displays a group of variables (items) that researchers use to measure the construct "market maven," defined as an individual who has a lot of information about products and who actively shares that information.

Relationship Association between two or more variables.

Relationships are associations between constructs or variables. Whether researchers rely on insights gained from conducting secondary research activities, including literature reviews on some topic, or qualitative exploratory research to determine subjects' attitudes or descriptive survey research, they are often seeking out *relationships* among data. The relationships between variables or constructs can be either independent or dependent in

eXHIBIT 8.1 Measuring the Marketing Maven Construct[3]

1. I like introducing new brands and products to my friends.
2. I like helping people by providing them with information about many kinds of products.
3. People ask me for information about products, places to shop, or sales.
4. If someone asked where to get the best buy on several types of products, I could tell him or her where to shop.
5. My friends think of me as a good source of information when it comes to new products or sales.
6. Think about a person who has information about a variety of products and likes to share this information with others. This person knows about new products, sales, stores and so on, but does not necessarily feel he or she is an expert on one particular product. How well would you say that this description fits you?

Independent variable The variable or construct that predicts or explains the outcome variable.

Dependent variable The variable or construct researchers are seeking to explain.

nature. An **independent variable** is the variable or construct that predicts or explains the outcome variable of interest. A **dependent variable** is the variable or construct researchers are seeking to explain. For example, if technology optimism and household income predict Internet adoption by seniors, then technology optimism and household income are independent variables, and Internet adoption is the dependent variable. Only after researchers have identified and defined their variables and constructs can they begin thinking about how variables may be related to each other and establish testable *hypotheses* that represent those relationships.

Framing a hypothesis about a relationship must always be based on prior knowledge. Suppose corporate management at Verizon is interested in being able to predict what type of consumer will quickly adopt the company's new FiOs Internet and TV fiber-optic network technologies. There is a great deal of existing research and theory on "new technological innovations." Past research suggests that more educated, higher income individuals who are open to learning are more likely to adopt new technologies. Consequently, several initial hypothesized relationships can be framed based on past research as follows:

- Individuals with more education are more likely to adopt the new fiber-optic technological innovation.
- Individuals who are more open to learning are more likely to adopt the new fiber-optic technological innovation.
- Individuals who have more income are more likely to adopt the new fiber-optic technological innovation.
- Individuals who have higher technology discomfort are less likely to adopt the new fiber-optic technological innovation.

Positive relationship An association between two variables in which they increase or decrease together.

Negative relationship An association between two variables in which one increases while the other decreases.

Null hypothesis A statement of the perceived existing relationship between two questions, dimensions, or subgroupings of attributes as being not significantly different.

Alternative hypothesis A statement that is the opposite of the null hypothesis, where the difference is not simply due to random error.

The first three hypotheses suggest positive relationships. A **positive relationship** between two variables is when the two variables increase or decrease together. **Negative relationships** suggest that as one variable increases, the other one decreases, or vice versa. For example, the last hypothesis above suggests that individuals exhibiting higher technology discomfort are less likely to adopt the new fiber-optic technological innovation.

In addition to available insights from past research and secondary information sources, experience within a *research context* can help a researcher develop hypotheses. An organization may accumulate a great deal of experience over time with a particular research context that is useful in understanding and conceptualizing relationships for future studies. For example, restaurant owners have a lot of insight about their restaurant patrons, as do managers of retail clothing stores about their customers. They learn over time by observing customers' behavior and listening to the questions they ask and so forth. Familiarity with a particular research context can suggest to the researcher a wealth of possible relationships among data.

To more effectively work with hypothesized relationships among variables, researchers typically prepare a diagram, referred to as a *conceptual model,* that visually represents the relationships under investigation. Using the Verizon fiber-optic technology adoption example, Exhibit 8.2 illustrates with a box and arrows diagram how hypothesized relationships can be visually expressed in a model.

Finally, in developing research hypotheses, researchers typically frame relationships in either the "null" or "alternative" format. The **null hypothesis** states that there is no relationship between the variables, or if there is one it is random. In many cases, the null hypothesis is the one that is tested by statisticians and market researchers. In contrast, the **alternative hypothesis** states that there is a relationship between two variables that is significant. If the null hypothesis is accepted, researchers conclude that the variables are not

eXHIBIT 8.2 Model of New Fiber-optic Technology Adoption

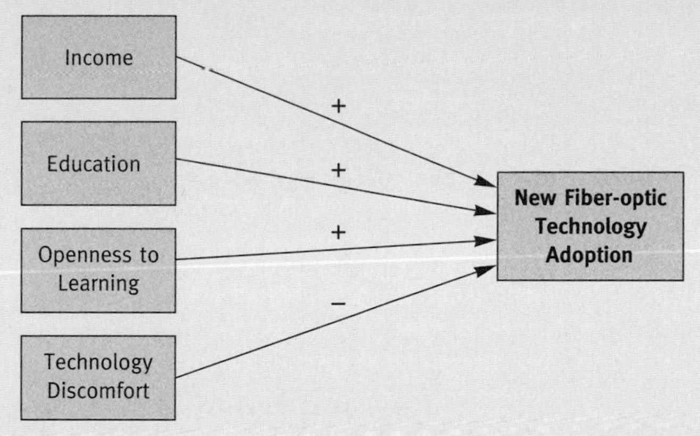

related in a meaningful way. If the null hypothesis is rejected, researchers find support for the alternative hypothesis, that the two variables are related in some way that may prove useful.

Overview of Survey Research Methods

Survey research methods Research procedures for collecting large amounts of data using question-and-answer formats.

Survey research methods are the mainstay of marketing research and are typically associated with descriptive and causal research situations. One distinguishing characteristic of survey research methods is the need to collect data from large samples of people (200 or more). This large sample size requires that individuals answer the same predetermined set of questions and that responses selected from a set of possible answers be recorded in a structured, precise manner.

Success in collecting primary *quantitative* data is move a function of correctly designing and administering a survey questionnaire than of relying on the communication and interpretive skills of an interviewer or observer. The main goal of quantitative survey research methods is to provide *specific facts and estimates* from a large, representative sample of respondents. The findings are then used to (1) make accurate predictions about relationships between market factors and customer behaviors; (2) understand the relationships and differences; and (3) validate the existing relationships. The advantages and disadvantages of quantitative survey research designs are summarized in Exhibit 8.3.

Advantages of Survey Methods

One major advantage of surveys is their ability to accommodate large sample sizes at relatively lower costs. Data collected from surveying large samples increases geographic flexibility of the research findings as well as the ability to make inferences about the target population. The resulting data can be analyzed in many different ways based on the diversity of the variables such as gender, income, occupation, or other variables included in the survey. Thus, another benefit of quantitative survey data is they can be used with advanced

eXHIBIT 8.3 Advantages and Disadvantages of Survey Research Designs

Advantages of Survey Methods

- Can accommodate large sample sizes so that results can be generalized to defined target population.
- Produce precise enough estimates to identify even small differences.
- Are easy to administer and record answers to structured questions.
- Facilitate advanced statistical analysis.
- Concepts and relationships not directly measurable can be studied.

Disadvantages of Survey Methods

- Questions that accurately measure respondent attitudes and behavior can be challenging to develop.
- Richness of detail, in-depth data and difficult to obtain.
- Timeliness of data collection is a challenge.
- Low response rates can be a problem.

statistical analysis to identify hidden patterns and trends. For example, an analysis of product purchasing behaviors among households headed by female single parents in the Northeast can be compared to purchasing behaviors among households headed by female single parents in the Southeast to reveal small differences in regional preferences that may not be apparent in simpler approaches.

Another advantage of surveys is their ease of administration. Typically, descriptive surveys are fairly easy to implement because there is less need for sophisticated devices to record actions and reactions, as with observations or experiments. Surveys facilitate the collection of standardized data since all respondents give answers to the same questions and have the same set of responses available to them. This allows direct comparisons among respondents.

A final advantage of surveys is their ability to tap into factors that are not directly observable (attitudes, feelings, preferences). Through both direct and indirect questioning techniques, people can be asked why they prefer one package design over another, for example. Structured questions can expose the thought process a customer uses to select a particular brand or how many brands were considered. In contrast, observation data show only that an individual selected a particular brand. Survey research methods enable researchers to collect all types of data (demographics, attitudes, preferences, emotions, behaviors) across any desired time frame (past, present, and future).

Disadvantages of Survey Methods

While implementation of surveys is relatively easy, developing the appropriate questions and answers that accurately measure respondents' attitudes and behaviors can be challenging. To ensure precision, researchers must resolve a variety of issues associated with construct development, scaling, and questionnaire design. Inappropriate treatment of these issues can produce many kinds of errors in survey findings. As the possibility of systematic error increases, so does the likelihood of collecting irrelevant or inaccurate data. The development, measurement and design issues associated with surveys are discussed in Chapters 11, 12, and 13.

Another disadvantage is the limited use of probing questions. Survey designs typically do not include probing questions and rarely use unstructured or open-ended questions.

Consequently, the data may lack the detail and richness researchers may need to define the research problem. A third potential weakness of surveys is the lack of control over timeliness in actually collecting the data. Depending on the administration method, some types of surveys take significantly longer to complete than others. Mail surveys require researchers to develop a questionnaire packet, disseminate the packets, and wait for them to be returned via the postal service. Researchers can only estimate how long it will take the postal service to actually get the questionnaire packet to each selected respondent, how long the respondents will take to complete the survey, and how long it will take the postal service to return the packets. Thus, researchers lose control of the timing in the process as soon as the questionnaire packets are given to the postal service. To illustrate, a researcher using a mail survey design might estimate the process will take 14 days to complete, yet mail designs often take 45 days or longer. Getting the surveys out and back within a reasonable amount of time remains a great challenge for researchers using mail surveys. Associated with the issue of response time is the problem of obtaining a high enough response rate (or return rate of completed surveys), depending on respondents' willingness to respond. As new data collection technologies emerge, timeliness and response rate issues should be alleviated.

Types of Errors in Survey Research

Errors reduce the accuracy and quality of the data collected by researchers. Survey research errors can be classified as being either sampling errors or nonsampling errors. Exhibit 8.4 provides an overview of the various forms of errors researchers must be aware of and attempt to either reduce or at least control.

Sampling Error

Sampling error The statistically measured difference between the actual sampled results and the estimated true population results.

Any survey research design that involves collecting primary data from a sample will have some error due to random fluctuations in the data. **Sampling error** is the difference between the findings based on the sample and the true values of the defined target population. Sampling error is caused by the method of sampling used and the size of the sample. This type of error can be reduced or controlled by increasing the sample size and using an appropriate sampling method. We learn more about sampling error in Chapter 10.

Nonsampling Errors

Nonsampling error A type of bias that occurs in a research study regardless of whether a sample or census is used.

Errors that occur in survey research design not related to sampling are called **nonsampling errors.** Most types of nonsampling errors stem from four major sources. They are respondent errors, measurement or questionnaire design errors, faulty or incorrect problem definition errors, and project administration errors.

Regardless of the survey method, there are several common characteristics among all sources of errors. First, they tend to create some form of "systematic variation" in the data that is not considered a natural occurrence of the surveyed respondents. Systematic variations usually result from imperfections in the survey design or mistakes in the execution of the research process. Second, nonsampling errors are controllable. They are the result of some type of human mistake in either the design or execution of a survey method. Consequently, the responsibility for reducing or eliminating such systematic errors falls on researchers and requires that controls be imposed during the design and execution processes of any type of survey research project. Third, unlike sampling error that can be statistically

EXHIBIT 8.4 Sources of Error in Survey Research Designs

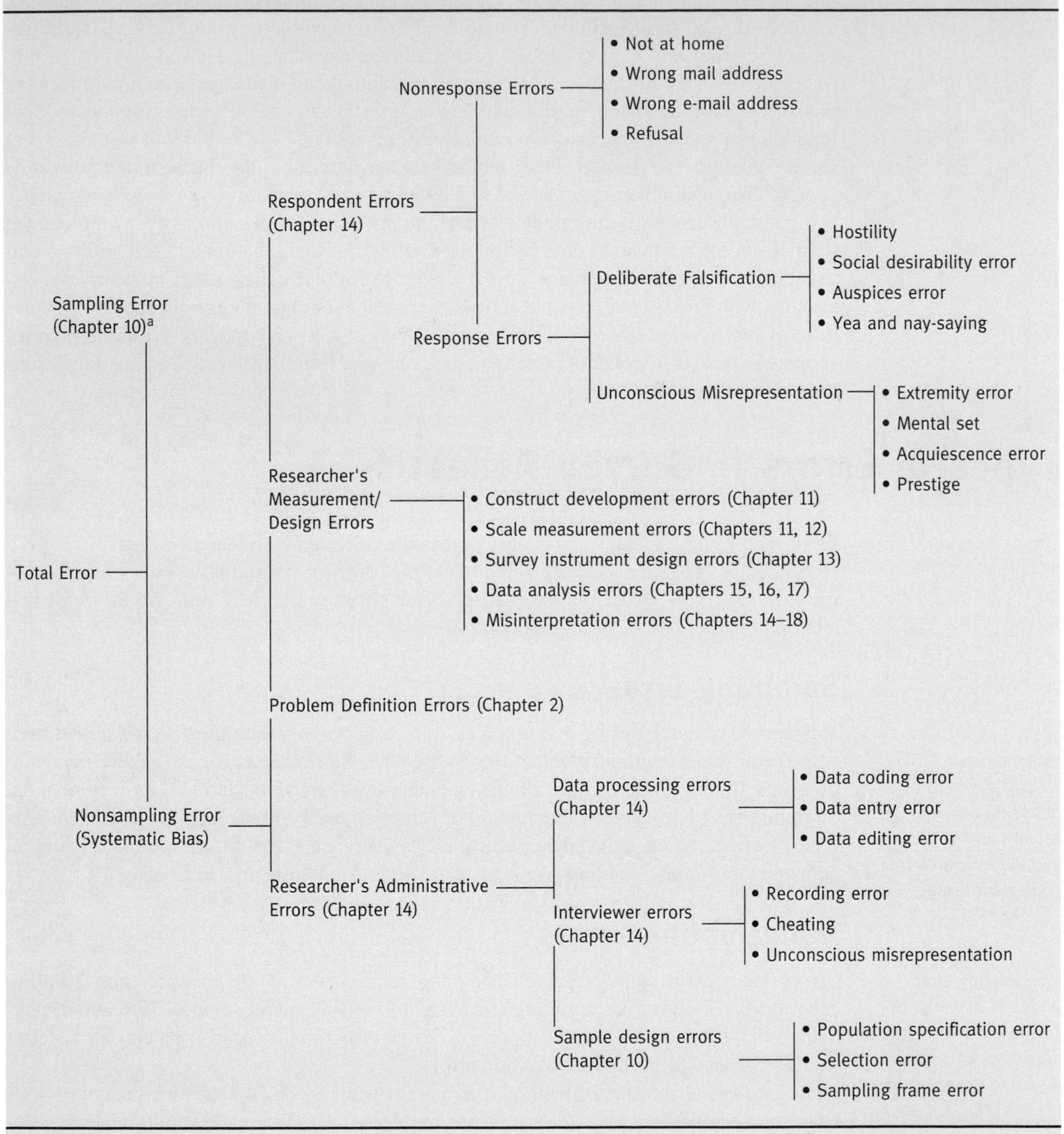

[a]Other chapters that discuss error.

measured, nonsampling errors cannot be directly measured. Finally, nonsampling errors are interactive in nature. One type of error can potentially allow other types of errors to enter the data collection process. For example, if researchers design a bad questionnaire, the errors can potentially cause respondent errors. Although difficult to accurately assess, nonsampling errors can only lower the quality level of the data being collected and therefore the information being provided to decision makers.

Respondent Errors

Systematic errors occur when respondents cannot be reached to participate in the survey process, do not cooperate, are unwilling to participate in the survey's question/answer exchange activities, or respond incorrectly or in an unnatural way to the questions asked in the survey. Exhibit 8.5 summarizes the major issues that lead to respondent error in survey research practices. The two major sources for respondent error are termed *nonresponse error* and *response error*.

Nonresponse error A systematic bias that occurs when the final sample differs from the planned sample.

Nonresponse error is a systematic bias that occurs when the final sample differs from the planned sample. This is likely to occur when a sufficient number of the prospective respondents in the sample cannot be reached for participation. The major reasons underlying this type of error are not at home, wrong postal mailing address or e-mail address, or wrong telephone numbers. Nonresponse error also can be caused when a sufficient number of the initial sampled respondents refuse to participate. Regardless of the cause, nonresponse errors can severely limit the generalizability of the findings, when individuals who do not respond have significantly different feelings from those who do respond. Typically, the higher the nonresponse rate, the greater the risk of biased results.

People choose to participate in a survey for a variety of reasons including social rewards, monetary incentives, boredom, and sometimes just for the experience. Nonresponse is also caused by many factors. For example, some people do not trust the research sponsor and/or have little commitment toward responding.[4] Some prospective respondents resent what is perceived as an invasion of privacy, or the subject matter may be too sensitive. The differences between people who do and do not respond can be striking. For example, some research has shown that for mail surveys, where the response rate tends to be lower than for most other primary data collection methods, respondents tend to be more educated than nonrespondents and have higher scores on other related variables such as income. In

EXHIBIT 8.5 Types of Respondent Errors in Survey Research Methods

Type of Errors	Error Sources
Nonresponse error	• Not at home • Wrong mailing address • Wrong phone number • Wrong e-mail address • Refusal
Response error	**Deliberate Falsification** • Feeling of hostility • Social desirability • Prestige responses • Yea- and nay-saying **Unconscious Misrepresentation** • Mental set errors • Extremity errors • Acquiescence errors

addition, respondents are more likely to be female.[5] The effect of other sociodemographic variables is not well understood. No matter the research method, community size, gender, age, education, and income of those who respond to second and third wave solicitations are often different from those of nonrespondents.[6]

To reduce the nonresponse rate, researchers attempt to be less intrusive in the respondent's life.[7] Other practices for improving response rates include multiple callbacks or mailing waves, building credibility of the research sponsor, and shorter questionnaires.[8]

Response error The tendency to answer a question in a particular and unique systematic way. Respondents may consciously or unconsciously distort their answers and true thoughts.

Faulty recall The inability of a person to accurately remember the specifics about the behavior under investigation.

Averaging assuming the norm behavior or belief to be the reality.

Response error is the tendency of respondents to answer a question in a particular and unique systematic way that distorts their answers and true thoughts. When researchers ask questions, one of two basic mechanisms begins operating. One mechanism is that respondents search their memory, retrieve their attitudinal recollection, and provide it as their response. If this doesn't happen automatically, however, or if individuals are not motivated to search their memory, the response may be biased in some manner. For example, respondents may give a socially desirable response—a response that enhances their ego—or they may simply guess.

The human memory is also a source of response error. People can have impaired memory and be unable to respond accurately; this is termed **faulty recall.** If the questions relate to a new attitude, respondents may answer on the basis of some combination of short-term memory and the context of the question.[9] Human memory is an inexact thing. It is subject to telescoping, selective perception, and the compression of time, such that respondents may think they recall things that happened when they actually do not. Another memory problem is termed *averaging.* **Averaging** refers to assuming the norm behavior or belief to be the reality. For example, individuals who commonly have fried chicken for Sunday dinner may be unable to recall that last week's Sunday dinner was pot roast. In some cases, respondents sometimes leave out information researchers would like to know about. While in most cases, respondents try to give more information rather than less, respondents may be tired or there may not be a good rapport with interviewers.

Some researchers find one approach that is useful to evaluate response bias is to measure the time between when a question is asked and the response is given. Responses that are expressed very fast and those that are given slowly may be biased. Fast responses are indicative of either a hurried response or a simple information request, while slow responses are indicative of a difficult question that requires a more extended thought process.[10]

Construct development error A type of nonsampling (systematic) error that is created when the researcher is not careful in fully identifying the concepts and constructs to be included in the study.

Scale measurement error Occurs when researchers do not develop or use the appropriate scales to measure the constructs.

Survey instrument error A type of error that occurs when the survey instrument induces some type of systematic bias in the response.

Measurement and Design Error

Researchers and decision makers must recognize that the quality of data can suffer from problems resulting from inappropriate design of the constructs, scales, and survey questionnaires.[11] Design errors make getting meaningful results from the data difficult. Exhibit 8.6 summarizes the five major sources of measurement and design errors researchers must reduce or control to improve data collection accuracy.

Construct development error occurs when researchers are not careful in identifying the constructs to be used in the study. Researchers must correctly identify and define the different data requirements (concepts, objects, topics, etc.) that are the focus of the investigation. When critical constructs are not completely defined, for example, there is a strong likelihood inappropriate dimensionality will occur resulting in underidentifying the construct subcomponents. When data requirements are not fully developed, data quality, reliability, validity, and ability to make generalizations about the defined target population become problematic.

Scale measurement error occurs when researchers do not develop or use the appropriate scales to measure the constructs. Moreover, measurement errors can be created several

eXHIBIT 8.6 Types of Measurement and Design Errors in Survey Methods

Type of Errors	Error Sources
Construct development error	Incomplete constructs
	Low reliability of construct
	Low construct validity
Scale measurement error	Lack of precision
	Lack of discriminatory power
	Ambiguity of question/setup
	Inappropriate use of scale descriptors
Survey instrument error	Improper sequence of questions
	Lack of or inadequate instructions
	Length of questionnaire
Data analysis error	Inappropriate analysis technique
	Predictive bias
Misinterpretation error	Interpretive bias
	Selective perception

Data analysis error A "family" of nonsampling errors that are created when the researcher subjects the data to inappropriate analysis procedures.

Misinterpretation error An inaccurate transformation of data analysis results into usable bits of information for the decision maker.

Interpretive bias Error that occurs when the wrong inference about the real world or defined target population is made by the researcher or decision maker due to some type of extraneous factor.

Selective perception bias A type of error that occurs in situations where researchers or decision makers use only a selected portion of the survey results to paint a tainted picture of reality.

ways, including inappropriate questions, scale attributes, or scale point descriptors. These problems result in (1) less precision in the measurement, (2) lower discriminatory power among the scale descriptors, (3) ambiguity of the scale's questions, or (4) use of inappropriate scale descriptors. These types of bias sources negatively impact the reliability and validity of the data.

Survey instrument error is the result of a poorly designed questionnaire and can result in several problems. In many cases, errors are a result of leading questions—ones that suggest an appropriate answer. Leading questions put words in respondents' mouths rather than drawing out what respondents actually think. For example, asking a respondent "Why do you think this is a high-quality product?" encourages only positive responses. Leading questions do not encourage respondents to give their true feelings about the topic being investigated but rather responses researchers want to hear. While careful design of the individual measurements can reduce bias, it does not guarantee it. For example, improper sequencing of scale measurements on a questionnaire (i.e., violation of the "Flower Pot" framework discussed in Chapter 13) can create systematic errors not directly related to scale measurement problems. Questionnaire design errors can result in both nonresponse and response errors.

Data analysis error occurs when researchers apply the wrong type of data analysis method. Incorrect statistical analysis prevents the researcher from accurately testing relationships.

Misinterpretation error is the inability to correctly or completely translate data analysis results into accurate findings or conclusions. The two main underlying sources are *interpretive error* and *selective perception error*. First, **interpretive bias** is created when the wrong inference is made by researchers about the real world or target population. For example, researchers might present the results in such a way that the findings appear to support the initial thoughts of researchers. **Selective perception bias** occurs when researchers

Faulty problem definition error An incorrect definition of what the marketing problem really is.

Project administration error Bias that can stem from data processing mistakes, interviewer distortion of the respondents' answers, or systematic inaccuracies created by using a faulty sampling design.

Data processing error A specific type of nonsampling error that can occur when researchers are not accurate or complete in transferring data from respondents to computer files.

Coding error is caused by assigning the wrong computer code to a response.

Data entry error The incorrect assignment of computer codes to their predesignated location on the computer data file.

Editing error The result of carelessness in verifying coding or data entry procedures.

use only a selected portion of the survey results to give support to a tainted picture of reality. For example, leaders in the tobacco industry for years manipulated test results of nicotine as an addictive substance to hide the truth about the effects of nicotine as an ingredient in cigarettes.

Faulty Problem Definition Errors

Survey research designs also can suffer when the initial problem is not clearly or correctly identified. **Faulty problem definition error** occurs when decision makers and/or researchers misinterpret the true nature of the problem situation. The main causes of creating this error are (1) management's lack of understanding of the real problem, (2) misinterpreting market performance factors (e.g., decrease in sales revenues) as being the problem rather than the symptom, or (3) researchers inaccurately transforming the problem into research questions. Regardless of the cause, incorrectly understanding the situation or the problems will make survey research results useless. For example, let's say the product manager for Nike requests a study to test the best media mix for athletic shoes. If the true problem is the company's pricing strategies, then any research conducted, no matter how technically correct, will not be helpful to the manager.

Project Administration Errors

In survey research, **project administration error** occurs from improper execution of the steps in gathering and processing data. In Exhibit 8.7 administration errors are grouped into three basic sources: data processing error, interviewer error, and sample design error.

Data processing errors occur when transferring respondents' answers to a computer data file. Data processing errors typically result from either data coding, entry, and/or editing problems. A **coding error** is caused by assigning the wrong computer code to a response. **Data entry errors** occur when response codes are incorrectly entered into their designated field in the computer's data file. **Editing errors** are the result of carelessness in verifying coding or data entry procedures. These errors can be minimized by executing control procedures that check each data processing step.

EXHIBIT 8.7 Types of Project Administration Errors in Survey Research

Type of Errors	Error Sources
Data processing error	Data coding errors
	Data entry errors
	Data editing errors
Interviewer/observer error	Unconscious misrepresentation
	Recording errors
	Cheating
Sample design error	Population specification error
	Sample selection errors
	Sampling frame error

Interviewer error A type of nonsampling bias that is created in situations where the interviewer distorts information in a systematic way from respondents during or after the interviewer/respondent encounter.

Unconscious misrepresentation Occurs when interviewers induce a pattern of responses that does not represent the target population.

Interviewer cheating *Deliberate falsification* of responses by incorrectly recording responses, by making up answers, or by filling in answers to questions that have been intentionally skipped by respondents.

Recording error Occurs when interviewers inadvertently check the wrong response or may be unable to write fast enough to capture the response verbatim.

Sample design error Occurs when the sampling plan does not select the "right" respondents.

Population specification error An incorrect definition of the true target population to the research question.

Sample selection error Occurs when incomplete or incorrect sampling procedures are used even when the target population is correctly specified.

Sampling frame error Occurs when an incomplete or inaccurate sampling frame is used.

Interviewer error is a result of an interaction between interviewers and respondents. Interviewer error distorts information from respondents in a manner similar to instrument bias. Three primary sources of interviewer error are *recording error*, *unconscious misrepresentation,* and *cheating*. **Unconscious misrepresentation** occurs when interviewers induce a pattern of responses that does not represent the target population. For example, respondents may interpret the interviewer's body language, facial expression, or tone of voice as a cue to how to respond to a question. Interviewers must remain as neutral as possible during interviews to reduce interviewer-induced bias. Proper training, supervision, and practice all help to reduce interviewer bias.

Interviewer cheating is *deliberate falsification* of responses by incorrectly recording responses, by making up answers, or by filling in answers to questions that have been intentionally skipped by respondents. In rare cases, interviewers cheat to finish interviews as quickly as possible to complete their assignment or to avoid asking sensitive topic questions. On the other hand, **recording errors** occur when interviewers inadvertently check the wrong response or may be unable to write fast enough to capture the response verbatim. Quality control techniques should be used to detect interviewer error, whether deliberate or inadvertent.

Sample design error occurs when the sampling plan does not select the "right" respondents. A key to capturing reliable and valid data is asking questions and recording responses from the "right" respondents. The "right" respondents are those who are representative of the target population. To achieve this goal, many survey research projects incorporate a sampling design process to determine the "right" respondents to represent the target population. Several types of sample design errors can occur, including population specification error, sample selection error, and sampling frame error.

Population specification error (also known as population frame error) is incorrect definition of the target population. Correctly defining the target population is a critical step in survey research. Imagine if researchers for Verizon design and conduct a study on alternative pricing plans of mobile phones with broadband capabilities thinking that only individuals earning more than $50,000 are interested and then discover that individuals earning $30,000 to $50,000 also use mobile phones with broadband capabilities. The entire segment of people earning $30,000 to $50,000 and their responses would not be represented. Population specification error is discussed more in Chapter 10.

Errors also can occur when an inappropriate sample is selected from the target population. **Sample selection error** occurs when incomplete or incorrect sampling procedures are used even when the target population is correctly specified. For example, interviewers may avoid some members of the target population in a mall-intercept survey because the individuals appear scruffy or unattractive. Quality controls should include checks on the sample selected to ensure the data is collected from randomly selected members of the target population.

In sample designs, the sampling frame is the list of population elements or members from which the prospective respondents (or sampling units) are selected. **Sampling frame error** occurs when an incomplete or inaccurate sampling frame is used. The main problem with frame error is that the sample selected is not likely to be representative of the target population. A classic example of a sample frame error is a sampling plan that uses a published telephone directory as the sample frame for a telephone survey. Many individuals or households either are not listed or not listed accurately in the current telephone directory because they (1) do not want to be listed, (2) have recently moved and missed the publication deadline date, (3) have recently changed their telephone number, or (4) use only a mobile phone. Research has shown that people listed in telephone directories are systematically different from those who are not listed.[12]

Types of Survey Methods

Many survey methods can be used to collect primary data. Continuous improvements in computer, multimedia, and telecommunication technologies have created new survey approaches. Nevertheless, almost all survey methods can be classified as *person-administered*, *telephone-administered*, or *self-administered* (including online). Exhibit 8.8 provides an overview of survey methods being used to collect data.

Person-administered surveys Data collection techniques that require the presence of a trained human interviewer who asks questions and records the subject's answers.

Person-Administered Surveys

Person-administered survey methods have trained interviewers (or observers) who ask questions and record respondent answers. Person-administered methods are used less often than other approaches because of the cost and longer completion time. Depending on

EXHIBIT 8.8 Types of Survey Research Methods

Type of Survey Research	Description
Person-Administered	
In-home interview	An interview takes place in the respondent's home or, in special situations, within the respondent's work environment (in-office).
Executive interview	A business executive is interviewed in person.
Mall-intercept Interview	Shopping patrons are stopped and asked for feedback during their visit to a shopping mall.
Purchase-intercept interview	The respondent is stopped and asked for feedback at the point of purchase.
Telephone-Administered	
Telephone interview	An interview takes place over the telephone. Interviews may be conducted from a central telephone location or the interviewer's home.
Computer-assisted telephone interview (CATI)	A computer is used to conduct a telephone interview; respondents give answers by pushing buttons on their phone.
Completely automated telephone surveys (CATS)	The survey is completely administered by a computer without the use of any human interviewer.
Self-Administered	
Mail panel survey	Surveys are mailed to a representative sample of individuals who have agreed in advance to participate.
Drop-off survey	Questionnaires are left with the respondent to be completed at a later time. The surveys may be picked up by the researcher or returned via mail.
Mail survey	Questionnaires are distributed to and returned from respondents via the postal service.
Computer-Assisted (Online)	
Fax survey	Surveys are distributed to and returned from respondents via fax machines.
E-mail survey	Surveys are distributed to and returned from respondents via electronic mail.
Internet survey	The Internet is used to ask questions and record responses from respondents.

EXHIBIT 8.9 Advantages and Disadvantages of Person-Administered Surveys

Advantages	**Comments**
Adaptability	Trained interviewers can *quickly adapt* to respondents' differences.
Rapport	Not all people are willing to talk with strangers when asked to answer a few questions. Interviewers can help establish a *comfort zone* during the questioning process.
Feedback	During the questioning process, interviewers can *answer respondents' questions* and increase the respondents' understanding of instructions and questions, and capture additional verbal and nonverbal information.
Quality of responses	Sometimes the interviewer must screen to qualify prospective respondents based on a set of characteristics like gender, age, etc. Interviewers can help ensure the *"right" respondents are correctly chosen.* Respondents tend to be more truthful in their responses when answering questions in a face-to-face situation.
Disadvantages	
Speed of data acquisition	Interviewers are sometimes *slow in recording responses.*
Possible recording error	Humans often *use selective perception* in listening to and recording responses to questions, which can cause inaccuracies in the respondent's answers.
Interviewer–respondent interaction error	Respondents may interpret the interviewer's *body language, facial expression, or tone of voice as a clue* to how to respond to a question.
High expense	Overall *cost* of data collection using an interviewer in a face-to-face environment *often is higher* than other data collection methods.

the research objectives and data requirements, different types of methods may be used. Exhibit 8.9 summarizes the advantages and disadvantages of person-administered surveys.

In-Home Interviews

In-home interview A structured question-and-answer exchange conducted in the respondent's home.

An **in-home interview** is a face-to-face question-and-answer exchange conducted in the respondent's home. Sometimes the interviewer–respondent exchange occurs in the respondent's work environment rather than in the home, in which case the term becomes *in-office interview.* This method has several advantages. Interviewers can explain confusing or complex questions, use visual aids or other stimuli to elicit responses, and assess contextual conditions. This helps generate more feedback from respondents. In addition, respondents are in a comfortable, familiar environment where they feel safe and secure, thus increasing the likelihood of respondents' willingness to answer survey questions.

Frequently, in-home interviewing is accomplished through door-to-door canvassing of geographic areas. This canvassing process is one of the disadvantages of in-home interviewing. Interviewers who are not constantly supervised may skip homes they find threatening or may simply fabricate interviews. To ensure the safety of interviewers, researchers provide training on how to avoid potentially threatening situations. In-home or in-office interviews are expensive and time-consuming.

Executive Interviews

Executive interview A personal exchange with a business executive conducted in his or her office.

An **executive interview** is a personal exchange with a business executive that typically takes place in the executive's office. The topics involve industrial products or service offerings because few executives are willing to share business hours to discuss nonbusiness or personal preferences.

Conducting executive interviews is expensive, not only in terms of interviewer compensation but also travel expenses. Also, securing an appointment with executives can be a time-consuming process and even then their agreement to be interviewed can be problematic. Finally, executive interviews require the use of well-trained and experienced interviewers because the topics often are technical.

Mall-Intercept Interviews

Mall-intercept interview A face-to-face personal interview that takes place in a shopping mall.

A **mall-intercept interview** is a face-to-face personal interview that takes place in a shopping mall. Mall shoppers are stopped and asked to complete a survey. Surveys take place in a common area of the mall or in the researcher's on-site offices. Mall-intercept interviews share the advantages of in-home and in-office interviews except for the familiarity of the environment for respondents. However, the mall-intercept is typically less expensive and more convenient for researchers. Interviewers spend little time and effort in securing individuals' agreement to participate in interviews because both are already at a common location. In addition, researchers benefit from reduced screening costs and time spent because interviewers can easily identify potential members of the target population by using their observation skills on location.

The disadvantages of mall-intercept interviews are similar to those of in-home or in-office interviews in terms of time, but as respondents are easy to recruit and travel time is nil, the total time investment is lower. However, mall patrons may not be representative of the general population or may shop at different stores or at different times of the day. Typically, mall-intercept interviews incorporate nonprobability sampling techniques for selecting prospective respondents. As you will learn later, nonprobability sampling can eliminate the ability to generalize survey results. Marketing researchers using mall-intercept interviews need to be sensitive to these issues.

Purchase-Intercept Interviews

Purchase-intercept interview A face-to-face interview that takes place immediately after the purchase of a product or service.

While similar to a mall-intercept, **purchase-intercepts** are different in that intercepts take place after interviewers have observed a behavior—usually the selection or purchase of a particular product. An advantage of this type of interview is that the recency of the behavior aids respondents' recall capabilities.

There are two major disadvantages to purchase-intercept interviews in addition to those mentioned regarding mall-intercepts already. First, many stores are not willing to let their customers be intercepted and their shopping interrupted in the store. Second, purchase-intercepts involve only those individuals who demonstrate some observable behavior. Thus, consumers who are considering a purchase but do not buy are excluded from this type of data collection technique.

Telephone-Administered Surveys

Traditional Telephone Interviews

Telephone interviews Question-and-answer exchanges that are conducted via telephone technology.

Telephone interviews are a major data collection method. Compared to face-to-face interviews, telephone interviews are less expensive, faster, and more suitable for gathering data from large numbers of respondents. **Telephone surveys** are personal interviews conducted via telephone. Individuals working from their homes or from central locations use telephones to ask questions and record responses.

Telephone surveys have a number of advantages over face-to-face surveys. One advantage is interviewers can be closely supervised if they work out of a central location. Supervisors can record calls and review them later and/or they can listen in on calls. Reviewing or listening to interviewers ensures quality control and can identify training needs. When interviewers work out of their own home, they can set hours that are convenient for them, within limits prescribed by the employer or the law.

Telephone interviews are less expensive than face-to-face interviews. Asking questions and recording responses over the phone enables interviewers to complete more surveys in a given time period and reduces travel and search time spent on locating respondents. This method also facilitates interviews with respondents across a wide geographic area.

Another advantage is interviewers can call back respondents who did not answer the telephone or respondents who found it inconvenient to be interviewed when first called. Callbacks are inexpensive compared to follow-up personal survey costs. A fourth advantage is that respondents perceive telephone surveys to be more anonymous and may feel less threatened and therefore be more candid. Anonymity also reduces the opportunity for interviewer bias. Finally, telephone surveys are useful in gathering data from busy executives. For example, business executives or hard-to-reach people (e.g., medical doctors) may not make time needed for conducting a face-to-face personal interview, but they often take time for a telephone call.

Traditional telephone-administered survey methods have several drawbacks. One disadvantage is that pictures or other nonaudio stimuli cannot be presented over the telephone. Also it is difficult for telephone respondents to perform complex tasks. For example, imagine the confusion in the mind of respondents asked to remember seven brands of a product category, each with multiple variations, throughout an entire interview. Another limitation is telephone surveys have to be kept shorter than personal interviews because people hang up on long telephone calls, resulting in less in-depth information on the topic. In some cases, telephone surveys are limited, at least in practice, by national borders. The telephone is still seldom used in international research. Probably the greatest limitation lies in the restrictions on the types of data that can be collected over the phone. For example, it is difficult to use multiple levels of agreement/disagreement, likes/dislikes, and so on, and all but impossible to accurately ask brand-image questions that would require respondents to answer using scales requiring visual responses.

Finally, many people have an unfavorable perception of telephone research due to the increased use of telemarketing practices. The nearby Ethics box describes the illegal and unethical act of "sugging," or selling under the guise of research, which no doubt contributes to this poor perception. The public has been vocal enough regarding sugging that it is against federal law. Yet other people are simply annoyed by telephone research because it interrupts their privacy, their dinner, or their relaxation time. The federal government has responded with not only legislation limiting the hours for conducting telephone interviews but also a federal "no call list registry" that restricts contacting prospective respondents. Today's advances in telecommunication technologies enable *call blocking* (also referred to as *gatekeeping*) including caller ID, answering services, and voice messaging so respondents can screen calls, decreasing the effectiveness of telephone survey methods.

A difficult aspect of conducting telephone-administered surveys is selecting the telephone number to be called. Using traditional or electronic telephone directories often does not produce a random sample because many people choose to have unlisted numbers or have only a mobile phone. In some cases, the client will supply researchers with a customer or calling list, but most descriptive research studies need a random sample. Over the years three dialing techniques have been used to select prospective respondents' telephone numbers: plus-one dialing, systematic random digit dialing, and random digit dialing.

ETHICS

Using Technology

Sugging Is a Federal Offense

Sugging is the term used for the illegal telemarketing practice of selling under the guise of research. Sugging has been described as the bane of telephone research and especially the researcher. Researchers are frequently forced to deal with respondents who challenge them to prove the call is a legitimate research effort and not a disguised sales solicitation.

Consumer outrage at the practice of sugging prompted the U.S. Congress to pass the Telemarketing Sales Act (TSA), which went into effect under Federal Trade Commission implementation rules. The final rules state:

> The legislative history of the Telemarketing Act noted the problem of deceptive telemarketers contacting potential victims under the guise of conducting a poll, survey, or other such type of market research. To address these problems, the Commission believes that in any multiple purpose call where the seller or telemarketer plans, at least in some of the calls, to sell goods or services, the disclosures required by this Section of Rule should be made "promptly," in the first part of the call, before the non-sales portion of the call takes place.

The TSA follows the Telephone Consumer Protection Act (TCPA), which prescribed the hours of 8:00 A.M. to 9:00 P.M. local time as the only hours during which telephone solicitations can be made. Under the provisions of both the TCPA and the TSA, the telephone research industry is clearly exempted. The new laws apply to telemarketers, those persons making calls to or receiving calls from a customer in connection with a sales transaction. A "telephone solicitation" is defined as "the initiation of a telephone call or message for the purpose of encouraging the purchase or rental of, or the investment in, property, goods, or services, which is transmitted to any person." Telemarketing and *marketing research using the telephone* are clearly different things.

The Direct Marketing Association, the National Association of Attorneys General, and the Council for Marketing and Opinion Research combined to support the outlawing of sugging. The intent of the law is to ensure that the recipient is informed about the nature of a call from someone he or she doesn't know. The call recipient can choose whether or not to participate in legitimate telephone survey research or make a purchase from a telemarketer.[13]

Plus-one dialing The method of generating telephone numbers to be called by choosing numbers randomly from a telephone directory and adding one digit.

Systematic random digit dialing The technique of randomly dialing telephone numbers, but only numbers that meet specific criteria.

In **plus-one dialing,** researchers generate telephone numbers to be called by choosing numbers randomly from a telephone directory and adding 1. For example, supposing the initial telephone number 727-7119 is selected from the directory, by adding 1 to the last digit, the interviewer would dial 727-7120. This method is easy and allows for the possibility of unlisted telephone numbers to be included in the sample. But researchers should remember any telephone directory is a weak sampling frame.

Systematic random digit dialing is a technique in which researchers randomly dial telephone numbers, but only numbers that meet specific criteria. For example, numbers that are not within a specified area code would be ignored. Assuming researchers are interested in consumer responses, all phone exchanges or numbers that are devoted to government or business organizations would also be ignored. To use this dialing method, researchers randomly select a telephone number as a starting point and use a constant, or "skip," pattern in the selection process. The starting point (seed number) is based on the sample interval. Specifically, the skip interval is added to the seed on the basis of the number of telephone numbers available divided by the number to be interviewed. For example, say that there are 10,000 telephone numbers in the 727 exchange area and researchers want to interview 500 households within that exchange area. Then the skip interval would be 10,000/500 = 20. The researcher would randomly choose an initial telephone number, say, between 727-0000 and 727-0020, and suppose it was 727-0009. To generate all the additional numbers, researchers would simply add the interval to each new number. The second number dialed in this example would be 727-0029, the third 727-0049, and so on.

Advantages of this method are that each number in an exchange has a known but not equal chance of being called. Thus, within an area, the selection of respondents is random. If the same number of calls is made in several exchanges, the sample tends to share the attributes of the area, having the same geographic dispersion. Also, this dialing method is fairly simple to set up and administer.

Random digit dialing A random selection of area code, exchange, and suffix numbers.

Random digit dialing refers to a random selection of area code, exchange, and suffix numbers. The advantage is that all numbers have an equal chance of being called—the unlisted numbers are just as likely to be called as listed numbers. However, random digit dialing is costly because many numbers either are not in service or are in use by people or organizations not included in the scope of the researcher's survey design.

Computer-Assisted Telephone Interviews

Computer-assisted telephone interview (CATI) Integrated telephone and computer system in which the interviewer reads the questions off a computer screen and enters respondents' answers directly into the computer program.

Advances in technology have revolutionized telephone survey methods. Research firms have computerized their central location telephone interviewing process. With faster, more powerful computers and affordable software, even small research firms can use **computer-assisted telephone interviewing (CATI)** systems. Although different systems are available, CATI systems basically integrate advanced telecommunication technologies with the traditional telephone survey methods. Interviewers are equipped with a "hands-free" headset and seated in front of a keyboard, "touch-screen" computer terminal, or personal computer. Upon activating the system, the computer dials the prospective respondent's phone number automatically and provides interviewers with the appropriate introduction screen. When qualified respondents are on the line, interviewers activate the interviewing process by pressing a key or series of keys on the computer's keyboard or touch screen. Following the introductory comments, another simple keystroke brings up to the screen the first question and a prelisted set of choice responses.

Many CATI systems have one question per screen. Interviewers read the question and record the answer. Note that depending on the question/scale design, interviewers might read not only the question but also a list of possible answer choices. By recording respondents' answers, the computer automatically skips ahead to the appropriate next question. For example, when Procter & Gamble conducts a clothes detergent purchasing behavior study using a CATI system, one question asked by interviewers might be "In the past 30 days have you purchased any clothes cleaning products?" If the answer is yes, a series of specific questions focusing on the types of clothes cleaning products the person buys might follow. If the answer is no, those questions might be inappropriate to ask respondents. The computer is programmed to skip to the next appropriate question on the basis of respondents' answers. Here, the next question might be something like "How often do you purchase clothes cleaning products?" When programmed to react in a predetermined way based on respondents' initial responses to the question, the computer can eliminate possible human errors that exist in surveys using the traditional paper-and-pencil telephone interview mode.

CATI systems can be used to customize questions. Consider a J. D. Power and Associates study focusing on new-car purchasers' satisfaction. In the early part of the survey, respondents are asked to provide the years, makes, and models of the cars owned in the past 10 years. Later in the interview, interviewers might be prompted to ask respondents to rate the safety features for a particular car owned. The question might appear as "You said you owned a 2009 Acura 3.2 TL. How would you rate each of the following safety features of that car?" Interviewers would first describe the scale and its use, then ask respondents to rate the first safety feature on the screen. The process would continue until all the prelisted safety features were rated. Although these types of questions can be handled in a traditional telephone interview mode, the computerized version handles them much more efficiently because interviewers do not have to physically flip questionnaire pages back and forth or remember respondents' previous answers. Today's CATI systems eliminate most of the problems associated with manual systems of callbacks, complex quotas, skip logic, rotations, and randomization.

Advantages of CATI. While many of the advantages of computer-assisted telephone interviews are based on lower costs per call, there are other advantages. In sophisticated systems, it is possible to switch from one questionnaire to another during the interview. Switching capabilities allow for interviewing family members other than the head of household, for example. The advantage is that common information is shared between all the questionnaires, saving the need for multiple calls. Another advantage is ownership of the call. Sometimes people need to stop in the middle of an interview but are willing to finish at another time. Computer technology has the capability of routing inbound calls to a particular interviewer who "owns" the interview. Not only is there greater efficiency in terms of labor per call, but there can be cost savings as well. A cost advantage, perhaps not so obvious, is the ability of computer systems to select the least expensive routing for a particular call.

CATI systems also eliminate the need for separate editing and data entry tasks associated with manual systems. Researchers eliminate the need for cross checking and cleaning complete questionnaires for errors or manually creating data computer files, because there is no physical questionnaire and the responses are automatically entered directly to a computer file at the end of the interview. Also, the likelihood of coding or data entry errors is eliminated with CATI systems because it is impossible to accidentally record an improper response from outside the set of prelisted responses established for a given question. Here is an easy example to remember that illustrates this point. The respondent is asked the question "How important is it for your new car to have an automatic seatbelt safety system?" The response choices are prelisted as (a) "Extremely important," (b) "Important," (c) "Somewhat important," and (d) "Not at all important." If interviewers, by mistake, enter any code other than one of the four established codes, the computer will ask for the answer to be reentered until an acceptable code is entered.

Given the sophistication of the CATI systems' software, tabulation of results can be run in real time at any point of the study. This was not possible using traditional paper-and-pencil methods. Quick preliminary results can be beneficial in determining when certain questions can be eliminated because enough information has been obtained or when some additional questions are needed because of unexpected patterns uncovered in the earlier part of the interviewing process. Overall, use of CATI systems continues to grow at a rapid rate because decision makers have embraced the cost savings, quality control, and timesaving aspects of these systems.

Disadvantages of CATI. CATI systems have two problem areas. Setting up and activating CATI systems require substantial initial investment and operating costs. The investment in computers, especially for large and sophisticated systems, remains high, considering how quickly a computer system becomes obsolete. Software to control the hardware, monitor calls, and record responses in real-time fashion is also expensive and rapidly changing, especially if customized, and can be very time-consuming to develop and debug. Another limitation is that interviewers must have specific computers in addition to traditional interpersonal communication skills to effectively administer this type of survey. As the costs of both computer hardware and software go down and more people develop better computer literacy, these problems will diminish.

Completely Automated Telephone Interviews

Completely automated telephone surveys (CATS) A telephone interviewing system in which a computer dials a phone number and a recording is used to introduce and administer the survey, leaving the subject to interact with the computer directly.

Going beyond CATI systems, some research companies have fully automated their telephone interviewing data collection process. This type of system is referred to as a **completely automated telephone surveys (CATS)** system and uses no human interviewer. Surveys are completely administered by a computer. After the system is activated, the computer dials a phone number and a recording is used to introduce the survey to prospective respondents and give directions. Surveys are actually conducted by the respondent by listening to the electronic voice and responding by pushing keys on the Touch-Tone telephone keypad. CATS has been successfully used in service quality monitoring, product/warranty registrations, customer satisfaction studies, in-home product tests, and election day polls.[14] One of the difficulties experienced in using fully automated systems is there is a high "disconnect" rate among prospective respondents. While research is under way to investigate this disconnect behavior, some informal evidence suggests invasion of home privacy and the impersonal, one-way communication involved in responding to an unsolicited electronic voice are problematic.

Wireless Phone Surveys

Wireless phone survey The method of conducting a marketing survey in which the data are collected on standard wireless phones.

Wireless data networking and advanced database technologies offer researchers a promising new data collection technique for doing marketing research studies—the wireless phone survey.[15] With **wireless phone surveys** data are collected from wireless phone users. Researchers can survey in either text-based or voice-based formats or a combination of both. In a text-based format, respondents can access the survey and display it as text messages on a wireless phone screen. Respondents use the phone's dial pad to answer the questions. Responses are sent in real time to a backend database through the wireless network. In contrast, voice-based surveys allow respondents to listen to the questions on their wireless phone and answer them by speaking. Survey questions and answers are automatically processed and analyzed by voice synthesis and recognition software on voice extensible markup language (VoiceXML) equipment. One of the unique characteristics of wireless phone surveys is their ability to deliver instant answers, anytime, anywhere. They also enable researchers to capture data from respondents in their natural shopping and consumption environments.

Wireless phone surveys provide immediacy in the sense that consumers can fill out surveys close to the moments of shopping, decision making, and consuming. For example, wireless phone surveys have been used to (1) capture impulse purchases as they are made and consumed, (2) collect data about side effects in real time from patients who are participating in pharmacological testing, and (3) survey wireless customers. A company named Kinesis Survey Research offers researchers the option of attaching a miniature bar code reader to a mobile phone that will discreetly collect and store bar codes of purchased items. Finally, wireless phone panels may be especially appropriate for surveying teens, early adopters, and impulse buyers.[16]

Researchers can use short messaging (SMS) formats for simple polling and very short surveys. In Europe, mobile phone penetration rates are high and SMS usage is higher than in the United States, so SMS is often preferred to wireless Web surveys.[17] In the United States, wireless Web surveys are used more often than SMS. As compared to SMS, the wireless Web facilitates a continuous session, with no time delay between questions and receipt of responses. Wireless Web surveys tend to be cheaper for both the recipient and administrator of the survey. Wireless Web surveys also permit some functionality associated with CATI and Internet surveys to be used, including conditional branching and display of images. When CATI abilities are added to wireless Web surveys, the result is called CAMI, or computer-aided mobile interviewing.[18]

Marketing researchers usually do not call wireless phone users to solicit participation as they do over landlines. One reason is that FCC regulations prevent the use of autodialing. Thus, when potential respondents are called, each one must be dialed by hand. Second, wireless phone respondents incur a cost when taking surveys. Third, wireless phone respondents could be anywhere when they are called, meaning they are likely to be distracted by other activities, and may disconnect in the middle of the call. Safety is a potential issue since respondents could be driving when they get the call from researchers.[19] Respondents typically are recruited using a solicitation method other than the mobile phone, such as landlines, the Internet, mall-intercept, or in-store. Wireless panels are created from participants who have "opted in" or agreed to participate in advance. Although this data collection method is relatively still new, there are a number of potential advantages over other online, telephone, and paper-pencil based methods. First, wireless phone surveys are contemporaneous in nature. That is, they capture consumers' real experiences at the moment of purchase or consumption. Another advantage is the mobility associated with wireless phones. Almost like a watch, wireless phones are always with the consumer wherever they go. This mobility factor brings a tremendous degree of convenience for respondents. Third, wireless surveys are less intrusive to respondents because they can be sent without interrupting respondents' lives. In turn, respondents have full control of the time and place to fill out the survey. In cases where respondents must complete the survey at a particular moment, such requirements are agreed upon by respondents prior to sending the survey and are not viewed as obtrusive.

Capturing data via wireless phones increases the potential of implementing longitudinal types of studies. Normally, a wireless phone is a personal belonging and can be associated with each individual, thus making it easier for researchers to keep track of each respondent over time. Another advantage relates to the flexibility of retrieving data from respondents. Wireless networks enable respondents to send their answers to a database in real time during the survey. The survey can be programmed similar to CATI and CATS surveys to branch questions automatically based on previous answers. Finally, wireless phone surveys provide geographic flexibility and facilitate completing surveys on location-sensitive topics like during a shopping trip at a particular mall or theme park.

There are several challenges facing the use of wireless phone surveys. First, there are limited display spaces on wireless phone screens. Therefore, the questions must be kept short and simple in both text-based and voice-based formats. Consequently, wireless phone surveys are not suitable for research that involves long and/or complex questions and responses. Second, wireless phones have limited capacity to handle graphics, but video-streaming technology is rapidly improving. Therefore, wireless surveys may not yet be appropriate for studies that require a lot of visual stimuli for answering certain types of research questions. Third, the initial technology costs (both hardware and software) required for implementing and maintaining wireless phone surveys remain very high. Finally, researchers conducting wireless phone surveys must be well trained in information technology skills in addition to other research skills.

Self-administered survey A data collection technique in which the respondent reads the survey questions and records his or her own answers without the presence of a trained interviewer.

Self-Administered Surveys

The third type of interviewing is the **self-administered survey.** A self-administered survey is a data collection method in which respondents read survey questions and record their own responses without the presence of trained interviewers. The advantages are low cost per survey and no interviewer bias, but the latter comes at a price since there are no interviewers to probe for deeper responses. For example, on a self-administered survey respondents may indicate they did not purchase a certain product, but also fail to answer "Why not?" Exhibit 8.10 highlights some of the advantages and disadvantages associated with self-administered data collection methods. We discuss three types of self-administered surveys: mail, mail panel, and drop-off.

Mail Surveys

Mail survey A self-administered questionnaire that is delivered to selected respondents and returned to the researcher by mail.

In situations where researchers decide that a **mail survey** is the best method, a questionnaire is developed and mailed to a list of people who return the completed surveys by mail. Researchers must be careful to select a list that accurately reflects the target population. Sometimes obtaining the required mailing addresses is an easy task. But in other cases, it can be time-consuming and difficult. In addition, there are production considerations. For example, envelopes need to be designed to stimulate potential respondents' interest enough that the questionnaire is not simply thrown out. Questionnaires need to be carefully

eXHIBIT 8.10 Advantages and Disadvantages of Self-Administered Surveys

Advantages	**Comments**
Low cost per survey	With no need for an interviewer or computerized assistance device, self-administered surveys are by far the least costly method of data acquisition.
Respondent control	Respondents are in total control of how fast, when, and where the survey is completed; thus the respondent creates his/her own comfort zone.
No interviewer–respondent bias	There is no chance of introducing interviewer bias or respondent interpretive error based on the interviewer's body language, facial expression, or tone of voice.
Anonymity in responses	Respondents are more comfortable in providing honest and insightful responses because their true identity is not revealed.
Disadvantages	
Minimal flexibility	The type of data collected is limited to the specific questions placed initially on the survey. It is impossible to obtain additional in-depth data, because of the lack of probing and observation capabilities.
High nonresponse rates	In some cases, it is impossible to guarantee that the respondent will complete and return the survey at all. The respondent may get frustrated with questions that need clarification.
Potential response errors	The respondent may not fully understand a survey question and provide an erroneous response or mistakenly skip sections of the survey, resulting in inaccurate answers. Without an interviewer, respondents may unconsciously commit numerous errors while believing they are properly responding.
Slow data acquisition	In many cases, the time required to acquire the data and enter it into a computer file for analysis is significantly longer than many other data collection methods.
Lack of monitoring capability	Not having an interviewer present could lead to increases in misunderstanding of questions and instructions on how to respond to certain questions.

designed to gather as much information as possible and still be short enough for people to complete in a reasonable length of time.

One advantage of mail surveys is they are inexpensive to implement. There are no interviewer-related costs such as compensation, training, travel, or search costs. Most of the production expenses are one-time costs that can be amortized over many surveys. The variable costs are primarily postage, printing, and the cost of the incentive. Another advantage is that mail surveys can reach even hard-to-interview people.

Mail surveys have several drawbacks. One major drawback is that response rates tend to be much lower than with person-administered methods or telephone interviews. The risk of nonresponse bias is very real with mail surveys since researchers give up control over who responds. Researchers are never exactly sure who filled out the questionnaire, leaving the question of whether someone else provided the answers instead of the intended person. For example, in sending a mail survey to Ms. Sasaki in Crete, Illinois, on Network Television Programming, researchers cannot determine precisely whether Ms. Sasaki or some other member of her household answered the survey.

Another problem is misunderstood or skipped questions. Mail surveys make it difficult to handle problems of both vagueness and potential misinterpretation in question-and-answer setups. People who simply do not understand a question may record responses researchers did not intend or expect or may skip one or more questions entirely. These are all problems associated with not having trained interviewers available to assist respondents. Finally, mail surveys are also slow as there can be a significant time lag between when surveys are mailed and when completed surveys are returned.

Mail Panel Surveys

Mail panel survey A questionnaire sent to a group of individuals who have agreed in advance to participate.

To avoid some of the drawbacks of the mail surveys, researchers may choose a mail panel survey method. A **mail panel survey** is a questionnaire sent to a group of individuals who have agreed in advance to participate. The panel can be tested prior to the survey so researchers know the panel is representative; prior agreements usually produce high response rates. Mail panel surveys allow for longitudinal research. The same respondents can be tested multiple times over an extended period. This enables researchers to observe changes in panel members' responses over time.

The major drawback to mail panels is that members are likely not to be representative of the target population. For example, individuals who agree to be on a panel may have a special interest in the topic or simply a lot of time available. There is little agreement among experts about whether these concerns distort the results of the research. Thus, researchers should be cautious in generalizing the findings.

It is important to remember that different survey methods are not necessarily mutually exclusive. It is common for several methods to be used on the same project. For example, researchers may contact potential in-home respondents via direct mail to help improve the response rate or as a part of the screening process. Telephone calls are used to inform people of mail surveys. Also, sending multiple copies of a mail survey to nonrespondents frequently is a useful way to increase response rates.

Drop-Off Surveys

Drop-off survey A self-administered questionnaire that a representative of the researcher hand-delivers to selected respondents; the completed surveys are returned by mail or picked up by the representative.

One survey method that combines both elements of personal interviews and self-administered methods is the **drop-off survey.** With this method the survey is hand-delivered to respondents by representatives of the researcher. Completed surveys are picked up at a later time by representatives, or in some cases returned by mail in a prestamped business envelope. The advantages of drop-off surveys include the availability of a person who can answer general questions, screen potential respondents, and spur interest in completing the questionnaire. The disadvantage to drop-offs is they are expensive in comparison to mail surveys.

Online Survey Methods

Methods used to collect primary data have changed dramatically in recent years. Descriptive survey methods have been revised by technology-savvy researchers to accommodate new "online" platforms. Although the main principles underlying traditional descriptive research surveys remain the same, the speed of data acquisition and reporting systems have created new benchmarks for how primary data will be collected in years to come. Many online advances that were just visions a few years ago are now reality. Exhibit 8.11

eXHIBIT 8.11 Online Computer Technology Integrates with Offline Survey Data Collection Methods

Offline Method	Online Method	Comments
Personal interview	Computer-assisted personal	The respondent sits with the interviewer, and the interviewer reads the respondent the questions from a laptop computer screen and enters the responses.
Handout self-administered	Computer-assisted self-interview	The researcher directs a respondent to a specified computer terminal where the respondent reads questions from the screen and directly enters responses.
Self-administered interview	Fully automated self-interview	The respondent independently reads and responds to the questions, all without researcher intervention.
Telephone interview	CATI	The interviewer calls the respondent at home or office, reads questions from a computer screen, and directly enters the responses into the computer system.
Telephone interview	CATS	The computer calls respondents and an electronic voice gives directions and asks questions. The respondent uses the keypad of a touch-tone telephone to enter responses.
Mail panel survey	Online panel survey	Groups of people agree to become members of a selected panel of consumers. Consumers fill out a form on background data such as demographic and purchase factors. Later, respondents are sent surveys via e-mail and they complete and return them via e-mail or direct mail.
Self-administered survey	e-mail survey	The batch feature available on most e-mail systems is used to send a "mass mailing" to potential respondents, and the respondent completes an opt-in/opt-out option. Respondents who opt in continue and complete the survey. Surveys are returned via e-mail.
Self-administered survey	Computer-generated fax survey	A computer is used to dial and send a survey to potential respondents via fax. Respondents complete the survey and return it via fax.
Self-administered survey	Internet/Web-based survey	The survey is placed on a Web site, and a respondent has to go to the specified site, complete the survey, then click the send button. Or the survey is placed on a Web site, the respondent is contacted separately by letter or e-mail about the survey and its online location and given a unique password in order to access the survey. Respondents complete the survey and return it by clicking the send button.

summarizes online data collection methods that are quickly replacing or augmenting traditional survey research methods. The following discussion focuses on online survey designs researchers increasingly are using to collect primary data.

Fax Surveys

Fax survey A self-administered questionnaire that is sent to the selected subject via fax.

A **fax survey** is essentially a mail survey sent by fax. The fax survey allows researchers to collect responses to visual cues, as in a mail survey, as well as semantic differential or constant sum scales, which are difficult to use in telephone interviews. The potential benefit of fax surveys is that the flexibility of mail can be combined, to an extent, with the speed of the telephone.

In comparison to mail surveys, the fax delivery facilitates faster delivery and response speed and may even be less expensive. Administrative and clerical functions also can be reduced because there is no need to fold surveys and stuff envelopes. Finally, fax surveys imply urgency and are not perceived as being junk mail by many recipients. Even in a regular mail survey, merely offering the option to respond by fax can increase the response rate.[20]

One disadvantage of fax surveys is that many consumers and small businesses do not have fax machines and therefore cannot be contacted. Also respondents have to pay to fax back their responses, which can reduce response rates. Another limitation is that fax surveys can be delayed or not delivered because of operator error, equipment malfunctions, or busy signals. These problems may be particularly acute in high-volume operations. The relative lack of privacy may cause response problems as well. Finally, fax surveys may lack the clarity of image of a printed mail survey, and a color fax may be too expensive.

Nevertheless, under proper conditions, fax surveys offer an attractive alternative to direct mail surveys. Fax surveys can provide relatively faster responses, higher response rates, and similar data quality. In addition, fax surveys can be cheaper due to low transmission and paper-handling costs. Still, the image-quality and limited-reach problems are not likely to be resolved in the foreseeable future.

E-Mail Surveys

E-mail survey A self-administered data collection technique in which the survey is delivered to and returned from the respondent by e-mail.

An **e-mail survey** is a self-administered data collection technique in which surveys are electronically delivered to and returned by e-mail. E-mail surveys have become one of the popular methods within the "family" of online surveys used by marketing researchers. Using the improvements of the batch feature associated with today's e-mail systems, researchers can create a standardized e-mail message, sometimes in the format of a cover letter, and append the online survey as an attachment. The e-mail message and survey are then electronically transmitted as a "mass mailing" to a large number of prospective respondents. Once respondents open the e-mail, they are given an opt-in or opt-out approval option that serves to gain the respondent's permission to participate in the study. The opt-in/opt-out option is required by federal consumer and data privacy laws to protect people from receiving "spam" or "sugging" mailings.[21] *Spam* and *sugg* are terms for the illegal marketing practice of selling unsolicited products or services under the guise of conducting research. By law, respondents who select the opt-out option do not participate in the attached survey, and their e-mail addresses are supposed to be automatically removed from researchers' mailing lists, so they receive no future e-mails from that originating source. In turn, respondents who select the opt-in option, granting permission, continue the survey following on-screen directions. After completing the survey, respondents return it via e-mail. Today, returning an e-mail survey is as easy as clicking a single "Submit" or "Return" button located at the end of the survey.

Proponents of e-mail surveys favor this method for its capabilities of collecting a variety of data at lightning speed at a very low cost-per-participant figure. In addition, as with other computer-assisted or online research methods, errors like data nonresponses caused by interviewer error, interviewer interaction bias, and data entry errors are eliminated by technology-based controls. E-mail surveys have grown in popularity as a method of conducting fast and inexpensive research for international consumer product and services studies.

Like any online survey method, there are still some difficulties that must be overcome. First, not everyone has access to the Internet. Experts estimate that 70 to 75 percent of individuals in the United States have access to the Internet. But in other global markets the percentage is much smaller. These percentages are expected to grow slowly in the United States, but increase significantly in most global markets, like Latin America, Europe, and the Pacific Rim.[22] Online researchers will have to continue their efforts to establish legitimacy in generalizing their results to large target populations. The second significant problem revolves around data privacy. Research firms have added opt-in/opt-out strategies in soliciting members of their online panels. Yet differences in strictness and enforcement of data privacy laws remain a sticking point, especially between global market governments.[23]

Internet/Web-based Surveys

Internet/Web-based survey A self-administered questionnaire that is placed on a Web site for prospective subjects to read and complete.

Some characteristics of Internet/Web-based surveys are similar to e-mail surveys, but there are some distinct differences. An **Internet/Web-based survey** is a self-administered questionnaire placed on a Web site for prospective respondents to read and complete. This survey method requires prospective respondents to first commit to becoming a member of a special club or advisory panel directly controlled by the organization conducting the survey. After agreeing to the opt-in membership requirements, prospective respondents then select unique "login" and "password" codes, which serve as entrance keys for participation. Following Web site instructions, respondents complete and submit their survey.

Another difference is that respondents have the option of accessing the results of the survey in real time. Some companies, like Procter & Gamble through its "Consumercorner.com" panel system, even encourage respondents to scroll through the results and have additional options that allow respondents to make and share testimonial comments about the products being surveyed with other group members. Internet/Web-based surveys are the most frequently used survey method (see Exhibit 8.12). Why has the administration of online surveys grown so rapidly in a relatively short time? There are several reasons. An important advantage for Internet/Web-based surveys is that they are cheaper per respondent than any other survey method. There is no cost of copying surveys or buying postage and no interviewer cost. Surveys are self-administered and no coding is necessary; thus the results are ready for statistical analysis almost immediately.

The ability of Internet/Web-based surveys to reach hard-to-reach samples is another important reason for their growth. Some market research firms maintain large panels of respondents that can be used to identify specific targets, for example, allergy sufferers or doctors. One of the largest online panels, Harris Interactive, has a worldwide panel that numbers in the millions, including specialty panels such as executives, teens, gays, lesbians, and transgender individuals. Access to hard-to-reach samples is also possible through community, blog, or social networking sites dedicated to specific demographic or interest groups, such as seniors, fans of *The Simpsons,* coffee lovers, or Texas Instrument calculator enthusiasts, just to name a few.[24]

EXHIBIT 8.12 Usage of Types of Survey Methods[25]

Internet/Web-based	36.8%
CATI	25.3
Hybrid (2 or more methods)	12.0
Face-to-face intercepts	11.5
Mail	3.3
Other	4.1

Other advantages of Internet/Web-based surveys include the improved functional capabilities of Web site technologies over pen and pencil surveys. One functional improvement is the ability to randomize the order of questions within a group, so that the effect of question order on responses is removed. Another important improvement over mail surveys is that missing data can be eliminated. Whenever respondents skip questions, they are prompted to answer them before they can move to the next screen. Third, marketing research firms are now learning how to use the improved graphic and animation capabilities of the Web. For example, the task of ranking questions (or responses) can be easily completed by clicking and dragging the items into an appropriate order. Words that might describe respondents such as personality, a brand, a product, or a retailer can be animated to move from left to right, with respondents clicking on the appropriate words as they pass by on their screen. Pictures and videos can be used, so that full-color 3D pictures and videos of store interiors, products, ads, or movie reviews can be shown in the context of online surveys.[26] Graphic improvements to survey design make tasks more realistic and more engaging for respondents.

In addition to using online panels created by marketing research firms, companies may survey their own customers using their existing e-mail lists to send out invitations to participate in surveys. Small businesses can use online survey creation software offered by businesses like Zoomerang.com and Surveymonkey.com to design an online survey and collect data relatively easily and inexpensively. Some online retailers use research contests both to gather information and to increase customer engagement with their company. For instance, graphic designers post pictures of possible T-shirts at www.Threadless.com. The designs that garner the most votes are printed and offered for sale on the site.

Propensity scoring Weighting underrepresented respondents more heavily in results.

While the benefits of Internet/Web-based surveys include low cost per completed interview, quick data collection, and the ability to use visual stimuli, Internet samples are rarely representative and nonresponse bias can be high. About 70 percent of individuals in the United State have home access to the Internet, which limits the ability to generalize to the general population. **Propensity scoring** can be used to adjust the results to look more like those a representative sample would have produced, but the accuracy of this procedure must be evaluated. With propensity scoring the responses of underrepresented sample members are weighted more heavily to adjust for sampling inadequacies. For example, if respondents 65 years of age or older are only half as likely to be in an Internet sample as their actual incidence in the population, each senior who responds would be counted twice in the sample. Read the nearby A Closer Look at Research (Using Technology) box to see

A Closer Look at Research

Virtual Reality in Marketing Research[27]

Tom Allison, president of Allison Hollander in Atlanta, Georgia, thinks that a computer program can do a better job of tabulating what customers will actually do rather than what the customers think they will do. The problem, according to Allison, is that people communicate in words but do not think or feel in words. People think and feel in pictures. Computer technology has the added bonus of reducing interviewer and consumer bias as well.

To illustrate the problem of consumer bias as a result of thinking in pictures and communicating in words, Allison asks audiences to think of the following sentence: "You are standing by the water's edge." Then, he produces four images: an ocean scene, a lake scene, a river scene, and a stream. Each image elicits different feelings, according to Allison. In practice, this consumer bias is the reason that people react differently to a can of Coca-Cola than they do to an old-style bottle of Coca-Cola.

The prescription, according to Allison, is to take the consumer to the McDonald's restaurant instead of simply talking about a McDonald's. In this way, the researcher can get a truer picture of the consumer's reactions than time-lagged thoughts and feelings allow. The way to take the consumer to McDonald's is by computer simulation.

By using full-scale electronic simulations, the consumer can be exposed to menus, store shelves, coolers, and vending machines. The realism of the simulations allows for accurate communications with respondents and also for meaningful data collection. Allison suggests that the simulation should be engaging and short enough to hold the respondent's attention. Letting the respondent do, observe, and question elicits the entire selection process. And the computer can track and record the mental process step by step.

Allison says that consumer companies can use simulations in many different ways. For example, a consumer might be asked to build a stereo system, spending only a given amount of money. The researcher using the computer simulation could see what the respondent would buy. Another example could be a sunglasses boutique. The consumer could have his or her face scanned into a computer and then electronically "try on" sunglasses by clicking a mouse.

Other researchers think that virtual reality may offer an exciting way of testing. The consumer could "shop" the store, picking up items from shelves as they would in an ordinary store. The computer could track the respondent's actions and reactions. This virtual reality testing would allow companies to very accurately pretest pricing changes, packaging, promotions, shelf layout, new-product interest, and substitution behaviors.

Proponents of the computer simulation research say the tests are becoming faster and the cost is decreasing as technology advances. Other benefits include a realistic context for the respondent; a controlled, low-risk environment; and no need for back data or norms.

how researchers use computer simulations as a creative method of integrating computer technologies with survey research.

While the benefits are many, there are still difficulties that result in nonresponse bias. In addition, response bias remains a problem because Internet/Web-based surveys are available to everyone without being targeted to anyone. Surveys are initially passive in nature: prospective respondents must seek out the Web site, and thus only those who have a prior interest are likely to even find the survey, let alone complete it. Exhibit 8.13 summarizes the benefits of using computer-assisted and online survey methods for collecting primary data.

EXHIBIT 8.13 Computer-Assisted Data Collection Methods[28]

	Personal	On-Site	On-Site	Telephone	Telephone	Mail	Online Panel	E-mail	Fax	Internet
	Computer-Assisted Personal Interview	Computer-Assisted Self-Interview	Fully Automated Self-Interview	Computer-Assisted Telephone Interview	Fully Automated Telephone Interview	Computer Disks by Mail	Online Panel Survey	Electronic-Mail Survey	Computer-Generated Fax Survey	Self-Administered Survey
Benefits										
No need for respondents to have computer-related skills	X			X	X		X		X	X
Allows respondents to choose own schedule for completing survey		X	X			X	X	X	X	X
Can incorporate complex branching questions into survey	X	X	X	X	X	X	X*	X*		X*
Can incorporate respondent-generated words in questions	X	X	X	X	X	X	X*	X*		X*
Can accurately measure response times to questions	X	X	X	X	X	X	X*	X*		X*
Can display graphics and directly relate them to questions	X	X	X			X	X*	X*		X*
Eliminates the need to encode data from paper survey forms	X	X	X	X	X	X	X*	X		X
Errors in data less likely compared to manual methods	X	X	X	X	X	X	X	X		X
Speedier data collection and encoding compared to manual methods	X	X	X	X	X	X	X	X	X	X

*Assumes interactive e-mail population specification.

Selecting the Appropriate Survey Method

Researchers must consider several factors when choosing a survey method. Selecting a descriptive method the researcher finds interesting or convenient may not produce usable, cost-efficient data. Instead consideration should be given to factors such as the situational, task difficulty, and respondent characteristics factors listed in Exhibit 8.14.

eXHIBIT 8.14 Factors to Consider in Selecting a Survey Method

Factors and Characteristics	Important Issues and Questions
Situational Characteristics	
Budget of available resources	What degree of appropriate resources can be committed to the project? What are the total dollars and worker-hours available for committing to the research project's activities of gathering raw data, developing data structures, and creating/presenting information? What is the cost of collecting the required data?
Completion time frame	How much time is needed for completing the research project? How quickly do data-gathering, analysis, and information-generation activities have to be completed?
Quality requirement	How accurate and representative is the derived information to the research problem?
Completeness of the data	How much information and what degree of detail are needed for the defined research problem?
Generalizability	What level of confidence does the researcher want to make inferences about the defined target population from the data results?
Precision	What is the acceptable level of error that the data results may have in representing true population parameters?
Task Characteristics	
Difficulty of the task	How much effort is required by the respondent to answer the questions? How hard does the subject have to work to answer the questions? How much preparation is required to create a desired environment for the respondents?
Stimuli needed to elicit a response	How much physical stimulus does a respondent need? Do specific stimuli have to be used to elicit a response? How complex do the stimuli have to be?
Amount of information	How detailed do the respondent's answers have to be? Will probing activities be needed? How many needed questions should there be? How long should the respondent expect to take?
Research topic sensitivity	To what degree are the survey's questions socially, politically, and/or personally sensitive?
Respondent Characteristics	
Diversity	What commonalities exist among the prospective respondents? How many and which common characteristics have to exist?
Incidence rate	What percentage of the defined target population has the key characteristics to qualify for being included in the survey?
Degree of survey participation	Are the respondents able to completely interact in the question-and-answer process? What is the person's ability to participate? What is the person's degree of willingness to participate? What is the knowledge-level requirement for a person to participate in the survey process?

Situational Characteristics

In an ideal situation, researchers' sole focus would be on collecting accurate data. However, we live in an imperfect world and researchers must evaluate the competing objectives of budget, time, and data quality. In most descriptive survey research methods, the goal is to produce usable data in as short a time as possible at the lowest cost. Finding the optimal balance among these three factors is frequently a ticklish task. It is easy to generate large amounts of data in a short time if quality is ignored. But excellent data quality often can be achieved only through expensive and time-consuming methods. In selecting the survey method, researchers commonly consider situational characteristics in combination.

Budget

The budget is the amount of resources available to the researcher. While budgets are commonly thought of in terms of dollar spending, other resources such as staff size can have similar constraining effects. The resources available for a study can greatly affect choice of the data collection method. For example, if only 500 hours are available in the research department, it would be impossible to conduct more than 1,000 personal interviews of 30 minutes each. In this situation, researchers might select a mail survey method because developing the survey form, mailing it, and collecting the responses would take much less time than personal interviews. In a similar light, a $20,000 budget for a 1,000-person study limits researchers to spending $20 per person. Given this constraint, researchers might elect a telephone survey method because the cost per response can be lower than in a personal interview. While total research budget dollars do not have to be completely spent, most researchers will try to keep the research design and activities cost-effective if at all possible. In practice, budget determinations are frequently much more arbitrary than researchers would prefer. However, budgets rarely are the sole determinant of the survey method. Much more commonly the budget is considered along with data quality and timing.

Completion Time Frame

For decisions to be effective, they often must be made within specified time periods. The time frame commonly has a direct bearing on the data-gathering method. Long time frames allow researchers greatest opportunity of selecting the research method that will produce the best data. Typically the affordable time frame is much shorter than desired, forcing researchers to choose a research method that may not be ideal. Some methods such as mail or personal interviews require relatively long time frames while other methods such as telephone surveys or mall-intercepts can be done more quickly.

Quality Requirements

Data *quality* is a complex issue that includes scale measurement, questionnaire design, sample design, and data analysis. A brief overview of three key issues will help explain the impact of data quality on the selection of survey methods.

The first issue is the completeness of the data. *Completeness* refers to the depth and breadth of the data. Complete data enable researchers to provide a total picture. In contrast, incomplete data lack detail, resulting in a picture that is vague or unclear. Another issue is generalizability. *Data generalizability* refers to the degree to which the data produce an accurate portrait of the defined target population. Data that are generalizable allow for accurate description of the population being studied. In contrast, data that are not generalizable cannot accurately reflect the population but only the respondents who supplied it. A third data quality issue is precision. *Data precision* is related to, but distinctively different from, completeness. Precision refers to the degree of exactness of the data in relation to some other possible response. For example, a car company may want to know what colors will be "hot" for their new models. Respondents may indicate their preference for a bright color for automobiles. The completeness issue refers to the respondents' preference for the red color. On the other hand, precision refers to the preference of red over blue by a two-to-one margin. If management needs to know only that bright colors are preferred, then fairly incomplete and imprecise data will suffice. But if management needs to know that red is preferred by a two-to-one margin, then both complete and precise data are required. For example, researchers know that mail surveys frequently deliver precise results, but may not always produce the most generalizable results. Telephone surveys may be generalizable but may lack precision due to short questions and short interview times.

Task Characteristics

Task characteristics refer to what respondents have to do in order to supply responses to questions, and these should influence the method used to collect data. Respondents' task characteristics can be categorized into four major areas: (1) the difficulty of the task; (2) the stimuli needed to elicit a response from the respondent; (3) the amount of information the respondent is asked to give; and (4) the sensitivity of the research topic.

Task difficulty How hard a survey respondent needs to work and how much preparation the researcher needs to do.

Task difficulty refers to how hard respondents need to work to supply a response. Some marketing research questions are easy to answer. For example, taste tests require respondents to sample foods prepared under very controlled conditions. The task difficulty lies primarily in creating exactly the same stimulus for each respondent. But in other cases, respondents have to work very hard to answer the questions. Take for example product or brand preference testing research that requires respondents to supply multiple responses to many similar products, making the overall response task very laborious for the respondents. As a general rule of thumb, the more complex the survey environment, the greater the need for trained interviewers to help respondents complete the interviews. Consequently, researchers should always try to make it easy for the respondent to fully answer the questions.

Respondents must be exposed to *some type of stimulus* in order to elicit a response. The stimuli may consist of products (as in taste tests), promotional visuals (as in advertising research), or some physical entity used to elicit respondents' preferences, attitudes, emotions, or behaviors. Personal involvement is when respondents are required to touch, see, or taste something. It is very difficult to maintain control over such situations without trained interviewers. For example, in product concept research, respondents frequently need to see and touch the product in order to form their responses to interviewers' questions. Another factor that impacts the difficulty of the response task is the *amount of information needed* from respondents. While researchers are always looking for ways to get more data, respondents have limits in time, knowledge, and patience. As a general rule, when researchers need large amounts of detailed information from respondents, the need for personal interaction with a trained interviewer increases. While some people are resistant to long mail surveys, this might not cause a dramatic drop in response rates. Although some people will terminate long interviews at shopping malls, others may not even agree to short interviews. People hang up on long telephone calls, too. Researchers' task is to achieve the best match between the survey method and the amount of information needed. Consequently, trade-offs between getting more information and risking respondent fatigue must be assessed.

Topic sensitivity The degree to which a survey question leads the respondent to give a socially acceptable response.

In some cases, the problem may require researchers to ask socially or personally sensitive questions. **Topic sensitivity** is the degree to which a specific survey question leads respondents to give socially acceptable responses. Topic sensitivity often relates to questions about income, but from time to time sensitive questions may be asked about racial issues, environmental issues, politics, religion, or personal hygiene. When asked about a sensitive issue, some respondents will give a socially acceptable response even if they actually feel or behave otherwise. Other respondents simply refuse to answer questions they consider too personal or sensitive and yet others will terminate the interview. Typically, less sensitive research topics relate to brand preference, shopping behaviors, and satisfaction levels. Such questions are usually viewed as being nonintrusive or otherwise not problematic.

Respondent Characteristics

Since most marketing research projects target specific people, another major factor to consider in selecting the appropriate survey method is respondent characteristics. The extent to which targeted respondents share common characteristics influences the survey method selected. Three of the key facets of respondent characteristics are *diversity, incidence,* and *participation.*

Diversity The degree to which the respondents share characteristics.

Diversity of respondents refers to the degree to which respondents share common demographic, socioeconomic, and cultural characteristics as well as selected attitudinal, emotional, and/or behavior characteristics. The more diverse the respondents the fewer similarities they share, and the less diverse the respondents the more similarities. For example, if the defined target population is specified as people who own or have access to fax machines, then diversity is low and fax surveys can be an effective and cost-efficient method. However, if the defined target population does not have convenient access to fax machine, then fax surveys will fail.

In other situations, researchers may assume that there is a particular personal characteristic or behavior that is shared by many people in the defined target population, when in fact very few share that characteristic. For example, the percentage rates of unlisted telephone numbers vary significantly by geographic area. In some areas (e.g., small rural towns in Illinois), the rate of unlisted numbers is very low (<10%), while in others (e.g., large cities like New York or Los Angeles) the rate is very high (>50%). If researchers select prospective respondents for telephone surveys from published numbers, there often are significant problems with the accuracy of the data. People who do not have listed numbers may be different from people with listed telephone numbers. The more diverse the defined target population, the greater the need for trained interviewer intervention. For example, public opinion polls on welfare reform, government spending, and education are commonly conducted via telephone surveys because most people have opinions on these issues. Compare that to a situation in which the Acura division of Honda America Motor Corporation wants to ask Acura TL 3.2 automobile owners about their satisfaction with the service provided with that car. With this less diverse target population, mail surveys or telephone interviews would most likely be the method chosen.

Incidence rate The percentage of the general population that is the subject of the market research.

Incidence rate refers to the percentage of the general population that is the subject of the research. Sometimes researchers are interested in a large portion of the general population and the incidence rate is high. For example, the incidence rate of auto drivers is very high in the general population. In contrast, if the defined target group is small in relation to the total general population, then the incidence rate is low. The incidence rate of airplane pilots in the general population is much lower than that of car drivers. Normally, the incidence rate is expressed as a percentage. Thus, an incidence rate of 5 percent means that 5 out of 100 members of the general population have the qualifying characteristics sought in a given study. Complicating the incidence factor is the persistent problem of contacting prospective respondents. For example, researchers may have taken great care in generating a list of prospective respondents for a telephone survey, but may then discover that a significant number of them have moved, changed their telephone number, or simply been disconnected (with no further information), resulting in the incidence rate being lower than initially anticipated. When incidence rates are very low, researchers will spend considerably more time and money in locating and gaining the cooperation of enough respondents. In low-incidence situations, personal interview surveys would be used very sparingly because it costs too much to find that rare individual who qualifies, and a direct mail survey may be the best choice. In other cases, telephone surveys can be very effective as a method of screening. Individuals who pass the telephone screen, for example, could receive a mail survey. In doing survey research, researchers have the goal of reducing search time and costs of qualifying prospective respondents while increasing the amount of actual, usable data.

Ability to participate The ability of both the interviewer and the respondent to get together in a question-and-answer interchange.

Respondent participation involves the respondent's ability to participate, the respondent's willingness to participate, and the respondent's knowledge level. **Ability to participate** refers to the ability of both interviewers and respondents to get together in a question-and-answer interchange. The ability of respondents to share thoughts with interviewers is an important selection consideration. It is frustrating to researchers to find qualified respondents willing to respond but for some reason unable to participate in the study. For example, personal interviews require uninterrupted time. Finding an hour to interview busy executives can present real problems for both researchers and executives. Similarly, while they might like to participate in a mall-intercept survey, some shoppers may be in a hurry to pick up children from day care or school. An optometrist may have only five minutes until the next patient. The list of distractions is endless. A method such as a mail survey, in which the time needed to complete the questions does not need to be continuous, may be an attractive alternative in such cases. As the above examples illustrate, the inability-to-participate problem is very common. To get around it, most telephone surveys, for example, allow for respondents to be called back at a more convenient time. This illustrates the general rule that marketing researchers make every possible effort to respect respondents' time constraints.

Willingness to participate The respondent's inclination or disposition to share his or her thoughts.

A second component of survey participation is prospective respondents' **willingness to participate** or their inclination to share their thoughts. Some people will respond simply because they have some interest in the subject. Others will not respond because they are not interested, wish to preserve their privacy, or find the topic objectionable for some reason. Nevertheless, a self-selection process is in effect. The type of survey method influences the self-selection process. For example, people find it much easier to ignore a mail survey or hang up on a telephone call than to refuse a person in a mall-intercept or personal in-home interview.

Knowledge level The degree to which the selected respondents feel they have knowledge of or experience with the survey's topics.

Knowledge level is the degree to which the selected respondents feel they have the knowledge or experience to answer questions about the survey topic. Respondents' knowledge levels play a critical role in whether or not they agree to participate and directly impacts the quality of data collected. For example, a large manufacturer of computer software wanted to identify the key factors small wholesalers use to decide what electronic inventory tracking system (EITS) they would need for improving their just-in-time delivery services to retailers. The manufacturer decided to conduct a telephone survey among a selected group of 100 small wholesalers who do not currently use any type of EITS. In the process of trying to set up the initial interviews, the interviewers noticed that about 80 percent of the responses were "not interested." In probing that response, they discovered that most of the respondents felt they were not familiar enough with the details of EITS to be able to discuss the survey issues. The more detailed the information needed, the higher respondents' knowledge level must be to get them to participate in the survey.

Through the years, researchers have developed "best practices" for increasing participation levels. One strategy is offering some type of incentive. Incentives can include both monetary "gifts" such as a dollar bill and nonmonetary items such as a pen, a coupon to be redeemed for a food product, or entry into a drawing. Another strategy is to personally deliver questionnaires to potential respondents. In survey designs involving group situations, researchers can use social influences to increase participation. But it is important that incentive strategies should not be promoted as "rewards" for respondent participation. Rewards can serve as the wrong motivator for people deciding to participate in a survey.

Researchers try to overcome as many of the above problems as possible in order to get as much participation as possible to avoid the dangers associated with nonresponse bias.

MARKETING RESEARCH IN ACTION

Continuing Case: Santa Fe Grill Mexican Restaurant

Developing Research Questions, Forming Hypotheses, and Selecting a Survey Method

The Santa Fe Grill owners have decided they need to know more about their customers, their main competitor (Jose's Southwestern Café), and the Dallas target market. After identifying several "Best Practices" guidelines on how restaurants should be run from their electronic literature search, they developed a list of issues that need to be addressed.

- If you do not have enough customers, first examine the quality of your food, the items on your menu, and the service.
- Examine and compare your lunch and dinner customers and menus for differences.
- Your wait staff should be consistent with the image of your restaurant. How your employees act and behave is very important. They must be well groomed, knowledgeable, polite, and speak clearly and confidently.
- Menu items should represent a good value for the money.
- Service should be efficient, timely, polished, and cordial.
- The cleanliness and appearance of your restaurant strongly influences the success of your business.
- Follow the marketing premise of "Underpromise and Overdeliver!"
- Empower your employees to make decisions to keep your customers happy. Train your employees on what to do to resolve customer complaints instead of coming to the manager.
- Create a pleasant dining atmosphere, including furniture and fixtures, decorations, lighting, music, and temperature.
- Learn more about your female customers. For family outings and special occasions, women make the decision on where to dine about 75 percent of the time.

Hands-On Exercise

Using the above insights and information, the Santa Fe Grill's owners now need to specify relevant research questions, variables, and relationships to examine as well as determine the most appropriate survey research method for collecting data in order to get the feedback they need to improve their operation. Help them by responding to the following questions:

1. What are key constructs that the owners should focus on? Why?
2. Develop a set of research questions that relate to each of these identified constructs.
3. Develop hypotheses that need to be tested.
4. What actual variables should primary data be collected on?
5. Now, using all your generated information, which descriptive survey method would be most appropriate in collecting the data? Why?

Summary of Learning Objectives

■ **Discuss the role of constructs, variables, and relationships in survey research.**

When one or more of your research questions require you to investigate relationships between variables, then you need to conceptualize these relationships. The conceptualization process is aided by developing a model that shows the predicted causal relationships between variables. You must understand the following terms: variables, constructs, and relationships. A *variable* is an observable item that is identified as a focus of study and used as a measure on a questionnaire. A *construct* is an unobservable concept that is measured by a group of related variables. Some examples of commonly measured constructs in marketing include service quality, value, customer satisfaction, and brand attitude. Constructs that represent characteristics of respondents may also be measured, for example, innovativeness, opinion leadership, and deal proneness. *Relationships* are associations between two or more variables. The relationships are often illustrated visually by drawing conceptual models such as arrow diagrams. Variables can be either *independent* or *dependent* variables. An independent variable is the variable or construct that predicts or explains the outcome variable of interest. A dependent variable is the variable or construct researchers are seeking to explain and is hypothesized as being affected by one or more independent variables. For example, if technology optimism and household income predict Internet adoption by seniors, then technology optimism and household income are independent variables, and Internet adoption is the dependent variable. A *hypothesis* is an empirically testable but yet unproven statement about relationships between variables. Hypotheses enable researchers to examine relationships between variables. The null hypothesis states that there is no meaningful relationship between variables in your conceptual model. The alternative hypothesis, the one you hope to prove, states that there is a relationship between two variables.

■ **Identify and explain the types of errors that occur in survey research.**

Researchers need to evaluate the errors in the research results. All errors are either random sampling errors or nonsampling errors. By far the greatest amount of error that can reduce data quality comes from nonsampling error sources. Four major sources of error are respondent error (nonresponse errors and response biases); measurement and design error (construct development, scale measurement, and survey instrument design errors); administrative error (data processing, interviewer, and sample design errors); and faulty problem definition error. In survey research, systematic errors decrease the quality of the data being collected.

■ **Describe the types of survey methods.**

Survey methods are generally divided into three generic types. One is the person-administered survey, in which there is significant face-to-face interaction between the interviewer and the respondent. Second is the telephone-administered survey. The telephone is used to conduct the question-and-answer exchanges. Computers are now used in many ways in telephone interviews, especially in data recording and telephone-number selection. Third is the self-administered survey, in which there is little, if any, actual face-to-face contact between the researcher and respondent. Respondents read the questions and record their answers.

■ **Assess the strengths and weaknesses of different survey methods.**

It is important to remember that all methods have strengths and weaknesses. No single method is the best choice under all circumstances. Nor are researchers limited to a single method. Innovative combinations of survey methods can produce excellent results, as the strengths of one method can be used to overcome the weakness of another. Some of the main advantages of using survey designs to collect primary data from respondents are the ability to accommodate large sample sizes; generalizability of results; ability to distinguish small differences between diverse sampled groups; ease of administering and recording questions and answers; increased capabilities of using advanced statistical analysis; and identifying latent factors and relationships. In contrast, the main disadvantages of survey research designs are potential difficulties of developing accurate survey instruments; inaccuracies in construct and scale measurements; and limits to the depth of the data structures. In addition, researchers can lack control over long time frames and potentially low response rates, among other problems.

■ **Explain the impact of technology on survey research designs.**

With the increasing advances in telecommunication and computer technologies, numerous new, fast techniques are available to researchers for collecting primary raw data from people. The range of new techniques continues to grow and includes such methods as computer-assisted telephone interviewing methods; fully automated self-administered and wireless cell phone methods; and e-mail, fax, and Internet/Web-based surveys. There is little doubt that the time requirements of collecting data will significantly decrease with these new methods.

■ **Discuss factors influencing the choice of survey methods.**

Three major factors affect the choice of survey method: situational characteristics, task characteristics, and respondent characteristics. Situational factors include available resources, completion time frame, and data quality requirements. Task requirements are reflected in questions like "How difficult are the tasks involved in completing a survey?" "What stimuli will be needed to evoke responses?" "How much knowledge is required in the respondent?" and "To what extent do the questions deal with sensitive topics?" Characteristics of the prospective respondents include diversity of the target group, willingness or ability to participate, the likely incidence rate in terms of the entire population, and the expected degree of survey participation.

Maximizing the quantity and quality of data that will be collected while minimizing the cost and time of the survey requires the researcher to make trade-offs while selecting a method and developing a survey.

Key Terms and Concepts

Ability to participate 265
Alternative hypothesis 234
Averaging 240
Coding error 242
Completely automated telephone surveys (CATS) 251
Computer-assisted telephone interview (CATI) 249
Construct 233
Construct development error 240
Data analysis error 241
Data entry error 242
Data processing error 242
Dependent variable 234
Diversity 264
Drop-off survey 254
Editing error 242
E-mail survey 256
Executive interview 245
Faulty problem definition error 242
Faulty recall 240
Fax survey 256
Incidence rate 264
Independent variable 234
In-home interview 245
Internet/Web-based survey 257
Interpretive bias 241
Interviewer cheating 243
Interviewer error 243
Knowledge level 265
Mail panel survey 254
Mail survey 253
Mall-intercept interview 246
Misinterpretation error 241
Negative relationship 234
Nonresponse error 239
Nonsampling error 237
Null hypothesis 234
Person-administered survey 244
Plus-one dialing 248
Population specification error 243
Positive relationship 234
Project administration error 242
Propensity scoring 258
Purchase-intercept interview 246
Random digit dialing 249
Recording error 243
Relationship 233
Response error 240
Sample design error 243
Sample selection error 243
Sampling error 237
Sampling frame error 243
Scale measurement error 240
Selective perception bias 241
Self-administered survey 252
Survey instrument error 240
Survey research methods 235
Systematic random digit dialing 248
Task difficulty 263
Telephone interviews 246
Topic sensitivity 263
Unconscious misrepresentation 243
Variable 233
Willingness to participate 265
Wireless phone survey 251

Review Questions

1. Discuss the advantages and disadvantages of using descriptive survey research methods to collect primary data in marketing research.
2. Describe the three critical components for determining data quality. How does achieving data quality differ in person-administered surveys and self-administered surveys?
3. Explain why survey designs that include trained interviewers are more appropriate than computer-assisted survey designs in situations where the task difficulty and stimuli requirements are extensive.
4. Explain the major differences between in-home interviews and mall-intercept interviews. Make sure you include their advantages and disadvantages.
5. A researcher develops hypotheses which suggest that consumers hold more favorable attitudes toward ads when they (1) are truthful, (2) are creative, and (3) present relevant information. Picture the conceptual model that would show these relationships. Which variables are independent and which are dependent?
6. What are relationships? What is a positive relationship? What is a negative relationship? Give an example of a positive and negative relationship.
7. How might measurement and design errors affect respondent errors?
8. Develop three recommendations to help researchers increase the response rates in direct mail and telephone-administered surveys.
9. What possible issues associated with customer behavior and consumption patterns might be extremely sensitive ones to directly question respondents about? How might researchers overcome the difficulties of collecting sensitive data?
10. What is "nonresponse"? Identify four types of nonresponse found in surveys.
11. How does a wireless phone survey differ from CATI and CATS surveys?
12. What are the advantages and disadvantages associated with online surveys?

Discussion Questions

1. Develop a list of the factors used by a researcher to decide between using person-administered, telephone-administered, self-administered, and computer-assisted survey designs. Specifically discuss the appropriateness of those selection factors across each type of survey design.
2. What impact, if any, will advances in telecommunication and computer technologies have on survey research practices? Support your thoughts.
3. Situation: The regional sales manager for Procter & Gamble interviews sales representatives in the Midwest and asks them questions about the percentage of their time they spend making presentations to potential new customers, talking on the telephone with

current customers, working on the computer, and engaging in on-the-job activities. What potential sources of error might be associated with the manager's line of questioning?

4. Look at Exhibit 8.4, which describes the different types of sampling and nonsampling errors in survey research designs, and identify five potential sources of error that have direct ethical implications. Write a short report that discusses the ethical issues associated with each type of error source and the strategies that a researcher should implement to resolve each issue.

5. **EXPERIENCE THE INTERNET.** Go to the latest Gallup Poll survey (www.gallup.com) and evaluate the survey design being used. Write a two-page report summarizing the design's strengths and weaknesses.

6. What types of research studies lend themselves to using e-mail as the communication method in surveying respondents? What are the advantages and disadvantages of using e-mail surveys?

7. Comment on the ethics of the following situations:
- A researcher plans to use invisible ink to code his direct mail questionnaires to identify those respondents who return the questionnaire.
- A telephone interviewer calls at 10:00 P.M. on a Sunday and asks to conduct an interview.
- A manufacturer purchases 100,000 e-mail addresses from a national e-mail distribution house and plans to e-mail out a short sales promotion under the heading of "We Want to Know Your Opinions."

8. Based on your experiences as a marketing major or minor, develop a conceptual model that shows the factors that led to your satisfaction (or dissatisfaction) with a marketing course you have taken.

9. Why is understanding marketing and consumer relationships so important to today's decision makers?

chapter 9

Causal Research Designs and Test Markets

Learning Objectives

After reading this chapter, you will be able to:

1. Explain experiments and the types of variables used in causal research designs.
2. Describe the theoretical importance and impact of validity measures in causal research designs.
3. Discuss the major types of experimental designs and explain the pros and cons of each.
4. Define test marketing and explain its usefulness in marketing research.
5. Compare the pros and cons of laboratory and field experiments.

"Experimental investigations that encourage development of more customized and tailored solutions should stimulate new ways of addressing issues in test marketing practices"[1]

—GORDON A. WYNER,
Executive Vice President of Strategy,
Millward Brown, Inc.

Test Marketing to Gauge New-Product Acceptance: Lee Apparel Company

The new-product development team at Lee Apparel Company was excited about their recent efforts in coming up with a new apparel line of jeans for females. The design team suggested the company go with the brand name "Riders" because it seemed a hip, stylish name for the new jeans. Based on past knowledge of launching other apparel lines, the company's marketing team decided to conduct a series of extensive market tests on Riders. After much discussion, a decision was made to test the product design and brand name in five major market areas in the United States. The overall objective of these tests was to gain greater insights into female purchase decisions, attitudes, motivations, and potential repeat purchase behavior for the new line of jeans. In addition the company was determined to create a complete customer database that would be shared by the manufacturer and all channel members.

Company officials were determined to test and evaluate the entire marketing program for Riders before any decision was made regarding a national launch of the product. In several test cities, design styles and colors were being manipulated. The brand name and different advertising strategies were monitored and evaluated based on customer sales. Even the colors of the product—brown, blue, red, and tan—were tested for customer reaction. Several different promotional themes and vehicles were evaluated for brand name awareness and test product positioning strategies. Point-of-sale coupons and price discounts were being varied across different retail stores as a way to monitor price sensitivity. Operating in conjunction with a battalion of data-collection personnel, Lee Apparel was attempting to determine customer intentions to purchase using different marketing programs for the new jeans apparel line. Based on initial results, company officials were hopeful the test marketing for Riders jeans would be highly successful. In addition to positive customer reaction indicated by early test results, Lee Apparel hoped to create a stronger information sharing process to enable the company to enjoy a successful product introduction.[2]

Make sure you read the Marketing Research in Action section at the end of the chapter to discover how the Lee Apparel Company successfully launched its Riders brand of female jeans and created partnerships with retailers.

Value of Experimentation and Test Marketing

As the chapter opener example suggests, a growing area in marketing research is test marketing using causal research designs. Test marketing consists of controlled field experiments usually conducted in limited market areas on specified market performance indicators. Its main objectives are to predict sales, uncover valuable market information, and anticipate any adverse consequences of a marketing program for a particular product. With growing popularity, experimental procedures and observational techniques are employed to investigate and collect cause–effect relationship data regarding new products or improvements of existing products. Test marketing is used to determine customer attitudes toward new-product ideas, service delivery alternatives, or marketing communication strategies. While exploratory and descriptive surveys are effective for collecting primary data, they do not establish causal links between variables and/or events. Causal research designs can provide data to understand *why* certain events occur. The primary focus of this chapter is introducing and discussing test marketing and experimental designs. We begin with an overview of causal research and a brief review of the variables and relationships underlying causal research and test marketing. We also discuss reliability and validity issues that are important to all research designs.

Overview of Causal Research Designs

Causal research designs differ from exploratory or descriptive research designs in several ways. First, the primary focus of causal research is to obtain data that enables researchers to assess "cause–effect" relationships between two or more variables. In contrast, data from exploratory and survey research designs enables researchers to assess noncausal relationships, or associations between variables The concept of *causality* between several independent variables (X) and one dependent variable (Y) in research specifies relationships that are investigated in causal research studies and stated as "If X, then Y."

There are three fundamental conditions that must exist in order to accurately conclude that a cause–effect relationship exists between variables. Researchers must establish that there is *temporal order* between the independent X and the dependent Y variables such that variable X (or a change in X) must occur prior to observing or measuring variable Y (or a change in Y). Second, researchers must establish that collected data confirm there is some type of meaningful association between variable X and variable Y. Finally, researchers must account for (or control for) all other possible variables other than X that might cause a change in variable Y.

Experiment Involves carefully designed data collection procedures in which researchers manipulate a proposed *causal* independent variable and observe (measure) the *effect* on a dependent variable, while controlling for all other influencing variables

Another difference between causal and descriptive research is that causal research requires researchers to collect data using experimental designs. An **experiment** involves carefully designed data collection procedures in which researchers manipulate a proposed *causal* independent variable and observe (measure) the *effect* on a dependent variable, while controlling for all other influencing variables. Exploratory and survey research designs lack the "control" mechanism of causal designs. Typically, researchers use either a *controlled laboratory environment* where the study is conducted in an artificial setting where the effect of all, or nearly all, uncontrollable variables is minimized. In a *field environment,* researchers use a natural setting in which one or more of the independent variables are manipulated under conditions controlled as carefully as the situation will permit.

A third difference is the framing of research questions for causal designs. In exploratory and survey research designs, initial research questions are typically framed broadly and hypotheses focus on the magnitude and/or direction of the association, and not on causality. To illustrate noncausal hypotheses, consider the example of a corporate merchandise VP of Macy's Department Stores who is concerned about decreased revenues generated by current marketing strategies. Several questions needing answers are framed as: "Should Macy's current marketing strategies (store, product, service, etc.) be modified to increase revenues and market share?" "Do merchandise quality, prices, and service quality significantly impact customer satisfaction, in-store traffic patterns and store loyalty?" and "Should Macy's expand its marketing efforts to include an e-commerce option?" While these questions suggest examining associations (or broad relationships) between the specified variables, none of the questions focus on determining the causality of the relationships. Consequently, researchers would use exploratory or descriptive survey research designs.

In contrast, questions examining causal relationships between variables are framed with the focus being on the specific impact (or influence) one variable causes on another variable. To illustrate, Macy's VP of merchandise might ask the following types of questions: "Will exchanging customer service policy A with customer service policy B lead to a significant increase in store loyalty among current customers?" "Can the profitability of the casual women clothing line be improved by increasing prices by 18 percent?" "Will decreasing the current number of brands of shoes from eight to four significantly lower sales in the shoe department?" and "Will offering storewide sales of 'buy one get a second one for half price' versus a '20 percent discount' lead to a marked increase in store traffic patterns?" Accurate answers to these questions can be obtained only through some type of controlled causal research design.

The Nature of Experimentation

Variable Any observable and measurable element (or attribute) of an item or event.

Marketing research requires the measurement of variables. **Variables** are the observable and measurable elements (or attributes) of an object or an event. They are the qualities the researcher specifies, studies, and draws conclusions about. They can vary in different situations and at different times. To illustrate this concept, let's take the vehicle you are currently driving. Your automobile, SUV, van, or truck is really a composite of many different attributes. The color, the make and model, the number of cylinders, the miles per gallon, and the price are all variables. Furthermore, different vehicles possess different variables, and any one vehicle has one given set of variables at any given time. Whenever an object, idea, or event is described, every element by which it could be observed and measured can be considered a variable, including where it is, how it is used, and what surrounds it.

When conducting an experiment, researchers attempt to identify the relationships among different variables. Let's consider, for example, the following research question: "How long does it take a customer to place and receive an order from the drive-through at

A Closer Look at Research

BehaviorScan: A Device Used for Testing New Products and Marketing Programs

BehaviorScan is a one-of-a-kind, in-market laboratory for testing new products and marketing programs under tightly controlled yet real-world conditions. The impact of the test program can be measured in terms of both total store sales and household-level purchasing behavior. BehaviorScan offers the only targetable TV service in the nation, capable of delivering different ad copy and/or media weight to two or three selected groups of households within a given market. In seven markets around the United States, Information Resources Inc. (IRI), the company providing BehaviorScan, has facilities optimally designed for test marketing. IRI handles everything from retail sell-in to product stocking and promotion execution to data collection and analysis. IRI can control the distribution, price, shelf placement, trade, consumer promotion, and TV advertising for each product in a test. This ability to control all the variables enables highly accurate evaluation of the test variable.

In each BehaviorScan market, a large, ongoing household panel is maintained, making it possible to track household purchasing behaviors on an item-by-item level over time. Panel data collection is passive: members need only present their "Shopper's Hotline ID" card at checkout in participating retailers. Scanner sales data are collected on an ongoing basis from groceries, drugstores, and mass merchandisers. In-store promotion activity in most categories is monitored as well as documented pricing, displays, and features by item. Data from other outlets, such as convenience stores or hardware stores, can be collected on a custom basis. More details on BehaviorScan can be obtained at www.infores.com.

a McDonald's restaurant?" The time it takes to receive a food order is a variable that can be measured quantitatively. That is to say, the different values of the time variable are determined by some method of measurement. But how long it takes a particular customer to receive a food order is complicated by a number of other variables. For instance, what if there were 10 cars waiting in line, or it was 12:00 noon, or it was raining? Additionally, such factors as the number of drive-up windows, the training level of order takers, and the number of patrons waiting inside are all variables. Consequently, all of these variables have some effect on the time variable.

To make all this a little clearer, the type of car a McDonald's customer is driving, the number of brothers or sisters she has, and the quantity of food she orders also are variables. But are the first two variables likely to have much effect on order time? No, but there *is* a relationship between the quantity of the order and the waiting time, because the more items in the order, the longer it takes to prepare. So the researcher must exclude extraneous variables. If it seems true that the quantity of food ordered increases one's wait at a drive-through, the researcher may hypothesize that there is a **functional relationship** between food quantity ordered and waiting time. It makes sense to hypothesize that waiting time at a fast-food drive-through is a function of the amount of food being ordered. In experiments, researchers investigate and measure likely functional relationships between variables. The focus is on discovering the systematic change in one variable as another variable changes. The nearby A Closer Look at Research (Using Technology) box illustrates a testing service called BehaviorScan that conducts controlled investigations "in the field."

Functional relationship An observable and measurable systematic change in one variable as another variable changes.

How Variables Are Used in Experimental Designs

When designing causal research experiments, researchers must understand the types of variables used in experiments: *independent, dependent, control,* and *extraneous* (see Exhibit 9.1).

Independent variables Variables whose values are directly manipulated by the researcher.

Independent variables are those whose values are directly manipulated by researchers in an experiment. They are also referred to as *causal, predictor,* or *treatment* variables. Researchers consider independent variables to be the causal factors in identifed functional relationships between independent and dependent variables. In many research experiments, marketing mix variables such as price levels, product/package designs, distribution channel systems, and advertising themes are treated as independent (causal) variables. For example, Procter & Gamble (P&G) recently wanted to determine the relationship between several new package designs for its Tide brand of laundry detergent and Tide's unit sales. Using experimental design procedures, researchers observed customers purchasing the product on four different occasions. On each occasion, researchers changed the package design from round to *square*, to *rectangular*, to *oval*. Every time the package design changed, sales were measured. Since the researchers directly manipulated package design, it served as the independent variable.

Dependent variables Measures of effect or outcome that occur during the experiment, or measures of change in the conditions that exist after the experiment is completed.

The values of **dependent variables** are measures of outcomes of an experiment. The point is to see how they will change depending on how the independent variables are manipulated. Values of independent variables are assigned *before* the experiment begins, and dependent variables are attributes or elements whose values may be affected *during* the process of the experiment. Dependent variables thus measure how conditions that existed before the experiment may have changed *after* the experiment. In marketing research dependent variables typically include such market performance factors as unit sales, profit levels, and market shares. The company is experimenting to see how they can improve these values. In the P&G package design example, the dependent variable is Tide's unit sales. This variable is measured under each manipulation of the package design. If the

EXHIBIT 9.1 Types of Variables Used in Experimental Research Designs

Type of Variable	Comments
Independent variable	Also called *cause, predictor,* or *treatment* variable (X). Represents an attribute (or element) of an object, idea, or event whose values are directly manipulated by the researcher. The independent variable is assumed to be the causal factor in a functional relationship with a dependent variable.
Dependent variable	Also called *effect, outcome,* or *criterion* variable (Y). Represents an observable attribute or element that is the outcome of specified tests that is derived from manipulating the independent variable(s).
Control variables	Variables the researcher controls so they do not affect the functional relationship between the independent and dependent variables included in the experiment.
Extraneous variables	Uncontrollable variables that should average out over a series of experiments. If not accounted for, they can have a confounding impact on the dependent variable measures that could weaken or invalidate the results of an experiment.

researchers wanted to state the results in terms of a functional relationship, they would say that Tide's unit sales (the dependent variable) are a function of package design (the independent variable).

Control variables Variables that the researcher does not allow to vary freely or systematically with independent variables; control variables should not change as the independent variable is manipulated.

Control variables are potential causal independent variables that researchers need to account for (control) during the experiment. Researchers do not allow them to vary freely or systematically with the independent variables under consideration. Thus, the average value of a control variable or its impact should not change as the independent variable is manipulated. Researchers must design the experiment so that control variables cannot systematically affect the causal relationship between the independent and dependent variables. Control variables present a major problem in using experimental designs to investigate hypothesized functional relationships. For example, if P&G wants to investigate the true relationship between Tide's unit sales and package design alternatives, researchers do not want any other variables to influence the measure of unit sales. They have to control them. They want to make sure the various other conditions surrounding Tide's unit sales (the dependent variable) are as similar as possible for each of the package design manipulations (the independent variable). In this experiment, the customers should (1) shop at the same store during each package design manipulation; (2) shop at the same time of day with the same amount of store crowding; and (3) shop on successive days without being exposed to any advertised message for Tide. The price and shelf location of Tide should remain the same for all successive package design manipulations. The problem is there are so many possible influences on Tide's unit sales that researchers cannot possibly control all of them, yet they must control as many of them as they can.

Extraneous variables Variables that cannot be controlled by researchers but that should average out over different trials and thus not systematically affect the results of the experiment.

Extraneous variables represent all potential factors other than the independent variable(s) that could impact the responses of the participants during the experiment. It is difficult and perhaps impossible for researchers to control these variables during an experiment. For example, how could one control changes in mood or health of shoppers or precise temperature or physical conditions of the store, to name a few. Researchers hope these uncontrollable variables average out over the different manipulations of the independent variables, resulting in their having little or no systematic influence on the dependent variable—that is, they will be merely extraneous. If extraneous variables cannot be accounted for or eliminated during the experiment, or if they do not average out, the result may be distorted or weak research conclusions, raising serious questions about the validity of the experiment. In the P&G example, one method researchers use to reduce the effects of extraneous variables is to *randomize* the same manipulation of the package design across a number of customers and then measure unit sales. Randomization has to be used across all of the package design manipulations until a significant number of customers are measured for Tide unit sales under each manipulation. This procedure is referred to as **complete randomization** of subjects. The desired outcome is that the influence of extraneous variables will average out over all manipulations of the independent variable. While the measured results under these conditions might not be very precise for any individual test subject, they should be precise enough across all individuals tested to show a fairly accurate relationship between the independent and dependent variables.

Complete randomization The procedure whereby many subjects are assigned to different experimental treatment conditions, resulting in each group averaging out any systematic effect on the investigated functional relationship between the independent and dependent variables.

Whether researchers design laboratory or field experiments to investigate cause–effect relationships, there are four important elements that need to be incorporated into experimental designs: (1) proper manipulation of the independent variable(s), (2) selection and appropriate measurement of the "effect" (dependent) variable, (3) selection and assignment of the "right" subjects, and (4) control of extraneous factors. Researchers must be able to create and categorize the independent variable into a minimum of two different treatment levels that are easily recognized by the subjects as being different. Typically, the independent variable is a nonmetric categorical variable such as a member of a set of colors like blue, green, red, gold; or some set of product/service characteristics like size, shape, brand name; or some set of consumer characteristics such as gender, occupation, or marital status that can be manipulated in the experiment.

In some experimental situations, researchers are faced with a *continuous variable* such as product prices or dollar expenditures, frequency of purchase, or use of products/services as the independent variable. When using an independent variable that may be manipulated along a continuum, researchers must decide which appropriate levels of the variable to use in the experiment. For example, let's say the owners of the Santa Fe Grill Mexican restaurant want to determine the relationship between price levels and sales of their 20-chicken-wing dinner they plan to add to the menu. In this situation, researchers are manipulating one continuous independent variable (price) to see how it affects sales revenue (the outcome or dependent variable). Price is a truly continuous variable, and researchers must decide how many different categorical levels of price ($8.99, $11.99, and $14.99, or others) should serve as the treatment levels to be manipulated, while controlling for the quantity level (i.e., 20 wings) for each price.

For an experimental design to be successful, researchers must carefully select and measure the dependent variable that is most relevant and representative of the outcome of interest. Selection of the right outcome variable is a direct result of the problem definition process. The choice of the dependent variable determines the type of answer given. In the Santa Fe Grill chicken wing dinner example, the owners need to think beyond consumers' initial reactions to the introduction of the new menu item. When the 20-wing meal was first introduced, initial trial rate was very high during the first three months, but only a small percentage of customers made repeat purchases over the next nine-month period. The 20-wing meal never achieved high repeat sales during that time period. Thus trial purchase and repeat purchase levels are both possible dependent variables in an experiment. Determining the most appropriate dependent variable needs to be done with care. Undertaking a complete problem definition procedure will help researchers select the most important dependent variable to include in the causal research design.

Theory A large body of interconnected propositions about how some portion of a certain phenomenon operates.

Experimental research An empirical investigation that tests for hypothesized relationships between dependent variables and manipulated independent variables.

Another key concern of researchers with experimental design research is the selection and assignment of the right test units. Typically test units are the human subjects responding to the independent variables (also referred to as treatments). Depending on the focus of the experiment, test units could be customers, consumers, employees, sales territories, product/service brands, specified stores, or market segments. Human subjects are the most common test units used in marketing or consumer behavior experiments. Researchers must understand the characteristics that identify members of the target population and use those characteristics in selecting the sample of subjects for the research. The qualifying characteristics can be demographic, psychographic, attitudinal, emotional or behavioral, or some combination. Regardless of the types of characteristics, researchers must use characteristics that will result in the sample of subjects accurately representing the individuals in the target population. Finally, in any causal research project researchers must ensure that subjects are randomly assigned to the specified treatment groups to control for possible effects of extraneous variables.

The Role of Theory in Experimental Designs

From an experimental design perspective, **theory** helps to explain and predict, and underpins the development of hypotheses about relationships that can be tested empirically. Hypotheses may be thought of as smaller versions of theories. **Experimental research** is a

Deductive research Experimental investigations that are undertaken to test hypothesized relationships.

Inductive research An investigation that uses causal design procedures to generate and test hypotheses that create new theories or extend existing theories.

hypothesis testing method that is a type of **deductive research.** Researchers derive a hypothesis from a theory, design an experiment, and gather data to test the hypothesis.

When researchers use causal designs to generate hypotheses in order to create new theories or extend existing theories about a phenomenon this is referred to as **inductive research.** In practice, researchers often use both deductive and inductive design methods. Researchers may begin an investigation using causal research procedures to test some hypotheses that focus on the cause–effect relationships between variables, but then develop new hypotheses based on the data results. Existing theoretical insights help researchers to identify the independent variables that might bring about changes in dependent variables. Experimental research designs are most appropriate when researchers want to find out *why* certain events occur and *why* they happen under certain conditions and not others. Identifying and being able to explain cause–effect relationships enable marketing researchers to be in a position to make reasonable predictions about marketing phenomena.

Laboratory and Field Experiments

Field experiments Causal research designs that manipulate the independent variables in order to measure the dependent variable in a natural setting of the test.

Laboratory experiments Causal research designs that are conducted in an artificial setting and have high internal validity but limited external validity.

When marketing experiments are conducted in a natural setting they are referred to as **field experiments.** In contrast, if the experiment is conducted in an artificial setting it is referred to as a **laboratory experiment.** In laboratory experiments researchers have control over the research setting, for the most part. For example, assume Apple wanted to obtain reactions to a series of advertisements about its iPhone. If it arranged with its advertising agency to recruit respondents to come to their facility, watch the new ads, and answer questions about the ads, this would be a lab experiment. The questions might be attitudinal, such as like or dislike the ads, or they might be behavioral intentions, such as how likely would they be to purchase the phone after seeing the ads.

Field experiments are conducted in real-life settings. An example of a field experiment would be if Apple placed the iPhone in its stores, but used different in-store advertising messages in different stores. It then could determine the effectiveness of the different in-store ad messages, assuming it had controlled for differences in the customers across the different stores in which the phone experiment was conducted. It is difficult and often impossible to control extraneous variables in a field setting. The value of field experiments is that they have high external validity, while lab experiments exhibit only internal validity. We discuss experimental validity in the next section.

Validity and Reliability Concerns with Experimental Designs

Validity The extent to which the conclusions drawn from the experiment are true.

To understand experimental research, we first must examine validity issues that directly affect research designs. Extraneous variables are numerous and difficult to control when using experimental research for testing hypothesized relationships. Their presence may result in contamination of the functional relationship being investigated. This contamination clouds the researcher's ability to conclusively determine whether the results of the experiment are valid. **Validity** refers to the extent to which the conclusions drawn from the experiment are true. That is, do the differences in the dependent variable found through experimental manipulations of the independent variables really reflect a cause–effect relationship? While there are many aspects of validity in causal research designs, we will discuss three important ones: *internal validity*, *external validity,* and *construct validity*.

Internal Validity

Internal validity The extent to which the research design accurately identifies causal relationships.

Internal validity refers to the extent to which the research design accurately identifies causal relationships. Internal validity exists when researchers can rule out other explanations for the observed conclusions about the functional relationship. Take for example an experiment on the effect of electricity. If you shock someone (experimental treatment) and he jumps (observed effect), and he jumps only because of the shock and for no other reason, then internal validity exists.

Why is establishing internal validity important to researchers? The following example illustrates the answer. Let's say a small bakery in Denver, Colorado, wants to know whether or not putting additional frosting on its new cakes would cause customers to like the cakes better. Using an experimental design, it tests the hypothesis that its customers like additional frosting on their cakes. As the "amount of frosting" (independent variable) is manipulated, the bakery discovers that additional frosting allows the cakes to stay moist longer. Consequently, it might be the moistness and not the frosting that causes customers' positive reaction to the new cakes. In assessing internal validity, control groups are developed consisting of customers who were not exposed to the independent variable but all other conditions were kept the same.[3] Adding the control group to the experimental design reduces the possibility that the observed effect of the new cakes is caused by some other factor other than the treatment. In this case, if it is the frosting, then the treatment group should like the new cake more than the control group. But if it were the moistness, then both groups would like the new cake equally.

Exhibit 9.2 displays the types of threats that can negatively affect internal, external, and construct validities of experiments. The latter two will be discussed in the next sections. Here we discuss the threats to internal validity. *History threats* involve events that occur between the first measurement of the dependent variable and the second measurement. If the objective of the manipulation is to measure changes in a person's attitude about political integrity (dependent variable) resulting from a political history course, the results can be strongly affected if a major political scandal occurs between the first and second manipulation treatments (while the person was taking the political history course).

People's attitudes and behaviors change as they get older over time, and these changes can also represent a *maturation threat* to internal validity. The *threat of testing* refers to the second administration of the treatment where the experience with the first administration may well affect scores on the second administration. Changes in observers' attitudes, reduced accuracy of scorers, or changed administration techniques are all examples of the *instrumentation threat* to internal validity.

When researchers do not randomly assign subjects to treatment groups or do not use control groups, then *selection bias* resulting in noncomparable groups can occur, threatening internal validity. *Mortality* involves the loss of subjects from groups due to natural causes, thereby creating groups of subjects that are no longer comparable. *Ambiguity* of causal direction may also be a problem. For instance, do higher family incomes result from higher education levels, or do higher income levels allow higher education levels? Such ambiguities reduce researchers' ability to differentiate between cause and effect.

Statistical regression is where subjects score differently on each trial in an experiment, with recorded scores regressing toward the true population mean, resulting in the errors balancing out. In other cases where subjects are selected for particular groups

eXHIBIT 9.2 Validity Types and Threats[4]

THREATS TO INTERNAL VALIDITY	
History	When extraneous factors that enter the experiment process between the first and later manipulations affect measures of the dependent variable.
Maturation	Changes in the dependent variable based on the natural function of time and not attributed to any specific event.
Testing	When learned understanding gained from the first treatment and measures of the dependent variable distort future treatments and measurement activities.
Instrumentation	Contamination from changes in measurement processes, observation techniques, and/or measuring instruments.
Selection bias	Contamination created by inappropriate selection and/or assignment processes of test subjects to experimental treatment groups.
Statistical regression	Contamination created when experimental groups are selected on the basis of their extreme responses or scores.
Mortality	Contamination due to changing the composition of the test subjects in the experiment.
Ambiguity	Contamination from unclear determination of a cause–effect relationship.
THREATS TO EXTERNAL VALIDITY	
Treatment vs. treatment	When test subjects in different treatment groups are exposed to different amounts of manipulations.
Treatment vs. testing	When the premeasurement process sensitizes test subjects to respond in an abnormal manner to treatment manipulations.
Treatment vs. selection	Generalizing the results to other categories of people beyond those types used in the experiment.
Treatment vs. setting	Generalizing the results to other environments beyond the one used in the experiment.
Treatment vs. history	Using the existing functional relationship to predict future phenomenon outcomes.
THREATS TO CONSTRUCT VALIDITY	
Inadequate	Contamination due to inadequate understanding of the complete makeup of the independent and preoperationalization dependent variables included in the experimental design.
Mono-operation bias	Contamination created by using only one method to measure the outcomes of the dependent variable.
Mono-method bias	Contamination due to assessing multiattribute treatment manipulations (independent variables) using single-item measuring instruments.
Hypothesis guessing	Contamination by test subjects believing they know the desired functional relationship prior to the manipulation treatment.
Evaluation apprehension	Contamination caused by test subjects being fearful that others will know their actions or responses.
Demand characteristics	Contamination created by test subjects trying to guess the true purpose behind the experiment, thus giving abnormal socially acceptable responses or behaviors.
Diffusion of treatment	Contamination due to test subjects discussing the treatment and measurement activities with individuals that have not received the treatment.

based on extreme pretreatment responses, the observed posttreatment measures will be even more biased.

The primary weapon against threats to internal validity is random selection of subjects from a heterogeneous target population and random assignment to treatment groups. This is considered standard practice in experimental research studies.

External validity The extent to which a causal relationship found in a study can be expected to be true for the entire target population.

External Validity

External validity refers to the extent to which a causal relationship found in a study can be expected to be true for the target population.[5] For example, let's say Kraft Foods, a global food company, wants to find out if its new "calci-yum" Jell-O Instant pudding dessert will appeal to a commercially viable percentage of U.S. citizens between the ages of 18 and 35. It would be too costly to ask each 18- to 35-year-old in the United States to taste the product. Therefore, using experimental design procedures, Kraft Foods can randomly select test subjects from the defined target population (18–35) and assign them to different treatment groups, varying one component of the dessert for each group. The subjects then taste the new dessert. If 60 percent indicate they will purchase the product, and if in fact 60 percent of the entire population did purchase the new product when it was marketed, then the results of the study can be considered externally valid. That is, they can be generalized to the target population.

Threats to external validity include interactions of treatment with history, setting, selection, testing, and treatment exposures. Interactions with *history* that lessen external validity could include testing on a special day such as Christmas or Halloween. If researchers are interested in charitable behavior, then treatment manipulation and effect measures administered on Christmas Day might give quite different results from those given at some other less notable time. After watching several movies emphasizing charity and love for our fellow man, the average subject might react significantly differently on that day than on some other. By the same token, polls on gun control will very likely be affected if taken immediately after the assassination of a major public figure. Generalizability to other time frames would be considerably reduced.

Similar reductions in external validity can occur if the location or setting of the experiment influences the observed results. Surely, a fear-of-heights scale administered on top of a mountain would have different results from one administered in a classroom. The final threat of selection bias occurs when the sample is not truly representative of the defined target population. Asking subjects to participate in an experiment requiring several hours will limit the actual sample to only those who have the spare time and may not generate a truly representative sample.

Another possible threat to external validity can occur when the test subjects experience more than one treatment in the experimental setting. The conclusions drawn could not be generalized to situations where individuals received fewer or more treatments. For example, if researchers for Home Depot design an experiment to study the effects of a 20 percent price reduction on one-gallon cans of Behr 1-Part Epoxy Concrete & Garage Floor Slate Gray Paint sales in which this paint is displayed in two separate store locations, the results cannot be generalized to situations where only one display was used. Here, the extra display competes with price reduction as an explanation for sales.

Construct Validity

Experimental research designs must accurately identify the independent and dependent variables in the study. Additionally, researchers must be able to accurately measure those variables in order to assess their true functional or cause–effect relationships. Consequently, researchers must assess the construct validity of both independent and dependent variables prior to executing the experiment. **Construct validity** is viewed as the extent to which the variables under investigation are completely and accurately identified prior to hypothesizing any functional relationships. Establishing construct validity for the variables can be an elusive goal. Of the many approaches to establishing construct validity, one that is used widely consists of three steps.[6]

Construct validity The extent to which the variables under investigation are completely and accurately identified prior to hypothesizing any functional relationships.

First, researchers must accurately identify the relationships between the constructs (or variables). To illustrate, let's assume researchers want to use a construct called "motivation to succeed" (MTS) as an independent variable in predicting the likelihood of individuals' life success. Subjects measuring the highest on the MTS construct would be those most likely to have succeeded in life. The fundamental question that must be addressed is "What are the observable, real-life indicators of such success?" Using a process referred to as specifying the *domain of observable subcomponents* related to the construct,[7] let's assume that peer respect, academic achievement, and personal financial security represent success in the society being investigated. The precise nature of this specification is necessary so that hypothesized relationships can be empirically tested with real data. Otherwise, the data collected will be insufficient to either support or refute the hypothesis.

Second, researchers execute an experiment that manipulates MTS and measures the outcome "life success." If the data are both positive and substantial in support of the hypothesized functional relationship, then evidence of construct validity exists. Researchers will attempt to determine what other constructs these observable subcomponents might be related to, such as social position, inherited wealth, or athletic prowess. In situations where the observable subcomponents are not related to MTS, but rather to other alternative constructs, the evidence in support of construct validity would be weakened. For example, peer respect and personal financial security might be the result of inherited wealth and have little to do with motivation to succeed. As a result, researchers will need to find other observable subcomponents that are more closely related to MTS and not generally caused by other variables.

Convergent validity When the researcher's measures of a construct are highly correlated with known existing measures of the same construct.

Discriminant validity The existence of a negative correlation between an experiment's measuring methods and those measurements of completely different constructs.

Finally prior to executing the experiment, researchers will compare their proposed measures of the independent and dependent variables with other similar measures. When existing measures of the same construct are highly correlated with researchers' measures, then there is evidence of **convergent validity** in support of the construct validity. Additional evidence, called **discriminant validity,** may come from a negative correlation between the experiment's measures and those designed to measure completely different constructs.[8]

Threats to Construct Validity

Inadequate operationalization When a construct is not carefully and completely defined.

Mono-operation bias Contamination created by using one method to measure the outcomes of the dependent variable.

Mono-method bias Contamination due to assessing multiattribute treatment manipulations (independent variables) using single-item measuring instruments.

Demand characteristic Contamination created by test subjects trying to guess the true purpose behind the experiment, thus giving abnormal socially acceptable responses or behaviors.

Construct validity can be threatened in many ways, including inadequate operationalization of constructs, mono-operation bias, mono-method bias, hypothesis guessing, demand characteristics, evaluation apprehension, and diffusion of treatment.

To avoid **inadequate operationalization,** researchers must carefully and completely define the construct. For example, "fear of heights" cannot simply be defined as a fear of high places, since some people are afraid of being on high mountain roads but not in an office in a high building or on an airplane. For researchers, it is essential that they know exactly what form of fear they are trying to measure. Then, once the definition has been refined in light of the purpose of the study, researchers can more precisely select measurable, observable constructs.

Mono-operation and **mono-method bias** can threaten construct validity through contamination created by using only one measuring method or single-item measurements. Whenever possible, researchers need to collect data using more than one measuring method (pen and pencil, interview, or physical reactions) and more than a single-item measure in each method.[9] Past research findings suggest that, in some cases, subjects try to guess the purpose of the research and respond as they feel researchers want them to respond to the **demand characteristic.** Researchers can control this type of threat by disguising the hypothesis, making it difficult to guess. For example, one clever psychologist invited people to participate in an experiment, had them wait in an outer office, and then took them into a room where they were asked several questions. In actuality, the experiment involved interpersonal conversational patterns and took place in the waiting room with the help of confederates posing as subjects (without the knowledge of the real subjects).[10]

Evaluation apprehension Contamination caused by test subjects being fearful that others will know their actions or responses.

Diffusion of treatment Contamination due to test subjects discussing the treatment and measurement activities with individuals who have not received the treatment.

Most people have exhibited **evaluation apprehension** before a college entrance exam, sports physical, or first job interview. Because such apprehension can seriously bias the results of many studies, researchers will reduce it as much as possible. One frequently used approach in marketing research involves ensuring the anonymity of subjects. Careful briefing of participants by the research team also can help reduce this threat.

The final threat to construct validity is **diffusion of treatment.** Since it is rarely possible to completely isolate subjects, the control group may exchange information with the treatment group, or participants who previously completed a questionnaire may discuss it with those who have yet to participate. Although researchers caution subjects not to discuss the research, such efforts are many times unsuccessful. Taking several samples from the target population at various locations and under different conditions usually reduces this threat. In fact, using different samples from the defined target population of interest is a good way to reduce threats to construct and other types of validity.

Reliability of Experimental Research Designs

Experimental design reliability The degree to which the design and its procedures can be replicated and achieve similar conclusions about hypothesized relationships.

Researchers also must understand reliability in experimental research designs. For **experimental design reliability** to exist, researchers must be able to demonstrate that their experiment can be repeated and similar conclusions will be reached. Although there tends to be little reward in repeating the experiments of other researchers, especially in academic studies, there are significant benefits in repeating the procedures used in causal research designs. For example, a company such as AT&T, which has many different types of telecommunication products, will standardize its design and testing procedures for investigating new-product acceptance. Such standardization of procedures leads to significant cost reductions within AT&T's research and development activities.

Improving the Internal and External Validity of Experimental Designs

The ultimate goal of experimental research is determining the true causal relationship between the independent and dependent variables. Researchers must minimize the extent to which extraneous variables confound experimental results. To do so, several techniques unique to experimental designs can be used to minimize threats to internal and external validity.

Use of Control Groups

When designing an experiment, researchers must randomly assign subjects to the groups that will be exposed to the manipulation(s) and to the control group that does not receive the manipulation. Control groups represent the greatest strength of the experiment and the best way to ensure internal validity.

Time Order of the Manipulation Exposure

Researchers must determine which variables, independent or dependent, will occur first. This can be accomplished by using experimental measures of the variables prior to manipulation or by establishing experimental treatment and control groups that do not differ in terms of influencing the dependent variable before the manipulation takes place.

Exclusion of Nonsimilar Test Subjects

To increase internal validity, researchers select only those test subjects who have similar and controllable characteristics. Let's say, for example, that Publix Supermarket researchers are interested in certain food-purchasing behaviors among "regular shoppers." The study's results might be confounded by differences in gender, age, and occupational status of the test subjects. To counter this possibility, researchers would select only those test subjects with gender, age, and occupational status characteristics similar to the "regular shopper" target market. By doing so, researchers are eliminating extraneous variation due to gender, age, and occupation.

Matching Extraneous Variables

Through the process of matching, researchers measure selected extraneous variables on an individual basis. Subjects who respond similarly to the variables are then allocated to the experimental and control groups. This process can control for selection bias and enhance internal validity.

Randomization of Test Subjects to Treatment Groups

Randomization in assigning test subjects to the experimental and control groups will help make the groups equivalent. The key to true randomization of test subjects is that the randomness must be secured in a carefully controlled manner. To enhance external validity, researchers can randomly select settings and times for the experiment based on the population or events under investigation. By following strict setup procedures when designing the experiment, researchers increase the experiment's ability to accurately identify true causal or functional relationships. Additionally, these procedures help researchers control for contamination of the relationships between the independent and dependent variables.

Types of Experimental Research Designs

Experimental designs can be classified into three groups: (1) pre-experiments, (2) true experiments, and (3) quasi-experiments (see Exhibit 9.3). The main difference among these groups is the degree of control researchers exercise in the design and execution. To facilitate understanding of the different types of experimental designs, we use the following set of symbols:[11]

X = The exposure of an independent variable (treatment manipulation) to a group of test subjects for whom the effects are to be determined.

O = The process of observation or measurement of the dependent variable (outcome) on the test subjects.

[R] = The random assignment of test subjects to separate treatment groups.

EG = The experimental group of test subjects.

CG = The control group of test subjects.

→ = A movement through time, normally displayed as left-to-right movement.

Note also that vertical alignment of symbols implies those symbols refer to activities that occur simultaneously at a prescribed point in time, and that horizontal alignment of symbols implies that all those symbols refer to a specific treatment group of test subjects.

eXHIBIT 9.3 Types of Experimental Research Designs in Marketing Research

Pre-experimental Designs	
One-shot study	A single group of test subjects is exposed to the independent variable treatment X, and then a single measurement on the dependent variable is taken (O_1).
One-group pretest-posttest	First a pretreatment measure of the dependent variable is taken (O_1), then the test subjects are exposed to the independent treatment X, and then a post treatment measure of the dependent variable is taken (O_2).
Static group comparison	There are two groups of test subjects: one group is the experimental group (EG) and is exposed to the independent treatment, and the second group is the control group (CG) and is not given the treatment. The dependent variable is measured in both groups after the treatment.
True Experimental Designs	
Pretest-posttest control group	Test subjects are randomly assigned to either the experimental or control group, and each group receives a pretreatment measure of the dependent variable. Then the independent treatment is exposed to the experimental group, after which both groups receive a post-treatment measure of the dependent variable.
Posttest-only control group	Test subjects are randomly assigned to either the experimental or the control group. The experimental group is then exposed to the independent treatment, after which both groups receive a posttreatment measure of the dependent variable.
Solomon Four Group	This design combines the "pretest-posttest control group" and "posttest-only control group" designs and provides both direct and reactive effects of testing. It is not used in marketing research practices because of complexity and lengthy time requirements.
Quasi-experimental Designs	
Nonequivalent control group	This design is a combination of the "static group comparison" and the "one-group pretest-posttest" pre-experimental designs.
Separate-sample pretest-posttest	Two different groups of test subjects are drawn; neither group is directly exposed to the independent treatment variable. One group receives a pretest measure of the dependent variable. Then after the insignificant independent treatment occurs, the second group of test subjects receives a posttest measure of the dependent variable.
Field experiment	This is a causal design that manipulates the independent variables in order to measure the dependent variable in the natural setting of the event or test.

Pre-experimental Designs

Three specific pre-experimental designs are available to marketing researchers: the *one-shot* study, the *one-group pretest-posttest,* and the *static group comparison.* These designs are commonly referred to as crude experiments and used only when a stronger experimental design is not possible. These designs are characterized by an absence of randomization of test subjects. Their major weakness is the inability to meet internal validity criteria due to a lack of equivalent group comparisons.[12]

One-Shot Study

The one-shot study can be illustrated as follows:

$$\text{(EG):} \quad X \rightarrow O_1$$

An example of this design would be when researchers wish to measure customers' reactions to a product display in a single store. This design does not control extraneous variables. It ignores the process of group comparisons that is fundamental in the experimental process. The only comparisons made are those based on common knowledge, past experiences, or general impressions of what the condition would have been had the manipulation not occurred. In this instance, even careful development of accurate measures will not compensate for the inadequate design.

One-Group Pretest-Posttest

The value of the one-group pretest-posttest design is its ability to provide researchers with a comparison measure. It is diagrammed as follows:

$$\text{(EG):}\quad O_1 \rightarrow X_1 \rightarrow O_2$$

The design is subject to the same extraneous confounding factors with the one-shot study. In addition, history contamination is a major weakness, given that events can occur between O_1 and O_2. Even environmental noise (sirens, thunder, phones) can affect results. The only way to control for the occurrence is to isolate the experiment in a controlled laboratory setting. Unfortunately, this is a widely used design in marketing research, often to measure advertising effects among consumers. Many advertisers take a pretest criterion measure of ad recall, product involvement, media habits, or purchase history. Then an experimental independent treatment manipulation is delivered (e.g., exposure to an ad during a TV program), followed by a posttest measure of the dependent variable, usually ad recall. An experimental design such as this is further affected by maturation and instrumentation problems. The effect of the pretest measure also introduces problems with the testing factor. One advantage of the "one-group pretest-posttest" design is its lack of selection bias. Since only one group exists, it automatically eliminates the problem of differential selection. Overall, this design has imperfect safeguards to internal validity and should be used only when nothing better is available.

Static Group Comparison

Static group comparison is a two-group experimental design consisting of an experimental group (EG) and a control group (CG) of subjects, but it lacks randomization. The experimental group receives the independent treatment manipulation, with the second operating as the control. It can be illustrated as follows:

$$\text{(EG):}\quad X \rightarrow O_1$$
$$\text{(CG):}\quad O_2$$

Selection bias is the major defect of this design mainly because the groups are formed on a nonrandom basis. For example, many studies look at two store settings or heavy users versus light users when comparing new-product trials or sales. Compared to other pre-experimental designs, the static group comparison is substantially less susceptible to history, maturation, instrumentation, and testing contaminations.

True Experimental Designs

There are three forms of true experimental designs: (1) *pretest-posttest, control group,* (2) *posttest-only, control group,* and (3) *Solomon Four Group.* The common denominator is that all three designs ensure equivalence between experimental and control groups by random assignment to the groups.[13]

Pretest-Posttest Control Group—Completely Randomized Design

The pretest-posttest control group design consists of one experimental group and one control group of test subjects, who are assigned to either group by the process of complete randomization. This process randomly assigns each experimental unit (subject) to the treatments. Randomization of experimental units is researchers' attempt to control all extraneous variables while manipulating a single treatment variable. It can be illustrated as follows:

$$\text{(EG):}\quad [R]\ O_1 \rightarrow X \rightarrow O_2$$

$$\text{(CG):}\quad [R]\ O_3 \longrightarrow O_4$$

with the treatment effect (TE) of the experimental manipulation being:

$$TE = (O_2 - O_1) - (O_4 - O_3)$$

This experimental design controls for extraneous factors that diminish internal validity, but does not ensure true internal validity. For example, if extraneous history events produce a difference between O_2 and O_1, and a difference between O_4 and O_3, it can be assumed researchers have controlled for history contamination. Yet researchers cannot directly determine whether the same exact history events occurred in both groups. Certain events may have taken place in the experimental group and not the other, even if the results suggest there is internal validity. This can occur due to some disturbance, diversion, or environmental factor influencing the subjects randomly assigned to the control group. To prevent this problem, researchers first randomly assign individuals into experimental and control groups, then have each individual tested for any such disturbance.

Regression, testing, and maturation threats are controlled since differences should be measured equally in experimental and control groups. An instrumentation problem might arise from researchers modifying the measuring instrument between the pretest and posttest measures of the dependent variable. Differences in dropout rates among group members can also develop into a mortality issue. Selection is adequately handled through the process of randomization, with matching techniques being employed to improve equivalency. Matching must only be used as a supplement to randomization.

Procedural operations of this design are straightforward. To illustrate this point, a Toyota dealership in Chicago, Illinois, considers testing the impact of a direct mail promotional message regarding customers' knowledge of automobiles. Researchers draw a random sample of individuals from the dealership's customer service records. Half are randomly assigned to the control group, the other half to the experimental group (the group that receives direct mail on automobiles). Everyone selected is measured on automobile knowledge. The experimental group then receives the promotional message, and after three weeks, the "automobile knowledge" measure is again administered to all subjects.

Sources of extraneous variation occur if there are differences between the measures of O_4 less O_3 (e.g., an actual product recall occurred during the experiment). However, if this type of extraneous effect did occur, it would be measured equally on those individuals in the experimental group. While the design produces adequate control for internal validity, it does not necessarily do so for external validity. Two factors serve as threats to the external validity of this design: testing and selection. Pretests run the risk of introducing bias into the design based on the mere topic area being pretested. This can cause unusual attitudes to develop among experimental group subjects that can ultimately bias the posttest measures. In addition, a high mortality rate of subjects can destroy the intentions of sound randomization procedures. If this is a factor, replication of the experiment over time among different groups is necessary to ensure external validity.

Posttest-Only Control Group

This experimental design is identical to the previous completely randomized design except the pretest measures of the dependent variable are absent. This type of experimental design works well if the process of randomization is totally assured. The design is illustrated as follows:

$$\text{(EG):} \quad [R]\ X \rightarrow O_1$$
$$\text{(CG):} \quad [R] \qquad O_2$$

Take for example a completely randomized posttest-only, control group design that might be used by a research company like J.D. Powers and Associates to examine the effects of various incentive alternatives used to increase the response rate of its direct mail new automobile owner satisfaction survey. The two experimental treatment incentive alternatives of interest are personal monetary payments of 10 dollars to prospective participants versus a 10-dollar contribution to a charitable organization selected by the participant. When a control group of participants is used, there are actually three treatment groups: (1) no incentive offered to the control group of participants, (2) $10 charity incentive, and (3) $10 personal incentive. Let's assume the researchers determine the overall sampling frame would need to be 1,500 new automobile owners resulting in 500 prospective participants (n) being randomly assigned to each of the three treatment groups. Below are the hypothetical results of the experiment:

	Response Rate Experimental Treatment Groups		
Groups	**$10 Personal Incentive**	**$10 Charity Incentive**	**Control: No Incentive**
Response Rates	39.4%	24.3%	25.7%
# of respondents (n)	500	500	500

In comparing the above response rate (dependent variable) of each of the three treatment groups, the results suggest that personal payment incentives have the strongest influence on response rate. From a managerial perspective, J.D. Power and Associates could expect a significantly higher survey response rate by including a $10 personal payment with each of the new automobile owner satisfaction surveys mailed.

Solomon Four Group

Although a highly complex design, the Solomon Four Group enables researchers to learn more about internal and external validity than any other experimental design does. But because of its complexity, marketing researchers do not use it as widely as the other design alternatives. It is illustrated as follows:

Design 1

$$\text{(EG):} \quad [R]\ O_1 \rightarrow X \rightarrow O_2$$
$$\text{(CG):} \quad [R]\ O_3 \longrightarrow O_4$$

Design 2

$$\text{(EG):} \quad [R] \qquad X \rightarrow O_5$$
$$\text{(CG):} \quad [R] \qquad\quad O_6$$

The design is a combination of the "pretest-posttest control group" and the "posttest only control group" experimental designs. It provides both direct and reactive effects of testing, based on $O_1 \rightarrow X \rightarrow O_2$ and $X \rightarrow O_5$, respectively. External validity is enhanced, along with true experimental effect assurance by comparing [O_2 less O_1], [O_2 less O_4], [O_5 less O_6], and [O_5 less O_3]. When these four comparisons agree, researchers' ability to infer that the resulting functional relationship between the dependent and independent variables is being caused by the experimental independent variable treatment dramatically increases.

Quasi-experimental Designs

Between the extremes of pre-experimental designs (which have little or no control) and true experimental designs (based on randomization), there are quasi-experimental designs. These designs are appropriate when researchers can control some variables (price level, media vehicle, package design) but cannot establish equal experimental and control groups based on randomization (store types or customer groups). While there are many different types of quasi-experimental designs available to marketing researchers, we will focus only on the two more widely used ones: (1) nonequivalent control group and (2) separate-sample, pretest-posttest (see Exhibit 9.4).[14]

EXHIBIT 9.4 Summary of Other Quasi-experimental Designs Used in Marketing Research

Nonequivalent dependent variable design	Single group of test subjects and pretest measures on two scales, one that is expected to change due to treatment manipulation and one that is not. This design is restricted to theoretical contexts where differential change is predicted. The design must be powerful enough to determine that the nontreated variable is reliably measured. These results are interpretable only when the two outcome measures are conceptually similar and both would be affected by the same nontreatment effect.
Removed treatment design with pretest and posttest	There could be an ethical problem in the removing of the treatment manipulation in the second scenario. There needs to be a noticeable discontinuity after the removal of the second treatment; otherwise, it could be that the initial treatment had no long-term effects.
Repeated treatment design	This design is most interpretable when the results of the first experiment occur in the same direction as the second experiment and the initial pretest measure differs from any of the following test measures. This design is best when there are unobservable treatments and long periods between a treatment and its reintroduction.
Reversed-treatment, nonequivalent control group design	This design requires both pretest and posttest measures and directional hypotheses. There is potential for high construct validity, but it depends on the research revealing the existence of an inverse relationship.
Cohort designs with cyclical turnover	Cohorts are test subjects who follow each other through a formal institutional environment such as school or work. In this type of design, the researcher pretests a group of test subjects, then gives the treatment manipulation to the next group and collects posttest measures from the second group. The major underlying premise of this type of quasi-experimental design is that the samples are drawn from the same population. This design can eliminate the threats of history and testing by stratifying the treatment groups.
Regression discontinuity design	This causal design is used when the experimental groups are given rewards or those in special need are given extra assistance. The regressed lines for the treatment and nontreatment groups should be different due to the effect of the treatment. Interpretation of the results becomes difficult with the possibility of curvilinear relationships. Knowledge of the reward could lead to extra actions in order to receive it.

Nonequivalent Control Group

Commonly used in marketing research, the "nonequivalent control group" design differs from true experimental designs in that the experimental and control groups are not equivalent. It can be illustrated as follows:

$$\text{Group 1 (EG): } O_1 \rightarrow X \rightarrow O_2$$
$$\text{Group 2 (CG): } O_3 \qquad\qquad O_4$$

This quasi-experimental design operates at two levels. The intact equivalent design allows experimental and control groups to be formed in natural settings. For example, many marketing research quasi-experiments recruit test subjects from established organizations such as church clubs or civic groups. They also use customers from similar stores. Ideally, the groups should be as similar as possible. In this self-selected experimental group design, group membership is based on subjects' interest or desire to participate. Many times, this is accomplished by selecting test subjects from a shopping mall, whereas control subjects are selected on the basis of availability. The difference between O_1 and O_3 becomes an indication of equivalency between the experimental and control groups. If pretest measures are significantly different, group compatibility must be seriously questioned. However, if the measures appear similar, then there is an increased certainty of internal validity. While this design may conform to sound validity practices, it is highly dependent on the circumstances that lead to the selection of test subjects.

Separate-Sample Pretest-Posttest

When it is virtually impossible to determine who is to receive the independent treatment manipulation, but when measures of the dependent variable can be determined, a "separate-sample pretest-posttest" design is an appropriate choice. This design can be illustrated as follows:

$$\text{Sample 1 } O_1 \rightarrow (X)$$
$$\text{Sample 2 } \qquad (X) \rightarrow O_2$$

When the experimental treatment manipulation (X) is insignificant to the research, it simply indicates the experimental group of test subjects cannot be controlled for treatment. Although this is a weak design, it is not an uncommon situation in marketing research practices. This type of quasi-design is most often used when the population is large, a pretest measure will not produce any meaningful information, and there is no way to control for application of the experimental manipulation. This quasi-experimental framework is commonly used in advertising research. For example, let's say the advertising agency for Home Depot, the "do-it-yourself" building supply chain, is launching a major image campaign. First, it draws two samples of test subjects. One sample is interviewed about their perception of Home Depot's image (dependent variable) prior to the image campaign. After the campaign ends, test subjects in the second group are interviewed about their perception of Home Depot.

Obviously, this design must deal with a number of threats to internal validity. History and mortality are the greatest concerns. Repetition of the experiment over several settings can reduce these effects somewhat. Yet this quasi-experimental design is considered superior to true experiments with regard to external validity. This occurs from its natural setting and the use of large samples of test subjects who are representative of the defined target group. Overall, the reason why quasi-experimental designs are practiced in marketing research is they are in a natural setting. Thus, they are a type of field experiment. Field experiments, which we discuss in the next section, provide valuable information to researchers because they allow both functional and causal relationships to be generalized to the target population.

Field Experiments

Field experiments are experimental research designs that manipulate the independent variables in order to measure the dependent variable in the natural setting. Field experiments are typically conducted in retail environments such as malls, supermarkets, or other retail stores. These settings tend to create a high level of realism. However, high levels of realism contribute to a lack of control of the independent variables and increase problems with extraneous variables. Problems with control can occur in several ways. For example, conducting a field experiment of a new product in a supermarket requires the retailer's commitment to authorize the product in the store. Today, retailers are becoming more hesitant about adding new products, given the large number of new-product introductions each year. Even if the product is authorized, proper display and retailer support are needed to appropriately conduct the experiment. Competition can also negatively influence a field experiment. In some field experiments of new products, competitors have negatively affected sales of the experimental product by using heavy price discounts and promotions to increase sales of their own products at the time of the test. When field experiments are used, there are two types of designs: *factorial* and *Latin square* designs.

Factorial Designs

In marketing, researchers are typically interested in investigating the simultaneous effects of two or more independent (treatment) variables on single or multiple dependent (outcome) variables. When the effects of two or more independent variables are investigated in a field experiment situation, researchers should use some type of factorial design. For example, Dell Computer's corporate vice president of marketing is interested in measuring the effects of the company's *sales training procedure* and the *compensation plan* (independent variables) on *sales performance* (dependent variable) for its online sales representatives. There are two different types of sales training procedures (STP): (1) sales manager's on-the-job training and (2) video-based off-the-job self-training. The compensation plan (CP) also has two different types of schemes: (1) straight commission of 9% and (2) salary plus a 4% commission. So in this example there are two independent variables each consisting of two alternatives resulting in what is called a 2 × 2 factorial design. This design has four cells (2 × 2 = 4) in the design matrix. Each cell can be considered a "treatment" group. The overall experimental design matrix would look as follows:

	Compensation Plan (CP)	
Training Procedure (STP)	**(CP_1) Combination Salary + 4%**	**(CP_2) Straight Commission**
(STP_1) On-the-job training	STP_1, CP_1	STP_1, CP_2
(STP_2) Video self-training	STP_2, CP_1	STP_2, CP_2

A factorial design enables researchers to measure the separate effects of each independent variable working alone. The *training procedure* (STP) effect is calculated similarly to that of a completely randomized design but researchers can also estimate the individual effect of the *compensation plans* (CP). The individual effects of each independent variable are referred to as the *main effects.* To illustrate the "main effect" concept, hypothetical numbers for online sales performance are used in the above design matrix. The results suggest that regardless of the compensation plan used, the on-the-job training program (STP_1) yields on average \$60,000 more than the video self-training program (STP_2). The main effect of STP_1 is \$60,000. In turn, the main effect of the combination salary plus 4% commission plan CP_1, regardless of the type of training program, yields on average \$90,000 more than the straight commission of 9% plan (CP_2). The total treatment effect STP_1, CP_2 is \$150,000 (\$60,000 + \$90,000 = \$150,000) and there is no interaction between sales training procedure and compensation plan.

	Compensation Plan (CP)	
Training Procedure (STP)	**(CP_1) Combination Salary + 4%**	**(CP_2) Straight Commission**
(STP_1) On-the-job training	\$280,000	\$190,000
(STP_2) Video self-training	\$220,000	\$130,000

The factorial design allows researchers to determine the magnitude of an *interaction effect* that may exist between the independent variables (STP and CP). This extra total effect combination of the independent variables working together is often greater than the sum of the variables' individual effects. An interaction effect occurs when the relationship between one of the independent variables, say STP, and the dependent variable (online sales representative performance) is different for different levels of the compensation plan (CP) independent variable. In the Dell Computer example, the relationship between online salespeople's performance and the type of sales training program may vary depending upon which compensation plan is used. The following design matrix illustrates the interaction effect between the independent variables.

	Compensation Plan (CP)	
Training Procedure (STP)	**(CP_1) Combination Salary + 4%**	**(CP_2) Straight Commission**
(STP_1) On-the-job training	\$280,000	\$220,000
(STP_2) Video self-training	\$220,000	\$130,000

Here the effect of the training procedure depends on the compensation plan used. The on-the-job training program (STP_1) is \$60,000 better than video self-training (STP_2) when the combination salary plus 4% commission compensation plan (CP_1) is used and \$90,000 when the straight commission of 9% compensation plan is employed. In turn, the combination of salary plus 4% commission (CP_1) is \$60,000 better than the straight commission plan (CP_2) when on-the-job training is used and is \$90,000 better when video self-training (STP_2) is the training program.

Latin Square Designs

The *Latin Square (LS)* design can be used in field experiment situations where researchers want to control the effects of two or more extraneous variables. Latin square designs manipulate one independent variable and control for two additional sources of extraneous variation by restricting randomization with respect to the row and column effects. In order to employ a

Latin square experimental design, several conditions must be met. First, the number of categories (levels) of each extraneous variable to be controlled must be equal to the number of treatments. For example, let's say Dell's management is now interested in three training procedures rather than two and wants to control for the "age of the sales representative" and the "potential dollar sales performances per year." Here STP_1 represents on-the-job training, STP_2 denotes video self-training, and STP_3 represents in-classroom training procedures. Because there are now three treatment groups based on type of training procedure, researchers have to make sure the selected "age" and "$ sales performance" variables also have only three categorical levels. If this condition is not met, then a Latin square design is not appropriate. In this situation, researchers would use a 3 × 3 design shown as follows:

	Sales Potential per Year (in thousands)		
Age of Salespersons	**$500–$999**	**$1,000–$3,999**	**$4,000–$6,999**
20–29	STP_1	STP_2	STP_3
30–45	STP_2	STP_3	STP_1
Over 45	STP_3	STP_1	STP_2

Another necessary condition for conducting a Latin Square design is the assignment of treatment levels in the cells of the square. While the assignment is random, each treatment can occur only once in each blocking situation. This means that because each row and column category defines a blocking situation, each type of training program (STP) must appear only once in each row and each column. In conducting this type of experiment, each test subject is exposed to all three treatments in a preset random order.

Considerations in Using Field Experiments

Besides realism and control, there are other issues to consider when deciding whether or not to use a field experiment, including *time frames, costs,* and *competitive reactions.* Field experiments take longer to complete than laboratory experiments. The planning stage—which can include determining which test market cities to use and which retailers to approach with product experiments, securing advertising time, and coordinating the distribution of the experimental product—adds to the length of time needed to conduct field experiments. Field experiments are more expensive to conduct than laboratory experiments because of the high number of independent variables that must be manipulated. For example, the cost of an advertising campaign alone can increase the cost of the experiment. Other items adding to the cost of field experiments are coupons, product packaging development, trade promotions, and product sampling. Because field experiments are conducted in a natural setting, competitors can learn about the new product almost as soon as it is introduced, and they can respond by using heavy promotional activity or by rushing similar products to market. If secrecy is desired, then laboratory experiments are generally more effective.

Validity Concerns

In deciding whether to use field experiments, researchers should consider the proposed experiment's internal validity and external validity. Although the ideal experiment would be high in both internal and external validity, this is difficult to achieve in a field setting and usually a trade-off must be made. Researchers who want to be able to generalize an experiment's results to other settings likely would select field experiments. If the lack of control over the independent variables associated with field experiments is a concern, then laboratory experiments are more appropriate to assess true functional relationships.[15] Researchers opting for field experiments can choose from several types depending on the objectives of the experiment and the considerations mentioned above. The next section discusses the most common type of field experiment—test marketing—and includes overviews of six different methods for conducting market tests.

Test Marketing

Test marketing Using controlled field experiments to gain information on specified market performance indicators.

Test marketing is the use of controlled field experiments to gain information on specified market performance indicators. Companies have several options available when choosing a test marketing method. Regardless of the method used, test marketing measures the sales potential of a product and evaluates variables in the product's marketing mix.[16] The cost of conducting test marketing experiments can be high. But with the failure rate of new consumer products estimated to be between 80 and 90 percent, many companies believe the expense of conducting test marketing can help them avoid the more expensive mistake of an unsuccessful product rollout. Exhibit 9.5 presents six of the more popular test marketing methods: *traditional, controlled, electronic, simulated, virtual,* and *Web-based TV*.[17]

Traditional Test Markets

The most frequently used form of test marketing is a *traditional test market.* This method tests a product's marketing mix variables through existing distribution channels. Companies select specific cities, or test markets, that have demographic and market characteristics similar to those of the targeted users of the product or service being tested. The most common use of a traditional test is to evaluate consumer acceptance of a new product or a variation of an existing product. For example, Procter & Gamble test marketed Sunny Delight Smoothies, a blend of Sunny Delight fruit beverage and milk, in Mobile, Alabama, and New Orleans, Louisiana.[18] Test marketing also is used to evaluate the potential of new marketing

eXHIBIT 9.5 Different Types of Test Marketing Used in Marketing Research

Types of Test Marketing	Comments
Traditional test markets	Also referred to as "standard" tests; these use experimental design procedures to test a product and/or a product's marketing mix variables through existing distribution channels.
Controlled test markets	Tests that are performed by an outside research firm that guarantees distribution of the test product through prespecified outlets in selected cities.
Electronic test markets	Tests that integrate the use of select panels of consumers who use a special identification card in recording their product-purchasing data.
Simulated test markets	Also referred to as "laboratory tests" or "test market simulations." These are quasi-experiments where test subjects are preselected, then interviewed and observed on their purchases and attitudes toward the test product.
Virtual test markets	Tests that are completely computerized, allowing the test subjects to observe and interact with the product as though they were actually in the test store's environment.
Web-based TV test markets	Similar to electronic test markets, these use broadband interactive TV (iTV) and advances in interactive multimedia communication technologies to conduct the field experiment. Preselected respondents are shown various stimuli and asked questions online through their iTV.

concepts. Spalding, a major sporting goods manufacturer, test marketed a women's theme shop in 58 stores of four national sporting goods retailers.[19]

Advantages and Disadvantages of Traditional Test Markets

The primary advantage of traditional tests is they are conducted in actual distribution channels. Other test marketing methods attempt to simulate distribution channels, while traditional test markets place products in actual distribution outlets, typically retail outlets. In addition to measuring consumer acceptance of a product, standard test markets can determine the level of trade support for the tested item. If retailers are reluctant to give a company additional shelf space or displays for the new product, then plans for the product rollout may need to be reevaluated. Even products that have a high level of consumer appeal will have difficulty succeeding if minimum levels of distribution cannot be attained.

The limitations of traditional test markets are cost, time, and exposure to competition. First, traditional test markets are much more expensive compared to laboratory experiments. Expenses incurred during a traditional test market include product development, packaging, distribution, and advertising and promotion. Second, traditional test markets require more time to conduct than other forms of test marketing. Most standard test markets take between 12 and 18 months to complete. Third, because traditional test marketing uses actual distribution channels, other companies are able to observe a competitor's activity and can take action to hurt a test market. The combination of time and competitive pressures has changed the way in which many companies introduce new products. The need to introduce products more quickly than competitors is leading to large-scale rollouts of new products. The traditional approach of beginning with a test market and then increasing distribution region by region is being replaced by introducing a product in multiple regions simultaneously. In addition, test marketing does not always mean success, as illustrated in the nearby A Closer Look at Research (In the Field) box, which describes the problems experienced by Coors.

Controlled Test Markets

Controlled test market A field experiment that guarantees the distribution of the test product through limited prespecified outlets in selected test cities.

A second type of test market is a controlled test market. A **controlled test market** is performed by an outside firm that guarantees distribution of the test product through outlets in selected cities. AC Nielsen and Audits & Surveys are two firms that offer controlled test marketing services. These companies provide financial incentives to distributors to allow the test product to be added to the product line. The outside firm handles all distribution functions for its client during the test market, including inventory, stocking, pricing, and billing. The research firm collects the necessary sales data. UPC scanner data and consumer surveys are used to compile information on trial and repeat rates, market penetration, and consumer characteristics.

Advantages and Disadvantages of Controlled Test Markets

Controlled test markets overcome many of the disadvantages of traditional test markets. One advantage is that distribution of the test products is assured by the outside firm handling the test market. Second, the cost of a controlled test market is less than that of a traditional test market. Third, monitoring by competitors of a controlled test market is somewhat difficult compared with traditional test markets, given the level of control that can be implemented.

Controlled test markets are not without drawbacks. First, the limited number of markets used makes accurate projections of sales and market penetration difficult. Second, the amount of actual trade support for a test product may be unclear if the research firm provided incentives to retailers to obtain shelf space. Will trade acceptance of the new product be the same

A Closer Look at Research

Good Test Market Results Do Not Guarantee New-Product Success: Coors Gives the Cold Shoulder to Wine Coolers[20]

Adolph Coors Company, manufacturer of Coors beer, has experienced a series of new-product disasters. When the company made a second attempt to enter the wine cooler market it relied on simulated test marketing to determine consumer acceptance for its new offering.

The company's test marketing woes began when it introduced Coors Light. By the time the Coors product reached the market, Miller Lite was firmly entrenched as the number one light beer. The slow rollout did not seem to bother the company. In fact, it was consistent with their philosophy. Pete Coors remarked that his company let other companies do the pioneering work, referring to product development. "Then we'll take what they've done, and do it better," he added. Another product failure, Killian's Irish Red Ale, was introduced using traditional test markets. The product stalled in the test marketing phase before national rollout could happen. Perhaps the worst experience was with Herman Josephs, a new beer positioned as a premium-priced beer that was supposed to compete with Michelob and Löwenbräu. Once again, Coors relied on traditional test marketing, planning to iron out bugs in the product and marketing mix before introducing the product in all markets. Coors abandoned the product after eight years in the test market.

Coors had made a previous attempt to enter the wine cooler market with its Colorado Chiller coolers. The failure of Colorado Chiller was attributed in part to not getting input from consumers about the product. Coors sought to correct this mistake when another cooler product, Crystal Springs Cooler, was tested. The company used simulated test marketing (STM) to find out how consumers would respond to the new product. Results of the STM were encouraging. Approximately 63 percent of cooler drinkers surveyed were interested in purchasing Crystal Springs Cooler, and 74 percent said they would buy the product after sampling it. Sales projections for Crystal Springs exceeded 300,000 barrels per year, which would have been Coors's third-largest product. But the company decided to discontinue its plans for Crystal Springs Cooler. Undoubtedly, previous new-product failures left Coors with little confidence about rolling out a new product like Crystal Springs Cooler despite strong test marketing results.

without incentives? Third, the effect of a proposed advertising program is difficult to evaluate. Despite these limitations, controlled test markets are beneficial for marketers. Many companies use controlled test markets to determine whether a product warrants a full-scale standard test market. Also, controlled test markets are used to test such pricing and promotional variables as coupons and displays. Read about Starbucks' recent test marketing of a new "fresh-pressed" coffee in the nearby A Closer Look at Research (In the Field) box.

Electronic test market A specific type of field experiment that requires the subject to use an electronic identification card and measures test product/service purchase results using universal product code scanner data.

Electronic Test Markets

An **electronic test market** gathers data from consumers who agree to carry an identification card they present when buying goods or services at participating retailers. An outside research firm such as AC Nielsen or Information Resources Inc. conducts the electronic test market experiment. An advantage of this method is that the identification card enables researchers to collect demographic data on consumers who purchase the test product. A primary disadvantage of this method is that the card-carrying consumers probably are not representative of the entire market because they are not chosen at random. Additionally, there is a

A Closer Look at Research

Starbucks Has Upscale Concept Percolating[21]

Starbucks Corp. recently began experimenting with a coffee concept for its stores that would add a new, premium product to help fight the first drop in U.S. customer visits in its 37-year history. In its hometown of Seattle and its Boston market, Starbucks is test marketing 12-ounce cups of "fresh-pressed" coffee at $2.50 each in Seattle and $2.25 in the Boston trial. Currently Starbucks charges $1.55 for a regular brew. What underscores these field experiments is the fact that McDonald's Corp. has been stealing Starbucks' customers with $1.39 coffee and their addition of espresso counters.

The new Starbucks drink, prepared in an $11,000 machine known as the "Clover," brews each cup individually using a vacuum piston system similar to a French press that allows the grind, water temperature, and other parameters to be set for each cup. This new drink may become part of CEO Howard Schultz's plan to increase customer traffic in the 15,000 stores of the world's largest coffee chain. Schultz is hoping the results from the two test markets will indicate no difference in consumption patterns from the two price levels, enabling Starbucks to price it just less than the lattes and cappuccinos that are among Starbucks' most expensive beverages at $2.55 for a 12-ounce cup.

high cost associated with the use of advanced technologies. As a result, small businesses normally cannot afford electronic test marketing.

Simulated Test Markets

Simulated test market A field experiment that uses computer models to estimate consumer responses to a new marketing program.

Another type of test market that uses computer models to estimate consumer response to a new marketing program is a **simulated test market** (STM). STMs project sales volume and evaluate the planned marketing mix. Some common STM services are Assessor, Bases II, ESP, and Litmus. While each of these methods uses its own approach to sampling, questionnaires, and modeling, the overall process includes the following steps:

1. Potential participants are screened to satisfy certain demographic and product usage criteria.
2. Participants are shown commercials or print advertisements for the test product, as well as for other competitive or noncompetitive products.
3. Participants are then allowed to purchase items in a simulated retail store. Regardless of whether the test item is selected, participants receive a free sample.
4. After a usage period, participants are contacted to gather information on the product as well as their repurchase intentions.[22]

Advantages and Disadvantages of Simulated Test Markets

STMs have several advantages. First, STMs offer substantial savings in cost and time. STMs can be conducted in four to six months, compared with a year or more for traditional test markets, and they cost approximately 5 to 10 percent of what a traditional test market costs. Second, a simulation can predict product trial rate, repurchase rate, and purchase cycle length with a great deal of accuracy. Third, computer modeling allows several alternative marketing mix plans to be tested for their effect on sales volume. Finally, exposure to competition is minimized because the test market is not conducted in normal channels of distribution.[23]

The isolation of STMs from the real-world environment leads to some weaknesses with this method. Trade acceptance of a new product cannot be measured using STMs—it must be assumed. A traditional test market would be more desirable if a company believes agreement for distribution with the trade will be difficult to secure. For example, Ore-Ida once conducted an STM for a new product in which it assumed a 90 percent distribution rate in the normal channels. However, the actual distribution rate was only 10 percent, making the sales volume projections from the STM impossible to attain. Second, broad-based consumer reaction to a new product is difficult to measure using STMs. A traditional test market allows a larger number of consumers the opportunity to try a new product. In addition, STMs are more effective in estimating trial rates than repurchase rates. However, a good estimate of repurchase intentions is needed to determine a new product's potential for success. Finally, although STMs cost less than traditional test markets, they are still expensive, costing $75,000 to $150,000. Only the largest of companies can afford to use STMs.[24]

STMs are an effective method for testing new products, especially variations of an existing brand or category of consumer package goods. For example, when Reynolds Metal Company introduced Reynolds Crystal Color plastic wrap, a variation of the traditional Reynolds clear plastic wrap, it used an STM to evaluate the potential of the new product. In the STM, 40 percent of the participants indicated they would definitely try it, which is double the average predicted trial rate for new products.[25]

STMs serve two important purposes. First, they can be used as either a substitute or a supplement to traditional test markets. STMs can be used as a substitute when the risk of product failure or cost is less than that for a traditional test market. They can be used as a supplement to test combinations of marketing mix variables prior to a traditional test market introduction, when making changes would be too costly, if not impossible. Second, STMs can serve as a pilot test to determine whether a particular concept or product has the potential for success. If not, the idea can be dropped before further testing increases the cost of the mistake.

Web-Based TV Test Markets

With consumers' growing acceptance of interactive TV (iTV), and the advances in multimedia communication technologies, larger technology-driven online research companies such as HarrisInteractive, Burke, Inc., Lieberman Research Worldwide, M/A/R/C Research, NFO WorldGroup, and smaller specialty research companies, such as Critical Mix, POPULUS, and DataStar, Inc., are investing heavily in the computer hardware and software to bring test marketing capabilities directly into the living rooms (or computer monitors) of consumers. **Web-based TV test markets** are a test market among consumers through Web-enabled television and Internet technology. This type of test market can literally bring consumers, manufacturers, and sponsors together into a convenient "living room" experience rather than a "desk" experience. Basically, iTV computerizes the consumer's TV set with a "set-top" box that has a hard drive for storing large amounts of data (a 60-second commercial, live or videotaped 30-minute interactive product demonstrations), allowing the consumer to watch at leisure for more in-depth product information.

Web-based TV test market The conducting of a test market among consumers through Web-enabled television technology.

Advantages and Disadvantages of Web-Based TV Test Markets

All the advantages associated with Web research practices are available through iTV. The big differences are the comfort of having the process delivered on a large screen versus the small PC screen, using larger fonts and bigger graphics, and having interactive products, ads, and other test stimuli delivered in a digital format. For now, applications of this alternative have been limited to advertising copy testing and some infomercial of consumer-oriented products.

Several factors are slowing the acceptance and use of iTV test markets. The most pressing are slow demand for iTV technology in the home, costs of the required hardware and software, and uncertainty among cable operators in supplying iTV services. Because iTV is still relatively in its infancy, many consumers lack full knowledge of the technologies. Without knowledge, acceptance of iTV will remain low. For example, Microsoft's MSN TV service subscriber base is only about 2 million after more than six years in the market.[26] AOL Time Warner Inc. has its version of iTV called AOLTV, which was tested more than eight years ago among 4,000 selected households in Orlando, Florida––but it has been slowed in introducing it because of low consumer demand. Although iTV service is comparatively inexpensive, its acceptance may be slow because iTV technology is still an expensive investment to many consumer segments.

Finally, this new technology is a difficult sell to many companies unfamiliar with Web-based TV test marketing. Complicating this situation is the fact that many cable providers have been slow to offer iTV services beyond just an interactive program guide. For example, AT&T Broadband dropped plans to introduce an advanced set-top box for its 18 million U.S. cable subscribers. Some experts feel the problem is that the iTV industry is based on the premise that the primary method of iTV distribution is the set-top boxes provided by cable operators. Nevertheless, this form of test marketing is definitely expected to grow with the government mandate that TV delivery systems all be digital by February 2009. Some experts believe it will overtake electronic test marketing.

Virtual Test Markets

Virtual test market A high-tech-driven field experiment that allows the subjects to manipulate different aspects of the test environment on a computer screen.

In **virtual test markets,** not only are different marketing mixes evaluated using computer modeling, but also the simulated store itself, as it appears on a computer screen. Using this method, participants view store shelves stocked with many different kinds of products. The shoppers can pick up an item by touching its image on the monitor, and examine the product by moving a tracking ball device (or click computer keys) that rotates the image. Products can be purchased by placing them in the participant's shopping cart, which appears on the screen. Information collected during this process includes the amount of time the participant spends shopping in each product category, the time the individual spends examining each side of a package, the quantity of product purchased, and the order of items purchased.[27]

Advantages and Disadvantages of Virtual Test Markets

Although virtual test markets are similar to simulated test markets, they do have some unique advantages. First, the "stores" that appear in virtual test markets more closely resemble actual stores than the ones created in simulated test markets. Second, researchers can make changes in the stores rather quickly. Different arrays of brands, pricing, packaging, promotions, and shelf space allocations can appear in a matter of minutes. Third, virtual test markets can be used for different purposes. They can be used to test entirely new concepts or products as well as to test for changes in existing products. Finally, as with simulated test markets, virtual test markets allow for these tests to be conducted without exposure to the competition.

The disadvantages of virtual test markets are similar to those of simulated test markets. The primary concern for many companies is whether consumers will shop in virtual stores using the same patterns they use in actual stores. However, research into this concern suggests there is a high degree of correlation between virtual store and actual store sales. For example, a study in which 300 consumers took six trips through a virtual store and an actual store to purchase cleaning and health-and-beauty-aid products revealed similar market

A Closer Look at Research

Goodyear Steps Out of Its Own Stores[28]

Goodyear Tire and Rubber Company used virtual test marketing to evaluate a major change in distribution strategy. For many years, the company sold its tires through its own retail outlets. The new strategy was to sell Goodyear tires through general merchandise stores and still maintain the current system of Goodyear stores. While such a move would no doubt allow Goodyear to reach more consumers, the new strategy would place Goodyear tires in direct competition with other brands in the general merchandise stores. Goodyear questioned whether this increased competition would dictate a change in marketing strategy. Specifically, the company needed to determine what the level of brand equity was for its products. Was it strong enough to be able to charge a premium over other brands, or would it be forced to reduce prices and/or extend warranties to be competitive?

Goodyear turned to virtual test marketing to find answers to its questions. The company conducted a study of 1,000 consumers who had recently bought or planned to purchase passenger tires, high-performance tires, or light-truck tires. Participants shopped several different virtual tire stores, each store offering a different assortment of products, pricing, and warranties. Goodyear believed it achieved brand equity if a consumer purchased a Goodyear product at a higher price than competitors' products, if it captured sales from competitors when Goodyear products were reduced in price, and if it maintained sales levels despite competitors' price cuts.

The results of the study assisted Goodyear in several ways. First, the company determined how shoppers in different product-market segments valued the Goodyear brand compared with competing brands. Second, the virtual market test allowed the company to test many different pricing strategies. This feature allowed Goodyear to evaluate how different prices, both its own and competitors' prices, affected consumer tendencies to switch brands. Third, major competitors were identified. Goodyear is now aware of the companies it should consider its major competitors in general merchandise stores.

shares. Correlations were .94 for the cleaning product and .90 for the health-and-beauty-aid product. Another concern is the cost of the computer hardware and software needed to conduct virtual test markets. While the cost is still high for many companies, improvements in technology should lower it in the future. Finally, in a virtual store, consumers cannot feel, smell, or touch a product. Items that involve special handling from consumers might not be suited for virtual test marketing. Virtual test markets can be used to study questions such as:

1. What is our brand equity in a new retail channel?
2. Do we offer a sufficient variety of products?
3. How should products be displayed?[29]

The nearby A Closer Look at Research (In the Field) box describes how one company used virtual test markets.

Other Issues in Test Marketing

Consumer versus Industrial Test Marketing

Our discussion of test marketing has centered on the evaluation of consumer products. However, manufacturers of industrial products also use test marketing practices, though with different methods. Rather than develop a product for trial in the market, industrial manufacturers seek input from customers to determine the features and technologies needed for new products. Manufacturers develop prototypes based on customers' input, then evaluate and test them using selected customers. The manufacturers receive feedback from customers involved in the product test and use the feedback to make further changes to the product before introducing it to the entire market. As with consumer test markets, industrial test markets can be lengthy. The longer a test market runs, the more likely it is a competitor will learn of the new product and respond by rushing a similar product to market or by becoming more competitive with existing products.

Matching Experimental Method with Objectives

When selecting a test marketing method, researchers should consider the research questions and objectives of the experiment. For example, if a company is test marketing an extension of its present product line, maybe a new color or flavor, it would be interested in the consumer acceptance of this new product. Therefore, it will want experimental results that can be generalized to all markets, not just the test markets. Also, it would want to observe how the new product performs in the market relative to the competition or how the distribution partners accept the new product. The decision for the company would be whether to use a standard test market or use a simulated or virtual test market. This decision is based on factors such as time, cost, and exposure to competition. Regardless of the method, the objective is to project the potential of the new product for the entire market.

Other field experiments may require more control over real-world variables. Consider a company that wants to evaluate the effectiveness of an advertising campaign for a new product. While the ability to generalize the results of the experiment to the entire market is important, the company must try to determine whether a relationship is present between the advertising campaign and customers' acceptance of the new product. In other words, did the promotional campaign influence sales, or did the influence come from other variables, such as pricing or competition? This objective requires that the experiment have high internal validity. An experimental design for this objective might be an electronic test market that can record information about the consumers' television viewing (did they view the advertisement?), and purchase and repurchase behaviors (did they buy the advertised product and, if so, how many times?), and determine whether a relationship exists between the advertising campaign and product sales. Such an experiment might not be generalizable to the complete target market, but the company can determine whether the advertising campaign has the intended effect on a small sample of consumers. If the results are positive, the company might roll out the advertising campaign to other areas or even nationwide. If the results are not positive, the company can make changes in the advertising campaign or drop it completely.

Each test marketing approach possesses certain strengths and weaknesses. Researchers must weigh these strengths and weaknesses with the objectives of the field experiment. Once researchers identify the objective of the experiment, they can select the method that offers the greatest amount of the desired validity, internal or external. Some of the difficulties associated with standard test markets are leading to new trends in new-product testing. First, companies that do not want to absorb the time and expense of standard test markets could turn to simulated and virtual test markets. Also, the growing resistance of retailers to adding thousands of new products may lead more companies to use some of the other test marketing methods discussed rather than standard test markets. Companies that find the standard test market process difficult but are not willing to try other methods may begin rolling out more products without any test marketing, especially if the risk of product failure is low. Read the nearby Marketing Research in Action box to see how the Lee Apparel Company used test marketing procedures to build a unique customer database to successfully launch a new brand of women's jeans.

MARKETING RESEARCH IN ACTION

Riders Fits New Database into Brand Launch

The Initial Launch

The Lee Apparel Company used market test data from a field experiment to build a customer database and help successfully launch a new brand of jeans. When Lee Apparel Company began marketing a new line of jeans under the name *Riders,* the brand's management team decided to build a customer database. Unlike the typical approach of building a customer database around promotions, merchandising, and advertising efforts that directly benefit retailers, their goal was to use marketing dollars to build both the brand and the database. The initial launch of the Riders apparel line went well with rollouts in the company's Midwest and Northeast regional markets. The initial positioning strategy called for the products to be priced slightly higher than competitive brands and marketed at mass-channel retailers like Ames, Bradlee's, Caldor, Target, and Venture. During the first year, the communication program emphasized the line's "comfortable fit," and within two years the rollouts went national, using major retail channels like Wal-Mart.

Initially, Riders used a spring promotion called "Easy Money" to generate product trial and to gather name, address, and demographic information about the line's first customers. This data was collected using a rebate card and certificate from the retailer. Upon completing and mailing the rebate card to Riders, the customer was rewarded with a check in the mail. This initial market test provided valuable data on each customer, such as the exact type of product purchased, how much was spent, whom they bought for, where they heard of the Riders brand, and their lifestyle interests. As part of the test market, Riders supported the effort with point-of-purchase (POP) displays and promotions in Sunday newspaper circulars. In addition, the management team funded the promotion and handled all development, redemption, and fulfillment in-house. Results of the first test market were as follows: a total of $1.5 million in certificates were distributed yielding a 2.1 percent response, or just over 31,000 customer names. About 20 percent of the buyers bought more than one item.

Another part of the test market design was the follow-up phone survey among new customers three months after the initial promotion. Of the customers surveyed, 62 percent had purchased Riders products. The survey provided detailed information to salespeople and consumers. Riders then repeated the test market design adding a postcard mailing to existing database names. The promotional effort netted over 40,000 new customer names and information for the database. It also proved the responsiveness of database customers—3.8 percent of the database customers who received the postcard promotion came into the store to make a purchase, compared to a 2.8 percent response to the POP and circular ads.

To build a successful customer database from test market designs, the critical first step is figuring out the most efficient way to gather the names. Next you must decide how you want to use the information with customers, prospects, and retailers. Finally, you begin the process of testing and evaluating the relationships, and applying what you have learned to build customer loyalty.

Focus on Retail Partnerships

The main goal of the test marketing was to create valuable information that could be used to build relationships with Riders consumers and those retail accounts Riders depended on for distribution. The growing philosophy within the Riders brand management team was

"The more we know about our customers, the better the decisions we'll be able to make in dealing both with them and with our retailers." Moreover, the detailed information such as hard dollar results of each promotion as well as the demographic profiles is shared with retailers, as is the research showing the consumer behavior benefits. For example, a tracking study found that purchase intent of database customers was twice that of nondatabase customers in a given trade area. Unaided brand awareness likewise was high (100 percent, compared to 16 percent of the general population), and awareness of Riders advertising was 53 percent compared to 27 percent.

The Riders team believed so strongly in tying database information with promotion efforts that they insisted that a database component be part of any chain-specific promotions. Management hoped to convince the retailers to build their own database capabilities to share their information. For example, retail account information can identify more product and promotion opportunities. Riders believed the real payoff comes when both manufacturer and retailer use data, from either source, to do a better job of attracting and keeping the key assets for both channel members—the customer. Riders must continue convincing retailers that putting Riders merchandise on their shelves is bringing people into their stores. From test marketing to creating complete customer databases, the Riders team has begun to put a major part of its marketing investment into image-building advertising strategies focused on print and television media.

For instance, they say, "The more we know about our customers and their preferences, the better we'll be able to hone our advertising messages and media buys, pinpoint what kind of promotions work best, and understand what new products we ought to be developing. As competitive pressures continue to mount, Riders expects detailed customer information to become more valuable in helping define the brand position clearly. Defining who we are and what's different about Riders products is going to be an increasingly important element in drawing customers who have a great many choices to stores where Riders products are on the shelves. Although it initially began with test markets guiding the development of a complete customer database program, it's now the databases that are guiding the inclusion of key elements in our test market research. Riders' ultimate goal is creating a tool that is going to make its products more attractive to retailers and to consumers."[30]

Hands-On Exercise

Using your knowledge from reading about market tests in the chapter and the above marketing research illustration about Riders, answer each of the following questions:

1. What was Lee Apparel Company's overall goal for conducting such an extensive test market of its new line of jeans under the brand name "Riders"? In your opinion did the company achieve its goal? Why or why not?
2. Identify and explain the strengths and weaknesses associated with the test market process used by the Lee Apparel Company.
3. In your opinion, should the company give consideration to the development and implementation of Web-based test marketing strategies? Why or why not?

Summary of Learning Objectives

■ **Explain experiments and the types of variables used in causal research designs.**

Experiments enable marketing researchers to control the research situation so that causal relationships among the variables can be examined. In a typical experiment the independent variable is manipulated (changed) and its effect on another variable (dependent variable) is measured and evaluated. During the experiment the researcher attempts to eliminate or control all other variables that might impact the relationship being measured. After the manipulation, the researcher measures the dependent variable to see if it has changed. If it has, the researcher concludes that the change in the dependent variable is caused by the manipulation of the independent variable.

To conduct causal research, the researcher must understand the four types of variables in experimental designs (independent, dependent, extraneous, control) as well as randomization of test subjects and the role that theory plays in creating experiments. The most important goal of any experiment is to determine which relationships exist among different variables (independent, dependent). Functional (cause–effect) relationships require measurement of systematic change in one variable as another variable changes.

■ **Describe the theoretical importance and impact of validity measures in causal research designs.**

Experimental designs are developed to control for any contamination that may distort the true relationship being studied. Internal, external and construct validity are the main tests of contamination to evaluate. Internal validity refers to the accuracy of conclusions the researcher draws about a demonstrated functional relationship. The question is "Are the experimental results truly due to the experimental variables?" External validity is concerned with the interaction of experimental variables with extraneous factors causing a researcher to question the generalizability of the results to other settings. Construct validity is important in the process of correctly identifying and understanding both the independent and the dependent variables in an experimental design. Several techniques unique to experimental designs are used to control for problems of internal and external validity. These techniques center on the use of control groups, pre-experimental measures, exclusion of subjects, matching subjects into groups, and randomization of group members. These dimensions, built into the experimental design, provide true power for controlling contamination.

■ **Discuss the major types of experimental designs and explain the pros and cons of each.**

Pre-experimental designs do not meet internal validity criteria due to a lack of group comparisons. Despite this weakness, three designs are used quite frequently in marketing research: the one-shot study, the one-group pretest-posttest design, and the static group comparison. True experimental designs ensure equivalence between experimental and control groups by random assignment of subjects into groups. Three forms of true experimental designs exist: pretest-posttest, control group; posttest-only, control group; and the Solomon Four Group. Quasi-experimental designs are appropriate when the researcher can control some of the variables but cannot establish true randomization of groups. While a multitude of these designs exist, two of the most common forms are the nonequivalent control group and the separate-sample pretest-posttest.

■ **Define test marketing and explain its usefulness in marketing research.**

Test markets are a specific type of field experiment commonly conducted in natural field settings. Most common in the marketing research field are traditional test markets, controlled test markets, electronic test markets, simulated test markets, Web-based TV test markets, and virtual test markets. Data gathered from test markets provide both researchers and practitioners with invaluable information concerning customers' attitudes, preferences, purchasing habits/patterns, and demographic profiles. This information can be useful in predicting new product/service acceptance levels and advertising and image effectiveness, as well as in evaluating current marketing mix strategies.

■ **Compare the pros and cons of laboratory and field experiments.**

Laboratory experiments are studies conducted in an artificial, controlled setting in which the effect of all, or nearly all, influential independent variables is kept to a minimum. Questions focus on understanding the causal relationships between variables and need to be framed on the specific impacts (or influences) one variable has on another variable. Since researchers can manipulate and control the independent variables, laboratory experiments typically yield results that have strong internal validity and reliability but limited external validity.

Field experiments are studies conducted in natural settings. The context focus of the study involves one or more independent variables that are manipulated under conditions controlled as carefully as the situation permits. Field experiments are typically conducted in retail environments such as malls, supermarkets, or other retail stores that create a high level of realism. But high levels of realism contribute to the lack of control of the independent variables and increase problems with extraneous variables. Field experiments have high external validity but lower internal validity and reliability.

Key Terms and Concepts

Complete randomization 278
Construct validity 283
Control variables 278
Controlled test market 297
Convergent validity 284
Deductive research 280
Demand characteristic 284
Dependent variables 277
Diffusion of treatment 285
Discriminant validity 284
Electronic test market 298
Evaluation apprehension 285
Experiment 274
Experimental design reliability 285
Experimental research 279
External validity 282
Extraneous variables 278
Field experiments 280
Functional relationship 276
Inadequate operationalization 284
Independent variables 277
Inductive research 280
Internal validity 281
Laboratory experiments 280
Mono-method bias 284
Mono-operation bias 284
Simulated test market 299
Test marketing 296
Theory 279
Validity 280
Variable 275
Virtual test market 301
Web-based TV test market 300

Review Questions

1. List the four types of experimental design variables and provide an explanation of each.
2. Identify the significant variables a consumer would consider when purchasing a computer.
3. Using college students as subjects for experimental studies is a common occurrence in marketing research. What possible problems could arise from this practice?
4. Identify the tests used for (a) pre-experimental testing and (b) true experimental testing. What advantages and disadvantages are associated with each?
5. Explain the difference between internal validity and external validity. Discuss the problems associated with of each type of validity.
6. When field experiments are used, what factors are detrimental to the observational techniques that could be used as a control aspect?
7. Identify the major differences between laboratory experiments and field experiments.
8. What are the advantages and disadvantages of traditional test market experiments compared to controlled test market designs?

9. What are the potential benefits of using Web-based TV test markets?
10. Under what conditions would a "posttest-only, control group experimental" design be better to use than a "pretest-posttest control group, completely randomized" design?

Discussion Questions

1. Which of the six types of test marketing are gaining acceptance with America's top advertisers? Why is this taking place?
2. Why do you feel that Adolph Coors Company has encountered so many problems in the past two decades concerning new-product introductions? What would you recommend that Coors do to solve these problems?
3. **EXPERIENCE THE INTERNET.** Go to the home page for the AC Nielsen research company (www.acnielsen.com). Examine the tools, procedures, and techniques the company uses for conducting test markets. Provide a brief explanation of the goals and objectives the company provides for its clients regarding test marketing.
4. The store manager of a local independent grocery association (I.G.A.) store thought that customers might stay in the store longer if slow, easy-to-listen-to music were played over the store's intercom system. After some thought, the manager considered whether he should hire a marketing researcher to design an experiment to test the influence of music tempo on shoppers' behaviors. Answer the following questions:
   - How would you operationalize the independent variable?
   - What dependent variables do you think might be important in this experiment?
   - Develop a hypothesis for each of your dependent variables.
5. Recall our continuing case about the Santa Fe Grill Mexican restaurant from other chapters. The owners are interested in increasing weekly sales of their Mexican chicken wings. Currently customers have three options for ordering these wings (10 wings for $5.99, 20 for $8.99, or 50 for $14.99). Management would like to know what impact various promotional incentives would have on the weekly sales of their Mexican wings. The two experimental treatment incentives are a 25%-off coupon to customers versus a coupon that sells wings for 25 cents each (with a 15-wing minimum order). On the advice of a marketing research expert, a control group would need to be included in the experiment, and thus there would be three treatment groups involved: (1) 25%-off coupon, (2) 25-cents per wing (minimum 15-wing order), and (3) no coupon. Design an experiment that would determine the impact of the proposed promotional incentives on weekly sales of Mexican chicken wings at the Santa Fe Grill restaurant. Make sure you address each of the following items:
   a. Identify and diagram your experiment.
   b. Indicate how you would conduct the experiment.
   c. Assess the internal and external validity of your experiment.
   d. What, if any, extraneous factors will you have to deal with?

part 3

Designing and Conducting Surveys

chapter 10

Sampling: Theories, Designs, and Plans

Learning Objectives

After reading this chapter, you will be able to

1. Distinguish between probability and nonprobability sampling.
2. Explain the advantages and disadvantages of probability sampling.
3. Compare the advantages and disadvantages of nonprobability sampling.
4. Describe the factors that influence the appropriate sample design.
5. Understand the steps in developing a sampling plan.

> **"A survey method is a valuable assessment tool in which a sample is selected and information from the sample can then be generalized to a larger population. Sampling is like taste-testing soup—a few spoonfuls tell what the whole pot tastes like."[1]**
>
> **—PAM HUNTER,**
> **Director of Survey Research,**
> **Pew Research Center**

Technology and Sampling Procedures—Can the Two Ever Co-exist?

Some pollsters say the Internet allows them to collect public attitudes more quickly and cheaply than the telephone. But others say surveys done strictly online don't measure up. They say Internet polling fails to survey people who don't have computers—people who tend to have lower income and less education, people more likely to be minorities. And they say it ignores some basic principles of survey research, especially the concept of random sampling. They raise the specter of 1936, when a famous survey miscalled the presidential election because it relied on lists of people who owned telephones and cars—at a time when those were luxuries.

As for Internet polling, Mike Traugott, president of the American Association for Public Opinion Research, has said, "Clearly, the Internet is the wave of the future. The turmoil running through the industry is similar to the anxiety faced by pollsters when they began to make the switch from face-to-face to telephone questioning." Traugott also said the number of American adults who go online, roughly half, is not high enough yet to provide a cross-section of the population. And no one has figured out how to draw a random sample of computer users the way traditional pollsters draw a probability sample of the population. Pollsters are working hard to figure out how to harness the speed, power, and efficiency of the Internet. Two different approaches are being debated.

InterSurvey of Menlo Park, California, is blending the methods of traditional research, starting by drawing a panel of respondents using a telephone poll. Anyone in the panel who doesn't have Internet access is given interactive television, at InterSurvey's expense, to file responses. When InterSurvey wants to conduct a poll, it contacts the respondents by lighting the boxes on top of their televisions, a technique less disruptive than a dinnertime phone call. "You don't have to abandon scientific sampling to poll on the Internet," said Doug Rivers, chief executive of the company. Traditional pollsters and major media outlets have used InterSurvey to get quick reaction on events such as the State of the Union address.

Another wave in Internet research is the collection of panels of potential respondents like those put together by Harris Interactive of Rochester, New York, Greenfield Online Inc., and other firms. Harris Interactive has built up a panel of 6.2 million people, most of whom volunteer through Web sites. As one supporter noted, "If they used unweighted data, their results would not be nearly so good. But by weighting data by demographics and the 'propensity' of people to be on the Internet, they stand by their surveys." Harris Interactive says its political polls have been largely successful, but traditional pollsters say they're worried about offers of inexpensive research they feel isn't scientific. Is it enough to survey 100 people or are you going to get useful results only if you survey 1,000 people? The answer depends on the questions you are asking, the likely results, and your preferred "margin of error" (the +/− 3% or +/− 4% reported with most survey results). This information enables you to determine whether that 4 percent difference between the two bars on your graph is meaningful.[2]

The Value of Sampling Methods in Marketing Research

As illustrated in the opening example, developing an accurate sampling method is important when a study uses interviewing or surveys for data collection. There are two basic sampling designs: probability and nonprobability. Exhibit 10.1 lists the different types of both sampling methods.

Probability sampling A technique of drawing a sample in which each sampling unit has a known probability of being included in the sample.

In **probability sampling,** each sampling unit in the defined target population has a known probability of being selected for the sample. The actual probability of selection for each sampling unit may or may not be equal depending on the type of probability sampling design used. Specific rules for selecting members from the population for inclusion in the sample are determined at the beginning of a study to ensure (1) unbiased selection of the sampling units and (2) proper sample representation of the defined target population. Probability sampling enables the researcher to judge the reliability and validity of data collected by calculating the probability that the sample findings are different from the defined target population. The observed difference can be partially attributed to the existence of sampling error. The results obtained by using probability sampling designs can be generalized to the target population within a specified margin of error.

Nonprobability sampling A sampling process where the probability of selecting each sampling unit is unknown.

In **nonprobability sampling,** the probability of selecting each sampling unit is not known. Therefore, sampling error is not known either. Selection of sampling units is based on some type of intuitive judgment or knowledge of the researcher. The degree to which the sample may or may not be representative of the defined target population depends on the sampling approach and how well the researcher executes and controls the selection activities. Although there is always a temptation to generalize findings of nonprobability samples to the target population, for the most part the results are limited to just the people who provided the survey data. Exhibit 10.2 provides a comparison of probability and nonprobability sampling methods.

EXHIBIT 10.1 Types of Probability and Nonprobability Sampling Methods

Probability Sampling Methods	Nonprobability Sampling Methods
Simple Random Sampling	Convenience Sampling
Systematic Random Sampling	Judgment Sampling
Stratified Random Sampling	Quota Sampling
Cluster Sampling	Snowball Sampling

EXHIBIT 10.2 Summary of Comparative Differences between Probability and Nonprobability Sampling Methods

Comparison Factors	Probability Sampling	Nonprobability Sampling
List of the Population Elements	Complete List Necessary	None Necessary
Information about the Sampling Units	Each Unit Identified	Need Detail on Habits, Activities, Traits, etc.
Sampling Skill Required	Skill Required	Little Skill Required
Time Requirement	Time-Consuming	Low Time Consumption
Cost per Unit Sampled	Moderate to High	Low
Estimates of Population Parameters	Unbiased	Biased
Sample Representativeness	Good, Assured	Suspect, Undeterminable
Accuracy and Reliability	Computed with Confidence Intervals	Unknown
Measurement of Sampling Error	Statistical Measures	No True Measure Available

Types of Probability Sampling Designs

Simple Random Sampling

Simple random sampling A probability sampling procedure that ensures every sampling unit in the target population has a known and equal chance of being selected.

Simple random sampling (SRS) is a probability sampling procedure. With this approach, every sampling unit has a known and equal chance of being selected. For example, let's say an instructor decided to draw a sample of 10 students ($n = 10$) from among all the students in a marketing research class that consisted of 30 students ($N = 30$). The instructor could write each student's name on a separate, identical piece of paper and place all of the names in a jar. Each student would have an equal, known probability of selection for a sample of a given size that could be expressed by the following formula:

$$\text{Probability of selection} = \frac{\text{Size of sample}}{\text{Size of population}}$$

Here, each student in the marketing research class would have a 10/30 (or .333) chance of being randomly selected in the sample.

When the defined target population consists of a larger number of sampling units, a more sophisticated method is used to randomly draw the sample. One of the procedures commonly used in marketing research is to have a computer-generated table of random numbers to select the sampling units. A table of random numbers is just what its name implies: a table that lists randomly generated numbers (see Exhibit 10.3). Many of today's computer programs can generate a table of random numbers.

Using the marketing research students again as the target population, a random sample could be generated (1) by using the last two digits of the students' social security numbers or (2) by assigning each student a unique two-digit code ranging from 01 to 30. With the first procedure, we would have to make sure that no two students have the same last two digits in their social security number; the range of acceptable numbers would be from 00 to 99. Then we could go to the table of random numbers and select a starting point, which

eXHIBIT 10.3 A Partial Table of Random Numbers

31 25	81 44	54 34	67 03
14 96	99 80	14 54	30 74
49 05	49 56	35 51	68 36
99 67	57 65	14 46	92 88
54 14	95 34	93 18	78 27
57 50	34 89	99 14	57 37
98 67	78 25	06 90	39 90
40 99	00 87	90 42	88 18
20 82	09 18	84 91	64 80
78 84	39 91	16 08	14 89

Source: M. G. Kendall and B. Babington Smith, "Table of Random Sampling Numbers," *Tracts for Computers* 24 (Cambridge, England; Cambridge University Press, 1946), p. 33.

can be anywhere on the table. Using Exhibit 10.3, let's say we select the upper-left-hand corner of the table (31) as our starting point. We would then begin to read down the first column (or across the first row) and select those two-digit numbers that matched the numbers within the acceptable range until 10 students had been selected. Reading down the first column, we would start with 31, then go to 14, 49, 99, 54, and so on.

If we had elected to assign a unique descriptor (01 to 30) to each student in class, we would follow the same selection procedure from the random number table, but use only those random numbers that matched the numbers within the acceptable range of 01 to 30. Numbers that fell outside the acceptable range would be disregarded. Thus, we would select students with numbers 14, 20, 25, 05, 09, 18, 06, 16, 08, and 30. If the overall research objectives call for telephone interviews, drawing the necessary sample can be achieved using a random-digit-dialing (RDD) technique.

Advantages and Disadvantages

Simple random sampling has several noteworthy advantages. The technique is easily understood and the survey's results can be generalized to the defined target population within a prespecified margin of error. Another advantage is that simple random samples allow the researcher to obtain unbiased estimates of the population's characteristics. This method guarantees that every sampling unit has a known and equal chance of being selected, no matter the actual size of the sample, resulting in a valid representation of the defined target population. The primary disadvantage of simple random sampling is the difficulty of obtaining a complete and accurate listing of the target population elements. Simple random sampling requires that all sampling units be identified. For this reason, simple random sampling often works best for small populations or those where computer-derived lists are available.

Systematic random sampling A probability sampling technique that requires the defined target population to be ordered in some way.

Systematic Random Sampling

Systematic random sampling (SYMRS) is similar to simple random sampling but requires that the defined target population be ordered in some way, usually in the form of a customer list, taxpayer roll, or membership roster. In research practices, SYMRS has become a popular alternative probability method of drawing samples. Compared to simple random sampling, systematic random sampling is less costly because it can be done relatively quickly. When executed properly, SYMRS can create a sample of objects or prospective respondents that is very similar in quality to a sample drawn using SRS.

To employ systematic random sampling, the researcher must be able to secure a complete listing of the potential sampling units that make up the defined target population. But unlike SRS, there is no need to give the sampling units any special code prior to drawing the sample. Instead, sampling units are selected according to their position using a skip interval. The skip interval is determined by dividing the number of potential sampling units in the defined target population by the number of units desired in the sample. The required skip interval is calculated using the following formula:

$$\text{Skip interval} = \frac{\text{Defined target population list size}}{\text{Desired sample size}}$$

For instance, if the researcher wants a sample of 100 to be drawn from a defined target population of 1,000, the skip interval would be 10 (1,000/100). Once the skip interval is determined, the researcher would then randomly select a starting point and take every 10th unit until he or she had proceeded through the entire target population list. Exhibit 10.4 lists the steps a researcher follows in drawing a systematic random sample.

eXHIBIT 10.4 Steps in Drawing a Systematic Random Sample

Step 1 → **Obtain a List of Potential Sampling Units That Contains an Acceptable Frame of the Target Population Elements.**
Example: Current list of students (names, addresses, telephone numbers) enrolled at your university or college from the registrar's office.

Step 2 → **Determine the Total Number of Sampling Units Making Up the List of the Defined Target Population's Elements and the Desired Sample Size.**
Example: 30,000 current student names on the list. Desired sample size is 1,200 students, for a confidence level of 95%, *P* value equal to 50%, and tolerance sampling error of ± 2.83 percentage points.

Step 3 → **Compute the Needed Skip Interval by Dividing the Number of Potential Sampling Units on the List by the Desired Sample Size.**
Example: 30,000 current student names on the list, desired sample of 1,200, so the skip interval would be every 25th name.

Step 4 → **Using a Random Number-Generation System, Randomly Determine a Starting Point to Sample the List of Names.**
Example: Select: Random number for starting page of the multiple-page listing (e.g., 8th page).
Select: Random number for name position on that starting page (e.g., Carol V. Clark).

Step 5 → **With Carol V. Clark as the First Sample Unit, Apply the Skip Interval to Determine the Remaining Names That Should Be Included in the Sample of 1,200.**
Example: Clark, Carol V. (Skip 25 names.)
Cobert, James W. (Skip 25 names.)
Damon, Victoria J. (Skip 25 names; repeat process until all 1,200 names are drawn.)

Note: The researcher must visualize the population list as being continuous or "circular"; that is, the drawing process must continue past those names that represent the Z's and include names representing the A's and B's so that the 1,200th name drawn will basically be the 25th name prior to the first drawn name (i.e., Carol V. Clark).

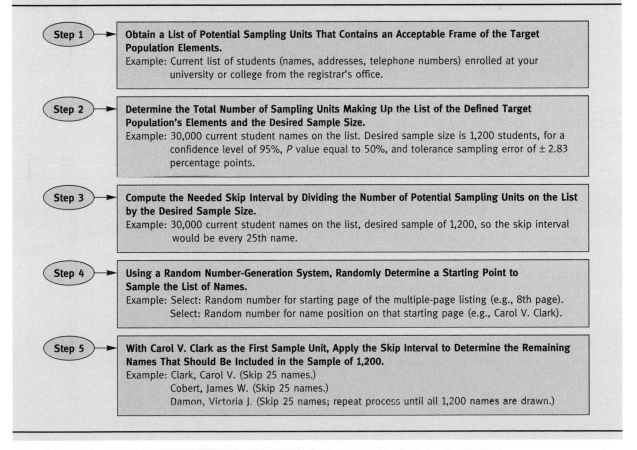

There are two important considerations when using systematic random sampling. First, the natural order of the defined target population list must be unrelated to the characteristic being studied. Second, the skip interval must not correspond to a systematic change in the target population. For example, if a skip interval of 7 were used in sampling daily sales or invoices from a retail store like Bloomingdale's, and Tuesday was randomly selected as the starting point, we would end up with data from the same day every week. We would not want to draw conclusions regarding overall sales performance based only on what happens every Tuesday.

Advantages and Disadvantages

Systematic sampling is frequently used because it is a relatively easy way to draw a sample while ensuring randomness. The availability of lists and the shorter time required to draw a sample versus simple random sampling makes systematic sampling an attractive, economical method for researchers. The greatest weakness of systematic random sampling is the potential for there to be hidden patterns in the data that are not found by the researcher. This could result in a sample that is not truly representative of the defined target population. Nonetheless, the potential small loss in overall representativeness of the target population is usually offset by larger savings in time, effort, and cost. Another difficulty is the researcher must know exactly how many sampling units make up the defined target population. When the size of the target population is extremely large or unknown, identifying the true number of units is difficult, and estimates may not be accurate.

Stratified Random Sampling

Stratified random sampling A probability sampling method in which the defined target population is divided into groups, called strata, and samples are selected from each stratum.

Stratified random sampling (STRS) involves the separation of the target population into different groups, called strata, and the selection of samples from each stratum. Stratified random sampling is useful when the divisions of the target population are skewed or when extremes are present in the probability distribution of the target population. The goal in stratifying is to minimize the variability within each stratum and maximize the differences between strata. STRS is similar to segmentation of the defined target population into smaller, more homogeneous sets of elements. Depending on the problem situation, there are cases in which the defined target population does not portray a normal symmetric distribution of its elements.

To ensure that the sample maintains the required precision, representative samples must be drawn from each of the smaller population groups (strata). Drawing a stratified random sample involves three basic steps:

1. Dividing the target population into homogeneous subgroups or strata.
2. Drawing random samples from each stratum.
3. Combining the samples from each stratum into a single sample of the target population.

As an example, if researchers are interested in the market potential for home security systems in a specific geographic area, they may wish to divide the homeowners into several different strata. The subdivisions could be based on such factors as assessed value of the homes, household income, population density, or location (e.g., sections designated as high- and low-crime areas).

Proportionate stratified sampling A stratified sampling method in which each stratum is dependent on its size relative to the population.

Disproportionate stratified sampling A stratified sampling method in which the size of each stratum is independent of its relative size in the population.

Two methods are commonly used to derive samples from the strata: proportionate and disproportionate. In **proportionate stratified sampling,** the sample size from each stratum is dependent on that stratum's size relative to the defined target population. Therefore, the larger strata are sampled more heavily because they make up a larger percentage of the target population. In **disproportionate stratified sampling,** the sample size selected from each stratum is independent of that stratum's proportion of the total defined target population. This approach is used when stratification of the target population produces sample sizes for subgroups that differ from their relative importance to the study. For example, stratification of manufacturers based on number of employees will usually result in a large segment of manufacturers with fewer than 10 employees and a very small proportion with, say, 500 or more employees. The obvious economic importance of those firms with 500 or more employees would dictate taking a larger sample from this stratum and a smaller sample from the subgroup with fewer than 10 employees than indicated by the proportionality method.

An alternative type of disproportionate stratified method is *optimal allocation.* In this method, consideration is given to the relative size of the stratum as well as the variability within the stratum. The basic logic underlying optimal allocation is that the greater the homogeneity of the prospective sampling units within a particular stratum, the fewer the units that have to be selected to accurately estimate the true population parameter (μ or P) for that subgroup. In contrast, the opposite would hold true for any stratum that has considerable variance among its sampling units or that is perceived as heterogeneous. Exhibit 10.5 displays the basic steps a researcher would take in drawing a proportionately stratified random sample.

Advantages and Disadvantages

Dividing the defined target population into homogeneous strata provides several advantages, including: (1) the assurance of representativeness in the sample; (2) the opportunity to study each stratum and make comparisons between strata; and (3) the ability to make estimates for the target population with the expectation of greater precision and less error. The primary difficulty encountered with stratified sampling is determining the basis for stratifying. Stratification is based on the target population's characteristics of interest. Secondary information relevant to the required stratification factors might not be readily available, therefore forcing the researcher to use less than desirable surrogate variables as the factors for stratifying the target population. Usually, the larger the number of relevant strata, the more precise the results. However, the inclusion of irrelevant strata will waste time and money without providing meaningful results. Read the nearby Ethics (Sampling Methods) box to learn about ethical issues that could impact stratified sampling methods.

Cluster Sampling

Cluster sampling A probability sampling method in which the sampling units are divided into mutually exclusive and collectively exhaustive subpopulations, called clusters.

Cluster sampling is similar to stratified random sampling, but is different in that the sampling units are divided into mutually exclusive and collectively exhaustive subpopulations, called clusters, rather than individually. Each cluster is assumed to be representative of the heterogeneity of the target population. Examples of possible divisions for cluster sampling include customers who patronize a store on a given day, the audience for a movie shown at a particular time (e.g., the matinee), or the invoices processed during a specific week. Once the cluster has been identified, the prospective sampling units are selected for the sample by either using a simple random sampling method or canvassing all the elements (a census) within the defined cluster.

EXHIBIT 10.5 Steps in Drawing a Stratified Random Sample

Step 1 → **Obtain a List of Potential Sampling Units That Contains an Acceptable Frame of the Defined Target Population Elements.**
Example: List of known performance arts patrons (names, addresses, telephone numbers) living in a three-county area from the current database of the Asolo Performing Arts Centre. Total number of known patrons in the current database is 10,500.

Step 2 → **Using Some Type of Secondary Information or Past Experience with the Defined Target Population, Select a Stratification Factor for Which the Population's Distribution Is Skewed (Not Bell-Shaped) and Can Be Used to Determine That the Total Defined Target Population Consists of Separate Subpopulations of Elements.**
Example: Using attendance records and county location, identify strata by county and number of events attended per season (i.e., regular, occasional, or rare). Total: 10,500 patrons with 5,900 "regular" (56.2%); 3,055 "occasional" (29.1%); and 1,545 "rare" (14.7%) patrons.

Step 3 → **Using the Selected Stratification Factor (or Some Other Surrogate Variable), Segment the Defined Target Population into Strata Consistent with Each of the Identified Separate Subpopulations. That is, use the stratification factor to regroup the prospective sampling units into their mutually exclusive subgroups. Then determine both the actual number of sampling units and their percentage equivalents for each stratum.**
Example: County A: 5,000 patrons with 2,500 "regular" (50%); 1,875 "occasional" (37.5%); and 625 "rare" (12.5%) patrons.
County B: 3,000 patrons with 1,800 "regular" (60%); 580 "occasional" (19.3%); and 620 "rare" (20.7%) patrons.
County C: 2,500 patrons with 1,600 "regular" (64%); 600 "occasional" (24%); and 300 "rare" (12%) patrons.

Step 4 → **Determine Whether There Is a Need to Apply a Disproportionate or Optimal Allocation Method to the Stratification Process; Otherwise, Use the Proportionate Method and Then Estimate the Desired Sample Sizes.**
Example: Compare individual county strata percentage values to overall target population strata values. Let's assume a proportionate method and a confidence level of 95% and a tolerance for sampling error of ±2.5 percentage points. Estimate the sample size for total target population with no strata needed and assuming P = 50%. The desired sample size would equal 1,537 people. Then proportion that size by the total patron percentage values for each of the three counties determined in step 2 (e.g., County A = 5,000/10,500 [47.6%]; County B = 3,000/10,500 [28.6%]; County C = 2,500/10,500 [23.8%]). New sample sizes for each county would be: County A = 732; County B = 439; County C = 366. Now for each county sample size, proportion the sample sizes by the respective within-county estimates for "regular," "occasional," and "rare" strata percentages determined in step 3.

Step 5 → **Select a Probability Sample from Each Stratum, Using either the SRS or SYMRS Procedure.**
Example: Use the procedures discussed earlier for drawing SRS or SYMRS samples.

Area sampling A form of cluster sampling in which the clusters are formed by geographic designations.

In marketing research, a popular form of cluster sampling is **area sampling.** In area sampling, the clusters are formed by geographic designations. Examples include metropolitan statistical areas (MSAs), cities, subdivisions, and blocks. Any geographical unit with identifiable boundaries can be used. When using area sampling, the researcher has two additional options: the one-step approach or the two-step approach. When deciding on a one-step approach, the researcher must have enough prior information about the various geographic clusters to believe that all the geographic clusters are basically identical with regard to the specific factors that were used to initially identify the clusters. By assuming that all the

ETHICS

Sampling Methods

U.S. Census Bureau Misleads Congress

Suppose the U.S. government is interested in gaining public support for its idea of investing budget surpluses in the stock market as the approach to ensure the stability of the country's ailing Social Security program in the future. The administration believes that members of the U.S. Congress respond in a predictable manner when they have American public opinion results in front of them. Government officials decide on using a quick telephone survey to ask the American people their opinions about three possible approaches: (1) invest a significant portion of government budget surpluses in the stock market; (2) use the surpluses to reduce overall income taxes of all Americans; or (3) use the surpluses to pay down the national debt. To conduct this study, the administration requests that U.S. Census Bureau researchers develop a sampling plan for the telephone survey to be administered to 5,000 randomly selected Americans that ensures representation across four age groupings described as (a) 20 to 35, (b) 36 to 50, (c) 51 to 65, and (d) 66 and older. Reminded of the importance of the study's main objective, the researchers choose to develop a disproportionate stratified random sampling plan that would place heavier emphasis on those Americans in the 36 to 50 and 51 to 65 age groupings than on those people in the other two groupings. To help ensure the desired outcome, interviewers will be encouraged to "work hard" on getting responses from respondents between ages 36 and 65. It is further determined that no matter the actual within-age-grouping response rates, only the study's overall response rate and normal error factor will be released to Congress, the media, and the general public.

- Is it ethical to conduct a study that knowingly misrepresents the true defined population for purposes of seeking a predetermined outcome?
- Is it ethical to encourage the interviewers to make disproportionate efforts to obtain completed interviews from less than all the defined sampled strata?
- Is it ethical to report only the overall response rate and error factor when a disproportionate stratified random sampling method is used to collect the data?
- Is it ethical not to report these facts to Congress, the media, and the general public, thereby causing these groups to misinterpret the results?
- Would it be more ethical to use a *proportionately* stratified random sampling approach?

clusters are identical, the researcher can focus his or her attention on surveying the sampling units within one designated cluster and then generalize the results to the population. The probability aspect of this particular sampling method is executed by randomly selecting one geographic cluster and performing a census on all the sampling units in that cluster.

As an example, assume the corporate vice president of merchandising for Dillard's Department Stores (www.dillards.com) wants to better understand shopping behaviors of people who shop at the 36 Dillard's stores located in Florida. Given budget constraints and a review of customer profile information in the database at corporate headquarters, the vice president assumes the same types of customers shop at Dillard's regardless of the store's geographic location or day of the week. The new Dillard's store located in University Mall in Tampa, Florida, is randomly selected as the store site for conducting in-store personal interviews, and 300 interviews are scheduled to be conducted on Wednesday, February 18, 2009.

The vice president's logic in using one store (a one-step cluster sampling method) to collect data on customers' shopping behaviors has several weaknesses. First, his assumption that customers at the University Mall store are similar to customers who shop at the other 35 stores in Florida might well be unfounded. Second, to assume that geographic differences in stores and consumers do not exist is a leap of faith. Limiting the sampling to only Wednesday also can create problems. To assume consumers' attitudes and shopping behaviors (such as traffic flow patterns) toward Dillard's Department Stores are the same on a weekday as they are on the weekend is likely to be very misleading.

Another option is to use a two-step cluster sampling approach. First, a set of clusters could be randomly selected and then a probability method could be used to select individuals within each of the selected clusters. Usually, the two-step approach is preferable to the one-step approach because there is a strong possibility a single cluster will not be representative of all other clusters. To illustrate the basics of the two-step cluster sampling approach, let's use the Dillard's Department Store example. In reviewing Dillard's database on customer profiles, assume the 36 stores can be clustered on the basis of annual sales revenue into three groups: (1) store type A (stores with gross sales under $2 million), (2) store type B (stores with gross sales between $2 million and $5 million), and (3) store type C (stores with over $5 million in gross sales). The result for the 36 stores operating in the Florida market is 6 stores can be grouped as being type A, another 18 stores as type B, and 12 stores as type C. In addition, sales were significantly heavier on weekends than during the week. Exhibit 10.6 shows the steps to take in drawing a cluster sample for the Dillard's situation.

Advantages and Disadvantages

Cluster sampling is widely used in marketing research because of its cost-effectiveness and ease of implementation, especially in area sampling situations. In many cases, the only representative sampling frame available to researchers is one based on clusters (states, counties, MSAs, census tracts). These lists of geographic regions, telephone exchanges, or blocks of residential dwellings usually can be easily compiled, thus avoiding the need for compiling lists of all the individual sampling units making up the target population. Clustering methods tend to be a cost-efficient way of sampling and collecting data from a defined target population.

Cluster sampling methods have several disadvantages. A primary disadvantage of cluster sampling is that the clusters often are homogeneous. The more homogeneous the cluster, the less precise the sample estimates. Ideally, the people in a cluster should be as heterogeneous as those in the population. When several sets of homogeneous clusters are uniquely different on the basis of the clustering factor (Dillard's store types A, B, and C), this problem may be lessened by randomly selecting and sampling a unit from each of the cluster groups. Exhibit 10.6 illustrates how researchers can overcome the problem of different homogeneous clusters within a defined target population.

Another concern with cluster sampling methods—one that is rarely addressed—is the appropriateness of the designated cluster factor used to identify the sampling units within clusters. Again let's use the Dillard's example to illustrate this potential weakness. Dillard's vice president of merchandising used a single geographic cluster designation factor (Florida) to derive one cluster consisting of 36 stores. By assuming that there was equal heterogeneity among all Dillard's shoppers, regardless of the store location, he randomly sampled one store to conduct the necessary in-store interviews. Then by changing the designated cluster factor to "annual gross sales revenue," he determined that there were three different sets of store clusters (store types A, B, and C) among the same 36 Dillard's stores located in Florida. This clustering method required a more complex sampling technique to ensure that the data collected would be representative of the defined target population of all Dillard's customers. The point is that while the defined target population remains constant, the subdivision of sampling units can be modified depending on the selection of the designation factor used to identify the clusters. This points out that caution must be used in selecting the factor to determine clusters in area sampling situations.

EXHIBIT 10.6 Steps in Drawing a Two-Step Cluster Sample

Step 1 → **Fully Understand the Information Problem Situation and Characteristics That Are Used to Define the Target Population. Then Determine the Clustering Factors to Be Used to Identify the Clusters of Sampling Units.**
Example: Initial sampling units would be the 36 known Dillard's stores located throughout Florida. Using secondary data of stores' annual gross sales revenue, establish the cluster categories (i.e., store types A, B, and C) and weekday versus weekend dollar sales figures.

Step 2 → **Determine the Number of Sampling Units That Make Up Each Cluster, Obtain a List of Potential Sampling Units for Each Cluster, and Assign Them a Unique Designation Code.**
Example: 6 type A stores—(01) Jacksonville; (05) Fort Lauderdale; (03) Gainesville; etc.
18 type B stores—(01) Tampa; (16) Sarasota; (07) Vero Beach; etc.
12 type C stores—(10) Miami; (02) West Palm Beach; (07) Orlando; etc.
Weekday sales—(01) through (52).
Weekend sales—(01) through (52).

Step 3 → **Determine Whether to Use a One-Step or Two-Step Cluster Sampling Method.**
Example: Given that both *store type* and *weekday/weekend sales* factors are being used to designate the clusters, a two-step clustering approach will be used to draw the sampling units.

Step 4 → **Determine How Many Sampling Units in Each Cluster Need to Be Sampled to Be Representative of That Cluster.**
Example: Given the perceived homogeneity within each cluster group of stores and cost considerations, let's assume that the researcher feels comfortable in sampling only one store in each store type over two weekday periods and four weekend periods.

Step 5 → **Using Random Numbers, Select the Sampling Unit (i.e., Store) within Each Cluster and the Weekday and Weekend Time Frames to Be Sampled.**
Example: For store type A: (01) Jacksonville; weekday periods for weeks (10) and (34); weekend periods for weeks (03), (14), (26), and (41).
For store type B: (12) Lakeland; weekday periods for weeks (33) and (45); weekend periods for weeks (09), (24), (29), and (36).
For store type C: (10) Miami; weekday periods for weeks (22) and (46); weekend periods for weeks (04), (18), (32), and (37).

Step 6 → **Determine the Needed Sample Sizes for Each Cluster by Weekday/Weekend Time Frames.**
Example: Let's assume a desired confidence level of 95% and a tolerance for sampling error of ±2.5 percentage points. Estimate the desired sample size for total target population with no cluster grouping needed and assuming $P = 50\%$. The desired sample size would equal 1,537 people. Then proportion that size by the percentage values for each type of store to total number of stores making up the defined target population frame (i.e., store type A = 6/36 [16.7%]; store type B = 18/36 [50.0%]; store type C = 12/36 [33.3%]). New sample sizes for each store type would be: store type A = 257; store type B = 769; store type C = 512. Now for each store type sample size, proportion the sample sizes by the respective within weekday and weekend estimates determined in step 4. As a result, the required sample sizes by store type by weekday/weekend time frames would be:
Store type A: Weekday periods 43 people in week (10), 43 people in week (34); Weekend periods 43 people in week (03) and the same number for weeks (14), (26), and (41).
Store type B: Weekday periods 43 people in week (33), 43 people in week (45); Weekend periods 43 people in week (09) and the same number for weeks (24), (29), and (46).
Store type C: Weekday periods 43 people in week (22), 43 people in week (46); Weekend periods 43 people in week (04) and the same number for weeks (18), (32), and (37).

Step 7 → **Select a Probability Sampling Method for Selecting Customers for In-Store Interviews.**
Example: Randomize the weekday interviews (i.e., Monday, Tuesday, Wednesday, and Thursday) as well as the weekend interviews (i.e., Friday, Saturday, and Sunday) so that the data are represented across shopping days and store operating hours.

Types of Nonprobability Sampling Designs

Convenience Sampling

Convenience sampling A nonprobability sampling method in which samples are drawn at the convenience of the researcher.

Convenience sampling is a method in which samples are drawn based on convenience. For example, mall-intercept interviewing of individuals at shopping malls or other high-traffic areas is a common method of generating a convenience sample. The assumptions are that the target population is homogeneous and the individuals interviewed at the shopping mall are similar to the overall defined target population with regard to the characteristic being studied. In reality, it is difficult to accurately assess the representativeness of the sample. Given self-selection and the voluntary nature of participating in the data collection, researchers should consider the impact of nonresponse error.

Advantages and Disadvantages

Convenience sampling enables a large number of respondents (e.g., 200–300) to be interviewed in a relatively short time. For this reason, it is commonly used in the early stages of research (construct and scale measurement development as well as pretesting of questionnaires). But using convenience samples to develop constructs and scales can be risky. For example, assume the researcher is developing a measure of service quality and in the preliminary stages uses a convenience sample of 300 undergraduate business students. While college students are consumers of services, serious questions should be raised about whether they are truly representative of the general population. By developing and refining constructs and scales using data from a convenience sample of college students, the construct's measurement scale might later prove to be unreliable when used in investigations of other defined target populations. Another major disadvantage of convenience samples is that the data are not generalizable to the defined target population. The representativeness of the sample cannot be measured because sampling error estimates cannot be calculated.

Judgment Sampling

Judgment sampling A nonprobability sampling method in which participants are selected according to an experienced individual's belief that they will meet the requirements of the study.

In **judgment sampling,** sometimes referred to as *purposive* sampling, sample respondents are selected because the researcher believes they meet the requirements of the study. In many industrial sales studies, the regional sales manager will survey sales representatives rather than customers to determine whether customers' wants and needs are changing or to assess the firm's product or service performance. Many consumer packaging manufacturers (for instance, Procter & Gamble) regularly select a sample of key accounts believed to be able to provide information about consumption patterns and changes in demand for selected products (Crest toothpaste, Cheer laundry detergent). The underlying assumption is that the opinions of a group of perceived experts are representative of the target population.

Advantages and Disadvantages

If the judgment of the researcher is correct, the sample generated by judgment sampling will be better than one generated by convenience sampling. However, as with all nonprobability sampling procedures, you cannot measure the representativeness of the sample. At best, the data collected from judgment sampling should be interpreted cautiously.

Quota Sampling

Quota sampling
A nonprobability sampling method in which participants are selected according to prespecified quotas regarding demographics, attitudes, behaviors, or some other criteria.

Quota sampling involves the selection of prospective participants according to prespecified quotas for either demographic characteristics (age, race, gender, income), specific attitudes (satisfied/dissatisfied, liking/disliking, great/marginal/no quality), or specific behaviors (regular/occasional/rare customer, product user/nonuser). The purpose of quota sampling is to assure that prespecified subgroups of the target population are represented in relevant sampling factors. Moreover, surveys frequently use quotas that have been determined by the nature of the research objectives. For example, if a research study is conducted about fast-food restaurants, the researcher may establish quotas using an age factor and the patronage behavior of prospective respondents as follows:

Age	Patronage Behavior
[1] Under 25	[1] Patronize a fast-food establishment an average of once a month or more
[2] 25 to 54	[2] Patronize fast-food establishments less frequently than once a month
[3] 55 and over	

Using these demographic and patronage behavior factors, the researcher identifies six different subgroups of people to be included in the study. Determining the quota size for each of the subgroups is a somewhat subjective process. The researcher might use sales information to determine whether the percentage size of each subgroup has contributed to the firm's total sales. This ensures the sample will contain the desired number in each subgroup. Once the individual percentage sizes for each quota are established, the researcher segments the sample size by those percentage values to determine the actual number of prospective respondents to include in each of the prespecified quota groups. Let's say, for example, that a fast-food restaurant wanted to interview 1,000 people and, using both industry-supplied sales reports and company sales records, determined that individuals aged 25 to 54 who patronize fast-food restaurants at least once a month make up 50 percent of its total sales. The researcher would probably want that subgroup to make up 50 percent of the total sample. Let's further assume that company records indicated that individuals aged 25 to 54 who frequent fast-food restaurants less than once a month make up only 6 percent of sales. This particular subgroup should consist of only 6 percent of the total sample size.

Advantages and Disadvantages

The greatest advantage of quota sampling is that the sample generated contains specific subgroups in the proportions desired by researchers. In research projects that require interviews, the use of quotas ensures that the appropriate subgroups are identified and included in the survey. Also, quota sampling should reduce selection bias by field workers. An inherent limitation of quota sampling is that the success of the study will again be dependent on subjective decisions made by the researchers. Since it is a nonprobability sampling method, the representativeness of the sample cannot be measured. Therefore, generalizing the results beyond the sampled respondents is questionable.

Snowball Sampling

Snowball sampling
A nonprobability sampling method in which a set of respondents is chosen and they help the researcher identify additional people to be included in the study.

Snowball sampling involves identifying and qualifying a set of initial prospective respondents who can, in turn, help the researcher identify additional people to include in the study. This method of sampling is also called *referral* sampling, because one respondent refers other potential respondents. Snowball sampling typically is used in situations where (1) the defined target population is small and unique, and (2) compiling a complete list of sampling units is very difficult. Consider, for example, researching the attitudes and behaviors of people who volunteer their time to charitable organizations like the Children's Wish Foundation. While traditional sampling methods require an extensive search effort (both in time and cost) to qualify a sufficient number of prospective respondents, the snowball method yields better results at a much lower cost. Here the researchers interview a qualified respondent, then solicit his or her help to identify other people with similar characteristics. While membership in these types of social circles might not be publicly known, intracircle knowledge is very accurate. The underlying logic of this method is that rare groups of people tend to form their own unique social circles.

Advantages and Disadvantages

Snowball sampling is a reasonable method of identifying respondents who are members of small, hard-to-reach, uniquely defined target populations. As a nonprobability sampling method, it is most useful in qualitative research practices. But snowball sampling allows bias to enter the study. If there are significant differences between people who are known in certain social circles and those who are not, there may be problems with this sampling technique. Like all other nonprobability sampling approaches, the ability to generalize the results to members of the target population is limited.

Determining the Appropriate Sampling Design

Selection of the most appropriate sampling design should consider the seven factors displayed in Exhibit 10.7.

EXHIBIT 10.7 Critical Factors in Selecting the Appropriate Sampling Design

Selection Factors	Questions
Research objectives	Do the research objectives call for the use of qualitative or quantitative research designs?
Degree of accuracy	Does the research call for making predictions or inductive inferences about the defined target population, or only preliminary insights?
Resources	Are there tight budget constraints with respect to both dollars and human resources that can be allocated to the research project?
Time frame	How quickly does the research project have to be completed?
Knowledge of the target population	Are there complete lists of the defined target population elements? How easy or difficult is it to generate the required sampling frame of prospective respondents?
Scope of the research	Is the research going be international, national, regional, or local?
Statistical analysis needs	To what extent are accurate statistical projections and/or testing of hypothesized differences in the data structures required?

Research Objectives

An understanding of the research problem and objectives provides the initial guidelines for determining the appropriate sampling design. If the research objectives include the desire to generalize the sample results to the target population, then the researcher must likely use some type of probability sampling method rather than a nonprobability sampling method. In addition, the stage of the research project and type of research (exploratory, descriptive, causal) influence the selection of the sampling method.

Degree of Accuracy

The degree of accuracy required will vary from project to project, especially when cost savings or other considerations are evaluated. If the researcher wants to make predictions about members of the defined target population, then a probability sampling method must be used. In contrast, if the researcher is interested only in preliminary insights about the target population, nonprobability methods might be as appropriate.

Resources

If financial and human resources are limited, this most certainly will eliminate some of the more time-consuming, complex probability sampling methods. If the budget is a substantial limitation, then a nonprobability sampling method likely will be used rather than conducting no research at all.

Time Frame

Researchers with short deadlines will be more likely to select a simple, less time-consuming sampling method rather than a more complex method. For example, researchers tend to use convenience sampling to gather data to test the reliability of a newly developed construct. While data from this sampling method might provide preliminary insights about the defined target population, there is no way to assess the representativeness of the results.

Knowledge of the Target Population

In many cases, a list of the population will not be available. Therefore, a preliminary study may be needed to develop a sampling frame for the study. To do so, the researcher must have a clear understanding of who is in the target population. Review the nearby A Closer Look at Research (Using Technology) box on using the Internet to gain valuable information on sampling using databases.

Scope of the Research

The scope of the research project, whether international, national, regional, or local, will influence the choice of the sampling method. The geographic proximity of the defined target population will influence not only the ability to compile lists of sampling units, but also the selection design. When the target population elements are known or unequally distributed geographically, a cluster sampling method may be more attractive than other methods. Generally, the broader the geographical scope of the research project, the more complex the sampling method becomes to ensure proper representation of the target population.

A Closer Look at Research

The Internet Provides Valuable Intelligence Information

As more businesses turn to online and database marketing research to solve marketing problems, sampling issues and procedures will play an increasing role in the success of obtaining the right information in a timely fashion. Advanced technologies used in creating and maintaining company-owned customer profile databases afford many businesses the opportunity to improve their capability to identify, understand, target, reach, and monitor customers. Increased availability of information from various online databases has enhanced the value of geodemographic segmentation and mapping practices. Business owners seeking to expand their markets can use the Internet to locate resources like Hoovers (www.hoovers.com), GeoPlace (www.geoplace.com), and the University of Virginia (http://fisher.lib.virginia.edu) to gain access to geodemographic information. For example, a business could use these resources to begin the process of determining where to expand and whether expansion would be economically feasible. Population size, demographic composite and lifestyle characteristics, competitive situation, media coverage and efficiency, media isolation, self-contained trading areas, and availability of scanner data all could be used to evaluate prospective target markets. The resulting information would be useful in assessing the feasibility of expansion as well as determining the appropriate marketing strategy for expansion. In addition, online geodemographic information provides opportunities for digital mapping, store location planning, demographic customer profiling, and gravity modeling activities.

Statistical Analysis

The need for statistical projections based on the sample results is often a criterion. Only probability sampling techniques enable the researcher to use statistical analysis for estimates beyond the immediate set of sampled respondents. While statistical analysis methods can be performed on data obtained from nonprobability samples, the ability to generalize the findings to the target population is suspect. Another important topic in deciding on the appropriateness of any proposed sample design is determining the sample size. Sample size has a direct impact on data quality, statistical precision, and generalizability of findings.

Steps in Developing a Sampling Plan

Sampling plan The blueprint or framework needed to ensure that the data collected are representative of the defined target population.

Sampling is much more than just finding some people to participate in a research study. As we have discussed, researchers must consider a number of different concepts and procedures to successfully gather data from a group of people that can be used to make inferential predictions about a larger target population. After understanding the key components of sampling theory, the methods of determining sample sizes, and the various designs available, the researcher is ready to use this knowledge to develop a sampling plan appropriate for the research situation. A **sampling plan** is the blueprint to ensure that the data collected are representative of the target population. A good sampling plan includes the following steps: (1) define the target population, (2) select the data collection method, (3) identify the

EXHIBIT 10.8 Steps in Developing a Sampling Plan

- Step 1 → Define the Target Population
- Step 2 → Select the Data Collection Method
- Step 3 → Identify the Sampling Frame(s) Needed
- Step 4 → Select the Appropriate Sampling Method
- Step 5 → Determine Necessary Sample Sizes and Overall Contact Rates
- Step 6 → Create an Operating Plan for Selecting Sampling Units
- Step 7 → Execute the Operational Plan

sampling frame(s) needed, (4) select the appropriate sampling method, (5) determine necessary sample sizes and overall contact rates, (6) create an operating plan for selecting sampling units, and (7) execute the operational plan.

Exhibit 10.8 presents these logical steps that make up a sampling plan, and the short discussions that follow allude to some of the key activities involved in each step. You are encouraged to revisit earlier parts of this chapter and also to preceding chapters to review your knowledge of these key activities.

Step 1: Define the Target Population

In any sampling plan, the first task of the researcher is to determine the group of people or objects that should be investigated. With the information problem and research objectives as guidelines, the target population should be identified using descriptors that represent the characteristics of the elements of the desired target population's frame. These elements become the sampling units from which a sample will be drawn. Clear understanding of the target population will help the researcher successfully draw a representative sample.

Step 2: Select the Data Collection Method

Using the information problem definition, the data requirements, and the research objectives, the researcher chooses a method for collecting the data from the target population elements. Choices include some type of interviewing approach (personal or telephone) or a self-administered survey. The method of data collection guides the researcher in identifying and securing the necessary sampling frame(s) to conduct the research.

Step 3: Identify the Sampling Frame(s) Needed

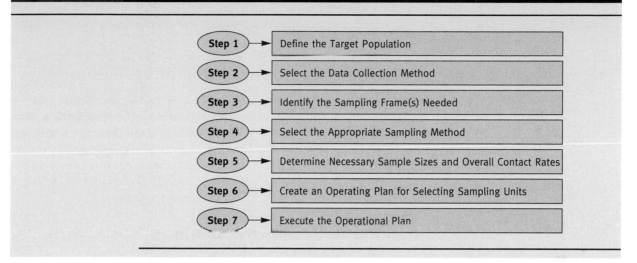

After deciding who or what should be investigated, the researcher must assemble a list of eligible sampling units. The list should contain enough information about each prospective sampling unit so the researcher can successfully contact them. Having an incomplete sampling frame decreases the likelihood of drawing a representative sample. Sampling frame lists can be created from a number of different sources (customer lists from a company's internal database, random-digit dialing, an organization's membership roster).

Step 4: Select the Appropriate Sampling Method

The researcher chooses between two types of sampling approaches: probability and nonprobability. If the data will be used to estimate target population parameters, using a probability sampling method will yield more accurate information about the target population than will nonprobability sampling methods. In determining the appropriateness of the sampling method, the researcher must consider seven factors: (1) research objectives, (2) desired accuracy, (3) availability of resources, (4) time frame, (5) knowledge of the target population, (6) scope of the research, and (7) statistical analysis needs.

Step 5: Determine Necessary Sample Sizes and Overall Contact Rates

The researcher needs to decide how precise the sample estimates must be and how much time and money are available to collect the data. To determine the appropriate sample size, decisions have to be made concerning (1) the variability of the population characteristic under investigation, (2) the level of confidence desired in the estimates, and (3) the precision required. The researcher also must decide how many completed surveys are needed for data analysis, recognizing that sample size often is not equal to the usable observations.

At this point the researcher must consider what impact having fewer surveys than initially desired would have on the accuracy of the sample statistics. An important question is "How many prospective sampling units will have to be contacted to ensure the estimated sample size is obtained, and at what additional costs?" To answer this, the researcher must be able to calculate the reachable rates, overall incidence rates, and expected completion rates for the sampling situation.

Step 6: Create an Operating Plan for Selecting Sampling Units

In this step, the researcher must determine how to contact the prospective respondents who were drawn in the sample. Instructions should be clearly written so that interviewers know what to do and how to handle any problems contacting prospective respondents. For example, if the study data will be collected using mall-intercept interviews, then instructions on how to select respondents and conduct the interviews must be given to the interviewer.

Step 7: Execute the Operational Plan

In some research projects, this step is similar to collecting the data (e.g., calling prospective respondents to do a telephone interview). The important thing in this stage is to maintain consistency and control.

MARKETING RESEARCH IN ACTION

Continuing Case: Santa Fe Grill

Developing a Sampling Plan for a New Menu Initiative Survey

The owners of the Santa Fe Grill realize that in order to remain competitive in the restaurant industry, new menu items need to be introduced periodically to provide variety for current customers and to attract new customers. Recognizing this, the owners of the Grill believe three issues need to be addressed using marketing research. First, should the menu be changed to include items beyond the traditional southwestern cuisine, for example, items that would be considered American, Italian, or European cuisine? Second, regardless of the cuisine to be explored, how many and what sort of new items (appetizers, entrees, desserts) should be considered and included on the survey? And third, what type of sampling plan should be developed for selecting respondents, and who should those respondents be (current customers, new customers, old customers)?

Understanding the importance of sampling and the impact it will have on the validity and accuracy of the research results, the owners have asked the local university if a marketing research class could assist them in this project. Specifically, the owners have posed the following questions that need to be addressed.

- How many questions should the survey contain to adequately address all possible new menu items, including the notion of assessing the desirability of new cuisines? In short, how can it be determined that all necessary items will be included on the survey so as not to ignore any menu items that may be desirable to potential customers?
- How should the potential respondents be selected for the survey? Should patrons be interviewed while they are dining? Should patrons be asked to participate in the survey upon exiting the restaurant? Or should a mail or telephone approach be used to collect information from patrons/nonpatrons?

Hands-On Exercise

Based on the questions outlined above, your task is to develop a procedure to address the following issues:

1. From the total domain of possible new items to include on the menu, how many items can be put on the survey? Remember, all menu possibilities should be assessed but you must have a manageable number of questions so the survey can be performed in a timely and reasonable manner. Specifically, from a list of all possible menu items that can be included on the survey, what is the optimal number of menu items that should be used? Is there a sampling procedure you can use to determine the maximum number of menu items to place on the survey?
2. Determine the appropriate sample design. Develop a sample design proposal for the Santa Fe Grill that addresses the following: Should a probability or nonprobabaility sample be used? Given your answer, what type of sampling design should be employed (simple random, stratified, convenience, and so on)? Given the sample design suggested, how will potential respondents be selected for the study? Finally, determine the necessary sample size and create an operating plan for selecting the sampling units.

Summary of Learning Objectives

■ **Distinguish between probability and nonprobability sampling.**
In probability sampling, each sampling unit in the defined target population has a known probability of being selected for the sample. The actual probability of selection for each sampling unit may or may not be equal depending on the type of probability sampling design used. In nonprobability sampling, the probability of selection of each sampling unit is not known. The selection of sampling units is based on some type of intuitive judgment or knowledge of the researcher.

■ **Explain the advantages and disadvantages of probability sampling.**
Probability sampling enables the researcher to judge the reliability and validity of data collected by calculating the probability that the findings based on the sample will differ from the defined target population. This observed difference can be partially attributed to the existence of sampling error. Each probability sampling method (simple random, systematic random, stratified, cluster) has its own inherent advantages and disadvantages.

■ **Compare the advantages and disadvantages of nonprobability sampling.**
In nonprobability sampling, the probability of selection of each sampling unit is not known. Therefore, potential sampling error cannot be accurately known either. Although there may be a temptation to generalize nonprobability sample results to the defined target population, for the most part the results are limited to the people who provided the data in the survey. Each nonprobability sampling method (convenience, judgment, quota, snowball) has its own inherent advantages and disadvantages.

■ **Describe the factors that influence the appropriate sample design.**
Selection of the most appropriate sampling design should incorporate the following seven factors: Research Objectives, Degree of Accuracy, Availability of Resources, Time Frame, Advanced Knowledge of the Target Population, Scope of the Research, and Statistical Analysis Needs.

■ **Understand the steps in developing a sampling plan.**
A sampling plan is the blueprint or framework needed to ensure that the data collected are representative of the defined target population. A good sampling plan will include, at least, the following steps: (1) define the target population, (2) select the data collection method, (3) identify the sampling frames needed, (4) select the appropriate sampling method, (5) determine necessary sample sizes and overall contact rates, (6) create an operating plan for selecting sampling units, and (7) execute the operational plan.

Key Terms and Concepts

Area sampling 318
Cluster sampling 317
Convenience sampling 322
Disproportionate stratified sampling 317
Judgment sampling 322
Nonprobability sampling 312
Probability sampling 312
Proportionate stratified sampling 317
Quota sampling 323
Sampling plan 326
Simple random sampling 313
Snowball sampling 323
Stratified random sampling 316
Systematic random sampling 314

Review Questions

1. Briefly discuss the differences between probability and nonprobability samples.
2. Explain the advantages and disadvantages of the following sampling methods:
   a. Simple random sampling
   b. Systematic random sampling
   c. Cluster sampling
   d. Convenience sampling
3. Identify the major steps involved in developing a two-step cluster sample.
4. Discuss the critical factors necessary for determining the appropriate sample design.
5. Briefly discuss the seven steps involved in developing a sampling plan.

Discussion Questions

1. **EXPERIENCE THE INTERNET.** Log on to the Internet and go to VACATION RENTALS by owners at www.vrbo.com/. This Web site consists of thousands of vacation rentals worldwide. After getting to this site, select and click on "Colorado." First, how many vacation rentals are available in each of the following towns (Breckenridge, Copper Mountain, Dillon, Frisco, Keystone, and Silverthorne)? Then using a systematic random sampling design, draw a representative sample of those vacation rentals within the six designated towns.
2. **EXPERIENCE THE INTERNET.** Go to the U. S. Census Bureau's home page at www.census.gov. Once there, select the population and housing option. Within this area, view all of the metropolitan areas (MSAs). Using a stratified random sampling approach, develop a sample of MSAs that could be used for distributing a survey on snowmobiles.
3. Many state lotteries require individuals to pick numbers between 1 and 10. Over the past ten weeks, the number 9 was a winning number 40 percent of the time. If you were to pick a number for the upcoming week, and you selected the number 9, would you be more or less likely to win the lottery? How would you explain your answer based on the concept of simple random sampling?
4. Outline the step-by-step process used to determine the following:
   a. A systematic random sample of 200 students at your university.
   b. A convenience sample of 150 shoppers at a local mall.
   c. A stratified random sample of 50 lawyers, 40 doctors, and 60 dentists who subscribe to your local newspaper.
5. A national cell phone company is interested in determining the heavy users of cell phones (airtime). What type of sampling method would be best suited for this situation? Why?

chapter 11

Overview of Measurement: Construct Development and Scaling

Learning Objectives

After reading this chapter, you will be able to:

1. Understand the role of measurement in marketing research.
2. Discuss validity and reliability issues in measurement and scaling.
3. Explain what scale measurement is and how to apply it.
4. Compare the four basic levels of scales.
5. Discuss scale development and its importance in gathering primary data.

"With iTV we can measure exactly what consumers are doing, how much time they are spending on the interactive domains and other metrics because it is entirely controlled and monitored, unlike the Internet."

—MICHELE BOGDAN,
Senior Vice President of Marketing,
Ensequence, Inc.[1]

Santa Fe Grill Mexican Restaurant: Predicting Customer Loyalty

About 18 months after opening their first restaurant close to the Cumberland Mall in Dallas, Texas, the owners of the Santa Fe Grill Mexican restaurant understood that while there was another Mexican theme restaurant direct competitor (Jose's Southwestern Café) located nearby, there were many more casual dining competitors within a three-mile radius including several well-established national chain restaurants like Chili's, Bennigan's, Applebee's, TGI Friday's, and Ruby Tuesday's, which also offered some Mexican food items. Concerned with growing a strong customer base in a very competitive restaurant environment, the owners had initially just focused on the image of offering the best, freshest "made-from-scratch" Mexican foods in hopes of creating strong satisfaction among their customers. Results from a series of informal satisfaction surveys with known customers indicated that many of the customers had a satisfying dining experience but intentions to revisit the restaurant on a regular basis were low. After reading a popular press article on customer loyalty, the owners' focus turned to being able to predict and understand elements of a restaurant operation leading to customer loyalty, that is, customers revisiting their restaurant more often.

To gain a better understanding of customer loyalty, the Santa Fe Grill owners sought help from Burke's (www.burke.com) Customer Satisfaction Division with its Customer Loyalty Index measures. New research objectives included measuring customer loyalty and its impact on the relationship between customer satisfaction, intention to recommend and revisit the restaurant, and sales, and then identifying any other criteria that would predict sales more accurately. New research quickly showed that assessing customer loyalty toward the Santa Fe Grill restaurant would directly influence the accuracy of sales potential estimates. A new study helped the owners see that while traffic density was a significant indicator of sales, the demographics of the surrounding area were less reliable indicators. Customers preferred locations where several casual dining establishments were clustered together so that more choice was available. The owners believed what they needed was a better understanding of the relationship between different aspects of consumers' satisfaction, positive word of mouth recommendations, and other levels of their behavioral intentions.

In short, customer loyalty to the Santa Fe Grill was a complex construct that needed to be carefully defined and measured.

Several insights about the importance of construct and measurement development can be gained from the Santa Fe Grill experience. First, not knowing the critical elements that influence customers' restaurant loyalty can lead to intuitive guesswork and counterproductive sales results. Second, creating loyal customers requires identifying and precisely defining and measuring the patronage constructs (their attitudes, emotions, behavioral factors) characterizing the Santa Fe Grill's customers' loyalty. After reading the discussion in this chapter, be sure to read the Marketing Research in Action at the end of the chapter about how Burke, Inc., defines and measures customer loyalty.

Value of Measurement in Information Research

Measurement is an integral part of the modern world, yet the beginnings of measurement lie in the distant past. Before a farmer could sell his corn, potatoes, or apples, both he and the buyer had to decide on units of measurement. Over time, one particular measurement became known as a bushel, or four pecks or, more precisely, 2,150.42 cubic inches. In the early days, measurement was simply achieved by using a basket or container of standard size that everyone agreed was a bushel.

From such simple everyday devices as the standard bushel basket, we have progressed in the physical sciences to such an extent that we are now able to measure the rotation of a distant star, the altitude of a satellite in micro-inches, or time in picoseconds (1 trillionth of a second). Today, such precise physical measurement is critical to airline pilots flying through dense fog or physicians controlling a surgical laser.

In most marketing situations, however, the measurements are applied to things that are much more abstract than altitude or time. For example, most decision makers would agree that information about whether or not a firm's customers are going to like a new product is critically important prior to introducing that product. In many cases, such information has made the difference between business success and failure. Yet, unlike time or altitude, people's preferences can be very difficult to measure accurately. As we described in an earlier chapter, the Coca-Cola Company introduced New Coke after inadequately measuring consumers' preferences, and thereby suffered substantial losses. Inadequate measurements of consumer attitudes quite often lead to the early cancellation of new television series, the withdrawal of new products, and sometimes the failure of entire companies.

Since accurate measurement of constructs is essential to effective decision making, the purpose of this chapter is to provide you with a basic understanding of the measurement of customers' attitudes and behaviors and other marketplace phenomena. We describe the measurement process and the central decision rules for developing scale measurements. The focus here is on basic measurement issues, construct development, and scale measurements. Chapter 12 continues the topic of measurement and discusses several popular attitudinal, emotional, and behavioral intention scales.

Overview of the Measurement Process

Measurement An integrative process of determining the intensity (or amount) of information about constructs, concepts, or objects.

Measurement is the process of determining the amount (or intensity) of information about persons, events, ideas, and/or objects of interest and their relationship to a business problem or opportunity. In other words, researchers use the measurement process by assigning either *numbers* or *labels* to (1) people's thoughts, feelings, behaviors, and characteristics; (2) the features or attributes of objects; (3) the aspects of ideas; or (4) any type of phenomenon or event, using specific rules to represent quantities and/or qualities of the factors being investigated. For example, to gather data that will offer insight about people who shop for automobiles online (a marketing phenomenon), researchers collect information on the demographic characteristics, attitudes, perceptions, past online purchase behaviors, and other relevant factors associated with these people.

Critical to the process of collecting primary data is the development of well-constructed measurement procedures. The measurement process consists of two distinctly different development processes: *construct development* and *scale measurement*. To achieve the overall goal of collecting high-quality data, researchers must understand what they are attempting to measure before developing the appropriate scale measurements. The goal of the construct development process is to precisely identify and define *what is to be measured*. In turn, the goal of the scale measurement process is to determine *how to precisely measure each construct*. We begin with construct development, then move to scale measurements.

Object Any tangible item in a person's environment that can be clearly and easily identified through his or her senses.

Researchers interpret and use the terms *objects* and *constructs* in several ways. First, the term **object** refers to any tangible item in a person's environment that can be clearly and easily identified through the senses (sight, sound, touch, smell, taste). Remember that researchers do not measure the object per se but rather the elements that make up the object. Any object has what is called *objective* (or concrete) *properties* or features that are used to identify and distinguish it from another object. These properties represent attributes that make up an object of interest and that are directly observable and measurable, such as the physical and demographic characteristics of a person (age, sex, income, occupation status, color of eyes), or the actual number of purchases made of a particular product, or the tangible features of the object (horsepower, style, color, stereo system of an automobile).

Construct A hypothetical variable made up of a set of component responses or behaviors that are thought to be related.

In turn, any object can also have *subjective* (or abstract) *properties* that are intangible characteristics that cannot be directly observed or measured because they are the mental images or emotions a person attaches to an object, such as attitudes, feelings, perceptions, expectations, or expressions of future actions regarding something (purchase intentions). Researchers refer to these intangible, subjective, or abstract properties as **constructs.** Measuring constructs requires researchers to ask people to translate these subjective features onto a continuum of intensity using carefully designed questions.

Construct Development

The necessity for precise definitions in marketing research may appear to be obvious, but it is an area where problems frequently arise. Precise definition of marketing constructs begins with defining the purpose of the study and providing clear expressions of the research problem. Without a clear initial understanding of the research problem before the study begins, researchers can end up collecting irrelevant or inaccurate data, thereby wasting a great deal of time, effort, and money. On the other hand the data may be accurate enough, but their purpose and meaning unclear.

Misguided research endeavors have resulted in many mistakes in industries such as music, fashion, and food. The U.S. auto industry provides a good example. Even after consumers became concerned with the trend of higher gas prices in the United States, most U.S. manufacturers continued to invest in factories designed to produce large, inefficient SUVs, trucks, and automobiles. Management ignored studies indicating that increasing fuel prices, highway congestion, and use of pollution controls favored more energy-efficient vehicles. Why was this? They lacked a clear understanding of how to define this research problem in a way that would accurately measure the likely impact on future purchase decisions. As a result, hundreds of millions of dollars in auto sales were lost to foreign competitors. Such cases show that a very careful definition of the purpose of the research study is essential.

Construct development An integrative process in which researchers determine what specific data should be collected for solving the defined research problem.

Construct development is an integrative process in which researchers identify the subjective properties or factors about which data should be collected to solve the defined research problem. Identifying properties to investigate requires understanding constructs and their dimensionality, validity, and operationalization.

Abstractness of the Construct

At the heart of construct development is the need to determine exactly what is to be measured. The objects that are relevant to the research problem are identified first. Then the objective and subjective properties of each object are specified. In cases where data are needed only about the concreteness of an object, the research focus is limited to measuring the object's objective properties. But when data are needed to understand an object's subjective properties, the researcher must identify measurable subcomponents that can be used to clarify the object's abstract, subjective properties.

For instance, a hammer can easily be thought of as a concrete object. Researchers can easily measure a hammer's physical characteristics: the hardness of its head, its length and weight, the composition of the handle, and so on. Yet the hammer can also have a set of subjective properties, such as its quality and performance, that are created from people's attitudes, emotions, and judgments toward the hammer. Due to level of abstractness associated with the hammer's intangible quality and performance features, there are no physical instruments that can directly measure these constructs. Exhibit 11.1 provides some examples of objects and their concrete, tangible properties and abstract, intangible construct properties, as well as some specific examples of marketing constructs. A rule of thumb is that if a feature of an object can be directly measured using physical instruments, then that feature is not a construct.

Determining Dimensionality of the Construct

In determining exactly what is to be measured, researchers must keep in mind the need to acquire relevant, high-quality data to support management's decisions. For example, if the purpose is to assess the service quality of an automobile dealership, then what exactly should be measured? Since dealer service quality is an abstract construct, perhaps the most appropriate way to begin to answer this question is to indirectly identify those dealership attributes that are important to customers.

Researchers in this case can use a variety of qualitative data collection methods (focus groups or in-depth interviews) to develop preliminary insights into service quality and its **domain of observables,** which is the set of identifiable and measurable components associated with an abstract construct.[2] To illustrate this point, researchers interested in identifying the domain of measurable components representing the service quality construct might conduct two types of exploratory research: a secondary literature review of past research on service quality and several focus groups. The results suggest that the service quality construct can be indirectly represented by the domain of a service provider's ability to (1) *communicate* and *listen* to consumers, (2) demonstrate *excellent interpretative skills,* (3) *sincerely empathize* with consumers in interpreting their needs and wants, (4) be *tactful in responding* to customers' questions, objections, and problems, (5) create an impression of *reliability in performing* the services, (6) create an *image of credibility* by keeping promises, (7) demonstrate *sufficient technical knowledge* and *competence,* and (8) exhibit *strong interpersonal skills* in dealing with consumers. In turn, this preliminary information can be used as a guideline for collecting data from a larger, more representative sample of customers about important service quality attributes. During the discovery process, researchers must be careful to include in the qualitative procedures people who are representative of the defined target

Domain of observables The set of identifiable and measurable components associated with an abstract construct.

eXHIBIT 11.1 Examples of Concrete Features and Abstract Constructs of Objects

Objects	
Airplane	**Concrete properties:** Number of engines, height, weight, length, seating capacity, physical characteristics of seats, type of airplane, etc.
	Abstract properties: Quality of in-flight cabin service, comfort of seating, smoothness of takeoff and landing, etc.
Consumer	**Concrete properties:** Age, sex, marital status, income, brand last purchased, dollar amount of purchase, types of products purchased, color of eyes and hair, etc.
	Abstract properties: Attitudes toward a product, brand loyalty, high-involvement purchases, emotions (love, fear, anxiety), intelligence, personality, risk taker, etc.
Organization	**Concrete properties:** Name of company, number of employees, number of locations, total assets, Fortune 500 rating, computer capacity, types and numbers of products and service offerings, type of industry membership, etc.
	Abstract properties: Competence of employees, quality control, channel power, competitive advantages, company image, consumer-oriented practices, etc.
Marketing Constructs	
Brand loyalty	**Concrete properties:** A particular purchase pattern exhibited toward a specific brand name product or service, the number of times a particular brand is purchased, the frequency of purchases of a particular brand, amount of time needed to select a brand.
	Abstract properties: The degree a person likes/dislikes a particular brand, the degree of satisfaction expressed toward a brand, a person's overall attitude toward the brand.
Customer satisfaction	**Concrete properties:** Identifiable attributes that make up a product, service, or experience.
	Abstract properties: The degree that a person is "delighted" with a specific experience; liking/disliking of the individual attributes making up the experience, product, or service; expressions of positive feelings toward the product, service, or experience.
Service quality	**Concrete properties:** Identifiable attributes (or dimensions) that make up a service encounter or experience (i.e., level of interaction, personal communications, service provider's knowledge, etc.).
	Abstract properties: Expectations held about each identifiable attribute, evaluative judgment of performance.
Advertising recall	**Concrete properties:** Factual properties of the ad (i.e., message, symbols, movement, models, text, etc.), aided and unaided recognition of the facts.
	Abstract properties: Interpretations of the factual elements in the ad, favorable/unfavorable judgments, degree of affective attachment to ad.

population. It is also necessary to evaluate the extent to which the actions taken as a result of the preliminary insights fit the organization's goals and objectives. For instance, most customers usually desire lower service prices. Yet, if the dealership is price-competitive in the marketplace, then it may not be in the best interests of the dealership to reduce prices.

Content validity The subjective yet systematic assessment of how well a construct's measurable components represent that construct.

Convergent validity When the researcher's measures of a construct are highly correlated with known existing measures of the same construct.

Assessing Construct Validity

It is essential to assess the *validity* of the construct, especially if the construct is believed to be multidimensional. It is important to note that assessing the validity of a construct is actually an after-the-fact activity because the process requires researchers to create a set of scale measurements for each of the construct's domain components and collect data on each of those components. Then researchers need to perform statistical analyses to test for content validity, convergent validity, and discriminant validity.[3] **Content validity** (sometimes referred to as *face validity*) is the systematic assessment of how well a construct's measurable components represent that construct. **Convergent validity** focuses on how well the construct's measurement positively correlates with different measurements of the same construct. For researchers to be able to evaluate convergent validity, they must use several different measurement approaches to evaluate the construct. For **discriminant validity,** researchers must determine whether the construct being investigated differs significantly from other constructs that are different. Finally, in some cases, researchers evaluate **nomological validity,** or how well one particular construct theoretically compares with other established constructs that are related yet different.

Discriminant validity The existence of a negative correlation between the measurement of one construct and those measures of another construct.

Nomological validity Assessment of how well one construct theoretically fits within a network of other established constructs that are related yet different.

Usually one of two approaches is used to collect data for assessing construct validity. If there are enough resources, researchers will conduct a pilot study among 50 to 100 people believed to be representative of the defined target population. In situations where resources are not available for a pilot study, researchers will attempt to approximate content validity by having a panel of experts independently judge the dimensionality of the construct. While these approaches have become common measurement practices, they contain several weaknesses.

Inappropriate Scale Measurement Formats

When after-the-fact data are used to assess construct validity, the scale point descriptors used in collecting the data can cause inaccuracies.[4] Thus, using untested or inappropriate scale measurement indicators to measure the construct creates measurement artifacts that lead to misinterpretations of the true components as well as the true dimensionality traits of the construct. In this situation, the data are driving the researcher's theoretical framework instead of theory driving the measurement process. A process to overcome this weakness is **direct cognitive structural analysis,** in which respondents are asked to determine whether an attribute is part of the construct and, if so, how important it is to that construct.[5]

Direct cognitive structural analysis A data analysis technique that assesses how well the identifiable attributes of a construct reflect that construct and their importance to it.

Another element that impacts assessment of construct validity but focuses more on scale measurement is **scale reliability.** Here researchers determine the extent to which the scale used to measure the construct consistently measured what it was intended to measure. While reliability of scale measurements is a necessary but not by itself a sufficient condition for accurately determining construct validity, scale reliability remains an important element in the process of collecting high-quality data.

Scale reliability The extent to which a scale can produce the same measurement results in repeated trials.

Inappropriate Set of Respondents

In academic research, researchers too often rely on college students' input to determine the components of the construct being investigated. Although college students are consumers and may have some knowledge and experience with certain products and services, in most cases their attitudes and buying behaviors are not representative of the general population or of many specifically defined target populations. A second problem relating to using college students in construct development is that student samples typically are drawn using convenience sampling. Convenience sampling does not guarantee true representation of a college student population, much less some other target population. As a result, the components originally thought to make up the construct may be different when the study is extended to another sample of the target population. The nearby A Closer Look at Research (In the Field) box provides an example of this problem as it occurred in a banking study.

Construct Operationalization

Operationalization Explaining a construct's meaning in measurement terms by specifying the activities or operations necessary to measure it.

Operationalization is when researchers explain a construct's meaning in measurement terms by specifying the activities or operations necessary to measure it. The process focuses on the design and use of questions and scale measurements to gather the needed data. Since many constructs, such as satisfaction, preferences, emotions, quality images, and

A Closer Look at Research

Problem in Construct Development

A marketing researcher wanted to identify the areas people might use in their process of judging banking service quality. The researcher conducted several focus groups among both undergraduate students in a basic marketing course and graduate students in a marketing management course to identify the service activities and offerings that might represent service quality. The researcher's rationale for using these groups was that they did have experience in conducting bank transactions, they were consumers, and the researcher had easy access to them for their opinions. The preliminary results of the focus group interviews revealed that the students used four dimensions for judging a bank's service quality: (1) interpersonal social skills of bank staff, (2) reliability of bank statements, (3) convenience of ATM delivery systems, and (4) diagnostic competence of bank tellers.

A month later, the researcher conducted four focus groups among known customers of one of the large banks in Charlotte, North Carolina. The preliminary results clearly suggested those customers used seven dimensions for judging a bank's service quality. Those dimensions were identified as the bank's ability to: (1) communicate with and listen to consumers; (2) demonstrate diagnostic competence in understanding the customer's banking needs and wants; (3) elicit sincere empathy by showing concern for how consumers interpret their requirements; (4) be tactful in responding to customers' questions, objections, or problems; (5) create an impression of reliability and credibility inherent in a bank service encounter; (6) demonstrate sufficient technological competence in handling the critical aspects of bank transactions; and (7) exhibit strong positive interpersonal social skills in conducting bank transactions.

The researcher was in a tentative position of not knowing for sure whether people perceive bank service quality as having four or seven critical components. Which qualitative source of information should be used to better understand the construct of bank service quality? Which preliminary information should the researcher rely on to conduct the empirical survey on bank service quality? These issues would directly affect the operationalization of construct development.[6]

brand loyalty cannot be directly observed or measured, researchers attempt to indirectly measure them through operationalization of their components.

For example, one researcher developed over 100 questions to determine if customers were satisfied with their recent automobile purchase and the dealer's service.[7] Using a variety of different measurement formats, customers were asked to rate a number of components, including the salesperson's listening skills; the reliability of the service; the appearance of the service facilities; and the serviceperson's interpersonal skills. They were also asked about attributes of the vehicle purchased, including road-holding ability, overall comfort, cost of routine maintenance, overall durability, overall exterior styling, visibility, steering precision, security features, fuel economy, and overall power. Exhibit 11.2 illustrates two different measurement approaches used to capture data about the construct of automobile dealership service satisfaction.

The examples in Exhibit 11.2 suggest that assessing what appears to be a simple construct of service satisfaction can be more involved than it might seem at first. Here, researchers are trying to fully capture information on all dimensions that may affect a customer's service satisfaction. Certainly this approach will give dealerships a more accurate basis for evaluating how successful they have been in satisfying customers. Moreover, this type of in-depth analysis provides a business with better opportunities to pinpoint areas of concern

EXHIBIT 11.2 Selected Question/Scales Used to Measure Service Satisfaction with Auto Dealerships

Example 1:

Now with all the knowledge, opinions, feelings, and personal experiences you have acquired as a customer with your primary *automobile service provider* (ASP), I would like to know how satisfied or dissatisfied you are concerning several service features. Using the scale described below, where

6 = Completely satisfied	4 = Somewhat satisfied	2 = Definitely dissatisfied
5 = Definitely satisfied	3 = Somewhat dissatisfied	1 = Completely dissatisfied

please write a number from 1 to 6 in the space provided that best expresses how satisfied or dissatisfied you are with each listed service feature.

____ Convenience of ASP's location	____ ASP's communication skills
____ Flexibility in ASP's operating hours	____ Availability of quality service offerings
____ Service provider's personal social skills	____ Overall reputation of your primary ASP
____ Personnel's understanding of customer needs	____ ASP's concern of putting its customers "first"
____ Reliability/credibility of ASP's service providers	____ ASP's listening skills
____ Service provider's technical knowledge/competence	____ Quality of the ASP's products (or services)

Example 2:

Using the educational letter grading system of "A," "B," "C," "D," and "F," please circle the one "letter grade" that best expresses the overall grade that you would give each of the following listed service factors at your primary ASP.

a. The communication skills of the service people at my primary ASP are . . .	A	B	C	D	F
b. The listening capabilities of the service people at my primary ASP are . . .	A	B	C	D	F
c. The ability of the service staff to understand my various repair/maintenance service needs is . . .	A	B	C	D	F
d. The ability of service employees to demonstrate understanding of my auto service needs (or requirements) from my point of view is . . .	A	B	C	D	F
e. The service personnel's ability to respond quickly to my objections (or problems, questions) is . . .	A	B	C	D	F
f. The reliability (or credibility) demonstrated by the service representatives are . . .	A	B	C	D	F
g. The technical knowledge (or understanding) demonstrated by the service personnel is . . .	A	B	C	D	F
h. The personal social skills used by the employees in dealing with me are . . .	A	B	C	D	F
i. The facilities/equipment/personnel all demonstrate that it is a "professional" organization to deal with . . .	A	B	C	D	F

and take corrective actions. With only a single-question approach, corrective action would be very difficult if not impossible since the researcher would not be able to determine the exact problem area. After constructs and their possible traits have been adequately identified and understood, researchers then need to create appropriate scale measurements.

Basic Concepts of Scale Measurement

Types of Data Collected in Research Practices

Regardless of whether researchers want to collect secondary or primary data, all information is drawn from question responses based on verifiable facts about people, objects, or phenomena; thoughts or feelings; past or current actions; or planned future actions of people or organizations. Thus, any response can be classified as belonging to one of four basic states of nature: verifiable facts, mental thoughts/emotional feelings, past or current behaviors, and planned future behavior intentions. To simplify discussion of these different states of nature, we will refer to verifiable facts as *state-of-being data,* mental thoughts and emotional feelings as *state-of-mind data,* past and current behaviors as *state-of-behavior data,* and planned future behavior intentions as *state-of-intention data.*

State-of-Being Data (Verifiable Facts)

State-of-being data The physical and/or demographic or socioeconomic characteristics of people, objects, and organizations.

When the problem requires researchers to collect responses that are relevant to the physical, demographic, or socioeconomic characteristics of individuals, objects, or organizations, the resulting data are considered verifiable facts, or state-of-being data. **State-of-being data** represent factual characteristics that can be verified through sources other than the person providing the responses. For example, researchers can directly ask respondents their sex, age, income level, education level, marital status, number of children, occupation, height, weight, color of eyes, and telephone number—or researchers can obtain these data through secondary sources such as birth certificates, loan applications, income tax returns, driver's licenses, public documents at a county courthouse, the telephone company, and so on. For organizations, data on total dollar/unit sales, computer capacity, number of employees, total assets, number and types of stores, and so on, often can be obtained through secondary sources, eliminating the need to ask direct questions about them. The same holds true for the physical characteristics of many objects. The main point to remember about state-of-being data is that researchers are not limited to collecting the data by only asking questions of subjects.

State-of-Mind Data (Mental Thoughts or Emotional Feelings)

State-of-mind data The mental attributes or emotional feelings of people.

State-of-mind data represent the mental attributes or emotional feelings of individuals that are not directly observable or available through some type of external source. State-of-mind data exist only within the minds of people. To collect such data, researchers have to ask a person to respond to questions. Verification through secondary or external sources is all but impossible. Some examples of state-of-mind data would be a person's personality traits, attitudes, feelings, perceptions, beliefs, cognitive decision processes, product/service preferences, awareness levels, and various images. Therefore, data quality and accuracy are limited to the degree of honesty of the person providing the responses to the researcher's questions.

State-of-Behavior Data (Past and Current Behaviors)

State-of-behavior data A person's or organization's current observable or recorded actions or reactions.

State-of-behavior data represent individuals' or organizations' current observable actions or recorded past actions. Researchers have several options available to obtain state-of-behavior data. A person can be asked questions about current or past behavior. For example, a person could be asked to respond to questions such as "In the past six months, how many times have you purchased dry cereal for your household?" or "In a typical week, how often do you go shopping at a mall?" To obtain current behavior, a person could be asked to respond to such questions as "Are you currently enrolled in college?" or "How many courses are you currently taking in marketing?"

Another option is to use either trained observers or mechanical/electronic devices to observe and record current behavior. For example, disguised observers or hidden cameras can be used to selectively observe and record customers' frozen-food selections at the local Safeway supermarket. Such behavioral data might include length of time in the frozen-food section of the store, the specific brands or types of frozen food inspected or selected, the number of units of a product that were placed in the shopping cart, and so on.

A third option useful for collecting data on past behavior is to find records of previously conducted behavior. For example, researchers helping the Santa Fe Grill owners can examine the restaurant's charge-card receipts over a specified period to determine how often a selected individual came in and ate at that particular restaurant. There are limitations to the quality and accuracy of data using this option, and in general verification of an individual's past behaviors through any type of external, secondary source is a difficult process in terms of time, effort, and accuracy. This method places heavy emphasis on the existence of well-documented behaviors.

State-of-Intention Data (Planned Future Behaviors)

State-of-intention data A person's or organization's expressed plans of future behavior.

State-of-intention data represent individuals' or organizations' expressed plans of future behavior. State-of-intention data are collected by asking people to respond to questions about behaviors that have yet to take place. For instance, researchers can ask such questions as "How likely are you to purchase a new Mazda in the next six months?" or "Do you plan to come and visit the Museum of Science and Industry next time you are in Chicago?" or "How likely would you be to buy Tide the next time you need laundry detergent?" Like state-of-behavior data, state-of-intention data are very difficult to verify through external, secondary sources, but verification sometimes is possible.

The Nature of Scale Measurement

Scale measurement The process of assigning descriptors to represent the range of possible responses to a question about a particular object or construct.

Scale points Designated degrees of intensity assigned to the responses in a given questioning or observation method.

To be successful in generating primary information to examine business problems, researchers must be able to gather the appropriate data. The quantity and quality of the responses associated with any question or observation technique depend directly on the scale measurements used by researchers. **Scale measurement** is the process of assigning a set of descriptors to represent the range of possible responses to a question about a particular object or construct.[8]

The focus of this process is on measuring the existence of various characteristics of a person's response. Scale measurement directly determines the amount of data that can be obtained from a given questioning or observation method. Scale measurement attempts to assign designated degrees of intensity to the responses. These degrees of intensity are commonly referred to as **scale points.** For example, a retailer might want to know how important a preselected set of store or service features is to consumers in deciding where to shop. The level of importance attached to each store or service feature would be determined by the researcher's assignment of a range of intensity descriptors (scale points) to represent the possible degrees of importance (definitely, moderately, slightly, not at all important) associated with each feature.

Properties of Scale Measurements

Researchers consider four properties in developing scales: *assignment, order, distance,* and *origin* (see Exhibit 11.3).

Assignment

Assignment property The employment of unique descriptors to identify each object in a set.

The **assignment property,** also referred to as *description* or *category property,* is where the researcher uses unique descriptors, or labels, to identify or assign each object within a set.[9] This property enables a researcher to categorize the responses into mutually exclusive groups, each with its own identity. Any descriptor can be used for a response. An everyday example would be the use of numbers (22, 34, 45, etc.) to identify the players on a basketball team so the scorekeeper can correctly record points scored or fouls committed. In research, examples would be yes and no responses to the question "Are you going to purchase a new automobile within the next six months?"; the use of colors (red, green, blue, etc.) to identify cars, clothes, or bathroom towels; and the use of size indicators (large, medium, small, etc.) to identify the quantity of soft drinks, or fitting of clothes, or amount of pizza people might purchase.

eXHIBIT 11.3 Four Scaling Properties: Description and Examples

Scaling Properties	Description and Examples
Assignment property	Use of unique descriptors to identify an object in a set. **Examples:** The use of numbers (10, 38, 44, 18, 23, etc.); the use of colors (red, blue, green, pink, etc.); yes and no responses to questions that identify objects into mutually exclusive groups.
Order property	Establishes "relative magnitudes" among the descriptors, creating hierarchical rank-order relationships among objects. **Examples:** 1st place is better than 4th place finish; a 5-foot person is shorter than a 7-foot person; a regular customer purchases more often than a rare customer.
Distance property	Enables the researcher and respondent to identify, understand, and accurately express absolute (or assumed) differences between objects. **Examples:** Family A with six children living at home, compared to family B with three children at home, has three more children than family B; differences in income ranges or age categories.
Origin property	Scale descriptor that is designated a unique starting point or as being a "true natural zero" or "true state of nothing." **Examples:** Asking a respondent his or her weight or current age; the number of times a person shops at a supermarket; or the market share of a specific brand of hand soap.

Order

Order property The relative magnitude assigned to each scale point descriptor.

The **order property** is the relative magnitude between the descriptors used as scale points.[10] Relative magnitude between descriptors is based on the relationships between two or more descriptors. For example, there are only three relationships between responses A and B: A can be *greater than* B; A can be *less than* B; or A can be *equal to* B. When respondents can identify and understand a "greater than" or a "less than" relationship between two or more objects or responses, the order scaling property is established and a meaningful rank order can be identified among the reported responses. Some examples of the order property include the following: 1 is less than 5; "extremely satisfied" is more intense than "somewhat satisfied"; "very important" is more important than "slightly important"; "somewhat disagree" involves less disagreement than "definitely disagree"; and a person holding a master of business administration (MBA) degree has more formal years of education than a person holding an associate of arts (AA) degree. When the order scaling property is included in a set of scale points, it enables the researcher to establish either a "highest to lowest" or a "lowest to highest" rank order among the responses. It is important to remember that the order scaling property, by itself, identifies only the relative differences between responses and not the absolute differences.

Distance

Distance property The measurement scheme that expresses the exact (or absolute) difference between each of the descriptors, scale points, or responses.

The **distance property** expresses the absolute difference between each of the descriptors or scale points.[11] In other words, the distance property shows the researcher knows the absolute magnitude that exists between each response to a question. For example, family A drives two cars, and family B drives four cars. Thus, family A has two fewer cars than family B. A student who has to travel 20 miles to school drives twice as many miles as a student who drives only 10 miles to the same school. The distance scaling property is restricted to situations where the responses represent some type of natural numerical answer.

In many cases researchers believe the scales associated with collecting state-of-mind data activate the distance property. This is a myth that causes misunderstanding of particular types of data and their structures. For example, some researchers believe that "extremely spicy" is one unit of spiciness away from "very spicy," or that "strongly agree" is two units of agreement away from "somewhat agree," or that "extremely important" is four units of importance away from "only slightly important." In all these examples, there is no way researchers can statistically verify that the assumed absolute relationships between those scale descriptors exist.

Origin

Origin property Having a unique starting point in a set of scale point descriptors that is designated as a true zero.

The **origin property** refers to the use of a unique starting point in a set of scale points that is designated as being a "true natural zero" or true state of nothing. The origin property relates to a numbering system where zero is the displayed starting point in a set of possible responses. It must be noted that a response of "don't know," "no opinion," "neither agree nor disagree," "don't care," "not at all important," "no response," and so on, to a question does not represent the zero origin property.[12] Rather, origin responses may be represented by answers to questions like current age; present income; number of dependent children living at home; number of miles one travels to go shopping at a supermarket; and number of times a person purchases a specific product or service in a week.

When developing scales, the more scaling properties that can be simultaneously activated in a scale design, the more complete the collected data. Note that each scaling property builds on the previous one. This means that any scale will have the assignment property. A scale that includes the order property automatically possesses the assignment property. If the researcher designs a scale with the distance property, the scale also has assignment and order. Scales that are built with the origin property also have assignment, order, and distance properties.

Basic Levels of Scales

Nominal scale The type of scale in which the questions require respondents to provide only some type of descriptor as the response.

While scaling properties determine the amount of data obtained from any scale design, all scale measurements can be logically and accurately classified as one of four basic scale levels: nominal, ordinal, interval, or ratio. There are specific relationships between the level of scale and which scaling properties are activated within the scale (see Exhibit 11.4).

Nominal Scales

A **nominal scale** is the most basic of scale designs. In this level of scale, questions require respondents to provide only some type of descriptor as the response. Responses do not

eXHIBIT 11.4 Relationships between Levels of Scales and Scaling Properties

	Scaling Properties			
Level of Scale	**Assignment**	**Order**	**Distance**	**Origin**
Nominal	**Yes**	No	No	No
Ordinal	**Yes**	**Yes**	No	No
Interval	**Yes**	**Yes**	**Yes**	No
Ratio	**Yes**	**Yes**	**Yes**	**Yes**

contain any level of intensity. Therefore, it is impossible to establish any form of rank order among the set of given responses. That is, nominal scales provide data that cannot be arranged in a "greater than/less than" or "bigger than/smaller than" hierarchical pattern. Nominal scales allow the researcher only to categorize the responses into mutually exclusive subsets that do not illustrate distances between them.[13] Examples of nominal scales are shown in Exhibit 11.5.

Ordinal Scales

Ordinal scale A scale that allows a respondent to express relative magnitude between the answers to a question.

An **ordinal scale** has both assignment and order scaling properties. This level of scale enables respondents to express relative magnitude between the answers to a question. The responses can be rank ordered into a hierarchical pattern.[14] Thus, it is easy to determine "greater than/less than," "higher than/lower than," "more often/less often," "more important/less important," or "less agreement/more agreement" types of relationships between the responses. But ordinal scales do not enable researchers to determine the absolute difference in any of the ordinal relationships. In practice, almost all state-of-mind data responses are collected using ordinal scales. Exhibit 11.6 provides several examples of ordinal scales.

Interval Scales

Interval scale A scale that measures absolute differences between each scale point.

An **interval scale** has not only assignment and order scaling properties but also the distance property. With the distance property, researchers can measure absolute differences between each scale point. When scales have the distance property, more powerful statistical

eXHIBIT 11.5 Examples of Nominal Scales

Example 1:
Please indicate your current marital status.
___ Married ___ Single ___ Separated ___ Divorced ___ Widowed

Example 2:
Do you like or dislike chocolate ice cream?
___ Like ___ Dislike

Example 3:
Please check those information and HCP service areas in which you have had a face-to-face or telephone conversation with a representative of your main HCP in the past six months. (Check as many as apply.)
___ Appointments ___ Treatment at home ___ Referral to other HCP
___ Prescriptions ___ Medical test results ___ Hospital stay
___ Some other service area(s); Please specify ______________________

Example 4:
Please indicate your gender:
___ Female ___ Male

Example 5:
Which of the following supermarkets have you shopped at in the last 30 days? (Please check all that apply.)
___ Albertson ___ Winn-Dixie ___ Publix ___ Safeway ___ Kash&Karry ___ I.G.A.

EXHIBIT 11.6 Examples of Ordinal Scales

Example 1:

Which category best describes your knowledge about the services offered by your main health care provider?

(Please check just one category.)

___ Complete knowledge of services
___ Good knowledge of services
___ Basic knowledge of services
___ Little knowledge of services
___ No knowledge of services

Example 2:

The following list of library services, activities, and resources may or may not be important to you when using a library. Using the scale provided below, for each listed item please check the box that best expresses how important you feel it is that a library provides that item.

Services, Activities, Resources	Extremely Important	Definitely Important	Somewhat Important	Not at All Important
Loans of books, CDs, videos, etc.	___	___	___	___
Availability of current magazines	___	___	___	___
Children's programs	___	___	___	___
Adult programs	___	___	___	___
Computer classes or assistance	___	___	___	___
Reference material for business	___	___	___	___
Online catalog of resources in region	___	___	___	___
General reference material	___	___	___	___

Example 3:

We would like to know your preferences for actually using different banking methods. Among the methods listed below, please indicate your top three preferences using a "1" to represent your first choice, a "2" for your second preference, and a "3" for your third choice of methods.

(Please write the numbers on the lines next to your selected methods.)

_____ Inside the bank
_____ Drive-in (drive-up) windows
_____ ATM
_____ Bank by mail
_____ Bank by telephone
_____ Internet banking

Example 4:

For each pair of retail discount stores, circle the store you would be more likely to patronize:

Kmart or Target   Target or Wal-Mart   Wal-Mart or Kmart

Example 5:

Which one statement best describes your opinion of the quality of an Intel Pentium processor?

(Please check just one statement.)

____ Higher than AMD's Athlon processor
____ About the same as AMD's Athlon processor
____ Lower than AMD's Athlon processor

techniques can be used to analyze the data.[15] With interval scales, researchers can identify not only some type of hierarchical order in the data but also the actual differences between the data points. Moreover, it is possible to calculate means and standard deviations for these scales. Interval scales are most appropriate when the researcher wants to collect state-of-behavior, state-of-intention, or certain types of state-of-being data. Exhibit 11.7 illustrates some examples of interval scales.

eXHIBIT 11.7 Examples of Interval Scales

Example 1:

For each of the brands of soft drinks listed below, please circle the number that best expresses your overall performance judgment of that brand.

Soft Drink Brands	Very Poor					Outstanding
Coke	1	2	3	4	5	6	7
Pepsi	1	2	3	4	5	6	7
Mountain Dew	1	2	3	4	5	6	7
A&W Root Beer	1	2	3	4	5	6	7
Sprite	1	2	3	4	5	6	7
Seven-Up	1	2	3	4	5	6	7

Example 2:

Using the scale provided below, select the number that best describes how important each of the attributes were in your deciding which restaurant to eat at. **(Please place your numerical response on the line provided next to each attribute.)**

Importance Scale

1 = Not at all important	3 = Somewhat important	5 = Definitely important
2 = Only slightly important	4 = Important	6 = Extremely important

Restaurant Attributes

____ Quality of the food	____ Dining atmosphere	____ Convenience of location
____ Wide variety in selection	____ Speed of service	____ Knowledgeable waitstaff
____ Takes reservations	____ Reasonably priced entrees	____ Valet parking

Example 3:

Consider the different banking methods you may or may not use. We would like to know your feelings toward these methods. Next to each of the banking methods shown below, please circle the number that best describes the degree to which you like or dislike using that method.

Banking Methods	Very Much Dislike Using								Very Much Like Using
Inside the bank	1	2	3	4	5	6	7	8	9	10
Drive-up window	1	2	3	4	5	6	7	8	9	10
24-hour ATM	1	2	3	4	5	6	7	8	9	10
Bank by mail	1	2	3	4	5	6	7	8	9	10
Bank by phone	1	2	3	4	5	6	7	8	9	10
Bank by Internet	1	2	3	4	5	6	7	8	9	10

eXHIBIT 11.8 Examples of Ratio Scales

Example 1:

Please circle the number of children under 18 years of age currently living in your household.

0 1 2 3 4 5 6 7 (If more than 7, please specify: ____.)

Example 2:

In the past seven days, how many times did you go shopping at a retail shopping mall?

_______ # of times

Example 3:

In whole years, what is your current age?

______ # of years old

Example 4:

When buying soft drinks for your household, approximately how many 12-ounce six-packs do you typically buy each week for each of the following brands?

____ Regular Pepsi	____ Regular Coke	____ Orange Crush
____ Diet Pepsi	____ Diet Coke	____ Sprite
____ A&W Root Beer	____ Mountain Dew	____ 7UP

Example 5:

In a typical 12-month period, how many miles do you drive your automobile and/or truck for personal activities?

____ # of miles driven in your car ____ # of miles driven in your truck

Ratio Scales

Ratio scale A scale that enables the researcher not only to identify the absolute differences between each scale point but also to make comparisons between the responses.

A **ratio scale** is the only scaling level that activates all four scaling properties. Ratio scales are the most sophisticated scales because they enable researchers not only to identify the absolute differences between each scale point but also to make absolute comparisons between the responses.[16] For instance, in collecting data about how many cars are driven by households in Atlanta, Georgia, researchers know that the difference between driving one car and driving three cars is always going to be two. Furthermore, when comparing a one-car family to a three-car family, researchers can assume that the three-car family will have significantly higher total car insurance and maintenance costs than the one-car family.

Remember that ratio scales are designed to enable a "true natural zero" or "true state of nothing" response to be a valid response to the question. Typically, ratio scales require respondents to provide a specific numerical value as their response, regardless of whether or not a set of scale points is used. Exhibit 11.8 shows several examples of ratio scales. For more examples of the various types of scales go to www.mhhe.com/hair4e and follow the links.

Developing and Refining Measurement Scales

The key to designing high-quality scales is: (1) understanding the problem, (2) establishing detailed data requirements, (3) identifying and developing constructs, and (4) understanding that measurement scales consist of three critical components (the question, the attributes, and the scale point descriptors). After the problem and data requirements are

EXHIBIT 11.9 Types of Question Phrasing

Information Requirement: To determine how often consumers purchase pizza from Papa John's.

NOMINAL QUESTION PHRASING:

When you are in the mood for pizza, do you usually purchase a pizza from Papa John's?

The logical response to this question would be a simple **YES** or **NO.**

ORDINAL QUESTION PHRASING:

When you are in the mood for pizza, how often do you purchase a pizza from Papa John's? **(Please check only one response.)**

___ Never ___ Seldom ___ Occasionally ___ Usually ___ Every time

OR

In a typical month, approximately how often do you purchase a pizza from Papa John's?

___ None ___ 1 to 3 times ___ 4 to 6 times ___ 7 to 10 times ___ more than 10 times

INTERVAL QUESTION PHRASING:

Thinking about your pizza purchases over the past six months, please circle the number that best expresses how often you have purchased a pizza from each of the listed pizza chains.

Pizza Chain	**Never**								**Every Time**
Lenny & Vinny's	0	1	2	3	4	5	6	7	8
Little Caesars	0	1	2	3	4	5	6	7	8
Papa John's	0	1	2	3	4	5	6	7	8
Pizza Hut	0	1	2	3	4	5	6	7	8
Westshore Pizza	0	1	2	3	4	5	6	7	8
Windy City	0	1	2	3	4	5	6	7	8

RATIO QUESTION PHRASING:

In the past three (3) months, how many times have you purchased a pizza from Papa John's? **(Please write the # of times on the line provided.)**

__________ # of times

understood, researchers must develop constructs. Next, the appropriate scale format (nominal, ordinal, interval, or ratio) must be selected. For example, if the problem requires interval data, but researchers ask the questions using a nominal scale, the wrong level of data will be collected and the final information that can be generated will not be helpful in resolving the initial problem. To illustrate this point, Exhibit 11.9 offers examples of the different levels of data that are obtained on the basis of how the question is phrased to a respondent. These examples show that how the questions are phrased will directly affect the amount of data collected. It should be clear that nominal scale questions provide the least amount of data and ratio scale questions provide the most specific data.

Criteria for Scale Development

Once the importance of question phrasing is understood, the researcher can now focus on developing the most appropriate descriptors for the scale points. Criteria for scale development are summarized in Exhibit 11.10.

EXHIBIT 11.10 Criteria for Scale Development

Scale Development Criteria	Description
Intelligibility of the questions	Use language in the questions and responses that is familiar to the respondents to ensure clarity and understanding.
Appropriateness of scale descriptors	Narrative scale point descriptors should accurately reflect the type of data being sought in the setup part of the scale measurement.
Discriminatory power of the scale descriptors	Make sure each scale point descriptor is understood by the respondent as being mutually exclusive from each of the other scale point descriptors as well as the use of the appropriate number of descriptors to accurately represent the intended intensity levels of the descriptors.
Reliability of the scale	Use a pretest to ensure that scale measures meet a desired minimum level of consistency in repeated trials.
Equal positive/negative scale descriptors	An equal number of both positive and negative descriptors should be used (balanced scale).
Inclusion of a neutral response choice	When attempting to capture state-of-mind or certain types of behavior-intention data, consideration must be given to including or excluding "neutral" or "not applicable" scale responses.
Measures of central tendency and dispersion	Consider the statistics and data analysis that will be used after the data are collected, and evaluate how different levels of scales determine the appropriate statistics (i.e., mode, median, mean, frequency distribution, range, and standard deviation).

Intelligibility of the Questions

Researchers must consider the *intellectual capacity* and *language ability* of those to whom the scale will be administered. Researchers should assume that prospective respondents do not know the research project's information requirements. This is, researchers must not automatically assume respondents understand the questions being asked or the response choices. The **intelligibility criterion** is the degree to which setup and questions are understood by respondents. Appropriate language must be used in both the questions and the answer choices.

Intelligibility criterion The degree to which the questions on a scale are understood by the respondents.

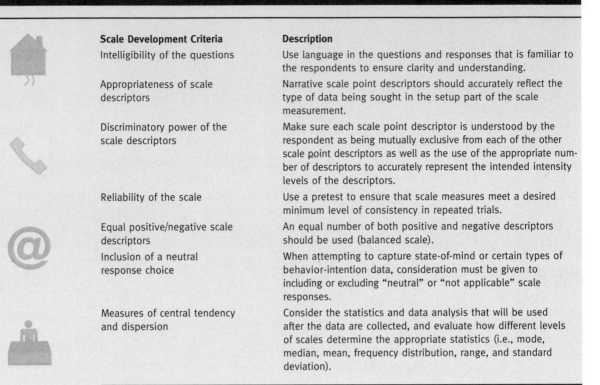

Researchers must try to eliminate guessing by respondents. Moreover, respondents should be able to understand what types of data are being asked for and how to respond. Referring back to the scale used in Example 3 of Exhibit 11.7, suppose that in the setup portion of that scale researchers used only the first portion of the setup ("Consider the different banking methods you may or may not use. We would like to know your feelings toward these methods."). This would suggest that the researchers assumed the respondents would automatically understand how to complete the scale question. Without the rest of the setup (the exact instructions), respondents might not know what to do. Such assumptions on the part of researchers can easily increase the likelihood of missing responses. The intelligibility factor thus promotes the use of "respondent instructions" in scaling designs, especially in self-administered surveys. For in-person or telephone interviews, "interviewer instructions" also may have to be included in the question/setup portion of the scale measurements.

Appropriateness of Scale Descriptors

Appropriateness of descriptors The extent to which the scale point elements match the data being sought.

Scale descriptors must match the type of data being collected. Thus, researchers must consider the **appropriateness of the descriptors.** That is, the adjectives or adverbs used to indicate the relative magnitudes must be related to the scale descriptors. Let's say, for example, researchers want to find out respondents' opinions about whether or not the Kroger supermarket has "competitive meat prices." The task becomes one of determining which scale descriptors best represent the notion of "competitive prices."

There are several creative ways of representing competitive prices. First, if researchers design the question/setup to ask the respondents to agree or disagree that "Kroger has competitive meat prices," then the appropriate set of scale descriptors would be levels of agreement/disagreement ("strongly agree," "agree," "neither agree nor disagree," "disagree," "strongly disagree"). Stating the question in terms of competitiveness would require an ordinal set of descriptors such as "extremely competitive," "definitely competitive," "generally competitive," "only slightly competitive," and "not at all competitive." In contrast, it would be inappropriate to try to represent respondents' opinions about "competitive prices" using a performance-oriented set of descriptors like "excellent," "very good," "good," "average," "fair," and "poor."

Discriminatory Power of Scale Descriptors

Discriminatory power The scale's ability to significantly differentiate between the responses.

This criterion relates to situations when either (1) the problem requires the inclusion of relative magnitudes to the set of possible responses or (2) the researcher decides to establish sizes of differences between the scale points. The **discriminatory power** of a scale is the scale's ability to significantly differentiate between the responses.[17] Researchers must decide how many scale points are necessary to represent the relative magnitudes of a response scale. Remember, the more scale points, the greater the discriminatory power of the scale.

There is no clear rule about the number of scale points that should be used in creating a scale. Some researchers believe scales should be between five and seven points[18] because some respondents find it difficult to make a choice when there are more than seven levels. To illustrate this point, suppose Marriott International is interested in determining which hotel features patrons consider important in their process of choosing a hotel. In developing an "importance" scale to capture the relative magnitude of importance attributed to each hotel feature, researchers must subjectively decide how many recognizable levels of importance exist in the minds of travelers. Researchers must first understand that the dichotomous scale descriptors are *"important"* and *"not important."* Second, researchers must decide how detailed or how varied the importance responses need to be to answer the research question.[19] For example, an importance scale may consist of five different levels of importance. The five differential degrees usually are expressed as "extremely," *"definitely," "generally," "somewhat,"* and *"slightly"* important. But an importance scale can also use seven points and sometimes more.

The more scale points researchers use, the greater the opportunity there is for variability in the data—an important consideration in data analysis. In the authors' experience, in most instances a 7-point scale is preferable and can be understood by most respondents. But one must always consider respondents' experience with scaled questions and their ability to discriminate when more scale points are used.

By understanding the makeup of the importance scale, researchers can include variations that may better fit the specific information requirements of different situations. When developing an importance scale, remember the scale descriptors are not simply *"important"* and *"unimportant."* In reality, most human beings *do not think or express* their "not at all important" feelings in degrees of "unimportant" (e.g., "extremely unimportant," "definitely unimportant," "generally unimportant"). In addition, there are times when attempting to incorporate too many degrees of relative magnitude into the scale can cause problems. Suppose in the above Marriott hotel example researchers design an importance scale that consists of 15 scale descriptors and presents the scale as follows:

IMPORTANCE SCALE

Not at All Important 0 1 2 3 4 5 6 7 8 9 10 11 12 13 14 15 Extremely Important

While this scale denotes "not at all important" as being a "0" and "extremely important" as being a 15, it is unlikely that researchers or respondents can accurately attach any meaningful interpretation to the scale points of 1 through 14. This potential discriminatory power problem can exist in any type of scale design.

Reliability of the Scale

Scale reliability refers to the extent to which a scale can reproduce the same measurement results in repeated trials. Random error produces inconsistency in scale measurements that leads to lower scale reliability. Two of the techniques that help researchers assess the reliability of scales are test-retest and equivalent form.

Test-retest A technique of measuring scale reliability by administering the same scale to the same respondents at two different times or to two different samples of respondents under similar conditions.

First, the **test-retest** technique involves repeating the scale measurement with either the same sample of respondents at two different times or two different samples of respondents from the same defined target population under as nearly the same conditions as possible. The idea behind this approach is simply that if random variations are present, they will be revealed by variations in the scores between the two sampled measurements.[20] If there are very few differences between the first and second administrations of the scale, the measuring scale is viewed as being stable and therefore reliable. For example, assume that determining the teaching effectiveness associated with your marketing research course involved the use of a 28-item scale designed to measure the degree to which respondents agree or disagree with each item. To gather the data on teaching effectiveness, your professor administers this scale to the class after the 7th week of the semester and again after the 12th week. Using a mean analysis procedure on the items for each measurement period, the professor then runs correlation analysis on those mean values. If the correlation is high between the mean value measurements from the two assessment periods, the professor concludes that the reliability of the 28-item scale is high.

There are several potential problems with the test-retest approach. First, some of the students who completed the scale the first time might be absent for the second administration of the scale. Second, students might become sensitive to the scale measurement and therefore alter their responses in the second measurement. Third, environmental or personal factors may change between the two administrations, thus causing changes in student responses in the second measurement.

Equivalent form A technique to establish scale reliability by measuring and correlating the measures of two equivalent scaling instruments.

Some researchers believe the problems associated with the test-retest reliability technique can be avoided by using the **equivalent form** technique. In this technique, researchers create two similar yet different (equivalent) scale measurements for the given construct (e.g., teaching effectiveness) and administer both forms to either the same sample of respondents or two samples of respondents from the same defined target population.[21] In the marketing research course "teaching effectiveness' xample, the professor would construct two 28-item scales whose main difference would lie in the wording of the item statements, not the agree/disagree scaling points. Although the specific wording of the statements would be changed, their meaning would remain constant. After administering each of the scale measurements, the professor calculates the mean values for each item and then runs correlation analysis. Equivalent form reliability is assessed by measuring the correlations between the scores on the t scale measurements. High correlation values are interpreted as meaning high scale measurement reliability.

There are two potential drawbacks with the equivalent form reliability technique. First, if the testing process suggests that equivalence can be achieved, it might not be worth the time, effort, and expense of determining that two similar yet different scales can be used to measure the same construct. Second, it is difficult and perhaps impossible to create two totally equivalent scale measurements. Questions may be raised as to which scale measurement is the most appropriate to use in measuring teaching effectiveness.

When investigating multidimensional constructs, summated scale measurements tend to be the most appropriate scales. In this type of scale, each dimension represents some aspect of the construct. Thus, the construct is measured by the entire scale, not just one component. **Internal consistency** refers to the degree to which the various dimensions of a multidimensional construct correlate with the scale. That is, the set of items that make up the scale must be internally consistent.

Internal consistency The degree to which the various dimensions of a multidimensional construct correlate with the scale.

There are two popular techniques used to assess internal consistency: split-half tests and coefficient alpha, also referred to as Cronbach's alpha. In a **split-half test,** the items in the scale are divided into two halves (odd versus even attributes, or randomly) and the resulting halves' scores are correlated against one another. High correlations between the halves indicate good (or acceptable) internal consistency. A **coefficient alpha** takes the average of all possible split-half measures that result from different ways of splitting the scale items.[22] The coefficient value can range from 0 to 1, and, in most cases, a value of less than 0.6 would typically indicate marginal to low (unsatisfactory) internal consistency.

Split-half test A technique used to evaluate the internal consistency of measurement scales that have multiple dimensions.

Coefficient alpha A technique of taking the average of all possible split-half coefficients to measure the internal consistency of multidimensional scales.

Researchers must remember that just because their scale measurement designs are reliable, the data collected are not necessarily valid. Separate validity assessments must be made on the constructs being measured.

Positive/Negative Scale Descriptors

This scale development criterion relates to the researcher's decision to maintain objectivity in a scale that is designed to capture both positive and negative responses. To maintain scale objectivity, the researcher must design both positive and negative descriptors as scale points. For example, let's assume that J. D. Power and Associates wants to add to its "New Vehicle Survey" a single-item scale that measures a purchaser's satisfaction with his or her new vehicle's overall performance. Since most people would consider the feeling of satisfaction to be positive and the feeling of dissatisfaction to be negative, J. D. Power and Associates would need to decide whether or not the scale measurement should be "objective" and not bias the respondent's feelings one way or the other. By having equal relative magnitudes of satisfaction (positive) and dissatisfaction (negative), the scale measure would maintain a level of objectivity. Such a *balanced* scale measurement design might look like the following:

Based on your experiences with your new vehicle since owning and driving it, to what extent are you presently satisfied or dissatisfied with the overall performance of the vehicle?

(PLEASE CHECK THE ONE APPROPRIATE RESPONSE)

____ Completely satisfied (no dissatisfaction)	____ Slightly dissatisfied (some satisfaction)
____ Definitely satisfied	____ Generally dissatisfied
____ Generally satisfied	____ Definitely dissatisfied
____ Slightly satisfied (some dissatisfaction)	____ Completely dissatisfied (no satisfaction)

With a balanced scale, objectivity is maintained in both the question/setup portion of the scale and the descriptors.[23]

Now let's assume that J. D. Power and Associates wants to assess new-vehicle purchasers' satisfaction with their vehicle's overall performance and that dissatisfaction data are not important. This type of data requirement might be better met by using an unbalanced scale measurement[24] that placed heavier emphasis on the positive (satisfaction) scale descriptors than on the negative (dissatisfaction) ones. The *unbalanced* scale measurement design might look like the following:

Based on your experiences with your new vehicle since owning and driving it, to what extent are you presently satisfied with the overall performance of the vehicle?

(PLEASE CHECK THE ONE APPROPRIATE RESPONSE)

____ Completely satisfied	____ Generally satisfied	____ Dissatisfied
____ Definitely satisfied	____ Slightly satisfied	

It is important to remember that with an unbalanced scale measurement, objectivity is lower in both the question/setup portion of the scale and the descriptors.

Including a Neutral Response Choice

Forced-choice scale A symmetrically designed polar scale that does not include a neutral response category.

Free-choice scale A symmetrically designed polar scale that includes a neutral response category.

In scale measurement design, the number of scale point descriptors becomes an important criterion only if the data requirements call for capturing either state-of-mind data or specific types of state-of-intention data that focus on positive/negative continuum ranges. The issue involves offering the respondent an opportunity to express a neutral response.[25] Having an even number of positive/negative descriptors tends to force the respondent to select either a positive or a negative answer only.

A symmetrical scale that does not have a neutral descriptor to divide the positive and negative domains is referred to as a **forced-choice scale.** In contrast, a symmetrical scale that includes a center neutral response is referred to as a **free-choice scale.** Exhibit 11.11 presents several examples of "even-point, forced-choice" and "odd-point, free-choice" descriptors.

EXHIBIT 11.11 Examples of "Even-Point" (Forced-Choice) and "Odd-Point" (Free-Choice) Scale Descriptors

"Even-Point, Forced-Choice" Itemized Rating Scale Descriptors

PURCHASE INTENTION (BUY/NOT BUY)

___ Definitely will buy ___ Probably will buy ___ Probably will not buy ___ Definitely will not buy

PERSONAL BELIEFS/OPINIONS (AGREEMENT/DISAGREEMENT)

Definitely agree	Generally agree	Slightly agree	Slightly disagree	Generally disagree	Definitely disagree
___	___	___	___	___	___

MODERNITY (MODERN/OLD-FASHIONED)

___ Very modern ___ Somewhat modern ___ Somewhat old-fashioned ___ Very old-fashioned

COST (EXPENSIVE/INEXPENSIVE)

Extremely expensive	Definitely expensive	Somewhat expensive	Somewhat inexpensive	Definitely inexpensive	Extremely inexpensive
___	___	___	___	___	___

"Odd-Point, Free-Choice" Itemized Rating Scales

PURCHASE INTENTION (BUY/NOT BUY)

Definitely will buy	Probably will buy	Neither will nor will not buy	Probably will not buy	Definitely will not buy
___	___	___	___	___

PERSONAL BELIEFS/OPINIONS (AGREEMENT/DISAGREEMENT)

Definitely agree	Generally agree	Slightly agree	Neither agree nor disagree	Slightly disagree	Generally disagree	Definitely disagree
___	___	___	___	___	___	___

MODERNITY (MODERN/OLD-FASHIONED)

Very modern	Somewhat modern	Neither modern nor old-fashioned	Somewhat old-fashioned	Very old-fashioned
___	___	___	___	___

COST (EXPENSIVE/INEXPENSIVE)

Definitely expensive	Somewhat expensive	Neither expensive nor inexpensive	Somewhat inexpensive	Definitely inexpensive
___	___	___	___	___

Some experts believe scales used to collect state-of-mind data should be designed as "odd-point, free-choice" scale measurements[26] since not all respondents will have enough knowledge or experience with the given topic to be able to accurately assess their thoughts or feelings. If those respondents are forced to choose, the scale may produce lower-quality data than the researcher desires. In free-choice scale designs, however, the so-called neutral scale point offers respondents an easy way to express their feelings about the given topic.

Some researchers believe there is no such thing as a neutral attitude or feeling—that these mental aspects almost always have some degree of a positive or negative orientation attached to them. A person either has an attitude or does not have an attitude about a given object. Likewise, a person will either have a feeling or not have a feeling. An alternative approach to handling situations in which respondents may feel uncomfortable about expressing their thoughts or feelings about a given object because they have no knowledge of or experience with it would be to incorporate a "not applicable" response choice that would not be part of the actual scale measurement. The following example illustrates the *not applicable* (NA) response:

Based on your experiences with your new vehicle since owning and driving it, to what extent are you presently satisfied or dissatisfied with the overall performance of the vehicle? If you feel that you lack enough experience with your vehicle or that the statement is not pertinent to you, please check the "NA" (Not Applicable) response.

(PLEASE CHECK THE ONE APPROPRIATE RESPONSE)

____ Completely satisfied (no dissatisfaction)	____ Generally dissatisfied
____ Definitely satisfied	____ Definitely dissatisfied
____ Generally satisfied	____ Completely dissatisfied (no satisfaction)
____ Slightly satisfied (some dissatisfaction)	____ NA (Not Applicable)
____ Slightly dissatisfied (some satisfaction)	

This approach enables the researcher to remove the "NA" responses from the data and ensures that only accurate data will be included in the data analysis.

Desired Measures of Central Tendency and Dispersion

In determining what levels of scale measurements should be developed, the researcher must consider the data analysis that will be used after the data are collected. Researchers must therefore have an understanding of the measures of central tendency and the measures of dispersion associated with different types of scale measurement designs. **Measures of central tendency** refer to the basic sample statistics that are generated through analyzing the collected data. These include the mean, the median, and the mode. The *mean* is the arithmetic average of all the data responses. The *median* represents the sample statistic that splits the data into a hierarchical pattern where half the data are above the statistic value and half are below. The *mode* is the response that is the most frequently given among all of the respondents.

Measures of central tendency The basic sample statistics that are generated through analyzing data; these are the mode, the median, and the mean.

Measures of dispersion relate to how the data are dispersed around a central tendency value. These sample statistics allow researchers to report the diversity of the responses to a particular scale measurement. They include the frequency distribution, the range, and the estimated sample standard deviation. A *frequency distribution* is a summary of how many times each possible response to a scale question/setup was recorded by the total group of respondents. This distribution can be easily converted into percentages or histograms for ease of comparison between raw data responses. The *range* represents the grouping of responses into mutually exclusive subgroups, each with an identifiable lower and upper boundary. The *sample standard deviation* is the statistical value that specifies the degree of variation in the data responses in such a way that allows the researcher to translate the

Measures of dispersion The sample statistics that allow a researcher to report the diversity of the data collected from scale measurements; they are the frequency distribution, the range, and the estimated sample standard deviation.

eXHIBIT 11.12 Relationships between Scale Levels and Measures of Central Tendency and Dispersion

	Basic Levels of Scales			
Measurements	**Nominal**	**Ordinal**	**Interval**	**Ratio**
Central Tendency				
Mode	**Appropriate**	Appropriate	Appropriate	Appropriate
Median	*Inappropriate*	**More Appropriate**	Appropriate	Appropriate
Mean	*Inappropriate*	*Inappropriate*	**Most Appropriate**	**Most Appropriate**
Dispersion				
Frequency Distribution	**Appropriate**	Appropriate	Appropriate	Appropriate
Range	*Inappropriate*	**More Appropriate**	Appropriate	Appropriate
Estimated Standard Deviation	*Inappropriate*	*Inappropriate*	**Most Appropriate**	**Most Appropriate**

variations into normal curve interpretations (e.g., 99 percent of the responses fall between the mean value plus or minus 3 standard deviations).

Given the important role these six basic sample statistics play in data analysis, understanding how different levels of scales influence the use of a particular statistic becomes critical in scale measurement design. Exhibit 11.12 displays these relationships. Remember that data collected with a nominal scale can be analyzed only by using modes and frequency distributions. For ordinal scales, you can analyze the data using medians and ranges as well as modes and frequency distributions. But for interval or ratio scales, the most appropriate analysis procedures would be those that involve means and standard deviations as the sample statistics. In addition, interval and ratio data can also be appropriately analyzed using modes, medians, frequency distributions, or ranges.

Now that the basics of construct development as well as the rules surrounding scale measurements have been presented, we are ready to move forward to the popular attitudinal, emotional, and behavior scales used by marketing researchers. Chapter 12 focuses on more advanced scales. The nearby A Closer Look at Research (Using Technology) box shows how a consulting firm integrates advanced technology to create high-quality segmentation measures.

A Closer Look at Research

Macro Consulting, Inc.

Deciding on a market segmentation strategy can be a difficult task for any manager or business owner. For small-business owners, the choice can be especially daunting. Macro Consulting, Inc. realizes that small-business owners and managers are forced to make most decisions with very little input or outside help. To provide guidance in this area, Macro Consulting publishes articles on its World Wide Web page (www.macroinc.com/articles/imageq. htm) that promote, among other options, innovative market segmentation strategies. Below is an excerpt from Macro Consulting's Internet page that describes ImageQ, a unique approach to measuring customer segmentation. By using Macro Consulting's Web site, small-business owners and managers have access to many innovative marketing ideas.

For example, ImageQ offers several advantages over other methods: (1) consumers are grouped together based not on how each of them perceives various brands but rather on which brand imagery attributes are most important to their individual purchase decisions; (2) the most important brand perceptions (as well as the least important) are clearly identified for each consumer segment; (3) brand imagery importance data do not need to be collected; and (4) virtually any existing brand imagery data can serve as the basis for this segmentation approach, making expensive data collection unnecessary.

These technical advantages of ImageQ provide marketers, advertisers, and anyone else needing to communicate to his or her customers several key benefits: (1) a completely new insight into the target market's motivations; (2) a customer-focused foundation for developing communications strategies; (3) a fresh perspective on how to best define the primary and secondary market segments; and (4) a new and deeper understanding of how brand imagery affects sales to specific market segments. The approach involves a unique and proprietary analytic protocol. It is an ideal tool for secondary analysis of existing data sets.

ImageQ uses McCullough's correlation measures (MCM), a family of nonparametric correlations that measure the relationships between a battery of brand imagery attributes and purchase interest at the individual respondent level. For virtually any data set that contains brand imagery data and some purchase interest or preference measure, one of these correlations can be calculated. MCMs reflect the importance of each brand imagery attribute to the purchase interest of all brands tested for each respondent in the sample. Cluster analysis is then conducted, using an MCM as its basis. Typically, several cluster solutions are examined and evaluated. The solution that offers the most interpretable and actionable results is selected for profiling and further analysis. The resulting segmentation provides a unique look at brand imagery-based market dynamics, on a segment-by-segment basis.

This is the only method that we are aware of that can segment the marketplace based on the relevance of various brand imagery attributes to individual consumers. In a dynamic marketplace it is essential to gather information and make decisions as quickly as possible. Getting the right message to the right consumer quickly is critical to success. This approach gleans additional and powerful information from existing data sets, saving time and money, while providing insights unattainable with other approaches or measures.

Source: Macro Consulting, Inc., www.macroinc.com/articles/imageq.htm.

MARKETING RESEARCH IN ACTION

Part 1

What You Can Learn from a Customer Loyalty Index

This application is presented in a two-part format. In Part 1 you will read how researchers at Burke Customer Satisfaction Associates (www.burke.com), a commercial research firm that specializes in customer satisfaction measurement and management programs, defines *customer loyalty* and how this construct is operationalized into a measurable index called the Secure Customer Index. The second part is presented in the Marketing Research in Action at the end of the next chapter and will focus on how this construct is actually measured by Burke Customer Satisfaction Associates.

The idea that loyal customers are especially valuable is not new to today's business managers. Loyal customers repeatedly purchase products or services. They recommend a company to others. And they stick with a business over time. Loyal customers are worth the special effort it may take to keep them. But how can you provide that special treatment if you don't know your customers and how their loyalty is won and lost?

Understanding loyalty—what makes your customers loyal and how to measure and understand loyal customers—enables your company to improve customer-driven quality. A customer loyalty index provides management with an easily understood tool that helps focus the organization toward improving satisfaction and retention, for a positive impact on the bottom line.

What Customer Loyalty Is and Isn't

To better understand the concept of customer loyalty, let's first define what customer loyalty is not. Customer loyalty is not customer satisfaction. Satisfaction is a necessary component of loyal or secure customers. However, the mere aspect of being satisfied with a company does not necessarily make customers loyal. Just because customers are satisfied with your company today does not mean they will continue to do business with you in the future.

Customer loyalty is not a response to trial offers or incentives. If customers suddenly begin buying your product or service, it may be the result of a special offer or incentive and not necessarily a reflection of customer loyalty. These same customers may be just as quick to respond to your competitors' incentives.

Customer loyalty is not strong market share. Many businesses mistakenly look at their sales numbers and market share and think, "Those numbers are surrogates for direct measures of customer loyalty. After all, we wouldn't be enjoying high levels of market share if our customers didn't love us." However, this may not be true. Many other factors can drive up market share, including poor performance by competitors or pricing issues. And high share doesn't mean low churn (the rate at which existing customers leave you—possibly to patronize your competition—and are replaced by new customers).

Customer loyalty is not repeat buying or habitual buying. Many repeat customers may be choosing your products or services because of convenience or habit. However, if they learn about a competitive product that they think may be less expensive or better quality, they may quickly switch to that product. Habitual buyers can defect; loyal customers usually don't.

Now that we know what does not constitute customer loyalty, we can talk about what does. Customer loyalty is a composite of a number of qualities. It is driven by customer

EXHIBIT 11.13 The Secure Customer Index

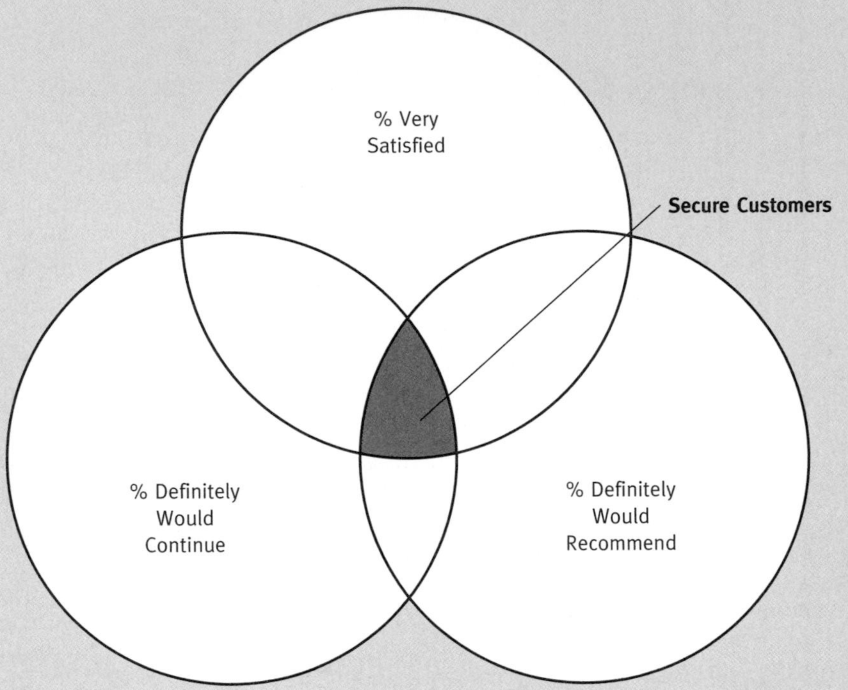

satisfaction, yet it also involves a commitment on the part of the customer to make a sustained investment in an ongoing relationship with a brand or company. Finally, customer loyalty is reflected by a combination of attitudes and behaviors. These attitudes include:

- The intention to buy again and/or buy additional products or services from the same company.
- A willingness to recommend the company to others.
- A commitment to the company demonstrated by a resistance to switching to a competitor.

Customer behaviors that reflect loyalty include:

- Repeat purchasing of products or services.
- Purchasing more and different products or services from the same company.
- Recommending the company to others.

Any one of these attitudes or behaviors in isolation does not necessarily indicate loyal customers. However, by recognizing how these indicators work together in a measurement system, we can derive an index of customer loyalty or, in a broader sense, customer security. Burke Customer Satisfaction Associates has developed a Secure Customer Index (SCI) using three major components to measure customer loyalty: overall customer satisfaction, likelihood of repeat business, and likelihood to recommend the company to others. Other elements may be included in the index depending upon the industry. In their experience, however, these three components are the core of a meaningful customer loyalty index. A visual representation of the SCI is shown in Exhibit 11.13.

Source: www.burke.com.

Hands-On Exercise

Using the material from the chapter and the above information, answer each of the following questions:

1. Identify and provide a meaningful definition of each of the three constructs that researchers at Burke Customer Satisfaction Associates believe are the driving forces behind measuring the concept of customer loyalty.
2. What is the dimensionality of each of these three constructs? That is, are the constructs unidimensional or multidimensional in nature? For each of those constructs that you believe is multidimensional, identify the possible domain of subcomponents that would be representative of that construct. Also, explain why you feel your proposed domain set represents that construct.
3. In your judgment, what level of scale design would be the most appropriate in creating the necessary scale measurements for collecting primary data on each construct?
4. For each construct, design an example of the measurement scale that could be used by Burke Customer Satisfaction Associates to collect the data for the owners of the Santa Fe Grill Mexican restaurant. As background, review the opening vignette for this chapter.

Summary of Learning Objectives

■ **Understand the role of measurement in marketing research.**

In creating meaningful information to solve business/marketing problems, researchers must be able to develop appropriate questions and record the responses to those questions. Not knowing exactly what it is that needs to be measured makes it difficult to design the appropriate measurement scales, so this is the first requirement. A construct can be viewed as any object that cannot be directly observed and measured yet about which information is needed (e.g., customer loyalty). In the instrument development process, researchers must consider the abstractness of the construct, its dimensionality, validity, and operationalization. After correctly defining the information problem, determining what type of data to collect is the second most critical aspect in information research. Gaining meaningful access to responses is achieved by the measurement scales used in the questioning process.

■ **Discuss validity and reliability issues in measurement and scaling.**

Regardless of the method of data collection, researchers must strive to collect the most accurate information possible. Data accuracy depends heavily on the validity of the constructs and the reliability of the measurements applied to those constructs. Constructs can be assessed for content, convergent, discriminant, and nomological validity. Testing for reliability of constructs is indirectly achieved by testing the reliability of the scale measurements used in data collection. Scale reliability methods available to researchers include test-retest, equivalent form, and internal consistency. Although measurement scales may be reliable, reliability alone does not guarantee construct validity.

■ **Explain what scale measurement is and how to apply it.**

Scale measurement is the process of assigning a set of descriptors to represent the range of possible responses a person gives in answering a question about a particular object, construct, or factor. This process helps determine the amount of data that can be obtained from asking questions, and therefore indirectly impacts the amount of primary information that can be derived from the data. Along with the amount of data, researchers must understand the four basic scaling properties (assignment, order, distance, and origin) that can be activated through scale measurements. The rule of thumb is that as researchers simultaneously activate more properties within the question/answering process, the greater the amount of data that can be gathered from people's responses. All data can be classified into one of four mutually exclusive types: state-of-being, state-of-mind, state-of-behavior, and state-of-intention. Understanding the categorical types of data that can be produced by individuals' responses to questions improves the researchers' ability to determine not only what questions should be asked, but also how to ask those questions.

■ **Compare the four basic levels of scales.**

The four basic levels of scales are nominal, ordinal, interval, and ratio. Nominal scales are the most basic and provide the least amount of data. They activate only the assignment scaling property; the data do not show relative magnitudes between the responses. The main data patterns that can be derived from nominal data are the modes and frequency distributions. Nominal scales ask respondents about their religious affiliation, gender, type of dwelling, occupation, or last brand of cereal purchased, and so on. The questions require yes/no, like/dislike, or agree/disagree responses.

Ordinal scales require respondents to express their feelings of relative magnitude about the given topic. Ordinal scales activate both assignment and order scaling properties and enable researchers to create a hierarchical pattern among the data responses (or scale points) that determine "greater than/less than" relationships. Data that can be derived from ordinal scales includes medians and ranges as well as modes and frequency distributions. An example of a set of ordinal scale descriptors would be "complete knowledge," "good knowledge," "basic knowledge," "little knowledge," and "no knowledge." While ordinal measurement scales are an excellent design for capturing the relative magnitudes in respondents' responses, they cannot measure absolute differences.

An interval scale activates not only the assignment and order scaling properties but also the distance property. Interval scales enable researchers to include scale elements that show the absolute differences between each scale point. The scale descriptors typically represent a distinct set of numerical ranges as the possible responses to a question. With interval data, researchers can develop a number of more meaningful measures including means and standard deviations, as well as the mode, median, frequency distribution, and range.

Ratio scales are the only scale measurements that simultaneously activate all four scaling properties (assignment, order, distance, and origin). Considered the most sophisticated scale design, they enable researchers to identify absolute differences between each scale point and to make absolute comparisons between the respondents' responses. Ratio scales are designed to allow "true natural zero" or "true state of nothing" responses. Typically, the respondent is requested to choose a specific numerical value. Data that can be derived from ratio scale measurements are basically the same as those for interval scale measurements. It is important to remember that the more scaling properties simultaneously activated, the greater the opportunity to derive more detailed and sophisticated data measures and therefore more information. Interval and ratio scale designs are most appropriate to use when researchers want to collect state-of-behavior or state-of-intention or certain types of state-of-being data.

■ **Discuss scale development and its importance in gathering primary data.**
In developing accurate scale measurements, there are three critical components to any complete scale: question/setup; dimensions (or attributes) of the object, construct, or behavior; and the scale point descriptors. Some of the criteria for scale development are the intelligibility of the questions, the appropriateness of the primary descriptors, the discriminatory power of the scale descriptors, the reliability of the scale, the balancing of positive/negative scale descriptors, the inclusion of a neutral response choice, and desired measures of central tendency (mode, median, and mean) and dispersion (frequency distribution, range, estimated standard deviation). If the highest quality data are to be collected and transformed into useful information, researchers and practitioners must understand construct development and measurement scales.

Key Terms and Concepts

Appropriateness of descriptors 351
Assignment property 342
Coefficient alpha 353
Construct 335
Construct development 336
Content validity 337
Convergent validity 337
Direct cognitive structural analysis 338
Discriminant validity 338
Discriminatory power 351
Distance property 343
Domain of observables 336
Equivalent form 352
Forced-choice scale 354
Free-choice scale 354
Intelligibility criterion 350
Internal consistency 353
Interval scale 345
Measurement 334
Measures of central tendency 356
Measures of dispersion 356
Nominal scale 344
Nomological validity 338
Object 335
Operationalization 338
Order property 343
Ordinal scale 345
Origin property 344
Ratio scale 348
Scale measurement 342
Scale points 342
Scale reliability 338
Split-half test 353
State-of-behavior data 341
State-of-being data 341
State-of-intention data 342
State-of-mind data 341
Test-retest 352

Review Questions

1. How does activating scaling properties determine the amount of data and information that can be derived from measurement scales?
2. Among the basic levels of scale measurements, which one provides researchers with the most data and information? Why is this particular scale the least used in research practices? Explain the main differences between interval and ratio scale measurements.

3. Identify and explain the components that make up any level of scale measurement. What are the interrelationships between these components?

4. When developing the scale point descriptors for a measurement scale, what rules of thumb should researchers follow?

5. What is scale measurement? In your response, explain the difference between an object's "concrete" properties and "abstract" properties. An example of an object you might consider using to answer this is a mobile phone.

6. In construct/scale measurement development, how does validity differ from reliability? Make sure you include definitions for each of these terms.

7. What are the major differences between nominal, ordinal, interval, and ratio scales? In your answer include an example of each type of scale.

8. Identify the differences between the four scaling properties that are used in scale measurement design, including an example illustrating each property.

Discussion Questions

1. What are some of the weaknesses of using college students as respondents when developing constructs like "retail store loyalty," "telecommunication service quality," or "attitudes toward kids' advertisements"?

2. For each of the scales below (A, B, and C), answer the following questions:
   a. What level of scale measurement is being used?
   b. What scaling properties are being activated in the scale?
   c. What is the most appropriate measure of central tendency?
   d. What is the most appropriate measure of variation (or dispersion)?
   e. What weakness, if any, exists with the scale?

   A. How often do you travel for business or pleasure purposes?

For Business	**For Pleasure**
___ 0–1 times per month	___ 0–1 times per year
___ 2–3 times per month	___ 2–3 times per year
___ 4–5 times per month	___ 4–5 times per year
___ 6 or more times per month	___ 6 or more times per year

   B. How do you pay for your travel expenses?

___ Cash	___ Company charge
___ Check	___ Personal charge
___ Credit card	___ Other ______________

   C. Please check the one category that best approximates your total family annual income, before taxes. (Please check only one category.)

___ Under $10,000	___ $30,001–$40,000	___ $60,001–$70,000
___ $10,000–$20,000	___ $40,001–$50,000	___ $70,001–$100,000
___ $20,001–$30,000	___ $50,001–$60,000	___ Over $100,000

3. For each of the listed concepts or objects, design a scale that would enable you to collect data on that concept/object.
   a. An excellent long-distance runner.
   b. A person's favorite Mexican restaurant.
   c. Size of the listening audience for a popular country and western radio station.
   d. Consumers' attitudes toward the Colorado Rockies professional baseball team.
   e. The satisfaction a person has in his or her automobile.
   f. Purchase intentions for a new tennis racket.

4. **EXPERIENCE THE INTERNET.** Using a browser of your choice, log on to the Internet and go to American Demographics' home page at www.demographics.com. Now surf the "hot spots" until you come across one of their segmentation questionnaires. Take the first five question/scales that appear on the questionnaire and evaluate each of them for the following five questions:
   a. What type of data is being sought?
   b. What level of scale measurement is being employed?
   c. What scaling properties are being activated?
   d. What would be the most appropriate measure of central tendency for analyzing the data?
   e. What would be the most appropriate measure of dispersion?

5. Identify and discuss the key issues researchers should consider when choosing a measurement scale for capturing customers' expressions of satisfaction?

6. AT&T is interested in obtaining evaluative judgments of its new wireless cell phone services. Determine and justify what service attributes should be used to capture the *performance* of its wireless cell phone service. Then design two scale measurements (one as an *ordinal* and the second scale as an *interval*) that would enable AT&T to accurately capture the necessary performance data.

7. The local Ford Dealership is interested in collecting data to answer the following information research question: "How likely are young adults to purchase a new automobile within a year after graduating from college?" Design a nominal, ordinal, interval, and ratio measurement scale that will enable the dealership to collect the required data. In your opinion, which one of your designs would be most useful to the dealership? Explain why.

8. Recall our continuing case about the Santa Fe Grill Mexican Restaurant. Management would like to collect some information from current customers to answer the following questions. (a) What type of Mexican-oriented food items do customers prefer? (b) How important are food prices, food quality, restaurant atmosphere, and service in selecting a restaurant to dine at? And (c) How often do customers dine out at Mexican theme restaurants each month? Use your understanding of scale development to do the following:
   - Develop an interval scale to determine what type of food items customers prefer.
   - Develop an ordinal scale to determine what is important in selecting a restaurant.
   - Develop an interval scale to measure how often customers dine at Mexican theme restaurants.

chapter 12

Advanced Measurement Designs for Survey Research

Learning Objectives

After reading this chapter, you will be able to:

1. Understand attitudes and their components.
2. Describe attitude and behavior scales and assess their strengths and weaknesses.
3. Recommend when noncomparative and comparative scale designs are appropriate.
4. Summarize measurement scale design issues.
5. Compare the trilogy and affect global approaches for explaining attitudes.

> **"While we know customer service is the main function of the library, capturing customers' evaluative judgments toward the service quality is very elusive."**
>
> **—CAROL V. LIVINGSTONE, Research Librarian, Hillsborough County Public Library System**

Attitude and Image Measurements in Marketing Research

Aca Joe, Inc., had been operating in the Tampa Bay metropolitan area for three years. Prior to opening the business, the owner decided to present the image of Aca Joe as being a men's casual-wear specialty store that was conveniently located, with a good reputation of offering a wide selection of high-quality fashionable men's casual apparel at competitive prices. In addition, the owner wanted Aca Joe to be known as having very knowledgeable sales associates and store staff who were committed to providing outstanding customer service and satisfaction.

The owner created and implemented marketing strategies to ensure that this image was communicated to actual and potential customers. Three years later, however, the sales and profit figures were lower than expected, causing the owner to question the effectiveness of the store's current marketing strategies. The owner was actually not sure how consumers viewed the store.

Realizing that he needed help, Aca Joe's owner consulted a marketing research expert. After several preliminary discussions, it was decided that a store image study should be conducted to gain insights into how Aca Joe's image compared with several competitors'. The ensuing information research process combined both qualitative and quantitative research methods in a two-phase study.

First, using qualitative research methods, the researcher completed several in-depth interviews with Aca Joe's owner and sales associates, a review of the retail literature, and four focus group sessions among known customers to identify the store dimensions and store service features that were most closely related to the store's desired image. The results from the qualitative research suggested that customers viewed 7 dimensions (quality, assortment, style, and prices of merchandise, the store's location, the store's overall reputation, and knowledge of sales staff) and 18 store service features as being relevant to Aca Joe's image. Once these critical store image dimensions and features were identified, the researcher had to determine the appropriate scale measurements needed to collect the second-stage data using quantitative information research practices.

Guided by the information research problem, the established list of information needs, and an understanding of the different types of scale measurements that could be used, the researcher developed and tested a seven-point semantic differential scale to measure the 7 recognized dimensions and a modified four-point, self-rating importance scale for the 18 service features. These scale measurements were included in an eight-page store image questionnaire which was administered to a randomly selected sample of 300 known Aca Joe customers using a direct mail survey. Interpretation of the findings from the semantic differential data structures revealed that customers perceived Aca Joe as having a good reputation as a retail men's specialty store that offered high-quality, stylish/fashionable merchandise but that its assortment of merchandise was only average and was somewhat high priced. In addition, customers viewed the store as being only somewhat conveniently located. The sales staff were considered generally knowledgeable and very helpful.

When cross-matched to the owner's desired store image, the image information created from the quantitative data structures identified several areas of concern. The results suggested that Aca Joe's overall desired store image was being compromised by the store's current merchandising and pricing strategies. The owners needed to further evaluate these particular strategies and be willing to modify them to change the current image held by customers toward the store's merchandise assortment and prices.

Value of Attitude Measurement

In today's business world, more and more marketers are attempting to better understand their customers' attitudes and feelings toward their products, services, and delivery systems, as well as those of their direct competitors. This chapter continues the discussion of measurement begun in Chapter 11. Moreover, it builds on the concepts discussed in earlier chapters and focuses on scales used to collect attitudinal, emotional, and behavior intention responses. These scales have a common link in that they are typically used to collect state-of-mind and state-of-intention data, and typically include both comparative and noncomparative measurements.

As mentioned in the last chapter, scale measurement consists of three components: the *question/setup,* the *scale dimensions* and *attributes,* and the *scale point descriptors.* If the overall goal is to collect high-quality data to transform into useful information, researchers and practitioners alike must have a full understanding of the relationships that exist among these three components.

Nature of Attitudes and Marketplace Behaviors

Today most businesses understand the importance of identifying customers' attitudes and feelings to determine the businesses' strengths and weaknesses. Identifying attitudes is useful in understanding consumers' and industrial buyers' observable marketplace behaviors. However, marketers have less precise scales to measure attitudes and related phenomena than the scales used in the physical sciences. Comprehensive coverage of the theory of attitudes is beyond the scope of this chapter. For those seeking additional information, we suggest either a consumer behavior textbook, the *Handbook of Consumer Behavior* by T. S. Robertson and H. H. Kassarjian,[1] or *Readings in Attitude Theory* by Martin Fishbein.[2]

Attitude A learned predisposition to react in a consistent positive or negative way to a given object, idea, or set of information.

An **attitude** is a learned predisposition to act in a consistent positive or negative way to a given object, idea, or set of information. Attitudes are state-of-mind constructs that are not directly observable. The true structure of an attitude lies in the mind of the individual holding that attitude. To accurately capture customers' attitudes, researchers must be able to understand the dimensions of the attitude construct.

Components of Attitudes

Attitudes have three components: *cognitive, affective,* and *behavioral.* Marketing researchers and decision makers must understand all three components.

Cognitive Component

Cognitive component The part of an attitude that represents a subject's beliefs, perceptions, and knowledge about a specified object.

The **cognitive component** of attitude is a person's beliefs, perceptions, and knowledge about an object and its attributes. For example, as a college student you may believe that your university:

- is a prestigious place to get a degree.
- has professors with excellent reputations.
- is a good value for the money.
- needs more and better computer labs.

These beliefs make up the cognitive component of your attitude toward your university. Your beliefs may or may not be true, but they represent reality to you. The more positive beliefs you have of your university and the more positive each belief is, the more favorable the overall cognitive component is assumed to be.

Affective Component

Affective component The part of an attitude that represents the person's emotional feelings held toward the given object.

The **affective component** of an attitude is the person's emotional feelings toward a given object. This component is most frequently revealed when a person is asked to verbalize his or her attitude toward some object, person, or phenomenon. For example, if you claim you "love your university" or your university "has the best athletes possible or smartest students around" you are expressing your emotional feelings. These emotional feelings are the affective component of your attitude about your university. Your overall feelings about your university may be based on years of observing it, or they may be based on little actual knowledge. Your attitude could change as you are exposed to more information (e.g., from your freshman to your senior year), or it may remain essentially the same. Finally, two individuals may have different affective responses to the same experience (one student may like a particular professor's teaching approach while another one may hate it).

Behavioral Component

Behavioral (conative) component The part of an attitude that represents a person's intended or actual behavioral response to the given object.

The **behavioral component,** also sometimes referred to as a *conative* component, is a person's intended or actual behavioral response to an object. For example, your decision to return to your university for the sophomore year is the behavioral component of your attitude. The behavioral component is an observable outcome driven by the interaction of a person's cognitive component (beliefs) and affective component (emotional strength of beliefs) as they relate to a particular object. The behavioral component may represent future intentions (your plan to get an MBA degree after you finish your BA), but it usually is limited to a specific time period. Recommendations also represent a behavioral component (such as recommending that another student take a class from a particular professor).

Attitudes are a complex area to understand fully. For those who wish to learn more we have included an appendix at the end of this chapter with more complete coverage. In the next section we discuss the different scales used to measure attitudes and behaviors.

Measuring Attitudes and Behaviors

Although the information problem and research objectives dictate which type of scale measurement researchers use, there are several types of attitudinal scaling formats that have proven to be useful in many different situations. The following section discusses three attitude scale formats: *Likert scales, semantic differential scales,* and *behavior intention scales.* Exhibit 12.1 shows the general steps in the construct development/scale measurement process.

Likert Scale

Likert scale A scale format that asks respondents to indicate the extent to which they agree or disagree with a series of mental belief or behavioral belief statements about a given object.

A **Likert scale** asks respondents to indicate the extent to which they either agree or disagree with a series of mental or behavioral belief statements about a given object. Typically the scale format is balanced between agreement and disagreement scale descriptors. Named after its original developer, Rensis Likert, this scale typically has five scale descriptors: "strongly agree," "agree," "neither agree nor disagree," "disagree," "strongly disagree." A series of hierarchical steps is followed in developing a Likert scale:

Step #1: Identify and understand the concept to be studied. For example, assume the concept is voting in Florida.

Step #2: Assemble a large number of belief statements (e.g., 50 to 100) concerning the general public's sentiments toward voting in Florida.

Step #3: Subjectively classify each statement as having either a "favorable" or an "unfavorable" relationship to the specific attitude under investigation. Then, the entire list of statements is pretested (e.g., through a pilot test) using a sample of respondents.

EXHIBIT 12.1 A General Construct Development/Scale Measurement Process

Process Steps	Key Activities
1. Identify and Define the Construct	Determine Dimensionality of Construct
2. Create Initial Pool of Attribute Items	Determine Theory, Secondary Data, Qualitative Research
3. Assess and Select a Reduced Set of Items	Perform Structural Analysis and Qualitative Judgments
4. Construct Initial Measurements and Pretest	Conduct Pilot Study, Collect Data from Pretest Sample
5. Do Appropriate Statistical Data Analysis	Conduct Construct Validity and Scale Reliability Tests
6. Refine and Purify Scale Measurements	Eliminate Irrelevant Attribute Items
7. Collect More Data on Purified Scale	Select New Sample of Subjects from Defined Target Population
8. Statistically Evaluate Scale Measurements	Conduct Reliability, Validity, Generalizability Tests
9. Perform Final Scale Measurement	Include Scale Measurement in Final Questionnaire

Step #4: Respondents decide the extent to which they either agree or disagree with each statement, using the intensity descriptors "strongly agree," "agree," "not sure," "disagree," "strongly disagree." Each response is then given a numerical weight, such as 5, 4, 3, 2, 1. For assumed favorable statements, a weight of 5 would be given to a "strongly agree" response; for assumed unfavorable statements, a weight of 1 would be given to a "strongly disagree" response.

Step #5: A respondent's overall-attitude score is calculated by the summation of the weighted values associated with the statements rated.

Step #6: Only statements that appear to discriminate between the high and low total scores are retained in the analysis. One possible method is a simple comparison of the top (or highest) 25 percent of the total mean scores with the bottom (or lowest) 25 percent of total mean scores.

Step #7: In determining the final set of statements (normally 20 to 25), statements that exhibit the greatest differences in mean values between the top and bottom total scores are selected.

Step #8: Using the final set of statements, steps 3 and 4 are repeated in a full study.

By using the summation of the weights associated with all the statements, researchers can tell whether a person's attitude toward the object is overall positive or negative. For example, the maximum favorable score on a 25-item scale would be 125 ($5 \times 25 = 125$). Therefore a person scoring 110 would be assumed to hold a positive (favorable) attitude. Another respondent who scores 45 would be assumed to hold a negative attitude toward the object. The total scores do not identify any of the possible differences that might exist on an individual statement basis between respondents.

Over the years researchers have extensively modified the design of the Likert scale. Today, the *modified Likert* scale expands the original five-point format to either a six-point forced-choice format with scale descriptors such as "definitely agree," "generally agree," "slightly agree," "slightly disagree," "generally disagree," "definitely disagree" or a seven-point free-choice format with these same descriptors plus "neither agree nor disagree" (sometimes labeled "not sure") in the middle. In addition, many researchers treat the Likert scale format as an interval scale.

Regardless of the actual number of scale descriptors that are used, Likert scales have several other unique characteristics. First, the Likert scale is the only summated rating scale that uses a set of agreement/disagreement scale descriptors. A Likert scale collects only cognitive-based or specific behavioral beliefs. Despite the popular notion that Likert scales can measure a person's complete attitude, they can capture only the cognitive components of a person's attitude and are therefore only partial measures. They also do not capture the different possible intensity levels of expressed affective or behavioral components of a person's attitude.

Likert scales are best for research designs that use self-administered surveys, personal interviewers, or most online methods to collect the data. It is difficult to administer a Likert scale over the telephone because respondents have trouble visualizing and remembering the relative magnitudes of agreement and disagreement that make up the scale descriptors. Exhibit 12.2 shows an example of a partial modified Likert scale in a self-administered survey.

To point out the interpretive difficulties associated with the Likert scale, in Exhibit 12.2 we have used boldface in each of the statements for the words that indicate a single level of intensity. For example, in the first statement (I buy many things with a credit card), the

eXHIBIT 12.2 Example of a Partial Modified Likert Scale

For each listed statement below, please check the one response that best expresses the extent to which you agree or disagree with that statement.

Statements	Definitely Agree	Generally Agree	Slightly Agree	Slightly Disagree	Generally Disagree	Definitely Disagree
I buy **many things** with a credit card.	___	___	___	___	___	___
I wish we had **a lot more** money.	___	___	___	___	___	___
My friends **often come** to me for advice.	___	___	___	___	___	___
I am **never influenced** by advertisements.	___	___	___	___	___	___

main belief focuses on **many things.** If respondents check the "generally disagree" response, it would be a leap of faith for researchers to interpret that response to mean that respondents buy only a few things with a credit card. In addition, it would be a speculative guess on the part of researchers to assume that the respondents' attitudes toward purchasing products or services with a credit card are unfavorable. The intensity levels assigned to the agree/disagree scale point descriptors do not truly represent the respondents' feelings associated with the belief response. The intensity levels used in a Likert scale identify only the extent to which respondents think the statement represents their own belief about credit card purchases.

Consider the last statement in Exhibit 12.2 (I am never influenced by advertisements) as another example. The key words in this statement are **never influenced.** If respondents check "definitely disagree," it would again be researchers' subjective guess that the response means that respondents are very much influenced by advertisements. In reality, all that the "definitely disagree" response indicates is that the statement is not one that respondents would make. No measure of feeling can be attached to the statement.

Likert scales can be used to identify and assess personal or psychographic (lifestyle) traits of individuals. To see how international marketing research companies, like the Gallup Organization, use attitude and psychographic scale measurements to profile consumers across Latin American countries, visit the book's Web site at www.mhhe.com/hair4e and follow the links.

Semantic Differential Scale

Semantic differential scale A bipolar scale format that captures a person's attitudes or feelings about a given object.

Another rating scale used quite often in marketing research projects is the **semantic differential scale.** This type of scale is unique in its use of bipolar adjectives and adverbs (good/bad, like/dislike, competitive/noncompetitive, helpful/unhelpful, high quality/low quality, dependable/undependable) as the endpoints of a symmetrical continuum. Typically there will be one object and a related set of factors (or attributes), each with its own set of bipolar adjectives to measure either a cognitive or an affective element. Because the individual scale descriptors are not identified, each bipolar scale appears to be a continuum. In most cases, semantic differential scales will use between five and seven scale descriptors, though only the endpoints are identified. Respondents are asked to select the point on the continuum that expresses their thoughts or feelings about the given object.

In most cases a semantic differential scale will use an odd number of scale points, thus creating a so-called neutral response that symmetrically divides the positive and negative poles into two equal parts. An interpretive problem that arises with an odd-number scale point format comes from the natural neutral response in the middle of the scale. A neutral response has little or no diagnostic value to researchers or decision makers. Sometimes it is interpreted as meaning "no opinion," "don't know," "neither/nor," or "average." None of these interpretations give much information to researchers. To overcome this problem, researchers can use an even-point (or forced-choice) format and incorporate a "not applicable" response out to the side of the bipolar scale.

A semantic differential scale is one of the few attitudinal scales that enable researchers to collect both cognitive and affective data for any given factor. But both types of data cannot be collected at the same time. For a given factor, a bipolar scale can be designed to capture either a person's feelings or cognitive beliefs. Although some researchers believe a semantic differential scale can be used to measure a person's complete attitude about an object or behavior, this scale type is best for identifying a "perceptual image profile" about the object or behavior of concern.

The actual design of a semantic differential scale can vary from situation to situation. To help understand the benefits and weaknesses associated with design differences, we present three different formats and discuss the pros and cons of each. In the first situation, researchers are interested in developing a credibility scale that can be used by Nike to assess the credibility of Tiger Woods as a spokesperson in TV or print advertisements for Nike brands of personal grooming products. Researchers determine the credibility construct consists of three factors—(1) expertise, (2) trustworthiness, and (3) attractiveness—with each factor measured using a specific set of five bipolar scales (see Exhibit 12.3).

EXHIBIT 12.3 Semantic Differential Scale for Tiger Woods as a Credibility Spokesperson[3]

Now with respect to Tiger Woods as the spokesperson for Nike golf apparel, we would like to know your opinions about the expertise, trustworthiness, and attractiveness that you believe he brings to the advertisement. Each dimension has five factors that may or may not represent your opinion. For each listed factor, please check the line that best expresses your opinion about that factor.

Expertise:								
Knowledgeable	___	___	___	___	___	___	___	Unknowledgeable
Expert	___	___	___	___	___	___	___	Not an Expert
Skilled	___	___	___	___	___	___	___	Unskilled
Qualified	___	___	___	___	___	___	___	Unqualified
Experienced	___	___	___	___	___	___	___	Inexperienced
Trustworthiness:								
Reliable	___	___	___	___	___	___	___	Unreliable
Sincere	___	___	___	___	___	___	___	Insincere
Trustworthy	___	___	___	___	___	___	___	Untrustworthy
Dependable	___	___	___	___	___	___	___	Undependable
Honest	___	___	___	___	___	___	___	Dishonest
Attractiveness:								
Sexy	___	___	___	___	___	___	___	Not Sexy
Beautiful	___	___	___	___	___	___	___	Ugly
Attractive	___	___	___	___	___	___	___	Unattractive
Classy	___	___	___	___	___	___	___	Not Classy
Elegant	___	___	___	___	___	___	___	Plain

Randomization of Positive and Negative Pole Descriptors

Halo effect bias
A generalization from the perception of one outstanding factor, attribute, or trait to an overly favorable evaluation on the whole object or construct.

While the semantic differential scale format in Exhibit 12.3 appears to be correctly designed, there are several technical problems that can create response bias. First, notice that all the positive pole descriptors are arranged on the left side of each scale and the negative pole descriptors are all on the right side. This approach can cause a **halo effect bias.**[4] That is, it tends to lead respondents to react more favorably to the positive poles on the left side than to the negative poles on the right side. To prevent this problem, researchers should randomly mix the positions of the positive and negative pole descriptors.[5]

Lack of Extreme Magnitude Expressed in the Pole Descriptors

A second response problem with the scale format displayed in Exhibit 12.3 is that the descriptors at the ends of each scale do not express the *extreme intensity* associated with end poles. Respondents are asked to check one of seven possible lines to express their opinion, but only the two end lines are given narrative meaning. Researchers can only guess how respondents are interpreting the other positions between the two endpoints. Consider, for example, the "dependable/undependable" scale for the trustworthiness dimension. Notice that the extreme left scale position represents "dependable" and the extreme right scale position represents "undependable." Because dependable and undependable are natural dichotomous phrase descriptors, the scale design does not allow for any significant magnitudes to exist between them. The logical question is what the other five scale positions represent, which in turn raises the question of whether or not the scale truly is a continuum ranging from dependable to undependable. This problem can be corrected by attaching a narratively expressed extreme magnitude to the bipolar descriptors ("extremely" or "quite" dependable, and "extremely" or "quite" undependable).

Use of Nonbipolar Descriptors to Represent the Poles

A third response problem that occurs in designing semantic differential scales relates to the inappropriate narrative expressions of the scale descriptors. In a good semantic differential scale design, the individual scales should be truly bipolar so that a symmetrical scale can be designed. Sometimes researchers will express the negative pole in such a way that the positive one is not really its opposite. This creates a skewed scale design that is difficult for respondents to interpret correctly.

Consider the "expert/not an expert" scale in the "expertise" dimension in Exhibit 12.3. While the scale is dichotomous, the words "not an expert" do not allow respondents to interpret any of the other scale points as being relative magnitudes of that phrase. Other than the one endpoint described as "not an expert," all the other scale points would have to represent some intensity of "expert," thus creating an unbalanced, skewed scale toward the positive pole. In other words, interpreting "not an expert" as really meaning "extremely" or "quite" not an expert makes little or no diagnostic sense.

Researchers must be careful when selecting bipolar descriptors to make sure that the words or phrases are truly extremely bipolar in nature and that they allow for creating symmetrically balanced scale designs. For example, researchers could use pole descriptors such as "complete expert" and "complete novice" to correct the above-described scale point descriptor problems.

Matching Standardized Intensity Descriptors to Pole Descriptors

The scale design used by Bank of America for a bank image study in Exhibit 12.4 eliminates the three problems identified in the example in Exhibit 12.3, as well as a fourth—it gives narrative expression to the intensity level of each scale point. Notice that all the separate poles and scale points in between them are anchored by the same set of intensity descriptors ("very," "moderately," "slightly," "neither one nor the other," "slightly,"

eXHIBIT 12.4 Semantic Differential Scale Used by Bank of America That Defines Each Scale Descriptor

For each of the following banking traits/features, please check the one line that best expresses your impression of that feature as it relates to Bank of America. **Make sure you give only one response for each listed feature.**

	Very	Moderately	Slightly	Neither One nor the Other	Slightly	Moderately	Very	
Courteous Employees	___	___	___	___	___	___	___	Discourteous Employees
Helpful Staff	___	___	___	___	___	___	___	Unhelpful Staff
Unattractive Exterior	___	___	___	___	___	___	___	Attractive Exterior
Competitive Rates	___	___	___	___	___	___	___	Noncompetitive Rates
Limited Service Offerings	___	___	___	___	___	___	___	Wide Variety of Service Offerings
Good Operating Hours	___	___	___	___	___	___	___	Bad Operating Hours
High-Quality Service	___	___	___	___	___	___	___	Low-Quality Service
Unreliable	___	___	___	___	___	___	___	Reliable
Successful Bank	___	___	___	___	___	___	___	Unsuccessful Bank
Makes You Feel at Home	___	___	___	___	___	___	___	Makes You Feel Uneasy

"moderately," "very"). In using standardized intensity descriptors, however, researchers must be extra careful in determining the specific phrases for each pole—each phrase must fit the set of intensity descriptors in order for the scale points to make complete sense to respondents. Consider the "makes you feel at home/makes you feel uneasy" scale in Exhibit 12.4. The intensity descriptor of "very" does not make much sense when applied to that scale ("*very makes* you feel at home" or "*very makes* you feel uneasy"). Thus, including standardized intensity descriptors in a semantic differential scale design may force researchers to limit the types of bipolar phrases used to describe or evaluate the object or behavior of concern. This can only raise questions about the appropriateness of the data collected using this type of scale design.

The fundamentals discussed in Chapter 11 can help researchers develop customized scales to collect attitudinal or behavioral data. To illustrate this point, Exhibit 12.5 shows a semantic differential scale used by Midas Auto Systems Experts to collect attitudinal data about the performance of Midas. Notice that each of the 15 different features that make up Midas's service profile has its own bipolar scale communicating the intensity level for the positive and negative poles. This reduces the possibility that respondents will misunderstand the scale.

Exhibit 12.5 also illustrates the use of an "NA"—not applicable—response as a replacement for the more traditional mid-scale neutral response. After the data are collected from this scale format, researchers can calculate aggregate mean values for each of the 15 features, plot those mean values on each of their respective scale lines, and graphically display the results using "profile" lines. The result is an overall profile that depicts Midas's service performance patterns (see Exhibit 12.6). In addition, researchers can use the same scale and collect data on several competing automobile service providers (Firestone Car Care, Sears Auto Center), then show each of the semantic differential profiles on one display.

eXHIBIT 12.5 Semantic Differential Scale for Midas Auto Systems Experts

From your personal experiences with Midas Auto Systems' service representatives, please rate the performance of Midas on the basis of the following listed features. Each feature has its own scale ranging from "one" (1) to "six" (6). Please circle the response number that best describes how Midas has performed on that feature. For any feature(s) that you feel is (are) not relevant to your evaluation, please circle the (NA)—Not applicable—response code.

Cost of Repair/Maintenance Work	(NA)	Extremely High	6	5	4	3	2	1	Very Low, Almost Free
Appearance of Facilities	(NA)	Very Professional	6	5	4	3	2	1	Very Unprofessional
Customer Satisfaction	(NA)	Totally Dissatisfied	6	5	4	3	2	1	Truly Satisfied
Promptness in Delivering Service	(NA)	Unacceptably Slow	6	5	4	3	2	1	Impressively Quick
Quality of Service Offerings	(NA)	Truly Terrible	6	5	4	3	2	1	Truly Exceptional
Understands Customer's Needs	(NA)	Really Understands	6	5	4	3	2	1	Doesn't Have a Clue
Credibility of Midas	(NA)	Extremely Credible	6	5	4	3	2	1	Extremely Unreliable
Midas's Keeping of Promises	(NA)	Very Trustworthy	6	5	4	3	2	1	Very Deceitful
Midas Services Assortment	(NA)	Truly Full Service	6	5	4	3	2	1	Only Basic Services
Prices/Rates/Charges of Services	(NA)	Much Too High	6	5	4	3	2	1	Great Rates
Service Personnel's Competence	(NA)	Very Competent	6	5	4	3	2	1	Totally Incompetent
Employees' Personal Social Skills	(NA)	Very Rude	6	5	4	3	2	1	Very Friendly
Midas's Operating Hours	(NA)	Extremely Flexible	6	5	4	3	2	1	Extremely Limited
Convenience of Midas's Locations	(NA)	Very Easy to Get to	6	5	4	3	2	1	Too Difficult to Get to

eXHIBIT 12.6 Midas Auto Systems' Performance Profile Compared with Two Competitors'

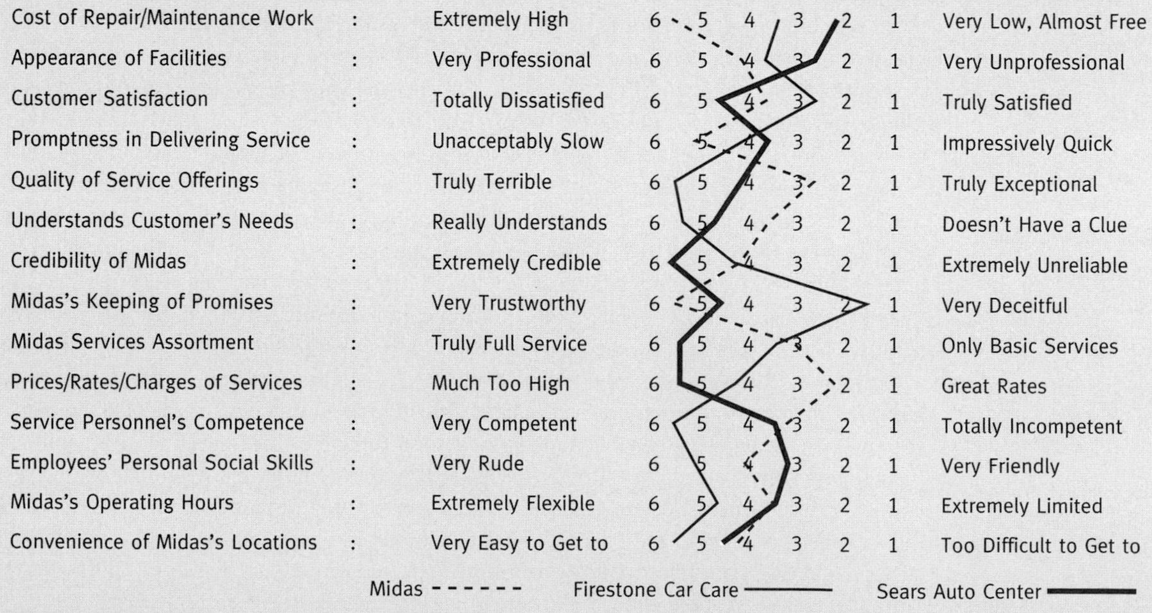
Cost of Repair/Maintenance Work : Extremely High 6 5 4 3 2 1 Very Low, Almost Free
Appearance of Facilities : Very Professional 6 5 4 3 2 1 Very Unprofessional
Customer Satisfaction : Totally Dissatisfied 6 5 4 3 2 1 Truly Satisfied
Promptness in Delivering Service : Unacceptably Slow 6 5 4 3 2 1 Impressively Quick
Quality of Service Offerings : Truly Terrible 6 5 4 3 2 1 Truly Exceptional
Understands Customer's Needs : Really Understands 6 5 4 3 2 1 Doesn't Have a Clue
Credibility of Midas : Extremely Credible 6 5 4 3 2 1 Extremely Unreliable
Midas's Keeping of Promises : Very Trustworthy 6 5 4 3 2 1 Very Deceitful
Midas Services Assortment : Truly Full Service 6 5 4 3 2 1 Only Basic Services
Prices/Rates/Charges of Services : Much Too High 6 5 4 3 2 1 Great Rates
Service Personnel's Competence : Very Competent 6 5 4 3 2 1 Totally Incompetent
Employees' Personal Social Skills : Very Rude 6 5 4 3 2 1 Very Friendly
Midas's Operating Hours : Extremely Flexible 6 5 4 3 2 1 Extremely Limited
Convenience of Midas's Locations : Very Easy to Get to 6 5 4 3 2 1 Too Difficult to Get to
Midas ------
Firestone Car Care
Sears Auto Center

Behavior Intention Scale

Behavior intention scale A type of rating scale designed to capture the likelihood that people will demonstrate some type of predictable behavior intent toward purchasing an object or service in a future time frame.

One of the most widely used scale formats in marketing research is the **behavior intention scale.** In using this scale, decision makers are attempting to obtain some idea of the likelihood that people will demonstrate some type of predictable behavior regarding the purchase of a product or service. In general, behavior intent scales have been found to be good predictors of consumers' choices of frequently purchased and durable consumer products.[6]

Behavior intention scales (purchase intent, attendance intent, shopping intent, usage intent) are easy to construct. Consumers are asked to make a subjective judgment on their likelihood of buying a product or service or taking a specified action. The scale descriptors typically used with a behavior intention scale are "definitely would," "probably would," "not sure," "probably would not," and "definitely would not." For example, for Vail Valley Foundation's interest in identifying how likely it is people will attend a variety of performing arts events at its new outdoor Ford Amphitheater in Vail, Colorado, see Exhibit 12.7, which illustrates the behavior intention scale the Vail Valley Foundation Management Team used to collect the

EXHIBIT 12.7 Behavior Intention Scale for Determining Attendance at Performing Arts Events In Vail, Colorado

Now with respect to the next six months, we would like to know the extent to which you would consider attending various types of entertainment/performing arts events if they were held in the Vail Valley area.

Next to each type of event, please check the one box that best expresses the extent to which you would consider attending within the next six months.

(PLEASE CHECK ONLY ONE BOX FOR EACH EVENT)

Type of Event	Definitely Would Consider Attending	Probably Would Consider Attending	Probably Would Not Consider Attending	Definitely Would Not Consider Attending
I. Music Concerts				
Popular Music	❑	❑	❑	❑
Jazz Music	❑	❑	❑	❑
Country Music	❑	❑	❑	❑
Bluegrass Music	❑	❑	❑	❑
Classical Music	❑	❑	❑	❑
Chamber Music	❑	❑	❑	❑
II. Theatrical Productions				
Drama	❑	❑	❑	❑
Comedy	❑	❑	❑	❑
Melodrama	❑	❑	❑	❑
Musical	❑	❑	❑	❑
III. Dance Productions				
Classical Dance	❑	❑	❑	❑
Modern Dance	❑	❑	❑	❑
Jazz	❑	❑	❑	❑
Folk Dance	❑	❑	❑	❑

intention data. Note that this scale uses a forced-choice design by not including the middle logical scale point of "not sure." It is important to remember when designing behavior intention scales that researchers should include a specific *time frame* ("would consider attending in the next six months") in the *question/setup* portion of the scale. Without an expressed time frame, researchers increase the possibility that respondents will bias their responses toward the "definitely would" or "probably would" scale categories.

To increase the clarity of the scale point descriptors, researchers can attach a percentage equivalent expression to each one. To illustrate this concept, let's assume that Sears is interested in knowing how likely it is that customers will shop at certain types of retail stores for men's casual clothing. The following set of scale points could be used to obtain the intention data: "definitely would shop at (90% to 100% chance)"; "probably would shop at (50% to 89% chance)"; probably would not shop at (10% to 49% chance)"; and definitely would not shop at (less than 10% chance)." Exhibit 12.8 shows what the complete shopping intention scale might look like.

For more examples of Likert, semantic differential, and behavior intention types of scale designs visit the book's Web site at www.mhhe.com/hair4e and follow the links.

Strengths and Weaknesses of Attitude and Behavior Intention Scales

Researchers and marketing practitioners alike must realize that no matter what types of scale measurements are used to capture people's attitudes and behaviors, there often is no

EXHIBIT 12.8 Retail Store Shopping Intention Scale for Men's Casual Clothes

When shopping for men's casual wear for yourself or someone else, how likely are you to shop at each of the following types of retail stores? **(Please check one response for each store type.)**

Type of Retail Store	Definitely Would Shop At (90–100% chance)	Probably Would Shop At (50–89% chance)	Probably Would Not Shop At (10–49% chance)	Definitely Would Not Shop At (less than 10% chance)
Giant Retail Stores (e.g., Sears, JC Penney)	❑	❑	❑	❑
Department Stores (e.g., Macy's, Dillard's, Nordstrom's)	❑	❑	❑	❑
Discount Department Stores (e.g., Marshall's, TG&Y, Target)	❑	❑	❑	❑
Retail Mall Outlets (e.g., Orlando Mall Outlet)	❑	❑	❑	❑
Men's Clothing Specialty Shops (e.g., Wolf Brothers, Surrey's Ltd.)	❑	❑	❑	❑
Men's Casual Wear Specialty Stores (e.g., The Gap, Banana Republic)	❑	❑	❑	❑

one best or guaranteed approach. While there are proven scale measurements for capturing the components that make up people's attitudes as well as behavioral intentions, the data provided from these scale measurements should not be interpreted as being facts about a given object or behavior. Instead, the data and any derived structures should be viewed as insights into what might be reality. For example, if the information problem involves predicting some type of shopping, purchase, or consumption behavior, then developing and administering behavioral intention scales might well be the best approach. Unfortunately, knowledge of individuals' attitudes is not always a good predictor of their behavior. Intentions are better than attitudes at predicting behavior, but the strongest predictor of actual behavior is past behavior.[7] Researchers have made significant advances in their predictive models using attitudes and intentions, but there is still much room for improvement.

In contrast, if the information problem is one of better understanding why consumers (or customers) behave or respond as they do in the marketplace, researchers need something other than a basic measurement of their buying intentions. Behavior can be explained, directly or indirectly, by measuring both the cognitive and affective elements of the consumers' attitudes. Read the nearby A Closer Look at Research (Small Business Implications) box to see how small-business owners might use the Internet and Opinion meters to measure their customers' satisfaction.

Other Types of Comparative and Noncomparative Scales

Besides the rating scales discussed earlier, several variations, both comparative and noncomparative, remain popular among commercial marketing research firms. Unfortunately, the terms used to identify these different scale formats vary from one researcher to the next. For example, some researchers refer to a *performance* rating scale format (see example B in Exhibit 12.9) as an *itemized* rating scale format. Other researchers refer to a similar format as a *numerical* scale, or maybe a *monadic* scale, or a *composite* scale, or a *category* scale. For now, to avoid confusion it is easiest to classify any type of rating or ranking scale format as being either comparative or noncomparative in nature.

Noncomparative rating scale A scale format that requires a judgment without reference to another object, person, or concept.

Comparative rating scale A scale format that requires a judgment comparing one object, person, or concept against another on the scale.

Graphic rating scales A scale measure that uses a scale point format that presents the respondent with some type of graphic continuum as the set of possible raw responses to a given question.

Overall, a **noncomparative rating scale** is used when the objective is to have respondents express their attitudes, emotions, actions, or intentions about a specific object (or person, or phenomenon) or its attributes without making reference to another object or its attributes. In contrast, a scale format is a **comparative rating scale** in nature when the objective is to have respondents express their attitudes, feelings, or behaviors about an object (or person, or phenomenon) or its attributes on the basis of comparison to some other object or its attributes.

Within the "family" of *noncomparative* scale descriptor designs, we describe the three types—*graphic rating* scales, *performance rating* scales, and *staple* scales—frequently used by researchers in their efforts to create noncomparative scales. Exhibit 12.9 provides examples that illustrate these types of scale descriptor designs. Additional examples can be viewed by visiting the book's Web site at www.mhhe.com/hair4e and following the links.

Graphic rating scales (also referred to as *continuous* rating scales) use a scaling descriptor format that presents respondents with a graphic continuum as the set of possible responses to a question/setup. For example, the first graphic rating scale (usage or quantity descriptors) displayed in Exhibit 12.9 is used in situations where researchers want to collect "usage behavior" data about an object (or person, or phenomenon). Let's say Yahoo! wants to determine how frequently Internet users employ its search engine without making reference to any other available search engine alternatives (e.g., Google or Ask.com). In using this type of scale design, respondents would simply place an "X" along the graphic "usage" line where the extreme endpoints of the line have narrative descriptors (Never Use and Use All the Time) and numerical descriptors (0 and 100), while

A Closer Look at Research

Small Business Implications

Instant On-Site Customer Satisfaction Feedback

Most small-business owners are constantly in search of different methods to evaluate customer satisfaction. An integral component of any small business, positive customer satisfaction is vital in building long-term relationships with valuable customers. Below is an excerpt taken from Direct Network Access, Inc.'s Web site (www.opinionmeter.com) that describes a tool small-business owners can use to quickly and efficiently evaluate customer satisfaction. We recommend browsing through some of the "hot links" to reveal other technologically advanced products that will improve small-business operations.

The Opinionmeter is a flexible, easy-to-use interactive survey system designed to collect customer satisfaction feedback at point-of-service. No more paper surveys or data entry—the Opinionmeter instantly tabulates responses and provides immediate on-site access to survey results. When placed in a business lobby, customers interact with the freestanding battery-operated Opinionmeter to self-administer their own surveys, anonymously. Opinionmeter takes advantage of customers' waiting time and captures feedback while opinions are still fresh. In addition, on-site surveying sends a powerful message about a company's commitment to customer satisfaction.

EASY TO USE Now you can have the questionnaire customized, the machine programmed, the data collected, and the formal report completed in a single day. Opinionmeter's unique questionnaire display system permits questions and answers printed in any language to be displayed in the easy-to-read Questionnaire Holder. Reprogramming for a new questionnaire takes only 2–3 minutes.

QUICK RESULTS Respondent answers are screened and tallied, and results made instantly available after any survey. Results can be called up on the screen, hard-copied by a handheld infrared printer or transmitted via serial cable to your PC for in-depth analysis using Opinionmeter's Opinion Analyzer statistical software package. Full cross-tabulations are available, including date and time bracketing of data.

the remainder of the line is sectioned and described in equal-appearing numerical intervals (10, 20, 30, and so on).

Another popular type of graphic rating scale descriptor design is the "Smiling Faces" (see the second example in Exhibit 12.9). The smiling faces are arranged in a particular order and depict a continuous range from "very happy" to "very sad" without providing narrative meaning of the two extreme positions. Typically, the design uses a symmetrical format having equal numbers of happy and unhappy faces with a "neutral" face in the middle position. This type of visual graphic rating design can be used to collect a variety of attitudinal and emotional data. It is most popular in collecting data from children. For example, let's say Mattel, Inc., the toy manufacturer, is product testing several new toys among children aged 6 to 10 years. Researchers can have the children play with the toys, then ask them questions about their likes and dislikes. The children would answer by pointing to the face that best expresses their feelings about the particular toy.

Graphic rating scales are easy to construct and simple to use. They allow the identification of fine distinctions between responses, assuming the respondents have adequate discriminatory abilities. Overall, graphic rating scales are most appropriate in self-administered surveys (both online and offline) or personal interviews and are difficult to use in telephone interviews.

eXHIBIT 12.9 Noncomparative Rating Scales Used in Marketing Research

A. Graphic Rating Scales

1. Usage (Quantitiy) Descriptors:

Never Use — Use All the Time

0 10 20 30 40 50 60 70 80 90 100

2. Smiling Face Descriptors:

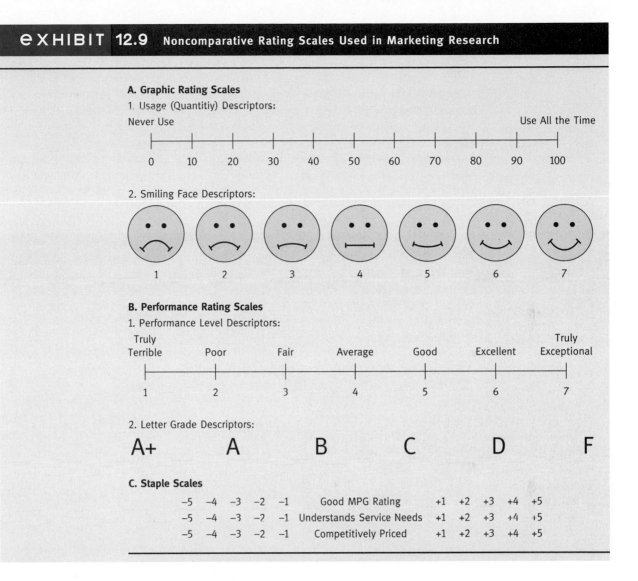

B. Performance Rating Scales

1. Performance Level Descriptors:

Truly Terrible	Poor	Fair	Average	Good	Excellent	Truly Exceptional
1	2	3	4	5	6	7

2. Letter Grade Descriptors:

A+ A B C D F

C. Staple Scales

−5	−4	−3	−2	−1	Good MPG Rating	+1	+2	+3	+4	+5
−5	−4	−3	−2	−1	Understands Service Needs	+1	+2	+3	+4	+5
−5	−4	−3	−2	−1	Competitively Priced	+1	+2	+3	+4	+5

Performance rating scales A scale measure that uses an evaluative scale point format that allows the respondent to express some type of postdecision or behavior evaluative judgment about an object.

Performance rating scales are types of itemized rating scales that use a scale point format that allows respondents to express some type of postdecision or evaluative judgment about the object under investigation. Although these scale descriptor designs have the initial appearance of being very similar to a graphic rating scale, the primary difference is that each scale point included is given narrative meaning and sometimes additional numerical meaning as well. The examples in part B of Exhibit 12.9 illustrate two design possibilities among many that researchers can use. When using performance-level descriptors, researchers ask respondents to select the response among a prelist of possible responses that best expresses their evaluative judgment toward the object or attribute of interest. The second design in part B of Exhibit 12.9 illustrates the letter-grade descriptor design. With this design, researchers ask respondents to express their performance judgments using a letter-grade scheme as commonly used in the United States. This type of design has an inherent flexibility factor in that researchers can easily expand the 6-point format as displayed in Exhibit 12.9 to a 13-point scale ranging from A+ down to F (A+, A, A−, B+, B, B−, C+, C, C–, D+, D, D−, F).

In contrast, this particular scale format has obvious limitations, making its use inappropriate in conducting international research studies. Performance rating scales are excellent for use in self-administered questionnaires or personal interviews, and generally poor for any type of telephone interview, unless the number of scale point descriptors is kept to three or four. An exception to this latter point would be the shorter form of the letter-grade design. Because of the inherent acceptance and understanding of this particular design, letter-grade descriptors are fairly easy to administer in both traditional and computer-assisted telephone interviews.

Turning now to *comparative* rating scales, Exhibit 12.10 illustrates some of the scales associated with *rank-order, paired-comparison,* and *constant sums* scale formats. A common characteristic among all comparative scale designs is that the scaling objective is to collect data that enable researchers to identify and directly compare similarities and

EXHIBIT 12.10 Comparative Rating Scales Used in Marketing Research

A. Rank-Order Scales

Thinking about the different types of music, please rank your top three preferences of types of music you enjoy listening to by writing in your first choice, second choice, and third choice on the lines provided below.

First Preference: ______________________

Second Preference: ______________________

Third Preference: ______________________

B. Paired-Comparison Scales

We are going to present you with several pairs of traits associated with a saleperson's on-the-job activities. For each pair, please circle either the "a" or "b" next to the trait you feel is more important for being a salesperson.

a. trust	b. competence
a. trust	b. communication skills
a. trust	b. personal social skills
a. competence	b. communication skills
a. competence	b. personal social skills
a. communication skills	b. personal social skills

Note: The researcher would want to scramble and reverse the order of these paired comparisons to avoid possible order bias.

C. Constant Sums Scales

Below is a list of seven banking features. Please allocate 100 points among those features such that the allocation represents the **importance** each feature had to you in selecting "your" bank. The more points you assign to a feature, the more important that feature was to your selection process. If the feature was "not at all important" in your process, you should not assign it any points. When you have finished, please double-check to make sure your total adds to 100.

Banking Features	Number of Points
Convenience/location	______
Banking hours	______
Good service charges	______
The interest rates on loans	______
The bank's reputation	______
The interest rates on savings	______
Bank's promotional advertising	______
	100 points

differences between *objects* (Mercedes versus Lexus cars), *people* (Hillary Clinton versus Barack Obama in the recent Democratic party primary elections), *marketing phenomena* (shopping online versus shopping offline), *concepts* (customer satisfaction versus service quality), or any of the *attributes* that underline objects, people, or phenomena (importance of salespeople's traits, for instance). In addition, comparative scale designs can be used to collect any type of data (state of being, mind, behavior, or intentions).

Rank-order scales These allow respondents to compare their own responses by indicating their first, second, third, and fourth preferences, and so forth, until all the desired responses are placed in a rank order.

Rank-order scales use a scale format that enables respondents to compare their own responses by indicating the first preference, second preference, third preference, and so forth, until all the desired responses are placed in either a "highest to lowest" or a "lowest to highest" rank order. For example, consider the rank-order scale design in Exhibit 12.10. Music.com, a new online music retailer, could use this rank-order scale design in an Internet user survey to determine the types of music prospective customers would most likely purchase online. This format allows for easy comparison of each possible response (e.g., type of music) that holds high importance or positive emotional feelings to the respondents.

Rank-order scales are easy to use in personal interviews and all types of self-administered surveys. Use of rank-order scales in traditional or computer-assisted telephone interviews may be difficult, but it is possible as long as the number of items being compared is kept to four or five. When respondents are asked to rank an object's attributes, problems can occur if respondents' preferred attributes are not part of the prelisted set of attributes being measured. Another limitation is that only ordinal data can be obtained using rank-order scales. Also, researchers cannot learn anything about the reasoning used by respondents in making their ranking choices.

Paired-comparison scales This format creates a preselected group of traits, product characteristics, or features that are paired against one another into two groups; respondents are asked to select which in each pair is more important to them.

Paired-comparison scales use a group of traits, product or service characteristics, or features that are paired against one another into two groups. Respondents are asked to select which trait, characteristic, or feature in each pair is more important to them. Consequently, respondents make a series of paired judgments between the attributes (features). It is important to remember that the number of paired comparisons increases geometrically as a function of the number of features being evaluated. For example, the paired-comparison scale shown in Exhibit 12.10 is one of several scales that Procter & Gamble's (P&G) recruiting team administers to new college graduates seeking employment in its consumer-products sales division. Here, P&G is concerned with the traits of communication skills, competence, and trust among its sales associates. By asking prospective applicants to make a series of paired judgments between these traits, the results are then compared with Procter & Gamble's standards to determine how well applicants match P&G's desired profile of a sales associate. A potential weakness of this type of scale design is that respondent fatigue can set in if too many attributes and paired choices are included.

Constant sums scales These require the respondent to allocate a given number of points, usually 100, among several attributes or features based on their importance to the individual; this format requires a person to evaluate each separate attribute or feature relative to all the other listed ones.

Constant sum scales require the respondent to allocate a given number of points, usually 100, among several attributes or features based on their importance or some other emotional feeling. This format requires respondents to determine the value of each separate feature relative to all the other listed features. Resulting value assignments indicate the relative magnitude of importance (or emotional feeling) that each feature has to respondents. This scaling format requires that the individual values must add up to 100. Consider the constant sum scale shown in Exhibit 12.10. Bank of America can use this type of scale design to identify which banking attributes are more important to customers in influencing their decision of where to bank. This type of comparative scale design is most appropriate for use in self-administered surveys and to a much lesser extent in personal interviews. Caution must be used with constant sum scales when too many (generally, more than seven) attributes are included for evaluation, since this design requires a lot of mental energy on the part of respondents.

For more examples of comparative and noncomparative scale designs, log on to the book's Web site at www.mhhe.com/hair4e and follow the links.

Comments on Single-Item and Multiple-Item Scales

Single-item scale design A scale format that collects data about only one attribute of an object or construct.

Multiple-item scale design A scale format that simultaneously collects data on several attributes of an object or construct.

Before concluding the discussion of advanced scale measures, several comments are needed about when and why researchers use single-item and multiple-item scaling formats. First, a scale design can be characterized as being a **single-item scale design** when the data requirements focus on collecting data about only one attribute of the object or construct being investigated. An easy example to remember is collecting "age" data. Here the object is "a person" and the single attribute of interest is that person's "age." Only one measure is needed to collect the required age data. Respondents are asked a single question about their age and supply only one possible response to the question. In contrast, most marketing research projects that involve collecting attitudinal, emotional, and behavioral data require some type of **multiple-item scale design.** Basically, when using a multiple-item scale to measure the object or construct of interest, researchers will have to measure several items simultaneously rather than measuring just one item. Most advanced attitude, emotion, and behavior scales are multiple-item scales.

The decision to use a single-item versus a multiple-item scale is made in the construct development stage. Two factors play a significant role in the process. First, researchers must assess the dimensionality of the construct under investigation. Any construct that is viewed as consisting of several different, unique subdimensions will require researchers to measure each of those subcomponents. Second, researchers must deal with the reliability and validity issues of the scales used to collect data. Consequently, researchers are forced to measure each subcomponent using a set of different scale items. To illustrate these two points, consider again the Tiger Woods as a spokesperson example in Exhibit 12.3. Here the main construct of interest was "credibility as a spokesperson." Credibility was made up of three key subcomponents (expertise, trustworthiness, and attractiveness). Each of the subcomponents was measured using five different seven-point scale items (e.g., expertise—knowledgeable/unknowledgeable, expert/not expert, skilled/unskilled, qualified/unqualified, experienced/inexperienced).

Formative composite scale A scale format that uses several individual scale items to measure different parts of the whole object or construct.

Reflective composite scale A scale format that uses multiple scale items to measure one component of an object or construct.

Another point to remember about multiple-item scales is that there are two types of scales: formative and reflective. A **formative composite scale** is used when each of the individual scale items measures some part of the whole construct, object, or phenomenon. For example, to measure the *overall image* of a 2010 Hummer, researchers have to measure the different attributes that make up that automobile's image, such as performance, resale value, gas mileage, styling, price, safety features, sound system, and craftsmanship. By creating a scale that measures each pertinent attribute, researchers can sum the parts into a complete (that is, formative) whole that measures the overall image held by respondents toward the 2010 Hummer. With a **reflective composite scale** design, researchers use multiple items to measure an individual subcomponent of a construct, object, or phenomenon. For example, in isolating the investigation to the *performance* dimension of the 2010 Hummer, researchers can use a common performance rating scale and measure those identified attributes (trouble-free, MPG rating, comfort of ride, workmanship, overall quality, dependability, responsiveness) that make up the performance dimension. Each of these attributes reflects performance and an average of the reflective scale items can be interpreted as a measure of performance.

Measurement Design Issues

The main design issues related to both construct development and scale measurement are reviewed below.

Construct Development Issues

Researchers must clearly define and operationalize constructs before they attempt to develop their scales. For each construct being investigated, researchers must determine its dimensionality characteristics (i.e., single versus multidimensional) before developing appropriate scales. In a multidimensional construct, all relevant dimensions must be identified as well as their related attributes.

Researchers also must not create *double-barreled dimensions*. That is, two different dimensions of a construct should not be represented as if they are one. For example, when investigating consumers' perceptions of *service quality,* do not combine the service provider's "technological competence" and "diagnostic competence" into a single competence dimension. Similarly, with a singular dimension, do not include double-barreled attributes. For example, avoid asking respondents to rate two attributes simultaneously (e.g., indicate to what extent you agree or disagree that Martha Stewart "perjured herself" and "should have been indicted"). For a multidimensional construct, use scale designs in which multiple attribute items are represented separately to measure each dimension independently from the other dimensions (see again the Tiger Woods example in Exhibit 12.3). Finally, construct validity must always be assessed before creating the final scales.

Measurement Scale Issues

When phrasing the question/setup element of a scale, use clear wording and avoid ambiguity. Also avoid using "leading" words or phrases in the question/setup part of any scale measurement.

Regardless of the data collection method (personal, telephone, or computer-assisted interviews, or any type of offline or online self-administered survey), all necessary instructions for both respondents and interviewers should be part of the scale measurement's setup. All instructions should be kept simple and clear. When using multiattribute items, make sure the items are phrased *unidimensionally* (avoid double-barreled item phrases). When determining the appropriate set of scale point descriptors, make sure the descriptors are relevant to the type of data being sought. Use only scale descriptors and formats that have been pretested and evaluated for scale reliability and validity. Scale descriptors should have adequate discriminatory power, be mutually exclusive, and make sense to respondents.

Screening Questions

Screening questions (also referred to as *screeners* or *filter questions*) should be used in any type of interview. Their purpose is to identify qualified prospective respondents and prevent unqualified respondents from being included in the study. It is difficult to use screening questions in many self-administered questionnaires, except for computer-assisted surveys. Screening questions need to be separately administered before the beginning of the main interview.

Skip Questions

Skip questions (also referred to as *conditional* or *branching questions*) should be avoided if at all possible. If they are needed, the instructions must be clearly communicated to respondents or interviewers. Skip questions can appear anywhere within the questionnaire and are used if the next question (or set of questions) should be responded to only by respondents who meet a previous condition. A simple expression of a skip command might be: "If you answered yes to Question 5, skip to Question 9." Skip questions help ensure that only specifically qualified respondents answer certain items.

Ethical Responsibility of Researchers

In the development of scale measurements, researchers must use the most appropriate scales possible. Intentionally using scale measurements to produce biased information raises questions about the professional ethics of researchers. Any set of scale point descriptors used to frame a noncomparative rating scale can be manipulated to bias the results in any direction. Inappropriate scale descriptors to collect brand-image data can be used to create a positive view of one brand or a negative view of a competitor's brand, which might not paint a true picture of the situation. To illustrate this point, let's revisit the Aca Joe example from the beginning of the chapter. Let's assume that in creating the seven-point semantic differential scale used to collect the image data for the seven dimensions of Aca Joe's store image (quality, assortment, style/fashion, prices of merchandise, store's location, overall reputation, and knowledgeability of sales staff), researchers decided not to follow many of the process guidelines for developing accurate scale measurements we have discussed, including no pretesting of the scales. Instead, they just used their intuitive judgment of what they thought the owner of Aca Joe's was hoping for. Consequently, the following semantic differential scale measurement was developed:

For each of the following attributes, please circle the number that best expresses how you would rate that attribute for the Aca Joe retail store.

Attributes									
Quality of Merchandise	Truly Terrible	1	2	3	4	5	6	7	Outstanding
Merchandise Assortment	Limited	1	2	3	4	5	6	7	Extremely Wide
Style of Merchandise	Very Stylish	1	2	3	4	5	6	7	Not Stylish
Merchandise Prices	Extremely High	1	2	3	4	5	6	7	Reasonable
Overall Store Reputation	Very Good	1	2	3	4	5	6	7	Extremely Poor
Store's Location	Very Inconvenient	1	2	3	4	5	6	7	Definitely Convenient
Sales Staff	Very Professional	1	2	3	4	5	6	7	Very Unprofessional

Now, select a retail store of your choice, assume it to be Aca Joe's, and rate that store using the above scale. Interpret the image profile that you create and compare it to Aca Joe's desired and actual images described in the chapter opener. What differences do you detect? How objective were your ratings? Did you find yourself rating your store positively like Aca Joe? What problems did you encounter on each dimension?

Using the above scale, researchers can negatively bias evaluations of competitors' image by providing mildly negative descriptors against strong descriptors or vice versa. For example, the adjective 'Truly Terrible" is much more negative than the positive impression of 'Outstanding.' Similarly, the adjective 'Extremely High' used with Merchandise Prices is much more negative than is the positive adjective of 'Reasonable.' Ethically, it is important to use balanced scales with comparable positive and negative descriptors. In addition, when researchers do not follow scale development guidelines, responses can be biased. This example also points out the need to pretest and establish scale measurements that have adequate reliability, validity, and generalizability. Remember, scales that are unreliable are invalid, or lack generalizability to the defined target population, and will provide misleading findings (garbage in, garbage out).

MARKETING RESEARCH IN ACTION

Part 2

Scale Measurements Used in Creating a Customer Loyalty Index[8]

This is Part 2 of the Marketing Research in Action introduced at the end of Chapter 11. Recall how researchers at Burke Customer Satisfaction Associates defined the three main components (overall customer satisfaction, likelihood of repeat business, and likelihood to recommend the company) making up their construct of the Secure Customer Index (SCI).

Measuring Customer Loyalty

At Burke Customer Satisfaction Associates, these three components (overall customer satisfaction, likelihood of repeat business, and likelihood to recommend the company) are measured by looking at the combined scores of three survey questions. For example, in examining the overall satisfaction of restaurant customers, respondents are asked, "Overall, how satisfied were you with your visit to this restaurant?" To examine their likelihood to recommend, they are asked, "How likely would you be to recommend this restaurant to a friend or associate?" And finally, to examine the likelihood of repeat visits (purchases), they are asked, "How likely are you to choose to visit this restaurant again?"

With these three components and the appropriate scales for each, *secure customers* would be defined as those giving the most positive responses across all three components. All other customers would be considered vulnerable or at risk of defecting to a competitor. The degree of vulnerability can be determined from responses to these questions.

When researchers interpret a company's SCI, they typically compare it to other relevant SCI scores, such as the company's SCI score in past years, the SCI scores of competitors, and the SCI scores of "best-in-class" companies. While a company should always strive for higher scores, understanding how "good" or "bad" a given score might be is best done in comparative terms.

Customer Loyalty and Market Performance

Increasingly, researchers are able to link customer satisfaction and customer loyalty to bottom-line benefits. By examining customer behaviors over time and comparing them to SCI scores, researchers see a strong connection between secure customers and repeat purchasing of products or services. For example, researchers examined the relationship between customer satisfaction survey data and repeat purchasing levels in the computer industry. Secure customers in this industry were twice as likely to renew contracts as were vulnerable customers. Secure customers also were twice as likely to expand their business with their primary vendor.

As researchers continued to look at cases across customer and industry types, they found other compelling illustrations that show a connection between the index scores and financial or market performance. These findings demonstrate the value of examining index scores not only across an industry but also over time within the same company to determine changes in the proportion of secure customers.

Competition, Customers, and Surveys

As with any measurement, a customer loyalty index may be influenced by other factors depending on the industry, market characteristics, or research methods. These factors must be considered when interpreting the meaning of any loyalty index. Industries with more than one provider of services tend to produce higher customer satisfaction scores than industries with limited choices. For example, the cable industry, which in many markets still tends to be monopolistic, generally has lower customer satisfaction scores in comparison to other industries. The notion that competition breeds more opportunities clearly affects customer satisfaction as well.

A second factor that may contribute indirectly to a customer loyalty index score is the type of market being examined. In specialty markets where the product is tailored or customized for customers, loyalty index scores tend to be higher than in general or noncustomized markets. For example, index scores for customers of specialized software or network configurations would likely be higher than scores for customers of airlines.

The type of customer being measured may influence the index scores. For example, business-to-business customers may score differently than general consumers. Again, the type of industry involved also will influence the type of customers being examined.

Finally, the data collection method may influence customers' responses. Researchers have long recognized that the different methods used to collect information, such as live interviews, mail surveys, and telephone interviews, may produce varying results.

Recognizing these factors is important not only in collecting information but also in interpreting an index. Learning how to minimize or correct these influences will enhance the validity or true "reading" of a customer loyalty index.

Using Data to Evaluate Your Own Efforts

Businesses committed to customer-driven quality must integrate the voices of customers into their business operations. A customer loyalty index provides actionable information by demonstrating the ratio of secure customers to vulnerable customers. An index acts as a baseline or yardstick for management to create goals for the organization and helps to focus efforts for continuous improvement over time. And as changes and initiatives are implemented in the organization, the index's score may be monitored as a way of evaluating initiatives. Using a customer loyalty index helps companies better understand their customers. By listening to customers, implementing change, and continuously monitoring the results, companies can focus their improvement efforts with the goal of winning and keeping customers.

Hands-On Exercise

Using your knowledge from the chapter and the information provided in this illustration, answer each of the following questions. Make sure you can defend your answers.

1. What are several weaknesses associated with how Burke Customer Satisfaction Associates measures its Secure Customer Index (SCI)? Make sure you clearly identify each weakness and explain why you feel it is a weakness.

2. If you were the head researcher, what types of scale measurement designs would you have used to collect the needed data for calculating SCI? Why? Design a sample of the scale measurements that you would use.

3. Do you agree or disagree with the Burke Associates' interpretation of the value they provide their clients using the Customer Loyalty Index? Support your response.

Summary of Learning Objectives

■ **Understand attitudes and their components.**

An attitude is a learned predisposition to act in a consistently positive or negative way to a given object, idea, or set of information. Attitudes are state-of-mind constructs that are not directly observable. Attitudes can be thought of as having three components: cognitive, affective, and behavioral. Marketing researchers and decision makers need to understand all three components. The cognitive component of an attitude is the person's beliefs, perceptions, and knowledge about an object and its attributes. The affective component of an attitude is the person's emotional feelings toward a given object. This component is the one most frequently expressed when a person is asked to verbalize his or her attitude toward some object, person, or phenomenon. The behavioral component, also sometimes referred to as a conative component, is a person's intended or actual behavioral response to an object.

■ **Describe attitude and behavior scales and assess their strengths and weaknesses.**

Likert scale designs uniquely employ a set of agreement/disagreement scale descriptors to capture a person's attitude toward a given object or behavior. Contrary to popular belief, a Likert scale format does not measure a person's complete attitude, but only the cognitive structure. Semantic differential scale formats are exceptional in capturing a person's perceptual image profile about a given object or behavior. This scale format is unique in that it uses a set of bipolar scales to measure several different yet interrelated factors (both cognitive and affective) of a given object or behavior.

Multiattribute affect scales use scale point descriptors that consist of relative magnitudes of an attitude ("very important," "important," "somewhat important," "not at all important," or "like very much," "like somewhat," "neither like nor dislike," "dislike somewhat," "dislike very much"). With respect to behavior intention scale formats, practitioners are interested in obtaining some idea of the likelihood that people (actual or potential consumers, customers, buyers) will demonstrate some type of predictable behavior toward purchasing an object or service. The scale point descriptors like "definitely would," "probably would," "probably would not," and "definitely would not" are normally used in an intentions scale format. If the information objective is collecting raw data that can directly predict some type of marketplace behavior, then behavior intention scales must be used in the study. In turn, if the objective is to understand why certain types of marketplace behaviors occur, then it is necessary to incorporate scale measurement formats that capture both the person's cognitive belief structures and feelings.

■ **Recommend when noncomparative and comparative scale designs are appropriate.**

The main difference is that comparative scale measurements require respondents to make a direct comparison between the attributes of the scale from the same known reference point, whereas noncomparative scales rate each attribute independently of the other attributes making up the scale measurement. The data from comparative scales must be interpreted in relative terms and only activate the assignment and order scaling properties. Noncomparative scale data are treated as interval or ratio, and more advanced statistical procedures can be employed in analyzing the data structures. One benefit of comparative scales is they allow for identifying small differences between the attributes, constructs, or objects. In addition, their comparative scale designs require fewer theoretical assumptions and are easier for respondents to understand and respond to than are many of the noncomparative scale designs. However, noncomparative scales provide opportunity for greater insights into the constructs and their components.

■ **Summarize measurement scale design issues.**

For organizations to make informed decisions regarding their customers, competitors, employees, suppliers, or organizational members, they must gather detailed, accurate information. To do so, they must design, pretest, and use valid and reliable constructs that accurately measure attitudes and behaviors. Moreover, the appropriate type of scale must be selected so that respondents can understand it and management can interpret the results. Finally, the constructs and scales must have instructions on how to evaluate them, and the necessary screening and skip questions to provide guidance to respondents on when and how to respond.

■ **Compare the trilogy and affect global approaches for explaining attitudes (Appendix 12.A).**

The trilogy approach is a model suggesting a person's attitude toward an object, a person, or a phenomenon and is based on cognitive, affective, and conative components that make up the attitude. It is the integration of these three components that allows a person to create an overall attitude of a given object. The *cognitive component* of an attitude represents the person's beliefs, perceptions, and knowledge about the specified object and its attributes. These are the key elements and outcomes of learning. An attitude's *affective component* represents the person's emotional feelings toward the given object. This is the component most frequently expressed when a person is asked to verbalize his or her attitude toward some object, person, or phenomenon. The *conative component* of an attitude relates to the person's intended or actual behavioral response to the given object. The conative component is also referred to as the behavioral component. Fishbein's attitude-toward-behavior model is a popular approach that captures a person's overall attitude toward his or her behavior with a given object rather than the attitude toward the object itself. This model more closely demonstrates the actual behavior of individuals than does the attitude-toward-object model. In contrast to the trilogy approach to attitude measurement, the affect global approach assumes an attitude is nothing more than a person's global (or overall) expression of favorable or unfavorable feelings toward a given object. The assumption is a person's feelings can have a dominant influence on his or her overall judgment of a given object. In other words, affect equals attitude. (A comprehensive explanation of these concepts is provided in the appendix to this chapter.)

Key Terms and Concepts

Affect global approach 397
Affective component 369
Attitude 368
Behavior intention scale 377
Behavioral (conative) component 369
Cognitive component 369
Comparative rating scale 379
Constant sums scales 383
Formative composite scale 384
Graphic rating scales 379
Halo effect bias 374
Likert scale 370
Multiple-item scale design 384
Noncomparative rating scale 379
Paired-comparison scales 383
Performance rating scales 381
Rank-order scales 383
Reflective composite scale 384
Semantic differential scale 372
Single-item scale design 384
Trilogy approach 392

Review Questions

1. Conceptually, what is an attitude? Is there one best method of measuring a person's attitude? Why or why not?
2. Explain the major differences between "rating" and "ranking" scales. Which is a better scale measurement technique for collecting attitudinal data on salesforce performance of people who sell commercial laser printers? Why?
3. When collecting importance data about the features business travelers use to select a hotel, should a researcher use a balanced or an unbalanced scale measurement? Why?
4. Explain the main differences between using "even-point" and "odd-point" scale measurement designs for collecting purchase intention data. Is one approach better than the other? Why?
5. If a semantic differential has eight attribute dimensions, should all the positive pole descriptors be on the left side and all the negative pole descriptors be on the right side of the scale continuum? Why or why not?

6. What are the benefits and limitations of comparative scale measurements? Design a paired-comparison scale that will allow you to determine brand preference between Bud Light, Miller Lite, Coors Light, and Old Milwaukee Light beers.

7. What are the weaknesses associated with the use of a Likert scale design to measure customers' attitudes toward the purchase of products at Wal-Mart?

Discussion Questions

1. Develop a semantic differential scale that can identify the perceptual profile differences between Outback Steakhouse and Longhorn Steakhouse restaurants.

2. Explain the differences between a Likert summated scale format and a numeric rating scale format. Should a Likert scale ever be considered an interval scale? Why or why not? Now develop a forced-choice Likert scale measurement that can be used to measure consumers' beliefs about the movie *Indiana Jones*.

3. Design a behavior intention scale that can answer the following research question: "To what extent are college students likely to purchase a new automobile within six months after graduating?" Discuss the potential shortcomings of your scale design.

4. Develop an appropriate set of attitudinal scales that would enable you to capture the cognitive and affective components of college students' overall attitudes concerning the presidential candidates John McCain and Barack Obama.

5. **EXPERIENCE THE INTERNET.** One company that relies heavily on asking Americans about their attitudes and values is SRI International. It has developed a unique segmentation technique that uses VALS-type data to classify people into different lifestyle categories. Get on the Internet and go to SRI's Web site at www.future.sri.com:/valshome.html. Take their short survey to determine your VALS (Values and Lifestyles) type. While you are taking the survey, evaluate what scale measurements are being used. What type of possible design bias might exist?

appendix 12.A

This appendix provides an overview of the trilogy and affect global approaches to explaining the structure of an attitude. The discussion illustrates how different attitude scaling formats yield different results about the same attitude construct.

The Trilogy Approach

Trilogy approach suggests that understanding of a person's complete attitude toward an object, a person, or a phenomenon requires an understanding of the *cognitive, affective,* and *conative* components that make up that attitude.

The **trilogy approach** suggests that understanding of a person's complete attitude toward an object, a person, or a phenomenon requires an understanding of the *cognitive*, *affective*, and *conative* components that make up that attitude. It is the integration of these three components that creates a person's overall perception of a given object. Exhibit 12.a.1 illustrates the integrative nature of these components.

The cognitive component of an attitude is made up of a person's beliefs, perceptions, and knowledge about the specified object and its attributes. These are outcomes of learning. For example, a series of TV ads for its wireless cell phone service sponsored by Alltel Communication had "Chad" comparing Alltel's wireless phone plans and benefits to its leading competitors (AT&T Wireless, Sprint, T-Mobile, and Verizon) and an "evil wizard" that popped out of the competitors' van. Research focusing on the "effectiveness" of those TV ads revealed that many people held a variety of different beliefs about them. Here is a sample of those beliefs:

- Alltel has a better pricing strategy than AT&T, Sprint, T-Mobile, and Verizon.
- Ads portray Alltel as a much more reliable wireless cell phone provider than its main competitors.

EXHIBIT 12.a.1 The Three Components of an Attitude

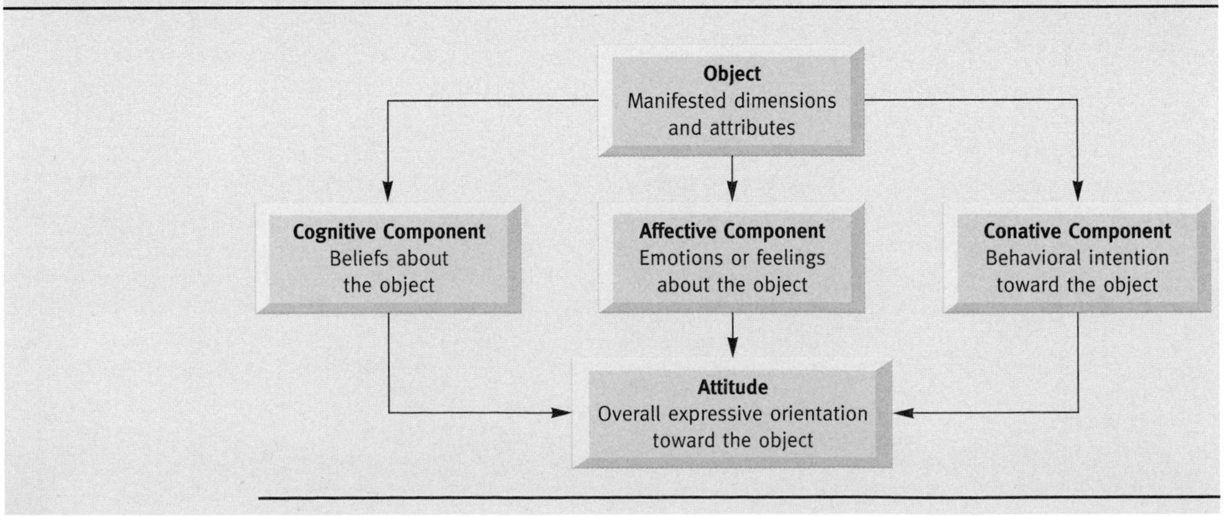

- AT&T, Sprint, T-Mobile, and Verizon are losing market share to Alltel.
- Alltel's customers are happier cell phone users than AT&T, Sprint, T-Mobile, or Verizon customers.
- Alltel is the innovative leader among wireless cell phone companies.
- AT&T, Sprint, T-Mobile, and Verizon are not consumer-friendly cell phone companies.
- Alltel is the only major cell phone company that understands consumers' wireless cell phone needs and wants.
- Even wizards have "circles" of friends that benefit from using Alltel as their wireless cell phone carrier.

These statements are selected beliefs about some of the attributes that people formed regarding Alltel as a wireless cell phone company compared to its leading competitors. Although any one of these beliefs by itself would provide a poor representation of the people's attitude concerning Alltel as a wireless cell phone company, in combination they form the basis for identifying people's overall attitude on the effectiveness of those specific TV commercials. A key point to remember here is that most state-of-mind objects or constructs investigated by researchers will most likely have a multidimensional aspect requiring researchers to include sets of attributes in their scale measurement designs. In reality, people have hundreds of beliefs about many different items, attributes, and objects that make up their everyday environment.

An attitude's affective component represents the person's emotional feelings toward the given object. This is the component most frequently expressed when a person is asked to verbalize his or her attitude toward some object, person, or phenomenon. A simple way to view this affective component is to think of it as being the amount of emotional feeling a person attaches to each of his or her individual beliefs. This component serves as a mechanism that enables a person to create some type of hierarchical order among a set of beliefs about an object or behavior. For example, a person considering the purchase of a new 2009 Acura 3.2 TL might identify several common factors about cars that in general are important in the selection process. The affective component of that person's attitude toward the Acura allows him or her to decide which of the car's attributes (engine power, safety system, sport option package, fuel economy, price, etc.) hold more importance (or less importance) with regard to that specific car. At this point, remember that people's emotional feelings toward an object are anchored to a set of recognizable beliefs about that object.

The conative component of an attitude relates to the person's intended or actual behavioral response to the given object. The conative component is also referred to as the behavioral component. This part of an attitude tends to be an observable outcome driven by the interaction of a person's cognitive component (beliefs) and affective component (emotional strength of those beliefs) as they relate to the given object. In the Acura example, the person's purchase intention decision to buy (conative component) a gold-colored 2009 Acura 3.2 TL with leather and wood interior, an antilock braking system, cruise control, automatic seat and side mirror adjustment, a high-performance six-cylinder engine, dual airbags, and a high-tech DVD sound system would be directly influenced by the set of beliefs (cognitive components) and the emotional feelings of importance (affective components) attached to those beliefs concerning each of the listed options that are part of the Acura car.

The key point to remember about the trilogy approach is that the complete measurement of attitudes cannot be achieved using a single-item or multiple-item global scale design but rather requires the development of some type of multiplicative-additive model. The fundamental reasons behind the need for a model are that most objects are really nothing more than a composite of many different parts (or attributes). People have the capability of developing a separate attitude toward each attribute, and attitudes themselves tend to consist of distinguishable components. In other words, to measure attitudes, researchers must collect several types of data (cognitive, affective, and conative) about the object and its attributes of interest and then, through a modeling process, derive a composite attitude score. Several types of multiplicative-additive model have been developed within the trilogy framework, but we will limit our discussion to two of the most frequently used models: attitude-toward-object and attitude-toward-behavior.

Attitude-toward-Object Model

One popular attitudinal model is Fishbein's *attitude-toward-object model,* which is normally presented in the form of the following equation:[9]

$$Attitude_O = \sum_{i=1}^{k} b_i\, e_i$$

where $Attitude_O$ is a separate, indirectly derived composite measure (sometimes considered a global measure) of a person's combined thoughts and feelings for or against the given object (product, service, brand, manufacturer, retail establishment); b_i is the strength of the belief that the person holds toward the *i*th attribute of the object (e.g., the 2009 Acura 3.2 TL has a satisfactory mileage rating); e_i is the person's affect evaluation (expressed feeling or importance) of the belief toward that *i*th attribute of the object (e.g., it is very important that my car has an excellent mileage rating); and $\sum$ indicates that there are k salient attributes making up the object over which the multiplicative combinations of b_i and e_i for those attributes are summated.

To illustrate the development processes for the scales researchers use to collect the data to capture a person's overall attitude toward an object through the attitude-toward-object modeling approach, we expand the 2009 Acura 3.2 TL example. Let's say the overall research objective is to collect data that will enable management to better understand the attitudes owners hold toward the *performance* of a 2009 Acura 3.2 TL. Acura's marketing experts worked with J. D. Power and Associates to develop a two-phase research plan that includes both qualitative and quantitative research activities to create the different scale measurements needed to collect the cognitive components (b_i) and corresponding affective components (e_i) that relate to assessing respondents' attitudes toward the performance of an automobile. First, using qualitative research practices, several general focus group interviews were conducted among a cross-section of people who were known to have purchased a new automobile within the past 12 months. One topic of those interviews was the elements people use to judge the performance of automobiles. This part of the research discovered and identified the following seven attributes:

1. The perception of the car as *trouble-free.*
2. The actual *miles per gallon* (MPG) *rating* of the automobile.
3. The *comfort* of the ride provided by the car.
4. The *craftsmanship* (or workmanship) built into the automobile.
5. The *overall quality* of the automobile.
6. The *dependability* (or reliability) of the automobile.
7. The *responsiveness* of the car in different weather conditions.

To validate these seven attributes as meaningful subfactors people use to assess their attitudes toward the performance of automobiles, researchers conducted a pilot study where

300 randomly selected respondents were given a survey that included these seven attributes and were asked to judge them using a four-point scale scheme where 4 = "*definitely* a factor of performance"; 3 = "*generally* a factor of performance"; 2 = "*only somewhat* a factor of performance"; and 1 = "*not at all* a factor of performance." The researchers then analyzed the data collected from the pilot study using direct cognitive structural (DCS) analysis. The results demonstrated that all seven attributes were considered factors people used in assessing the performance of automobiles, all having mean values of 3.5 or higher.

Using the information generated from the first phase of the research project, researchers planned and executed the second phase by conducting a more elaborate quantitative study where surveys were administered to 1,500 known Acura 3.2 TL owners who were randomly selected from an Acura (Honda American) Corporation's customer data bank. To capture these respondents' emotional importance (e_i) associated with each of the seven performance attributes, the affective scale measurement displayed in Exhibit 12.a.2 was developed and

EXHIBIT 12.a.2 Scale Measurements Used in Determining the Attitude toward the *Performance* of a 2009 Acura 3.2 TL

AFFECTIVE (IMPORTANCE) SCALE MEASUREMENT

Using the scale below, please write a number from one (1) to six (6) in the space provided that best expresses how emotionally important you feel each listed attribute is to you in assessing the performance of an automobile.

Not at All Important	Only Slightly Important	Somewhat Important	Generally Important	Definitely Important	Extremely Important
(1)	(2)	(3)	(4)	(5)	(6)

ATTRIBUTES

____ The perception of the car as trouble-free (or practically defect-free).
____ The actual miles per gallon (MPG) rating of the automobile.
____ The comfort (or smoothness) of the ride provided by the car.
____ The craftsmanship (or workmanship) built into the automobile.
____ The overall quality of the automobile.
____ The dependability (or reliability) of the automobile.
____ The responsiveness of the car in different weather conditions.

COGNITIVE (BELIEF) SCALE MEASUREMENT

Thinking about all experiences with driving your 2009 Acura 3.2 TL, we would like to know your opinion about each of the following factors. For each factor, please circle the number that best expresses how you believe your 2009 Acura 3.2 TL has performed on that factor. For any factor(s) that are not relevant to your assessment, please circle the "zero" (0), which means "not applicable" (N/A).

2009 Acura 3.2 TL	Truly Terrible	Fair	Average	Good	Excellent	Truly Exceptional	(N/A)
Trouble- (practically defect-) free	1	2	3	4	5	6	0
Miles per gallon (MPG) rating	1	2	3	4	5	6	0
Comfort (smoothness) of the ride	1	2	3	4	5	6	0
Craftsmanship (or workmanship)	1	2	3	4	5	6	0
Overall quality	1	2	3	4	5	6	0
Dependability (or reliability)	1	2	3	4	5	6	0
Responsiveness (or handling)	1	2	3	4	5	6	0

tested for reliability (internal consistency). Using this scale measurement, respondents were asked to write a number from 1 to 6 in the space provided that best expressed how emotionally important they felt each listed factor was to them in assessing the performance of a new automobile. In contrast, the six-point cognitive scale measurement displayed in the exhibit was developed, tested for reliability (internal consistency), and used to capture the respondents' evaluative performance beliefs (b_i) about the 2009 Acura 3.2 TL. In applying the cognitive scale measurement, respondents' were asked to circle a number from 1 to 6 that best expressed how well the 2009 Acura 3.2 TL performed on each listed factor. In those cases where a particular factor might not be relevant in their assessment, respondents were instructed to circle the zero (0) response, which meant "not applicable" (N/A).

After collecting the cognitive (b_i) and corresponding affective (e_i) data on the seven attributes, researchers can apply the multiplicative-additive model to determine respondents' overall composite attitude toward the performance of the 2009 Acura 3.2 TL or respondents' individual attitudes for each of the separate seven attributes. To see how researchers can determine an individual attitude toward a particular attribute, let's use attribute 1, perception of the *car as being a trouble-free* automobile. We simply multiply the respondent's belief score (b_i) assigned to this factor by the corresponding importance score (e_i), resulting in a possible score range of 1 ($1 \times 1 = 1$) to 36 ($6 \times 6 = 36$). The score would be interpreted to mean that the lower the value, the weaker the attitude and the higher the value, the stronger the attitude. In determining respondents' overall attitude toward the *performance* of the 2009 Acura 3.2 TL, researchers would take each of the individually derived attitude scores for each factor and add them together into one composite score that could range between 7 (7 attributes $\times$ 1 = 7) on the low end and 252 (7 attributes $\times$ 36 = 252) at the high end. Again, interpretation of the composite scores would be that the lower the composite value, the weaker the overall attitude and the higher the score, the stronger the attitude.

This modeling approach also enables researchers to determine the average attitudes held by all the respondents included in the study for each attribute as well as the comprehensive performance attitude held toward the 2009 Acura 3.2 TL. To analyze the group attitude toward a particular attribute, researchers with the use of a computer would calculate the 1,500 individual attitude scores for that attribute, then add those scores together, then divide that total by the total number of respondents who contributed in deriving that total score. The average group attitude score for any of the individual attributes would range between 1 and 36 and be interpreted similarly to an individual attitude score. A similar procedure would be used to determine the group's overall composite performance attitude toward the 2009 Acura 3.2 TL. Researchers would have the computer calculate the individual composite scores for each of the seven attributes among the 1,500 respondents, add those scores together, then divide that total by the sample size of respondents used to derive the total attitude score. Interpretation of the group's average composite attitude score would be the same as the interpretation of an individual's composite score described earlier.

It is important to remember that in this measurement approach, equal emphasis is given to measuring both a person's beliefs (cognitive) and a person's feelings (affective) toward the attributes of the object under investigation. This modeling approach provides researchers and decision makers with a lot of diagnostic insight into the components that make up the consumer's attitude. Decision makers can learn how and what the customer used to evaluate either the potential or actual performance of a given object (e.g., a 2009 Acura 3.2 TL).

Attitude-toward-Behavior Model

Another popular multiplicative-additive attitude model is Fishbein's *attitude-toward-behavior model*.[10] This model captures a person's attitude toward his or her *behavior* with a given object rather than the attitude toward the object itself. One benefit of this approach is that it gives researchers a picture that more closely demonstrates the actual behavior of individuals than does the attitude-toward-object model. Normally, the attitude-toward-behavior model is presented by the following equation:

$$Attitude_{(beh)} = \sum_{i=1}^{n} b_i\, a_i$$

where $Attitude_{(beh)}$ is a separate, indirectly derived composite measure (sometimes considered an overall or global measure) of a person's combined thoughts and feelings for or against carrying out a specific action or behavior (the purchase and/or driving of an Acura 3.2 TL); b_i is the strength of the person's belief that the ith specific action will lead to a specific outcome (e.g., that driving a 2009 Acura 3.2 TL will increase the person's social standing in the community); a_i is the person's expressed feeling (affect) toward the ith action outcome (the "favorableness feeling" of knowing friends admire the 2009 Acura 3.2 TL); and Σ indicates that there are n salient action outcomes making up the behavior over which the multiplicative combinations of b_i and a_i for those outcomes are summated.

Exhibit 12.a.3 illustrates the scales and procedures that might be used in an attitude-toward-behavior model to capture a person's overall attitude toward *purchasing* a 2009 Acura 3.2 TL. The key thing to remember here is that behavior-oriented beliefs are used and that greater emphasis is placed on measuring the person's affective evaluation of the behavioral outcome. This approach can help the researcher or decision maker understand why customers might behave as they do toward a given object. For example, collecting this type of attitudinal data offers the researcher insights into how and why customers judge the "service quality" construct associated with purchasing a new automobile.

From a scaling perspective, deciding which affective or cognitive descriptors to use for an attitudinal measurement can be difficult. To make that decision easier, we suggest the following rules for designing cognitive or affective scales:

1. If the measurement objective is one of collecting data that enable you to describe *how the respondent is thinking,* then the focus should be on using scale descriptors that emphasize the *cognitive component.*

2. If the measurement objective is one of collecting data that enable you to identify *how the respondent is feeling,* then the focus should be on using scale descriptors that reflect the *affective component.*

The Affect Global Approach

Affect global approach Maintains that an attitude is a person's global (or overall) expression of favorable or unfavorable feelings toward a given object or event.

In contrast to the trilogy approach to attitude measurement, the **affect global approach** maintains that an attitude is nothing more than a person's global (or overall) expression of favorable or unfavorable feelings toward a given object. The idea here is that a person's *feelings* can have dominant influence on his or her overall judgment of a given object. In other words, affect equals attitude. Within this approach, heavy emphasis is placed on capturing a person's global evaluative feeling of an object as being either positive or negative (liking/disliking, good/bad, satisfied/dissatisfied). Rating scale formats use a set of affective scale descriptors to capture the necessary responses. A limitation to the affect global approach is that it does not give researchers insight into what beliefs contribute to the

EXHIBIT 12.a.3 Scales Used in Determining Attitude toward Purchasing a 2009 Acura 3.2 TL

In this example, both qualitative and quantitative research activities were employed to create the different scale measurements needed to collect both the cognitive components (b_i) and the affective components (a_i) that relate to assessing respondents' attitude toward the purchasing of automobiles (attitude-toward-behavior).

I. Qualitative research activities

A. Several general focus group interviews were conducted among a cross-section of people who were known to be considering the purchase of a new automobile within the next six months. One of the topics of those interviews was the elements people deemed as factors in purchasing a new automobile. The study discovered and identified the following 15 factors.

1. The car is viewed as being a trouble-free (or practically defect-free) automobile.
2. The car's miles per gallon (MPG) rating.
3. The comfort (or smoothness) of the car's ride.
4. The craftsmanship (or workmanship) built into the car.
5. The overall quality of the car.
6. The dependability (or reliability) of the car.
7. The car will have responsiveness in different weather conditions.
8. The car's potential resale value.
9. The warranty guarantee program associated with the car.
10. The car must have the styling features (or options) I want.
11. The car's price is affordable.
12. Overall reputation of the dealership.
13. Reputation of the dealer's service department.
14. The car's safety features.
15. The quality reputation of the manufacturer.

B. To validate the 15 factors as the meaningful items that people consider in their purchase of a new automobile, 250 randomly selected respondents were given a survey that included those 15 factors and were asked to express the degree to which each one was a factor of consideration they would use in purchasing a new automobile, using the following five-point scale: (5) "a critical factor"; (4) "definitely a factor"; (3) "generally a factor"; (2) "only somewhat of a factor"; (1) "not at all a factor." With direct cognitive structural (DCS) analysis, the results demonstrated that all 15 factors were reasonable elements of consideration that people used in their process of purchasing a new automobile, all having mean values of 3.5 or higher.

[Importance Scale]

Not at All Important	Only Slightly Important	Somewhat Important	Generally Important	Definitely Important	Extremely Important
(1)	(2)	(3)	(4)	(5)	(6)

Buying a car . . .

___ that is *trouble- (or practically defect-) free.*

___ with an *acceptable miles per gallon (MPG) rating.*

___ that provides a *comfortable (or smooth) ride.*

___ that has *craftsmanship (or workmanship)* built into it.

___ that is built with *overall quality.*

___ that is *dependable (or reliable).*

___ that will have *responsiveness* in different weather conditions.

___ that keeps its *resale value.*

___ that is backed by a solid *warranty (or guarantee) program.*

___ that has the *styling features (or options)* I want.

___ that has a *price that is affordable.*

___ from a dealership having an *overall reputation of excellence.*

___ from a dealership whose service department is *reputable.*

___ that has the *safety features* I want.

___ that is made by a manufacturer with a *quality reputation.*

(continued)

EXHIBIT 12.a.3 Scales Used in Determining Attitude toward Purchasing a 2009 Acura 3.2 TL, *continued*

II. Quantitative research activities

A. To capture respondents' emotional importance (a_i) associated with each of the 15 purchasing attributes, the following scale measurement was developed and tested for internal consistency.

Using the affective (importance) scale below, please write a number from 1 to 6 in the space provided that best expresses how emotionally important you feel each listed factor is to you in purchasing a new automobile.

B. To capture respondents' evaluative expectation beliefs (b_i) about the 2009 Acura 3.2 TL being able to meet the individual's needs/wants, the following scale measurement was developed and tested for internal consistency.

Regarding all your expectations about a new car, we would like to know your opinions about each of the following factors as they relate to the 2009 Acura 3.2 TL. For each factor please circle the number that best expresses the extent to which you agree or disagree that buying a 2009 Acura 3.2 TL will meet that factor. For any factor(s) that are not relevant to your assessment, please circle "zero" (0), which means "not applicable" (NA).

Buying a 2009 Acura 3.2 TL Will . . .	**Definitely Agree**	**Generally Agree**	**Slightly Agree**	**Slightly Disagree**	**Generally Disagree**	**Definitely Disagree**	**(NA)**
	(6)	**(5)**	**(4)**	**(3)**	**(2)**	**(1)**	**(0)**
Give me a *trouble-free (or practically defect-free)* mode of transportation	6	5	4	3	2	1	0
Give me a car with acceptable *miles per gallon (MPG)* rating	6	5	4	3	2	1	0
Allow me a *comfortable (smooth) ride*	6	5	4	3	2	1	0
Give me a car with *great craftsmanship*	6	5	4	3	2	1	0
Give me a car with the *overall quality* I was looking for	6	5	4	3	2	1	0
Give me a car that is *dependable (reliable)*	6	5	4	3	2	1	0
Give me a car that has *responsiveness* in different weather conditions	6	5	4	3	2	1	0
Give me a car that keeps its *resale value*	6	5	4	3	2	1	0
Give me a solid *warranty (guarantee) program*	6	5	4	3	2	1	0
Give me a car that has the *styling features (or options)* I want	6	5	4	3	2	1	0
Give me a car I can *afford*	6	5	4	3	2	1	0
Give me a car from a dealership with an *overall reputation of excellence*	6	5	4	3	2	1	0
Give me a car from a dealership whose service department is *reputable*	6	5	4	3	2	1	0
Give me a car that has the *safety features* I want	6	5	4	3	2	1	0
Be a car made by a manufacturer with a *quality reputation*	6	5	4	3	2	1	0

EXHIBIT 12.a.4 Examples of Affect Scale Formats for Measuring Attitudes

Example 1:

For each of the following listed items, please *fill in* the box that best expresses the extent to which you were satisfied or dissatisfied with that item at the time you purchased or leased your vehicle.

Items	Very Satisfied	Somewhat Satisfied	Somewhat Dissatisfied	Very Dissatisfied
Availability of parts and service	❑	❑	❑	❑
Trouble-free operation	❑	❑	❑	❑
Quality of workmanship	❑	❑	❑	❑
Reputation of manufacturer	❑	❑	❑	❑
Low purchase price	❑	❑	❑	❑
High resale value	❑	❑	❑	❑

Example 2:

Now we would like you to think about your driving experiences, then read each of the following statements and *fill in* the box that best expresses your feelings about that statement.

Statement	Like Very Much	Like Somewhat	Neither Like nor Dislike	Dislike Somewhat	Dislike Very Much
Selecting option for my car	❑	❑	❑	❑	❑
Changing the oil myself	❑	❑	❑	❑	❑
Driving on an extended trip	❑	❑	❑	❑	❑
Letting someone else do the driving	❑	❑	❑	❑	❑
Observing the speed limit at all times	❑	❑	❑	❑	❑

Example 3:

Overall, how angry or happy were you with the outcome of the 2008 Presidential election? (Please check only one response.)

Very Angry	Somewhat Angry	Neither Angry nor Happy	Somewhat Happy	Very Happy
❑	❑	❑	❑	❑

formation of the overall attitude. At best, researchers can only speculate about the beliefs underlying the expressed emotional ratings. Exhibit 12.a.4 displays several affect-based attitude scale formats.

Links between Measurements of Cognitive, Affective, and Actual or Intended Behavior

Researchers have mixed feelings about the strength of the relationships between the cognitive and affective components as they are used to explain or predict marketplace behaviors. Some researchers have found that when people's beliefs toward an object (e.g., the 2009

Acura 3.2 TL) coincide with their associated feelings, then attitude consistency exists and behavior is more likely to be predictable.[11] Yet others have found only limited relationships among the three components.[12] Marketers should be aware of several factors that can operate to reduce the consistency between measures of beliefs, feelings, and observations of marketplace behavior.[13] Factors that might create attitude measurement bias are the following:

1. A favorable attitude requires a need or motive before it can be translated into action.
2. Translating favorable beliefs and feelings into ownership requires ability.
3. Some attitude scales measure only one concept, construct, or object at a time.
4. If the cognitive and affective components are weakly held when the consumer obtains additional information in the shopping process, then the initial attitudes may give way to new ones.
5. Researchers typically measure attitudes of an isolated member of the family and the other members may affect purchase behavior.
6. Researchers generally measure brand attitudes independent of the purchase action.
7. In reality, it is difficult to measure all of the relevant aspects of an attitude.

chapter 13

Questionnaire Design: Concepts and Issues

Learning Objectives

After reading this chapter, you will be able to:

1. Describe the process of questionnaire design.
2. Discuss questionnaire development using the "flowerpot" approach.
3. Summarize the characteristics of good questionnaires.
4. Understand the role of cover letters.
5. Explain the importance of other documents used with questionnaires.

"Having recently completed our test trial of Time Warner's Interactive Cable System, we now need an accurate tool to collect the participants' attitudes, feelings, and behaviors toward this new system. Predicting future acceptance rates and usage patterns of such an interactive cable system is the next critical step in determining its long-term success as well as the development and marketing of potential product offerings."

—KEVIN NOLAN,
Former Vice President,
Marketing and Customer Operations,
Time Warner Cable–FSN

Can Surveys Be Used to Develop University Residence Life Plans?

University administrators implemented a "Residence Life" program to identify and better understand the factors relevant to enriching the academic and social experiences of its on-campus students. The program's main goals were to ensure that the university offered high-quality on-campus living experiences with facilities and programs for attracting new students to the university, increasing on-campus housing occupancy rates to 100 percent, and improving retention levels of students, thus increasing the likelihood that students would renew their on-campus housing contracts for multiple years. The MPC Consulting Group, Inc., a national firm that specializes in assessing on-campus housing programs, was retained to oversee the project. While it has an excellent reputation, the firm was not known for conducting primary marketing research.

After clarifying the objectives of the project, MPC determined that a self-administered survey instrument would be used to obtain students' information, attitudes, and feelings regarding on-campus living experiences. The survey would be administered using the university's newly acquired "Blackboard" electronic e-mail system. The rationale for using this method was that all 43,000 students had access and it would save time and costs. MCP's consulting team brainstormed a list of 59 questions to be asked of both on-campus and off-campus students currently enrolled at the university. The questionnaire's design began by asking about personal demographic characteristics followed by some questions concerning students' current housing situations and an evaluation of housing conditions. Next, questions were asked about the importance of a list of preselected housing characteristics, then questions about students' intentions of living on-campus versus off-campus and reasons for those intentions. There were questions about marital status and children, and the desirability of different types of housing structures and amenities. The survey ended with a request for personal thoughts about the need for child care services.

When placed on "Blackboard" for access, the questionnaire took 24 screens with six different "screener" questions requiring respondents to skip back and forth between computer screens depending on how they responded to the screening questions. After being in the field three weeks, only

17 students had responded, and eight of those surveys were incomplete. University officials were disappointed in the response rate and asked MPC three simple but critical questions: (1) "Why such a low response rate?" (2) "Was the survey a good or bad instrument for capturing the needed information?" and (3) "What was the value of the data for addressing the given goals?"

Based on your knowledge and understanding of good information research practices to this point, give your answer to the three questions and identify the potential problems created by MPC's process.

Value of Questionnaires in Marketing Research

The opening example above shows that designing a single questionnaire for collecting a specific type of data is different from using a set of scale measurements to create a good scientific questionnaire. A researcher's ability to design a good scale is, by itself, not enough to guarantee that the appropriate data will automatically be collected.

This chapter focuses on developing a clear understanding of the importance of questionnaire designs and the process that should be undertaken in the development of most data collection instruments. Understanding questionnaire designs will require you to integrate many of the concepts discussed in earlier chapters.

As a future marketing or business decision maker, you may never personally design a questionnaire, but most certainly you will be in a client's position of determining whether a survey is good or bad. Therefore, you should know about the considerations, preliminary activities, and processes that are undertaken in designing scientific questionnaires.

Much of the primary data necessary to create new information for resolving business and marketing problems requires the researcher to ask people questions and record their responses. If business problems were simple and required only one bit of raw data, questionnaires would not be necessary. A researcher could develop a single question measurement and administer it to a sample of respondents, collect the data, analyze it, and derive meaningful information from the data structure. For example, let's say a retailer like Target wanted to know if having a "50 percent off" sale on Saturday, January 9, 2010, would increase sales revenues that day. A researcher could identify 1,000 consumers representative of the general population and send them the following question: "If Target had a storewide 50 percent off sale on all merchandise Saturday, January 9, 2010, would you come to Target and buy at least one item? ___YES ___NO." Let's assume that 650 people replied yes (65 percent) and 350 people replied no (35 percent) to the above question and the researcher interprets the results as being "the majority (65 percent) of shoppers would come to Target and buy merchandise." By having this one bit of information, does Target have enough information to decide whether or not to hold the sale?

It is highly unlikely that a single item of information would be a good predictor of actual shopping behavior. Some of the other factors that also directly affect a person's decision to shop at Target might be (1) attitude toward Target and its merchandise, (2) other obligations or activities on the day of the sale, (3) lack of a means of transportation on that particular day, or (4) limited financial resources. The point is that many business situations or problems are not unidimensional, and therefore a single piece of information about a problem often is not sufficient to resolve them.

Questionnaire A formalized framework consisting of a set of questions and scales designed to generate primary data.

A **questionnaire** is a formalized framework consisting of a set of questions and scales designed to generate primary data. Questionnaire construction involves taking established sets of scale measurements and formatting them into an instrument for collecting data from respondents. Prior to discussing questionnaire designs, there are several key insights about questionnaires worth noting. First, the purpose of designing a "good" survey instrument is to increase the probability of collecting high-quality data that can be transformed into reliable and valid information for marketing managers and/or researchers. Yet actual construct and scale measurement reliability and validity issues should be addressed and assessed during the construct development stage by researchers prior to finalizing the questionnaire. The *layout* of the scale measurements used to collect data can influence any particular measurement's ability to provide reliable and valid data.

Second, advancements in communication systems, the Internet, and computer software programs have impacted the methods of asking questions and recording responses. Yet the critical decisions and processes that underlie the construction of good questionnaires basically remain unchanged. That is, whether designing a survey instrument for "online" methods (Internet, Websurvey) or "offline" methods (personal, telephone, direct mail), the rules and process steps researchers need to follow in designing questionnaires are essentially the same. Finally, questionnaires are the key instruments used in collecting data, regardless of the type of research (exploratory, descriptive, causal) study.

Questionnaire Design

A major weakness of questionnaire design in the field is that many researchers do not understand questionnaire development theory. Many researchers believe designing questionnaires is an art rather than a science. While there is some creativity involved in designing questionnaires, the process itself should be a scientific one based on established rules of logic, objectivity, and systematic procedures.[1] Most individuals understand that words go into questions and that questions go into questionnaires, but not everyone understands that writing questions does *not* automatically result in a good questionnaire.

Theoretical Components of a Questionnaire

Theoretically, a questionnaire consists of several components—words, questions, formats, and hypotheses—that are integrated into a recognizable, hierarchical layer system.[2] We discuss each in this section.

Words

The most obvious component is words. Researchers must carefully consider which words to use in creating the questions and scales for collecting data from respondents. A few examples of wording problems include ambiguity, abstraction, and connotation. The words selected by the researcher can influence a respondent's answer to a given question. The following examples illustrate this point:

1. Do you think anything *could* be done to make it more convenient for students to register for classes at your University or College?
2. Do you think anything *should* be done to make it more convenient for students to register for classes at your University or College?
3. Do you think anything *might* be done to make it more convenient for students to register for classes at your University or College?

The different answers each of these questions would generate show how "word phrasing" variations can become significant in questionnaire designs. Slight changes in wording can introduce different concepts or emotional levels into the questionnaire.

Questions/Setups

The next component is the question/setup used in a particular scale to collect raw data from the respondent. Two important issues relating to question phrasing that have a direct impact on survey designs are (1) the type of question format (unstructured or structured) and (2) the quality of the question (good or bad).[3]

Unstructured questions Open-ended questions formatted to allow respondents to reply in their own words.

Unstructured questions are open-ended questions that allow respondents to reply in their own words. There is no predetermined list of responses available to aid or limit the respondents' answers. This type of question requires more thinking and effort on the part of respondents. In most cases, a trained interviewer asks follow-up probing questions. If administered correctly, unstructured questions can provide the researcher with a rich array of information. The actual format of open-ended questions might vary depending on the data collection method (personal interviews, traditional and computer-assisted telephone interviews, online and offline self-administered surveys). Exhibit 13.1 provides several examples to illustrate these format differences.

eXHIBIT 13.1 Examples of Unstructured Question/Setup Designs

Personal or Telephone Interviews

What toppings, if any, do you usually add to a pizza other than cheese when ordering a pizza for yourself from Pizza Hut? **(Interviewer: Record all mentioned toppings in the space provided below. Make sure you probe for specifics and clarity of responses.)**

____

____

____

or

What toppings, if any, do you usually add to a pizza other than cheese when ordering a pizza for yourself from Pizza Hut? **(Interviewer: DO NOT read the listed toppings; just record the toppings by checking the box next to the mentioned toppings below. Make sure you probe for specifics and clarity of responses.)**

❑ anchovies	❑ bacon	❑ barbecue beef
❑ black olives	❑ extra cheese	❑ green olives
❑ green peppers	❑ ground beef	❑ ham
❑ hot peppers	❑ mushrooms	❑ onions
❑ pepperoni	❑ sausage	❑ some other topping: ________

Self-Administered Survey (Online or Offline)

In the space provided below, please write the types of toppings, if any, that you usually add to a pizza other than cheese when ordering a pizza for yourself from Pizza Hut. **(Please indicate as many toppings as apply.)**

____

____

____

____

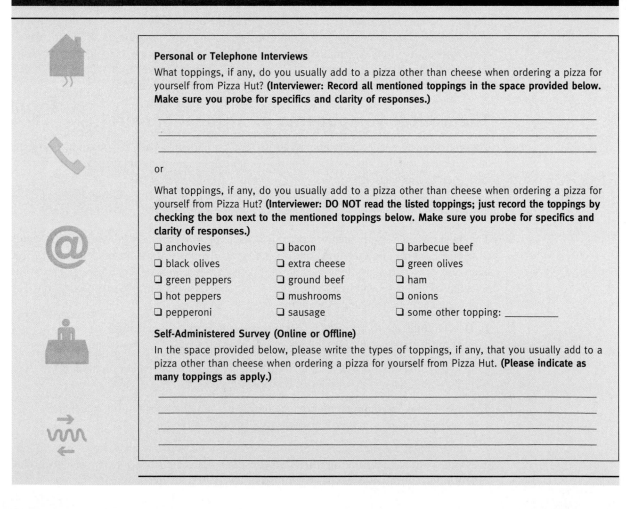

Structured questions Closed-ended questions that require the respondent to choose from a predetermined set of responses or scale points.

Bad questions Any questions that prevent or distort the fundamental communication between the researcher and the respondents.

Structured questions are closed-ended questions that require the respondent to choose a response from a predetermined set of responses or scale points. This question format reduces the amount of thinking and effort required by respondents. In general, structured questions are more popular than unstructured ones. Interviewer bias is eliminated because either (1) the interviewer simply checks a box or line, circles a category, hits a key on a keyboard, points and clicks a computer mouse, or records a number or (2) the respondents themselves check a box or line, circle a category, hit a key on a keyboard, point and click a computer mouse, or record a number that best represents their response to the question.[4] In many ways, structured formats give the researcher greater opportunities to control the thinking respondents must do in order to answer a question. Exhibit 13.2 shows some examples.

Bad questions *are any questions that prevent or distort the fundamental communication between the researcher and the respondent.* A researcher may think an excellent question

EXHIBIT 13.2 Examples of Structured Question/Setup Designs

Personal Interview

(HAND RESPONDENT CARD.) Please look at this card and tell me the letters that indicate what toppings, if any, you usually add to a pizza other than cheese when ordering a pizza for yourself from Pizza Hut. **(Interviewer: Record all mentioned toppings by circling the letters below, and make sure you probe for any other toppings.)**

[a] anchovies	[b] bacon	[c] barbecue beef
[d] black olives	[e] extra cheese	[f] green olives
[h] green peppers	[i] ground beef	[j] ham
[k] hot peppers	[l] mushrooms	[m] onions
[n] pepperoni	[o] sausage	[p] some other topping: ________

Telephone Interview (Traditional or Computer Assisted)

I'm going to read you a list of pizza toppings. As I read each one, please tell me whether or not that topping is one that you usually add to a pizza when ordering a pizza for yourself from Pizza Hut. **(Interviewer: Read each topping category slowly and record all mentioned toppings by circling their corresponding letter below, and make sure you probe for any other toppings.)**

[a] anchovies	[b] bacon	[c] barbecue beef
[d] black olives	[e] extra cheese	[f] green olives
[h] green peppers	[i] ground beef	[j] ham
[k] hot peppers	[l] mushrooms	[m] onions
[n] pepperoni	[o] sausage	[p] some other topping: ________

Self-Administered Survey (Online or Offline)

Among the pizza toppings listed below, what toppings, if any, do you usually add to a pizza other than cheese when ordering a pizza for yourself from Pizza Hut?

(Please check as many boxes as apply.)

❑ anchovies	❑ bacon	❑ barbecue beef
❑ black olives	❑ extra cheese	❑ green olives
❑ green peppers	❑ ground beef	❑ ham
❑ hot peppers	❑ mushrooms	❑ onions
❑ pepperoni	❑ sausage	❑ some other topping: ________

has been written because it accurately conveys a point of view or interest to the respondent, but if the respondent cannot answer it in a meaningful way, it is a bad question. Some examples of bad questions are those that are:

1. **Incomprehensible to the respondent** *because the wording, the concept, or both cannot be understood.* An example would be "What is your attitude about the linkage between the war on the al-Qaida terrorists in Afghanistan and the Democrats decrying of sexual McCarthyism toward improving the environment in Arizona?"
2. **Unanswerable** *either because the respondent does not have access to the information needed or because none of the answer choices apply to the respondent.* An example would be: "What was your parents' exact annual income two years ago?"
3. **Leading (or loaded)** *in that the respondent is forced or directed into a response that would not ordinarily be given if all possible response categories or concepts were provided, or if all the facts of the situation were provided.* An example of this would be: "Do you believe that Republicans who loved George W. Bush agreed he did a good job as president of the United States?"
4. **Double-barreled** *in that they ask the respondent to address more than one issue at a time.* An example would be: "To what extent do you agree or disagree that Monica Lewinsky **and** Representative Henry Hyde, R-Ill., were responsible for the impeachment vote against President Clinton?"

For more examples of bad questions go to the book's Web site at www.mhhe.com/hair4e and follow the links.

Questionnaire Format

This component does not directly relate to the process of developing the individual questions but rather the layout of sets of questions or scale measurements into a systematic instrument. The questionnaire's format should allow for clear communication. Later in the chapter, we discuss the "flowerpot" approach to designing scientific questionnaires, which improves the researcher's ability to collect accurate data.

Hypothesis Development

Hypothesis A formalized statement of a testable relationship between two or more constructs or variables.

Questionnaires are designed for collecting meaningful data to test a **hypothesis** rather than merely to gather facts. Theoretically, each of the questions used in a questionnaire should either directly or indirectly relate to a research hypothesis that is relevant to the research objectives. Hypotheses can relate to:

1. The nature of the respondent.
2. The relationship between the expressed attitudes and behavior of the respondent (e.g., motivation).
3. The sociological structures and their influence on the respondent.
4. The meaning of words and the respondent's grasp of language and/or concepts.
5. The relationships among a respondent's knowledge, attitudes, and marketplace behaviors.
6. The descriptive and predictive capabilities of attributes of the constructs (e.g., customer satisfaction, product or service quality, and behavioral intentions).[5]

EXHIBIT 13.3 Examples of Different Types of Hypotheses Used in Information Research

Type	Examples
Null Hypothesis	There is ***no significant difference*** between the preferences toward specific banking methods exhibited by white-collar customers and blue-collar customers. ***No significant differences*** will be found to exist in the requests for specific medical treatments from emergency medical walk-in clinics between users and nonusers of annual physical preventive health care progams.
Nondirectional Hypothesis	***Significant differences*** do exist in the sexual behavior profiles of academically strong and weak male and female students. There is a ***significant difference*** in the satisfaction levels among 2002 Mazda Millenia owners according to how much they have driven the car.
Inverse (Negative) Directional Hypothesis	Those students who exhibit ***high levels*** of self-confidence and knowledge toward the topic and ***positive*** overall study habits will demonstrate ***low profiles*** of introverted social behavior. The ***greater the amount*** of outside-classroom studying done by marketing majors, the ***less chance*** there is that they will turn to cheating to improve their grades.
Direct (Positive) Directional Hypothesis	***Positive*** study habits are related ***positively*** to GPA. College students who tend to ***worry a lot about*** what other students think of them will tend to be ***more conservative*** in their overall classroom and social behavior than those students who don't worry much about their self-image.

By identifying the hypothesis associated with each of the questions on a questionnaire, researchers can improve their ability to determine which measurements are necessary for collecting primary data and which ones are nice but not necessary. Collecting "nice but not necessary" data only increases the length of the questionnaire and the likelihood of bias. Exhibit 13.3 displays some examples of different types of hypotheses a researcher can develop about the questions on a questionnaire.

Description versus Prediction

While all good questionnaires are systematically structured, most surveys are designed to be either descriptive or predictive.[6] A *descriptive* design allows the researcher to collect raw data that can be turned into facts about a person or object. For example, the U.S. Census Bureau uses questionnaires that collect primarily state-of-being or state-of-behavior data that can be translated into facts about the U.S. population (income levels, marital status, age, occupation, family size, usage rates, consumption quantities). In contrast, *predictive* questionnaires force the researcher to collect a wider range of state-of-mind and state-of-intention data that can be used in predicting changes in attitudes and behaviors as well as in testing hypotheses.

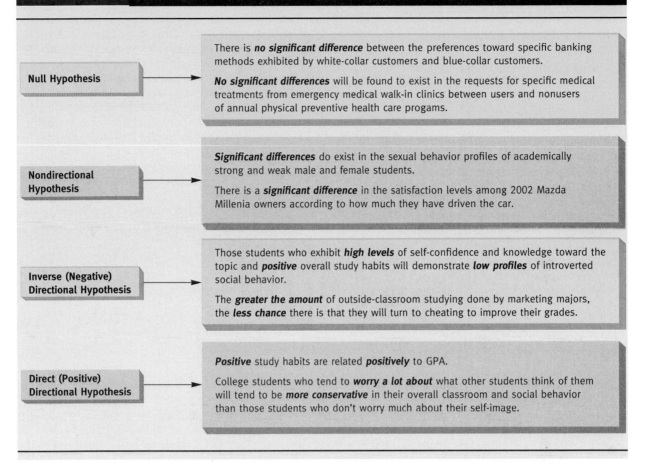

A Closer Look at Research

Computerized Questionnaires

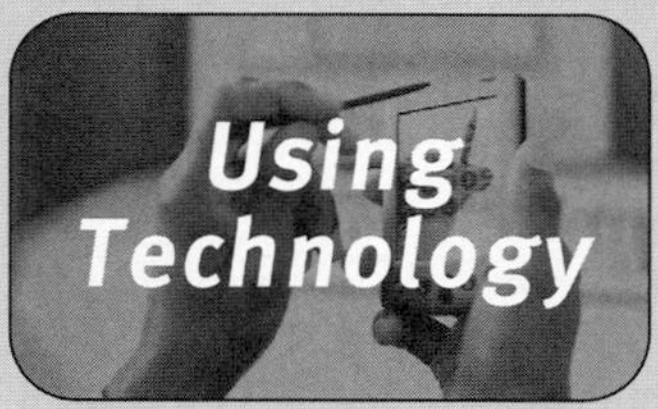

"Smart" questionnaires are a very important development in marketing research. These questionnaires are structured with a mathematical logic that enables the computer to customize them for each respondent as the interview progresses. Through the use of interactive software, the computer constantly evaluates new information and presents the respondent with a new decision to make. In this type of survey, different respondents taking the same questionnaire would answer different sets of questions, each custom-designed to provide the most relevant data.

For global corporations with diverse product lines, computerized questionnaires can provide information related to each product line. Before computerized questionnaires, corporations had to rely on survey data that used scripted questions that often did not provide relevant data. However, with computerized questionnaires, the information obtained is relevant to the needs of the organization.

Important advantages of computerized questionnaires over pen-and-paper surveys include increased ease of participation, decreased time requirements, and a reduction in resources needed to conduct the survey, thereby reducing the overall cost of survey administration. For corporations faced with constantly increasing time demands, computerized questionnaires are a natural choice for meeting their data collection needs.

Accuracy versus Precision

Accuracy The degree to which the data obtained from a questionnaire provide the researcher with a description of the true state of affairs.

Questionnaire design precision The extent to which a questionnaire design can reproduce similar results over repeated usages.

Another theoretical principle that should guide the design of questionnaires is *accuracy*, meaning that a true report is obtained of the respondent's attitudes, preferences, beliefs, feelings, intentions, and/or actions. Also, questions and scales must be used that enable the researcher to gain an overall picture rather than just a fragment.[7] **Accuracy** refers to the degree to which the data provide the researcher with a description of the true state of affairs. In contrast, **questionnaire design precision** focuses on whether questions or scales are narrowly defined.

Value of a Good Survey Instrument

The value of a well-constructed questionnaire cannot be overestimated by researchers and marketing practitioners. How a survey instrument is developed is critical in the process of creating information that can be used to solve business problems. The main function of a questionnaire is to capture people's true thoughts and feelings about different issues or objects. Data collected with a questionnaire can be viewed as the key to unlocking understanding and truth about a problem situation.[8]

In contrast, a bad questionnaire can be costly in terms of time, effort, and money. It produces nothing more than "garbage" data that, if used by decision makers, results in inappropriate or incorrect marketing actions.[9] New technologies are providing alternatives for designing good questionnaires. Read the nearby A Closer Look at Research (Using Technology) box for a discussion of computerized questionnaire designs. For examples of "good" and "bad" questionnaires, visit this book's Web site at www.mhhe.com/hair4e and follow the links.

Flowerpot Approach to Questionnaire Design

The process researchers follow to develop a questionnaire is systematic. While the specific steps may vary, most researchers follow established rules. Exhibit 13.4 shows a set of steps for developing survey instruments. Note that some of the activities in each step are critically necessary but not part of the actual layout. For example, some questionnaires call for the development of separate screening questions that are used to qualify the prospective respondents. Other activities are pertinent to the actual design task.

Flowerpot approach A specific framework for integrating sets of question/scale measurements into a logical, smooth-flowing questionnaire.

With all these steps to understand, the development process can seem overwhelming at first. To simplify the questionnaire development process, we present the **flowerpot approach.** This scientific approach involves a series of activities that have a logical, hierarchical order.[10] The flowerpot notion is symbolically derived from the natural shape associated with a clay pot used for growing flowers. The shape is wide at the top and narrower at the bottom—symbolizing a natural flow of data from general to specific. Although this approach is primarily used to create a good questionnaire structure, it has direct impact on steps 1 and 3 of the development process outlined in Exhibit 13.4. The flowerpot approach helps the researcher make decisions regarding (1) construct development, (2) object attributes, (3) various question/scale formats, (4) wording of questions, and (5) scale points. In situations where there are multiple research objectives, each objective will have its own pot of data. To reduce the likelihood of creating biased data, the size and width of the data requirements must be determined for each objective, with the most general data requirements going into the biggest flowerpot and the next most general set of data going into a smaller pot. As illustrated in Exhibit 13.5, when multiple pots are stacked, the larger pot is always placed on top of a smaller pot to ensure that the overall general to specific flow of data is maintained.

Someone just learning to develop a scientific questionnaire might raise this fundamental question: *"Why should the questioning layout in the overall questionnaire as well as individual flowerpots always create a directional flow from general to more specific information?"* The answer is threefold. First, logic has to be used in collecting data when the researcher (or the interviewer) and respondent begin the process as "strangers" to each other. A survey that begins with general information questions promotes the development of the necessary "comfort zone" between the two parties. This comfort zone is similar to the one that has to be established in either focus group or in-depth interviews. When respondents feel comfortable, the question/answer exchange process goes more smoothly and respondents are more thoughtful and honest with their responses.

Second, data quality is critical in any research study. Researchers run the risk of collecting low-quality data by asking respondents questions about an object or construct in an illogical order. For example, expecting respondents to be able to accurately express their evaluative judgments toward the performance of a particular object (e.g., an Apple iPod) is illogical if they have no knowledge of or personal experience with that particular object. A more general question about MP3 ownership or experience must be asked prior to the evaluative performance question. In some cases, asking a specific question about the attributes or purchasing behaviors associated with an object and then following up with more general questions about the object can cause ambiguity, confusion, and possibly response bias. For example, let's say the researcher, in conducting a retail store study in Chicago, asks several questions concerning the respondent's *intentions* of shopping at Macy's for children's clothes, then asks a question about what the respondent likes or dislikes about shopping at Macy's. Further let's assume the respondent indicated he or she *definitely plans to*

EXHIBIT 13.4 Steps in the Development of Survey Instruments

Step 1 → **Transform Research Objectives into Information Objectives**
- Establish hierarchical order of the objectives.
- Establish research hypotheses within each objective.

Step 2 → **Determine the Appropriate Data Collection Method**
- Determine who the sampled respondents are.

Step 3 → **Determine Information Requirements for Each Objective**
- Establish hierarchical order of requirements.

Step 4 → **Develop Specific Question/Scale Measurement Formats**
- Decide needed type of raw data.
- Decide needed question/scale measurement format.
- Decide needed question and scale point wording.
- Decide what type of data analysis is desired.

Step 5 → **Evaluate Question/Scale Measurements**
- Test for reliability and validity of scales.

Step 6 → **Establish Flowerpot Format and Layout**
- Determine the number of information flowerpots needed.
- Determine the sizes of the flowerpots needed.
- Determine the type of base needed.

Step 7 → **Evaluate the Questionnaire and Layout**
- Check the type of scale format, scaling properties, measures of central tendencies, and variations.
- Check the information flow of general to specific within each flowerpot, and the identification questions.

Step 8 → **Obtain the Client's Approval**
- Revise questionnaire layout if needed.

Step 9 → **Pretest and Revise the Questionnaire**
- Check for specific ambiguity of words, phrases, instructions.
- Check for completion time and difficulties of answering questions.

Step 10 → **Finalize Questionnaire Format**

Step 11 → **Implement the Survey**

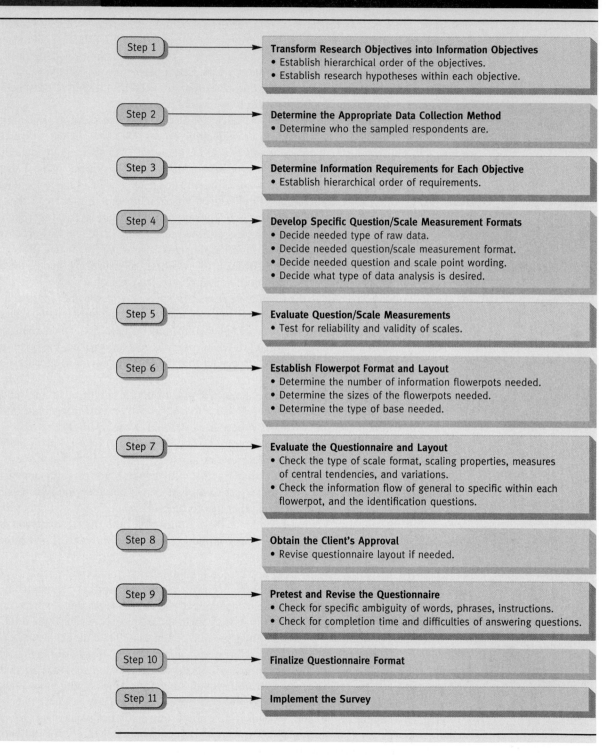

EXHIBIT 13.5 The Flowerpot Approach

This diagram illustrates the overall flowerpot design of a questionnaire that fits a research survey that has two defined information objectives and calls for an identification base that contains both psychographic and demographic-socioeconomic traits about the respondent.

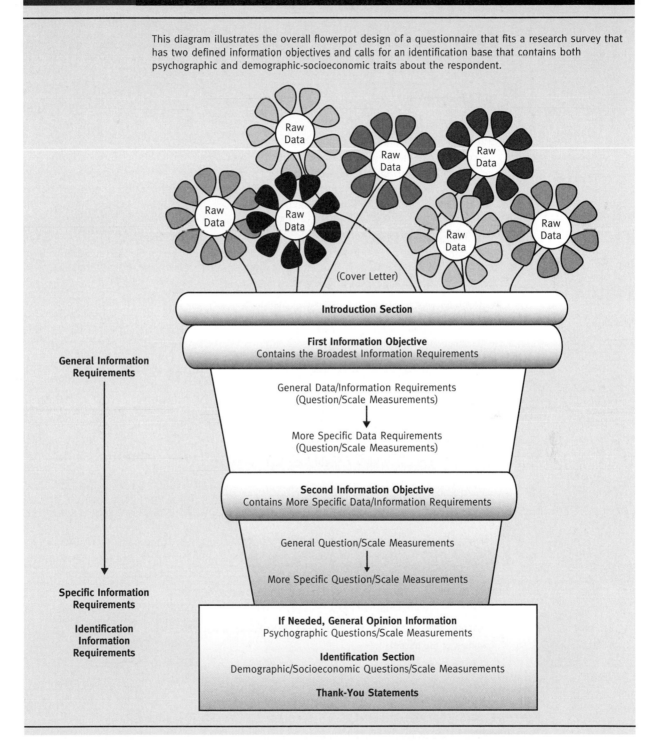

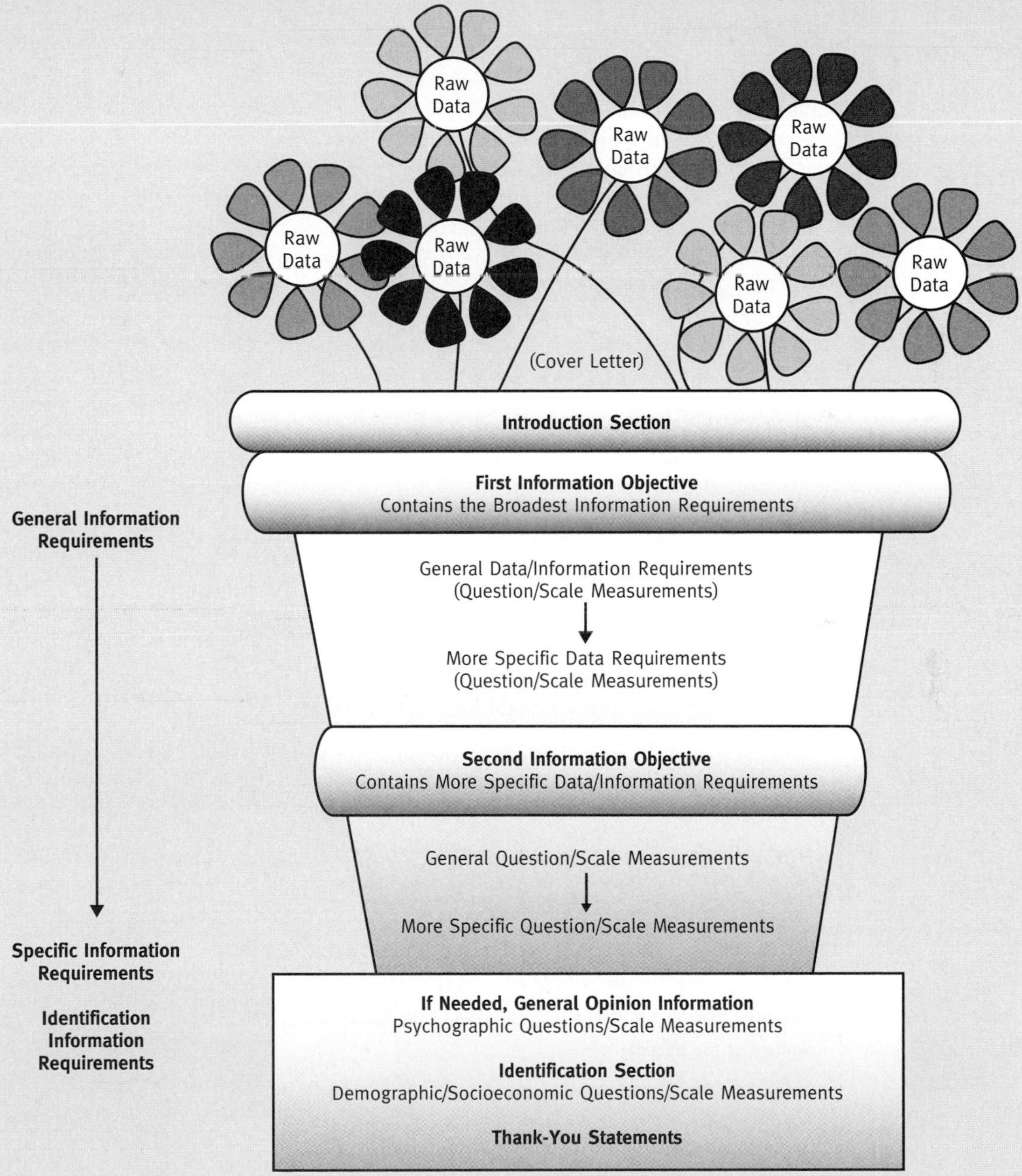

shop at Macy's the next time they shop for children's clothing. The respondent's answer here could influence his or her response pattern to the liking/disliking question in that the responses given will justify the intentions-to-shop response. What a respondent likes and dislikes about the store should be established prior to finding out the respondent's intentions to shop at that store.

Finally, the general-to-specific sequence helps ensure the appropriate sequence of questions will be maintained so the respondent or interviewer does not have to jump back and forth between different pages of the instrument in order to respond to questions. If the questionnaire appears to be complex, there is a greater chance that the respondent will not complete the survey. An inappropriate response is a potential problem in any type of self-administered questionnaire.

According to the flowerpot concept, in a good questionnaire design, the data will flow from a general information level, down to a more specific information level, and end with identification data. A questionnaire begins with an introductory section that gives the respondent a basic idea of the main topic of the research. This section also includes general instructions for filling out the survey. The introduction's appearance will vary with the desired data collection method (e.g., self-administered or interview). For example, the introduction needed for a self-administered questionnaire in a restaurant study might look as follows:

Thank you for your participation in this study. Your participation will aid us in determining what people in our community think about the present products and services offered by restaurants. The results of the study will provide the restaurant industry with insights into how to better serve the needs of people in the Cincinnati Metropolitan community.

Your attitudes, preferences, and opinions are important to this study; they will be kept strictly confidential.

DIRECTIONS: Please read each question carefully. Answer the question by checking the appropriate box(es) that represent your response or responses.

In contrast, an introduction for a Hillsborough County housing survey using computer-assisted telephone interviews might look as follows:

Hillsborough County Housing Study

Verified	Phone # ______________________
By: ______	Call Back Date: ______ Time: ______
Date: _____	Time Started: _______ (a.m.) (p.m.)
	Serial # ____________

MARKETS: [1] NW Hillsborough [2] NE Hillsborough [3] Brandon

INTERVIEWER: Ask to speak with the man of the house. If not available or none, ask for the woman of the house.

Hello, I'm **(Your Name)** representing the Marketing Resources Group here in Tampa. Today, we are conducting an interesting study on housing in Hillsborough County and would like to include your opinions in it.

As it was explained in the letter mailed to your residence about a week ago, we are not interested in selling you anything. We are only interested in your honest opinions about housing structures in the Hillsborough area.

Notice how the two introductions differ. A computer-assisted telephone interview requires specific interviewer instructions.

Next, the researcher must determine how many different information objectives there are (the number of flowerpots needed to construct the questionnaire) and the true breadth and depth of the information requirements (the different pot sizes).

First, working with the largest flowerpot (the most general information), the researcher must identify the specific information requirements and arrange them from general to more specific. Then, going to the next largest flowerpot, the researcher again arranges the information requirements from general to specific. Because stacking the larger pots on top of smaller pots tends to create an unstable, top-heavy structure, a good questionnaire design will also end with demographic and socioeconomic questions about the respondent to form a solid identification base. All questionnaires produced by the flowerpot approach will end with a thank-you statement.

The reasons underlying the placement of demographic and socioeconomic characteristics at the end of a questionnaire are twofold. First, in most research studies, the primary information research objectives focus on collecting attitudinal, emotional, and/or behavioral data about objects, people, and marketing phenomena. Demographic, socioeconomic, and physical characteristics about people and organizations, although important, are collected to add a "face" to those attitudes, feelings, and behaviors. In most cases that require a cover letter or letter of introduction, seldom if ever is the purpose of the research expressed in terms of wanting to obtain demographic information about people. Demographic and socioeconomic factors are neither the stated primary objective nor directly used to achieve a person's willingness to participate in the study. Second, these types of characteristics are direct facts about a respondent often of a personal nature. In general, people are initially unwilling to provide these facts to strangers (the researcher or interviewer). This unwillingness stems from the fact that most respondents do not understand their relevancy to the study's main information objectives and view them as inappropriate. Until the "comfort zone" is established between the interviewer and respondent, asking personal questions could easily bring the interviewing process to a halt. To illustrate this point, suppose when you leave this class a student you don't know stops you and begins asking questions relating to your age, income, family members, occupation, marital status, and so on. How would you react? Without knowing why this stranger was asking these types of questions and how the information was going to be used, this awkward situation would create uneasy feelings for you—powerful reasons for not responding and for ending the question/answer process.

Impact of the Flowerpot Approach on Questionnaire Development

Although the flowerpot approach is primarily used to determine the appropriate sequential order of the questions and scale measurements, it has a direct impact on several of the other development activities.

Determining the Information Objectives

After transforming the research objectives into information objectives, the researcher must evaluate each information objective for its broadness. This activity achieves two things for the researcher. First, it helps the researcher decide which information objectives truly represent a flowerpot of information. Second, it helps the researcher to determine how many flowerpots, and in what sizes, will need to be stacked up in the questionnaire design.

Determining the Information Requirements

Rather than using general brainstorming techniques to develop all the data requirements for the information objectives, the flowerpot approach focuses on one information topic at a time. This decreases the likelihood of generating irrelevant or "nice but not necessary" data. It also enhances the researcher's ability to determine the necessary order (e.g., general to specific) among the data requirements within a given pot.

Developing a Flowerpot-Designed Questionnaire

This section describes how the flowerpot approach influences the activities in the survey instrument development process described in Exhibit 13.4. It is important to remember that the "flowerpot" approach to questionnaire designs is very workable regardless of the method used to collect primary data. The discussion is based on an actual study conducted for American Bank and Trust.

The Situation

The American Bank and Trust Company was located in Baton Rouge, Louisiana. The primary goal of the survey was to provide the marketing team with relevant information regarding banking habits and patterns, as well as demographic and lifestyle characteristics of the bank's current customers.

Transform Research Objectives into Information Objectives

In the initial phase of the development process, the flowerpot approach guides the researcher not only in transforming the research objectives into information objectives but also in determining how many information objectives to include (the number of pots), along with parts of the base stand and those objectives which represent testable hypotheses. The order of the information objectives (the size of the pots) also is determined. The initial research objectives (in bold) were rewritten into information objectives (in italics) as follows:

1. **To obtain a demographic profile of American Bank's current customers.** *(To collect data on selected demographic characteristics that can be used to create a profile of people who are current American Bank customers.)*
2. **To obtain a partial lifestyle profile of people who currently bank with American Bank, with particular emphasis on financial dimensions.** *(To collect data on selected financial-oriented lifestyle dimensions that can be used to create a profile that further identifies people who currently bank at American Bank.)*
3. **To determine banking habits and patterns of these customers.** *(To collect data to identify and describe desired and actual banking habits and patterns exhibited by customers, as well as their selected attitudes and feelings toward those banking practices.)*
4. **To investigate the existence of possible differences between the psychological and demographic dimensions associated with customers' perceptions of being either a blue-collar or white-collar person.** *(To collect data that will enable the researcher to (1) classify customers as being either "blue collar" or "white collar" and (2) test for significant demographic and lifestyle profile differences between these two social classes.)*

5. **To determine the various geographic markets now being served by American Bank on the basis of customers' length of residence in the area.** *(To collect selected state-of-being data that will enable the researcher to identify and describe existing geographic service markets.)*

After transforming the research objectives into information objectives, the researcher determined that objectives 1 and 2 directly related to data that would be part of the questionnaire's basic structure. Objective 3 represents an information flowerpot. In contrast, objectives 4 and 5 do not represent information flowerpots but rather hypotheses about data structures that will be derived from data obtained within either the basic structure or the identified information flowerpot. Although there were five initial information objectives, the actual structure consists of only one information flowerpot and its base.

Determine the Appropriate Data Collection Method

On the basis of the information objectives and target population (American Bank's own current customers), bank management and the researcher jointly decided that a direct mail survey approach would be the most efficient method of collecting data from the randomly selected respondents. This step has a direct influence on creating the individual questions and scales, although these are designed only after the specific information items are determined for each objective.

Determine Information Requirements for Each Objective

The flowerpot approach has a significant impact on this step of the development process. Here the researcher interacts with bank management to determine what specific data are needed to achieve each of the information objectives as well as the respondent classification information. The researcher must establish the general-to-specific order among the identified data. The study's data and flow are detailed as follows:

1. **Flowerpot 1** *(third objective):* To collect data that can identify and describe desired and actual banking habits and patterns exhibited by customers as well as their selected attitudes and feelings toward those banking practices.
   a. Consideration toward the bank used most often.
   b. Bank characteristics believed important in selecting a bank (e.g., convenience/location, banking hours, good service charges, interest rates on savings accounts, knew a person at the bank, bank's reputation, bank's promotional advertisements, interest rates on loans).
   c. Considerations toward having personal savings accounts at various types of financial institutions.
   d. Preference considerations toward selected banking methods (e.g., inside the bank, drive-up window, 24-hour ATM, electronic banking, bank by mail, bank by phone).
   e. Actual usage considerations toward various banking methods (e.g., inside the bank, drive-up window, 24-hour ATM, electronic banking, bank by mail, bank by phone).
   f. Frequency of balancing a checkbook as well as the number of not-sufficient-funds (NSF) charges.

2. **Flowerpot base—lifestyle dimensions** *(second objective):* To collect data on selected financial-oriented lifestyle dimensions that can be used to create a descriptive profile that further identifies people who currently bank at American Bank.

Belief statements that will classify the customer's lifestyle as being financial optimist, financially dissatisfied, information exchanger, credit card user, advertising viewer, family oriented, price conscious, blue/white-collar oriented.

3. **Flowerpot base—demographic characteristics** *(first objective):* To collect data on selected demographic characteristics that can be used to create a descriptive profile identifying people who are current American Bank customers.

   Include characteristics of gender, years in area, years at current residence, present employment status, present marital status, spouse's current employment status, number of dependent children, education level, age, occupation, nature of work, union membership, income level, and zip code.

Notice that the fourth and fifth objectives have no direct bearing on determining the data requirements because they include factors that are covered either in the information flowerpot or its base. Therefore, the researcher does not have to integrate them into this particular aspect of the development process.

Develop Specific Question/Scale Measurement Formats

The flowerpot approach does not impact the activities that take place in this part of the development process. Nevertheless, these activities remain a critical part of questionnaire design. Researchers must use their construct and scale measurement knowledge to develop appropriate scales *(question/setup, dimension/attributes, scale points/responses)* for each individual data requirement. To do so, the researcher must make three key decisions: (1) *the type of data* (e.g., state of being, mind, behavior, intention); (2) *question/scale format* (e.g., open-ended or closed-ended format and nominal, ordinal, interval, or ratio structure); and (3) the question and *specific scale point wording*.

The flowerpot approach advocates that when designing the specific question/scale measurements, researchers should act as if they are two different people, one thinking like a technical, logical researcher and the other like a respondent. The results of this step can be seen in the final questionnaire displayed in Exhibit 13.6.

Evaluate Question/Scale Measurements

The flowerpot approach also does not impact the activities that take place in this aspect of the development process. Prior to laying out the actual survey instrument, the researcher should have already examined each question and scale measurement for reliability and validity. Now the focus is on evaluating any needed instructions and revisions. See Exhibit 13.7 for a summary of the guidelines for evaluating the adequacy of questions.

Establish Flowerpot Format and Layout

The activities undertaken here are at the center of the flowerpot approach to questionnaire designs. Taking all the individual questions and scales previously developed and tested, the researcher must present them in a specific, logical order. After creating a title for the questionnaire, the researcher must include a brief introductory section and any general instructions prior to asking the first question. The questions that make up the first information flowerpot must be asked in a natural general-to-specific order to reduce the potential for sequence bias.

In any type of research design that uses questioning as the data collection method (personal interviews, computer-assisted or regular telephone interviews, self-administered questionnaires), all instructions should be included within each question or scale, where

EXHIBIT 13.6 Consumer Banking Opinion Survey: Baton Rouge, Louisiana

THANK YOU for your participation in this interesting study. Your participation will aid us in determining what people in our community think about the present products and services offered by banks. The results will provide the banking industry with additional insights on how to better serve the needs of people in the Baton Rouge community. Your attitudes, preferences, and opinions are important to this study; they will be kept strictly confidential.

DIRECTIONS: PLEASE READ EACH QUESTION CAREFULLY. ANSWER THE QUESTION BY FILLING IN THE APPROPRIATE BOX(ES) THAT REPRESENT YOUR RESPONSE OR RESPONSES.

I. GENERAL BANKING HABITS SECTION

1. Which one of the following banks would you consider the one that you use most often in conducting banking or financial transactions? **(PLEASE FILL IN THE ONE APPROPRIATE BOX)**

❑ American Bank ❑ Capital Bank ❑ Fidelity National Bank

❑ Baton Rouge Bank ❑ City National Bank ❑ Louisiana National Bank

❑ Some other bank; please specify: ____________________

2a. To what extent were each of the following bank items an important consideration to you in selecting your bank mentioned in Q.1 above? **(PLEASE BE SURE TO FILL IN ONLY ONE RESPONSE FOR EACH BANK ITEM.)**

Banking Items	**Extremely Important**	**Somewhat Important**	**Not at All Important**	**Important**
Convenience of location	❑	❑	❑	❑
Banking hours	❑	❑	❑	❑
Good service charges	❑	❑	❑	❑
Interest rates on savings	❑	❑	❑	❑
Personally knew someone at the bank	❑	❑	❑	❑
Bank's reputation	❑	❑	❑	❑
Bank's promotional advertising	❑	❑	❑	❑
Interest rate on loans	❑	❑	❑	❑

2b. If there was some other reason (or bank item) you deemed important in selecting your bank mentioned in Q.1, please write it in the space below. ____________________

____

3. At which of the following financial institutions do you or some member of your immediate household have a personal savings account? **(PLEASE FILL IN AS MANY OR AS FEW AS ARE NECESSARY.)**

Financial Institutions	**Both You and Some Other Member**	**Some Other Member**	**Yourself**
A credit union	❑	❑	❑
Savings & loan	❑	❑	❑
American Bank	❑	❑	❑
Baton Rouge Bank	❑	❑	❑
Capital Bank	❑	❑	❑
City National Bank	❑	❑	❑
Fidelity National Bank	❑	❑	❑
Louisiana National Bank	❑	❑	❑
Another institution: __________ (Please specify)	❑	❑	❑

continued

eXHIBIT 13.6 Consumer Banking Opinion Survey: Baton Rouge, Louisiana, *continued*

4. Concerning the different banking methods which you may or may not use, we would like to know your feeling toward these methods. For each listed banking method, please fill in the appropriate response that best describes your desire for using that method. **(PLEASE FILL IN ONE RESPONSE FOR EACH BANKING METHOD)**

Banking Methods	Definitely Like Using	Somewhat Like Using	Somewhat Dislike Using	Definitely Dislike Using
Inside the bank	❑	❑	❑	❑
Drive-in (Drive-up)	❑	❑	❑	❑
24-hour machine	❑	❑	❑	❑
Bank by phone	❑	❑	❑	❑
Bank by mail	❑	❑	❑	❑
Electronic banking	❑	❑	❑	❑
Third-person banking	❑	❑	❑	❑

5. Now we would like to know to what extent you actually use each of the following banking methods. **(PLEASE FILL IN THE APPROPRIATE RESPONSE FOR EACH LISTED BANKING METHOD.)**

Banking Methods	Usually	Occasionally	Rarely	Never
Inside the bank	❑	❑	❑	❑
Drive-in (Drive-up)	❑	❑	❑	❑
24-hour machine	❑	❑	❑	❑
Bank by phone	❑	❑	❑	❑
Bank by mail	❑	❑	❑	❑
Electronic banking	❑	❑	❑	❑
Third-person banking	❑	❑	❑	❑

6. Thinking about your monthly bank statement, approximately how often do you balance your checkbook with the aid of your statement?

❑ Always (every statement) ❑ Rarely (once or twice a year)
❑ Occasionally (every 2 or 3 months) ❑ Never

7. Approximately how many overdrawn charges on your checking account (NSF checks) has your bank imposed on your account in the past year?

❑ None ❑ 1–2 ❑ 3–7 ❑ 8–15 ❑ 16–25 ❑ More than 25

II. GENERAL OPINION SECTION

In this section, there is a list of general opinion statements for which there are no right or wrong answers. As such, the statements may or may not describe you or your feelings.

8. Next to each statement, please fill in the one response box that best expresses the extent to which you agree or disagree with the statement. Remember, there are no right or wrong answers—we just want your opinions.

Statements	Definitely Agree	Generally Agree	Somewhat Agree	Somewhat Disagree	Generally Disagree	Definitely Disagree
I often seek out the advice of my friends regarding a lot of different things.	❑	❑	❑	❑	❑	❑
I buy many things with credit cards.	❑	❑	❑	❑	❑	❑

EXHIBIT 13.6 *continued*

Statements	Definitely Agree	Generally Agree	Somewhat Agree	Somewhat Disagree	Generally Disagree	Definitely Disagree
I wish we had a lot more money.	❑	❑	❑	❑	❑	❑
Security for my family is most important to me.	❑	❑	❑	❑	❑	❑
I am definitely influenced by advertising.	❑	❑	❑	❑	❑	❑
I like to pay cash for everything I buy.	❑	❑	❑	❑	❑	❑
My neighbors or friends often come to me for advice on many different matters.	❑	❑	❑	❑	❑	❑
It is good to have charge accounts.	❑	❑	❑	❑	❑	❑
I will probably have more money to spend next year than I have now.	❑	❑	❑	❑	❑	❑
A person can save a lot of money by shopping around for bargains.	❑	❑	❑	❑	❑	❑
For most products or services, I try the ones that are most popular.	❑	❑	❑	❑	❑	❑
Unexpected situations often catch me without enough money in my pocket.	❑	❑	❑	❑	❑	❑
Five years from now, the family income will probably be a lot higher than it is now.	❑	❑	❑	❑	❑	❑
Socially, I see myself more as a blue-collar person rather than a white-collar one.	❑	❑	❑	❑	❑	❑

III. CLASSIFICATION DATA SECTION

Now just a few more questions so that we can combine your responses with those of the other people taking part in this study.

9. Please indicate your gender. ❑ Female ❑ Male

10. Please fill in the one response that best approximates how long you have lived in the Baton Rouge area.
    ❑ Less than 1 year ❑ 4 to 6 years ❑ 11 to 20 years
    ❑ 1 to 3 years ❑ 7 to 10 years ❑ Over 20 years

11. Approximately how long have you lived at your current address?
    ❑ Less than 1 year ❑ 4 to 6 years ❑ 11 to 20 years
    ❑ 1 to 3 years ❑ 7 to 10 years ❑ Over 20 years

12. Please indicate your current employment status.
    ❑ Employed full-time ❑ Employed part-time ❑ Not currently employed ❑ Retired

continued

EXHIBIT 13.6 Consumer Banking Opinion Survey: Baton Rouge, Louisiana, *continued*

13. Please indicate your current marital status.
❑ Married ❑ Single (never married) ⟶ **PLEASE SKIP TO Q.15**
❑ Single (widowed, divorced, or separated) ⟶ **PLEASE SKIP TO Q.15**

14. **IF MARRIED,** please indicate your spouse's current employment status.
❑ Employed full-time ❑ Employed part-time ❑ Not currently employed ❑ Retired

15. **IF YOU HAVE CHILDREN,** please indicate the number of children under 18 years of age in your household.

0	1	2	3	4	5	6	7	8	More than 8; please specify: _____	❑ Do not have children
❑	❑	❑	❑	❑	❑	❑	❑	❑		

16. Which one of the following categories best corresponds with your last completed year in school?
❑ Post-graduate studies or advanced degree ❑ Completed high school
❑ Graduate studies or degree ❑ Some high school
❑ Completed college (4-year degree) ❑ Completed grammar school
❑ Some college or technical school ❑ Some grammar school

17. Into which one of the following categories does your current age fall?
❑ Under 18 ❑ 26 to 35 ❑ 46 to 55 ❑ 66 to 70
❑ 18 to 25 ❑ 36 to 45 ❑ 56 to 65 ❑ Over 70

18. What is your occupation; that is, in what kind of work do you spend the major portion of your time?
____

19. Which one of the following categories best describes the nature of your work?
❑ Government (Fed., State, City) ❑ Legal ❑ Financial ❑ Insurance
❑ Petrochemical ❑ Manufacturing ❑ Transportation ❑ Consulting
❑ Educational ❑ Medical ❑ Retailing ❑ Wholesaling
❑ Some other area, please specify: ______________________

20. Are you a non-union or union worker? ❑ Non-union worker ❑ Union worker

21. Into which of the following categories does your total (approximate) family income, before taxes, fall?
❑ Under $10,000 ❑ $30,001 to $50,000
❑ $10,000 to $15,000 ❑ $50,001 to $75,000
❑ $15,001 to $20,000 ❑ $75,001 to $100,000
❑ $20,001 to $30,000 ❑ Over $100,000

22. What is your residence address five-digit zip code? ❑ ❑ ❑ ❑ ❑

THANK YOU VERY MUCH FOR PARTICIPATION IN THIS STUDY! YOUR TIME AND OPINIONS ARE GREATLY AND DEEPLY APPRECIATED.

appropriate. After completing the information flowerpot, the researcher must stabilize the structure by building a base. In the American Bank example, there is a two-part base. The lifestyle belief (general opinions or psychographics) section is presented first, and then the more standardized classification section (demographics). The final part of any base is the thank-you statement.

EXHIBIT 13.7 Guidelines for Evaluating the Adequacy of Questions

1. Questions should be *simple* and *straightforward* whenever possible.
2. Questions should be *expressed clearly* whenever possible.
3. Questions should avoid *qualifying phrases* or *extraneous references,* unless they are being used as a qualifying (screening) factor.
4. *Descriptive words* should be avoided, unless absolutely necessary.
5. Questions/setups, attribute statements, and data response categories should be *unidimensional,* except when there is a need for a *multiple-response question.*
6. Data response categories (scale points) should be *mutually exclusive.*
7. The questions/setups and the response categories should be *meaningful to the respondent.*
8. Questions/scale measurement formats should avoid *arrangement* of response categories that *might bias* the respondent's answer.
9. Unless called for, question/setups should avoid *undue stress* of particular words.
10. Questions/setups should avoid *double negatives.*
11. Questions/scale measurements should avoid *technical* or *sophisticated language,* unless necessary.
12. Where possible, questions/setups should be phrased in a *realistic setting.*
13. Questions/scale measurements should be designed to *read logically.*
14. Questions/scale measurements should always avoid the use of *double-barreled items.*

Note: For examples, go to the book's Website (www.mhhe.com/hair4e) and follow the links.

At the beginning of the classification section is this statement: *"Now just a few more questions so that we can combine your answers with those of the other people taking part in this study."* This is a "transition phrase," which serves three basic purposes. First, it communicates to the respondents that a change in their thinking process is about to take place. No longer do they have to think about their specific belief structures. They can clear their minds before thinking about their personal data. Second, it hints that the task of completing the survey is almost over. Third, it assures the respondent that the information she or he gives will be used only in aggregate combinations—that is, it will be blended with information from other respondents participating in the survey.

Evaluate the Questionnaire and Layout

After drafting the questionnaire, but before submitting it to the management team for approval, the researcher should review the layout to make sure the questionnaire meets all the information objectives. Typically the researcher would focus on determining whether each question is necessary and whether the overall length is acceptable. In contrast, the flowerpot approach gives more attention to (1) checking whether the instrument meets the overall objectives; (2) checking the scale format and scaling properties; and (3) checking general-to-specific order.

An easy method of evaluating any questionnaire design is to answer the following five questions for each question or scale measurement:

1. What types of data (state of being, mind, behavior, or intention) are being sought in the question, and for what purpose?
2. What types of questions or scale measurements (nominal, ordinal, interval, ratio) are being used?

3. What scaling properties (assignment, order, distance, origin) are being activated in the scale measurement?
4. What is the most appropriate measure of central tendency (mode, median, mean)?
5. What is the most appropriate measure of dispersion (frequency distribution, range, standard deviation)?

Obtain the Client's Approval

The flowerpot concept does not impact this aspect of the overall development process. Copies of the questionnaire draft should be made and distributed to all parties that have authority over and interest in the project. Realistically, the client may step in at any time in the design process to express a need for some type of modification.

Nevertheless, it is important to get final approval of the questionnaire prior to pretesting it. The logic behind client approval is that it commits management to the body of data and eventually to the information that will result from the specific questionnaire design. In addition, it helps reduce unnecessary surprises and saves time and money. If changes are necessary, this is where they should occur. The researcher must make sure that any changes adhere to the design requirements.

Pretest and Revise the Questionnaire

While fine-tuning of the questionnaire can take place via discussions between the researcher and client, the final evaluation should come from people representing the individuals who will be asked to actually fill out the survey. Remember, pretesting the questionnaire does not mean that one researcher administers the questionnaire to another researcher, or to the client's management or staff. Furthermore, it does not mean that the pretest is done with college students unless they are representative of the study's target population.

An appropriate pretest involves giving the survey to a small, representative group of respondents. How many respondents should be included in a pretest is open to debate. Some researchers will use as few as 10 respondents, while others might use as many as 50 depending on the purpose of the pretest, the method of administering the survey, and how the survey was developed. For example, if the questions were not properly tested for reliability and validity during the construct/scale measurement development process, then the pretest should include at least 50 respondents so that the researcher can address reliability and validity issues.[11] In contrast, if the main purpose of the pretest is to check for specific wording problems, then only about 10 respondents are needed in the pretest.[12] In a pretest respondents are asked to pay attention to such elements as words, phrases, instructions, and question flow patterns and point out anything they feel is confusing, difficult to understand, or otherwise a problem.

When using the flowerpot approach, the researcher should not find reliability/validity or wording issues at this point, since those issues should have been handled in earlier development procedures. Rather, the pretest should help the researcher determine how much time respondents will need to complete the survey, whether to add any instructions, and what to say in the cover letter. If any problems or concerns arise in the pretest, modifications must be made and approved by the client prior to moving to the next step. The American Bank study questionnaire was pretested on 25 randomly selected bank customers and revealed no surprises.

Finalize the Questionnaire Format

The questionnaire is now converted to final format. Decisions are made about typing instructions, spacing, numbers for questions and pages, folding, and stapling—all of which relate to the professional appearance of the questionnaire. Quality in appearance is more important in self-administered surveys than in personal or telephone interviews. Repro duction of documents also must be considered here. Support materials—such as interviewer instructions, cover letters, rating cards, mailing and return envelopes—are finalized and reproduced for distribution.

Another set of decisions relates to the precoding of the response categories used to represent the scaling points. In the American Bank study, the questionnaire was formatted as a four-page booklet with a separate cover letter and a self-addressed, stamped return envelope. (See Exhibit 13.10 for the cover letter used by American Bank.)

Implement the Survey

The focus here is on the processes that must be followed to begin the collection data. These will vary based on the collection method. Although the American Bank example illustrates how the flowerpot approach plays a useful role in the development process of survey instruments, no single study can exemplify all of the numerous factors researchers must consider when designing a questionnaire. We offer a general summary of the major considerations in questionnaire designs in Exhibit 13.8. Firms are also faced with new challenges as they expand into global markets. One question they must address is whether the research techniques they used in their own country can be directly applied in foreign countries. To illustrate this point log on to the book's Web site at www.mhhe.com/hair4e, follow the links to the Global Insight, read the Holiday Inn Resort example, and answer the questions.

eXHIBIT 13.8 Considerations in Questionnaire Design

- Confirm research objectives before designing the questionnaire.
- Determine the data requirements, and organize the flowerpots from largest to smallest.
- Use simple words or phrases—avoid technical references, if possible.
- Include a general description of the study in the introduction section—make sure instructions are clearly expressed.
- Begin with simple questions and then progress to more difficult ones—topics move from general to specific and follow a logical sequence to the respondents.
- Ask personal or sensitive questions toward the end, unless the question is for screening purposes.
- Questions that involve psychological aspects, such as lifestyle issues, should be toward the end of the questionnaire.
- Make response categories mutually exclusive—do not use double-barreled questions/responses.
- Avoid asking questions using a different measurement format in the same section of the questionnaire.
- Classification (demographic) questions come at the end of the questionnaire, unless for screening purposes.
- End with a thank-you.

Developing Cover Letters

This section covers considerations and guidelines in developing cover letters. Many of the issues also apply to introductions used in surveys that rely on Internet data collection.

The Role of a Cover Letter

Cover letter A separate written communication to a prospective respondent designed to enhance that person's willingness to complete and return the survey in a timely manner.

A critical aspect associated with good questionnaire design is the development of an appropriate cover letter. Many marketing research textbooks offer little discussion of cover letter development. Usually, a **cover letter** is viewed as a letter accompanying a self-administered questionnaire that explains the nature of the survey. With personal or telephone interviews, researchers generally do not use a cover letter. But cover letters play several important roles in the successful collection of data with several collection methods. A cover letter is neither the same as the introductory section on the actual questionnaire nor the same as a screener.

The main role of the cover letter should be that of winning over the respondent's cooperation and willingness to participate in the research project. In other words, the cover letter should help persuade a prospective respondent to fill out the questionnaire and return it in a timely fashion. With self-administered surveys, many times a research project falls short of its goal because the response rate is low (25 percent or less). Usually when the response rate is low, the researcher can only guess at why. With either telephone or personal interviewing, similar problems occur when large numbers of prospective respondents decline to participate.

Secondary roles of a cover letter include (a) introducing the respondent to the research project and the researcher, (b) informing the respondent of the importance of the study, and (c) communicating the study's legitimacy and other particulars such as the deadline for returning the completed survey, and where to return it.[13]

Having a standardized cover letter that will fit all survey or interviewing situations is highly unlikely, but there are several factors that should be included in any cover letter. Exhibit 13.9 presents guidelines for developing cover letters. Each of these is discussed in the next section.

Guidelines for Developing Cover Letters

Regardless of a research project's method of data collection, the researcher should include a well-developed cover letter that relates to the survey instrument. For self-administered questionnaires, a separate cover letter should be sent with the questionnaire. For most telephone surveys and some types of personal interviews, a cover letter should be mailed to each prospective respondent before the initial contact by the interviewer.

Prior mailing of cover letters in interviewing situations is not a common practice among researchers, but this procedure can increase respondents' willingness to participate.[14] The reason for this comes from an understanding of human behavior. For example, the prospective respondent and interviewer are strangers to each other. People are more hesitant to express their opinions or feelings about a topic to a stranger than to someone they know, even to a limited extent. Mailing a cover letter to prospective respondents enables the researcher to break the ice prior to the actual interview.

The cover letter should introduce the potential respondent to the research project, stress its legitimacy, encourage participation, and let respondents know that a representative will be contacting them in the near future. Using a cover letter in interviewing situations increases the initial cost of data collection, but the resulting increase in the response rate can reduce the overall cost of the project.

While the exact wording of a cover letter will vary from researcher to researcher and from situation to situation, any cover letter should include the factors displayed in Exhibit 13.9.

EXHIBIT 13.9 Guidelines for Developing Cover Letters

Factors	Description
1. Personalization	Cover letter should be addressed to the specific *prospective respondent;* use research firm's professional letterhead stationery.
2. Identification of the organization	Clear identification of the name of the research firm conducting the survey or interview; decide on disguised or undisguised approach of revealing the actual client (or sponsor) of the study.
3. Clear statement of the study's purpose and importance	Describe the general topic of the research and emphasize its importance to the prospective respondent.
4. Anonymity and confidentiality	Give assurances that the prospective respondent's name will not be revealed. Explain how the respondent was chosen, and stress that his or her meaningful input is important to the study's success.
5. General time frame of doing the study	Communicate the overall time frame of the survey or interview.
6. Reinforcement of the importance of the respondent's participation	Where appropriate, communicate the importance of the prospective respondent's participation.
7. Acknowledgment of reasons for nonparticipation in survey or interview	Point out "lack of leisure time," "surveys classified as junk mail," and "forgetting about survey" as reasons for not participating, and defuse them.
8. Time requirements and the compensations	Clearly communicate the approximate time required to complete the survey; discuss incentive program, if any.
9. Completion date and where and how to return the survey	Communicate to the prospective respondent all instructions for returning the completed questionnaire.
10. Advance thank-you statement for willingness to participate	Thank the prospective respondent for his or her cooperation.

Factor 1: Personalization

Whenever possible, the cover letter should be addressed to the person who was randomly selected as a prospective respondent. The cover letter should be typed on professional letterhead that represents the research organization's affiliation, not the client's.

Factor 2: Identification of the Organization Doing the Study

The first comments should identify the research company conducting the survey but not necessarily the sponsor. If the sponsor wants or needs to be identified, then the researcher can choose one of two options: an undisguised or a disguised approach. With an undisguised approach, the actual sponsor's name will appear as part of the introduction statement. For example, the opening statement might read as follows:

> The Nationwide Opinion Research Company in New York is conducting a study for Verizon on people's cell phone practices.

In contrast, a disguised approach would not divulge the sponsor's identity to the respondent and would appear like this:

> The Nationwide Opinion Company in New York is conducting a study on people's cell phone habits and would like to include your opinions.

The sponsorship approach to use will be determined by the research objectives or mutual agreement between the researcher and client regarding the possible benefits and drawbacks of revealing the sponsor's name to the respondent. One reason for using a disguised approach is that it prevents competitors from finding out about the survey.[15]

Factor 3: Clear Statement of the Study's Purpose and Importance

One or two statements must be included in any cover letter to describe the general nature or topic of the survey and emphasize its importance. In the American Bank survey example, the researcher might use the following statements:

> Consumer banking practices are rapidly changing in 2009. With more bank locations, many new bank services, new technologies, the growth of credit unions, and the increased complexity of people's financial needs and wants, financial institutions are indeed changing. These changes are having important effects on you and your family. We would like to gain insights into these changes and their impact from the consumer's perspective by better understanding your opinions about different banking services, habits, and patterns. We believe you will find the survey interesting.

When you state the purpose of the study, it is important that you introduce the general topic of the survey in an interesting manner using words that are familiar to most members of the target audience. The purpose of the study should be followed by a statement that conveys the importance of the respondent's opinions on the topic. Some researchers like to follow up the purpose by adding a disclaimer that strongly emphasizes (1) the company is not trying to sell anything and (2) the respondent's name will not be added to any type of mailing list.

Factor 4: Anonymity and Confidentiality

After describing the purpose of the survey, the researcher must let the respondent know how and why people were selected for the study. The researcher can use a statement like this:

> Your name was one of only 1,500 names randomly selected from a representative list of people living in the Chicago area. Because the success of the survey depends upon the cooperation of all people who were selected, we would especially appreciate your willingness to help.

The phrasing should emphasize the importance of the respondent's participation to the success of the study and indirectly suggest that the respondent is special.

Anonymity The assurance that survey respondents will in no way be matched to their responses.

Confidentiality The assurance that the respondent's identity will not be divulged to a third party, including the client of the research.

If the researcher and client decide that assurances about anonymity and confidentiality are necessary, those factors should be incorporated at this point. **Anonymity** assures that the respondent's name or any identifiable designation will not be associated with his or her responses. Among the different data collection methods, anonymity statements are most appropriately associated with self-administered questionnaires. The researcher might use the following as an anonymity statement:

> The information obtained from the survey will in no way reflect the identities of the people participating in the study.

When an interview is used to collect data, an anonymity statement can appear in the letter of introduction that is mailed prior to the interviewer's initial contact with a prospective respondent.

A statement of **confidentiality** assures the prospective respondent that his or her name, while known to the researcher, will not be divulged to a third party, especially the client. Regardless of the data collection method, a confidentiality statement should always be included in a cover letter. A confidentiality statement might be phrased as follows:

> Your cooperation, attitudes, and opinions are very important to the success of the study and will be kept strictly confidential. Your opinions and responses will only be used when grouped with those of the other people participating in the survey.

Once the prospective respondent is promised confidentiality, it is the researcher's responsibility to keep that promise.

Factor 5: Time Frame

The cover letter should identify the general time frame for the survey. To encourage a prospective respondent to participate, it should state the actual completion time and any compensation that might be offered. When using an interview, for example, the researcher would include a statement or phrase like the following:

> In the next couple of days, one of our trained representatives will be contacting you by phone . . . The survey will only take a few moments of your time.

The key consideration with this factor is not to use a question format that requires a simple yes or no response. For example, "May I have one of our trained representatives contact you in the next couple of days?" or "May we have a few moments of your time?" If prospective respondents can answer *"no"* to a question asked in the cover letter, they are less likely to participate in the study.

Factor 6: Reinforcement of the Importance of the Respondent's Participation

The researcher can incorporate simple phrases into any part of the cover letter to reinforce the point that the respondent's participation is critical to the success of the study. Such phrases should be worded positively, not negatively.

Factor 7: Acknowledgment of Reasons for Not Participating in the Study

People offer numerous reasons when declining the role of being a respondent in a survey. Research among a variety of different groups has identified three of the most common reasons for not participating in a survey: (1) not having enough time, (2) seeing surveys as junk mail, and (3) forgetting about the survey.

First, people treasure their leisure time and feel they do not have enough of it. Therefore, when they receive a survey or telephone call or are asked on the spot to answer a few questions, potential respondents tend to use "do not have the time" as a reason not to participate. Since people are more likely to take the time to answer questions from someone they know, or are at least aware of, than from a stranger, the researcher has to acknowledge the time factor in the cover letter. To do this, a researcher should use a statement like this:

> We realize that to most of us in the community our leisure time is scarce and important and that we do not like to spend it filling out a questionnaire for some unknown person's or organization's study. Please remember that you are among a few being asked to participate in this study and your opinions are very important to the success of it.

This type of statement can easily be combined with statements about time requirements and compensation to effectively negate the time objection. Second, many people have the tendency to classify surveys received through regular mail or e-mail as "junk mail" or a telephone interviewer's call as an attempt to sell them something they do not need or want. To acknowledge this, something like the following statement could be used:

> We realize that many of us in the community receive a lot of things through regular mail or e-mail which we classify as "junk mail" and not important to respond to, but please do not consider the attached survey as being "junk mail." Your opinions, attitudes, and viewpoints toward each question are very important to us as well as the success of this study.

And for regular telephone interviews or CATI, the researcher should incorporate a statement like the following:

> We realize that many of us in the community receive a lot of phone calls from strangers trying to sell us some product or service that we neither need nor want. Let me assure you that I am not trying to sell you anything. I would just like to get your honest opinions on several questions pertaining to your banking habits and preferences; they are important to the success of this study.

Third, the issue of forgetting the survey primarily relates to direct mail or e-mail surveys. To help eliminate this problem, the researcher should incorporate a statement in the cover letter something like this:

> Past research has suggested that many questionnaires received through the mail or e-mail, if not completed and returned within the first 36 hours, have a tendency to get misplaced or forgotten about. Upon receiving this survey, please take the time to complete it. Your opinions are very important to us.

By taking away these three main reasons for not participating in a research study, the researcher significantly improves the likelihood that the prospective respondent will complete and return the direct mail, e-mail, or Web survey or cooperate in a telephone interview.

Factor 8: Time Requirements and Compensation

In an effort to win over a prospective respondent, the researcher might emphasize in the cover letter that the survey will not take much time or effort. For a self-administered survey, the researcher can incorporate statements like the following:

> We have designed the questionnaire to include all the directions and instructions necessary to complete the survey without the assistance of an interviewer. The survey will take approximately 15 minutes to complete. Please take your time in responding to each question. Your honest responses are very important to the success of the study.

For any type of interview, the researcher could incorporate the following statement into the letter of introduction: *"The interview will take approximately 15 minutes to complete."* These types of statements reinforce the notion that the survey will not take up much of the person's time.

The researcher and client may decide that some form of compensation is needed to encourage the respondent's participation. The type of compensation will depend on the study's topic and the data collection method. A token dollar amount (e.g., $1 or $5) can be offered to each prospective respondent and be included in the questionnaire packet. The idea is that giving respondents a reward up front for participating will make them feel obligated to complete the survey and return it as requested.[16] Experience with this method, however, suggests that people tend to assign a higher price than $1 or even $5 to their time. In other situations, nonmonetary incentives (a sample product, tickets to a movie, a certificate redeemable for specific products or services) might be used to encourage a respondent's participation.

Lottery incentive approach The pooling of individual incentive offerings into a significantly larger offering for which those people who participate have an equal chance of receiving the incentive.

An alternative to the individual reward system is the **lottery incentive approach** in which the incentive money forms a significantly larger dollar amount and everyone who completes and returns the survey has a chance of receiving the incentive. A significant reward is most likely to increase the response rate. The lottery approach is not, however, restricted to direct monetary rewards. Alternative rewards might be the chance to win an expense-paid trip somewhere. For example, the JP Hotel Corporation has used a "three-day, two-night, all-expenses-paid weekend stay for two people" at one of its luxury hotel complexes as the incentive for respondents who completed and returned their questionnaire by the specified date.

Among the different incentive programs available to the researcher, the lottery incentive system is advocated whenever possible. When a lottery is used, extra effort is required by the researcher to develop and include a separate identification form in the questionnaire packet that can be filled out and returned with a respondent's completed questionnaire. This incentive system tends to be most appropriate for self-administered surveys. Comments concerning incentives in a cover letter might be phrased as follows:

> To show our appreciation for your taking the time to participate in this study, we are going to hold a drawing for $500 among those who complete this survey. The drawing procedure has been designed in such a way that everyone who completes and returns the questionnaire will have an equal opportunity to receive the appreciation gift of $500.

Factor 9: Completion Date and Where and How to Return the Survey

In studies that collect data using a self-administered mail method, the researcher must give the respondents instructions for how, where, and when to return their completed survey. The how and where instructions can be simply expressed through the following type of statement:

> After completing all the questions in the survey, please use the enclosed stamped, addressed envelope to return your completed survey and appreciation gift card.

To deal with the return deadline date, the researcher should include a statement like this:

> To help us complete the study in a timely fashion, we need your cooperation in returning the completed questionnaire and incentive drawing card by no later than Friday, June 26, 2009.

For cover letters used with e-mail or Internet-based surveys, the researcher must communication the notion that after completing the survey the respondent only needs to click the "submit" button to send the completed survey to the researcher.

Factor 10: An Advanced Thank You

Prior to closing the cover letter with a thank-you statement, the researcher might want to include a final reassurance that she or he is not trying to sell the prospective respondent anything. In addition, the legitimacy of the study can be reinforced by supplying a name and telephone number if there are any concerns or questions, as follows:

> Again, let me give you my personal guarantee that we are not trying to sell you something. If you have any doubts, concerns, or questions about this survey, please give me a call at (504) 974-XXXX. Thank you in advance. We appreciate your cooperation in taking part in our study.

The researcher should sign the cover letter and include his or her title.

A Closer Look at Research

MARKETING RESOURCES GROUP
2305 Windsor Oaks Drive, Suite 1105
Baton Rouge, Louisiana 70814

CONSUMER BANKING OPINION STUDY
BATON ROUGE, LOUISIANA
(June 10, 2009)

If you have a bank account—

We need your opinion.

With more bank locations, new banking services, and the growth of credit unions and savings and loans, financial institutions are indeed changing. These changes will have an effect on you and your family, and that's why your opinion is important.

Your name has been selected in a sample of Baton Rouge residents to determine what people in our community think about the present products and services offered by banks. Your individual opinions in this survey can never be traced back to you, and all results will be held strictly confidential. The results of the study will provide the banking industry with insight into how to better serve the needs of its customers.

The brand-new quarter enclosed with this letter is not enough to compensate you for your time, but it may brighten the day of a youngster you know.

Thank you for your assistance.

Sincerely,

Thomas L. Kirk
MRG Project Director

P.S. Please return no later than June 24, 2009. A postage-paid envelope is enclosed.

A good cover letter entails as much thought, care, and effort as the questionnaire itself. While the actual factors will vary from researcher to researcher, these 10 are standard elements of any good cover letter. The specific examples given above should not be viewed as standardized phrases that must be included in all cover letters, but they do show how a researcher might increase a prospective respondent's willingness to participate in a given study. To see how these factors fit together in a cover letter, see Exhibit 13.10. The bold number inserts in the cover letter refer to the guidelines listed in Exhibit 13.9 of the chapter.

Cover Letter Length

A rarely discussed design question that affects the development of a cover letter is "How long should the cover letter be?" There is no simple answer that is correct in all situations, and in fact there are two opposing views. First, many researchers believe that the cover letter should be simple, to the point, and no longer than one page. The nearby A Closer Look at Research (In the Field) box illustrates a hypothetical cover letter for the American Bank and Trust survey that follows the direct, one-page approach.

While the one-page cover letter includes some of the factors we have discussed for influencing a prospective respondent's willingness to participate, it tends to lack the intensity level and clarity needed to win over a stranger. Still, many researchers go with a one-page

eXHIBIT 13.10 Cover Letter Used with the American Bank Survey

MARKETING RESOURCES GROUP
2305 Windsor Oaks Drive, Suite 1105
Baton Rouge, Louisiana 70814

June 10, 2009

[1]
Ms. Caroline V. Livingstone
873 Patterson Drive
Baton Rouge LA 70801

Dear Ms. Livingstone:

[2]We at Marketing Resources Group here in Baton Rouge are conducting an interesting study on people's banking habits and services **[5]**this month and would like to include your opinions.

[3]As you know, consumer banking practices are rapidly changing in the new millennium. With more bank locations, many new bank services, new technologies, the growth of credit unions and savings and loans, and the increased complexity of people's financial needs and wants, financial institutions are indeed changing. These changes are having important effects on you and your family. We would like to gain insights into these changes and their impact from the consumer's perspective by better understanding your opinions about different banking services, habits, and patterns.

We think you will find the survey interesting.

[4]Your name was one of only 600 names randomly selected from a representative list of people currently living in the Baton Rouge community. **[6]**Because the success of the survey depends upon the cooperation of all the people who were selected, we would especially appreciate your willingness to help us in this study.

[4]The information obtained from the survey will in no way reflect the identities of the people participating. Your cooperation, attitudes, and opinions are very important to the success of the study and will be kept strictly confidential. Your response will only be used when grouped with those of the other people taking part in the study.

[7]We realize that many of us in the community receive a lot of things through the mail which we classify as "junk mail" and not important to respond to, but please do not consider the attached survey as being "junk mail." **[6]**Your opinions, attitudes, and viewpoints toward each question are very important to us.

[7]To most of us in the community our leisure time is scarce and important, and we do not like to spend it filling out a questionnaire for some unknown organization's survey. Please remember that you are among a few being asked to participate in this study and **[6]**your opinions are very important to the success of it. **[8]**We have designed the questionnaire to include all the directions and instructions necessary to complete the survey without the assistance of an interviewer. You will find that the survey will take only about 15 minutes of your time. Please take your time in responding to each question. **[6]**Your honest responses are what we are looking for in the study.

[8]To show, in part, our appreciation for your taking the time to participate in this important study, we are going to hold a drawing for $500 among those of you who donate some of your leisure time to help us in completing this survey. The drawing procedure has been designed in such a way that everyone who completes and returns the questionnaire will have an equal opportunity to receive the appreciation gift of $500.

[7]Past research has suggested that many questionnaires that are received through the mail, if not completed and returned within the first 36 hours, have a tendency to be misplaced or forgotten about. Upon receiving this survey, please take the time to complete it. **[6]**Your opinions are very important to us.

[9]After completing all the questions in this survey, please use the enclosed stamped and addressed envelope to return your completed survey and appreciation gift card. To help us complete the study in a timely fashion, we need your cooperation in returning the survey and gift card by no later than **Friday, June 24, 2009.**

Again, let me give you my personal guarantee that we are not trying to sell you something. If you have any doubts, concerns, or questions about this survey, please give me a call at (504) 974-6236.

[10]Thank you in advance. We deeply appreciate your cooperation in taking part in our study.

Sincerely,

Thomas L. Kirk
MRG Project Director

ETHICS

Telephone Survey Goes Sour

In the spring of 2009, the Quality A-1 Rainbow Rug Cleaners, a new franchised carpet cleaning business, began operations in San Diego, California. This company was a member of San Diego's chamber of commerce. The owners of this franchised carpet cleaning business were struggling to get customers. They turned to a telemarketing firm for help. After several conversations with the telemarketing experts, a joint decision was made to use a disguised approach to solicit prospective customers by phone. The telemarketing firm developed what it called a telephone survey that would capture the necessary information to identify people in need of carpet cleaning services. Upon determination of the need, the survey was designed for the telephone interviewer to activate the customized sales pitch for Quality A-1 Rainbow Rug Cleaners' services. The survey started out by informing prospective respondents that they were randomly selected to participate in a short survey about cleaning products. Once it was determined that the individual qualified, the survey became a sales pitch, telling the qualified prospective customers that Quality A-1 Rainbow Rug Cleaners would be in their neighborhood that week and asking when they would like to schedule an appointment. Those unsuspecting respondents who agreed were scheduled on the spot by the telemarketing interviewer. The telemarketing firm convinced the owners that the survey process should run for one month at a cost of $4,000. Two weeks into the project, Quality A-1 Rainbow's owners received a call from San Diego's chamber of commerce notifying them that it had received about 100 calls from residents complaining about unwanted sales solicitations for Quality A-1 Rainbow's carpet cleaning services. Identify the ethical problems Quality A-1 Rainbow Rugs created for itself through their research program. How might the cleaning company have avoided those problems?

design because of the cost factor and because they believe people do not like to read correspondence from unknown commercial organizations like a research company. It is true that it costs less to develop, reproduce, and mail a one-page cover letter than a multiple-page letter, but if the one-page cover letter does not produce an adequate response rate, the study will cost more in the long run. The notion that people do not like to read correspondence from unknown commercial senders is basically true and is one of the reasons people use to justify not participating in a survey.

The contrasting view focuses on the need to deliver an emotion-laden story that compels the prospective respondent to cooperate. If a cover letter is well crafted and interesting, the prospective respondent will read not only the first page but the complete cover letter and move on to the questionnaire.

As always, the researcher should keep in mind the importance of ethical behavior. The nearby Ethics box discusses a carpet cleaning company's misuse of a telephone survey to gain new sales.

Other Documents Associated with Survey Instrument Designs

Although the main focus of this chapter is the development process and flowerpot approach to designing questionnaires, several supplemental documents required to execute the fieldwork activities in marketing research are worthy of discussion. When the decision is made to collect data by means of either personal, CATI, or telephone interviews, there is a need to develop good supervisor and interviewer instructions as well as screening forms, rating cards, and call record sheets. These types of documents help ensure that the process of collecting high-quality data will be successful. We discuss the highlights of each of these forms in this section.

Supervisor Instructions

Supervisor instruction form A form that serves as a blueprint for training people on how to execute the interviewing process in a standardized fashion; it outlines the process by which to conduct a study that uses personal and telephone interviewers.

Many commercial research companies collect much of their data using interviews that are conducted by specialty field interviewing companies located in selected geographic test markets. These companies are the production line for collecting data within the research industry. Usually, this type of company completes the interviews and sends them to the research company for processing. A **supervisor instruction form** serves as a blueprint for training people on how to complete the interviewing process in a standardized fashion. The instructions outline the process for conducting the study and are vitally important to any research project that utilizes personal or telephone interviews. They include detailed information about the nature of the study, start and completion dates, sampling instructions, number of interviewers required, equipment and facility requirements, reporting forms, quotas, and validation procedures. Exhibit 13.11 displays a sample page from a set of

EXHIBIT 13.11 Example of Supervisor Instructions for a Retail Bank Study Using Personal Interviews

Purpose:	To determine from students their banking practices and attitudes toward bank service quality across several different types of financial institutions.
Number of interviewers:	A total of 90 trained student interviewers (30 interviewers per class, three different classes).
Location of interviews:	Interviews will be conducted over a two-week period beginning October 10 and ending October 24, 2010. They will be conducted between the hours of 8:00 A.M. and 9:00 P.M., Monday through Friday. The locations of the interviews will be outside the campus buildings housing the 14 colleges making up the university plus the Library and Student Union. There will be three shifts of interviewers, 30 interviewers per shift, working the time frames of 8:00 A.M. to 12:00 noon or 12:01 P.M. to 5:00 P.M. or 5:01 P.M. to 9:00 P.M.
Quota:	Each interviewer will conduct and complete 30 interviews, with a maximum of 5 completed interviews for each of the following named retail banks: Bank of America, Sun Trust Bank, Citicorp, Capital One, First Union, and any five "Other Banks." All the completed interviews should come from their assigned location and time period. For each shift of 30 interviewers, there will be a minimum of 150 completed interviews for each of the five named banks in the study and a maximum of 150 completed interviews representing the set of "Other Banks."
Project materials:	For this study, you are supplied with the following materials: 2,701 personal questionnaires, 91 interviewer instruction-screening-quota forms, 91 sets of "Rating Cards" with each set consisting of six different rating cards, 91 "Verification of Interview" forms, and 1 interviewer scheduling matrix form.
Preparation:	Using your set of materials, review all material for complete understanding. Set a two-hour time frame for training your 90 student interviewers on how they should select a prospective respondent, screen for eligibility, and conduct the interviews. Make sure each interviewer understands the embedded "interviewer's instructions" in the actual questions making up the survey. In addition, assign each interviewer to a specified location and time frame for conducting the interviews, making sure all locations and time frames are appropriately covered.

supervisor instructions for a retail banking study that uses trained student interviewers to administer personal interviews for collecting the data.

Interviewer Instructions

Interviewer instructions The vehicle for training the interviewer on how to select prospective respondents, screen them for eligibility, and conduct the actual interview.

To ensure data quality, the interviewing process must be consistent. Thus, it is very important to train the people who will actually be conducting the interviews. **Interviewer instructions** serve as the vehicle for training the interviewers to (1) correctly select a prospective respondent for inclusion in the study, (2) screen prospective respondents for eligibility, and (3) properly conduct the actual interview. Although these instructions cover many of the same points found in the supervisor's instructions, they are designed to be pertinent to the actual interview. The instructions include detailed information about the nature of the study; start and completion dates; sampling instructions; screening procedures; quotas; number of interviews required; guidelines to asking questions, using rating cards, and recording responses; reporting forms; and verification form procedures. Exhibit 13.12 displays a sample page from a set of interviewer instructions for a retail banking study that used personal interviews to collect the data.

While not shown in Exhibit 13.12, many interviewer instructions list separately each general instruction as well as those within each question of the survey. In addition, the instructions include specific comments on procedures for asking each question and recording responses. The primary purpose of interviewer instructions is to ensure that all the interviews are conducted in basically the same fashion. It is critical for all interviewers to read each survey question as it was written, with no modifications. The interviewer instructions constitute a training tool to enhance the likelihood that all interviews will be conducted in the same manner, thus reducing the possibility that potential interviewer bias will enter the study and negatively impact the quality of the data.

Screening Forms

Screening forms A set of preliminary questions that are used to determine the eligibility of a prospective respondent for inclusion in the survey.

Although screening forms are not involved in all surveys, when used they play an important role in ensuring that the sampled respondents of a study are representative of the defined target population. Determining the eligibility of a prospective respondent up front increases the likelihood that the resulting data will be of high quality. **Screening forms** are a set of preliminary questions used to determine the *eligibility* of a prospective respondent for inclusion in the survey. Normally, the researcher and the client group determine the set of special characteristics a person must have in order to be included in the pool of prospective respondents. Almost any characteristics of an individual can be used as a screener. For example, a person's age, marital status, education level, number of purchases in a given time frame, or level of satisfaction toward a product or service might serve as a useful screener in a particular survey.

Screening forms should also be used to ensure that certain types of respondents are *not* included in the study. This means there are many marketing situations where it is desirable to have a good cross section of individuals, yet within the cross section there are particular types of individuals that should be excluded from the group. This occurs most frequently when a person's direct occupation or a family member's occupation in a particular industry would eliminate the person from inclusion in the study. For example, let's assume that J. D. Power and Associates was hired to conduct a study among the general population on the impact of advertising on perceived quality of automobiles manufactured by the Ford Motor Company. To ensure objectivity in the results, J. D. Power and Associates would want to automatically exclude people who themselves or whose immediate family members work for a marketing research firm, an advertising firm, the Ford Motor Company, or an

EXHIBIT 13.12 Example of Interviewer Instructions for a Retail Bank Study Using Personal Interviews

Purpose:	To determine from students their banking practices and attitudes toward bank service quality across several different types of financial institutions.
Method:	All interviewing will be conducted in person at your assigned designated locations within your assigned interviewing time frames. These locations and times will be assigned to you by your supervisor.
Location and time of interviews:	Your interviews will be conducted over a two-week period beginning October 10 and ending October 24, 2009. You will conduct the interviews during your assigned shift between the hours of 8:00 A.M. and 9:00 P.M., Monday through Friday. The locations of the interviews will be outside the campus buildings assigned to you by your supervisor.
Number of interviews/quota:	You will conduct and complete 30 interviews, with a maximum of 5 completed interviews for each of the following named retail banks: Bank of America, Sun Trust Bank, Citicorp, Capital One, First Union, and any five "Other Banks." All your completed interviews should come from your assigned location and time period.
Project materials:	For this study, you are supplied with the following materials: 30 personal questionnaires, 1 interviewer instruction-screening-quota form, 1 set of "Rating Cards" consisting of six different rating cards, 1 "Verification of Interview" form, and 1 interviewer scheduling matrix form.
Sampling procedure:	Once you are at your assigned location during your assigned interviewing shift (e.g., College of Education, 8:00 A.M. to 12:00 noon), randomly select a person in that area and follow the "introduction" instructions on your Introduction-Screening-Quota sheet. (First, politely walk up to that individual and introduce yourself. Then, politely explain to the person that: [read the given introduction statement on your *Introduction-Screening-Quota* sheet].) Follow the exact instructions. If the person is willing to be interviewed, continue to ask the "screening" questions to determine that person's eligibility and quota requirements. Follow the instructions on your *Introduction-Screening-Quota* sheet. If the person qualifies, begin the actual survey. If you determine that the person is not eligible, follow the instructions for terminating the interview and selecting your next prospective respondent. All interviewer instructions will be denoted in **FULL CAPS** on your Introduction-Screening-Quota sheet.
Screening factors:	Prospective respondents will be eligible if: 1. They are a current university student this current fall semester. 2. They have not already participated in this survey. 3. They are needed to fill any of the designated "quotas" for the five specific named banks or the "Other Banks" group.
Guidelines for actual interview:	Once the prospective respondent is determined eligible, you should begin the actual survey starting with question 1. Make sure you read each question as it is written on the questionnaire. All your instructions will appear in **FULL CAPS;** follow them carefully. After completing the interview, you must have the respondent fill out the required information on the "Verification of Interview" form. Then randomly select your next prospective respondent and follow the procedures and instructions on your Introduction-Screening-Quota sheet.
Preparation:	Using your set of materials, review all material for complete understanding. Prior to beginning the actual interviews, do at least three practice interviews to become familiar with the procedures for selecting a prospective respondent, screening for eligibility, and conducting the interviews. Make sure you understand the embedded "interviewer instructions" in the actual questions making up the survey.

automobile dealership that sold Ford vehicles. The reason behind excluding people who have an association with these particular types of occupations is that they normally hold inherent biases toward Ford vehicles or they have knowledge about the advertising industry. Thus, their opinions, attitudes, and feelings about the impact of advertising and/or quality of Ford vehicles *are not representative* of the people who make up the general population.

Screening forms are used mainly with personal or telephone interviews rather than with self-administered surveys. The reason for this is researchers often need a human being to control the screening process and make the final judgment about eligibility.

Self-administered questionnaires prevent this type of control. This does not mean that screening of prospective respondents is not possible in self-administered surveys. But it does require an additional process prior to administering the questionnaires. This process involves conducting a separate screening procedure either by telephone or with a personal interviewer before the prospective respondent receives his or her questionnaire. An exception to the need for a human being to serve as the control mechanism would be a survey that is self-administered through a computer or a television network (e.g., a hotel-guest survey that is programmed on the TV in a guest's room). In these methods, the questionnaire can be preprogrammed to automatically terminate the survey depending on how respondents themselves answered the prelisted screening questions. Exhibit 13.13 illustrates the screening form used in the retail banking study among college students.

Quota Sheets

Quota sheets A tracking form that enhances the interviewer's ability to collect data from the right type of respondents; the form helps ensure that representation standards are met.

In any type of research study there are situations when the researcher and client decide the prospective respondents should automatically represent specifically defined subgroups or categories of prespecified sizes (or quotas). **Quota sheets** are a simple tracking form that enhances the interviewer's ability to collect data from the right type of respondents. This form ensures that the identifiable respondent groups meet the prespecified requirements. Quotas also help an interviewer determine who is eligible for inclusion in the study. When a particular quota for a subgroup of respondents is filled, it indicates to the interviewer that although a respondent might qualify on the basis of all the screening factors, she or he is not needed for the specific subgroup of respondents. Therefore, the interview would be terminated at that point.

In the retail banking example, it was noted that 90 interviewers were used to collect the data for the study. Each interviewer was required to complete 30 interviews, for a total of 2,700 interviews. Among that total, overall quotas of 16.67 percent were established for Bank of America, Sun Trust Bank, Citicorp, Capital Bank, and First Union as well as for "Other Banks." Once the quota was reached for a particular bank, let's say Capital One, any prospective respondent who qualified on the screening questions but indicated that Capital One was his or her primary bank would be terminated from the survey. Exhibit 13.13 illustrates how the quota system worked for the retail banking survey.

Rating Cards

Rating cards Cards used in personal interviews that represent a reproduction of the set of actual scale points and descriptions used to respond to a specific question/setup in the survey. These cards serve as a tool to help the interviewer and respondent speed up the data collection process.

When collecting data by means of personal interviews, the researcher needs to develop another type of support document, referred to as a *rating card.* These cards serve as a tool to help the interviewer and respondent speed up the process of asking and answering the questions that make up the actual survey instrument. A **rating card** represents a reproduction of the set of actual scale points and their descriptions for specific questions on the survey. Whenever there is a question that asks the respondent to express some degree of intensity as part of the response, the interviewer provides the respondent with a rating card that reflects the possible scale responses. Before asking the survey question, the interviewer would hand the respondent the rating card and explain how to use the information on the card to respond to the question. Then the interviewer would read the question and each prelisted attribute to the respondent and record the person's response. Typically, the respondent's answer would be in the form of a letter or numerical descriptor that was specifically assigned to represent each response on the card. Exhibit 13.14 offers a specific example of a question and the appropriate rating card used in a retail banking survey administered using personal interviews.

EXHIBIT 13.13 Example of an Introduction-Screening-Quota Sheet for a Retail Bank Study Using Personal Interviews

INTRODUCTION-SCREENING-QUOTA SHEET
FOR THE UNIVERSITY STUDENT BANKING OPINION SURVEY

Approach to Randomly Selecting a Student

A. Politely walk up to an individual and introduce yourself.

B. Politely explain to the person that:

Your Marketing Research class is conducting an interesting class project this semester on students' banking attitudes and habits and you would like to include their opinions in the study.

- IF THEY SAY **"NO"** or **"DON'T WANT TO PARTICIPATE,"** politely thank them and move on to randomly select another person and repeat steps A and B.
- IF THEY ARE WILLING TO BE INTERVIEWED, ASK:

Q1. **Are you currently a university student this semester?**

If **YES,** continue with Q2.

If **NO,** thank them and **DISCONTINUE** the survey.

Q2. **Have you already participated in this survey?**

If **YES,** thank them and **DISCONTINUE** the survey.

If **NO,** continue with Q3.

Q3. **Thinking about the various banking systems which you may or may not use, please tell me the name of the one bank that you would generally consider as being "YOUR" primary bank.**

(CHECK TO SEE IF THE RESPONDENT'S CHOICE FITS YOUR NEEDED QUOTA OF BANK TYPES BELOW)

Quota		Possible "Other" Banks
1 2 3 4 5	Bank of America	☐ Beneficial Savings
1 2 3 4 5	Sun Trust Bank	☐ Glendale Federal
1 2 3 4 5	Citicorp	☐ USF Credit Union
1 2 3 4 5	Capital One	☐ Southeast Bank
1 2 3 4 5	First Union	☐ Wells Fargo
1 2 3 4 5	Some Other Bank ⟶	☐ Write In ______________

- IF THE ANSWER FITS A NEEDED QUOTA AREA,
  - (a) cross out one of the respective quota counts, and
  - (b) record the answer in Question 1 of the survey and continue with Question 2 of the survey.
- IF THE ANSWER **DOES NOT FIT** A NEEDED QUOTA AREA,
  - (a) politely thank them and **DISCONTINUE** the survey, and
  - (b) go back and repeat Steps A and B.

Call record sheet A recording document that gathers basic summary information about an interviewer's performance efficiency (e.g., number of contact attempts, number of completed interviews, length of time of interview).

Call Record Sheets

Call record sheets, also referred to as either *reporting or tracking sheets,* are used to help the researcher estimate the efficiency of interviewers' performance. While there is no one best format for designing a call record sheet, the form usually indicates some basic summary information regarding the number of contacts (or attempts) made by each interviewer and the results of those attempts. Typically, record sheets are used in data collection methods that require the use of an interviewer. Examples of the types of information gathered from a call record sheet would include number of calls or contacts made per hour, number of contacts per completed interview, length of time of the interview, completions by quota

eXHIBIT 13.14 Example of the Question/Scale Format and Rating Card Used in Collecting Raw Data in a Retail Banking Survey

RATING CARD A
(Importance Scale for Q2)

Rating Numbers	Description
6___	**Extremely Important** Consideration to Me
5___	**Definitely Important** Consideration to Me
4___	**Generally Important** Consideration to Me
3___	**Somewhat Important** Consideration to Me
2___	**Only Slightly Important** Consideration to Me
1___	**Not At All Important** Consideration to Me

Q2 Let's begin. I am going to read to you some bank features which may or may not have been important to you in selecting "YOUR" bank.

Using this rating card **(HAND RESPONDENT RATING CARD A),** please tell me the number that best describes how important you feel the bank feature was to you in helping select "YOUR" bank.

To what extent was **(READ FIRST FEATURE)** an important consideration to you in selecting "YOUR" bank?

(INTERVIEWER: MAKE SURE YOU READ AND RECORD THE ANSWER FOR ALL LISTED FEATURES)

Rating Number	Features	Rating Number	Features
___	Convenience of branch locations	___	Competitive minimum service charges
___	Flexibility of banking hours	___	Free checking availability
___	Friendly/courteous bank personnel	___	Interest rates on saving type accounts
___	No minimum balance requirement	___	Competitive interest rates on loans
___	Availability of credit card services	___	Credibility of the bank's reputation
___	Availability of ATM services	___	Bank's promotional advertisements

(UPON COMPLETION TAKE BACK RATING CARD A)

categories, number of terminated interviews, basic reasons for termination, and number of callback attempts (see Exhibit 13.15).

A researcher or supervisor can examine the information in an effort to assess an interviewer's efficiency in gathering the required data or to identify potential problem areas in the data collection process. For example, if the supervisor notices an interviewer's number of contacts per completed survey is significantly above the average of all interviewers, he or she should investigate the reasons behind it. Perhaps the interviewer was not appropriately trained or is not using the proper approach in securing the prospective respondents' willingness to participate. From a cost perspective, the researcher might find that the high cost per interview associated with a particular field service operation was due to a larger number of contacts needed to get a completed interview. Further investigation might indicate that the field service company did a poor job in either selecting the needed interviewers or provided inadequate training.

Your understanding of the activities needed to develop a scientific survey instrument completes the third phase of the information research process—gathering and collecting accurate data—and prepares you to journey into the last phase—data preparation and

eXHIBIT 13.15 Example of an Interviewer's Call Record Sheet

Interviewer Code Number 076		Date 10/11	Date 10/13	Date 10/16	Date 10/18	Date 10/19	Date 10/20	Date 10/23
Total Contact Attempts		20	22	24	18	14	20	8
Number of initial attempts		8	12	10	8	12	14	4
Number of callbacks		12	10	14	10	2	6	4
Total Number of Noncontacts		4	2	5	0	6	2	2
No answer		1		1				
Reached a recording		2		1		3		1
Wrong phone number			1			1		
Phone no longer in service		1		3			1	1
Specific person not available						2		
Other reasons			1				1	
Total Number of Actual Contacts		4	10	5	8	6	12	2
Number of Completed Interviews		4	8	5	6	3	2	2
Bank of America		2	1		1	1		
Sun Trust Bank			2	1	2			
Citicorp		1	1	2			1	
Capital One		1	1		3			
First Union			3			1		1
Other Banks				2		1	1	1
Contacts per Completed Interview		1	1.25	1	1.3	2	6	0
Number of Terminated Interviews		0	2	0	2	3	10	0
Screening ineligibility						1	2	
Refused participation					1		1	
Respondent break-off			1		1			
Quota requirement filled						3	7	
Language/hearing problems			1					
Some other reason								
Interviewing hours		4	4	4	5	4	4	4
Training hours	2							
Travel hours	4.5							
Mileage to interviewing center	35							

analysis. Chapter 14 focuses on activities involved with coding, editing, and preparing data for analysis.

But before leaving this chapter, you are encouraged to revisit the chapter's opening example and reassess your original answers to the university officials' three critical questions:

1. Why such a low response rate (9 completed surveys out of a possible 28,000)?
2. Was the survey a "good" or "bad" instrument for collecting the needed primary information?
3. Is there any diagnostic value of the data for addressing the given objectives?

In addition, remember to visit the book's Web site (www.mhhe.com/hair4e) for more useful information and examples pertinent to questionnaire designs.

marketing research in action

Continuing Case

Designing a Questionnaire to Assess the Dining Habits and Patterns of the Santa Fe Grill's Customers

This illustration extends the chapter's discussion on questionnaire development via the flowerpot approach using our Continuing Case about the Santa Fe Grill Mexican restaurant. Read through this restaurant example and using the actual Screening Questions (Exhibit 13.16) and Questionnaire (Exhibit 13.17), answer the questions at the end.

Background of the Situation

The Santa Fe Grill Mexican restaurant was started 18 months ago by two former business students at the University of Nebraska, Lincoln. They had been roommates in college and both had an entrepreneurial desire. After graduating they wanted to start a business instead of working for someone else. The students worked in restaurants while attending college, both as waiters and one as an assistant manager, and felt they had the knowledge and experience necessary to start their own business.

During their senior year they prepared a business plan in their entrepreneurship class for a new Mexican restaurant concept. They initially intended to start the restaurant in Lincoln, Nebraska. After a demographic analysis of that market, however, they decided that Lincoln did not match their target demographics as well as they initially thought it would.

After researching the demographic and competitive profile of several markets, they decided Dallas, Texas, would be the best place to start their business. In examining the markets, they were looking for a town that would best fit their target market of singles and families in the age range of 25 to 50. The population of Dallas was almost 5.5 million people,

eXHIBIT 13.16 Screening and Rapport Questions for the Restaurant Survey

Hello. My name is ____ and I work for DSS Research. We are talking to individuals today (tonight) about dining out habits.

1. Do you regularly eat out at casual dining restaurants? Yes = 1; No = 0
2. Have you eaten at more than one Mexican restaurant in the last six months? Yes = 1; No = 0
3. Is your gross annual household income $15,000 or more? Yes = 1; No = 0
4. What is your favorite Mexican restaurant to eat at?
   - **a.** Santa Fe Grill—Yes, continue.
   - **b.** Jose's Southwestern Café—Yes, continue.
   - **c.** Other—thank them and select another respondent.

If respondent answers Yes to the first three questions, and indicates either the Santa Fe Grill or Jose's Southwestern Café, then say:

We would like you to answer a few questions about yourself and your experiences eating at the ___??? restaurant. The questions will take only a few minutes and your answers will be very helpful in better serving customers.

If individual says yes, give them a clipboard with the questionnaire on it, briefly explain the questionnaire, and show them where to complete the questions.

EXHIBIT 13.17 Restaurant Dining Out Questionnaire

DINING OUT SURVEY

Please read all questions carefully. If you do not understand a question, ask the interviewer to help you. In the first section a number of statements are given about interests and opinions. Using a scale from 1 to 7, with 7 being "Strongly Agree" and 1 being "Strongly Disagree," please indicate the extent to which you agree or disagree that a particular statement describes you. Circle only one number for each statement.

Section 1: Lifestyle Questions

	Strongly Disagree						Strongly Agree
1. I often try new and different things.	1	2	3	4	5	6	7
2. I like parties with music and lots of talk.	1	2	3	4	5	6	7
3. People come to me more often than I go to them for information about products.	1	2	3	4	5	6	7
4. I try to avoid fried foods.	1	2	3	4	5	6	7
5. I like to go out and socialize with people.	1	2	3	4	5	6	7
6. Friends and neighbors often come to me for advice about products and brands.	1	2	3	4	5	6	7
7. I am self-confident about myself and my future.	1	2	3	4	5	6	7
8. I usually eat balanced, nutritious meals.	1	2	3	4	5	6	7
9. When I see a new product in stores, I often buy it.	1	2	3	4	5	6	7
10. I am careful about what I eat.	1	2	3	4	5	6	7
11. I often try new brands before my friends and neighbors do.	1	2	3	4	5	6	7

Section 2: Perceptions Measures of Your "Favorite" Mexican Restaurant

Listed below is a set of characteristics that could be used to describe the restaurant you just identified as your favorite Mexican restaurant. Using a scale from 1 to 7, with 7 being "Strongly Agree" and 1 being "Strongly Disagree," to what extent do you agree or disagree your favorite Mexican restaurant:

	Strongly Disagree						Strongly Agree
12. Has friendly employees	1	2	3	4	5	6	7

continued

EXHIBIT 13.17 Restaurant Dining Out Questionnaire, *continued*

13. Is a fun place to eat	Strongly Disagree 1 2 3 4 5 6 7	Strongly Agree
14. Has large size portions	Strongly Disagree 1 2 3 4 5 6 7	Strongly Agree
15. Has fresh food	Strongly Disagree 1 2 3 4 5 6 7	Strongly Agree
16. Has reasonable prices	Strongly Disagree 1 2 3 4 5 6 7	Strongly Agree
17. Has an attractive interior	Strongly Disagree 1 2 3 4 5 6 7	Strongly Agree
18. Has excellent food taste	Strongly Disagree 1 2 3 4 5 6 7	Strongly Agree
19. Has knowledgeable employees	Strongly Disagree 1 2 3 4 5 6 7	Strongly Agree
20. Serves food at the proper temperature	Strongly Disagree 1 2 3 4 5 6 7	Strongly Agree
21. Has quick service	Strongly Disagree 1 2 3 4 5 6 7	Strongly Agree

Section 3: Relationship Measures

Please indicate your view on each of the following questions:

22. How satisfied are you with your favorite Mexican restaurant?	Not Satisfied At All 1 2 3 4 5 6 7	Very Satisfied
23. How likely are you to return to your favorite Mexican restaurant in the future?	Definitely Will Not Return 1 2 3 4 5 6 7	Definitely Will Return
24. How likely are you to recommend your favorite Mexican restaurant to a friend?	Definitely Will Not Recommend 1 2 3 4 5 6 7	Definitely Will Recommend

25. How often do you eat at your favorite Mexican restaurant?

1 = Very Infrequently
2 = Somewhat Infrequently
3 = Occasionally
4 = Somewhat Frequently
5 = Very Frequently

Section 4: Selection Factors

Listed below are some factors (reasons) many people use in selecting a restaurant where they want to dine. Think about your visits to casual dining restaurants in the last three months and please rank each

eXHIBIT 13.17 *continued*

attribute from 1 to 4, with 1 being the most important reason for selecting the restaurant and 4 being the least important reason. There can be no ties so make sure you rank each attribute with a different number.

Attributes	Ranking
26. Prices	
27. Food Quality	
28. Atmosphere	
29. Service	

Section 5: Classification Questions

Please circle the number that classifies you best.

30. Distance Driven
1 Less than 1 mile
2 1–5 miles
3 More than 5 Miles

31. Do your recall seeing any advertisements in the last 60 days for your favorite Mexican restaurant?
0 No
1 Yes

32. Your Gender
0 Male
1 Female

33. Number of Children at Home
1 None
2 1–2
3 More than 2 children at home

34. Your Age in Years
1 18–25
2 26–34
3 35–49
4 50–59
5 60 and Older

35. Your Annual Gross Household Income Please specify ____________

Thank you very much for your help. Please give your questionnaire back to the interviewer.

Interviewer: Check answers to questions 22, 23, and 24. If respondent answers 1, 2, or 3, ask the following questions.

You indicated you are not too satisfied with your favorite Mexican restaurant. Could you please tell me why?

Record answer here:

You indicated you are not likely to return to your favorite Mexican restaurant. Could you please tell me why?

Record answer here:

---

continued

eXHIBIT 13.17 Restaurant Dining Out Questionnaire, *continued*

You indicated you are not likely to recommend your favorite Mexican restaurant. Could you please tell me why?

Record answer here:

____

Could I please have your name and phone number for verification purposes?

______________	______________
Name	**Phone #**

I hereby attest that this is a true and honest interview and complete to the best of my knowledge. I guarantee that all information relating to this interview shall be kept strictly confidential.

______________	______________
Interviewer's Signature	**Date and Time completed**

of which about 50 percent were between the ages of 25 and 60. This indicated there were a lot of individuals in their target market in the Dallas area. They also found that about 55 percent of the population earned between $35,000 and $75,000 a year, which indicated the market would have enough income to eat out regularly. Finally, 56 percent of the population was married and many of them had children at home, which was consistent with their target market.

The new restaurant concept was based upon offering exciting Mexican fare made with the freshest ingredients, complimented by a festive atmosphere, friendly service, and cutting-edge advertising and marketing strategies. The key would be to prepare and serve the freshest "made-from-scratch" Mexican foods possible. Everything would be prepared fresh every single day. In addition to their freshness concept, they wanted to have a fun, festive atmosphere and fast, friendly service. The atmosphere would be open, brightly lit, and bustling with activity. Their target market would be mostly families with children, between the ages of 18 and 49. Their marketing programs would be ahead of the pack, with the advertising designed to provide an appealing, slightly off-center, unrefined positioning in the market.

The Santa Fe Grill promised to be successful but not as quickly as the owners had anticipated. To improve the restaurant operations, the owners needed to understand what aspects of the restaurant created customer satisfaction and loyalty, and where they were falling short in the minds of the customers. They came up with a few questions that could be researched: "Are the customers satisfied, and if not, why are they not satisfied? Is the problem the food or the atmosphere or something else (e.g., employees or service)? Is the target market correctly defined or do they need to focus on a different niche? What are the common characteristics of the satisfied customers?" The owners determined that answering these questions and other similar questions would help them to focus their marketing efforts to generate more success in the restaurant.

Despite the slow start for the restaurant, they managed to break even and have enough money to conduct a customer survey. The restaurant was located on an outparcel on the east side near the main entrance of the Cumberland Mall, which has 75+ stores in it and is considered very successful for the area. A market research company was located in the mall so they decided to use a mall intercept approach to collect data. Another Mexican restaurant that had been in business longer and appeared to be more successful was also on an outparcel at the same mall, but its location was on the west side of the mall. Their goal was to complete interviews with 250 individuals who considered the Santa Fe Grill their favorite Mexican restaurant and 150 individuals who considered Jose's Southwestern Café their favorite Mexican restaurant. Over a period of two weeks, a total of 405 interviews were completed—152 for Jose's and 253 for the Santa Fe Grill.

The owners believe the survey will help them to identify the restaurant's strengths and weaknesses, enable them to compare their restaurant to a nearby competitor, and develop a plan to improve the restaurant's operations. The questionnaire began with four screening questions (see Exhibit 13.16), including lifestyle, restaurant experience, and classification questions. The following six research objectives were used to guide the design of the questionnaire shown in Exhibit 13.17:

1. To develop a psychographic/demographic profile of the customers of the Santa Fe Grill and Jose's Southwestern Café.
2. To identify the factors people feel are important in selecting casual dining restaurants.
3. To determine the characteristics customers use to describe the Santa Fe Grill and Jose's Southwestern Café.
4. To determine the dining frequency and advertising recall for the Santa Fe Grill restaurant and Jose's Southwestern Café.
5. To assess the likelihood of customers returning to the Santa Fe Grill and Jose's Southwestern Café in the future.
6. To assess the degree to which customers are satisfied with and likely to recommend the Santa Fe Grill and Jose's Southwestern Café.

Hands-On Exercise

Using your knowledge and understanding of the material in Chapter 13, prepare answers to each of the following questions:

1. Based on the research objectives, does the questionnaire, in its current form, correctly illustrate the "Flowerpot" survey design approach? Please explain why or why not.
2. Overall, is the current survey design able to obtain the required data needed to address all the stated research objectives? Why or why not? If changes are needed, how would you change the survey's design?
3. Evaluate the "screener questions" used to qualify the respondents. Are there any changes needed? Why or why not?
4. Redesign questions #26–29 on the survey using a "rating" scale that will enable you to capture the "degree of importance" that a customer might attach to each of the four listed attributes in selecting a restaurant to dine at.

Summary of Learning Objectives

■ Describe the process of questionnaire design.

Questionnaire development is much more than just writing a set of questions and asking people to answer them. Designing good surveys goes beyond just developing reliable and valid scales. A number of design factors, systematic procedural steps, and rules of logic must be considered in the development process. The process requires knowledge of sampling, construct development, scale measurement, and types of data. A questionnaire is a set of questions/scales designed to generate enough data to allow the researcher and decision maker to develop information to solve the business problem.

Many researchers believe that questionnaire design is an art rather than a science. Questionnaires consist of four different components: words, questions, formats, and hypotheses. Most surveys use descriptive instruments that rely heavily on the collection of state-of-being or state-of-behavior data. Others use predictive instruments that focus on collecting state-of-mind and state-of-intention data. Good questionnaires enable researchers to gain a true report of the respondent's attitudes, preferences, beliefs, feelings, behavioral intentions, and actions/reactions in a holistic manner, not just a fragment. By understanding good communication principles, researchers can avoid bad questioning procedures that might result in unrealistic information requests, unanswerable questions, or leading questions that distort the meaning of a person's responses.

■ Discuss questionnaire development using the "flowerpot" approach.

Once research objectives are transformed into information objectives, determining the specific information requirements plays a critical role in the development of questionnaires. Using their knowledge of construct development and scale measurement (Chapter 11) and attitude measurement (Chapter 12), researchers can follow an 11-step process to develop scientific survey instruments. See Exhibit 13.4 which lists these steps. The flowerpot approach serves as a unique framework for integrating different sets of questions and scales into a scientific structure for collecting high-quality data. This ordered approach helps researchers make critical decisions regarding (1) construct development, (2) the appropriate dimensions and attributes of objects, (3) question/scale formats, (4) wording of actual questions and directives, and (5) scale points and descriptors. Following the flowerpot approach assures that the data flow will correctly move from a general information level to a more specific level.

■ Summarize the characteristics of good questionnaires.

Survey information requirements play a critical role in the development of questionnaires. For each objective, the researcher must choose types of scale formats (nominal, ordinal, interval, or ratio); question formats (open-ended and closed-ended); and the appropriate scaling. Researchers must be aware of the impact that different data collection methods (personal, telephone, self-administered, computer-assisted) have on the wording of both questions and response choices. With good questionnaires, the questions are simple, expressed clearly, logical, meaningful to the respondent, and move from general to specific topics.

■ Understand the role of cover letters.

While the main role of any cover letter should be winning over a prospective respondent, a set of secondary roles ranges from initial introduction to communicating the legitimacy and other important factors about the study. Ten critical factors should be included in most, if not all, cover letters. Including these will help the researcher counteract the three major reasons prospective respondents use to avoid participating in self-administered surveys and personal interviews. A lottery-based compensation system can significantly improve a prospective respondent's willingness to participate.

■ Explain the importance of other documents used with questionnaires.

When data are collected using interviews, supervisor and interviewer instructions must be developed as well as screening forms, rating cards, and call record sheets. These documents ensure the data collection process is successful. Supervisor instructions serve as a blueprint for training people to complete the interviewing process in a consistent fashion. The instructions outline the process for conducting the study and are important to any research project that uses personal or telephone interviews. Interviewer instructions are used to train interviewers to correctly select a prospective respondent for inclusion in the study, screen prospective respondents for eligibility, and properly conduct the actual interview. Screening forms are a set of preliminary questions used to confirm the eligibility of a prospective respondent for inclusion in the survey. Quota sheets are tracking forms that enable the interviewer to collect data from the right type of respondents. Rating cards help respondents to better understand scaling, and call record sheets enable interviewers' performance to be evaluated. All of these documents help improve data collection and accuracy.

Key Terms and Concepts

Accuracy 410
Anonymity 428
Bad questions 407
Call record sheet 439
Confidentiality 428
Cover letter 426
Flowerpot approach 411
Hypothesis 408
Interviewer instructions 436
Lottery incentive approach 431
Questionnaire 404
Questionnaire design precision 410
Quota sheets 438
Rating cards 438
Screening forms 436
Structured questions 407
Supervisor instruction form 435
Unstructured questions 406

Review Questions

1. What are the advantages and disadvantages of using unstructured (open-ended) and structured (closed-ended) questions in developing an online, self-administered survey instrument?
2. Explain the role of a questionnaire in the information research process. What should be the role of the client during the questionnaire development process?
3. Identify the guidelines for deciding the form and layout of a questionnaire. Discuss the advantages and disadvantages of using the flowerpot approach in developing survey instruments.
4. What are the factors that constitute bad questions in questionnaire design? Develop three examples of bad questions. Then, using the information in Exhibit 13.7, rewrite your examples so they could be judged as good questions.
5. What are the main benefits of including a brief introductory section in a questionnaire?
6. Unless needed for screening purposes, why shouldn't classification questions be presented up front in most questionnaire designs?
7. What are the critical issues involved in pretesting a questionnaire?

Discussion Questions

1. Identify and discuss the guidelines for developing cover letters for a survey research instrument. What are some of the advantages of developing good cover letters? What are some of the costs of a bad cover letter?
2. Using the guidelines for developing questionnaires (see Exhibit 13.8), evaluate the Santa Fe Grill restaurant questionnaire at the end of this chapter. Write a one-page assessment report.
3. **EXPERIENCE THE INTERNET.** Using any browser of your choice, go to www.opentext.com and type in the search phrase "questionnaire design." Browse the various listings until you find a questionnaire of your liking. Evaluate the extent to which your selected questionnaire follows the flowerpot approach and write a two-page summary of your findings. (Make sure you include in your report the exact Web site address used for reaching your selected questionnaire.)
4. **EXPERIENCE THE INTERNET.** Get on the Net and go to Visual Research's site at www.vrcinc.com. Browse through the site and evaluate the various new technologies being offered for conducting surveys via the Internet. Write a one-page summary that focuses on the advantages and disadvantages associated with collecting survey data through the Internet.

part 4

Data Preparation, Analysis, and Reporting Results

chapter 14

Preparing Survey Data for Analysis

Learning Objectives

After reading this chapter, you will be able to:

1. Describe the process of data preparation for analysis.
2. Discuss validation, editing, and coding of survey data.
3. Explain data entry procedures as well as how to detect errors.
4. Describe data tabulation approaches.

"The rapid proliferation of computer technology has made the procedure for raw data entry appear almost second nature for many data analysts. Yet everyone in this field understands the fundamental concept behind this task—GIGO: garbage in, garbage out."[1]

—ROBERT W. KNEEN,
Senior Systems Analyst,
Union Bancorporation

Wal-Mart and Scanner Technology

Each item you purchase in almost any retail store is scanned into a computer. The bar code enables each store to know exactly what products are selling and when. Store managers can also keep accurate control of inventory, so they can easily order more products when they run low. Probably the ultimate example of scanning use is Wal-Mart, where scanners have been vital. Wal-Mart does not own the products on its shelves; they remain there on consignment by the manufacturers. With its scanning system, however, Wal-Mart always knows what is there, what is selling, and what needs replenishment. The scanner has pushed back the law of diminishing returns and made it possible to build and manage larger inventories than would have been possible a few years ago.

The same equipment that scans product codes can also scan a bar-coded customer card so the customer is associated with his or her purchase in a central database. This process takes a second or two per transaction, and requires only that the customer produce the card at purchase time.

Scanner technology is widely used in the marketing research industry. Questionnaires can be prepared through any of a number of word processing software packages and printed on a laser printer. Respondents can complete the questionnaire with any type of writing instrument. With the appropriate software and scanning device, the researcher can scan the completed questionnaires and the data are checked for errors, categorized, and stored within a matter of seconds. When a researcher expects to receive 400 to 500 completed surveys, scanner technology can be worth its weight in gold.[2]

Value of Preparing Data for Analysis

Converting information from a questionnaire so it can be transferred to a data warehouse is referred to as data preparation. This process usually follows a four-step approach, beginning with data validation, then editing and coding, followed by data entry and data tabulation. Error detection begins in the first phase and continues throughout the process. The purpose of data preparation is to take data in its raw form and convert it to establish meaning and create value for the user.

The process of data preparation and analysis starts after the data is collected. Several interrelated tasks must be completed to ensure the data is accurately reported. The stages of data preparation and analysis are shown in Exhibit 14.1. This chapter discusses the data preparation process and Chapters 15, 16 and 17 provide an overview of data analysis for quantitative research.

EXHIBIT 14.1 Overview of Data Preparation and Analysis

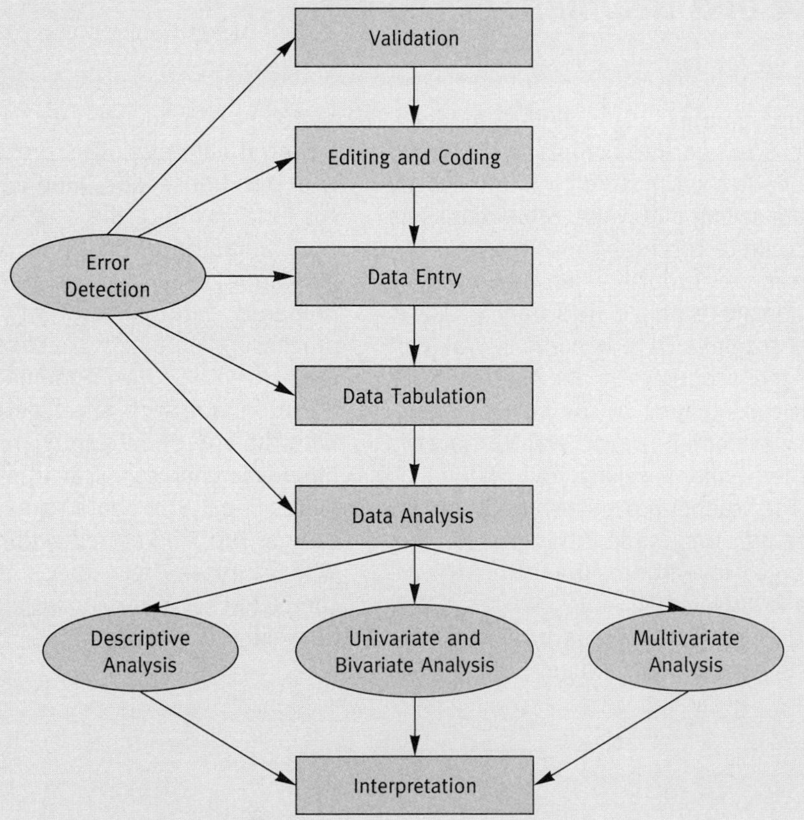

Data Validation

Data validation The process of determining, to the extent possible, whether a survey's interviews or observations were conducted correctly and are free of fraud or bias.

Curbstoning Cheating or falsification in the data collection process.

The purpose of **data validation** is to determine if surveys, interviews, and observations were conducted correctly and free of bias. Data collection often is not easy to monitor closely. To facilitate accurate data collection, each respondent's name, address, and phone number may be recorded. While this information is not used for analysis, it does enable the validation process to be completed.

In the marketing research industry submitting false data is referred to as curbstoning. As the name implies, **curbstoning** is when interviewers find an out-of-the-way location, such as a curbstone, and fill out the survey themselves rather than follow procedures with an actual respondent. Because of the potential for such falsification, data validation is an important step in the data acquisition process.

Most marketing research professionals will target between 10 and 30 percent of completed interviews for "callbacks." Specifically for telephone, mail, and personal interviews, a certain percentage of respondents from the completed interviews will be recontacted by the research firm to make sure the interview was conducted correctly. Normally through telephone recontact, respondents will be asked several short questions as a way of validating the returned interview. Generally, the process of validation covers five areas:

1. *Fraud.* Was the person actually interviewed, or was the interview falsified? Did the interviewer contact the respondent simply to get a name and address, and then proceed to fabricate responses? Did the interviewer use a friend to obtain the necessary information?

2. *Screening.* Many times an interview must be conducted only with qualified respondents. To ensure accuracy of the data collected, many respondents will be screened according to some preselected criteria, such as household income level, recent purchase of a specific product or brand, or even sex or age. For example, the interview procedure may require that only female heads of households with an annual household income of $25,000 or more be interviewed. In this case, a validation callback would verify each of these factors.

3. *Procedure.* In many marketing research projects it is critical that the data be collected according to a specific procedure. For example, many customer exit interviews must occur in a designated place as the respondent leaves a certain retail establishment. In this particular example a validation callback may be necessary to ensure the interview took place at the proper setting, not some social gathering or area like a party or a park.

4. *Completeness.* In order to speed through the data collection process, an interviewer may ask the respondent only a few of the requisite questions. In such cases, the interviewer asks the respondent a few questions from the beginning of the interview form and then skips to the end, omitting questions from other sections. The interviewer may then make up answers to the remaining questions. To determine if the interview is valid, the researcher could recontact a sample of respondents and ask about questions from different parts of the interview form.

5. *Courtesy.* Respondents should be treated with courtesy and respect during the interviewing process. Situations can occur, however, where the interviewer may

inject a tone of negativity into the interviewing process. To ensure a positive image, respondent callbacks are common to determine whether the interviewer was courteous. Other aspects of the interviewer checked during callbacks include appearance, communication, and interpersonal skills.

Editing and Coding

Editing The process in which the raw data are checked for mistakes made by either the interviewer or the respondent.

Following validation, the data must be edited for mistakes. **Editing** is the process of checking the data for mistakes made by either the interviewer or the respondent. By scanning each completed interview, the researcher can check several areas of concern: (1) asking the proper questions, (2) accurate recording of answers, (3) correct screening of respondents, and (4) complete and accurate recording of open-ended questions.

Asking the Proper Questions

One aspect of the editing process especially important to interviewing methods is to make certain the proper questions were asked of the respondent. As part of the editing process, the researcher will check to make sure all respondents were asked the proper questions. In cases where they were not, respondents are recontacted to obtain a response to omitted questions.

Accurate Recording of Answers

Completed questionnaires sometimes have missing information. The interviewer may have accidentally skipped a question or not recorded it in the proper location. With a careful check of all questionnaires, these problems can be identified. In such cases, if it is possible, respondents are recontacted and the omitted responses recorded.

Correct Screening Questions

The first four items on the questionnaire in Exhibit 14.2 are actually screening questions that determine whether the respondent is eligible to complete the survey. During the editing phase, the researcher will make certain that only qualified respondents were included. It is also critical in the editing process to establish that the questions were asked and (for self-administered surveys) answered in the proper sequence. If the proper sequence is not followed, the respondent must be recontacted to verify the accuracy of the recorded data.

Responses to Open-Ended Questions

Responses to open-ended questions often provide very meaningful data. Open-ended questions may provide greater insight into the research questions than forced-choice questions. A major part of editing the answers to open-ended questions is interpretation.

eXHIBIT 14.2 The Santa Fe Grill Questionnaire

Hello. My name is ____ and I work for DSS Research. We are talking to individuals today/tonight about dining out habits.

1. "Do you regularly eat out at casual dining restaurants?" __ Yes __ No

2. "Have you eaten at more than one Mexican restaurant in the last six months?" __ Yes __ No

3. "Is your gross annual household income $15,000 or more?" __ Yes __ No

4. What is your favorite Mexican restaurant to eat at?

a. Santa Fe Grill—Yes, continue.

b. Jose's Southwestern Café—Yes, continue.

c. Other—thank them and select another respondent.

If respondent answers 'Yes' to first three questions, and indicates either the Santa Fe Grill or Jose's Southwestern Café, then say:

We would like you to answer a few questions about yourself and your experiences eating at the ___???___ restaurant. The questions will only take a few minutes and it will be very helpful in better serving customers.

If the individual says yes, give them a clipboard with the questionnaire on it, briefly explain the questionnaire, and show them where to complete the survey.

DINING OUT SURVEY

Please read all questions carefully. If you do not understand a question, ask the interviewer to help you. In the first section a number of statements are given about interests and opinions. Using a scale from 1 to 7, with 7 being "Strongly Agree" and 1 being "Strongly Disagree," please indicate the extent to which you agree or disagree a particular statement describes you. Circle only one number for each statement.

Section 1: Lifestyle Questions

1. I often try new and different things. Strongly Disagree 1 2 3 4 5 6 7 Strongly Agree

2. I like parties with music and lots of talk. Strongly Disagree 1 2 3 4 5 6 7 Strongly Agree

3. People come to me more often than I go to them for information about products. Strongly Disagree 1 2 3 4 5 6 7 Strongly Agree

4. I try to avoid fried foods. Strongly Disagree 1 2 3 4 5 6 7 Strongly Agree

5. I like to go out and socialize with people. Strongly Disagree 1 2 3 4 5 6 7 Strongly Agree

6. Friends and neighbors often come to me for advice about products and brands. Strongly Disagree 1 2 3 4 5 6 7 Strongly Agree

continued

EXHIBIT 14.2 The Santa Fe Grill Questionnaire, *continued*

7. I am self-confident about myself and my future.
Strongly Disagree 1 2 3 4 5 6 7 Strongly Agree

8. I usually eat balanced, nutritious meals.
Strongly Disagree 1 2 3 4 5 6 7 Strongly Agree

9. When I see a new product in stores, I often buy it.
Strongly Disagree 1 2 3 4 5 6 7 Strongly Agree

10. I am careful about what I eat.
Strongly Disagree 1 2 3 4 5 6 7 Strongly Agree

11. I often try new brands before my friends and neighbors do.
Strongly Disagree 1 2 3 4 5 6 7 Strongly Agree

Section 2: Perceptions Measures

Listed below is a set of characteristics that could be used to describe the Santa Fe Grill Mexican restaurant. Using a scale from 1 to 7, with 7 being "Strongly Agree" and 1 being "Strongly Disagree," to what extent do you agree or disagree the Santa Fe Grill:

12. Has friendly employees
Strongly Disagree 1 2 3 4 5 6 7 Strongly Agree

13. Is a fun place to eat
Strongly Disagree 1 2 3 4 5 6 7 Strongly Agree

14. Has large size portions
Strongly Disagree 1 2 3 4 5 6 7 Strongly Agree

15. Has fresh food
Strongly Disagree 1 2 3 4 5 6 7 Strongly Agree

16. Has reasonable prices
Strongly Disagree 1 2 3 4 5 6 7 Strongly Agree

17. Has an attractive interior
Strongly Disagree 1 2 3 4 5 6 7 Strongly Agree

18. Has excellent food taste
Strongly Disagree 1 2 3 4 5 6 7 Strongly Agree

eXHIBIT 14.2 *continued*

19. Has knowledgeable employees
Strongly Disagree 1 2 3 4 5 6 7 Strongly Agree

20. Serves food at the proper temperature
Strongly Disagree 1 2 3 4 5 6 7 Strongly Agree

21. Has quick service
Strongly Disagree 1 2 3 4 5 6 7 Strongly Agree

Section 3: Relationship Measures

Please indicate your view on each of the following questions:

22. How satisfied are you with your favorite Mexican restaurant?
Not Satisfied At All 1 2 3 4 5 6 7 Very Satisfied

23. How likely are you to return to your favorite Mexican restaurant?
Definitely Will Not Return 1 2 3 4 5 6 7 Definitely Will Return

24. How likely are you to recommend your favorite Mexican restaurant to a friend?
Definitely Will Not Recommend 1 2 3 4 5 6 7 Definitely Will Recommend

25. How often do you eat at your favorite Mexican restaurant?
1 = Very Infrequently
2 = Somewhat Infrequently
3 = Occasionally
4 = Somewhat Frequently
5 = Very Frequently

Section 4: Selection Factors

Listed below are some factors (reasons) many people use in selecting a restaurant where they want to dine. Think about your visits to casual dining restaurants in the last three months and please rank each attribute from 1 to 4, with 1 being the most important reason for selecting the restaurant and 4 being the least important reason. There can be no ties so make sure you rank each attribute with a different number.

Attribute	Ranking
26. Prices	
27. Food Quality	
28. Atmosphere	
29. Service	

continued

eXHIBIT 14.2 The Santa Fe Grill Questionnaire, *continued*

Section 5: Classification Questions

Please circle the number that classifies you best.

30. Distance Driven
- 1 Less than 1 mile
- 2 1–5 miles
- 3 More than 5 Miles

31. Do your recall seeing any advertisements in the last 60 days for the Santa Fe Grill?
- 0 No
- 1 Yes

32. Your Gender
- 0 Male
- 1 Female

33. Number of Children at Home
- 1 None
- 2 1–2
- 3 More than 2 children at home

34. Your Age in Years
- 1 18–25
- 2 26–34
- 3 35–49
- 4 50–59
- 5 60 and Older

35. Your Annual Gross Household Income Please specify ________

Thank you very much for your help.

____

Interviewer: Check answers to questions 22, 23, and 24. If respondent answers 1, 2, or 3, ask the following questions.

You indicated you are not too satisfied with your favorite Mexican restaurant. Could you please tell me why?

Record answer here:

____

You indicated you are not likely to return to your favorite Mexican restaurant. Could you please tell me why?

Record answer here:

____

You indicated you are not likely to recommend your favorite Mexican restaurant. Could you please tell me why?

Record answer here:

____

Could I please have your name and phone number for verification purposes?

________________ ________________

Name **Phone #**

I hereby attest that this is a true and honest interview and complete to the best of my knowledge. I guarantee that all information relating to this interview shall be kept strictly confidential.

________________ ________________

Interviewer's Signature **Date and Time Completed**

eXHIBIT 14.3 Responses to an Open-Ended Question

10. Why are you eating at the Santa Fe Grill more often?

- They have good service.
- Found out how good the food is.
- I enjoy the food.
- We just moved here and where we lived there were no good Mexican restaurants.
- That part of town is building up so fast.
- They have a couple of offers in the newspaper.
- It is right beside where my husband works.
- Tastes better—grilled.
- They started giving better value packages.
- We really like their chicken sandwiches, so we go more often now.
- The good food.
- Only because they only put one in within the last year.
- Just opened lately.
- It is located right by Wal-Mart.
- Just moved into area and they have good food.
- There is one in the area where I work.

Exhibit 14.3 shows some typical responses to an open-ended question and thus points to problems associated with interpreting these questions. For example, one response to the question "Why are you eating at the Santa Fe Grill more often?" is simply "They have good service." This answer by itself is not sufficient to determine what the respondent means by "good service." The interviewer needed to probe for a more specific response. For example, are the employees friendly, helpful, courteous? Do they appear neat and clean? Do they smile when taking an order? Probes such as these would enable the researcher to better interpret the "good service" answer. In cases such as these, the individual doing the editing must use judgment in classifying responses. At some point the responses must be placed in standard categories. Answers that are incomplete are considered useless.

The Coding Process

Coding Grouping and assigning value to various responses from the survey instrument.

Coding involves grouping and assigning values to responses to the survey questions. It is the assignment of numerical values to each individual response for each question on the survey. Typically, the codes are numerical (a number from 0 to 9) because numbers are quick and easy to input and computers work better with numbers than alphanumerical values. Like editing, coding can be tedious if certain issues are not addressed prior to collecting the data. A well-planned and -constructed questionnaire can reduce the amount of time spent on coding and increase the accuracy of the process if it is incorporated into the design of the questionnaire. The Santa Fe Grill questionnaire shown in Exhibit 14.2 has built-in coded responses for all questions except the open-ended ones asked by the interviewer at the end of the survey. In the "Lifestyle Questions," for example, a respondent has the option of responding from 1 to 7, based on his or her level of agreement or disagreement with a particular statement. Thus, if the respondent circled "5" as his or her choice, then the value of "5" would become the coded value for a particular question.

When questionnaires do not have coded responses, a master code sheet is prepared showing the assigned numeric values for each response. Exhibit 14.4 is an example of a master code sheet. Question 1 has all the coded values for responses to "fast-food establishments visited in the past two months." These values range from 01 to 13, with Taco Bell having the value of 01, Hardee's 02, Kentucky Fried Chicken 03, and so on. An additional statement in question 1, "Other, please specify," has different coding properties. "Other, please specify" will have a separate set of codes based on all possible answers that may have been provided by the respondents. For example, a respondent may have specified "White Castle" in this response category. Since "White Castle" is not on the list of possible responses for question 1, a separate and unique value will have to be coded

eXHIBIT 14.4 An Illustration of a Master Code Sheet

Master Code Sheet

Questionnaire Identification Number 000 (1–3)

FAST-FOOD OPINION SURVEY

This questionnaire is being used by a marketing research class at Kennesaw State University. The purpose of the project is to better understand the attitudes and opinions of consumers toward fast-food restaurants. The questionnaire will take only 10–15 minutes to complete, and all responses will remain strictly confidential. Thank you for your help on this project.

1. **Below is a listing of various fast-food restaurants. How many of these restaurants have you eaten at in the past two months? Check as many as may apply.**

Taco Bell	01	Church's Fried Chicken	08
Hardee's	02	McDonald's	09
Kentucky Fried Chicken	03	Burger King	10
Wendy's	04	Back Yard Burgers	11 ✓
Rally's	05	Arby's	12
Popeye's Chicken	06	Sonic	13
Krystal's	07	Other, please specify →	see code sheet.
		Have not visited any of these establishments	20

2. **In a typical month, how many times do you eat at a fast-food restaurant, such as the ones listed in question #1? (X ONE BOX)**

One ☐	Two ☐	Three ☑	Four ☐	Five ☐	Six ☐	Seven or more ☐
1	2	3	4	5	6	7

3. **On your last visit to a fast-food restaurant, what was the approximate dollar amount you spent on food and beverages?**

Under $2	☐ 1	$8.01–$10.00	☐ 5
$2.01–$4.00	☐ 2	$10.01–$12.00	☐ 6
$4.01–$6.00	☑ 3	More than $12	☐ 7
$6.01–$8.00	☐ 4	Don't remember	☐ 8

for "White Castle" that is different from the other values in question 1. These coded values are usually stored and listed on a separate code sheet identified as "Code sheet for 'Other' responses."

Another example of a coded response can be seen in question 3. In this case, if the respondent checked "$4.01–$6.00" in question 3, the coder would assign the value of 3 to that response. If a respondent checked "more than $12," the coder would assign a value of 7 to the category. Such closed-ended questions as these are typically precoded at the time of questionnaire design. The use of a master code is an additional safeguard to be sure the coding process is followed correctly.

In contrast, open-ended questions pose unique problems to the coding process. An exact list of potential responses cannot be prepared ahead of time for open-ended questions. Thus, a coding process must be prepared after data is collected. But the value of the information obtained from open-ended questions often outweighs the problems of coding the responses.

Researchers typically use a four-step process to develop codes for responses. The procedure begins by generating a list of as many potential responses as possible. Responses are then assigned values within a range determined by the actual number of separate responses identified. When reviewing responses to the open-ended questions, the researcher attaches a value from the developed response list. If responses do not appear on the list, the researcher adds a new response and corresponding value to the list or places the response into one of the existing categories.

Consolidation of responses is the second phase of the four-step process. Exhibit 14.5 illustrates several actual responses to the question "Why are you dining less frequently at

eXHIBIT 14.5 Illustration of Response Consolidation for Open-Ended Questions

Q10a. Why are you dining less frequently at the __________ restaurant?

Respondent # 72113

- I am a state employee. I look for bargains. Need more specials.
- Because I'm no longer close to a __________.

Respondent # 72114

- I do not like the food.

Respondent # 72116

- They never get my order right.
- I got tired of the hamburgers. I don't like the spices.
- Prices are too high.
- Family doesn't like it.
- My husband didn't like the way the burgers tasted.
- They should give more with their combos than they do. More fries.
- Because they always got our orders wrong and they are rude.
- The order is never right.
- Health reasons.
- I work longer hours and don't think about food.
- Cannot eat the food.
- We started eating at __________.
- The location of my work moved so I am not near a __________.

the __________ restaurant?" Four of these related to not liking the food can be consolidated into a single response category because they all have the same shared meaning. Developing consolidated categories is a subjective decision that should be made only by an experienced research analyst with input from the project's sponsor.

The third step of the process is to assign a numerical value as a code. While at first this may appear to be a simple task, the structure of the questionnaire and the number of responses per question need to be considered. For example, if a question has more than 10 responses, then double-digit codes need to be used, such as "01," "02," . . . "12." Another good practice is to assign higher-value codes to positive responses than to negative responses. For example, "no" responses are coded 0 and "yes" responses coded 1; "dislike" responses are coded as 1 and "like" responses coded as 5. Coding of this nature makes subsequent analysis easier. For example, the researcher will find it easier to interpret means or averages if higher values occur as the average moves from "dislike" to "like."

If correlation or regression will be used in data analysis, then for categorical data there is another consideration. The researcher may wish to create "dummy" variables in which the coding is "0" and "1."

Assigning a coded value to missing data is very important. For example, if a respondent completes a questionnaire except for the very last question and a recontact is not possible, how do you code the response to the unanswered question? A good practice in this situation is to first consider how the response is going to be used in the analysis phase. In certain types of analysis, if the response is left blank and has no numerical value, the entire questionnaire (not just the individual question) will be deleted. The best way to handle the coding of omitted responses is first to check on how your data analysis software treats missing data. This should be the guide for determining whether omissions are coded or left blank.

The fourth step in the coding process is to assign a coded value to each response. This is probably the most tedious process because it is done manually. Unless an optical scanning approach is used to enter the data, this task is almost always necessary to avoid problems in the data entry phase.

Each questionnaire is assigned a numerical value. The numerical value typically is a three-digit code if there are fewer than 1,000 questionnaires to code, and a four-digit code if there are 1,000 or more. For example, if 452 completed questionnaires were returned, the first would be coded 001, the second 002, and so on, finishing with 452. Questionnaire coding is discussed again when we cover data entry.

Data Entry

Data entry Those tasks involved with the direct input of the coded data into some specified software package that ultimately allows the research analyst to manipulate and transform the data into useful information.

Data entry follows validation, editing, and coding. **Data entry** is the procedure used to enter the data into a computer file for subsequent data analysis. Data entry is the direct input of the coded data into a file that enables the research analyst to manipulate and transform the data into useful information.

There are several ways of entering coded data into an electronic file. With CATI and Internet surveys, the data are entered simultaneously with data collection and a separate step is not required. However, if the data is entered manually, it is most likely to be entered using a personal computer (PC) and a spreadsheet interface. But other approaches are available. Some terminals have touch-screen capabilities that enable the analyst to touch an area of the terminal screen to enter a data element. A similar technique uses a light pen—a handheld electronic pointer that enters data through the terminal screen.

Scanning technology also can be used to enter data. Exhibit 14.6 shows a questionnaire that has been designed for optical character recognition. This approach enables the

eXHIBIT 14.6 Example of Optical Character Recognition Questionnaire

WELLNESS ASSESSMENT QUESTIONNAIRE

Risk Assessment Systems, Inc.
5846 Distribution Drive
Memphis, Tennessee 38141

INSTRUCTIONS

To ensure an accurate Personal Wellness Assessment, please answer all of the following questions as accurately and completely as possible.

USE A NO. 2 PENCIL ONLY | Example: ☐ ☐ ■ ☐ ☐ | Erase *completely* to change

Name ____________

Street address ____________

City ____________

State ____________

Phone # ( ) ____________

Zip Code: ☐☐☐☐☐ (0–9 for each digit)

Social Security Number: ☐☐☐ – ☐☐ – ☐☐☐☐ (0–9 for each digit)

PHYSICAL DATA/CURRENT HEALTH STATUS

Sex: ☐ Male ☐ Female

Date of Birth: Month – Day – Year

Height: ☐ ft. ☐☐ in.

Weight: ☐☐☐ lbs.

Blood Pressure: If you know your Blood Pressure, enter it here ------> Systolic (High) ☐☐☐ Diastolic (Low) ☐☐☐

If not, which best describes it? ☐ High ☐ Normal or Low ☐ Don't Know

1. In general, would you say your current state of health is:
☐ Excellent ☐ Very Good ☐ Good ☐ Fair ☐ Poor

2. During the past 12 months, how many days of work have you missed due to your own injury or sickness?
☐ None ☐ 1 to 3 ☐ 4 to 6 ☐ 7 or more ☐ Does not apply

PERSONAL/FAMILY MEDICAL HISTORY

3. How often are you given a routine physical examination by a physician?
☐ More than once a year ☐ Once a year ☐ Once every 2 years ☐ Every 3 years or longer ☐ Never had one

4. How long has it been since your last electrocardiogram (EKG)?
☐ Less than 1 year ago ☐ 1 to 2 years ago ☐ 2 to 3 years ago ☐ 3 or more years ago ☐ Never had one

5. Have you or has anyone in your family (parents, grandparents, brother or sister) had any of the following health problems? If so, please mark the corresponding box. *(Please mark all that apply.)*

	Self	Brother	Sister	Father	Mother	Father's side Grandfather	Father's side Grandmother	Mother's side Grandfather	Mother's side Grandmother
Heart disease before age 55	☐	☐	☐	☐	☐	☐	☐	☐	☐
Heart disease age 55 to 64	☐	☐	☐	☐	☐	☐	☐	☐	☐
Heart disease age 65 or later	☐	☐	☐	☐	☐	☐	☐	☐	☐
High blood pressure	☐	☐	☐	☐	☐	☐	☐	☐	☐
Stroke	☐	☐	☐	☐	☐	☐	☐	☐	☐
Diabetes	☐	☐	☐	☐	☐	☐	☐	☐	☐
Breast cancer	☐	☐	☐	☐	☐	☐	☐	☐	☐
Colon cancer	☐	☐	☐	☐	☐	☐	☐	☐	☐
Cancer (except breast/colon)	☐	☐	☐	☐	☐	☐	☐	☐	☐
Kidney disease	☐	☐	☐	☐	☐	☐	☐	☐	☐
Tuberculosis	☐	☐	☐	☐	☐	☐	☐	☐	☐
Mental illness	☐	☐	☐	☐	☐	☐	☐	☐	☐
Suicide	☐	☐	☐	☐	☐	☐	☐	☐	☐
Drug/alcohol addiction	☐	☐	☐	☐	☐	☐	☐	☐	☐

Continued on Page 2

 1 SCANTRON FORM NO. F-5414-RAS P4 3593-C C1520- 5 4 3 2

computer to read alphabetic, numeric, and special character codes through a scanning device. On the questionnaire in Exhibit 14.6, the respondent uses a number two pencil to fill in responses, which are then scanned directly into a computer file.

Online surveys are becoming increasingly popular for completing marketing research studies. Indeed, online surveys now represent almost 40 percent of all data collection approaches. Not only are they often faster to complete, they also eliminate entirely the data entry process.

Error Detection

Error detection identifies errors from data entry or other sources. The first step in error detection is to determine whether the software used for data entry and tabulation performs "error edit routines" that identify the wrong type of data. For example, say that for a particular field on a given data record, only the codes of 1 or 2 should appear. An error edit routine can display an error message on the data output if any number other than 1 or 2 has been entered. Such routines can be quite thorough. A coded value can be rejected if it is too large or too small for a particular scaled item on the questionnaire. In some instances, a separate error edit routine can be established for every item on the questionnaire.

Another approach to error detection is for the researcher to review a printed representation of the entered data. Exhibit 14.7, for example, shows the coded values for observations

eXHIBIT 14.7 SPSS Data View of Coded Values for Santa Fe Grill Observations

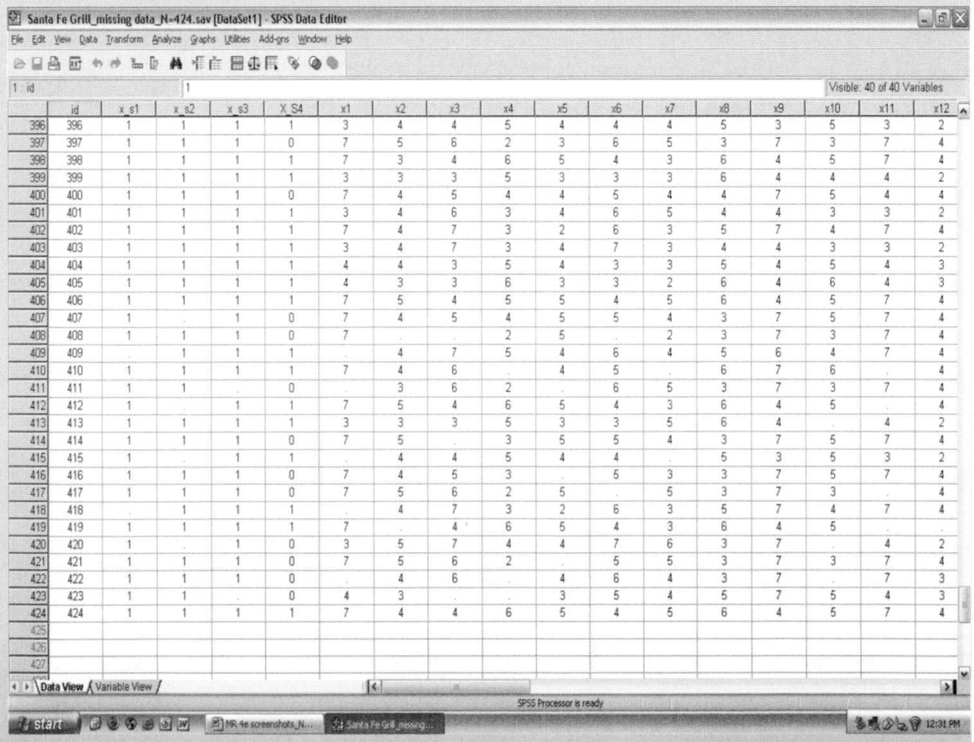

	id	x_s1	x_s2	x_s3	X_S4	x1	x2	x3	x4	x5	x6	x7	x8	x9	x10	x11	x12
396	396	1	1	1	1	3	4	4	5	4	4	4	5	3	5	3	2
397	397	1	1	1	0	7	5	6	2	3	6	5	3	7	3	7	4
398	398	1	1	1	1	7	3	4	6	5	4	3	6	4	5	7	4
399	399	1	1	1	1	3	3	3	5	3	3	3	6	4	4	4	2
400	400	1	1	1	0	7	4	5	4	4	5	4	4	7	5	4	4
401	401	1	1	1	1	3	4	6	3	4	6	5	4	4	3	3	2
402	402	1	1	1	1	7	4	7	3	2	6	3	5	7	4	7	4
403	403	1	1	1	1	3	4	7	3	4	7	3	4	4	3	3	2
404	404	1	1	1	1	4	4	3	5	4	3	3	5	4	5	4	3
405	405	1	1	1	1	4	3	3	6	3	3	2	6	4	6	4	3
406	406	1	1	1	1	7	5	4	5	5	4	5	6	4	5	7	4
407	407	1	.	1	0	7	4	5	4	5	5	4	3	7	5	7	4
408	408	1	1	1	0	7	.	.	2	5	.	2	3	7	3	7	4
409	409	.	1	1	1	.	4	7	5	4	6	4	5	6	4	7	4
410	410	1	1	1	1	7	4	6	.	4	5	.	6	7	6	.	4
411	411	1	1	.	0	.	3	6	2	.	6	5	3	7	3	7	4
412	412	1	.	1	1	7	5	4	6	5	4	3	6	4	5	.	4
413	413	1	1	1	1	3	3	3	5	3	3	5	6	4	.	4	2
414	414	1	1	1	0	7	5	.	3	5	5	4	3	7	5	7	4
415	415	1	.	1	1	.	4	4	5	4	4	.	5	3	5	3	2
416	416	1	1	1	0	7	4	5	3	.	5	3	3	7	5	7	4
417	417	1	1	1	0	7	5	6	2	5	.	5	3	7	3	.	4
418	418	.	1	1	1	.	4	7	3	2	6	3	5	7	4	7	4
419	419	1	1	1	1	7	.	4	6	5	4	3	6	4	5	.	.
420	420	1	.	1	0	3	5	7	4	4	7	6	3	7	.	4	2
421	421	1	1	1	0	7	5	6	2	.	5	5	3	7	3	7	4
422	422	1	1	1	0	.	4	6	.	4	6	4	3	7	.	7	3
423	423	1	1	.	0	4	3	.	.	3	5	4	5	7	5	4	3
424	424	1	1	1	1	7	4	4	6	5	4	5	6	4	5	7	4
425																	
426																	
427																	

eXHIBIT 14.8 Example of Data/Column List Procedure

Data Field	1	2	3	4	5	6	7
40	50	20	33	81	0	2	1
41	5	9	82	77	36	8	0
42	10	12	11	15	0	0	0
43	15	16	17	80	1	3	5
44	0	0	7	100	2	11	0
45	17	42	71	62	1	3	5
46	100	2	5	18	16	2	12
47	22	25	62	90	10	30	15
48	0	0	25	18	13	17	35
49	61	40	23	30	18	22	17
50	10	11	62	73	10	21	0
51	7	11	21	17	52	47	5
52	82	46	80	20	30	6	7

396–424 in the Santa Fe Grill restaurant survey. In this example the top row indicates the variable names assigned to each data field (i.e., "id" is the label for the questionnaire number, "x_s1" represents the first screening question, x1 is the first question on the survey after the four screening questions, etc.). The numbers in the columns are the coded values that were entered. The dots indicate missing responses. While the process is somewhat tedious, the analyst can view the actual data for accuracy and can tell where errors occurred.

The final approach to error detection is to produce a data/column list for the entered data. A sample data/column list is shown in Exhibit 14.8. The rows of this output indicate the fields of the data record. The columns indicate the frequency of responses for each particular field. In data field 40, for example, 50 responses of 1 were entered, 20 responses of 2 were entered, and so on. A quick viewing of this data/column list can indicate whether inappropriate codes were entered into the data fields. The analyst can then find the corresponding questionnaire and correct the error as needed.

Tabulation The process of counting the number of observations (cases) that are classified into certain categories.

By scanning actual data input and producing a data/column list table, the researcher should be confident of error-free data entry. At this point the data should be ready for preliminary tabulation and data analysis. The nearby A Closer Look at Research (In the Field) box addresses additional issues of error detection.

Data Tabulation

One-way tabulation Categorization of single variables existing in a study.

Tabulation is counting the number of responses in categories. Two common forms of tabulation are used in marketing research projects: one-way tabulation and cross-tabulations. A **one-way tabulation** looks at single variables in the study. In most cases, a one-way tabulation shows the number of respondents who gave each possible answer to each question

A Closer Look at Research

Data Collection Should Not Be Manual Labor

With the computerization of survey design and Internet data collection, manual questionnaires are being used much less frequently. Computer-based surveys can handle large amounts of data, increasing the capacity for data collection and substantially reducing confusion and errors by interviewers and respondents. Three of the major benefits are as follows:

1. **Encoding data without transcribing from paper.** The interviewer or respondent enters data directly into an electronic file. Hours of tedious effort can be eliminated by avoiding the use of paper surveys.
2. **Minimizing errors in data.** Errors in data are less likely with computer data collection than with paper surveys. Researchers no longer have to decipher illegible interviewer or respondent handwriting.
3. **Speeding up data collection and coding.** Computer surveys speed data collection at several points in the data collection process, including: (a) getting questions to the respondent, (b) asking questions of the respondent, (c) recording the respondent's answers, (d) getting the answers back to the researcher, and (e) entering the answers into an electronic file. Clearly, these all result in time savings and potential cost savings.

on the questionnaire. The number of one-way tabulations is determined by the number of variables measured in the study.

Cross-tabulation Simultaneously treating two or more variables in the study; categorizing the number of respondents who have answered two or more questions consecutively.

Cross-tabulation simultaneously compares two or more nominal variables in the study. Cross-tabulations categorize the number of responses to two or more questions, thus showing the relationship between those two variables. For example, a cross-tabulation could show the number of male and female respondents who spent more than $7.00 eating at McDonald's versus those who spent less. We show you how to use software to develop cross-tabulations in the next chapter.

One-Way Tabulation

One-way tabulations serve several purposes. First, they can be used to determine the amount of nonresponse to individual questions. Based on the coding scheme used for missing data, one-way tabulations identify the number of respondents who did not answer various questions on the questionnaire. Second, one-way tabulations can be used to locate simple blunders in data entry.

If a specific range of codes has been established for a given response to a question, say 1 through 5, a one-way tabulation can illustrate if an inaccurate code was entered, say, a 7 or 8. It does this by providing a list of all responses to the particular question. In addition, means, standard deviations, and related descriptive statistics often are determined from a one-way tabulation. Finally, one-way tabulations are also used to communicate the results of the research project. One-way tabulations can profile sample respondents, identify characteristics that distinguish between groups (heavy users versus light users), and show the

eXHIBIT 14.9 Example of One-Way Frequency Distribution

Output23 - SPSS Viewer

File Edit View Insert Format Analyze Graphs Utilities Window Help

Restaurant

		Frequency	Percent	Valid Percent	Cumulative Percent
Valid	Superior Grill	99	20.1	20.1	20.1
	Mamacitas	74	15.0	15.0	35.1
	Ninfa's	110	22.3	22.3	57.4
	Moe's southwestern Grill	47	9.5	9.5	66.9
	Santa Fe Grill	38	7.7	7.7	74.6
	Jose's	36	7.3	7.3	81.9
	Papacita's	32	6.5	6.5	88.4
	Other	24	4.9	4.9	93.3
	None	23	4.7	4.7	98.0
	Dont Remember	10	2.0	2.0	100.0
	Total	493	100.0	100.0	

percentage of respondents who respond differently to different situations (percentage of people who purchase fast food from drive-thru windows versus those who use dine-in facilities).

The most basic way to illustrate a one-way tabulation is to construct a one-way frequency table. A one-way frequency table shows the number of respondents who answered each possible response to a question given the available alternatives. An example of a one-way frequency table is shown in Exhibit 14.9, which shows which Mexican restaurants the respondents dined at in the last 30 days. The information indicates that 99 individuals (20.1 percent) ate at Superior Grill in the last 30 days, 74 (15.0 percent) ate at Mamacita's, 110 (22.3 percent) ate at Ninfa's, and so on. Typically, a computer printout will be prepared with one-way frequency tables for each question on the survey. In addition to listing the number of responses, one-way frequency tables also identify missing data and show valid percentages and summary statistics.

1. **Indications of missing data.** One-way frequency tables show the number of missing responses for each question. As shown in Exhibit 14.10, a total of 19 respondents, or 4.5 percent of the sample, did not respond to how frequently they patronized the Santa Fe Grill. It is important to recognize the actual number of missing responses when estimating percentages from a one-way frequency table. In order to establish valid percentages, missing responses must be removed from the calculation.

2. **Determining valid percentages.** To determine valid percentages one must remove incomplete surveys or particular questions. For example, the one-way frequency table in

Exhibit 14.10 actually constructs valid percentages (the third column). While the total number of responses for this particular question was 424, only 405 are used to develop the valid percentage of response across categories because the 19 missing responses were removed from the calculations.

3. **Summary statistics.** Finally, SPSS also provides summary statistics from the frequency table option. In Exhibit 14.10 the summary statistics for question X25 are the mean, median, mode, standard deviation, and range. These statistics help the researcher better understand the patterns of the responses. For example, the mode of

eXHIBIT 14.10 One-Way Frequency Table Illustrating Missing Data

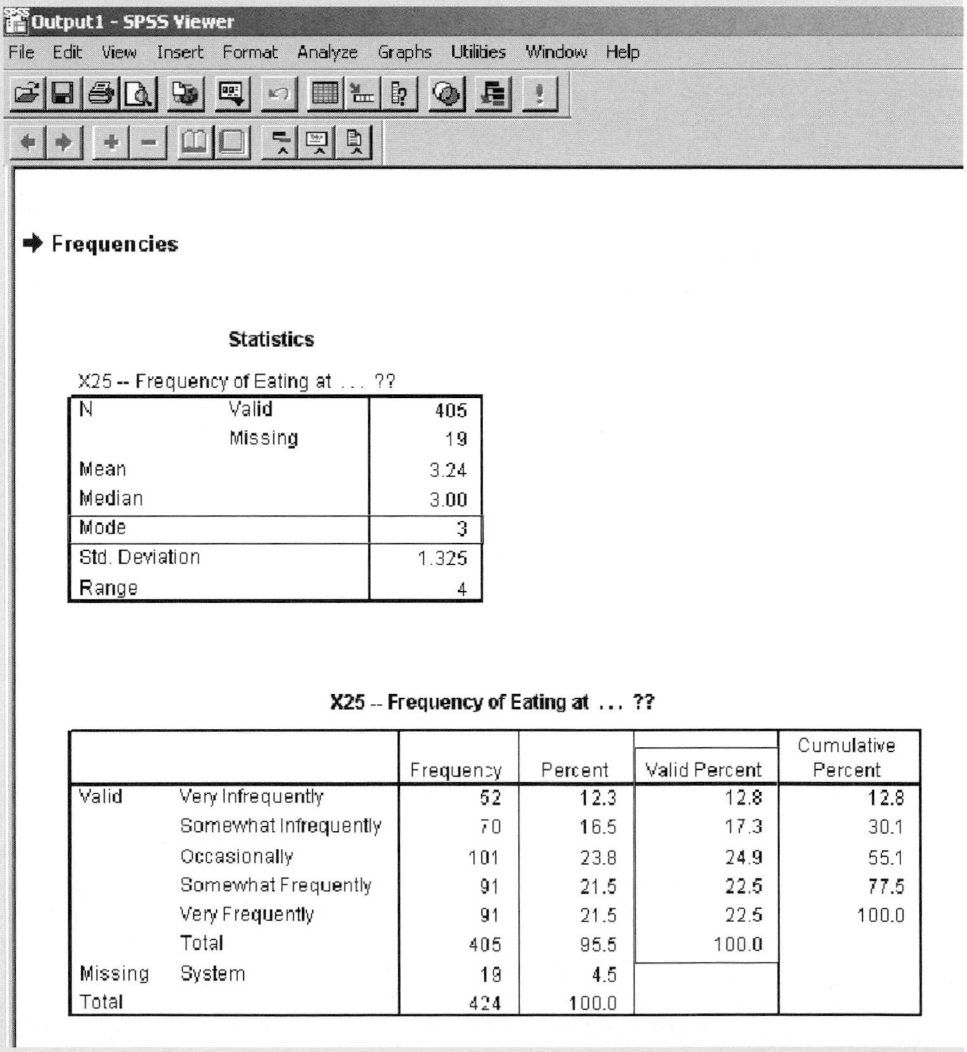

➜ **Frequencies**

Statistics

X25 -- Frequency of Eating at . . . ??

N	Valid	405
	Missing	19
Mean		3.24
Median		3.00
Mode		3
Std. Deviation		1.325
Range		4

X25 -- Frequency of Eating at . . . ??

		Frequency	Percent	Valid Percent	Cumulative Percent
Valid	Very Infrequently	52	12.3	12.8	12.8
	Somewhat Infrequently	70	16.5	17.3	30.1
	Occasionally	101	23.8	24.9	55.1
	Somewhat Frequently	91	21.5	22.5	77.5
	Very Frequently	91	21.5	22.5	100.0
	Total	405	95.5	100.0	
Missing	System	19	4.5		
Total		424	100.0		

3.0 indicates "Occasional" visits to either the Santa Fe Grill or Jose's Southwestern Café are the response given most often. Note that variable X25 ranges from one to five, with larger numbers indicating higher frequency.

Descriptive Statistics

Descriptive statistics are used to summarize and describe the data obtained from a sample of respondents. Two types of measures are often used to describe data. One of those is measures of central tendency and the other is measures of dispersion. Both are described in detail in the next chapter. For now we refer you to Exhibit 14.11 which provides an overview of the major types of descriptive statistics used by marketing researchers.

Graphical Illustration of Data

The next logical step following development of frequency tables is to translate them into graphical illustrations. Graphical illustrations can be very powerful for communicating key research results generated from preliminary data analysis.

EXHIBIT 14.11 Overview of Descriptive Statistics

To clarify descriptive statistics, we use a simple data set to illustrate each of the major ones. Assume that data has been collected from ten students about satisfaction with their Apple iPOD. Satisfaction is measured on a 7-point scale with the end points labeled "Highly Satisfied = 7" and "Not Satisfied at All = 1." The results of this survey are shown below by respondent.

Respondent	Satisfaction Rating
1	7
2	5
3	6
4	4
5	6
6	5
7	7
8	5
9	4
10	5

Descriptive Statistics

Frequency = the number of times a number (response) is in the data set.

To compute it, count how many times the number is in the data set. For example, the number 7 is in the data set twice.

Frequency distribution = a summary of how many times each possible response to a question appears in the data set.

continued

eXHIBIT 14.11 Overview of Descriptive Statistics, *continued*

To develop a frequency distribution, count how many times each number appears in the data set and make a table that shows the results. For example, create a chart like the one shown below:

Satisfaction Rating	Count
7	2
6	2
5	4
4	2
3	0
2	0
1	0
Total	10

Percentage distribution = the result of converting a frequency distribution into percentages.

To develop a percentage distribution, divide each frequency count for each rating by the total count.

Satisfaction Rating	Count	Percentage
7	2	20
6	2	20
5	4	40
4	2	20
3	0	0
2	0	0
1	0	0
Total	10	100%

Cumulative percentage distribution = each individual percentage added to the previous one to get a total.

To develop a cumulative percentage distribution, arrange the percentages in descending order and sum the percentages one at a time and show the result.

Satisfaction Rating	Count	Percentage	Cumulative Percentage	
7	2	20	20	
6	2	20	40	
5	4	40	80	← median
4	2	20	100%	
3	0	0		
2	0	0		
1	0	0		
Total	10	100%		

Mean = the arithmetic average of all the raw responses.

To calculate the mean, add up all the values of a distribution of responses and divide the total by the number of valid responses.

The mean is: (7 + 5 + 6 + 4 + 6 + 5 + 7 + 5 + 4 + 5) = 54 / 10 = 5.4

Median = the descriptive statistic that splits the data into a hierarchical pattern where half the data is above the median value and half is below.

To determine the median, look at the cumulative percentage distribution and find either where the cumulative percentage is equal to 50 percent or where it includes 50 percent. The median is marked in the table above.

Mode = the most frequently occurring response to a given set of questions.

To determine the mode, find the number which has the largest frequency (count). In the responses above, the number 5 has the largest count and is the mode.

eXHIBIT 14.11 *continued*

Range = a statistic that represents the spread of the data and is the distance between the largest and the smallest values of a frequency distribution.

To calculate the range, subtract the lowest rating point from the highest rating point and the difference is the range. For the above data, the maximum number is 7 and the minimum number is 4 so the range is 7 − 4 = 3.

Standard deviation = the measure of the average dispersion of the values in a set of responses about their mean. It provides an indication of how similar or dissimilar the numbers are in the set of responses.

To calculate the standard deviation, subtract the mean from the square of each number and sum them. Then divide that sum by the total number of responses minus one, and then take the square root of the result.

MARKETING RESEARCH IN ACTION

Examining Data

Deli Depot

In this chapter we have shown you simple approaches to examining data. In later chapters, we show you more advanced statistical techniques to analyze data. The most important consideration in deciding how to analyze data is to remember your purpose—to enable businesses to use data to make better decisions. To help students more easily understand the best ways to examine data, we have prepared several databases that can be applied to various research problems. This case is about Deli Depot, a sandwich restaurant. The database is available at www.mhhe.com/hair4e.

Deli Depot sells cold and hot sandwiches, soup and chili, yogurt, and pies and cookies. The restaurant is positioned in the fast-food market to compete directly with Subway and similar sandwich restaurants. Its competitive advantages include special sauces on sandwiches, supplementary menu items like soup and pies, and quick delivery within specified zones. As part of their marketing research class, students conducted a survey for the owner of a local restaurant near their campus.

The students obtained permission to conduct interviews with customers inside the restaurant. Information was collected for 17 questions. Customers were first asked their perceptions of the restaurant on six factors (variables X1–X6) and then asked to rank the same six factors in terms of their importance in selecting a restaurant where they wanted to eat (variables X12–X17). Finally, respondents were asked how satisfied they were with the restaurant, how likely they were to recommend it to a friend, how often they ate there, and how far they drove to eat a meal at Deli Depot. The variables, sample questions, and their coding are shown below.

Performance Perceptions Variables

The performance perceptions were measured as follows. Listed below is a set of characteristics that could be used to describe Deli Depot. Using a scale from 1 to 10, with 10 being "Strongly Agree" and 1 being "Strongly Disagree," to what extent do you agree or disagree that Deli Depot has:

X1—Friendly Employees

X2—Competitive Prices

X3—Competent Employees

X4—Excellent Food Quality

X5—Wide Variety of Food

X6—Fast Service

If a respondent chose a 10 for Friendly Employees, this would indicate strong agreement that Deli Depot has friendly employees. On the other hand, if a respondent chose a 1 for Fast Service, this would indicate strong disagreement and the perception that Deli Depot offers very slow service.

Classification Variables

Data for the classification variables was requested at the end of the survey, but in the database it is recorded as variables X7–X11. Responses were coded as follows:

X7—Gender (1 = Male; 0 = Female)

X8—Recommend to friend (7 = Definitely recommend; 1 = Definitely not recommend)

X9—Satisfaction Level (7 = Highly satisfied; 1 = Not very satisfied)

X10—Usage Level (1 = Heavy user [eats at Deli Depot 2 or more times each week]; 0 = Light user [eats at Deli Depot fewer than 2 times a week])

X11—Market Area (1 = Came from within 1 mile; 2 = Came from 1–5 miles; 3 = Came from more than 5 miles)

Selection Factor Rankings

Data for the selection factors were collected as follows. Listed below is a set of attributes (reasons) many people use when selecting a fast-food restaurant to eat at. Regarding your visits to fast-food restaurants in the last 30 days, please rank each attribute from 1 to 6, with 6 being the most important reason for selecting the fast-food restaurant and 1 being the least important reason. There can be no ties, so make sure you rank each attribute with a different number.

X12—Friendly Employees

X13—Competitive Prices

X14—Competent Employees

X15—Excellent Food Quality

X16—Wide Variety of Food

X17—Fast Service

The questionnaire for the Deli Depot survey is shown in Exhibit 14.12.

Hands-On Exercise

1. How would you improve the Deli Depot survey and questionnaire?
2. Which questions should be analyzed by looking at the means?
3. Which questions should be analyzed by looking only at the medians?

EXHIBIT 14.12 Deli Depot Questionnaire

SCREENING AND RAPPORT QUESTIONS

Hello. My name is ____ and I work for Decision Analyst, a market research firm in Dallas, Texas. We are talking to people today/tonight about eating out habits.

1. "How often do you eat out?" __ Often __ Occasionally __Seldom

2. "Did you just eat at Deli Depot?" __ Yes __ No

3. "Have you completed a restaurant questionnaire on Deli Depot before?" __ Yes __ No

If respondent answers "Often or Occasionally" to the first question, "Yes" to the second question, and "No" to the third question, then say:

We would like you to answer a few questions about your experience today/tonight at Deli Depot, and we hope you will be willing to give us your opinions. The survey will only take a few minutes and it will be very helpful to management in better serving its customers. We will pay you $5.00 for completing the questionnaire.

If the person says yes, give them a clipboard with the questionnaire on it, briefly explain the questionnaire, and show them where to complete the survey.

DINING OUT SURVEY

Please read all questions carefully. If you do not understand a question, ask the interviewer to help you.

Section 1: Perceptions Measures

Listed below is a set of characteristics that could be used to describe Deli Depot. Using a scale from 1 to 10, with 10 being "Strongly Agree" and 1 being "Strongly Disagree," to what extent do you agree or disagree that Deli Depot has: (Circle the correct response.)?

1. Friendly employees — Strongly Disagree 1 2 3 4 5 6 7 8 9 10 Strongly Agree

2. Competitive prices — Strongly Disagree 1 2 3 4 5 6 7 8 9 10 Strongly Agree

3. Competent employees — Strongly Disagree 1 2 3 4 5 6 7 8 9 10 Strongly Agree

4. Excellent food quality — Strongly Disagree 1 2 3 4 5 6 7 8 9 10 Strongly Agree

5. Wide variety of food — Strongly Disagree 1 2 3 4 5 6 7 8 9 10 Strongly Agree

6. Fast service — Strongly Disagree 1 2 3 4 5 6 7 8 9 10 Strongly Agree

Section 2: Classification Variables

Circle the response that describes you.

7. Your Gender
1 Male
0 Female

8. How likely are you to recommend Deli Depot to a friend? — Definitely Not Recommend 1 2 3 4 5 6 7 Definitely Recommend

continued

eXHIBIT 14.12 Deli Depot Questionnaire, *continued*

9. How satisfied are you with Deli Depot?	Not Very Satisfied ... Highly Satisfied 1 2 3 4 5 6 7
10. How often do you patronize Deli Depot?	1 = eat at Deli Depot 2 or more times each week. 0 = eat at Deli Depot fewer than 2 times each week.
11. How far did you drive to get to Deli Depot?	1 = came from within one mile 2 = 1–5 miles 3 = came from more than 5 miles

Section 3: Selection Factors

Listed below is a set of attributes (reasons) many people use when selecting a fast-food restaurant to eat at. Regarding your visits to fast-food restaurants in the last 30 days, please rank each attribute from 1 to 6, with 6 being the most important reason for selecting the restaurant and 1 being the least important reason. There can be no ties so make sure you rank each attribute with a different number.

Attribute	Ranking
12. Friendly employees	
13. Competitive prices	
14. Competent employees	
15. Excellent food quality	
16. Wide variety of food	
17. Fast service	

Thank you very much for your help. Please give your questionnaire to the interviewer and you will be given your $5.00.

Summary of Learning Objectives

■ Describe the process of data preparation for analysis.

The value of marketing research is its ability to provide accurate decision-making information to the user. To accomplish this, the data must be converted into usable information or knowledge. After collecting data through the appropriate method, the task becomes one of ensuring the data provides meaning and value. Data preparation is the first part of the process of transforming data into useful knowledge. This process involves several steps: (1) data validation, (2) editing and coding, (3) data entry, (4) error detection, and (5) data tabulation. Data analysis follows data preparation and facilitates proper interpretation of the findings.

■ Discuss validation, editing, and coding of survey data.

Data validation attempts to determine whether surveys, interviews, or observations were conducted correctly and are free from fraud. In recontacting selected respondents, the researcher asks whether the interview (1) was falsified, (2) was conducted with a qualified respondent, (3) took place in the proper procedural setting, (4) was completed correctly and accurately, and (5) was accomplished in a courteous manner. The editing process involves scanning of interviews or questionnaire responses to determine whether the proper questions were asked, the answers were recorded according to the instructions given, and the screening questions were executed properly, as well as whether open-ended questions were recorded accurately. Once edited, the questionnaires are coded by assigning numerical values to all responses. Coding is the process of providing numeric labels to the data so they can be entered into a computer for subsequent statistical analysis.

■ Explain data entry procedures as well as how to detect errors.

There are several methods for entering coded data into a computer. First is the PC keyboard. Data also can be entered through terminals having touch-screen capabilities, or through the use of a handheld electronic pointer or light pen. Finally, data can be entered through a scanner using optical character recognition. Data entry errors can be detected through the use of error edit routines in the data entry software. Another approach is to visually scan the actual data after it has been entered.

■ Describe data tabulation approaches.

Two common forms of data tabulation are used in marketing research. A one-way tabulation indicates the number of respondents who gave each possible answer to each question on a questionnaire. Cross-tabulation provides categorization of respondents by treating two or more variables simultaneously. Categorization is based on the number of respondents who have responded to two or more consecutive questions.

Key Terms and Concepts

Coding 461

Cross-tabulation 468

Curbstoning 455

Data entry 464

Data validation 455

Editing 456

One-way tabulation 467

Tabulation 467

Review Questions

1. Briefly describe the process of data validation. Specifically discuss the issues of fraud, screening, procedure, completeness, and courtesy.
2. What are the differences between data validation, data editing, and data coding?

3. Explain the differences between establishing codes for open-ended questions and for closed-ended questions.
4. Briefly describe the process of data entry. What changes in technology have simplified this procedure?
5. What are the three approaches to error detection? In your discussion be sure to describe the data/column list procedure.
6. What is the purpose of a simple one-way tabulation? How does this relate to a one-way frequency table?

Discussion Questions

1. **EXPERIENCE THE INTERNET.** Go to the Web site for the Acxiom Corporation, at www.acxiom.com, and select the topic Case in Point. Once there, select the topic Newsletters and select the newsletter for vol. 2, issue 1. Read the passage on cluster coding systems and comment on how they apply to preliminary data analysis.
2. **EXPERIENCE THE INTERNET.** At the Acxiom site select newsletter vol. 2, issue 3. Select the article on data warehousing and comment on how it relates to the coding of marketing data.
3. Obtain a copy of a marketing research questionnaire and on the basis of your knowledge of developing codes, convert the questionnaire into a master code illustrating the appropriate values for each question and corresponding responses.
4. Look back at the quote at the beginning of this chapter. On the basis of what you now know about preparing data for analysis, explain what Robert W. Kneen meant by "garbage in, garbage out."
5. **SPSS Exercise.** Using SPSS and the Deli Depot database, provide frequencies, means, modes, and medians for all the relevant variables on the Deli Depot questionnaire. You should have read about Deli Depot and the questionnaire in the Marketing Research in Action section at the end of this chapter. The database is available at this book's Web site.

chapter 15

Data Analysis: Testing for Significant Differences

Learning Objectives

After reading this chapter, you will be able to:

1. Explain measures of central tendency and dispersion.
2. Describe how to test hypotheses using univariate and bivariate statistics.
3. Apply and interpret analysis of variance (ANOVA).
4. Utilize perceptual mapping to present research findings.

"The more I know,
the more I know I don't know."

—ANONYMOUS

Statistical Software Makes Data Analysis Easy

Firms of all sizes increasingly are collecting and storing data relevant to their business activities. These data may come from surveys of customers or be internally generated by sales force contact software and stored in the company's data warehouse. But to be useful for decision making, the data must be organized, categorized, analyzed, and shared among company employees. Tom Peters, in his book *Thriving on Chaos,* said, "We are drowning in information and starved for knowledge." To convert this ocean of information into knowledge, we need user-friendly, powerful software packages. Many software packages can help us accomplish this conversion, including the popular Excel program that is part of Microsoft Windows. But as the amount of information increases exponentially, we need comprehensive, sophisticated packages that are relatively inexpensive and easy to use. Fortunately, at least two are available and can be used with most PCs: SPSS and SAS. Both are very powerful and provide statistical processing capabilities for a variety of tasks, from calculating means and modes to executing neural networking and other sophisticated data mining tasks. Each package is briefly described below. We rely on SPSS in many chapters in this text to analyze and evaluate data collected in a customer survey of a local restaurant (our continuing case about the Santa Fe Grill).

SPSS

The SPSS, Inc., software package is designed to be user-friendly, even for novice computer users. Released in the Microsoft Windows format and touted as "Real Stats. Real Easy," SPSS delivers easy data access and management, highly customizable output, complete just-in-time-training, and a revolutionary system for working with charts and graphs. The producers of SPSS proudly claim that "you don't have to be a statistician to use SPSS," an important characteristic for individuals who are somewhat afraid of computers and their power. Available in almost any format, SPSS provides immense statistical analysis capability while remaining one of the most user-friendly statistical packages available today. Information concerning SPSS is available online at www.spss.com.

SAS

The SAS (rhymes with class) system provides extensive statistical capabilities, including tools for both specialized and enterprisewide analytical needs. Research institutes, laboratories, marketing research firms, universities, pharmaceutical companies, government agencies, and banks all take advantage of the statistical capabilities of SAS. From traditional analysis of variance to exact methods of statistical visualization, the SAS system provides the tools required to analyze data and help organizations make the right statistical choices. Many heavy users of statistical software packages feel that SAS offers greater statistical analysis capability than SPSS. However, this increased statistical power is sometimes compromised by applications less user-friendly than those of SPSS. Information concerning SAS is available online at www.sas.com.

Value of Testing for Differences in Data

Once the data have been collected and prepared for analysis, several statistical procedures can help to better understand the responses. It is difficult to understand the entire set of responses because there are "too many numbers" to look at. Consequently, almost all data needs summary statistics describing the information it contains. Basic statistics and descriptive analysis achieve this purpose.

Some of the statistics common to almost all research projects are described in this chapter. First we describe measures of central tendency and dispersion. The advantages and pitfalls of each measure need to be understood so the information can be summarized. Next, we discuss the Chi-square statistic to examine cross-tabulations, and then the *t*-statistic for testing differences in means. Finally, the chapter closes with an introduction to analysis of variance, a powerful technique for detecting differences between three or more sample means.

Analyzing the Santa Fe Grill Database

The Santa Fe Grill database has an important new feature in this edition. Interviews were completed with customers from the Santa Fe Grill and its major competitor, Jose's Southwestern Café. To help you analyze the new database, we introduce you to some features of the SPSS software. These features are available under the Data pull-down menu and help you to divide the database into groups, such as males and females, and customers of the Santa Fe Grill versus those of Jose's Southwestern Café.

Analyzing Groups

To split the sample into two groups so you can compare them, you can use the options under the Data pull-down menu. For example, to compare the customers of the Santa Fe Grill and the customers of Jose's Southwestern Café, the click-through sequence is: DATA → SPLIT FILE → Click on Compare Groups. Now highlight the fourth screening question (Favorite Mexican restaurant—x_s4) and move it into the "Groups Based on:" window, and then click OK. Your results will now be computed for each restaurant separately. The same procedure can be used with any variable. To do so, you insert the variable of choice into the "Groups Based on:" window, and then click OK. A word of caution, however, is that until you remove this instruction all data analysis will be based on separate groups as defined by the "Groups Based on:" window.

Select Cases Analysis

Sometimes you may wish to select a smaller subset of your total sample to analyze. This can be done using the "Select Cases" option under the Data pull-down menu. For example, to select customers from only the Santa Fe Grill, the click-through sequence is DATA → SELECT CASES → IF CONDITION IS SATISFIED → IF. Next, highlight x_s4 Favorite Mexican restaurant and move it into the window; click the = sign and then 1. This instructs the SPSS software to select only questionnaires coded 1 in the x_s4 column (the fourth screening question on the survey), which is the Santa Fe Grill. If you wanted to analyze only the Jose's Southwestern Café respondents, then you would do the same except after the = sign, put a 0.

Measures of Central Tendency

Frequency distributions can be useful for examining the different values for a variable. Frequency distribution tables are easy to read and provide a great deal of basic information. There are times, however, when the amount of detail is just too much. In such situations the researcher needs a way to summarize and condense all the information in order to get at the underlying meaning. Descriptive statistics are commonly used to accomplish this task. The mean, median, and mode are measures of central tendency. These measures locate the center of the distribution. For this reason, the mean, median, and mode are sometimes also called *measures of location.*

We use variable X25—Frequency of Eating to illustrate the measures of central tendency (Exhibit 15.2). Looking first at the frequency distribution, note that 405 respondents indicated how frequently they eat at their favorite Mexican restaurant using a 5-point scale, with 1 = Very Infrequently, 2 = Somewhat Infrequently, 3 = Occasionally, 4 = Somewhat Frequently, and 5 = Very Frequently. The total sample was 424, but 19 respondents did not answer this question and therefore are considered missing data. The numbers in the Percent column are calculated using the total sample size of 424, while the numbers in the Valid % and Cumulative % columns are calculated using the total sample size minus the number of missing responses to this question (424 − 19 = 405).

Mean

Mean The arithmetic average of the sample; all values of a distribution of responses are summed and divided by the number of valid responses.

The **mean** is the average value within the distribution and is the most commonly used measure of central tendency. The mean tells us, for example, the average number of cups of coffee the typical student may drink during finals to stay awake. The mean can be calculated when the data scale is either interval or ratio. Generally, the data will show some degree of central tendency, with most of the responses distributed close to the mean.

The mean is a very robust measure of central tendency. It is fairly insensitive to data values being added or deleted. The mean can be subject to distortion, however, if extreme values are included in the distribution. For example, suppose you ask four students how many cups of coffee they drink in a single day. Respondent answers are as follows: Respondent A = 1 cup; Respondent B = 10 cups; Respondent C = 5 cups; and Respondent D = 6 cups. Let's also assume that we know that respondents A and B are males and respondents C and D are females and we want to compare consumption of coffee between males and females. Looking at the males first (Respondents A and B), we calculate the mean number of cups to be 5.5 (1 + 10 = 11/2 = 5.5). Similarly, looking at the females next (Respondents C and D), we calculate the mean number of cups to be 5.5 (5 + 6 = 11/2 = 5.5). If we look only at the mean number of cups of coffee consumed by males and females, we would conclude there are no differences in the two groups. If we consider the underlying distribution, however, we must conclude there are some differences and the mean in fact distorts our understanding of coffee consumption patterns among males and females.

Mode

Mode The most common value in the set of responses to a question; that is, the response most often given to a question.

The **mode** is the value that appears in the distribution most often. For example, the average number of cups of coffee students drink per day during finals may be 5 (the mean), while the number of cups of coffee that most students drink is only 3 (the mode). The mode is the value that represents the highest peak in the distribution's graph. The mode is especially useful as a measure for data that have been somehow grouped into categories. The mode of the data distribution in Exhibit 15.2 is Occasionally because when you look in the Frequency column you will see the largest number of responses is 111 for the "Occasionally" label, which has a value of 3.

Median

Median The middle value of a rank-ordered distribution; exactly half of the responses are above and half are below the median value.

The **median** is the middle value of the distribution when the distribution is ordered in either an ascending or a descending sequence. For example, if you interviewed a sample of students to determine their coffee-drinking patterns during finals, you might find that the median number of cups of coffee consumed is 4. The number of cups of coffee consumed above and below this number would be the same (the median number is the exact middle of the distribution). If the number of data observations is even, the median is generally considered to be the average of the two middle values. If there are an odd number of observations, the median is the middle value. The median is especially useful as a measure of central tendency for ordinal data and for data that is skewed to either the right or left. For example, income data is skewed to the right because there is no upper limit on income.

Each measure of central tendency describes a distribution in its own manner, and each measure has its own strengths and weaknesses. For nominal data, the mode is the best measure. For ordinal data, the median is generally best. For interval or ratio data, the mean is generally used. If there are extreme values within the interval or ratio data, however, the mean can be distorted. In those cases, the median and the mode should be considered. SPSS and other statistical software packages are designed to perform such types of analysis.

SPSS Applications—Measures of Central Tendency

The Santa Fe Grill database can be used with the SPSS software to calculate measures of central tendency. The SPSS click-through sequence is ANALYZE → DESCRIPTIVE STATISTICS → FREQUENCIES. Let's use X25—Frequency of Eating as a variable to examine. Click on X25 to highlight it and then on the arrow box for the Variables window to use in your analysis. Next open the Statistics box and click on Mean, Median, and Mode, and then Continue and OK. Recall that if you want to create charts, open the Charts box. Your choices are Bar, Pie, and Histograms. For the Format box we will use the defaults, so

eXHIBIT 15.1 Dialog Boxes for Calculating the Mean, Median, and Mode

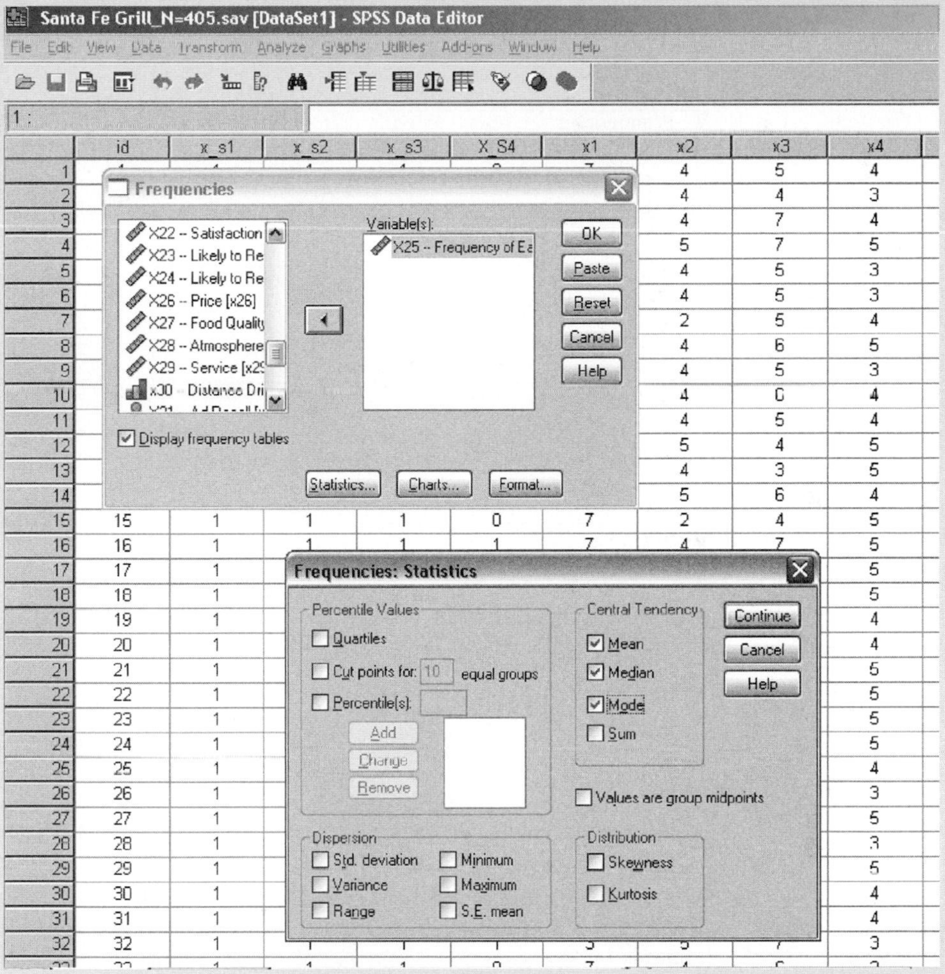

click on OK to execute the program. The dialog boxes for this sequence are shown in Exhibit 15.1.

Let's look at the output for the measures of central tendency shown in Exhibit 15.2. In the Statistics table we see the mean is 3.24, the median is 3.00, the mode is 3. Recall that this variable is measured on a 5-point scale, with lower numbers indicating lower frequency of patronage and larger numbers indicating higher frequency. The three measures of central tendency can all be different within the same distribution, as described above in the coffee-drinking example. But it also is possible that all three measures can be the same. In our example here the median and the mode are the same, but the mean is different.

eXHIBIT 15.2 Output for Mean, Median, and Mode for X25–Frequency of Eating at . . .

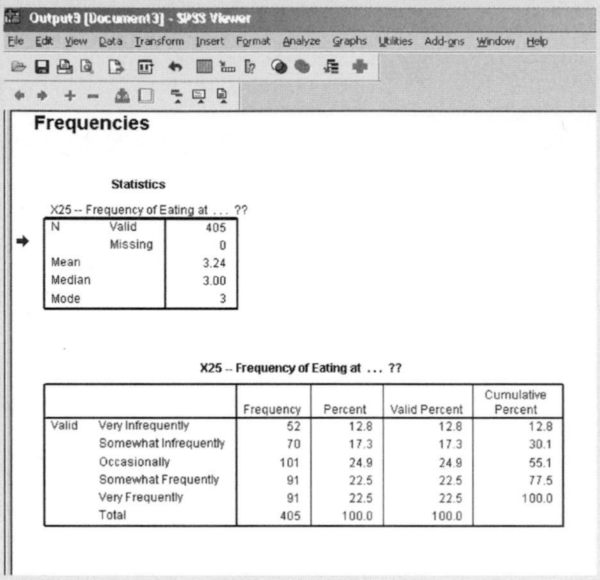

Frequencies

Statistics

X25 -- Frequency of Eating at . . . ??

N	Valid	405
	Missing	0
Mean		3.24
Median		3.00
Mode		3

X25 -- Frequency of Eating at . . . ??

		Frequency	Percent	Valid Percent	Cumulative Percent
Valid	Very Infrequently	52	12.8	12.8	12.8
	Somewhat Infrequently	70	17.3	17.3	30.1
	Occasionally	101	24.9	24.9	55.1
	Somewhat Frequently	91	22.5	22.5	77.5
	Very Frequently	91	22.5	22.5	100.0
	Total	405	100.0	100.0	

Measures of Dispersion

Measures of dispersion Describe how close to the mean or other measure of central tendency the other values in the distribution fall.

Range The distance between the smallest and largest values in a set of responses.

Measures of central tendency often do not tell the whole story about a distribution of responses. For example, if data have been collected about consumers' attitudes toward a new brand of a product, you could find out the mean, median, and mode of the distribution of answers, but you might also want to know if most of the respondents had similar opinions. One way to answer this question would be to examine the measures of dispersion associated with the distribution of responses to your questions. **Measures of dispersion** describe how close to the mean or other measure of central tendency the other values in the distribution fall. Two measures of dispersion used to describe the variability in a distribution of numbers are the *range* and the *standard deviation.*

Range

The **range** defines the spread of the data. It is the distance between the smallest and largest values of the variable. Another way to think about it is that the range identifies the endpoints of the distribution of values. For variable X25—Frequency of Eating, the range is the difference between the response category 5 (largest value) and response category 1 (smallest value); that is, the range is 4. In this example, since we defined a narrow range of response categories in our survey, the range doesn't tell us much. However, many questions have a much wider range. For example, if we asked how often in a month respondents rent DVDs, or how much they would pay to buy a DVD player that also records songs, the range would be quite informative. In this case, the respondents, not the researchers, would be defining the range by their answers. For this reason, the range is more often used to describe the variability of open-ended questions such as our DVD example. For variable X25—Frequency of Eating, the range is calculated as the distance between the largest and smallest values in the set of responses and equals 4 (5 − 1 = 4).

Standard Deviation

Standard deviation The average distance of the distribution values from the mean.

The estimated **standard deviation** describes the average distance of the distribution values from the mean. The difference between a particular response and the distribution mean is called a deviation. Since the mean of a distribution is a measure of central tendency, there should be about as many values above the mean as there are below it (particularly if the distribution is symmetrical). Consequently, if we subtracted each value in a distribution from the mean and added them up, the result would be close to zero (the positive and negative results would cancel each other out).

The solution to this difficulty is to square the individual deviations before we add them up (squaring a negative number produces a positive result). To calculate the estimated standard deviation, we use the formula below.

$$\text{Standard deviation} = \sqrt{\frac{\sum_{i-1}^{n}(X_1 - \bar{X})^2}{n-1}}$$

Once the sum of the squared deviations is determined, it is divided by the number of respondents minus 1. The number 1 is subtracted from the number of respondents to help produce an unbiased estimate of the standard deviation. The result of dividing the sum of the squared deviations is the average squared deviation. To convert the result to the same units of measure as the mean, we take the square root of the answer. This produces the **estimated standard deviation** of the distribution. Sometimes the average squared deviation is also used as a measure of dispersion for a distribution. The *average squared deviation,* called the **variance,** is used in a number of statistical processes.

Estimated standard deviation Describes the average distance of the distribution values from the mean.

Variance The average squared deviation about the mean of a distribution of values.

Since the estimated standard deviation is the square root of the average squared deviations, it represents the average distance of the values in a distribution from the mean. If the estimated standard deviation is large, the responses in a distribution of numbers do not fall very close to the mean of the distribution. If the estimated standard deviation is small, you know that the distribution values are close to the mean.

Another way to think about the estimated standard deviation is that its size tells you something about the level of agreement among the respondents when they answered a particular question. For example, in the Santa Fe Grill database, respondents were asked to rate the restaurant on the friendliness and knowledge of its employees (X12 and X19). We will use the SPSS program later to examine the standard deviations for these questions.

Together with the measures of central tendency, these descriptive statistics can reveal a lot about the distribution of a set of numbers representing the answers to an item on a questionnaire. Often, however, marketing researchers are interested in more detailed questions that involve more than one variable at a time. The next section, on hypothesis testing, provides some ways to analyze those types of questions.

SPSS Applications—Measures of Dispersion

The Santa Fe Grill database can be used with the SPSS software to calculate measures of dispersion, just as we did with the measures of central tendency. Note that to calculate the measures of dispersion we will be using the database with a sample size of 405 so we

eXHIBIT 15.3 Output for Measures of Dispersion

Output4 - SPSS Viewer

File Edit View Insert Format Analyze Graphs Utilities Window Help

Frequencies

Statistics

X22 -- Satisfaction

N	Valid	405
	Missing	0
Std. Deviation		1.118
Variance		1.251
Range		4
Minimum		3
Maximum		7

X22 -- Satisfaction

		Frequency	Percent	Valid Percent	Cumulative Percent
Valid	3	38	9.4	9.4	9.4
	4	148	36.5	36.5	45.9
	5	95	23.5	23.5	69.4
	6	93	23.0	23.0	92.3
	7 = Highly Satisfied	31	7.7	7.7	100.0
	Total	405	100.0	100.0	

have eliminated all respondents with missing data. The SPSS click-through sequence is ANALYZE → DESCRIPTIVE STATISTICS → FREQUENCIES. Let's use X222—Satisfaction as a variable to examine. Click on X22 to highlight it and then on the arrow box to move X22 to the Variables box. Next open the Statistics box, go to the Dispersion box in the lower-left-hand corner, and click on Standard deviation, Variance, Range, Minimum and Maximum, and then Continue. If you would like to create charts, then open the Charts box. Your choices are Bar, Pie, and Histograms. For the Format box we will use the defaults, so click on OK to execute the program.

Let's look at the output for the measures of dispersion shown in Exhibit 15.3 for variable X22. First, the highest response on the 7-point scale is 7 (maximum) and the lowest response is 3 (minimum). The range is 4 ($7 - 3 = 4$), the standard deviation is 1.118, and the variance is 1.251. A standard deviation of 1.118 on a 7-point scale tells us the responses are dispersed fairly widely around the mean of 3.24.

Analyzing Relationships in Sample Data

Chi-square analysis Assesses how closely the observed frequencies fit the pattern of the expected frequencies and is referred to as a "goodness-of-fit" test.

Researchers often wish to test hypotheses about proposed relationships in the sample data. In this section we will discuss several methods used to test hypotheses. We first introduce **Chi-square analysis,** a statistic used with nominal and ordinal data. We then discuss the *t*-distribution and describe its function for testing hypotheses using interval and ordinal data. Before discussing these methods of testing hypotheses, we review some basic statistical terminology.

Sample Statistics and Population Parameters

The purpose of inferential statistics is to make a determination about a population on the basis of a sample from that population. As we explained in Chapter 10, a sample is a subset of the population. For example, if we wanted to determine the average number of cups of coffee consumed per day by students during finals at your university, we would not interview all the students. This would be costly, take a long time, and might be impossible since we may not be able to find them all or some would decline to participate. Instead, if there are 16,000 students at your university, we may decide that a sample of 200 females and 200 males is sufficiently large to provide accurate information about the coffee-drinking habits of all 16,000 students.

You may recall that sample statistics are measures obtained directly from the sample or calculated from the data in the sample. A population parameter is a variable or some sort of measured characteristic of the entire population. Sample statistics are useful in making inferences regarding the population's parameters. Generally, the actual population parameters are unknown since the cost to perform a true census of almost any population is prohibitive.

A frequency distribution displaying the data obtained from the sample is commonly used to summarize the results of the data collection process. When a frequency distribution displays a variable in terms of percentages, then this distribution is representing proportions within a population. For example, a frequency distribution showing that 40 percent of the people patronize Burger King indicates the percentage of the population that meets the criterion (eating at Burger King). The proportion may be expressed as a percentage, a decimal value, or a fraction.

Univariate Statistical Tests

Marketing researchers often form hypotheses regarding population characteristics based on sample data. The process typically begins by calculating frequency distributions and averages, and then moves on to actually test the hypotheses. When the hypothesis testing involves examining one variable at a time, it is referred to as a *univariate statistical test.* When the hypothesis testing involves two variables it is called a *bivariate statistical test.* We first discuss univariate statistical tests.

Suppose the owners of the Santa Fe Grill believe customers think their menu prices are very reasonable. Respondents have answered this question using a 7-point scale where 1 = "Strongly Disagree" and 7 = "Strongly Agree." The scale is assumed to be an interval scale, and previous research using this measure has shown the responses to be approximately normally distributed.

A couple of tasks must be completed before answering the question posed above. First, the hypotheses to be compared (the null and alternative hypotheses) have to be developed. Then the **level of significance** for rejecting the null hypothesis and accepting the alternative hypothesis must be selected. At that point, the researcher can conduct the statistical test and determine the answer to the research question.

Level of significance The amount of risk regarding the accuracy of the test that the researcher is willing to accept.

In this example, the owners think the customers consider the prices of food at the Santa Fe Grill to be very reasonable. The question is measured using a 7-point scale with 7 = Strongly Agree. The marketing research consultant has indicated that expecting a 7 on a 7-point scale is unreasonable. Therefore, the owners have defined "reasonable prices" by saying that perceptions of the prices at Santa Fe Grill will not be significantly different from 6 = Very Favorable. The null hypothesis is that the mean of the X166—Reasonable Prices will not be significantly different from 6. Recall that the null hypothesis asserts the status quo: any difference from what is thought to be true is due to random sampling. The alternative hypothesis is: the mean response to X166—Reasonable Prices will not be 6—there is in fact a true difference between the sample mean and the mean we think it is (6).

Assume also the owners want to be 95 percent certain the mean is not different from 6. Therefore, the significance level will be set at .05. Using this significance level means that if the survey of Santa Fe Grill customers is conducted many times, the probability of incorrectly rejecting the null hypothesis when it is true would happen less than 5 times out of 100 (.05).

SPSS Application—Univariate Hypothesis Test

Using the SPSS software, you can test the responses in the Santa Fe Grill database to find the answer to the research question posed above. Before running this test, however, you must split the sample into two groups: the customers of the Santa Fe Grill and the customers of Jose's Southwestern Café. Recall that to do this, the click-through sequence is DATA → SPLIT FILE → Click on Compare Groups. Now highlight the fourth screening question (Favorite Mexican Restaurant—x_s4) and move it into the "Groups Based on:" window, and then click OK. Your results will now be computed for each restaurant separately.

To complete this test, the click-through sequence is ANALYZE → COMPARE MEANS → ONE-SAMPLE T-TEST. When you get to the dialog box, click on X166—Reasonable Prices to highlight it. Then click on the arrow to move X16 into the Test Variables box. In the box labeled Test Value, enter the number 6. This is the number you want to compare the respondents' answers against, because your null hypothesis is that the mean of X16 will not be significantly different from 6. Click on the Options box and enter 95 in the confidence interval box. This is the same as setting the significance level at .05. Then, click on the Continue button and OK to execute the program.

The SPSS output is shown in Exhibit 15.4. The top table is labeled One-Sample Statistics and shows the mean, standard deviation, and standard error for X16—Reasonable Prices for the two restaurants (mean of 4.47 for Santa Fe Grill and standard deviation of 1.384). The One-Sample Test table below shows the results of the *t*-test for the null hypothesis that the average response to X16 is not significantly different from 6 (Test Value = 6). The *t*-test statistic is –25.613, and the significance level is .000. This means that the null hypothesis can be rejected and the alternative hypothesis accepted with a high level of confidence from a statistical perspective.

From a practical standpoint, in terms of the Santa Fe Grill, the results of the univariate hypothesis test indicate respondents perceived that menu prices were significantly below a 6 (defined as very reasonable by the owners). The mean of 4.47 is substantially below 6 (7 = Strongly Agree prices are reasonable). Thus, the Santa Fe Grill owners can conclude that their prices are not perceived very favorably. Indeed, there is a lot of room to improve between the mean of 4.47 on the 7-point scale and the highest value of 7. This is definitely an area that needs to be examined. Of course, compared to Jose's restaurant the Santa Fe Grill is perceived slightly more favorably.

Bivariate Statistical Tests

In many instances marketing researchers test hypotheses that compare the characteristics of two groups or two variables. For example, the marketing researcher may be interested in determining whether there is a difference between older and younger new car purchasers

eXHIBIT 15.4 Univariate Hypothesis Test Using X16—Reasonable Prices

Output34 [Document34] - SPSS Viewer

File Edit View Data Transform Insert Format Analyze Graphs Utilities Add-ons Window Help

→T-Test

One-Sample Statistics

Favorite Mexican Restaurant		N	Mean	Std. Deviation	Std. Error Mean
0 Jose's Southwestern Cafe	X16 -- Reasonable Prices	152	4.12	.906	.073
1 Santa Fe Grill	X16 -- Reasonable Prices	253	4.47	1.384	.087

One-Sample Test

		Test Value = 6					
						95% Confidence Interval of the Difference	
Favorite Mexican Restaurant		t	df	Sig. (2-tailed)	Mean Difference	Lower	Upper
0 Jose's Southwestern Cafe	X16 -- Reasonable Prices	-25.613	151	.000	-1.882	-2.03	-1.74
1 Santa Fe Grill	X16 -- Reasonable Prices	-17.574	252	.000	-1.530	-1.70	-1.36

in terms of the importance of a 6-disk DVD player. In situations where more than one group is involved, bivariate tests are needed. In the following section we first explain the concept of cross-tabulation, which examines two variables. We then describe three bivariate hypothesis tests: Chi-square, which is used with nominal data; and the *t*-test (to compare two means) and analysis of variance (compares three or more means), both of which are used with either interval or ratio data.

Cross-Tabulation

In Chapter 14 we introduced one-way frequency tables to report the findings for a single variable. The next logical step in data analysis is to perform cross-tabulation using two variables. Cross-tabulation is useful for examining relationships and reporting the findings for two variables. The purpose of cross-tabulation is to determine if differences exist between subgroups of the total sample. In fact, cross-tabulation is the primary form of data analysis in some marketing research projects. To use cross-tabulation you must understand how to develop a cross-tabulation table as well as how to interpret the outcome.

EXHIBIT 15.5 Dialog Boxes for Crosstab

*Santa Fe Grill_4e_N=405.sav [DataSet1] - SPSS Data Editor

File Edit View Data Transform Analyze Graphs Utilities Add-ons Window Help

1 : id 1

Crosstabs

Row(s): x31
Column(s): x32
Layer 1 of 1

Display clustered bar charts
Suppress tables

Statistics... Cells... Format...

OK Paste Reset Cancel Help

Crosstabs: Cell Display

Counts
☑ Observed
☑ Expected

Percentages
☑ Row
☐ Column
☐ Total

Residuals
☐ Unstandardized
☐ Standardized
☐ Adjusted standardized

Noninteger Weights
◉ Round cell counts ○ Round case weights
○ Truncate cell counts ○ Truncate case weights
○ No adjustments

Continue Cancel Help

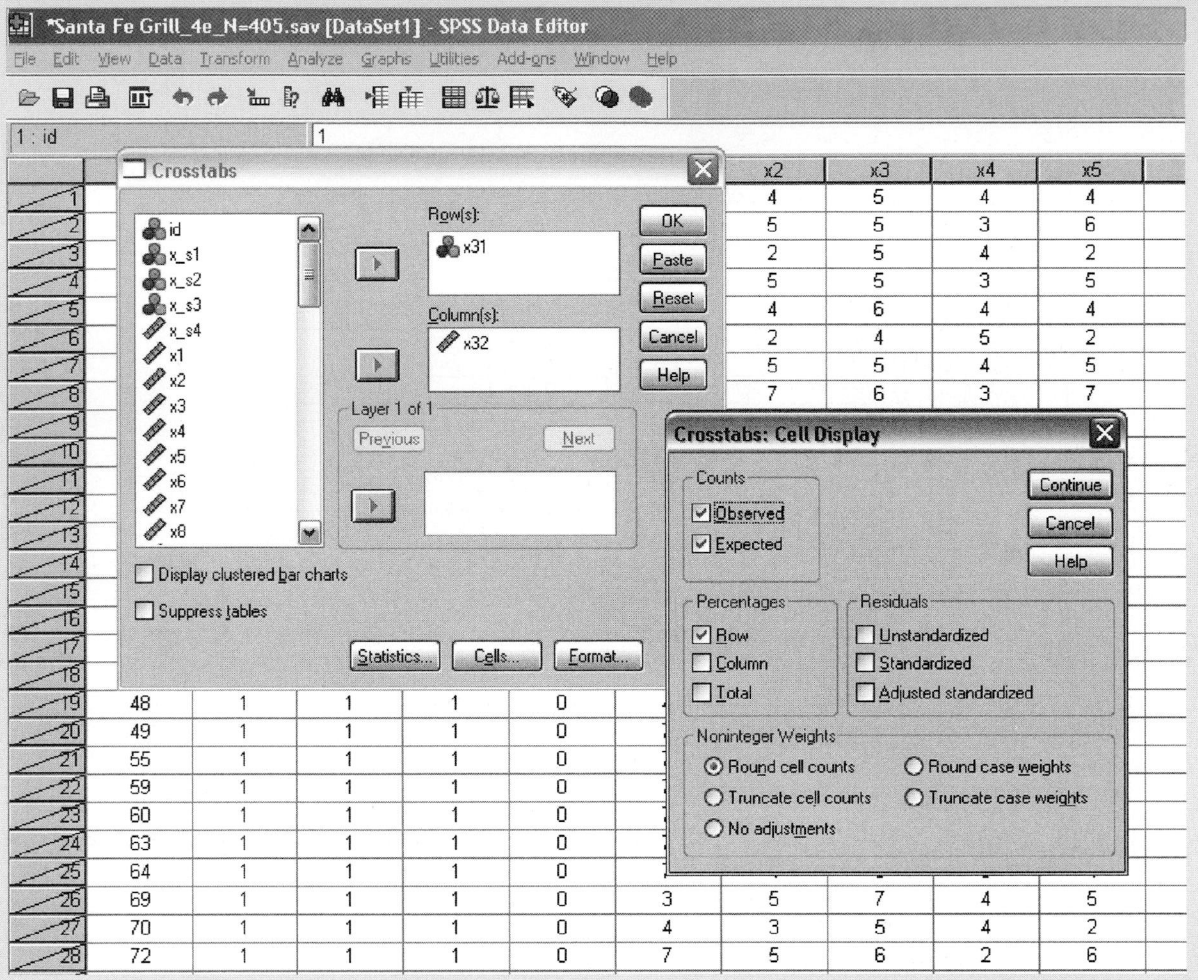

Note that to simplify this example we will run this crosstab only for customers of the Santa Fe Grill. To select just customers from the Santa Fe Grill, the click-through sequence is DATA → SELECT CASES → IF CONDITION IS SATISFIED → IF. Highlight x_s4 Favorite Mexican restaurant and move it into the window. Then click the = sign and next the 1. This instructs the SPSS software to select only questionnaires coded 1 in the x_s4 column, which is the Santa Fe Grill. If you wanted to analyze only the Jose's Southwestern Café respondents, then do the same except after the = sign put a 0.

To run the crosstab using SPSS, the click-through sequence is ANALYZE → DESCRIPTIVE STATISTICS → CROSSTABS. This will get you the set of dialog boxes shown in Exhibit 15.5. Insert X31 in the Rows window and X32 in the Columns window. Now click on the Cells box and check the Row box under Percentages, and then the Expected box under Counts. Then click Continue and OK to get the results.

EXHIBIT 15.6 Example of a Cross-Tabulation: Gender by Ad Recall

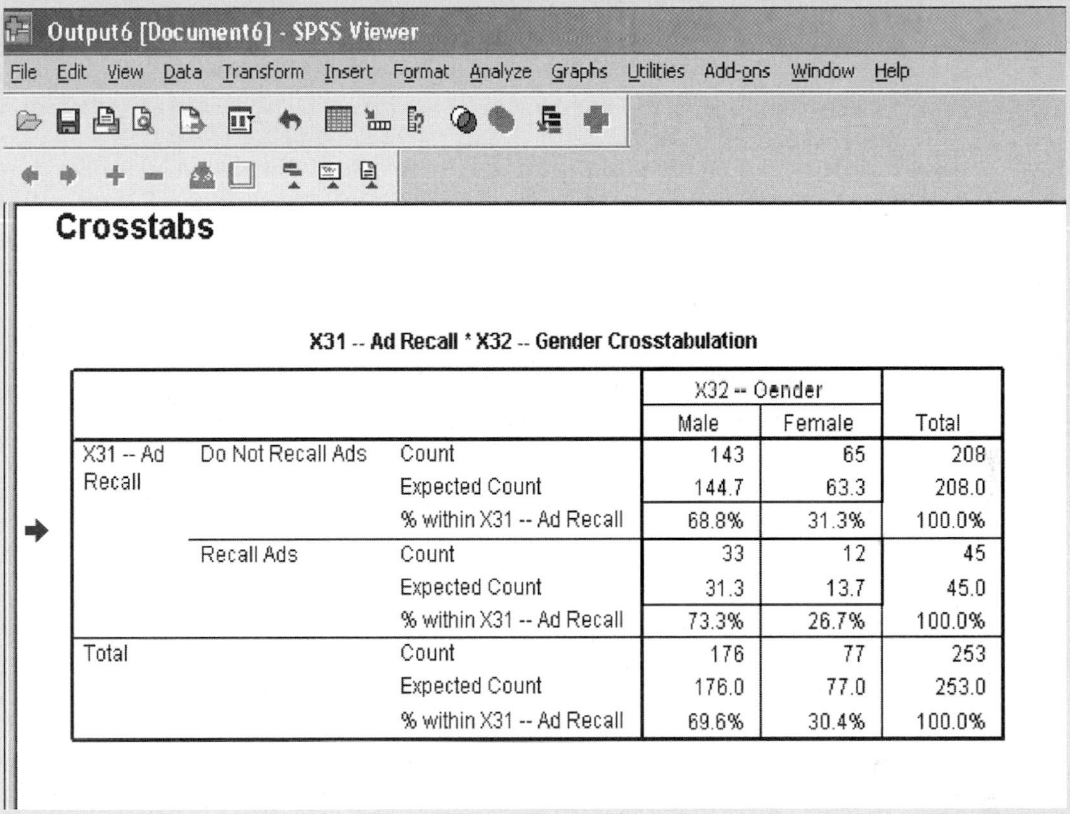

Crosstabs

X31 -- Ad Recall * X32 -- Gender Crosstabulation

			X32 -- Gender		
			Male	Female	Total
X31 -- Ad Recall	Do Not Recall Ads	Count	143	65	208
		Expected Count	144.7	63.3	208.0
		% within X31 -- Ad Recall	68.8%	31.3%	100.0%
	Recall Ads	Count	33	12	45
		Expected Count	31.3	13.7	45.0
		% within X31 -- Ad Recall	73.3%	26.7%	100.0%
Total		Count	176	77	253
		Expected Count	176.0	77.0	253.0
		% within X31 -- Ad Recall	69.6%	30.4%	100.0%

Exhibit 15.6 shows the cross-tabulation between X31—Ad Recall and X322—Gender for the Santa Fe Grill customers ($N = 253$). The cross-tabulation shows frequencies and percentages, with percentages shown only for rows. One way to interpret this table, for example, would be to look at the Observed Count versus the Expected Count. As you can see, the numbers are not very different. Thus, our preliminary interpretation suggests that males and females do not differ in their recall of Santa Fe Grill ads.

In constructing a cross-tabulation table, the researcher selects the variables to use when examining relationships. Selection of variables should be based on the objectives of the research project. Demographic variables typically are the starting point in developing cross-tabulations. These variables usually are the columns of the cross-tabulation table, and the rows are variables like purchase intention, usage, or other categorical response questions. Cross-tabulation tables show percentage calculations based on column or row totals. Thus, the researcher can make comparisons of behaviors and intentions for different categories of predictor variables such as income, sex, and marital status.

As a preliminary technique, cross-tabulation provides the market researcher with a powerful tool to summarize survey data. It is easy to understand and interpret, and can provide a description of both total and subgroup data. Yet the simplicity of this technique can create problems. Analysis can result in an endless variety of cross-tabulation tables. In developing these tables, the analyst must always keep in mind both the project objectives and specific research questions the study is designed to answer.

Chi-Square Analysis

Marketing researchers often analyze survey data by means of one-way frequency counts and cross-tabulations. One purpose of cross-tabulations is to study relationships among variables. The research question is "Do the numbers of responses that fall into different categories differ from what is expected?" The null hypothesis is always that the two variables are not related. Thus, the null hypothesis in the previous example would be that the number of men and women customers who recall Santa Fe Grill ads is the same. The alternative hypothesis is that the two variables are related, or that men and women differ in their recall of Santa Fe Grill ads. This question and similar ones can be answered using Chi-square analysis. Below are some other examples of research questions that could be examined using Chi-square statistical tests:

- Is usage of the Internet (low, moderate, and high) related to gender?
- Does frequency of eating out (infrequent, moderately frequent, and very frequent) differ between males and females?
- Do part-time and full-time workers differ in terms of how often they are absent from work (seldom, occasionally, frequently)?
- Do college students and high school students differ in their preference for Coke versus Pepsi?

Chi-square (X^2) analysis enables researchers to test for statistical significance between the frequency distributions of two (or more) nominally scaled variables in a cross-tabulation table to determine if there is any association. Categorical data from questions about gender, education, or other nominal variables can be examined with this statistic. Chi-square analysis compares the observed frequencies (counts) of the responses with the expected frequencies. The Chi-square statistic tests whether or not the observed data are distributed the way we expect them to be, given the assumption that the variables are not related. The expected cell count is a theoretical value, while the observed cell count is the actual cell count based on your study. For example, if we observe that women recall ads more so than men, we would compare the observed value with the frequency we would expect to find if there is no difference between women's and men's ad recall. Thus, the chi-square statistic helps to answers questions about nominally scaled data that cannot be analyzed with other types of statistical analysis, such as ANOVA or *t*-tests.

Calculating the X^2 Value

To help you to better understand the Chi-square statistic, we will show you how to calculate it. The formula is shown below:

$$\text{Chi square formula } X^2 = \sum_{i-1}^{n} \frac{(\text{Observed}_i - \text{Expected}_i)^2}{\text{Expected}_i}$$

where

Observed_i = observed frequency in cell i

Expected_i = expected frequency in cell i

n = number of cells

eXHIBIT 15.7 SPSS Chi Square Crosstab Example

Output41 [Document41] - SPSS Viewer

File Edit View Data Transform Insert Format Analyze Graphs Utilities Add-ons Window Help

Crosstabs

x30 -- Distance Driven * X32 -- Gender Crosstabulation

			X32 -- Gender		
			0 Male	1 Female	Total
x30 -- Distance Driven	1 Less than 1 mile	Count	74	12	86
		Expected Count	59.8	26.2	86.0
		% within X32 -- Gender	42.0%	15.6%	34.0%
	2 1 -- 5 miles	Count	45	31	76
		Expected Count	52.9	23.1	76.0
		% within X32 -- Gender	25.6%	40.3%	30.0%
	3 More than 5 miles	Count	57	34	91
		Expected Count	63.3	27.7	91.0
		% within X32 -- Gender	32.4%	44.2%	36.0%
Total		Count	176	77	253
		Expected Count	176.0	77.0	253.0
		% within X32 -- Gender	100.0%	100.0%	100.0%

Chi-Square Tests

	Value	df	Asymp. Sig. (2-sided)
Pearson Chi-Square	16.945[a]	2	.000
Likelihood Ratio	18.390	2	.000
Linear-by-Linear Association	11.153	1	.001
N of Valid Cases	253		

a. 0 cells (.0%) have expected count less than 5. The minimum expected count is 23.13.

When you apply the above formula to the Santa Fe Grill survey data shown in Exhibit 15.7, you get the following:

Calculation of Chi-square value

$$\frac{(74-59.8)^2}{59.8}+\frac{(12-26.2)^2}{26.2}+\frac{(45-52.9)^2}{52.9}+\frac{(31-23.1)^2}{23.1}+\frac{(57-63.3)^2}{63.3}+\frac{(34-27.7)^2}{27.7}=\text{Chi square value}=16.945$$

As above equation indicates, the expected frequency is subtracted from the observed frequency and then squared to eliminate any negative values before the results are used in further calculations. After squaring, the resulting value is divided by the expected frequency to take into consideration cell size differences. Then each of these calculations, which are performed for each cell of the table, are summed over all cells to arrive at the

Chi-square value. The Chi-square value tells you how far the observed frequencies are from the expected frequencies. Conceptually, the larger the Chi-square is, the more likely it is that the two variables are related. This is because Chi-square is larger whenever the number actually observed in a cell is much different than what we expected to find, given the assumption that the two variables are not related. The computed Chi-square statistic is compared to a table of Chi-square values to determine if the differences are statistically significant. If the calculated Chi-square is larger than the Chi-square reported in standard statistical tables, then the two variables are related for a given level of significance, typically .05.

Some marketing researchers call Chi-square a "goodness of fit" test. That is, the test evaluates how closely the actual frequencies "fit" the expected frequencies. When the differences between observed and expected frequencies are large, you have a poor fit and you reject your null hypothesis. When the differences are small, you have a good fit.

One word of caution is necessary, however, in using Chi-square. The Chi-square results will be distorted if more than 20 percent of the cells have an expected count of less than 5, or if any cell has an expected count of less than 1. In such cases, you should not use this test. SPSS will tell you if these conditions have been violated. One solution to small counts in individual cells is to collapse them into fewer cells to get larger counts.

SPSS Application—Chi Square

Based on their conversations with customers, the owners of the Santa Fe Grill believe that female customers are coming to the restaurant from farther away than are male customers. The Chi-square statistic can be used to determine if this is true. The null hypothesis is no difference in distance driven (X30) between male and female customers of the Santa Fe Grill.

To conduct this analysis we examine only the responses for the Santa Fe Grill ($N = 253$). The SPSS click-through sequence is ANALYZE → DESCRIPTIVE STATISTICS → CROSSTABS. Click on X30—Distance Traveled for the Row variable and on X32—Gender for the Column variable. Click on the Statistics button and the Chi-square box, and then Continue. Next click on the Cells button and on Expected frequencies (Observed frequencies is usually already checked). Then click Continue and OK to execute the program.

The SPSS results are shown in Exhibit 15.7. The top table shows the actual number of responses (count) for males and females for each of the categories of X300—Distance Driven: less than 1 mile, 1–5 miles, and more than 5 miles. For example, 74 males drove a distance of less than 1 mile while 12 females drove from this same distance. The expected frequencies (count) are also shown in this table, right below the actual count.

The expected count is calculated on the basis of the proportion of the sample represented by a particular group. For example, the total sample of Santa Fe Grill customers is 253, and 176 are males and 77 are females. This means 69.6 percent of the sample is male and 30.4 percent is female. When we look in the Total column for the distance driven category labeled "Less than 1 mile" we see that there are a total of 86 male and female respondents. To calculate the expected frequencies, you multiply the proportion a particular group represents times the total number in that group. For example, with males you calculate 69.6 percent of 86 and the expected frequency is 59.8. Similarly, females are

30.4 percent of the sample so the expected number of females = 26.2 (.304 × 86). The other expected frequencies are calculated in the same way.

Look again at the observed frequencies and note that a higher count than expected of female customers of Santa Fe Grill drive more than 5 miles. That is, we would expect only 27.7 women to drive to the Santa Fe Grill from more than 5 miles, but actually 34 women drove from this far away. Similarly, there are fewer male customers than expected who drive from more than five miles away (expected = 63.3 and actual only 57). This pattern is similar for the distance of 1–5 miles. That is, a higher proportion of females are driving from this distance than would be expected.

Information in the Chi-Square Tests table shows the results for this test. The Pearson Chi-Square value is 16.945 and it is significant at the .000 level. Since this level of significance is much less than our standard criterion of .05, we can reject the null hypothesis of no difference in distance driven with a high degree of confidence. The interpretation of this finding suggests that female customers are indeed driving from farther away than expected to get to the Santa Fe Grill. At the same time, the males are driving shorter distances than expected to get to the Santa Fe Grill.

Comparing Means: Independent versus Related Samples

Independent samples Two or more groups of responses that are tested as though they may come from different populations.

Related samples Two or more groups of responses that originated from the sample population.

In addition to examining frequencies, marketing researchers often want to compare the means of two groups. There are two possible situations when means are compared. The first is when the means are from **independent samples,** and the second is when the samples are related. An example of an independent sample comparison would be the results of interviews with male and female coffee drinkers. The researcher may want to compare the average number of cups of coffee consumed per day by male students with the average number of cups of coffee consumed by female students. An example of the second situation, **related samples,** is when the researcher compares the average number of cups of coffee consumed per day by male students with the average number of soft drinks consumed per day by the same sample of male students.

In a related sample situation, the marketing researcher must take special care in analyzing the information. Although the questions are independent, the respondents are the same. This is called a *paired sample.* When testing for differences in related samples the researcher must use what is called a paired samples *t*-test. The formula to compute the *t*-value for paired samples is not presented here. Students are referred to more advanced texts for the actual calculation of the *t*-value for related samples. The SPSS package contains options for both the related-samples and the independent samples situations.

Using the *t*-Test to Compare Two Means

***t*-test** A hypothesis test that utilizes the *t*-distribution; used when the sample size is smaller than 30 and the standard deviation is unknown.

Just as with the univariate *t*-test, the bivariate *t*-test requires interval or ratio data. Also, the ***t*-test** is especially useful when the sample size is small ($n < 30$) and when the population standard deviation is unknown. Unlike the univariate test, however, we assume that the samples are drawn from populations with normal distributions and that the variances of the populations are equal.

Essentially, the *t*-test for differences between group means can be conceptualized as the difference between the means divided by the variability of the means. The *t*-value is a ratio of the difference between the two sample means and the standard error. The *t*-test provides a mathematical way of determining if the difference between the two sample means occurred by chance. The formula for calculating the t-value is:

$$Z = \frac{\overline{X}_1 - \overline{X}_2}{S\overline{x}_1 - \overline{x}_2}$$

where

$\overline{X}_1$ = mean of sample 1

$\overline{X}_2$ = mean of sample 2

$S\overline{x}_1 - \overline{x}_2$ = standard error of the difference between the two means

SPSS Application—Independent Samples *t*-Test

To illustrate the use of a t-test for the difference between two group means, let's turn to the Santa Fe Grill database. The Santa Fe Grill owners want to find out if there are differences in the level of satisfaction between male and female customers. To do that we can use the SPSS Compare Means program.

The SPSS click-through sequence is Analyze → Compare Means → Independent-Samples t-Test. When you get to this dialog box, move variable X22—Satisfaction into the Test Variables box and variable X32—Gender into the Grouping Variable Box. For variable X32 you must define the range in the Define Groups box. Enter a 0 for Group 1 and a 1 for Group 2 (males were coded 0 in the database and females were coded 1) and then click Continue. For the Options we will use the defaults, so just click OK to execute the program.

Results are shown in Exhibit 15.8. The top table shows the Group Statistics. Note that 176 male customers and 77 female customers were interviewed. The mean satisfaction level for males was a bit higher at 4.70, compared with 4.18 for the female customers. Also, the standard deviation for females was smaller (.823) than for the males (1.034).

To find out if the two means are significantly different, we look at the information in the Independent Samples Test table. The statistical significance of the difference in two means is calculated differently if the variances of the two means are equal versus unequal. In the column labeled Sig. (2-tailed) you will note that the two means are significantly different ($<$ .000), whether we assume equal or unequal variances. Thus, there is no support for the null hypothesis that the two means are equal, and we conclude that male customers are significantly more satisfied than female customers. There is other information in this table, but we do not need to concern ourselves with it at this time.

SPSS Application—Paired Samples *t*-Test

Sometimes marketing researchers want to test for differences in two means for variables in the same sample. For example, the owners of the Santa Fe Grill noticed that the taste of their food was rated 4.78 while the food temperature was rated only 4.38. Since the two food variables are obviously related, they want to know if the ratings for taste really are significantly higher (more favorable) than for temperature. To examine this, we use the paired samples test for the difference in two means. This test examines whether two means from two different questions using the same scaling and answered by the same respondents are significantly different. The null hypothesis is that the mean ratings for the two food variables (X18 and X20) are equal. Note that in this example we are looking only at the responses of the Santa Fe Grill customers.

eXHIBIT 15.8 Comparing Two Means with the Independent-Samples *t*-Test

Output8 [Document8] - SPSS Viewer

File Edit View Data Transform Insert Format Analyze Graphs Utilities Add-ons Window Help

→T-Test

Group Statistics

	X32 -- Gender	N	Mean	Std. Deviation	Std. Error Mean
X22 -- Satisfaction	Male	176	4.70	1.034	.078
	Female	77	4.18	.823	.094

Independent Samples Test

		Levene's Test for Equality of Variances		t-test for Equality of Means					95% Confidence Interval of the Difference	
		F	Sig.	t	df	Sig. (2-tailed)	Mean Difference	Std. Error Difference	Lower	Upper
X22 -- Satisfaction	Equal variances assumed	19.800	.000	3.882	251	.000	.517	.133	.255	.779
	Equal variances not assumed			4.241	179.954	.000	.517	.122	.276	.758

To test this hypothesis we use the SPSS paired-samples *t*-test. The click-through sequence is Analyze → Compare Means → Paired-Samples *t*-Test. When you get to this dialog box, highlight both X188—Food Taste and X20—Food Temperature and then click on the arrow button to move them into the Paired Variables box. For the Options we will use the defaults, so just click OK to execute the program.

Results are shown in Exhibit 15.9. The top table shows the Paired Samples Statistics. The mean for food taste is 4.78 and for food temperature is 4.38. The *t*-value for this comparison is 8.421 (see Paired Samples Test table) and it is significant at the .000 level. Thus we can reject the null hypothesis that the two means are equal and conclude that Santa Fe Grill customers definitely have more favorable perceptions of food taste than food temperature.

Analysis of variance (ANOVA) A statistical technique that determines whether three or more means are statistically different from each other.

Analysis of Variance (ANOVA)

Analysis of variance (ANOVA) is used to determine the statistical difference between three or more means. For example, if a sample finds that the average number of cups of coffee consumed per day by freshmen during finals is 3.7, while the average number of cups of coffee consumed per day by seniors and graduate students is 4.3 cups and 5.1 cups,

eXHIBIT 15.9 Paired Samples *t*-Test

File Edit View Data Transform Insert Format Analyze Graphs Utilities Add-ons Window Help

T-Test

Paired Samples Statistics

		Mean	N	Std. Deviation	Std. Error Mean
Pair 1	X18 -- Excellent Food Taste	4.78	253	.881	.055
	X20 -- Proper Food Temperature	4.38	253	1.065	.067

Paired Samples Correlations

		N	Correlation	Sig.
Pair 1	X18 -- Excellent Food Taste & X20 -- Proper Food Temperature	253	.721	.000

Paired Samples Test

		Paired Differences					t	df	Sig. (2-tailed)
					95% Confidence Interval of the Difference				
		Mean	Std. Deviation	Std. Error Mean	Lower	Upper			
Pair 1	X18 -- Excellent Food Taste - X20 -- Proper Food Temperature	.395	.747	.047	.303	.488	8.421	252	.000

respectively, are these observed differences statistically significant? The ability to make such comparisons can be quite useful for the marketing researcher.

The technique is really quite straightforward. In this section we describe a one-way ANOVA. The term one-way is used since there is only one independent variable. ANOVA can be used in cases where multiple independent variables are considered, which enables the analyst to estimate both the individual and joint effects of the several independent variables on the dependent variable.

An example of an ANOVA problem may be to compare light, medium, and heavy drinkers of Starbucks coffee on their attitude toward a particular Starbucks advertising campaign. In this instance there is one independent variable, consumption of Starbucks coffee, but it is divided into three different levels. Our earlier *t*-statistics won't work here since we have more than two groups to compare.

ANOVA requires that the dependent variable, in this case the attitude toward the Starbucks advertising campaign, be metric. That is, the dependent variable must be either interval or ratio scaled. A second data requirement is that the independent variable, in this case the coffee consumption variable, be categorical.

The null hypothesis for ANOVA always states that there is no difference between the dependent variable groups—in this situation, the ad campaign attitudes of the groups of Starbucks coffee drinkers. In specific terminology, the null hypothesis would be:

$$\mu_1 = \mu_2 = \mu_3$$

ANOVA examines the variance within a set of data. Recall from the earlier discussion of measures of dispersion that the variance of a variable is equal to the average squared deviation from the mean of the variable. The logic of ANOVA is that if the variance between the groups is compared to the variance within the groups, we can make a logical determination as to whether the group means (attitudes toward the advertising campaign) are significantly different.[1]

Determining Statistical Significance in ANOVA

_F_-test The test used to statistically evaluate the differences between the group means in ANOVA.

Total variance Consists of the between-group and within-group variance added together.

Between-group variance Measures how much the sample means of the groups differ from one another.

Within-group variance Measures how much the observations within each group differ from one another.

_F_-ratio is the between groups variance divided by the within groups variance.

Follow-up test A test that flags the means that are statistically different from each other; follow-up tests are performed after an ANOVA determines there are differences between means.

In ANOVA, the ***F*-test** is used to statistically evaluate the differences between the group means. For example, suppose the heavy users of Starbucks coffee rate the advertising campaign 4.4 on a five-point scale, with 5 = Very favorable. The medium users of Starbucks coffee rate the campaign 3.9, and the light users of Starbucks coffee rate the campaign 2.5. The *F*-test in ANOVA tells us if these observed differences are meaningful.

The **total variance** in a set of responses to a question is made up of between-group and within-group variance. The **between-group variance** measures how much the sample means of the groups differ from one another. In contrast, the **within-group variance** measures how much the observations within each group differ from one another. The *F*-distribution is the ratio of these two components of total variance and can be calculated as follows:

$$F\text{-ratio} = \frac{\text{Variance between groups}}{\text{Variance within groups}}$$

The larger the difference in the variance between groups, the larger the ***F*-ratio.** Since the total variance in a data set is divisible into between and within components, if there is more variance explained or accounted for by considering differences between groups than there is within groups, then the independent variable probably has a significant impact on the dependent variable. Larger *F*-ratios imply significant differences between the groups. The larger the *F*-ratio, the more likely it is that the null hypothesis will be rejected.

ANOVA, however, is able to tell the researcher only that statistical differences exist between at least one pair of the group means. The technique cannot identify which pairs of means are significantly different from each other. In our example of Starbucks coffee drinkers' attitudes toward the advertising campaign, we could conclude that differences in attitudes toward the advertising campaign exist among light, medium, and heavy coffee drinkers, but we would not be able to determine if the differences are between light and medium, or between light and heavy, or between medium and heavy, and so on. We would be able to say only that there are significant differences somewhere among the groups. Thus, the marketing researcher still must determine where the mean differences lie. Follow-up "post-hoc" tests have been designed for just that purpose.

There are several **follow-up tests** available in statistical software packages such as SPSS and SAS. All of these methods involve multiple comparisons, or simultaneous assessment of confidence interval estimates of differences between the means. All means are compared two at a time. The differences between the techniques lie in their ability to control the error rate. We shall briefly describe the Scheffé procedure, although a complete discussion of these techniques is well beyond the scope of this book. Relative to the other follow-up tests mentioned, however, the Scheffé procedure is a more conservative method of detecting significant differences between group means.

The Scheffé follow-up test establishes simultaneous confidence intervals, which hold the entire experiment's error rate to a specified α level. The test exposes differences between all pairs of means to a high and low confidence interval range. If the difference between each pair of means falls outside the range of the confidence interval, then we reject the null hypothesis and conclude that the pairs of means falling outside the range are statistically different. The Scheffé test might show that one, two, or all three pairs of means in our Starbucks example are different. The Scheffé test is equivalent to simultaneous two-tailed hypothesis tests, and the technique holds the specified analysis significance level. Because the technique holds the experimental error rate to α, the confidence intervals tend to be wider than in the other methods, but the researcher has more assurance that true mean differences exist. Recall that the Scheffé test is very conservative so you may wish to look at one of the other tests available in your statistical software.

SPSS Application—ANOVA

To help you understand how ANOVA is used to answer research questions, we refer to the Santa Fe Grill database to answer a typical question. The Santa Fe Grill owners want to know how their restaurant compares to their major competitor, Jose's Southwestern Café. They are particularly interested in comparing satisfaction and related variables as well as gender. The purpose of the ANOVA analysis is to see if the differences that do exist are statistically significant. To examine the differences, an *F*-ratio is used. The larger the *F*-ratio, the more difference there is among the means of the various groups with respect to their likelihood of recommending the restaurant. Note that this application of ANOVA examines only two groups: the two restaurant competitors Santa Fe Grill and Jose's Southwestern Café. But ANOVA can be used to examine three, four, or more groups, to identify statistical differences if they exist.

SPSS can conduct the statistical analysis to test the null hypothesis. To compare male and female customers from the two restaurants, we first must split the sample into two groups—the male and female customers. To do this, the click-through sequence is DATA → SPLIT FILE → Click on Compare Groups. Now highlight the variable X322—Gender and move it into the "Groups Based on:" window, and then click OK. Your results will now be computed for male and female customers separately.

Next we want to test whether the two restaurants are viewed differently on selected variables. The click-through sequence is ANALYZE → COMPARE MEANS → ONE-WAY ANOVA. Highlight X22—Satisfaction, X23—Likely to Return, and X24—Likely to Recommend by highlighting them and moving to the Dependent List window. Next, highlight x_s4 Favorite Mexican restaurant and move it to the Factor window. This tells the SPSS software to statistically test the differences in the responses on the three variables selected. Next click on the Options box, then on Descriptive (to get group means), and then continue. Now click OK to run the test.

The results for the ANOVA are shown in Exhibit 15.10. The two restaurants differ significantly on four of the six variables compared (see Sig. column). In the top of the table are the comparisons of males and they differ on only one variable: X24—Likely to Recommend. That is, the mean perceptions of males between the two restaurants do not differ significantly on satisfaction or likelihood of returning. But the male customers of the Santa Fe Grill are more likely to recommend (X24) the restaurant (mean = 3.78) than are the male customers of Jose's Southwestern Café (mean = 3.23).

EXHIBIT 15.10 ANOVA Comparing Two Restaurants on Selected Variables

Gender	Variable	Restaurant	Mean	F	Sig.
Male	X22—Satisfaction	Jose's Southwestern Cafe	4.75	.149	.700
		Santa Fe Grill	4.70		
	X23—Likely to Return	Jose's Southwestern Cafe	4.32	.058	.810
		Santa Fe Grill	4.29		
	X24—Likely to Recommend	Jose's Southwestern Cafe	3.23	19.28	.000
		Santa Fe Grill	3.78		
Female	X22—Satisfaction	Jose's Southwestern Cafe	6.08	174.59	.000
		Santa Fe Grill	4.18		
	X23—Likely to Return	Jose's Southwestern Cafe	5.84	152.59	.000
		Santa Fe Grill	3.88		
	X24—Likely to Recommend	Jose's Southwestern Cafe	5.23	134.24	.000
		Santa Fe Grill	3.22		

The female customers feel very differently about the two restaurants, and indeed there are significant differences on all three variables (<.000). The female customers are more favorable about Jose's Southwestern Café, particularly in terms of satisfaction and likelihood of returning. The females are likely to recommend Jose's restaurant (mean = 5.23 on a 7-point scale), but not likely to recommend the Santa Fe Grill (mean = 3.22).

n-Way ANOVA

Discussion of ANOVA to this point has been devoted to one-way ANOVA in which there is only one independent variable. In the examples, the usage category (consumption of Starbucks coffee) or the restaurant competitors (Santa Fe Grill and Jose's Southwestern Café) was the single independent variable. It is not at all uncommon, however, for the researcher to be interested in several independent variables simultaneously. In such cases an *n*-way ANOVA would be used.

Often researchers are interested in the region of the country where a product is sold as well as consumption patterns. Using multiple independent factors creates the possibility of an interaction effect. That is, the multiple independent factors can act together to affect group means. For example, heavy consumers of Starbucks coffee in the Northeast may have different attitudes about advertising campaigns than heavy consumers of Starbucks coffee in the West, and there may be still further differences between the various coffee-consumption-level groups, as shown earlier.

Another situation that may require *n*-way ANOVA is the use of experimental designs, where the researcher uses different levels of a stimulus (for example, different prices or ads) and then measures responses to those stimuli. For example, a marketer may be interested in finding out whether consumers prefer a humorous ad to a serious one and whether that preference varies across gender. Each type of ad could be shown to different groups of customers (both male and female). Then, questions about their preferences for the ad and the product it advertises could be asked. The primary difference between the groups would be the difference in ad execution (humorous or nonhumorous) and customer gender. An *n*-way ANOVA could be used to find out whether the ad execution differences helped cause differences in ad and product preferences, as well as what effects might be attributable to customer gender.

From a conceptual standpoint, *n*-way ANOVA is similar to one-way ANOVA, but the mathematics is more complex. However, statistical packages such as SPSS will conveniently allow the marketing researcher to perform *n*-way ANOVA.

Perceptual Mapping

Perceptual mapping A process that is used to develop maps showing the perceptions of respondents. The maps are visual representations of respondent's perceptions of a company, product, service, brand, or any other object in two dimensions.

Perceptual mapping is a process that is used to develop maps that show the perceptions of respondents. The maps are visual representations of respondents' perceptions of a company, product, service, brand, or any other object in two dimensions. A perceptual map typically has a vertical and a horizontal axis that are labeled with descriptive adjectives. Possible adjectives for our restaurant example might be food temperature and/or freshness, speed of service, good value for the money, and so on.

Several different approaches can be used to develop perceptual maps. These include rankings, medians, and mean ratings. To illustrate perceptual mapping, data from an example involving ratings of fast-food restaurants are shown in Exhibit 15.11. Customers are given a set of six fast-food restaurants and asked to express how they perceive each restaurant. The perceptions of the respondents are then plotted on a two-dimensional map using two of the adjectives, freshness of food and food temperature. Inspection of the map, shown in Exhibit 15.12, illustrates that Wendy's and Back Yard Burgers were perceived as quite similar to each other, as were McDonald's and Burger King. Arby's and Hardee's were also perceived as somewhat similar, but not as favorable as the other restaurants. However, Back Yard Burgers and McDonald's were perceived as very dissimilar.

Perceptual Mapping Applications in Marketing Research

While our fast-food example illustrates how perceptual mapping grouped pairs of restaurants together based on perceived ratings, perceptual mapping has many other important applications in marketing research. Other applications include

- *New-product development.* Perceptual mapping can identify gaps in perceptions and thereby help to position new products.

EXHIBIT 15.11 Ratings of Six Fast-Food Restaurants

	Food Freshness	Food Temperature
McDonald's	1.8	3.7
Burger King	2.0	3.5
Wendy's	4.0	4.5
Back Yard Burger	4.5	4.8
Arby's	4.0	2.5
Hardee's	3.5	1.8

Key: Food temperature, 1 = Warm, 5 = Hot; Food freshness, 1 = Low, 5 = High.

EXHIBIT 15.12 Perceptual Map of Six Fast-Food Restaurants

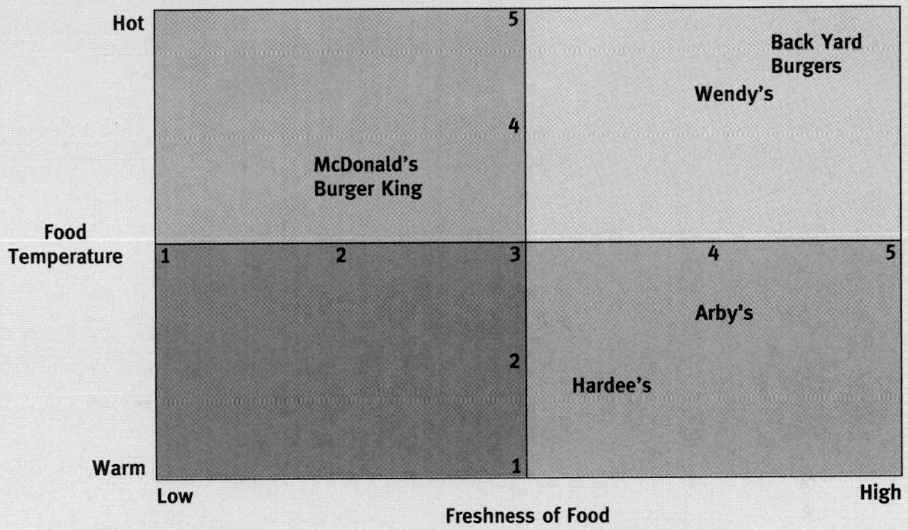

- *Image measurement.* Perceptual mapping can be used to identify the image of the company to help to position one company relative to the competition.
- *Advertising.* Perceptual mapping can assess advertising effectiveness in positioning the brand.
- *Distribution.* Perceptual mapping can be used to assess similarities of brands and channel outlets.

Continuing Case: The Santa Fe Grill

With the survey completed, edited, and entered into an electronic file, a decision has to be made regarding the best way to analyze the data to understand the individuals interviewed, and how the information can be used to improve the restaurant's operations. The data analysis should be based on the research objectives. The researcher and the owners have been brainstorming on how to best analyze the data to better understand the situation.

1. Draw several conceptual models to represent relationships that could be tested with the customer survey?
2. Which statistical techniques would be appropriate to test the proposed relationships?
3. Give examples of relationships that could be tested with Chi-square? with ANOVA?

marketing research in action

Examining Restaurant Image Positions

Remington's Steak House

About three years ago, John Smith opened Remington's Steak House, a retail theme restaurant located in a large Midwestern city. Smith's vision for his restaurant was for customers to perceive his restaurant as being a unique, theme-oriented specialty restaurant with an excellent reputation for offering a wide assortment of high-quality yet competitively priced entrees and services, and having knowledgeable employees who understand customers' needs and place heavy emphasis on satisfying the customer.

Smith used this vision to guide the development and implementation of his restaurant's positioning and marketing strategies. Although Smith knows how to deliver dining experiences, he does not know much about developing, implementing, and assessing marketing strategies.

Recently, Smith began asking himself some fundamental questions about his restaurant's operations and the future of his business. Smith expressed these questions to an account representative at a local marketing research firm and, as a result, decided to do some research to better understand his customers' attitudes and feelings. More specifically, he wanted to gain some information and insights into the following set of questions:

1. What are the major factors customers use when selecting a restaurant to dine at, and what is the relative importance of each of these factors?
2. What image do customers have of Remington's and its two major competitors?
3. Is Remington's providing quality and satisfaction to its customers?
4. Do any of Remington's current marketing strategies need to be changed, and if so in what ways?

To address Smith's questions, the account representative recommended completing an image survey using an Internet panel approach. Initial contact was made with potential respondents using a random digit dialing telephone survey to screen for individuals who were patrons of Remington's as well as customers of similar restaurants (i.e., Remington's main competitors: Outback Steakhouse and Longhorn Steak House) within the market area. Respondents also must have a minimum annual household income of $20,000, and be familiar enough with one of the three restaurant competitors to accurately rate them. If an individual correctly answered the screening questions, they were directed to a Web site where they completed the survey.

Since this was the first time Smith had conducted any marketing research, it was considered exploratory and the consultant recommended a sample size of 200. She said that if the results of the initial 200 surveys were helpful, then increasing the sample size would be evaluated to increase the precision of the findings. The questionnaire collected data on the importance ratings of restaurant selection factors, perceptions of the images of the three restaurant competitors on the same factors, and selected classification information on the respondents. When the quota of 200 usable completed questionnaires was reached, the sample included 86 respondents most familiar with Outback, 65 most familiar with Longhorn, and 49 most familiar with Remington's. This last criterion was used to determine which restaurant competitor a respondent evaluated. A database for the questions in this case is available in SPSS format at www.mhhe.com/hair4e. The name of the database is Remington's MRIA_4e.sav. A copy of the questionnaire is in Exhibit 15.13.

EXHIBIT 15.13 The Remington's Steakhouse Questionnaire

Screening and Rapport Questions

Hello. My name is ____ and I work for DSS Research. We are talking to individuals today/tonight about dining out habits.

1. "Do you regularly dine at casual dining restaurants?" __ Yes __ No
2. "Have you eaten at other casual restaurants in the last six months?" __ Yes __ No
3. "Is your gross annual household income $20,000 or more?" __ Yes __ No
4. There are three casual steakhouse restaurants in you neighborhood—Outback, Longhorn, and Remington's. Which of these restaurants are you most familiar with?
   - **a.** Outback __
   - **b.** Longhorn __
   - **c.** Remington's __
   - **d.** None __

If respondent answers Yes to first three questions, and is familiar with one of the three restaurants, then say:

We would like you to answer a few questions about your recent dining experiences at Outback/Longhorn/Remington's restaurant. The survey will only take a few minutes and it will be very helpful in better serving restaurant customers in this area.

If the person says yes, give them instructions on how to access the Website and complete the survey.

DINING OUT SURVEY

Please read all questions carefully. If you do not understand a question, stop the survey and e-mail us so we can help you to understand it.

In the first section a number of factors are listed that people use in selecting a particular restaurant to dine at. Using a scale from 1 to 7, with 7 being "Very Important" and 1 being "Not Important at All," please indicate the extent to which a particular selection factor is important or unimportant. Circle only one number for each selection factor.

Section 1: Importance Ratings

How important is/are __________ in selecting a particular restaurant to dine at?

	Not Important At All						Very Important
1. Large Portions	1	2	3	4	5	6	7
2. Competent Employees	1	2	3	4	5	6	7
3. Food Quality	1	2	3	4	5	6	7
4. Speed of Service	1	2	3	4	5	6	7
5. Atmosphere	1	2	3	4	5	6	7
6. Reasonable Prices	1	2	3	4	5	6	7

continued

EXHIBIT 15.13 The Remington's Steakhouse Questionnaire, *continued*

Section 2: Perceptions Measures

Listed below is a set of characteristics that could be used to describe Outback/Longhorn/Remington's. Using a scale from 1 to 7, with 7 being "Strongly Agree" and 1 being "Strongly Disagree," to what extent do you agree or disagree that Remington's—Outback—Longhorn's: (a particular restaurant's name appeared on the screen based on the familiarity question on the telephone screening question)

Item	Strongly Disagree						Strongly Agree
7. has large portions	1	2	3	4	5	6	7
8. has competent employees	1	2	3	4	5	6	7
9. has excellent food quality	1	2	3	4	5	6	7
10. has quick service	1	2	3	4	5	6	7
11. has a good atmosphere	1	2	3	4	5	6	7
12. has reasonable prices	1	2	3	4	5	6	7

Section 3: Relationship Measures

Please indicate your view on each of the following questions:

13. How satisfied are you with ________?

Not Satisfied At All						Very Satisfied
1	2	3	4	5	6	7

14. How likely are you to return to ________ in the future?

Definitely Will Not Return						Definitely Will Return
1	2	3	4	5	6	7

15. How likely are you to recommend ________ to a friend?

Definitely Will Not Recommend						Definitely Will Recommend
1	2	3	4	5	6	7

16. Frequency of Patronage
How often do you eat at ________?

1 = Occasionally (Less than once a month)
2 = Frequently (1–3 times a month)
3 = Very Frequently (4 or more times a month)

Section 4: Classification Questions

Please circle the number that classifies you best.

17. Number of Children at Home

1 None
2 1–2
3 More than 2 children at home

EXHIBIT 15.13 The Remington's Steakhouse Questionnaire

18. Do your recall seeing any advertisements in the last 60 days for Outback/Longhorn/Remington's?
0 No
1 Yes

19. Your Gender
0 Male
1 Female

20. Your Age in Years
1 18–25
2 26–34
3 35–49
4 50–59
5 60 and Older

21. Your Annual Gross Household Income
1 $20,000–$35,000
2 $35,001–$50,000
3 $50,001–$75,000
4 $75,001–$100,000
5 More than $100,000

22. Competitors: Most familiar with _______?
1 Outback
2 Longhorn
3 Remington's

Thank you very much for your help. Click on the submit button to exit the survey.

The initial analysis of the data focused on the importance ratings for the restaurant selection factors. The importance ratings are variables X1–X6 in the Remington's database. Exhibit 15.14 shows that food quality and speed of service are the two most important factors. To derive this exhibit, the click-through sequence is ANALYZE → DESCRIPTIVE STATISTICS → FREQUENCIES. Highlight variables X1–X6 and move them to the Variable(s) box. Then go to the Statistics box and check Mean, and then click Continue and

EXHIBIT 15.14 Importance Ratings for Restaurant Selection Factors

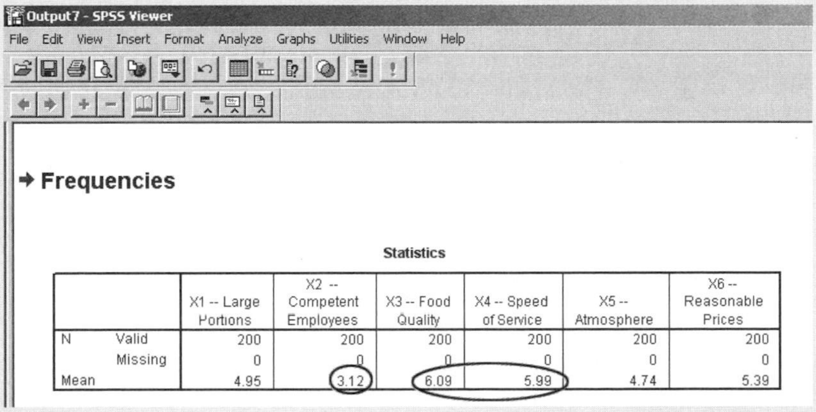
Output7 - SPSS Viewer
File Edit View Insert Format Analyze Graphs Utilities Window Help

→ **Frequencies**

Statistics

		X1 -- Large Portions	X2 -- Competent Employees	X3 -- Food Quality	X4 -- Speed of Service	X5 -- Atmosphere	X6 -- Reasonable Prices
N	Valid	200	200	200	200	200	200
	Missing	0	0	0	0	0	0
Mean		4.95	3.12	6.09	5.99	4.74	5.39

OK. The least important factor was competent employees (mean = 3.12). This does not mean employees aren't important. It simply means they are relatively less important compared to the other factors respondents were asked about in the survey. In sum, these respondents wanted good food, fast service, and reasonable prices.

The next task was to examine the perceptions of the three restaurant competitors. Using the restaurant image factors, the consultant conducted an ANOVA to see if there were any differences in the perceptions of the three restaurants (Exhibits 15.15 and 15.16). To derive these exhibits, the click-through sequence is ANALYZE → COMPARE MEANS → ONE-WAY ANOVA. Highlight variables X1–X6 and move them to the Dependent List box, and then highlight variable X22 and move it to the Factor box. Next go to the Options box and check Descriptive, and then click Continue and OK.

Results are shown in Exhibits 15.15 and 15.16. An overview of the findings presented in Exhibits 15.14 through 15.16 is provided in Exhibit 15.17.

The findings of the survey were quite revealing. On the most important factor (food quality), Remington's rated the highest (mean = 6.86; see Exhibit 15.15), but Outback was a close second (mean = 6.42). Remington's was also rated the highest on atmosphere

eXHIBIT 15.15 One-Way ANOVA for Three Restaurant Competitors

Output3 - SPSS Viewer

File Edit View Insert Format Analyze Graphs Utilities Window Help

Descriptives

		N	Mean	Std. Deviation	Std. Error	95% Confidence Interval for Mean Lower Bound	95% Confidence Interval for Mean Upper Bound	Minimum	Maximum
X7 -- Large Portions	Outback	86	3.57	.805	.087	3.40	3.74	2	4
	Longhorn	65	2.77	.880	.109	2.55	2.99	1	4
	Remington's	49	3.39	.862	.123	3.14	3.64	1	4
	Total	200	3.27	.910	.064	3.14	3.39	1	4
X8 -- Competent Employees	Outback	86	5.15	.623	.067	5.02	5.28	4	6
	Longhorn	65	3.25	.919	.114	3.02	3.47	2	5
	Remington's	49	2.49	.617	.088	2.31	2.67	2	4
	Total	200	3.88	1.355	.096	3.69	4.07	2	6
X9 -- Food Quality	Outback	86	6.42	.659	.071	6.28	6.56	5	7
	Longhorn	65	5.12	.839	.104	4.92	5.33	4	7
	Remington's	49	6.86	.354	.051	6.76	6.96	6	7
	Total	200	6.11	.969	.069	5.97	6.24	4	7
X10 -- Speed of Service	Outback	86	4.35	.943	.102	4.15	4.55	3	6
	Longhorn	65	3.02	.857	.106	2.80	3.23	2	5
	Remington's	49	2.27	.670	.096	2.07	2.46	1	3
	Total	200	3.41	1.216	.086	3.24	3.57	1	6
X11 -- Atmosphere	Outback	86	6.09	.890	.096	5.90	6.28	4	7
	Longhorn	65	4.35	.799	.099	4.16	4.55	3	6
	Remington's	49	6.59	.537	.077	6.44	6.75	5	7
	Total	200	5.65	1.210	.086	5.48	5.82	3	7
X12 -- Reasonable Prices	Outback	86	5.50	.763	.082	5.34	5.66	4	6
	Longhorn	65	5.00	.810	.100	4.80	5.20	4	6
	Remington's	49	5.49	.767	.110	5.27	5.71	4	6
	Total	200	5.34	.810	.057	5.22	5.45	4	6

eXHIBIT 15.16 One-Way ANOVA of Differences in Restaurant Perceptions Variables

Output1 - SPSS Viewer

File Edit View Insert Format Analyze Graphs Utilities Window Help

Oneway

ANOVA

		Sum of Squares	df	Mean Square	F	Sig.
X7 -- Large Portions	Between Groups	24.702	2	12.351	17.349	.000
	Within Groups	140.253	197	.712		
	Total	164.955	199			
X8 -- Competent Employees	Between Groups	259.779	2	129.889	242.908	.000
	Within Groups	105.341	197	.535		
	Total	365.120	199			
X9 -- Food Quality	Between Groups	98.849	2	49.425	110.712	.000
	Within Groups	87.946	197	.446		
	Total	186.795	199			
X10 -- Speed of Service	Between Groups	150.124	2	75.062	102.639	.000
	Within Groups	144.071	197	.731		
	Total	294.195	199			
X11 -- Atmosphere	Between Groups	169.546	2	84.773	136.939	.000
	Within Groups	121.954	197	.619		
	Total	291.500	199			
X12 -- Reasonable Prices	Between Groups	10.810	2	5.405	8.892	.000
	Within Groups	119.745	197	.608		
	Total	130.555	199			

eXHIBIT 15.17 Summary of ANOVA Findings from Exhibits 15.14–15.16

		Competitor Means			
Attributes	**Rankings[a]**	**Outback**	**Longhorn**	**Remington's**	**Sig.**
X7—Large portions	4	3.57	2.77	3.39	.000
X8—Competent employees	6	5.15	3.25	2.49	.000
X9—Food quality	1	6.42	5.12	6.86	.000
X10—Speed of service	2	4.35	3.02	2.27	.000
X11—Atmosphere	5	6.09	4.35	6.59	.000
X12—Reasonable prices	3	5.50	5.00	5.49	.000
N = 200 total		86	65	49	.000

[a]*Note:* Rankings are based on mean importance ratings.

eXHIBIT 15.18 Importance-Performance Chart for Remington's Steak House

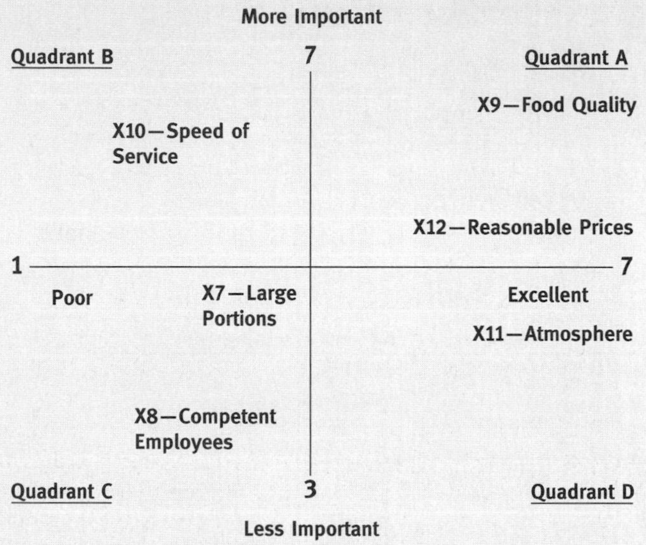

(mean = 6.59) but that factor was fifth most important. For speed of service (2nd most important) and competent employees (least important), Remington's was rated the lowest of the three competitors.

An easy way to convey the results of an image analysis is to prepare an importance performance chart (IPC). An IPC has quadrants (A–D) that are described as follows:

Quadrant A: Modifications are needed.

Quadrant B: Good job—no need to modify.

Quadrant C: Don't worry—low priority.

Quadrant D: Rethink—a possible overkill.

The IPC for Remington's Steak House is shown in Exhibit 15.18. The chart shows that in terms of food quality and prices, Remington's is doing well. But there are several areas for improvement, particularly in comparison to the competition.

Hands-On Exercise

1. What are other areas of improvement for Remington's?
2. Run post hoc ANOVA tests between the competitor groups. What additional problems or challenges did this reveal?
3. What new marketing strategies would you suggest?

Summary of Learning Objectives

■ **Explain measures of central tendency and dispersion.**

The mean is the most commonly used measure of central tendency and describes the arithmetic average of the values in a sample of data. The median represents the middle value of an ordered set of values. The mode is the most frequently occurring value in a distribution of values. All these measures describe the center of the distribution of a set of values. The range defines the spread of the data. It is the distance between the smallest and largest values of the distribution. The standard deviation describes the average distance of the distribution values from the mean. A large standard deviation indicates a distribution in which the individual values are spread out and are relatively farther away from the mean.

■ **Describe how to test hypotheses using univariate and bivariate statistics.**

Marketing researchers often form hypotheses regarding population characteristics based on sample data. The process typically begins by calculating frequency distributions and averages, and then moves on to actually test the hypotheses. When the hypothesis testing involves examining one variable at a time, it is referred to as a univariate statistical test. When the hypothesis testing involves two variables it is called a bivariate statistical test. The Chi-square statistic permits us to test for significance between the frequency distributions of two or more groups. Categorical data from questions about gender, race, profession, and so forth can be examined and tested for statistical differences. In addition to examining frequencies, marketing researchers often want to compare the means of two groups. There are two possible situations when means are compared. In independent samples the respondents come from different populations, so their answers to the survey questions do not affect each other. In related samples, the same respondent answers several questions, so comparing answers to these questions requires the use of a paired-samples *t*-test. Questions about mean differences in independent samples can be answered by using a *t*-test statistic.

■ **Apply and interpret analysis of variance (ANOVA).**

ANOVA is used to determine the statistical significance of the difference between two or more means. The ANOVA technique calculates the variance of the values between groups of respondents and compares it with the variance of the responses within the groups. If the between-group variance is significantly greater than the within-group variance as indicated by the *F*-ratio, the means are significantly different. The statistical significance between means in ANOVA is detected through the use of a follow-up test. The Scheffé test is one type of follow-up test. The test examines the differences between all possible pairs of sample means against a high and low confidence range. If the difference between a pair of means falls outside the confidence interval, then the means can be considered statistically different.

■ **Utilize perceptual mapping to present research findings.**

Perceptual mapping is used to develop maps that show perceptions of respondents visually. These maps are graphic representations that can be produced from the results of several multivariate techniques. The maps provide a visual representation of how companies, products, brands, or other objects are perceived relative to each other on key attributes such as quality of service, food taste, and food preparation.

Key Terms and Concepts

Analysis of variance (ANOVA) 499
Between-group variance 501
Chi-square analysis 488
Estimated standard deviation 487
Follow-up test 501
***F*-ratio** 501
***F*-test** 501
Independent samples 497
Level of significance 489
Mean 483
Measures of dispersion 486
Median 484
Mode 484
Perceptual mapping 504
Range 486
Related samples 497
Standard deviation 487
Total variance 501
***t*-test** 497
Variance 487
Within-group variance 501

Review Questions

1. Why are graphic approaches to reporting marketing research better than simply reporting numbers?
2. Explain the differences between the mean, the median, and the mode.
3. Why and how would you use Chi-square and *t*-tests in hypothesis testing?
4. Why and when would you want to use ANOVA in marketing research?
5. What will ANOVA tests not tell you, and how can you overcome this problem?

Discussion Questions

1. The measures of central tendency discussed in this chapter are designed to reveal information about the center of a distribution of values. Measures of dispersion provide information about the spread of all the values in a distribution around the center values. Assume you were conducting an opinion poll on voters' approval ratings of the job performance of the mayor of the city where you live. Do you think the mayor would be more interested in the central tendency or the dispersion measures associated with the responses to your poll? Why?
2. If you were interested in finding out whether or not young adults (21–34 years old) are more likely to buy products online than older adults (35 or more years old), how would you phrase your null hypothesis? What is the implicit alternative hypothesis accompanying your null hypothesis?
3. The level of significance (alpha) associated with testing a null hypothesis is also referred to as the probability of a Type I error. Alpha is the probability of rejecting the null hypothesis on the basis of your sample data when it is, in fact, true for the population you are interested in. Since alpha concerns the probability of making a mistake in your analysis, should you always try to set this value as small as possible? Why or why not?
4. Analysis of variance (ANOVA) allows you to test for the statistical difference between two or more means. Typically, there are more than two means tested. If the ANOVA results for a set of data reveal that the four means that were compared are significantly different from each other, how would you find out which individual means were statistically different from each other? What statistical techniques would you apply to answer this question?
5. **EXPERIENCE THE INTERNET.** Nike, Reebok, and Converse are strong competitors in the athletic shoe market. The three use different advertising and marketing strategies to appeal to their target markets. Use one of the search engines on the Internet to identify information on this market. Go to the Web sites for these three companies (www.Nike.com; www.Reebok.com; www.Converse.com). Gather background information on each, including its target market and market share. Design a questionnaire based on this information and survey a sample of students. Prepare a report on the

different perceptions of each of these three companies, their shoes, and related aspects. Present the report in class and defend your findings.

6. **SPSS EXERCISE.** Form a team of three to four students in your class. Select one or two local franchises to conduct a survey on, such as Subway or McDonald's. Design a brief survey (10–12 questions) including questions like ratings on quality of food, speed of service, knowledge of employees, attitudes of employees, and price, as well as several demographic variables such as age, address, how often individuals eat there, and day of week and time of day. Obtain permission from the franchises to interview their customers at a convenient time, usually when they are leaving. Assure the franchiser you will not bother customers and that you will provide the franchise with a valuable report on your findings. Develop frequency charts, pie charts, and similar graphic displays of findings, where appropriate. Use statistics to test hypotheses, such as "Perceptions of speed of service differ by time of day or day of week." Prepare a report and present it to your class; particularly point out where statistically significant differences exist and why.

7. **SPSS EXERCISE.** Using SPSS and the Santa Fe Grill database, provide frequencies, means, modes, and medians for the relevant variables on the questionnaire. The actual questionnaire is presented in Chapter 14. In addition, develop bar charts and pie charts where appropriate for the data you analyzed. Run an ANOVA using the lifestyle and restaurant perceptions variables to identify any group differences that may exist. Be prepared to present a report on your findings.

8. **SPSS EXERCISE.** Review the Marketing Research in Action case for this chapter. There were three restaurant competitors: Remington's, Outback, and Longhorn. Results for a one-way ANOVA of the restaurant image variables were provided. Now run post hoc ANOVA follow-up tests to see where the group differences are. Make recommendations for new marketing strategies for Remington's compared to the competition.

chapter 16

Data Analysis: Testing for Associations

Learning Objectives

After reading this chapter, you will be able to:

1. Understand and evaluate the types of relationships between variables.
2. Explain the concepts of association and covariation.
3. Understand the differences between Pearson correlation and Spearman correlation.
4. Explain the concept of statistical significance versus practical significance.
5. Know when and how to use regression analysis.

"By far the most important things to a statistician are the quality of the data, the dimensionality of the data, and the completeness of the data."

—RANDY HLAVAC,
President,
Marketing Synergy, Inc.

Data Mining Helps Rebuild Procter & Gamble as a Global Powerhouse

Procter & Gamble (P&G) is a global player in consumer household products, with 20 world-ranking brands such as Tide, Folgers, Febreze, Mr. Clean, and Pringles, to name a few. Three billion times a day, P&G products touch the lives of consumers around the world. Yet, several years ago the company saw its status in jeopardy. While many businesses, including P&G, pursue three overall marketing objectives—to get customers, to keep customers, and to grow customers—P&G realized it had to change its traditional marketing strategies and tactics in order to rebuild its global image and practices. The new approach was based on answering three key questions: Who are the targeted consumers for each brand? What is the company's desired brand equity or positioning? and How should it be achieved—what should be the mechanics of execution?

P&G, known as the leader of brand management, turned to information technology and customer relationship management to develop their new brand building strategy. Although the company's leaders understood that most CRM programs focus on helping to find and attract new customers, keep current customers happy (satisfied), and grow customers to maximize their lifetime value to P&G, they learned through internal surveys they needed to recommit P&G employees to consumers. For example, analysis of employees' attitudes regarding what P&G was doing "right" and "wrong" aided in reestablishing five fundamental focus points to serve as operating objectives: (1) respecting the consumer as the "boss" and delivering superior consumer value, (2) making clear strategic choices about where to compete and how to win, (3) being a leader in innovation and branding, (4) leveraging P&G's unique, global operating structure, and (5) executing with excellence as well as more rigorous financial and operating discipline.

P&G mines the information in its data warehouse to retool customer models for its global brand and distributor markets. One of the objectives of the brand models is to acquire new customers worldwide for its brands as well as cross selling the brands to current customers. Another objective is to use product innovation and acquisition to expand the type of products sold worldwide. Statistical models with high predictive capability were modified and validated for each of the brands' market segments. The models considered factors such as household purchasing power, length of residence, family size, age, gender, attitudes toward a brand, media habits, purchase frequencies, and so on. Today, the results suggest that P&G has made progress in its rebuilding efforts. Brand equity in 19 of its 20 major brands is growing, and 30 million times a day consumers are purchasing P&G brand products over competitors. Internally, employee confidence in P&G is growing—56 percent of all P&G employees believe P&G is moving in the right direction compared to only 26 percent a year ago. To learn more about P&G's turnaround go to www.pg.com.

Examining Relationships between Variables

Relationships between variables can be described in several ways—with the concepts of *presence, direction, strength of association,* and *type.* We will describe each of these concepts in turn.

The first issue is whether two or more variables are related at all. If a systematic relationship exists between two or more variables, then a relationship is present. To measure whether a relationship exists, we rely on the concept of statistical significance. If we test for statistical significance and find that it exists, then we say that a relationship is *present.* Stated another way, we say that knowledge about the behavior of one variable enables us to make a useful prediction about the behavior of another. For example, if we find a statistically significant relationship between perceptions of the quality of Santa Fe Grill food and overall satisfaction, we would say a relationship is present.

If a relationship is present between two variables, it is important to know the *direction,* which can be either positive or negative. Using the Santa Fe Grill example, we could say that a positive relationship exists if respondents who rate the quality of the food high are also very satisfied. Similarly, a negative relationship exists if respondents say the speed of service is slow (low rating) but they are still satisfied (high rating).

An understanding of the strength of association also is important. We generally categorize the *strength of association* as no relationship, weak relationship, moderate, or strong. If a consistent and systematic relationship is not present, then there is no relationship. A weak association means the variables may have something in common but not much. A moderate or strong association means there is a consistent and systematic relationship, and the relationship is much more evident when it is strong.

Linear relationship The strength and nature of the relationship between the independent and dependent variable remains the same over the range of both variables, and can be represented best by a straight line.

Curvilinear Relationship A relationship between two variables whereby the strength and/or direction of their relationship changes over the range of both variables.

A fourth concept that is important to understand is the *type* of relationship. If we say two variables are related, then we would pose this as a question: "What is the nature of the relationship?" How can the link between Y and X best be described? There are a number of different ways in which two variables can share a relationship. Variables Y and X can have a **linear relationship,** which means that the strength and nature of the relationship between them remain the same over the range of both variables, and can best be described using a straight line. Conversely, Y and X could have a **curvilinear relationship,** which would mean that the strength and/or direction of their relationship changes over the range of both variables (perhaps Y's relationship with X first gets stronger as X increases, but then gets weaker as the value of X continues to increase).

A linear relationship is much simpler to work with than a curvilinear relationship. That is, if we know the value of variable X, then we can apply the formula for a straight line ($Y = a + bX$) to determine the value of Y. But when two variables have a curvilinear relationship, the formula that best describes the linkage is more complex. Therefore, most marketing researchers work with relationships they believe are linear.

Marketers are often interested in describing the relationship between two variables they think make a difference in purchases of their product(s). There are four basic questions to ask about a possible relationship between two variables. First, "Is there a relationship between the two variables we are interested in?" If there is a relationship, then you are interested in knowing "How strong is that relationship? What is the direction of the relationship?" and "Is the relationship linear or nonlinear?" Once these questions have been answered, the researcher can interpret results, make conclusions, and recommend managerial actions based on the analysis.

Covariation and Variable Relationships

Covariation The amount of change in one variable that is consistently related to the change in another variable of interest.

Since we are interested in finding out whether two variables describing our customers are related, the concept of covariation is a very useful idea. **Covariation** is defined as the amount of change in one variable that is consistently related to a change in another variable of interest. For example, if we know that DVD purchases are related to age, then we want to know the extent to which younger persons purchase more DVDs. Another way of stating the concept of covariation is that it is the degree of association between two items (e.g., the attitude toward Starbucks coffee advertising is more favorable among heavy consumers of Starbucks coffee than it is for light consumers). If two variables are found to change together on a reliable or consistent basis, then we can use that information to make predictions that will improve decision making about advertising and marketing strategies.

Scatter diagram A graphic plot of the relative position of two variables using a horizontal and a vertical axis to represent the values of the respective variables.

One way of visually describing the covariation between two variables is with the use of a **scatter diagram.** A scatter diagram plots the relative position of two variables using horizontal and vertical axes to represent the variable values. Exhibits 16.1 through 16.4 show some examples of possible relationships between two variables that might show up on a scatter diagram. In Exhibit 16.1, the best way to describe the visual impression left by the dots representing the values of each variable is probably a circle. That is, there is no particular pattern to the collection of dots. Thus, if you take two or three sample values of variable *Y* from the scatter diagram and look at the values for *X*, there is no predictable pattern to the values for *X*. Knowing the values of *Y* or *X* would not tell you very much (maybe nothing at all) about the possible values of the other variable. Exhibit 16.1 suggests that there is no systematic relationship between *Y* and *X* and that there is very little or no covariation shared by the two variables. If we measured the amount of covariation shared by these two variables (something you will learn how to do in the next section), it would be very close to zero.

eXHIBIT 16.1 No Relationship between X and Y

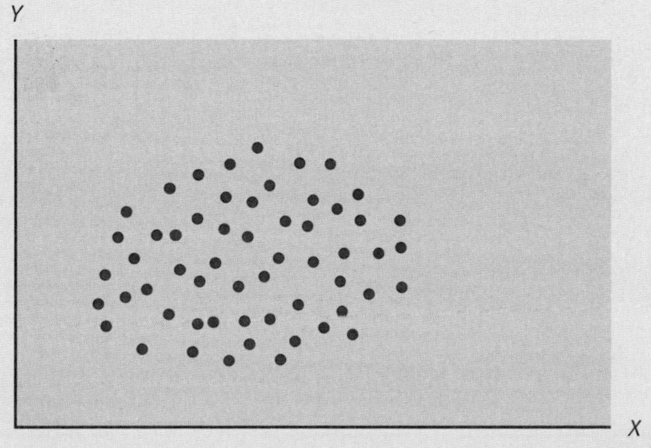

eXHIBIT 16.2 Positive Relationship between *X* and *Y*

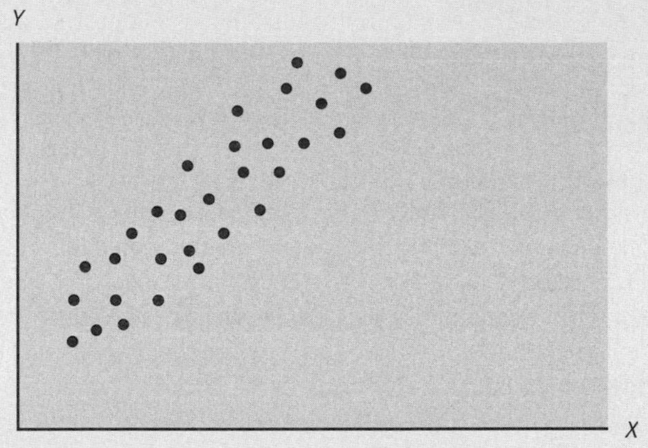

In Exhibit 16.2, the two variables present a very different picture from that of Exhibit 16.1. There is a distinct pattern to the dots. As the values of *Y* increase, so do the values of *X*. This pattern could be described as a straight line or an ellipse (a circle that has been stretched out from both sides). We could also describe this relationship as positive, because increases in the value of *Y* are associated with increases in the value of *X*. That is, if we know the relationship between *Y* and *X* is a linear, positive relationship, we would know that the values of *Y* and *X* change in the same direction. As the values of *Y* increase, so do the values of *X*. Similarly, if the values of *Y* decrease, the values of *X* should decrease as well. If we try to measure the amount of covariation shown by the values of *Y* and *X*, it would be relatively high. Thus, changes in the value of *Y* are systematically related to changes in the value of *X*.

Exhibit 16.3 shows the same type of distinct pattern between the values of *Y* and *X*, but the direction of the relationship is the opposite of Exhibit 16.2. There is a linear

eXHIBIT 16.3 Negative Relationship between *X* and *Y*

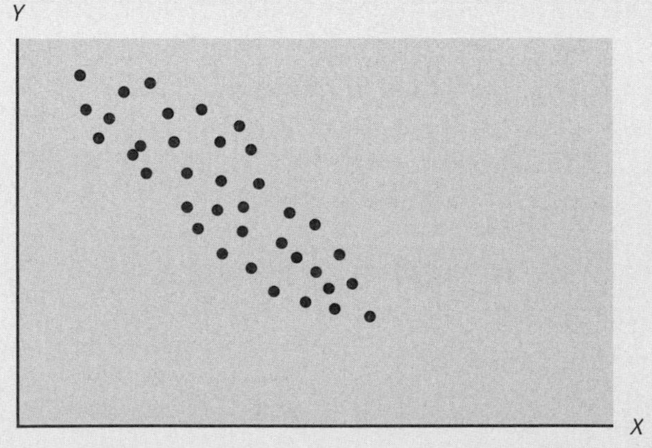

eXHIBIT 16.4 Curvilinear Relationship between X and Y

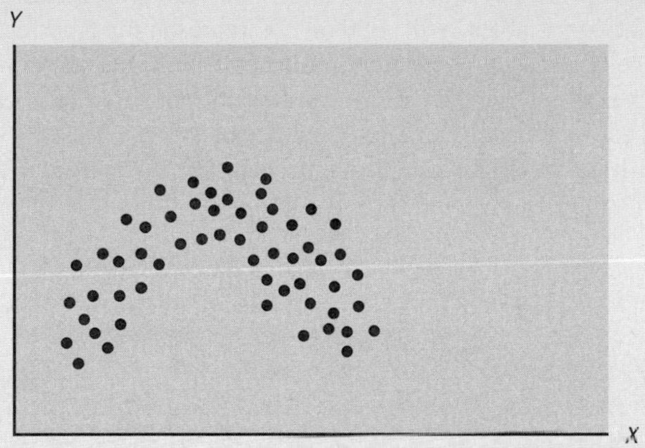

pattern, but now increases in the values of *Y* are associated with decreases in the values of *X*. This type of relationship is known as a negative relationship. The amount of covariation shared between the two variables is still high, because *Y* and *X* still change together, though in a direction opposite from that shown in Exhibit 16.2. The concept of covariation refers to the amount of shared movement, not the direction of the relationship between two variables.

Finally, Exhibit 16.4 shows a more complicated relationship between the values of *Y* and *X*. This pattern of dots can be described as curvilinear. That is, the relationship between the values of *Y* and the values of *X* is different for different values of the variables. Part of the relationship is positive (increases in the small values of *Y* are associated with increases in the small values of *X*), but then the relationship becomes negative (increases in the larger values of *Y* are now associated with decreases in the larger values of *X*).

This pattern of dots cannot be described as a linear relationship. Many of the statistics marketing researchers use to describe association assume the two variables have a linear relationship. These statistics do not perform well when used to describe a curvilinear relationship. In Exhibit 16.4, we can still say the relationship is strong, or that the covariation exhibited by the two variables is strong. But now we can't talk very easily about the direction (positive or negative) of the relationship, because the direction changes. To make matters more difficult, many statistical methods of describing relationships between variables cannot be applied to situations where you suspect the relationship is curvilinear.

Correlation Analysis

Scatter diagrams are a visual way to describe the relationship between two variables and the covariation they share. For example, a scatter diagram can tell us that as age increases the average consumption of Starbucks coffee increases too. But even though a picture is worth a thousand words, it is often more convenient to use a quantitative measure of the covariation between two items.

Pearson correlation coefficient A statistical measure of the strength of a linear relationship between two metric variables.

The **Pearson correlation coefficient** measures the degree of linear association between two variables. It varies between –1.00 and 1.00, with 0 representing absolutely no association between two variables, and –1.00 or 1.00 representing a perfect link between two variables. A large correlation coefficient indicates a higher level of association between two variables. The correlation coefficient can be either positive or negative, depending on the direction of the relationship between two variables.

The null hypothesis for the Pearson correlation states that there is no association between the two variables and the correlation coefficient is zero. For example, we may hypothesize there is no relationship between Starbucks coffee consumption and income levels. If you take measures of coffee consumption and income from a sample of the population and estimate the correlation coefficient for that sample, the basic question is "What is the probability that I would get a correlation coefficient of this size in my sample if the correlation coefficient in the population is actually zero?" That is, if you calculate a large correlation coefficient between the two variables in your sample, and your sample was properly selected from the population of interest, then the chances the population correlation coefficient is really zero are relatively small. Therefore, if the correlation coefficient is statistically significant, the null hypothesis is rejected, and you can conclude with some confidence that the two variables you are examining do share some association in the population. In short, Starbucks coffee consumption is related to income.

If you remember, earlier in the chapter we stated that the first question of interest was "Does a relationship between *Y* and *X* exist?" This question is equivalent to asking whether a correlation coefficient is statistically significant. If this is the case, then you can move on to the second and third questions: "If there is a relationship between *Y* and *X*, how strong is that relationship?" and "What is the best way to describe that relationship?"

The size of the correlation coefficient can be used to quantitatively describe the strength of the association between two variables. Many authors have suggested some rules of thumb for characterizing the strength of the association between two variables based on the size of the correlation coefficient.

As Exhibit 16.5 suggests, correlation coefficients between .81 and 1.00 are considered very strong. That is, covariance is shared between the two variables under study. At the other extreme, if the correlation coefficient is between .00 and .20, there is a good chance the null hypothesis won't be rejected (unless you are using a large sample). You should

eXHIBIT 16.5 Rules of Thumb about the Strength of Correlation Coefficients

Range of Coefficient	Description of Strength
±.81 to ±1.00	Very strong
±.61 to ±.80	Strong
±.41 to ±.60	Moderate
±.21 to ±.40	Weak
±.00 to ±.20	Weak to No Relationship

realize that these numbers are only suggestions and other ranges and descriptions of relationship strength are possible.

In addition to the size of the correlation coefficient, we also must consider its significance level. How do we do this? Most statistical software, including SPSS, shows you the significance level for a computed correlation coefficient. The SPSS software indicates significance as the probability the null hypothesis is true and in the output is identified as the "Sig." value. For example, if the null hypothesis is no association between Starbucks Coffee consumption and income, and the correlation coefficient is .71 with a statistical significance of .05, then there are only five chances out of 100 that there is not a relationship between the two variables. Thus, we reject the null hypothesis of no association.

Pearson Correlation Coefficient Assumptions

The Pearson correlation coefficient makes several assumptions about the nature of the data you are applying it to. First, we assume the two variables have been measured using interval- or ratio-scaled measures. If this is not the case, there are other types of correlation coefficients that can be computed which match the type of data on hand. A second assumption is the relationship we are trying to measure is linear. That is, a straight line describes the relationship between the two variables of interest.

Use of the Pearson correlation coefficient also assumes the variables you want to analyze come from a normally distributed population. The assumption of normal distributions for the variables under study is a common requirement for many statistical techniques. But determining whether it holds for the sample data you are working with is sometimes difficult and often taken for granted.

SPSS Application—Pearson Correlation

The Santa Fe Grill database can help us better understand the Pearson correlation. Assume the owners anticipate the relationship between satisfaction and likelihood to recommend the restaurant would be significant and positive. Looking at the database variables you note that information was collected on Likely to Recommend (variable X24) and Satisfaction (variable X22). With SPSS it is easy to compute a Pearson correlation between these two variables and test this assumption.

Before testing the assumption that satisfaction is related to likelihood of recommending, one consideration is "Should this assumption be tested for both restaurants combined or for each restaurant separately?" Logic suggests that examining the restaurants separately is the best approach since the Santa Fe owners would like to test this relationship for their restaurant compared to Jose's. To split the sample into two groups to compare the restaurants, you can use the options under the Data pull-down menu. For example, to compare the customers of the Santa Fe Grill and the customers of Jose's Southwestern Café, the click-through sequence is: DATA → SPLIT FILE → Click on Compare Groups. Now highlight the fourth screening question (Favorite Mexican Restaurant) and move it into the "Groups Based on:" window, and then click OK. Your results will now be computed for each restaurant separately.

Now we can test the assumption that satisfaction is related to likelihood of recommending. To do so, the SPSS click-through sequence is ANALYZE → CORRELATE → BIVARIATE, which leads to a dialog box where you select the variables. Transfer variables X22 and X24 into the Variables box. Note that we will use all three default options shown

eXHIBIT 16.6 SPSS Pearson Correlation Example

Output11 [Document11] - SPSS Viewer

File Edit View Data Transform Insert Format Analyze Graphs Utilities Add-ons Window Help

Correlations

Descriptive Statistics

Favorite Mexican		Mean	Std. Deviation	N
Jose's Southwestern Cafe	X22 -- Satisfaction	5.31	1.141	152
	X24 -- Likely to Recommend	4.07	1.474	152
Santa Fe Grill	X22 -- Satisfaction	4.54	1.002	253
	X24 -- Likely to Recommend	3.61	.960	253

Correlations

Favorite Mexican Restaurant			X22 -- Satisfaction	X24 -- Likely to Recommend
Jose's Southwestern Cafe	X22 -- Satisfaction	Pearson Correlation	1	.837**
		Sig. (2-tailed)		.000
		N	152	152
	X24 -- Likely to Recommend	Pearson Correlation	.837**	1
		Sig. (2-tailed)	.000	
		N	152	152
Santa Fe Grill	X22 -- Satisfaction	Pearson Correlation	1	.776**
		Sig. (2-tailed)		.000
		N	253	253
	X24 -- Likely to Recommend	Pearson Correlation	.776**	1
		Sig. (2-tailed)	.000	
		N	253	253

**. Correlation is significant at the 0.01 level (2-tailed).

below: Pearson correlation, two-tailed test of significance, and flag significant correlations. Next go to the Options box, and after it opens click on Means and Standard Deviations and then continue. Finally, when you click on OK at the top right of the dialog box it will execute the Pearson correlation.

The Pearson correlation results are shown in Exhibit 16.6. As you can see in the Correlations table, the correlation between variable X24—Likely to Recommend and X22—Satisfaction is .837 for Jose's and .776 for the Santa Fe Grill, and the statistical significance of both correlations is .000. Thus, we have confirmed our hypothesis that satisfaction is positively related to likely to recommend. When we examine the means of the two variables, we see that satisfaction (4.54 = Santa Fe Grill) is somewhat higher than likely to recommend (3.61 = Santa Fe Grill) but the pattern of responses to these questions is very similar. That is, there is covariation between the responses to the two variables. What we also know is there is room for improvement in both measures, for both restaurants, because they are measured on a 7-point scale and except for satisfaction with Jose's the means are close to the mid-point.

Substantive Significance of the Correlation Coefficient

When the correlation coefficient is strong and significant, you can be confident the two variables are associated in a linear fashion. In our Santa Fe Grill example, we can be reasonably confident that likelihood to recommend is in fact related to satisfaction. When the correlation coefficient is weak, two possibilities must be considered: (1) there is no consistent, systematic relationship between the two variables; or (2) the association exists, but it is not linear, and other types of relationships must be investigated further.

Coefficient of determination (r^2) A number measuring the proportion of variation in one variable accounted for by another. The r^2 measure can be thought of as a percentage and varies from 0.0 to 1.00.

When you square the correlation coefficient, you arrive at the **coefficient of determination,** or r^2. This number ranges from .00 to 1.0 and shows the proportion of variation explained or accounted for in one variable by another. In our Santa Fe Grill example, the correlation coefficient was .776. Thus, the $r^2 = .602$, meaning that approximately 60.2 percent of the variation in likelihood to recommend the Santa Fe Grill is associated with the customer's satisfaction. If the size of the coefficient of determination is large (closer to 1), then the linear relationship between the two variables being examined is stronger. In our example, we have accounted for almost one-half of the variation in likelihood to recommend by relating it to satisfaction.

There is a difference between statistical significance and substantive significance. Thus, you need to assess the substantive significance (that is, do the numbers you calculate provide useful information for management?). Since the statistical significance calculation for correlation coefficients depends partly on sample size, it is possible to find statistically significant correlation coefficients that are too small to be of much practical use. This is possible because large samples result in more confidence that a relationship exists, even if it is weak. For example, if we had correlated satisfaction with the likelihood of recommending the Santa Fe Grill to others, and the correlation coefficient was .20 (significant at the .05 level), the coefficient of determination would be .04. Can we conclude that the results are meaningful? It is unlikely they are since the amount of shared variance is only 4 percent. Remember you must always look at both types of significance (statistical and substantive) before you develop conclusions.

Influence of Measurement Scales on Correlation Analysis

A common occurrence in marketing research studies is that the questions marketing researchers are most interested in can be measured only with ordinal or nominal scales. For example, if we are interested in learning more about Starbucks coffee consumption, we might consider consumption patterns of female versus male coffee drinkers. In these cases, applying the Pearson correlation coefficient to the data and assuming the gender measures have interval or ratio scale properties (when they do not) will produce misleading or overstated results.

Spearman rank order correlation coefficient A statistical measure of the linear association between two variables where both have been measured using ordinal (rank order) scales.

What options are available to the researcher when ordinal scales are used to collect data, or when the data simply cannot be measured with an interval scale or better? The **Spearman rank order correlation coefficient** is the recommended statistic to use when two variables have been measured using ordinal scales. If either one of the variables is represented by rank order data, the best approach is to use the Spearman rank order correlation coefficient, rather than the Pearson product moment correlation.

In addition to the Spearman rank order correlation coefficient, there are other correlation coefficients that may be used to take into consideration the scale properties inherent in the data. For example, if you think the gender of your customers makes a difference in the amount of your product they purchase, it would be possible to correlate customer gender (male/female) with product purchases (dollars) to answer your question. To do so, you would use a biserial correlation coefficient to make this calculation. You must use the appropriate statistic to match the characteristics of your data, and there are formulas available to calculate almost any type of correlation coefficient to match the situation.

SPSS Application—Spearman Rank Order Correlation

The Santa Fe Grill customer survey collected data that ranked four restaurant selection factors. These data are represented by variables X26 to X29. Management is interested in knowing whether "Food Quality" is a significantly more important selection factor than is "Service." Since these are ordinal (ranking) data, the Pearson correlation is not appropriate. The Spearman correlation is the appropriate coefficient to calculate. Variables X27—Food Quality and X29—Service are the variables we will use.

To conduct this analysis, we will use the database for the two restaurants combined. This is based on the logic that the owners are interested in knowing the results for dining customers in general and not for the two restaurants' customers separately. The SPSS click-through sequence is ANALYZE → CORRELATE → BIVARIATE, which leads to a dialog box where you select the variables. Transfer variables X27 and X29 into the Variables box. You will note the Pearson correlation is the default along with the two-tailed test of significance, and flag significant correlations. "Unclick" the Pearson correlation and click on Spearman. Then click on OK at the top right of the dialog box to execute the program.

The SPSS results for the Spearman correlation are shown in Exhibit 16.7. As you can see in the Correlations table, the correlation between variable X27—Food Quality and X29—Service is –.130, and the significance value is .009. Thus, we have confirmed that there is a statistically significant relationship between the two restaurant selection factors, although the correlation is very small. The negative correlation indicates that a customer who ranks food quality high in importance tends to rank service significantly lower. Thus, these customers select restaurants to eat in more on the basis of food quality than service.

SPSS Application—Calculating Median Rankings

To better understand the Spearman correlation findings, we need to calculate the median rankings of the four selection factors. To do this, the SPSS click-through sequence is

eXHIBIT 16.7 SPSS Spearman Rank Order Correlation

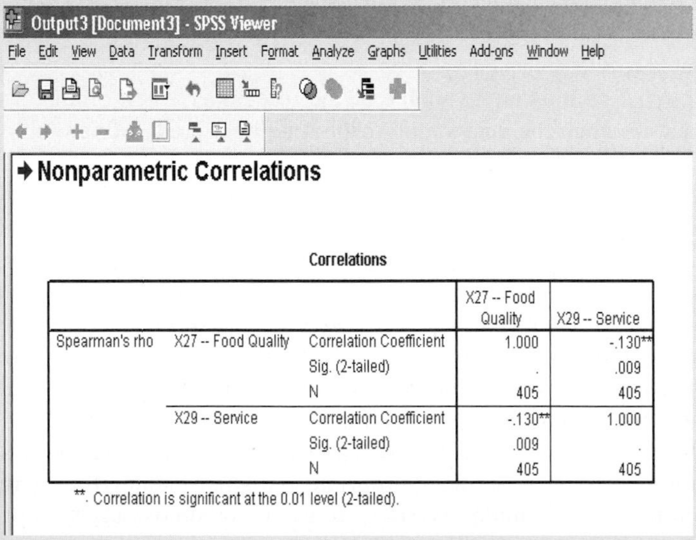

Nonparametric Correlations

Correlations

			X27 -- Food Quality	X29 -- Service
Spearman's rho	X27 -- Food Quality	Correlation Coefficient	1.000	-.130**
		Sig. (2-tailed)	.	.009
		N	405	405
	X29 -- Service	Correlation Coefficient	-.130**	1.000
		Sig. (2-tailed)	.009	.
		N	405	405

**. Correlation is significant at the 0.01 level (2-tailed).

EXHIBIT 16.8 SPSS Median Example for Restaurant Selection Factors

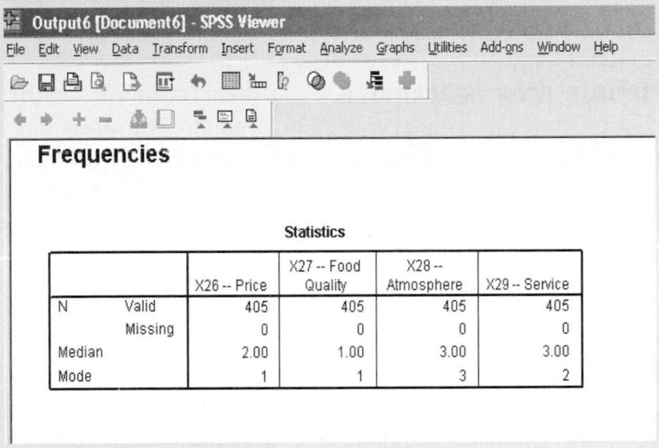

		X26 -- Price	X27 -- Food Quality	X28 -- Atmosphere	X29 -- Service
N	Valid	405	405	405	405
	Missing	0	0	0	0
Median		2.00	1.00	3.00	3.00
Mode		1	1	3	2

ANALYZE → DESCRIPTIVE STATISTICS → FREQUENCIES. Click on variables X26–X29 to highlight them and then on the arrow box for the Variables box to use them in your analysis. We use all four selection factors because this will enable us to examine the overall relative rankings of all the restaurant selection factors. Next, open the Statistics box and click on median and mode, and then Continue. For the Charts and Format options we will use the defaults, so click on OK to execute the program.

The SPSS results for median rankings are shown in the Statistics table in Exhibit 16.8. Recall that medians are descriptive data and can only be used to describe respondents. The variable with the lowest median is ranked the highest and is the most important, and the variable with the highest median is the least important, since the four selection factors were ranked from 1 to 4, with 1 = most important, and 4 = least important. Food quality is ranked as the most important (median = 1.0) while atmosphere and service are the least important. The modal response for atmosphere is 3 and for service it is 2. Thus, since the median is the same for the two variables we can use the mode to break the median tie, and conclude that atmosphere is ranked as less important than service. Moreover, the previously calculated Spearman rank correlation compared food quality (median = 1) with service (median = 3.00), so food quality is significantly more important in restaurant selection than service.

Regression Analysis

Correlation can determine if a relationship exists between two variables. The correlation coefficient also tells you the overall strength of the association and the direction of the relationship between the variables. Sometimes, however, managers still need to know how to describe the relationship between variables in greater detail and *regression analysis* is one method.

A marketing manager may want to predict future sales or how a price increase will affect the profits or market share of the company. There are a number of ways to make such predictions: (1) extrapolation from past behavior of the variable; (2) simple guesses; or

(3) use of a regression equation that compares information about related variables to assist in the prediction. Extrapolation and guesses (educated or otherwise) usually assume that past conditions and behaviors will continue into the future. They do not examine the influences behind the behavior of interest. Consequently, when sales levels, profits, or other variables of interest to a manager differ from those in the past, extrapolation and guessing do not explain why.

Bivariate regression analysis A statistical technique that analyzes the linear relationship between two variables by estimating coefficients for an equation for a straight line. One variable is designated as a dependent variable and the other is called an independent or predictor variable.

Bivariate regression analysis is a statistical technique that uses information about the relationship between an independent or predictor variable and a dependent variable to make predictions. Values of the independent variable are selected, and the behavior of the dependent variable is observed using the formula for a straight line. For example, if you wanted to find the current level of your company's sales volume, you would apply the following straight-line formula:

$$\text{Sales volume } (Y) = \$0 + (\text{Price per unit} = b) * (\text{Number of units sold} = X)$$

You would not expect any sales volume if nothing were sold. Thus, the constant or x-intercept is \$0. Price per unit (b) determines the amount that sales volume (Y) increases with each unit sold (X). In this example, the relationship between sales volume and number of units sold is linear (it is consistent over the values of both Y and X).

Once a regression equation has been developed to predict values of Y, we want to find out how good that prediction is. A place to begin is to compare the values predicted by our regression model with the actual values we collected in our sample. By comparing this actual value Y_i with our predicted value (Y), we can tell how well our model predicts the actual value of our dependent variable. In fact, comparing actual values from a sample with predicted values from a regression equation is a commonly used method of determining the accuracy of a regression equation.

A couple of points should be made about the assumptions behind regression analysis. First, just like correlation analysis, regression analysis assumes a linear relationship is a good description of the relationship between two variables. If the scatter diagram showing the positions of the values of both variables looks like the scatter plots in Exhibits 16.2 or 16.3, this assumption is a good one. If the plot looks like Exhibits 16.1 or 16.4, however, then regression analysis isn't a good choice.

Second, even though the common terminology of regression analysis uses the labels *dependent* and *independent* for the variables, those names don't mean that we can say one variable *causes* the behavior of the other. Regression analysis uses knowledge about the level and type of association between two variables to make predictions. Statements about the ability of one variable to cause changes in another must be based on conceptual logic or information other than just statistical techniques.

Finally, the use of a simple regression model assumes (1) the variables of interest are measured on interval or ratio scales (except in the case of dummy variables, which we discuss later); (2) the variables come from a bivariate normal population (the same assumption made in correlation analysis); and (3) the error terms associated with making predictions are normally and independently distributed.

Fundamentals of Regression Analysis

A fundamental basis of regression analysis is the assumption of a straight line relationship between the independent and dependent variables. This relationship is illustrated in Exhibit 16.9. The general formula for a straight line is:

$$Y = a + bX + e_i$$

eXHIBIT 16.9 The Straight Line Relationship in Regression

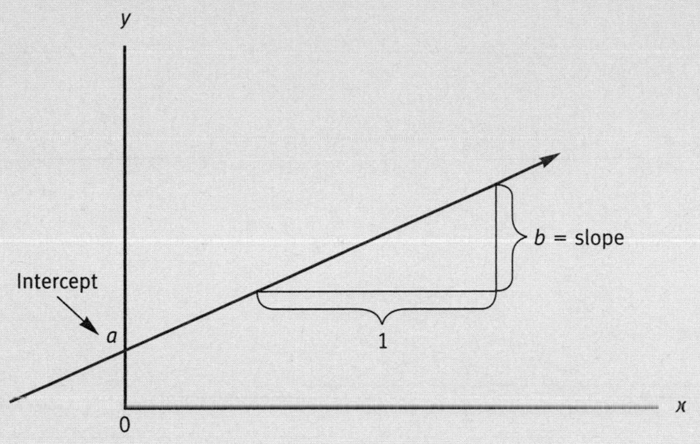

where

Y = the dependent variable

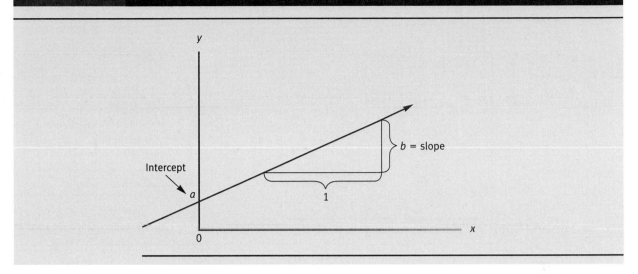

a = the intercept (point where the straight line intersects the y-axis when $x = 0$)

b = the slope (the change in y for every 1-unit change in x)

X = the independent variable used to predict y

e_i = the error for the prediction

In regression analysis, we examine the relationship between the independent variable X and the dependent variable Y. To do so, we use the known values of X and Y and the computed values of a and b. The calculations are based on the least squares procedure. The **least squares procedure** determines the best-fitting line by minimizing the vertical distances of all the points from the line, as shown in Exhibit 16.10. The best-fitting line is the regression line. Any point that does not fall on the line is the result of **unexplained variance,** or the variance in Y that is not explained by X. This unexplained variance is called *error* and is represented by the vertical distance between the regression straight line and the points not on the line. The distances of all the points not on the line are squared and added together to determine the **sum of the squared errors,** which is a measure of the total error in the regression.

Least squares procedure Determines the best-fitting line by minimizing the vertical distances of all the points from the line.

Unexplained variance The variance in Y that is not explained by X, referred to as error variance.

Sum of the squared errors is a measure of the total error in the regression.

After we compute the values of a and b, we must test their statistical significance. The calculated a (intercept) and b (slope) are sample estimates of the true population parameters α (alpha) and β (beta). The t-test is used to determine whether the computed intercept and slope are significantly different from zero. In the SPSS regression examples discussed later, the significance of these tests is reported in the Sig. column for each of these coefficients. The a is referred to as a "Constant" and the b is associated with each independent variable.

In the case of bivariate regression analysis, we are looking at one independent variable and one dependent variable. Managers frequently want to look at the combined

EXHIBIT 16.10 Fitting the Regression Line Using the "Least Squares" Procedure

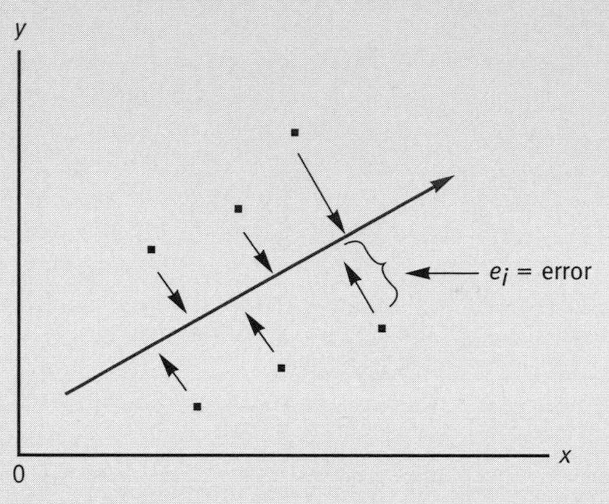

influence of several independent variables on one dependent variable. For example, are DVD purchases related only to age, or are they also related to income, ethnicity, gender, geographic location, education level, and so on? Similarly, referring to the Santa Fe Grill database, we might ask whether customer satisfaction is related only to perceptions of the restaurant's food taste (X18), or is satisfaction also related to perceptions of friendly employees (X12), reasonable prices (X16), and speed of service (X21)? Multiple regression is the appropriate technique to measure these relationships. We discuss bivariate or simple regression analysis before moving on to multiple regression analysis.

Developing and Estimating the Regression Coefficients

The regression equation examining the relationship between two variables is based on the equation for a straight line. The slope coefficient *b* tells us how much we can expect *Y* to change, given a 1-unit change in *X*. Once this equation is developed from sample data, we can use it to make predictions about *Y*, given different values of *X*.

Regression uses an estimation procedure called ordinary least squares (OLS) that guarantees the line it estimates will be the best-fitting line. We said earlier that the best prediction would be one in which the difference between the actual value of *Y* and the predicted value of *Y* was the smallest. **Ordinary least squares** is a statistical procedure that results in equation parameters (*a* and *b*) that produce predictions with the lowest sum of squared differences between actual and predicted values.

Ordinary least squares A statistical procedure that estimates regression equation coefficients that produce the lowest sum of squared differences between the actual and predicted values of the dependent variable.

Error in Regression

The differences between actual and predicted values of *Y* are represented by e_i (the error term of the regression equation). If we square these errors for each observation (the difference between actual values of *Y* and predicted values of *Y*) and add them up, the total would represent an aggregate or overall measure of the accuracy of the regression equation.

eXHIBIT 16.11 Random Pattern of Residuals

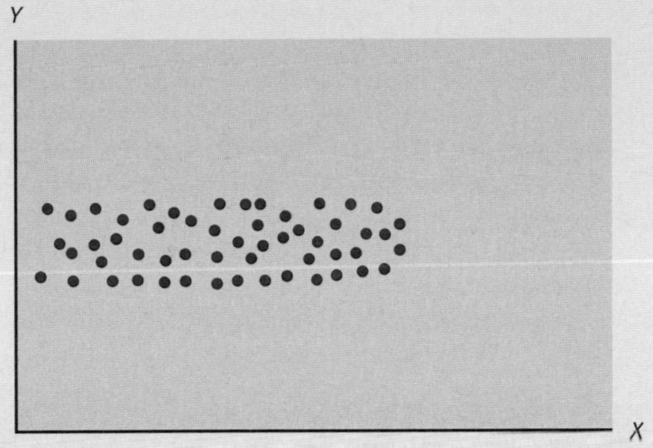

Regression equations calculated using ordinary least squares will always give the lowest squared error totals, and this is why both bivariate and multiple regression analysis are sometimes referred to as OLS regression.

Besides enabling the researcher to evaluate the quality of the regression equation prediction, the error terms also are used to diagnose problems that arise when the regression analysis assumptions are not met. The pattern of errors produced by comparing actual Y values with predicted Y values can tell you whether the errors are normally distributed and/or have equal variances across the range of X values. Exhibits 16.11, 16.12, and 16.13 show several possible patterns of residuals (another term for the error between actual and predicted Y values).

eXHIBIT 16.12 Increasing Pattern of Residuals

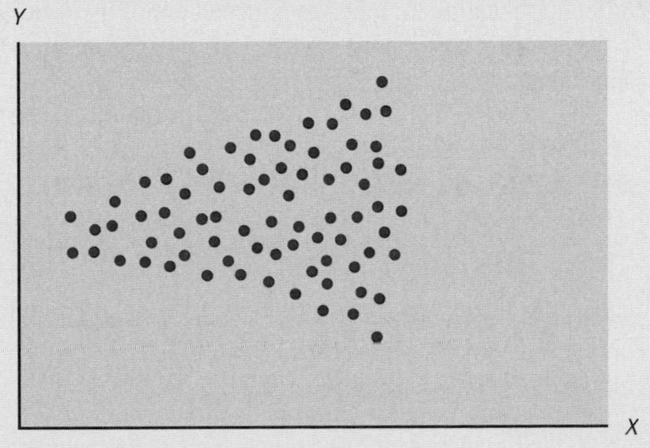

eXHIBIT 16.13 Nonlinear Pattern of Residuals

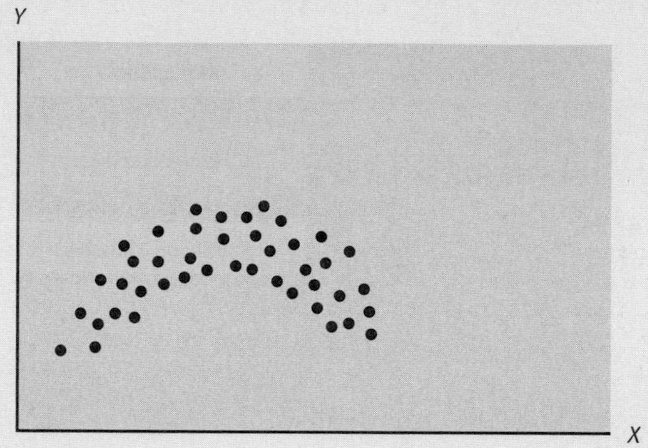

In Exhibit 16.12, there is no discernible pattern to the error terms when you plot the predicted values against the residuals. In Exhibit 16.13, there is an apparent pattern. The predictions made for small values of *Y* are more precise (spread is narrower) than the predictions made for large values of *Y* (spread is wider). As a result, the regression equation is more accurate for some values of the independent variable *X* than for others. There are transformation techniques that can be applied to the data, which may reduce this problem.[1] These techniques are beyond the scope of this text.

Exhibit 16.13 portrays a pattern to the error terms that suggests a nonlinear relationship between *Y* and *X*. In this case, the researcher's initial assumption that a straight line would be the best way to describe the potential relationship may need to be changed. The best approach may be a nonlinear relationship–based technique.

Examination of the error terms and the pattern obtained by comparing the predicted values of *Y* against the residuals can tell us whether our initial assumptions about the appropriateness of using regression analysis to examine variable relationships are correct. This type of evidence also can suggest other types of analysis given the characteristics of the data. While other statistical techniques may occasionally be more appropriate, regression analysis is widely used, very robust, and often an appropriate statistical technique for analysis of metric data.

SPSS Application—Bivariate Regression

Suppose the owners of the Santa Fe Grill want to know if more favorable perceptions of their prices are associated with higher customer satisfaction. The obvious answer would be "of course they would." But how much improvement would be expected in customer satisfaction if the owners improved the perceptions of prices? Moreover, does the relationship between prices and satisfaction differ between the Santa Fe Grill and Jose's Southwestern Café? Bivariate regression provides answers to these questions.

In the Santa Fe Grill database X22 is a measure of customer satisfaction, with 1 = Not Satisfied At All and 7 = Highly Satisfied. Variable X16 is a measure of whether the respondents perceive the restaurants' prices as reasonable (1 = Strongly Disagree, 7 = Strongly Agree). The null hypothesis is there is no relationship between X22—Satisfaction and X16—Reasonable Prices. The alternative hypothesis is that X22 and X16 are significantly related. To complete this analysis, we need to split the sample and analyze customers of the Santa Fe Grill and Jose's separately, as explained before.

After you split the sample, the SPSS click-through sequence is ANALYZE → REGRESSION → LINEAR. Click on X22—Satisfaction and move it to the Dependent Variable box. Click on X16—Reasonable Prices and move it to the Independent Variables box. We use the defaults for the other options so click OK to run the bivariate regression.

Exhibit 16.14 contains the results of the bivariate regression analysis. The table labeled Model Summary has three types of "*R*s" in it. The *R* on the far left is the correlation coefficient (.157 for Jose's; .479 for Santa Fe Grill). The R-square for Jose's is very small (.025)—you get it by squaring the correlation coefficient (.157) for this regression model. The R-square for the Santa Fe Grill is moderately strong .230—you get it by squaring the correlation coefficient (.479) for this regression model. The R-square shows the percentage of variation in one variable that is accounted for by another variable. In this case,

eXHIBIT 16.14 SPSS Results for Bivariate Regression

Model Summary

Favorite Mexican Restaurant	Model	R	R Square	Adjusted R Square	Std. Error of the Estimate
Jose's Southwestern Cafe	1	.157[a]	.025	.018	1.130
Santa Fe Grill	1	.479[a]	.230	.227	.881

a. Predictors: (Constant), X16 -- Reasonable Prices

ANOVA[b]

Favorite Mexican Restaurant	Model		Sum of Squares	df	Mean Square	F	Sig.
Jose's Southwestern Cafe	1	Regression	4.820	1	4.820	3.772	.054[a]
		Residual	191.647	150	1.278		
		Total	196.467	151			
Santa Fe Grill	1	Regression	58.127	1	58.127	74.939	.000[a]
		Residual	194.688	251	.776		
		Total	252.814	252			

a. Predictors: (Constant), X16 -- Reasonable Prices

b. Dependent Variable: X22 -- Satisfaction

Coefficients[a]

Favorite Mexican Restaurant	Model		Unstandardized Coefficients B	Unstandardized Coefficients Std. Error	Standardized Coefficients Beta	t	Sig.
Jose's Southwestern Cafe	1	(Constant)	4.497	.428		10.502	.000
		X16 -- Reasonable Prices	.197	.102	.157	1.942	.054
Santa Fe Grill	1	(Constant)	2.991	.188		15.951	.000
		X16 -- Reasonable Prices	.347	.040	.479	8.657	.000

a. Dependent Variable: X22 -- Satisfaction

customer perceptions of the Santa Fe Grill's prices accounts for 23.0 percent of the total variation in customer satisfaction with the restaurant. We also look at the Std. Error of the Estimate—a measure of the accuracy of the predictions of the regression equation. The smaller the standard error of the estimate, the better the fit of the regression line and therefore the better the predictive power of the regression.

The ANOVA table shows the *F*-ratio for the regression models and the associated statistical significance. The *F*-ratio is calculated the same way for regression analysis as it was for the ANOVA techniques described in Chapter 15. The variance in X22—Customer Satisfaction that is associated with X16—Reasonable Prices is referred to as explained variance. The remainder of the total variance in X22 that is not associated with X16 is referred to as unexplained variance. The ***F*-ratio** compares the amount of explained variance to the unexplained variance. The larger the *F*-ratio, the more variance in the dependent variable that is associated with the independent variable. In our example, the *F*-ratio for the Santa Fe Grill is 58.127. The statistical significance is .000—the "Sig." value on the SPSS output—so we can reject the null hypothesis that no relationship exists between the two variables for the Santa Fe Grill. In contrast, there is not a statistically significant relationship (.054) for Jose's, although it is very close. Even if it were significant, the correlation for the two variables for Jose's is so small that the relationship is not meaningful.

F-ratio Compares the amount of explained variance to the unexplained variance. The larger the *F*-ratio, the more variance in the dependent variable that is associated with the independent variable.

The Coefficients table shows the regression coefficient for X16 (reasonable prices). The column labeled Unstandardized Coefficients indicates the Santa Fe Grill unstandardized regression coefficient for X16 is .347. The column labeled Sig. shows the statistical significance of the regression coefficient for X16, as measured by the *t*-test. The *t*-test examines the question of whether the regression coefficient is different enough from zero to be statistically significant. The *t*-statistic is calculated by dividing the regression coefficient by its standard error (labeled Std. Error in the Coefficients table). If you divide .347 by .040, you will get a *t*-value of 8.657, which is significant at the .000 level.

The Coefficients table also shows the result for the Constant component in the regression equation. This item is a term in the equation for a straight line we discussed earlier. It is the *X*-intercept, or the value of *Y* when *X* is 0. If the independent variable takes on a value of 0, the dependent measure (X22) would have a value of 2.991. Considering only the Santa Fe Grill results, and combining the results of the Coefficients table into a regression equation, we have:

$$\text{Predicted value of X22} = 2.991 + .347 * (\text{value of X16}) + .881\ (\text{standard error of the estimate})$$

For the Santa Fe Grill, the relationship between customer satisfaction and reasonable prices is positive and moderately strong. The regression coefficient for X16 is interpreted as "For every unit that X16 (the rating of reasonable prices) increases, X22 (satisfaction) will increase by .347 units." Recall the Santa Fe Grill owners asked: "If the prices in our restaurant are perceived as being reasonable, will this be associated with improved customer satisfaction?" The answer is yes, because the model was significant at the .000 level. But how closely are they related? For every unit increase in X16, X22 goes up .347 units.

One additional note must be mentioned. The Coefficients table contained a column labeled Standardized Beta Coefficients. This number is the same in a bivariate regression as the Correlation Coefficient (similarly, with only one independent variable a squared standardized beta coefficient is the same as the coefficient of determination). However, as you will see later in this chapter, when there are several independent variables as in multiple regression, the standardized coefficients represent the relative contribution of each of the several independent variables.

Significance

Once the statistical significance of the regression coefficients is determined, we have answered the first question about our relationship: "Is there a relationship between our dependent and independent variables?" In this case, the answer is yes. But recall our discussion of statistical versus substantive significance. The logic of that discussion also applies when we evaluate whether regression coefficients are meaningful. A second question to ask is: "How strong is that relationship?" The output of regression analysis includes the coefficient of determination, or r^2, which describes the amount of variation in the dependent variable associated with the variation in the independent variable. The regression r^2 also tells you what percentage of the total variation in your dependent variable you can explain by using the independent variable. The r^2 measure varies between .00 and 1.00, and is calculated by dividing the amount of variation you have been able to explain with your regression equation by the total variation in the dependent variable. In the previous Santa Fe Grill example that examined the relationship between reasonable prices and satisfaction, the r^2 was .23. That means approximately 23.0 percent of the variation in customer satisfaction is associated with the variation in respondents' perceptions of the reasonableness of prices. Remember, we cannot say that perceptions about the reasonableness of prices cause changes in satisfaction, only that changes in perceived prices tend to be reliably associated with changes in satisfaction.

When examining the substantive significance of a regression equation, you should look at the size of the r^2 for the regression equation and the size of the regression coefficient. The regression coefficient may be statistically significant, but still relatively small, meaning that your dependent measure won't change very much for a given unit change in the independent measure. In our Santa Fe Grill example, the unstandardized regression coefficient was .347, which is a moderately strong relationship. When regression coefficients are significant but small, we say a relationship is present in our population, but that it is weak. In this case, the Santa Fe Grill owners have confirmed a relationship, but they still need to consider additional independent variables that will help them to better understand and predict customer satisfaction.

Multiple Regression Analysis

Multiple regression analysis A statistical technique that analyzes the linear relationship between a dependent variable and multiple independent variables by estimating coefficients for the equation for a straight line.

In most problems faced by managers, there are several independent variables that need to be examined for their influence on a dependent variable. **Multiple regression analysis** is the appropriate technique to use for these situations. The technique is an extension of bivariate regression. Multiple independent variables are entered into the regression equation, and for each variable a separate regression coefficient is calculated that describes its relationship with the dependent variable. The coefficients enable the marketing researcher to examine the relative influence of each independent variable on the dependent variable. For example, the Santa Fe Grill owners want to examine not only reasonable prices, but also perceptions of employees, atmosphere, service, and so forth. This gives them a more accurate picture of what to focus on in developing marketing strategies.

The relationship between each independent variable and the dependent measure is still linear. Now, however, with the addition of multiple independent variables we have to think of multiple independent dimensions instead of just a single one. The easiest way to analyze the relationships is to examine the regression coefficients for each independent variable, which represent the average amount of change expected in Y given a unit change in the value of the independent variable you are examining. For example, assume the dependent variable in a multiple regression is number of cups of Starbucks coffee consumed by students per day during final exams compared to other times. The two independent variables are number of hours studied per day during finals and number of exams on a particular day. Students are likely to study more hours on exam days and with more exams per day study longer hours, so they also are likely to drink more cups of coffee. We therefore would expect the regression coefficients for both independent variables to be large enough to suggest a relationship because both are logically related to the number of cups of coffee consumed.

With the addition of more than one independent variable, we have some new issues to consider. One is the possibility that each independent variable is measured using a different scale. For example, let's assume a group of students was asked by the local Canon copier distributor to predict the distributor's annual sales revenue. To predict the dependent variable, sales revenue, we use size of sales force (X1), amount of advertising budget (X2), and customer attitude toward the distributor's products (X3). Each of these independent variables is likely to be measured using a different scale, that is, different units. The size of the sales force would be measured by the number of salespeople, the amount of the advertising budget would be in dollars, and the customer attitude might be measured on a five-point scale from "Very poor" to "Excellent." When several independent variables are measured with different scales, it is not possible to make relative comparisons between regression coefficients to see which independent variable has the most influence on the dependent variable.

Standardized regression coefficient Referred to as a beta, it shows the change in the dependent variable for each unit change in an independent variable.

Beta coefficient An estimated regression coefficient that has been recalculated to have a mean of 0 and a standard deviation of 1. Such a change enables independent variables with different units of measurement to be directly compared on their association with the dependent variable.

To solve this problem, we calculate the **standardized regression coefficient.** It is called a **beta coefficient,** and it shows the change in the dependent variable for each unit change in the independent variable. Standardization is a method of removing the units of measure from each variable and placing all the predictors on the same scale. After standardization, regression coefficients have a mean of 0 and a standard deviation of 1. Standardization removes the effects of using different scales of measurement (for example, years of age and annual income are measured on different scales). Beta coefficients will range from .00 to 1.00, and can be either positive or negative. A *positive beta* means as the size of an independent variable increases, then the size of the dependent variable increases. A *negative beta* means as the size of the independent variable increases, then the size of the dependent variable gets smaller. Use of the beta coefficient allows direct comparisons between several independent variables to determine the relative influence of each independent variable on the dependent variable. This is because the values of beta coefficients are partial in that they represent the effect of one independent variable controlling for all the other independent variables.

Statistical Significance

After the regression coefficients have been estimated, you must examine the statistical significance of each coefficient. This is done in the same manner as with bivariate regression. Each regression coefficient is divided by its standard error to produce a *t*-statistic, which is compared against the critical value to determine whether the null hypothesis can be rejected. The basic question is still the same: "What is the probability we would get a coefficient of this size if the real regression coefficient in the population were zero?" You should examine the *t*-test statistics for each regression coefficient. Many times, not all the independent variables in a regression equation will be statistically significant. If a regression coefficient is not statistically significant, that means the independent variable does not have a relationship with the dependent variable and the slope describing that relationship is relatively flat (i.e., the value of the dependent variable does not change at all as the value of the statistically insignificant independent variable changes).

When using multiple regression analysis, it is important to examine the overall statistical significance of the regression model. The amount of variation in the dependent variable you have been able to explain with the independent measures is compared with the total variation in the dependent measure. This comparison results in a statistic called a **model *F*-statistic** which is compared against a critical value to determine whether or not to reject the null hypothesis. If the *F*-statistic is statistically significant, it means the chances of the regression model for your sample producing a large r^2 when the population r^2 is actually 0 are acceptably small.

Model *F*-statistic
A statistic that compares the amount of variation in the dependent measure "explained" or associated with the independent variables to the "unexplained" or error variance. A larger *F*-statistic indicates that the regression model has more explained variance than error variance.

Substantive Significance

Once we have estimated the regression equation, we need to assess the strength of the association. The multiple r^2 or multiple coefficient of determination describes the strength of the relationship between all the independent variables in our equation and the dependent variable. If you recall our discussion of r^2 from the section on correlation analysis, the coefficient of determination is a measure of the amount of variation in the dependent variable associated with the variation in the independent variable. In the case of multiple regression analysis, the r^2 measure shows the amount of variation in the dependent variable associated with (or explained by) all of the independent variables considered together.

The larger the r^2 measure, the more of the behavior of the dependent measure is associated with the independent measures we are using to predict it. For example, if the multiple r^2 in our Canon copier example above were .78, it would mean that we can account for, or explain, 78 percent of the change in sales revenue by examining the variable sales force size, advertising budget, and customer attitudes toward our copier products. Higher values for r^2 mean stronger relationships between the group of independent variables and the dependent measure. As before, the measure of the strength of the relationship between an individual independent variable and the dependent measure of interest is shown by the regression coefficient or the beta coefficient for that variable.

To summarize, the elements of a multiple regression model to examine in determining its significance include the r^2; the model *F*-statistic; the individual regression coefficients for each independent variable; their associated *t*-statistics; and the individual beta coefficients. The appropriate procedure to follow in evaluating the results of a regression analysis is: (1) assess the statistical significance of the overall regression model using the *F*-statistic and its associated probability; (2) evaluate the obtained r^2 to see how large it is; (3) examine the individual regression coefficients and their *t*-statistics to see which are statistically significant; and (4) look at the beta coefficients to assess relative influence. Taken together, these elements give you a comprehensive picture of the answers to our basic three questions about the relationships between your dependent and independent variables.

SPSS Application—Multiple Regression

Regression can be used to examine the relationship between a single metric dependent variable and one or more metric independent variables. If you examine the Santa Fe Grill database you will note that the first 21 variables are metric independent variables. They include lifestyle variables and perceptions of the two restaurants, measured using a 7-point Likert-type rating scale with 7 representing the positive dimension and 1 the negative dimension. Variables X22, X23, and X24 are metric dependent variables measured on a

7-point Likert-type rating scale. Variables X25—Frequency of Patronage, X30—Distance Driven, X31—Ad Recall, and X32—Gender are nonmetric. Variables X26 to X29 also are nonmetric variables because they are ranking data and cannot therefore be used in regression.

One relationship to examine with multiple regression would be to see if customers' perceptions of their experience eating at the Santa Fe Grill are related to satisfaction. Variables X12 to X21 in the database measure customer perceptions of dining experiences in the restaurant. As a specific example, let's use X22—Satisfaction as the single metric dependent variable, and X12—Friendly Employees, X13—Fun Place to Eat, and X15—Fresh Food as three metric independent variables. The null hypothesis would be that there is no relationship between the three independent variables and X22—Satisfaction. The alternative hypothesis would be that X12, X13, and X15 are significantly related to X22—Customer Satisfaction.

To test this hypothesis, let's look only at the experiences of the Santa Fe Grill customers. To do so, we need to select the customer responses for the Santa Fe Grill from the sample and analyze them separately. This can be done using the "Select Cases" option under the Data pull-down menu. For example, to select customers from only the Santa Fe Grill, the click-through sequence is DATA → SELECT CASES → IF CONDITION IS SATISFIED → IF. Next, highlight x_s4 Favorite Mexican restaurant and move it into the window, click the = sign and then 1. This instructs the SPSS software to select only questionnaires coded 1 in the x_s4 column (the fourth screening question on the survey), which is the Santa Fe Grill. If you wanted to analyze only the Jose's Southwestern Café respondents, then follow the same steps except after the = sign put a 0.

After you select the Santa Fe Grill customers, the SPSS click-through sequence to examine this relationship is ANALYZE → REGRESSION → LINEAR. Highlight X22 and move it to the Dependent Variables box. Highlight X12, X13, and X15 and move them to the Independent Variables box. We will use the defaults for the other options so click OK to run the multiple regression.

The SPSS output for the multiple regression is shown in Exhibit 16.15. The Model Summary table shows the R-square for this model is .602. This means that 60.2 percent of the variation in satisfaction (dependent variable) can be explained from the three independent variables. The results in the ANOVA table indicate that the overall model is significantly different from zero (*F*-ratio = 125.749; probability level ("Sig.") = .000). This probability level means there are .000 chances the regression model results come from a population where the R-square actually is zero. That is, there are no chances out of 1000 that the correlation coefficient is zero.

To determine if one or more of the independent variables is a significant predictor of the dependent variable satisfaction we examine the information provided in the Coefficients table. Looking at the Standardized Coefficients Beta column reveals that X12—Friendly Employees has a beta coefficient of .471 which is significant (.000). Similarly, X15—Fresh Food has a beta coefficient of .722 (Sig. = .000). The Beta for X13—Fun Place to Eat is –0.020 and not significant (.655). These findings indicate that we can reject the null hypothesis that the independent variables are not related to X22—Customer Satisfaction with the Santa Fe Grill, at least for two of the variables. Thus, this regression analysis tells us that customer perceptions of the friendliness of employees (X12) and food freshness (X15) in the Santa Fe Grill are predictors of the level of satisfaction with the restaurant. Insignificant Beta coefficients (X13) are not interpreted.

Examination of the SPSS output reveals that there is a lot of information provided we did not discuss. Experts in statistics may use this information, but managers typically do not. One of the challenges for you will be to learn which information from the SPSS output is most important to analyze and present in a report.

eXHIBIT 16.15 Multiple Regression Example

Model Summary

Model	R	R Square	Adjusted R Square	Std. Error of the Estimate
1	.776[a]	.602	.598	.635

a. Predictors: (Constant), X15 -- Fresh Food, X12 -- Friendly Employees, X13 -- Fun Place to Eat

ANOVA[b]

Model		Sum of Squares	df	Mean Square	F	Sig.
1	Regression	152.294	3	50.765	125.749	.000[a]
	Residual	100.521	249	.404		
	Total	252.814	252			

a. Predictors: (Constant), X15 -- Fresh Food, X12 -- Friendly Employees, X13 -- Fun Place to Eat

b. Dependent Variable: X22 -- Satisfaction

Coefficients[a]

Model		Unstandardized Coefficients		Standardized Coefficients		
		B	Std. Error	Beta	t	Sig.
1	(Constant)	-.043	.309		-.138	.890
	X12 -- Friendly Employees	.498	.045	.471	11.135	.000
	X13 -- Fun Place to Eat	-.028	.062	-.020	-.447	.655
	X15 -- Fresh Food	.622	.038	.722	16.421	.000

a. Dependent Variable: X22 -- Satisfaction

At this point we recommend that you start with simple problems and learn from there. For example, the next problem you may want to examine is changing the dependent variable from X22—Satisfaction to X23—Likely to Return, and run regression with the same independent variables. Another possibility is to keep X22—Satisfaction as the dependent variable and use either the lifestyle variables or the other restaurant perceptions as independent variables. By doing this you will learn how to use the SPSS package and also see if any relationships exist between the variables. Have fun!

Multicollinearity and Multiple Regression Analysis

Multicollinearity A situation in which several independent variables are highly correlated with each other. This characteristic can result in difficulty in estimating separate or independent regression coefficients for the correlated variables.

A common problem in regression analysis is when the independent variables are highly correlated among themselves. This characteristic of the data, referred to as **multicollinearity,** is often a substantial problem. The **regression coefficient** describes the relationship between each independent variable and the dependent variable and indicates the average amount of change in the dependent variable associated with a unit change in the independent variable, assuming all other independent variables in the equation remain the same.

The effect of high levels of multicollinearity is to make it difficult or impossible for the regression equation to identify the separate contributions of the independent (predictor) variables. The practical impact of multicollinearity relates to the statistical significance of the individual regression coefficients, as well as their signs (negative or positive).

Regression coefficient An indicator of the importance of an independent variable in predicting a dependent variable. Large coefficients are good predictors and small coefficients are weak predictors.

Multicollinearity increases the standard error of the coefficient and lowers the t-statistic associated with it (recall that the regression coefficient is subtracted from the null hypothesis coefficient and divided by its standard error to calculate the t-statistic). Therefore, it may be possible, if the multicollinearity is severe enough, for your regression model to have a significant F-statistic, a reasonably large r^2, and still have no regression coefficients that are statistically significant.

Multicollinearity problems do not have an impact on the size of the r^2 or your ability to predict values of the dependent variable. But they can influence the statistical significance of the individual regression coefficients. Another outcome of multicollinearity is that the signs of the individual coefficients may be reversed. When results look suspicious, always check the signs using a bivariate correlation procedure, as discussed earlier in this chapter.

SPSS Application—Multicollinearity

The Santa Fe Grill can be used as an example to demonstrate the potential problems of multicollinearity among regression independent variables. First, select only the Santa Fe Grill customers to analyze, as described earlier. After selecting them, the click-through sequence is ANALYZE → REGRESSION → LINEAR. Highlight X22 and move it to the Dependent Variable box. Next, highlight the three food perceptions variables—X15, X18, and X20—and move them to the Independent Variables box. In the Methods box we will keep Enter, which is the default. Next, click on the Statistics button below and keep Estimates in the Regression Coefficients box and Model Fit as defaults (already checked). Now click Collinearity Diagnostics, then Continue, and OK.

The results are shown in Exhibit 16.16. First, note that the R^2 for this regression model is .417 and it is significant at the .000 level. Next, we look at the information in the Coefficients table. Looking at the Standardized Coefficients Beta column reveals that X15—Fresh Food has a beta coefficient of .767 which is significant (.000). Similarly, X18—Food Taste has a beta coefficient of –0.267 (Sig. = .002). The Beta for X20—Food Temperature is 0.096 and not significant (.191). These findings indicate that we can reject the null hypothesis that the independent variables are not related to X22—Customer Satisfaction with the Santa Fe Grill, at least for two of the variables. Thus, this regression analysis tells us that customer perceptions of food freshness (X15) and food taste (X18) at the Santa Fe Grill are predictors of the level of satisfaction with the restaurant. The Beta coefficient for the third independent variable (X20) is not significant (.191) and therefore not interpreted.

A word of caution is needed at this point regarding the interpretation of Beta coefficients in regression. Recall that the size of the individual coefficients shows how strongly each independent variable is related to the dependent variable. The signs (negative or positive) also are important. A positive sign indicates a positive relationship (higher independent variable values are associated with higher dependent variable values). A negative sign indicates a negative relationship. But when multicollinearity is present among the independent variables, the beta coefficients and signs must be interpreted very cautiously.

The negative sign of X18—Excellent Food Taste (–0.267, sig. = .002) suggests that less favorable perceptions of food taste are associated with higher levels of satisfaction. This result is clearly not logical and points out one of the weaknesses of multiple regression. When the independent variables are highly correlated with each other, the signs of the beta coefficients may be reversed in a regression model, which happened in this case.

Because multicollinearity creates problems when using regression, you must always examine the logic of the signs for the regression betas. When a relationship is different from what is anticipated (i.e., wrong sign), one must look at a simple bivariate correlation of the two variables. For example, in Exhibit 16.17 the information clearly shows that satisfaction

eXHIBIT 16.16 SPSS Results for Multicollinearity

Model Summary

Model	R	R Square	Adjusted R Square	Std. Error of the Estimate
1	.646[a]	.417	.410	.770

a. Predictors: (Constant), X20 -- Proper Food Temperature, X15 -- Fresh Food, X18 -- Excellent Food Taste

ANOVA[b]

Model		Sum of Squares	df	Mean Square	F	Sig.
1	Regression	105.342	3	35.114	59.288	.000[a]
	Residual	147.472	249	.592		
	Total	252.814	252			

a. Predictors: (Constant), X20 -- Proper Food Temperature, X15 -- Fresh Food, X18 -- Excellent Food Taste

b. Dependent Variable: X22 -- Satisfaction

Coefficients[a]

Model		Unstandardized Coefficients		Standardized Coefficients			Collinearity Statistics	
		B	Std. Error	Beta	t	Sig.	Tolerance	VIF
1	(Constant)	2.144	.269		7.984	.000		
	X15 -- Fresh Food	.660	.068	.767	9.642	.000	.371	2.698
	X18 -- Excellent Food Taste	-.304	.095	-.267	-3.202	.002	.337	2.971
	X20 -- Proper Food Temperature	.090	.069	.096	1.312	.191	.438	2.283

a. Dependent Variable: X22 -- Satisfaction

and food taste (X18) are positively correlated (.393) and the relationship is statistically significant (.000). Moreover, the information in the exhibit also shows that food temperature (X20) is indeed positively and significantly related to satisfaction (.430, sig. = .000). Thus, in addition to reversing the signs of the coefficients, the regression model may indicate that a variable is not significant when in fact it is—if multicollinearity is present.

How can we anticipate and deal with multicollinearity among independent variables? One way is to look at the bivariate correlations, as shown in Exhibit 16.17. Note that the correlations between the three food variables range from .686 to .770. These high correlations (multicollinearity) between the three independent variables are the reason for the problems in interpreting the Betas in this regression model. Using this type of information enables you to confirm the true relationship when multicollinearity is present.

Another way to assess multicollinearity is to request collinearity diagnostics from the SPSS software. Look back at Exhibit 16.16. In the columns labeled Tolerance and VIF, under the heading Collinearity Statistics on the right side of the Coefficients table, there are some measures we need to consider. These are both measures of multicollinearity among the independent variables (VIF stands for variance inflation factor). These measures—Tolerance and VIF—show the degree to which each independent variable is explained by

eXHIBIT 16.17 Bivariate Correlations of Food Variables with Satisfaction

Output4 [Document4] - SPSS Viewer

File Edit View Data Transform Insert Format Analyze Graphs Utilities Add-ons Window Help

Correlations

Correlations

Favorite Mexican Restaurant			X22 -- Satisfaction	X15 -- Fresh Food	X18 -- Excellent Food Taste	X20 -- Proper Food Temperature
Santa Fe Grill	X22 -- Satisfaction	Pearson Correlation	1	.627**	.393**	.430**
		Sig. (2-tailed)		.000	.000	.000
		N	253	253	253	253
	X15 -- Fresh Food	Pearson Correlation	.627**	1	.770**	.686**
		Sig. (2-tailed)	.000		.000	.000
		N	253	253	253	253
	X18 -- Excellent Food Taste	Pearson Correlation	.393**	.770**	1	.721**
		Sig. (2-tailed)	.000	.000		.000
		N	253	253	253	253
	X20 -- Proper Food Temperature	Pearson Correlation	.430**	.686**	.721**	1
		Sig. (2-tailed)	.000	.000	.000	
		N	253	253	253	253

**. Correlation is significant at the 0.01 level (2-tailed).

the other independent variables and can be used to assess whether multicollinearity is likely a problem in regression.

Multicollinearity is indicated by the sizes of the Tolerance and VIF. The rules of thumb or "threshold sizes" for Tolerance and VIF can vary, depending on the sample size and other issues. The following guidelines are based on the author's experiences in the application of regression models for samples in the range of 200 to 500 observations. For Tolerance, values smaller than .75 generally indicate multicollinearity is likely a problem. In contrast, if the tolerance value is larger than .75, multicollinearity is likely not a problem. These guidelines can be extended when examining simple bivariate correlations of the independent variables. The result indicates that if bivariate correlations are .50 or larger, multicollinearity is likely a problem in regression models.

The VIF is the inverse of Tolerance (VIF = 1/Tolerance). Using a similar threshold value as with Tolerance, the maximum threshold for VIF is typically a value of 1.33 (1/.75). Thus, values larger than 1.33 indicate multicollinearity is likely a problem, and values below 1.33 indicate multicollinearity is not a problem. But researchers should use their own judgment in choosing criteria for Tolerance and VIF, as the levels suggested here may differ in other research contexts. In the Santa Fe Grill output, the tolerance for X15 is .371, for X18 it is .337, and X20 tolerance is .438. Moreover, the VIF for all three variables is above 2.0. Since the tolerance value is substantially below .75 and the VIF is much larger than 1.33, we conclude that multicollinearity among the independent variables is definitely a serious problem for this regression model. Therefore, action is necessary if the researcher wants to use several independent variables exhibiting multicollinearity similar to that of the Santa Fe Grill database.

To avoid the problem of multicollinearity in regression, you should examine the correlations between the independent variables ahead of time. If they are too high (>.50), then you should consider removing one or more of the highly correlated variables. To do so, you can select one of your independent variables as a representative variable (proxy variable) for the highly correlated variables and use only that variable in your regression model. But there are other solutions to consider that overcome the problem of multicollinearity. A second solution is to combine the variables (in our example, variables X15, X18, and X20) into a summated composite variable. The third solution is to apply factor analysis to the set of independent variables. These last two solutions are considered better for most regression models and are therefore discussed in the next chapter.

Dummy Variables and Multiple Regression

Dummy variable An artificial variable introduced into a regression equation to represent the categories of a nominally scaled variable.

Sometimes the particular independent variables you may want to use to predict a dependent variable are not measured using interval or ratio scales (a basic assumption for the use of regression analysis). It is still possible to include such variables through the use of **dummy variables.** For example, if you wanted to include the gender of customers of the Santa Fe Grill restaurant to help explain their satisfaction with the restaurant, it is obvious your measure for gender would include only two possible values, male and female.

The use of dummy variables involves choosing one category of the variable to serve as a reference category and then adding as many dummy variables as there are possible values of the variable, minus that reference category. The categories are coded as either 0 or 1. In the example above, if you choose the male category as the reference category, you would have one dummy variable for the female category. That dummy variable would be assigned the value of 1 for females and 0 for males. In the Santa Fe Grill database, X32—Gender is already coded as a dummy variable for gender, with males as the reference category.

SPSS Application—Use of Dummy Variables in Regression

To see how multiple regression works with dummy variables, let's again use the customer responses for the Santa Fe Grill. Let's examine the relationship between satisfaction of customers and X12—Friendly Employees, X17—Attractive Interior, and the dummy variable Gender (X32). The null hypothesis would be that X22—Customer Satisfaction is not related to X12, X17, or X32.

After you select the Santa Fe Grill customers, the SPSS click-through sequence is ANALYZE → REGRESSION → LINEAR. Click on X22—Satisfaction and move it to the Dependent Variables box. Highlight X12—Friendly Employees, X17—Attractive Interior, and X32—Gender and move them to the Independent Variables box. Now click OK to run the multiple regression.

The SPSS results are shown in Exhibit 16.18. In the Model Summary table, you can see the R^2 for the model is .147. Thus, approximately 14.7 percent of the total variation in X22 is associated with X12—Friendly Employees, X17—Attractive Interior, and X32—Gender. The ANOVA table indicates the regression model is significant. The "Sig." value indicates a probability level of .000.

The Coefficients table shows that the variable X12—Friendly Employees is a significant predictor of satisfaction, with a beta coefficient of .286. Attractive Interior (X17) with a beta of .080 is not significantly related to customer satisfaction (i.e., probability level of .181). Now, the question of interest is: "Does the satisfaction level of Santa Fe Grill customers differ depending on whether they are male or female?" According to the results in the

EXHIBIT 16.18 SPSS Multiple Regression with a Dummy Variable

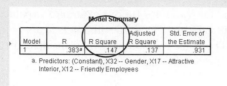

Model Summary

Model	R	R Square	Adjusted R Square	Std. Error of the Estimate
1	.383[a]	.147	.137	.931

a. Predictors: (Constant), X32 -- Gender, X17 -- Attractive Interior, X12 -- Friendly Employees

ANOVA[b]

Model		Sum of Squares	df	Mean Square	F	Sig.
1	Regression	37.156	3	12.385	14.300	.000[a]
	Residual	215.658	249	.866		
	Total	252.814	252			

a. Predictors: (Constant), X32 -- Gender, X17 -- Attractive Interior, X12 -- Friendly Employees

b. Dependent Variable: X22 -- Satisfaction

Coefficients[a]

Model		Unstandardized Coefficients		Standardized Coefficients	t	Sig.
		B	Std. Error	Beta		
1	(Constant)	3.343	.361		9.258	.000
	X12 -- Friendly Employees	.302	.064	.286	4.748	.000
	X17 -- Attractive Interior	.086	.065	.080	1.340	.181
	X32 -- Gender	-.371	.131	-.171	-2.839	.005

a. Dependent Variable: X22 -- Satisfaction

Coefficients table, the beta coefficient of –.171 for X32—Gender is significant (Sig. level of .005). This means the female and male customers exhibit significantly different levels of satisfaction with the Santa Fe Grill. The negative beta coefficient means that lower numbers for gender are associated with higher values for satisfaction. Since males were coded 0 in our database this means males are more satisfied with the Santa Fe Grill than are females.

It is also possible to use categorical independent variables with more than just two categories. Let's say you wanted to use consumers' purchase behavior of Starbucks coffee to help predict their purchase behavior for Maxwell House, and you had separated your sample into nonusers, light users, and heavy users. To use dummy variables in your regression model, you would pick one category as a reference group (nonusers) and add two dummy variables for the remaining categories. The variables would be coded as follows, using 0 and 1:

Category	D_1	D_2
Nonuser	0	0
Light user	1	0
Heavy user	0	1

The use of dummy variables in regression models allows different types of independent variables to be included in prediction efforts. The researcher must keep in mind the difference in the interpretation of the regression coefficient and the identity of the reference category that is represented by the intercept term.

MARKETING RESEARCH IN ACTION

Customer Satisfaction Survey

The Role of Employees in Developing a Customer Satisfaction Program

The plant manager of QualKote Manufacturing is interested in the impact his year-long effort to implement a quality improvement program is having on the satisfaction of his customers. The plant foreman, assembly-line workers, and engineering staff have closely examined their operations to determine which activities have the most impact on product quality and reliability. Together, the managers and employees have worked to better understand how each particular job affects the final delivered quality of the product as the customer perceives it.

To answer his questions about customer satisfaction, the plant manager conducted an internal survey of plant workers and managers using a 7-point Likert scale (endpoints: 1 = Strongly Disagree and 7 = Strongly Agree). His plans are to get opinions from within the company first and then do a customer survey on similar topics. He has collected completed surveys from 57 employees. The following are examples of the topics covered in the questionnaire:

- Data from a variety of external sources (customers, competitors, suppliers, etc.) are used in the strategic planning process. Independent variable A10.
- Customers are involved in the product quality planning process. Independent variable A12.
- Customer requirements and expectations of the company's products are used in developing strategic plans and goals. Independent variable A17.
- There is a systematic process to translate customer requirements into new/improved products. Independent variable A23.
- There is a systematic process to accurately determine customers' requirements and expectations. Independent variable A31.
- The company's product quality program has improved the level of customer satisfaction. Dependent variable A36.
- The company's product quality program has improved the likelihood that customers will recommend us. Dependent variable A37.
- Gender of the employee responding: Male = 1; Female = 0. Classification variable A40.

A multiple regression was run using SPSS with responses of the 57 employees as input to the model. The output is shown in Exhibits 16.19 and 16.20. There is an actual database of QualKote employee responses to these questions available in SPSS format at www.mhhe.com/hair4e. The database is labeled Qualkote MRIA_4e.sav.

The results indicate that there is a statistically significant relationship between the metric dependent variable (A36—Satisfaction) and at least some of the five metric independent variables. The R^2 for the relationship is 67.0 and it is statistically significant at the .000 level. This suggests that when employees have more favorable perceptions about some

eXHIBIT 16.19 Descriptive Statistics and Correlations for Variables

Descriptive Statistics

	Mean	Std. Deviation	N
A36	4.81	.953	57
A10	5.00	1.414	57
A12	3.60	1.334	57
A17	2.28	1.176	57
A23	4.53	1.104	57
A31	2.89	.838	57

Correlations

		A36	A10	A12	A17	A23	A31
Pearson Correlation	A36	1.000	.490	.626	.065	.472	.354
	A10	.490	1.000	.435	-.494	-.080	-.030
	A12	.626	.435	1.000	-.188	.171	.073
	A17	.065	-.494	-.188	1.000	.324	.266
	A23	.472	-.080	.171	.324	1.000	.736
	A31	.354	-.030	.073	.266	.736	1.000
Sig. (1-tailed)	A36	.	.000	.000	.315	.000	.003
	A10	.000	.	.000	.000	.277	.412
	A12	.000	.000	.	.080	.102	.295
	A17	.315	.000	.080	.	.007	.023
	A23	.000	.277	.102	.007	.	.000
	A31	.003	.412	.295	.023	.000	.
N	A36	57	57	57	57	57	57
	A10	57	57	57	57	57	57
	A12	57	57	57	57	57	57
	A17	57	57	57	57	57	57
	A23	57	57	57	57	57	57
	A31	57	57	57	57	57	57

eXHIBIT 16.20 Multiple Regression of Qualkote Satisfaction Variables

Model Summary

Model	R	R Square	Adjusted R Square	Std. Error of the Estimate
1	.819[a]	.670	.638	.574

a. Predictors: (Constant), A31, A10, A12, A17, A23

ANOVA[b]

Model		Sum of Squares	df	Mean Square	F	Sig.
1	Regression	34.095	5	6.819	20.723	.000[a]
	Residual	16.782	51	.329		
	Total	50.877	56			

a. Predictors: (Constant), A31, A10, A12, A17, A23

b. Dependent Variable: A36

Coefficients[a]

Model		Unstandardized Coefficients		Standardized Coefficients		
		B	Std. Error	Beta	t	Sig.
1	(Constant)	.309	.496		.624	.535
	A10	.314	.068	.466	4.587	.000
	A12	.294	.066	.411	4.451	.000
	A17	.208	.080	.257	2.614	.012
	A23	.296	.108	.343	2.744	.008
	A31	.020	.136	.017	.145	.885

a. Dependent Variable: A36

aspects of the implementation of the quality improvement program they also believe that the program has improved customer satisfaction (dependent variable = A36).

Hands-On Exercise

1. Will the results of this regression model be useful to the QualKote plant manager? If yes, how?
2. Which independent variables are helpful in predicting A36—Customer Satisfaction?
3. How would the manager interpret the mean values for the variables reported in Exhibit 16.19?
4. What other regression models might be examined with the questions from this survey?

Summary of Learning Objectives

■ **Understand and evaluate the types of relationships between variables.**

Relationships between variables can be described in several ways, including presence, direction, strength of association, and type. Presence tells us whether a consistent and systematic relationship exists. Direction tells us whether the relationship is positive or negative. Strength of association tells us whether we have a weak or strong relationship, and the type of relationship is usually described as either linear or nonlinear.

Two variables may share a linear relationship, in which changes in one variable are accompanied by some change (not necessarily the same amount of change) in the other variable. As long as the amount of change stays constant over the range of both variables, the relationship is termed linear. Relationships between two variables that change in strength and/or direction as the values of the variables change are referred to as curvilinear.

■ **Explain the concepts of association and covariation.**

The terms *covariation* and *association* refer to the attempt to quantify the strength of the relationship between two variables. Covariation is the amount of change in one variable of interest that is consistently related to change in another variable under study. The degree of association is a numerical measure of the strength of the relationship between two variables. Both these terms refer to linear relationships.

■ **Understand the differences between Pearson correlation and Spearman correlation.**

Pearson correlation coefficients are a measure of linear association between two variables of interest. The Pearson correlation coefficient is used when both variables are measured on an interval or ratio scale. When one or more variables of interest are measured on an ordinal scale, the Spearman rank order correlation coefficient should be used.

■ **Explain the concept of statistical significance versus practical significance.**

Because some of the procedures involved in determining the statistical significance of a statistical test include consideration of the sample size, it is possible to have a very low degree of association between two variables show up as statistically significant (i.e., the population parameter is not equal to zero). However, by considering the absolute strength of the relationship in addition to its statistical significance, the researcher is better able to draw the appropriate conclusion about the data and the population from which they were selected.

■ **Know when and how to use regression analysis.**

Regression analysis is useful in answering questions about the strength of a linear relationship between a dependent variable and one or more independent variables. The results of a regression analysis indicate the amount of change in the dependent variable that is associated with a one-unit change in the independent variables. In addition, the accuracy of the regression equation can be evaluated by comparing the predicted values of the dependent variable to the actual values of the dependent variable drawn from the sample.

Key Terms and Concepts

Beta coefficient 536

Bivariate regression analysis 528

Coefficient of determination (r^2) 525

Covariation 519

Curvilinear relationship 518

Dummy variables 543

***F*-ratio** 534

Least squares procedure 529

Linear relationship 518

Model *F*-statistic 537

Multicollinearity 539

Multiple regression analysis 535

Ordinary least squares 530

Pearson correlation coefficient 522

Regression coefficient 540

Scatter diagram 519

Spearman rank order correlation coefficient 525

Standardized regression coefficient 536

Sum of the squared errors 529

Unexplained variance 529

Review Questions

1. Explain the difference between testing for significant differences and testing for association.
2. Explain the difference between association and causation.
3. What is covariation? How does it differ from correlation?
4. What are the differences between univariate and bivariate statistical techniques?
5. What is regression analysis? When would you use it?
6. What is the difference between simple regression and multiple regression?

Discussion Questions

1. Regression and correlation analysis both describe the strength of linear relationships between variables. Consider the concepts of education and income. Many people would say that these two variables are related in a linear fashion. As education increases, income usually increases (although not necessarily at the same rate). Can you think of two variables that are related in such a way that their relationship changes over their range of possible values (i.e., in a curvilinear fashion)? How would you analyze the relationship between two such variables?
2. Is it possible to conduct a regression analysis on two variables and obtain a significant regression equation (significant *F*-ratio), but still have a low r^2? What does the r^2 statistic measure? How can you have a low r^2 yet still get a statistically significant *F*-ratio for the overall regression equation?
3. The ordinary least squares (OLS) procedure commonly used in regression produces a line of "best fit" for the data to which it is applied. How would you define best fit in regression analysis? What is there about the procedure that guarantees a best fit to the data? What assumptions about the use of a regression technique are necessary to produce this result?
4. When multiple independent variables are used to predict a dependent variable in multiple regression, multicollinearity among the independent variables is often a concern. What is the main problem caused by high multicollinearity among the independent variables in a multiple regression equation? Can you still achieve a high r^2 for your regression equation if multicollinearity is present in your data?

5. **EXPERIENCE THE INTERNET.** A trend in marketing is to shop for products and services on the Internet. In the last decade or so, traditional retailers have begun selling through catalogs. More recently, they also are selling over the Internet. To learn more about this, go to www.catalogsite.com. At this site, many retailers are listing their merchandise and hoping to sell it. Review the catalogs. Compare the information on the Website with traditional catalogs and retail stores. Prepare a questionnaire covering the common elements of these three approaches to selling. Select a retailer students are familiar with. Compile a sample of catalogs that offer similar merchandise. Then

ask a sample of students to visit catalogs on the Web site, look at the catalogs you have brought to class, and then complete the questionnaire. Enter the data into a software package and assess your finding statistically. Prepare a report and be able to defend your conclusions.

6. **SPSS EXERCISE.** Choose one or two other students from your class and form a team. Identify the different retailers from your community where DVD players, TVs, and other electronics products are sold. Team members should divide up and visit all the different stores and describe the products and brands that are sold in each. Also observe the layout in the store, the store personnel, and the type of advertising the store uses. In other words, familiarize yourself with each retailer's marketing mix. Use your knowledge of the marketing mix to design a questionnaire. Interview approximately 100 people who are familiar with all the retailers you selected and collect their responses. Analyze the responses using a statistical software package such as SPSS. Prepare a report of your findings, including whether the perceptions of each of the stores are similar or different, and particularly whether the differences are statistically or substantively different. Present your findings in class and be prepared to defend your conclusions and your use of statistical techniques.

7. **SPSS EXERCISE.** The Marketing Research in Action case in Chapter 15 for Remington's Steakhouse and two competitors included numerous categorical variables. Run a Chi-square analysis to compare the three competitors on the categorical segmentation variables (X16–X21) and prepare a profile of each restaurant's customers. Next, run a multiple regression between the restaurant selection factors and satisfaction. Be prepared to present your findings. A database for the Remington's Steakhouse case is available in SPSS format at www.mhhe.com/hair4e. The database is labeled Remingtons_MRIA_4e.sav.

8. **SPSS EXERCISE.** The Santa Fe Grill owners believe one of their competitive advantages is that the restaurant is a fun place to eat. Use the Santa Fe Grill database and run a bivariate correlation analysis between X13—Fun Place to Eat and X22—Satisfaction to test this hypothesis. Could this hypothesis be further examined with multiple regression?

appendix 16.A

Formulas for Calculating Correlation and Regression Issues

Marketing researchers seldom calculate statistics. We provide the formulas below for those who wish to better understand the computational process.

Pearson Product Moment Correlation

$$r_{xy} = \frac{\sum_{i=1}^{n} (x_i - \bar{x})(y_i - \bar{y})}{n s_x s_y}$$

where

X_i = the X values

Y_i = the Y values

$\overline{X}$ = mean of the X values

$\overline{Y}$ = mean of the Y values

n = number of paired cases

$s_x s_y$ = standard deviation of X and Y

Regression

The general equation for regression is:

$$y = a + bx + e_i$$

where

Y = the dependent variable

a = the intercept for the regression line, or constant (point where the straight line intersects the y-axis when $x = 0$)

b = the slope of the regression line, or regression coefficient (the change in y for every 1-unit change in x)

x = the independent variable used to predict y

e_i = the error for the prediction (the difference between the predicted value and the true value)

Values for a and b can be calculated using the following formulas:

The formula for computing the regression parameter b is:

$$b = \frac{n\sum_{i=1}^{n} x_i y_i - \left(\sum_{i=1}^{n} x_i\right)\left(\sum_{i-1}^{n} y_i\right)}{n\sum_{i=1}^{n} x_i^2 - \left(\sum_{i=1}^{n} x_i\right)^2}$$

where

x_i = an x variable value

y_i = a y value paired with each x_i value

n = the number of pairs

The formula for computing the intercept is:

$$a = \bar{y} - b\bar{x}$$

appendix 16.B

Examining Residuals

Earlier in the chapter we discussed the need to examine error terms (residuals) in order to diagnose potential problems caused by data observations that do not meet the assumptions of regression. Remember, residuals are the difference between the observed value of the dependent variable and the predicted value of the dependent variable produced by the regression equation. We can use SPSS to examine the residuals.

To examine the regression residuals, let's look only at the Santa Fe Grill customers. To do so, we need to select the customer responses for the Santa Fe Grill from the sample and analyze them separately. This can be done using the "Select Cases" option under the Data pull-down menu. For example, to select customers from only the Santa Fe Grill, the click-through sequence is DATA → SELECT CASES → IF CONDITION IS SATISFIED → IF. Next, highlight x_s4 Favorite Mexican restaurant and move it into the window, click the = sign and then 1. This instructs the SPSS software to select only questionnaires coded 1 in the x_s4 column (the fourth screening question on the survey), which is the Santa Fe Grill. If you wanted to analyze only the Jose's Southwestern Café respondents, then you would follow the same steps except after the = sign put a 0.

The click-through sequence is ANALYZE → REGRESSION → LINEAR. Highlight X22 and move it to the Dependent Variable box. Highlight X15 and X16 and move them to the Independent Variable box. In the Methods box we will keep Enter, which is the default. This is the same sequence as earlier regression SPSS applications, but now we also must click on the Plots button. To produce plots of the regression residuals to check on potential problems, click on ZPRED and move it to the Y box. Then click on ZRESID and move it to the X box. These two items stand for Standardized Predicted Dependent Variable and Standardized Residual. Comparing these two quantities allows us to determine whether the hypothesized relationship between the dependent variable X22 and the independent variables X15 and X16 is linear, and also whether the error terms in the regression model are normally distributed (one of the basic assumptions of a regression model).

To fully evaluate the regression results, we need to examine two other graphs. To do so, go to the lower left-hand portion of the dialog box where it says Standardized Residual Plots. Click on the Histogram and Normal probability options. Now click on Continue and then OK to run the regression procedure.

The SPSS output is shown in Exhibit 16.B.1. The information in the Model Summary table shows the R-square is .477. From the ANOVA table you can see that this R-square is significant at the .000 level. Finally, in the Coefficients table we see that both independent variables have significant betas and are positively related to the dependent variable satisfaction.

Now go to the Charts section at the end of the output to evaluate whether the data we used in the regression model violated any of the basic assumptions (linear relationship, normally distributed errors, etc.). Exhibits 16.B.2 to 16.B.4 present information about the distribution of the residuals. If the regression model predicts equally well over the entire range of the independent variables, there should be no discernible pattern or shape to the residuals and their

eXHIBIT 16.B.1 Examining Residuals in Multiple Regression

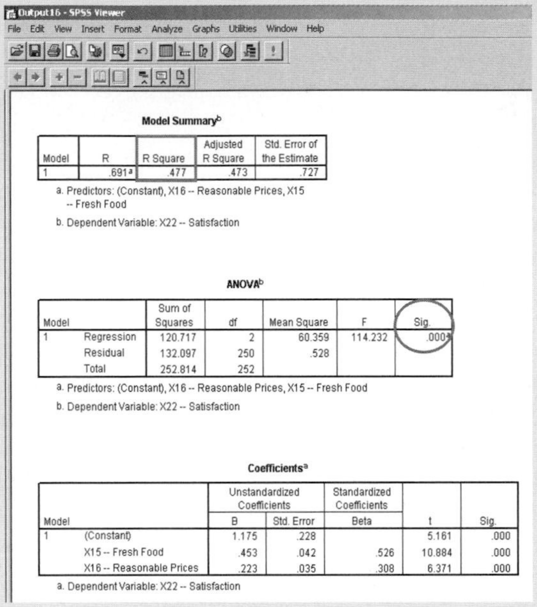

Output16 - SPSS Viewer

File Edit View Insert Format Analyze Graphs Utilities Window Help

Model Summary[b]

Model	R	R Square	Adjusted R Square	Std. Error of the Estimate
1	.691[a]	.477	.473	.727

a. Predictors: (Constant), X16 -- Reasonable Prices, X15 -- Fresh Food

b. Dependent Variable: X22 -- Satisfaction

ANOVA[b]

Model		Sum of Squares	df	Mean Square	F	Sig.
1	Regression	120.717	2	60.359	114.232	.000[a]
	Residual	132.097	250	.528		
	Total	252.814	252			

a. Predictors: (Constant), X16 -- Reasonable Prices, X15 -- Fresh Food

b. Dependent Variable: X22 -- Satisfaction

Coefficients[a]

Model		Unstandardized Coefficients		Standardized Coefficients		
		B	Std. Error	Beta	t	Sig.
1	(Constant)	1.175	.228		5.161	.000
	X15 -- Fresh Food	.453	.042	.526	10.884	.000
	X16 -- Reasonable Prices	.223	.035	.308	6.371	.000

a. Dependent Variable: X22 -- Satisfaction

distribution should be normal. The results shown in these residual charts will help you determine whether the residuals produced by our regression analysis conform to this standard.

Exhibit 16.B.2 shows the frequency distribution of the standardized residuals compared to a normal distribution. As you can see, most of the residuals are fairly close to the normal

eXHIBIT 16.B.2 Standardized Residuals versus Normal Distribution

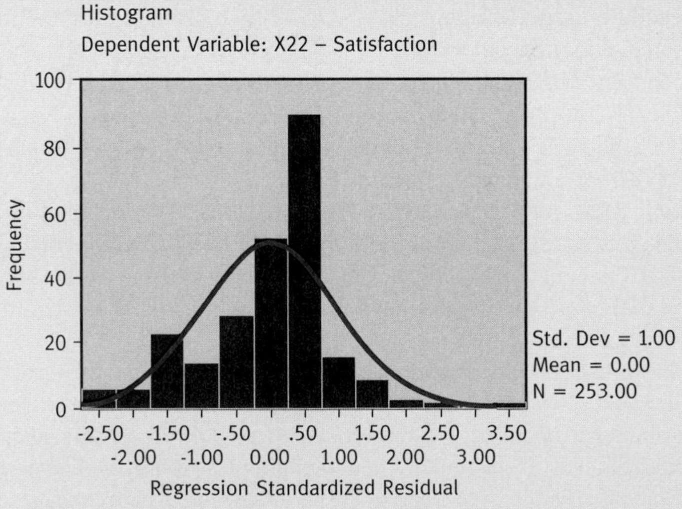

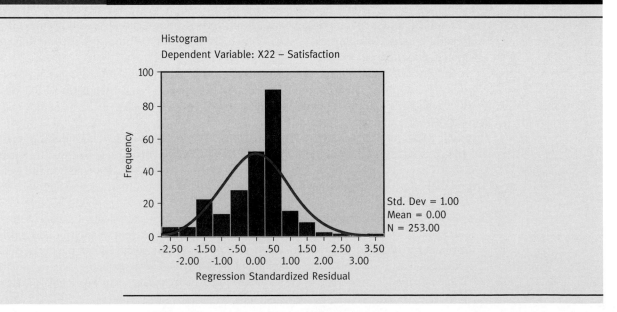

eXHIBIT 16.B.3 Observed versus Expected Standardized Residuals

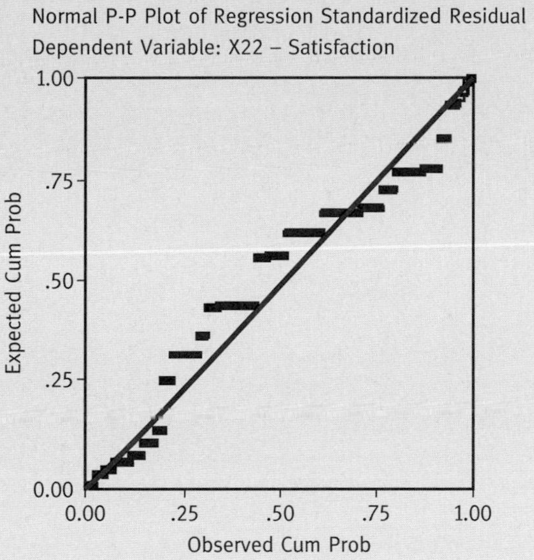

curve. There are some observations at –1.50 and +.5 and +3.50 that exceed the curve, but this result is not of significant concern at this point. Examination of only this table does not suggest there is a significant problem—but you need to look at all three tables to make a final judgment.

Exhibit 16.B.3 shows the observed standardized residuals compared against the expected standardized residuals from a normal distribution. If the observed residuals are normally distributed, they will fall directly on the 45° line shown on the graph. As you can see, the residuals from our regression model vary somewhat below and above the line, but again there does not seem to be a major problem. Finally, Exhibit 16.B.4 compares the standardized predicted values of the dependent variable with the standardized residuals from the regression equation. The scatter plot of residuals shows some variation in spread at the left and right ends of the diagram. But the difference in the spread of the residuals is not substantial as you look from left to right on the chart. Again, this result suggests the relationship we are trying to predict is linear and that the error terms are normally distributed.

Thus, from an examination of the information presented in all three exhibits we conclude that there are no significant data problems that would lead us to say the assumptions of multiple regression have been seriously violated. As a final note we can say that regression is a robust statistical method and substantial violations of the assumptions are necessary to create problems.

There is one last issue to examine from the printout, the Residual Statistics table (see Exhibit 16.B.5). Note that it includes columns across the top for the minimum, maximum, mean, and standard deviation of the predicted value of the dependent variable, X22. Down the left side are references to the predicted value of X22, the residual, the standardized predicted value, and the standardized residual value. Since the standardization process produces scores with a mean of 0 and a standard deviation of 1.00, you should look most closely at the Minimum and Maximum columns. The numbers in

eXHIBIT 16.B.4 Standardized Predicted Values versus Standardized Residuals

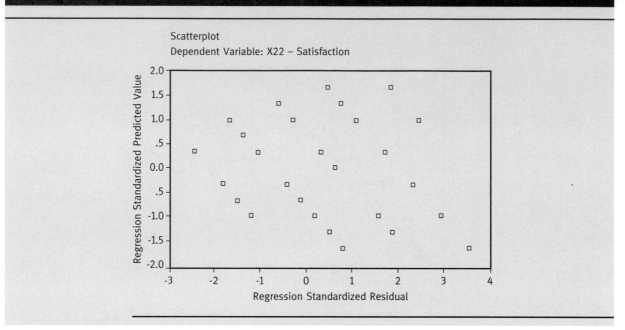

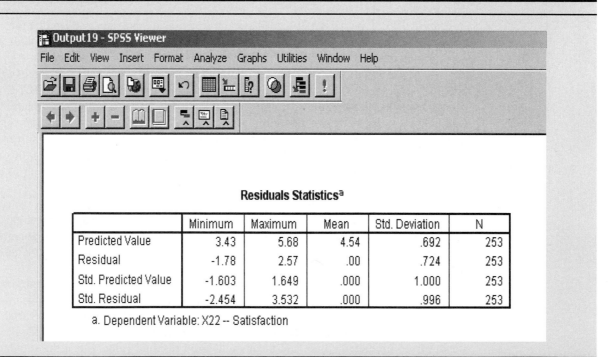

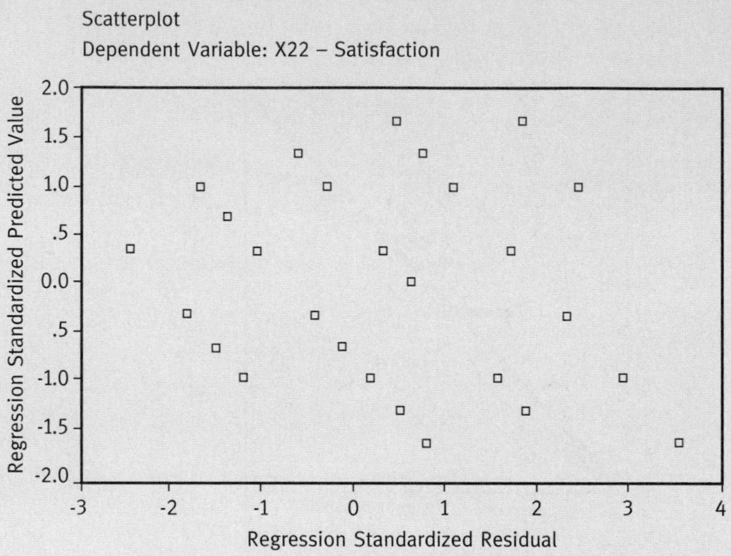

eXHIBIT 16.B.5 Residual Statistics for Regression

Output19 - SPSS Viewer

File Edit View Insert Format Analyze Graphs Utilities Window Help

Residuals Statistics[a]

	Minimum	Maximum	Mean	Std. Deviation	N
Predicted Value	3.43	5.68	4.54	.692	253
Residual	-1.78	2.57	.00	.724	253
Std. Predicted Value	-1.603	1.649	.000	1.000	253
Std. Residual	-2.454	3.532	.000	.996	253

a. Dependent Variable: X22 -- Satisfaction

eXHIBIT 16.B.6 Frequencies for Multiple Regression Dependent Variable

Frequencies

X22—Satisfaction

		Frequency	Percent	Valid Percent	Cumulative Percent
Valid	3	32	12.6	12.6	12.6
	4	112	44.3	44.3	56.9
	5	52	20.6	20.6	77.5
	6	54	21.3	21.3	98.8
	7 = Highly Satisfied	3	1.2	1.2	100.0
	Total	253	100.0	100.0	

these columns will tell you if the data have any distinctive outliers (i.e., individual responses that probably are valid responses, but quite different from the rest of the responses to a particular question). The entries in the Minimum and Maximum columns for the standardized predicted value and standardized residual value represent the number of standard deviations from the mean of 0. For example, the largest value (absolute size) of the standardized predicted value for X22 is 1.649 standard deviations above the mean value of 0. Likewise, the largest value of the standardized residual is –3.532 standard deviations above its mean of 0. The best way to utilize these numbers is to look for minimum and maximum values greater than 3.0. That would mean that some of the predicted values and residuals are further than three standard deviations away from their means and could indicate the presence of outliers in the data. The maximum value of 3.532 suggests the possibility of one or more outliers in the data for X22 so you need to examine this further.

We ran a frequency count for the multiple regression dependent variable. The results are shown in Exhibit 16.B.6. Note that there are three responses of 7 on the 7-point scale, whereas all other responses range from 3 to 6. It is possible these are true outliers, but more likely individuals who truly are satisfied with the Santa Fe Grill. To resolve this, look at the other responses for these individuals and if they are very favorable then it is not likely these three individual responses are outliers.

chapter 17

Overview of Multivariate Analysis Methods

Learning Objectives

After reading this chapter, you will be able to:

1. Define multivariate analysis.
2. Understand when and why you should use multivariate analysis in marketing research.
3. Distinguish between dependence and interdependence methods.
4. Apply factor analysis, cluster analysis, discriminant analysis, and conjoint analysis to examine marketing research problems.

"The unique yet ironic element associated with statistics is that they can be used to produce evidence to support any conclusions the researcher may make."

—HAROLD AUSTIN
President,
Beta Dynamics, Inc.

Multivariate Methods Impact Our Lives Every Day

The amount of information available for business decision making has grown tremendously over the last decade. Until recently, much of that information just disappeared. It either was not used or was discarded because collecting, storing, extracting, and interpreting it was not economical. Now, decreases in the cost of data collection and storage, development of faster data processors and user-friendly client–server interfaces, and improvements in data analysis and interpretation made possible through data mining enable businesses to convert what had been a "waste by-product" into a great new resource to provide added value to customers and to improve business decisions.

Data mining facilitates the discovery of interesting patterns in databases and data warehouses that are difficult to identify and have a high potential for improving decision making and creating knowledge. It does this first through an automated process involving "machine-learning" methods which emerged mostly from work on artificial intelligence. Examples include neural networking and genetic algorithms. After this first phase, the identified relationships are confirmed using "human-learning" approaches such as multiple regression, discriminant analysis, and factor analysis. The use of data mining and related approaches will continue to expand because data will increase exponentially, applications will become real-time, the quality of data will improve, and data mining tools will be more powerful and easier to use.

Multivariate methods are widely used today for commercial purposes. The business model of Fair Isaac & Co. (www.fairisaac.com) is based on the commercial use of multivariate techniques. The firm is perhaps best known for its complex analytical model that can accurately predict who will pay bills on time, who will pay late, who will not pay at all, who will file for bankruptcy, and so on. Its predictive models are useful for both the consumer and the business-to-business markets. Similarly, the IRS uses discriminant analysis to identify which returns to audit and which to pass on. State Farm uses multivariate statistics to decide whom to sell insurance to, and Progressive Insurance combines multivariate methods with global positioning technology to identify where and how fast you drive and then to raise your auto insurance premiums if you drive in a hazardous manner.

To make accurate business decisions in today's increasingly complex environment, we must analyze intricate relationships with many intervening variables. Multivariate methods are powerful analytical techniques made for addressing such issues.

Value of Multivariate Techniques in Data Analysis

In recent years we have seen remarkable advances in computer hardware and software. The speed and storage capability of PCs have been doubling every 18 months while prices have tumbled. Statistical software packages with Windows user interfaces have taken many tasks into the "click-and-point" era. We can now analyze large quantities of complex data with relative ease. For many years data came mostly from surveys. Data warehouses are now stocked with mountains of internal data that can be mined to identify valuable relationships about customers and employees. Some of these data can be analyzed using simple statistics like those discussed in earlier chapters. But in many situations we need more complex techniques. Indeed, many market researchers believe that unless we use more complex multivariate techniques we are only superficially examining marketing problems.

Today most of the problems marketing researchers are interested in understanding involve more than two variables and therefore require multivariate statistical techniques. Moreover, business decision makers as well as consumers tend to use a lot of information to make choices and decisions. Consequently, potential influences on consumer behavior and business reactions abound.

Multivariate techniques arose partially out of the need of businesses to address such complexity. The ability to determine the relative influence of different independent variables, as well as to assess the behavior of groups of dependent measures simultaneously, has become an important asset in the marketing researcher's toolbox. In addition, tremendous increases in computing power and portability have encouraged the adoption of multivariate analysis by individuals who were unable to realistically consider such approaches in earlier years.

Multivariate analysis A group of statistical techniques used when there are two or more measurements on each element and the variables are analyzed simultaneously. Multivariate analysis is concerned with the simultaneous relationships among two or more phenomena.

What is multivariate analysis? **Multivariate analysis** refers to a group of statistical procedures that simultaneously analyze multiple measurements on each individual or object being investigated. The multivariate statistical procedures we will highlight in this chapter are extensions of the univariate and bivariate statistical procedures that were discussed in previous chapters. It should be emphasized that we can provide only a very brief overview of some of these techniques in this chapter. The reader is referred to other more advanced texts for a more complete coverage of all the techniques.[1]

Multivariate analysis is extremely important in marketing research because most business problems are multidimensional. Corporations and their customers are seldom described on the basis of one dimension. An individual's decision to visit a fast-food restaurant is often dependent on such factors as the quality, variety, and price of the food; the restaurant's location; and the service. When corporations develop databases to better serve their customers, the database often includes a vast array of information—such as demographics, lifestyles, zip codes, purchasing behavior—on each customer. As marketing researchers become increasingly aware of the power of multivariate analysis, they will use multivariate techniques more and more in solving complex business problems. The nearby A Closer Look at Research (Small Business Implications) box illustrates how these techniques can aid the small-business owner.

A Closer Look at Research

XLSTAT

Many small businesses cannot afford the rather expensive statistical packages like SPSS or SAS. XLSTAT is an affordable and user-friendly statistical package designed for small businesses that utilize Microsoft Excel. XLSTAT is an add-on for Excel. It allows the small-business user, working mainly in an Excel worksheet, to transfer stored data into the program for data analysis purposes.

XLSTAT offers more than 40 different functions to empower Excel and make it an everyday statistical solution package for small businesses. The package can perform very simple techniques like box plots, frequencies, and other descriptive statistics. But it also can perform many of the more complex statistical techniques, such as factor analysis, cluster analysis, discriminant analysis, and multiple regression. To see examples of data analyzed, and how XLSTAT performs various statistical analysis functions, consult the XLSTAT Web page at www.xlstat.com.

Classification of Multivariate Methods

One challenge facing marketing researchers is determining the appropriate statistical method for a given problem. Several approaches have been suggested. A useful classification of most multivariate statistical techniques is presented in Exhibit 17.1. The multivariate procedures presented in this text are briefly described in Exhibit 17.2.

EXHIBIT 17.1 Classification of Multivariate Methods

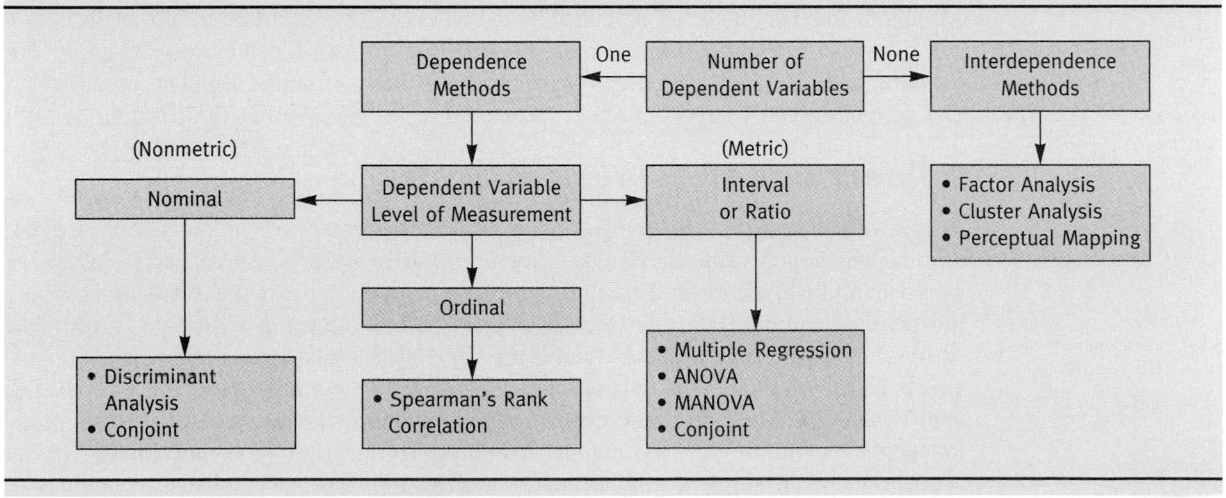

EXHIBIT 17.2 Summary of Selected Multivariate Methods

Multiple regression enables the marketing researcher to predict a single dependent metric variable from two or more metrically measured independent variables.

Multiple discriminant analysis can predict a single dependent nonmetric variable from two or more metrically measured independent variables.

Factor analysis is used to summarize the information contained in a large number of variables into a smaller number of subsets called factors.

Cluster analysis is used to classify respondents or objects (e.g., products, stores) into groups that are homogeneous, or similar within the groups but different between the groups.

Conjoint analysis is used to estimate the value (utility) that respondents associate with different product and/or service features, so that the most preferred combination of features can be determined.

Perceptual mapping is used to visually display respondents' perceptions of products, brands, companies, and so on. Several multivariate methods can be used to develop the data to construct perceptual maps.

Dependence and Interdependence Methods

Dependence method Multivariate technique appropriate when one or more of the variables can be identified as dependent variables and the remaining as independent variables.

If we use multivariate techniques to explain or predict the dependent variable on the basis of two or more independent variables, we are attempting to analyze and understand dependence. A **dependence method** can be defined as one in which a variable is identified as the dependent variable to be predicted or explained by other independent variables. Dependence techniques include multiple regression analysis, discriminant analysis, and MANOVA. For example, many businesses today are very interested in predicting dependent variables like customer loyalty, or high-volume customers versus light users (e.g., heavy vs. light consumers of Starbucks coffee), on the basis of numerous independent variables. Multiple discriminant analysis is a dependence technique that predicts customer usage (frequent beer drinker vs. nondrinker) based on several independent variables, such as how much is purchased, how often it is purchased, and age of purchaser.

Interdependence method Multivariate statistical technique in which the whole set of interdependent relationships is examined.

In contrast, an **interdependence method** is one in which no single variable or group of variables is defined as being independent or dependent. In this case, the multivariate procedure involves the analysis of all variables in the data set simultaneously. The goal of interdependence methods is to group respondents or objects together. In this case, no one variable is to be predicted or explained by the others. Cluster analysis, factor analysis, and multidimensional scaling are the most frequently used interdependence techniques. For example, a marketing manager who wants to identify various market segments or clusters of fast-food customers (burgers, pizza, chicken customers) might utilize these techniques.

Influence of Measurement Scales

Just as with other approaches to data analysis, the nature of the measurement scales will determine which multivariate technique is appropriate to analyze the data. Selection of the appropriate multivariate method requires consideration of the types of measures used for both independent and dependent sets of variables. When the dependent variable is measured nonmetrically, the appropriate method is discriminant analysis. When the dependent variable is measured metrically, the appropriate techniques are multiple regression, ANOVA, and MANOVA. Multiple regression and discriminant analysis typically require metric independents, but they can use nonmetric dummy variables. ANOVA and MANOVA are appropriate with nonmetric independent variables. The interdependence techniques of

GLOBAL INSIGHTS

Analysis from Global Research May Yield Interesting Findings

Just Kids Inc., a marketing research firm specializing in the 2- to 12-year-old market, uncovered some interesting findings among youngsters in Great Britain. Kids in Great Britain seem to shed their childhood much earlier than their peers elsewhere. McDonald's and Coke are universally loved, but the same advertising that attracts a 9-year-old Yank does not appeal to the 9-year-old Brit. Asked to identify their favorite TV programs, kids in Great Britain named adult shows. Their responses also demonstrated more teen behavior than those of kids from other countries. For example, most of the 9-year-olds around the globe said they wanted to be like their mom and dad when they grow up. In Britain, 9-year-olds want to be rock stars and entertainers. The conclusion: If you're a marketer with a clown and a happy meal, you may have a problem in England.

factor analysis and cluster analysis are most frequently used with metrically measured variables, but nonmetric adaptations are possible.

We covered multiple regression in Chapter 16. In this chapter we will consider factor analysis, cluster analysis, discriminant analysis, and conjoint analysis. These statistical techniques help us to analyze marketing problems that have multiple variables.

Multivariate statistical techniques help marketers make better decisions than is possible with univariate or bivariate statistics. But regardless of which type of technique is selected, the outcome of the analysis is key. Review the nearby Global Insights box to see how outcomes can change across markets.

Interdependence Methods

We begin our discussion of specific multivariate techniques with an analysis of interdependence methods. The purpose of techniques such as factor analysis and cluster analysis is not to predict a variable from a set of independent variables, but to summarize and better understand a large number of variables or objects.

Factor Analysis

Factor analysis A class of procedures primarily used for data reduction and summarization.

Factor analysis is a multivariate statistical technique that is used to summarize the information contained in a large number of variables into a smaller number of subsets or factors. The purpose of factor analysis is to simplify the data. With factor analysis there is no distinction between dependent and independent variables; rather, all variables under investigation are analyzed together to identify underlying factors.

Many problems facing businesses today are often the result of a combination of several variables. For example, if the local McDonald's franchisor is interested in assessing customer satisfaction, many variables of interest must be measured. Variables such as freshness of the food, speed of service, taste, food temperature, cleanliness, and how friendly and courteous the personnel are would all be measured by means of a number of rating questions.

Let's look at an intuitive example of factor analysis. Customers were asked to rate a fast-food restaurant on six characteristics. On the basis of the pattern of their responses, these

EXHIBIT 17.3 A Factor Analysis Application to a Fast-Food Restaurant

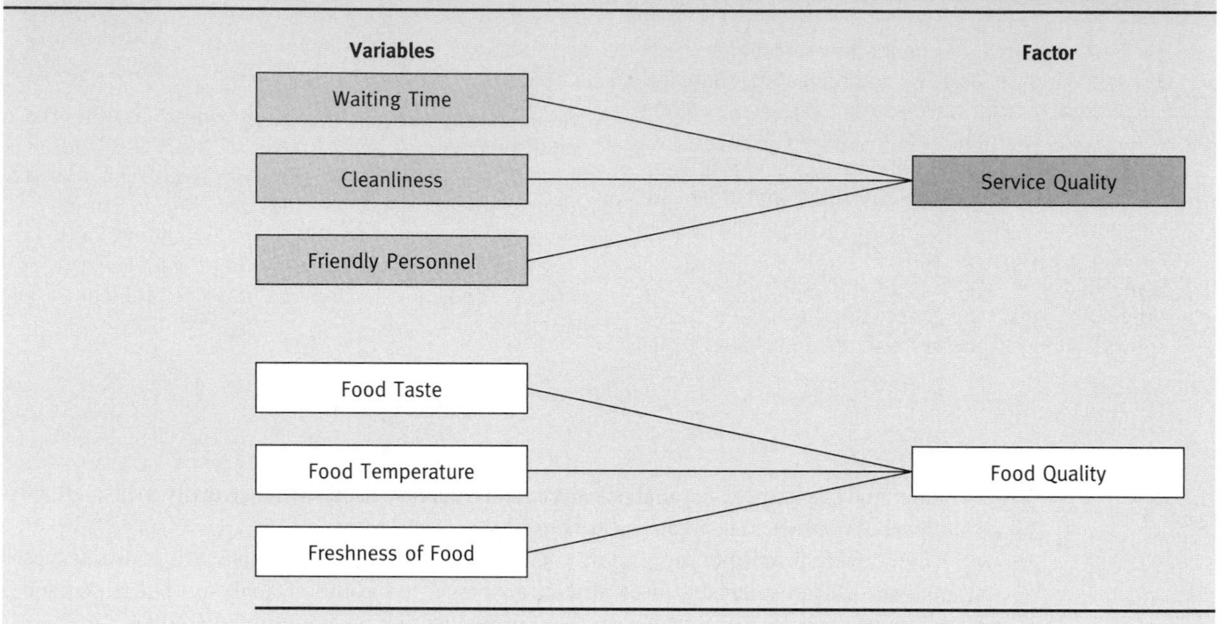

six measures were combined into two summary measures, or factors: service quality and food quality (see Exhibit 17.3). Marketing researchers use factor analysis to summarize the information contained in a large number of variables into a smaller number of factors. The result is that managers can then simplify their decision making because they have to consider only two broad areas—service quality and food quality—instead of six. Our example has reduced six variables to two factors, but in typical business situations marketing researchers use factor analysis to reduce, for example, 50 variables to only 10 or fewer factors, a much simpler problem to handle.

Factor loading
A simple correlation between the variables and the factors.

The starting point in interpreting factor analysis is factor loadings. **Factor loading** refers to the correlation between each of the original variables and the newly developed factors. Each factor loading is a measure of the importance of the variable in measuring each factor. Factor loadings, like correlations, can vary from +1.0 to –1.0. If variable A_4 (food taste) is closely associated with factor 2, the factor loading or correlation would be high. The statistical analysis associated with factor analysis would produce factor loadings between each factor and each of the original variables. An illustration of the output of this statistical analysis is given in Exhibit 17.4. Variables A_1, A_2, and A_3 are highly correlated with factor 1 and variables A_4, A_5, and A_6 are highly correlated with factor 2. An analyst would say that variables A_1, A_2, and A_3 have "high loadings" on factor 1, which means that they help define that factor. Similarly, an analyst would say that variables A_4, A_5, and A_6 have "high loadings" on factor 2.

The next step in factor analysis is to name the resulting factors. The researcher examines the variables that have high loadings on each factor. There often will be a certain consistency among the variables that load high on a given factor. For example, the ratings on waiting time (A_1), cleanliness (A_2), and friendly personnel (A_3) all load on the same factor. We have chosen to name this factor *service quality* because the three variables deal with some aspect of a customer's service experience with the restaurant. Variables A_4, A_5, and A_6 all load highly on factor 2, which we named *food quality.* Naming factors is often a subjective process of combining intuition with an inspection of the variables that have high loadings on each factor.

EXHIBIT 17.4 Factor Loadings for the Two Factors

	Correlation with:	
Variable	**Factor 1**	**Factor 2**
A_1 (waiting time)	.79	.07
A_2 (cleanliness)	.72	.10
A_3 (friendly personnel)	.72	.05
A_4 (food taste)	.09	.85
A_5 (food temperature)	.11	.70
A_6 (freshness of food)	.04	.74

A final aspect of factor analysis concerns the number of factors to retain. While our restaurant example dealt with two factors, many situations can involve anywhere from one factor to as many factors as there are variables. Deciding on how many factors to retain is a very complex process because there can be more than one possible solution to any factor analysis problem. A discussion of the technical aspects of this part of factor analysis is beyond the scope of this book, but we will provide an example of how an analyst can decide how many factors to retain.

An important measure to consider in deciding how many factors to retain is the percentage of the variation in the original data that is explained by each factor. A factor analysis computer program will produce a table of numbers that will give the percentage of variation explained by each factor. A simplified illustration of these numbers is presented in Exhibit 17.5. In this example, we would definitely keep the first two factors, because they explain a total of 75.7 percent of the variability in the five measures. The last three factors combined explain only 24.3 percent of the variation, and each accounts for only a small portion of the total variance. Thus, they contribute little to our understanding of the data and would not be retained. Most marketing researchers stop factoring when additional factors no longer make sense, because the variance they explain often contains a large amount of random and error variance.

Factor Analysis Applications in Marketing Research

While our fast-food example illustrated the power of factor analysis in simplifying customer perceptions toward a fast-food restaurant, the technique has many other important applications in marketing research:

- *Advertising.* Factor analysis can be used to better understand media habits of various customers.

EXHIBIT 17.5 Percentage of Variation in Original Data Explained by Each Factor

Factor	Percentage of Variation Explained
1	50.3%
2	46.5
3	1.8
4	0.8
5	0.6

- *Pricing.* Factor analysis can help identify the characteristics of price-sensitive and prestige-sensitive customers.
- *Product.* Factor analysis can be used to identify brand attributes that influence consumer choice.
- *Distribution.* Factor analysis can be employed to better understand channel selection criteria among distribution channel members.

SPSS Application—Factor Analysis of Restaurant Perceptions

The value of factor analysis can be demonstrated with our Santa Fe Grill database. When we look at our database we have many variables that are measured metrically. Let's look first at variables X12 to X21, which are customers' perceptions of the Santa Fe Grill and its competitor Jose's on 10 dimensions. The task is to determine if we can simplify our understanding of the perceptions of the restaurant by reducing the number of restaurant perceptions variables to fewer than 10. If this is possible, the owners of the Santa Fe Grill can simplify their decision making by focusing on fewer aspects of the restaurants in developing competitive profiles as well as appropriate marketing strategies.

The SPSS click-through sequence is ANALYZE → DATA REDUCTION → FACTOR, which leads to a dialog box where you select variables X12–X21. After you have put these variables into the Variables box, look at the data analysis options below. First click on the Descriptives box and unclick the Initial Solution box because we do not need it at this point. Now click Continue to return to the previous dialog box. Next go to the Extraction box. In this one you leave the default of principal components and unclick the unrotated factor solution under Display. We will keep the other defaults, so now click the Continue box. Next go to the Rotation box. The default is None. We want to rotate, so click on Varimax as your rotational choice and then Continue. Finally, go to the Options box and click Sorted by Size, and then change the Suppress Absolute Values from .10 to .30. These last choices eliminate unneeded information, thus making the solutions printout much easier to read. We do not need Scores at this point, so we can click on OK at the top of the dialog box to execute the factor analysis. Exhibit 17.6 shows examples of some of the dialog boxes for running this factor analysis.

The SPSS output for a factor analysis of the restaurant perceptions is shown in Exhibit 17.7. The first table you will see on the output is the Rotated Component Matrix table. Labels for the 10 variables analyzed (X12–X21) are shown in the left column. To the right are four columns of numbers containing the factor loadings for the four factors that resulted from the factor analysis of restaurant perceptions. By suppressing loadings under .30 we see only three numbers under column one (Component 1, or factor 1), three numbers under column two (Component 2, or factor 2), and two numbers under columns three and four (Components 3 and 4). For example, X12—Friendly Employees has a loading of .923 on factor 1, and X18—Excellent Food Taste has a loading of .895 on factor 2. We prefer a factor solution in which each original variable loads on only one factor, as in our example. But in many cases this does not happen.

Before trying to name the factors we must decide if four factors are enough or if we need more. Our objective here is to have as few factors as possible yet account for a reasonable amount of the information contained in the 10 original variables. To determine the number of factors, we look at information in the Total Variance Explained table (bottom of Exhibit 17.7). It shows that the four factors accounted for 83.600 percent of the variance in the original 10 variables. This is a substantial amount of the information to account for, and we have reduced the number of original variables by two-thirds, from 10 to four. So let's consider four factors acceptable and see if our factors seem logical.

eXHIBIT 17.6 SPSS Dialog Box Examples for Factor Analysis

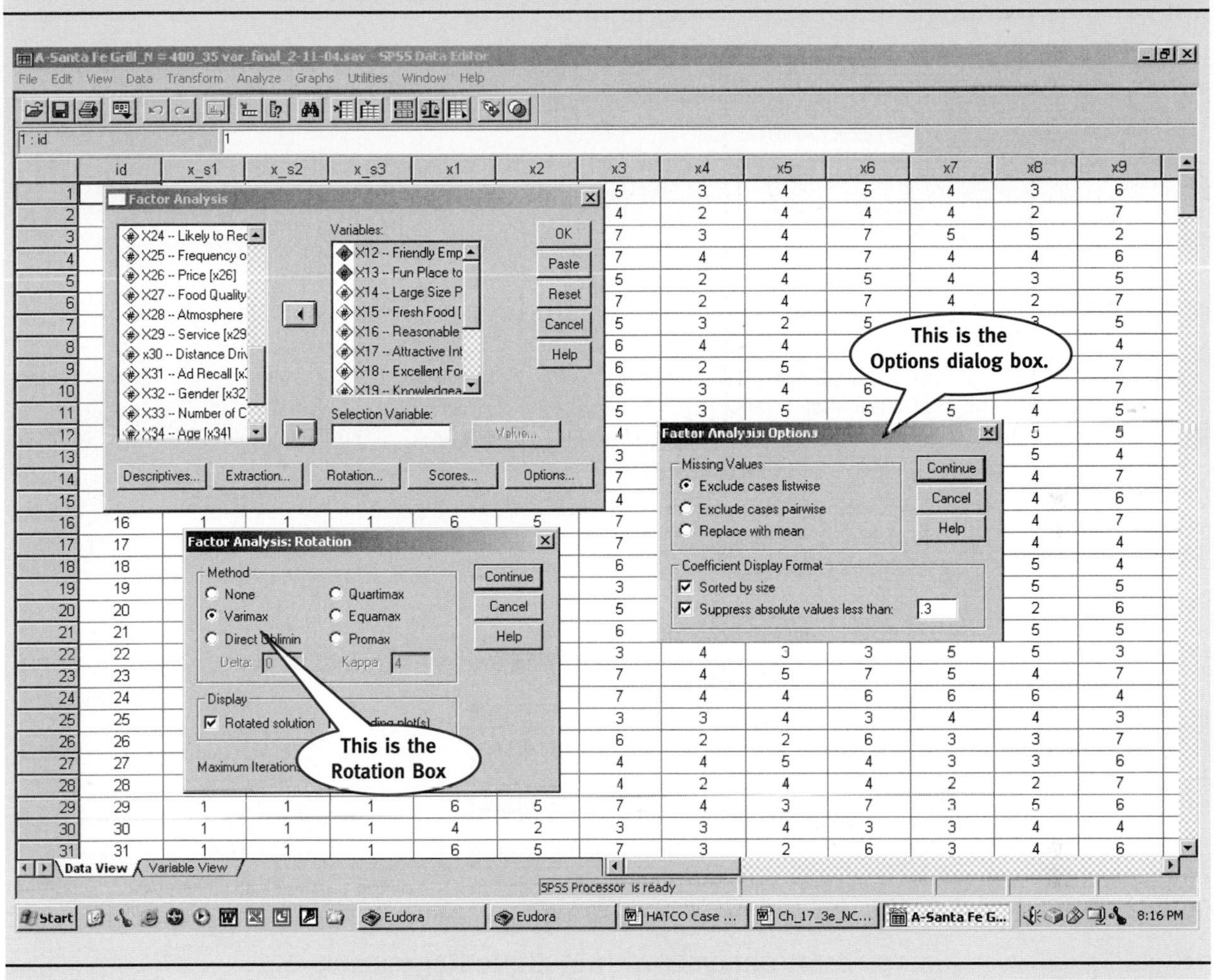

To determine if our factors are logical, look at the information in the Rotated Component Matrix (Exhibit 17.7). First, examine which original variables combine to make each new factor. Factor 1 is made up of X12—Friendly employees, X21—Speed of Service, and X19—Knowledgeable Employees. Factor 2 is made up of X18—Excellent Food Taste, X15—Fresh Food, and X20—Proper Food Temperature. Factor 3 is made up of X14—Large Size Portions and X16—Reasonable Prices. Factor 4 is made up of X17—Attractive Interior and X13—Fun Place to Eat. To analyze the logic of the combinations we look at the variables with the highest loadings (largest absolute size). That is why we suppressed loadings less than .30. Factor 1 seems to be related to service, whereas factor 2 is related to food. Similarly, factor 3 seems to be related to value, whereas factor 4 is related to atmosphere. Thus, we have developed a four-factor solution that accounts for a substantial amount of variance and shows logic in the combinations of the 10 original variables. With this four-factor solution, instead of having to think about 10 separate variables, the owners of the Santa Fe Grill can now think about only four variables—service, food, value, and atmosphere—when they are developing their marketing strategies.

eXHIBIT 17.7 SPSS Output for Factor Analysis of Restaurant Perceptions

Rotated Component Matrix[a]

	Component			
	1	2	3	4
X12 -- Friendly Employees	.923			
X21 -- Speed of Service	.907			
X19 -- Knowledgeable Employees	.744			
X18 -- Excellent Food Taste		.895		
X15 -- Fresh Food		.858		
X20 -- Proper Food Temperature		.807		
X14 -- Large Size Portions			.969	
X16 -- Reasonable Prices			.968	
X17 -- Attractive Interior				.916
X13 -- Fun Place to Eat				.860

Extraction Method: Principal Component Analysis.
Rotation Method: Varimax with Kaiser Normalization.
a. Rotation converged in 5 iterations.

Total Variance Explained

	Rotation Sums of Squared Loadings		
Component	Total	% of Variance	Cumulative %
1	2.327	23.275	23.275
2	2.310	23.103	46.378
3	1.979	19.793	66.171
4	1.743	17.428	83.600

Extraction Method: Principal Component Analysis.

Using Factor Analysis with Multiple Regression

Sometimes we may want to use the results of a factor analysis with another multivariate technique, such as multiple regression. This is most helpful when we use factor analysis to combine a large number of variables into a smaller set of variables. We can demonstrate this with the previous example, where we combined the 10 restaurant perceptions into four factors.

Without factor analysis, we must consider customer perceptions on 10 separate characteristics. But if we use the results of our factor analysis we have to consider only the four characteristics (factors) developed in our factor solution. To use the resulting four factors in a multiple regression, we first must calculate factor scores. Factor scores are composite scores estimated for each respondent on each of the derived factors. Return to the SPSS dialog box for the four-factor solution (if you have left the previous factor solution, follow the same instructions as before to get to this dialog box). Looking at the bottom of this dialog box you see the Scores box, which we did not use before. Click on this box and then click Save as Variables. When you do this there will be more options, but just click the Regression option. Now click Continue and then OK and you will calculate the factor scores. The result will be four factor scores for each of the 405 respondents. They will appear at

eXHIBIT 17.8 Factor Scores for Restaurant Perceptions

Santa Fe Grill_new class test - 5 expanded_Nov 27_N=405.sav - SPSS Data Editor

File Edit View Data Transform Analyze Graphs Utilities Window Help

31 :

	fac1_1	fac2_1	fac3_1	fac4_1	var	var
1	.40533	.48619	-.51450	1.35933		
2	-1.29543	1.40070	-1.29942	.60775		
3	-1.74419	-1.08350	1.59215	-1.13164		
4	.35381	-.42437	1.18151	.22402		
5	-1.24036	.64092	-.22915	-.77495		
6	-.68291	1.56728	1.01214	.32439		
7	-.12460	.18962	-.53141	1.39211		
8	.44839	-1.36806	.60254	-.73064		
9	.76047	.94640	-.10818	.38988		
10	.45279	1.31488	.12629	1.42220		
11	-1.35313	.00031	-.43757	.48331		
12	.26070	-1.30121	-1.02469	-.51249		
13	.08139	-1.16261	-1.67707	-1.37936		
14	.31457	.48156	1.20660	.28846		
15	1.14978	-.97800	-1.13135	.50573		
16	.99248	-.34137	.70742	.54304		
17	-.49178	-.82680	1.23548	.20540		
18	.52178	-1.38451	-.00463	.48504		
19	-1.10610	-.32936	-2.17115	.86072		
20	1.08607	-.02794	-.24655	.15135		
21	-.70349	-1.15043	.48209	-.22685		
22	-.61848	-1.33787	-1.61439	-1.02686		
23	1.26023	-1.05323	1.12192	1.39241		
24	-1.18793	-2.15848	1.04185	.07556		
25	-.67450	-.35519	-1.99872	.64860		
26	1.33731	.61802	.18691	1.49992		
27	.83359	.40333	-1.09525	-.55797		
28	1.43831	1.43540	-1.57044	1.91791		

the far right side of your original database and will be labeled fac1_1 (scores for factor 1), fac2_1 (scores for factor 2), and so on. See Exhibit 17.8 to view the factor scores.

Now we want to see if perceptions of the restaurant customers, as measured by the factors, are related to satisfaction. In this case, the single dependent metric variable is X22—Satisfaction and the independent variables are the factor scores. The SPSS click-through sequence is ANALYZE → REGRESSION → LINEAR, which leads you to a dialog box where you select the variables. You should select X22 as the dependent and fac1_1, fac2_1, fac3_1, and fac4_1 as the independents. Note that the fac1_1, fac2_1, fac3_1, and fac4_1 are the factor scores of the new variables you created in the previous example. Now click on the Statistics button and check Descriptives. There are several additional types of analysis that can be selected, but at this point we will use the program defaults. Click OK at the top right of the dialog box to execute the regression. The dialog boxes for this regression are shown in Exhibit 17.9.

The Descriptive Statistics and bivariate correlations for the SPSS regression with factor scores are shown in Exhibit 17.10. Note that the factor scores are standardized with a mean of zero and a standard deviation of one. Moreover, in the correlations table you can see that the factor scores have correlations of zero with each other, but in all cases are significantly related to dependent variable satisfaction.

EXHIBIT 17.9 SPSS Dialog Boxes for Regression with Factor Scores

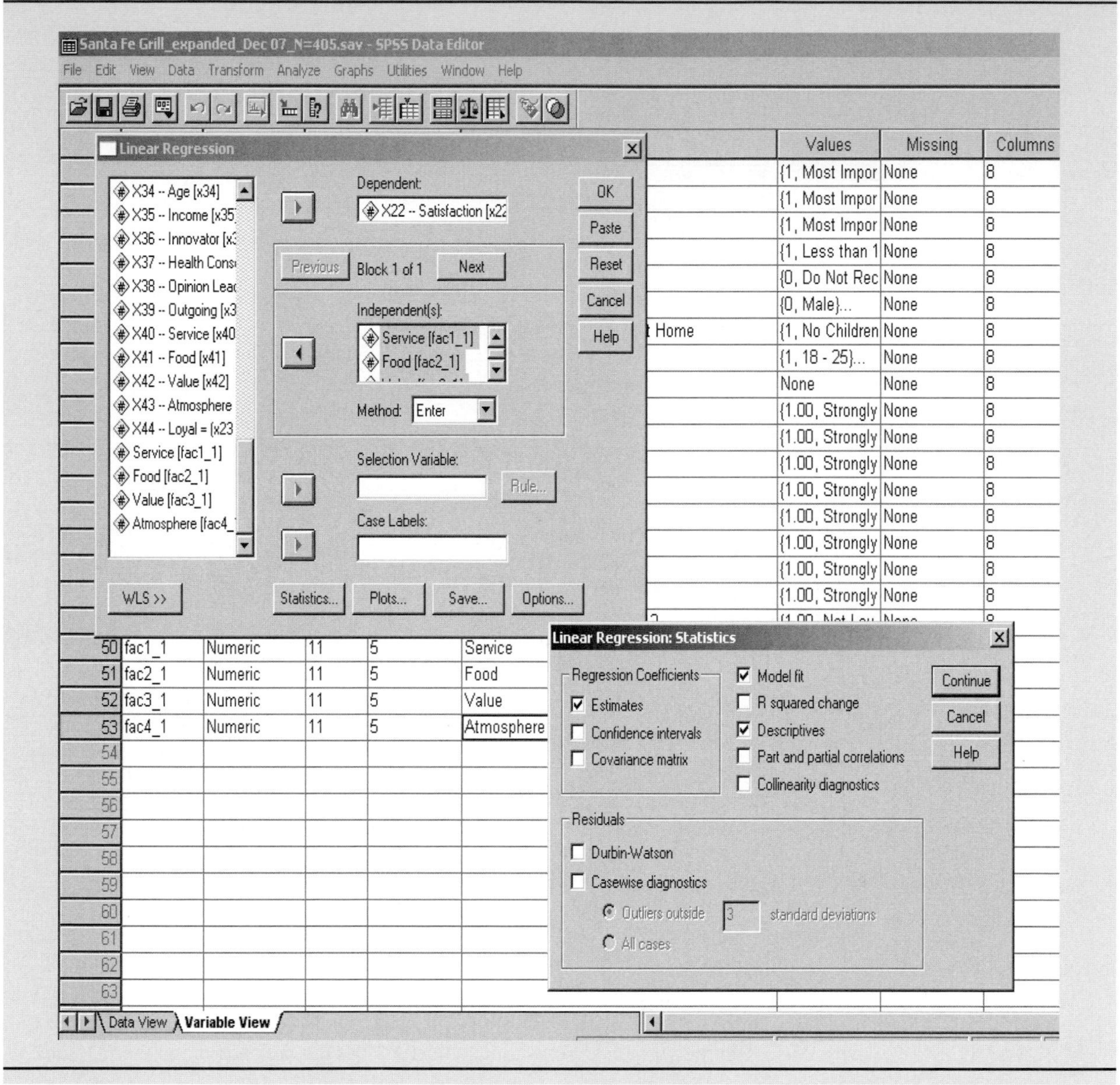

The Model Summary table in Exhibit 17.11 reveals that the R-square is .490 and the ANOVA table indicates it is statistically significant at the .000 level. This means that 49 percent of the variation in satisfaction (dependent variable) can be explained from the four independent variables—the factor scores. Footnote *a* underneath the table tells you that the regression equation included a constant and that the predictor (independent) variables were factor scores for the four variables (Atmosphere, Value, Service, and Food).

To determine if one or more of the factor score variables are significant predictors of satisfaction we must examine the Coefficients table (Exhibit 17.11). Looking at the Standardized Coefficients Beta column reveals that Factor 1—Service is .388, Factor 2—Food

eXHIBIT 17.10 Multiple Regression with Factor Scores—Descriptive Statistics

Output6 - SPSS Viewer

File Edit View Insert Format Analyze Graphs Utilities Window Help

Regression

Descriptive Statistics

	Mean	Std. Deviation	N
X22 -- Satisfaction	4.83	1.118	405
Service	.0000000	1.00000000	405
Food	.0000000	1.00000000	405
Value	.0000000	1.00000000	405
Atmosphere	.0000000	1.00000000	405

Correlations

		X22 -- Satisfaction	Service	Food	Value	Atmosphere
Pearson Correlation	X22 -- Satisfaction	1.000	.388	.498	.238	.186
	Service	.388	1.000	.000	.000	.000
	Food	.498	.000	1.000	.000	.000
	Value	.238	.000	.000	1.000	.000
	Atmosphere	.186	.000	.000	.000	1.000
Sig. (1-tailed)	X22 -- Satisfaction	.	.000	.000	.000	.000
	Service	.000	.	.500	.500	.500
	Food	.000	.500	.	.500	.500
	Value	.000	.500	.500	.	.500
	Atmosphere	.000	.500	.500	.500	.
N	X22 -- Satisfaction	405	405	405	405	405
	Service	405	405	405	405	405
	Food	405	405	405	405	405
	Value	405	405	405	405	405
	Atmosphere	405	405	405	405	405

is .498, Factor 3—Value is .238, and Factor 4—Atmosphere is .186. The statistical significance is .000 for all four factors. Thus, we know from this regression analysis that perceptions of all restaurant factors are strong predictors of satisfaction with the two restaurants, with Factor 2 being somewhat better than the other three factors since the size of the Factor 2 Beta is the largest. Furthermore, interpreting only four variables in developing a marketing strategy is much easier than is dealing with the original 10 independent variables.

In this section we have demonstrated how you can use one multivariate technique—factor analysis—with another technique—regression—to better understand your data. It is also possible, however, to use other multivariate techniques in combination. For example, if your dependent variable is nonmetric, such as gender, then you could use discriminant

eXHIBIT 17.11 Multiple Regression with Factor Scores—Model Results

Output6 - SPSS Viewer

File Edit View Insert Format Analyze Graphs Utilities Window Help

Model Summary

Model	R	R Square	Adjusted R Square	Std. Error of the Estimate
1	.700[a]	.490	.485	.802

a. Predictors: (Constant), Atmosphere, Value, Food, Service

ANOVA[b]

Model		Sum of Squares	df	Mean Square	F	Sig.
1	Regression	247.799	4	61.950	96.253	.000[a]
	Residual	257.445	400	.644		
	Total	505.244	404			

a. Predictors: (Constant), Atmosphere, Value, Food, Service

b. Dependent Variable: X22 -- Satisfaction

Coefficients[a]

Model		Unstandardized Coefficients		Standardized Coefficients	t	Sig.
		B	Std. Error	Beta		
1	(Constant)	4.830	.040		121.152	.000
	Service	.434	.040	.388	10.872	.000
	Food	.557	.040	.498	13.962	.000
	Value	.267	.040	.238	6.681	.000
	Atmosphere	.208	.040	.186	5.217	.000

a. Dependent Variable: X22 -- Satisfaction

analysis in a manner similar to our use of regression. Also, you could use cluster analysis in combination with regression or discriminant analysis. This will be clearer after we have covered these other techniques in this chapter.

Cluster analysis A multivariate interdependence technique whose primary objective is to classify objects into relatively homogeneous groups based on the set of variables considered.

Cluster Analysis

Cluster analysis is another interdependence multivariate method. As the name implies, the basic purpose of cluster analysis is to classify or segment objects (customers, products, market areas) into groups so that objects within each group are similar to one another on a variety of variables. Cluster analysis seeks to classify segments or objects such that there will be as much similarity within segments and as much difference between segments as possible. Thus, this method strives to identify natural groupings or segments among many variables without designating any of the variables as a dependent variable.

We will start our discussion of cluster analysis with this intuitive example. A fast-food chain wants to open an eat-in restaurant in a new, growing suburb of a major metropolitan area. Marketing researchers have surveyed a large sample of households in this suburb and collected data on characteristics such as demographics, lifestyles, and expenditures on eating out. The fast-food chain wants to identify one or more household segments that are likely to visit its new restaurant. Once this segment is identified, advertising and services will be tailored to them.

A target segment can be identified by conducting a cluster analysis of the data researchers have gathered. Results of the cluster analysis will identify segments, each containing households that have similar characteristics but differing considerably from the other segments. Exhibit 17.12 identifies four potential clusters or segments for our fast-food chain. As our intuitive example illustrates, the growing suburb contains households that seldom visit restaurants at all (cluster 1), households that tend to frequent dine-in restaurants exclusively (cluster 2), households that tend to frequent fast-food restaurants exclusively (cluster 3), and households that frequent both dine-in and fast-food restaurants (cluster 4). By examining the characteristics associated with each of the clusters, management can decide which clusters to target and how best to reach them through marketing communications.

Statistical Procedures for Cluster Analysis

Several cluster analysis procedures are available, each based on a somewhat different set of complex computer programs. The general approach in each procedure is the same, however, and involves measuring the similarity between objects on the basis of their ratings on the various characteristics. The degree of similarity between objects is usually determined

eXHIBIT 17.12 Cluster Analysis Based on Two Characteristics

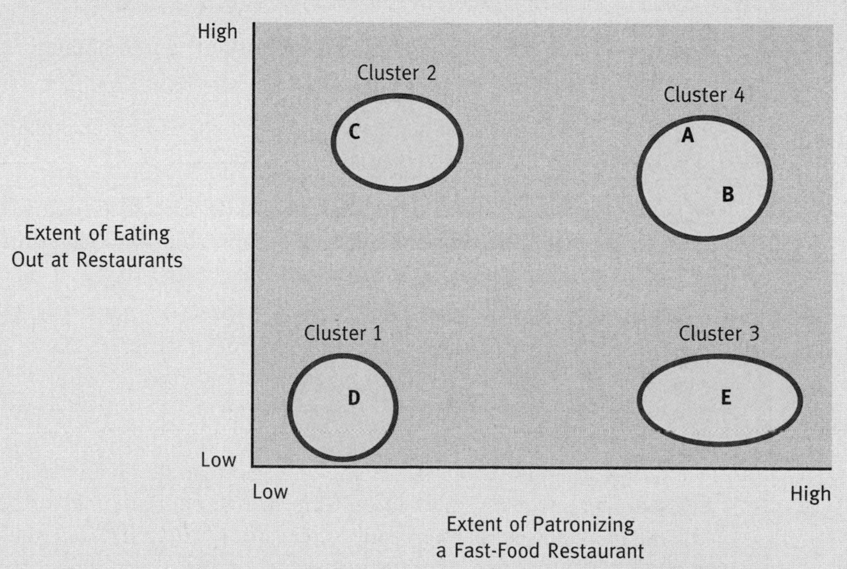

through a distance measure. This process can be illustrated with our earlier example involving two variables:

V1 = Frequency of eating out at restaurants

V2 = Frequency of eating out at fast-food restaurants

Data on V1 and V2 are shown on the two-dimensional plot in Exhibit 17.12. Five individuals are plotted with the letters A, B, C, D, and E. Each letter represents the position of one consumer with regard to the two variables V1 and V2. The distance between any pair of letters is positively related to how similar the corresponding individuals are when the two variables are considered together. Thus, individual A is more like B than like either C, D, or E. As can be seen, four distinct clusters are identified in the exhibit.

This analysis can inform marketing management of the proposed new fast-food restaurant that customers are to be found among those who tend to eat at both fancy and fast-food restaurants (cluster 4). To develop a marketing strategy to reach this cluster of households, management would like to identify demographic, psychographic, and behavioral profiles of the individuals in cluster 4.

Clusters are often developed from scatter plots, as we have done with our fast-food restaurant example. This is a complex trial-and-error process. Fortunately, computer algorithms are available and must be used if the clustering is to be done in an efficient, systematic fashion. While the mathematics are beyond the scope of this chapter, the algorithms are all based on the idea of starting with some arbitrary cluster boundaries and modifying the boundaries until a point is reached where the average distances within clusters are as small as possible relative to the average distances between clusters.

Cluster Analysis Applications in Marketing Research

While our fast-food example illustrated how cluster analysis segmented groups of households, it has many other important applications in marketing research:

- *New-product research.* Clustering brands can help a firm examine its product offerings relative to competition. Brands in the same cluster often compete more fiercely with each other than with brands in other clusters.
- *Test marketing.* Cluster analysis groups test cities into homogeneous clusters for test marketing purposes.
- *Buyer behavior.* Cluster analysis can be employed to identify similar groups of buyers who have similar choice criteria.
- *Market segmentation.* Cluster analysis can develop distinct market segments on the basis of geographic, demographic, psychographic, and behavioral variables.

SPSS Application—Cluster Analysis

The value of cluster analysis can be demonstrated easily with our restaurant database. The task is to determine if there are subgroups/clusters of the 405 respondents to the customer surveys of the two restaurants. In selecting the variables to use in cluster analysis, we must use only variables that are metrically measured and logically related. There are three logical sets of metric variables to consider for the cluster analysis: the life style questions (x1–X11), the restaurant perceptions questions X12–X21), and the three relationship questions (X22–X24; X25 is nonmetric).

The owners of the Santa Fe Grill have been asking if there are subgroups of customers that exhibit different levels of loyalty to the restaurant. To answer this question, we must define what we mean by loyalty. The loyalty construct could consist of variables X22–X24, or it could include only X23 and X24, based on the assumption that satisfaction (X22) differs from loyalty. While the definition of loyalty can be debated, let's use only variables X23 and X24 as our measure of the loyalty construct. Thus, we will apply cluster analysis using variables X23 and X24 to find loyalty clusters for the restaurant customers.

The SPSS click-through sequence is ANALYZE → CLASSIFY → HIERARCHICAL CLUSTER, which leads to a dialog box where you select variables X23 and X24. After you have put these variables into the Variables box, look at the other options below. Unclick the Plots check in the Display window; this is not needed and will speed up the processing time. You do not need to change anything in the Statistics and Plots options below. Click on the Method box and select Ward's under the Cluster Method (you have to scroll to the bottom of the list), but use the default of squared euclidean distances under Measure. We do nothing with the Save option at this point, so you can click OK at the top of the dialog box to execute the cluster analysis. Exhibit 17.13 shows two of the SPSS dialog boxes for running the cluster analysis.

The SPSS output has a table called Agglomeration Schedule, a portion of which is shown in Exhibit 17.14. This table has lots of numbers in it, but we look only at the numbers in the Coefficients column (middle of table). Go to the bottom of the table and look at the numbers

eXHIBIT 17.13 SPSS Dialog Boxes for Cluster Analysis

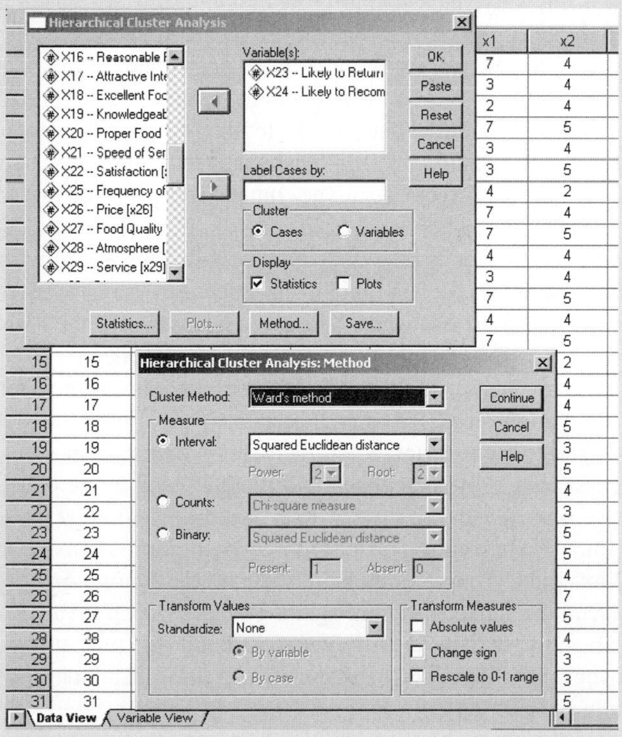

EXHIBIT 17.14 Cluster Analysis Agglomeration Schedule

390	40	175	.800	300	0	392
391	186	296	2.133	94	101	393
392	11	40	6.813	385	390	399
393	9	186	11.766	372	391	395
394	7	58	17.099	386	282	398
395	9	10	22.692	393	364	402
396	1	15	29.142		325	401
397	26	33	41.121	368	359	400
398	5	7	59.787	377	394	403
399	2	11	86.047	388	392	401
400	6	26	117.019	384	397	402
401	1	2	179.094	396	399	403
402	6	9	245.556	400	395	404
403	1	5	420.974	401	398	404
404	1	6	1073.042	403	402	0

Coefficients

in the Coefficients column (inside the box). The number at the bottom will be the largest, and the numbers get smaller as you move up the table. The bottom number is 1073.042, the one right above it is 420.974, and the next above is 245.556. The coefficients in this column show how much you reduce your error by moving from one cluster to two clusters, from two clusters to three clusters, and so on. As you move from one cluster to two clusters there always will be a large drop (difference) in the coefficient of error, and from two clusters to three clusters another drop. Each time you move up the column the drop (difference) in the numbers will get smaller. What you are looking for is where the difference between two numbers gets substantially smaller. This means that going from, say, three clusters to four clusters does not reduce your error very much. You will note that in this case the change is from 245.556 to 179.094. For this solution, we definitely would choose three clusters over four because the difference between the numbers as you go from three clusters to four clusters is getting much smaller. We might also choose to use only two clusters instead of three. We could do this because the error is reduced a large amount (>50%) by going from one to two clusters, and two clusters likely will be easier to understand than three.

Let's focus on the two-cluster solution because it is easier to understand. Before trying to name the two clusters, let's make sure they are significantly different. To do so, you must first create a new variable that identifies which cluster each of the 405 respondents has been assigned to by the cluster analysis. Go back to the Cluster dialog box and click on the Save box. When you do this, you can choose to create a new cluster membership variable for a single solution or for a range of solutions. Choose the single solution, put a 2 in the box, and a group membership variable for the two-group solution will be created when you run the cluster program again. The new group membership variable will be the new variable in your data set at the far-right-hand side of your data labeled clu2_1. It will show a 1 for respondents in Cluster One and a 2 for respondents assigned to Cluster Two, as shown in Exhibit 17.15.

Now you can run a one-way ANOVA between the two clusters to see if they are statistically different. The SPSS click-through sequence is ANALYZE → COMPARE MEANS

eXHIBIT 17.15 New Cluster Variable to Identify Group Membership

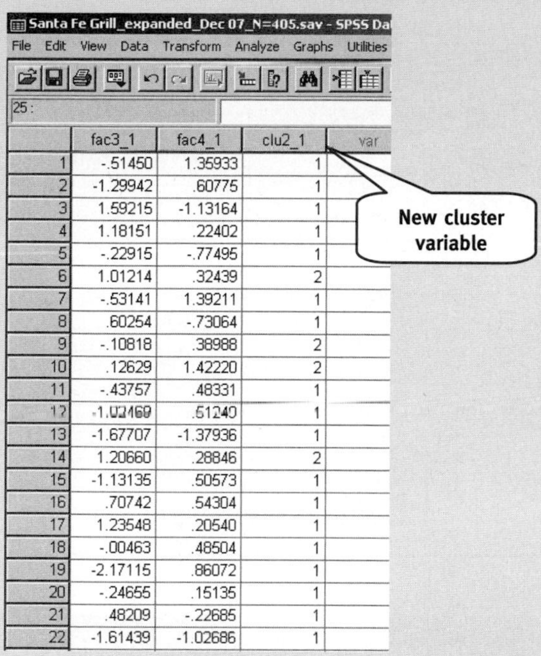

	fac3_1	fac4_1	clu2_1	var
1	-.51450	1.35933	1	
2	-1.29942	.60775	1	
3	1.59215	-1.13164	1	
4	1.18151	.22402	1	
5	-.22915	-.77495	1	
6	1.01214	.32439	2	
7	-.53141	1.39211	1	
8	.60254	-.73064	1	
9	-.10818	.38988	2	
10	.12629	1.42220	2	
11	-.43757	.48331	1	
12	-1.02469	.51240	1	
13	-1.67707	-1.37936	1	
14	1.20660	.28846	2	
15	-1.13135	.50573	1	
16	.70742	.54304	1	
17	1.23548	.20540	1	
18	-.00463	.48504	1	
19	-2.17115	.86072	1	
20	-.24655	.15135	1	
21	.48209	-.22685	1	
22	-1.61439	-1.02686	1	

→ ONE-WAY ANOVA. Next you put variables X23 and X24 in the Variables box and the new Cluster Membership variable in the Factor box. This will be the new variable in your data set labeled clu2_1. Next click on the Options box and then on Descriptive under Statistics, and Continue. Now click OK and you will get an output with a Descriptives and an ANOVA table. The dialog boxes for running this procedure are shown in Exhibit 17.16.

The SPSS output for the ANOVA of the cluster solution is shown in Exhibit 17.17. When you look at the Descriptives table you will see the sample sizes for each cluster (N) and the means of each variable for each cluster, as well as a lot of other numbers we will not use. For example, the sample size for Cluster One is 271 and for Cluster Two it is 134. Similarly, the mean for likely to return in Cluster One is 3.86 and in Cluster Two it is 5.68, and the mean for likely to recommend in Cluster One is 3.13 and in Cluster Two it is 5.12.

We interpret the two clusters by looking at the means of the variables for each of the groups. By looking at the means we see that respondents in Cluster One are relatively less likely to return and less likely to recommend (lower mean values), and therefore less loyal. In contrast, Cluster Two respondents are relatively more likely to return and more likely to recommend the restaurants (higher mean values), and therefore more loyal. Thus, Cluster Two respondents have much more favorable perceptions of the restaurants than do respondents in Cluster One. We therefore can define Cluster Two as the more highly loyal group. A final interesting conclusion is that there are substantially more customers that are not loyal ($N = 271$) than there are loyal customers ($N = 134$).

Next, look at the ANOVA table to see if the differences between the group means are statistically significant. You will see that for all three variables the differences between the

eXHIBIT 17.16 Comparing Cluster Means Using ANOVA

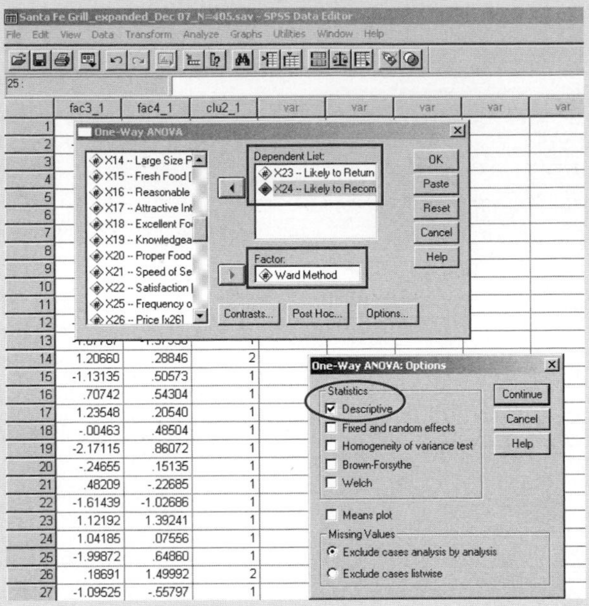

eXHIBIT 17.17 SPSS ANOVA Output—Results for Cluster of X23–X24

Descriptives

		N	Mean	Std. Deviation	Std. Error	95% Confidence Interval for Mean Lower Bound	95% Confidence Interval for Mean Upper Bound	Minimum	Maximum
X23 -- Likely to Return	1	271	3.86	.740	.045	3.77	3.95	2	6
	2	134	5.68	.608	.053	5.58	5.78	5	7
	Total	405	4.46	1.104	.055	4.36	4.57	2	7
X24 -- Likely to Recommend	1	271	3.13	.747	.045	3.04	3.22	2	4
	2	134	5.12	.736	.064	4.99	5.25	4	7
	Total	405	3.79	1.196	.059	3.67	3.90	2	7

ANOVA

		Sum of Squares	df	Mean Square	F	Sig.
X23 -- Likely to Return	Between Groups	295.581	1	295.581	604.206	.000
	Within Groups	197.150	403	.489		
	Total	492.731	404			
X24 -- Likely to Recommend	Between Groups	355.169	1	355.169	643.095	.000
	Within Groups	222.569	403	.552		
	Total	577.738	404			

means of the two clusters are highly significant (Sig. = .000) and therefore statistically different. Thus, we have two very different groups of restaurant customers with Cluster Two being relatively loyal to the restaurants and Cluster One much less loyal. Based on the mean values and significance levels, we will name Cluster One "Low Loyalty" and Cluster Two "Moderately High Loyalty."

Dependence Methods

We now focus our discussion on the multivariate techniques that deal with analysis of dependence (see Exhibit 17.1). The purpose of dependence techniques is to predict a dependent variable from a set of independent variables. The dependence techniques we cover in this book include multiple regression, discriminant analysis, and conjoint analysis. We covered regression in Chapter 15, and we cover discriminant and conjoint analysis in this chapter.

Discriminant Analysis

Discriminant analysis A technique for analyzing marketing research data when the criterion or dependent variable is categorical and the predictor or independent variables are interval.

Discriminant analysis is a multivariate technique used for predicting group membership on the basis of two or more independent variables. There are many situations where the marketing researcher's purpose is to classify objects or groups by a set of independent variables. Thus, the dependent variable in discriminant analysis is nonmetric or categorical. In marketing, consumers are often categorized on the basis of heavy versus light users of a product, or viewers versus nonviewers of a media vehicle such as a television commercial. Conversely, the independent variables in discriminant analysis are metric and often include characteristics such as demographics and psychographics. Additional insights into discriminant analysis can be found in the nearby A Closer Look at Research (Using Technology) box.

Let's begin our discussion of discriminant analysis with an intuitive example. A fast-food restaurant, Back Yard Burgers (BYB), wants to see whether a lifestyle variable such as eating a nutritious meal (X_1) and a demographic variable such as household income (X_2) are useful in distinguishing households visiting their restaurant from those visiting other fast-food restaurants. Marketing researchers have gathered data on X_1 and X_2 for a random sample of households that eat at fast-food restaurants, including Back Yard Burgers. Discriminant analysis procedures would plot these data on a two-dimensional graph, as shown in Exhibit 17.18.

The scatter plot in Exhibit 17.18 yields two groups, one containing primarily Back Yard Burgers' customers and the other containing primarily households that patronize other fast-food restaurants. From this example, it appears that X_1–Lifestyle and X_2–Income are critical discriminators of fast-food restaurant patronage. Although the two areas overlap, the extent of the overlap does not seem to be substantial. This minimal overlap between groups, as in Exhibit 17.18, is an important requirement for a successful discriminant analysis. What the plot tells us is that Back Yard Burgers customers are more nutrition conscious and have relatively higher incomes.

Discriminant function The linear combination of independent variables developed by discriminant analysis which will best discriminate between the categories of the dependent variable.

Let us now turn to the fundamental statistics of discriminant analysis. Remember, the prediction of a categorical variable is the purpose of discriminant analysis. From a statistical perspective, this involves studying the direction of group differences based on finding a linear combination of independent variables—the **discriminant function**—that shows large differences in group means. Thus, discriminant analysis is a statistical tool for determining linear combinations of those independent variables, and using this to predict group membership.

A linear function can be developed with our fast-food example. We will use a two-group discriminant analysis example in which the dependent variable, Y, is measured on a nominal

A Closer Look at Research

Discriminant Analysis—SPSS

Discriminant analysis is used primarily to classify individuals or experimental units into two or more uniquely defined populations. An example of the use of discriminant analysis could include a credit card company that would like to classify credit card applicants into two groups: (1) individuals who are considered good credit risks, and (2) individuals who are considered poor credit risks.

On the basis of this classification, individuals considered good credit risks would be offered credit cards, while individuals considered poor credit risks would not be offered credit cards. Different factors that could help the credit card company in determining which of the two groups that applicants would fall into include salary, past credit history, level of education, and number of dependents. The statistical software package SPSS could be used to determine where the line should be drawn between these two groups.

To learn more about the use of discriminant analysis in SPSS, go to the SPSS Web site at www.spss.com.

scale (i.e., patrons of Back Yard Burgers versus other fast-food restaurants). Again, the marketing manager believes it is possible to predict whether a customer will patronize a fast-food restaurant on the basis of lifestyle (X_1) and income (X_2). Now the researcher must find a linear function of the independent variables that shows large differences in group means. The plots in Exhibit 17.18 show this is possible.

EXHIBIT 17.18 Discriminant Analysis Scatter Plot of Lifestyle and Income Data for Fast-Food Restaurant Patronage

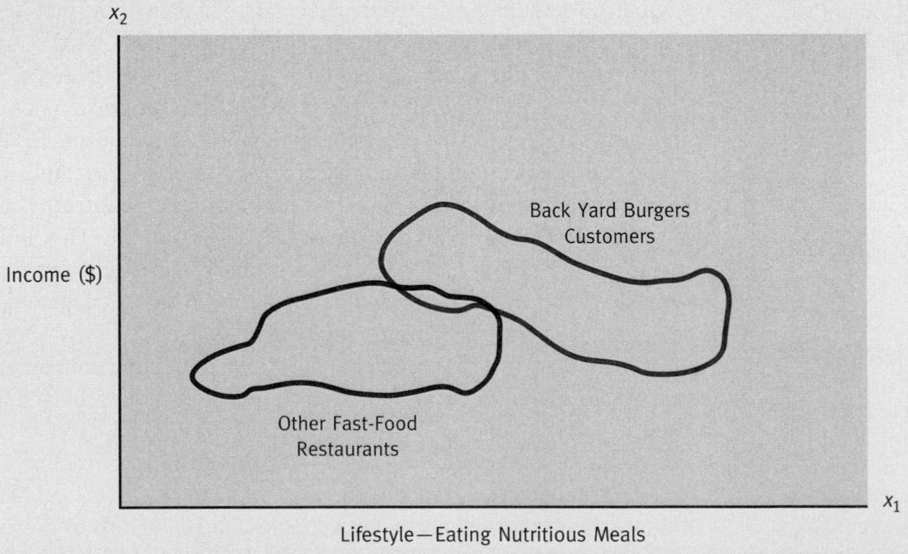

The discriminant score, or the Z score, is the basis for predicting to which group a particular individual belongs and is determined by a linear function. This Z score will be derived for each individual by means of the following equation:

$$Z_i = b_1X_{1i} + b_2X_{2i} \ldots + b_nX_{ni}$$

where

Z_i = ith individual's discriminant score

b_n = Discriminant coefficient for the nth variable

X_{ni} = Individual's value on the nth independent variable

Discriminant weights (b_n), or discriminant function coefficients, are estimates of the discriminatory power of a particular independent variable. These coefficients are computed by means of the discriminant analysis software, such as SPSS. The size of the coefficients associated with a particular independent variable is determined by the variance structure of the variables in the equation. Independent variables with large discriminatory power will have large weights, and those with little discriminatory power will have small weights.

Returning to our fast-food example, suppose the marketing researcher finds the standardized weights or coefficients in the equation to be

$$Z = b_1X_1 + b_2X_2$$
$$= .32X_1 + .47X_2$$

These results show that income (X_2) with a coefficient of .47 is the more important variable in discriminating between those patronizing Back Yard Burgers and those who patronize other fast-food restaurants. The lifestyle variable (X_1) with a coefficient of .32 also represents a variable with good discriminatory power.

Another important goal of discriminant analysis is classification of objects or individuals into groups. In our example, the goal was to correctly classify consumers into Back Yard Burgers patrons and those who patronize other fast-food restaurants. To determine whether the estimated discriminant function is a good predictor, a classification (prediction) matrix is used. The classification matrix in Exhibit 17.19 shows that the discriminant function correctly classified 214 of the original BYB patrons (99.1%) and 80 of the nonpatrons (100%). The classification matrix also shows that the number of correctly classified consumers (216 patrons and 80 nonpatrons) out of a total of 296 equals 99.3 percent correctly classified. This resulting percentage is much higher than would be expected by chance.

Discriminant Analysis Applications in Marketing Research

While our example illustrated how discriminant analysis helped classify users and nonusers of the restaurant based on independent variables, other applications include the following:

- *Product research.* Discriminant analysis can help to distinguish between heavy, medium, and light users of a product in terms of their consumption habits and lifestyles.
- *Image research.* Discriminant analysis can discriminate between customers who exhibit favorable perceptions of a store or company and those who do not.
- *Advertising research.* Discriminant analysis can assist in distinguishing how market segments differ in media consumption habits.
- *Direct marketing.* Discriminant analysis can help in distinguishing characteristics of consumers who respond to direct marketing solicitations and those who don't.

eXHIBIT 17.19 Classification Matrix for BYB Patrons and Nonpatrons

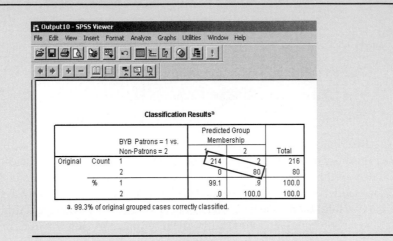

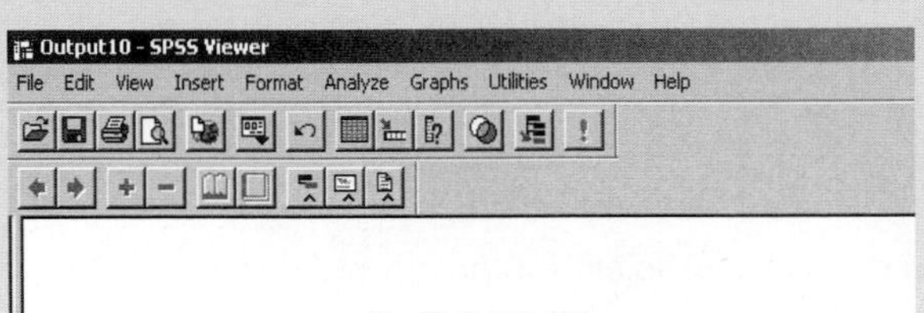

Classification Results[a]

		BYB Patrons = 1 vs. Non-Patrons = 2	Predicted Group Membership		Total
			1	2	
Original	Count	1	214	2	216
		2	0	80	80
	%	1	99.1	.9	100.0
		2	.0	100.0	100.0

a. 99.3% of original grouped cases correctly classified.

SPSS Application—Discriminant Analysis

The usefulness of discriminant analysis can be demonstrated with our Santa Fe Grill database. Remember that with discriminant analysis the single dependent variable is a nonmetric variable and the multiple independent variables are measured metrically. In the classification variables of the database, variables X30—Distance Driven, X31—Ad Recall, and X32—Gender are nonmetric variables. The screening variable of Favorite Mexican Restaurant is also a nonmetric variable. Variables X31 and X32 are two-group variables and X30 is a three-group variable. We could use discriminant analysis to see if there are differences between perceptions of the Santa Fe Grill by male and female customers or by ad recall, or we could see if the perceptions differ depending on how far customers drove to eat at the Santa Fe Grill.

The Santa Fe Grill owners want to know how its food and service compare to Jose's. In looking at variables X12–X21, there are three variables associated with food: variables X15, X18, and X20, and one variable measuring speed of service (X21).

The task is to determine if customer perceptions of the food and service are different between the two restaurants. Another way of stating this is "Can perceptions of food and service predict which restaurant a customer ate at?" This second question is based on the primary objective of discriminant analysis: to predict group membership. In this case, can the food and service perceptions predict restaurant customer groups?

The SPSS click-through sequence is ANALYZE → CLASSIFY → DISCRIMINANT, which leads to a dialog box where you select the variables (see Exhibit 17.20). The dependent, nonmetric variable is Favorite Mexican Restaurant (screening question 4) and the independent, metric variables are X15, X18, X20, and X21. The first task is to move the favorite Mexican restaurant variable to the Grouping Variable box at the top, and then click on the Define Range box just below it. You must tell the program what the minimum and maximum numbers are for the grouping variable. In this case the minimum is 0 = Jose's and the maximum is 1 = Santa Fe Grill, so just put these numbers in and click on Continue. Next you must transfer the food and service perceptions variables into the Independents box (X15, X18, X20, and X21). Then click on the Statistics box at the bottom and check Means, Univariate ANOVAS, and Continue. The Method default is Enter, and we will use this. Now click on Classify and Compute from group sizes. We do not know if the sample

eXHIBIT 17.20 SPSS Dialog Boxes for Discriminant Analysis Comparing Two Restaurants

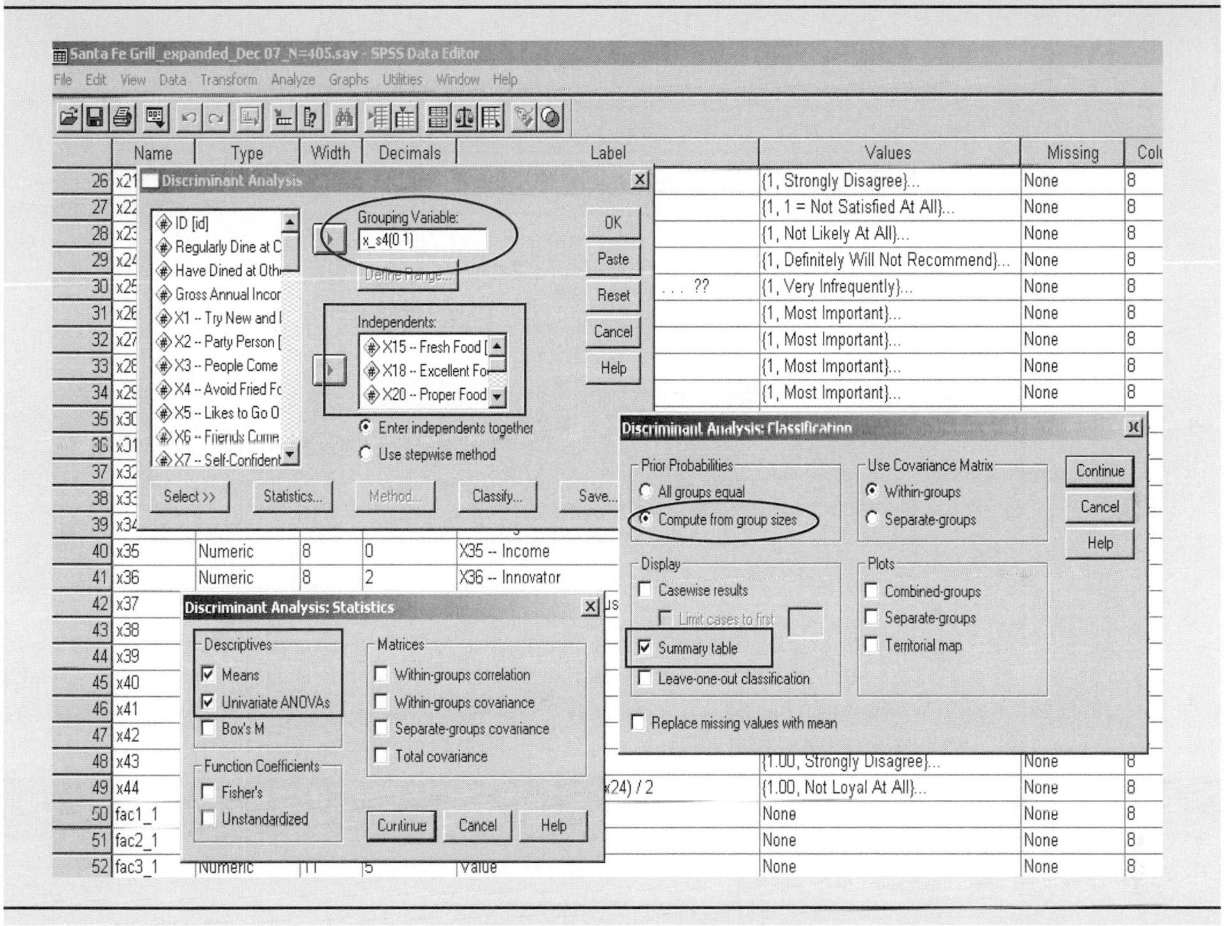

sizes are equal, so we must check this option. You should also click Summary Table and then Continue. We do not use any options under Save so click OK to run the program. Exhibit 17.20 shows the SPSS screen where you move the dependent and independent variables into their appropriate dialog boxes as well as the Statistics and Classification boxes.

Discriminant analysis is an SPSS program that gives you a lot of output you will not use. We will look at only five tables from the SPSS output. Information from two tables is shown in Exhibit 17.21. The first important information to consider is in the Wilks' Lambda table. The Wilks' Lambda is a statistic that assesses whether the discriminant analysis is statistically significant. If this statistic is significant, as it is in our case (.000), then we next look at the Classification Results table. At the bottom we see that the overall ability of our discriminant function to predict group membership is 90.4 percent. This is good because without the discriminant function we could predict with only 62.5 percent accuracy (our sample sizes are Santa Fe Grill = 253 and Jose's = 152, so if we placed all respondents in the Santa Fe Grill group, we would predict with 253/405 = 62.5% accuracy).

To find out which of the independent variables help us to predict group membership we look at the information in the two tables shown in Exhibit 17.22. Results shown in the table labeled Tests of Equality of Group Means show which food perceptions variables differ

eXHIBIT 17.21 SPSS Discriminant Analysis of Favorite Mexican Restaurant

Output6 - SPSS Viewer

File Edit View Insert Format Analyze Graphs Utilities Window Help

Wilks' Lambda

Test of Function(s)	Wilks' Lambda	Chi-square	df	Sig.
1	.393	374.986	4	.000

Classification Results[a]

		Favorite Mexican Restaurant	Predicted Group Membership: Jose's Southwestern Cafe	Santa Fe Grill	Total
Original	Count	Jose's Southwestern Cafe	132	20	152
		Santa Fe Grill	19	234	253
	%	Jose's Southwestern Cafe	86.8	13.2	100.0
		Santa Fe Grill	7.5	92.5	100.0

a. 90.4% of original grouped cases correctly classified.

between the two restaurants on a univariate basis. Note that variables X15, X18, X20, and X21 are all highly statistically significant (look at the numbers in the Sig. column). Thus, on a univariate basis all four food perceptions variables differ significantly between the restaurant customer groups.

eXHIBIT 17.22 Discriminant Output for Favorite Mexican Restaurant (continued)

Output7 - SPSS Viewer

File Edit View Insert Format Analyze Graphs Utilities Window Help

Tests of Equality of Group Means

	Wilks' Lambda	F	df1	df2	Sig.
X15 -- Fresh Food	.672	196.473	1	403	.000
X18 -- Excellent Food Taste	.597	271.499	1	403	.000
X20 -- Proper Food Temperature	.976	9.909	1	403	.002
X21 -- Speed of Service	.799	101.494	1	403	.000

Structure Matrix

	Function 1
X18 -- Excellent Food Taste	.660
X15 -- Fresh Food	.561
X21 -- Speed of Service	.403
X20 -- Proper Food Temperature	.126

Pooled within-groups correlations between discriminating variables and standardized canonical discriminant functions
Variables ordered by absolute size of correlation within function.

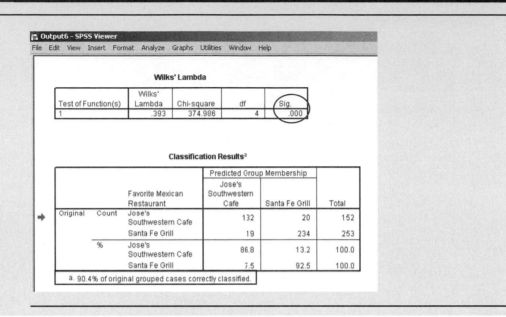

eXHIBIT 17.23 Group Means for Favorite Mexican Restaurants (continued)

Output8 - SPSS Viewer

File Edit View Insert Format Analyze Graphs Utilities Window Help

Group Statistics

Favorite Mexican Restaurant		Mean	Std. Deviation
Jose's Southwestern Cafe	X15 -- Fresh Food	6.64	.557
	X18 -- Excellent Food Taste	6.20	.764
	X20 -- Proper Food Temperature	4.76	1.292
	X21 -- Speed of Service	6.39	1.213
Santa Fe Grill	X15 -- Fresh Food	5.23	1.164
	X18 -- Excellent Food Taste	4.78	.881
	X20 -- Proper Food Temperature	4.38	1.065
	X21 -- Speed of Service	4.50	2.107
Total	X15 -- Fresh Food	5.76	1.195
	X18 -- Excellent Food Taste	5.31	1.084
	X20 -- Proper Food Temperature	4.52	1.168
	X21 -- Speed of Service	5.21	2.039

To consider the variables from a multivariate perspective (discriminant analysis), we look at the information in the Structure Matrix table. First we compare the sizes of the numbers in the Function column. The variables with the largest numbers are the best predictors. Food taste and food freshness help predict group membership the most, but speed of service is a moderately strong predictor, and even food temperature helps predict somewhat. These findings are similar to the univariate results, in which all four perceptions variables are statistically different between the two restaurants.

To further interpret the discriminant analysis we look at the group means in the Group Statistics table (Exhibit 17.23). For all four variables (X15, X18, X20, and X21) we see that customers had more favorable perceptions of Jose's Southwestern Café than of the Santa Fe Grill (mean values for Jose's are all higher). Thus, perceptions of food and service are significantly more favorable for Jose's customers than for the Santa Fe Grill's. This finding can definitely be used by the owners of the Santa Fe Grill to further develop their plan to improve restaurant operations.

SPSS Application—Combining Discriminant Analysis and Cluster Analysis

We can use discriminant analysis in combination with other multivariate techniques. Remember the cluster analysis example earlier in the chapter in which we identified customer loyalty groups using variables X23 and X24. Of the two clusters, Cluster One respondents were least loyal while Cluster Two respondents were most loyal. We can use the results of this cluster analysis solution as the dependent variable in a discriminant analysis.

Now we must identify which of the database variables we might use as metric independent variables. We have used the restaurant perceptions variables (X12–X21) in an earlier example but we have not used the lifestyle variables (X1–X11). Let's, therefore, see if we can find a relationship between the metric lifestyle variables and the nonmetric customer loyalty clusters.

There are eleven lifestyle variables that could be used as independent variables. Three of the variables are related to nutrition: X4–Avoid Fried Foods, X8–Eat Balanced Meals, and X10–Careful about What I Eat. If we use these three variables as independents, the objective will be to determine whether nutrition is related to customer loyalty. That is, can nutrition predict whether a customer is loyal or not?

The SPSS click-through sequence is ANALYZE → CLASSIFY → DISCRIMINANT, which leads to a dialog box where you select the variables. The dependent, nonmetric variable is clu2_1, and the independent, metric variables are X4, X8, and X10. First transfer variable clu2_1 to the Grouping Variable box at the top, and then click on the Define Range box just below it. Insert the minimum and maximum numbers for the grouping variable. In this case the minimum is 1 = Cluster One and the maximum is 2 = Cluster Two, so just put these numbers in and click on Continue. Next you must transfer the food perceptions variables into the Independents box (X4, X8, and X10). Then click on the Statistics box at the bottom and check Means, Univariate ANOVAS, and Continue. The Method default is Enter, and we will use this. Now click on Classify and Compute from group sizes. We do not know if the sample sizes are equal, so we must check this option. You should also click Summary Table and then Continue. We do not use any options under Save so click OK to run the program.

Remember the SPSS discriminant analysis program gives you a lot of output you will not use. We again will look at only five tables. The first two tables to look at are shown in Exhibit 17.24. Note that the discriminant function is highly significant (Wilks' Lambda of .000) and that the predictive accuracy is good (77.3% correctly classified). Recall that group 1 of our cluster analysis solution had relatively fewer customers than did group 2. The mean level of loyalty of the customers is shown in the Classification Results section of the exhibit.

eXHIBIT 17.24 Discriminant Analysis of Customer Loyalty Clusters and Nutrition Lifestyle Variables

Output12 - SPSS Viewer

File Edit View Insert Format Analyze Graphs Utilities Window Help

Wilks' Lambda

Test of Function(s)	Wilks' Lambda	Chi-square	df	Sig.
1	.678	155.871	3	.000

Classification Results[a]

		Loyal - 2 Group	Predicted Group Membership: Least Loyal (mean=3.5)	Predicted Group Membership: Most Loyal (mean=5.4)	Total
Original	Count	Least Loyal (mean=3.5)	228	43	271
		Most Loyal (mean=5.4)	49	85	134
	%	Least Loyal (mean=3.5)	84.1	15.9	100.0
		Most Loyal (mean=5.4)	36.6	63.4	100.0

a. 77.3% of original grouped cases correctly classified.

eXHIBIT 17.25 Discriminant Analysis—Customer Loyalty Clusters

Output13 - SPSS Viewer

File Edit View Insert Format Analyze Graphs Utilities Window Help

Tests of Equality of Group Means

	Wilks' Lambda	F	df1	df2	Sig.
X4 -- Avoid Fried Foods	.730	148.744	1	403	.000
X8 -- Eat Balanced, Nutritious Meals	.845	74.058	1	403	.000
X10 -- Careful about What I Eat	.759	128.008	1	403	.000

Structure Matrix

	Function
	1
X4 -- Avoid Fried Foods	.882
X10 -- Careful about What I Eat	.818
X8 -- Eat Balanced, Nutritious Meals	.622

Pooled within-groups correlations between discriminating variables and standardized canonical discriminant functions
Variables ordered by absolute size of correlation within function.

To find out which of the independent variables help us to best predict group membership we look at the information in two tables (shown in Exhibit 17.25). Results shown in the table labeled Tests of Equality of Group Means show which nutrition lifestyle variables differ on a univariate basis. Note that all three predictor variables are highly significant. To consider the variables from a multivariate perspective, use the information from the Structure Matrix table. The structure matrix numbers are all quite large and can therefore be considered to be helpful in predicting group membership. Like the univariate results, all of the variables help us to predict group membership. The strongest nutrition variable is X4 (.882), the second best predictor is X10 (.818), and the least predictive but still helpful is X8 (.622).

To interpret the meaning of the discriminant analysis results we examine the means of the nutrition variables shown in the Group Statistics table of Exhibit 17.26. Note that the means for all three nutrition variables in the Most Loyal group are lower than the means in the Least Loyal group. Moreover, based on the information provided in Exhibit 17.25 we know all of the nutrition variables are significantly different. Thus, customers in the Most Loyal group are significantly less "nutrition conscious" than those in the Least Loyal group.

Recall that Cluster One was not very loyal (mean = 3.5 on a 7-point scale) and Cluster Two (less nutrition conscious) was relatively loyal (based on a combination of variables X23 and X24). Thus, the results indicate the most loyal customers are less nutrition conscious. One interpretation of this finding might be that the owners of the Santa Fe Grill should consider putting some "Heart Healthy" entrees on their menu. But before doing that they need to look at loyalty as it relates only to the Santa Fe Grill. Up to this point the analysis has been with both restaurants combined.

Conjoint analysis A multivariate technique that estimates the relative importance consumers place on different attributes of a product or service, as well as the utilities or value they attach to the various levels of each attribute.

Conjoint Analysis

Conjoint analysis is a multivariate technique that estimates the relative importance consumers place on different attributes of a product or service, as well as the utilities or value they attach to the various levels of each attribute. This dependence method assumes that

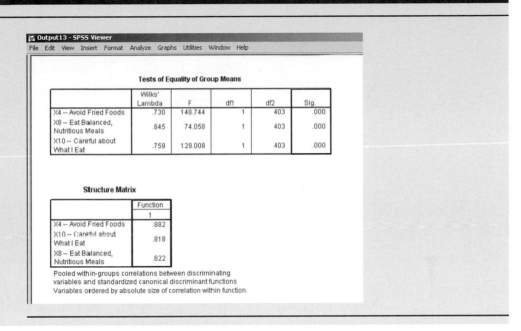

eXHIBIT 17.26 Nutrition Variable Means for Customer Loyalty Clusters

Output14 - SPSS Viewer

File Edit View Insert Format Analyze Graphs Utilities Window Help

Group Statistics

Loyal - 2 Group		Mean	Std. Deviation
Least Loyal (mean=3.5)	X4 -- Avoid Fried Foods	4.59	1.167
	X8 -- Eat Balanced, Nutritious Meals	4.91	1.123
	X10 -- Careful about What I Eat	4.81	.993
Most Loyal (mean=5.4)	X4 -- Avoid Fried Foods	3.15	1.015
	X8 -- Eat Balanced, Nutritious Meals	3.88	1.144
	X10 -- Careful about What I Eat	3.66	.902
Total	X4 -- Avoid Fried Foods	4.11	1.308
	X8 -- Eat Balanced, Nutritious Meals	4.57	1.228
	X10 -- Careful about What I Eat	4.43	1.105

consumers choose or form preferences for products by evaluating the overall utility or value of the product. This value is composed of the individual utilities of each product feature or attribute. Conjoint analysis tries to estimate the product attribute importance weights that would best match the consumer's indicated product choice or preference.

For example, assume that our fast-food restaurant wants to determine the best combination of features to attract customers. A marketing researcher could develop a number of descriptions or restaurant profiles, each containing different combinations of features. Exhibit 17.27 shows two examples of what these profiles might look like. Consumers would then be surveyed, shown the different profiles, and asked to rank the descriptions in order of their likelihood of patronizing the restaurant. Note that with the conjoint analysis technique, the researcher has to do a lot more work than the survey respondent. The researcher must choose the attributes that are likely to affect consumer choice or preference, and must also pick the levels of each attribute to include in the survey. All that is required of the consumer is to rank order the profiles in terms of preference.

Part-worth estimate A number showing the preference for each level of each attribute evaluated in the conjoint procedure.

If each of the four attributes shown in Exhibit 17.27 had two levels or values (e.g., price level: inexpensive versus moderate), there would be 16 possible combinations for consumers to rank ($2 \times 2 \times 2 \times 2 = 16$). Once those data were collected, applying conjoint analysis to the responses would produce a **part-worth estimate** for each level of each attribute.

eXHIBIT 17.27 Sample Conjoint Survey Profiles

Attribute	Restaurant Profile A	Restaurant Profile B
Price Level	Inexpensive ($3–$6)	Moderate ($7–$10)
Atmosphere	Family style	Upscale
Menu type	Sandwiches	Salad, entrée, dessert
Service level	Self-service	Table service

The statistical process underlying conjoint analysis uses the customer ranking of the profiles as a target. The process then assigns a part-worth estimate for each level of each attribute. The overall utility is estimated using the following formula:

$$U(X) = \alpha_{11} + \alpha_{12} + \alpha_{21} + \alpha_{22} + \cdots + \alpha_{mn}$$

where

$U(X)$ = Total worth for product

α_{11} = Part-worth estimate for level 1 of attribute 1

α_{12} = Part-worth estimate for level 2 of attribute 1

α_{21} = Part-worth estimate for level 1 of attribute 2

α_{22} = Part-worth estimate for level 2 of attribute 2

α_{mn} = Part-worth estimate for level n of attribute m

Once the total worths of the product profiles have been estimated, the process compares it to the consumer's actual choice ranking. If the predictions are not accurate, then the individual part-worth estimates are changed and the total worths recalculated. This process continues until the predictions are as close to the consumer's actual rankings as possible. The ability of the estimated part-worth coefficients to accurately predict the consumer rankings can be determined through inspection of the model statistics, such as r^2. Just as in regression, a high r^2 indicates a good fit to the data (i.e., the model predictions closely match the consumer rankings).

Returning to our fast-food example above, Exhibit 17.28 shows graphs of the part-worth estimates for the various levels of the four attributes. The importance of each attribute across its different levels is indicated by the range of the part-worth estimates for that attribute, that is, by subtracting the minimum part-worth for the attribute from the maximum part-worth. Looking at the graphs, we see the "price" attribute is the most important because the difference between the highest and lowest plotted part-worths is the greatest. Similarly, menu type is second most important and the two lowest are atmosphere and service level.

Attribute importance estimate An estimate that shows the relative importance of each attribute as a percentage of the total importance scores of all the attributes in the model.

Once the **attribute importance estimate** has been determined, the relative importance of each attribute can be calculated as a percentage of the total importance scores of all the attributes in the model. The formula for the attribute importance is:

$$I_i = \{\text{Max}(\alpha_{ij}) - \text{Min}(\alpha_{ij})\} \text{ for each attribute } i$$

EXHIBIT 17.28 Conjoint Part-Worth Estimates for Restaurant Survey

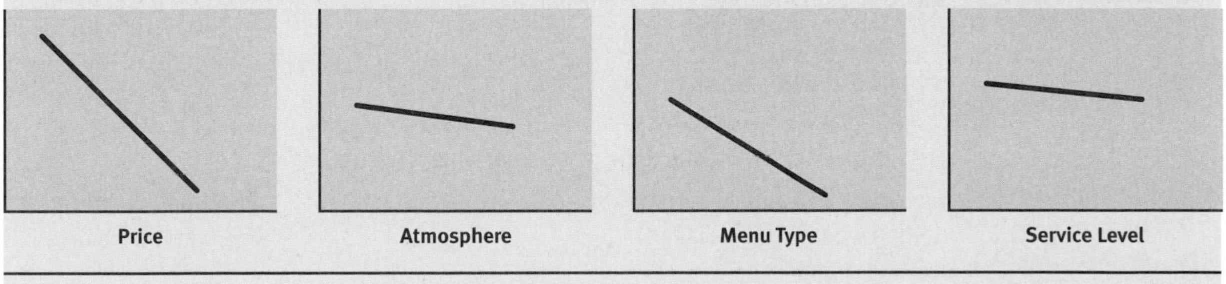

eXHIBIT 17.29 Importance Calculations for Restaurant Data

Attribute	Description	Part-Worth	Attribute Importance	Relative Importance
Price Level 1	Inexpensive ($3–$6)	1.762		
Price Level 2	Moderate ($7–$10)	−1.762	3.524	0.600
Atmosphere 1	Family style	0.244		
Atmosphere 2	Upscale	−0.244	0.488	0.083
Menu type 1	Sandwiches	0.598		
Menu type 2	Salad, entrée, dessert	−0.598	1.196	0.203
Service 1	Self-service	0.337		
Service 2	Table service	−0.337	0.674	0.115

And the formula for the relative attribute importance is:

$$R_i = \frac{I_i}{\Sigma I_i}$$

If we take the part-worth estimates shown in Exhibit 17.28 and calculate the importance of each attribute and its relative importance, we get the results shown in Exhibit 17.29. As you can see, the price level of the potential restaurant is the most important attribute to consumers in choosing a place to eat, followed by menu type.

Once the importance weights of the attributes have been estimated, it is relatively easy to make predictions about the overall preference for particular combinations of product features. Comparisons of alternative products can then be made to determine the most feasible alternative to consider bringing to market.

The main advantages of conjoint analysis techniques are (1) the low demands placed on the consumer to provide data; (2) the ability to provide utility estimates for individual levels of each product attribute; and (3) the ability to estimate nonlinear relationships among attribute levels. The limitations placed on the researcher by conjoint analysis are (1) that the researcher is responsible for choosing the appropriate attributes and attribute levels that will realistically influence consumer preferences and choice; and (2) that consumers may have difficulty making choices or indicating preferences among large numbers of profiles. Therefore, the number of attributes and levels used cannot be too large.

Conjoint Analysis Applications in Marketing Research

The fast-food example in this discussion illustrates one possible use of conjoint analysis to identify the important attributes that influence consumer restaurant choice. There are other important applications of this technique in marketing research, however, such as the following:

- *Market share potential.* Products with different combinations of features can be compared to determine the most popular designs.
- *Product image analysis.* The relative contributions of each product attribute can be determined for use in marketing and advertising decisions.
- *Segmentation analysis.* Groups of potential customers who place different levels of importance on the product features can be identified for use as high and low potential market segments.

MARKETING RESEARCH IN ACTION

Cluster and Discriminant Analysis

DVD Recorders Remain Popular

The latest DVD recorders do a lot more than just record material on DVDs. The latest models let you play and record video, while others include hard drives and programming guides to give you TiVo-like functionality. Stand-alone DVD recorders use the same drive technology as PCs, only they provide a home theater platform. The DVD discs take up less physical space than bulky tapes, plus they have menus that let you easily jump to a specific point within a recording. Moreover, the quality is much better and so is the storage capacity.

The DVD market is huge and rapidly getting much larger. No longer limited to home entertainment playback boxes, it is being combined with increasing numbers of consumer electronics products: computers, portable devices, appliances, and industrial systems—DVD is everywhere!

DVDs have enjoyed phenomenal growth in recent years, as evidenced by meteoric U.S. sales since mass-market introduction. Indeed, DVD has enjoyed the most rapid rise of any consumer electronics technology ever introduced. The total market for all types of DVD systems (players, recorders, set-tops, PCs, etc.) is expected to exceed 500 million units by 2008.

DVD player/recorders have caught the imagination and interest of consumers. DVD set-top box players have boomed in sales due not only to their functionality, but also to their rapidly falling prices. The average selling price fell from about $500 when first introduced to about $100 in major retail outlets in early 2009, with some units selling for much lower. The most popular brands of DVD recorders are Apex, Panasonic, Philips, Samsung, Toshiba, Sharp, and Sony.

Two of the biggest challenges for today's marketers are (1) the successful introduction of new technology-based product innovations into consumer markets, and (2) stimulating the diffusion of those innovations to higher penetration levels. To meet these challenges, the companies must know the key factors consumers use in deciding whether to adopt technology innovations in consumer electronics.

A study recently was completed to investigate opinions of potential purchasers of DVDs. The study focused on comparing the innovator and early adopter segments with regard to product usage, DVD purchase likelihood, demographics, and related issues. The primary questions addressed were: "Are there attitudinal and behavioral differences between consumers who are innovators versus early adopters?" and "Can these differences be associated with purchase likelihood of DVDs?" A copy of the questionnaire is shown in Exhibit 17.30.

Data were collected using an Internet panel approach from a sample of 200 individuals. The sample frame was consumers with annual household incomes $20,000 or more and ages 18 to 35 years. Data were collected over a two-week period. Participants had to be living in North America since the market study was limited to that geographic area. The questionnaire included topics on innovativeness, lifestyles, product and brand image, and classification questions. Some of the questions were intervally measured while others were nominal and ordinal. There is a database for the questions in this case available in SPSS format at www.mhhe.com/hair4e. The database is labeled DVD Survey MRIA_4e.sav.

EXHIBIT 17.30 Electronics Products Opinion Survey

This is a project being conducted by a marketing research class at The University of Oklahoma. The purpose of this project is to better understand the attitudes and opinions of consumers toward electronics products. The questionnaire will take only a few minutes to complete, and all responses will remain strictly confidential. Thank you for your help on this project.

I. Attitudes

The following questions relate to your attitudes about electronics products, things you like to do, and so forth. On a scale of 1 to 7, with 7 being Strongly Agree and 1 being Strongly Disagree, please circle the number that best expresses the extent to which you agree or disagree with each of the following statements.

	Strongly Disagree						Strongly Agree
1. The Internet is a good place to get lower prices.	1	2	3	4	5	6	7
2. I don't shop for specials.	1	2	3	4	5	6	7
3. People come to me for advice.	1	2	3	4	5	6	7
4. I often try new brands before my friends and neighbors.	1	2	3	4	5	6	7
5. I would like to take a trip around the world.	1	2	3	4	5	6	7
6. My friends and neighbors come to me for advice and consultation.	1	2	3	4	5	6	7
7. Coupons are a good way to save money	1	2	3	4	5	6	7
8. I seldom look for the lowest price when I shop.	1	2	3	4	5	6	7
9. I like to try new and different things.	1	2	3	4	5	6	7

10. To what extent do you believe you need a DVD player? Please indicate on the scale provided below:

Product I Definitely Do Not Need						Product I Would Like to Try
1	2	3	4	5	6	7

11. How likely are you to purchase a DVD player? Please indicate whether you are moderately likely or highly likely to purchase a DVD player. (Note: respondents who were not likely to purchase a DVD player were screened out of the survey.)

0 = Moderately Likely
1 = Highly Likely

II. Classification Information

We need some information for classification purposes. Please tell us a little about yourself.

12. What is the highest level of education you have attained? (Check only ONE box.)

__ High school graduate
__ College graduate

13. Electronics Products Ownership. Please indicate the level of electronics products ownership that best describes you.

__ Own few electronics products
__ Own a moderate amount of electronics products
__ Own lots of electronics products

eXHIBIT 17.30 Electronics Products Opinion Survey, *continued*

14. Please check the category that best indicates your total annual household income before taxes. (Check only ONE box.)
__ $20,000–$35,000
__ $35,001–$50,000
__ $50,001–$75,000
__ $75,001–$100,000
__ More than $100,000

15. Innovators vs. Early Adopters—this classification was developed using the statistical technique called cluster analysis. In the database, participants were classified as shown below:
0 = Early Adopters
1 = Innovators

16. Price Conscious—this classification was developed using questions 1, 2, 7, and 8 from the survey. In the database, participants were classified as shown below:
0 = Less Price Conscious
1 = More Price Conscious

THANK YOU FOR SHARING YOUR OPINIONS WITH OUR MARKETING RESEARCH CLASS.

To examine the main question, it was necessary to classify respondents as either an innovator or an early adopter. The Innovativeness scale consisted of five variables: X3, X4, X5, X6, and X9. A cluster analysis was run to identify respondents who rated themselves higher on these scales, that is, relatively more innovative. The result was 137 Innovators and 63 Early Adopters. This categorical variable (X15) was then used as the dependent categorical variable in a discriminant analysis. The independent variables were X10—DVD Product Perceptions, X11—Purchase Likelihood, X12—Education, X13—Electronics Products Ownership, X14—Income, and X16—Price Consciousness.

The results are shown in Exhibit 17.31. Based on the Wilks' Lambda, the discriminant function is highly significant in predicting innovators versus early adopters. Moreover, the Classification Results indicate that the predictive accuracy of the discriminant function is 92.0 percent.

The significant independent variable predictors are shown in Exhibit 17.32. On a univariate basis (see Tests of Equality of Group Means table), all of the independent variables are highly significant. Looking at the information in the Structure Matrix table, variables X11, X10, and X14 are the most significant in predicting innovators versus early adopters.

The comparison of group means is shown in Exhibit 17.33. The group means indicate that for all variables except X16–Price Consciousness, the means are higher for innovators than they are for early adopters. This can be interpreted as follows. Innovators:

- Have more positive perceptions of DVD Player-Recorders.
- Are more likely to purchase a DVD Player-Recorder.
- Are more highly educated.
- Own relatively more electronic products.
- Have higher incomes.

EXHIBIT 17.31 Discriminant Analysis of Innovators vs. Early Adopters

Output17 - SPSS Viewer

File Edit View Insert Format Analyze Graphs Utilities Window Help

Wilks' Lambda

Test of Function(s)	Wilks' Lambda	Chi-square	df	Sig.
1	.323	220.177	6	.000

Classification Results[a]

		X15 -- Innovators vs. Early Adopters	Predicted Group Membership: Early Adopters	Predicted Group Membership: Innovators	Total
Original	Count	Early Adopters	60	3	63
		Innovators	13	124	137
	%	Early Adopters	95.2	4.8	100.0
		Innovators	9.5	90.5	100.0

a. 92.0% of original grouped cases correctly classified.

EXHIBIT 17.32 Significant Predictors of Innovators vs. Early Adoptors

Output18 - SPSS Viewer

File Edit View Insert Format Analyze Graphs Utilities Window Help

Tests of Equality of Group Means

	Wilks' Lambda	F	df1	df2	Sig.
X10 -- DVD Product Perceptions	.527	178.053	1	198	.000
X11 -- Purchase Likelihood	.512	188.856	1	198	.000
X12 -- Education	.921	17.006	1	198	.000
X13 -- Electronic Products Ownership	.954	9.505	1	198	.002
X14 -- Income	.615	123.915	1	198	.000
X16 -- Price Conscious	.968	6.643	1	198	.011

Structure Matrix

	Function 1
X11 -- Purchase Likelihood	.675
X10 -- DVD Product Perceptions	.655
X14 -- Income	.547
X12 -- Education	.203
X13 -- Electronic Products Ownership	.151
X16 -- Price Conscious	-.127

Pooled within-groups correlations between discriminating variables and standardized canonical discriminant functions
Variables ordered by absolute size of correlation within function.

eXHIBIT 17.33 Mean Profiles of Innovators vs. Early Adopters

Output19 - SPSS Viewer

File Edit View Insert Format Analyze Graphs Utilities Window Help

Group Statistics

X15 -- Innovators vs. Early Adopters		Mean	Std. Deviation
Early Adopters	X10 -- DVD Product Perceptions	3.17	1.115
	X11 -- Purchase Likelihood	.10	.296
	X12 -- Education	.40	.493
	X13 -- Electronic Products Ownership	1.49	.669
	X14 -- Income	2.48	.965
	X16 -- Price Conscious	.59	.496
Innovators	X10 -- DVD Product Perceptions	5.45	1.124
	X11 -- Purchase Likelihood	.83	.375
	X12 -- Education	.69	.463
	X13 -- Electronic Products Ownership	1.82	.727
	X14 -- Income	4.04	.906
	X16 -- Price Conscious	.39	.490
Total	X10 -- DVD Product Perceptions	4.74	1.542
	X11 -- Purchase Likelihood	.60	.491
	X12 -- Education	.60	.491
	X13 -- Electronic Products Ownership	1.72	.724
	X14 -- Income	3.55	1.177
	X16 -- Price Conscious	.46	.499

The price conscious mean is lower for innovators than for early adopters (0 = less price conscious; 1 = more price conscious). The interpretation of this is: Innovators are less price conscious than early adopters.

Overall, discriminant analysis can help today's DVD marketers gain a better understanding of their potential market segments. This study demonstrated that DVDs have left the innovation stage of the diffusion process and are making inroads into the early adopter phase. But DVD manufacturers and retail marketers alike must focus on developing strategies that can attract more potential early adopters as well as create awareness and desire among the early majority.

Hands-On Exercise

1. What other topics should be examined with this survey?
2. What problems do you see with the questionnaire? (See Exhibit 17.30 for the questionnaire.)

Summary of Learning Objectives

■ Define multivariate analysis.

Multivariate analysis refers to a group of statistical procedures used to simultaneously analyze three or more variables. Factor analysis, cluster analysis, multidimensional scaling, discriminant analysis, and conjoint analysis are commonly used multivariate statistical techniques.

■ Understand when and why you should use multivariate analysis in marketing research.

Multivariate analysis is extremely important in marketing research because most business problems are multidimensional. Marketing managers are often concerned with various aspects of the consumer (e.g., demographics, lifestyles); consumers' purchasing process (e.g., motives, perceptions); and competition. Thus, techniques such as factor analysis, cluster analysis, and discriminant analysis assist marketing managers in simultaneously assessing a set or sets of important variables.

■ Distinguish between dependence and interdependence methods.

Multivariate data analysis techniques can be classified into dependence and interdependence methods. A dependence method is one in which a variable or set of variables is identified as the dependent variable to be predicted or explained by other, independent variables. Dependence techniques include multiple regression analysis, discriminant analysis, and conjoint analysis. An interdependence method is one in which no single variable or group of variables is defined as being independent or dependent. The goal of interdependence methods is data reduction, or grouping things together. Cluster analysis, factor analysis, and multidimensional scaling are the most commonly used interdependence methods.

■ Apply factor analysis, cluster analysis, discriminant analysis, and conjoint analysis to examine marketing research problems.

Factor analysis and cluster analysis are both interdependence methods. Factor analysis is used to summarize the information contained in a large number of variables into a smaller number of factors. Cluster analysis classifies observations into a small number of mutually exclusive and exhaustive groups. In cluster analysis, these groups should have as much similarity within each group and as much difference between groups as possible.

Multiple discriminant analysis and conjoint analysis are dependence methods. The purpose of techniques such as discriminant and conjoint analysis is to predict a variable from a set of independent variables. Discriminant analysis uses independent variables to classify observations into mutually exclusive categories. Discriminant analysis can also be used to determine whether statistically significant differences exist between the average discriminant score profiles of two or more groups. Conjoint analysis uses customer ranking or preference ratings of a group of products or service profile descriptions to estimate attribute importance coefficients through the use of part-worth estimates. Each level of each attribute in the product description is given a weight, and the weights are added together to form a product utility. Conjoint analysis can be used to compare customer preferences for different product attribute combinations.

Key Terms and Concepts

Attribute importance estimate 589
Cluster analysis 572
Conjoint analysis 587
Dependence method 562
Discriminant analysis 579
Discriminant function 579
Factor analysis 563
Factor loading 564
Interdependence method 562
Multivariate analysis 560
Part-worth estimate 588

Review Questions

1. Why are multivariate statistical analysis methods so important to managers today? How do multivariate methods differ from univariate methods?
2. What is the difference between dependence and interdependence multivariate methods?
3. What is the goal of factor analysis? Give an example of a marketing situation that would call for factor analysis.
4. How does cluster analysis differ from factor analysis? Give an example of how cluster analysis is used in marketing research.
5. What is the purpose of discriminant analysis? How might it be used to solve a marketing problem or identify a marketing opportunity?

Discussion Questions

1. Cluster analysis is a commonly used multivariate analysis technique in segmentation studies. Its primary objective is to classify objects into relatively homogeneous groups based on a set of variables. Once those groups are identified by a cluster analysis, what is the next logical analysis step a marketer might want to take? Will the results of a cluster analysis also reveal the characteristics of the members in each group? Why or why not?
2. Discriminant analysis is a frequently used multivariate technique when the objective is to identify important variables in identifying group membership of some type. What is the role of the discriminant function coefficients in identifying these important variables? In the chapter on regression, multicollinearity among the independent variables in a regression equation was highlighted as a potential problem for interpretation of the results. Do you think multicollinearity would also pose a problem for interpreting discriminant analysis results? Why or why not?

3. **EXPERIENCE THE INTERNET.** Access the Internet and select a particular search engine. Use various keywords and identify five major market research providers listed on the Web. Compare and contrast their Web sites and suggest the strengths and weaknesses of each. Which would you choose to conduct a marketing research project for yourself? Why? Prepare a report for class so you can share your findings with other students.
4. **SPSS EXERCISE.** Using the Santa Fe Grill data set and the questionnaire found in Chapter 14, conduct the following tasks:
   a. Submit the data for questions 22, 23, and 24 to an SPSS cluster analysis. Create a new variable called "Customer Commitment." Develop a three-group cluster solution identifying three levels of commitment.
   b. Using these new clusters as the dependent variable and questions 12 to 21 (restaurant perceptions variables) as the independent variables, perform a three-group discriminant analysis.
5. **SPSS EXERCISE.** Using the Santa Fe Grill dataset and questionnaire, perform a factor analysis on the lifestyle variables. Are the results of the factor analysis acceptable, and if so why?

chapter 18

Preparing and Presenting Marketing Research Reports

Learning Objectives

After reading this chapter, you will be able to:

1. Understand the objectives of a research report.
2. Describe the format of a marketing research report.
3. Discuss several techniques for graphically displaying research results.
4. Clarify problems encountered in preparing reports.
5. Understand the importance of presentations in marketing research.

"Many times what you say may not be as important as how you say it."

—ANONYMOUS

It Takes More than Numbers to Communicate

Visual display of data is not easy and even research experts do not always do it well. After all, the kinds of people who are good at statistics are not necessarily the ones that are good at visual presentation. Nevertheless, the ability to present data visually in a way that is illuminating is important in writing research reports.

The person most known for his expertise in presenting visual data is Professor Edward Tufte. The author of several books on the topic, including *The Display of Quantitative Information,* Professor Tufte hails from the field of political science but his advice applies to any field. Business graphics have the same goals as any other graphics: to convey information, to summarize reasoning, and to solve problems. Tufte explains the importance of visual displays of data: "Good design is clear thinking made visible, and bad design is stupidity made visible. . . . So when you see a display filled with chart junk, there's a deeper corruption: they don't know what they're talking about."[1]

Tufte has implicated poor presentation of statistics and information in the Challenger disaster. A NASA PowerPoint slide show buried statistics revealing that rubber O-ring seals in the boosters tended to leak at low temperatures. The failure of an O-ring ultimately resulted in the death of seven astronauts. Of course, poor graphic presentations rarely have such dramatic consequences. Instead, business opportunities are missed, time is wasted, and audiences are bored.

The New York Times calls Tufte the Leonardo da Vinci of data presentation. But Professor Tufte emphasizes that presenting statistics well is not about creating slick graphics. "The task is not to have 'high-impact' presentations," or 'point, click, wow,' or 'power pitches.' The point is to explain something. . . . The right metaphor for presentations is not power or PowerPoint," and "It's not television or theater. It's teaching."[2]

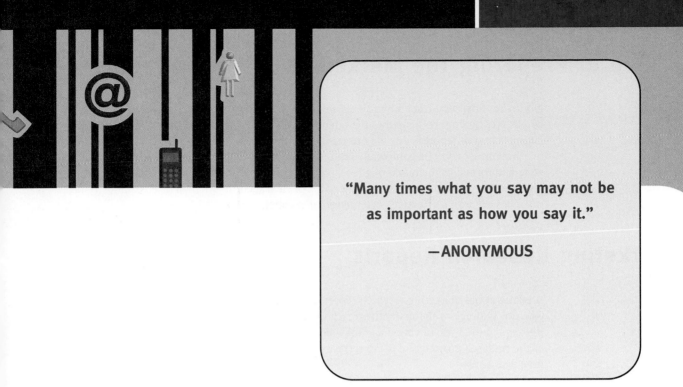

Value of Preparing the Marketing Research Report

No matter how well research projects are designed and implemented, if the results cannot be effectively communicated to the client, the project is not a success. An effective marketing research report is one way to ensure the time, effort, and money that went into the research project will be completely realized. The purpose of this chapter is to introduce the style and format of the marketing research report. We identify how the marketing research report is designed and explain the objectives of each section. We then discuss industry best practices regarding effective presentation of research reports.

Marketing Research Reports

A professional marketing research report has four objectives: (1) to effectively communicate the findings of the marketing research project, (2) to provide interpretations of those findings in the form of sound and logical recommendations, (3) to establish the credibility of the research project, and (4) to serve as a future reference document for strategic or tactical decisions.

The first objective of the research report is to effectively communicate the findings of the marketing research project. Since a major purpose of the research project is to obtain information to answer questions about a specific business problem, the report must explain both how the information was obtained and what relevance it has to the research questions. A detailed description of the following topics should be communicated to the client:

1. The research objectives.
2. The research questions.
3. Literature review and relevant secondary data.
4. A description of the research methods.
5. Findings displayed in tables, graphs, or charts.
6. Interpretation and summary of the findings.
7. Conclusions and recommendations.

In Chapter 7, we explained how to write a qualitative research report. Quantitative reports include the same general information as do qualitative reports. But some of the issues faced in developing a research report are different. The objectives and questions in qualitative research tend to be broader, more general, and more open-ended than in quantitative research. The literature review and relevant secondary data may be integrated in the analysis of findings in qualitative data analysis, rather than being presented separately from other findings. The description of research methods in both qualitative and quantitative research helps to develop credibility for both kinds of research projects, but different kinds of evidence are offered in developing credibility in quantitative and qualitative analyses. Data display is important in both methods. Qualitative researchers rarely present statistics, but they are the bread and butter of a quantitative presentation. Writing conclusions and recommendations is the final step in both qualitative and quantitative reports.

Too often quantitative researchers are so concerned about doing statistical analyses they forget to provide a clear, logical interpretation of their results. Researchers must recognize that clients are seldom knowledgeable about sampling methods and statistics. Thus, researchers must present technical or complex information in a manner that is understandable to all parties. Many words used to teach research to students are not necessary in a marketing research report. For example, the word "hypothesis" seldom appears in a marketing research report. When Crosstabs, ANOVAs, *t*-tests, correlation, and regression are used, they are presented with simplicity and clarity. The name of the analysis technique may not even be used in the presentation and discussion of results. Most market researchers do not even include information about statistical significance in their reports, although we recommend that you do so.

In writing a report, researchers must cross the gap from doing and understanding statistics to communicating findings in a way that is completely understandable to nontechnical readers. Most researchers are comfortable with statistics, computer outputs, questionnaires, and other project-related material. In presenting results to the client, researchers should keep the original research objectives in mind. The task is to focus on the objectives and communicate how each part of the project is related to the completion of those objectives.

For example, Exhibit 18.1 illustrates a research objective that focused on identifying senior Internet adoption and use. While a great deal of numerical data was necessary to prepare the chart, the data have been reduced to a format that is compact and easy to understand. In this chapter, we show you how to use graphics to summarize the statistical analyses covered in our text. The PowerPoint slide in Exhibit 18.1 summarizes a number of statistical analyses that show predictors of senior Internet adoption (self-adoption, helped adoption, or

eXHIBIT 18.1 Pictorial Representation of Senior Internet Adoption Segments

SENIOR INTERNET ADOPTION SEGMENTS

	Light Use	Heavy Use
Self-Adoption	**Demographics** High Income and education, more male **Self-Directed Values** Low curiosity and proactive coping **Technology Attitudes/Behavior** Low technology discomfort Medium technology optimism, innovativeness 12%	**Demographics** High income and education, younger, more male **Self-Directed Values** High curiosity and proactive coping **Technology Attitudes/Behavior** Earliest adoption Low technology discomfort High technology optimism, innovativeness 8%
Helped Adoption	**Demographics** Medium education and income, more female **Self-Directed Values** Medium curiosity and proactive coping **Technology Attitudes/Behavior** Latest adoption High technology discomfort Medium technology optimism, innovativeness 13%	**Demographics** Medium income and education, more female **Self-Directed Values** High curiosity and proactive coping **Technology Attitudes/Behavior** High technology discomfort High technology optimism, innovativeness 8%
Non-Adopters, 59%	**Demographics** Low income and education, more female, older **Self-Directed Values** Low curiosity and high proactive coping **Technology Attitudes/Behavior** High technology discomfort, low technology optimism and low innovativeness	

nonadoption) and resulting usage behavior (heavy and light usage). The slide also shows that a segment of highly motivated senior adopters were nevertheless high in technology discomfort and thus waited longer to adopt. But eventually they got help to adopt and became heavy users (see the quadrant that shows heavy users by helped adoption). Researchers are always looking for ways to summarize information in a meaningful and compact way. They must be careful, however, that results are still easy to interpret and provide text (even in a PowerPoint slide show) to help readers focus on important points. In this chapter, we provide suggestions on how to present various kinds of analysis. But there are always multiple ways to present the same data, and researchers must use their creativity and continually think about if and how their presentation makes the points they want to make.

Credibility The quality of a report that is related to its accuracy, believability, and professional organization.

In addition to presenting results in an easy-to-understand fashion, a third objective of the research report is to establish **credibility** for the research methods, findings, and conclusions. This can be accomplished only if the report is accurate, believable, and professionally organized. These three dimensions cannot be treated separately, for they collectively operate to build credibility in the research document. For the report to be accurate, all of the input must be accurate. No degree of carelessness in handling data, reporting statistics, or incorrect interpretation can be tolerated. Errors in mathematical calculations, grammatical errors, and incorrect terminology diminish the credibility of the entire report.

Believability The quality of a report that is based on clear and logical thinking, precise expression, and accurate presentation.

Clear and logical thinking, precise expression, and accurate presentation create **believability.** When the underlying logic is fuzzy or the presentation imprecise, readers may have difficulty understanding what they read. If readers do not understand what they read, they may not believe what they read. It is important to note that whenever findings are surprising, or are different from what the client expects, research analysts can expect to be questioned. The methodology will be scrutinized to find an explanation that explains away the surprising findings. Sampling method, question wording, and nonresponse error are some of the most common ways of explaining away surprising findings. Researchers must anticipate these questions and have clear explanations for all findings.

Finally, the credibility of the research report is affected by the quality and organization of the document itself. The report must be clearly developed and professionally organized. The overall look of the report must not only clearly communicate results, but convey the professionalism of the research effort. Also, the document must reflect the preferences and technical sophistication of the reader. Reports are written to reflect three levels of readers: (1) readers who will read only the executive summary, (2) readers who will read the executive summary and look at the body of findings more closely, and (3) readers with some technical expertise, who may read the entire report and look to the appendix for more detailed information.

It is helpful to prepare an outline of all major points, with supporting details in their proper position and sequence. The report should have sections that address each of the research objectives. Use short, concise sentences and paragraphs. Always select wording consistent with the background and knowledge of readers. Rewrite the report several times. This will force you to remove clutter and critically evaluate the document for improvements.

The fourth objective of the research report is to be a reference. Most marketing research studies cover a variety of different objectives and seek to answer several research questions. This is accomplished in the report using both statistical and narrative formats. To retain all of this information is virtually impossible for the client. As a result, the research report becomes a reference document that is reviewed over an extended period.

Many marketing research reports become a part of a larger project conducted in various stages over time. It is not uncommon for one marketing research report to serve as a baseline for additional studies. Also, many reports are used for comparison purposes. For example, they are used to compare promotional changes, image building tactics, or even strengths and weaknesses of the firm.

Format of the Marketing Research Report

Every marketing research report is unique in that it is based on the needs of the client, the research purpose, and the study objectives. Yet all reports contain some common elements. Although the terminology may differ among industries, the basic format discussed in this section will help researchers plan and prepare reports for various clients. The parts common to all marketing research reports are the following:

1. Title page
2. Table of contents
3. Executive summary
    a. Research objectives
    b. Concise statement of method
    c. Summary of key findings
    d. Conclusion and recommendations
4. Introduction
5. Research methods and procedures
6. Data analysis and findings
7. Conclusions and recommendations
8. Limitations
9. Appendices

Title Page

The title page indicates the subject of the report and the name of the recipient, along with his or her position and organization. Any numbers or phrases to designate a particular department or division also should be included. Most important, the title page must contain the name, position, employing organization, address, telephone number of the person or persons submitting the report, and date the report is submitted.

Table of Contents

The table of contents lists the topics of the report in sequential order. Usually, the contents page will highlight each topical area, the subdivisions within each area, and corresponding page numbers. It is also common to include tables and figures and the pages where they can be found.

Executive Summary

Executive summary The part of a marketing research report that presents the major points; it must be complete enough to provide a true representation of the document but in summary form.

The **executive summary** is the most important part of the report. Many consider it the soul of the report, insofar as many executives read only the report summary. The executive summary presents the major points of the report. It must be complete enough to provide a true representation of the entire document but in summary form. Make sure your executive summary can stand alone. The rest of your report supports the key findings included in the summary, but the overview provided by the executive summary must nevertheless seem complete. While the executive summary comes near the front of the report, it should

EXHIBIT 18.2 Research Objectives

Research Objectives
- Measure and model the impact of Apex advertising on employees
  - Measure employees' perceptions of
    - effectiveness, organizational accuracy, promise exaggeration, and value-congruence of Apex ads
  - Measure outcome variables after viewing Apex ads
    - pride, trust, organizational identification, organizational commitment, customer focus
- Measure the effect of pre-existing employee organizational identification and customer focus on response to Apex ads

actually be written last. Until all the analyses are done, researchers cannot determine which findings are most important.

The executive summary has several purposes: (1) to convey how and why the research was undertaken, (2) to summarize the key findings, and (3) to suggest future actions. In other words, the executive summary must contain the research objectives, a concise statement of method, a summary of the findings, and specific conclusions and recommendations.

Research objectives should be as precise as possible, but not longer than approximately one page. The research purpose along with the questions or hypotheses that guided the project should also be stated in this section. Exhibit 18.2 shows a PowerPoint slide that summarizes research objectives for a project in which employees' reactions to their company's consumer ads were measured. After explaining the research purpose and objectives, a brief description of the sampling method, the research design, and any procedural aspects are addressed in one or two paragraphs. Following this is a statement of key findings.

Exhibit 18.3 shows a slide that summarizes a few of the key findings from a research project. The findings presented in the summary must agree with those found in the findings section of the full report. Only key findings that relate to the research objectives should be included.

EXHIBIT 18.3 Selected Key Findings from a Research Project

Key Findings
- Apex employees identify strongly with Apex, averaging 6.3 on a 7-point scale across all organizational identity items.
- Perceived advertising effectiveness with consumers has strong effects on all outcome variables. Employees thus "care" about the effectiveness of advertising. In particular, effectiveness is very strongly associated with employee pride.
- The perception that ads portray the organization accurately has moderate to strong effects on all outcome variables. Employees thus desire for Apex to be portrayed in ads consistent with how they see their company.

Finally, the summary contains a brief statement of conclusions and recommendations. The conclusion section of the report summarizes your findings. Conclusions concisely explain research findings and the meaning that can be attached to the findings. Recommendations, in contrast, are for appropriate future actions. Recommendations focus on specific marketing tactics or strategies the client can use to gain a competitive advantage. Conclusions and recommendations typically are stated in one to two paragraphs.

Introduction

The **introduction** contains background information necessary for a complete understanding of the report. Definition of terms, relevant background information, and the study's scope and emphasis are communicated in the introduction. The introduction also lists specific research objectives and questions the study was designed to answer, as well as hypotheses, length of the study, and any research-related problems. Usually hypotheses are not stated formally. They are stated in everyday language. For example, a research team can summarize their hypotheses about the variables they believe will affect senior Internet adoption as follows: "We expected the following factors to be positively related to senior adoption: income, education, curiosity, and technology optimism." Upon reading the introduction, the client should know exactly what the report is about, why the research was conducted, and what relationships exist between the current study and past or future research endeavors.

Research Methods and Procedures

Methods-and-procedures section Communicates how the research was conducted.

The objective of the **methods-and-procedures section** is to communicate how the research was conducted. Issues addressed in this section include the following:

1. The research design used: exploratory, descriptive, and/or causal.
2. Types of secondary data included in the study, if any.
3. If primary data were collected, what procedure was used (observation, questionnaire) and what administration procedures were employed (personal, mail, telephone, Internet).
4. Sample and sampling processes used. The following issues are usually addressed:
   - **a.** How the sample population was defined and profiled?
   - **b.** Sampling units used (for example, businesses, households, individuals)?
   - **c.** The sampling list (if any) used in the study?
   - **d.** How was the sample size determined?
   - **e.** Was a probability or nonprobability sampling plan employed?

Many times when writing the methods-and-procedures section, the writer gets bogged down in presenting too much detail. If on completion of this section, the reader can say what was done, how it was done, and why it was done, the objective of the writer has been fulfilled. A slide summarizing the methodology used in the senior adoption of the Internet study appears in Exhibit 18.4.

Data Analysis and Findings

The body of the marketing research report consists of the study's findings. Data analysis requirements differ for each project, so the presentation of findings will be somewhat different for each project. No matter how complicated the statistical analysis, the challenge for researchers is to summarize and present the analysis in a way that makes it easy to understand for nonspecialists. Findings should always include a detailed presentation with supporting tables, figures, and graphs. All results must be logically arranged to correspond

eXHIBIT 18.4 Slide Summarizing Research Methodology

CRITO *Consortium*
University of California, Irvine

Research Methodology

- National telephone survey of seniors 65+
- Questions appended to IDC's technology panel
- 200 internet users and 245 non-users (random sample)
- Questions measured:
  - Values
    - Curiosity and self-efficacy (proactive coping)
  - Technology attitudes/behavior
    - Technology optimism, technology discomfort, technology innovativeness
  - Internet use
    - Amount and variety of use; attitudes toward use
  - Demographics
    - Age, Education, Income, Sex

CENTER FOR RESEARCH ON INFORMATION TECHNOLOGY AND ORGANIZATIONS

with each research objective or research question listed in the report. This portion of the report is not simply an undifferentiated dump of the findings. When reporting results, no writer should claim the results are "obvious," or "self-evident." Rather, report writers both present and interpret their results. The researcher must decide how to group the findings into sections that facilitate understanding. Best practices suggest that tables, figures, and graphs be used when results are presented. Graphs and tables should provide a simple summation of the data in a clear, concise, and nontechnical manner.

When writing the report, the information must be explained in the body of the report in a straightforward fashion without technical output and language. Technical information most readers will have trouble understanding is best suited for the appendix section of the report. Below are several strategies for presenting analyses using graphs and tables. There is probably no one best way to present a particular analysis. Instead there often are several effective ways to portray a particular finding or set of findings. We discuss some specific methods to illustrate frequencies, crosstabs, *t*-tests, ANOVAs, correlations, and regressions. With some patience, you can master the simpler presentation techniques in this chapter. If you become comfortable working with the chart editor in SPSS, you will find there are many more options we have not covered. Once you have mastered the basic techniques, you can teach yourself more by experimenting with the chart editor in SPSS. In addition, you can convert your SPSS data into an Excel spreadsheet and use the graphing functions from Excel to present your findings.

Reporting Frequencies

Frequencies can be reported in tables, bar charts, or pie charts. For example, Exhibit 18.5 contains a table illustrating the results for the research question "How frequently do you patronize the Santa Fe Grill?" This table illustrates the data output in a simple and concise manner, enabling the reader to easily view how often respondents eat at the Santa Fe Grill. Notice that all digits past the decimal point have been removed. This is common practice in reporting percentages in marketing research. The extra digits create clutter without providing very much information. Moreover, because most research involves sampling error, carrying percentages out past the decimal point is misleading. Researchers usually cannot estimate the results with the degree of precision the extra decimal points imply.

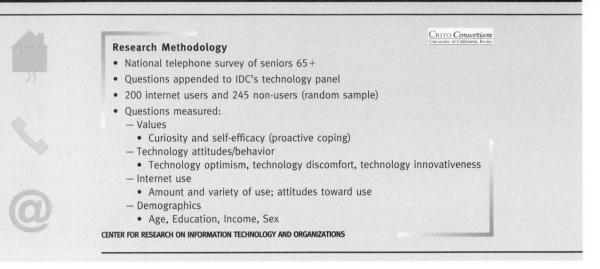

eXHIBIT 18.5 Findings Illustrating Simple Readable Results of Frequencies

How often do you eat at the Santa Fe Grill?

	Frequency	Percent	Cumulative Percent
Very Infrequently	49	19	19
Somewhat Infrequently	62	25	44
Occasionally	43	17	61
Somewhat Frequently	59	23	84
Very Frequently	40	16	100%
Total	253	100%	

Using Bar Charts to Display Frequencies

Exhibit 18.6 shows the simplest type of bar chart that can be made in SPSS. While you will see more options on the screen in the chart editor interface in SPSS Version 14.0 (which was used to make the charts in this chapter), most of the same command sequences we show here will work in versions 12 and 13 chart editors. If your version of SPSS is 12 or 13, you will see that your chart editor is similar to the one in version 14, but that the interface occasionally offers fewer options. To make a bar chart, the SPSS "click-through"

eXHIBIT 18.6 Example of a Bar Chart

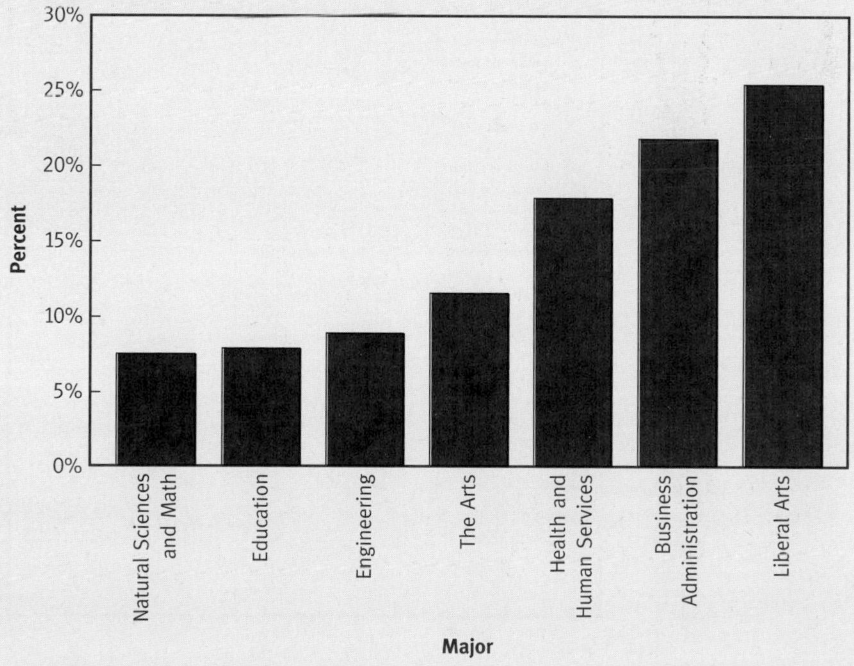

sequence is GRAPH → BAR. Leave the default on "Simple" and under "Data in chart are," you also use the default of "Summaries for groups of cases." On the next screen (shown in Exhibit 18.7), you will usually want to change the default choice from "N of cases" to "% of cases." On the left side of your screen, highlight the name of the variable you want in your bar graph (in this case, the variable is "Major") and move it across to the space that says "Category Axis," and click "OK." SPSS will then generate your bar graph.

To make changes to the graph, you double click the chart in the output which will take you to a chart editor. There you will find several options for the chart. Double clicking on any of the elements in your chart brings up the relevant menu for customizing that particular element. For example, double clicking on the bars in the chart will bring up a "Properties" menu with several tabs. To produce the graph shown in Exhibit 18.6 we chose the "Categories" tab on the Properties menu. On the categories menu, we selected the "sort by" option and then "statistic/ascending." This option arranges the graph by lowest percent to highest percent, which makes the graph easier for readers to understand.

By experimenting with various tabs on the Properties menu, students will find they can change the color, font, and font size on the graph. It is often desirable to enlarge the font if the graph will be exported to either Word or PowerPoint. The orientation of the bar labels can be changed as well. If you click on the bar labels while in the chart editor, the Properties

eXHIBIT 18.7 Using SPSS to Prepare a Bar Graph

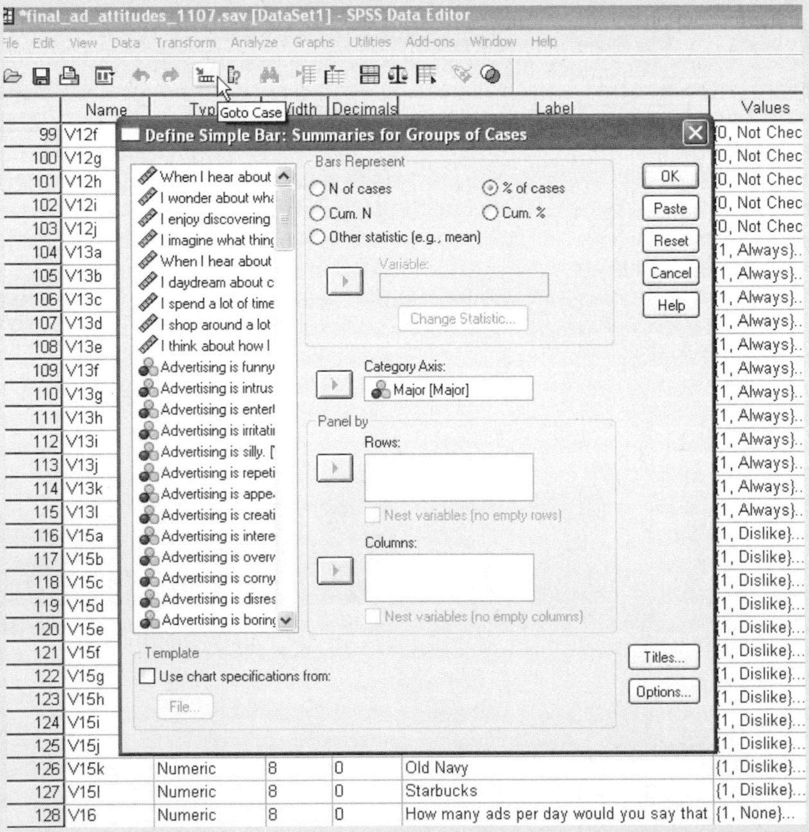

menu will appear, and one of the tabs will be "Labels and Ticks." Using this menu, the orientation of labels can be chosen: vertical, horizontal, or staggered. You should experiment with options until everything on your graph is clear and readable. Then, you can right click on your finished chart, choose the "copy chart" option, and cut and paste the result to a Word or PowerPoint document. The finished result is shown in Exhibit 18.6.

Portraying Frequencies Using Pie Charts

Pie charts are particularly good at portraying the relative proportion of response to a question. The process for creating a pie chart is similar to that used for creating the bar chart. From the SPSS menu, choose GRAPH → PIE. A menu will appear with three radio buttons. The default choice "Summaries for groups of cases" is the correct option for a simple pie chart. Click "Define" and a new menu will appear. On this menu, although "N of cases" is the default option, in most cases you will be more interested in reporting percentages, so click the button next to "% of cases." Move the variable name from the variable list (in this case "V16," which is labeled "How many ads per day do you pay attention to?") into the blank next to "Define Slices by." Then click "OK." SPSS will now create your chart in an output file.

As with the bar chart, when you double click on the pie chart in the output file, you will open the chart editor in SPSS. From the toolbar in the editor, you can choose "Elements → Show Data Labels" and the percentages will be displayed on the pie chart for each slice. However, you want to remove any extra digits after the decimal place from the percentages displayed in your chart. You can double click on the percentages box, which will give you a Properties menu. Choose the "Number Format" tab and next to decimal places, enter "0" (see Exhibit 18.8). Note that if you don't click in the right place, the Properties menu may

eXHIBIT 18.8 Changing the Properties of a Pie Chart in the SPSS Chart Editor

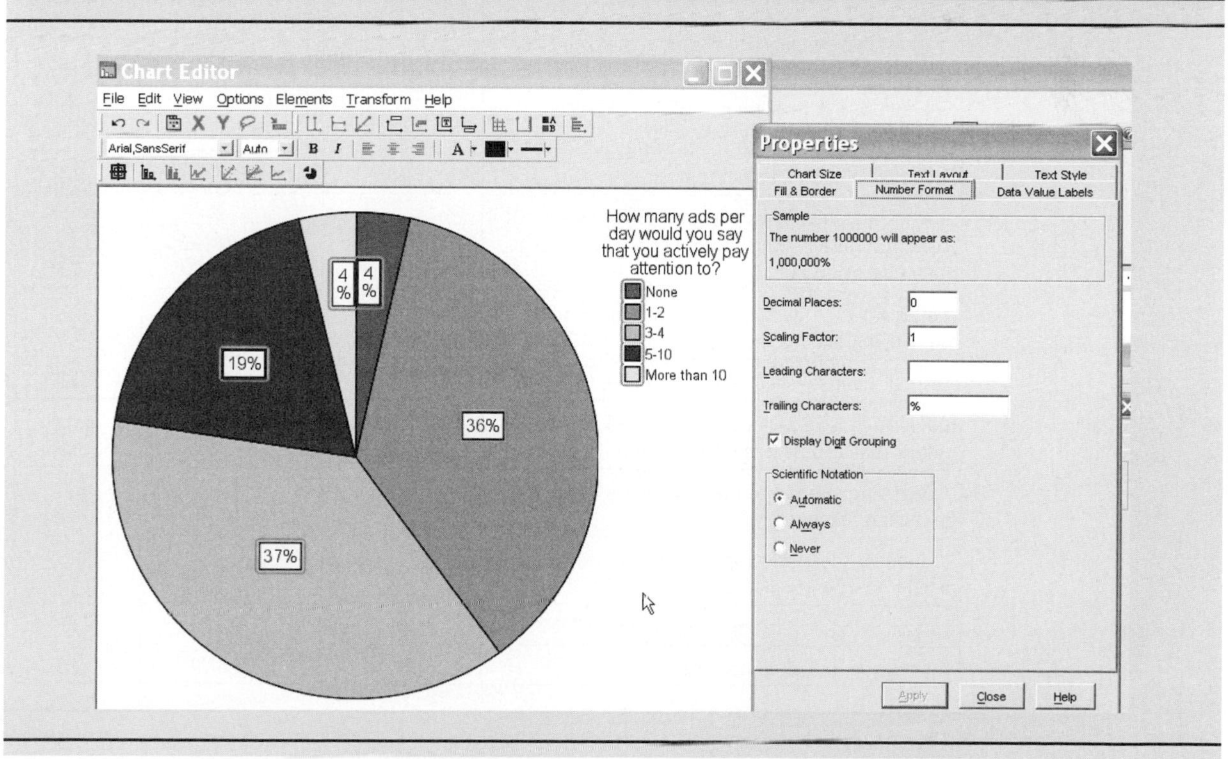

not show the appropriate tab. If you don't see the tab you want on the Properties menu, try double clicking the relevant part of the chart that you want to change again.

If you spend some time investigating the Options and Properties menus, you will see that you can make fonts bigger, change the font style, and alter the color and appearance of the slices in the pie. When you are done, you can right click on the chart and copy and paste it to Word or PowerPoint.

Reporting Means of Thematically Related Variables

Researchers may want to report the means of several thematically related variables in the same chart or table. This can be accomplished with either a bar chart or a table. A table may be preferred when a researcher feels that the entire question needs to be portrayed in order to fully understand the findings. Exhibit 18.9 shows a table that was constructed in PowerPoint using the table function. The results shown in the table are based on SPSS output, using the command sequence Analyze → Descriptive Statistics → Frequencies. A menu will appear, and then you click the "Statistics" button near the bottom of that menu. Then choose "Mean" and "Standard Deviation." Click "OK," and the results will be generated by SPSS.

Note that the items in the table have been ordered from the highest to the lowest average. Sorting responses in this manner often facilitates reader understanding. There are

EXHIBIT 18.9 A Table Summarizing Means of Thematically Related Items

COLLEGE STUDENTS' ATTITUDES TOWARD ADVERTISING

Item	Number of Responses	Average 7 = Strongly Agree	Standard Deviation
Ads can be a good way to learn about products.	312	5.2	1.5
The purpose of marketing is to attract customers by learning what they want.	308	5.2	1.5
Advertising is an interesting business.	308	5.2	1.5
Advertising sometimes encourages me to seek out more information about products I am interested in.	312	5.0	1.5
I think it would be fun to work for an advertising agency.	306	4.5	1.9
Overall, I am satisfied with advertising.	308	4.3	1.3
Advertising is usually designed to sell things that people don't really need.	310	4.3	1.8
Advertising appeals to the selfishness in human beings.	303	3.6	1.8
If there was less advertising, the world would be a better place.	304	3.4	1.7
I try to avoid advertising whenever possible.	304	3.3	1.7
Advertising is bad for society.	310	2.6	1.5

two other important elements of the table to note: (1) the maximum value of 7 is clearly indicated so that readers can easily compare the mean to the maximum possible score, and (2) the mean and standard deviations are shown with only one digit past the decimal. While percentages should have no decimals past the decimal point, means should generally display one digit past the decimal point.

It is also possible to portray thematically related means on a bar chart in SPSS. In order to do so, you begin as you did when portraying one variable by choosing Graphs → Bar from the toolbar and leaving the default bar chart type "Simple" selected. However, you will change the default at the bottom of the menu from "Summaries of groups of cases" to "Summaries of separate variables." Then click "Define." From there, move the variables you want in the graph from the variable list on the left into the window labeled "Bars Represent" (see Exhibit 18.10). The default is "Mean" so you will not have to change any options. Once you click "OK" the bar graph will be created. When you double click on the bar chart in the output, this will take you to the chart editor. As we explained earlier in the chapter, you can double click elements within the chart and change the properties and the appearance of the bar

eXHIBIT 18.10 Using the Bar Chart Function in SPSS to Summarize Thematically Related Means

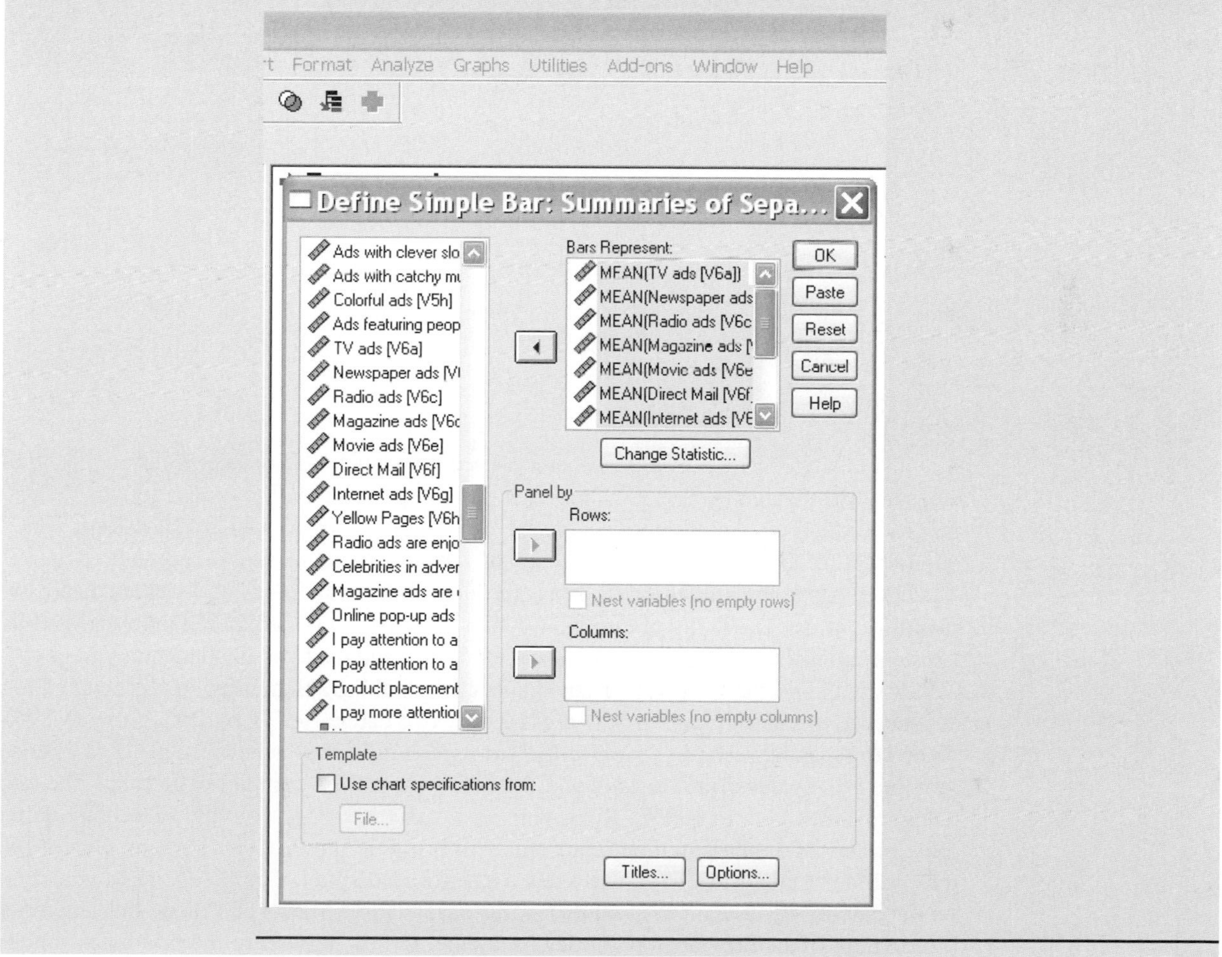

eXHIBIT 18.11 Bar Chart Displaing Multiple Thematically Related Means

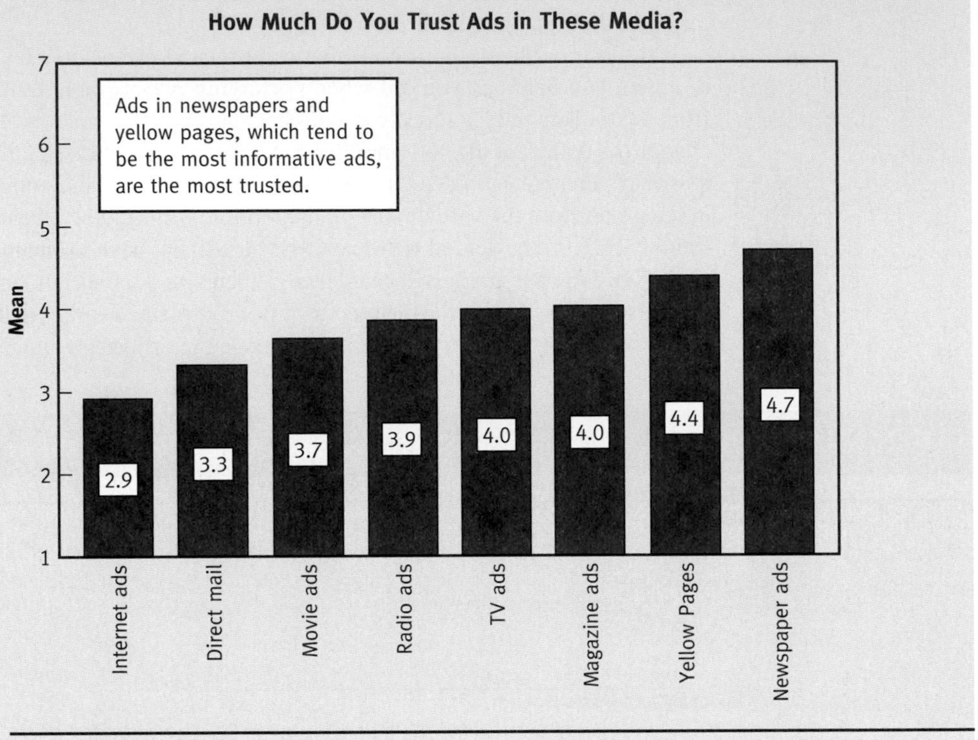

chart. Exhibit 18.11 shows a finished image that has been cut and pasted to a PowerPoint slide. An interpretation has been added to the slide to facilitate reader comprehension.

Reporting Crosstabs (Bar Charts)

The bar chart function in SPSS can be used to display Crosstabs. Once again, you can start with Graphs → Bar → Summaries for groups of cases. From there, choose "Cluster" rather than the default option "Simple" and click "Define." Under "Bars Represent," choose "% of cases." Your independent or causing variable should be entered in the "Category Axis" blank. In this case, sex is the independent variable. The variable you are explaining, in this case, liking of the Carl's Junior Paris Hilton ad, is entered in to the "Define Clusters" blank (see Exhibit 18.12). Then click "OK," and the Crosstab bar chart will be created. As with the other charts, you can double click on the graph to bring up the chart editor.

Because this particular Crosstab crosses only two categories by two categories, we excluded the bars representing "don't like" from the graph. This is because in a 2 × 2, once you know the values for one category, the other category is completely defined (the two categories must add to 100%). Removing a category is straightforward. You can double click on any of the bars in the graph. This will bring up the Properties menu. One of the tabs will be "Categories." You will see the categories displayed on the menu. If you click on the category you want to exclude (in this case "Don't Like") and then click the red x button next to the box labeled "Order," the label will be moved to the box below under

eXHIBIT 18.12 Using the SPSS Bar Chart Function to Show Crosstabs

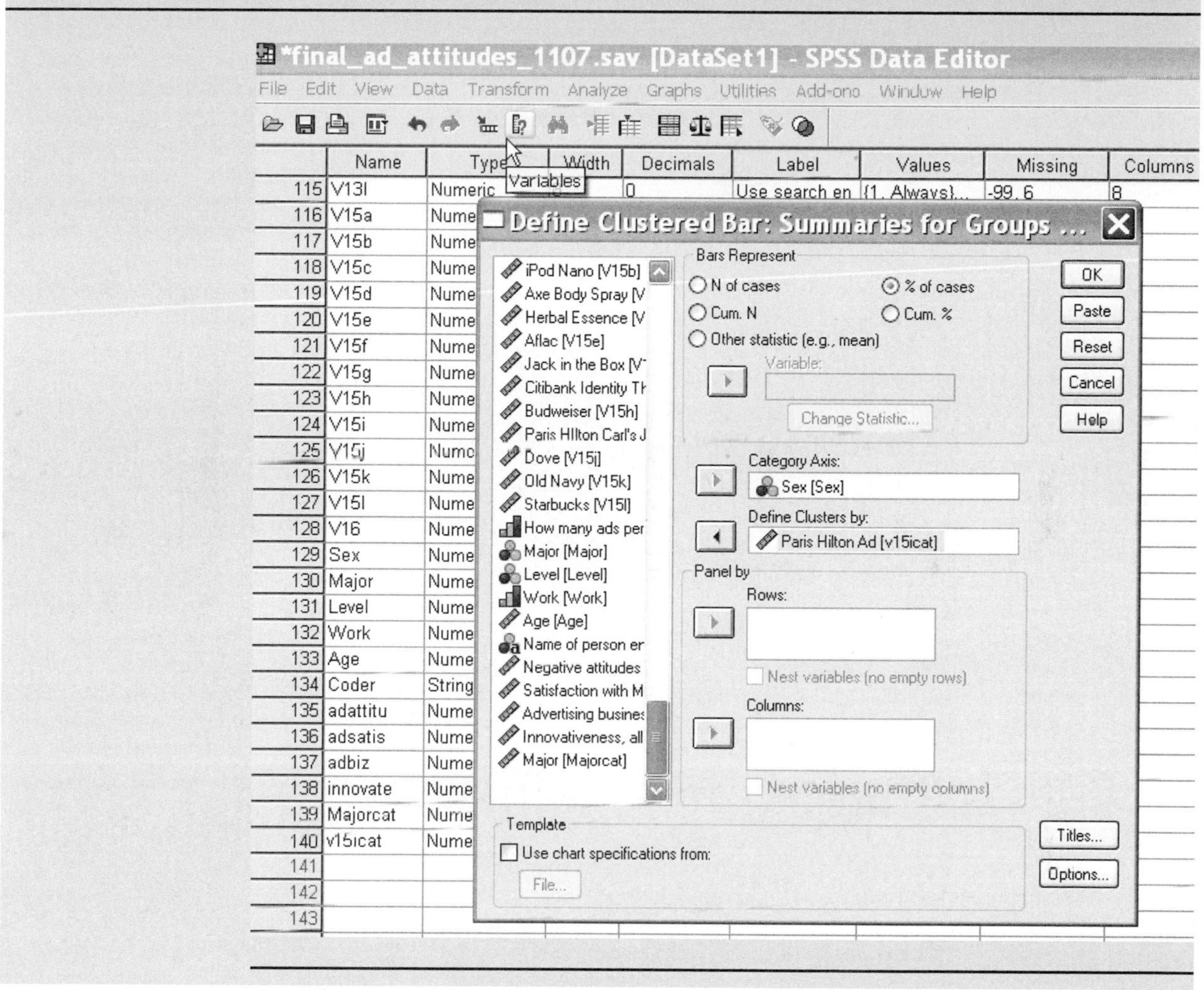

"Excluded." Click "Apply" and your Crosstab will now display only one category of the outcome variable, in this case, the percentage of respondents within each sex who liked the Carl's Junior Paris Hilton ad. The resulting graph is displayed in Exhibit 18.13.

Reporting *t*-Tests and ANOVAs (Bar Charts)

Exhibit 18.14 shows a table created in PowerPoint that pictures the results of four different *t*-tests that are thematically related. Each *t*-test compares outcome measures for two groups: employees with low and high identification with their company. The average for each group of employees for each variable appears in the cells, along with the number of employees in each group. Again, significant *p*-values are indicated.

Both *t*-tests and ANOVAs can be displayed on bar charts created in SPSS. Our example will focus on using the bar charts for an ANOVA, but the command sequence within SPSS is the same. Start with Graphs → Bar → Simple. Leave the box chosen next to

EXHIBIT 18.13 Bar Chart Showing a Crosstab

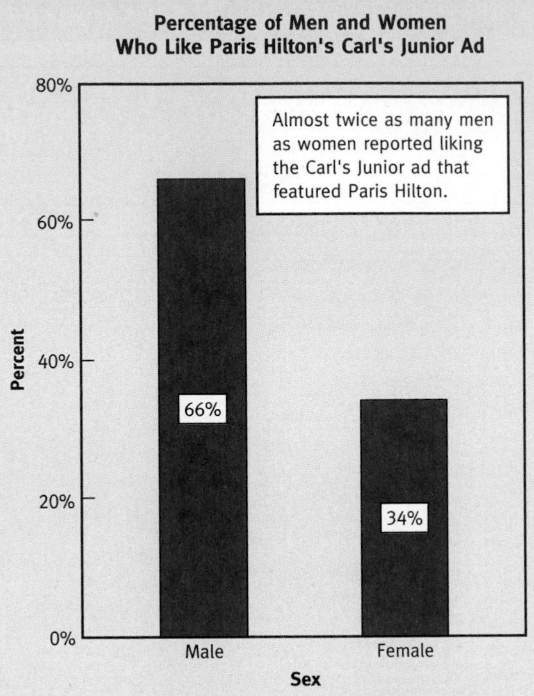

*$p < .05$

EXHIBIT 18.14 A Table Showing *t*-Tests

PRE-EXISTING ORGANIZATIONAL IDENTIFICATION AFFECTED ALL AD EVALUATIONS

Constructs	Less Identified Employees	More Identified Employees	Standard Deviation
Organizational Accuracy (max = 35)	21.6 (n = 341)	24.0* (n = 209)	Lo = 6.1 Hi = 7.0
Promise Exaggeration (max = 21)	9.2 (n = 351)	8.1* (n = 207)	Lo = 8.1 Hi = 8.8
Value Congruence (max = 21)	12.6 (n = 345)	14.5* (n = 208)	Lo = 3.8 Hi = 4.1
Ad Effectiveness (max = 28)	19.2 (n = 355)	20.2* (n = 218)	Lo = 5.7 Hi = 6.1

Employees more strongly identified with Apex rated the ads as more accurate in presenting the organization, less exaggerated, and more consistent with their values, and believed the ads to be more effective. Despite the fact that on average more strongly identified individuals were more predisposed to see the ads positively, they also varied more in their responses than did the less identified employees.

*All differences significant at $p < .05$

EXHIBIT 18.15 Using SPSS to Create Bar Charts to Display ANOVA Results

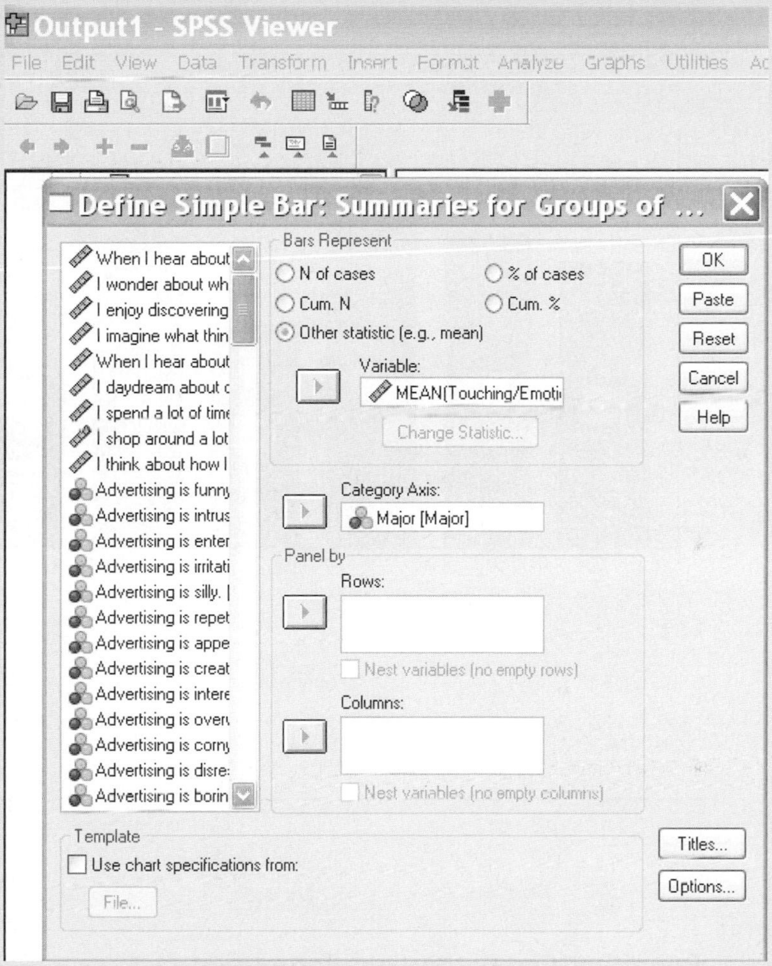

"Summaries are groups of cases," and click "Define." On the next screen (pictured in Exhibit 18.15), under "Bars Represent," choose "other" and enter the outcome variable (in this case, "Liking for Touching/Emotional ads) into the blank under "Variable." For "Category Axis," enter the independent variable (in this case "Major"). Then click "OK" and the graph will be produced. Using "Options" we added a title and a footnote to the graph. Click on the *y*-axis, which shows the scale that we used in the survey, and you get the Properties menu along with a tab labeled "Scale." In that menu, we changed the minimum to 1 and the maximum to 7 (the endpoints in the actual scale). SPSS will often change the scale points represented to maximize the space in the chart, but the resulting default chart may distort your findings. In many cases, you will want to change the axis to show the actual endpoints of your scale. A footnote shows an ANOVA analysis performed separately using Scheffé's post hoc test to examine the significance of categorical differences. The final graph is displayed in Exhibit 18.16.

EXHIBIT 18.16 Bar Chart Portraying ANOVA Results

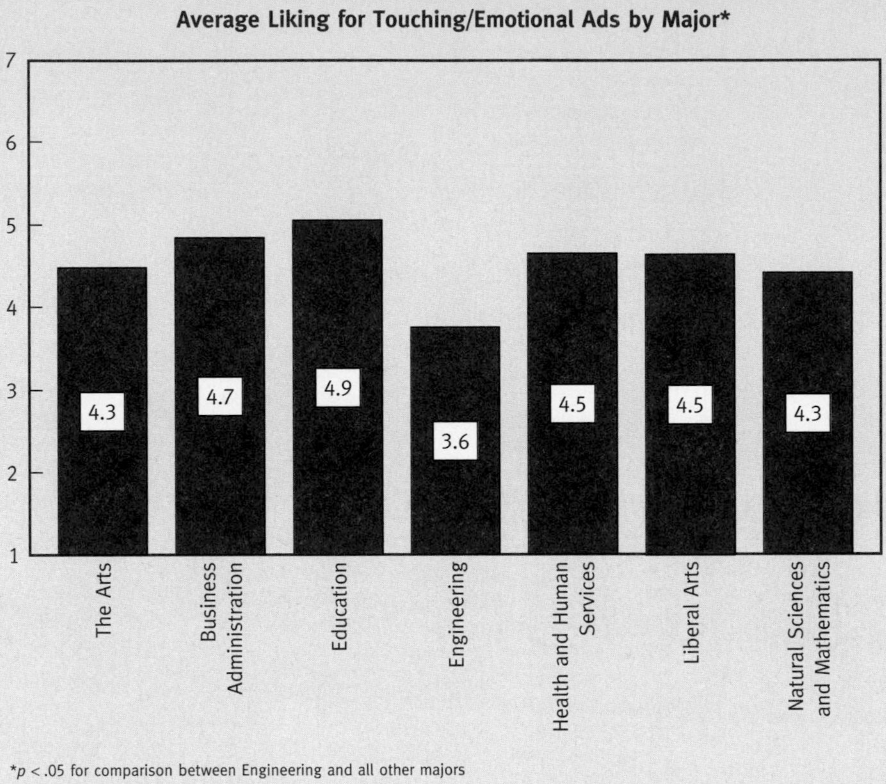

Reporting Correlation and Regression

Correlations may be included in a report to illustrate relationships between several variables that are later used in a regression or to show the relationship of several variables to an outcome variable of interest. Exhibit 18.17 is a table showing the correlation of several variables with overall satisfaction for a retailer named Primal Elements. To facilitate comparison of the sizes of the correlations, they are arranged from strongest to mildest. Note that the negative correlation is sorted by its strength because the negative value indicates the direction of the relationship only. The significance levels are once again indicated with a star.

Recall that regression is a multivariate technique that estimates the impact of multiple explanatory or independent variables on one dependent variable. One of the simplest ways to present regression findings is to create a diagram in Word or in PowerPoint that pictures the predictor and the outcome variables with arrows showing the relationships between the variables (see Exhibit 18.18). These diagrams were referred to as conceptual models in Chapter 6. The title of the analysis clearly describes the picture. The standardized Betas are portrayed above the appropriate arrow because the Beta shows the strength of

EXHIBIT 18.17 Correlations of Item Ratings with Overall Satisfaction with Primal Elements

Item	Correlation
Store atmosphere	.59*
How intimidating the store is	–.30*
Expense of products	–.25*
Interior appearance of store	.25*
Quantity of information workers provide about products	.21*
Exterior appearance of store	.16

the relationship between the independent and dependent variables. As in the other pictured analyses, a star may be used to indicate statistical significance. The R^2 appears in the diagram and is briefly explained in the accompanying text. The text summarizes the information provided by the regression analysis in the picture.

EXHIBIT 18.18 Displaying Regression Findings

How Employee Ratings of Consumer Ad Characteristics Affect Pride in Their Company

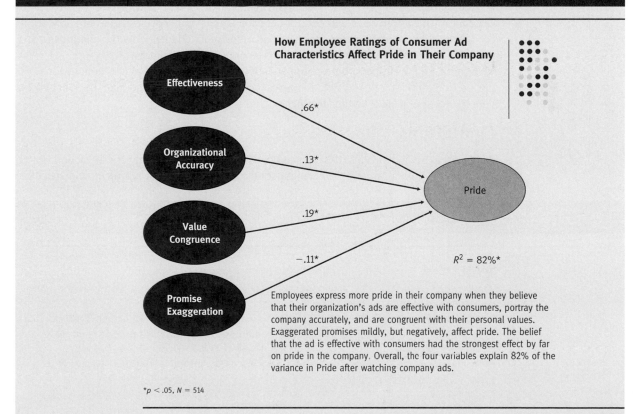

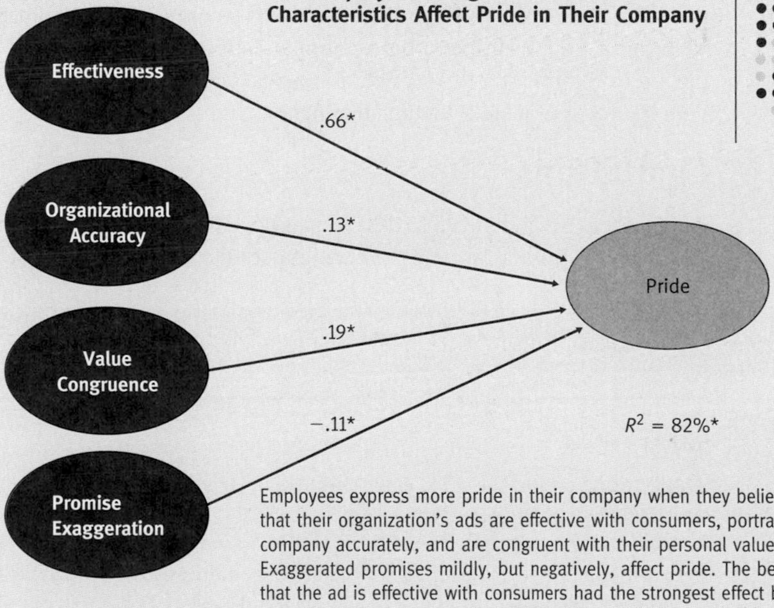

Employees express more pride in their company when they believe that their organization's ads are effective with consumers, portray the company accurately, and are congruent with their personal values. Exaggerated promises mildly, but negatively, affect pride. The belief that the ad is effective with consumers had the strongest effect by far on pride in the company. Overall, the four variables explain 82% of the variance in Pride after watching company ads.

*$p < .05$, $N = 514$

eXHIBIT 18.19 Illustration of Conclusions in a Marketing Research Report

Conclusions

- Four primary factors are related to satisfaction with and patronage of the Santa Fe Grill: food quality, service, value, and atmosphere.
- Food quality is the most important factor influencing satisfaction with and patronage of the Santa Fe Grill.
- Service at the Santa Fe Grill is the second most important factor influencing satisfaction with and patronage of the restaurant.
- Perceptions of Santa Fe Grill food quality and service are favorable.
- Perceptions of value and atmosphere are relatively less favorable.
- Perceptions of the Santa Fe Grill on all four factors—food, service, value, and atmosphere—are significantly less favorable for the less frequent patrons.
- More frequent patrons of the Santa Fe Grill have lifestyles that characterize them as Innovators and Influencers.

Conclusions and Recommendations

Conclusions and recommendations are derived specifically from the findings. As illustrated in Exhibit 18.19, conclusions are descriptive statements generalizing the results, not necessarily the numbers generated by statistical analysis. Each conclusion directly references research objectives.

Recommendations are generated by critical thinking. The task is one where the researcher must critically evaluate each conclusion and develop specific areas of applications for strategic or tactical actions. Recommendations must address how the client can solve the problem at hand through the creation of a competitive advantage.

Exhibit 18.20 outlines the recommendations that correspond to the conclusions displayed in Exhibit 18.19. You will notice that each recommendation, unlike the conclusions, is in the form of a clear action statement.

Limitations

Researchers always strive to develop and implement a flawless study for the client. But all research has limitations. Researchers must note the limitations of a project, and speculate

eXHIBIT 18.20 Illustration of Recommendations in a Marketing Research Report

Recommendations

- Advertising messages should emphasize food quality and service, since these are the most important factors influencing satisfaction.
- If advertisements include people, they should be characterized as innovative in their lifestyles.
- Focus group research needs to be conducted to learn why perceptions of value and atmosphere are less favorable than perceptions of food quality and service.
- The focus group research also needs to examine why perceptions of less frequent patrons of the Santa Fe Grill are significantly less favorable than those of more frequent patrons.
- The current study collected data from customers of the Santa Fe Grill. In the future, data should be collected from noncustomers.

Limitations Extraneous events that place certain restrictions on the report and are normally mentioned when results are being compared.

intelligently about if and how the limitations may have affected their conclusions. Common **limitations** associated with marketing research include sampling bias, financial constraints, time pressures, and measurement error.

Every study has limitations and the researcher has to make the client aware of them. Researchers should not be embarrassed by limitations but rather admit openly that they exist. However, limitations should not be stated in a way that undermines the credibility of the entire project. Researchers cover limitations, but do so in a way that develops reasonable confidence in the conclusions made in the report. Treatment of limitations in the research report usually involves a discussion of results and accuracy. For example, researchers should tell clients about the generalizability of the results beyond the sample used in the study. Any weaknesses in specific scales should be addressed, along with other potential sources of nonsampling error. If limitations are not stated and are later discovered by the client, mistrust and skepticism toward the entire report may result. When properly reported, limitations rarely diminish the credibility of the report but instead improve client perceptions of the quality of the project.

Appendix A section following the main body of the report; used to house complex, detailed, or technical information.

Appendices

An **appendix,** often referred to as a "technical appendix," contains complex, detailed, or technical information not necessary for the formal report. Common items contained in appendices include the questionnaire or data collection instrument used for the research project, interviewer forms, statistical calculations, and detailed sampling maps.

Problems in Preparing the Marketing Research Report

Industry best practices suggest five problem areas that may arise in writing a marketing research report:

1. **Lack of data interpretation.** In some instances, researchers get so involved in constructing results tables that we fail to provide proper interpretation of the data in the tables. The researcher always provides unbiased interpretation of any findings.

2. **Unnecessary use of complex statistics.** To impress clients, many researchers unnecessarily use sophisticated multivariate statistical techniques. In many research reports, the most sophisticated statistical technique required will be a Chi-square test. Avoid using statistical methods unless they are essential to derive meaning from the data.

3. **Emphasis on packaging instead of quality.** Many researchers go out of their way to make reports look classy or flamboyant using sophisticated computer-generated graphics. While professional graphic representation of the results is essential in the report, never lose sight of the primary purpose: to provide valid and credible information to the client.

4. **Lack of relevance.** Reporting data, statistics, and information that are not consistent with the study's objectives can be a major problem when writing the report. Always develop the report with the research objectives clearly in focus. Avoid adding unnecessary information just to make the report longer. Always remain in the realm of practicality. Suggest ideas that are relevant, doable, and consistent with the results of the study.

5. **Placing too much emphasis on a few statistics.** Never base all conclusions or recommendations on one or a few statistically significant questions or results, but on the weight of evidence from your literature review, secondary data, and the pattern of results in your entire report. Always attempt to find substantial supporting evidence for any recommendation or conclusion.

The final research document is the end product of the researcher. Individual credibility can be enhanced or damaged by the report, and credibility is what helps a researcher gain repeat business and referrals from clients. The quality, dedication, and honesty one invests in the report have the potential to generate future business, career promotions, and salary raises.

The Critical Nature of Presentations

Presentation of marketing research results can be as important as, if not more important than, the results of the research itself. This is true for several reasons. First, any research, no matter how well done or how important, cannot be properly acted upon if the results are not effectively communicated to those who will use the information in making decisions. Managers need accurate information if they are going to make good decisions, and if they do not understand the marketing research findings, they may well make poor decisions that lead to difficulty not only for the organization but also for individuals in the organization affected by those decisions. Second, the report or presentation is often the only part of the marketing research project that will be seen by those commissioning the report. Senior managers often do not have the time to review all aspects of a research project, so they rely on the researcher to carry out the research properly and then present the findings clearly and concisely. Third, the content and presentation form of the research are closely intertwined. Poorly organized presentations presented in an unclear, lengthy, difficult-to-access format often lead audiences to discount the content.

Guidelines for Preparing the Visual Presentation

The visual presentation is a separate but equal component of the marketing research report and has one primary goal: to provide a visual summary of the marketing research report, designed in a manner that will complement and enhance oral communication of the written marketing research report. In many cases, Microsoft PowerPoint is the preferred method of preparing the visual marketing research presentation. Given the versatility of PowerPoint, the visual presentation may employ graphics as simple as those in this chapter. But these presentations may also employ a full multimedia array of techniques, including sound, animation, color graphics, and video. Regardless of the complexity in the presentation, industry practices suggest the following guidelines:

1. Begin with a slide showing the title of the presentation and the individual(s) doing the presentation. In addition, the client and the marketing research firm should also be identified.
2. A sequence of slides should be developed indicating the objectives of the research and the specific research questions to be addressed, followed by the research methodology employed and a description of the sample surveyed.
3. Additional slides should be developed that highlight the research findings or particular results of the study that the researcher deems important for communication purposes.
4. Finally, the presentation should conclude with recommendations, conclusions, and research implications as they pertain to the study at hand.

MARKETING RESEARCH IN ACTION

Reporting Research Findings

Writing the Marketing Research Report for a Focus Group Interview

This illustration uses a focus group report to demonstrate many of the concepts addressed in this chapter.

Introduction

This focus group report is prepared for the area known as the Jackson community, located in the north-central section of Memphis, Tennessee. The purpose of the report is to communicate findings that were revealed in a focus group interview. Elements of discussion centered on the trends and market dynamics of the business environment within the Jackson community.

Research Purpose

Issues pertaining to the business climate of the Jackson community will be explored. The purpose of the study is twofold: first, to explore the business trends, market dynamics, and growth potential of the Jackson community for the purpose of providing insights into future business development in the area; second, to obtain data on market characteristics to be used in a subsequent survey to determine residents' buying power and spending habits within the community. To address these issues, the following research objectives were developed.

Research Objectives

To obtain accurate data pertaining to future business development in the Jackson area, the following research objectives were agreed upon:

1. To determine the current level of saturation and possible oversaturation of business activities in the Jackson community.
2. To assess opportunities for new and emerging businesses regarding trends and potential of the Jackson market.
3. To discover potential barriers to entry and growth in such areas as capital, markets, banking, and suppliers.
4. To explore related business issues such as supplier/vendor relations, receivables, financial variables, leasing, and location, along with selling strategies.
5. To assess positive city-delivered services to the Jackson community.
6. To explore business and neighborhood relations.
7. To discuss what can be done to improve the Jackson community business environment.
8. To learn how businesses in the Jackson community market themselves.
9. To address the future of the economy and business climate regarding customer segments, spending behavior, and consumer decision making.

Sample Characteristics

On the basis of a random sample of the university business community, eight business owners/managers participated in the focus group:

Mr. Harry Grayden	Johnson Supply
Mr. Warren Bowling	Plastic Fabrication
Ms. Emma Roberson	Temporary Employment
Ms. Anna Hogan	Sheet Metal Services, Inc.
Mr. Tom Brockway	Target Medical, Inc.
Mr. Sam Jorce	Retail Glass Co.
Mr. Andy Hammond	Retail Auto Parts
Mr. Hilliard Johnson	Carpet Cleaning

Research Findings

To best illustrate the findings of this focus group interview, results will be categorized in narrative form as they pertain to each research objective, following a general overview of the Jackson community.

General Overview of the Jackson Community

Major Positive Aspects Jackson is a centralized location with easy access to all areas of the city and surrounding communities. It also is a good area in which to locate manufacturing or wholesaling businesses. Stable, yet dependent on the economy, Jackson is the first area to lose jobs when the economy softens. Major competitive advantage is the central location.

Major Negative Aspects Major problems in the area are sales of illegal drugs centering around two motels and an adult bookstore. Also, crime is relatively high—all participants in the study were victims of break-ins during the past two years. In addition, the uncertainty of the Sam Cooper Expressway extension has created a lot of anxiety among businesses.

1. Saturation and Oversaturation of Business Activities

Not unlike other areas of the city, Jackson is oversaturated in low-entry-barrier businesses. These include:

Pawn shops	Title companies
Used-car lots	Small, home-based businesses
Credit agencies	Medium-sized distribution businesses

A major concern of the participants was the increased number of small mom-and-pop–type businesses. The Jackson area has low-cost rental space that makes it attractive for many small, novice businesses to operate with a severe level of undercapitalization. The Broad/Tillman area is an example of undercapitalized businesses that often fail in the first year, leading to distressed commercial property.

2. Opportunity Assessment and Market Trends

Growth in the Jackson area is uncertain, given the uncertainty of the extension of the Sam Cooper Expressway. High level of business turnover leads to both distressed commercial and residential property.

Several participants labeled Jackson as a good "incubation" area for small businesses, given its central location and low rent for commercial property.

Business Trends and Market Potential The Jackson area has an excellent opportunity for growth due to the high level of business turnover and low cost of rental property. Certain businesses can take advantage of a low barrier to entry but need to understand how to operate a business successfully without intensifying the level of saturation. Businesses that were identified by the participants include:

Hardware stores	Large manufacturing plants
Grocery stores	Warehousing and logistical businesses
Movie theaters	Fast-food restaurants
Entertainment businesses	Discount stores

All participants were in agreement that the Jackson area is a great magnet area due to the high level of employment that brings working people into the area.

3. Potential Barriers to Entry and Growth

The area is good for business growth if certain conditions exist. A neglected area that needs to be cleaned up is distressed property resulting from evicted tenants. There appears to be little code enforcement in the area. Drugs are keeping many businesses out.

4. Related Business Issues

- **Supplier/vendor relations.** No problems with suppliers because of the high volume of warehousing, distribution, and manufacturing in the community.
- **Controlling receivables.** Heavy inflow of dollars into the community from all parts of the metropolitan statistical area. Most accounts are large, high volume. Receivables are usually paid within 30 days; typical business cycles.
- **Financial variables.** Most financial institutions have moved out of the area due to crime. The level of financial support is still good in the community, but more so for service businesses and not as supportive for retail.
- **Leasing and location.** Low rent, convenient access, and central location are the major positives of the area. Yet many facilities are in the process of relocating because large spaces are not available in the area. Office space is high priced relative to other areas, retail space is average, and warehousing and distribution space is very cheap in the community.
- **Selling strategies.** The community is excellent for business-to-business activity; not so good, given current conditions, for retail trade. Appeal to drive-up business, not a conducive area for pedestrian traffic. No real community support for retail business.

5. Negative Aspects of City Services

Businesses in the community are very disgruntled with city officials. Aside from electricity and water they feel the community is ignored by the city—especially a lack of concern from the department of public works. Lack of city services detracts from the community, making it unappealing for consumers to shop in the area. The city has done nothing to promote the area in general, and nothing to promote business growth. The infrastructure of the community is deteriorating; high level of break-ins in the community.

6. Business and Neighborhood Relationships

Community commitment is low among both residential and business entities. The community has no sense of identity. Low community support for retail businesses. Heavy migration to East Memphis for shopping/specialty goods due to a lack of discount stores in the area and unpleasant shopping centers. The lack of adequate retailers is forcing people to other communities, specifically to the east.

Curb appeal of many businesses is low. Unsightly areas need to be cleaned up, with emphasis on distressed property, both commercial and residential.

7. How to Improve the Business Environment in the Jackson Community

- Clean up distressed property; enforce city codes on property.
- Resolve the problems with the rail tracks.
- Provide some certainty as to the Sam Cooper Expressway extension.
- Add more foliage; make the streets look more attractive.
- Start enforcing housing codes for both residential and commercial property.

8. How Do Businesses Market Themselves?

- Focus on the business-to-business market, not on retail.
- Have good labor supply; provide security for the employees.
- Provide a safe, appealing, and convenient environment for customers and employees.
- Train employees.
- Take advantage of any form of low-cost advertising and promotions.
- Provide quality service; don't promise what you can't deliver.

9. Future Direction of the Economy and Business Community in the Jackson Area

- It is a static area—will probably go unchanged for the immediate future. Possibly a slow decline in the area due to larger businesses relocating to other parts of the city.
- Perception of the area needs to change if businesses are to remain there.
- Major opportunity for the community is to position it as a warehousing/distribution park.
- Not a good area for retail—too many distressed neighborhoods, too many home-based businesses.
- Sam Cooper Expressway extension will determine the future of the community; need better leadership by the city to correct crime problems.
- Area is ideally suited for small manufacturing businesses or transportation businesses. Not really conducive to retail—bad pedestrian traffic area.
- Provide the area with a focus of what it should be—industrial, residential, etc. Develop much of the vacant land with businesses that reinforce that focus.

Hands-On Exercise

1. Did the report effectively communicate the situation?
2. What conclusions can be drawn from this focus group report?
3. Can strategy decisions be made for the Jackson community using this focus group report, or will more research be necessary? If more research is necessary, what kind?

Summary of Learning Objectives

■ **Understand the objectives of a research report.**
The key objective of a marketing research report is to provide the client with a clear, concise interpretation of the research project. The research report is a culmination of the entire study and therefore must communicate the systematic manner in which the study was designed and implemented. Secondary objectives of the report are to provide accurate, credible, easy-to-understand information to the client. The end result of the report is its ability to act as a reference document to guide future research and serve as an information source.

■ **Describe the format of a marketing research report.**
The research report generally includes the following: a title page, a table of contents, and an executive summary, which includes a statement of the research objectives, a detailed statement of the research method and procedures, a brief statement of findings, and conclusions and recommendations. Following the executive summary are the introduction of the report, a description of the methodology employed, and a discussion of data analysis techniques and findings. The final elements are conclusions and recommendations, and a description of limitations. An appendix may include technical explanations or documentation.

■ **Discuss several techniques for graphically displaying research results.**
A vast array of graphic techniques is available to display research results. A variety of bar charts can be used to display analyses from simple frequencies to Crosstabs, *t*-tests, and ANOVA. As well, pie charts can be used to display the results of frequencies. Tables are especially helpful for portraying related results, including means, *t*-tests, and correlations. Diagrams with arrows showing relationships between variables are often used to portray regression results.

■ **Clarify problems encountered in preparing reports.**
Problem areas that may arise in the preparation of the research report are (1) lack of data interpretation, (2) unnecessary use of multivariate statistics, (3) emphasis on packaging rather than quality, (4) lack of relevance, and (5) placing too much emphasis on a few statistical outcomes.

■ **Understand the importance of presentations in marketing research.**
Presentations are important because research results must be effectively communicated to those seeking to use the information in decision making. The report or presentation may be the only part of the research project that will be seen by those commissioning the report. The content of the research and the presentation form of the research are closely intertwined.

Key Terms and Concepts

Appendix 619
Believability 602
Credibility 602
Executive summary 603
Limitations 619
Methods-and-procedures section 605

Review Questions

1. What are the primary objectives of the marketing research report? Briefly discuss each objective and why it is so important.
2. In the the marketing research report what is the primary goal of the executive summary?
3. What is the primary purpose of the research methods-and-procedures section of a marketing research report?

4. Why are conclusions and recommendations included in a marketing research report?
5. What are the common problems associated with the marketing research report?
6. Why is it important to explain limitations in your marketing research report?

Discussion Questions

1. **EXPERIENCE THE INTERNET.** Go to the following Web site: www.microsoft.com/Education/Tutorials.aspx. Complete the Tutorials dialog box by typing in higher education in the Grade Level box, technology in the Learning Area box, and PowerPoint in the Product box. After selecting and completing the tutorial, provide written comments on the benefits you received by taking this tutorial.
2. Select the Santa Fe Grill data or one of the other databases provided with this text (see Deli Depot MRIA_4e, Chapter 14; Remington's MRIA_4e, Chapter 15; DVD Survey MRIA_4e, Chapter 16; or Qualkote MRIA_4e, Chapter 17), analyze the data using the appropriate statistical techniques, prepare a PowerPoint presentation of your findings, and present it to your research class.
   a. Select an appropriate variable from the data set and prepare a simple bar chart of the findings in SPSS.
   b. Select an appropriate variable from the data set and prepare a simple pie chart of the findings in SPSS.
   c. Select a group of thematically related items that are on metric scales. Present the results in a table and also in a bar chart using SPSS.
   d. Find two categorical items that are appropriate for a Crosstab and present your results in a bar chart made with SPSS.
   e. Find a categorical independent variable and a metric dependent variable. Present the results in a bar chart made with SPSS.
   f. Choose an outcome variable that can be explained by two or more independent variables. Run a regression and then develop a diagram (using PowerPoint or Word) that displays your findings.
3. There are several PowerPoint presentations on the book's Web site at www.mhhe.com/hair4e that are based on the Santa Fe Grill restaurant study. The presentations demonstrate how findings from a statistical analysis of data from a survey can be reported. Review the presentations and select the one you believe most effectively communicates the findings. Justify your choice.

glossary

ability to participate The availability of both the interviewer and the respondent to get together in a question-and-answer interchange.

abstraction Collapsing some categories or themes into a larger category or higher order conceptual construct.

accuracy The degree to which the data obtained from a questionnaire provide the researcher with a description of the true state of affairs.

acquiescence error A specific type of response bias that can occur when the respondent perceives what answer would be the most desirable to the sponsor.

active data Data acquired by a business when customers interact with the business's Web site.

administrative error Bias that can stem from data processing mistakes, interviewer distortion of the respondents' answers, or systemic inaccuracies created by using a faulty sampling design.

affect global approach Maintains that an attitude is a person's global (or overall) expression of favorable or unfavorable feelings toward a given object or event.

affective component That part of an attitude which represents the person's feelings toward the given object, idea, or set of information.

alpha factor The desired or acceptable amount of difference between the expected and the actual population parameter values; also referred to as the *tolerance level of error* (α).

alternative hypothesis A statement that is the opposite of the null hypothesis, where the difference is not simply due to random error.

ambiguity Contamination of internal validity measures due to unclear determination of cause–effect relationships between investigated constructs.

analysis of variance (ANOVA) A statistical technique that determines whether two or more means are statistically different from each other.

anonymity The assurance that the prospective respondent's name or any identifiable designation will not be associated with his or her responses.

appendix A section at the end of the final research report used to house complex, detailed, or technical information.

appropriateness of descriptors The extent to which the scale point elements match the data being sought.

archives Secondary sources of recorded past behaviors and trends.

area sampling A form of cluster sampling where clusters are formed by geographic designations such as cities, subdivisions, and blocks. Any geographic unit with boundaries can be used, with one-step or two-step approaches.

articulative interview A face-to-face questioning technique for listening for and identifying key conflicts in a person's orientation values toward products and services.

assignment The scaling property that allows the researcher to employ any type of descriptor to identify each object (or response) within a set; this property is also known as *description* or *category.*

assignment property The employment of unique descriptors to identify each object in a set.

attitude A learned predisposition to react in some consistent positive or negative way to a given object, idea, or set of information.

attitude-toward-behavior model A multiplicative-additive model approach that attempts to capture a person's attitude toward a behavior rather than to the object itself; where the attitude is a separate, indirectly derived composite measure of a person's combined thoughts and feelings for or against carrying out a specific action or behavior.

attitude-toward-object model A multiplicative-additive model approach that attempts to capture a person's attitude about a specific object; where the attitude is a separate, indirectly derived composite measure of a person's combined thoughts and feelings for or against a given object.

attribute-importance estimate The importance of an attribute of an object as estimated by conjoint analysis. It is calculated by subtracting the minimum part-worth estimate from the maximum part-worth estimate.

auspices error A type of response bias that occurs when the response is dictated by the image or opinion of the sponsor rather than the actual question.

automatic replenishment system (ARS) A continuous, automated inventory control system designed to analyze inventory levels, merchandise order lead times, and forecasted sales.

availability of information The degree to which the information has already been collected and assembled in some type of recognizable format.

averaging Assuming the normal behavior or belief to be the reality.

awareness The degree to which subjects consciously know their behavior is being observed and recorded.

axial coding Specifying the conditions, context, or variables that lead to a particular category or construct, and the outcomes from the construct.

bad questions Any question or directive that obscures, prevents, or distorts the fundamental communications between respondent and researcher.

balancing positive/negative scale descriptors The researcher's decision to maintain objectivity in a scale that is designed to capture both positive and negative state-of-mind raw data from respondents; the same number of relative magnitudes of positive and negative scale descriptors are used to make up the set of scale points.

bar code A pattern of varied-width electronic-sensitive bars and spaces that represents a unique code of numbers and letters.

behavioral (conative) component The part of an attitude that represents a person's intended or actual behavioral response to the given object.

behavior intention scale A type of rating scale designed to capture the likelihood that people will demonstrate some type of predictable behavior toward purchasing an object or service.

believability The quality achieved by building a final report that is based on clear, logical thinking, precise expression, and accurate presentation.

benefit and lifestyle studies Studies conducted to examine similarities and differences in needs; used to identify two or more segments within a market for the purpose of identifying customers for the product category of interest to a particular company.

beta coefficient An estimated regression coefficient that has been recalculated to have a mean of 0 and a standard deviation of 1. This statistic enables the independent variables with different units of measurement to be directly compared on their association with the dependent variable.

between-group variance Measures how much the sample means of the groups differ from one another.

bias A particular tendency or inclination that skews results, thereby preventing accurate consideration of a research question.

bivariate regression analysis A statistical technique that analyzes the linear relationship between two variables by estimating coefficients for an equation for a straight line. One variable is designated as a dependent variable, and the other as an independent (or predictor) variable.

Boolean operators Key words that form a logic string to sort through huge numbers of sites on the World Wide Web.

brand awareness The percentage of respondents having heard of a designated brand; brand awareness can be either unaided or aided.

business ethics The moral principles and standards that guide behavior in the world of business.

business intelligence A procedure for collecting daily operational information pertinent to the company and the markets it serves.

buying power index (BPI) A statistical indicator that provides weighted-average population, retail sales, and effective buying income data on different geographic areas of the United States.

call record sheet A recording document that gathers basic summary information about an interviewer's performance efficiency (e.g., number of contact attempts, number of completed interviews, length of time of interview).

cardinal numbers Any set of consecutive whole integers.

cartoon (balloon test) A qualitative data collection method in which the subject is given a cartoon drawing and suggests the dialogue in which the character(s) might engage.

case study An exploratory research technique that intensively investigates one or several existing situations similar to the current problem/opportunity situation.

categorization Placing portions of transcripts into similar groups based on their content.

causal research Enables decision-makers to determine cause and effect relationships between two or more variables.

census Questioning or observing all the members of a defined target population.

central limit theorem (CLT) The theoretical backbone of sampling theory. It states that the sampling distribution of the sample mean ($\bar{x}$) or the sample proportion ($\bar{p}$) value derived from a simple random sample drawn from the target population will be approximately normally distributed provided that the associated sample size is sufficiently large (e.g., when n is greater than or equal to 30). In turn, the sample mean value ($\bar{x}$) of that random sample with an estimated sampling error (S_g) (estimated standard error) fluctuates around the true population mean value (μ) with a standard error of σ/n and has a sampling distribution that is approximately a standardized normal distribution, regardless of the shape of the probability frequency distribution curve of the overall target population.

cheating The deliberate falsification of respondents' answers on a survey instrument.

Chi-square analysis Assesses how closely the observed frequencies fit the pattern of the expected frequencies and is referred to as a "goodness-of-fit" test.

Chi-square (X^2) statistic The standardized measurement of the observed difference squared between two frequency distributions that allows for the investigation of statistical significance in analyzing frequency distribution data structures.

Claris Home Page A specific software program that can be used to create Web pages that can integrate both text and graphics with other types of computer files.

classification (or prediction) matrix The classification matrix in discriminant analysis that contains the number of correctly classified and misclassified cases.

cluster analysis A multivariate interdependence technique whose primary objective is to classify objects into relatively homogeneous groups based on the set of variables considered.

clusters The mutually exclusive and collectively exhaustive subpopulation groupings that are then randomly sampled.

cluster sampling A method of probability sampling where the sampling units are selected in groups (or clusters) rather than individually. Once the cluster has been identified, the elements to be sampled are drawn by simple random sampling or all of the units may be included in the sample.

code of ethics A set of guidelines that states the standards and operating procedures for ethical decisions and practices by researchers.

code sheet A sheet of paper that lists the codes for different themes or categories for a particular study.

codes Labels or numbers that are used to track categories in a qualitative study.

coding The activities of grouping and assigning values to various responses from a survey instrument.

coding error Caused by assigning the wrong computer code to a response.

coefficient alpha See Cronbach's alpha.

coefficient of determination (r^2) A statistical value (or number) that measures the proportion of variation in one variable accounted for by another variable; the r^2 measure can be thought of as a percentage and varies from .00 to 1.00.

cognitive component That part of an attitude which represents the person's beliefs, perceptions, preferences, experiences, and knowledge about a given object, idea, or set of information.

commercial/syndicated data Data that have been compiled and displayed according to some standardized procedure.

company ethics program The framework through which a firm establishes internal codes of ethical behavior to serve as guidelines for doing business.

comparative ranking scale A scale format that requires a judgment comparing one object, person, or concept against another on the scale.

comparative scale Scale used when the scaling objective is to have a respondent express an attitude, feeling, or behavior about an object (or person, or phenomenon) or its attributes on the basis of some other object (or person, or phenomenon) or its attributes.

comparison The process of developing and refining theory and constructs by analyzing the differences and similarities in passages, themes, or types of participants.

competitive intelligence analysis Specific procedures for collecting daily operational information pertaining to the competitive companies and markets they serve.

completely automated telephone survey (CATS) A survey administered by a computer with no human interviewer. The computer dials a telephone number and the respondent listens to the electronic voice, responding by pushing keys on the Touch-Tone telephone pad.

completeness The depth and breadth of the data.

complete randomization The procedure whereby many subjects are assigned to different experimental treatment conditions, resulting in each group averaging out any systematic effect on the investigated functional relationship between the independent and dependent variables.

completion deadline date Part of the information included in a cover letter that directly communicates to a prospective respondent the date by which his or her completed questionnaire must be returned to the researcher.

complexity of the information One of the two fundamental dimensions used to determine the level of information being supplied by the information research process; it relates to the degree to which the information is easily understood and applied to the problem or opportunity under investigation.

computer-administered survey A survey design that incorporates the use of a computer to ask questions and record responses.

computer-assisted personal interviewing An interview in which the interviewer reads respondents the questions from a computer screen and directly keys in the response.

computer-assisted self-interviewing An interview in

which respondents are directed to a computer where they read questions from the computer screen and directly enter their responses.

computer-assisted telephone interview (CATI) The computer controls and expedites the interviewing process.

computer-assisted telephone survey A survey that uses a fully automated system in which the respondent listens to an electronic voice and responds by pushing keys on a Touch-Tone telephone keypad.

computer disks by mail A survey procedure in which computer disks are mailed to respondents; the respondents complete the survey on their own computer and return the disk to the researcher via the mail.

computer-generated fax survey A survey procedure in which a computer is used to send a survey to potential respondents via fax; the respondent completes the survey and returns it via fax or mail.

computerized secondary data sources Data sources designed by specific companies that integrate both internal and external data with online information sources.

conative component That part of an attitude which refers to the person's behavioral response or specific action/reaction toward the given object, idea, or set of information; it tends to be the observable outcome driven by the interaction of a person's cognitive and affective components toward the object or behavior.

concept and product testing Information for decisions on product improvements and new product introductions.

confidence interval A statistical range of values within which the true value of the target population parameter of interest is expected to fall based on a specified confidence level.

confidence levels Theoretical levels of assurance of the probability that a particular confidence interval will accurately include or measure the true population parameter value. In information research, the three most widely used levels are 90 percent, 95 percent, and 99 percent.

confidentiality to client The agreement between a researcher and the client that all activities performed in the process of conducting marketing research will remain private and the property of the client, unless otherwise specified by both parties.

confidentiality to respondent The expressed assurance to the prospective respondent that his or her name, while known to the researcher, will not be divulged to a third party, especially the sponsoring client.

confirmation/invitation letter A specific follow-up document sent to prospective focus group participants to encourage and reinforce their willingness and commitment to participate in the group session.

conformance to standards The researcher's ability to be accurate, timely, mistake free, and void of unanticipated delays.

conjoint analysis A multivariate technique that estimates the utility of the levels of various attributes or features of an object, as well as the relative importance of the attributes themselves.

connectors Logic phrases and symbols that allow search terms to be linked together in a Boolean logic format.

connect time The length of time, frequently measured in minutes and seconds, that a user is logged on to an electronic service or database. The amount of connect time is generally used to bill the user for services.

consent forms Formal signed statements of agreement by the participants approving the taping or recording of the information provided in group discussions and releasing that data to the moderator, researcher, or sponsoring client.

constant sums rating scale A scale format that requires the respondents to allocate a given number of points, usually 100, among several attributes or features based on their importance to the individual; this format requires a person to value each separate feature relative to all the other listed features.

construct Hypothetical variables composed of a set of component responses or behaviors that are thought to be related.

construct development An integrative process of activities undertaken by researchers to enhance understanding of what specific data should be collected for solving defined research problems.

construct development error A type of nonsampling (systematic) error that is created when the researcher is not careful in fully identifying the concepts and constructs to be included in the study.

construct Hypothetical variables composed of a set of component responses or behaviors that are thought to be related.

construct validity The degree to which researchers measure what they intended to measure, and to which the proper identification of the independent and dependent variables was included in the investigation.

consumer panels Large samples of households that provide certain types of data for an extended period of time.

content analysis The technique used to study written or taped materials by breaking the data into meaningful aggregate units or categories using a predetermined set of rules.

content validity That property of a test which indicates that the entire domain of the subject or construct of interest was properly sampled. That is, the identified factors are truly components of the construct of interest.

control group That portion of the sample which is not subjected to the treatment.

controlled test markets Test markets performed by an outside research firm that guarantees distribution of the test product through prespecified outlets in selected cities.

control variables Extraneous variables that the researcher is able to account for according to their systematic variation (or impact) on the functional relationship between the independent and dependent variables included in the experiment.

convenience sampling A method of nonprobability sampling where the samples are drawn on the basis of the convenience of the researcher or interviewer; also referred to as *accidental sampling*. Convenience sampling is often used in the early stages of research because it allows a large number of respondents to be interviewed in a short period of time.

convergent validity The degree to which different measures of the same construct are highly correlated.

cost analysis An analysis of alternative logistic system designs that a firm can use for achieving its performance objective at the lowest total cost.

covariation The amount of change in one variable that is consistently related to the change in another variable of interest.

cover letter A separate letter that either accompanies a self-administered questionnaire or is mailed prior to an initial interviewer contact call and whose main purpose is to secure a respondent's willingness to participate in the research project; sometimes referred to as a *letter of introduction*.

cover letter guidelines A specific set of factors that should be included in a cover letter for the purpose of increasing a prospective respondent's willingness to participate in the study.

credibility The quality that comes about by developing a final report that is accurate, believable, and professionally organized.

critical questions Questions used by a moderator to direct the group to the critical issues underlying the topics of interest.

critical tolerance level of error The observed difference between a sample statistic value and the corresponding true or hypothesized population parameter.

critical *z* value The book *z* value and the amount of acceptable variability between the observed sample data results and the prescribed hypothesized true population values measured in standardized degrees of standard errors for given confidence levels.

Cronbach's alpha A widely used measurement of the internal consistency of a multi-item scale in which the average of all possible split-half coefficients is taken.

cross-researcher reliability The degree of similarity in the coding of the same data by different researchers.

cross-tabulation The process of simultaneously treating (or counting) two or more variables in the study. This process categorizes the number of respondents who have responded to two or more questions consecutively.

curbstoning Cheating or falsification of data during the collection process that occurs when interviewers fill in all or part of a survey themselves.

curvilinear relationship An association between two variables whereby the strength and/or direction of their relationship changes over the range of both variables.

customer-centric approach Use of granular data to anticipate and fulfill customers' desires.

customer interaction The relationship between the enterprise and the customer.

customer knowledge The collection of customer interaction information used to create customer profiles that can be used to tailor interactions, segment customers, and build strong customer relationships.

customer knowledge data Information volunteered by customers that might be outside the marketing function of an organization.

customer relationship management (CRM) Management of customer relationships based on the integration of customer information throughout the business enterprise in order to achieve maximum customer satisfaction and retention.

customer satisfaction studies Studies designed to assess both the strengths and weaknesses customers perceive in a firm's marketing mix.

customer-volunteered information Data provided by the customer without solicitation.

cycle time The time that elapses between taking a product or service from initial consumer contact to final delivery.

cycle time research A research method that centers on reducing the time between the initial contact and final delivery (or installation) of products.

data Facts relating to any issue or subject.

data analysis error A "family" of nonsampling errors that are created when the researcher subjects the data to inappropriate analysis procedures.

database A collection of secondary information indicating what customers are purchasing, how often they purchase, and how much they purchase.

database technology The means by which data are transformed into information.

data coding errors The incorrect assignment of computer codes to the raw responses.

data editing errors Inaccuracies due to careless verifying procedures of raw data to computer data files.

data enhancement The process of weaving data into current internal data structures for the purpose of gaining a more valuable categorization of customers relative to their true value to the company.

data entry The direct inputting of the coded data into some specified software package that will ultimately allow the research analyst to manipulate and transform the data into data structures.

data entry errors The incorrect assignment of computer codes to their predesignated location on the computer data file.

data field A basic characteristic about a customer that is filled in on a database.

data interaction matrix A procedure used to itemize the type and amount of data required by each functional area of the company regardless of the cost of data collection.

data mining The process of finding hidden patterns and relationships among variables/characteristics contained in data stored in the data warehouse.

data processing error A specific type of nonsampling error that can occur when researchers are not accurate or complete in transferring data from respondents to computer files.

data silo Collection of data by one area of a business that is not shared with other areas.

data structures The combination of raw responses into groups of data using quantitative or qualitative analysis to reveal patterns or trends.

data validation A specific control process that the researcher undertakes to ensure that his or her representatives collected the data as required. The process is normally one of recontacting about 20 percent of the selected respondent group to determine that they did participate in the study.

data warehouse A central repository for all significant pieces of information that an organization collects.

debriefing analysis The technique of comparing notes, thoughts, and feelings about a focus group discussion between the moderator, researcher, and sponsoring client immediately following the group interview.

decision opportunity The presence of a situation in which market performance can be significantly improved by undertaking new activities.

decision problem A situation in which management has established a specific objective to accomplish and there are several courses of action that could be taken, each with its own risks and potential benefits.

deductive research Experimental investigations that are undertaken to test hypothesized relationships.

defined target population A specified group of people or objects for which questions can be asked or observations made to develop the required data structures and information; also referred to as the *working population*. A precise definition of the target population is essential when undertaking a research project.

degree of manipulation The extent to which data structures and results have been interpreted and applied to a specific situation.

deliberate falsification When the respondent and/or interviewer intentionally gives wrong answers or deliberately cheats on a survey.

demand analysis The estimating of the level of customer demand for a given product as well as the underlying reasons for that demand.

demand characteristics Contamination to construct validity measures created by test subjects trying to guess the true purpose behind the experiment and therefore give socially acceptable responses or behaviors.

demographic characteristics Physical and factual attributes of people, organizations, or objects.

deontologists Individuals who emphasize good intentions and the rights of the people involved in an action; they are much less concerned with the results from any ethical decision.

dependence techniques Appropriate multivariate procedures when one or more of the variables can be identified as dependent variables and the remaining as independent variables.

dependent variable A singular observable attribute that is the measured outcome derived from manipulating the independent variable(s).

depth The overall number of key data fields or variables that will make up the data records.

description The process of discovering patterns, associations, and relationships among key customer characteristics.

descriptive questionnaire design A questionnaire design that allows the researcher to collect raw data that can be turned into facts about a person or object. The questions and scales primarily involve the collecting of state-of-being and state-of-behavior data.

descriptive research Provides answers to who, what, when, where, and how questions.

diffusion of treatment Contamination to construct validity measures due to test subjects discussing the treatment and measurement activities with individuals yet to receive the treatment.

direct cognitive structural analysis A data analysis procedure in which respondents are simply asked to determine the extent to which an attribute is part of the construct's structural makeup and its importance to the construct.

direct (positive) directional hypothesis A statement about the perceived relationship between two questions, dimensions, or subgroups of attributes that suggests that as one factor moves in one direction, the other factor moves in the same direction.

directed data Comprehensive data about customers collected through the use of computers.

direct mail survey A questionnaire distributed to and returned from respondents via the postal service.

directness of observation The degree to which the researcher or trained observer actually observes the behavior/event as it occurs; also termed *direct observation.*

direct observation The process of observing actual behaviors or events and recording them as they occur.

direct self-administered questionnaire A survey instrument designed to have the respondent serve as both an interviewer and a respondent during the question-and-answer encounter.

discretion of primary descriptors The carefulness that a researcher must use in selecting the actual words used to distinguish the relative magnitudes associated with each of the primary descriptors in a scale design.

discriminant analysis A multivariate technique for analyzing marketing research data when the dependent variable is categorical and the independent variables are interval.

discriminant function The linear combination of independent variables developed by discriminant analysis which will best discriminate between the categories of the dependent variable.

discriminant function coefficient The multipliers of variables in the discriminant function when the variables are in the original units of measurement.

discriminant score In discriminant analysis, this represents the score of each respondent on the discriminant function.

discriminant validity The degree to which measures of different constructs are uncorrelated.

discriminatory power The scale's ability to significantly differentiate between the responses (or points).

disguised observation An observation technique in which the test subjects are completely unaware that they are being observed and recorded.

disguised sponsorship When the true identity of the person or company for which the research is being conducted is not divulged to the prospective respondent.

disproportionate stratified sampling A form of stratified sampling in which the size of the sample drawn from each stratum is independent of the stratum's proportion of the total population.

distance property The scaling property that when activated allows the researcher and respondent to identify, understand, and accurately express in a unit measurement scheme the exact (or absolute) difference between each of the descriptors, scale points, or responses.

diversity The degree to which the respondents share characteristics.

diversity of respondents The degree to which the respondents in the study share some similarities.

domain of observables The set of observable manifestations of a variable that is not itself directly observable. A domain represents an identifiable set of components that indirectly make up the construct of interest.

drop-off survey A questionnaire that is left with the respondent to be completed at a later time. The questionnaire may be picked up by the researcher or returned via some other mode.

dummy variables Artificial variables introduced into a regression equation to represent the categories of a nominally scaled variable (such as sex or marital status). There will be one dummy variable for each of the nominal categories of the independent variable, and the values will typically be 0 and 1, depending on whether the variable value is present or absent for a particular respondent (e.g., male or female).

editing The process in which the interviews or survey instruments are checked for mistakes that may have occurred by either the interviewer or the respondent during data collection activities.

editing error The result of carelessness in verifying coding or data entry procedures.

effective buying income (EBI) The measure of personal income less federal, state, and local taxes.

electronic database A high-speed, computer-assisted information source or library.

electronic data interchange (EDI) A specific system designed to speed the flow of information as well as products from producer to distributor to retailer.

electronic test markets Test procedures that integrate the use of selected panels of consumers who use a special identification card in recording their product purchasing data.

element The name given to the object about which information is sought. Elements must be unique, countable, and, when added together, make up the whole of the target population.

e-mail survey A survey in which electronic mail is used to deliver a questionnaire to respondents and receive their responses.

emic validity An attribute of qualitative research that affirms that key members within a culture or subculture agree with the findings of a research report.

empirical testing The actual collection of data in the real world using research instruments and then subjecting that data to rigorous analysis to either support or refute a hypothesis.

empowerment Employees can solve problems immediately without requesting permission.

ending questions Questions used by a focus group moderator to bring closure to a particular topic discussion; they encourage summary-type comments.

enterprise The total business unit, including all facets of the business as well as suppliers and retailers.

environmental forecasting The projection of environmental occurrences that can affect the long-term strategy of a firm.

environmental information Secondary information pertaining to a firm's suppliers and/or distributors.

equivalent form A method of assessing the reliability associated with a scale measurement; the researcher creates two basically similar yet different scale measurements for the given construct and administers both forms to either the same sample of respondents or two samples of respondents from the same target population.

error The difference between the true score on a research instrument and the actual observed score.

estimated sample standard deviation A quantitative index of the dispersion of the distribution of drawn sampling units' actual data around the sample's arithmetic average measure of central tendency; this sample statistical value specifies the degree of variation in the raw data responses in a way that allows the researcher to translate the variations into normal curve interpretations.

estimated sample variance The square of the estimated sample standard deviation.

estimated standard deviation Describes the average distance of the distribution values from the mean.

estimated standard error of the sample statistic A statistical measurement of the sampling error that can be expected to exist between the drawn sample's statistical values and the actual values of all the sampling units' distributions of those concerned statistics. These indexes are referred to as *general precision.*

estimates Sample data facts that are transformed through interpretation procedures to represent inferences about the larger target population.

ethical dilemmas Specific situations in which the researcher, decision maker, or respondent must choose between appropriate and inappropriate behavior.

ethics The field of study that tries to determine what behaviors are considered to be appropriate under certain circumstances by established codes of behavior set forth by society.

ethnography A form of qualitative data collection that records behavior in natural settings to understand how social and cultural influences affect individuals' behaviors and experiences.

evaluation apprehension Contamination to construct validity measures caused by test subjects being fearful that their actions or responses will become known to others.

executive dashboard An interactive computer terminal or screen that organizes and presents information in a way that is easy for executives to read and understand.

executive interview A person-administered interview of a business executive. Frequently, these interviews will take place in the executive's office.

executive summary The part of the final research report that illustrates the major points of the report in a manner complete enough to provide a true representation of the entire document.

expected completion rate (ECR) The percentage of prospective respondents who are expected to participate and complete the survey; also referred to as the *anticipated response rate.*

experience interview A face-to-face questioning technique to gather opinions from people considered to be knowledgeable on the issues of the research problem.

experience surveys An informal gathering of opinions and insights from people who are considered to be knowledgeable on the issues surrounding the defined research problem.

experimental design reliability The degree to which the research design and its procedures can be replicated and achieve similar conclusions about hypothesized relationships.

experimental research An empirical investigation that tests for hypothesized relationships between dependent variables and manipulated independent variables.

expert systems Advanced computer-based systems that function in the same manner as a human expert, advising the analyst on how to solve a problem.

explained variance In multivariate methods, it is the amount of variation in the dependent construct that can be accounted for by the combination of independent variables.

exploratory research Generates insights that help define the problem and increase the understanding of consumer motivations, attitudes, and behavior.

external secondary data Data collected by outside agencies such as the federal, state, or local government; trade associations; or periodicals.

external validity The extent to which the measured data results of a study based on a sample can be expected to hold in the entire defined target population. In addition, it is the extent that a causal relationship found in a study can be expected to be true for the entire defined target population.

extraneous variables All variables other than the independent variables that affect the responses of the test subjects. If left uncontrolled, these variables can have a confounding impact on the dependent variable measures that could weaken or invalidate the results of an experiment.

extremity error A type of response bias when the clarity of extreme scale points and ambiguity of midrange options encourage extreme responses.

eye tracking monitor A device that observes and records a person's unconscious eye movements.

facilitating agencies Businesses that perform a marketing research function as a supplement to a broader marketing research project.

factor analysis A class of statistical procedures primarily used for data reduction and summarization.

factor loadings Simple correlations between the variables and the factors.

factor scores Composite scores estimated for each respondent on the derived factors.

facts Pieces of information that are observable and verifiable through a number of external sources.

faulty problem definition error An incorrect definition of what the marketing problem really is.

faulty recall The inability of a person to accurately remember the specifics about the behavior under investigation.

fax survey A questionnaire distributed to the sample via fax machines.

field experiments Causal research designs that manipulate the independent variables in order to measure the dependent variable in a natural test setting.

finite correction factor (fcf) An adjustment factor to the sample size that is made in those situations where the drawn sample is expected to equal 5 percent or more of the defined target population. The fcf is equal to the overall square root of $N - n/N - 1$.

flowerpot approach A specific, unique framework or blueprint for integrating different sets of questions and scale measurements into an instrument that is capable of collecting the raw data needed to achieve each of the established information objectives.

focus group facility A professional facility that offers a set of specially designed rooms for conducting focus group interviews; each room contains a large table and comfortable chairs for up to 13 people, with a relaxed atmosphere, built-in audio equipment, and normally a one-way mirror for disguised observing by the sponsoring client or researcher.

focus group incentives Specified investment programs to compensate focus group participants for their expenses associated with demonstrating a willingness to be a group member.

focus group interview An interactive group discussion on selected topic issues.

focus group moderator A special person who is well trained in interpersonal communications; listening, observation, and interpretive skills; and professional mannerisms and personality. His or her role in a session is to draw from the participants the best and most innovative ideas about an assigned topic or question.

focus group research A formalized qualitative data collection method for which data are collected from a small group of people who interactively and spontaneously discuss one particular topic or concept.

follow-up test A statistical test that flags the means that are statistically different from each other; follow-up tests are performed after an ANOVA determines there are differences between means.

forced-choice scale measurements Symmetrical scale measurement designs that do not have a logical "neutral" scale descriptor to divide the positive and negative domains of response descriptors.

formal rating procedures The use of structured survey instruments or questionnaires to gather information on environmental occurrences.

formative composite scale Scale used when each of the individual scale items measures some part of the whole construct, object, or phenomenon.

***F*-ratio** The statistical ratio of between-group mean squared variance to within-group mean squared variance; the *F* value is used as an indicator of the statistical difference between group means in an ANOVA.

free-choice scale measurements Symmetrical scale measurement designs that are divided into positive and negative domains of scale-point descriptors by a logical center "neutral" response.

frequency distributions A summary of how many times each possible raw response to a scale question/setup was recorded by the total group of respondents.

***F*-test** The test used to statistically evaluate the difference between the group means in ANOVA.

full-text Option of having the entire document, news story, article, or numerical information available for downloading.

fully automated self-interviewing A procedure in which respondents independently approach a central computer station or kiosk, read the questions, and respond—all without researcher intervention.

fully automated telephone interviewing A data collection procedure in which the computer calls respondents and asks questions; the respondent records his or her answers by using the keypad of a Touch-Tone telephone.

fully automatic devices High-tech devices that interact with respondents without the presence of a trained interviewer during the question/response encounter.

functional relationship An observable and measurable systematic change in one variable as another variable changes.

garbage in, garbage out A standard phrase used in marketing research to represent situations where the process of collecting, analyzing, and interpreting data into information contains errors or biases, creating less than accurate information.

gatekeeper technology Automated screening and/or answering devices that protect an individual against instrusive business practices.

generalizability The extent to which the data are an accurate portrait of the defined target population; the representativeness of information obtained from a small subgroup of members to that of the entire target population from which the subgroup was selected.

generalizability of data structures The degree to which sample data results and structures can be used to draw accurate inferences about the defined target population, that is, the extent to which the research can extrapolate results from a sample to the defined target population.

general precision The amount of general sampling error associated with the given sample of raw data that was generated through some type of data collection activity; no specific concern for any level of confidence.

granular data Highly detailed, highly personalized data specifically structured around an individual customer.

graphic rating scale descriptors A scale point format that presents respondents with some type of graphic continuum as the set of possible raw responses to a given question.

group dynamics The degree of spontaneous interaction among group members during a discussion of a topic.

halo effect bias A generalization from the perception of one outstanding factor, attribute, or trait to an overly favorable evaluation on the whole object or construct.

hits The number of documents or other items that meet the search terms in an online search.

human observation Data collection by a researcher or trained observer who records text subjects' actions and behaviors.

hypertext markup language (HTML) The language used to create Web pages for communicating the research results as well as other information on the Internet.

hypothesis A yet-unproven proposition or possible solution to a decision problem that can be empirically tested using data that are collected through the research process; it is developed in order to explain phenomena or a relationship between two or more constructs or variables.

hypothesis guessing Contamination to construct validity measures due to test subjects' believing they know the desired functional relationship prior to the manipulation treatment.

iceberg principle The general notion indicating that the dangerous part of many marketing decision problems is neither visible nor well understood by marketing managers.

importance-performance analysis A research and data analysis procedure used to evaluate a firm's and its competitors' strengths and weaknesses, as well as future actions that seek to identify key attributes that drive purchase behavior within a given industry.

inadequate operationalization When a construct is not carefully and completely defined.

inadequate preoperationalization of variables Contamination to construct validity measures due to inadequate understanding of the complete makeup of the independent and dependent variables included in the experimental design.

inappropriate analysis bias A type of data analysis error that creates the wrong data structure results and can lead to misinterpretation errors.

incentives Monetary or nonmonetary compensation for an individual's willingness to participate in a focus group session.

incidence rate The percentage of the general population that is the subject of the marketing research.

independent samples Two or more groups of responses that are tested as though they may come from different populations.

independent variable An attribute of an object whose measurement values are directly manipulated by the researcher, also referred to as a *predictor* or *treatment variable.* This type of variable is assumed to be a causal factor in a functional relationship with a dependent variable.

in-depth interview A formalized, structured process of a subject's being asked a set of semistructured, probing questions by a well-trained interviewer usually in a face-to-face setting.

indirect observation A research technique in which researchers or trained observers rely on artifacts that, at best, represent specific reported behavioral outcomes from some earlier time.

inductive research An investigation that uses causal design procedures to generate and test hypotheses that create new theories or extend existing theories.

information Data used by researchers to create knowledge for decision-making.

informational data Data collected through On-Line Analytical Processing (OLAP) software for analysis purposes as a decision-making tool for marketing programs.

information objectives The clearly stated reasons why raw data must be collected; they serve as the guidelines for determining the raw data requirements.

information requirements The identified factors, dimensions, and attributes within a stated information objective for which raw data must be collected.

information research process A systematic approach to collecting, analyzing, interpreting, and transforming data into decision-making information.

information research questions Specific statements that address the problem areas the research study will attempt to investigate.

Information sharing All functional areas of the business have the information they need to improve decision-making.

in-home interview A person-administrated interview that takes place in the respondent's home.

instrumentation Contamination to internal validity measures from changes in measurement processes, observation techniques, and/or measuring instruments.

integration The process of moving from the identification of themes and categories to the development of theory.

intelligibility The degree to which questions can be understood by the respondents making up the defined target population to whom the scale will be administered.

intelligibility criterion The degree to which the questions on a scale are understood by the respondents.

intention to purchase A person's planned future action to buy a product or service.

interdependence techniques Multivariate statistical procedures in which the whole set of interdependent relationships is examined.

internal consistency reliability The extent to which the items of a scale represent the same domain of content and are highly correlated with both each other and summated scale scores. It represents the degree to which the components are related to the same overall construct domain.

internal quality movement One of the underlying factors for which many organizations are restructuring away from old traditional functional control/power systems of operating to new cross-functional structures where team building, decision teams, and sharing of information and responsibility are the important factors, not control and power.

internal secondary data Facts that have been collected by the individual company for accounting and marketing activity purposes.

internal validity The certainty with which a researcher can state that the observed effect was caused by a specific treatment; exists when the research design accurately identifies causal relationships.

Internet A network of computers and technology linking computers into an information superhighway.

Internet survey The method of using the Internet to ask survey questions and record responses of respondents.

interpersonal communication skills The interviewer's abilities to articulate the questions in a direct and clear manner so that the subject understands what she or he is responding to.

interpretive bias Error that occurs when the wrong inference about the real world or defined target population is made by the researcher or decision maker due to some type of extraneous factor.

interpretive skills The interviewer's capabilities of accurately understanding and recording the subject's responses to questions.

interval scales Any question/scale format that activates not only the assignment and order scaling properties but also the distance property; all scale responses have a recognized absolute difference between each of the other scale points (responses).

interviewer error A type of nonsampling error that is created in situations where the interviewer distorts information, in a systematic way, from respondents during or after the interviewer/respondent encounter.

interviewer instructions The vehicle for training the interviewer on how to select prospective respondents, screen them for eligibility, and conduct the actual interview.

interviewer/mechanical devices The combination of highly skilled people who are aided by high-technology devices during the questioning/responding encounters with respondents.

introductory questions Questions used by a focus group moderator to introduce the general topic of discussion and opportunities of reflecting their past experiences.

inverse (negative or indirect) directional hypothesis A statement about the perceived relationship between two questions, dimensions, or subgroupings of attributes that suggests that as one factor moves in one direction, the other factor moves in an opposite fashion.

iteration Working through the data several times in order to modify early ideas and to be informed by subsequent analyses.

judgment sampling A nonprobability sampling design that selects participants for a sample based on an experienced individual's belief that the participants will meet the requirements of the research study.

junk mail A categorical descriptor that prospective respondents attach to surveys that are administered through the direct mail delivery system or an unwanted telephone interview that is viewed as being nothing more than a telemarketing gimmick to sell them something they do not want or need.

knowledge A combination of information and judgment used to make decisions that emerges after data has been collected, analyzed, and interpreted.

knowledge level of respondent The degree to which the selected respondents feel they have experience (or knowledge) with the topics that are the focus of the survey's questioning.

laboratory experiments Causal research designs that are conducted in an artificial setting and have high internal validity but limited external validity.

lead country test markets Field test markets that are conducted in specific foreign countries.

leading question A question that tends to purposely elicit a particular answer.

least squares procedure Determines the best-fitting line by minimizing the vertical distances of all the points from the line.

level of significance The amount of risk regarding the accuracy of the test that the researcher is willing to accept.

library A large group of related information.

lifetime value models Procedures developed using historical data, as well as actual purchase behavior, not probability estimates, to predict consumer behavior.

Likert scale A scale format that asks respondents to indicate the extent to which they agree or disagree with a series of mental belief or behavioral belief statements about a given object; it is a cognitive-based scale measurement.

limitations A section of the final research report in which all extraneous events that place certain restrictions on the report are fully communicated.

linear relationship An association between two variables whereby the strength and nature of the relationship remain the same over the range of both variables.

listening skills The interviewer's capabilities of understanding what the respondent is communicating.

logistic assessment Information in logistics that allows market researchers to conduct total cost analysis and service sensitivity analysis.

lottery approach A unique incentive system that pools together either individual small cash incentives into a significantly larger dollar amount or a substantial nonmonetary gift and then holds a drawing to determine the winner or small set of winners. The drawing procedure is designed so that all respondents who complete and return their survey have an equal chance of receiving the larger reward.

mail panel survey A representative sample of individual respondents who have agreed in advance to participate in a mail survey.

mail survey A self-administered questionnaire that is delivered to selected respondents and returned to the researcher by mail.

mall-intercept interview An interview technique in which mall patrons are stopped and asked for feedback. The interview may take place in the mall's common areas or in the research firm's offices at the mall.

managerial function software system A computer-based procedure that includes forecasting, brand management, and promotional budget capabilities.

marketing The process of planning and executing pricing, promotion, product, and distribution of products, services, and ideas in order to create exchanges that satisfy both the firm and its customers.

marketing decision support system (MDSS) A computer-based system intended for use by particular marketing personnel at any functional level for the purpose of solving information and/or semistructured problems. Within this system databases are developed and used to analyze the firm's performance as well as control its marketing activities.

marketing knowledge A characteristic that complements a researcher's technical competency.

marketing research The function that links an organization to its market through the gathering of information. The information allows for the identification and definition of market-driven opportunities and problems. The information allows for the generation, refinement, and evaluation of marketing actions.

market intelligence The use of real-time customer information (customer knowledge) to achieve a competitive advantage.

market performance symptoms Conditions that signal the presence of a decision problem and/or opportunity.

maturation Contamination to internal validity measures due to changes in the dependent variable based on the natural function of time and not attributed to any specific event.

mean The arithmetic average of all the raw responses; all values of a distribution of responses are summed and divided by the number of valid responses.

measurement Rules for assigning numbers to objects so that these numbers represent quantities of attributes.

measurement/design error A "family" of nonsampling errors that result from inappropriate designs in the constructs, scale measurements, or survey measurements used to execute the asking and recording of people's responses to a study's questions.

measures of central tendency The basic sample statistics that could be generated through analyzing the collected raw data; they are the mode, the median, and the mean.

measures of dispersion The sample statistics that describe how all the raw data are actually dispersed around a given measure of central tendency; they are the frequency distribution, the range, and the estimated sample standard deviation.

mechanical devices High-technology instruments that can artificially observe and record either current behavioral actions or physical phenomena as they occur.

mechanical/electronic observation Data collection using some type of mechanical device to capture human behavior, events, or marketing phenomena.

mechanical observation Some type of mechanical or electronic device is used to capture human behavior, events, or marketing phenomena.

median The sample statistic that splits the raw data into a hierarchical pattern where half the raw data is above the median statistic value and half is below.

media panels Selected households that are primarily used in measuring media viewing habits as opposed to product/brand consumption patterns.

member checking Asking key informants to read the researcher's report to verify that the analysis is accurate.

memoing Writing down thoughts as soon as possible after each interview, focus group, or site visit.

method bias The error source that results from selecting an inappropriate method to investigate the research question.

misinterpretation error An inaccurate transformation of data analysis results into usable bits of information for the decision maker.

mode The most frequently mentioned (or occurring) raw response in the set of responses to a given question/setup.

model *F* statistic A statistic which compares the amount of variation in the dependent measure "explained" or associated with the independent variables to the "unexplained" or error variance. A larger *F*-statistic value indicates that the regression model has more explained variance than error variance.

moderator's guide A detailed document that outlines the topics, questions, and subquestions that serve as the basis for generating the spontaneous interactive dialogue among the focus group participants.

modified Likert scale Any version of the agreement/disagreement-based scale measurement that is not the original five-point "strongly agree" to "strongly disagree" scale.

monetary compensation An individual cash incentive used by the researcher to increase the likelihood of a prospective respondent's willingness to participate in the survey.

monomethod bias A particular type of error source that is created when only a single method is used to collect data about the research question.

mono-operation bias Contamination created by using one method to measure the outcomes of the dependent variable.

moral philosophy A person's basic orientation toward problem solving. Within the ethical decision-making process, philosophical thinking will come from teleology, deontology, and/or relativity orientations.

mortality Contamination to internal validity measures due to changing the composition of the test subjects in the experiment.

multicollinearity A situation in which several independent variables are highly correlated with each other. This characteristic can result in difficulty in estimating separate or independent regression coefficients for the correlated variables.

multiple-item scale designs Method used when the researcher has to measure several items (or attributes) simultaneously in order to measure the complete object or construct of interest.

multiple regression analysis A statistical technique that analyzes the linear relationships between a dependent variable and multiple independent variables by estimating coefficients for the equation for a straight line.

multivariate analysis (techniques) A group of statistical techniques used when there are two or more measurements on each element and the variables are analyzed simultaneously.

mystery shopper studies Studies in which trained, professional shoppers visit stores, financial institutions, or companies and "shop" for various products and assess service quality factors or levels.

negative case analysis Deliberately looking for cases and instances that contradict the ideas and theories that researchers have been developing.

negative relationship An association between two variables in which one increases while the other decreases.

netnography A research technique that draws on ethnography but uses "found data" on the Internet that is produced by virtual communities.

nominal scales Question/scale structures that ask the respondent to provide only a descriptor as the raw response; the response does not contain any level of intensity.

nomological validity The extent to which one particular construct theoretically networks with other established constructs which are related yet different.

nonapplicable response descriptor The alternative response attached to even-point (or forced-choice) scale designs that allows respondents not to directly respond to a given scale dimension or attribute if they feel uncomfortable about expressing thoughts or feelings about a given object because they lack knowledge or experience.

noncomparative scale Scale used when the scaling objective is to have a respondent express an attitude, emotion, action, or intention about one specific object (person, phenomenon) or its attributes.

nondirectional hypothesis A statement regarding the existing relationship between two questions, dimensions, or subgroupings of attributes as being significantly different but lacking an expression of direction.

nonequivalent control group A quasi-experimental design that combines the static group comparison and one-group, pretest-posttest preexperimental designs.

nonmonetary compensation Any type of individual incentive excluding direct cash (e.g., a free T-shirt) used by the researcher to encourage a prospective respondent's participation.

nonparticipant observation An ethnographic research technique that involves extended contact with a natural setting, but without participation by the researcher.

nonprobability sampling Sampling designs in which the probability of selection of each sampling unit is not known. The selection of sampling units is based on the judgment or knowledge of the researcher and may or may not be representative of the target population.

nonresponse error An error that occurs when the portion of the defined target population not represented or underrepresented in the response pool is systematically and significantly different from those that did respond.

nonsampling error A type of bias that occurs in a research study regardless of whether a sample or census is used.

North American Industry Classification System (NAICS) Codes numerical industrial listings designed to promote uniformity in data reporting procedures for the U.S. government.

not at home A specific type of nonresponse bias that occurs when a reasonable attempt to initially reach a prospective respondent fails to produce an interviewer/respondent encounter.

null hypothesis A statement of the perceived existing relationship between two questions, dimensions, or subgroupings of attributes as being not significantly different; it asserts the status quo condition, and any change from what has been thought to be true is due to random sampling error.

object Any tangible item in a person's environment that can be clearly and easily identified through the senses.

objectivity The degree to which a researcher uses scientific procedures to collect, analyze, and create nonbiased information.

observation The systematic process of witnessing and recording the behavioral patterns of objects, people, and occurrences without directly questioning or communicating with them.

observation methods The tools researchers use to collect primary data about human behavior and marketing phenomena.

observing mechanism How the behaviors or events will be observed; *human observation* is when the observer is either a person hired and trained by the researcher or the researcher himself; *mechanical observation* refers to the use of a technology-based device to do the observing rather than a human observer.

odd or even number of scale points When collecting either state-of-mind or state-of-intention data, the researcher must decide whether the positive and negative scale points need to be separated by a neutral scale descriptor; even-point scales (known as *forced-choice scales*) do not require a neutral response, but odd-point scales (known as *free-choice scales*) must offer a neutral scale response.

one-group, pretest-posttest A pre-experimental design where first a pretreatment measure of the dependent variable is taken (O_1), then the test subjects are exposed to the independent treatment (X), then a posttreatment measure of the dependent variable is taken (O_2).

one-shot study A single group of test subjects is exposed to the independent variable treatment (X), and then a single measurement on the dependent variable is taken (O_1).

one-way tabulation The categorization of single variables existing in the study.

online focus groups A formalized process whereby a small group of people form an online community for an interactive, spontaneous discussion on one particular topic or concept.

online services Providers of access to electronic databases and other services in real time.

opening questions Questions used by a focus group moderator to break the ice among focus group participants; identify common group member traits; and create a comfort zone for establishing group dynamics and interactive discussions.

operational data Data collected through online transaction processing (OLTP) and used for the daily operations of the business.

operationalization The process of precisely delineating how a construct is to be measured. The variables are specified in such a manner as to be potentially observable or manipulable.

opportunity assessment The collection of information on product-markets for the purpose of forecasting how they will change in the future. This type of assessment focuses on gathering information relevant to macroenvironments.

optical scanner An electronic device that optically reads bar codes; this scanner captures and translates unique bar code numbers into product information.

order property The scaling property that activates the existence of relative magnitudes between the descriptors used as scale points (or raw responses); it allows the researcher to establish either a higher-to-lower or lower-to-higher rank order among the raw responses.

ordinally interval scales Ordinal questions or scale formats that the researcher artificially redefines as being interval by activating an assumed distance scaling property into the design structure; this hybrid-type scale format incorporates both primary ordinal scale descriptors and a secondary set of cardinal numbers used to redefine the original primary descriptors.

ordinal scales A question/scale format that activates both the assignment and order scaling properties; the respondent is asked to express relative magnitudes between the raw responses to a question.

ordinary least squares A statistical procedure that estimates regression equation coefficients that produce the lowest sum of squared differences between the actual and predicted values of the dependent variable.

origin property The scaling property that activates a unique starting (or beginning) point in a set of scale points that is designated as being a "true zero" or true state of nothing.

overall incidence rate (OIR) The percentage of the defined target population elements who actually qualify for inclusion into the survey.

overall reputation The primary dimension of perceived quality outcomes. Quality of the end product can be gauged in direct proportion to the level of expertise, trust, believability, and contribution the research brings to the client.

overregistration When a sampling frame contains all of the eligible sampling units of the defined target population plus additional ones.

paired-comparison rating scale A scale format in which preselected groups of product characteristics or features are paired against one another and the respondents are asked to select which feature in each pairing is more important to them.

participant observation An ethnographic research technique that involves extended observation of behavior in natural settings in order to fully experience cultural or subcultural contexts.

part-worth estimates Estimates of the utility survey that respondents place on each individual level of a particular attribute or feature.

passive data Data supplied to a business when a consumer visits the company's Web site.

Pearson correlation coefficient A statistical measure of the strength and direction of a linear relationship between two metric variables.

peer review A process in which external qualitative methodology or topic area specialists are asked to review the research analysis

People Meter A technology-driven TV rating and data collection system.

perceptual map A graphic representation of respondents' beliefs about the relationship between objects with respect to two or more dimensions (usually attributes or features of the objects).

perceptual mapping A process that is used to develop maps showing the perceptions of respondents. The maps are visual representations of respondent's perceptions of a company, product, service, brand, or any other object in two dimensions.

performance rating scale descriptors A scale that uses an evaluative scale point format that allows the respondents to express some type of postdecision evaluative judgment about an object.

person-administered survey A survey in which an individual interviewer asks questions and records responses.

phantom respondents A type of data falsification that occurs when the researcher takes an actual respondent's data and duplicates it to represent a second (nonexisting) set of responses.

physical audits (or traces) Tangible evidence (or artifacts) of some past event or recorded behavior.

picture test A qualitative interviewing method where the subjects are given a picture and instructed to describe their reactions by writing a short narrative story about the picture.

plus-one dialing The method of generating telephone numbers to be called by choosing numbers randomly from a telephone directory and adding one digit.

population The identifiable total set of elements of interest being investigated by a researcher.

population mean value The actual calculated arithmetic average parameter value based on interval or ratio data of the defined target population elements (or sampling units).

population proportion value The actual calculated percentage parameter value of the characteristic of concern held by the target population elements (or sampling units).

population size The determined total number of elements that represent the target population.

population specification error An incorrect definition of the true target population to the research question.

population standard deviation A quantitative index of the dispersion of the distribution of population elements' actual data around the arithmetic average measure of central tendency.

population variance The square of the population standard deviation.

positioning The desired perception that a company wants to be associated with its target markets relative to its products or brand offerings.

positive relationship An association between two variables in which they increase or decrease together.

posttest-only, control group A true experimental design where the test subjects are randomly assigned to either the experimental or control group; the experimental group is then exposed to the independent treatment after which both groups receive a posttreatment measure of the dependent variable.

PowerPoint A specific software package used to develop slides for electronic presentation of the research results.

precise precision The amount of measured sampling error associated with the sample's raw data at a specified level of confidence.

precision The degree of exactness of the raw data in relation to some other possible response of the target population.

prediction Uses patterns and relationship to predict future trends and behaviors.

predictive bias A specific type of data analysis error that occurs when the wrong statistical facts and estimates invalidate the researcher's ability to predict and test relationships between important factors.

predictive questionnaire design A design that allows the researcher to collect raw data that can be used in predicting changes in attitudes and behaviors as well as testing hypothesized relationships. The question/scales primarily involve the collecting of state-of-mind and state-of-intention data.

predictive validity The extent to which a scale can accurately predict some event external to the scale itself.

pre-experimental designs A family of designs (one-shot study, one-group pretest-posttest, static group comparison) that are crude experiments characterized by the absence of randomization of test subjects; they tend not to meet internal validity criteria due to a lack of equivalent group comparisons.

pretesting The conducting of a simulated administering of a designed survey (or questionnaire) to a small, representative group of respondents.

pretest-posttest, control group A true experimental design where the test subjects are randomly assigned to either the experimental or the control group and each group receives a pretreatment measure of the dependent variable. Then the independent treatment is exposed to the experimental group, after which both groups receive a posttreatment measure of the dependent variable.

primary data Information specifically collected for a current research problem or opportunity.

primary information Firsthand facts or estimates that are derived through a formalized research process for a specific current problem situation.

probability distribution of the population The relative frequencies of a population's parameter characteristic emulating a normal bell-shaped pattern.

probability sampling Sampling designs in which each sampling unit in the sampling frame (operational population) has a known, nonzero probability of being selected for the sample.

probing questions The outcome of an interviewer's taking the subject's initial response to a question and using that response as the framework for asking the next question.

problem definition A statement that seeks to determine precisely what problem management wishes to solve and the type of information necessary to solve it.

product analysis Methods that identify the relative importance of product selection criteria to buyers and rate brands against these criteria.

project administration error Bias that can stem from data processing mistakes, interviewer distortion of the respondents' answers, or systematic inaccuracies created by using a faulty sampling design.

project costs The price requirements of doing marketing research.

projective hypothesis The belief that a good deal of thoughts and emotions are processed in images and metaphors rather than just words.

projective method An indirect method of questioning that enables a subject to project beliefs and feelings onto a third party, into a task situation, or onto an inanimate object.

projective techniques A family of qualitative data collection methods where subjects are asked to project themselves into specified buying situations and then asked questions about those situations.

propensity scoring Weighting underrepresented respondents more heavily in results.

proportionate stratified sampling A form of stratified sampling in which the sample size from each stratum is dependent on that stratum's size relative to the total population.

protocol interviewing A technique that takes respondents into a specified decision-making situation and asks them to verbally express the process and activities considered when making the decision.

psychogalvanometer A device that measures a subject's involuntary changes in the electronic resistance of his or her skin, referred to as galvanic skin response (GVR).

pupilometer A device that observes and records changes in the diameter of a subject's pupils. Changes are interpreted as the result of unobservable cognitive activity.

purchase intercept interview An interview similar to a mall intercept except that the respondent is stopped at the point of purchase and asked a set of predetermined questions.

qualitative research Selective types of research methods used in exploratory research designs where the main objective is to gain a variety of preliminary insights to discover and identify decision problems and opportunities.

quality of the information One of the two fundamental dimensions that is used to determine the level of information being provided by the research process; it refers to the degree to which the information can be depended on as being accurate and reliable.

quantitative research Data collection methods that emphasize using formalized, standard, structured questioning practices where the response options have been predetermined by the researcher and administered to significantly large numbers of respondents.

quasi-experimental designs Designs in which the researcher can control some variables in the study but cannot establish equal experimental and control groups based on randomization of the test subjects.

query Part of an MDSS that enables the user to retrieve

information from the system without having to have special software requirements.

questionnaire A set of questions and scales designed to generate enough data for accomplishing the information requirements that underlie the research objectives.

questionnaire design precision The extent to which a questionnaire design can reproduce similar results over repeated usages.

questionnaire development process A specific yet integrative series of logical activities that are undertaken to design a systematic survey instrument for the purpose of collecting primary raw data from sets of people (respondents).

questionnaire format/layout The integrative combination of sets of question/scale measurements into a systematic structured instrument.

question/setup element The question and/or directive that is asked of the respondent for which the respondent is to supply a raw response; it is one of the three elements that make up any scale measurement.

quota sampling The selection of participants based on specific quotas regarding characteristics such as age, race, gender, income, or specific behaviors. Quotas are usually determined by specific research objectives.

quota sheets A tracking form that enhances the interviewer's ability to collect data from the right type of respondents; the form helps ensure that representation standards are met.

random-digit dialing A random selection of area code, exchange, and suffix numbers.

random error An error that occurs as the result of chance events affecting the observed score.

randomization The procedure whereby many subjects are assigned to different experimental treatment conditions, resulting in each group's averaging out any systematic effect on the investigated functional relationship between the independent and dependent variables.

random sampling error The statistically measured difference between the actual sampled results and the estimated true population results.

ranges Statistics that represent the grouping of raw data responses into mutually exclusive subgroups with each having distinct identifiable lower and upper boundary designation values in a set of responses.

rank-order rating scale A scale point format that allows respondents to compare their responses to each other by indicating their first preference, then their second preference, then their third preference, etc., until all the desired responses are placed in some type of rank order, either highest to lowest or lowest to highest.

rating cards Cards used in personal interviews that represent a reproduction of the set of actual scale points and descriptions used to respond to a specific question/setup in the survey. These cards serve as a tool to help the interviewer and respondent speed up the data collection process.

ratio scales Question/scale formats that simultaneously activate all four scaling properties; they are the most sophisticated scale in the sense that absolute differences can be identified not only between each scale point but also between individuals' raw responses. Ratio scales request that respondents give a specific singular numerical value as their response to the question.

raw data Actual responses obtained about a topic of investigation by asking questions or observing actions.

reachable rate (RR) The percentage of active addresses on a mailing list or other defined population frame.

reader-sorter An electronic mechanism located at the point-of-purchase (POP) that resembles a miniature automated bank teller machine. This device enables consumers to pay for transactions with credit cards, ATM cards, or debit cards.

real-time transactional data Data collected at the point of sale.

recording error Occurs when interviewers inadvertently check the wrong response or may be unable to write fast enough to capture the response verbatim.

recursive A relationship in which a variable can both cause and be caused by the same variable.

reflective composite scale Scale used when a researcher measures an individual subcomponent (dimension) of a construct, object, or phenomenon.

refusal A particular type of nonresponse bias that is caused when a prospective respondent declines the role of a respondent, or simply is unwilling to participate in the question/answer exchange.

regression coefficient The statistical measure of the slope coefficient (b) of an independent variable (x) that tells how much the researcher can expect the dependent variable (y) to change, given a unit change in (x).

related samples Two or more groups of responses that originated from the sample population.

relational database system A database in table format of rows and columns, with tables (not data fields) being linked together depending on the output requirements.

relationship marketing A management philosophy that focuses on treating each customer as uniquely different with the overall goal of building a long-term, interactive relationship and loyalty with each customer.

relationships The degree (relative magnitude) and direction of a consistent and systematic linkage (dependence) between two or more variables; this type of information can be derived from either facts or sample data estimates; in special cases, the researcher can determine the existence of cause–effect associations between two or more variables.

relativists Individuals who let present practice set the standard for ethical behavior.

reliability The extent to which the measurements taken with a particular instrument are repeatable.

reliability of data Data structures that are consistent across observations or interviews.

reliability of the scale The extent to which the designed scale can reproduce the same measurement results in repeated trials.

reliability of service The researcher's ability to be consistent and responsive to the needs of the client.

reputation of the firm The culmination of a research firm's ability to meet standards, reliability of service, marketing knowledge, and technical competency for purposes of providing quality outcomes.

research instrument A microscope, radiation meter, ruler, questionnaire, scale, or other device designed for a specific measurement purpose.

research objectives Statements that the research project will attempt to achieve. They provide the guidelines for establishing a research agenda of activities necessary to implement the research process.

research proposal A document that serves as a written contract between the decision-maker and the researcher regarding the research to be conducted.

respondent characteristics The attributes that make up the respondents being included in the survey; three important characteristics are diversity, incidence, and participation.

respondent error The type of nonsampling errors that can occur when selected prospective respondents cannot be initially reached to participate in the survey process, do not cooperate, or demonstrate an unwillingness to participate in the survey.

respondent participation The overall degree to which the selected people have the ability and the willingness to participate as well as the knowledge of the topics being researched.

response error The tendency to answer a question in a particular and unique systematic way. Respondents may consciously or unconsciously distort their answers and true thoughts.

response rate The percentage of usable responses out of the total number of responses.

retailing research Research investigations that focus on topics such as trade area analysis, store image/perception, in-store traffic patterns, and location analysis.

role-playing interviews A technique in which participants are asked to take on the identity of a third person and are placed into a specific predetermined situation. They are then asked to verbalize how they would act in the situation.

sales forecasting A research method that uses variables that affect customer demand to provide estimates of financial outcomes for different price strategies.

sample A group of people or objects selected from the target population.

sample design error A family of nonsampling errors that occur when sampling plans are not appropriately developed and/or the sampling process is improperly executed by the researcher.

sample mean value The actual calculated arithmetic average value based on interval or ratio data of the drawn sampling units.

sample percentage value The actual calculated percentage value of the characteristic of concern held by the drawn sampling units.

sample selection error A specific type of sample design bias that occurs when an inappropriate sample is drawn from the defined target population because of incomplete or faulty sampling procedures or because the correct procedures have not been carried out.

sample size The determined total number of sampling units needed to be representative of the defined target population; that is, the number of elements (people or objects) that have to be included in a drawn sample to ensure appropriate representation of the defined target population.

sampling The process of selecting a relatively small number of elements from a larger defined group of elements so that the information gathered from the smaller group allows one to make judgments about that larger group of elements.

sampling distribution The frequency distribution of a specific sample statistic value that would be found by taking repeated random samples of the same size.

sampling error Any type of bias in a survey study that is attributable to mistakes made in either the selection process of prospective sampling units or determining the size of a sample required to ensure its representativeness of the larger defined target population.

sampling frame A list of all eligible sampling units for a given study.

sampling frame error An error that occurs when a sample is drawn from an incomplete list of potential or prospective respondents.

sampling gap The representation difference between the population elements and sampling units in the sample frame.

sampling plan The blueprint or framework used to ensure that the raw data collected are, in fact, representative of a larger defined target population structure.

sampling units Those elements that are available for selection during the sampling process.

satisfaction of experience A person's evaluative judgment about his or her postpurchase consumption experience of a specified object.

scale dimensions and attributes element The components of the object, construct, or concept that is being measured; it identifies what should be measured and is one of the three elements of a scale measurement.

scale measurement The process of assigning a set of descriptors to represent the range of possible responses that an individual gives in answering a question about a particular object, construct, or factor under investigation.

scale measurement error Occurs when researchers do not develop or use the appropriate scales to measure the constructs.

scale points The set of assigned descriptors that designate the degrees of intensity to the responses concerning the investigated characteristics of an object, construct, or factor; it is one of the three elements that make up scale measurements.

scale reliability The extent to which a scale can produce the same measurement results in repeated trials.

scanner based-panel A group of participating households that have a unique bar-coded card as an identification characteristic for inclusion in the research study.

scatter diagram A graphic plot of the relative position of two variables using a horizontal and a vertical axis to represent the values of the respective variables.

scientific method Research procedures are logical, objective, systematic, reliable, and valid.

scoring models Procedures that attempt to rank customer segments by their potential profitability to the company.

screening forms A set of preliminary questions that are used to determine the eligibility of a prospective respondent for inclusion in the survey.

screening questions/scales Specific questions or scales that are used to qualify prospective respondents for a survey or eliminate unqualified respondents from answering questions/scales in a study.

search A computer-assisted scan of the electronic databases.

search engine An electronic procedure that allows the researcher to enter keywords as search criteria for locating and gathering secondary information off the Internet.

search words The terms that the computer looks for in electronic databases.

secondary data Information previously collected for some other problem or issue.

secondary information Information (facts or estimates) that has already been collected, assembled, and interpreted at least once for some other specific situation.

selection bias Contamination of internal validity measures created by inappropriate selection and/or assignment processes of test subjects to experimental treatment groups.

selective coding Building a storyline around one core category or theme; the other categories will be related to or subsumed to this central overarching category.

selective perception bias A type of error that occurs in situations where the researcher or decision maker uses only a selected portion of the survey results to paint a tainted picture of reality.

self-administered survey A survey in which respondents read the survey questions and record their responses without the assistance of an interviewer.

semantic differential scale A bipolar scale format that captures respondents' cognitive and affective components of specified factors and creates perceptual image profiles relating to a given object or behavior.

semistructured question A question that directs the respondent toward a specified topic area, but the responses to the question are unbounded; the interviewer is not looking for any preconceived right answer.

sentence completion test A projective technique where subjects are given a set of incomplete sentences and asked to complete them in their own words.

separate sample, pretest-posttest A quasi-experimental design where two different groups of test subjects are drawn for which neither group is directly exposed to the independent treatment variable. One group receives the pretest measure of the dependent variable; then after the insignificant independent treatment occurs, the second group of test subjects receives a posttest measure of the dependent variable.

sequential database system A sorting procedure that displays data in a very simple pattern, usually where the data are organized by a simple path, linkage, or network.

service quality studies Studies designed to measure the degree to which an organization conforms to the quality level expected by customers; they concentrate on attributes determined to be most important to customers.

service sensitivity analysis A procedure that helps an organization in designing a basic customer service program by evaluating cost-to-service trade-offs.

silo Data in one functional area of a business not shared with other areas of the business.

similarity judgments A direct approach to gathering perceptual data for multidimensional scaling; where the respondents use a Likert scale to rate all possible pairs of brands in terms of their similarity.

simple random sampling (SRS) A method of probability sampling in which every sampling unit has an equal, nonzero chance of being selected. Results generated by using simple random sampling can be projected to the target population with a prespecified margin of error.

simulated test markets Quasi-test market experiments where the test subjects are preselected, then interviewed and observed on their purchases and attitudes toward the test products; also referred to as *laboratory tests* or *test market simulations.*

single-item scale descriptors A scale used when the data requirements focus on collecting data about only one attribute of the object or construct being investigated.

single-item scale design A scale format that collects data about only one attribute of an object or construct.

situation analysis A tool that focus on gathering background information to familiarize the researcher with the overall complexity of the research problem.

situational characteristics Factors of reality such as budgets, time, and data quality that affect the researcher's ability to collect accurate primary data in a timely fashion.

skip interval A selection tool used to identify the position of the sampling units to be drawn into a systematic random sample design. The interval is determined by dividing the number of potential sampling units in the defined target population by the number of units desired in the sample.

skip questions/scales Questions designed to set the conditions which a respondent must meet in order to be able to respond to additional questions on a survey; also referred to as *conditional* or *branching questions.*

snowball sampling A nonprobability sampling method that involves the practice of identifying a set of initial prospective respondents who can, in turn, help in identifying additional people to be included in the study.

social desirability A type of response bias that occurs when the respondent assumes what answer is socially acceptable or respectable.

Solomon Four Group A true experimental design that combines the pretest-posttest, control group and posttest only, or control group designs and provides both "direct" and "reactive" effects of testing.

Spearman rank order correlation coefficient A statistical measure of the linear association between two variables where both have been measured using ordinal (rank-order) scale instruments.

split-half test A technique used to evaluate the internal consistency reliability of scale measurements that have multiple attribute components.

standard deviation The measure of the average dispersion of the values in a set of responses about their mean.

standard error of the population parameter A statistical measure used in probability sampling that gives an indication of how far the sample result lies from the actual population measure we are trying to estimate.

standard industrial classification (SIC) codes The numerical scheme of industrial listings designed to promote uniformity in data reporting procedures for the U.S. government.

staple scales Considered a modified version of the semantic differential scale; they symmetrically center the scale point domain within a set of plus (+) and minus (–) descriptors.

state-of-behavior data Raw responses that represent an individual's or organization's current observable actions or reactions or recorded past actions/reactions.

state-of-being data Raw responses that are pertinent to the physical and/or demographic or socioeconomic characteristics of individuals, objects, or organizations.

state-of-intention data Raw responses that represent an individual's or organization's expressed plans of future actions/reactions.

state-of-mind data Raw responses that represent the mental attributes or emotional feelings of individuals which are not directly observable or available through some type of external source.

static group comparisons A pre-experimental design of two groups of test subjects; one is the experimental group (EG) and is exposed to the independent treatment; the second group is the control group (CG) and is not given the treatment; the dependent variable is measured in both groups after the treatment.

statistical conclusion validity The ability of the researcher to make reasonable statements about covariation between constructs of interest and the strength of that covariation.

statistical regression Contamination to internal validity measures created when experimental groups are selected on the basis of their extreme responses or scores.

statistical software system A computer-based system that has capabilities of analyzing large volumes of data and computing basic types of statistical procedures, such as means, standard deviations, frequency distributions, and percentages.

store audits Formal examinations and verifications of how much of a particular product or brand has been sold at the retail level.

strata The subgroupings that are derived through stratified random sampling procedures.

stratified random sampling (STRS) A method of probability sampling in which the population is divided into different subgroups (called strata) and samples are selected from each stratum.

structured observation The degree to which behaviors or events are specifically known prior to observing them.

structured questions Questions that require the respondent to make a choice among a limited number of prelisted responses or scale points; they require less thought and effort on the part of the respondent; also referred to as closed-ended questions.

structuredness of observation The degree to which the behaviors or events are specifically known to the researcher prior to doing the observations.

subjective information Information that is based on the decision maker's or researcher's past experiences, assumptions, feelings, or interpretations without any systematic assembly of facts or estimates.

subject's awareness The degree to which subjects consciously know their behavior is being observed; *disguised observation* is when the subject is completely unaware that he or she is being observed, and *undisguised observation* is when the person is aware that he or she is being observed.

supervisor instructions A form that serves as a blueprint for training people on how to execute the interviewing process in a standardized fashion; it outlines the process by which to conduct a study that uses personal and telephone interviewers.

survey instrument design error A "family" of design or format errors that produce a questionnaire that does not accurately collect the appropriate raw data; these nonsampling errors severely limit the generalizability, reliability, and validity of the collected data.

survey instrument error A type of error that occurs when the survey instrument induces some type of systematic bias in the response.

survey research methods Research design procedures for collecting large amounts of data using interviews or questionnaires.

symptoms Conditions that signal the presence of a decision problem or opportunity; they tend to be observable and measurable results of problems or opportunities.

syndicated (or commercial) data Data and information that have been compiled according to some standardized procedure which provides customized data for companies such as market share, ad effectiveness, and sales tracking.

systematic error The type of error that results from poor instrument design and/or instrument construction causing scores or readings on an instrument to be biased in a consistent manner; creates some form of systematic variation in the raw data that is not a natural occurrence or fluctuation on the part of the surveyed respondents.

systematic random-digit dialing The technique of randomly dialing telephone numbers, but only numbers that meet specific criteria.

systematic random sampling (SYMRS) A method of probability sampling that is similar to simple random sampling but requires that the defined target population be naturally ordered in some way.

table of random numbers A table of numbers that have been randomly generated.

tabulation The procedure of counting the number of observations, or data items, that are classified into certain categories.

target market analysis Information for identifying those people (or companies) that an organization wishes to serve.

target population A specified group of people of whom questions will be asked or observations made to obtain the desired information.

task characteristics The requirements placed on the respondents in their process of providing answers to questions asked.

task difficulty How hard the respondent needs to work to respond, and the level of preparation required to create an environment for the respondent.

technical competency The degree to which the researcher possesses the necessary functional requirements to conduct the research project.

teleologists Individuals who follow a philosophy that considers activities to be ethical if they produce desired results.

telephone-administered survey A survey in which individuals working out of their homes or from a central location use the telephone medium to ask participants questions and record the responses.

telephone interview A question-and-answer exchange that is conducted via telephone technology.

test marketing A controlled field experiment conducted for gaining information on specified market performance indicators or factors.

test-retest A procedure used to assess the reliability of a scale measurement; it involves repeating the administration of the scale measurement to either the sample set of sampled respondents at two different times or two different samples of respondents from the same defined target population under as nearly the same conditions as possible.

test-retest reliability The method of accumulating evidence of reliability by using multiple administrations of an instrument to the same sample. If those administrations are consistent, then evidence of test-retest reliability exists.

thematic apperception test (TAT) A specific projective technique that presents the subjects with a series of pictures and asks them to provide a description of or a story about the pictures.

theory A large body of interconnected propositions about how some portion of a certain phenomenon operates.

thick description An ethnographic research report that contextualizes behavior within a culture or subculture.

topic sensitivity The degree to which a specific question or investigated issue leads the respondent to give a socially acceptable response.

topographically integrated geographic encoding and referencing (TIGER) system The U.S. government's new system that provides the researcher with the ability to prepare detailed maps of a variety of areas within the United States.

total variance Consists of the between-group and within-group variance added together.

touchpoint Specific customer information gathered and shared by all individuals in an enterprise.

traditional test markets Test markets that use experimental design procedures to test a product and/or a product's marketing mix variables through existing distribution channels; also referred to as *standard test markets.*

trained interviewers Highly trained people, with excellent communication and listening skills, who ask research participants specific questions and accurately record their responses.

trained observers Highly skilled people who use their various sensory devices to observe and record either a person's current behaviors or physical phenomena as they take place.

transactional data Secondary information derived from transactions by consumers at the retail level.

transition questions Questions used by a moderator to direct a focus group's discussion toward the main topic of interest.

triangulation Addressing the topic analysis from multiple perspectives, including using multiple methods of data collection and analysis, multiple data sets, multiple researchers, multiple time periods, and different kinds of relevant research informants.

trilogy approach The theoretical approach of viewing a person's attitude toward an object as consisting of three distinct components: cognitive, affective, and conative.

true experimental designs Designs that ensure equivalence between the experimental and control groups of subjects by random assignment of subjects to the groups ("pretest-posttest, with control group," "posttest-only, with control group," Solomon Four Group).

***t*-test (also referred to as *t* statistic)** A hypothesis test procedure that uses the *t*-distribution: *t*-tests are used when the sample size of subjects is small (generally less than 30) and the standard deviation is unknown.

Type I error The error made by rejecting the null hypothesis when it is true; represents the probability of alpha error.

Type II error The error of failing to reject the null hypothesis when the alternative hypothesis is true; represents the probability of beta error.

unconscious misrepresentation Occurs when interviewers induce a pattern of responses that does not represent the target population.

underregistration When eligible sampling units are left out of the sampling frame.

undisguised observation Data recording method where the subjects are aware that they are being watched.

undisguised sponsorship When the true identity of the person or company for which the research is being conducted is directly revealed to the prospective respondent.

unexplained variance In multivariate methods, it is the amount of variation in the dependent construct that cannot be accounted for by the combination of independent variables.

unstructured observation Data recording format that does not place any restrictions on the observer regarding what behaviors or events should be recorded.

unstructured questions Question/scale formats that require respondents to reply in their own words; this format requires more thinking and effort on the part of respondents in order to express their answers; also called *open-ended questions*.

usability study A study that combines observation and interviewing in which a moderator gives participants activities to complete at a Web site, and then talks with them about any problems they are having in completing their task.

validity The degree to which a research instrument serves the purpose for which it was constructed; it also relates to the extent to which the conclusions drawn from an experiment are true.

validity of data The degree to which data structures actually do represent what was to be measured.

variability A measure of how data are dispersed; the greater the dissimilarity or "spread" in data, the larger the variability.

variable Any observable, measurable element (or attribute) of an event.

variance The average squared deviations about a mean of a distribution of values.

verbatims Quotes from research participants that are used in research reports.

virtual test markets Completely computerized systems that allow the test subjects to observe and interact with the product as though they were actually in the test store's environment.

voice pitch analyzer A computerized system that measures emotional responses by changes in the subject's voice.

Web-based TV test markets Use of broadband interactive TV (iTV) and advances in interactive multimedia communication technologies to conduct field experiments. Preselected respondents are shown various stimuli and asked questions online through their iTV.

Web home page The guide to a Web site; generally the home page is the first Web page accessed at the Web site.

Web page A source of secondary information that is likely to be linked to other complementary pages; includes text, graphics, and even audio.

Web site An electronic location on the World Wide Web.

width The total number of records contained in the database.

willingness to participate The respondent's inclination or disposition to share his or her thoughts and feelings.

wireless phone survey The method of conducting a marketing survey in which the data are collected on standard wireless phones.

within-group variance Measures how much the observations within each group differ from one another.

word association test A projective technique in which the subject is presented with a list of words or short phrases, one at a time, and asked to respond with the first thoughts or word that comes in mind.

World Wide Web (WWW) A graphical interface system that allows for text linkage between different locations on the Internet.

wrong mailing address A type of nonresponse bias that can occur when the prospective respondent's mailing address is outdated or no longer active.

wrong telephone number A type of nonresponse bias that can occur when the prospective respondent's telephone number either is no longer in service or is incorrect on the sample list.

ZMET (Zaltman Metaphor Elicitation Technique) A visual research technique used in in-depth interviewing that encourages research participants to share emotional and subconscious reactions to a particular topic.

***z*-test (also referred to as *z* statistic)** A hypothesis test procedure that uses the *z* distribution; *z*-tests are used when the sample size is larger than 30 subjects and the standard deviation is unknown.

endnotes

Chapter 1

1. *Annual Report*, Dillard's Department Stores, Little Rock, Arkansas, 1997.

2. Scott Berinato, "Take the Pledge—The CIO's Code of Ethical Data Management," *CIO Magazine,* July 1, 2002, www.cio.com, accessed April, 2008.

3. American Marketing Association, *Official Definition of Marketing Research*, www.marketingpower.com, accessed April, 2008.

4. Michael R. Solomon, *Consumer Behavior,* 6th ed. (Upper Saddle River, NJ: Pearson/Prentice Hall, 2004), pp. 242–45.

5. *Research Topics in Cycle Time Research* (Memphis, TN: Center for Cycle Time Research, University of Memphis, 2003).

6. C. Lamb, J. Hair, and C. McDaniel, *Marketing,* 9th ed. (Cincinnati: Southwestern Publishing, 2008).

7. Kevin Lane Keller, *Strategic Brand Management,* 2nd ed. (Upper Saddle River, NJ: Prentice Hall, 2003).

8. Steven Rutan, "Market Research: An Update on Sources and Techniques for Your Strategic Planning Efforts," www.inc.com, July 2001, accessed April, 2008.

9. "Honomichl 50," *Marketing News,* American Marketing Association, August 15, 2007.

10. "Survey of Top Marketing Research Firms," *Advertising Age*, June 27, 1997.

11. "Fostering Professionalism," *Marketing Research*, Spring 1997.

12. AMA Code of Ethics, www.marketingpower.com, accessed April, 2008.

Chapter 2

1. R. K. Wade, "The When/What Research Decision Guide," *Marketing Research: A Magazine and Application* 5, no. 3 (Summer 1993), pp. 24–27; and W. D. Perreault, "The Shifting Paradigm in Marketing Research, *Journal of the Academy of Marketing Science* 20, no. 4 (Fall 1992), p. 369.

2. Coca-Cola Company, Form 10-K (Washington, DC: Securities and Exchange Commission, September 16, 1996); and Mitchell J. Shields, "Coke's Research Fizzles, Fails to Factor in Customer Loyalty," *Adweek*, July 15, 1985, p. 8.

3. This example is adapted from a project conducted by one of the text's authors for the Ford Foundation's Amphitheater Design Team in Vail, Colorado.

Chapter 3

1. "The Net's Good Fortunes," *Wired*, March 2004, p. 57.

2. Gabriel Kahn and Cris Prystay, "Charge It, Your Cell Phone Tells Your Bank," *The Wall Street Journal,* August 13, 2003, p. B1.

3. Anne Chen, "Harrah's Places Its CRM Bet," www.e-week.com, accessed April 18, 2008.

4. "Harley-Davidson on the Path to Success," www.peoplesoft.com, accessed April 13, 2008.

5. Ulric Gelinas, Steve Sutton, and Jane Fedorwicz, *Business Processes and Information Technology* (Thomson, 2004), pp. 69–71.

6. Ibid.

7. Kevin Kelleher, "Budnet: 66,207,896 Bottles of Beer on the Wall," *Business 2.0,* February 2004.

8. Ibid.

9. "1000 Executives' Best Skillset," *The Wall Street Journal,* July 15, 2003.

10. K. Jain, P. Flynn, and A. Ross, *Handbook of Biometrics* (Springer, 2007).

11. Ibid.

12. David Utter, "Biometrics Comes to Disney World," September 1, 2006, www.securitypronews.com, accessed April 3, 2008.

13. Chen, "Harrah's Places Its CRM Bet."

14. "Web Surveys Target Too Few, Leading Software Firm Says," SPSS Press Release, July 24, 2007, www.spss.com, accessed April 10, 2008.

15. Katie Fehrenbacher, "Embrace Mobile: Surveys via Cell Phones," October 12, 2006, www.gigaom.com, accessed April 4, 2008.

16. Ibid.

17. www.MBuzzy.com, accessed April 17, 2008.

18. www.netfluential.com/qual, accessed April 17, 2008.

19. www.technorati.com, accessed April 17, 2008.

20. "Online Options for Focus Group Research," www.thefreelibrary.com, accessed April 10, 2008.

21. "VNU Unites BuzzMetrics, Intelliseek," January 18, 2006, www.cymfony.com/news, accessed April 17, 2008.

22. "Emerging Mobile Pursuits: The Future of Mobile Media Consumption," March 2008, www.neilsen.com/consumer_insights, accessed April 3, 2008.

23. Scott Berianato, "Take the Pledge," *CIO Magazine,* www.cio.com, accessed April 20, 2008.

24. "Surfing with Sega," *Forbes,* November 4, 2002, p. 58.

Chapter 4

1. Louis Fickle, "Know Your Customer," *CIO Magazine,* April 15, 1999.

2. *The Business Intelligence and Data Warehousing Glossary, www.sdgcomputing.com,* June 2004.

3. Charles Lamb, Joseph F. Hair, Jr., and Carl McDaniel, *Marketing,* 7th ed. (Cincinnati, OH: Southwest, 2004), pp. 685–86.

4. Ibid., p. 687.

5. Bill Inmon, "Building the Data Warehouse," *The Data Warehousing Information Center,* June 21, 2001.

6. Peter Nolan, "Getting Started and Finishing Well," *Intelligence Enterprise Magazine,* May 7, 2001.

7. This is a Case-in-Point Report based on client files of Acxiom (www.acxiom.com) and other sources, including www.gemini.com, www.trustmark.com, www.netbank.com, and www.fingerhut.com.

Chapter 5

1. Thomas W. Miller, "At the Junction," *Marketing Research Magazine,* Winter 2007, pp. 8–14.

2. "The Dollar Sign: Secondary Data," *Database,* May 1997.

3. Jakob Nielsen, "Usability 101: Intro to Usability," 2001, http://www.useit.com/alertbox/20010805.html; "Quantitative Studies: How Many Users to Test," 2005, http://www.useit.com/alertbox/20050815.html; "Putting A/B Testing Methods in Its Place," 2005, http://www.useit.com/alerbox/20050214.html; "Risks of Quantitative Studies," 2004, http://www.useit.com/alertbox/20040301.html; "First Rule of Usability? Don't Listen to Users," 2001, http://www.useit.com/alertbox/20010805.html; all accessed August 26, 2006.

4. Adapted from Jose L. Galvan, *Writing Literature Reviews,* 3rd ed. (Glendale, CA: Pyrczak Publishing, 2005).

5. Sally Barr Ebest, Gerald J. Alred, Charles T. Brusaw, and Walter E. Oliu, *Writing from A to Z: An Easy-to-Use Reference Handbook,* 4th ed. (Boston: McGraw-Hill/Irwin, 2002), pp. 36–37.

6. Marketing Sherpa.com, "Marketing Sherpa's Top 10 Best Blogs and Best Podcasts of 2006: Readers' Choice Award Results," June 27, 2006, accessed January 14, 2008.

7. Ibid., pp. 44–46 and 54–56.

8. Edward Forrest, *Internet Marketing Intelligence* (Burr Ridge, IL: McGraw-Hill/Irwin, 2003), p. 31.

9. Ibid., p. 59.

10. Chun Wei Choo, "Information Management for the Intelligent Organization: The Art of Scanning the Environment," *ASIS Monograph Series,* 1995, http://choo.fis.utoronto.ca/FIS/IMIO/IMIO4/archive.html, accessed January 2008.

11. Adapted from Forrest, *Internet Marketing Intelligence,* p. 72.

12. Ibid., p. 92.

13. Ibid.; also see D. Simmons, "Competitive Intelligence: Can You Manage without It?" *Business Information Review* 14, no. 4 (December 1997), pp. 173–77.

14. Adapted from Forrest, *Internet Marketing Intelligence,* pp. 94–107.

15. "Secondary Research," *Marketing Research Magazine,* Fall 1997.

16. William Pride and O. C. Ferrell, *Marketing,* 11th ed. (Boston: Houghton Mifflin, 2006).

17. *Sourcebook of Demographics and Buying Power for Every Zip Code in the U.S.A.,* C.A.C.I., Gale Research, Detroit, MI, 2006.

18. *The Wall Street Journal Index,* www.wsj.com, accessed March 2008.

19. NPD Group, www.npdgroup.com, accessed March 2008.

20. AC Nielsen Media Research, www.nielsenmedia.com, accessed February 2008.

21. Arbitron, www.arbitron.com, accessed April 2008.

Chapter 6

1. Clotaire Rapaille, *The Culture Code: An Ingenious Way to Understand Why People around the World Buy and Live as They Do* (2006), pp. 1–11.

2. Yvonne Lincoln and Egon G. Guba, "Introduction: Entering the Field of Qualitative Research," in *Handbook of Qualitative Research,* ed. Norman Denzin and Yvonne Lincoln, (Thousand Oaks, CA: Sage Publication, 1994), pp. 1–17.

3. Gerald Zaltman, *How Customers Think: Essential Insights into the Mind of the Market* (Boston: Harvard Business School Press, 2003).

4. Melanie Wallendorf and Eric J. Arnould, "We Gather Together: The Consumption Rituals of Thanksgiving Day," *The Journal of Consumer Research* 19, no. 1 (1991), pp. 13–31.

5. Dennis W. Rook, "The Ritual Dimension of Consumer Behavior," *The Journal of Consumer Research* 12, no. 3 (1985), pp. 251–64.

6. Alfred E. Goldman and Susan Schwartz McDonald, *The Group Depth Interview: Principles and Practice* (Englewood Cliffs, NJ: Prentice Hall, 1987), p. 161.

7. Mary Modahl, *Now or Never: How Companies Must Change Today to Win the Battle for Internet Consumers* (New York: HarperCollins, 2000).

8. Power Decisions Group, "Market Research Tools: Qualitative Depth Interviews," 2006, http://www.powerdecisions.com/qualitative-depth-interviews.cfm, accessed March 2008.

9. Richard A. Krueger, *Focus Groups: A Practical Guide for Applied Research,* 2nd ed. (Thousand Oaks, CA: Sage Publications, 1994), p. 233; T. L. Greenbaum, "It's Possible to Reduce Cost of Focus Groups," *Marketing News,* August 29, 1988, p. 43; also see T. C. Kinnear and J. A. Taylor, *Marketing Research: An Applied Approach,* 5th ed. (New York: McGraw-Hill, 1996), p. 312.

10. David J. Ortinau and Ronald P. Brensinger, "An Empirical Investigation of Perceived Quality's Intangible Dimensionality through Direct Cognitive Structural (DCS) Analysis," in *Marketing Perspectives for the 1990s,* ed. Robert L. King (Richmond, VA: Society for Marketing Advances, 1993), pp. 214–19.

11. Adapted from suggestions offered in Krueger, *Focus Groups,* pp. 79–82; also see Joe L. Welch, "Research Marketing Problems and Opportunities with Focus Groups," *Industrial Marketing Management* 14 (1985), p. 248.

12. Peter Cooper, "Comparison between the UK and US: The Qualitative Dimension," *Journal of the Marketing Research Society* 31, no. 4 (1991), pp. 509–20.

13. Alvin A. Achenbaum, "When Good Research Goes Bad," *Marketing Research,* Winter 2001, pp. 13–15; B. G. Yovovick, "Focusing on Consumers' Needs and Motivations," *Business Marketing,* March 1991, pp. 41–43.

14. Krueger, *Focus Groups,* pp. 149–51.

15. Ibid., pp. 165–66.

16. Thomas L. Greenbaum, "Understanding Focus Group Research Abroad," *Marketing News* 30, no. 12 (June 2, 1996), pp. H16, H36.

17. M. Zinchiak, "Online Focus Groups FAQs," *Quirk's Marketing Research Review,* July/August 2001, pp. 38–46; FocusVision Worldwide, "FocusVision Products and Services," August 18, 2001, http://focusvision.com/products/index.htm; "A Feedback on the Phone," *Business Marketing,* March 1991, p. 46; and Harris Interactive, "Online Qualitative Research," 2006, http://www.harrisinteractive.com/services/qualitative.asp, accessed April 2008.

18. S. Jarvis and D. Szynal, "Show and Tell," *Marketing News,* November 19, 2001, pp. 1,13; K. Lonnie, "Combine Phone and Web for Focus Groups," *Marketing News,* November 19, 2001, pp. 15–16; Rebecca Piirto Heather, "Future Focus Groups," *American Demographics,* January 1, 1994, p. 6; and Tibbert Speer, "A Nickelodeon Puts Kids Online," *American Demographics,* January 1, 1994, p. 16.

19. G. Beistell and D. Nitterhouse, "Asking All the Right Questions," *Marketing Research,* Fall 2001, pp. 14–20; B. Wansink, "New Techniques to Generate Key Marketing Insights," *Marketing Research,* Summer 2000, pp. 28–36; David Ensing, "Web-based Reporting Makes for Easy Info," *Marketing News,* August 14, 2000, p. 15; and Berni Stevens, "Save Money with Online Analysis," *Marketing News,* November 6, 2000, pp. 27–28.

20. Marie Flores Letelier, Charles Sinosa, and Bobby J. Calder, "Taking an Expanded View of Consumers' Needs: Qualitative Research for Aiding Innovation," *Marketing Research,* Winter 2000, pp. 4–11; Gordon A. Wyner, "Anticipating Customer Priorities," *Marketing Research,* Spring 1999, pp. 36–38.

21. Clifford Geertz, *Interpretation of Cultures* (New York: Basic Books, 2000).

22. Richard L. Celsi, Randall L. Rose, and Thomas W. Leigh, "An Exploration of High-Risk Leisure Consumption through Skydiving," *The Journal of Consumer Research* 20, no. 1 (1993), pp. 1–23.

23. Jennifer McFarland, "Margaret Mead Meets Consumer Fieldwork: The Consumer Anthropologist," *Harvard Management Update,* September 24, 2001, http://hbswk.hbs.edu/archive/2514.html, accessed May 2008.

24. Robert V. Kozinets, "The Field behind the Screen: Using Netnography for Marketing Research in Online Communities," *Journal of Marketing Research* 39 (February 2002), p. 69.

25. Ibid., pp. 61–72.

26. Gerald Zaltman, "Rethinking Market Research: Putting People Back In," *Journal of Marketing Research* 34, no. 4 (1997), pp. 424–37.

27. Emily Eakin, "Penetrating the Mind by Metaphor," *New York Times,* February 23, 2002, p. B11; Zaltman, *How Consumers Think.*

28. Eakin, "Penetrating the Mind by Metaphor."

29. William Rathje and Cullen Murphy, "Garbage Demographics," *American Demographics,* May 1992, pp. 50–53; Eugene J. Webb, Donald T. Campbell, Richard D. Schwartz, and Lee Sechrest, *Unobtrusive Measures: Nonreaction Research in the Social Sciences* (Chicago: Rand-McNally, 1971), pp. 113–14; and Joseph A. Cote, James McCullough, and Michael Reilly, "Effects of Unexcepted Situations on Behavior-Intention Differences: A Garbology Analysis," *The Journal of Consumer Research,* September 1985, pp. 188–94.

30. B. Becker, "Guidelines to Direct Observation," *Marketing News,* September 27, 1999, pp. 20, 29, 31, and 33.

31. See Bernie Whalen, "Marketing Detective Reveals Competitive-Intelligence Secrets," *Marketing News,* September 16, 1983, p. 1; and Witold Rybeznski, "We Are What We Throw Away," *New York Times Book Review,* July 5, 1992, pp.5–6.

32. Webb et al., *Unobtrusive Measures,* chap. 2.

33. P. Kephart, "The Spy on Aisle 3," *American Demographics Marketing Tools,* October 1996, pp. 15–17.

34. James M. Sinkula, "Status of Company Usage of Scanner Based Research," *Journal of the Academy of Marketing Science,* Spring 1986, pp. 63–71; and "Some Factors Affecting the Adoption of Scanner-Based Research in Organizations," *Journal of Advertising Research,* April/May 1991, pp. 50–55.

35. S. J. Helleburschh, "Don't Read Research by the Numbers," *Marketing News,* September 11, 2000, pp. 19, 25, and 34.

Chapter 7

1. Barney G. Glaser and Anselm Strauss, *The Discovery of Grounded Theory: Strategies for Qualitative Research* (Chicago: Aldine Publishing, 1967); and Anselm Strauss and Juliet M. Corbin, *Basics of Qualitative Research: Grounded Theory Procedures and Techniques* (Newbury Park, CA: Sage, 1990).

2. Alfred E. Goldman and Susan Schwartz McDonald, *The Group Depth Interview: Principles and Practice* (Englewood Cliffs, NJ: Prentice Hall, 1987), p. 161.

3. Matthew B. Miles and A. Michael Huberman, *Qualitative Data Analysis: An Expanded Sourcebook* (Thousand Oaks, CA: Sage, 1994).

4. Clifford Geertz, *Interpretation of Cultures* (New York: Basic Books, 2000); and Eric J. Arnould and Craig J. Thompson, "Consumer Culture Theory (CCT): Twenty Years of Research," *Journal of Consumer Research* 31, no. 2 (2005), pp. 868–82.

5. Miles and Huberman, *Qualitative Data Analysis.*

6. Susan Spiggle, "Analysis and Interpretation of Qualitative Data in Consumer Research," *The Journal of Consumer Research* 21, no. 3 (1994), pp. 491–503.

7. Mary Wolfinbarger and Mary Gilly, "Shopping Online for Freedom, Control and Fun," *California Management Review* 43, no. 2 (Winter 2001), pp. 34–55.

8. Spiggle, "Analysis and Interpretation of Qualitative Data in Consumer Research," pp. 491–503; Miles and Huberman, *Qualitative Data Analysis.*

9. Mary Wolfinbarger, Mary Gilly, and Hope Schau, "A Portrait of Venturesomeness in a Later Adopting Segment," Working Paper, 2006.

10. Spiggle, "Analysis and Interpretation of Qualitative Data in Consumer Research"; Miles and Huberman, *Qualitative Data Analysis.*

11. Mary C. Gilly and Mary Wolfinbarger, "Advertising's Internal Audience," *Journal of Marketing* 62 (January 1998), pp. 69–88.

12. Wolfinbarger and Gilly, "Shopping Online for Freedom, Control and Fun."

13. Richard L. Celsi, Randall L. Rose, and Thomas W. Leigh, "An Exploration of High-Risk Leisure Consumption through Skydiving," *The Journal of Consumer Research* 20, no. 1 (1993), pp. 1–23.

14. Robin A. Coulter, Linda L. Price, and Lawrence Feick, "Rethinking the Origins of Involvement and Brand Commitment: Insights from Postsocialist Central Europe," *The Journal of Consumer Research* 31, no. 2 (2003), pp. 151–69.

15. Spiggle, "Analysis and Interpretation of Qualitative Data in Consumer Research"; and Strauss and Corbin, *Basics of Qualitative Research.*

16. Hope Jensen Schau and Mary C. Gilly, "We Are What We Post? Self-presentation in Personal Web Space," *The Journal of Consumer Research* 30, no. 3 (2003), pp. 385–404; Albert M. Muniz and Hope Jensen Schau, "Religiosity in the Abandoned Apple Newton Brand Community," *The Journal of Consumer Research* 31, no. 4 (2005), pp. 737–47; Wolfinbarger, Gilly, and Schau, "A Portrait of Venturesomeness in a Later Adopting Segment"; and Lisa Penaloza, "Atravesando Fronteras/Border Crossings: A Critical Ethnographic Exploration of the Consumer Acculturation of Mexican Immigrants," *The Journal of Consumer Research* 21, no. 1 (1993), pp. 32–54.

17. Strauss and Corbin, *Basics of Qualitative Research.*

18. Goldman and McDonald, *The Group Depth Interview: Principles and Practice;* and Miles and Huberman, *Qualitative Data Analysis.*

19. Miles and Huberman, *Qualitative Data Analysis.*

20. Goldman and McDonald, *The Group Depth Interview: Principles and Practice.*

21. Barney G. Glaser and Anselm L. Srauss, *The Discovery of Grounded Theory: Strategies for Qualitative Research* (Hawthorne, NY: Aldine de Gruyter, 1967); and Strauss and Corbin, *Basics of Qualitative Research.*

22. Yvonne S. Lincoln and Egon G. Guba, *Naturalistic Inquiry* (Beverly Hills, CA: Sage, 1985), p. 290.

23. Caroline Stenbecka, "Qualitative Research Requires Quality Concepts of Its Own," *Management Decision* 39, no. 7 (2001), pp. 551–55.

24. Glaser and Strauss, *The Discovery of Grounded Theory: Strategies for Qualitative Research;* also see Strauss and Corbin, *Basics of Qualitative Research.*

25. Goldman and McDonald, *The Group Depth Interview: Principles and Practice.*

26. Ibid., p. 147.

27. Ibid., p. 175.

28. Rebekah Nathan, *My Freshman Year: What a Professor Learned by Becoming a Student* (Ithaca, NY: Cornell University Press, 2005).

Chapter 8

1. Michael R. Czinkota and Ilkka A. Ronkainen, "Conducting Primary Market Research: Market Research for Your Export Operations, Part 2," *International Trade Forum*, January 1995, p. 18.

2. Adapted from Beth Bulik, "How the Male of the Species Shops," *Advertising Age*, March 3, 2008, http://adage.com/article?article_id=125376, accessed March 9, 2008.

3. Terry L. Childers and Steven J. Skinner, "Toward a Conceptualization of Mail Survey Response Behavior," *Psychology and Marketing* 13, no. 2 (March 1996), pp. 185–225.

4. Lawrence F. Feick and Linda L. Price, "The Marketing Maven: A Diffuser of Marketplace Information," *Journal of Marketing* 51 (1987), pp. 83–97.

5. Kathy E. Green, "Sociodemographic Factors and Mail Survey Response Rates," *Psychology and Marketing* 13, no. 2 (March 1996), pp. 171–84.

6. M. G. Dalecki, T. W. Ilvento, and D. E. Moore, "The Effect of Multi-Wave Mailings on the External Validity of Mail Surveys," *Journal of Community Development Society* 19 (1988), pp. 51–70.

7. Arthur Saltzman, "Improving Response Rates in Disk-by-Mail Surveys," *Marketing Research: A Magazine of Management and Applications* 5 (Summer 1993), pp. 32–39.

8. Richard P. Bagozzi, "Measurement in Marketing Research: Basic Principles of Questionnaire Design," in *Principles of Marketing Research*, Richard P. Bagozzi, ed. (Cambridge, MA: Blackwell Publishers, 1994), pp. 1–49.

9. Ibid., p. 35.

10. Ibid., p. 40

11. Fred N. Kerlinger and Howard B. Lee, *Foundations of Behavioral Research,* 4th ed. (Wadsworth/Thomson Learning, Cincinnati, OH, 2000), pp. 629–30.

12. Patricia E. Moberg, "Biases in Unlisted Phone Numbers," *Journal of Advertising Research,* August–September 1982, p. 55; also see Richard Curtin, Stanley Presser, and Eleanor Singer, "Changes in Telephone Survey Nonresponse over the Past Quarter Century," *Public Opinion Quarterly* 56, no. 3 (2005), pp. 65–76.

13. Diane K. Bowers, "Sugging Banned, at Last," *Marketing Research* 7, no. 4 (Fall 1995), p. 40.

14. Leif Gjestland, "Net? Not Yet: CATI Is Still Superior to Internet Interviewing but Enhancements Are on the Way," *Marketing Research: A Magazine of Management and Applications* 8, no. 1 (1996), pp. 26+; also see Peter J. DePaulo and Rick Weitzer, "Interactive Phone Technology Delivers Survey Data Quickly," *Marketing News* 28, no.1 (January 4, 1994), p. 15.

15. Ju Long, Andrew B. Whinston, and Kerem Tomak, "Calling All Customers," *Marketing Research: A Magazine of Management and Applications*, Fall 2002, pp. 28–33.

16. "Mobile Memoir: The Power of the Thumb," Mobile Memoir LLC 2004, April 2004, www. kinesissurvey.com/phonesolutions.html, accessed January 18, 2008.

17. Leslie Townsend, "The Status of Wireless Survey Solutions: The Emerging Power of the Thumb," *Journal of Interactive Advertising,* Fall 2005, http://jiad.org/vol6/no1/townsend/index.htm, accessed February 2008.

18. "Mobile Memoir."

19. Townsend, "The Status of Wireless Survey Solutions."

20. Paul R. Murphy and James M. Daley, "Mail Surveys: To Fax or Not to Fax," *Proceedings of the Association of Marketing Theory and Practice Annual Meetings* (Chicago: American Marketing Association, 1995), pp. 152–57.

21. Bowers, "Sugging Banned, at Last."

22. Lisa Bertagnoli, "Middle East Muddle," *Marketing* News, July 16, 2001, pp. 1 and 9; "World's Online

Population," *Nua Internet Surveys 2000*, as reported in *Marketing News*, July 3, 2000, p.15; and Anja S. Goritz, "Recruitment for On-line Access Panels," *International Journal of Marketing Research* 46, no. 4 (2004), pp. 411–25.

23. Steve Jarvis, "U.S., EU Still Don't Agree on Data Handling," *Marketing News*, August 13, 2001, pp. 5–6; Maxine Lans Retsky, "Staying in Line with New Contest Legislation," *Marketing News,* July 31, 2000, p. 9; "Do-Not-Call List Reduces Telemarketing, Poll Finds," *The Wall Street Journal,* January 12, 2006, http://online.wsj.com.

24. Kevin B. Wright, "Research Internet-Based Populations: Advantages and Disadvantages of Online Survey Research, Online Questionnaire Authoring Software Packages, and Web Survey Services," *Journal of Computer-Mediated Communication* 10 (article 11, 2005), http://jcmc.indiana.edu/vol10/issue3/wright.html, accessed March 2008.

25. *Research Industry Trends 2006 Report,* Pioneer Marketing Research, GreenBook, Dialtek and Rockhopper Research.

26. Maryann Jones Thompson, "Market Researchers Embrace the Web," *The Industry Standard,* January 26, 1999, http://www.thestandard.com/article/0,1902,3274,00.html, accessed September 17, 2006.

27. Chad Rubel, "Researcher Praises On-Line Methodology," *Marketing News* 30, no. 12 (June 3, 1996), p. H18.

28. Scot Dacko, "Data Collection Should Not Be Manual Labor," *Marketing News* 29 no. 18 (August 28, 1995), p. 31; and Michael Kraus, "Research and the Web: Eyeballs and Smiles," *Marketing News*, December 7, 1998, p. 18.

Chapter 9

1. Adapted from Gordon A. Wyner, "Truth or Consequences—Go Beyond Tradition in Assessing Research's Validity and Reliability," *Marketing Research Magazine* 18, no. 3 (Fall 2006), pp. 7–8.

2. This vignette was prepared by the authors.

3. Thomas D. Cook and Donald T. Campbell, *Quasi-Experimentation: Design and Analysis Issues for Field Settings* (Boston: Houghton Mifflin, 1979), pp. 39–41, 51, 59, 64, 70–73.

4. Edward G. Carmines and Richard A. Zeller, *Reliability and Validity Assessment* (Newbury Park, CA: Sage, 1979), pp. 9–48; also see Donald T. Campbell and Julian C. Stanley, *Experimental Designs for Research* (Skokie, IL: Rand-McNally, 1966).

5. B. J. Calder, L. W. Phillips, and A. M. Tybour, "The Concept of External Validity," *Journal of Consumer Research,* December 1992, pp. 240–44.

6. Gilbert A. Churchill, Jr., "A Paradigm for the Development of Better Measures of Marketing Constructs," *Journal of Marketing Research* 16 (February 1979), pp. 64–73.

7. William D. Crano and Marilyn B. Brewer, *Principles and Methods of Social Research* (Boston: Allyn and Bacon, 1986), pp. 23–38.

8. Churchill, "A Paradigm."

9. Carmines and Zeller, *Reliability and Validity Assessment;* Campbell and Stanley, *Experimental Designs for Research;* and Fred N. Kerlinger and Howard B. Lee, *Foundations of Behavior Research,* 4th ed. (Wadsworth-Thomson Learning, Cincinnati, OH, 2000), pp. 324–26, 461–63.

10. Martin Fishbein, "Attitude and the Prediction of Behavior," in *Readings in Attitude Theory and Behavior,* M. Fishbein, ed. (New York: John Wiley and Sons, 1967), pp. 477–92.

11. S. Banks, *Experimentation in Marketing* (New York: McGraw-Hill, 1965), pp. 168–79.

12. Kerlinger and Lee, Foundations of Behavior Research.

13. Ibid.

14. Ibid.

15. Cook and Campbell, Quasi-Experimentation.

16. L. Brennan, "Test Marketing," *Sales and Marketing Management Magazine,* March 1988, pp. 140, 150–52.

17. Betsy Peterson, "Trends Turn Around," *Marketing Research* 7 no. 3 (Summer, 1995).

18. Mark Gleason, "P&G Tests Smoothie," *Advertising Age* 66 (October 30, 1995).

19. Andrew Bernstein, "Spalding and Four Major Chains Launch Women's Theme Shops," *Sporting Goods Business* 28 (November 1985).

20 Robert Burgess, "Coors Chiller Fiasco Costs Brewer Dearly," *The Denver Business Journal* 44, no. 32 (April 23, 1993), p. 1A.

21. Adapted from Peter Robinson, "Premium Brew a Bid to Boost Sales," *Bloomberg News,* reported in the *Tampa Tribune,* February 15, 2008, p. 3.

22. Melvin Prince, "Choosing Simulated Test Marketing Systems," *Marketing Research* 4 (September 1992), pp. 14–16.

23. Ibid.

24. Raymond Burke, "Virtual Shopping: Breakthrough in Marketing Research," *Harvard Business Review* (March/April 1996).

25. Ibid.

26. Steve Jarvis, "iTV Finally Comes Home," *Marketing News,* August 27, 2001, pp. 1, 19, and 20.

27. Burke, "Virtual Shopping."

28. Ibid.

29. Ibid.

30. This vignette was prepared by the authors.

Chapter 10

1. Pam Hunter, "Margin of Error and Confidence Levels Made Simple," www.isixsigma.com/library, accessed April 2008.

2. "How Big Should Your Sample Be?" December 9, 2006, www.marketresearchtech.com, accessed April 2008.

Chapter 11

1. See Jonathan Lemonnier, "Most Americans Ready for ITV—Harris Study: Interactivity Is Already Here," January 25, 2008, http://adage.com/article_id=12335, accessed January 28, 2008.

2. William D. Crano and Marilyn B. Brewer, *Principles and Methods of Social Research* (Boston: Allyn and Bacon, 1986), pp. 23–38; Edward G. Carmines and Richard A. Zeller, *Reliability and Validity Assessment* (Newbury Park, CA: Sage Publications, 1979), pp. 9–48; and Paul E. Spector, *Summated Rating Scale Construction: An Introduction* (Newbury Park, CA: Sage Publications, 1992), pp. 12–17, 46–65.

3. Gilbert A. Churchill, Jr., "A Paradigm for the Development of Better Measures of Marketing Constructs," *Journal of Marketing Research* 16 (February 1979), pp. 64–73.

4. Jum C. Nunnally, *Psychometric Theory,* 2nd ed., (New York: McGraw-Hill, 1978), p. 102.

5. David J. Ortinau and Ronald P. Brensinger, "An Empirical Investigation of Perceived Quality's Intangible Dimensionality through Direct Cognitive Structural (DCS) Analysis," in Robert L. King, ed., *Marketing: Perspectives for the 1990s* (New Orleans, LA: Southern Marketing Association, 1992), pp. 214–19.

6. These studies were conducted by one of the authors. Part of the results were reported in Ortinau and Brensinger, "An Empirical Investigation of Perceived Quality's Intangible Dimensionality."

7. Ronald P. Brensinger, "An Empirical Investigation of Consumer Perceptions of Combined Product and Service Quality: The Automobile," unpublished doctoral dissertation, Tampa, FL: The University of South Florida, 1993, pp. 54–60.

8. Nunnally, *Psychometric Theory*, p. 3.

9. Stanley S. Stevens, "Mathematics, Measurement and Psychophysics," in S. S. Stevens, ed., *Handbook of Experimental Psychology* (New York: John Wiley and Sons, 1951).

10. Fred N. Kerlinger and Howard B. Lee, *Foundations of Behavioral Research,* 4th ed. (Wadsworth-Thomas Learning, Cincinnati, OH, 2000), p. 403; also see Stanley S. Stevens, "On the Theory of Scales of Measurement," *Science* 103 (June 7, 1946), pp. 677–80.

11. Melvin R. Crask and Richard J. Fox, "An Exploration of the Interval Properties of Three Commonly Used Marketing Research Studies: A Magnitude Estimation Approach," *Journal of the Marketing Research Society* 29, no. 3 (1987), pp. 317–39.

12. Wendell R. Garner and C. D. Creelman, "Problems and Methods of Psychological Scaling," in Helson Bevan and William Bevan, eds., *Contemporary Approaches to Psychology* (New York: Van Nostrand, 1967), p. 4.

13. Stevens, "On the Theory of Scales of Measurement."

14. Kerlinger and Lee, *Foundations of Behavioral Research,* p. 405.

15. Ibid., p. 411.

16. Garner and Creelman, "Problems and Methods of Psychological Scaling," p. 7; also see E. T. Goetz, P. A. Alexander, and M. J. Ash, *Educational Psychology* (New York: Macmillan, 1992), pp. 670–74.

17. Nunnally, *Psychometric Theory*, pp. 3–30, 86–90, 102, 225–40.

18. Albert R. Wildt and Michael B. Mazis, "Determinants of Scale Response: Labels versus Position," *Journal of Marketing Research* 15 (May 1978), pp. 261–67; also see Jacob Jacoby and Michael S. Matell, "Three Point Likert Scales Are Good Enough," *Journal of Marketing Research* 8 (November 1971), pp. 495–506.

19. "Measuring the Importance of Attributes," *Research on Research* 28 (Chicago, IL: Market Facts, Inc., undated).

20. Gilbert A. Churchill and J. Paul Peter, "Research Design Effects on the Reliability of Rating Scales: A Meta-Analysis," *Journal of Marketing Research* 21 (February 1984), pp. 360–75.

21. M. N. Segal, "Alternate Form Conjoint Reliability," *Journal of Advertising Research* 4 (1984), pp. 31–38.

22. L. J. Cronbach, "Coefficient Alpha and Internal Structure of Tests," *Psychometrika* 16 (1951), pp. 297–334.

23. H. Schuman and S. Pesser, *Questions and Answers in Attitude Survey* (New York: Academic Press, 1981), pp. 179–201.

24. Ibid., p. 192.

25. G. J. Spagna, "Questionnaire: Which Approach Do You Use?" *Journal of Advertising Research,* February–March 1984, pp. 67–70; also see E. A. Holdaway, "Different Response Categories and Questionnaire Response Patterns," *Journal of Experimental Education,* Winter 1971, p. 59.

26. K. C. Schneider, "Uninformed Response Rate in Survey Research," *Journal of Business Research,* April 1985, pp. 153–62; also see Del I. Hawkins and K. A. Coney, "Uninformed Response Error in Survey Research," *Journal of Marketing Research* 18 (August 1981), pp. 370–74.

Chapter 12

1. Thomas S. Robertson and Harold H. Kassarjian, *Handbook of Consumer Behavior* (Englewood Cliffs, NJ: Prentice Hall, 1991).

2. Martin Fishbein, *Readings in Attitude Theory* (New York: John Wiley and Sons, 1967).

3. Roobina Ohanian, "Construction and Validation of a Scale to Measure Celebrity Endorsers' Perceived Expertise, Trustworthiness, and Attractiveness," *Journal of Advertising* 19, no. 3 (1990), pp. 39–52.

4. Robert T. W. Wu and Susan M. Petroshius, "The Halo Effect in Store Image Management," *Journal of Academy of Marketing Science* 15 (1987), pp. 44–51.

5. Rajendar K. Garg, "The Influence of Positive and Negative Wording and Issues Involvement on Response to Likert Scales in Marketing Research," *Journal of the Marketing Research Society* 38, no. 3 (July 1996), pp. 235–46.

6. Tony Siciliano, "Purchase Intent: Facts from Fiction," *Marketing Research* 21 (Spring 1993), p. 56.

7. Michael R. Solomon, *Consumer Behavior,* 7th ed. (Upper Saddle River, NJ: Pearson/Prentice Hall, 2007), pp. 240–48.

8. www.burke.com; and Amanda Prus and D. Randall Brandt, "Understanding Your Customers—What You Can Learn from a Customer Loyalty Index," *Marketing Tools,* July/August 1995, pp. 10–14, and www.burke.com, accessed June 2008.

9. Martin Fishbein, "Attitude and the Prediction of Behavior," in *Readings in Attitude Theory and Behavior,* ed. M. Fishbein (New York: Wiley, 1967); also see Martin Fishbein, "An Investigation of the Relationships between Beliefs about an Object and the Attitude toward That Object," *Human Relations* 16 (1983), pp. 233–40.

10. Icek Ajzen and Martin Fishbein, *Understanding and Predicting Social Behavior* (Englewood Cliffs, NJ: Prentice Hall, 1980), pp. 53–89; and Icek Ajzen and

Martin Fishbein, "Attitude-Behavior Relations: A Theoretical Analysis and Review of Empirical Research," *Psychological Bulletin* 84 (September 1977), pp. 888–948.

11. Y. Tsai, "On the Relationship between Cognitive and Affective Processes," *Journal of Consumer Research* 12, no. 3 (December 1985), pp. 358–62; also see P. A. Dabholkar, "Incorporating Choice into an Attitudinal Framework," *Journal of Consumer Research* 21, no. 1 (June 1994), pp. 100–18.

12. Sharon E. Beatty and Lynn R. Kahle, "Alternative Hierarchies of the Attitude-Behavior Relationship," *Journal of the Academy of Marketing Science,* Summer 1988, pp. 1–10; A. Sahni, "Incorporating Perceptions of Financial Control in Purchase Prediction," in *Advances in Consumer Research XXI,* Chris T. Allen and Debbie R. John, eds. (Provo, UT: Association for Consumer Research, 1994), pp. 442–48; and J. A. Cote, J. McCullough, and M. Reilly, "Effects of Unexpected Situations on Behavior-Intention Differences," *Journal of Consumer Research* 12, no. 3 (September 1985), pp. 188–95.

13. These factors were adopted from the discussion in Del I. Hawkins, Roger J. Best, and Kenneth A. Coney, *Consumer Behavior: Building Marketing Strategy,* 7th ed. (New York: Irwin/McGraw-Hill, 1998), pp. 401–3.

Chapter 13

1. These characteristics are known as the cornerstones for conducting scientific inquiries into many different types of marketing phenomena. An excellent overview can be obtained by reading Stanley Payne's classic book *The Art of Asking Questions* (Princeton, NJ: Princeton University Press, 1951).

2. Ibid., pp. 8–9.

3. Maria Elena Sanchez, "Effects of Questionnaire Design on the Quality of Survey Data," *Public Opinion Quarterly* 56 (1992), pp. 208–17.

4. Pamela L. Alreck and Robert B. Settle, *The Survey Research Handbook*, 2nd ed. (New York: McGraw-Hill/Irwin, 1995), pp. 120–22.

5. Robert A. Peterson, *Constructing Effective Questionnaires* (Thousand Oaks, CA: Sage, 2000), pp. 1–2.

6. Ibid., p. 53.

7. Sanchez, "Effects of Questionnaire Design on the Quality of Survey Data," p. 209; also see James H. Barns and Michael J. Dotson, "The Effects of Mixed Grammar Chains on Response to Survey Questions," *Journal of Marketing Research* 26, no. 4 (November 1989), pp. 468–72.

8. Alreck and Settle, *The Survey Research Handbook*, pp. 97–100.

9. Susan Carroll, "Questionnaire's Design Affects Response Rate," *Marketing News* 28 (January 3, 1994), pp. 14, 23.

10. The "Flowerpot" design approach is a symbolic model developed in 1974 by David J. Ortinau while teaching at Illinois State University, Normal, Illinois.

11. M. Patten, *Questionnaire Research* (Los Angeles, CA: Pyrczak, 2001), pp. 8–12.

12. A. Diamantopoula, B. Schlegelmilch, and N. Wilcox, "The Pretesting in Questionnaire Design: The Impact of Respondent Characteristics on Error Detection," *Journal of Marketing Research Society* 35 (April 1994), pp. 295–314.

13. Carroll, "Questionnaire's Design Affects Response Rate," p. 23; also see D. Dillman, M. Sinclair, and J. Clark, "Effects of Questionnaire Length, Respondent Friendly Design, and a Difficult Question on Response Rates for Occupant-Addressed Census Mail Surveys," *Public Opinion Quarterly* 57 (1993), pp. 289–304.

14. Dillman et al., "Effects of Questionnaire Length," p. 294.

15. Patten, *Questionnaire Research*, p. 78.

16. R. Hubbard and E. Little, "Cash Prizes and Mail Response Rates: A Threshold Analysis," *Journal of the Academy of Marketing Science* (Fall 1988), pp. 42–44.

Chapter 14

1. Barry Deville, "The Data Assembly Challenge," *Marketing Research Magazine*, Fall/Winter 1995, p. 4.

2. Ibid., p. 15.

CHAPTER 15

1. For a more detailed discussion of analysis of variance (ANOVA), see Gudmund R. Iversen and Helmut Norpoth, *Analysis of Variance* (Newbury Park, CA: Sage, 1987); and John A. Ingram and Joseph G. Monks, *Statistics for Business and Economics* (San Diego, CA: Harcourt Brace Jovanovich, 1989).

CHAPTER 16

1. For a more detailed discussion of transformations see Chapter 2 of Hair, J. F., W. Black, B. Babin, R. Anderson, and R. Tatham, *Multivariate Data Analysis,* Upper Saddle River, NJ, Prentice-Hall, 2006.

CHAPTER 17

1. For a conceptual discussion of these techniques, see Hair, J. F., W. Black, B. Babin, R. Anderson, and R. Tatham, *Multivariate Data Analysis,* Upper Saddle River, NJ, Prentice-Hall, 2006.

Chapter 18

1. David Corcoran, "Talking Numbers with Edward R. Tufte; Campaigning for the Charts that Teach," *New York Times,* February 6, 2000, www.NYTimes.com, accessed January 20, 2008.

2. Ibid.

name index

A

Achenbaum, Alvin A., 651
Adams, Larry, 122
Ajzen, Icek, 657
Alexander, P. A., 657
Allen, Chris T., 658
Allison, Tom, 259
Alreck, Pamela L., 658
Alred, Gerald J., 650
Ambrosino, Al, 101
Anderson, R., 659
Arnould, Eric J., 651, 653
Ash, M. J., 657
Austin, Harold, 559

B

Babin, B., 659
Bagozzi, Richard P., 654
Banks, S., 655
Barns, James H., 658
Beatty, Sharon E., 658
Becker, B., 652
Beistell, G., 652
Bengen, Robert, 113
Berianato, Scott, 649, 650
Bernstein, Andrew, 656
Bertagnoli, Lisa, 654
Best, Roger J., 658
Black, W., 659
Blinkoof, Robbie, 205
Bogdan, Michele, 333
Boggs, Chris, 122
Bowers, Diane K., 654
Brandt, D. Randall, 657
Brennan, L., 655
Brensinger, Ronald P., 651, 656
Brewer, Marilyn B., 655, 656
Brusaw, Charles T., 650
Bulik, Beth, 654
Burgess, Robert, 656
Burke, Raymond, 656

C

Calder, Bobby J., 652, 655
Calvan, Jose L., 650
Campbell, Donald T., 652, 655
Carey, Morgan, 122
Carmines, Edward G., 655, 656
Carroll, Brian, 122
Carroll, Susan, 658
Carter, Dan, 35
Celsi, Richard L., 217, 652, 653
Chen, Anne, 649, 650
Childers, Terry L., 654
Choo, Chun Wei, 651
Churchill, A. Gilbert, Jr., 655, 656, 657
Clark, J., 658
Claymore, Clayton, 122
Coney, Kenneth A., 657, 658
Cook, Thomas D., 655
Cooper, Peter, 651
Coors, Pete, 298
Corbin, Juliet M., 653
Corcoran, David, 659
Cote, J. A., 658
Cote, Joseph A., 652
Coulter, Robin A., 219, 653
Crano, William D., 655, 656
Crask, Melvin R., 656
Creelman, C. D., 657
Cronbach, L. J., 657
Curtin, Richard, 654
Czinkota, Michael R., 231, 654

D

Dabholkar, P. A., 658
Dacko, Scot, 655
Dalecki, M. G., 654
Daley, James M., 654
Denzin, Norman, 651
DePaulo, Peter J., 654
Deville, Barry, 658
Diamantopoula, A., 658
Dillard, William, Sr., 3

Dillman, D., 658
Dotson, Michael J., 658

E

Eakin, Emily, 652
Ebest, Sally Barr, 650
Ensing, David, 652

F

Fedorwicz, Jane, 649
Fehrenbacher, Katie, 650
Feick, Lawrence, 219, 653, 654
Ferrell, O. C., 651
Fickle, Louis, 650
Fishbein, Martin, 368, 394, 396, 655, 657, 658
Flynn, P., 649
Fontova, Al, 3
Forrest, Edward, 650, 651
Fournier, Susan, 216
Fox, Richard J., 656

G

Gallagher, Sean, 198
Garcia, Anthony C., Jr., 122
Garg, Rajendar K., 657
Garner, Wendell R., 657
Gautheir, Laura W., 151
Geertz, Clifford, 652, 653
Gelinas, Ulric, 649
Gilly, Mary C., 218, 653
Gjestland, Leif, 654
Glaser, Barney G., 653
Gleason, Mark, 656
Godin, Seth, 122
Goetz, E. T., 657
Goldman, Alfred E., 224, 651, 653, 654
Goodstein, Anastasia, 122
Goritz, Anja S., 655
Green, Kathy E., 654
Greenbaum, Thomas L., 651, 652
Guba, Egon G., 651, 653

H

Hair, Joseph F., Jr., 649, 650, 659
Hall, Steve, 122
Hawkins, Del, 657, 658
Heather, Rebecca Pinto, 652
Hellerbusch, S. J., 652
Hernandez, Ignacio, 122
Hilton, Paris, 613–614
Hlavac, Randy, 519
Hogan, Shawn, 122
Holdaway, E. A., 657
Hubbard, R., 658
Huberman, A. Michael, 208, 221, 653
Hudson, Jonathan, 122
Hullar, Bob, 35
Hunter, Pam, 656

I

Ilvento, T. W., 654
Ingram, John A., 659
Inmon, Bill, 650
Isabella, Joan, 122
Iversen, Gudmund R., 659

J

Jacoby, Jacob, 657
Jain, K., 649
Jantsch, John, 122
Jarvis, Steve, 652, 655, 656
John, Debbie R., 658
Jolley, Craig, 75

K

Kahle, Lynn R., 658
Kahn, Gabriel, 649
Kaplan, Howard, 122
Kassarjian, H. H., 368, 657
Kelleher, Kevin, 649
Keller, Kevin Lane, 649
Kendall, M. G., 314
Kephart, P., 652
Kerlinger, Fred N., 654, 655, 656, 657
King, Robert L., 651, 656

Kinnear, T. C., 651
Kneen, Robert W., 453
Kozinets, Robert V., 185, 652
Kraus, Michael, 655
Krause, Kim, 122
Krueger, Richard A., 651

L

Lamb, Charles, 649, 650
Lee, Howard B., 654, 655, 656, 657
Leigh, Thomas W., 217, 652, 653
Lemmonier, Jonathan, 656
Letelier, Marie Flores, 652
Likert, Rensis, 370
Lincoln, Yvonne, 651, 653
Little, E., 658
Livingstone, Carol V., 367
Long, Ju, 654
Lonnie, K., 652

M

Matell, Michael S., 657
Mazis, Michael B., 657
McCullough, James, 652, 658
McDaniel, Carl, 649, 650
McDonald, Susan Schwartz, 224, 651, 653, 654
McFarland, Jennifer, 652
Mick, David Glen, 216
Miles, Matthew B., 208, 221, 653
Miller, Thomas, 117, 650
Moberg, Patricia E., 654
Modahl, Mary, 651
Monks, Joseph G., 659
Moore, D. E., 654
Muniz, Albert M., 653
Murphy, Cullen, 652
Murphy, Paul R., 654

N

Nathan, Rebekah, 654
Nielsen, Jakob, 650
Nitterhouse, D., 652
Nolan, Kevin, 403
Nolan, Peter, 650
Norpoth, Helmut, 659
Novo, Jim, 122
Nunnally, Jum C., 656, 657

O

Ogilvy, David, 83
Ohanian, Roobina, 657
Oliu, Walter E., 650
Ortinau, David J., 651, 656, 658

P

Patten, M., 658
Payne, Stanley, 658
Penaloza, Lisa, 653
Perreault, W. D., 649
Pesser, S., 657
Peter, J. Paul, 657
Peters, Tom, 205
Peterson, Betsy, 655
Peterson, Robert A., 658
Petroshius, Susan M., 657
Pfeiffer, Benjamin, 122
Phillips, L. W., 655
Pick, Tom, 122
Presser, Stanley, 654
Price, Linda, 219, 653, 654
Pride, William, 651
Prince, Melvin, 656
Prus, Amanda, 657
Prystay, Cris, 649

R

Rapaille, Clotaire, 151–152, 651
Rathje, William, 652
Reilly, Michael, 652, 658
Retsky, Maxine Lans, 655
Rivers, Doug, 311
Robertson, T. S., 368, 657
Robinson, Peter, 656
Romero, Donna, 185
Ronkainen, Ilkka A., 231, 654
Rook, Dennis W., 651
Rose, Randall L., 217, 652, 653
Ross, A., 649
Rubel, Chad, 655

Rutan, Steven, 649
Rybeznski, Witold, 652

S

Sahni, A., 658
Saltzman, Arthur, 654
Sanchez, Maria Elena, 658
Schau, Hope Jensen, 653
Schlegelmilch, B., 658
Schneider, K. C., 657
Schultz, Howard, 299
Schuman, H., 657
Schwartz, Barry, 122
Schwartz, Richard D., 652
Sechrest, Lee, 652
Segal, M. N., 657
Settle, Robert B., 658
Shields, Mitchell J., 649
Shulby, Rob, 35
Siciliano, Tony, 657
Simmons, D., 651
Sinclair, M., 658
Singer, Eleanor, 654
Sinkula, James M., 652
Sinosa, Charles, 652
Skinner, Steven J., 654
Sloan Brothers, 122
Smith, Alex, 60
Smith, B. Babington, 314
Smith, John, 506
Solomon, Michael R., 649, 657
Spagna, G. J., 657
Spector, Paul E., 656
Speer, Tibbert, 652
Spiggle, Susan, 653
Stanley, Julian C., 655
Stenbecka, Caroline, 653
Stevens, Berni, 652, 657
Stevens, Stanley S., 656
Stewart, Martha, 385
Strauss, Anselm, 653
Sutton, Steve, 649
Szynal, D., 652

T

Tatham, R., 659
Taylor, J. A., 651
Thies, Dan, 122
Thompson, Craig J., 653
Thompson, Maryann Jones, 655
Tomak, Kerem, 654
Townsend, Leslie, 654
Traugott, Mike, 311
Tsai, Y., 658
Tufte, Edward, 599
Tybour, A. M., 655

U

Utter, David, 650

W

Wade, R. K., 649
Wallendorf, Melanie, 651
Wansink, B., 652
Webb, Eugene J., 652
Weitzer, Rick, 654
Welch, Joe L., 651
Welsh, Joel, 122
Whalen, Bernie, 652
Whinston, Andrew B., 654
Wibbels, Andy, 122
Wilcox, N., 658
Wildt, Albert R., 657
Wolfinbarger, Mary, 218, 653
Woods, Tiger, 373, 385
Wright, Kevin B., 655
Wu, Robert T. W., 657
Wyner, Gordon A., 652, 655

Y

Yin, Sandra, 198
Young, Dave, 122
Yovovick, B. G., 651

Z

Zaltman, Gerald, 188, 220, 651, 652
Zeller, Richard A., 655, 656
Zinchiak, M., 652

subject index

Note: Entries in **bold face** indicate definitions.

A

ABI/Inform, 121, 138
Ability to participate, 265
Abstraction, 209–211
AC Nielsen, 17, 78, 127, 143, 190, 194, 297
  customized data from, 18
  tracking system for blogs, 76
Aca Joe, Inc., 367–368, 386
Accuracy of data, **410**
Activity-based cost information system, 13
Acura, 394–401
Acxiom Corporation, 105, 106
Ad-Ware, 125
Advertising Age, 16
Advertising agencies, 19
Advertising effectiveness studies, 14
  discriminant analysis and, 581
  factor analysis and, 565
Affect global approach, 397–400
Affective component of attitude, 369
Allison, Hollander, 259
Alltel Communication, 392, 393
AltaVista, 117, 143
Alternative delivery systems studies, 12
Alternative hypothesis, 234
Alto Lakes Golf and Country Club, 44
Amazon.com, 182
Ambiguity threats to validity, 281, 282
America Online, 194
American Association for Public Opinion Research, 311
American Bank and Trust Company, 416–422, 432, 433
American Consumer Satisfaction Index (ACSI), 127
American Demographics (AD), 198, 225
American Demographics/Marketing Tools, 144
American Express, 98, 154
American Law Sources Online, 126
American Marketing Association, 4
  Code of Ethics, 21–24
American Multi-Cinema Inc. (AMC), 129
Ames, 304
Analysis of variance (ANOVA), 499–504, 562
  between-group variance, 501
  cluster analysis and, 576–579
  follow-up tests, 501–502
  F-ratio, 501
  F-test, 501
  n-way, 503–504
  reporting, 613–616
  SPSS application, 502–503
  total variance, 501
  within-group variance, 501
Analytical customer data, 68
  benefits of, 68–69
Analyzing relationships in sample data, 488–504
  ANOVA. *See* Analysis of variance (ANOVA)
  bivariate statistical tests, 490–504
  chi-square analysis, 488, 494–497
    SPSS application, 496–497
  independent samples, 497
  population parameters, 489
  related samples, 497
  sample statistics, 489
  t-test. *See t*-test
  univariate statistical tests, 489–490
    SPSS application, 490
Anheuser-Busch (AB), 68
Anonymity, 428
AOL, 67, 301
Apex, 591
Appendix, 619
Apple Computer, 5, 76, 85, 280
Appropriateness of descriptors, 351
Arbitron Ratings, 17, 127, 142
Area sampling, 318
Arm & Hammer, 164
Articulative interviews, 183–184
Ask.com, 379
Assignment property, 342, 343

Association analysis, 518–557
correlation analysis. *See* Correlation analysis
learning objectives, 518, 548
regression analysis. *See* Regression analysis
multiple. *See* Multiple regression analysis
relationships between variables, 518–521
covariation, 519–521
curvilinear, 518, 521
linear, 518
negative, 518, 520
positive, 518, 520
presence and, 518
questions to ask about, 518–519
scatter diagrams and, 519–521
strength of association, 518
type, 518
AT&T, 85, 285, 301, 392, 393
Atlas/ti, 208
Atomica.com, 125
Attitude measurement, 366–401
behavior intention scale, 377–379
comparative rating scales. *See* Comparative rating scales
components of, 369
design issues, 384–386
construct development, 385
ethical responsibility and, 386
measurement scale, 385
screening questions, 385
skip questions, 385
formative composite scale, 384
image measurement and, 367–368
learning objectives, 366, 389–390
Likert scale, 370–372
multiple-item scale design, 384
noncomparative rating scales. *See* Noncomparative rating scales
reflective composite scale, 384
semantic differential scale. *See* Semantic differential scale
single-item scale design, 384
value of, 368
Attitude measurement
trilogy approach to understanding, 392–397
affect global approach to, 397–400
links between cognitive affective behavior and, 400–401
toward-behavior model, 396–397
toward-object model, 394–396
Attitudes, 368
affective component of, 369
behavioral component of, 369
cognitive component of, 369
nature of, 368–369
Attitudinal data, 91
Attitudinal research, 14
Attribute importance estimate, 589–590
Audits and Surveys, Inc., 143, 297
Automatic replenishment systems, 11–12
AutoZone, 143
Average squared deviation, 487
Averaging, 240
Awareness, 192
ethics and, 197
Axial coding, 212

B

Bad questions, 407–408
examples of, 408
Balloon tests, 188
Bank of America, 37, 86, 383, 438
semantic differential scale used by, 374, 375
Bar charts
ANOVAs, 613–616
crosstabs, 612–163
displaying frequencies with, 607–609
example of, 607
thematically related means, 611–612
t-tests, 613–614
Barnett Bank of Pasco County, 151
Behavior intention scale, 377–379
example of, 378
strengths and weaknesses of, 378–379
Behavioral component of attitude, 369
BehaviorScan, 276
Believability, 602
Benefit and lifestyle studies, 8
Best Buy, 87, 116
Beta coefficient, 536
Beta Dynamics, Inc., 559
Between-group variance, 501
Bias
halo effect, 374
interpretive, 241
mono-method, 284
mono-operation, 284
in research designs, 197
selection, 281, 282
selective perception, 241–242
of sources, 131
Biometrics, 69–70

Bivariate regression analysis, 528
developing and estimating coefficients, 530–532
F-ratio, 534
SPSS application, 532–534
Bivariate statistical tests, 490–504
ANOVA. *See* Analysis of variance (ANOVA)
chi-square analysis, 488, 494–497
cross-tabulation, 491–494
independent samples, 497
related samples, 497
t-test. *See* *t*-test
Black & Decker, 49
Blogs, 74–76
marketing, 121–123
Boeing, 65
Bookmarking tools, 123
Boolean logic, 132, 145
Bradlee's, 304
Branching questions, 385
BRINT, 144
Broker research firms, 19
BudNet, 68
Bureau of Labor Statistics (BLS), 126, 127
Burke Market Research, 17, 127, 194, 300, 333–334
Secure Customer Index of, 359–361, 387–388
Business 2.0, 121
Business Periodical Index, 139
BusinessWeek, 121, 139
BUSLIB-L, 144
"Buzzmetrics," 76

C

Caldor, 304
Call blocking, 247
Call record sheets, 439–441
example of, 441
Callbacks
data validation and, 455
telephone interviews and, 247
Calloway Golf, 69
Canon, 536, 537
Capital Bank, 438
Capital One, 87, 438
Carl's Junior, 613–614
Carolina Consulting Company, 35
Cartoon (balloon) tests, 188
Case studies, 182, 183
Categorization, 209
Category scale, 379
Causal research, 52
experimental research. *See* Experimental research
learning objectives, 272, 306–307
overview of, 274–275
test marketing. *See* Test marketing
value of, 274
Census, 52
Chi-square analysis, 488, 494–497
calculation, 494–496
SPSS application, 496–497
Chili's, 186–187
Chip card, 70
Chrysler, 151–152
CI Resource Index, 144
CitiBank, 98, 438
Claritas, 127
Click-stream data, 69, 194–195
Click-to-Call alliance, 119
Clickz-com, 121
Cluster analysis, 562–563, **572**–579
based on two characteristics, 573
combining discriminant analysis with, 585–587
example of, 591–595
marketing research applications, 574
SPSS application, 574–579
statistical procedures for, 573–574
Cluster sampling, 317–321
advantages and disadvantages of, 320
area, 318
steps in, 321
Coca-Cola, 37, 85, 89, 188–189, 334
new Coke, 46
Code of Ethics, 21–24
Code sheet, 209
example of, 210
Codes, 209
in the margins, 211
theory building and, 212–213
Coding. *See* Data coding
Coding error, 242
Coefficient alpha, 353
Coefficient of determination (r^2), **525**
Cognitive component of attitude, 369
Commercial data, 140
Company Sleuth, 143
Comparative rating scales, 379
constant sums scales, 382, 383
paired-comparison scales, 382, 383
rank-order scales, 382, 383

Comparison, 211–212
Competitive analysis, 9
Competitive intelligence, 126, 128
steps in conducting research, 128
Complete randomization, 278
Completely automated telephone surveys (CATS), 251
Composite scale, 379
CompuServe, 75
Computer-assisted telephone interviews (CATI), 249–251
advantages of, 250
disadvantages of, 250–251
Conative component of attitude, 369
Concept of product testing, 10
Conceptual model, 234
examples of, 235
Conditional questions, 385
Confidentiality, 428–429
Conjoint analysis, 562, **587**–590
advantages of, 590
attribute importance estimate, 589–590
formula for, 589
marketing research applications, 590
part-worth estimate, 588
sample survey profiles, 588
Constant development error, 240
Constant sums scale, 383
example of, 382
Construct development, 335–**336**
general steps in, 370
goal of, 335
measurement design and, 385
problem in, 338, 339
Construct validity, 283–284
threats to, 284–285
Constructs, 233, 335–340
abstractness of, 336
dimensionality of, 336–337
direct cognitive structural analysis and, 338
domain of observables and, 336–337
inappropriate set of respondents and, 338
operationalization of, 338–340
scale measurement formats and, 338
scale reliability and, 338
validity of, 337–338
Consumer intelligence, 125–126
sources of, 127
Consumer panels, 140–142
data source examples, 141
media panel, 141–142
Consumer Report on Eating Share Trends (CREST), 141
Consumer test marketing, 302–303
Consumer Trends Institute, 127
Content analysis, 175
future of for-profit higher education, 198
interpretive factors in, 176
Content validity, 337
Context-Based Research Group, 205
Continuous rating scales, 379–381
Control variables, 277, **278**
Controlled laboratory environment, 275
Controlled test markets, 296, **297**–298
advantages and disadvantages of, 297–298
Convenience sampling, 322
Convergent validity, 284, 337–338
Coors beer, 298
CoreStates Bank, 105–106
Corporate Communications and Marketing, Inc., 49
"Corporate Information," 143
Correlation analysis, 521–527
measurement scales and, 525
Pearson. *See* Pearson correlation coefficient
reporting, 616–617
rules of thumb concerning, 522
Spearman rank order, 525
Cost-to-service trade-offs, 13
Council for Marketing and Opinion Research, 248
Covariation, 519–521
Cover letters, 426–434
example of, 432, 433
guidelines for developing, 426–432
advanced thank you, 431–432
anonymity, 428
compensation, 430–431
completion date, 431
confidentiality, 428–429
identification of the study organization, 427–428
importance of respondent's participation, 429
incentive programs, 431
personalization, 427
purpose and importance of study, 428
reasons for not participating, 429–430
returning survey, 431
summary of, 427
time frame, 429
time requirements, 430
length of, 432, 434
role of, 426
Creative and Response Research Services, 141

Credibility, 218, **221, 602**
of research reports, 602
of sources, 131
Critical Mix, 300
Cronbach's alpha, 353
Cross-researcher reliability, 221
Cross-tabulation, 468, 491–494
dialog boxes for, 492
by gender, 493
Culture codes, 151–152
Curbstoning, 21, **455**
Curvilinear relationship, 518
scatter diagram of, 521
Customer-centric approach, 85–**86**
Customer information, 86–87. *See also* Databases
cluster analysis and, 574
Customer knowledge, 84–85, 114, **115**
Customer loyalty
in the financial services industry, 106–107
index of, 359–361
scale measurements used in creating an, 387–388
predicting, 333–334
Customer/market knowledge, 6
Customer profiles, 6
Customer relationship management (CRM), 4, 5–**6, 84**–85
secondary data and, 116
Customer retention, 83–84
Customer satisfaction studies, 11, 52
instant on-site, 380
role of employees in, 545–547
Customer-volunteered data, 97, 114
Customized research firms, 17
example of, 18
Cycle time research, 11–12

D

Dashboards, 67
Data, 93. *See also specific types of data*
Data accuracy, 131
Data analysis
of associations. *See* Association analysis
multivariate. *See* Multivariate analysis
preparation for. *See* Preparing data for analysis
qualitative. *See* Qualitative data analysis
quantitative, 206–207
of significant differences. *See* Significant difference analysis
Data analysis error, 241
Data coding, 461–464
consolidation of responses, 463–464
errors in, 242
master code sheet, 462–463
Data collection methods, 54–55
technology and primary, 70–76
nontraditional methods, 73
social networking and, 73–76
Data completeness, 262–263
Data conversion, 130–131
Data dictionary, 93, 95
Data editing, 456
errors in, 242
open-ended questions, 456, 461
proper questions, 456
recording of answers, 456
screening questions, 456, 457
Data enhancement, 90–92
advantages of, 90
attitudinal data, 91
geodemographic data, 91–92
motivational data, 91
target market characteristics and, 91
Data entry, 464–466
Data entry error, 242
Data falsification, 21
Data generalizability, 262
Data integration, 6
Data marts, 76
Data mining, 76–77, **98**–100
approaches to, 99, 100
description and, 98
implementation of, 99
marketing research questions, 98
prediction and, 98
at Procter & Gamble, 519–520
visual product of, 99
Data overload, 98
Data precision, 262–263
Data preparation. *See* Preparing data for analysis
Data processing error, 242
Data reduction, 208–215, **209**
abstraction, 209–211
axial coding, 212
categorization, 209
coding, 209–211
comparison, 211–212
integration, 212–213
iteration, 213
memoing, 213
negative case analysis, 213
recursive relationship, 212

Data reduction—*Cont.*
selective coding, 212–213
tabulation, 213–215
theory building, 212–213
Data relevancy, 130
Data structures, 42–43
Data tabulation, 467–473
cross-tabulation, 468
descriptive statistics, 471
overview of, 471–473
graphical illustration of data, 471
one-way. *See* One-way tabulation
in qualitative analysis, 213–215
examples of, 214, 215
Data validation, 455–456
callbacks, 455
completeness, 455
courtesy, 455–456
curbstoning and, 455
fraud, 455
procedure, 455
screening, 455
Data warehouses, 37, **76,** 86, **96**–97
customer-volunteered information and, 97
informational data and, 96–97
marketing-related data and, 97
operational data and, 96
purposes of, 96–97
real-time transactional data and, 97
Database America, 101
Database depth, 93
Database development, 92–93
affinity and, 92
amount and, 92
depth and, 93
frequency and, 92
profitability and, 92–93
recency and, 92
width and, 93
Database management system, 93
typical output of, 94
Database modeling, 100–104, **101**
company engaged in, 101
lifetime value models, 103–104
scoring models, 102–103
Database processing system, 93–96
Database technology, 93–96
data dictionary and, 93, 95
database management system and, 93, 94
relational, 95–96
sequential, 95
Database width, 93
Databases, 88–110
as customer profile, 88–89
customer relationship management and, 84–85
customer retention and, 83–84
decision making and, 83–84
development of. *See* Database development
enhanced, 90–92
function of, within the financial services industry, 105–108
counting profitable customers, 105–106
data enhancement, 106
loyalty connection, 106–107
RFM segmentation, 106
win-win situations, 107
interactive components of, 91
learning objectives, 82, 109
market intelligence and, 84–85
mining. *See* Data mining
modeling. *See* Database modeling
operational, 88
purposes of, 89–90
questions answered by, 90
technology. *See* Database technology
value of, 84
warehouses. *See* Data warehouses
DataStar, Inc., 300
Debriefing analysis, 175
Decision making, 7–8
consumer databases and, 83–84
researchers and, 38–41
research-related tasks and, 7
Decision trees in data mining, 100
Deductive research, 280
Deli Depot, 474–477
Del.icio.us.com, 123
Delivery expense studies, 12
Dell Computers, 37, 89, 183, 293
Demand analysis, 13
Demand characteristics, 284
Department of Transportation (DOT), 194
Dependence methods, 562, 579–590
conjoint analysis. *See* Conjoint analysis
discriminant analysis. *See* Discriminant analysis
Dependent variable, 234, 277–278
Depth of the database, **93**
Description, 98
Descriptive research, 51–52
causal research and, 274–275
construct and, 233
hypotheses and, 234–235
quantitative research, 232–233
relationships and, 233–234

using surveys. *See* Surveys
variables and, 233, 234
Diffusion of treatment, 285
Dillard's Department Stores, 3, 319–320
Direct cognitive structural analysis, 338
Direct directional hypothesis, 409
Direct marketing, 581
Direct Marketing Association, 248
Direct observation, 191
Discovery Group, 186
Discriminant analysis, 579–587
combining cluster analysis with, 585–587
discriminant function and, 579
example of, 591–595
marketing research application, 581
scatter plot for, 579–581
SPSS application, 580, 582–587
Discriminant function, 579
Discriminant validity, 284, 338
Discriminatory power, 351–352
Disguised observation, 192
Disney World, 70
Disproportionate stratified sampling, 317
Distance property, 343–344
Distribution decisions, 11–13
cycle time research, 11–12
factor analysis and, 566
logistics assessment, 13
retailing research, 12–13
Diversity, 264
Domain of observables, 336–337
subcomponents, 284
Double-barreled dimensions, 385
Double-barreled questions, 408
Drive dimension, 91–92
Drop-off surveys, 254–255
Du Pont, 13
Dummy variables, 543–544
SPSS application, 543–544
DVD recorders, 591–595

E

E-commerce, 36
E-mail surveys, 256–257
eBay, 119
EconData, 144
Editing. *See* Data editing
Editing error, 242
Editors and Publishers Market Guide, 138
Electronic data interchange, 11–12
Electronic inventory tracking system (EITS), 265
Electronic searches, 121–124
online. *See* Online electronic data searches
popular sources, 121–123
scholarly research, 123–124
Electronic test markets, 296, **298**–299
eMarketer, 127
Embrace Mobile, 73
Emic validity, 221
Employees
empowerment and teamwork, 5
training programs, 5
Empowerment, 5
eNotes, 125
Ensequences, Inc., 333
Enterprise Informational Portal (EIP), 67
Environmental forecasting, 16
Environmental intelligence, 124
sources of, 126
Environmental scans, 124–125
Equivalent form, 352–353
Error detection, 466–467
benefits of computer-based surveys and, 468
Estimated standard deviation, 487
Ethics, 20–24
client/research user and, 20
code of, 21–24
measurement design and, 386
observational methods and, 196, 197
research provider and, 20–21
respondent and, 21
stratified random sampling and, 319
telephone interviews and, 248, 434
unethical activities, 20–21
Ethnography, 184–185, 207
European Research Gateways, 144
European Union in the U.S., 113
Eurostat, 126
Evaluation apprehension, 285
Excelsior Hotels, 43, 164
research proposal, 58–60
Excite, 67, 143, 144
Executive dashboard, 6
Executive interviews, 245–246
Executive summary, 603–605
conclusion and recommendations, 605
key findings, 604
purposes of, 604
research objectives, 604
Experience interviews, 182
Experiment, 274–275
field, 280
laboratory, 280

Experimental design reliability, 285
Experimental research, 272–308, **279**
complete randomization and, 278
deductive, 280
elements incorporated into, 278–279
field experiments. *See* Field experiments
functional relationship and, 276
inductive, 280
laboratory experiments, 280
learning objectives, 272, 306–307
nature of, 275–276
reliability of, 285
symbols used in, 286
test marketing and. *See* Test marketing
theory and, 279–280
types of, 286–292
pre-experimental designs, 287–288
quasi-experimental designs, 291–292
true experimental designs, 287, 288–291
validity and. *See* Validity
value of, 274
variables and. *See* Variables
Exploratory research, 51, 150–203
causal research and, 274–275
learning objectives, 150, 199–200
observation. *See* Observational methods of data collection
qualitative. *See* Qualitative research methods
quantitative. *See* Quantitative research methods
value of, 152
External research providers, 17
External secondary data, 115
sources of, 133–139
business information, 137–139
government documents, 136–137
NAICS codes, 134, 136
syndicated. *See* Syndicated sources of secondary data
at the Santa Fe Grill, 139
variables sought in, 135
External validity, 282–283
improving, 285–286
threats to, 282, 283
Extraneous variables, 277, **278**
Eye tracking monitor, 195

F

Face validity, 337
Facilitating agencies, 19
Fact-finding projects, 124
Factor analysis, 562–572, **563**
example of, 563–564
factor loading and, 564–565
marketing research applications, 565–566
SPSS application, 566–572
use of, with multiple regression, 568–572
Factor loading, 564–565
Factoral designs, 293–294
Fair Credit Reporting Act, 107
Fair Isaac & Co., 559
Fast Search, 117
Faulty problem definition error, 242
Faulty recall, 240
Fax surveys, 256
Federal Express (FedEx), 12
careers in marketing research at, 31–32
FedStats, 126
Field environment, 275
Field experiments, 280, 293–296
considerations in using, 295
factoral designs, 293–294
Latin Square designs, 294–295
validity concerns, 295–296
Field searches, 132
Filter questions, 385
Fingerhut, 107
First Union, 438
Flowerpot approach to questionnaire design, **411**–425
development process, 411, 412
example of, 416–425
client's approval, 424
data collection method, 417
develop question/scale measurement format, 418, 419–422
establish format and layout, 418, 422–423
evaluate questionnaire and layout, 423–424
evaluate question/scale measurement format, 418, 423
evaluate question/scale measurements, 418, 423
finalize the format, 425
implement the survey, 425
information requirements for each objective, 417–418
pretest and revise, 424
research objectives into information objectives, 416–417
situation, 416
illustrated, 413
information objectives and, 415
information requirements and, 416
summary of, 425

Focus group interviews, 165–182
advantages of, 177–178
breadth of topics covered, 178
client participation, 1778
new ideas, 177–178
special market segments, 178
underlying reasons for behavior, 178
analyzing and reporting the results, 175–177
content analysis, 175, 176
debriefing analysis, 175
format of report, 177
conducting discussions, 171–175
beginning the session, 174
closing the session, 175
main session, 174–175
moderator, 171–172
moderator's guide, 172–174
disadvantages of, 178–179
high cost per participant, 179
inability to generalize results, 178–179
questions of data reliability, 179
subjectivity of interpretations, 179
group incentives, 170–171
online options for, 75
planning the study, 165–171
confirmation/invitation letter, 169, 170
location of group, 171
number of sessions, 171
participants, 166–168
sampling procedures, 169
social networks and, 74–76
three-phase process for developing, 166
Focus group moderator, 171–174
guide for, 172–174
interaction bias, 179
traits of, 172
Focus group research, 161–182
abroad, 180
cost of, 161
goal of, 161
idea behind, 161
interviews. *See* Focus group interviews
nature of, 161
new technologies and, 179–182
offline focus groups, 180–182
online focus groups, 179–182
objectives of, 163–165
changing consumer preference and, 164–165
hidden information and, 163
marketing problems and, 163
new constructs and measurement methods and, 164
new ideas and, 164
quantitative statistics and, 163–164
subconscious feelings and, 164
reports for, 621–624
FocusVision Worldwide, 180–181, 194
Follow-up tests, 501–502
For-profit higher education, 198
Forbes, 121, 139
Forced-choice scale, 354–356
Ford Foundation of the Performing Arts, 50, 163
Ford Motor Company, 98
Forecasting
environmental, 16
sales, 13–14
Formative composite scale, 384
Forrester Research, 157
Fortune, 139
Fortune 500, 115
***F*-ratio, 501, 534**
Free-choice scale, 354–356
Freeedgar.com, 145
Frequency distribution, 356
***F*-test, 501**
Functional relationship, 276
Fuzzy logic in data mining, 100

G

Gains tables, 102, 103
Galvanic skin response (GSR), 195
Gatekeeper technologies, 36, **37**
Gatekeeping, 247
Gator, 125
Gemini Consulting, 108
General Motors, 17
Genetic algorithms in data mining, 100
Geodemographic data, 91–**92**
Global market expansion, 36, 37
GlobalEdge, 126
Goodyear Tire and Rubber Company, 302
Google, 65, 85, 117, 119, 121, 143, 194, 379
Google Scholar, 123
Government documents, 136–137
Granular data, 85
Graphic rating scales, 379–381
illustration of, 381
Greenfield Online, Inc., 311
Grounded theory, 207
Group depth interview. *See* Focus group interviews

H

Halo effect bias, 374
Hand City, 143
Harley-Davidson, 67
Harrah's, 67, 70
Harris Info Service, 144
HarrisInteractive, 194, 231–232, 257, 300, 311–312
Harvard Business Review, 121
Hawthorne effect, 179
History threats to validity, 281, 282
Hitachi, 65
Home Depot, 283
Honda, 264
Hypotheses, 234–235, **408**
  experimental research and. *See* Experimental research
  questionnaires and, 408–409
  testing. *See* Analyzing relationships in sample data
  theories and, 279–280
  used in information research, 409

I

IBM, 37
Iceberg principle, 46, 47
Image assessment surveys, 52, 367–368
  conjoint analysis and, 590
  discriminant analysis and, 581
ImageQ, 358
Importance-performance analysis, 9
In-depth interviews, 158–161
  advantages of, 161
  disadvantages of, 161
  primary objectives of, 159
  probing questions and, 159–160
  skills required for conducting, 159–160
  steps in conducting, 161, 162
In-home interviews, 245
In-office interview, 245
Inadequate operationalization, 284
Incentives, 171
  focus group, 170–171
  participation levels and, 266
Incidence rate, 264–265
Incomprehensible questions, 408
Independent samples, 497
  SPSS application, 498
Independent variable, 234, 277–279
Indirect observation, 192
Inductive research, 280
Industrial test marketing, 302–303
Information, 43, 66
Information analysis, 16
Information driven technology, 6, 64–81
  analytical customer data and, 68–69
  biometrics and, 69–70
  data analysis and, 76–77
  disseminating research results through portals, 77–78
  learning objectives, 64, 80
  market intelligence and, 87–88
  marketing research process and, 66–67
    dashboards and, 67
    portals and, 67
    problems, objectives, and, 66–67
  primary data collection and, 70–76
    nontraditonal methods of, 73
    social networking and, 73–76
  research designs and, 68–70
  smart cards and, 70
  transactional customer data and, 68–69
  value of, 66
Information exchange, 89–90
Information research process, 38
  communicating the research results, 56
  decision makers and, 38–41
  determining the need for, 38–41
  determining the problem, 45–51
    information needs, 45–48
    objectives of research, 50–51
    purpose of research, 45–46
    redefining the problem as a research question, 48–50
    relevant variables, 48
    symptoms, 47–48
    understanding the complete situation, 46–47
    unit of analysis, 48
    value of information, 51
  executing the research design, 54–56
    analysis of data, 56
    collection of data, 54–55
    creating knowledge, 56
    preparing of data, 55
  final report, 56
  interrelatedness of the steps in, 44
  learning objectives, 61
  overview of, 42–44
  research proposal, 56–60
  selecting the research design, 51–54
    causal research, 52
    descriptive research, 51–52

exploratory research, 51
measurement and scaling issues, 53–54
questionnaire design and pretest, 54
sampling, 52–53
secondary and primary data sources, 52
summary of, 44
transforming data into knowledge, 42–43
value of measurement in, 334
Information Resources Inc. (IRI), 143, 276
Information sharing, 6
Informational data, 96–**97**
Infoscan, 143
Instrumentation threats to validity, 281, 282
Integrated circuit card (ICC), 70
Integrated marketing communications, 14
Integration, 212–213
Intellectual capacity, 350
Intellifacts.com, 144
Intelligibility criterion, 350–351
Intelliseek, 225
Interactive marketing technologies (IMTs), 179–181
Interactive Tracking Systems, 181
Interactive TV (iTV), 300–301
Interdependence methods, 562, 563–579
cluster analysis. *See* Cluster analysis
factor analysis. *See* Factor analysis
Internal consistency, 353
Internal research providers, 17
Internal secondary data, 115
sources of, 131–133, 134
Internal validity, 281–282
improving, 285–286
threats to, 282–283
International Business Research, 144
International Business Resource, 144
Internet, 36–37, 67, 87
characteristics of U.S. users, 72
electronic observation and, 194–195
intelligence information and, 326
for primary data collection, 70–76
secondary data and, 117–118, 143–145
secondary research on. *See* Online electronic data searches
senior adoption study, 209–215
traditional data collection compared to, 71
Internet Advertising Bureau (IAB), 118, 123
Internet for Competitive Intelligence, The, 144
Internet Intelligence Index, 144
Internet/Web-based surveys, 257–260
Interpersonal communication skills, 159
Interpretive bias, 241
Interpretive skills, 160
InterSurvey, 311
Interval scales, 345, 347
examples of, 347
Interview cheating, 243
Interview error, 243
Interview instructions, 436
example of, 437
Interviewing techniques, 158. *See also specific techniques*
ethics and, 21
Inverse directional hypothesis, 409
iRemember, 125
IRS, 559
ISL, 141
Iteration, 213
itracks, 180, 194

J

J. D. Power and Associates, 141, 154, 249–250, 353–354, 394
JC Penney, 138
Jeep, 151–152
Jose's Southwestern Café, 482, 483, 490, 502, 503
bivariate regression, 532–534
discriminant analysis, 583–585
Pearson correlation, 523–524
JP Hotel Corporation, 431
JSTOR, 123
Judgment sampling, 322
Just Kids, Inc., 563

K

Katiesoft, 125
Key customers, 16
Key performance indicators (KPIs), 6
Kinesis Survey Research, 251
Knowledge, 42
transforming data into, 42–43, 56, 98–100
Knowledge level, 265
Knowledge Networks, 205
KnowThis, 143
Kodak, 17
Kraft Foods, 17, 98, 282–283
Kroger, 143

L

Laboratory experiments, 280
Land's End, 89, 138
Language ability, 350
Latin Square (LS) designs, 294–295
Leading (or loaded) questions, 408
Least square procedure, 529
  ordinary, 530
Lee Apparel Company, 304–305
Level of significance, 489
Lexis/Nexis, 121
Lieberman Research Worldwide, 300
Lifetime value models, 103–104
Likert scale, 370–372
  modified, 371, 372
Lillian Vernon Corp., 68–69
Limitations of reports, 618–**619**
Limiting, 132
Linear relationship, 518
Linksnarf.com, 123
Listening skills, 159
Literature reviews, 48, 51, **118**–121
  Click-to-Call alliance, 119
  divergent perspectives in, 124
  guidelines for conducting, 120–121
  reasons for conducting, 118–119
Logistics assessment, 13
Lottery incentive approach, 431
Lowe's Home Improvement Inc., 49

M

Macro Consulting, Inc., 358
Macy's, 275, 414
Mail panel surveys, 254
Mail surveys, 253–254
Mall shopping, 231–232
Mall-intercept interviews, 246
MANOVA, 562
Marcive, Inc., 137
M/A/R/C Research, 300
Market analysis, 8
Market Facts, Inc., 141
Market intelligence, 84
  customer-centric approach and, 85–86
  databases and, 84–85
  in the financial services industry, 86
  learning objectives, 82, 109
  secondary data and, 138
  transforming marketing research into, 85–88
    companywide approach, 87
    strategic use of customer information, 86–87
    technology support, 87–88
    transactional focus and, 87
  value of, 84
Market intelligence culture, 85
Market knowledge, 5
Market maven, 233
Market Opinion Research (MOR), 180
Market segmentation, 8–9
  cluster analysis and, 574
  conjoint analysis and, 590
Market share potential, 590
Marketing, 4
  test, 574
Marketing databases, 88–90. *See also* Databases
Marketing decision support system (MDSS), 16
Marketing plan, 15
Marketing planning, 7–8
Marketing program
  development of, 10–15
    distribution decisions, 11–13
    integrated marketing communications, 14–15
    pricing decisions, 13–14
    product portfolio analysis, 11
  implementation and control, 15–16
  information analysis and, 16
  marketing plan and, 15
Marketing research, 2–24, **3**
  careers in, 31–32
  cluster analysis and, 574
  conjoint analysis and, 590
  data enhancement and, 90–92
  discriminant analysis and, 581
  employees engaged in, 19
  ethics issue, 20–24
  factor analysis and, 565–566
  learning objectives, 2, 28
  process of. *See* Marketing research process
  relationship marketing and, 4–6
  reports. *See* Reports
  transforming into market intelligence, 85–88
  value of information generated by, 4
Marketing research industry, 16–19
  changing skills for the, 19
  types of firms, 17–19

Marketing research process, 34–63
  changing view of, 36–41
  environmental factors affecting, 36–38
  information research process and. *See* Information research process
  learning objectives, 34, 61
  solving marketing problems with, 35
  technology and, 66–67
    dashboards and, 67
    portals and, 67
    problems, objectives, and, 66–67
  value of, 36
Marketing research suppliers, 17
  proposal from, 58–60
Marketing Resource Group (MRG), 60
Marketing strategy design, 9–10
  new product planning, 10
  positioning, 9–10
  research and, 37
  target marketing, 9
Marketing Synergy, Inc., 519
MarketingSherpa.com, 122–123
Marketplace behaviors, 368–369. *See also* Attitude measurement
Marriott Hotels, 37, 159, 351
Marshall Fields, 411
MasterCard International, 105
Maturation threats to validity, 281, 282
McCullogh's correlation measures (MCM), 358
McDonald's, 37, 299
Mead Data Central, 75
Mean, 483–484
Means of thematically related variable, 610–612
Measurement, 332–365, **334**
  advanced. *See* Attitude measurement
  constructs and. *See* Constructs
  learning objectives, 332, 362–363
  numbers or labels and, 334–335
  objects and, 335
  overview of, 334–340
  predicting customer loyalty, 333–334
  scale. *See* Scale measurement
  value of, in information research, 334
Measurement and design error, 240–242
Measurement of dispersion, 356–357, **486**–488
  range, 486–487
  SPSS applications, 487–488
  standard deviation, 487
    estimated, 487
  variance, 487
Measures of central tendency, 356–357, 483–486
  mean, 483–484
  median, 484
  mode, 484
  SPSS applications, 484–486
Mechanical/electronic observation, 193–195
Media panels, 141
Median, 484
Member checking, 207
Memoing, 213
Men's Health Magazine, 231
Methodological appropriateness, 131
Methods-and-procedures section, 605, 606
Microsoft, 301, 481
  Excel, 561
  PowerPoint, 599, 601, 602, 608–610, 612, 613, 616
  Windows, 560
  Word, 608–610, 616
Midas Auto Systems, 375
  semantic differential scale used by, 376
MIECO, 86
Miller beer, 97, 298
Misinterpretation error, 241
Mobile phones, 73, 205–206
Mobile Transit Authority, 73
Mode, 484
Model F-statistics, 537
Moderator's guide, 172
  example of, 173–174
Monadic scale, 379
Mono-method bias, 284
Mono-operation bias, 284
Mortality threat to validity, 281, 282
Motivation to succeed (MTS), 283–284
Motivational data, 91
MPC Consulting Group, 403–404
MSN Search, 117, 121, 194
MTV/Nickelodeon, 73
Multicollinearity, 539–543
  regression coefficient, 539–540
  SPSS application, 540–543
Multiple discriminant analysis, 562
Multiple-item scale design, 384
Multiple regression analysis, 535–557
  beta coefficient, 536
  dummy variables and, 543–544
  examining residuals, 553–557
  factor analysis with, 562, 568–572
  multicollinearity and, 539–543
  regression coefficient, 539–540

Multiple regression analysis—*Cont.*
SPSS applications, 537–547, 568–572
standardized regression coefficient, 536
statistical significance, 536–537
Multivariate analysis, 558–597, **560**
classification of methods, 561–563
cluster analysis. *See* Cluster analysis
conjoint analysis. *See* Conjoint analysis
dependence methods. *See* Dependence methods
discriminant analysis. *See* Discriminant analysis
every day impact of, 559–560
factor analysis. *See* Factor analysis
global research and, 563
interdependence method. *See* Interdependence methods
learning objectives, 558, 598
measurement scales and, 562–563
for small businesses, 561
summary of methods, 562
value of, 560
Music.com, 383
Mystery shopper study, 192
Mystery shoppers, 11

N

NAICS codes, 134
sample list of, 136
Namestormers, 17
NASA, 599
National Association of Attorneys General, 248
National Eating Trends, 141
National Family Opinion (NFO), 141
National Total Market Audits and Surveys, 143
National Trade Data Bank, 113
Negative beta, 536
Negative case analysis, 213
Negative directional hypothesis, 409
Negative relationship, 234
Nesting, 132
Netnography, 185
NetSonic, 125
Neural networking in data mining, 100
Neutral response choice, 354–356
New-product planning, 10
cluster analysis and, 574
New York Times, The, 121, 599
Newsweek, 139
NEXIS, 75
Nextel, 65
NFO (National Family Opinion Worldwide, Inc.), 37, 300
Nielsen Media Research, 17, 142, 144
Nielsen Retail Index, 143
Nielsen Television Index (NTI), 190, 194
Nike, 89, 130
Nokia, 98
Nominal scales, 344–345
examples of, 345
Nomological validity, 338
Noncomparative rating scales, 379
graphic rating scales, 379–381
performance rating scales, 381–382
staple scales, 381
Nondirectional hypothesis, 409
Nonequivalent control group, 292
Nonparticipant observation, 185
Nonprobability sampling, 53, **312,** 322–324
convenience sampling, 322
judgment sampling, 322
probability sampling and, 313
quota sampling, 323
snowball sampling, 323–324
Nonresponse error, 239–240
Nonsampling error, 237–239
North American Industry Classification System (NAICS) codes, 134
sample list of, 136
Northern Light, 117
Northwest Airlines, 16
NPD Group, 141
Null hypothesis, 234–235, 409
Numerical scale, 379

O

Objective properties, 335
Objects, 335
concrete features and abstract constructs of, 337
Observation, 190
Observation mechanism, 193
Observational methods of data collection, 54–55, 152–153, **189**–197
benefits of, 196–197
ethical issues, 196, 197
eye tracking monitor, 195
information condition, 190
limitations of, 196–197

mechanical/electronic, 193–195
People Meter, 194
psychogalvanometer, 195
pupilometer, 195
scanner-based panels, 194
selecting the appropriate, 195–196
setting, 191
time-frame condition, 190–191
type-of-data condition, 190
types of behavior observed, 189–190
unique characteristics of, 191–195
direct observation, 191
disguised observation, 192
indirect observation, 192
mechanisms for observation, 193–195
mystery shopper study, 192
structural observation, 192–195
subjects' awareness, 192, 197
undisguised observation, 192
unstructured observation, 193
usability studies, 190
voice pitch analysis, 195
weakness of, 190
Ogilvy & Mather, 83
Olson Zaltman Associates, 188
One-group pretest-posttest, 287, 288
One-shot study, 287–288
One-way tabulation, 467–471
frequency table, 469
missing data, 469, 470
summary statistics, 470–471
valid percentages, 469–470
Online analytical processing (OLAP), 97
Online electronic data searches, 121–128
blogs, 121–123
competitive intelligence, 126, 128
consumer intelligence, 125–126, 127
environmental intelligence, 124, 126
environmental scans, 124–125
personal intelligence, 124, 125
popular sources, 121–123
scholarly research, 123–124
tools and strategies used in, 132
Online focus groups, 179–182
offline groups versus, 181–182
Online Intelligence Project, 126
Online survey methods, 255–260
e-mail, 256–257
fax, 256
Internet/Web-based, 257–260
offline method and, 255
Online transaction processing (OLTP), 96
Open-ended questions
data editing of, 456, 461
response consolidation for, 463–464
typical responses to, 461
Operational data, 96
Operationalization, 338–340
example of, 340
Opportunity assessment, 8
portals and, 67
Optical scanning, 12
Order property, 343
Ordinal scales, 345
examples of, 346
Ordinary least squares, 530
Ore-Ida, 300
Origin property, 343, **344**
Outback Steakhouse, 41

P

P-Shat, Inc., 19
Paired sample, 497
SPSS application, 498–499
t-test, 498–499
Paired-comparison scales, 383
example of, 382
Panasonic, 591
Participant observation, 184–185
Part-worth estimate, 588
Pay By Touch, 69–70
Pay-per-action, 14
Pay-per-click, 14
Pearson correlation coefficient, 522–523
assumptions of, 523
coefficient of determination, 525
formula for, 551
SPSS application, 523–524
substantive significance of, 524–525
Peer review, 221
People Meter, 194
Perceptual mapping, 9–10, **504**–505, 562
Performance rating scales, 379, **381**–382
illustration of, 381
Person-administered surveys, 244–246
advantages and disadvantages of, 245
executive interviews, 245–246
in-home interviews, 245
mall-intercept interviews, 246
purchase-intercept interviews, 246
Personal digital assistants (PDAs), 73

Personal intelligence, 124
customizing, 125
Personal selling, promotion mix and, 14
Personal service, 89
Philips, 591
Picture tests, 187
Pie charts, 609–610
Piggly Wiggly, 69–70
Pizza Hut, 116
Planetfeedback, 225–226
Plus-one dialing, 248
Population specification error, 243
POPULUS, 300
Portals, 67
pull, 77–78
push, 77–78
Positioning, 9–10
Positive beta, 536
Positive directional hypothesis, 409
Positive relationship, 234
Posttest-only control group, 287, 290
Powerize.com, 144
PR Webpress Database, 144
Pre-experimental designs, 287–288
one-group pretest-posttest, 287, 288
one-shot study, 287–288
static group comparison, 287, 288
Prediction, 98
Preparing data for analysis, 55, 452–479
data coding. *See* Data coding
data editing. *See* Data editing
data entry, 464–466
data tabulation. *See* Data tabulation
data validation. *See* Data validation
error detection, 466–467, 468
examples of questionnaires, 457–460, 476–477
learning objectives, 452, 478
overview of, 454
scanner technology and, 453, 464–466
value of, 454
Presentation of results, 620
Pretest-posttest control group, 287, 289
Pricing decisions, 13–14
factor analysis and, 566
Primary data, 37
collection of, 150–308
sources of, 52
technology and, 70–76
nontraditional collection methods, 73
social networking and, 73–76
Prior data manipulation, 130
PRIZM, 127
Probability sampling, 53, **312,** 313–321
cluster sampling, 317–321
nonprobability sampling and, 313
simple random sampling, 313–314
stratified random sampling, 316–317
systematic random sampling, 314–316
Probing questions, 159–160
Procter & Gamble, 17, 65, 86, 89, 115, 116, 178–179, 182, 249, 257, 277–278, 296, 322, 383
data mining by, 519–520
Product analysis, 16
factor analysis and, 566
Product portfolio analysis, 11
Product research, 581
Professional focus group facility, 171
Progressive Insurance, 559–560
Project administration error, 242–243
Projective hypothesis, 188–189
Projective interviewing methods, 185–189
cartoon (balloon) test, 188
picture test, 187
role-playing, 188
sentence completion test, 186–187
thematic apperception test, 187–188
word association test, 185–186
ZMET, 188–189
Promotional activities, 14
Propensity scoring, 258
Proportionate stratified sampling, 317
Protocol interviews, 183
Proximity operators, 132
Psychogalvanometer, 195
Publix Supermarket, 285–286
Pull portal, 77–78
Pupilometer, 195
Purchase-intercept interviews, 246
Purposive sampling, 322
Push portal, 77–78

Q

QSR NVIVO, 208
Qualitative data analysis, 204–229
components of, 208
conclusion drawing/verification, 217–221
credibility, 218, 221
cross-researcher reliability, 221
emic validity, 221
peer review, 221
triangulation, 221

data display, 215–217
examples of, 216–220
data reduction. *See* Data reduction
goal of, 207
of hotel travelers, 225–226
as inductive process, 207
interactive model of, 208
learning objectives, 204, 227–228
managing, 208
member checking and, 207
nature of, 206
quantitative versus, 206–207
writing the report, 222–224
analysis of the data/findings, 223
conclusions and recommendations, 223–224
introductory portion of, 222–223
Qualitative forecasting, 14
Qualitative research methods, 152, **154**–189
advantages of, 156–157
analyzing data produced by. *See* Qualitative data analysis
articulative interviews, 183–184
case studies, 182, 183
common objective of, 155
differences between quantitative and, 153
disadvantages of, 156, 157
ethnography, 184–185
experience interviews, 182
focus group research. *See* Focus group research
guidelines for using, 155
in-depth interviews. *See* In-depth interviews
interviewers and observers for, 157
multistage, 151–152
netnography, 185
nonparticipant observation, 185
participant observation, 184
projective interviews. *See* Projective interviewing methods
protocol interviews, 183
richness data and, 156
sample size issue, 157
subconscious motivation and, 156–157
uses of, 154–155
Quality A-1 Rainbow Rug Cleaners, 434
QualKote Manufacturing, 545–547
Quantitative forecasting, 14
Quantitative research methods, 152, **154**
analyzing data produced by, 206–207
differences between qualitative and, 153
focus group interviews and, 163–164
guidelines for using, 154
main goals of, 154
surveys and, 232–233. *See also* Surveys
Quasi-experimental designs, 291–292
nonequivalent control group, 292
separate-sample pretest-posttest, 292
summary of, 291
Questioning/recording approaches to data collection, 54–55, 152–153
scale measurement and, 349–357
Questionnaire design, 405–425
example of, 442–447
flowerpot approach to. *See* Flowerpot approach to questionnaire design
learning objectives, 402, 448–449
supplemental documents. *See* Supplemental documents for survey instruments
theoretical components of, 405–409
accuracy versus precision, 410
bad questions, 407–408
description versus prediction, 409
hypothesis development, 408–409
structured questions, 407
unstructural questions, 406
words, 405
value of a good instrument, 410
Questionnaire design precision, 410
Questionnaires, 402–450, **404**
computerized, 410
cover letters and. *See* Cover letters
design of. *See* Questionnaire design
development process, 411, 412
ethics and, 434
learning objectives, 402, 448–449
university residence life plans and, 403–404
value of, 404–405
value of good, 410
Quota sampling, 323
Quota sheets, 438
example of, 439

R

Radio Frequency Identification tags (RFID), 92
Random digit dialing, 249
Random sampling
simple, 313–314
stratified, 316–317
systematic, 314–316
table of random numbers, 314
Random sampling error, 237
Randomization, 278

Range, 486–487
Rank-order scales, 383
example of, 382
Rating cards, 438
example of, 440
Ratio scales, 348
Raw data, 42
Real time, 69
Real-time communication, 87
Real-time transactional data, 97
Recording error, 243
Recursive relationship, 212
Referral sampling, 323–324
Reflective composite scale, 384
Regression analysis, 527–535
assumptions behind, 528
bivariate, 528
developing and estimating coefficients, 530–532
error in regression, 530–532
formula for, 551–552
fundamentals of, 528–530
least squares procedure, 529
multiple. *See* Multiple regression analysis
reporting, 616–617
significance, 535
SPSS application, 532–534
straight line relationship, 528–529
unexplained variance, 529
Regression coefficient, 539–**540**
Related samples, 497
Relationship building, 4
Relationship database system, 95–96
Relationship marketing, 4–6, **5**
customer relationship management and, 5–6
marketing research process and, 4–5
Relationships, 233–234
negative, 234
positive, 234
Remington's Steak House, 506–512
ANOVA findings for, 510, 511
importance ratings for, 509
importance-performance chart for, 512
questionnaire of, 507–509
Report format, 603–619
data analysis and findings, 605–619
ANOVAS, 613–616
appendices, 619
bar charts, 607–609, 612–616
conclusions and recommendations, 618
correlation, 616–617
crosstabs, 612–613, 614
limitations, 618–619
means of thematically related items, 610–612
pie charts, 609–610
regression, 616–617
reporting frequencies, 606–607
t-tests, 613–164
executive summary. *See* Executive summary
introduction, 605
methods-and-procedures section, 605, 606
table of contents, 603
title page, 603
Reporting sheets, 439–441
Reports, 598–626
believability and, 602
credibility and, 602
effective communication and, 600
for a focus group interview, 621–624
format of. *See* Report format
future reference and, 602
learning objectives, 598, 625
levels of readers, 602
logical interpretation of results and, 600–602
presentations, 620
problems in preparing, 619–620
qualitative data analysis, 222–224
analysis of the data/findings, 223
conclusions and recommendations, 223–224
introductory portion of, 222–223
value of, 600
visual display of data, 599
Research design, 51–52
analysis of data, 56
causal, 52
collection of data, 54–55
creating knowledge, 56
descriptive, 51–52
executing the, 54–56
exploratory, 51
measurement and scaling issues, 53–54
preparation of data, 55
questionnaire design and pretest, 54
sample size, 52–53
sampling plans, 53
secondary and primary data sources, 52
Research proposal, 56–60
example of, 58–60
outline of, 57
Research Publishers LLC, 117
Research reports. *See* Reports
Respondent errors, 239–240
Responsive error, 240
Retailing research, 12–13
Reynolds Metals, 300

Rich Focus, 74
Rocking-chair interviewing, 21
Role-playing interviews, 188
Rolex, 11
Roper Starch Worldwide, 141
Rosetta Technologies, 35
Ruf Strategic Solutions, 77
Rule induction in data mining, 100

S

Saab Cars USA, 3–4, 5
Sales and Marketing Management's Survey of Buying Power, 138
Sales forecasting, 13–14
Sales tracking, 14–15
SalesLeads, 101
Sample, 53
Sample design error, 243
Sample frame error, 243
Sample selection error, 243
Sample size, 157
Sample standard deviation, 356–357
Sampling, 310–331
  determining the appropriate design, 324–326
    degree of accuracy, 325
    Internet and, 326
    knowledge of target population, 325, 326
    research objectives, 325
    resources, 325
    scope of research, 325
    statistical analysis, 326
    time frame, 325
  learning objectives, 310, 330
  nonprobability. *See* Nonprobability sampling
  plan. *See* Sampling plan
  probability. *See* Probability sampling
  technology and, 311–312
  value of, 312
Sampling design, 52–53
Sampling plan, 326–329
  appropriate sampling method, 328
  contact rates, 328
  data collection method, 327
  example of, 329
  execute the operating plan, 328
  operating plan for selecting sample units, 328
  sample size, 328
  sampling frame(s) needed, 327–328
  target population, 327
Samsonite Corporation, 83–84, 113
Samsung Electronics, 66–67, 591
Santa Fe Grill Mexican Restaurant, 25
  analyzing the database, 482–483. *See also* Significant difference analysis
  bivariate regression, 532–535
  considering expansion, 146
  direction of relationship, 518
  discriminant analysis, 582–587
  dummy variables, 543–544
  experimental design and, 279
  exploratory research for, 189
  multicollinearity, 540–543
  multiple regression analysis, 530, 535, 537–538
  Pearson correlation and, 523–524
  predicting customer loyalty, 333–334
  qualitative research for, 224
  questionnaire for
    coded responses, 461–463
    designing a, 442–447
    example of, 457–461
    open-ended questions on, 461
    response consolidation, 463–464
    SPSS data view of, 466–467
  reports and, 606, 618
  research questions, hypotheses, and survey method, 267
  sampling plan for, 329
  secondary data and, 139, 146
  Spearman rank order correlation, 526
  state-of-behavior data and, 341–342
  target demographics and, 26–27
  technology and, 79
SAS statistical software, 482
Scale descriptors
  appropriateness of, 351
  discriminatory power of, 351–352
  positive/negative, 353–354
Scale measurement, 340–365, **342**
  attitude measurement and. *See* Attitude measurement
  developing and refining, 348–358
    appropriateness of descriptors, 351
    criteria for, 349–357
    discriminatory power, 351–352
    importance scale, 351–352
    intelligibility of questions, 350–351
    measures of central tendency, 356–357
    measures of dispersion, 356–357
    neutral response choice, 354–356
    positive/negative scale descriptors, 353–354
    reliability of the scale, 352–353
    types of question phrasing, 349

Scale measurement—*Cont.*
direct cognitive structural analysis, 338
forced-choice, 354–356
free-choice, 354–356
goal of, 335
high-quality segmentation measures, 358
inappropriate formats, 338
learning objectives, 332, 362–363
levels of scales, 344–348
interval, 345, 347
nominal, 344–345
ordinal, 345, 346
ratio, 348
relationship between scaling properties and, 344
multivariate methods and, 562–563
nature of, 342
properties of, 342–344
assignment, 342
distance, 343–344
order, 343
origin, 343, 344
summary of, 343
reliability of, 338
scale points and, 342
types of data collected and, 340–342
state-of-behavior, 341–342
state-of-being, 341
state-of-intention, 342
state-of-mind, 341
Scale measurement error, 240–241
Scale points, 342
Scale reliability, 338
Scanner-based panels, 194
Scatter diagrams, 519
of curvilinear relationship, 521
of negative relationship, 520
of patterns of residuals, 531, 532
of positive relationship, 520
Schefflé test, 502
Scholarly research, 123
Scientific method, 42
Scoring models, 102–103
gains tables and, 102, 103
key variables in, 102–103
Screening
correct questions, 456
examples of, 456
data validation and, 455
Screening forms, 436–438
Search engines, 121, 143–144
Secondary data, 37, 114
advantages of, 129–130
customer relationship management and, 16
customized, 145
external. *See* External secondary data
internal, 115, 131–133
Internet for, 117–118, 143–145
limitations of, 130–131
online searches for. *See* Online electronic data searches
role of, in marketing research, 116–118
sources of, 52, 115
syndicated sources of, 140–143
characteristics of, 140
consumer panels, 140–142
store audits, 142–143
uses of, 117–118
Secondary research, 112–149
data produced by. *See* Secondary data
designs, 118–124
electronic searches, 121–124
globalization of, 113
learning objectives, 112, 147–148
literature reviews, 118–121, 124
nature and scope of, 114–115
scholarly research, 123–124
steps in, 115
value of, 114
Secure Customer Index (SCI), 359–361, 387–388
Sega, 77
Selection bias, 281, 282
Selective coding, 212–213
Selective perception bias, 241–242
Self-administered surveys, 252–253
advantages and disadvantages of, 253
Semantic differential scale, 372–376
examples of, 373, 375, 376
halo effect bias, 374
pole descriptor problems with, 374–375
Senior Internet adoption study, 209–215
pictorial representation of, 601–602
slide summarizing the methodology, 606
Sentence completion tests, 186–187
Separate-sample pretest-posttest, 292
Sequential database system, 95
Service Intelligence, 127
Service quality studies, 11
Service sensitivity analysis, 13
Seven-Eleven, 87
Sharp, 591
Short messaging (SMS) formats, 251
Significant difference analysis, 480–515
central tendency. *See* Measures of central tendency
dispersion. *See* Measurement of dispersion
learning objectives, 480, 513

perceptual mapping, 504–505
relationships. *See* Analyzing relationships in sample data
restaurant image positions, 506–512
for the Santa Fe Grill, 482–483
select case analysis, 483
statistical software and, 481–482
value of, 482
Simple random sampling (SRS), 313–314
advantages and disadvantages of, 314
Simulated test markets (STM), 299
advantages and disadvantages of, 299–300
example of, 298
Single-item scale design, 384
Situation analysis, 8–9, **46**
competitive analysis, 9
market analysis, 8
market segmentation, 8–9
research problems and, 46–47
Skip questions, 385
Smart card, 70
"Smart questionnaires," 410
Snowball sampling, 323–324
advantages and disadvantages of, 324
Social networks, 73
focus group interviews and, 74–76
as a marketing research tool, 73–74
Society of Competitive Intelligence Professionals, 117–118, 140
Solomon Four Group, 287, 290–291
Sony, 37–38, 591
Source Book of Demographics and Buying Power . . ., 138–139
Spam, 256
Spearman rank order correlation coefficient, 525–527
calculating median rankings, 526–527
SPSS applications, 526–527
Split-half test, 353
Sprint, 392, 393
SPSS (Statistical Product and Service Solutions)
ANOVA, 502–503
bivariate regression, 532–534
chi square, 495, 496–497
cluster analysis, 574–579
described, 481
discriminant analysis, 580, 582–587
dummy variables, 543–544
error detection and, 466–467
factor analysis, 566–572
independent samples *t*-test, 498
measures of central tendency, 484–486
measures of dispersion, 487–488
median ranking, 526–527
multicollinearity, 540–543
multiple regression, 537–547, 568–572
paired-samples *t*-test, 498–499
Pearson correlation, 523–524
reports and, 606–615
residuals, 553–557
select cases analysis, 483
Spearman rank order correlation, 526
tasks performed by, 72–73
univariate hypothesis test, 490
Standard deviation, 487
estimated, 487
Standardized regression coefficient, 536
Standardized research firms, 17
Starbucks, 299, 500, 503, 519, 562
correlation analysis of, 521–523
dummy variables and, 544
multiple regression and, 536
State Farm, 559
State-of-behavior data, 341–342
State-of-being data, 341
State-of-intention data, 342
State-of-mind data, 341
Static group comparison, 287, 288
Statistical regression, 281–282
Store audits, 142–143
Stratified random sampling (STRS), 316–317
advantages and disadvantages of, 317
disproportionate, 317
ethics and, 319
proportionate, 317
steps in, 318
Structured observation, 192–**193**
Structured questions, 407
Subconscious consumer motivations, 155, 156–157, 164, 188
Subjective properties, 335
Subjects' awareness, 192, 197
Sugging, 247, 248, 256
Sum of the squared errors, 529–530
Sun Trust Bank, 438
Supervisor instruction form, 435–436
example of, 435
Supplemental documents for survey instruments, 434–441
call record sheets, 439–441
interviewer instructions, 436, 437
quota sheets, 438, 439
rating cards, 438, 440
screening forms, 436–438
supervisor instructions, 435–436
Survey instrument error, 240, 241

Survey research errors, 237–243
averaging, 240
coding error, 242
construct development error, 240
data analysis error, 241
data entry error, 242
data processing error, 242
detection of, 466–467
editing error, 242
faulty problem definition error, 242
faulty recall, 240
interpretive bias, 241
interviewer cheating, 243
interviewer error, 243
measurement and design error, 240–242
misinterpretation error, 241
nonresponse error, 239–240
nonsampling error, 237–239
population specification error, 243
project administration errors, 242–243
random sampling error, 237
recording error, 243
respondent error, 239–240
response error, 240
sample design error, 243
sample frame error, 243
sample selection error, 243
scale measurement error, 240
selective perception bias, 241–242
sources of, 238
summary of, 239, 241, 242
survey instrument error, 240, 241
unconscious misrepresentation, 243
Survey research methods, 235–237
advantages of, 235–236
disadvantages of, 236–237
goal of, 235
measurement of. *See* Attitude measurement; Constructs; Scale measurement
questionnaires. *See* Questionnaires
selecting the appropriate, 260–266
ability to participate, 265
budget, 262
completion time frame, 262
diversity, 264
incidence rate, 264–265
knowledge level, 265
quality requirements, 262–263
respondent characteristics, 261, 264–266
situational characteristics, 261–263
summary of, 261
task characteristics, 261, 263–264
task difficulty, 263
topic sensitivity, 263–264
willingness to participate, 265, 266
supplemental documents. *See* Supplemental documents for survey instruments
usage of, 258
value of, 232
Survey Sampling International, 17
Surveymonkey.com, 258
Survey-Net, 127
Surveys, 230–271
construct and, 233
drop-off, 254–255
errors in. *See* Survey research errors
hypothesis and, 234–235
learning objectives, 230, 268–269
mail, 253–254
mail panel, 254
online. *See* Online survey methods
person administered. *See* Person-administered surveys
quantitative research and, 232–233
relationships and, 233–234
sampling and. *See* Sampling
self-administered, 252–253
in shopping malls, 231–232
summary of computer-assisted, 260
telephone. *See* Telephone interviews
types of, 244
value of, 232
variables and, 233, 234
virtual reality and, 258–259
Syndicated business services, 17
Syndicated (commercial) data, 140
Syndicated sources of secondary data, 140–143
characteristics of, 140
consumer panels, 140–142
store audits, 142–143
Systematic random-digit dialing, 248–249
Systematic random sampling (SYMRS), 314–316
advantages and disadvantages of, 316
steps in, 315

T

T-Mobile, 392, 393
***t*-test, 497**–499
to compare two means, 497–498
independent samples, 498, 499
paired-samples, 498–499, 500
reporting, 613–614
SPSS application, 498–499

Tabulation. *See* Data tabulation
Target, 88, 92, 143, 304, 404
Target market analysis, 9
  key variables of, 10
Target market characteristics, 91
Target population, 52
Task difficulty, 263
Teamwork, 5
Tech Data, 192
Technology
  adapting new, 209–215, 234–235
  error detection and, 468
  information driven. *See* Information driven technology
  Internet. *See* Internet
  paradoxes of, 216
  primary data collection and, 70–76
  sampling and, 311–312
  scanner, 453, 464–466
Telemarketing Sales Act (TSA), 248
Telephone Consumer Protection Act (TCPA), 248
Telephone interviews, 246–252
  completely automated, 251
  computer-assisted, 249–251
  ethics and, 248, 434
  traditional, 246–249
  wireless, 251–252
TeleSessions, 180
Temporal order, 274
Test marketing, 10, 296–305, 574
  advantages and disadvantages of, 300–301
  consumer versus industrial, 302–303
  controlled, 297
    advantages and disadvantages of, 297–298
  customer database and, 304–305
  electronic, 298–299
  matching experimental method with objectives, 303
  problems with, 298
  simulated, 299
    advantages and disadvantages of, 299–300
  summary of, 296
  traditional, 296–297
    advantages and disadvantages of, 297
  value of, 274
  virtual, 301
    advantages and disadvantages of, 301–302
  Web-based TV, 300
    advantages and disadvantages of, 300–301
Testing threats to validity, 281, 282
Test-retest, 352
Thematic apperception test (TAT), 187–188
Theory, 279–280
Thick description, 207
Time, 139
Time Warner, 301, 403
Timeliness, 69
Topic sensitivity, 263–264
Toshiba, 591
Total cost analysis, 13
Total variance, 501
Touchpoint, 87
Tracking sheets, 439–441
Traditional test markets, 296–297
Training programs, employee, 5
Transactional customer data, 68
  benefits of, 68–69
  market intelligence and, 87
Triangulation, 221
Trilogy approach, 392–397
  attitude-toward-behavior model, 396–397
  attitude-toward-object model, 394–396
  illustrated, 392
True experimental designs, 287, 288–291
  posttest-only control group, 287, 290
  pretest-posttest control group, 287, 289
  Solomon Four Group, 287, 290–291
Truncation, 132
Trustmark National Bank, 105, 107

U

Unanswerable questions, 408
Unconscious misrepresentation, 243
Undisguised observation, 192
Unexplained variance, 529
Union Bancorporation, 453
United Nations Global Trends, 126
U.S. Census Bureau, 127, 129, 130, 137, 144, 319, 409
U.S. Department of Commerce, 137
U.S. Department of Defense, 133
U.S. Postal Service, 12
Units of measurement, 130–131
Univariate statistical tests, 489–490
  level of significance and, 489
  SPSS application, 490
  using X16, 490, 491
University of South Florida, 165
Unstructured observation, 193
Unstructured questions, 406
UPS, 12, 130
USA Data, 127, 144
Usability study, 190

V

Vail Valley Foundation Management Team, 377–378
Validity, 280–286
  construct, 283–285, 337–338
    threats to, 284–285
  content, 337
  convergent, 284, 337–338
  discriminant, 284, 338
  external, 282–283
    threats to, 282, 283
  face, 337
  field experiments and, 295–296
  improving, 285–286
    control groups, 285
    exclusion of nonsimilar test subjects, 285–286
    matching extraneous variables, 286
    randomization of test subjects, 286
    time order of the manipulation exposure, 285
  internal, 281–282
    threats to, 282–283
  nomological, 338
Variables, 233, 275
  association analysis and, 518–521
  complete randomization and, 278
  control, 277, 278
  dependent, 234, 277–278
  experimentation and, 275–279
  extraneous, 277, 278
  independent, 234, 277–279
  multiple. *See* Multivariate analysis
  problem determination and, 48
Variance, 487
  analysis of. *See* Analysis of variance (ANOVA)
  unexplained, 529
Venture, 304
Verbatims, 223
Verizon, 86, 118–119, 234, 243, 392, 393
Virgin Mobile Cell Phone, 187
Virtual test markets, 296, **301**
  advantages and disadvantages of, 301–302
  example of, 302
Voice pitch analyzer, 195

W

Wachovia National Bank, 93
Wal-Mart, 37, 92, 97, 143, 192, 304
  scanner technology and, 453
Wall Street Journal, The, 115, 121
Web-based TV test markets, 296, **300**
  advantages and disadvantages of, 300–301
Web sites. *See also* Internet
  portals as, 77–78
  social networking and, 73–74
Web traffic analysis, 69
Whirlpool, 185
Width of the database, **93**
Wilks' Lambda, 583
Willingness to participate, 265
Wireless communication, 205–206
Wireless phone surveys, 251–252
Within-group variance, 501
Word association tests, 185–186
World Factbook, 113, 126
World Opinion, 144

X

Xerox, 65
XLSTAT, 561

Y

Yahoo!, 17, 67, 117, 121, 143, 194, 379
  customized data from, 18
Yahoo!/AC Nielson Internet Confidence Index, 18

Z

Zaltman metaphor elicitation technique (ZMET), 188–189
ZDNet.com, 125
Zoomerang.com, 258